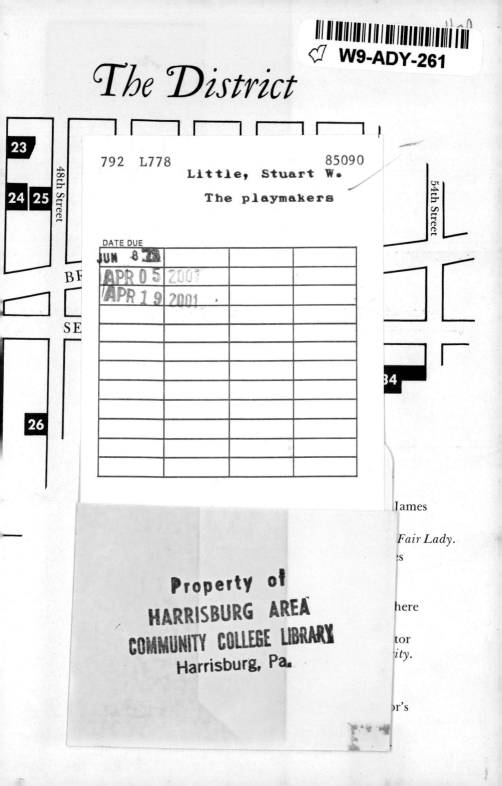

The District

W9-ADY-261

792 L778   85090

Little, Stuart W.

The playmakers

DATE DUE

JUN 8 73			
APR 05 2001			
APR 19 2001			

Property of
HARRISBURG AREA
COMMUNITY COLLEGE LIBRARY
Harrisburg, Pa.

James

Fair Lady.
s

here

tor
ity.

r's

The Playmakers

The Playmakers

Stuart W. Little & Arthur Cantor

W · W · NORTON & COMPANY · INC ·
NEW YORK

Copyright © 1970 by Stuart W. Little and Arthur Cantor

SBN   393   04315   0

Library of Congress Catalog Card No. 72-90987

Lyric lines from "There's No Business Like Show Business"
on page 89 © copyright 1946 Irving Berlin.
Reprinted by permission of Irving Berlin Music Corporation.

ALL RIGHTS RESERVED

Published simultaneously in Canada
by George J. McLeod Limited, Toronto

Printed in the United States of America

2   3   4   5   6   7   8   9   0

For Anastazia and Deborah

85090

Contents

Photographs follow pages 96 and 192

Foreword

Carl Van Doren once defined a classic as a book that "didn't need to be written again," meaning it was all-encompassing, definitive. Surely this is true of *The Playmakers*. Even though I have been in and out of the theater for fifty years, both as participant and spectator, I learned something new on nearly every page.

Did you know that Lee and J. J. Shubert, brothers, didn't speak to each other, even if they passed on the street? And did you know of the many magnificent (and sometimes diabolic) devices by which David Merrick promotes his many enterprises?

When two men as knowledgeable about their subject as Arthur Cantor and Stuart Little sit down to tell about actors, writers, directors, producers, stagehands, choreographers, and night watchmen, you know you have a book that doesn't "need to be written again" because it is so all-encompassing and completely fascinating.

In reading *The Playmakers* one is constantly aware of the fact that it would make an excellent textbook for anyone giving an overall course on the Theater (with a capital T), past and present. What would astound and please a student, however, is that while the ordinary textbook on any subject often tends to be very dry, exceedingly academic, this one has humor throughout and is a pure joy.

Actors aren't usually asked to write forewords to books. It is common knowledge that I have never been on a best-seller list and my last attempt to put pen to paper, as I recall, was in the fourth grade when I wrote a masterful essay entitled "My Kitty."

However, as anyone who has ever been connected with the theater in any capacity knows, it is always a joy to be associated with a quality production.

—Fredric March

The Playmakers

CHAPTER ONE

Another Country

For sixty years the heart of the American theater, the district known colloquially as Broadway, has been a narrow rectangular plot of ground measuring twenty-six square blocks in the very center of New York City. In 1969, along side streets branching off Times Square, were to be found all thirty-four of Broadway's legitimate theaters.

The district is a shabby, untidy neighborhood of souvenir shops, third-class hotels, and garish neon signs which blind by night and gather grime by day. It is an area of pokerino halls, penny arcades, record stores, hot dog stands, and pornographic bookshops which show dubious physical-culture magazines in the windows and advertise "peep shows" for a quarter inside. It is an area of freak exhibits and taxi-dance halls, some of which have turned to topless entertainment and some of whose girls still affect the Rita Hayworth longhair look of a 1940 movie.[1]

---

[1] A few years ago the recidivous world of the dance hall and the Broadway theater met when Gwen Verdon opened at the Palace in the musical *Sweet Charity* as a dance hall hostess—that most elegant of Broadway euphemisms. To the left of the Palace entrance was the staircase to one of the dance halls that had been used as a model for the show.

It is a district, too, of morose, heavily bewigged prostitutes who gather day or night in uncertain clusters along West 47th Street looking for a "fast trick," and of street drifters who shuffle vaguely within the crowds, past movie theaters and office buildings, begging for handouts or staring dumbly out of alleyways.

The district is bounded on the south by West 41st Street, on the north by West 54th, on the west by Eighth Avenue, and on the east by Sixth Avenue. Clamorous Broadway runs down the middle of the district like a shabby express train in the night. Within this crowded area east and west of Broadway are rehearsal halls, prop shops, costume lofts, photo studios, union headquarters, and the offices of producers, theater owners, theatrical publications, and press agents. The district has its own sharp ambience which distinguishes it from other Manhattan working districts—the garment district immediately to the south, or Wall Street, or advertising's Madison Avenue, where normal commuter hours, habits, and modes of dress are the rule.

But the distinctions would not strike a stranger visiting the theater district for the first time. Some kind of infrared vision or inner eye is needed to separate theater offices and theater people from the jarring distractions of penny arcades, pornography shops, over-the-counter juiceries, and "giftorama" stands and to find among the shadow people of Times Square the authentic theatrical types: stage managers, wardrobe attendants, wig fitters, box-office treasurers, backstage doormen—the infantrymen and combat specialists of the theatrical army.

The theater is a nation to itself, with its own citizens and imperatives of behavior, its own laws and customs, its clan absorption and kindred solidarity. It has its own job-classification systems and work routines, money games, class structure, power centers, hierarchies of influence. It has its own mode of dress and manner of speech. It has its own mores, sex habits, rituals, superstitions, fetishes, and folkways. To the eye of the stranger this world looks undisciplined, capricious, and lax. In fact, it moves inexorably in its own way of life, a different way from most, to be sure, but definable, classifiable, and nonpareil.

The theater keeps time by a different clock. In the garment district and on Madison Avenue the lights are out by seven P.M., just when the theater is coming to life. The work sounds of the theater fade around three A.M., after the rest of the city has quieted.

By midnight, theater marquees have gone dark. The actors gather in such beery hangouts as Joe Allen's, a popular actors' restaurant on 46th Street west of Eighth Avenue where performers from a dozen shows crowd the long bar and red-checkered tables and talk shop until closing. On Saturday nights Catholic actors attend midnight mass in the Actors Chapel in the basement of St. Malachy's Roman Catholic Church on West 49th Street. In the vestibule the bulletin board lists reserved masses for the theater's dead, and on the nights of Broadway openings the blue flames of votive candles glow with special brightness.

In most of the district the streets are empty and dark when the Shubert "roundsman" starts on his early-morning route to check the darkened theaters. He picks the keys off the board in the tiny stage-doorman's office at the Booth Theatre on Shubert Alley, a private walkway between West 44th and 45th streets. He has clocks to punch in each theater's basement, at stage level, in the balcony, and on the topmost dressing-room floor. He heaves his shoulder against each exit door to be sure the lock has caught. He checks the front of the house and the back. Out on the stage he peers into the emptied hall. His flashlight points a path through pull ropes and rigging lines, and he prepares to leave. There is an eerie silence. Then, behind him, a creaking sound passes along the stage floor. A forgotten actor making a final exit? It is only the rising stage, a particular sound, primitive and complaining, especially common in winter when the heat is off and the wood floor contracts, a wood sound in a city of glass, steel, and concrete. Although the roundsman has heard it before, the sound is startling in the dark of morning. He glances over his shoulder and sweeps his flashlight around. But there is no intruder, only the rising stage.

At eight o'clock in the morning the day crew is swabbing the sidewalk in front of Sardi's, the theatrical restaurant. The doors are open, revealing the dim, maroon-carpeted interior. Upturned chairs rest on bare table tops. The normal workday for theater professionals does not begin before ten or eleven o'clock, but across from Sardi's, in an office on the top floor of the Shubert Theatre building, right on Shubert Alley, one producer, Alexander H. Cohen, may already be at work, talking on the transatlantic wire to London.[2]

At ten o'clock the box offices open. No roomier than a closet, the box office is the principal means of distribution, and many thousands of dollars a day flow into these tiny ticket rooms. At least a third of the Broadway audience comes to the theater in person to buy tickets in advance of show time. Thousands of mail orders, particularly for the big musicals, flow into the district. The "broker phones" (direct lines to the box-office ticket offices in the Times Square area or in hotels and clubs in other parts of the city) begin to ring at ten o'clock.[3]

The box office gets the action when the theater has a smash hit. Lines form in three waves—before the ten o'clock opening in the morning, again during the lunch hour, and finally later in the afternoon, after office hours. In a year Broadway boasts no more than two or three shows of such impact. Theater pros can look at a box-office line on the day after a hit opens and tell you to the month how long the play will run. For the first few high-fever days after a hit explodes, it is common for its producer, playwright, and director to "go down to watch the line" and gloat at a

[2] Two other Broadway producers, Richard Rodgers and Harold Prince, have London offices, but Cohen is alone among his colleagues in producing full-time in both cities.

[3] Brokers' sales amount to $20 million a year. Electronic box-office systems to sell seats in distant outlets, in much the same way as airline tickets are sold, are fast being perfected.

queue that runs out of the lobby and down the street where everyone in the business will be sure to see it.

At ten o'clock David Merrick, Broadway's plenipotentiary producer, takes a tiny elevator to the top of the St. James Theatre building on West 44th Street, a few doors west of Sardi's, steps into a red-carpeted, red-walled office, and glances at his huge Bernard Buffet painting. Simultaneously, in other offices not quite so grand, other producers sit at their desks chasing the day's rainbows—opening mail, reading scripts, phoning agents, lawyers, landlords, playwrights, and directors, and preparing to stem a theatrical tide of visitors welcome and not so welcome. There are actors looking for work, out-of-towners asking help in getting tickets to hit shows, visionary types with make-a-million projects, and the solid visitors who collaborate on past, present, and future productions. The late Alexander Sandor Ince, a colorful Hungarian producer who was forever announcing plays but never quite getting them on, used to say, "The joy of theater is in dreaming, planning, imagining—when you have to do something, that's when you're in trouble."

About a hundred individual producers and producing organizations are active on Broadway, and a quarter of them are based in six theatrical office buildings within a few blocks of each other in the district.

The most distinctive is the Sardi Building, which takes its name from the restaurant. In this eleven-floor structure of shabby grandeur much of Broadway's business is done at one time or another. The executive offices of the Shubert theaters are on the sixth floor; the anteroom has huge portraits of departed Shuberts on its walls. In the penthouse, which looks like the court of Versailles, are the luxurious offices of the powerful Dramatists Guild. On the eighth floor is the most active theatrical advertising agency in New York, the Blaine-Thompson Company, a beehive in crisis buzzing with account executives, artists, and messengers. Producers and press agents, agents and actors, managers and treasurers meet in the airless elevators of the Sardi Building; the conversation is relentlessly tradey. "That was a fast one at the Belasco" . . . "The show sold out for a month in Washington" . . . "How did you like what that son of a bitch said in the *Times?*" . . . "We decided to switch to Sunday matinees instead of playing Monday nights." Even the elevator operators are turned on to show business, repeating the latest rumor of triumph or disaster in the district.

Other major theatrical office buildings dot Times Square. The Palace, at 47th Street and Broadway, has become a new power center in the last few years. The Nederlander theater interests of Detroit took title to Broadway's famous vaudeville house in August 1965 and renovated not only the theater, where they began to book musicals, but also the office tower. Today the building rivals the Sardi Building in influence, prestige, and the single-mindedness of its tenancy. The once-shabby Palace was the talent headquarters of the vaudeville circuit—head office of the Keith-Albee chain—in the 1920's and 1930's. Roger L. Stevens, real estate man and Broadway producer and chairman of the National Endowment for the Arts during its first years, keeps an office there. Producers Michael Myerberg, Morton Gottlieb, and Eugene Wolsk are also there, as is the Theatre Development Fund, Inc., a nonprofit organization formed in 1967 to assist worthwhile drama in the commercial theater. The Fund operates primarily through ticket-subsidy plans that assure a producer of audiences in the crucial first weeks of a Broadway run.

At 1545 Broadway producers Robert Whitehead and Kermit Bloomgarden and director Elia Kazan head the roster in a building that had all its windows blocked off by the largest billboard in New York some years ago. At 165 West 46th Street, directly across Times Square, are Actors Equity, the weekly trade publication *Backstage,* and producers Richard Barr and Edward Albee. At 226 West 47th Street, above the redolent Gaiety Delicatessen, are the Theatre Guild, the American Theatre Society, and the League of New York Theatres. Over the years the directory listings in lobbies may change, but the parochial quality of the district remains. In New York City there is one West Side street devoted solely to buttons—button makers, button jobbers, button buyers—and in the theater district theater people work, eat, and transact business with their own kind in their own inbred enclave.

Elegance is not the hallmark of theatrical offices, and they are usually poorly furnished and carelessly equipped. Until a short time ago the Shuberts ran their headquarters with proud penury; most of their furnishings were from their warehouse of stage props. The late Jack Small, general manager for the Shuberts, was once asked if a chair in his office was from *The Student Prince,* and he replied, "We ran out of *Student Prince* furniture last year." Many show people, particularly producers, are too frantic worrying about the way their shows look to give any thought to the way their offices look. Producer Alfred de Liagre, Jr. has not been inhibited by the size of his postage-stamp office in a 42nd Street building overlooking Bryant Park from overseeing such outstanding Broadway successes as *The Voice of the Turtle, The Madwoman of Chaillot,* and *J.B.* The late dean of Broadway press agents, Richard Maney, ran his office for years in mare's-nest clutter in the old Empire Theatre building (long since torn down). "A theatrical office should be shabby," comments a director. "The real life of the theater belongs on the stage."

The tendency to congregate in the old rabbit warrens around Times Square and shun decorativeness in one's office is changing, however. Saint-Subber, the successful producer of Neil Simon's comedies, including *Barefoot in the Park, The Odd Couple,* and *Plaza Suite,* has homelike offices in an East Side town house. Harold Prince, producer of *Fiddler on the Roof, Cabaret,* and *Zorbá,* has a tastefully decorated suite in Rockefeller Center. Leland Hayward, producer of *South Pacific, Gypsy,* and *The Sound of Music,* works out of a penthouse suite at Madison Avenue and 60th Street. Scenic designer Jo Mielziner works in an office-apartment at the Dakota on Central Park West and 72nd Street; costume designer Patricia Zipprodt works in a handsome studio com-

plete with skylights on the top floor of a five-story loft
building on University Place.

No one occupies more elegant space than Richard Rodgers
—a quiet, curtained room only four floors above the busy in-
tersection of Madison Avenue and 57th Street. There is a
Lautrec poster of Jane Avril in the entrance foyer. Visitors
are passed through a buzzer-operated door into a long narrow
hallway, off which are the richly furnished offices of the people who work for Rodgers, many of them long-term
employees. At the end of the hall is Rodgers' door. In the
far sanctum the walls are softly gray, the carpet a thick,
solid brown. Facing the entrance is an illuminated Egyptian bas relief dated 1320 B.C., and in a corner is the obligatory grand piano. (Rodgers rarely plays it, but is sometimes
photographed at the keyboard.) On the far wall are oils by
abstract expressionists Gottlieb and Goldberg. In another
corner is a drawing-room sofa where Rodgers seats his guests,
and above it hangs a Soulages.

There is no working desk as such in the room, no file
cabinets, no such obvious office machine as a typewriter. Instead, in the southwest corner there is a small, fine round
table with neatly arranged objects and a few of the well-
sharpened twenty-five-cent Blackwing 602 pencils Rodgers
uses for composing. Four graceful chairs surround the table.
Here Rodgers, a superb businessman, dictates letters to his
secretary—he is as punctilious as a corporation lawyer about
answering mail. The office is a necessity. For the "office stuff"
he is on the job early, although he does most of his composing in his country home in Fairfield County, Connecticut.

By late morning, actors have awakened and fill the theater
district, some to rehearse, some to audition, some merely to
visit casting offices, leave their pictures and résumés, and
demonstrate their availability. There are two kinds of auditions. At regular auditions actors attend by invitation of
the producer and their names are registered with the stage
manager, who times their appointments. The second is the
"open call," required by the rules of Actors Equity to make
sure all willing performers are given a chance to be heard.

There is no more bizarre and colorful occasion in the theater than the open call for dancers for a large Broadway musical. Only ten dancers may be required but hundreds will show up to audition, heedless of the terrible odds.

In the district, dancers are known as "gypsies" because of their habit of traveling from show to show. Even when they are settled in a hit, they fly to fresh auditions as if from some uncontrollable dancer's reflex. They arrive at the stage door in a great variety of costumes, improvising on the basic black uniform of leotard and tights by tying a scarf around the waist or using contrasting colors on top and bottom. By midmorning the line of pretty, leggy girls that has formed just inside the stage door is divided into groups of four, and each group dances across the stage to the jumpy tunes of the rehearsal piano. The choreographer, director, and producer sit in the darkened auditorium. Intermittently a voice calls out a cryptic command: "One and four stay, two and three go." In this way the choreographer reduces the field, and after a couple of hours of auditioning only half the girls are left. The process is then repeated. The remaining girls are assigned a new audition step and given a change of tempo. The voice from the auditorium calls out, "Number-two girl wait. The others, thank you." The same matter-of-fact voice repeats politely, "Thank you . . . thank you . . . thank you . . ."

Finally, when all remaining dancers have been seen a second time, the choreographer clears the stage for the final judging: "Will the 'thank-you's' please leave." Then the final ten are chosen. The mass audition has achieved its purpose, and the impersonality of selection has taken some sting out of the disappointment for the rejected ones.

As morning rehearsals continue, dancers and actors flock to empty theaters and oddly cloistered rehearsal halls throughout the district. One such retreat is the New Amsterdam Theatre. Now a grind movie house with a faded Byzantine décor, it was once a showplace for Ziegfeld musicals. Above this theater in 1928, when *Whoopee* starred Eddie Cantor in blackface, Ziegfeld opened a rooftop theater with after-hours entertainment called the Midnight Frolics, featuring Cantor, Maurice Chevalier, and Ruth Etting. The Ziegfeld Roof was briefly famous, and the small, perfectly designed theater fell into disuse until television's early days when it was put into service for live shows. The narrow camera ramp [4] dating from those days still juts out into the audience.

For the last fifteen years the theater has rented the roof as rehearsal space, and many Broadway casts have filed through the rococo lobby of the movie theater to the elevator, which takes them past floors of long-forgotten theatrical offices. (In one of them the young Moss Hart worked as an office boy.) Through swinging doors at the end of a bare upstairs lobby is a cameo playhouse, dusty and neglected. Out on the camera ramp in 1959 Elia Kazan and Tennessee Williams sat to watch Geraldine Page and Paul Newman run through scenes from Williams' *Sweet Bird of Youth*. Moss Hart, up from office boy, used the same platform to direct Julie Andrews and Rex Harrison in *My Fair Lady* and Miss Andrews and Richard Burton in *Camelot*.

In dozens of similar half-darkened rooms around the district morning rehearsals are over, and it is time for the lunch break. Rehearsing casts send out for coffee and corned-beef sandwiches from the Gaiety Delicatessen on West 47th Street or Harry and Ben's across the street or Act IV on 44th Street. The luncheon crowd shows up at Sardi's or at Dinty Moore's on West 46th Street, where the specialty is Irish stew and the atmosphere is businesslike and not familial as it is at Sardi's.

Sardi's is the inevitable theater restaurant and has retained its popularity through the years, despite its high prices. Its location at the crossroads of the district is unbeatable. It is eating place, greeting place, meeting place. To be seen lunching at Sardi's at a good front table downstairs ("the A-group of the east wall" is the expression used

---

[4] The platform on which a television camera is rolled in and out of the set. In a legitimate theater converted to television, the camera ramp usually pre-empts the center aisle.

by director Tyrone Guthrie) is to have arrived—a goal for the striving set, a blessing to be bestowed by the management. Productions frequently have caught fire because of a chance encounter between producer and playwright or director and actor across the crowded room. For an actor badly needing work, exposure at Sardi's may remind someone— anyone—of an opportunity, and nobody is more conscious of such unspoken drama than Vincent Sardi, who runs the restaurant and once wanted to be an actor.

Middle-rank actors are more apt to eat at Jim Downey's bluff Irish bistro on Eighth Avenue and leave Sardi's to the stars, or to visit less expensive places in the mid-40's west of Eighth Avenue.

Top names zip into the Twenty-One Club at 21 West 52nd Street, a gleaming establishment that caters to the rich and super-rich in all fields and makes no special fuss over theater people unless the name is Fonda or Brando or Streisand. Twenty-One's following is a many-splendored elite, whereas Sardi's clientele is solidly theatrical.

Between noon and one o'clock the dining rooms of theatrical clubs fill up. Only one is located within the theater district proper—the venerable Lambs on 45th Street east of Broadway. The old order is changing fast at the Lambs. Once staunchly restricted to showfolk, the club woke up one day to find its membership rolls composed of aging actors and vaudevillians past their prime. Nostalgia tried hard to compete with rising costs, and failed. Now the Lambs welcomes commercial types, and at night the once all-male club allows women guests. Many blocks south on Gramercy Park, the theater's most distinguished club—The Players—still survives. The food is not quite as top-drawer as the company, but the ambiance is timeless. Once the home of Edwin Booth, The Players is alive with memorabilia and has a splendid library, and such are the hours and employment uncertainties of theater that one can always find good company at The Players at any time of day or night.

There are other theatrical clubs, of a sort, in the headquarters of the ten theatrical unions in the district. The largest in membership (16,500) is the Actors Equity Association on two floors at 165 West 46th Street. Equity has a substantial treasury with assets of $2.5 million and receipts from annual membership dues of a half a million.[5] In the afternoon the membership lounge at Equity is a popular place for actors to gather and exchange gossip, read trade papers, scan the bulletin board for job opportunities, and swap information. At the reception desk there is a stack of free tickets donated by producers who need to "paper the house"—the trade phrase for flooding a theater with passes.

Most of the profession's unions have headquarters within the district: Local 802 of the American Federation of Musicians on West 52nd Street just west of the ANTA Theatre; the Association of Theatrical Press Agents and Managers on West 47th Street; Local B-183 of the Legitimate Theatre Employees in Amusement and Cultural Buildings at 1650 Broadway; the Society of Stage Directors and Choreographers at 1619 Broadway; Local 1 of the Theatrical Protective Union (stagehands) on West 54th Street; Local 764 of the Theatrical Wardrobe Attendants Union on West 57th Street; Local 751 of the Treasurers and Ticket Sellers in the Hotel Paramount on West 46th Street.

Two craft organizations, under the terms of the federal labor law, cannot be described as unions because their members are "individual contractors" and are not considered "employees" subject to collective-bargaining agreements. These are the Dramatists Guild and Local 829 of the United Scenic Artists of America on West 47th Street. "They may not be unions," says a producer who deals with these two potent cabals, "but God help you if you cross them."

The tightness of labor organization in the theater and the wide publicity given to its frequent labor difficulties have given the impression that the industry is much larger than it is. It is really a small world, the theater, incredibly

---

[5] By comparison, the assets of the industry organization, the League of New York Theatres, are less than $100,000 and the receipts from the annual membership dues are around $125,000.

small—so small, in fact, that almost everyone knows every-one else, and half a dozen key people in the district whose paths cross a half a dozen times a day know all the answers.

At any one moment the most knowledgeable people in the theater may be a couple of Shubert executives and Vir-ginia Burkhardt, who handles theater parties for the Shu-berts and has a sixth sense about the strength of incoming shows; Irving W. Cheskin and Ruth Green, the two execu-tives at the League of New York Theatres; Ernest Rawley, head of the Independent Booking Office, who is the first to know when a new show is set or when a production cancels out; and a cadre of business managers and producers—only they know all the answers at any one time.

No other industry of comparable significance in America is controlled or managed by so small a group. Perhaps a dozen people who keep in touch by telephone or at informal meet-ings throughout the day control the business life of the theater. This power elite—steeped in the theater's prob-lems and its tortuous techniques of solving them—deter-mines by its experience and judgment what happens in the thirty-four theaters from 41st to 54th streets. The theater district is not much bigger than the Vatican, and the centralization of power is just as acute.

To land a desirable theater or negotiate a favorable talent contract, to book the most lucrative out-of-town subscription tour or find the most promising script requires access to accurate information, and quickly. Power in the theater coalesces around those who can get this information speedily and who can act on it unequivocally. The flow of information is facilitated by the compactness of the area, and indeed is one reason for its ethnocentricity. News travels like radar within the district, especially bad news.

After lunch there is a lull in the theater district. Trea-surers, managers, and others who play the market drop in to watch the broad tape run out at closing time in Sartorius & Company, a brokerage office at 1540 Broadway. On Tues-days the sixty-five-member Equity Council is in session all afternoon. Tuesday is also the day that *Variety,* the trade newspaper that is the Bible of the industry, goes to press for Wednesday publication. *Variety*—its logotype appears in green lettering in every window of its five-story headquarters—is located in a little building with creaking stairs on 46th Street east of Broadway, adjoining the stage door of the Lyceum Theatre. All day Tuesday *Variety* staff members are unreachable; to "break" a big theatrical story in *Variety,* one must have copy in by Monday afternoon.

At 5:30 P.M. general managers and treasurers begin gathering at Fornos, a Spanish restaurant on West 52nd Street a few doors east of the Alvin Theatre. The dovecote principle in the district is at work. Huddled at the bar, the men pass a dice shaker back and forth to determine who pays for the drinks. Fornos regulars stay until 7:30, when they fan out like a flight of birds to check their theaters in the critical hour before the curtain rises. At dusk the marquee lights are switched on, and the tempo of the district changes. Life drains out of rehearsal halls and offices and into the theaters.

In no city does a theater building seem more out of scale than it does in New York. The odd disparity between the size of theaters and the adjacent structures grows steadily greater as tall office towers invade the Times Square area. Once again, as in other years, the geographical integrity of the theater district is threatened by real estate developers on the move.

The first theater in Manhattan was erected in 1753 on a site occupied by an old Dutch church on Nassau Street not far from the Battery. A group of players who had performed the year before in Williamsburg, Virginia, opened the Nassau Street Theatre on September 17, 1753. In the two centuries since then, the theater district has taken quantum jumps uptown. An early nineteenth-century move brought it to Union Square on 14th Street. In the 1880's the district was relocated near Madison Square at 23rd Street along a stretch of Broadway known as the Rialto, which extended from Madison Square to the old Metropolitan Opera House at 39th Street. In the twentieth century the district reached the side streets of Times Square.

Each generation has brought change to the shape, size, and location of the theater district, and there are to be drastic changes in the immediate future. The trend is still northward. In the 1880's people confidently predicted that the northernmost theater, at 41st Street, was too far uptown to do business. Today the southernmost theater, the Billy Rose, is on 41st Street, next door to the old Herald Tribune Building, and few would say that the northernmost theater, the George Abbott (formerly the 54th Street), is too far uptown.

Not all thirty-four of Broadway's present complement of legitimate theaters are lit at all times.[6] Broadway's business is cyclical, varying with weather, holidays, the vagaries of the stock market, labor disturbances, and transportation crises. In general the district is active from Labor Day through the Fourth of July, subject to predictable lulls (for instance, the night before a holiday will bring more people to the box office than the night of the holiday itself, and weekends are better for business than the early part of the week). Summer is a period of estivation and dark houses, with almost two-thirds of the theaters inactive.

At the high point of theatrical real estate in 1931 there were sixty-six first-run Broadway houses. In the thirty-year period from 1930 to 1960, while population increased by 45 per cent and personal income increased six times, there was a 50 per cent decline in the number of Broadway theaters. In the 1930's the theater lost houses to films, particularly along West 42nd Street, and in the late 1940's and 1950's it lost more theaters to television, although some of these have since been reclaimed.

Broadway theaters as they exist today may be distinctive and quaint, but they are certainly old. In 1969, the youngest—the Ethel Barrymore—was forty. The oldest—the Hudson—was a doddering sixty-six and ready for the wrecking crews. In 1969 the average age of a Broadway theater was

---

[6] It is customary to say a theater is "lit" rather than open, and that it is "dark" rather than closed.

forty-nine and a half years.

The life of the Hudson as it draws to a close (it is part of a real estate assembly for a high-rise office building) illustrates the life and changing fortunes of the district.

The Hudson was opened in the fall of 1903 by Henry B. Harris, one of the foremost producers and theater operators of his time. Nine years later he went down on the *Titanic,* and his widow, Renée Harris, a remarkably bright-eyed lady who died in 1969 at the age of ninety-three, carried on gallantly in his place, keeping the Hudson lit, seeing to his other theatrical interests, and becoming the first woman producer in New York. As an early employer of Moss Hart and the producer of his first play, she was the heroine of the first part of Hart's autobiographical *Act One.* In the Depression most of what remained of her husband's theatrical fortune was lost. The Hudson, which Renée Harris clung to desperately as a memorial to her husband went too. Possibly the last chance to save the theater came when she was offered the booking of Marc Connelly's *The Green Pastures,* but for technical reasons the Hudson stage was unable to accommodate the production and it went instead to the Mansfield (now Brooks Atkinson) Theatre, where it had a long, prosperous run. *Variety* falsely accused Mrs. Harris of refusing to book a play with a Negro cast, a charge that rankled her for years.

Hard times have befallen the Hudson. In latter years it has housed few legitimate attractions, and it may never see a play again. A succession of owners, primarily real estate operators, have pursued an erratic booking policy that has included tawdry burlesque shows and Andy Warhol's film *My Hustler,* an epic of male prostitution.[7]

In the fall of 1968 Mrs. Harris, then ninety-two and alert as ever but uncertain of step, took a small party of friends, including the author Walter Lord, who had written about the loss of her husband on the *Titanic* in *A Night to*

---

[7] Under a "blue movie" policy, the Hudson, with weekly expenses of $6,000, was reported to be grossing $36,000 in 1969, for a net profit of $30,000 —an unheard-of figure for any legitimate attraction.

Remember, to dinner at the Lambs Club, just across the street from the Hudson. Once again she talked about losing the Hudson, one of the sorrows of her life. As the party left the Lambs, Mrs. Harris, leaning on Lord's arm, carefully kept her eyes lowered. She said, "I haven't let myself look at the theater since I lost it in 1930."

Built in a day of theatrical panache, the Hudson has luxurious living quarters upstairs. So does the Lyceum Theatre, which is one block north of the Hudson and was opened by Daniel Frohman a few weeks after Harris opened the Hudson. The public was astounded by the Lyceum's spaciousness, its mechanical air-conditioning, and the generous backstage facilities built for a full repertory company. Frohman put in seven dressing rooms on either side of the stage and fourteen more behind, which to this day are the most generous accommodations for actors in any legitimate theater in New York except for the $8 million Vivian Beaumont Theatre in Lincoln Center. In the rear of the Lyceum, where the building rises six stories in a narrow chimneylike column that can be seen on 46th Street, a space was set aside for a two-story "paint frame" where set "drops" fifty to sixty feet high could be treated by scenic artists standing on two levels. In the front of the theater Frohman had his own office-apartment, with a peep-hole window from which the audience could be seen. To Frohman, according to James Barrie, "The playhouse was the real universe; outside, all was wearying and bothersome."

In 1903 Frohman had built a theater for repertory but by the time it was constructed fashions had changed and repertory was out. It was not until sixty-three years later that the theater was fully put to its intended use by the APA-Phoenix repertory company, which had three seasons at the Lyceum before the enormous costs of repertory on Broadway drove it out. Once again the doors to all those dressing rooms were closed and the Lyceum was returned to its owners, the Shuberts.

Including the Lyceum, the Shuberts own seventeen Broadway theaters outright and have a half ownership with composer Irving Berlin in the Music Box. The Shuberts own the largest theater, the Broadway, with a capacity of 1,788, and the smallest, the Booth, with a capacity of 781. The sixteen non-Shubert Broadway theaters are owned by thirteen different managements.

Despite the emphasis on musicals in the Broadway theater, there are more dramatic houses than musical houses. Twenty theaters are essentially drama-oriented, although in recent seasons half of them have become what are known in the trade as "swing houses," which can shift over to a musical if a play is not available for booking, and have booked small-scale musicals such as *Irma La Douce* at the Plymouth in 1960, *Hair* at the Biltmore in 1968, and *Celebration* at the Ambassador in 1969. There are twelve musical houses as such, some of which have occasionally housed dramatic attractions or even one-man shows. Marlene Dietrich, for example, performed solo in the cavernous Mark Hellinger Theater in 1968, and John Gielgud delivered *Ages of Man* in 1959 alone from the stage of the 1,400-seat 46th Street Theatre. Two theaters—the Broadhurst and the Martin Beck—book dramas as often as musicals.

For plays, the most intimate and desirable theaters are the Booth, the Golden, the Biltmore, Henry Miller's, and the Lyceum, all with a capacity of under a thousand. The Golden in recent seasons has booked a succession of small revues: Comden and Green, Flanders and Swann, Nichols and May, *Beyond the Fringe,* and *Wait a Minim.*

Each theater has its own character, personality, and even individual smell, and a producer will try to match his show with a theater that seems to suit the show's special qualities even though the exigencies of booking often get in the way. Theater owner Michael Myerberg redecorated the old Mansfield Theatre on West 47th Street and renamed it the Brooks Atkinson, after *The New York Times'* distinguished drama critic emeritus. "I wanted a comedy theater," he said, and he used gay colors inside and installed cloth-of-gold walls. Announcing that it had exactly the right tone and feel for comedy, he said, "It would be hard to imagine a tragedy in it." Nevertheless, one of the theater's first bookings was the heavy semidocumentary drama, *The Deputy,* which dealt with the wartime neutrality of Pope Pius XII in the face of Hitler's atrocities against the Jews. On opening night angry pickets marched in front of Myerberg's comedy theater.

Names have a certain indefinable influence on theater personality. Nine theaters are named for theatrical producers, managers, or directors: the George Abbott, the Alvin,[8] the Martin Beck, the (David) Belasco, the (John) Golden, Henry Miller's, the (Oliver) Morosco, the Billy Rose, and the (Sam S.) Shubert. Four are named for actors and actresses: the Ethel Barrymore, the (Edwin) Booth, the Helen Hayes, and the Lunt-Fontanne. Two are named for newspapermen: the Brooks Atkinson and the Mark Hellinger, and only one, the Eugene O'Neill, for a playwright.

Two blocks—44th and 45th streets *west* of Broadway—are the prime theater blocks. In 1969 eleven of the thirty-four Broadway houses were clustered along these precious few square feet of Manhattan real estate, and producers vie for these houses. To have a hit on 45th Street is to have arrived; more pragmatically, it assures a show of longer life because of "walk-in" trade, the impulse-buyers who go from show to show looking for tickets. These streets, however, whose theaters command higher rentals because of location, do not necessarily guarantee brisk attendance; the crowds, almost by telepathy, ignore the flop, and failure on 45th Street is as ignominious as anywhere else.

Some theaters are known as "jinx" houses because they never seem to get a hit, only a succession of quick closers. The jinx theaters by and large are on the fringe—the outer edges of the district. Ironically, only a few hundred yards separate the "fringe" from the magnetic middle. The George Abbott on 54th Street, the Longacre on 48th Street

[8] The acronymous Alvin on 52nd Street opened in 1927 and took its name from the first two syllables of the first names of two partners in musical-comedy production who also controlled the theater, Alex A. Aarons and Vinton Freedley.

west of Broadway, and the Cort on 48th Street east of Broadway are considered the least desirable theaters to book, and in the competitive booking scramble they are allotted the least promising plays. For many years the Ambassador on 49th Street just west of Broadway was considered a jinx house until *You Know I Can't Hear You When the Water's Running* by Robert Anderson changed its luck by running there two seasons. In 1969 the Ambassador was back to "jinx" status.

In an expanding economy, theaters are dismayingly inelastic. Extra seats and rows have been crowded into theaters in an effort to upgrade dramatic houses into musical houses or to improve the weekly gross in other ways, but there is a limit to this stretching. Theaters can be expanded only so far and remain effective, because if the line of contact between live actor and live audience is too greatly attenuated the meaning of live theater is destroyed.[9]

Theater owners either have their offices in the theaters they own or only a few blocks away. For example, the Shuberts manage their theaters and their extensive real estate holdings from a suite of offices on the sixth floor of the Sardi Building, which they own. The Shubert lawyers, Bernard B. Jacobs and Gerald Schoenfeld, who have a hand in almost every major decision affecting the chain—even to the booking of individual shows—are in the Shubert Theatre building. Their names never appear on the marquees or in the programs and outside of theater circles they are unknown, but great theatrical power rests in their hands.

Their offices occupy two rooms of what was once Lee Shubert's baronial apartment. A tiny three-passenger elevator ascends to the fifth floor, where a narrow corridor opens into a large, square reception room in which there is an oriental rug and an unused ornamental piano in one

[9] The O'Keefe Center, a 3,000-seat auditorium in Toronto, is a glaring example of architecture destroying impact by increasing capacity irrationally. At the O'Keefe, which actors call the "football field" or the "charnel house," the distance between stage and audience is so vast that the link between them is gone. Acoustically, emotionally, psychologically, and geographically the O'Keefe is an anti-theater theater.

corner with a vase of artificial flowers. On the walls are two large oil portraits of Sam S. Shubert, the talented Shubert brother who was killed in a train wreck in 1905 at the age of twenty-nine and whose picture is also in the lobby of every Shubert theater in America.

A hallway to the right leads into Lee Shubert's former living quarters. The large room at the back, once Lee's bedroom, now serves as Gerald Schoenfeld's office. His partner, Jacobs, is next door in what was Lee's living room. The two lawyers and the other Shubert executives work together harmoniously, unlike the founders of the empire they now administer. The brothers, Lee and J. J. Shubert, ruled their holdings for many years on a fifty-fifty basis without speaking to each other except through intermediaries. Lee had his office next to his apartment in a small oval room in the corner of the building while J. J. set up his command post in the Sardi Building across the way. Each looked straight past the other when they passed on the street. The divided-office setup survives to this day, although there is no family rancor left. (There is no family left.)

When dusk falls on the district the theater wakes up. At about seven an actress comes out of the 47th Street exit of the BMT subway on her way to work, a white scarf knotted under her chin, her pale face scrubbed clean of make-up, a leather pouch bag large enough to hold a script and a change of clothing swinging at her side as she strides down the street. She must sign in on the stage-door bulletin board at "half hour"—thirty minutes before the curtain goes up— and only after the performance, when everyone goes home, does her free time begin. On Broadway, the night of the tourist is the day of the actor, and the actor's own night extends past midnight into the day ahead.

An hour after the casts gather in their dressing rooms, theatergoers crush down Broadway and into the side streets like bargain hunters at a fire sale. Traffic jams up, custom limousines line the district, and the affluent audiences from New York and out of town—sweet-smelling, well dressed, and shining with anticipation—push into the theaters.

The heaviest theatergoing months are from October through mid-June, when 35,000 to 40,000 theatergoers invade the district each night. These people absorb and incubate the attitudes, styles, and messages of the plays and musicals they see, and they function on the upper levels of American life. The district exerts enormous influence locally, nationally, and even on a world scale. The industry grosses $60 million a year, which is insignificant when compared to other industries, and yet the theater holds an acknowledged place of importance in the total economy of New York City. Tourism, for example, is New York's second largest industry; in 1968 New York City entertained 16.5 million visitors who spent $1.5 billion in the city, and at the top of the list of popular attractions for the visitor was the Broadway theater district, an area whose character and function cannot be duplicated in any other city in the country.

Broadway has learned from strike experience that when theaters are dark, restaurants are poorly patronized, hotels have vacancies, and peripheral industries—garages, specialty shops, nightclubs, and the like—languish. "Without the theater," said Mayor Robert F. Wagner during the actors' strike of 1960, "what's the point of visiting New York City?"

Socially and culturally the theater transmits the group instinct far beyond its immediate audience. If a play opens on Broadway, if it captures the attention of its first audiences, if the critics endorse it, if it succeeds in gathering momentum and fresh audiences, if it survives, it becomes a part of history. It will take its place in dramatic literature and will travel widely for years, decades, perhaps for generations. The plays of Edward Albee, Tennessee Williams, Arthur Miller, Paddy Chayefsky, William Inge, Murray Schisgal, and Neil Simon (to mention only some obvious leaders) are performed the world over in many languages and on countless stages. From Broadway the word spreads, the play earns royalties—in money and in the power of word and thought. Fame, fortune, and influence spin off. Other media—television, film, the novel—await the successful playwright, actor, director, producer. The theater district is a central power station in the circuitry of communications.

For sixty years a twenty-six-square-block area in midtown Manhattan has been the home of show business and the creative core of the American theater. Once fashionable, then blighted, it is no longer either, but it has become choice real estate for high-rise builders and its future as the home of the theater is in jeopardy. Brownstones and low-rent stores have vanished from Sixth Avenue, which is lined today with sheathed skyscrapers. The Broadway area seemed immune from the developers—"Too far west," real estate men said. Then in 1966 the Allied Chemical Company took over the Times tower at 42nd Street and Broadway. Next the stolid Hotel Astor, which anchored the theater district in place, fell to the wreckers and became rubble in 1968. (The sturdy Astor did not yield without a fight—two wrecking companies went broke trying to tear it down.) It is clear that the district in its present form is doomed. In another ten years, a major theater operator predicts, half the present Broadway houses will be gone. The district trembles daily to the sounds of pneumatic drills and the thud of dynamite charges going off in the bedrock of the West Side.

Mayor John V. Lindsay and his administration have taken special steps to preserve the character of the theater district in the face of encroaching real estate interests. The City Planning Commission now offers special waivers and easements to builders for putting theaters into new office towers. The first developer to take advantage of the new regulations was Sam Minskoff & Sons, which planned the One Astor Plaza Theatre, a fifty-story office building on the Astor site that includes a 1,600-seat musical house in the ground-floor plan. Other theater-office buildings are projected, and the City Planning Commission is promoting a "mix" of such theaters, combining off-Broadway-size drama theaters with the larger musical houses, and open-stage theaters with conventional proscenium stages.

There are also indications that the theater district may become more fragmented, moving into other locations in the city, possibly to the west and north of Times Square, continuing the historic pattern of uptown movement. No one in 1969 could be quite sure of the direction, but no one denied that physical change could no longer be contained, not even by the strongest sentimental attachment to things as they were.

However deep the change, certain things will remain unchanged. The essence of theater is revealed only at night when the curtains are up. The English director John Dexter once remarked, "Something's got to happen along about nine o'clock in a musical." He meant that by that time the opening numbers are out of the way, the characters have been introduced, the exposition has been laid out, and now something has to *happen*. The confirmed bachelor Henry Higgins must begin to realize the unsettling effect of having a woman in his life, especially a common Cockney flower girl. The irrepressible matchmaker Dolly Levi, having picked one Horace Vandergelder for herself, must begin to clear the field of all rivals—except Mrs. Irene Molloy. The good father Tevye must begin to realize that his marriageable daughter Tzeitel, breaking ancient tradition, will refuse the rich husband he has chosen in favor of a poor tailor named Motel.

The laws of dramatic construction call for a turning point about thirty minutes into the evening. By nine o'clock the in-gathering of traffic into the district has subsided, and the bumper-to-bumper procession of cabs and limousines has dispersed. The streets have quieted. The audience sits in warm darkness before the lit stage. In the box office the treasurers straighten their ticket racks and count up the day's receipts. A few ushers converse in undertones in the drafty lobby. The backstage doorman puts his feet up for a smoke, the early-evening edition of the *Daily News,* open to the racing page, in his lap. And then, in the thirty darkened theaters of the district, almost at once, it begins to happen.

CHAPTER TWO

The Vanishing Producer

"Everything that happens on Broadway happens *because* of the producer. He has the ideas. He goes out and finds the scripts. He gets the people together to put them on."

This definition is from David Merrick, producer, commanding and controversial figure in the American theater. His evaluation of the producer's role may seem self-serving, but it is fundamentally accurate.

What is a producer? What does a producer do? The general public, which may understand the function of a stockbroker or automobile dealer or manufacturer of machine tools, has trouble grasping the meaning of a theater producer's existence. What does a producer do? Most producers don't really know. They just get the show on.

In sociological terms, the producer is the superordinate of the world of the playmakers. He must be an effective fund raiser, unless he possesses a substantial personal fortune. Since he leads battalions of theatrical subordinates, he must be able to command and deserve authority, subject to the rigors of powerful unions. Prodigious energy and basic taste are important, if not vital. Failure is endemic to his profession, and the producer must learn to transcend it, but success is almost as difficult to live with. In getting the show on, the producer must be innovator, talent scout, catalyst, and promoter.

The best producers generally possess most if not all of these diverse attributes. They are, on the whole, a colorful and exasperating lot. There is a touch of the poet and of the charlatan in them. They feed their own impressive egos while decrying the egos of their fellows.

When the show opens, it is the producer who bears the final responsibility—praise or blame—for what is on the stage. Out of the raw materials of script, live actors, scenery, costumes, and lights, he has supervised the creation of a world in microcosm. He is creator and *Ubermensch*.

The Broadway producer is a product of the last sixty or seventy years. A century ago the theater in America was an actor's theater—he was his own manager and leading man, and frequently his own playwright, director, and designer. Actor-managers like Dion Boucicault and Edwin Booth had their counterparts in every country.

As theater became more complex, the men who concentrated on producing emerged—Charles Frohman and his brother Daniel, Florenz Ziegfeld, Gilbert Miller, David Belasco, Max Gordon, Sam Harris, and a hundred others. His power was sweeping, and he generally financed his plays from his own exchequer or with the help of a few friends.

Gradually, writers' guilds developed, craft unions expanded, production costs grew, and the producer became less a lone operator and more a chairman of the board. His powers as employer dwindled, and in time his only unchallenged right has become the right to close the show. All else—wage minimums, employment tenure, control of material—is subject to approval from others.

In the era of bigness and mass communication, the theater producer persists. His ranks are depleted regularly, but just as regularly they are filled up. There are no examinations, applications, or quotas for producers—anyone who can find a script and raise the money to finance its production is *ipso facto* a producer. In many ways it is easier to be a producer than to get a job as a stagehand.

"The problem," producer Alexander H. Cohen says, "is not how to become a producer. The problem is how to stay alive as a producer."

The vague public image of the theater producer is an amalgam of notions that go back many years in the mass memory. The image is overdrawn, absurd, inaccurate, and unfair—but there is a lot of truth in it.

In novels, plays, and films about the theater, the producer rarely comes off as a fully rounded character. References to him are usually pejorative and more often than not he is a figure to be patronized, ridiculed, or disdained. His ethics are considered questionable, his personal appearance flamboyant but less than debonair, his literacy marginal. Movies, particularly the now-camp epics of the 1930's, are probably most responsible for the producer myth, portraying an *arriviste* complete with cigar and casting couch, ready to fleece elderly angels and exploit young playwrights. In the Sunday *New York Times* in March 1969 Walter Kerr wrote, "You see, [the theatrical investor] still has the old image in his head, the image of a producer making a get-rich-quick pitch to a possible investor at razzle-dazzle speed, painting beautiful pictures of the profits to come while promising him a spare blonde just to keep him comfy in the meantime." Zero Mostel's hilarious portrayal of the Broadway producer in the film *The Producers* is the cliché at its ultimate. Nothing is too scruffy for Max Bialystock, the character Mostel plays. He seduces dowagers to raise money; he sells 500 per cent of the play, hoping the play will flop and 400 per cent will fall into his lap; and he puts on a musical comedy with Adolf Hitler as a sympathetic character. Extreme though it is, the concept mirrors what many people, including Mel Brooks, the scriptwriter, think of producers and producing.

The obvious sources of the myth were the Shuberts, the Klaws, and the Erlangers, and a hundred grubby imitators of these ferocious pioneers of early-twentieth-century Broadway. The myth of the producer as untutored, unethical, and ungentle is the fruit of early struggles and, like all myths, it has ballooned beyond reality.

It is hard to assess the producer's role in the contemporary Broadway theater because so few producers actually make a living from producing. Of the hundred producer-members of the League of New York Theatres, not more than a dozen or so are active on a sustained basis, and not more than a dozen can be said to derive all or most of their income from producing. They are the competent (and lucky) survivors who parlay one hit into another, who produce enough hits to carry the flops, or for whom one blockbuster (it must be a musical in today's theatrical economy) has piled up enough subsidiary income to see them through a year or more of disaster. Most of the other producers either have an independent income or other, more reliable, employment. It is significant that when the producers interviewed were asked if they would recommend producing as a career to others, none said yes, and most of them mentioned outside income as a prerequisite.

This means that most producers operate on a part-time basis, and the trouble with producing part-time is that the theater demands total concentration. The really successful producers—men like David Merrick, Harold Prince, Saint-Subber, Stuart Ostrow, Alexander H. Cohen, Robert Whitehead, Theodore Mann, Kermit Bloomgarden, and Edgar Lansbury—devote both waking and sleeping hours to producing. They may waste time and energy on false leads and aborted projects, but at least they are working toward a definite goal. Even the most total concentration, however, cannot guarantee success or a consistent income.

Any survey of working producers must be unscientific, because the profession is so fluid and volatile, but in examining the roster of the dozen or so leaders of the producing fraternity, some insights may be gained.

Producers are a diverse group mainly in background and tastes, but they have a few characteristics in common. They are all devoted to the theater even as they deprecate it. All have something of the promoter in their make-up. All fluctuate drastically between bleak pessimism and wild optimism, depending on the state of the play they're involved with. All of them have a strong gambling streak. A Broadway producer is a picaresque combination of idealism and pragmatism; he resents being treated as a merchant, but he rages at the alleged impracticality of the "artists" he employs.

Very few top Broadway producers are what you might call "trained businessmen." The backgrounds of America's corporate oligarchy reveal specific and orderly patterns of education and training, but the theater has no school for producers. As for the producers discussed in this chapter, one was originally a theater accountant, two were attorneys, two were stage managers, one was a designer, one an actor, one a music publisher, and one a public-relations counsel—not one was a "trained businessman." Spectacular business careers, in fact, do not guarantee spectacular producing careers, for the rules of the marketplace do not apply in the world of the playmaker. Theater can only be learned from the inside out, not from the outside in.

Yet it would be a mistake to assert that because the business aspects of theater have lunatic overtones—there is no even flow of capital into theater and no possible way of predicting income—it can then function without scrupulous regard to the balance sheet. In the crucible of Broadway a producer, whatever his past experience, must become a businessman to survive; if he does not learn the business rhythms of the theater, exotic though they may be, he is doomed.

The producer participates in every phase of playmaking. Handling prosaic business details, sharing in delicate artistic decisions, he alone deals with every department and every person, from the backer to the star. All productions must start with a producer's go-ahead. He supplies the capital and he must spark the production and breathe life into it, first by assembling the creative staff and cast, then by making sure they work together productively, and finally by setting an artistic tone for the project. He must promote the show, presell it to parties and mail-order patrons, guide it safely past the tumultuous Broadway opening, coax it through its critical first weeks, help it to establish a run, and make sure as the weeks go by that the morale of the cast is kept up and the performances hold shape. Into the space of months, the producer must crowd the parental duty of a lifetime.

The first truth about the producer is that no credentials are needed for the job. And the second truth is that no matter how impressive one's credentials, they are never adequate to the demands of the job. The theoretical possibility of anyone breaking into producing is part of its great allure. In 1950 Theodore Mann, a lawyer by training, and José Quintero, a young Panama-born director, founded off-Broadway's landmark theater, the Circle in the Square, with capital of under a thousand dollars. Mann says, "All you need are whatever ingenuity, novelty, and originality you can bring to it. New people are forever breaking in. You pick up the ball game from wherever you are."

Mann's early legal background counts for little in his present work, since there was no precedent for establishing the Circle in the Square, and no precedent for its success. He says, "The way to be part of the theater is to create your own." Since he began in 1950, Mann has produced about fifty plays, including the major modern revivals of Eugene O'Neill, at the Circle in the Square and on Broadway.[1]

Alexander Cohen started at the top as a producer in 1941 on the strength of a $55,000 trust fund turned over to him on his twenty-first birthday. All but $4,000 disappeared immediately in a four-day flop entitled *Ghosts for Sale*. Within

---

[1] Mann keeps a bound volume of each script he has produced in a bookcase in his office above the Circle in the Square in Greenwich Village. The fattest volume is *Long Day's Journey Into Night* and the slimmest is *Hughie*—both plays, fittingly, by Eugene O'Neill.

a few months, without a backward glance, Cohen put the $4,000 into *Angel Street,* which turned into a hit, and his lifetime career was settled.

Few professions offer such freedom and such scope for self-expression. In many ways the producer is the ultimate embodiment of the free-thinking individualist who is accountable only to himself. For Edgar Lansbury, who produced and designed films and television shows before he came into the theater on the success of Frank D. Gilroy's *The Subject Was Roses,* theater means escape from dependency on the studio or network front office. And for Stuart Ostrow, who got into producing from the music-publishing business and had a hit at age thirty-six with the musical *1776,* theater is an attractive profession partly because the limited-partnership form of agreement under which Broadway shows are financed gives the backers no artistic control over a production. There is no sponsor as there is in television and no bank as in films to pre-empt the power of decision—the "let's do it" choice that is precious and unique to the theater producer.

Producing is a full-time activity requiring a full day in the office and theatergoing at night. Producers must keep up not only with regularly opening commercial shows but also with tryouts, workshop productions, and new work being done out of town. The time burden is enormous—there is a never-ending list of chores awaiting the producer each day and the demands upon his energy are prodigious.

Very few persons survive as producers. Approximately 40 per cent of each season's crop of shows bear the names of new producers—that is, each year there are between fifteen and twenty new producers, of whom the vast majority retire in confusion after the baptism of chaos that attends a resounding flop. Four or five, cheered by initial success, will go on to produce again, but only one or two will continue to produce year after year. Failure—repeated failure—dries up the will to produce and the "angel" money that backs plays.

Statistics in the theater are incomplete but relentless.

Of the forty-five to fifty productions each season on Broadway, no more than one out of four or five will be hits; of these, no more than two or three will bear the names of new producers, and, in most cases, these men will have teamed with a veteran to get the play or musical on the boards.

Broadway producers are generally men ("Even when they're women," quips one theatrical-company manager). A number of lady producers have distinguished themselves over the years—Irene Mayer Selznick, who produced *A Streetcar Named Desire*, *The Chalk Garden*, and *Bell, Book and Candle;* Cheryl Crawford, whose credits include *Brigadoon* and *Sweet Bird of Youth;* and Claire Nichtern, the sponsor of *Luv* and *Jimmy Shine*. But in 1969, out of approximately a hundred producer-members of the League of New York Theatres, only seven were women and only one or two are consistently active as producers. The theater jungle seems fittest for men, and most women who succeed as producers usually shuck femininity for the abrasive and mannish cynicism of their brother impresarios. Off-Broadway, the percentage of women producers is sharply higher; at least 30 per cent of the 1969 off-Broadway shows were produced by women. But these ladies are generally younger and fresher than their uptown sisters.

For the most part, producers are well aware of their psychological motivations. Some are in the business because of a frustrated desire to write or perform, others partly because of the gratification that comes from close association with the greatly talented, and still others for the notoriety. Alexander Cohen admits that his desire for public attention is so intense that the reduction of daily newspapers in New York and the resulting diminished theatrical news coverage is a personal hardship.

"When I first came into the business there were ten newspapers in New York," said Cohen. "John Jones of the *Daily News* would call up and beg you not to tell Tom Smith of the *Evening Sun* what your next play was going to be. If I called up Lou Calta on *The New York Times* and told him

I had a script in my hand called *The Big Tickle* there would be a headline in the *Times* the next day and a story saying Cohen is reading a new script entitled *The Big Tickle.* You couldn't take a script to the bathroom without a report appearing in some newspaper.

"I don't know how many people recognize the yearning for publicity in themselves. Part of the reason for my being in the business in the old days was the publicity. You were constantly in the public mind. We counted it a triple if we got the lead in the theater-news column of the *Times* three days in a row. It was a home run if you got Thursday, Friday, Saturday, and Funke on Sunday.[2] Part of my disenchantment with the business today is that there are only three papers left and the major one, the *Times,* doesn't give a damn about the theater."

With newsprint for theater so drastically curtailed, Cohen started his own TV program. "When I get a play I think of its potential as a ballyhoo," he says. He is so adept at preselling a show that sometimes the long run that only grows out of quality material eludes him. "I've always had a line for all of my productions *before* the show opened," he once said ruefully. A precise administrator of great energy, Cohen floods his confreres in his Shubert Theatre office with memos, push-button phones, and sophisticated office gadgetry. He is a master of the proper gesture—opening-night telegrams, engraved party invitations, red-carpet proprieties, all the traditions that display the folkways of the theater in the grand manner.

Whatever the subsidiary satisfactions, the actual production gives the producer the greatest enjoyment. Fully realized work is the pay-off for the long make-ready period—the months of searching for the right script, of casting, rehearsing, and polishing, often of heart-breaking delays. Kermit Bloomgarden, a distinguished Broadway producer for nearly thirty years, says, "The only time I have any fun is when I'm producing a play. Just reading and looking for plays

[2] See Chapter 9 for the influence of Lewis Funke's Sunday *Times* column, "News of the Rialto."

is not any fun. Living with the play, watching rehearsals, watching as the actors begin to catch hold, finally watching the whole play emerge—this is the fun of it for me. The most exciting part of all is the last week of rehearsals. With the first run-throughs, the whole thing comes alive."

The notion that producers are creatures of insolvency is inaccurate. Successful producing has corollary financial rewards. A smash hit in the theater can bring the producer huge profits that continue for many years. *The Music Man,* produced by Kermit Bloomgarden, which opened in 1957 and ran for nearly three and a half years (1,375 performances) on Broadway, has so far earned $4.5 million on a $300,000 investment and paid backers almost eight dollars for every dollar invested. The producer and his co-producers, who have already received $2.25 million, will continue to receive profits, as will investors, for seventeen years from the date of the Broadway opening, or through 1974. (This seventeen-year period of subsidiary payments is part of the original agreement between the producer and the authors.) *Fiddler on the Roof* is an even bigger financial bonanza. It opened in 1964 and by the end of 1969 had realized a total profit in excess of $5 million and was still going strong.

These are blockbusters. Every producer longs for one, and when it comes, if it comes, it repays agonizing months of inaction or failure. "I don't know why we become producers," says David Merrick. "It isn't the money. Theater is practically a nonprofit business now.[3] Sure, you can hit with a big one. But you can lose it all on the others. For the investor we have to hold out the hope of that big one coming along and we try to make them money. But we can't always. I suppose we're in the business because of the fame or because we're frustrated artists ourselves and like to work with creative people. I don't really know why we become producers."

The frequency of production varies from producer to pro-

[3] Merrick's personal profits in twenty years of Broadway production are estimated on good authority to be "pretty close to $5 million."

ducer. Merrick, who may be responsible for as many as five shows a season, expresses the catholicity of Broadway, balancing dramas with musicals, alternating musicals with comedies, and working on all of them at once. Other producers, such as Kermit Bloomgarden, who has presented such fine dramas as Arthur Miller's *Death of a Salesman* and Lillian Hellman's *The Autumn Garden,* deplore the assembly-line routine of mass production and will only deal with one play at a time. Whatever the method, few theatrical projects, from the time the script is optioned to opening night, can be realized in less than a year, and for musicals it is longer. Harold Prince, keeping to a precise timetable, allows six months to decide on a project ("That's six months examining and rejecting material and finding it and picking it," he says) and another year to get it on. Prince opened his musical *Zorbá* almost exactly two years after *Cabaret.* His next musical should be ready about two years after *Zorbá's* opening night.

In a career that began with a hit *(Pajama Game)* and spans sixteen productions, Prince has had only six failures (four musicals and two plays). Most producers have had to survive early failure to achieve later success. Bloomgarden had *Heavenly Express,* a quick failure, in 1941 before he had *Deep Are the Roots* in 1945. David Merrick had the innocuous *Clutterbuck* in 1949 before he hit with his second show, *Fanny,* in 1954. Stuart Ostrow closed a musical called *We Take the Town* during its tryout in Philadelphia in 1961, and waited eight years for his first big musical success, *1776,* in 1969. Whitehead's *Medea* in 1947 and his next show, *Crime and Punishment,* the same year were artistic successes but financial failures, and it was not until 1950 that he scored his first big success with *The Member of the Wedding,* winning the Drama Critics Circle Award.

For the successful, the driving compulsion to produce rarely weakens, and producers frequently commit themselves and move into the production phase before a project is ready or when it is an unwise project to begin with. It is easier to get in than to turn back. Clive Barnes, the *Times* drama critic, observes, "The producer is going to produce and if he hasn't got a good show he's going to produce a bad show. He's going to do the best he can do. Very often they put on shows that they know aren't going to last the week out, but they can't go to their backers and say, 'Well, the reason this was a failure was that it was a bad show to start with, and we did the best with it, kids, but it was lost in New Haven.' Some producers have a great and lucky ability for deceiving themselves. On the other hand, I think deep down where it matters some of them have a pretty shrewd idea of what they've really got."

Plays are submitted to producers in an unending flow—mimeographed scripts bound in red, blue, green, gray, or black imitation-leather covers, mount higher and higher on their desks, spill out of bookcases, pile up in odd corners, more than they can possibly read themselves. Alexander Cohen's office logs in some 500 scripts a year, a figure that is standard for name producers. Cohen keeps several readers on the payroll to weed out obviously hopeless material and to flag scripts of possible merit. Whitehead has a script or two beside his bed for nighttime reading and gets through sixty to seventy-five a year. Mann reads between five and ten a week and his staff another ten. Ostrow and producer Leland Hayward religiously scan the galleys of new books before publication.

Cohen won't bother with scripts unless they are sent by reputable agents. Merrick, on the other hand, ferrets out new material personally and says he has never received a good idea from an agent.[4] "I've called somebody. I've seen something off-Broadway and asked a writer to show me his next work. I get a lot of scripts sent to me that are not produceable. The only one I've turned down that became a hit was *You Know I Can't Hear You When the Water's Running* by Robert Anderson."

Producers perennially complain about the scarcity of good material, to the dismay, disbelief, and anger of playwrights. Still, for the most part in disappointment, producers hunt

[4] There are agents who would dispute Merrick on this point.

for a play that is new but not too far ahead of the audience, a play of quality that will redound to their credit and yet will be commercial, a play that won't be too difficult to cast nor costly to mount and yet will be instantly promotable.

The producer finds the play, or he may commission it. "I never wait until the play comes to me," says Saint-Subber. He thinks of subjects for possible dramatization and spends large sums optioning plays and having writers rework scripts. They don't all work out. In 1968 Saint-Subber spent $30,000 on options, all to no purpose.

"I attempt twice as many projects as I put on," he said. He spent a year and a half on *The Grass Harp* by Truman Capote, two and a half years on Capote's *House of Flowers,* and another two and a half years on *The Square Root of Wonderful* by Carson McCullers. Three plays, seven years of work, all failures. Sometimes a play gets on more quickly. *Dark at the Top of the Stairs* by William Inge took only four months from the time Saint-Subber decided to do it until opening night, but that was partly because the dynamic Elia Kazan was the director and Inge was a "hot" playwright at the time.

Most of the ideas for musicals come from producers rather than writers. Leland Hayward visualized a musical after he read James Michener's *Tales of the South Pacific.* Rodgers and Hammerstein, as producers, took the idea of Ethel Merman playing Annie Oakley to Irving Berlin and got *Annie Get Your Gun.* Harold Prince and the late Robert E. Griffith, backed by George Abbott, saw a musical in Richard Bissell's *7½¢*, and it became *Pajama Game.* All of David Merrick's eighteen musicals—with the exception of four imports—originated with Merrick personally. It is a source of frequent irritation to producers that they come up with ideas for musicals but don't get program credit (or pride of authorship) for their trouble. As Merrick points out, "The phrase 'Conceived by David Merrick' isn't covered by the Dramatists Guild."

Merrick's greatest commercial musical-comedy success was his own brainchild, and proof supreme of the theory of the producer's creative initiative. ("You start with an idea, you tell them how you would do it, invariably they turn it down the first time, but you keep at it.") In 1962, Merrick conceived the idea of making a musical out of Thornton Wilder's play *The Matchmaker,* which he had presented on Broadway in 1956. He called in composer-lyricist Jerry Herman, who had written *Milk and Honey,* his only previous Broadway credit; Michael Stewart, who had written *Carnival* for Merrick; and Gower Champion, *Carnival's* director. They were skeptical at the first conference, but Merrick persisted, and signed Carol Channing, who had had indifferent luck after her early success in *Gentlemen Prefer Blondes.* The concept knitted, and the end result was *Hello Dolly!,* which has brought millions to all concerned.

With the straight play, the producer's creativeness is more subdued. He does not usually beget the project, although he may buy a book he likes and find a playwright to adapt it (Leland Hayward and *Mr. Roberts,* for example, or Fred Coe and *A Death in the Family,* which became *All the Way Home.)* In most cases, a producer will find a straight play in a foreign or out-of-town production or buy a script that comes full-blown or half-baked over his desk, submitted either by an agent or by the playwright himself. Frequently, in lasting producer-playwright relationships, ideas that originate in real-life stories or from casual observation or conversations are swapped and discussed and grow into Broadway productions.

All producers hate raising money but some find it less burdensome than others. For established producers it is almost routine. David Merrick has a small list of backers who have been with him since the early days, sharing in his good fortune. Harold Prince has had no problem raising money since his first show, *Pajama Game,* in 1953. To bring production money rolling in he simply mails out a chatty form letter to a list of about 150 people who invest with him regularly. Considering his overall record, the rate of return to his investors is extremely high. By the beginning of 1969 the sixteen Prince-produced shows had made a profit of nearly $13 million, and the 164 investors in *Pajama Game* have so far gained $7.56 for every dollar they spent on it. A few investors drop out and a few die. To allow for attrition the Prince office adds a dozen new names a year. Money-raising didn't bother Prince at the start when he was twenty-five and had nothing to lose. Now he is more successful but less carefree, and if unforeseen circumstances forced him to go out once more with hat in hand he might give up producing and concentrate on directing.

Money-raising, for other reasons, has not been such a problem to Stuart Ostrow, who has had no more than half a dozen backers on most of his shows, one of whom, Edgar M. Bronfman, of the Seagram family, put up $250,000 for *1776*.

Not everyone has a Bronfman for a friend. Producer Edgar Lansbury and author Frank D. Gilroy exhausted their list of friends in nearly two years to raise the $40,000 required for the three-character *The Subject Was Roses* in 1964, and it came in in dribs and drabs. "I'm not a huckster," said Lansbury, "and you have to be a huckster to raise money."

A run of bad luck erodes the confidence of old investors. Then, unless you have a well-known star, a name director, and everything going for you, raising money, according to Kermit Bloomgarden, can become a "hammer-and-tongs" affair.

Although production costs have mounted steeply and rising running costs have prolonged the period required for a show to pay back its initial investment, there still seems to be no lack of money for Broadway shows. In 1969 Merrick had to capitalize "a simple little play" (Woody Allen's one-set show with modest costumes, *Play It Again, Sam*) for $175,000 and he estimates that the same kind of play will require a capitalization of $200,000 in 1970. At the same time he expects a musical to become an $800,000 production in 1970 and to reach an even million by 1974. "I don't know why commercial people put up that kind of money," he says. "The interesting thing is that there is always financing. They always get the money." (*He* always gets the money.)

If costs on Broadway have doubled in the past fifteen

years, so, in some cases, have profits. With *Pajama Game* in 1954 Harold Prince was able to gross $52,000 a week and realize a profit of $12,000. With *Zorbá* in 1969 he was able to gross $104,000 a week and realize a profit of $24,000—both figures exactly doubled.

Producers "buy" the chief item on their shopping list—talent—through agents. The biggest producers—Merrick, Cohen, and Prince—all have their own casting departments which are kept busy finding replacements for running shows or casting new ones. Other producers appeal to agents to help them out of their casting dilemmas.

In the sensitive area of talent procurement David Merrick has a reputation for being rough. He does most of his contract negotiating for talent (stars, featured players, directors, choreographers, writers, designers, etc.) at arm's length through his general manager, Jack Schlissel, or his attorney, Ben Aslan of the firm of Fitelson & Mayers. Aslan, chunky, tough-talking and pugnacious, is a hard bargainer, feared and respected by agents and other lawyers. Merrick's terms are hard and Aslan interprets them rigidly. As one lawyer observes, "David will not let anyone—actors, directors, playwrights—get anything out of him easily." Where Merrick is tough, Aslan is tougher. An agent once attempted to negotiate what he felt would be a fair contract for his client, a director. He asked no more than his client had received on his last three shows. Aslan refused. "Everyone takes less with Merrick," he said.

Sometimes it is easier to deal with Merrick personally if Aslan can be bypassed. The great man can afford concessions; Aslan as the front man must stand firm. But, as one agent puts it, "Merrick would have to want you very badly to be generous." Merrick's need to employ talent for less money is part sharp business sense and part personal vanity—it pleases him to have people work for him for less.

It is this toughness that makes businessmen in the theater grudgingly admire Merrick while actors and playwrights dislike him, or at least have an ambivalent attitude toward him. Merrick is the busiest producer in the theater and the largest employer of talent. His record of success is some guarantee of length of employment in a notoriously short-term-employment business, and his reputation for getting good runs out of weak shows the ordinary producer would have long since abandoned is widely admired within the profession. Authors especially are beholden to him for his tenacity, because their income continues so long as Merrick keeps the show running. But for all these benefits Merrick exacts his own ego-bruising payment at contract time.

When the producer options a script and engages a director, the play in an artistic sense ceases to be the exclusive property of the playwright and becomes a collaborative project in which the original idea is interpreted by the director and is communicated by the actor. In the necessary and often uncomfortable collaboration among writer, director, actors, and the other theater artists, the producer must act as catalyst.

Kermit Bloomgarden describes the process: "The producer works with the author until the script is ready to go. Then producer and writer agree on a director. If the director wants changes in the script, producer and author work them out with the director. Then producer, author, and director choose a set and costume designer and the cast. Of course, contractually, the author has the final say on the creative people, but usually everyone is in agreement."

As author, director, and actors become deeply immersed in technical problems and frequently in differences of interpretation, the custodial producer must preserve objectivity. As Stuart Ostrow says, "Establishing and preserving the vision is his job. He has to remind everyone why they started to do it in the first place. The worst thing that can happen in a show is when people start to say, 'Let's try it this way instead.' Then the producer is urgently needed to step in and remind them of what everyone had in mind to start with and to keep them at it."

Most producers tend to keep their distance from actors, but they cannot avoid dealing directly with their stars. The actor who was hired in the first place partly because of his drawing power at the box office needs the constant attention of the producer to reaffirm that fact to himself.

Ziegfeld's lavishness with his stars is legendary—the garlands of dressing-room flowers, the cases of champagne, the banquets and limousines. Today's producers are generally less flamboyant, but the protocol of obeisance to stars is inviolable. A star requires and receives constant physical and emotional solicitude beyond the call of contract—or else.

The star must have the best dressing room and the right to decorate the dressing room to individual taste. When Rosalind Russell moved into the Broadhurst for *Auntie Mame,* her dressing room was refurbished from carpet to ceiling. When Greer Garson replaced Miss Russell after a year, the dressing room was redecorated lavishly and in a different style.[5]

The conscientious producer visits his star frequently, entertains him on off-stage occasions, remembers birthdays, anniversaries, and infirmities, and procures special favors with speed and good humor. A producer must also be able to listen patiently and at length to his star. ("I frequently think of myself as an unpaid combination psychiatrist-nursemaid," says producer Morton Gottlieb.)

On Broadway very few stars live up to the commercial excuse for their stardom—their drawing power. "Sure, he's a name; but will he sell tickets?" is the question producers must constantly ask themselves. In the old days before the media explosion, this was a cut-and-dried matter. The star had a ready-made public who would come to see him in any play that was tolerable for an evening—"He'll sell out reading the telephone book" was a Broadway cliché. But that day is over.

Only a few stars will draw box-office lines as soon as their names are announced for a Broadway show. Those few, whose charisma is heightened by other media (films, television,

---

[5] Ironically, the new paint job did not dry thoroughly enough and Miss Garson got a bad throat from the paint fumes and had severe laryngitis during the first fortnight of her run in the play.

recordings, or just plain notoriety), are worth the inflated prices they demand. Barbra Streisand, Richard Burton, Marlene Dietrich, Ingrid Bergman, Katharine Hepburn are some examples. But most actors who star on Broadway need hit reviews for their plays to last, and producers actively resent the money they get. "You can't get a star today for less than $3,000 a week against a percentage of the gross," says Jack Schlissel, general manager for David Merrick, "and that doesn't include the fringe benefits"—such as a limousine or daily hair styling at the production's expense. Producer Joel Schenker sought a male lead for his musical, *Darling of the Day,* in 1968. "We were offered a real no-draw guy," he recalls, "who had played Henry Higgins in a third road company of *My Fair Lady.* He wanted $2,500 a week and a percentage; he meant nothing, but he could play the part, so we agreed. Then he asked for free dinners on Saturdays between the matinee and evening performances. We blew the deal. Later we had to settle for someone who got $5,000 a week and wasn't a draw, either. I guess we should have paid for the dinners."

As shows cost more to produce, they must run longer to pay off, and as they run longer, producers want their stars to stay longer. Understandably, stars resist long runs, hoping to restrict their contracts to six months or at most a year. Merrick is nearly alone among producers who can today insist upon two-year commitments from major names. (Judy Holliday played over four years in *Born Yesterday,* but such devotion to the stage is unknown along Broadway now.) A dissenting note is struck by Harold Prince, who says, "Stars don't interest me and I don't interest them." He prefers shows to create their own stars, as *West Side Story* did for Carol Lawrence, *Fiorello!* for Tom Bosley, *A Funny Thing Happened on the Way to the Forum* for Zero Mostel (as a musical star), and *Zorbá* for Herschel Bernardi.

Except for the stars, producers prefer to deal with actors through intermediaries. Merrick refers to actors as children not to be trusted with such grown-up matters as politics or money management. Stuart Ostrow expresses similar views: "They are childlike, capricious, and better to watch from afar. I appreciate their talent and I am willing to pay for them, but I don't want to be involved in their problems and vanities. That's why I hire a director. Handling the actors is part of his job."

The relationship between producer and working actor has caused considerable resentment on both sides. Producers are annoyed by actors' egotism. Actors, fired by insecurity and the business agents of their unions, look on producers as money-grubbing exploiters; the late Ben Irving, a highly respected and aggressive Actor's Equity official, said reflexively of producers, "They ride on the backs of the actors." But supply and demand work in favor of the producers. The actor needs the producer more than the producer needs the actor, so the producer can afford to be high-handed.

The distance a producer keeps from his actors is necessary in another, more practical way. A good producer must be objective and protect his authority. He is chairman of the board, responsible for the "big picture"; the day-by-day minutiae of the company are the responsibility of his foremen and personnel directors.

By tradition, the hit play opens, is hailed by the critics, and settles down to a long run accompanied by acclaim and lasting dividends. But Broadway plays do not operate on a perpetual-motion principle, and producers cannot survive or be judged solely as men who put the play together and get it on. It also has to keep running—at a profit, both in New York and on the road. Once the product emerges for public consumption, the modern producer must become salesman and merchandiser. Merchandising techniques have become more urgent and sophisticated—and expensive. Building up the play's advance sale, nursing it to run through fair weather and foul, strikes and emergencies, are producers' responsibilities which are not very glamorous but are crucial to the work.

It is common for producers to have general managers— men or women who tend strictly to the play's business and leave top-echelon decisions to the boss. Some general managers stay in this "vice president in charge of sales and operations" category indefinitely; others graduate to become producers themselves.

The producer's dealings with ticket brokers and theater-party agents begin early in the life of the play. He will try to interest brokers in a "buy"—a block purchase of thousands of tickets in advance of opening—which commits the broker to push the show.[6] And if he can stimulate the interest of theater-party agents, who in turn act for charity-benefit committees, he may be able to dispose of full-house theater parties long before the show opens and the reviews—good or bad—are in.

Producers don't really like theater parties, but they need them to fight mixed reviews. When a producer feels most insecure about his play, his campaign to book parties and woo party agents reaches peak intensity. The love-hate relationship of producers and party agents is abiding and sometimes amusing. The charities want hit shows and will flock to the "sure things"—the big-name plays or musicals that will help them assuage the pain of inflated prices ($50 and $100 surcharges on regular $10, $12, and $15 tickets are usual). When a producer has a "sure thing" show, he plays hard to get with the parties. When the party agents know they are dealing with a show their charities will not sell easily, they play hard to get with the producers. The minuet is endless, and it is particularly ironic when the "sure thing," swollen with parties, opens to disastrous reviews, and the "sleeper," partyless and patronized, becomes a smash hit and doesn't need the parties after all.

While parties and "buys" are helpful, all producers concede that parties alone can never provide the margin between success and failure or offset significantly the devastating financial effects of bad notices. "We make the mistake of booking far too many parties," says Harold Prince. "We should have more faith in our shows." Every producer will agree that theater parties are unnecessary with a hit and

---

[6] It also forces him to "eat" the tickets if the show is a failure and the public simply refuses to buy the seats at any price.

can't save a flop, but it's a form of insurance, and parties
continue to be sought and booked, administered by a covey
of colorful middle-aged ladies who are treated by producers
with a mixture of fear and affection.

As employers, producers must deal not only with the
unions and guilds which represent the "creative echelon"—
the actors, playwrights, directors, designers, and composers
—but with a bewildering array of tightly organized craft
unions. These unions blanket every facet of production. The
stagehands are organized, as are the managers and press
agents, the musicians and the wardrobe mistresses and
dressers, the truckers and the painters of scenery, the treasurers and ushers and backstage doormen and engineers,
and even the boys who sell orange drinks and souvenir books
in the lobby.

Theatrical unions are aggressive in their demands, rigid
in their bargaining, and their work rules are restrictive. Long
before the inflationary cycle began, the theatrical unions
were exerting their powers against the loosely organized
producers. There is no doubt that the extraordinary rise in
stage production and operating costs—far higher than the
rise in other fields of business—has been triggered by the
incessant wage inflation of the theater craft unions.

"Featherbedding!" is a favorite battle cry of the producers, particularly where musicians are involved. A musical
comedy in a Broadway house must employ a minimum of
twenty-five musicians, regardless of the composer's wishes.
Most composers don't complain too strenuously, on the
theory that the more musicians the better the music
sounds, but it is not uncommon for intimately orchestrated
shows that require no more than six or eight musicians to
employ the full complement of twenty-five simply because
they have to pay for them anyway, or to use only the six or
eight called for by the show while the others sit around
backstage and do nothing, or, which is more common, never
show up at all except to get paid. The trade phrase for such
absent players is "walking" musicians—they take their wages

and walk away, never to be seen again until next payday.[7]

The musicians' Broadway contract stipulates "contract" and "penalty" houses. If a theater is designated a contract house, it pledges to employ at least four musicians at regular pay (double pay for the conductor) even if a straight play without music is booked. If it is designated a penalty house, it need not hire any musicians except for musical attractions, but—and it is an expensive "but"—the wage scale for musicians in a contract house is considerably lower than in a penalty house. If a musical plays a penalty house its musicians' salary list is many hundreds of dollars a week (and thousands of dollars a year) more! [8] Each stagehand also represents about $10,000 per year, and some lavish musicals may be forced to hire five, six, or more stagehands than they actually need.

Considerable lagniappe accrues to unionists from various codified gradations of overtime. For instance, a stagehand working after midnight is on "golden time," or double his regular hourly wage. If a magazine photographer, with the management's approval, takes candid pictures of a show during an actual performance, the show must pay the entire stage crew, down to the lowliest grip, a minimum of three hours' extra pay even though the crew is being paid anyway to "work" the show for the regular audience.

Equity has a steadily lengthening list of rules prescribing extra pay for equivalent circumstances, although Equity is generally much more reasonable in its demands than some of its fellow unions. One Equity wrinkle for squeezing extra dollars from a work situation: only one record album—the

---

[7] "Walking" musicians are, like working musicians, entitled to vacation pay, which one Broadway manager refers to as "compensation for fatigue arising from idleness."

[8] The musicians' contract has other intriguing features, notably the demand for the payment of musicians when recorded music is used in a straight play and the arbitrary rule that a show with more than twenty-five minutes of music in it is considered a musical. In tryout towns, the musicians' unions are even more predatory. Once in Philadelphia an angry producer made his unnecessary orchestra play "The Star-Spangled Banner" in the men's lounge. The following year the union ruled that no musician could be required to play anywhere except onstage or in the orchestra pit.

"original cast" album—may use a photograph from a show without payment. All other albums using pictures from a show must pay a week's salary to each actor in the photograph, and the producer is held responsible for such payment. A union press agent now receives a week's pay for any recording session of a show he represents, although he literally has nothing to do at the session. Such extras—which amount to a kind of residual payment—have hardened by precedent into contract clauses, and go on and on and expensively on.

Producers complain in private about featherbedding but are fatalistic in public about the practice. "I take the attitude that if the play's any good it's going to carry everything," says Saint-Subber. "If it's no good, featherbedding is going to hurt the hell out of it."

Saint-Subber had a big hit in *Barefoot in the Park* but a flop subsequently in *Dr. Cook's Garden*. While *Barefoot* was running he used to play pinochle with the stagehands by the hour beneath the stage of the Biltmore Theatre, but when he saw stagehands idly playing pinochle during the wobbly run of *Dr. Cook's Garden* his attitude changed. Watching them playing on his time, like secretaries gossiping casually in the hall in the midst of an office crisis, irritated him unbearably.

Producers complain of inflexibility and endless escalation of demands on the part of unions, and, in truth, producers are virtually helpless in bargaining. But the basic laws of economics are inexorable, and for every gain made by unions, producers have to cut another corner. It is now economically unfeasible for musicals to have large choruses, so they have small choruses or, in some cases, like the new hit *1776,* no chorus at all. As scenery gets more expensive to build, producers make do with less scenery. Large-scale dramas are avoided in favor of small-cast, one-set plays (*The Great White Hope,* a success with a cast of sixty, is an exception). "Fewer are getting more and most are getting less," one producer notes wryly. Another producer specializes in one-man shows; he would cheerfully present a show with no cast at all if he could find one.

Building the scenery is usually the costliest single operation in a production, unless the show is a lavish multi-costume affair. The set designer picks the scenic shop, just as the costume designer decides which shoemaker, wig fitter, and costume house to use. A handful of shops quartered in lofts and warehouses in the city's fringe neighborhoods execute designs of such artists as William and Jean Eckart, Oliver Smith, David Hays, William Ritman, Jo Mielziner, and Ming Cho Lee. The labor costs of the carpenters and painters used by these shops run high (close to $60 a day), and frequently scenery will cost as much as 25 per cent of a show's total capitalization. Designers traditionally overspend. The late Herman Bernstein, for years an astute labor negotiator for producers, used to say, "Never tell a designer what you really want to spend. If you do, you're dead. You must give him a figure from 30 to 50 per cent lower than your limit. You say you'll spend $2,000 knowing you'll wind up spending $3,000. If you say $3,000, you'll wind up spending $5,000."

The brotherhood of organized labor is a great leveler. Oddly enough, the gifted scenic designers, along with lighting designers and costume designers, cannot work in the theater unless they are accredited members of the Brotherhood of Painters, Decorators, and Paperhangers of America, of which the United Scenic Artists is a local. And, like the Dramatists Guild, this union after almost a decade of desultory negotiations does not yet have a collective bargaining agreement with the League of New York Theatres. Nevertheless, it enforces arbitrary minimums, pay rates, and working conditions on an individual show-by-show basis that no producer dares violate.

The League of New York Theatres is in a constant state of crisis negotiation. If it isn't one contract, it's nine others. If it isn't the stagehands, it's the wardrobe attendants. If it isn't the treasurers, it's the directors. If it isn't the press agents and managers, it's the ushers. Long before the United States began negotiating with North Korea or with North Vietnam, the League discovered the secret to perpetual negotiation.

In all fairness to the unions, their lot is not always a happy

one either. Theater is only occasional work for most unionists and, unlike actors, designers, and directors, craft-union
members expect and get no billing. "We have to make the
hits pay for the flops; we can't live on glory," says one business agent for backstage workers. "We were exploited for
years," recalls a veteran stagehand who is over seventy. "I
remember when we got fifty cents a show." Of course, that
was fifty years ago, and he now averages $300 a week and
perquisites as a "house property man." By and large, the
craft unions don't care much about their public image. "The
public don't care about us," says the same business agent
quoted above, "and public relations don't buy groceries for
my guys."

A Broadway general manager sums up the union situation
in the theater: "You have to do business with unions. They
have a gun at your head. They can destroy you with a couple
of telephone calls. But they are still not as bad to bargain
with as, say, steamfitters or longshoremen. Many of them
really enjoy the glamour of the theater. And a really dedicated stagehand can save you a fortune. I wish I could say
the same for the musicians."

In day-to-day dealings with theatrical unions, the disu-
nited producers remain largely impotent. Only when a massive challenge faces them does any kind of solidarity develop
in their normally shattered ranks. Competitors at every
other level, the producers unite grandly during a labor crisis.
Joint action is taken through the League of New York Theatres, which, on most industrywide matters, can only suggest a course of action. Like an international-treaty proposal
that must be ratified individually by each sovereign state, a
League recommendation lacks binding force unless each producer individually gives consent, and the fraternity of producers is a congress of anarchists.

A rare insight into what producers really think of themselves was afforded during one of the bitter negotiating
sessions of the ten-day actors' strike of 1960.[9] The two op-

---

[9] It was the first such strike since 1919, six years after the union was organized. It was the forerunner of two more—in 1964 for one day and in
1968 for three days.

posing teams, a dozen on each side, shrilled abuse at each other in private and issued apocalyptic statements to the press. Into this overheated atmosphere attorney Herman E. Cooper dropped an incendiary remark: "What is a producer? What is a producer?" he demanded in a voice rising in sarcasm. And then he answered himself: "A producer is a businessman with artistic pretensions."

Kermit Bloomgarden, a member of the League of New York Theatres negotiating team, rose to his feet, shaking in anger. "I resent Mr. Cooper's statement and the narrowness behind it. What is a producer? What is a producer? A producer is an *artist with business pretensions!*"

Saint-Subber represents the producer as artist without any business pretensions at all. He fastidiously avoids business detail, leaving all that side of the job entirely to C. Edwin Knill, his general manager for more than twenty years. Saint-Subber devotes his time to the artistic side, finding and shaping the material for the stage. He studiously avoids industrywide affairs and stays out of the theater district. He keeps very much to himself, working in an exotically furnished office at the top of his cream-colored town house on East 64th Street just off Park Avenue.

Dressed in dark slacks and a turtleneck jersey, Saint-Subber—a slight, intense man in his midforties—sits on a low brown leather sofa with a white four-button phone beside him. He hates to talk to anyone who is not in the business —nontheater people bore him, especially the ubiquitous sort that knows his own business *and* show business. Saint-Subber appears to know everything there is to know about his business. Alone among the major producers, he grew up in the theater; his parents were ticket brokers. As a boy he remembers being dragged to New Haven to see such shows as *Sailor Beware* and *Getting Gertie's Garter*. From an early age his parents cautioned him against a worldly vice—investing in shows. He says he vowed to stay out of the business end of theater, but he nevertheless lost no time in becoming a producer. Precocious, eager, intelligent, at nineteen he persuaded Max Gordon to join with him in presenting a dramatized John Cheever story, *Town House*. The first show to carry his own exotic name (he was christened Arnold Saint-Subber, but dramatic instinct told him to drop his first name) was *Kiss Me, Kate* in 1948.

Saint-Subber has an almost eccentric devotion to theater. He is immersed in theater seven days a week, reading scripts, turning over ideas, consulting agents, talking to writers. He insulates himself with the phones and the files in a room decorated with tall potted plants and large framed posters. The scripts and the production folders are piled up on a low white-lacquered coffee table. "Without passion, nothing is accomplished," he says.

Saint-Subber's meal ticket is the playwright Neil (Doc) Simon, and he has produced all of Simon's hits since *Barefoot in the Park* in 1963. Their working relationship is close, and Simon lives only a few blocks away. "Doc lets me see the first seven pages of the script and every seven pages thereafter," says Saint-Subber. "He sits there while I read them and watches my face." Saint-Subber has an ascetic face with a high forehead and burning eyes that seem surprised by everything and nothing. He doesn't necessarily say anything as the readings continue intermittently, seven pages at a time. There is no need to. The writing relationship between this playwright and his producer is as close as that of husband and wife.

"The theater," says Saint-Subber, "is made up at best of maverick talent. The more maverick, the better. I can't explain what the hell I do. I produce."

Another producer is Robert Whitehead. "To me the relationship to the play is the most important thing," says Whitehead. "I enjoy it most when there is some relationship between me and the material."

Today Whitehead is identified with the later work of Arthur Miller. When he was co-director of the Lincoln Center Repertory Company with Elia Kazan, Whitehead produced Miller's *After the Fall* and *Incident at Vichy*. Since leaving Lincoln Center he has produced Miller's *The Price* on Broadway. The producer-playwright relationship is personally close. Miller likes to read sections of his play aloud as he finishes them and, much as Simon uses Saint-Subber, he uses Whitehead as a sounding board. Whitehead may or may not comment or make suggestions; the fact of his initial attention during the lonely, tedious creative process is gratifying to Miller.

Slight and good-looking, Whitehead is the only major Broadway producer who could reasonably be mistaken for a leading man. In his early fifties, he comes from a prosperous Canadian family (the actor Hume Cronyn is his cousin) and moves easily within New York's monied class. He is married to actress Zoe Caldwell. His polished good looks and background belie his essential seriousness as a producer; he is no dilettante. Without being pedantic, he is earnest about artistic goals, and there is a bedrock of idealism in his work. To such qualities, so rare along Broadway, Whitehead adds the normal business agility and promotional persuasiveness to be found among the majority of his colleagues. He is the man of ideas who is also a doer.

Whitehead's background is in acting. He arrived in the United States from Canada at twenty and enrolled in drama school in New York. He got a one-line part with a visiting French acting company and later was in three Broadway plays whose names have been forgotten. "I had to produce a play to get one that lasted longer than two weeks," he says. He got into producing after military service in World War II. "I felt a little old to be going around from office to office looking for a job. That kind of thing is all right when you're young, but it's hard to take when you're thirty. I realized if I wanted employment I would have to create it for myself."

For $500 he took out an option on the Robinson Jeffers version of *Medea* and was able to interest Judith Anderson and John Gielgud in playing it. In the 1940's and 1950's Whitehead, sometimes in combination with Roger L. Stevens and Robert W. Dowling, developed a considerable producing reputation on Broadway. Winning the Drama

Critics Circle Award became habit: *The Waltz of the Torea-
dors* in 1957, *The Visit* in 1958, *A Man for All Seasons* in
1962.

In 1960 Robert Whitehead and Elia Kazan were appointed to head the Lincoln Center Repertory Theater. Both
were ready for the assignment because each in his way was
fed up with the commercial struggles and saw in Lincoln
Center new hope for the American theater. It was a short-
lived hope. Their forced separation from Lincoln Center after less than two seasons is one of the scandals of the modern
American theater and illuminates a recurring dilemma—the
operational gulf between the artists and those responsible
for the financial control of large institutional theaters. In
Whitehead's case, the split occurred over what was essentially an artistic choice, and, indirectly, it involved Arthur
Miller.

In 1961 Whitehead and Kazan heard that Miller was working on his first play since *A View from the Bridge* in 1955.
They wanted that play to open their new theater—a major
American playwright for the new American theater. One
year later enough of the play was down on paper for them to
decide to go ahead with it, but the theater building was
nowhere near ready. The ground had been broken and construction work commenced for the $8 million Vivian Beau-
mont Theatre in Lincoln Center, but clearly it would not
be opened for several more seasons. Whitehead and Kazan
were impatient to break in a company and give it at least
one shakedown season in a less exacting environment than
the brand-new theater, and, furthermore, if they did not
open on schedule they would lose both Miller's new play
and another by S. N. Behrman.

The theater's board of directors, consisting of two bankers, two lawyers, a television executive, a businessman-phi-
lanthropist who invested in Broadway shows, and a theater
producer, was headed by George D. Woods, then president
of the International Bank for Reconstruction and Development. Whitehead incurred the ire of the board by deciding
to go ahead with a season in a temporary location well out-

side the Broadway environment. When the board withheld its support, Whitehead found the backing himself.

The ANTA-Washington Square Theatre—a temporary steel "tent" theater erected in Greenwich Village on ground provided by New York University [10]—was opened January 20, 1964, with Arthur Miller's *After the Fall*. The play, largely autobiographical and containing a clearly stated characterization of the playwright's ex-wife Marilyn Monroe, was a substantial success, but with this success Whitehead had made an enemy of George Woods. Miller later said of the actions that followed that Whitehead had been "betrayed" by the board—"there is no other word for it."

That first season, partly due to anticipation of the Miller play, the theater had 46,500 subscribers. But in the next season subscription fell off sharply to 27,000, and the next three productions were disappointing, critically and commercially. (Miller also blames the newspaper critics for not comprehending the problems and aims of a national repertory theater in formation and the board for reading the newspapers instead of watching the theater.) Miller's subsequent *Incident at Vichy* helped redeem the second season but it was already too late. The deficits, predictably, were large, as Whitehead had forewarned the directors they would be. Then, the disastrous critical reception of the Jacobean drama *The Changeling* gave the theater's board of directors an excuse for taking action. After a season and a half, Whitehead, who had spent six years preparing and planning for the Lincoln Center theater, was out of a job. Miller and Kazan quit with him. After an extended period of introspection during which he traveled and stayed away from the New York theater, Whitehead re-established himself as a Broadway producer with *The Prime of Miss Jean Brodie* and Miller's *The Price* in 1967.

"There is always another thing, another idea, another

---

[10] The required half a million dollars in financing was secured from ANTA and the First National City Bank of New York through the good offices of Whitehead's friend Robert W. Dowling, then chairman of ANTA and also the city's Cultural Administrator.

play," Whitehead says of producing. "The great satisfaction for a producer is watching the play grow and making what's on the page come to life. A new problem crops up with every production just when you least expect it, right in the place where you felt most secure. It doesn't matter how many times you have produced a play; there will be some new unforeseen problem every time.

"You have to have the money, the stage, and the theater to put it in," he continues. "Then when you have it all done, and you're tired out from all those headaches, you have to shift gears entirely, because the only thing that matters is what's there when the curtain goes up. The producer reaches that point of exhaustion getting everything ready for that first night in New Haven, and then you discover everybody forgot about the play. It doesn't matter if you postpone, it doesn't matter when you open, it only matters what's there when the curtain goes up."

Harold Prince is a producer who is not only an artist but a phenomenally successful businessman who in his midthirties had already amassed a personal fortune of over a million dollars in the theater. In recent years he has directed his own musicals—the latest are *Cabaret* and *Zorbá*. Along Broadway, people argue over the relative merits, as businessmen, of Prince and Merrick, Broadway's most successful showmen. Each has his partisans and the argument develops obscurantist overtones. A Merrick admirer suggests, for example, that Prince's *Fiddler on the Roof,* which has had cyclical dips in its long run, would have had fewer ups and downs had David Merrick been the producer. Merrick's *Hello Dolly!* still leads *Fiddler* in the long-run sweepstakes.[11] And *West Side Story,* one of the landmarks of modern American musical theater, would have had an even longer run under the aegis of Merrick, the same admirer asserts.[12]

[11] Merrick gave fresh impetus to his long-run *Hello, Dolly!*, which is thirty-three weeks older than *Fiddler,* by starring Pearl Bailey at the head of an all-black cast in 1967.

[12] *West Side Story* opened on Broadway on September 26, 1957. *The Music Man,* which opened nearly two months later and ran for 1,375 performances,

Balanced against this implied criticism is Prince's unrivaled producing record (he attempts fewer shows but has a higher ratio of big hits than anyone) and his more recent work as director of his own productions of *She Loves Me, Superman, Cabaret,* and *Zorbá.*

Prince is an ebullient producer, quick-witted, enthusiastic, and as cocky as a boxer acknowledging cheers after scoring a first-round knockout. He has a working knowledge of backstage theater because he began at the age of twenty as a "gofer" boy ("Go for some coffee") for George Abbott and then became an assistant stage manager on Abbott shows. At the age of twenty-five he teamed as a producer with the late Robert E. Griffith, a genial and popular veteran stage manager whose experience added balance to Prince's brash impulsiveness. After their first success, *Pajama Game,* Prince and Griffith continued with four successive musical hits: *Damn Yankees, New Girl in Town, West Side Story,* and *Fiorello!*

The boyishness of Prince, a veteran now at forty-one, has disappeared in recent years behind a bristly gray beard, but his youthful enthusiasm still runs strong and his bumptious good spirits infect his colleagues with the same will to succeed. Enjoying constant success, Prince is like the promising only child; the public has hardly ever said "no" to him. For investors and for audiences his name connected with a show spells hit.

Prince's success has not affected his highly developed business sense. He operates out of a small, simply furnished office in Rockefeller Center. His desk is modest and uncluttered and he talks briskly and to the point, discouraging long conversations. He wears "mod" clothes, such as three-quarter-length brown leather coats with broad belts. He is married to the former Judith Chaplin, daughter of Holly-

---

won the major awards for a musical that season. Only later did *West Side Story* receive full critical and popular recognition as a musical of exceptional artistic merit. The show had 734 performances through June 27, 1959, and was brought back to Broadway on April 27, 1960, for another 249 performances.

wood composer and producer Saul Chaplin, and they have two small children.

"I am known as a man who is tight with a buck," Prince once confessed. This self-appraisal has been widely verified.

For all his aggressive "sell," Prince is proud, sensitive, and touchy. A leading attorney who often deals with him says, "He seems to feel nowadays that his role in a production is more important than that of the talent." The attorney once represented a writer Prince wanted for a musical. The Prince office refused to pay his going rate, on the theory that to work on a Prince show a writer should be willing to accept less. Negotiations broke off with the two sides within a quarter of a percentage point of each other. "I'm a good businessman not because I enjoy it but because I have to be," says Prince.

After observing George Abbott and Jerome Robbins—the theater's two most successful musical directors—Prince turned to directing on his own eight years ago. He now regards directing as more fulfilling than producing because it gives him artistic control over a production, and now people talk about his shows having "the Harold Prince look."

Prince is a restless, driven man in a restless business. "Success doesn't make you any more secure," he says. "To some extent, the more success you have, the more insecure you become. With the work you do you wonder more and more whether it will meet an audience. In fourteen years in this business I'm . . . well, older. I'm more vulnerable than I was. When creative people lose the sense of what people want in the theater they should get out. The world of theater is moving quickly like everything else that has to do with communications. In twenty years I may not understand what the public will respond to. I hope I'll know enough to get out."

The universally accepted example of the producer as wheeler-dealer publicist and prototypical showman is, of course, David Merrick. Judging by Merrick, the public expects all producers to be colorful, quotable, and newsworthy.

Not all producers can live up to the image, but Merrick acts out in real life what would be wildest fantasy to the inhibited producer, and his skill and nonchalance infuriate his competitors. His publicity stunts, feats of self-exploitation, and open quarrels with critics have won him a place beside Belasco, Ziegfeld, Mike Todd, and Billy Rose.

The direction his career would take began to be evident with *Clutterbuck*, in 1949. After the play opened, Merrick paid telephone operators and bellboys to page "Mr. Clutterbuck" during the busy hours between five and six in the lobbies of midtown hotels. The show also trained Merrick in the intricacies of discount-ticket merchandising. Although *Clutterbuck* was a failure, it ran for six months on "two-for-one" tickets. Merrick's "twofer" campaigns, initiated when a show is nearing the end of its run, are marvels of milking an attraction to the ultimate patron.

Five years were to elapse before Merrick had another show for Broadway, the musical *Fanny*, which featured a belly-dancer named Nejla Ates. This time Merrick had a Greenwich Village sculptor make a life-size nude statue of Miss Ates and one night he had it placed on a vacant pedestal in Central Park, being careful, of course, to scatter enough clues so that police and press could find their way to the spot in the morning.

For his next show Merrick hired an English cab with a set of dual controls fitted in the back seat. Behind a dummy wheel in front sat a live monkey grinning inanely at the dumbfounded pedestrians. The sign on the side of the cab read, "I am driving my master to see *The Matchmaker*."

During this period Merrick had become friends with a crafty publicist named Jim Moran, whose brainstorms were ideally suited to Merrick's wildest publicity needs. In the winter of 1956 the huge signboard above the block-long Bond clothing store in the middle of Times Square was blank, and it presented a tempting opportunity to Moran and Merrick. Delightedly, they prepared slides for two Merrick shows, *Fanny* and *The Matchmaker*, and hired a room on the fifth floor of the Astor Hotel with windows facing the sign directly across Times Square. Piece by piece they smuggled cumbersome electrical equipment up to the room, installed a projector, and were almost ready to commence operations when Moran had to inquire about the electrical current. The hotel staff became suspicious, and Moran and Merrick were thrown out of the Astor before they had a chance to project a single slide.

When box-office business slowed for John Osborne's *Look Back in Anger*, Merrick paid $250 to a young woman to climb up on the stage from her planted location in a second-row seat and assault Kenneth Haigh, the actor who was playing Jimmy Porter, an unfaithful husband. The newspapers, as Merrick intended, played up the story as a bizarre but real incident involving an inflamed playgoer overwhelmed by the emotion of a powerful play, and the uncertain life of the drama was extended seven months, by the producer's calculation. The more outré the joke, the better. For his French musical *Irma La Douce* Merrick had sandwich-board men walk the streets in portable cardboard *pissoirs*.

When Merrick's production of *Forty Carats*, starring Julie Harris, opened in 1968, Clive Barnes, *The New York Times* daily critic, dismissed it, but Walter Kerr raved about it on Sunday. Knowing that the daily paper has more impact than the Sunday paper, Merrick set out about creating his own daily *Times* review. He got his advertising agency to reset Kerr's *Forty Carats* critique in the same type face as the daily *Times,* and ran an ad in the theater section on a weekday. It looked exactly like a brand-new review, and the play was a sell-out within a few days. Merrick was elated not only at the play's success, but at having outwitted *The New York Times*.

Merrick says he finds the promotional side of his work something of a chore—desirable, even necessary, perhaps, but not really in line with what producing is all about. "I know people think I like doing this," he has said. "But I think it's a bore. I've created a public image and now I have to live up to it. Producers used to be able to create a little excitement because they were colorful themselves—take Arthur Hopkins, or Frohman, or Belasco. Now the producers are drab." Merrick's enemies are always waiting for him to overstep. At times they are exultant, thinking that he has gone too far, but they are always proven wrong, because success inevitably sweetens the worst behavior. It doesn't matter what Merrick says or does; if his shows are hits, pragmatism triumphs. One of his most elaborate stunts was a full-page advertisement in January 1962 to publicize the musical *Subways Are for Sleeping*. Merrick had been turning the idea over in his mind for months. Painstakingly assembling the pieces, he created an ad that looked remarkably like a conventional critics' quote ad, except that every comment was one of ecstatic praise for a show that had opened to universally dismal notices. There were small captioned pictures of each critic down the left-hand margin of the ad, but they looked peculiar. The pictures were not those of the city's then familiar seven daily newspaper critics although the names were correct: Howard Taubman, Walter Kerr, John Chapman, John McClain, Richard Watts, Jr., Norman Nadel, and Robert Coleman. For one thing, the Richard Watts in the ad was a black man.

Merrick and his zealous publicity agents had located seven persons with the same names as the critics, and each was provided with a pair of good tickets to the show and stimulated to favorable reactions afterward. The bogus quote ad was sent late in the business day to the *Times*, the *Tribune*, and the *News*. The *Times* and the *News*, spotting the fraud, rejected it, but under pressure of its deadline the *Tribune* let it slip past and it appeared in 30,000 copies of the city edition before it was caught and killed. But by that time Merrick had accomplished all he wanted to—even the *Tribune* ran a blushing story about its own slip-up.

Merrick has been guilty of provoking the critics outrageously. He tried once to bait Walter Kerr by attacking him through his wife, Jean Kerr, the playwright and author of *Mary, Mary* and a collection of humorous family stories, *Please Don't Eat the Daisies*. Merrick said Kerr formed his opinions of a play only when his wife "nudged" him. Kerr sidestepped Merrick's invitation to a public quarrel. In a Sunday piece, he admitted to having a wife who nudged him, but went on to say that it was nice to be nudged and he was sorry for Merrick if he had no one to give him the same attention.

A reasonably gentle thrust by Merrick, and a sportsman-like parry by Kerr. But a few years later, in the spring of 1963, there was no sport when Merrick appeared on NBC's *Tonight Show* and called Howard Taubman "an incompetent hack" and "a blind idiot" and spoke a prayer for his "removal" by the *Times*. Theater people for the first time were uneasy over Merrick's peevishness: he had gone too far, for this time the insult, far from being confined to the parochial press as a family quarrel, had been aired before a national television audience of 22 million. Something new and distasteful had been injected into the rancorous running dispute between the producers and the critics.

With every fresh season and every new critic, Merrick manages to renew his feud. Shortly after Clive Barnes took over as drama critic of the *Times* in 1967 and had panned his first Merrick show, Merrick cabled him ominously, "The honeymoon is over." Barnes shot back his reply, "Had no idea we were married. Did not even imagine you were the type."

To his colleagues as to the general public, Merrick has survived such episodes of public approbation and remains the most fascinating character on Broadway today. A loner among loners, he has more than once described his character in a self-revealing phrase, "I have the soul of an alley cat." And again, in another interview, "My attitude is that of the alley cat—the alley cat that's not quite trustful, that's always watching for someone to leap on him."

He has no visible personal life. His work is a day-and-night affair all year long with frequent overnight trips to Philadelphia, Washington, New Haven, or Boston when a show is trying out (usually three or four months out of the year), and some six business trips abroad and the same number to the West Coast. He is divorced from his second wife, Jeanne Gilbert, once publicity director for two of London's first-class hotels, the Savoy and Claridge's, and more recently a part-time press agent on Broadway. In September 1969 he was married for the third time—to a young Swedish model. He has one child, a daughter, by his second wife.

Merrick's other children are his shows, and in a totally unsentimental way his true family is probably his office staff. Whatever reputation for ferocity Merrick has among actors, unions, drama critics, and his colleagues must be balanced against the loyalty of those who work for him. His hyperkinetic, capable general manager, Jack Schlissel, has been with him since the beginning. He has had only two principal production assistants for the greater part of his career. The first was Neil Hartley, who left after many years to become assistant producer to the English film and stage director Tony Richardson in Woodfall Productions. Since Hartley's departure Samuel (Biff) Liff, once the production stage manager of *My Fair Lady*, has held that key job. Merrick hired him for the same reason he hired Hartley—as the best available production man in the business. Everyone on Merrick's staff works overtime. Their compensation, in addition to good pay, is to be working for the best.

Merrick, in his late fifties, dresses like a Londoner in dark suits with vests or occasionally a rich tailored tweed. It is impossible to imagine him with his coat off and his sleeves rolled up as he sits in his office in the St. James Theatre building and talks theater. His voice is pitched low, but it is purposeful. He never hesitates, never fumbles for words. At the outset of a business conversation, Merrick will be difficult, contrary, uncooperative, a manner calculated to throw his visitor offstride; imperceptibly Merrick takes the initiative and restructures the interview to suit his own purposes. He sends out a conversational jab here and there. He drops in an occasional remark of pure malice, like a line of dialogue in an Edward Albee play, and the visitor is kept at a disadvantage. Having once established himself on higher ground, Merrick will be pleasant and helpful. The sudden flashing anger is frequently a put-on.

Even those close to Merrick do not always find it easy to tell what is on his mind. Is the anger real or feigned? Is the insult self-serving or does it spring from genuine pique? Is his attitude toward critics the result of actual moral outrage or is it simply a put-up job designed to provoke the enemy, create a synthetic dispute, and gain publicity? In Merrick's case it is often a little of each. In his own defense Merrick says he plays a role in order to protect his shows, and critic baiting is just part of the job. But to what extent are his productions extensions of his own ego? Merrick barely conceals a feeling of almost physical oneness with his shows, and therefore when a critic bad-mouths his show he is bad-mouthing Merrick, and the reaction is fury. In fact, Merrick's personal life is so umbilical to his producing career that his plays become part of him and he expects public recognition of his right of self-protection even when that involves attacks against the critics uncomfortably tinged with personal pique.

Each of the producers we have discussed in some detail— Merrick, Prince, Whitehead, and Saint-Subber—represents, in his own way, a traditional pattern of producing. One might ask how well these men and their methods will survive the changes in theater that clearly lie ahead, changes coming from the unfavorable economics of producing, from the challenge of film, which has claimed the under-thirty audience, and from impatience with the formula plays and musicals of Broadway as being no longer "relevant."

Theater costs, which have climbed relentlessly, are driving the serious play from the Broadway theater at worst, and at the very least they are influencing the dramatic work Broadway producers can risk attempting. Economics, combined with the type of audience attracted to Broadway, are strong restraints on the theater. In 1940 it cost less than $20,000 to produce a play. In successive decades, straight-play costs rose to $60,000 by 1950 and to $125,000 by 1960. In 1970 the figure should be in the neighborhood of

$200,000.

Live theater is, in Robert Whitehead's phrase, the last of the "handmade articles." Script, performances, costumes, scenery, handling of stage equipment—nothing very much can be mechanized or automated. This is a personal-service industry imprisoned within an expanding, and increasingly automated, mass society.

The theater producer has no way to pass along his costs to the consuming public except through higher ticket prices. The course open to almost all businessmen—that of reducing unit costs through increased production and greater sales volume—is closed to the producer. His product is ephemeral and inflexible—a stage performance. Live actors, even if there were unlimited public demand, cannot crowd more than eight performances into the week, nor can seating capacity be expanded beyond certain optimum theater sizes, about 1,200 seats for drama, 1,800 for musicals.

What are the chances for closing the economic gap by higher prices or subsidies? Either course assumes that the public created by the new leisure-time society will learn to place a higher value on theater and its cultural importance. But at the moment, theater exists in a shadow time of transition between the old craft-dominated economy of traditional capitalism and the new craftless economy of automation. It cannot participate in the economic benefits of the automated society, and the automated society has yet to produce a class fully awakened to the uses of leisure.

The commodity most in demand in the American theater is the musical. The public accepts the necessarily high ticket prices for musicals, which today reach to fifteen dollars for an orchestra seat down front. In 1940 it cost about $80,000 to produce a musical; these costs rose to $200,000–$250,000 by 1950 and to $350,000–$450,000 by 1960. In 1970 the figure, optimistically, will be $600,000–$750,000 and, pessimistically, $1 million. Operating costs have climbed similarly and ticket prices in recent years have nowhere kept pace.

When will the converging lines of rising costs and diminishing returns meet and demolish the producer?

Serious drama has been severely affected. The artistic odds against good drama emerging are so unfavorable that many plays must be attempted for one good one to appear. Since costs have the effect of contracting production, the chances for drama grow slimmer and slimmer. And when drama falls off, the whole theater suffers.

The character of the audience also acts as a deterrent and prevents theater from changing to meet the times. Saint-Subber bemoans the everlasting sameness of the typical Broadway audience. "They are always forty years old. Forty years ago they were forty. They are forty today." [13] Broadway theater is "an artificial institution based on snob appeal," according to Edgar Lansbury, whose office has developed special college and school ticket plans to encourage theatergoing among young people. Other producers are alarmed at the shrinkage of the audience ("We're losing them by the thousands," says Stuart Ostrow), and there are no longer any moderately successful shows—only big hits and quick flops.

Despite his own success, Merrick can also be pessimistic. "The public isn't interested any more," he says. "Theater used to be a glamorous business. The young people are not interested in it. Some of that is related to the high price of the ticket, but they don't even go if you give them twofers. They're interested in film. Theater is for the middle-aged and the old people."

The competition of film, the natural medium of the younger generation, is part of the theater's problem, and some of the producers are joining up. One of the first to go was Henry T. Weinstein, a Theatre Guild producer, who left for the West Coast in the late 1950's and hasn't been near the theater since. Frank Perry also left the Theatre Guild for films and today the Guild's own Philip Langner

---

[13] Saint-Subber's intuition is correct. According to William J. Baumol and William G. Bowen's 1966 survey, *Performing Arts: The Economic Dilemma*, for the Twentieth Century Fund, the median age of the Broadway audience is thirty-nine. Few people under twenty or over sixty attend. Broadway appears to draw more heavily from the aging managerial class, and fewer members of the professions, than do other arts.

devotes more time to film than theater. Director choreographers such as Herb Ross and Michael Kidd today work almost full-time in film. William Inge has repeatedly given up theater to do film scripts. A number of Broadway producers have worked into film by seeing their shows transferred to the screen. Robert Fryer, veteran producer of *Redhead, Auntie Mame,* and *Sweet Charity,* now produces films (*The Boston Strangler* and *The Prime of Miss Jean Brodie*), and Harold Prince has committed himself to film projects. Even Merrick talks about abandoning the theater for the cinema. "I'm talking to film people," he mutters from time to time; "I'm waiting for the right deal." But he always has half a dozen projects in various stages of readiness for Broadway.

Theater used to be the most daring medium, the freest from censorship, the least inhibited in topics treated. Says Merrick, "It used to be that we could handle subject matter that couldn't be done in film—homosexuality and nudity. Now we can't be so astounding. The films do sex and nudity better than we do."

Broadway also feels the challenge from off-Broadway and from the new nonprofit theatrical establishment of regional repertory companies and institutional theaters. In the emerging theater of the 1970's all of them will have a greater role to play.

Off-Broadway production costs are substantially lower. By remaining small (299 seats or under), off-Broadway theaters have so far avoided some harsh union regulations and Broadway wage scales. In 1969 the off-Broadway production budget for a moderate-size straight play was $25,000, which included the required six-week theater rental, bonds, a four-week printing of tickets, insurance, programs, and other preopening items that disappear into running expenses if the show becomes a hit. If the show flops, the entire $25,000 disappers; if it runs it should have cost the producer only about $13,000 or so to open. For musicals off-Broadway the comparable figures are a production budget of $40,000 to $50,000 and an actual cost through opening night of $25,000 to $30,000.

To some extent, off-Broadway is being affected by the
same economic problems besetting uptown theater. In the
last five years production costs have risen approximately 50
per cent. Only a few years ago off-Broadway producers were
hiring actors as carpenters at two dollars an hour to build
sets in theater basements; in the late 1960's they were having sets built in union scenic shops where labor, for the
moment, gets eight dollars an hour.

Off-Broadway's growing professionalism and some of its
startling successes of recent season (*Scuba Duba, Little
Murders,*[14] *The Boys in the Band,* and the musicals *You're a
Good Man, Charlie Brown, Promenade,* and *Salvation*) have
shaken old-line Broadway. A growing national acceptance of
off-Broadway theater and respect for what it can do has
paid off in sales of subsidiary rights to the films (practically
unheard of ten years ago but increasingly common today)
and in lucrative national tours. The profit picture has
brightened and for a hit such as *Charlie Brown,* which has
had more touring productions than almost any show in recent history, profits have surpassed many a grown-up Broadway hit. And there is no theatrical phenomenon in the city
to equal *The Fantasticks,* Tom Jones's and Harvey Schmidt's
never-ending musical, which is already ten years old and the
longest-running production in American theatrical history.

The Broadway producers regard all this as unfair competition. They become incensed when off-Broadway's profits,
based on lower labor costs in every department, approach
their own. "I'm going to demand of Equity a most-favored-
nation clause," says Merrick. The hierarchy which runs the
Shubert empire also fulminates regularly against off-Broadway and its "cheap labor."

To a Broadway producer (Merrick) who raised $175,000
in 1968 to put on Woody Allen's *Play It Again, Sam,* the
economic profile of an off-Broadway hit such as *The Boys in
the Band* is offensive. *The Boys,* budgeted at $20,000, was

[14] Jules Feiffer's play was a failure on Broadway in 1967. With a new cast
and a new director (Alan Arkin), it became a hit at the Circle in the Square
in 1969.

actually brought in for $10,500, paid back this investment in ten days, and began showing a weekly profit of better than $6,000.[15] Even worse for the Broadway crowd, it earned almost unanimous critical acclaim. Brendan Gill, critic for *The New Yorker*, regards it as the best play of the 1967–68 season—in fact, the best new American play since *Who's Afraid of Virginia Woolf?*

The anti-off-Broadway animosity of Broadway producers erupts noisily in meetings of the Play Selection Committee of the Theatre Guild-American Theatre Society. This argumentative group, which includes key members of the Broadway establishment who meet around the long black-walnut table at the Theatre Guild, decides which plays will get the financially advantageous Guild subscription in tryout and touring cities, worth many thousands of dollars a week in advance sales. Time after time, off-Broadway candidates of worth or reputation are turned down. The rationale is always that Broadway-sponsored candidates should receive first consideration since it is the risk-taking Broadway producer who supplies most of the product for the road. To the Broadway producer, subscription for an incoming show in Philadelphia, Washington, and Boston can often mean the difference between a serious preopening loss and a manageable one.

The virulence of Broadway's attacks on off-Broadway mirrors not so much the dominance of the uptown theater as its impotence and the general decline of such traditionally sturdy Broadway offshoots as the pre-Broadway tryout and the road tour following the Broadway run. The focus has shifted not only to off-Broadway but to such anti-Broadway manifestations as the regional theater and the nonprofit institutional theater. The road is dying, and regional the-

---

[15] Special circumstances account for the low cost and quick pay-off figures of *The Boys in the Band*. The play was first put on in the Richard Barr-Edward Albee Playwrights Unit, a workshop for new writers into which, over a period of years, Barr and Albee have put $250,000—and therefore it was introduced off-Broadway when it was only partially ready. It required only a ten-day rehearsal instead of the usual three-week period, resulting in a considerable cost saving.

aters are taking its place. And it is those theaters, furthermore, which in years to come may be supplying many of the
new plays for Broadway.

Broadway seems increasingly destined to become a showcase theater. For many years Merrick has treated it as such,
bringing in pretested productions from England.[16] In 1968
a new trend began. Broadway producers, hitherto the principal originators of new shows in America, began to accept
developed and tested shows from nonprofit foundation-sup-
ported repertory theaters around the country. A new kind
of theatrical entity came into being that could be called
the quasi noncommercial profit-making Broadway production. It starts pure and becomes tainted. A prime example
is *The Great White Hope,* the Howard Sackler drama about
Jack Johnson starring James Earl Jones. Originating in the
nonprofit Arena Stage in Washington, it was brought to
Broadway under commercial auspices by Herman Levin, best
known as the producer of *My Fair Lady.* A smash hit and
Pulitzer Prize winner of the 1968–69 season, it became heavily tainted—with profit. Another Arena Stage production,
Arthur Kopit's *Indians,* opened on Broadway in the fall of
1969.

When a play follows such a path to Broadway it can be
said that tax-free contributions indirectly have come to the
assistance of the commercial theater. The Broadway producer's costs are less because he is able to bring in a completed production and his risks are reduced because the play
has already been tested at someone else's expense before
paying audiences.

Increasingly, the institutional theater will become the
theater of origination for new plays. This is true in New
York of Joseph Papp's Shakespeare Festival Public Theater
and of Lincoln Center, which in 1968–69 put on William
Gibson's *A Cry of Players* and a Los Angeles production of
In the Matter of J. Robert Oppenheimer which had been

[16] Twenty-one of the fifty-nine productions David Merrick presented on
Broadway from June, 1949, through June, 1969 originated in England; five
others were Irish or French.

turned down for Broadway as too risky.

While Broadway declines as the creative core of the American theater and Broadway's tough-minded producers diminish in power and influence, the importance of producers such as Jules Irving at Lincoln Center, Joseph Papp at the Public Theater, Zelda Fichandler of Washington's Arena Stage, Peter Zeisler of Minneapolis' Tyrone Guthrie Theater, Robert Brustein at Yale, and others is bound to rise.

In many ways forty-eight-year-old Joseph Papp may be the prototype of the producer of the future. He has been the most successful at combining private and public sources of funds to keep a large theater running. The theater of the future is going to depend on this multisource subsidy, as theater already is in every other country in the world. The bulk of the annual operating budget of the New York Shakespeare Festival must come from municipal appropriation, but the theater has also enjoyed federal assistance through the National Council on the Arts and state help through the New York State Council on the Arts. Further funds have come from foundations, private contributors, the Mayor's "Audience Sponsors" committee, and general contributions. Papp is adroit at political manipulation, and keeps all channels to funds open and free-flowing.

The old formulas are under heavy challenge. Paradoxically, the Broadway producer is one of the greatest forces for continuity in the theater. The writer is perhaps most vulnerable, then the director. Today it is difficult for writers to keep up with events, let alone reflect on them and give them dramatic meaning. Says Stuart Ostrow, "The front page of *The New York Times* every day is filled with more drama and more emotion than anything they could think up." [17] Producer David Susskind, who produces liberally in all media, says he derives all his ideas for production from spending two full hours every morning reading "every line in *The New York Times*." The director is once removed from the writer. The producer, twice removed, can choose among

[17] "This wide and universal theater presents more woeful pageants than the scene wherein we play in."—*As You Like It*, Act II: Scene 7.

writers and directors. and pick those who best express what is happening or who have made the best accommodation to cataclysmic change. "The producer," says Harold Prince, "has a better chance of staying around because he lives off the younger talent."

The producers do not expect to be left behind. Most of them took the surprise success of the musical *Hair* with bad grace, and when it came time in 1969 to pass out the annual Tony Awards, the theater's Oscars, there was virtually nothing for *Hair* because it was not a regular Broadway producer but an "outsider," Michael Butler, who brought *Hair* from Joseph Papp's Public Theater to Broadway. None of the Broadway producers had foreseen the enormous popularity, even with the regular audience, of a show based on folk and rock music and performed in an informal, almost disorganized, fashion by young, not fully trained actors to whom the life style of their generation, with its exaggeratedly shaggy appearance and its militantly antiwar sentiment, was not acting but indigenous.

It is easy to malign the producer. His name is above the title and the enterprise is his "baby." Therefore he is the logical, obvious, and available scapegoat for disaster. And since disaster is the lifeblood of the theater and 80 per cent of every season's shows go down the drain, there are ample opportunities for scapegoatism. Additionally, many producers are unfitted by training, background, or temperament for their roller-coaster lives. The dilettante producer, fussing over trivia and ignoring basics, is familiar to all theater professionals. "To me, the automatic sign of an idiot producer," says one press agent, "is to spend days or weeks fussing over the design of the window-card while the show goes to hell in a barrel. People are walking out in droves in Philadelphia, and this guy is wondering whether apple-green or fuchsia is the right background for the play's title on the window-card. I tell all my producers, 'Critics don't review window-cards. Audiences watch the show!'"

For other producers, the opening-night party is a major fix-ation—the proper restaurant, the appropriate guest list, the fitting seat location at the premiere. Running a show is a split-second on Olympus for the producer; godlike, he distributes largesse or poises the thunderbolt. "You have to understand," says a veteran company manager, "that the producer is Mr. Helpless. He's Samson without hair. He has to sweat for everything—the play, the theater, the money, the right cast, the reviews. Yet he fights with both hands tied behind his back. The playwright controls the script, the director controls the actors, the unions run their own turf, the critics ignore him, the theater owner throttles him. All the poor bastard can do is close the show! And then they louse him up for not having the guts to keep it running."

Why does he do it? Most producers will tell you, "If I were in any other business but the theater, I'd be a millionaire." In truth, the dedication, initiative, and numbing volume of man-hours worked would probably bring far greater rewards to the average producer in the marts of trade than along Broadway.

But David Merrick is a millionaire, and so is Harold Prince, and so are Feuer and Martin and a few others, and they made their pile in the theater. Every season, eight or ten hits will explode, on or off Broadway, and the dollars will pour out in the heady cash flow of a slot machine that has hit the jackpot.

The power and the glory—and the money. These motivate the producer, an artist with business pretensions, unabashed egotist, celebrity hunter, and stage-struck patron of the arts. "Where else," David Merrick once asked, "could I associate with such creative people on a day-to-day, minute-to-minute basis?"

Not in Monte Carlo or in Las Vegas or at the racetrack, certainly. However, it is the logic of the gaming table that ultimately prevails. For the logic of the producer's life—like the rationale of the horse player and the crap shooter—is that it doesn't matter how long or how hard he plays the game, unless he wins.

CHAPTER THREE

The Naked Actor

Every day, somewhere in the United States, somebody says, "I want to be an actor." The rolls of Actors Equity increase by 500 names a year; hundreds more never get that far. Usually the decision requires a person to leave a stable job, come to New York, and present himself at a series of strangely public and humiliating talent-evaluation sessions known as auditions. There is no other way to do it.

Four years ago a young man named Terry Kiser was living in his home state of Nebraska and working in the office of a civil engineer. He had, to be sure, some background in acting. As a boy, encouraged by his mother, he had appeared in children's plays at Northwestern University. Later on, Kansas University accepted Kiser on a combined football and drama scholarship. He took his degree in engineering and eventually wound up in an Omaha office. On the side he acted at the Omaha Community Playhouse, an institution remarkable for a body of alumni including Marlon Brando, Montgomery Clift, Henry Fonda, and Sandy Dennis.

As an engineer Kiser was vaguely discontented. A stage

career was always in the back of his mind, but he knew this meant leaving Omaha for New York, and he was apprehensive. He knew only one person in New York, an old Nebraska friend who had just returned to Omaha, leaving one month's rent paid in advance on his Manhattan apartment. The friend offered Kiser the key. "Right there I decided," Terry said. "I had a place to land." Within two weeks he sold his car and abandoned Omaha. His only assets were $1,500 from the car and the key to the apartment. A week after landing in New York he auditioned for and won his first professional acting job "in a theater so far off Broadway you could hardly find it." The job paid only $40 a week, but Kiser was on his way.

Four struggling years in the theater can seem a lifetime, but now Terry Kiser is one of Broadway's promising "new breed." His colleagues consider him a coming star, and Kiser, in all candor, agrees with them. In sessions with Lee Strasberg at the Actors Studio, in off-Broadway plays, in stock, in an occasional film, and on television he is learning more about Terry Kiser the actor, and more about the audience for whom the actor exists.

In the world of the playmakers the ultimate experience can be summed up in these two terms—"actor" and "audience." It is for the actor who performs and the audience who watch that the whole lumbering, gasping, cumbersome mechanism of theater is conceived. Out of the direct emotional contact between actor and audience comes catharsis, and the purpose of living theater is fulfilled. And when that "miracle" occurs, when communication between actor and audience is achieved, then it is easier to understand the ferocity of the drives that inflame the strange small world of the Broadway stage.

In this world, the actor is especially exposed because he is "up there" under lights in a performance rite which at once appalls and uplifts him, which he both longs for and dreads. Again and again, when questioned about their life styles, actors allude to the feelings of exposure and nakedness that accompany stage appearances. The expressions they use are remarkably similar.

A young actress says, "You're naked. You're stripped down. You're put out there to fall flat on your face or triumph."

An experienced Broadway actress who has played many leads says, "Most people are really very frightened. Getting out there on stage is like walking a tightrope. It's like walking on stage naked—naked and looking awful!"

A Broadway star says, "All the other collaborators are in the audience or safely in the wings or in the orchestra pit. The producer or the author or the director may be outside having a drink—or in London. But the actors are all alone with a thousand strangers."

But the loneliness can have affirmative compensations. Applause quickly overcomes fright. The warmth of admiration, affection, and respect that radiates from an attentive audience, the sheer delight of taking curtain calls ("Nowhere could you get that happy feeling/When you are stealing that extra bow," wrote Irving Berlin in "There's No Business Like Show Business" [1]), all these and the anticipation of adulation offstage—*being recognized by strangers*—are what makes the actor's life as pleasant as it can be painful.

A middle-aged character actor who has never played a lead admits, "When I go out there, that's when I'm happiest."

A great star says, "To have a thousand people waiting on your every move. To get to that climactic point when you can hear a pin drop. And it's you they're watching. You're ruling the roost!"

Another star says, "When you feel you have them, when you know you've got them, what a wonderful feeling!"

The artificial nature of the actor's experience is self-evident but bears repeating in detail. An actor on a stage is saying someone else's lines, wearing clothes that belong to the evening's identity, and walking and behaving according to directions imposed on him by others. The audience he plays to is composed of strangers who will cough and fall asleep and make impolite noises when they are bored; and,

[1] © Copyright 1946 Irving Berlin. Reprinted by permission of Irving Berlin Music Corporation.

conversely, will laugh and cheer when they are stirred, or, in special moments, will stay thrillingly silent. It is to please these ill-assorted strangers that the actor deliberately fantasizes and exhibits himself. A child seeking to please his parents, a lover wooing his mistress, a soldier going to battle, the actor will do almost anything for the favors of these strangers. It is a brief glory he enjoys, but it is unique, and actors are unique people.

Implicit in the relationship of actor and audience are violence and hostility: the cliché phrases associated with this relationship abound in references to destruction, death, and sexual conquest. *"Merde"* and "Break a leg"[2] are common actor's telegrams. The victory shouts of actors after triumphant performances are filled with violent images:

"I killed them tonight."

"We mowed 'em down."

"I laid them in the aisles."

Conversely, if the show goes poorly, an actor will say, "We died out there tonight" or "We bombed" or "It just laid there."

Blythe Danner, an actress in her early twenties, has her own milder schoolgirl counterpart of these aggressive expressions. Before a performance she rallies her spirits by telling herself to "go out there and maim them!"

For some actors the act of performance has pronounced sexual implications and the conquest of the audience relates itself directly to the rituals of love-making. Burgess Meredith says, "The audience is the dragon to be slain, the woman to be raped." Terry Kiser describes his hours on stage as "complete stimulation." He says, "It has something to do with power and with love. . . . The great feeling the actor gets on stage is the ability to control the audience. It is power; and it is beyond power."

An actress active on Broadway for fifteen years in top featured and starring roles describes the acting experience in frankly sexual terms: "At the end of a performance I'm in a state of heightened emotional and physical awareness. My

[2] Originally, *Hals und Beinbruchi,* from the German.

dream at the end of a performance is to be greeted at the stage door by a great stud. It's depressing to go home without a single date. I want to rush into the arms of someone."

For another actress, the expression of the actor's love relationship to the audience is more muted. Rae Allen, who has a cheerful, unrepressed openness about her work, says of audiences, "I love them—if I've rehearsed correctly, if it's really rolling well. Some actors feel antagonized by audiences. I never do."

The reverse side of the audience as lover and beloved is the audience as enemy, and for all the emanations of affection felt by an actor in a successful show there are many chilling experiences of dismissal for the times he dared go before them in a flop. Burgess Meredith says, "If you're in a hit, there's so much love around you can't stand it. And if it's a flop, the audience is merciless and there's very little you can do about it."

Blythe Danner, who is serious and clearly has star potential, describes feelings akin to fury. "You feel all kinds of strong emotions when you are acting. I get furious. If things aren't going well, I feel I'm not liked."

Part of the complex affinity between actor and audience is that most actors face the nightly exposure with varying degrees of terror. Anyone who has ever appeared in public is aware of stage fright: the triphammer pulse, the dry mouth, the preternatural stammer. One would suppose that professional actors were immune to these fears, but to a man, whether beginner or veteran, actors confront a spectrum of jitters on playing nights—all playing nights—particularly in the endless seconds before the curtain rises and the audience awaits, pitiless and expectant.

Opening night, which is climactic in many senses, is particularly hard on actors. The first-night audience is invariably tougher than most (despite the presence of hand-picked well-wishers): a squadron of critics lies in wait; weeks of long, arduous work schedules crowded with rewrites and changes lie behind. Maureen Stapleton calls opening night "a nightmare, an absolute nightmare. I black out on opening nights." Laurence Olivier traditionally arrives early, stands behind the closed curtain, and bolsters his confidence by calling inaudibly in the direction of the lying-in-wait critics, "You bastards!" Rex Harrison arrives only a few minutes before curtain on opening nights, just in time to get into costume and rush onstage, so there's no time to worry about the critics.

For actors, the worst part of judgment night is that they can justly assume only partial responsibility for what audiences see and judge. The actor is the medium, but the message was created by others; when things go wrong in a play it is the actor who is the immediate scapegoat; and it is the actor as instrument who has no possible way to explain what makes him look so bad. Actress Marian Seldes, describing a special small hazard of opening night, says, "I can't tell the critics, 'Look, this is the very first time I'm wearing this dress.' "

As conscious as actors are of critics in an opening-night audience, they are even more conscious of their fellow actors sitting in almost parental judgment before them. Rosemary Murphy points out, "I always am more aware of the members of the profession in the audience. Previews are just as bad as opening nights, too, because the professionals come to previews."

For all its terrors, many actors feel opening-night excitement enhances their performances. It gets the adrenalin going. Rae Allen optimistically says, "I don't feel there are any audiences that can't somehow be won—even the cold, commercial Broadway first-night audience. I've enjoyed every opening night I've ever had." Blythe Danner says, "Everyone's up. If it goes great you have a ball."

For some actors openings create such euphoria that when the reviews come out in the morning papers before the cast has gone to bed, it hardly matters how they read, good or bad. Fredric March remembers receiving a terrific critical drubbing after opening in a Broadway flop. He had a bad leg at the time and after the performance took a few drinks to ease the pain. When the reviews were read at midnight, he remembers nodding and smiling delightedly at every adjective. The next day he read them again. They were all pans, especially of his performance.

Even after opening night is over and the play is launched, the jitters remain. The nightly ordeal may never again be as acute, but it persists for most actors even after long, long runs.

March has been acting for half a century, but he is always scared for the first few minutes. He quotes Belasco's maxim, "I wouldn't give a nickel for an actor who isn't nervous." He regularly does ten minutes of vocal exercises prior to his entrance, humming and articulating to banish the butterflies.

Making that first entrance is the hardest part of all, in March's estimation. He recalls his entrance in Eugene O'-Neill's *Long Day's Journey Into Night* when he had to "boom on" from offstage. In the next line, fortunately, the stage directions called for him to light a cigar. "Lighting the cigar," March remembers, "kept my hands from shaking." Handling props and performing ordinary physical chores on stage, such as picking up the phone or straightening a chair, traditionally are good for calming stage jitters.

Other actors devise complex preperformance rituals for exorcising fright and anxiety. Kiser describes his fixed routine as follows: "I get to the theater a little earlier than half hour, usually about an hour before, but not really to prepare for the role—mostly to get the subway ride out of my mind. I need to clear my mind of all those things—the subway, the telephone, the bills. When I get to my dressing room, I do the same thing every night. I always have a cup of coffee. I shine my shoes. I put on cologne for freshness. I shave at the theater. I wash my hair every day. My hair tends to be greasy. I like it fluffed up. It gives me a different look.

"I always go on stage about five or ten minutes before the curtain. I listen to the audience. I sing to myself, and I try to make my mind very specific. I free-associate. I start my mind going. I'm ready, now, to go on stage and face the audience."

Endless hours of preparation, minute personal adjust-
ments, and unique, individualistic exercises precede the moment of contact between actor and audience—the contact
whose ultimate justification and fulfillment is communication. The moment is one of power and also humility to Miss
Allen, and also "self-revelation and the satisfaction of com-
municating that self-revelation to an audience. That's the
ultimate meaning of acting. That's what it's all about.
You communicate *with*, not *to*, an audience."

Within the frame of this two-way exchange, for theater
to have any kind of emotional impact, a necessary transference of identity must take place between audience and
actor. The man in the audience projects himself into the
person the actor is portraying on the stage, experiencing
the conflicts and emotions almost as if they were his own.

But another sort of transference very commonly takes
place, which makes the actor an object of timeless fascination in the civilian world. The audience identifies with the
actor as actor as well. When Richard Burton plays *Hamlet,*
the audience not only becomes Hamlet, it also becomes
Richard Burton playing Hamlet. This stems from an old universal urge—to stand up before the admiring crowd and perform first before the family, then one's friends, and finally,
by a light, easy leap of the imagination, before the world at
large. This is why one experiences an unidentified tremor
of excitement when walking into a theater, a shiver of anticipation, and then an unspoken series of questions ad-
dressed to oneself: What if *I* were up there? Will the actors
(would I?) remember the lines? What is it like for the leading man (for me!) to be watched step by step moving across
the stage?

The actor personifies theater not only to the public but
to everyone, actor and nonactor, who works in the theater.
When the stage curtain parts and the first actor steps forth
to speak the first lines, the meaning of theater is fulfilled—
and it is the actor who fulfills it. It is for the actor that the

play is written, and through the actor that the play achieves the shocks of recognition, empathy, and catharsis. The script, the set, the costumes, the director, the author, the lighting, the whole apparatus of production seems to recede at curtain time, and the actors, like infantrymen, must bear the brunt of battle. The play may be the thing, but the actor is the visible instrument.

All theater people secretly or openly envy the actor, and many of them yearn for the actor's life. Spiritually we are all actors, says one producer. Playwright Arthur Miller once observed, "The full-blown actors are merely the completed types of secret actors who are called producers, backers, directors, yes, and playwrights. . . . The actor himself is the lunacy in full profusion—the lunacy which in others is partially concealed." [3]

This lunacy has shining, if transitory, awards. For actors in a successful play, everything glows—the applause during the show, curtain calls, backstage attention from a corps of attendants and technicians, one's name on the marquee, and one's pictures blown up to heroic size on the houseboards out front. After the performance, the parade of visitors, autograph fans at the stage door, conspicuous suppers in theatrical restaurants. During the day there are interviews, photographs, appointments, and the expectancy of the evening's repeated attentions.

This lunacy has a fascination that attracts and repels simultaneously. If the actor's status is desirable because of the attention, adulation, and self-fulfillment it provides, it also contains the savage appeal of the cockpit.

"As a profession it's a ghastly one," says Rosemary Murphy. "It's a vicious cutthroat business. I realize that other professions have their drawbacks. Now that I have friends in the magazine business, I realize there's an awful lot of backstage politics and maneuvering on magazines, too. It's just that it's so open in the theater. The competition is so

[3] From a 1955 piece Miller wrote for *Holiday* reprinted in *The Passionate Playgoer*, George Oppenheimer's collection of essays on the theater (Viking Press, 1958).

public."

Even husbands and wives in acting families can't escape the spirit of mutual competitiveness that pervades the theater. When actress Jessica Tandy found herself keeping house in Hollywood while her husband Hume Cronyn made three pictures in a row, she wryly observed, "Hume is working. I am just sitting here perfecting cooking recipes—and getting worse and worse at it all the time."

If annoyance can arise when one partner in a marriage is working and another is not, arguments can result when couples work together. Eli Wallach and Anne Jackson, partners on stage and in marriage, confess to a certain tension rehearsing together in a play. Wallach is a "fast study," mastering his lines early in rehearsal; Miss Jackson "feels" her way into a part. Such seemingly slight differences can trigger monumental stage quarrels. Rehearsals with the Wallachs have never produced any permanent breach, but they have occasionally been spirited and noisy.

The endless competitiveness of an actor's life stems from the basic condition of his existence in the theater—the lack of employment and the endless search for jobs. At any one time, 75 per cent of all Actors Equity members cannot find employment in the theater. Equity is an open union: the labor pool increases by hundreds every month. Only at the top does the work seek the actor; for the most part, the actor seeks the work.

An actor's rounds—from agent to producer to audition and back—can be harrowing. This circuit of rejection hardens the actor's approach to life and his career.

The search for work is sometimes carried to ridiculous extremes by Broadway musical chorus dancers, the "gypsies" [4] who are the most restless actors of all. Even when dancers have jobs in established shows, they audition automatically for the next one coming in. In one year on Broadway there were 143 replacements in a cast of thirty-nine in *West Side Story,* the dancers' musical.

[4] There is no comparable, affectionately derogatory word for singers or straight-play actors.

8 A.M.
The theatrical day begins with the sweeping of the sidewalk in front of Sardi's.

10 A.M.
The box office gets the action when the theater has a smash hit.

*All photographs
in this section by
Christopher Little*

2 P.M.
Rehearsal break backstage at the Barrymore for *A Patriot for Me.*

5 P.M.
Programs are delivered for the evening's performance.

7:30 P.M.
Virginia Vestoff of the cast
of *1776* on her way to work.

Half-Hour

The actress must sign in on the stage-door bulletin board at 'half-hour'—thirty minutes before the curtain goes up.

8:30 P.M.
Curtain Time

9 P.M.

At the 46th Street Theatre Virginia Vestoff plays her scene with William Daniels.

11:30 P.M.

2 A.M.
 The streets are empty and dark when the Shubert 'roundsman' starts on his early-morning route to check the darkened theaters.

In a strange way, the search for work imposes more order and discipline in an actor's life than the mythology of the theater world would lead one to believe. Nina Vance, the founder and director of Houston's famous Alley Theatre, once suggested that tracing the footsteps of an actor making his rounds week in and week out would reveal a recurring pattern: so many hours spent at lessons, so many at auditions; certain times for seeing agents; certain times for visiting the casting offices; certain days seeing people in the theater, and others for checking with friends in film and television.

Theatrical employment greatly depends on accidents of place, time, and contact. To some extent, one can make one's own accidents. For example, Miss Murphy got her first Broadway part in the following manner. She was babysitting for Maureen Stapleton, who was married at the time to Max Allentuck, general manager for producer Kermit Bloomgarden, who was casting *Look Homeward, Angel*. Allentuck recommended her to the director, George Roy Hill, who inquired about her talent and was told, "She's the best babysitter in New York."

The remark brought the chance to read. Miss Murphy found herself backstage in a theater with other young actresses waiting to read. She let everyone go ahead so she could study the part more thoroughly. Finally, late in the day, it was her turn, and she was given just six lines to speak. There was never any question in her mind about the outcome. "I was determined to get the part and I got it," she said.

The actor today must be open to job opportunities on a variety of fronts. Soap operas, commercials, "voice-overs" (the use of an actor's voice for narration behind a visual commercial), a "spot" in a continuing television series, and films—today's actor must seek multiple opportunities. An off-Broadway part may lead to a role on Broadway, the Broadway role to a film job. Soap operas today supply important exposure to the high middle-rank actor. Starring in a "soap" gives the actor the kind of prominence he needs, for example, to qualify for a summer-stock "package." These traveling productions frequently play to huge audiences pre-conditioned by the impact of television.

Yet the need to diversify—to meet the needs of various acting markets—inevitably breeds resentment, particularly in those actors who prefer to concentrate on perfecting their theater careers. Miss Danner resents agents, for example, because she feels they are more interested in moving careers than in developing talent. "You're a commodity to be sold," she says. "That's just how you're dealt with. And I don't think I'm being paranoid or insecure. If you can be sold and sold well, you'll get attention."

Young actresses take outside jobs as models, waitresses, and sales girls in New York in order to remain at the center of theatrical employment. It's hard for an actor who must train, take lessons, and report for auditions to accept a steady nine-to-five job.

The constant search for work and the heavy percentage of turndowns create morale problems. One must soon learn not only to live with rejection but to build on it. Lucille Ball, a graduate of the American Academy of Dramatic Arts, returned as guest lecturer and showed, for all her success, that she had not forgotten and could sympathize with the relentless realities of job-seeking. She said, "I see the defeat, the defeat, the defeat that goes on when kids go looking for jobs. But you must not feel rejected or defeated. Resiliency is important. You've got to keep buoyed up constantly."

Auditions are the worst humiliations of all. Young unknown actors must audition endlessly, conscious of impossible odds against landing a part, lining up along with the untalented and the hopeless to be judged. "You feel like cattle," one actress says, discussing the daily ritual performed in dreary rehearsal halls or darkened theaters. "There is no place to sit. It's either too hot or it's freezing. You're given a time to appear and generally you're not called until at least forty-five minutes after you're scheduled, and you always have another audition scheduled for right after. Of course the smart way to do it is to say, 'I'm sorry, I have another reading at four. Would you be sure I'm out on time?' Then they let you go ahead."

After an actor attains a certain status, he resents being asked to audition or read for a part. With a given number of credits an actor assumes that his work is well enough known within the profession to preclude auditions or "reading for roles" again. He feels a producer or director should know whether he wants the actor or not. Some actors bridle at having to read even when the circumstances are reasonable.

For example, an established actress was offered a good Shakespearean role for the summer at the American Shakespeare Festival in Stratford, Connecticut, a part she had always wanted and one for which she would be too old in another year or so. Salary and billing were satisfactory and she had no other plans for the summer. She met the director and was charmed by him. But since he was English and did not know her work, he asked her to read as a formality. She hadn't been required to read for a part in five years and was outraged at the request, recalling past humiliations. She did not show up for the reading, although the part was clearly hers.

Only the well-established actor can afford to be this choosy, and it is generally the star actor of middle years who insists upon the prerogatives of status. Such conventions mean little to the rising generation of actors, the new breed which is not only transforming the stage but all other entertainment media. The world of the playmakers is swiftly and surely moving into the control of these complex young people.

The young actor of today is further distinguished from older performers by his attitude toward training and by the demands of the new media. Young actors today face the necessity of working with the multimedia world and are prepared to handle off-Broadway, commercial work, television, Broadway, repertory, and films. Older actors owe their allegiance to the school of experience—tours and long runs.

The young actor, studying the work of his seniors, augments his lessons with his own more varied exposure to the theatrical arts in an attempt to graft psychological insight onto technique.

Consider Mr. Kiser, thirty years old, on his way up. He frankly admits to using every method—including openly borrowing other actors' tricks—to improve his own technique. Thievery is the beginning of creativity, he likes to say. "I steal a lot. I like to work with the older men in the theater who have worked with the Group Theatre.[5] I study their technique. I can interpolate the new ideas."

"In the beginning I worked at the Actors Studio all the time. I had raw instinct. I learned technique, how to work on roles, how to repeat the same things without growing stale, how to make things come alive."

It is Kiser's credo that an actor who stops training and learning destroys himself artistically. He cites Marlon Brando, the most promising stage actor of his generation, who has not appeared on Broadway since *A Streetcar Named Desire* more than twenty years ago. "So often I've seen an actor quit learning and then have only himself to fall back on, like Brando."

Kiser is confident of becoming a star. He recognizes the need for patience to permit development and the artistic obligation to be judged by his peers. This means dutifully reporting back to the theater, harsh taskmaster that it is, between lucrative film assignments. "It's quite simple: when you stop developing, you fall; you don't stay at the same level."

The younger actors and actresses today are more academically inclined. Rae Allen has studied at the American Academy of Dramatic Arts and with Stella Adler, Morris

[5] The Group Theatre was founded in 1931 by Harold Clurman, Cheryl Crawford, and Lee Strasberg, and produced plays by Clifford Odets and Sidney Kingsley, among others. It survived for a decade as one of the most vigorous institutions in American theater history, and was the seminal organization for many of the dramatic ideas of the 1940's and 1950's. Its story is told by Harold Clurman in *The Fervent Years* (Alfred A. Knopf, 1948, and Hill & Wang, 1957).

Carnovsky, Harold Clurman, Hiram Sherman, Uta Hagen, and the Polish director Jerzy Grotowski. She sets herself reading tasks: all of Chekhov, all of Strindberg, all of Shakespeare (which took her a couple of years), and all of the new plays she can get her hands on.

Most actors prefer studying human behavior to reading books. Kiser, for example, reads newspapers but never novels. He regularly sees all the new movies and plays, but he never "sees" the movie or play as would an ordinary viewer, in terms of character and story; he goes to watch actors and study performances.

A new breed of actor is emerging from the theater of the 1960's and is flexing his muscles in other media. The movies are beginning to discard physical perfection as a standard for actors. Such New York-trained actors as the "ordinary"-looking Walter Matthau, Dustin Hoffman, Martin Balsam, and Richard Benjamin and such stage-trained actresses as Barbra Streisand and Estelle Parsons are big names in films today. Their success has created a breakthrough in films for the stage actor who is long on talent, training, character, and realism but short on flawless features.

The situation is changing so rapidly in favor of the less idealized-looking actor that conventional leading men are becoming obsolete. Kiser sees new opportunities for his style of actor. "The pretty boys are out," he says. "We're getting away from the Tab Hunters. There is a move toward greater reality. I'm going to be in demand."

Most of the new breed of actors lead more sensibly ordered lives than many of their predecessors. As the theatrical profession gains respectability the actor takes a more respectful view of his work and seeks to separate his work from his personal life. He approves of the life style of an acting couple such as Paul Newman and Joanne Woodward, who live in a secluded country place in Westport, Connecticut, deliberately isolating their home life and children from the public demands of their profession. Such actors no longer depend wholly on the society of other actors, and they actively seek friends outside the theater.

The new generation scoffs at the old myths of the profession. It is symptomatic of the new skepticism that they ignore such venerable actor superstitions as not whistling in the dressing room, never wishing a performer good luck, or not putting your shoes on a shelf above your head.[6] There is less romanticizing. Kiser says, "Acting today is more of a business than the 'glorious' thing it used to be. Actors are more rounded, more professional than they were. They're not like those kooky Barrymores or like Tallulah Bankhead. They are more stable."

The new actor can become affluent quickly in the multimedia world. Like other affluent Americans of his generation, he is increasingly sophisticated in the economics of his profession. In his first Broadway play, *Jimmy Shine,* Dustin Hoffman earned $150,000 in a six-month run in 1968. Films, which require an average of eight weeks of shooting, pay many times that amount to a star like Hoffman, who can command half a million dollars for a film assignment. But if the young actor today is not eager to sign for a long run on Broadway, for fear of losing a chance at a film, neither is he likely to commit himself to a long-run film contract and give up the stage.

One young actor expresses this loyalty as follows: "Theater means a lot to me. It means stretching your instrument.[7] You can have a hysterical girl in front of the camera and it will be great and she'll look like a great actress on film. But she can't do it more than once. An actor doesn't realize the mental loss when he cuts himself off from the stage."

The new actor was made for the modern renaissance of film as the new film expresses the spirit of the modern actor. Films, as they have matured in content and technique, require actors whose talent is sufficiently sturdy and flexible

---

[6] Still, actors habitually consult astrologers, and for some New York actors a palmist at the Fifth Avenue Hotel north of Washington Square near off-Broadway territory has become an irresistible consultant.

[7] This unusual phrase is common actor jargon. "Instrument" signifies the physical embodiment of an actor's talent.

to accommodate the new themes and the serious treatment of those themes. At the same time, actors have become serious students of their craft. The fusion of the new breed of film and the new breed of actor is inexorable and historic, and it is a major reason for the unquestioned flowering of the modern cinema as a serious art form, far superior to television drama and most stage drama in its sophistication, its daring, its openness to experiment, and its technical virtuosity.

The older actor stood for discipline and technique; the new actor stands for intelligence. Perceptiveness of character, a higher reality, and psychological insight are qualities the new breed of actor values above the outward physical show of technique favored by classically trained actors—the good diction, the mannered walk, the controlled gesture. Even John Gielgud, an old master of stagecraft, is regarded with suspicion by some young actors. Says Miss Allen, "Gielgud is an actor whose outer technique is more important than his inner technique."

Inner technique! To the new-breed actor, inner technique is paramount. It is not enough for him to speak the speech trippingly or to give his characterization "outer" plausibility. True technique for him means getting inside the character, not just as a mimic or copyist or tape recorder but internally and without shame. The old-timer created brilliant effects but he was always *playing* the part. The new actor more completely *becomes* the character.

Such an actor physically and emotionally dissects the character he will play even before he begins rehearsing. He can say, "When the curtain goes up, the actor knows more about the character than the writer ever did.[8] He knows deep intimacies of the character's identity—how he lives, what his schooling was, what his I.Q. is, what he does in his spare time, in specific detail."

Type-casting is anathema to the new actor; he seeks experimental theater, is unafraid of roles which may not seem

[8] This statement was vehemently refuted by a playwright to whom it was referred for comment.

"right" for him. He thinks of stardom as artistic fulfillment rather than merely public acclaim. The two attitudes—resentment of stereotype casting and the desire for stardom on artistic terms—are closely related. Miss Danner, young, pretty, blonde, and blue-eyed—the typical ingenue—says, "I'd rather not be typecast and see if I can make the stretch. So many of the stars you see can't act their way out of a paper bag. I don't really want to be a star. What I really want to be is a true artist—as good an artist as I can be." The artist may "arrive" later but is likely to stay longer.

The new young actors coming out of universities in increasing numbers have more thorough academic training than their predecessors of the experience-and-instinct school. They expect slower development, they resist the temptation to cut corners, and they are skeptical of sudden stardom.

The belief that an actor can reach stardom in one lightning performance has always been alluring to the public. It has always been repellent to actors. They know better.

Overnight success is an indestructible cliché of show business. There is no more hallowed rite than that of the understudy waiting in the wings who goes on for the ailing star and triumphs, as Judy Holliday did for Jean Arthur in *Born Yesterday* in 1946, as Lainie Kazan did for Barbra Streisand in *Funny Girl* in 1964, and as Harold Gary did for David Burns in *The Price* in 1968. That all three of these performers had waited and worked long years for their moments is easily glossed over.

Show business itself perpetuates the mystique of sudden stardom; some actors even subscribe to it. The notion is a staple of the movies, particularly in the Busby Berkeley musicals of the campy 1930's from *42nd Street* onward, when Ruby Keeler was the shy hopeful who was hurried onstage to replace the absent leading lady as the curtain rose.

The occasional truth of the legend only accents the reality that in show business *there are almost no overnight successes*. Sudden recognition can come in films because of accidents of lucky casting, but rarely in theater, where seasoning is a prerequisite of success.

To be "discovered" in fairy-tale fashion seems patronizing and specious to serious actors. They are only too aware of the months and years of lessons, rounds, auditions, rejections, part-time work, bit parts, and incessant waiting for the break to believe in miracles. How could they be "discovered"? They were "there" all along!

Even worse for the actor than simple discovery is compound discovery—to be discovered not once but over and over again. In 1960 Angela Lansbury, a respected film actress but not quite a star, made an important Broadway debut in *A Taste of Honey*. She didn't work in the theater again until *Anyone Can Whistle,* a musical of the 1963–64 season, when she was again reviewed admiringly even though the show died quickly. When she was cast for the title role of the musical *Mame* in 1966, she was considered a competent casting choice, but not in the box-office bravura tradition. *Mame* and her performance made Miss Lansbury—for the third time in six years—a "discovery," but this time for good.

Kim Stanley was a busy but largely unnoticed actress in New York for many years before her "discovery" in *Bus Stop* in 1955. Between roles she was a receptionist, a salesgirl, and a waitress in a Lexington Avenue cocktail bar. She acted frequently but in out-of-the-way plays and places—off-Broadway, summer stock, the "subway circuit" of Brooklyn and the Bronx. The trade knew her work and readings got her jobs, but it was in *Bus Stop* that she finally arrived—nine years of incessant striving had made her an "overnight" success.

Making a name for oneself is a never-ending process even for established stars. Actors must justify themselves every time the show goes on. In show business, public acclaim resounds all too briefly. Miss Murphy puts it this way: "In acting there's no such thing as 'going ahead.' It's always 'back and forth.'"

John Gielgud's first success in New York occurred in 1936 in *Hamlet;* for a quarter of a century he was a major star in London, and his occasional Broadway visits were uniformly well received. Yet his reputation was in eclipse in America until the evening of December 28, 1958, when he walked on-stage at the 46th Street Theatre and for two hours en-thralled his audience with readings of Shakespeare in his one-man show, *Ages of Man*. At the age of fifty-four, he was "discovered" all over again.

Actors work with each other and their collaborators in the theater according to very specific, largely unwritten, and universally recognized commandments. If one were to codify the major actors' commandments they might read something like this:

Thou shalt not "upstage" a fellow actor;

Nor interrupt his speeches;

Nor move conspicuously on his lines;

Nor ruin another actor's laugh by any means, motivated or otherwise;

Honor thy playwright and read the lines as they are written.

Such rules are elementary, recognized by all actors. And they are broken all the time.

Since an actor is instinctively tempted to think a play is about him and that his role is the key part,[9] he frequently "improves" on his lines. As an actress acknowledges, "This abuses the material, abuses the other actors, abuses the di-rectorial concept." The older playwrights find improvisa-tion intolerable and "Method" actors the worst offenders; Paddy Chayefsky doesn't appreciate spontaneous line-readings by actors. He says, "I really wouldn't mind, if only most actors didn't improvise such lousy lines."

It is the director's job to hold the actors not only to the words but to the theme of the play, and not allow them to go wandering off into quixotic self-expression. A good direc-tor must resolve the conflict between his higher allegiance

[9] A 1938 *New Yorker* short story by Patricia Collinge entitled "The Play's the Thing" depicted each member of a newly assembled cast at a cocktail party as describing the play in terms of himself, which leaves a nontheatrical lady puzzled as to what the play is all about.

to the overall concept and the actor's fierce drive to interpret the play in terms of his own part.

Actors need firmness and self-confidence in a director, who is often a father-surrogate to the members of his cast. A confident director can permit a certain freedom of experimentation at the outset of rehearsals, knowing he can get control later. Miss Allen says, "I like a director who experiments. If he comes along with nothing—with his own fears, his own insecurities, his own ambitions—it's a pain in the neck."

Strong-willed actors, however, favor permissive directors. Miss Murphy says, "My main requirement for a director now is that he doesn't interfere with me. If he was right in casting me in the first place, then he should trust me with the part and leave me alone. A good director can heighten your performance but he can't make it happen. That has to come from yourself." She described rehearsing for a workshop production where the director was interfering. "I wasn't enjoying it any more. Finally, I told him to stop explaining. 'If you tell me nine different ways to do something then I'm not free, free to have any ideas of my own. So just shut up, and don't say anything for three days.'" Since they were friends, the confrontation worked.

Actors respond best to directors who have themselves been actors. Actor-directors recognize the need to experiment and to make one's own choice of gesture, behavior, and movement in building a characterization. Many top directors, including Elia Kazan, Joseph Anthony, Ellis Rabb, and Mike Nichols, have begun as performers.

When the directors depart, soon after opening night, actors are left pretty much on their own; it is then the assignment of the stage manager, as the director's representative, to become the new father-surrogate. The stage manager is comparable to the foreman in the factory. Operationally, he is more management than union, but socially he is less employer than employee. As management, he is sometimes suspect in the eyes of the cast. He is frequently a martinet, but he has to be. He must keep the show running smoothly.

He checks attendance. He cues the cast and crew. He oversees company morale. And he times the show, scene by scene, night after night. Running time is a sure measure of the shape of the show. Henri Caubisens, a veteran Broadway stage manager, times a play as clinically as a nurse watches a fever chart. "Three minutes over what it should be," he says, "and I call a brush-up rehearsal. Actors always stretch their speeches. When the play runs long, it's a signal for me to get rid of the 'improvements.' "

But stage managers can divide as well as conquer. They can be troublemakers rather than healers, holding on to authority by creating divisions within a company. It is not uncommon for a stage manager to be obsequious to the star and brutal to the understudy. Some stage managers are tyrants who publicly castigate an actor for being two minutes late for "half hour" or for not returning a prop ashtray to within an inch of its designated place.

Such pettiness can be understood only in terms of the frustrated aspirations of many stage managers. As one actor says, "They want to direct or they want to act, but they're not doing either, and they want you to pay for it."

Actors relate to all their fellow workers in the theater with varying degrees of volatility, but it is in the actor's relationships with other actors—onstage before an actual audience—that the codes of behavior are religiously heeded or wantonly flouted.

"Upstaging" is the most obvious breach of conduct. Literally, it means that an actor moves "up" (toward the back of) the stage while another actor is addressing him, thus keeping his own face conspicuously in view of the audience and forcing his fellow to turn his back to the audience. Older actors who have learned all the tricks are past masters of the art of upstaging.

Competition, especially between star actress and young male lead, can be vicious. Terry Kiser describes an experience in a West Coast production of *Sweet Bird of Youth*. He was young, the leading lady was an aging film star, and this was his chance for "experience." Curiously, the real-life situation paralleled the make-believe situation Tennessee Williams had put in his play—repulsion and attraction, rivalry and complicity, between the fading screen beauty Alexandra De Lago and the ambitious young stud Chance Wayne. In a preview performance before an audience, the actress behaved like her stage character. In the first scene, Kiser, following the exit of another character, dared to turn his eyes away from his leading lady, who was reclining on a bed. She leaped up in profane fury. Audience or no audience, she turned to the director sitting in the front row and screamed, "What the —— does this ——— actor think he's doing!" The audience was horrified by the exhibition and Kiser very nearly gave up his career on the spot. The lady in question is notorious for such behavior, and rarely works with any actor or director more than once.

There is also the story of a grande dame of the English stage who was behaving with outrageous highhandedness toward a young juvenile in the cast. In his big scene he was on his knees in front of her, pleading. Instead of remaining seated as the stage directions required during his long speech, the actress took to walking up and down the stage in her full flowing costume. Naturally, the juvenile's speech was ruined. Finally he decided to act. Kneeling firmly on the hem of her dress, he at last prevented her from getting up until he had finished his speech. The scene—now clearly his scene—won applause. Ever the star, the lady leaned down and hissed in his ear, "You're learning."

Some modern directors—Tyrone Guthrie, for instance—actually encourage actors to turn their backs occasionally on an audience; Guthrie calls the always-facing-front tradition "dreary" and ridicules it as "C-major-to-the-balcony stuff." This technique, while it may be interesting, is useful only in direct relation to the actor's audibility. Regardless of how they are directed, however, actors will always avoid and resent being upstaged, and Guthrie was always amused and understanding when he revisited his production of *The Tenth Man* to find that the actor he had instructed to deliver a speech with back to audience had revolved 180 degrees and was now squarely facing the audience.

Fredric March tells the story of his appearance in Thornton Wilder's *The Skin of Our Teeth* with Montgomery Clift, a young Method-trained actor. They had a scene together in the third act. Several weeks after the play opened, Clift began to jump his cue and overrun March's speech, coming in as much as four or five words before March stopped speaking and spoiling lines for the older actor night after night. "Tradition says you wait three times before you say anything," recalls March. "I waited three times and then spoke to him."

Clift's excuse was that at that moment it "felt right" for him to come in. "That's divine afflatus," March muttered to himself, and to Clift he said, "You may feel it, but it hurts my line. You didn't do this before. You're doing it out of the blue."

Clift still maintained his timing was the natural outgrowth of his role. "I see no reason why I should change," he declared.

"I'll tell you why you should change," said March. "You should change because I as an older actor ask you to change."

Where reason had failed, the prerogatives of age succeeded. Clift never jumped the speech again.

Actors can become paranoid about audience attention and the popularity of stage rivals, and resort to crude stage stratagems when they are not center-stage themselves—making extraneous movements, coughing, or indulging in sly stage business such as pulling out a handkerchief or picking up a stage prop and studying it intensely. Vaudeville-trained actors are the worst offenders. It is an old vaudeville trick for an actor to slap his thigh in exaggerated response to another actor's laugh line—but just a second too soon. The effect is more devastating to the laughed-at actor than a slap across the face. In the summer of 1969 off-Broadway's nude revue *Oh! Calcutta!* threw the art of upstaging into a whole new ballpark. How could five men and five girls appearing together on stage totally nude possibly gain any advantage from resorting to the old stratagems?

Immediate retaliation for rudeness from other actors can backfire. No actor can be angry on stage and still perform satisfactorily, but the offense can't go unnoticed and there are various ways to restrain the wrongdoer. Faced with the willful interference of another actor, Rae Allen performs what she calls "the laying on of hands." When another actor gets out of line and infringes on her own performance, she places her hands on his arm, gently but firmly, as if to say, "No, don't do that." Actors quickly get the point. Another actor simply relaxes and stays stock still while his stage rivals compete energetically for notice. In effect this is up-staging in reverse and the audience's attention frequently shifts back to the motionless actor.

The mood of a company is linked strongly to the code of onstage behavior. Company morale also fluctuates as it reflects the onstage tensions and private problems of actors. Monday night—the beginning of the performance week—is usually the worst night of the week, emotionally and artistically, for actors. The relaxation of a day off dulls technique and reaction, and audiences are generally slower to respond, for much the same reason. Actors learn to watch out for Monday nights.

Before and during the actual performance, actors are notoriously idiosyncratic about resisting the pressures of the outside world. Paul Muni would fly into a rage if anyone spoke to him before a show, particularly if he were told in advance of a celebrity in the audience. During the run of *Inherit the Wind* he issued an edict forbidding anyone to speak to him until the end of the play. In greeting him at the start of the evening, his fellow actors would learn to wave at him mutely. Ruth Gordon invariably paces in the wings like a caged lioness, waiting for show time, muttering to herself; she is going over her lines, which she repeats to herself every night of the run in the same methodical restlessness.

Self-insulation during the show is equally vital for most actors; backstage becomes a cocoon. "You've got to protect yourself as much as you can from things going wrong," says one actress. She learned her lesson while making personal telephone calls during stage waits. One night she called her sister "in one of our more hostile periods. I went on stage afterward in tears."

On the other hand, there are actors who can switch their double lives on and off without any appreciable trauma. Jason Robards, who had an hour offstage in the second act of *Long Day's Journey into Night,* used to slip out of the stage door to a nearby delicatessen where he would sit in costume and make-up drinking coffee. As his cue approached, he would amble into the wings with a container of strong coffee, usually a split second before his time. He would gulp a mouthful, plunge on stage totally in character, a lurching, agonized member of the Tyrone family, then exit. Without missing a beat, he would retrieve his coffee. He occasionally caused the stage manager near fits of apoplexy but he never once missed a cue.

Basically, the world of the actor in a given play is a sort of commune, a kibbutz in which a group of hectic individualists temporarily pool their lives for the common purpose of getting the show on and off. The nobility of communal life expresses itself in many ways; just as man often shows his finest attributes under enemy fire, so actors often rise to their highest levels of perception, discipline, artistry, and comradeship in meeting and vanquishing their common foe —the audience.

A company becomes a family soon after rehearsals start, and especially out of town, when the company can be compared to a platoon of infantry scouting in enemy territory. As a family, the actors fall swiftly into affectionate patterns and relationships. Despite the backbiting and gossipmongering that are common to productions, particularly when they are in trouble, there is generally an overall "one-for-all, all-for-one" unity that occurs when sensitive mortals are thrown together on unfamiliar terrain in chancy circumstances and have only each other to cling to as the venture moves doggedly ahead to success or failure. Even the special language of the stage sharpens a separation from the world and creates internal cohesiveness. "If you talk acting," Miss Murphy says, "you have to talk to actors; nobody else will understand what the hell you're talking about."

Some shows develop a closer company solidarity than others. *Fiddler on the Roof* is a case in point. When "Places!" is called just before curtain, all cast members go out on stage and circulate quietly, talking. The ceremony, which began spontaneously soon after the show opened, strengthens friendship and communal spirit and is akin to religious ritual. With other shows, when places are called, the actors usually gather in the wings to await the curtain and their cues. But with *Fiddler* this semimystical expression of group identity, a quiet assertion of faith and belief in the work, is made before every performance.

It is erroneous to suppose that because actors lead lives that seem glamorous to nonactors the little world of actors can never be dull or commonplace to those who inhabit it. Trade talk among actors becomes just as parochial and monotonous as trade talk in any other calling and no one is more conscious of how narrow theater can be than the sensitive actor.

"To talk theater, theater, theater drives me up the wall," says Miss Danner, impatient with the ingrown nature of a society which tends to feed on itself. Miss Allen says, "If you're smart you don't always associate with other actors. It's stultifying and boring."

Inevitably, then, the actor must live in two worlds. When his own proscenium world goes dark he must join another world, the outside society which applauds him at the curtain and views him oddly when he emerges from the stage door and moves among them. The actor must make a place for himself outside, as the outside world must make a place for the actor.

The community of actors within the larger community of the playmakers is an intense society of siblings, often at each others' throats and beset by fierce pressures. A chasm of misunderstanding, opened centuries ago, separates the actor from the "square" world—the world of the "normal" breadwinner with regular hours and conforming life styles. For actors, respectability and social acceptance have come only recently.

Even now, in 1969, actors are not altogether accepted as "regular" human beings by the civilian world which applauds them for their art. For many nonactors in modern times the actor is still an inferior and incomplete being. "We are the dock rats, the deformed children of the world," Maureen Stapleton once told an interviewer.

Miss Stapleton is of course dramatizing the legend that actors are strange beings. The legend dies hard. It has persisted for a thousand years, and, as with all legends, there is some truth to it. As one of the oldest professions, acting has never been quite proper in the eyes of the establishment, of whatever time or place. In one of his satires Horace called actors *mendici, mimae, balatrones, hoc genus omne* (Beggars, mimics, buffoons, and all that sort). In fourth-century Spain a sacerdotal council made it a sin to marry or entertain actors or comedians and mandated excommunication for offenders. In England an act of Parliament in 1597 stated: "All bearwards, common players of interludes, counterfeit Egyptians, etc. shall be taken, adjudged and deemed rogues, vagabonds and sturdy beggars."

Actors were forbidden the sacraments by the Bishop of Arras in France in 1695, couldn't be married in respectable American churches as recently as the turn of the twentieth century, and were denied burial in consecrated ground in New York City as recently as 1870.

In 1969 a stockbroker whose son had left Columbia to study at the American Academy of Dramatic Arts inquired plaintively, "What did I do wrong? How can that boy want to be an actor, how can he want to mess around with actors? When I tell him this, he asks me how could I want to be a stockbroker!" In the eighteenth century Alexander Pope expressed the same upper-class point of view in "The Dunciad" when he described actors as "peel'd, patch'd, and piebald, linsey-woolsey brothers, grave mummers . . . sleeveless some and shirtless others." Samuel Johnson told Boswell that players were "no better than creatures set upon tables and stools to make faces and produce laughter like dancing dogs." St. John Chrysostom, certainly no stockbroker, wrote, "Spending time in theaters produces fornication, intemperance and every kind of impurity," and in 1775 the British parson Charles Churchill called actors "a strolling tribe; a despicable race."

The concept of the actor as rogue and vagabond—shiftless, irresponsible, immoral, irreverent, unstable, improper—has persisted. In story and song, in TV and film, he comes through as the eternal outsider, childlike and egomaniacal and not worthy of trust.

Reflecting the judgment of society, families rarely give their blessings to children who want to enter the theater. The theme of parental rejection runs through actors' reminiscences. Fredric March recalls that his father, a midwestern businessman, pleaded with him to go into the banking business, ultimately "forgave" him, still urged him not to marry a "painted actress." (He did.[10]) Rosemary Murphy had a continental upbringing and her childhood was spent abroad in foreign capitals. She was schooled by Sacred Heart nuns. "They taught that no nice woman could become anything but a wife and mother. For me there was always a conflict between what my family wanted and the nuns taught and what I wanted to be. I never remember thinking it could be both. I got no encouragement from my family. They made excuses about it being such a tough profession, but they simply didn't want me to act. Now, they don't mind. In fact, they're rather proud of me."

Why are actors suspected, feared, so frequently condemned through the ages and in so many different cultures and countries? Modern insights supply a few clues.

The actor *is* different; his work and his habits are different. He is part of an unconventional minority amid a con-

---

[10] She is the actress Florence Eldridge, and the marriage has lasted forty years.

formist majority, and he is therefore "not quite right." Actors have never been shy about flaunting their apartness from the Establishment; therefore, they have faced legal, societal, and emotional repression.

An actor's craft is hard for most people to fathom. He can move an audience to tears and laughter, but they do not understand how he does it. It smacks somehow of sorcery and deceit; it is not quite truthful since it is obvious pretending. Most people value what is tangible and can be bartered or exchanged. By this standard the output of the actor has little value and the meaning of his life is ephemeral and meretricious. How can one equate the worth of an evening's memory with a painting, a book, a building, or a business that can be handed down? Stage actors cannot bequeath anything of their worth to posterity. Their performances may stir their contemporaries but their art does not survive, which is probably why actors cherish clippings and scrapbooks as tangible proofs of their accomplishments. Theater is illusion and the actor's art illusory.

Television and films have relieved the actor's built-in sense of impermanence to some extent. Since the turn of the century it has been possible to record their work for the future, and thus the craft has greater meaning because it lives beyond the life-span of the performer. The fact that actors have gained so much prestige and acceptance in recent years is unquestionably due to the lasting impact of the new media.

The "rogue and vagabond" image of the actor has been linked through the ages to his chronic insolvency. Actors from time immemorial have been poor risks for tradesmen and landlords. Wandering minstrels, things of shreds and patches, ready to sacrifice salaries for applause, actors were notoriously impoverished throughout history. It is hard to believe that actors' unions have existed in the Western world for barely fifty years! The neediness of actors is one reason for the perpetual militancy of actors' unions. The late Ben Irving, an Actors' Equity executive, used to say, "An actor is the only human being who will work for nothing—if you let him." One of Actors' Equity's most extraordinary funds still supplies shoes free to any actor who cannot afford to buy them, and hundreds of pairs are given away every year.

But the modern actor is beginning to assert his worth to society more positively than ever before, working with increasing confidence in an environment in which the acceptance of all the arts, including theater, has grown. The affluence of the 1960's, with its emphasis on leisure-time pursuits, has given theater more prominence. This is reflected in the proliferation of new urban cultural centers, the multiplicity of resident professional theater companies in city after city, the fact that actors are hired the year round, and the growing emphasis on the dramatic arts on university campuses across the country. In short, the demand for culture has risen in the affluent society, and the value of the actor has risen with it.

At the same time the unions have bolstered the actor's uncertain economic position. The once-starvation wage of the actor has been driven steadily up in successive triennial negotiations by Actors' Equity to the level of sustenance if not luxury, and the union was even able to win pensions for its members after the ten-day actors' strike of 1960.[11]

With affluence and social security, the actor's image is changing. Many actors now commute to the theater from mortgaged suburban homes and talk taxes and the stock market in the wings while waiting to go on. In the Broadway musical *Redhead* a principal actor once was asked, "How's everything with the show?" and replied, "Never mind the show! How about that Texas Instruments?" In or out of a show he is still speculating in the stock market.

Burgess Meredith sums up the new image, "Actors are not outcasts now. I know no place where actors are not welcome, in Buckingham Palace, in the White House, in cafe society. Actors are senators and governors now—look at Ron-

[11] Before the Equity strike of 1960 the minimum weekly wage for a Broadway actor was $103.50; the strike boosted it to $111. As of June 1969 the weekly minimum for a Broadway actor was $150.

ald Reagan and George Murphy; and they're big-money men—look at Robert Montgomery and Richard Burton."

Hobe Morrison, the veteran drama reporter and critic for *Variety*, is even more emphatic about the stability of the working actor and show people in general. "Theater people," he says, "are basically about the same as everyone else. If they are different—and perhaps they are a little bit —it's because of the contrasts in the conditions under which they live and work. The real professionals in the theater are, I firmly believe, less egocentric, vain, shallow, petty, or spiteful than nontheatrical people. . . . Comparatively speaking, show-business people are squares."

Serious actors repeat insistently, "The actor is his own instrument." The artist disappears behind canvas, the novelist behind the pages of his book. But the actor, unassisted, exposed, alone, works in full public view with his body, his voice, and his personality as the direct expression of the ideas he must convey. This is why an actor talks about how helplessly vulnerable he feels on the stage. He is his one and only weapon, his own instrument.

Playing many roles, an actor exhibits or expresses many aspects of himself. Before the audience can "identify" with the actor, the actor must first "identify" with the character he is playing.

In 1963, when the first directors of the Lincoln Center Repertory Company were looking for an actress combining sensuality with innocence to play the part of Maggie in Arthur Miller's long autobiographical play *After the Fall,* they turned to a young, relatively unknown member of their own company, Barbara Loden. She was an apprentice player who left her Asheville, North Carolina, home at seventeen and came north alone to become a model or actress. Her baptism in show business was to be shot out of a cannon in a carnival. Elia Kazan, co-director of the company, had spotted her in several quick-closing Broadway shows and had cast her in small parts in two of his films. Now she was with the Lincoln Center group, a young, physically magnetic unknown.

Miller intended the part of Maggie, it became clear later, to represent his ex-wife, Marilyn Monroe. During casting in 1963 Miss Loden had a long talk with the playwright before she had read a line of the script. "He talked to me about everything," she recalled. "I told him all about my life. I had the impression he was a quiet man. But he likes to talk. He told me many things about his life, and that spurred me to talk about mine."

The conversation lasted two hours. At the time Miss Loden was nine months pregnant, and soon after the baby came she auditioned for the role. Reading the script for the first time, she was immediately struck by certain resemblances between herself and the character, and she saw herself in the part. "I was so sure of it that I thought Miller must have written these lines after our talk. They sounded exactly like my life."

Did that mean she was comparing herself to Marilyn Monroe? "Let's say our lives ran parallel to each other," she answered, "but at a great distance."

Parallel lives at a great distance. Parallel experience between performer and part—it is this that creates the fusion between a gifted actor and a great role. The result is called many things—charismatic, bravura, electric.

Katharine Cornell was asked to define "star quality." She hesitated. "It's a magic. It's a God-given thing, that's all. In the end it's something from the stars."

But it will not happen unless the part is there to begin with and the actor as instrument can realize the part's dynamics.

It is virtually impossible for people outside the actor's world to understand how complex the actor's relationship to his past can be, and how much research and self-discovery the creative actor must employ. Even people in the theater frequently underestimate the actor's crisis of identity. Jerome Chodorov, an experienced playwright-director, says, "An actor's favorite line is 'I really can't say that.' When you ask why, they tell you, but it's unintelligible—an avalanche of vagueness. There's a neurotic compulsion to change for the sake of change. Comics are the worst—it has to be *their* joke. Method actors don't want to be actors; they want to be creators."

The gifted Florence Eldridge, actress-wife of Fredric March, calls acting "a schizophrenic experience. You're working on two levels. You try to recapture fantasy each night. And then the editorial part of your mind begins to function, coolly monitoring the fantasy part of you and making intellectual comments on your performance."

With every role, an actor must look into himself unflinchingly. From his own inner life and experience, he must dredge up the sense material of his new identity. The period of self-exposure can be painful, but out of it the actor gains a new sense of power and authority. Cloaked in the new identity of his stage character, he no longer needs to be so protective of self. Many actors are painfully shy and withdrawn in real life while on stage they are outgoing and aggressive. Many who stammer offstage speak with bell-like clarity onstage. The armor of the new personality confers a quicksilver power. It is common for actors who perform smoothly onstage to become mute and terrified at the thought of speaking in public on their own behalf.

Rehearsing a role, actors frequently suppress or relinquish their own personality traits and assume new ones. These changes of identity can cause feelings of rejection and alienation in those who know them best in private life—husbands or wives or lovers. Blythe Danner says, "When I work on roles I tend to change. This caused a problem with a boyfriend I had. When I started to work on the part of Lily—the neurotic young wife in *Toys in the Attic*—he could see me becoming involved in the part. It's not that I was Lily twenty-four hours a day, but things do creep out when I begin to investigate a part. I become a little more like the role. And my boy friend, all he says is, 'Oh, no, here we go again!' "

For Terry Kiser, a new life commences the instant rehearsals begin. His first move is to put on the specific pair of shoes he will use in the play; he likes to work on the part from the ground up. As rehearsals progress, he digs deeper and deeper into the role, and his concentration begins to affect outside relationships, even his relationship with a young actress who is his girl friend. "To me, the stage and my life become the same. I am thoroughly engrossed in the part. I try my role out all day long in the rehearsal hall and away from it. When I was working in an engineering firm and acting nights, a fellow in my office would say, 'I see another part of your character coming into this office every time you get a new part.' I take a lot of this out on my girl friend. I withdraw into the part and cut her out of my life."

In building characterizations, the actor becomes an "identity magpie," borrowing from himself and from both casual and close acquaintances. No one is spared. Fredric March becomes, in his own words, "a human tape recorder," classifying voice shadings, lisps, stammers, tics and winks and lifted eyebrows, studying people everywhere. When asked about a specific onstage mannerism, March will say, "I got that from an old fellow in Racine, Wisconsin," or "Elia Kazan has this habit, and I find it's right for certain moments."

Sometimes the search for new identity causes understandable confusion within the actor himself. Rosemary Murphy was assigned the part of a corporation executive's wife in a television drama, and she said of the experience, "I saw the part in terms of the wife of a general my family knows and decided to copy her. But I had just had a fight with a friend, and suddenly I wasn't the executive's wife at all, but my friend." The conscious choice of one set of characteristics had given way to the subconscious adoption of others with a deeper private meaning. Since the part was that of a dictatorial, argumentative woman, the actress was evidently giving vent to her private feud without quite realizing it.

Borrowing identities can be acutely painful, psychologically, in the "emotional recall" scenes performed in the classes of Lee Strasberg, the acting teacher and theoretician who is head of the Actors Studio. In these classes an actor methodically re-creates an emotional scene out of his own life, step by step, reconstructing the physical circumstances and sense data of the actual happening—the size and shape of the room, the placement of the furniture, the time of day, the quality of sunlight—until the original emotional impact returns in full force. Actors, helpless in the grip of recollection, are temporarily reduced to emotional "basket cases" right before the eyes of an audience.

Psychosomatic quirks also develop. An actress started to have headaches several weeks into rehearsal. She mentioned her indisposition to her male co-star, who admitted to having horrid nightmares. They were rehearsing two one-act plays. "In both of them he was trying to kill me," said the actress later. "In both of them I ended up killing him. Both of us had been going around for a month with murder in our hearts." [12]

Theoretically, by opening night an actor has determined his stage identity, but the conscientious actor never stops refining characterization. Lynn Fontanne is famous for having worked on a line in *Reunion in Vienna* until the very last performance (it ran for 264 showings), when the labor paid off in a huge laugh. It had been there all the time, but it took her eight months to find it.

The new breed of actor is equally persistent, although his technique is more self-consciously oriented to "feeling" the characterization than to working on the delivery of lines. Kiser attacks his assignments in terms of character rather than story. "I try to find the flow of the character, not the play." After he "sets" a role—that is, freezes the patterns of behavior of his characters—he maintains a looseness in the playing. Within the tight framework set in rehearsal he varies his performance from night to night to keep it fresh and flexible. He calls himself a very "specific" actor—every stage movement has to be motivated, there

[12] The film *A Double Life* (1950), starring Ronald Colman and Shelley Winters dealt with the problem of an actor playing Othello. Filled with homicidal urges toward Desdemona, he re-creates the stage situation in real life and strangles a blonde girl friend he believes is unfaithful to him.

must be a reason for each action. This does not necessarily oblige him to think what the character is supposed to be thinking, but thought must be running through his mind. If the actor's mind is blank, the audience will notice it immediately and stop believing in the character.

Kiser gave an example: "In my last play there was a point where I had to look up at the ceiling reflectively and think about when I would get out of prison. What I was actually looking at was a grate in the wall with one unpainted board in it. Every night I would look up and see the board and ask myself why was it unpainted.

"I remember seeing the wonderful actor James Earl Jones in *Blood Knot* and I was fascinated because thought was obviously running through his mind when he was just sitting and not speaking. You could almost see it. Now I know what he was doing. When he picked up a match book he would be reading the inside of the cover, word for word."

For a character to be totally convincing on stage, the actor must make him not only physically but psychologically consistent. Using analytical powers, the actor must delve into the subconscious thought of the character and express it in terms of physical behavior. Suppose an actor is playing John Jones, a character suffering from a neurosis. The actor decides that one way to convey the character's nervousness is with an eye twitch, but if the twitch is so marked that the audience is constantly aware of it, he overdoes the effect and spoils it. However, if the twitch is so subtle that it becomes subliminal and a part of his character, he has achieved a level of artistry.

It is this carefully jeweled detail that actors relish in the performance of other actors. To an actor as audience, there is no professional experience quite so pleasurable as to explore the tricks and devices a great performer uses, and it takes an actor to appreciate the subtle play of the subconscious at work in a fellow actor's performance.

Despite their jealousy of each other, actors need heroes, and they are unabashed idolaters of such renowned actors as the Lunts, Katharine Hepburn, John Gielgud, and Laurence Olivier. Most actors watch, study, and steal from brilliant performances, taking technique, ideas, and inspiration. Young actors are especially struck when older actors take great risks with their careers by accepting roles foreign to their own experience or attempting radically new interpretations of familiar parts, such as Olivier did with Othello in the British National Theatre.

Actors are their own best audiences, and actors give their best performances when other actors are present. On Broadway, it is a tradition for a show to give periodic benefit performances to aid the Actors' Fund, which cares for ill and needy members of the profession. The Actors' Fund Benefit is an extra performance scheduled on a Sunday night when other working members of the profession can attend, and it is the most exhilarating performance of the season. The cast is "up," the audience is eager. It is a gala affair with curtain calls and bravos—actors being accepted warmly by their peers.

Another extraordinary performance in the life cycle of a show is the "gypsy run-through," so named because it is also held at a time when the gypsies and the other working members of the profession can attend. This performance, usually held in late afternoon, is the last performance a rehearsing cast gives before going out of town in tryout. There is no scenery or costumes; they have been sent on ahead. The actors are in work clothes, without make-up, on a bare stage under crude lighting: all there is are actors and words. The invited audience consists of theater people: actors, bit players, chorus dancers, theatrical office workers.

The audience reacts to everything. The just-rehearsed company, which has still to meet its first paying audience, responds. For sheer brilliance of performance the gypsy run-through, primitive and preliminary as it is, is hardly ever surpassed.

Actors encourage each other because they recognize their own deep-lying fears and insecurities and the constant need for encouragement and praise. A beginning actor will mistake the apparent self-control of an older actor for confidence. He feels the veteran has somehow overcome the doubts, misgivings, and indecisions of apprenticeship, but it is not long before he recognizes the elemental truth of his profession and can say, "I don't know an actor who isn't insecure."

When actress Marian Seldes worked in a play with John Gielgud, she was heartened and relieved to find that even a great actor makes mistakes. "To hear Gielgud stammer over a line—it's not like watching a bad actor stumble," she said. "You watch him work things out and you say to yourself, 'So that's the way a great actor meets a problem.' And you learn."

Chronic underemployment, the wild improbability of job hunting, the uncertainty of audience response, the vagaries of public taste—all these trigger the actor's insecurity. Every part, every rehearsal, every performance is a new start, a new challenge. Actors are obsessed with the fear of being all acted out and unable to act again. "I'm always terrified when I start a new play," confesses Terry Kiser. "In rehearsal I feel I'm dried up, that I can't do it. It happens every rehearsal period, but I get over it."

Of the three-week rehearsal period Eli Wallach says, "I know I'll develop voice trouble in the third week. And I know I'll get over it."

The insecurity is endless. It is not surprising that actors crave praise and acclaim, beginning immediately after the performance. It is obligatory to visit an actor backstage after the show and obligatory to say something nice. "Always tell an actor he was marvelous," says one producer. "Lie in your teeth."

Opening nights call for bravura flattery. There is no such thing as too much adulation. Nothing is really enough after a smashingly successful opening, not even a full-dress parade through Times Square with a band, cheering crowds, and the victorious star throwing kisses in triumph.

But the parade is another fantasy.

Whatever the rewards of acting—and they can be immense—the majority of actors are doomed to be also-rans. Stardom and affluence are elusive to all but a very few. Burgess Meredith is philosophical, even optimistic about the actor's life. "Actors," he says, "have to get over feeling inferior, that they're puppets, secondary or tertiary figures. If an actor doesn't make a star of himself, there's still room for him—he can be a clerk, not a president."

Other actors are less ebullient. Veteran character man Merrill Joels says, "No matter who an actor is, after he's done the job he's unemployed again. You go out of town, you open up in town, and you close in a week. Getting a job is a heartbreak, keeping it is a heartbreak, and losing it is a heartbreak."

The question inevitably comes up—Why be an actor? Why do actors persist? How did they get into the profession in the first place?

The reasons are diverse and do not lend themselves to easy generalization. Some actors, such as Katharine Cornell, the Barrymores, and Jason Robards, are from acting families. Others take up the profession as an act of rebellion, flouting parental discipline by escaping into "bohemia." For Burgess Meredith, acting was *"reductio ad absurdum.* I had failed in everything else." Maureen Stapleton went to movies where "the actors all looked nice, made money, and were loved. I was a poor kid and had an unhappy home life." Emery Battis, who quit a professorship at Rutgers University after twenty years of teaching to act in a regional theater in Minneapolis, says, "I wanted to be an actor by the time I was thirteen or fourteen, but the depression made things so disheartening that I gave it up." Fredric March acted in a civic theater as a youth and abandoned his bank job in adult life when the routine palled.

In every case the actor has an unusual gift for fantasy. This ability to fantasize is true of all children, and, in an affirmative sense, carries over with actors into adult life. "They're all children!" a producer will say frequently and with annoyance. And he is right. Actors have retained the child's ability to improvise without shame.

Living in fantasy, actors learn to tell stories early. Like the actor, the child is constantly playing greater-than-life roles. In fantasy the child lives the role of the grownup. In performance the grown-up actor becomes the warrior king, the brave soldier, the great lover. And by some perverse logic the stern and disapproving parent often stimulates this drive to fantasy by driving his child to express artistic impulses previously buried under family discipline.

Herschel Bernardi says, "Actors have retained their childhood. They will not give it up, which makes them very unhappy people, which makes them conflicted all the time. At the same time, it makes it possible for them to convey and interpret life to an audience—that childlike quality makes them look at the world as if for the first time, with wonder and freshness and beauty, and they see things. Actors are able to see things that an ordinary adult cannot see, because he's lost that childishness. The actor has not lost it, and though it's a curse, it's the only thing that makes him worth anything."

Unique gratification can come to the actor through the stage, because onstage an actor becomes more fully realized than he could in real life. "I find myself in theater," is a common actor's expression. The actress-daughter of a celebrity says, "Having a well-known father was no answer. Oddly enough, only by playing other parts did I find myself."

An overwhelming fear of self-betrayal keeps an actor returning again and again to the stage. Rae Allen says, "If you stand still, you will petrify. If you don't feed your talent, it will die."

The actor's life has such irresistible fascination that every year all over America dozens of people leave well-established jobs and break up apparently orderly lives to become actors. They are usually in their middle years and some are quite successful, but they are obviously unfulfilled in what they are doing, and acting supplies long-felt needs.

Consider Joel Fredericks. Until the age of forty-two Fred-

ericks was a podiatrist in St. Joseph, Missouri, making $30,-
000 a year. His appointment book was filled a year in advance and he had three examination rooms constantly in
use.

"I had an active social and community life," he recalls.
"I was president of Kiwanis, active in the Shrine and United
Fund drive. I joined the community theater in 1952. My
first part was Inspector Rough in *Angel Street*. I did twenty
plays in ten years with the local drama group. I drove a
Thunderbird, I had closets full of clothes, I belonged to the
country club. I had everything."

Fredericks was single and lived with his widowed father.
In 1962 his father died. He began to question his life, to
ask himself what he really wanted. It burst upon him that
acting was what he enjoyed most, and within two weeks he
had abandoned his practice and left for Glenwood Springs,
Colorado, to act in melodramas. Then he came to New York.

"I've never been happier," he says. "In seven years I've
done two Broadway shows. I've toured, done summer stock,
two industrials, a dozen movies mostly as an extra. I had a
bit in the elevator in *Barefoot in the Park* with Jane Fonda
and Robert Redford. I was a court stenographer with Kirk
Douglas and Eli Wallach in *A Lovely Way to Die* and I was
in the delicatessen scene in *The Night They Raided Min-
sky's.*

"I've run into a lot of antagonism from other people because I'm an actor. Motel and restaurant people resent actors; they think we're pushy and demanding and conceited.
Some of us are.

"All my friends in St. Joe want to know if I've got acting
out of my system yet. So I asked one of them, an attorney,
if he's got the law out of his system yet.

"I guess there was something about my old life that I
didn't like. When I'm onstage, I'm somebody else—it's a
great catharsis. Now I'm onstage twenty-four hours a day.
I'm very fulfilled. I want to be free, and I'm free."

CHAPTER FOUR

The Odd Couple: Playwright and Director

On the eleventh floor of the Sardi Building the elevator opens into a narrow lobby whose walls are covered with autographed pictures. Facing the elevator, a heavy iron door opens into a huge room. The ceiling is sky-blue with an oval design and gilt decoration; a thick blue rug covers the parquet floor. In front of a marble fireplace two black leather sofas face each other across a glass-topped coffee table opposite French windows opening onto a roof balcony. At the near end of the room is a writing desk. At the far end, beyond the grand piano, the drawn curtains filter out the harsh electrics of Times Square. In this magnificent room the stage is set for a modern comedy of manners.

This is the figurative home of the playwright—the office

of the powerful Dramatists Guild. The photographs in the lobby gallery are of senior Guild members whose collective earnings in the theater are incalculable. The iron door, a nineteenth-century Italian trophy, is an immovable relic of earlier Shubert occupancy, for these rooms were once J. J. Shubert's penthouse apartment. In his later years, white-haired and bent, he would limp home on the arm of his much younger wife after an opening in the Shubert Theatre across the street and pass through the long drawing room to his bedroom, there to gaze with dim eye upon his molded ceiling. The former Shubert bedroom, now fitted with an antique table-desk, is now the office of David E. LeVine, the brisk young executive secretary of the Dramatists Guild. A dressing room, the kitchen pantry, and two small maid's rooms in the rear hold records, files, and secretaries. The Shubert dining room has become the Guild Council room where once a month from September through June eighteen to twenty dramatists meet around the long table under the chairmanship of Frank D. Gilroy, the Guild's twelfth president, to discuss the affairs of the theater and the condition of the playwright.

The baronial splendor of Guild headquarters matches the status of the playwright and suits an aristocracy of achievement whose public image is that of a cocktail-party hero, witty, world-weary, and wealthy—the handsome, urbane writer of hit comedies with a duplex apartment in midtown Manhattan and a summer home in Maine, or the tall, distinguished dramatist who lunches at the St. Regis between rehearsals, or the lyricist whose chauffeured Rolls waits outside the Oak Room of the Plaza. One floor below the Guild penthouse, the plain rooms of the companion Authors Guild attest to the lower earning power of the writer of books as opposed to the writer of plays.

The Guild is a prosperous organization even though most playwrights cannot make a living in the theater. Its income in dues and assessments may be estimated conservatively as well in excess of a quarter of a million dollars a year, derived from a handful of thriving members. There are

only 515 active members in the Dramatists Guild (as opposed to more than 3,000 in the Authors Guild), comprised
of composers, musical-book writers, and lyricists as well as
playwrights. For all practical purposes the Guild dictates
contract terms for all scripts produced on Broadway. The
standard Dramatists Guild contract, thirty-five pages of
closely packed legal strictures, must be countersigned by producers, playwrights, and the Guild before a production
can begin. The agreement gives the dramatist absolute control over his material and approval of director, designer, and
cast. Curiously enough, the League of New York Theatres
and the Dramatists Guild do not have an official agreement
between them on these basic terms. Producers resent the
unilateral authority of the Guild and mutter periodically
about its "monopolistic" practices, but nothing is ever
really done about negotiating a new collective agreement.
A producer technically does not have to sign a Dramatists
Guild contract to produce a play, but no playwright will
deal with him without a contract. And there the matter
rests, uneasily.

An author's minimum royalties are figured at about 10
per cent of the gross. A few playwrights of international
stature may command higher royalties as well as a percentage of the show's profits. Active members of the Guild—
those who have had a "first-class" production of a play, usually on Broadway—pay a $20 annual membership plus a
percentage of weekly royalties (2 per cent on royalties under $3,000, 3 per cent on royalties over $3,000). Suppose a
play grosses $50,000. The playwright's weekly royalty will
amount to $5000. He will turn back 3 per cent of this
amount, or $150, to the Dramatists Guild. There are 1,325
associate members of the Guild—those who have had a play
optioned for first-class production but not yet produced—
who pay a $10 annual membership fee, with 2 per cent of
their option earnings going to the Guild. In the spring of
1969 the Guild, for the first time, asserted jurisdiction over
off-Broadway and began to admit off-Broadway playwrights.

The life style of the working playwright, however, bears

little relation to the image of the opulence and noble insulation projected by the Dramatists Guild headquarters. In real life he is neither opulent nor insulated. He inhabits two distinct worlds—the private, inner world of creation in which he works, and the public world of audiences and critics and interviews in which the work has meaning and is fulfilled.

Israel Horovitz is a young playwright who supported himself in advertising before a first notable success off Broadway. Horovitz lives in an uptown Manhattan apartment with his wife and three children, but his mornings are spent in a friend's apartment in Greenwich Village where he buries himself in long sessions at the typewriter. (Horovitz has his own system for finding cheap studio space to write in. He locates a friend who is going out of town and asks to use the apartment in the friend's absence. When he offers to pay the cleaning lady, the deal is usually clinched.) Like all writers, Horovitz works in isolation, but he accepts the need to promote himself and his ideas in all possible media as part of his life. Periodically he goes on television interview shows to augment his audience.

Brought up in an electronic environment, the modern young playwright understands the pressures and uses of this environment more readily than do his older colleagues. He sees himself as a solitary artist, but he also knows that the public will only take notice of him if he is successful. Horovitz says, "To me, to be a playwright is to write plays. That's all. To the world, it means to write plays, to have them produced, to have them reviewed favorably, and then, after the first play, and the second, and maybe the third succeeds, they accept you as a playwright."

No one knows for sure just how many persons there are who fit the definition of a playwright as someone who has written a play, but it is obviously many times the membership of the Dramatists Guild. Somebody somewhere is always writing a play. Broadway producers receive hundreds of unsolicited scripts a year, even though plays that aren't submitted through an agent or that aren't recommended by someone in the theater practically never reach Broadway. In ten years play agent Leah Salisbury has found, among all the scripts that have come in "cold" to her office, only one or two of any interest at all, and none strong enough for Broadway. Even when a script is accepted by an agent and bought by a producer, it may never get on. The Dramatists Guild estimates that for every four plays optioned for Broadway, only one gets produced, and off-Broadway the odds are five to one. Of the plays that do reach Broadway, according to long-established odds, only one out of five will become a hit.[1] That means that in a Broadway season of fifty plays not more than ten will succeed.

No playwright, young or old, produced or unproduced, can escape the brutal economics of his trade. In no other field except perhaps wildcat oil drilling are the swings between success and failure so enormous, so capricious, and so abrupt. Some playwrights find these odds unplayable. Paddy Chayefsky is widely regarded as a highly successful playwright and yet he will no longer write for Broadway even though three of his four Broadway plays were hits: *Middle of the Night, The Tenth Man,* and *Gideon.* Chayefsky's last Broadway show, *The Passion of Josef D.,* closed after fifteen performances in 1964. "The dramatic writer has become unnecessary," says Chayefsky. "The most significant people writing today, in the words of Seymour Krim, are creative non-fiction writers such as Norman Mailer. The noble theater is gone. If drama is to persist at all it will be in university theater or on television, and the chances of the latter are minimal."

Chayefsky, short, bearded, and built like a wrestler, works in a Seventh Avenue studio just north of the theater district but no longer on plays for Broadway. "I'm taking one last crack at television," he says, "even though it's a pretty lousy whorehouse to be working in. They tell you they're interested in drama, but they're not. They'd just as soon run *Bonanza* forever.

"In the theater what you find now is the instant play, and

[1] A hit is defined as a show that has returned its production cost and shows a profit.

the playwright doesn't matter. I don't approve of this because I'm a writer, and I want to matter. We pretend we're living by industrial age values but we don't. We're living in a technotronic society and the dramatist is unnecessary. Somebody should do a piece on the function of art in the post-industrial world."

Working two years on a play that runs fifteen performances is heartbreaking emotionally and financially, and yet one Broadway hit can make its author a millionaire. At the age of twenty-seven Herb Gardner saw his first comedy, *A Thousand Clowns,* become successful. It played in New York in 1962–63 for 429 performances—a comfortable, but not exceptional run—and then ran a season on the road. It was sold to the movies and has been performed extensively in stock. With his royalties from Broadway and touring, the film sale and foreign rights, and an expected generation of stock performances on tap, *A Thousand Clowns* will earn Gardner a minimum of $750,000. The incredible Neil Simon, whose first play, *Come Blow Your Horn,* was produced in New York less than ten years ago, is estimated to have earned some $4 million in royalties from the five plays and three musicals he has so far turned out. Even unsuccessful plays can make handsome profits for their authors. Alec Coppel saw his comedy, *The Gazebo,* end a season's run in New York in 1961 having repaid only 50 per cent of its investment, and yet he made $54,000 in royalties just from the Broadway run plus another $60,000 from the movie sale. For the lucky dramatist, a hit is an annuity.[2]

With such huge profits within reach, everyone involved in a production, including the playwright, is susceptible to Broadway's much-deplored "hit" psychology. However pure

[2] Stock and foreign rights can be enormously profitable. John Patrick's play, *The Curious Savage,* which ran for a few weeks on Broadway, has earned him hundreds of thousands of dollars in stock. Several of Patrick's plays have detoured Broadway altogether, premiering in stock and living out their lives without a New York production. He has also made millions from Broadway—*Teahouse of the August Moon, The Hasty Heart,* etc. It might also be noted that writing a hit play leads to lucrative writing assignments in other fields, notably films.

an artist's motives may be at the outset, the pressures may
be corrupting. No matter how many rights and approvals a
playwright has in his contract, as one writer points out, they
mean nothing unless the play is successful. "You give up all
to get a hit," he says. "If you don't have a hit, you have
nothing." He cites this example: one producer always starts
out with the best artistic intentions, but halfway through
production, obsessed by fear of failure, he changes course
and veers toward what seems "commercial," disillusioning
his writers and ultimately himself.

Because the stakes are high, playwrights and their collaborators become neurotic about quick success, according to
director Alan Schneider. In the summer of 1969, after a
disheartening season in which he had directed four failures
in a row, Schneider toured Eastern Europe, visiting Moscow, Budapest, Bucharest, and Prague. He returned refreshed. "In that society—and there's a lot wrong with it—
theater people are a lot less neurotic than we are, and there's
a simple answer. No one there makes a million bucks fast.
No one becomes a success fast. No one gets destroyed fast.
Our problem is that every time you do a show you're laid
bare in front of a thousand people a night. Everybody's
naked. You're either a son-of-a-bitch nothing or you're a great
genius. There's no in-between."

The pressure-cooker conditions of commercial theater torment all but the hardiest writers at one time or another.
Creative inhibitions, writer's block, and manic-depressive
states recur so commonly in playwrights that they become
part of life, particularly after a galling failure.[3]

William Murray, a young dramatist who has had several
productions off-Broadway and on the West Coast but never
on Broadway, has given up on the theater numberless times
only to come back again. He loathes the theater experience
even while he craves it: "In the theater, win or lose, you

[3] Psychiatrist Philip Weissman holds that writer's depression stems from
deeper causes than mere lack of success. He feels that the serious dramatist
is always searching for solutions of unresolved traumatic childhood experiences. See Weissman's *Creativity in the Theater* (Basic Books, 1965).

lose—time, health, peace of mind, temper, confidence, even, for weeks and months, the desire or the ability to write anything else ever again." For Mary Rodgers, daughter of Richard Rodgers, herself a produced composer, the sensation of failure is like dying. "You decide you can't do anything about it. You try to do it as gracefully and with as much good humor as possible." This attitude of philosophic resignation is not the norm, however.

The younger playwrights are less apt to despair. Israel Horovitz has conceived a ritual for opening nights in order to persuade himself that the fate of the world does not necessarily hang upon the outcome of his play. For an hour before curtain he takes a walk around the Bowery looking at the defeated figures that move along the street dragging their irreversible lives like shadows. "Then I say to myself whether they love my play or hate it, nothing is going to change the conditions I see around me on the Bowery. Surely not a play."

By the nature of things, playwrights and drama critics are doomed to be enemies, and yet today's dramatists for the most part suffer the abuse of critics in silence, venting their anger only in private conversation. Public outbursts are rare, and it has been many years since Maxwell Anderson dismissed the whole newspaper reviewing fraternity as "the Jukes family of journalism." Generally, hostility to critics is expressed more subtly. In the early years of the Lincoln Center Repertory Theater, the productions and leadership of Elia Kazan and Robert Whitehead came under ferocious attack from some critics who deplored the choice of plays and the level of acting while the theater was still struggling to find itself. Arthur Miller blamed the critics for "incomprehension" of the aims and problems of the theater, but he also detected dark motives behind the attacks: "Some of the critics had ambitions of their own. They wanted to become producers, directors, impresarios. There was a terrific mendacity in those attacks."

The playwright suspects that the critic is more interested

in serving himself than the work under review or the public. To the wounded playwright, a flippantly negative notice is flagrant exhibitionism. Many playwrights maintain they have never gained anything from reading a review. The only worthwhile criticism, in the judgment of Paddy Chayefsky, is that which (1) is revelatory and points out something the audience may have missed, (2) shows taste and discretion, and (3) helps manufacture an appetite for theater. "For example," he says, "Brooks Atkinson loved lyrical drama and as a result there was good lyrical drama when he was reviewing. How much lyrical drama have you seen since then?"

When a playwright feigns indifference to critics and says he never reads a notice, it is a clear sign of intense hostility, equivalent to the suppressed fury of the tight-lipped child who makes no outward protest on being punished but simply refuses to speak to his parents or teachers. The hostility of the playwright increases as his play nears its Broadway opening. During the out-of-town tryout he listens readily to audience and critic, for they are early collaborators in the new work. Neil Simon, who rarely gets a bad notice, finds this collaboration indispensable. During the writing and rehearsal periods, he applies tests of his own devising to determine the worth of his play. Then other forces take over. "Once the play is exposed to the public, the audience, the critics, and the people involved with the production will tell you what is wrong, and they rarely lie." And yet the same old ambivalence of the author toward his ultimate judges crops up in Simon, too. As a beginning playwright he felt that only two rules applied to the work: what the critics liked and what the audience liked. Later, as success bred confidence, he substituted one rule for the other two—what the author likes. "I learned that if you please yourself, the chances are you will please others."

George S. Kaufman had a formula for evaluating plays: "Don't watch the play; watch the audience." When his plays were being tried out in Boston and Philadelphia he would mingle with the audience during intermissions, listening for reactions and comments. Other playwrights, however, are not convinced that audiences know best, particularly today's audiences, and particularly where serious drama is concerned. They feel that Broadway theatergoers are middle-aged, affluent, emotionally homogeneous, change-resistant. Arthur Miller once apostrophized the audience as an amorphous mass waiting to be shaped by the playwright. "They are the *tabula rasa,* the blank sheet on which the artist must write. They are the raw lump of clay to be formed by the artist." Miller now ascribes his own misgivings about today's theater to the erosion of the concerned audience. "I have become personally depressed about the theater," he says. "The audience is limited by its make-up. This affects the kinds of plays that are written, the way they are written, the way they are staged—everything."

For heterogeneous and responsive audiences many playwrights prefer off-Broadway. Lonne Elder III is a black playwright whose drama of Harlem life, *Ceremonies in Dark Old Men,* was first presented by the Negro Ensemble Company in the spring of 1969 to an excellent press. After a limited run at the St. Marks Playhouse, Elder had a chance to transfer his play either to Broadway or to another off-Broadway theater, and he chose the latter. "The main reason," he explains, "was that I couldn't reach the audience I wanted at Broadway prices. The play works for me because it attracts black people, and it requires a black audience. There are certain colors, tones, and shapes that only they understand. And when they understand, the white part of the audience understands too. As a playwright, I must get this satisfaction out of the play or I feel frustrated."

Elder works out of an established, subsidized theater with continuity of policy and program and has been able to reach the audience he wants. This is the relationship—the clear affinity between play and audience—that playwrights long for. Arthur Miller still wants to be part of a public theater in America. Like other playwrights plagued by the uncertainties of Brodway, he wants permanency, a sense of belonging, a feeling of community. He says, "The playwright's position today is probably at its lowest ebb. He can't be said to be using his talents properly in the Broadway marketplace. Before, costs were lower. You didn't need to drive in a massive hit every time you pulled up the curtain. Sure, for the writer there's more opportunity in other media today. But that's scriptwriting, not playwriting. There is no playwriting life. There are no ongoing reverberations between one play and another. I'm in a totally lonely position, I'm afraid."

For the rare playwright the rare producer once provided security, continuity, and the means for an ongoing career. In the early 1960's producer Roger L. Stevens demonstrated his faith in a young British actor-playwright—Harold Pinter— who had just had a massive failure on the London stage. The critics had just rejected Pinter's *The Birthday Party* and he was penniless when Stevens advanced him option money to write three plays. Pinter is now a playwright of international stature.

Such one-to-one relationships between producer-patron and playwright-protégé are growing scarce. The parental function has been taken over by publicly financed workshops and foundation-financed institutional theaters. The new tradition of patronage is developing in different places at different rates of growth and with varying degrees of sophistication. In New York's off-off-Broadway world, the mother-figure for a sudden generation of young playwrights is Ellen Stewart of Cafe La Mama, an appropriately named theater in the East Village. Among the dozens of writers who have benefited by her warm and unremitting care are Israel Horovitz, Jean-Claude van Itallie, Rochelle Owens, Leonard Melfi, Megan Terry, Paul Foster, Lanford Wilson, and Sam Shepard. She finances two new productions a week for forty weeks a year, at $200 a play. Most of the plays are unsuccessful by commercial standards, but she is not trying for success. She is trying to encourage playwrights, and in this she succeeds.

Miss Stewart is a handsome woman for whom the writer is all. "I call them my children, my babies, my biddies. My

playwrights. I possess them until they don't need me any-
more. Playwrights should be treated with utmost care, you
know; they can die. They are such delicate, perishable creatures." [4]

Half a dozen different organizations, none so maternalis-
tic as La Mama, are set up for the care and feeding of new
playwrights. The New Dramatists Committee was established twenty years ago in the conviction that the health of
the theater depended upon a steady supply of new writers.
Financed annually with industry funds, the Committee
stages readings of scripts by selected writers for which actors
volunteer their services, as well as fully rehearsed productions of more advanced work before invited audiences. Scores
of playwrights—including Joe Masteroff (*Cabaret*) and William Gibson (*The Miracle Worker*)—have passed through
the hands of the New Dramatists, and a number of Broadway
productions have originated here.

Another organization that gives writers a chance to see
their work onstage is the Albee-inspired playwriting workshop, which operates out of an off-Broadway house. Now a
nonprofit foundation, it was financed at first out of the
profits of *Who's Afraid of Virginia Woolf?* by Edward Albee,
Richard Barr, and Clinton Wilder, the author and producers.[5] Dozens of new young playwrights have worked here
in cross-pollination with La Mama.

The American Place Theater was formed in Hell's Kitchen
by a former minister, Sidney Lanier, and director Wynn
Handman at St. Clement's Church, which gave it a stage
and an auditorium. In five seasons the American Place has
produced some remarkable new works, including Robert
Lowell's *The Old Glory*, Ronald Ribman's *Harry, Noon and
Night* and *The Journey of the Fifth Horse,* and William Alfred's *Hogan's Goat.*

During the winter the Playwrights' Unit of the Actors

---

[4] From an interview with Patricia Bosworth, *The New York Times,* March
30, 1969.
[5] Barr has been amply rewarded for his efforts by one commercial success,
The Boys in the Band, which came out of the workshop.

Studio puts on partial productions by new authors which are then analyzed by the "class" under the direction of a moderator who may be critic Harold Clurman or such Studio regulars as actor Fred Stewart, director Arthur Storch, or Lee Strasberg himself. In the summer the Eugene O'Neill Foundation, in Waterford, Connecticut, runs a three-week conference of playwrights, importing critics to view the work without reviewing it.

Ford Foundation funds have been granted to the playwright. Ten years ago W. McNeil Lowry, the Foundation executive who has given many millions to nonprofit theater, thought up a resident-playwright program among professional repertory theaters to see if new work could take root outside New York. The results of the program are disappointing so far, and New York remains the richest spawning ground. Another productive environment for new playwrights has been Joseph Papp's New York Public Theater, housed in the old Astor Library. This resolutely nonprofit institution draws a heterogeneous audience, dares to offer the different play, and mixes the media—films, music, dance, drama.

For all this ferment, Broadway is still the center ring, and draws the attention, the applause—and the money. And Broadway exacts the severest price, for the only real way a "commercial" playwright can build a career is to move from hit to hit to hit.

No one has mastered this magic progression with more sureness than Neil Simon, the outstanding comedy writer of his generation. His *Come Blow Your Horn* has led to *Plaza Suite* and *Promises, Promises* by way of *Barefoot in the Park, The Odd Couple, Little Me* and *Sweet Charity.* Any one of them would have made a writer rich. A former associate says of Simon: "He has the kind of face that always seems to be saying, 'Who, me?' " He would probably cast himself as Felix Unger (Art Carney) rather than Oscar Madison (Walter Matthau) in *The Odd Couple,* and as the telephone man in *Barefoot in the Park,* and yet the mention of his name with a project has galvanizing effect. Before Simon commits a scene to paper he can commit an entire Broadway production, even to booking a choice theater a season in advance, and with a two-sentence synopsis he can write his own ticket on a multi-million-dollar motion picture deal.[6] He started out diffidently in 1961, not even daring to question a set design for *Come Blow Your Horn* although he hated it. A graduate of television, where he had worked with such masters of comedy as Billy Friedberg and Nat Hiken (*The Show of Shows*), Simon thought theater was different, and he waited to be told. He felt, conscientiously, that he should heed the wishes of an experienced producer, director, and a designer "who had designed more plays than I had seen." But Simon waits no more. Modest but self-assured, he says, "Today, I do what I want. There are no problems. The only problems are my own." He wrote twenty different versions of *Come Blow Your Horn,* only one rewrite of *Plaza Suite,* and none of his latest big hit, *Last of the Red Hot Lovers.*

Success confers order and continuity on Simon's life. In any given week he knows exactly what he'll be doing a year ahead. In early summer he will write a new play for the winter. In late summer he will draft a screenplay based on his current hit. In early fall he'll do a rewrite on the new play. In late fall he'll block out another new play. In winter the first new play goes into production. After it opens he'll do a rewrite of the screenplay. In spring he'll work on a second new play. The following fall it will go into production. By then it is time to write another screenplay. Simon spends seven months writing, five months in production.

This schedule is arduous, but Simon is only doing what comes naturally. His method makes playwriting seem easy: "I usually write a three-sentence synopsis and then the plays grow by themselves. I never say, 'Today I'm going to sit

---

[6] Simon sold an original film, *The Out-of-Towners,* as follows: "Two people from out of town come to New York where the man is looking for a job. They come in the night before and every disastrous thing that can happen to people in New York happens to them, and he has to make that nine o'clock appointment in the morning."

down and write a play.' I say, 'Today I'm going to sit down and write four pages.' I don't know that I'm going to be able to write a play, but I know I can write four pages in a day. If the main idea is good, if the characters are good, I can start. I don't believe in starting with a scene-by-scene outline. I write the whole play instead of the outline. I don't like heavily plotted plays. I write characters and let them go off on their own."

Since 1961 Simon has averaged more than $5,000 a week in royalties from the Broadway theater, and in this same period he has had eight movie sales, seven London productions, and probably the largest stock and amateur royalties of any playwright. He is a millionaire many times over, but he has never read a book on playwriting.

Lyric writing however, is a form of dramatic composition that apparently can be taught. Stephen Sondheim, lyricist and composer, says writing lyrics is not a mysterious art but a practical craft. "Like any craft, lyric writing has absolute rules that cannot be broken. They can be taught, and really quite easily. If you learn the rules and follow them conscientiously, I maintain you can write good lyrics."

Sondheim learned about musicals personally from Oscar Hammerstein 2nd. Sondheim wrote his first musical at the age of fifteen and showed it to Hammerstein, a family friend, and asked for a frank opinion. Hammerstein said it was awful and that Sondheim hadn't learned the rules. A decade later, Sondheim wrote the lyrics for *West Side Story,* followed by *Gypsy* and *A Funny Thing Happened on the Way to the Forum,* for which he wrote both lyrics and music.

The first rule Sondheim learned was that the lyric must follow the music. "Where there's a pause in the music, there must be a pause in the lyric. Lyric writing, like music itself, is an art that exists in time. It's not like poetry printed on a page which you can read at your own speed, referring back, if you wish, to earlier allusions and thoughts. A lyric goes from here to there in a direct line and you must make yourself understood absolutely at every line." In other words, it's much like following the moving news sign in Times Square.

A playwright, on the other hand, makes up his own rules. "There is stuff I write that I know will work," says Neil Simon, "and even if people tell me it's wrong, I won't change it. Then there is other material people may say is marvelous, but deep down inside me a radar tells me something is wrong. When that happens, the people are wrong, and the radar is right.

"Usually, when there is a flow to my writing and when it comes easy, it's right," he continues, "but when it's a passage I have to sweat over, when it doesn't come easily, it's going to look that way on the stage. It's almost as though you can hear the typewriter keys pounding on the stage. The lines should sound as if the characters are speaking them for the first time."

After he writes the play, Simon puts it away for a month or two. "When I pick it up again, I read it more objectively, as if for the first time. If I find myself enjoying it, I *know* it's right." (But, as we shall see, that isn't necessarily so.) Once the author's test is passed, the next test is the first reading by the actors. "Hearing it spoken for the first time is different," says Simon. "What looks good on paper may sound bad on stage."

The night before *The Odd Couple* went into rehearsal in 1964 Simon checked everything through for one last time with producer Saint-Subber and then asked director Mike Nichols if he wanted anything in the script to be changed. Everyone, including Simon, thought the script was fine, but a warning buzzer went off in the playwright's head and he said to Nichols, "Then how come after the first reading tomorrow we're going to find out we're in desperate trouble in the third act?"

The next day Walter Matthau, Art Carney, and the rest of the cast assembled for the first rehearsal. The first two acts rolled by and Saint-Subber, a delighted producer, got up and left. "You obviously don't need me here," he said.

In the third act everything went wrong. All through the next three weeks of rehearsal Simon fussed with the script. He was still working on it when the show went out of town. He wrote three different versions of the third act before everything fell into place—another "easy" Simon success.

Unfortunately for the playwriting business, there is only one Neil Simon. But any playwright who means to survive must keep writing, writing, writing, even when the producers are not buying. Israel Horovitz is an obviously prolific dramatist. "I write enough to throw away," he says. "To me, that's the secret of writing." (The late composer Frank Loesser put it another way—"I don't work slowly, I throw away fast.") Horovitz is a wiry, long-limbed leader of the new avant-garde Establishment. He made his name in 1968 with a long one-act play, *The Indian Wants the Bronx,* which probes the meaningless violence of city existence. Counting *Indian,* Horovitz had four plays produced in his first season, but the unseen body of his work, like the submerged part of an iceberg, includes an "embarrassing" number of scripts starting with *Comeback,* produced in Boston when Horovitz was seventeen. At one period, when he was allied with the Poets' Theater in Boston, he wrote a play a week, manufacturing scripts to order. It is a habit he dares not break. "I just keep working. I always have another play working, another play to push out over the counter. Keep them coming and get them out when they're fresh."

The musical theater cannot support such frequency and facility. A play is the product of one man and an idea. A musical is the product of many men and many ideas, and the cumbersome and costly machinery of the musical slows the rate of production. Rodgers and Hart, in a simpler day, turned out twenty-six musicals in twenty-three years. Even today, Jerry Bock, the composer of *Fiddler on the Roof* and *Fiorello!,* feels that writers could easily create two musicals a season. In practice, they are lucky to have one show produced every two years.

Like the play, the musical is a literary property, but the musical can spark even more lucrative spinoffs for the writer. Alan Jay Lerner and Frederick Loewe sold a partial share of

My Fair Lady (all but the first-class performing rights) to CBS for a reported $3.6 million.[7] Richard Rodgers, who retains the ownership of everything he has ever written, has an annual income of well over a million dollars from the performing rights of the shows in the Rodgers and Hammerstein library. The successful writer in a society of growing leisure is a capitalist and a man of property, no matter what his political persuasion. A sincere left-wing liberal such as lyricist E. Y. ("Yip") Harburg (*Bloomer Girl, Finian's Rainbow, The Wizard of Oz*) emerges as a reluctant plutocrat from the torrent of royalties and fees which accrue to him from his work. He takes the sting out of it all by contributing generously to liberal causes.

Plays not only must be written to become "properties," they must be directed. It is the director, through the actors he controls, who transmits the words and ideas of the playwright to the audience.

Numerically, at least, there is a director for every playwright. The Society of Stage Directors and Choreographers, in contrast to the Dramatists Guild, occupies a plain four-room suite in the sleazy Brill Building on Broadway, a rabbit warren of music publishers and song players whose pianos bang away through the halls. The SSD&C lists 450 active members, of whom sixty-five are choreographers or choreographer-directors. In addition to a $100 initiation fee, members pay annual dues of $60 and a 1 per cent assessment on fees and royalties.

The English director Peter Brook has made the following formulation: in performance the relationship is actor/subject/audience. In rehearsal the relationship is actor/subject/director.[8] Until the play is ready the director is stand-in for the audience. Once the playwright entrusts his script to the director, a major collaboration of the theater develops

[7] Fritz Loewe is said to have framed a canceled check for $1.8 million on his wall. On seeing it, a friend suggested, "But how much more chic it would have been, Fritz, if the check were uncanceled!"

[8] *The Empty Space* by Peter Brook (Atheneum, 1969).

which has been likened to the partnerships of husband and wife, editor and author, master and servant, composer and conductor. If the collaboration takes, the play lives.

The relationship between playwright and director, the most complex in the theater, is founded on an uneasy interdependence. They cannot live without each other but all too often they discover they cannot live with each other either. Today Arthur Miller has absolute faith in Robert Whitehead as a producer, but there is no director, he says, with the possible exception of Harold Clurman, who directed his *Incident at Vichy*, to whom he would entrust his future work. It would not surprise Miller to find himself directing all of his own plays from now on.

The playwright instinctively resents the director from the moment rehearsals start. It is as though a mother has given up a child for adoption and cannot forgive herself. Writers and directors are natural enemies, according to Robert Whitehead, who as producer often finds himself in the middle, acting as an arbiter. The writer writes out of his own sense of memory, Whitehead says. His material comes from deep within, from a buried unconscious. But the director brings his own different memory sense to the material, drawing upon his own unconscious language to interpret the playwright's innermost feelings and ideas. The two tangle on the battleground of their unconscious minds. An irreparable break is sometimes averted only by an aware producer who knows what both are after and has the patience to separate contentious egos.

William Murray describes the trauma of relinquishment: ". . . the actors mindlessly questioning every line and every motivation, eventually subtly rewording their speeches to suit themselves; the dawning aloofness of the director as he begins to find his own creative meanings in the text and makes changes he proclaims will only serve to illuminate the author's real intentions; the increasingly worried look of the producer, who continues to demand only one change, the complete elimination of the author's favorite scene . . ."

Some playwrights, however, have nothing but praise for

their directors. Chayefsky, for example, is willing to ascribe some of his own success to Tyrone Guthrie, who came to the United States in 1959 to direct *The Tenth Man,* Chayefsky's play about a modern dybbuk set in a synagogue in Queens. "I was spoiled by Guthrie," he says. "He improved *The Tenth Man* at least 25 per cent." Chayefsky felt "inspirited" by the Irish director and lost no time getting into his next play. "I went out and wrote another one fast because of him," Chayefsky says.

The avant-garde writer Eugene Ionesco describes the relationship in absurdist terms. When he came to the United States in the summer of 1969 to work with American theater director Arthur Storch on a production of his play, *Hunger and Thirst,* Ionesco said the author's function "is not to tell the director what to do but to tell him what not to do." Edward Albee recently observed, "A fine line exists between creative interpretation and usurpation" by a director.

For their part, most directors seem happiest when the writer isn't around; for them, a dead author is an ideal author. Most directors firmly assert their purpose is to interpret the author, but they insist upon being left alone to interpret him. When the author sees his work on stage for the first time, he may hardly recognize it. The director may be aware of the discrepancy, but if he knows what he is about, he is working toward the author's goal in his own way, like a traveler who knows where he must go and when he must arrive, but prefers his own itinerary.

Gerald Freedman, the artistic director of the Shakespeare Festival in New York's Central Park in the summer and of the Public Theater in the winter, tracks the misunderstanding between playwright and director to its source. "It's fine for Arthur Miller to say he knows of no director he wants to direct a play of his today. When he writes a bad scene, Arthur Miller can crumple up a piece of paper and throw it away. But when I as a director put together a bad scene it's right there to be seen. The playwright sees it and is horrified. 'That's not my play!' he says. I know it isn't his play, but maybe I had to make that mistake to find the right way."

All theater craftsmen who collaborate on a show must find the "right way" but few can judge each other's work until it is completed. This is especially true of musicals, which are highly departmentalized—though finally all departments must answer to the director. Each department head —the set designer, the lighting director, the choreographer, the costume designer—starts with a common aim and hopes to achieve a unified result, but each follows a different path to reach the goal.[9] At midpoint everyone's work may seem hopelessly disorganized or unfinished to an outsider. The costume designer, for example, is most likely to be misunderstood during a ceremony known as the dress parade, held late in the production schedule. This comes long after many early conferences among designer, director, and producer to fix the "overall look" of the show. After that, the designer goes off to do her sketches—creating as many as a hundred a week—and to choose the fabrics and visit costume shops, jewelry shops, hat makers, wig makers, and shoemakers. Finally the costumes are sewn and fitted and at the dress parade, for the first time, they are modeled by the cast.

The parade takes place in the cramped fitting rooms of the costume shop, where the costumes can be rushed back to the workroom if something looks wrong. The star may dislike the color of her dress. The playwright may feel the cut of a costume violates the characterization he intended. For the costume designer the dress parade is just plain purgatory. "There are no lights," says designer Patricia Zipprodt, "there are racks and hangers everywhere, and you want to soap over those three-way mirrors." Costumes are designed to be seen from a distance against the specific color background of the set under artificial lighting conditions, but of course neither producers nor directors take this into consideration during the dress parade. Costume after

[9] In her own adaptation of the medieval riddle "How many angels can stand on the head of a pin?" designer Patricia Zipprodt says everyone has to be standing on the head of the pin in New Haven.

costume is rejected—the color, the fabric, the cut—and all for the wrong reasons. The designer must plead with her bosses to withhold judgment until the costumes can be viewed under proper conditions.

Miss Zipprodt, a prize-winning designer of scores of shows, works only with outstanding directors and producers, and still she is misunderstood. She cites the case of the bride's costume for the wedding scene in *Fiddler on the Roof*. "In costuming we're dealing with relative color values all the time. You have to be particularly careful of white on white. It's brighter than the human skin, and when you put lights on it, it spreads all over the stage, like a burning ball. I knew if I made the dress white it would bloom."

Working against the blue-green-black palette that set designer Boris Aronson had picked for the wedding scene, Miss Zipprodt took an Oxford-weave silk and dyed it almost a robin's-egg blue, which she felt would survive the amber lighting. When director Jerome Robbins saw the wedding gown he exploded. "You've got a blue bride!" he said. "She should be in white. A blue bride! She looks awful."

Miss Zipprodt tried to pacify Robbins, asking him not to reject the costume until he had seen it under stage conditions when the show got to Detroit. It would turn out to be white, she promised. Miss Zipprodt had tested swatches of her costume material under the lights, but the lighting designer, the late Jean Rosenthal, had not. At the first dress rehearsal in Detroit, Robbins saw the bride radiantly arrayed in white. In front of Miss Zipprodt, he turned to Miss Rosenthal and asked innocently, "Why does that dress look white, Jean?" Miss Rosenthal replied, "Because it's white, that's why."

Few Broadway directors have achieved a comedy style so distinctive and so sure as that of Mike Nichols, who matches gesture to emotion. Because he works with skillful comedy writers, he has managed to come up with some outrageously funny bits of stage business in every show from *Barefoot in the Park*, his first on Broadway, to *Luv, The Odd Couple*, and *Plaza Suite*. In *Luv*, Murray Schisgal's three-character comedy of marriage set entirely on a Manhattan bridge, the biggest laugh comes when the woman throws her mink coat into the river. In a sense, it was Nichols alone who invented the gag and it was Nichols' comedy invention which the critics praised. Actually Nichols is ill served as a director by this sort of praise. In his own view, action flows naturally from the demands of the script, and the disposition of the mink coat was simply a director's logical solution to the author's stage direction, which specified that the woman wear a mink with her first man and a raincoat with her second. Nichols gave a directorial twist to this change of heart.

"Mike never, never, never makes a suggestion from outside the play or imposes a gag on the play," says Nichols' agent, Robert Lantz. "The great director is always a great servant of the work. Leonard Bernstein is a composer in his own right, but the fact that he conducts Mahler's Seventh Symphony better than anyone doesn't mean that he's added a couple of bars to the score. Everything Nichols does is within the intention of the author." And unlike some directors, Nichols prefers to have his authors present at rehearsals.

In new musicals it is impossible for rehearsals to proceed without the authors. If the director decides a scene isn't working and has to be cut, other scenes before and after will be affected, and this may cause changes in set and costume design. The book must be revised; the actors' movements must be reblocked; a new musical "bridge" may have to be composed on the spot, and additional songs and lyrics created. A railroad switching yard has been bombed, and every train must be rerouted.

Sometimes changes must conform to awkward reality. Simply because a given set exists, a scene will have to be written for it. In the musical *Fiorello!* Jerome Weidman and George Abbott wrote a precinct-house scene where party workers played poker while discussing politics. Composer Jerry Bock and lyricist Sheldon Harnick felt the scene was clumsy, but in such situations good writers must be flexible. A precinct set had already been built, so Bock and Harnick wrote a number to fit—"Politics and Poker." As sung by Howard DaSilva and the chorus, it was the big hit of the show.

With musicals, the collaboration between director and authors must begin early. Some directors even conceive the show; the idea for *West Side Story,* for example, came from director Jerome Robbins. Lyricist Alan Jay Lerner prefers his director to pick the principals before he begins to write the show so that he will have real people to write for, and director Moss Hart cast Rex Harrison and Julie Andrews in *My Fair Lady* before Lerner wrote their parts. Of course, the show will already "exist" in outline-synopsis form. Lerner's new musical *Coco* was written after Katharine Hepburn agreed to play the part. Many directors will not agree to direct a musical unless they are in on the project from the very beginning.

On *America Hurrah,* a recent off-Broadway hit, director Jacques Levy met regularly with author Jean-Claude van Itallie during the writing process. A section entitled "TV" was set in the viewing room of a television-rating company with three testers sitting downstage at a console making comments while other performers upstage enacted fragments of television programs. Van Itallie originally wrote the passages in linear fashion. First one group spoke and then the other. The section ran ninety minutes and seemed tedious. Why not interrupt the dialogues, suggested Levy, and run the speeches simultaneously? Van Itallie agreed, and the scene was thus pared to a bristling thirty minutes without losing a word.

Some directors make substantial *written* contributions to plays and musicals and thus feel entitled to a share of the writer's royalties and co-author's program credit. Several cases of this nature have come up before the Dramatists Guild, which has stoutly resisted any nibbling away at the playwright's status (and income). Such conflicts are omens of impending economic battles between playwrights and directors. Directors historically earn less from plays than their authors and they don't share in the cornucopia of subsidiary rights. "If I have contributed extensively to a play's success," says one director (who does not wish to be quoted by name, since authors may resent his presumptions), "why shouldn't I benefit from the money that accrues to a hit made possible by my direction? Those movie sales, those stock deals, they're partially or largely due to me. They use my direction and yet I don't get anything out of it." Sooner or later, thanks to his aggressive union, the director will get a slice of the subsidiary pie; it may come out of the producer's share, but it may also be granted—reluctantly—by the author. It is only a matter of time.[10]

The director will use subordinate terms—"servant," "interpreter," "means," "editor," and "collaborator"—to suggest his relationship to the playwright. Alan Schneider, who has directed most of Edward Albee's work and is Samuel Beckett's chief interpreter in America, says, "I think of myself as serving the playwright. That's my function. Sometimes I can serve him by arguing with him. Sometimes I can serve him by objecting violently. Trying to rate a director's contribution to a production is abstract and mathematical. I am a means to an end. I'm the chief collaborator. I'm not there to put something over on the playwright or to take credit from the playwright or to do something apart from the playwright."

In the next breath, Schneider adopts the nomenclature of the familial hierarchy, with actors as the children who embody the play and author and director together as the parents. The author transmits the words to the actors, the director the meaning and movement. Alan Schneider compares playwright and director to husband and wife, although he is not sure sometimes which is which and the roles may

[10] Choreographers also feel victimized, since their dance creations are cribbed shamelessly in revivals. A breakthrough in establishing the choreographer's property rights in his work was quietly scored by the SSD&C in 1969, when it won for Agnes De Mille a token choreographer's residual royalty in the Lincoln Center revival of *Oklahoma!* twenty-six years after Miss De Mille had first choreographed the show.

reverse under stress.[11] Schneider says the relationship is also analogous to the editor-novelist, a process of chopping, adding to, intensifying, underlining, cutting. The familiar conflict arises when the director wants to cut a scene and the playwright won't let him. But often, according to Schneider, the reverse occurs. "Sometimes Edward Albee wants to cut something and I think it's great, and I have to fight like mad to keep him from cutting it. We argue a lot, but we've built up mutual trust over several productions, so Edward will say, 'Okay, if you think so, Alan.' I've had some arguments with playwrights, but I've never had a knock-down, drag-out fight on a serious level with a serious playwright."

Ultimately the director leaves the playwright behind and moves closer to the actor when the time comes for the child (the play) to leave its mother (the playwright). When he walked into the first rehearsal of *Tenderloin*, composer Jerry Bock, arriving with his partner, lyricist Sheldon Harnick, saw the performers assembled and the director bustling about. He said, "This is a sad day for us. The work is no longer our work."

At this point the playwright becomes an onlooker. His solitary ego merges into a collective ego. Written speeches must become spoken words. Writer-director Abe Burrows says, "People shouldn't be aware of the writer. They shouldn't go out of the theater and say, 'That was great Burrows' or 'That was great Tennessee Williams.' Once the actor has learned the line, it's his."

Playwright Sidney Kingsley agrees. At rehearsal, he says, "The one-man phase is ended. Now twenty to thirty artists will be working together. Whatever is created will be new, unexpected. When two people have a baby, the baby is a bit of a surprise. In the theater we have a marriage of many people. I can't really tell how the baby will turn out."

---

[11] Director Morton Da Costa uses almost exactly the same terminology. "To me it's a wheedling, cajoling relationship on both sides. I suppose it's like husband and wife, but which is which, and when?"

The director, previously occupied in a marital role with the playwright, now becomes a parent to actors. The playwright has "disappeared," the producer is absent, and the director is left alone for long hours in a darkened hall with his charges. Like it or not, he is authority and he wears many faces. The actors regard him as a boss and they accept him as a father figure, and he may also be confessor, judge, analyst, and referee.

"I prefer the father-figure idea," says Gerald Freedman. "In a real family you establish an atmosphere in which everyone knows what is expected of him and how to behave. With actors you draw a fine line of permissiveness which, I imagine, is rather like the permissiveness of a parent. The father establishes a kind of line. The children know it is there, but the father doesn't always tell the children to do this or not to do that."

Just as in a real family, the strong father (director) derives much of his authority from past success. Actors are vulnerable souls when rehearsals start—receptive, childlike, in search of security. A director fresh from a hit or a string of hits is living proof, for the moment, that their trust is well placed and that the father will not fail them.

"Sometimes actors demand that you act as a boss, that you give them orders," Freedman says. "They literally want you to whip them and beat them until they do something. In the end you have to give them what they want."

The director pledges himself to get the best out of his actors. "I don't tell the actor what to do," says Alan Schneider. "I stimulate him to his highest creativity. I'm there somehow to make him do what he can do best. I edit the actor. I say, give me a comma here instead of a period, or there are too many short sentences, or this chapter is fine but it should be cut in half."

The rehearsal period for a Broadway play is about a month (three and a half weeks for plays, four and a half weeks for musicals), and it is an authentic prenatal period during which the play, hermetically sealed in the rehearsal hall, moves steadily toward the day of delivery. As Herman

Shumlin says, it follows a curious cyclical path in which the first few days and the last few days are the most critical. Shumlin—producer, director, and playwright—is one of Broadway's remarkable survivors; he has seen great success and also known long stretches of failure. Starting out as a press agent in the 1920's, he became general manager for the producer Jed Harris, from whom he may have picked up his fiercely independent manner. His own producing career goes back to *Grand Hotel* in 1931, and his productions include *The Children's Hour, The Little Foxes, Watch on the Rhine, Inherit the Wind,* and *The Deputy.* He wrote his first play, *Spofford,* at the age of sixty-nine. Shumlin is bullet-bald, has piercing brown eyes, is unsmiling and tenacious, and he has seen it all. On his office wall is a picture of Ethel Barrymore at the age of eight; Miss Barrymore gave Shumlin this signed memento when she was sixty-three and the star of his production of *The Corn Is Green.*

Shumlin finds that a special atmosphere obtains when rehearsals commence. All is euphoric, the cast and collaborators are alight with optimism. There is a great coming together with single purpose, says Shumlin: "Everyone involved throws himself into the pot: flesh, bones, color of hair disappear. . . . It is a remarkable thing that takes place. It happens right away, and in my experience it always happens. People are not conscious of it at all. I recognize it, because as the director I have already shaped the play in my own mind. Maybe something will be a little wrong—something about the play, an actor in his part. But spiritually the thing will still happen. Each will have cast himself into the forge in which the metal, the amalgam, will be made, as they are modified by the play and as they themselves modify the play."

As rehearsals continue, euphoria dissolves and a change comes over the members of the cast. Shumlin notices that the actors begin to rely on their own judgments. They begin to question, to criticize, to analyze, as they grow more confident of their own abilities. At this stage, by thinking of himself at the expense of the group, an actor can be destructive. "Now," Shumlin says, "the director must hold a firm hand over the cast. He can be rewarded by the creativity that comes out of the actor exploring his own way, but he must find a tolerable level of permissiveness. You very quickly recognize when an actor has more to offer than you originally expected of him."

In the last days of rehearsal, the great coming together of the early days must repeat itself. The end meets the purpose of the beginning as the deadline approaches. "This factor creates its own dynamic," says Shumlin. "Time is rapidly diminishing. And this works to re-create the spirit that existed on the first day." The cycle is complete, and a show is born.

CHAPTER FIVE

Men of Property

The Shuberts are the classic landlords of the Broadway world—and their image is a legendary mixture of grandeur and penny-pinching. For two generations they ran the theater—in New York and on the road. At the highwater mark, in the late 1920's, the Shuberts owned or controlled 75 per cent of all theaters in the United States. They gave weekly employment to 3,500 actors, singers, and musicians, and hundreds of electricians, carpenters, costumers, ushers, stagehands, and painters. Just before the Depression of 1929 their holdings were valued at $400 million.

As Broadway's dominant landlord since the early 1900's the Shubert empire has survived threatened holocaust and imminent disaster on an almost daily basis. The Shuberts have endured slashing family feuds. They have initiated and defended endless lawsuits. They have beaten off sorties of rival theater raiders, survived bankruptcy and receivership during the Depression, and emerged little scathed out of a federal anti-trust action in the 1950's that forced them to divest themselves of twelve theaters in six cities, including four of their least desirable ones in New York City. That action left them with their seventeen theaters and a half interest in an eighteenth, all in the heart of the theater district. In 1969 the Shubert interests owned 51 per cent of Broadway's legitimate theaters, an even higher percentage of the total than before anti-trust proceedings. The last of the Shubert brothers, J. J., died in 1963 (he had been predeceased by his only son, John) and control of the empire passed collaterally to Lawrence Shubert Lawrence, Jr., a grandnephew of J. J.

Outgoing, gregarious, fun-loving, the tall, lanky Lawrence, now in his early fifties, is much more at home with company managers and treasurers than with Broadway producers. During a prolonged apprenticeship he filled sideline managerial posts in Shubert theaters. He was kept out of higher councils and was not consciously groomed for leadership. Then, unexpectedly, in 1963, Lawrence woke up an emperor. But he does not rule alone; he has surrounded himself with a quartet of ubiquitous advisers: Howard Teichmann, a slight, talkative playwright and professor of drama at Barnard who wrote *The Solid Gold Cadillac* and other comedies and who handles the philanthropic activities of the Sam S. Shubert Foundation, repository for the bulk of the twin fortunes amassed by the Shubert brothers; Warren Caro, a former Theatre Guild executive who oversaw Guild subscription in a dozen cities and now handles the Shubert bookings; and Gerald Schoenfeld and Bernard B. Jacobs, the two sharp-witted Shubert attorneys who are involved in all major decisions involving any of the far-flung Shubert interests.

Presiding over the old empire, these gentlemen are really engaged in a long-run holding action. For the first time in sixty years the Shuberts face a force greater than their own —the surge of office-building construction that is battering down the old landmarks of the theater district. The Shuberts' theaters are all written off, fully depreciated, mortgage-free, and in the overall design they are supposed to become part of the Sam S. Shubert Foundation once all challenges and counterchallenges to the Shubert wills have been met. Fresh legal problems await them. For example, should the Shubert Foundation be allowed to function in the business or must the Foundation divest itself of Shubert theaters the way the Ford Foundation was forced to divest itself of Ford stock? From the beginning the Shuberts have lived with controversy and litigation—and totally without public affection. The future holds the promise of more of the same.

After the Shuberts on the ownership rolls of the Broadway theater come a dozen or so independent owners with minor holdings. The one management with hope of Shubert-like aggrandizement is the Nederlander family of Detroit, who built up a chain of theaters outside of New York before invading the heartland itself. They now own the Palace on Broadway and a half interest in the Brooks Atkinson Theatre on West 47th Street. Outside the city they own or lease theaters in Detroit, Chicago, Baltimore, San Francisco, and Phoenix. They are acquisition-hungry.

The patriarchal founder of the Nederlander theaters, David T. Nederlander, who was a Shubert partner in 1914, died at eighty-one in October 1967. He has five surviving sons in the business—Harry, James, Joseph, Fred, and Robert. New York business agent and chief booker for the clan is James Nederlander, second oldest, a bluff, good-natured man in his late forties. He is direct in his business dealings, pragmatic in his judgments. "My test of a good show is did I have a good time at it," he says from his high corner office in the Palace Theatre building with windows looking out over Times Square display signs.

Nederlander's major decisions in 1969 reflect the instability of the real estate economy of the theater. Lacking a musical for his Palace Theatre, he booked hard-ticket movies. After losing $150,000 in two years on Henry Miller's Theatre on West 43rd Street, he sold the handsome but too-small (938 seats) house of the late Gilbert Miller to real estate operators who plan to tear it down. Next, Nederlander signed with the Uris Building Corporation to lease a combined office building and 1,700-seat theater designed by Ralph Alswang for the skyscraper rising in 1970 at the corner of Broadway and 51st Street. "You can't stop progress," says Jimmy Nederlander. "The only answer to the theater is new theaters. We found that out in Detroit. Everyone wants to go to a new comfortable theater with parking and restaurant facilities. I'm all in favor of the new buildings, even if the theaters in them aren't mine."

The Nederlanders and the Shuberts together accounted for all but fourteen of Broadway's thirty-four legitimate theaters in 1969. All the other theater owners who were not simply real estate speculators are rich men, including Lester Osterman, who has had tough luck as a producer, but exceptional booking success with his three theaters—the Morosco, the Helen Hayes and the 46th Street; Konrad Matthaei, a young actor-producer from Michigan who owns the Alvin; playwright Neil Simon, who owns the Eugene O'Neill; Albert W. Selden, producer of *Man of La Mancha,* who will have a long term lease on the new One Astor Plaza Theater; and multimillionaire William L. McKnight, a principal owner of the Minnesota Mining and Manufacturing Company, who with Samuel H. Schwartz as his operating partner owns the St. James and the Martin Beck theaters in New York and others in Boston and Philadelphia. These gentlemen look at their theatrical real estate as J. P. Morgan looked at his yacht: they own theaters because they don't have to stop and ask themselves how much it will cost to run them.

One attractive trait unites both the gentlemen theater owners and the business owners—a true devotion to theater and a fascination with show people that transcend the profit motive. There are no absentee landlords in the theater. They invariably show up for their own opening nights and usually for each other's. "The Shuberts always invite me to their openings," says Sam Schwartz affectionately, "and I invite them to mine." Theater owners are likely to come around on closing nights too, with a sadness both fiscal and sentimental.

Although they are members of the propertied class, theater landlords identify more readily with theater than with
real estate, and are not just rent collectors. They are caught
up in the glamour of a hit; they haunt tryout and preview
performances of their tenants' shows and press their suggestions on harried producers. Lee Shubert would weep real
tears at out-of-town break-ins of dramas heading for his
Broadway houses. "There he goes, crying again," theater
cynics would say; "he's worried about what to book when
this turkey closes." On opening night of the flop musical
Saratoga at the Winter Garden, a diffident press agent approached J. J. Shubert at the final curtain. "What do you
think, Mr. J. J.?" he inquired. J. J. leaned over conspira-
torially. "Tell the people to stop smoking in the lobby during intermission," he said.

Theater landlords are more interested in scouting new
shows than in soliciting takeover bids for their valuable
properties. When they sell, even at huge profits, they sell
with regret. Of the Palace, Jimmy Nederlander says, "I get
an offer a week on this building, but it's the flagship of our
fleet. I want to keep it as a theater."

For years the Shuberts have held out against this kind
of temptation. All of their business expertise has gone into
preserving their theaters, hunting strong attractions to fill
their 18,000 seats each night. The Shuberts and the Nederlanders chronically invest in shows, and threaten to become
producers when product is in short supply. "We've invested
for years," says Jimmy Nederlander, "and the main reason
is to help out the producers. In the last ten years we have
invested in more than fifty shows. Now we have to become
producers to make sure our theaters are filled." Nederlander
has set up a special producing unit[1] and plans to increase
his producing activity, which already embraces the road companies of several plays and musicals.

Real estate men seem to be drawn irresistibly to the
theater. Roger L. Stevens was known as the man who bought

---

[1] Nederlander-Steinbrenner Productions, in which his partner is George
Steinbrenner of the American Shipbuilding Company in Cleveland.

(and later sold) the Empire State Building before he became a prolific Broadway producer, in the late 1950's rivaling David Merrick (and occasionally surpassing him) in the number and quality of his productions. Manhattan real estate man Robert W. Dowling bought up Broadway theaters after the war through his City Investing Company. One goal of the City Playhouses was to give Broadway's producers an "alternative" to the Shuberts and break that ancient monopolistic hold on the industry.[2] Dowling also has been a steady show investor, particularly in the productions of Roger Stevens and Robert Whitehead, and for a time the three of them were united formally in the Producers Theater.

The West Side developer Irving Maidman, who owns blocks of property between Times Square and the Hudson River, once created a string of four off-Broadway theaters on 42nd Street west of Ninth Avenue. A driven and humorless man, Maidman named the first theater after himself and the names of all the rest began with M—the Midway, the Mermaid, and the Masque. For a time his own Silver Cloud Rolls Royce led a procession of unlikely theater patrons to artificially inflated first-night occasions in this theatrically unfamiliar part of town. Maidman's little theaters adjoined the teeming West Side Airlines Terminal (he owns that, too) and were within whistling distance of the North River piers, but he was never able to book a really substantial hit and his efforts to create a little Rialto on a barren wind-blown stretch of West 42nd Street never jelled. The theaters are still there, playing sex movies and "skin shows."

Another real estate operator, the fantastic William Zeckendorf, at the height of his own real estate career was a highly visible and beaming first-nighter and an expansive investor as well. His firm, Webb & Knapp, contributed a notable executive to the theater in Joel W. Schenker, once

[2] These theaters were unloaded one by one in the 1960's. In 1968 Dowling's company sold its Broadway block between 45th and 46th streets, including the Helen Hayes and the Morosco, to Peter Sharp & Company, Inc., realty brokers, for a reported $14 million. Sharp has sublet these two theaters to Lester Osterman.

president of Webb & Knapp Construction Corporation, now a full-time Broadway producer and theater owner.

What attracts them? What natural affinity seems to exist between the seemingly dissimilar worlds of real estate and theater? One obvious link is the actual physical property, the investment in land and buildings. Notoriously uneconomic as income-producing buildings and wasteful of space, theaters traditionally occupy land of marginal use and worth; today, however, this land has skyrocketed in value in Manhattan's current real estate boom. The possibility of dramatic land appreciation has always been present in Manhattan theatrical property, but the speculative streak in most real estate men is also fulfilled by gambling in theatrical production. Temperamentally, real estate men are well equipped for producing. The same creative drive and ingenuity spark both real estate deals and playmaking. Who can say that creating a skyscraper is not to be compared with creating a smash hit on Broadway?

The theater offers the real estate man certain psychological gratifications—with its use of color, design, and ornamentation, theater appeals to the decorative sense of builders, and it appeases their acquisitive sense. Instead of land and buildings, the real estate man on the Broadway turf collects actors and actresses and constructs cardboard worlds in which they come to life. In this country the arts have always been a suspect activity for men to engage in and are thought more suitable for women to practice and enjoy. Suspicions of frivolity, homosexuality, and worthlessness hang over the male who is involved in the arts, but the real estate man can embrace this world with impunity. His background is one of proven masculinity, asserting itself in the acquisition of solid property and in the construction of tall buildings.[3]

[3] The reverse of the real estate man's interest in theater is the actor's interest in real estate. Actors who achieve success are likely to put their money into real estate. June Havoc, for example, has property in New York City, Connecticut, and California. The stability of property helps compensate for the abiding sense of insecurity that plagues all members of the acting profession.

One might think that the theater owner's first concern is the ticket buyer, but it is the producer who is his natural tenant and customer. Only after he has "sold" the theater to the producer does he turn his attention, jointly with the producer, to the job of selling tickets to the public and filling the seats in his house. He needs producers exactly as the proprietor of a rooming house needs tenants, and thereafter he suffers all the routine worries and complaints of any landlord. Even the most stable landlord-tenant relationships in the theater are subject to strains. With the exception of one seven-month run,[4] the affable, rotund Samuel Schwartz has booked only David Merrick productions[5] in his St. James Theatre for the past ten years, and the two men are office neighbors on the same floor in the St. James Theatre building, making Merrick a Schwartz tenant twice over. Yet not a week goes by that Schwartz doesn't have a gripe from Merrick about the St. James—the air conditioning, the heat, the ashtrays—something. These problems are usually settled amicably, but Merrick is a demanding tenant and Schwartz a giving landlord.

The theater owner today must pay more attention to producer demands that affect stage arrangement and backstage space because as shows become more complex, more platform area and more storage potential are needed. (One theater owner believes that an overelaborate production is related to the poverty of dramatic inventiveness in much the same way as the heaviness of a woman's make-up is often related to the plainness of her face.) Modern producers seek to work free of the restrictions of the proscenium stage, the universal Broadway model, in favor of a thrust stage, which juts out into the auditorium, making for closer contact between actor and audience.

Since the real customer of the theater owner is the producer, negotiations are conducted on a highly personal basis; everyone knows everyone else not only from prior dealings

[4] Irving Berlin's *Mr. President,* which opened on October 20, 1962, and closed on June 8, 1963.
[5] *Becket, Do Re Mi, Subways Are for Sleeping, Luther,* and *Hello, Dolly!*

but from daily associations. Sam Schwartz says, "All the people I do business with are my friends, my lifelong friends. Theater is really a family. Somewhere along the line we have all done things together. We're all nice people. We're not gypsies any more."

Booking the play is the most delicate and telling decision a theater owner can make. Until the booking is absolutely secure, the producer dares not proceed. A theater-booking contract involves a percentage division of the gross box-of-fice receipts. For a play the division is usually 30 per cent to the theater, 70 per cent to the producer, or 25-75 in the case of musicals. Out of his share the theater owner has to pay mortgage interest, taxes, insurance, repairs and maintenance, and the usual house help—box-office treasurers, doormen, ticket takers, ushers, porters, cleaners, and janitors. The theater owner is also responsible for a proportionate share of the stagehands and of the musicians. And finally, the theater assumes a percentage share of the advertising expenses in proportion to its percentage share of the box-office receipts. The landlord, in effect, becomes a partner to the producer.

It is possible, even with present heavy costs, for a theater to show huge profits for its owners, and huge losses when the theater is dark. A hit play that grosses $50,000 weekly gives roughly $13,500 of this to the theater. Of this sum, about 40 per cent, or $5,500, is net profit. Assuming the cost of the theater is $1 million,[6] it is therefore possible—with a smash hit—to recoup the entire cost of a straight-play theater in fewer than four years. This does not include subsidiary revenue from concessions which—again assuming a smash hit —can add $25,000 to $50,000 a year in profits. And this from buildings in use only twenty-four hours out of the 168 hours in a week!

[6] Musical theaters are more expensive to buy and operate, but since they hold more people they can gross more and earn substantial profits. A musical house with a smash hit can handily spin off $15,000 a week profit, or $750,000 a year.

Shrewd booking is the key to smart theater management. For Sam Schwartz many old friendships are involved and the process is pleasant for him because he doesn't usually call producers; they call him. "I started in this business as an office boy for Channing Pollock in 1923," says Schwartz. "I had my first lunch at the Players Club with Pollock in 1926." By such landmarks is the theater defined. For James Nederlander, much newer to the game, good booking means dealing with people and knowing your man. "Hal Prince can write a blank check with me any time he wants to book one of my theaters," Nederlander says. He believes in playing winners.

"Close booking" is the trick theater owners must try to master—booking one show on top of another to avoid the dreaded dark house. When the show itself closes, the set is burned, the costumes are sold, and the production is forgotten. But the dark theater stays, and taxes, mortgage payments, insurance, help, and maintenance go on. "A dark house is a terrible thing," says Sam Schwartz.

In booking plays, personal taste is paramount. Nederlander is pragmatic, like all bookers. "I book people," he says. "Look at *Sweet Charity*.[7] It had Gwen Verdon, Bob Fosse, a score by Coleman and Fields, and a book by Neil Simon. Take *George M.* It had Joel Grey, Cohan's music, and Joe Layton as director. How far wrong could I go? And at the Brooks Atkinson I bet on the stars, Albert Finney and Dustin Hoffman."[8]

Booking shows is so competitive (there is always a scramble for the likely hits) that decisions have to be made early on only partial evidence. The booking process calls for a blend of bargaining skill, artistic judgment, and a sixth sense of anticipation about shows, a magic touch. Hairtrigger timing is vital; sometimes a week, a day, an hour or two in fixing a contract are crucial. Tensions flourish on both sides of the table. Not the least of the producer's wor-

---

[7] Nederlander used this show to reopen the refurbished Palace Theatre in 1965.

[8] In *Joe Egg* and *Jimmy Shine,* respectively.

ries is the suitability of the theater. Is it too large for the mood the play projects, too small for the expense of operating the play? Is it on the right side of the street? Is it near enough to an established hit so it will attract overflow? Is the treasurer polite or boorish?

On his side of the table, the landlord is equally apprehensive. Will the play look as promising on stage as in script form? Contrariwise, will the star make up for what appear to be the play's deficiencies? Does the producer have financial resources to keep the play running to bad or mixed notices? Will the theater-party ladies like the theme? What will *The New York Times* think? Is it dirty enough, or clean enough? If the play has been a hit in England or elsewhere, that is a plus, but foreign plays are known to travel badly. How to figure the odds? "In the end," says general manager Jack Schlissel, a veteran of booking encounters, "it's the guy with the aces who wins."

One of the unwritten rules of successful booking is never to book a show that isn't yet written. In 1968 the Shuberts had an opportunity to sign a musical involving four gifted artists: Leonard Bernstein, Stephen Sondheim, Jerome Robbins, and Zero Mostel, as composer, lyricist, director and star respectively. But the show, based on Brecht's *The Exception and the Rule,* wasn't written and the odds against getting such talents together at the same time to meet all the production dates were bound to be great. For that season the Shuberts had a choice of booking either *The Great White Hope* or Dustin Hoffman in *Jimmy Shine* into their desirable Broadhurst Theatre on West 44th Street. Instead they held out for the unwritten Bernstein-Sondheim-Robbins-Mostel show. Their unfortunate decision painfully illustrated another rule of thumb in booking: one mistake usually leads to another. *The Great White Hope* went to the Alvin and *Jimmy Shine* to the Brooks Atkinson, both to become hits in that season, both in theaters that were non-Shubert houses. And then the Bernstein musical was canceled.

Only for a musical by Richard Rodgers or a comedy by

Neil Simon, according to a Shubert official, should an exception be made to the rule against booking unwritten shows—at least in today's theatrical market. As always, shadow areas exist. This same official, for example, would favor booking a half-written show by a procrastinating writer if David Merrick were its producer. A notorious arm-twister, Merrick can get reluctant writers to work, where the same show in the hands of a weaker producer might not come in on schedule.

The Shubert booker, with his seventeen and a half theaters to fill, sits at a three-dimensional chess game. He must balance factors of time, openings, and show availabilities. He must have the chess player's ability to look ahead several jumps and anticipate what will happen to his advance man. To change the metaphor, the booker must try to fit the square pegs into the square holes and the round pegs into the round holes. Some theaters are right for one kind of show, some for another, and often round pegs end up in square holes.

The case of *Hair,* a surprise hit of the 1968 spring season, illustrates the quixoticism of theater booking. *Hair* was first displayed for a limited run in the heavily subsidized Public Theater off-Broadway. Optioned by Michael Butler, a new face to producers and theater owners, it was moved to a nightclub, Cheetah, at Broadway and 53rd Street, where it failed. Butler, the eccentric heir to a midwest fortune (he is known as "the world's richest hippie") decided to open *Hair* yet a third time—on Broadway.

He ran smack into the last great booking jam of 1968. No theater suitable for the hippie musical was available, and landlords were loath to push tenants out for a show with a rock score, four-letter words, and paeans to acid, sex, and nudity. How wrong they were! One theater—the intimate Biltmore on West 47th Street—finally agreed to book *Hair,* on stiffer-than-usual terms. The musical's opening in May 1968 coincided with the Great American Breakthrough of permissiveness in the arts. Its anti-establishment rhythms were aided by a lyrical, free-swinging rave from Clive Barnes, the anti-establishment critic of *The New York Times*. *Hair* and its nude scene became obligatory viewing for the same middle class the musical savaged.

Ideally, the consummate booker[9] never misses a good show, but Alvin Cooperman, booker for the Shuberts in the early 1960's, a supremely self-confident businessman of theatrical talent who came out of television, missed one good show. Unfortunately for his record, it was *Hello, Dolly!* David Merrick, the producer, offered the Shuberts a double booking, the first show being contingent upon the second. First, *Luther*, the John Osborne historical drama starring Albert Finney in a limited engagement. Second, a musical based on Thornton Wilder's *The Matchmaker*. But *Hello, Dolly!*, a show that was really made on the road, wasn't written yet. That compounded the risk, and Cooperman, following a good rule, turned the show down. Schwartz accepted *Luther* for the St. James and later got the promised *Dolly!*—a box-office bonanza in the modern Broadway theater bigger even than *My Fair Lady*.

Playing the booking game, Merrick is in a driving position because of the number and variety of his shows—if one fails, he has another ready to throw into the breach. The "back-up" booking is a favorite and convenient Merrick ploy. He will use a limited-run dramatic show with doubtful drawing power to hold a big, desirable theater for a Merrick musical ready to come in. Thus Merrick, often criticized as blatantly commercial, is actually helping the theater vary its product. By dangling the carrot of the big, slick musical before the nose of the landlord, he persuades him to lease his house to the uncommercial art play. Since the theater habitually confounds the most skillful soothsayer, it sometimes happens that the art play is the blockbuster and the "commercial" show the disaster. Merrick booked the literary *Rosencrantz and Guildenstern Are Dead* into the Alvin with

[9] The Shuberts had one consummate booker in its modern history in the late Jack Small, and a Shubert official feels that his successor, Alvin Cooperman, now in charge of events at Madison Square Garden, might have surpassed him had he remained in the job.

the promise that the lavish musical *Mata Hari* would follow. *Rosencrantz* was a sleeper hit; when Merrick offered to continue the run at the Alvin, the theater booker insisted on the original deal, smelling fat profits from a top-grossing song-and-dance show. *Mata Hari* closed on the road.

The Shuberts, naturally, have the edge on other theater owners because of the variety and location of their theaters and their ability to juggle bookings to accommodate the most intricate gambits of theatrical chess.

Knowing when to move a show out is as important as the initial booking. Theater-booking contracts always include what is known in the business as a "stop clause," which sets a minimum weekly gross figure. If the show drops below this figure for a stated period of time—usually two consecutive weeks—the theater owner may exercise his option to serve notice on the show. In a celebrated court case in the winter of 1962, the owners of the Mark Hellinger Theatre won a suit to evict the waning *My Fair Lady* on an interpretation of the stop clause. Ironically, the show, which had just gone on half-price tickets, or "twofers," was reviving, but the Mark Hellinger owners had their eye on the new Richard Rodgers musical, *No Strings*. *My Fair Lady* changed theaters and continued to run to good business, but Rodgers was nervous about the lawsuit and refused to sign with the Hellinger, which went dark for months. The decision to push out a show is double-edged. Before evicting the show that is running out of steam, the judicious theater owner should have a new one on deck.

The Broadway theater is as vulnerable to the laws of supply and demand as any other commodity. In recent years there have been at least three "waves" of production during the season, when theater availability was at a premium. First comes the fall season, technically beginning right after Labor Day, but in practice subject to the vagaries of Rosh Hashanah and Yom Kippur. ("When Yom Kippur falls on a Saturday," one theater owner says, "you might just as well go to synagogue and repent, even if you're not Jewish. Nobody will come on Friday night, Yom Kippur eve; Saturday matinee, Yom Kippur day, is death on toast; and Saturday night, the one night you can always count on, is post-operative surgery, because all of the Jewish customers are home eating up a storm after fasting all day.") By tradition, the best time for a show to open in New York is after the Jewish holidays, preferably between mid-October and early November. The first fast flops are in and out, the weather is tangy, lots of people are in town. For some occult reason—which some show people blame on moon tides or zodiacal fallout—it is rare for the first few plays or musicals to be successful, possibly because expectations run high after the summer lull and critics, refreshed by their hiatus, swing with both fists at the early starters. By October, when the season appears dismal beyond repair, critical standards are less rigid, the public is poised for the arrival of a hit, and—almost as though it knew it was being expected—the smash will open.

By November the theaters that booked failures are available for the second wave—the January and February shows. The second booking jam then occurs, and productions are postponed or called off because theaters are not available. But March brings vacancies again, and the third wave and the third booking jam come in midspring. It is now or never for the dark house. If the April or May booking comes a cropper, the theater is doomed to shadows until the next fall season.

This, then, is the cycle. Book a show in September. If it runs, hurrah. If it flops, book a show in December, January, or early February. If it flops, book a show for April or May. Three chances to land a winner.

Or at least it used to be that way. But in the 1968–69 season something was happening, and it spelled trouble for the landlords of Broadway. Almost as if by prearrangement, the number of Broadway-bound productions dwindled. Booking jams thinned. Dark weeks, especially in marginal houses, added up.

There were good and sufficient reasons for the dry-up. Production and operating costs were higher, so plays and musicals were more costly to finance. Theater rentals had escalated; landlords blamed higher taxes and higher salaries for maintenance personnel (said one landlord, "Even ushers get cradle-to-the-grave benefits now").

But the real culprit was off-Broadway. There have always been "little" theaters in New York—Eugene O'Neill's early plays were produced in the 182-seat Provincetown Playhouse on Macdougal Street in Greenwich Village, for example—but they were mainly for semiprofessional or dilettante operators. There was the Cherry Lane Theatre, also in the Village, where the Gilmores, a Dickensian father-mother-daughter repertory theater, played to empty houses for years.[10] And there was the Davenport Free Theatre on East 27th Street, where a couple of show-struck brothers performed their own plays and passed the hat in lieu of admission. And from time to time a few starveling troupes rented other halls or lofts and prayed for big-time drama critics to notice them.

Until the early 1950's off-Broadway was a down-at-the-heels changeling, patronized by the big boys uptown. Vanity productions abounded—the rich Boston dowager would subsidize her grandson's costume drama in blank verse, or the college girls who had majored in drama would present revivals of Sheridan or Aeschylus. The meager productions could be financed at $3,000 or less; actors and technicians worked for nothing or coffee money. And most drama critics passed them by.

Brooks Atkinson of the *Times* did not. A theater-in-the-round in Sheridan Square, aptly called Circle in the Square, which was managed by director José Quintero and producer Theodore Mann, had distinguished itself with a revival of Tennessee Williams' *Summer and Smoke* with Geraldine Page in the lead. Atkinson traveled to the Circle to see the production and gave it an enthusiastic notice that sent audiences scurrying downtown. From that moment on, off-Broadway became a force to be reckoned with in the New

---

[10] The Gilmores gave Carl Reiner the inspiration for his comedy, *Enter Laughing*, which was a hit of the 1962–63 season.

York theater. In 1953 T. Edward Hambleton and Norris Houghton opened the Phoenix Theatre on Second Avenue. Then the Circle had a revival of O'Neill's *The Iceman Cometh* with Jason Robards, and off-Broadway could no longer be ignored by any critic.

As Broadway raised its prices and its salaries, off-Broadway expanded and new theaters opened. Actors' Equity set a double standard; since off-Broadway was valuable to actors as a showcase, the union consented to less-than-subsistence minimums (Equity first permitted actors to work off-Broadway in 1949 for five dollars a week plus 5 per cent of the gross receipts over $1,000.) A rag-tag network of playhouses opened, the most lavish of which was the 299-seat Theatre de Lys, which promptly made history by booking a revival of *The Threepenny Opera* that lasted six years. Long runs were rare, however; even though ticket prices were low, off-Broadway theaters were dingy, out-of-the-way, and uncomfortable. New plays were also rare, because Equity insisted on a percentage of eventual movie rights for actors who had originated the roles. Revivals were easier and safer, and young writers had their hearts set on Broadway.

In the 1960's off-Broadway's pulse quickened. Equity rescinded its fiat on sharing subsidiary rights. It was so much easier to produce plays downtown. Actors enjoyed the easy off-Broadway experimentation and the relaxed atmosphere. There were no craft unions with exorbitant salaries and medieval work rules. Hordes of youngsters were available to work backstage and out front, anxious to supplement daytime jobs with nighttime labor. And most of all, unlike the surly stagehands of Broadway, they were *willing*. Equity minimums downtown were (and still are) half of uptown minimums. Off-Broadway landlords rented their shabby properties at relatively reasonable rates. One could put on a play at 25 per cent of its cost uptown.

The off-Broadway audience was young, interested, tolerant, intelligent. While the expense-account crowd and fur-coated theater parties yawned and glittered on Times Square, earnest showgoers in cloth coats and loafers listened and *reacted* downtown. The League of New York Theatres, meeting in plush offices, paid no attention to off-Broadway. David Merrick has led his colleagues in looking down his nose at the little theaters, calling a trip downtown "a visit to the lower depths" to theaters that "smell like gyms."

They are now beginning to smell more like money. The off-Broadway breakthrough into the echelon of big business is about three seasons old. Suddenly, as Broadway theaters turned out manicured flop after flop, the unkempt cellars of off-Broadway turned out hit after hit. *Your Own Thing,* a rock-musical version of *Twelfth Night,* became a hot "broker ticket" and was sold to the films for $500,000. *The Boys in the Band,* a breakthrough comedy-drama about homosexuals, opened in an out-of-the-way converted church on 55th Street west of Ninth Avenue, fascinated the city— and the world—and is making its creators rich. *You're a Good Man, Charlie Brown* was the first attraction at the new 80 St. Marks Place Theatre in 1967; it is still running. The list grows every month. Off-Broadway turned a play that had failed in Broadway production—Jules Feiffer's *Little Murders*—into a big hit. Black playwrights were coming strongly to the fore off-Broadway, including Lonne Elder III with *Ceremonies in Dark Old Men* and Charles Gordone at the New York Public Theater with *No Place to Be Somebody.*

As Brooks Atkinson had for an earlier generation of off-Broadway landlords and producers, in the late 1960's Clive Barnes gave extra encouragement to the newer generation by his visits and his appraisals and reappraisals of off-Broadway work. In summary pieces, Barnes found that the sound new musicals should make was the very off-Broadway sound of *Hair.* He praised Israel Horovitz' *The Indian Wants the Bronx,* put on in a narrow little theater on Astor Place, as one of the most hopeful works on the New York stage of 1967.

Uptown landlords are only beginning to realize what has hit them. "Just imagine," said one of them in the summer of 1969, "if you want to book an off-Broadway theater, you have to stand in line. There are fifty plays waiting for forty off-Broadway houses; there are thirty-four theaters on Broadway, and eight are still unbooked for the fall. It's crazy."

Crazy, perhaps, but completely understandable. Because it is easier to do plays downtown than uptown, more plays are written, acted, produced, and directed in the scruffy tenement-theaters than in the gingerbread castles off Times Square. History repeats itself endlessly in show business. Avarice and achievement will lead to more off-Broadway theaters, more expensive productions, and higher ticket prices. Off-Broadway will therefore become (indeed, is already becoming) "establishment" theater, pocked with guilds, regulations, and commercial pressures.[11] Ergo, economic rigidity will induce scarcity, and the young Turks, the new rebellious writers, actors, directors, and producers who want to be "free," will search out new low-rent areas and shabby buildings, and the whole process will start all over again. Theater, like water, finds its own level.

There was good reason in 1969 for theater owners uptown and down to be watching the real estate trends. Billy Rose had a theory that theaters could be built only on "gypsy ground"—that is, land of only marginal worth and low-class tenants—and history bears him out all the way back to Shakespeare's Globe Theatre, built on marshland in Southwark outside the city limits of London. Rose had bought the Ziegfeld Theatre at Sixth Avenue and 54th Street when it stood on what might have been considered gypsy ground, but he held it while land values rocketed all around him. He paid $525,000 at auction for the Ziegfeld in 1944, using what he called his "ill-gotten Aquacade money." Like a rising tide, skyscrapers shot up along the avenue, pressing against Rose's Ziegfeld property.[12] Long before the event,

[11] Theater parties in significant numbers are beginning to book off-Broadway houses for the first time.

[12] The Time-Life Building at 51st Street, the J. C. Penney and CBS buildings at 52nd Street, the ABC Building at 53rd Street, and the New York Hilton Hotel at 54th Street.

Rose had foreseen that Sixth Avenue was destined to become a commercial artery, and he began assembling around the Ziegfeld a building plot suitable for a skyscraper. "Can this land afford a theater?" Rose asked himself and the answer was negative even before the builder's bids began coming in for his property. When finally he sold the Ziegfeld and the adjoining parcels, in 1966, he got $18 million for them.

In the 1970's the furious thrust of new construction will veer westward through Times Square. The office-building boom has exhausted the land possibilities farther east and now the Times Square area is the target. Part of the pressure is coming from the theater's nearest southern neighbor—the dress industry. William Zeckendorf, Manhattan's postwar real estate seer, once predicted that the garment district could not be contained along Seventh Avenue below 42nd Street forever, and the natural path of expansion lay through Times Square. In the late 1960's Broadway frontage in the area commanded $300 a foot, double what it had been only five years before.

During the early phase of the boom the Shuberts guarded their theatrical empire while other owners responded to zooming land prices as if oil had been discovered under 42nd Street. The Shuberts, in fact, were caught between an ancient vow and a glittering promise. On behalf of the family, in the late 1950's John Shubert had promised that the Shubert Foundation would hold the theaters "in perpetuity." But in 1969 a Shubert official commented, "The property is becoming ever more valuable, almost in geometric progression. We've had lots of offers. It's a question of how long you can resist them." And another overseer of Shubert interests remarked that in ten years half the present Broadway theaters will be gone. Many of them, riddled by age and structural failings, are probably not worth saving anyway.

Apparently no amount of sentimental attachment to the old theaters can prevail against the trend. In practical real estate terms, as Joel Schenker remarks, New York has become "a shrunken land mass, a tiny island. It is no longer possible to build buildings beautifully in the nineteenth-century tradition. There is only one way to go—up. A free-standing theater is an uneconomic and wasteful use of land in today's real estate economy." The only possible mortgage obtainable on a theater in New York is on the land.

Certainly no free-standing theater will ever again be constructed in the theater district. Richard Weinstein, a brilliant young architect who in 1969 headed the Urban Design Group in the City Planning Commission, has little patience with the preservationists. "The theater will have to ally itself with the economic thrust of our times and accommodate itself to existing forces," he says. "It may not be ideal but the alternatives are worse. Churchill once remarked that democracy as a means of government is full of faults, but what system is better?"

As the demolition crews advanced on Times Square, Mayor John V. Lindsay's first order to Urban Design was to find out how to save the theater district. Recognizing the complete futility of trying to oppose the boom, Weinstein's department studied ways to control and direct it so that the interests of theater would be served. Urban Design produced a plan that offered builders special inducements in the form of waivers and modifications of building requirements if they would agree to integrate new theaters into their buildings to replace the old theaters that inevitably would be torn down. Weinstein's Urban Design Group established a special T (for theater) District running from 40th to 57th streets and from Sixth to Eighth avenues. Within the T District a new building would be allowed up to 20 per cent more tower space in exchange for putting in a theater that fully met Equity standards for backstage facilities and city standards for the auditorium, including the number of seats, the spacing, the exit locations, the lobby area, and all the rest. The allowable extra rental space, which would depend upon the size and expense of the theater, would be calculated by computer, taking into account the extra dollar of profit the developer would gain through having the extra space upstairs against the dollar he would lose through loss of rental space below, where the theater, or in some cases theaters, would be located.

"No actor, director, designer, or producer I have talked to wants to save the present theaters," says Weinstein. "The actors want showers, the designers want more fly space, the producer wants better seating facilities." The City Planning Commission is doing nothing actively to see that the present theaters are torn down but neither is it doing anything to see that they are preserved. Weinstein feels that a few—a very few—deserve to be preserved, but he feels that eventually the theater district would have disappeared entirely if the present formula had not been adopted.

The city is in a strong position to influence not only the construction but also the size and type of the new theaters. Urban Design intends to promote a "mix" of theaters which will, for one thing, have the effect of breaking down the old geographical barriers between Broadway and off-Broadway. Large theaters and small, experimental stages, standard proscenium stages, and open stages that can be converted to the proscenium type will be constructed side by side, sometimes with one of each in the same building.

The Lindsay administration has had a vision of a new theater district to be superimposed on the old. Broadway would look different but its function and spiritual identity would remain triumphantly intact. It is Weinstein's belief that the city plan avoids a painful error made by the founders of Lincoln Center, who proceeded on the assumption that the richest city in the country, with the Rockefellers leading the way, could easily support a citadel of culture in which all the performing arts would be represented and interconnected. "Now," Weinstein says, "they are trapped inside an Acropolis format." They built their gleaming marble theaters around a prodigally spacious plaza to enshrine an already outmoded system of culture, and they never stopped to think how to support them financially. Already those theaters stand on land too dear for them to occupy alone, and a kind of cultural-financial obsolescence has set in. The performing palaces have increased the cost of doing business in culture without providing any additional means of financial support to keep them going.

Equally wrong, to Weinstein's way of thinking, is the Medici approach. Patronage of artists is obsolete, and for the city to subsidize an individual playwright, manager, or theater group in acquiring a theater would be an unworkable return to an outmoded form of cultural assistance. Instead, a middle course is being followed. The theaters are to be constructed by the real estate industry but to specifications the city can influence. In this way the city can assist theatrical organizations such as Theodore Mann's Circle in the Square and Wynn Handman's American Place Theater, housed in St. Clement's Church on West 46th Street, to acquire new theaters suitable to their needs and purposes and, therefore, to co-exist in the Broadway environment.

When the T District building modifications were originally proposed, the Shuberts opposed them as subsidized competition. Nothing in the plan gave any encouragement to the owners of existing theaters, and there was no help for the producer or renting theater manager, who would simply have a more expensive theater to help maintain. But the new plan had even more far-reaching implications for the Shuberts. In time it would break the Shuberts' monolithic hold over the Broadway theater.

The Shuberts, of course, have the same opportunity to build or lease the new theaters as anyone else. Structurally it is not possible for the Shuberts to allow overbuilding on their existing theaters by selling the air rights and allowing a skyscraper on stilts to rise over the crowded theatrical block between 44th and 45th Streets. But the Shuberts have enough other land in the T District to take advantage of the new regulations alone or in partnership with a builder.

If this concept works, the theater district will be held together and a Broadway better and bigger than before will be fashioned. Directly to the west of Times Square, toward the Hudson River in Hell's Kitchen, where the land is 20 per cent vacant and eminently suited for development, the city will build a large convention center and film-studio complex. New York at last will become a truly integrated entertainment-industry capital, with film, theater, and television co-existing laterally across the center of Manhattan, each feeding the other. Geographically, the plan recognizes the economic need of theater artists to work simultaneously or alternately in several of the media. Out of the communications explosion has come the multimedia artist, and under the new plan all careers can be pursued in one locale so that an actor or director or writer will no longer have to take a cross-country jet but only a cross-town subway ride to move from television to theater to films.

New York's planners propose to lace the three media together in the bosom of the city by running a crosstown subway line under 48th Street to link all the professional groups directly involved in the entertainment industry—lawyers on the East Side with agents and television people on Sixth Avenue with the theater district in Times Square with the new film center near the Hudson River. Most important of all, the film industry will be easily accessible to theater and television workers instead of 3,000 miles away in Hollywood.

Looking even further ahead, Richard Weinstein has still another plan that may assist the theater, especially the producer. He proposes a City Cultural Authority as a non-profit organization empowered like the present Port of New York Authority to buy and sell property, and specifically to buy the new combined office buildings and theaters going up. Within the next ten to fifteen years, Weinstein estimates, the new theater real estate in the Times Square area will have an assessed worth of $200 million. From property such as this the city can realize perhaps $20 million in taxes. Let the Cultural Authority, says Weinstein, take over ownership of the buildings, since the building owners have neither the desire nor the competence to run them themselves. The Cultural Authority can then rent the air space above the theater back to the building owner and rent out the theater itself to the Broadway or off-Broadway producer. Under private ownership a large Broadway theater normally rents for $300,000 a year, but if the City Cultural Authority owns the theater, the Authority could collect $100,000 a year for the air rights and rent the theater to the producer for a saving of $200,000 annually. There is more than one way to skin the cultural cat.

For the moment this scheme is nothing more than a planner's daydream. But even if it is still a figment, enough other changes are reality to insure that present patterns of theater ownership in the Broadway world as we have known it for so many years may shortly become unrecognizable. And yet certain things will always remain the same wherever theaters are built and whoever owns them. The old Broadway saying will still apply: nobody goes to see the theater, they go to see the show. And whatever problems future landlords encounter, the adage holds, there's nothing a hit won't cure.

CHAPTER SIX

"Let's Go to Contract"

On the Broadway opening night of *The Glass Menagerie* in the spring of 1945 only one other person in the audience besides the author, Tennessee Williams, understood fully the despair and toil that preceded the shining moment of triumph. Williams' devoted agent Audrey Wood had worked seven years for her client's success.

From the beginning of their long association she recognized in the shy, soft-spoken Williams a writer of exceptional gifts. When they met he was writing only one-act plays, and when she urged him to attempt the longer form, he countered with, "But Audrey, how can I do that when my drama professor at Iowa writes nothing but one-act plays himself and teaches me to write one-act plays?" She persisted, and parceled $25 a week to the struggling playwright from small grants and fellowships, and kept him going through unending disappointments with encouragement and care until the night of *The Glass Menagerie.*

There were twenty-six curtain calls for the actors, and then the thirty-four-year-old Williams, with a button missing from the jacket of his gray flannel suit, was led to the stage. There he made his brief bows to Laurette Taylor and the cast. "When Williams stood up in the theater to take a bow," says Audrey Wood, "if I had died that night, I would have been a completely fulfilled woman."

The best agents are selfless individuals.[1] They are in a parent relationship to their clients—writers, actors, directors—and the children come running to them with questions, complaints, pleas for understanding and approval —and money. Agents, to be effective, must submerge their egos in the interests of their clients. As Audrey Wood says, "I enjoy the creativity of other people. I get enormous satisfaction out of making something happen, out of helping talented people accomplish what you hope they will do." Her client roster overflows with talented people: besides Williams, there are William Inge, Robert Anderson, Truman Capote, Arthur Kopit, Michael Gazzo, Jerome Chodorov. A pert bright-eyed woman, she looks as though Grant Wood had designed her with much affection.

Agenting can be pleasurable as well, in gratifying a need for creature comfort, participatory glamour, and *involvement.* Good agents thrive on the controlled chaos of show business. To visit Charles Baker, chief of the theatrical-agent division of the giant William Morris office, is to understand the real appeal of agentry. Baker is a former actor; his office is forty stories high and has a panoramic view of the city. He is in his late forties, impeccable in dress and appearance, with a graying brush mustache and clothes from Saville Row. His conversation is punctuated with first-name references ("I told Maggie Leighton the play was all wrong for her, and Maggie agrees with me". . . Never saw Ingrid better in my life" . . . "If only we could get Marlon

---

[1] In negotiations, some agents never use the word "I" but rather the collective "we." "We don't like that costume for us," an agent will tell a producer at a dress rehearsal (one producer answered, "We do for us").

back to Broadway, my God!").[2] His days are filled with meetings, business luncheons, teas and cocktails, fast flights to everywhere, and above all, impassioned telephone negotiations ("That's the least we'll take, David, and if you want us, that's what it will cost you" . . . "Cheryl, darling, we're going to sign for the other play this afternoon unless you up the ante"). Baker is a supremely fulfilled agent, complete with cables, teletypes, and weekend trips to London.

The theater is knotted together with contracts—talent contracts, service contracts, theater contracts, investment contracts. Contracts mean money. To make things happen in the theater, contracts must be negotiated, drawn up, and signed. The signers of contracts are highly visible people—producers, playwrights, directors, theater owners, stars. Those who negotiate contracts and those who draw up contracts are less visible but equally powerful. They are the agents and the lawyers, the middlemen of the industry —secretive, maneuvering, and indispensable.

The agent's power comes from his control of the availability of talent, which is really due to a mutation in traditional theater relationships. In the old days negotiation between talent and its employer was clear-cut. If Charles Frohman wanted Maude Adams for a play, he spoke to her directly and negotiated on a face-to-face basis. The old theater relationships were enduring. The Theatre Guild could always be sure of getting the next Shaw play, the next S. N. Behrman, the next Philip Barry. If Katharine Hepburn wanted to do a Broadway play, she went to Lawrence Langner; George S. Kaufman was produced by Max Gordon. The producer ran the show. Producers became parentally involved in the lives of their artists, writers, and directors —the Gilbert Millers, Brock Pembertons, Lawrence Langners, and Sam Harrises of forty years ago bypassed the agents

[2] Comedian Shelley Berman has a routine in which, impersonating an agent, he signs Albert Schweitzer for a TV appearance and refers to Schweitzer throughout the routine as "Al, baby."

fearlessly and rendered them sometimes powerless.

Today, in a world of many media, it is the agent who steers the talent through theater, films, television, and commercial work. Today the Broadway producer needs the agent to locate and funnel the talent to the theater. The client needs the agent to cope with the thousand and one details of the new contracts with their riders on taxes, options, subsidiary rights, picture deals. To exploit his opportunities, a star may have a business entourage of five —personal manager, agent, lawyer, accountant, and press agent. The press agent will be on a weekly retainer, the accountant will charge a fee. The lawyer may take 5 per cent, the agent 10 per cent of the actor's net earnings. A $2,000-a-week actor with an army of such mercenaries behind him ends up with less than a thousand a week for himself before taxes.

There isn't enough money in theater to support many personal managers, but there are many agents handling actors—ninety-two Equity-franchised agents in New York, sixty-eight more in California. By comparison, the list of agents for playwrights is tiny—a score in all. One-man agencies generally are vertically organized, handling one type of client—only actors or only playwrights. But the big agencies such as Ashley-Famous,[3] William Morris, and General Artists Corporation are horizontal, employing their own legal and accounting departments and handling not only actors of all skills in all fields but directors, designers, playwrights, composers, lyricists, and choreographers, anybody and anything that can be sold in show business. On the twenty-ninth floor of the J. C. Penney Building on Sixth Avenue, in a choice northwest-corner office, Audrey Wood deals for her playwrights and on the same floor in a choice southwest-corner office Milton Goldman deals for his actors. Each works for Ashley-Famous. Each is major league. Each personally shepherds twenty to thirty of the biggest names in the

[3] In late 1969, Ashley-Famous was rechristened International-Famous when one of its founders, Ted Ashley, became president of Warner Bros. The trade still insists on referring to the firm by its old name.

business and is responsible for career guidance on a grand scale. A hit play can make a tidy sum for an author's agent. If the play runs two years at an average gross of $30,000, the author receives $3,000 a week, or $300,000 over two years. The play agent gets 10 per cent, or $30,000. If the play goes on the road for a year, the author nets another $150,000; chalk up another $15,000 for the play agent (the road company and the New York company may be running simultaneously). If the play sells to films for $300,000, the agent gets another $30,000. Most Broadway hits bring in at least $200,000 in stock and amateur royalties to the dramatist over a twenty-year period; that's another $20,000 for the agent. If the play is then adapted for a musical, or revived, the gold mine starts producing again. In effect, a Broadway smash means an approximate income of $100,000 for the writer's agent. A hit is the annuity all play agents dream of.

Audrey Wood's love of theater goes beyond the money. Her writers vary in their needs, work habits, and the frequency with which they write plays. "It's like being a doctor," she says. "You go when the patient needs help. When he doesn't, you mind your manners." Miss Wood started as an independent agent, later joined forces (maritally and professionally) with William Liebling, a courtly gentleman who dresses with Old World formality in stiff collar and vest, and handles actors. She sold her agency to the Music Corporation of America and moved to Ashley-Famous when MCA had to divest itself of talent clients for anti-trust reasons in order to stay in film production. Similarly, a dozen years ago Milton Goldman was in business for himself but moved into Ashley-Famous on a capital-gains arrangement, also availing himself of the facilities of an agency with offices in Hollywood and around the world, film and television specialists, and a staff of six agents to work on the legitimate theater.[4]

---

[4] In our high-tax society, the small agent's goal is to accumulate a stable of thriving clients and then to sell his business to a larger, preferably publicly owned agency. Ashley-Famous is now owned by Marvin Josephson, who has

Goldman is a brisk, fast-talking operator, a passionate theater enthusiast, and a tireless one-man claque for his clients. They can do no wrong. He handles many leading British actors and is considered by producers to be an authority on West End theater. Many English actors come to him on a referral basis—"Look up Milton when you get to New York" is a password. Goldman finds the English easier to deal with than his American clients because the English actor will have played more roles and is surer of "the dimensions of his talent" and is more secure about career moves. By comparison, American actors are more dependent upon their agents for career guidance. "In this country," says Goldman, "an actor plays one part and overnight he's a Hollywood star. He hasn't done his apprenticeship."

Actor's agents can make a lot of money from their customary 10 per cent, not so much from the theater, but from other media influenced by success on Broadway. An actor fresh from a New York hit can earn a fortune in pictures. His agent, who makes a pittance on theater work, can cash in heavily on the high Hollywood pay.[5] Ironically, some actors desert their agents when they reach the winner's circle. "I need special representation," an actor will say, or another agent may have freer access to Hollywood studios than his original agent. This happens all the time and nothing angers agents more than ungrateful clients. One literary agent who lost a much-coddled writer to a high-powered Holly-

---

"gone public." Creative Management Associates (CMA), a high-powered agency with a list of expensive movie stars, has merged with GAC (General Artists Corporation), which is traded in the over-the-counter stock market. GAC had previously taken over the Baum-Newborn Agency in a transaction involving six figures and stock options.

[6] Actor's agents do not get a commission on off-Broadway salaries unless the salary is up to the on-Broadway minimum ($150 weekly). It is common for an agent to earn nothing whatever on a busy off-Broadway actor, hoping to be rewarded when the actor signs for a TV series or a "big picture." An actor can jump from absolute minimum wage to thousands of dollars weekly within a few months. From an off-Broadway wage in *Eh?* Dustin Hoffman, thanks to the success of the film *The Graduate,* appeared a year later as the star of *Jimmy Shine* on Broadway at a salary of $4,000 weekly against 12½ per cent of the gross plus a percentage of the profits.

wood agent said flatly, "It became a conflict between loyalties and royalties—and guess which won."

While money is not the only factor in the agent-client relationship, it is the ultimate factor, and clients will not stay with an agent who isn't getting them the money they feel their talents deserve. This is especially true of actors, whose fees are so much more flexible than those of playwrights, directors, and designers, whose basic terms are within more standard limits.

An agent's services to an actor range from negotiating the billing to shaping the actor's career. Billing is never a small matter because it symbolizes an actor's importance within the tribal unit and to the public. To the profession it says, in effect, "I'm making top money and I'm worth it." Billing determines choice of dressing room and order of curtain calls the way diplomatic rank determines table seating. In negotiating actors' contracts, the question of money is frequently routine. Actors demand billing clauses, dressing rooms, dressers, approval of publicity releases and photographs, opening-night tickets, house seats, and special vacation arrangements. Lawyers add their own wrinkles, changing "ands" to "buts" and performing other feats of pettifoggery. The dressing room must be on the stage level; after the eighth consecutive performance—proof that the show is in for a run—the dressing room must be repainted; air conditioning between April and November; "out clauses" (free time) to make a pilot TV film or a feature movie; a car and chauffeur at the show's expense to get to and from the theater.

For most actors the problem is simply to find work, but for the rare actor in great demand, such as Jason Robards, it means deciding which of the concurrent offers to accept, knowing that the choice of one will preclude the others and may rule out future opportunities. Peter Witt, an actor's agent who now operates more in Hollywood than in New York, handles Robards and says, "The only kind of role I can't get him is an ingenue role."

An agent likes to be considered a "creative agent," one who doesn't just sit around waiting for business to come to him but is in constant motion, dreaming up projects for his clients. If he is a play agent, he will suggest themes and milieus to the writer; if he handles actors, he will call a producer or director and suggest a property "right" for his client; if he represents a designer, he will circularize the producers of incoming shows, suggesting they look at his client's portfolios. "It's all in the air," Robert Sanford says. "You pull a deal out of the air sometimes, just by looking at a newspaper story. I read a review of a book. I call a movie producer and tell him why doesn't he buy the book and I'll get him Chayefsky to do the screenplay. Then I call Chayefsky and ask him if he'll do the screenplay for the book if the producer buys it to begin with. By the time it all ends, I might wish I hadn't read the review. But then again, I might have a solid deal going for me."

In the theater "representation" has psychological significance. "To have an agent is to have a kind of reassurance that you exist," Arthur Miller has written. So much is at stake in every outing in the theater today, with theatrical fashions changing as rapidly as advertising slogans, that the decision to take on a Broadway assignment is a crucial one. More and more the agent has moved into the area of "career guidance." As Milton Goldman says, "In this business, an actor's career is made on the roles that are turned down."

Actor's agents are in the middle between the casting producer and their client. Producers often ring up agents for suggestions when they have a script in front of them and roles to fill, but the more usual routine is for the agent to sell the producer his clients when casting is underway. Robert Sanford, who handles Fredric March, Delbert Mann, Florence Eldridge, Burgess Meredith, and Paddy Chayefsky, says agentry is a matter of double selling: "First you have to sell your client to the buyer. Then you have to turn around and sell the deal to your client. And by the time that's over you're ready for a psychiatric institution."

The stereotyped attributes of agents—as presented in

Christopher Little

Herman Shumlin

Press agent
Harvey Sabinson

Christopher Little

Life Magazine, Time Inc. © *1969*

Director Harold Clurman

Husband and wife agents
Audrey Wood and William Liebling

Life Magazine, Time Inc. © 1969

Director Alan Schneider with Nobel-prizewinning playwright Samuel Beckett on film location in New York.

Walter Kerr

Clive Barnes

Life Magazine, Time Inc. © 1969

Life Magazine, Time Inc. © 1969

David Merrick

Friedman-Abeles

Producer Harold Prince (center) with choreographer Ronald Field and Associate Producer Ruth Mitchell at a rehearsal of *Zorbá*

Playwright Neil Simon (left) and director Mike Nichols (right) with the stars of *Plaza Suite,* Maureen Stapleton and George C. Scott

Martha Swope

Blythe Danner in *Summertree*

Theatrical lawyer
John F. Wharton

Saint-Subber in his
Manhattan town-house
office off Park Avenue

Jack Mitchell

Inge Morath

Arthur Miller with NBC drama critic Edwin Newman

Life Magazine, Time Inc. © 1969

films and novels—are materialism and avarice. Agents drive hard bargains with employers. "The goddamn agents are driving the prices up," a producer will say, because it's easier for him to blame an agent for a tough deal than to blame himself for agreeing to it. The truth about agents, however, is that most of them are hard-working, dedicated, and practical. Their hours are long, the pressures are fierce. Their phones ring incessantly with nuisance calls from demanding clients. They must travel to check talent in try-out towns, showcase performances in off-Broadway lofts, auditions, and readings. Night work is the rule.

And agents are more compassionate than they are pictured. The veteran Robert Sanford occupies a small office in the Sardi Building. From Monday through Thursday ("I wouldn't work on Friday if I handled the Messiah," he says) a stream of petitioners visit him, and his anteroom is always filled with people waiting to be discovered—singers from army camps, playwrights carrying heavy scripts in shopping bags, other agents with quick-buck ideas for TV series, acting beginners looking for the Broadway break. He sees them all, always understanding and helpful. He's not completely altruistic, because there may be a winner in the crowd, but he says, with New York wryness, "If I find a needle in the haystack, it's sure to give me blood poisoning." A former producer-director-choreographer in burlesque, he is a master of the throwaway gag and the argot of the district. "Sometimes I feel more like a dog catcher than an agent," he says, surveying the waiting throng.

In negotiations, two different postures, two distinct tones of voice are used. The agent sweet-talks his nervous client, hard-mouths the bargaining producer. Audrey Wood wears pillbox hats at her desk and gently coaxes her clients. In a single brief telephone conversation with her most famous client, Tennessee Williams, she refers to him variously as "Mr. Williams," "Ten," "ducky," "love," and "sweetheart." But at the negotiating table she is a fierce protectress of her cubs.

Miss Wood considers herself a servant of the theater, as do

the best agents. Milton Goldman says, "In seeking to guide his client into the best possible work the agent makes it difficult for bad shows to get good people." Better the worst agent than none at all, says Robert Lantz. "If it's the children who keep difficult marriages together, it's the agents who keep artists in the theater working together. An agent can be loyal to his client and still keep in mind the overall project. Most agents who work for the key elements in a production do have this overall view and they keep their perspective."

The agent can also serve as a lightning rod for disputes; he is someone both sides can yell at instead of each other.

A producer once asked an actor to attend a post-performance function in Philadelphia "for the good of the show." The actor smilingly assented, and the producer went back to his hotel, where a call was waiting for him from the actor's agent. "It's absolutely impossible for Max to go to that publicity thing you scheduled," said the agent. "He's tired, he's worried about the script, and it's not in his contract."

"But why did he say yes when I asked him?" the producer demanded.

"Don't ask me," said the agent, "and if you want a straight answer, don't ask him, either."

Robert Lantz is a kind of superagent who is becoming less and less involved in theater *per se*. He recently joined with the up-and-coming literary agent Candida Donadio and together they handle about a hundred clients, including Mike Nichols, Leonard Bernstein, Philip Roth, Jules Feiffer, Peter Shaffer, José Quintero, Alfred Drake, Lillian Hellman, James Baldwin, Mary Rodgers, Elizabeth Taylor, and Richard Burton. By himself Mike Nichols is an entire industry—hardly an hour in the Lantz office day goes by without some piece of business involving Nichols; hardly a day goes by without four or five matters involving Bernstein.

The fusion of actor and play creates theater, and the agent is an annealing instrument in this process. It is such a focal role that heavyweight agents easily evolve into packagers or subproducers, particularly when they represent several production elements at once. (We shall see that this is even truer of theatrical lawyers.) These agents make no apology for not knowing their place—"Agents are some of the best producers I know," says Audrey Wood. Many agents actually do become producers—Leland Hayward, David Susskind, Richard Halliday, Hillard Elkins—and wind up being clients to their own agents.

When David Merrick presented a Tennessee Williams play he told Miss Wood he felt she was really the co-producer, and during the most recent Williams play, produced off-Broadway, Miss Wood found herself okaying the poster for ticket-broker windows. Whole productions sometimes fall into place in the agent's offices because the talent is available there. Miss Wood, for example, was handling the script of Giraudoux's *Ondine,* which was under option to Roger L. Stevens. Casting the play seemed insurmountable until Miss Wood got a letter from an old friend, Mel Ferrer, saying he and Audrey Hepburn wanted to do something together in the theater. Then *Ondine* suddenly came alive. When Milton Goldman was representing Cyril Ritchard and Claudette Colbert he got Ritchard to direct and Miss Colbert to star in an English comedy entitled *The Irregular Verb To Love* and took the package to producer Alfred de Liagre, Jr. It was also Goldman who persuaded Maureen Stapleton to do a revival of *The Glass Menagerie* in 1965 with Piper Laurie and Pat Hingle, which rekindled her career after a long absence from the theater.

A major distinction must be drawn between an ordinary literary agent and a drama agent. Both have a fiduciary relationship to their clients and both share the duty to negotiate the sale or lease of rights in the literary work and collect the monies due, but the work of the literary agent handling a novelist is almost finished when the manuscript is delivered to the publisher. When the playscript is completed, the work of the drama agent is just beginning. The good play agent will actively follow the script through casting, rehearsal, and opening, while at the same time negotiating film, foreign, stock, amateur, and print and reprint rights.

Because he must keep in touch with so many aspects of production the agent ingests information automatically, and information is power. Goldman, Wood, Baker, Lantz, Witt, Sanford, and others continually read scripts, attend theater, and commune with producers, actors, directors, writers, and publicists. Their offices are clearinghouses of information. They know what scripts are being cast, what options have been picked up, which actors are available, when the right director is free, and what happened last night in New Haven. They know when to move.

And they move fast when the time is right. There may be days of back-and-forth bargaining over the telephone, and hours when the gulf between bids seems unbridgeable, but the moment will come when the deal can be made and one side will sing out, "Let's go to contract!"

Enter the lawyer, whom the agent seldom welcomes with enthusiasm. Lawyers are slow and cautious and quick with caveats, and agents feel inhibited and worry that they will upset the deal. "A deal is only hot for so long," says Robert Lantz. "If Mike Nichols says, yes, he'll do a deal, you want his signature on the contract tomorrow morning. Otherwise, he'll hear of something better he wants to do."

Deep down inside, agents feel they can do everything lawyers can do and do it better, and that lawyers are unnecessary—especially in disputes between actor and producer. "Once people begin to work together," says Robert Lantz, "if they have to go to the drawer and pull out the contract, the situation is already over. It's like a marriage. The minute one party feels he has to go to the lawyer, that's the end of the marriage."

The agent who was the marriage broker now becomes the marriage counselor. "For example," says Lantz, "if a producer wants Alfred Drake to accept a new leading lady and if Alfred has approval of his leading lady in his contract, I'll go to him and say, 'Barbra Streisand is ill, Julie Andrews is having an operation, Ethel Merman is really a little too old for you. Now why don't you play it with So-and-So?' But if I went to him and said, 'Stick to your contract, you have approval of the leading lady in your contract and the only girl you should accept is So-and-So,' then all is lost. If the star and the producer have to meet in a room with a legal document over a problem, you might as well cancel the show and go home."

But the root complaint agents have about lawyers is that lawyers have slid into agenting. Some theatrical lawyers have become the biggest deal makers of all—hyperagents bigger than the biggest agents. Some are accused of playing both ends against the middle and controlling the middle.

A few years ago, according to a familiar Broadway story, a contract dispute arose between the creators of a new musical. The lawyers for the producer, the composer, the director-choreographer, the lyricist, the designer, and the star were to meet to negotiate a settlement. When the meeting began only one man showed up, with an attaché case and six hats. His law firm represented all six parties to the dispute. He argued passionately, wearing a different hat each time he pled the case of each client, sitting in a different chair at the conference table as he negotiated with himself. It was a fruitful session. All sides were heard, all hats were worn, a decision was unanimously agreed on. The show was a big hit, and all parties to the dispute, including the lawyer, prospered.

This story is completely apocryphal. No such meeting ever took place. Yet Broadwayites like to repeat it, partly because of envy, partly because there is an inner truth in this imaginary picture of the *modus operandi* of influential, active, and hard-to-hire theatrical attorneys in New York.

H. William (Bill) Fitelson is a founding partner of Fitelson & Mayers, legal powerhouse of the theater which is housed in a plain, businesslike suite of offices on the twenty-second floor of the Longines-Wittnauer Building at Fifth Avenue and 47th Street. He is an intriguing show-business veteran who stays out of the spotlight but makes his presence felt in key transactions that affect Broadway's balance of power.

Fitelson is a short man who wears dark suits and bow ties and might be overlooked in a first-night audience. But the black shock of hair that curls Napoleonically above his forehead and the piercing brown eyes under black brows accent his persuasiveness and power. The voice rings with firebrand assurance, and knowing theater people do not ignore it.

Fitelson is a man of contradictions. A hard negotiator, he is a connoisseur of art, owning works by Henry Moore, Picasso, Degas, and Giacometti, and his plainly furnished office displays some distinctive wood sculpture. Few people are aware of his charity work and sponsorship of liberal causes, but he contributes heavily of his time to the American Civil Liberties Union.[6]

He has been active for forty years but his face is youthful and his step is spry. Born in Bridgeport, Connecticut, bantam-proud of his achievements, Fitelson is a very wealthy man. He owns a town house in Greenwich Village and a country home, and he recently sold a theater he owned on West 58th Street to a television network for $1 million. And, more than anyone else, Fitelson is the man to see to get things moving on Broadway.

In addition to Fitelson, the theatrical bar consists of a handful of firms and a few individual practitioners who are fascinated by the irregularities and the peculiarities of its people. The seventy-five-year-old dean of theatrical law is John F. Wharton, a corporation attorney, founding partner of his firm, representative of the Marshall Field interests, and frequent writer on the theater. He became involved with Broadway in the 1920's through his friend and client, producer Dwight Deere Wiman.

Behind Wharton's Yankee manner and easy laughter is a

---

[6] During the McCarthy witchhunt in the early 1950's Fitelson was criticized by some theater people, because a number of his clients with radical political backgrounds admitted past membership in "subversive" organizations, naming names of fellow-members. While these expedient actions may not have sat well with everyone, they were eminently pragmatic, enabling the friendly witnesses to keep working. Others who remained silent were blacklisted and made unemployable for years.

stern intelligence, a keen esthetic sense, strong principles, and a fine legal mind. He can be blunt when opposed, and although he is habitually skeptical, he is also an incurable idealist. Wharton's firm—Paul, Weiss, Goldberg, Rifkind, Wharton & Garrison,[7] at 345 Park Avenue—is busy in theatricals and represents producers Robert Whitehead, Roger L. Stevens, T. Edward Hambleton, Albert W. Selden, directors Arthur Penn and Gower Champion, playwrights Arthur Miller and Robert Anderson, and many others. Wharton was a founder of the Playwrights Company and of the Producers Theater and is a long-time advocate of ticket reform, an architect of the Theatre Development Fund, Inc., and a passionate playgoer. Now technically retired, he is still active in theater. His firm's theatrical affairs are managed by four partners—Robert Montgomery, John C. Taylor 3rd, Norman Zelenko, and Richard R. Davidson—and six associates.

Weissberger & Frosch, 120 East 56th Street, has in Arnold Weissberger a theatrical attorney who seems more theatrical than lawyerish. Weissberger, a tall man, is an elegant dresser, never without a red or white carnation in his buttonhole. He patronizes the best restaurants, throws fashionable show-business parties, travels eagerly, and goes to the theater all the time. Weissberger has been an amateur photographer for years and takes countless 35-mm color photos at parties, first nights, and theatrical outings. His subjects are show people, and only show people.[8] He is hopelessly stage-struck. He once took *New York Times* critic Clive Barnes to task for being too harsh on the producers of shows Barnes didn't like. The producers, Weissberger felt, shouldn't get all the blame when things go wrong.

[7] Goldberg is former Supreme Court Justice and former U.S. Representative to the United Nations Arthur J. Goldberg, and Rifkind is former U.S. District Court Judge Simon H. Rifkind. Other members of the firm include Theodore Sorensen and former Attorney General Ramsey Clark.

[8] The Weissberger Collection was recently donated and displayed at the Theater Collection of the Museum of the City of New York. It covered the walls of many large rooms, depicted almost every theatrical celebrity in the U.S. and England. It is valued by Weissberger in six figures.

He represents movie producer Otto Preminger, composers Burton Lane and Igor Stravinsky, and international stars whose names still dazzle him: Rex Harrison, Richard Burton, Elizabeth Taylor, Beatrice Lillie, Helen Hayes, Orson Welles, John Gielgud, and Laurence Olivier. The Weissberger practice is 90 per cent show business.

A lawyer with a reputation for toughness and shrewdness is Edward E. Colton, of Colton, Fernbach, Weissberg & Yamin, at 745 Fifth Avenue, who represents, among others, producers Harold Prince, Fred Coe, Saint-Subber, and Alexander H. Cohen, and agent Audrey Wood and is the negotiator for the Dramatists Guild. In this key capacity he handles the sale of motion-picture rights to every Broadway play and musical, for which he receives $20,000 a year plus $15,000 expenses and a percentage of the gross proceeds. In a good year this means $100,000 plus for Colton.[9]

A firm with an extensive literary and theatrical practice is Greenbaum, Wolff & Ernst at 437 Madison Avenue, whose partner Alan U. Schwartz represents Tennessee Williams and the American Place Theatre. The firm of Schoenfeld & Jacobs on Shubert Alley is unique in being the only West Side theatrical law firm. Representing the Shuberts, it deals with everybody on Broadway, including the unions. Just plain propinquity has turned this firm into a kind of legal-aid society for the business.

With these firms and a few more individuals—Irving Cohen, who represents Alan Jay Lerner and producers Feuer and Martin; Howard Reinheimer, Cohen's former partner who is now counsel to Weissberger & Frosch; and Albert I. Da Silva, who handles Neil Simon—the theatrical bar would seem to be complete. But new blood enters the profession continually as young lawyers break away from established firms to go out on their own. Although theatrical law is chancy and payments erratic, particularly from newcomers to the theater, the practice is perennially attractive.

Legal fees in the theater vary, as in other fields, with the

---

[9] In 1968 the proceeds of the sales of film rights to Broadway properties amounted to approximately $6 million.

availability and experience of the lawyer and the financial resources of the client. Formerly it was usual for a theatrical attorney to charge a flat fee—ranging from $2,500 to $5,000 for a play and from $5,000 to $7,500 for a musical—for supervising the legal procedures for a forthcoming production. Now initial fees are 25 per cent to 50 per cent higher for shows, and seasoned theatrical lawyers demand a weekly retainer or a piece of the producer's profits. Off-Broadway fees are token by comparison.

Just as agents overstep their functional limits, so lawyers sometimes venture beyond strictly legal responsibilities. It is characteristic of the theater that everyone wants to put his two cents' worth in. Saint-Subber tells the story of holding some eighty auditions to interest backers in the musical *Kiss Me, Kate,* as no one could see the sense in a musical-comedy marriage between Cole Porter and Shakespeare. Saint-Subber was represented by a firm which had agreed to do all his legal work for 12½ per cent of the show's profits. At one of the last auditions, the lawyers suddenly anounced that two of the songs—"I've Come to Wive It Wealthily in Padua" and "Were Thine That Special Face" —weren't working, and if they were to remain as counsel the songs would have to be cut from the score. Saint-Subber did not agree, and the firm got out.

Lawyers really cannot help intervening in matters technically beyond their province, even matters of artistic concern. Often they are so close to the heart of the production that their roles are reversed and they act as shadow producers. Theatrical lawyers are constantly solicited on such extralegal problems as what director to hire or what actor to cast or what theater to book. They are asked to read and judge scripts, and sometimes they locate producers for these scripts. At least five scripts a week cross the desk of lawyer Robert Montgomery, and Bill Fitelson is never without a pile of scripts in his office. "A lawyer doesn't exist in a vacuum," says Arnold Weissberger. "It's all very well to know about tax regulations and contracts, but he should also know something about his client's world. It's important for me to read scripts."

Weissberger is forthright in advising his clients on the suitability of scripts for production. "Where we go wrong," he says, "is not with things we dislike but with things we like. For the most part we are right when we reject scripts, because most scripts are rejectable anyway. It's when we like a script that it's hard to let go."

In the money-raising area, lawyers can be invaluable, particularly the powerhouse lawyers. Some attorneys have instant access to big investors, Wall Street moneymen, and corporate tycoons. It's a delicate balance when one client invests in another client's play, but it's one reason why some lawyers have an edge over others.

The lawyer's intervention is not always cheerfully received. Theatrical attorney Jack Perlman once confessed to getting rebuffed when he made a suggestion during a rehearsal to the director. The producer, his client, was outraged at this breach of etiquette. "Tell me first, and I'll tell the director," the producer said. He was angry with Perlman not so much for making a suggestion as for not going through channels. Perlman forswore artistic intervention from that moment on. "It's the business of other people to express opinions in the play or the movie," he said. "My judgment is a very private matter."

Frequently lawyers are at odds with agents although, theoretically, there should be no overlap. The agent negotiates the money; the lawyer writes the contract. But as agents tend to become subproducers lawyers tend to become superagents. The Fitelson firm, for example, will negotiate almost everything for a client such as Mary Martin. A glance at the names on the client list of Fitelson & Mayers shows how easily the lawyer can absorb an agent's historical function. The firm, which has represented more than a thousand Broadway productions, represents the following: David Merrick, Leland Hayward, Joshua Logan, the Theatre Guild, Richard Barr, Edward Albee, Theodore Mann, Mary Martin, Richard Halliday, Elia Kazan, Cheryl Crawford, Elliot Martin, Jerome Robbins, Dore Schary, Philip Lang-

ner, Jule Styne. The list goes on, but we'll stop here. Stir
the pot of names, and another show is cooking within the
Fitelson office. To take just one example: *Gypsy,* produced
by David Merrick and Leland Hayward, book by Arthur
Laurents, music by Jule Styne, lyrics by Stephen Sondheim,
directed by Jerome Robbins, concerning Gypsy Rose Lee—
all but Laurents and Sondheim are Fitelson clients.

It is not hard to understand why the power of some theatrical lawyers is envied and feared, justly or not, in many
quarters of the theater world, but that power is an unalter-
able fact of the business. "You hear of an author giving his
play to So-and-So," said one producer not represented by a
large firm, "and then you hear that both the author and the
producer and the director are represented by the same lawyer. That puts other producers in an inferior position."

A multiple-client list with possibly competing interests
imposes the need for Solomon's wisdom. What happens, for
example, in Weissberger's office if half his clients all happen
to call on Friday afternoon with a problem? "You have to
remain calm," Weissberger says calmly, "and show no favorit-
ism. You can't say to a $500 client that he'll have to wait
while you take care of a $50,000 client first. He won't accept
that. If you decide to take on a new client you have to treat
him just the same as you do all your other clients."

The theatrical bar must cope with continual conflict-of-
interest problems. This was admitted by virtually every
lawyer questioned. One lawyer has this approach: "I try to
be fair. If I represent a producer in the morning and a director in the afternoon, and if I ask for every last penny for
the producer, it's going to hit back at me in the afternoon
when I'm representing the director."

Occasionally a theatrical lawyer is accused of favoring one
client over another. During Attorney General Louis J. Lefkowitz' investigation of ticket-selling irregularities in 1963,
one attorney, to protect a vulnerable major client, informed
the Attorney General that none of his clients would cooperate with the investigation, but he had not consulted
his less important clients before taking this step and at

least one resented it enough to leave him, particularly after
he was subpoenaed. In another case, a producer claims to
have made a deal with an author's agent to translate a book
into a musical. The producer and the agent shook hands on
the deal in front of the lawyer but no contract was signed.
A few days later another producer announced the project
in the papers. The flabbergasted first producer appealed to
his lawyer to be witness to the agreement and sue, but the
lawyer also represented the agent who made the deal, and
the handshake producer was out of luck.

"When I was just starting out," one lawyer said, "an actress came to me from another firm which had drawn up
an employment contract for her that clearly favored the
producer, whom the firm also represented. This was clear
conflict of interest. But the firm had evidently decided to
favor the client that would do it the most good. Actresses
come and go, but a big producer stays around."

On the subject of possible conflict of interest, Fitelson
explains the attitude taken by his firm as follows: "Frequently,
we represent various interests in the same project. Our
clients are always advised whom we represent in every transaction; it is never a secret from them. Most of our clients
are pleased to have us represent the various interests and
often we represent as many as five or six parties to a contract, and in the same project. Each party always has opportunity to engage other counsel if he feels there is serious
conflict or that it may in some way be disadvantageous to
him. Of course, we also have the opportunity to withdraw or
suggest the engagement of other counsel if we feel that the
representation of any party is disadvantageous to him. And
from time to time we do."

A classic example of how one law firm initiated and organized one hugely successful Broadway project—*The Sound of
Music*—is described by William Fitelson.

"The libretto was based on a German motion picture. A
print was first screened by someone at Paramount to a bright
client of ours, the stage director, Vincent Donehue, to see if
he would be interested in directing a motion picture remake

of it. Vincent thought it would make an excellent musical for the stage. He arranged to have the picture screened for Mary Martin and Richard Halliday. They enthusiastically agreed with him and arranged to have the picture screened for Leland Hayward who also agreed about its potential for the musical stage. Leland Hayward screened it for the late Lindsay and Crouse and later for Richard Rodgers and Oscar Hammerstein 2nd. The basic rights were extremely complicated, involving many people, including the producer of the German motion picture, authors, the Baroness Trapp and her children, etc. Leland Hayward and I flew to Munich in connection with the clearance of the basic rights. There were negotiations with all those parties, as well as with everyone else one has to negotiate with in connection with the production of a musical. One of the most successful stage musicals and probably the largest grossing motion picture to date was the result. In reply to your question, we represented the following parties: Richard Halliday, Mary Martin, Leland Hayward, Vincent Donehue and The Sound of Music Company."

Fitelson also represented the production when Rodgers and Hammerstein joined Halliday and Hayward as producers. There were many problems during that production, which Fitelson handled without crisis, but there was one major problem afterward that caused a serious split between Rodgers and the other two producers. Rodgers and Hammerstein had made an agreement with Twentieth Century Fox to control the soundtrack album of the film. Hayward and Halliday charged in court that they had not been informed of this agreement, and they sued to share in the sizable royalties that were piling up. Hayward and Halliday won a unanimous decision in the Appellate Division. They won the appeal in the Court of Appeals, New York State's highest court. And they won the largest arbitration award on record—$1.1 million. They were represented by Fitelson & Mayers.

To some extent, conflicts of interest occur in law firms specializing in other business fields because as soon as a law

The Sound of Money

American business has led the world in creating ingenious debt machinery to ease the ways of trade. Corporations issue bonds, debentures, promissory notes, and warrants. The American economy floats on an ocean of credit, and when credit is tightened, the resulting "crunch" is heard around the world. Americans, more than others, eat, travel, buy, study, sicken, and die on "time."

But the Broadway theater lives by cash alone. It is a hard-ticket, hard-cash society. Theater unions demand cash bonds in advance before they permit their members to work. "I like your looks and your ideas," Lee Shubert would say to young producers, "but are you sure you have the cash?" Ticket selling is a cash operation.[1] Cash receipts are totted up each night and twice on matinee days. Ticket brokers and landlords settle up weekly, in cash. "The theater is C.O.D.," says business manager Jack Schlissel, "and its re-

---

[1] The credit-card clubs have made sporadic forays into selling theater tickets, without apparent success. Some ticket brokers honor credit cards, but "cash on the line" is preferred. Treasurers in most theaters will not accept checks except by mail, and then only with sufficient advance notice to enable the checks to clear.

ligion is here today, gone tomorrow, and don't trust your mother for a dollar!"

In the 1968–69 season the Broadway theater grossed approximately $60 million. Note the word "approximately." No other word can be used. The theater is one of the few industries in America which does not supply accurate statistics on its operations to anyone, including itself. Accurate fiscal data on Broadway shows has never been compiled in one place, is not now being compiled, and—barring government control of theaters and productions—probably never will be compiled. To arrive at total figures for the industry, or a significant part of it, one would have to check a hundred different sources.[2]

The industry acknowledges the importance of truth in its financial accounting and must, of course, give public, state, and federal figures in the case of a public offering, but theater producers and managers simply will not otherwise tell the truth about their shows unless the shows are smash hits. Irving W. Cheskin, executive director of the League of New York Theatres, has tried vainly for years to establish a central information bureau for figures on production and operating costs, profit margins, and the like. "The producers simply won't cooperate," complains Cheskin. "They have a meeting," he says, "they vote to authorize a businesslike study of industry finances; then they go back to the office and if anyone asks for information they say, 'Why should I tell you? My show is my business. I guess we'll have to take it up again at the next meeting.' "

Producers are ambivalent about their secrecy. One observer calls it "fair-weather honesty." The closed-mouth policy dates back to the ruggedly entrepreneurial days when shows were financed privately and full disclosure was literally nobody's business but the producer's. Yet most shows are now financed through public offering, and eventually the financial statements of such offerings are available to the

---

[2] By not considering enough sources, *The New York Times* incurred the wrath of theater people in May 1963 when it described that season as "disastrous." See Chapter 9.

public. With odd contrariness, producers will not hesitate to disclose and usually exaggerate their receipts or their profits —*when it suits their convenience.* In general, producers will only talk about business when it's good.

An implacable foe of this double standard is Hobe Morrison, drama editor of *Variety,* who feels financial privacy has no place in the theater. "The public has a right to know what's happening on Broadway," he says.

Morrison wages vendettas with producers who give him "phony" figures, overstating their grosses when business is bad.[3] Occasionally a play will be "overquoted" for weeks before Morrison learns through his network of tipsters that he has been gulled. He will then "underquote" the play's gross in the next issue of *Variety.* At this, the producer who has kept a smug silence while his fake high grosses were publicized will fly into a tantrum at having his fake low grosses circulated. During David Merrick's early days as a producer, he feuded with Morrison on the issue of full disclosure. On one musical, *Fanny,* Merrick was caught with his grosses up. Morrison then printed extra-low grosses for the show to prove that he knew what had been going on. Merrick was furious. He sent a telegram to *Variety* on August 8, 1955, imparting a mystical Merrickian formula to determine exact grosses of Merrick shows.

> Knowing of your melancholy preoccupation with box-office grosses and since you have been guessing the "Fanny" grosses erroneously of late, here is the way you can determine "Fanny" grosses for last week and henceforth. Whenever the average high temperature for the preceding week is 63° or less, the gross for "Fanny" is $63,000. Thereafter, the gross recedes in inverse ratio to the rise in the average high temperature for the week. For example, if the average high temperature is 64° then our gross is $62,000 and if the average high temperature for the week is 75° then our gross is

[3] There is a half-affectionate Broadway story about the producer whose show took in only four dollars at one performance. The following day while lunching with another producer, he was asked the inevitable "How did you do last night?" and replied, "It was brutal. Worst business in my experience. Would you believe it—we took in only *eight* dollars!"

$51,000. This will make it easy for you and if any change in this trend occurs, I will keep you informed.

> Your obedient servant,
> David Merrick

This was one battle Merrick could not win. In one of his rare surrenders, he gave up the fight and ever since has been dutifully supplying figures that are accurate to the penny. With success and millions of dollars to sustain him, a mellowed Merrick can now afford to admit that his shows occasionally do not sell out.

Some producers justify prevarication by claiming that *Variety*'s reports of declining business endanger the future property value of a show. How can you expect to negotiate a decent price for film rights, they ask, when a film company can look at *Variety* and see a show gasping for life; how can you maneuver a London production or touring company or a stock-rights sale on the basis of low grosses? "I don't think my show's gross is a proper concern of *Variety*," says a major producer. "*Variety* doesn't give a damn about me or my investors or the future of a show into which I've poured my blood. If my show doesn't do business, I'm not going to destroy its chances for the sake of *Variety* and if *Variety* catches me, so what. Maybe by that time I'll have made the film sale." The same producer will shamelessly solicit *Variety* for a "puff" story when riding the crest of a sell-out hit, and will delightedly trumpet the news of capacity grosses.

In their whirling little world on the West Side of New York, show people tend to inflate the fiscal dimensions of their industry, but the Broadway theater is insignificant when compared to other American businesses. In terms of dollar value, the theater is in the lowest percentile of industry.

An obscure paper-products company in Illinois annually grosses $120 million—twice the Broadway gross. A regional grocery chain has an annual sales volume of $1.5 billion, twenty-five times the Broadway gross. One film, *The Graduate,* is expected to gross $80 million, $20 million more than the total Broadway gross. The "road" adds a scant $40 million annually. Off-Broadway grosses a minuscule $1.5 million.

The money needed to finance Broadway each year is even less impressive. It costs $17 million a year to pay for the entire product of the Broadway stage—musicals, revues, dramas, comedies, special productions.[4]

The $17 million figure is arrived at as follows. About fifty shows open on Broadway each year; forty are straight plays at an average cost of $200,000 each; the remaining ten are musicals at an average cost of $600,000 each. Total cost of all productions: $14 million.

Add ten plays that close out of town before they get to New York and assume arbitrarily that seven are straight plays at $200,000 each and three are musicals at $600,000 each. Total cost of productions closing out of town: $3.2 million. Total cost of all sixty productions: $17.2 million.

Seventeen million dollars! Seventeen million is what one tobacco company spends in one year to advertise one brand of cigarettes. It represents the cost of four F-111 fighter planes. It is slightly more than half the cost of waging the Vietnam War for one day. It will buy a twenty-story office building. It cost twice as much to produce one film, *Cleopatra*.

A half century of rapid changes in American life has altered the structuring of Broadway finance. In those old days sentimentally recalled by company managers sitting around the Lambs, producers financed themselves or persuaded a handful of stage-struck plutocrats to "angel" their plays. "Angels" were authentic multimillionaires. Men such as Otto Kahn, Jules Brulatour, and Jules Bache played Maecenas, subsidizing plays out of Wall Street fortunes. In the 1920's and 1930's an angel, in Billy Rose's words, was "a guy who liked to wear a black hat and meet blondes." Income taxes were low, and straight plays cost $5,000 to produce and musicals $25,000. The theater was a pretty plaything

---

[4] In these calculations, allowance is made for inflation. In 1970 most producers expect production costs to approximate those used in this chapter. Costs in 1969 were 20 per cent lower, on the average.

festooned with girls. One angel could back an entire production painlessly; a couple of phone calls did the trick.

"Everybody makes fun of the old movies about the theater," recalls Irving Cooper, whose career as a business manager spans five decades. "But that's really how it was. It was like Ruby Keeler and Dick Powell playing in the movie *42nd Street* with all the stereotypes. You could do a play within a week after you got the script. Buy it on Monday, get the dough from your backer on Tuesday, sign the star and director on Wednesday, and go into rehearsal the next Monday, probably with your backer's girl friend in the cast. Now you have to count on a three-month wait for your backers' prospectus to be approved by the Attorney General's office before you can accept a dollar from an investor legally."

It was usual in those days for producers to solicit mobster money. One gangster angel was the notorious "Waxey" Gordon, who backed the musical *Red, Hot and Blue* starring Jimmy Durante and Ethel Merman in 1934. A mobster preferred musicals because they were loud and lavish and had lots of chorus girls, but some racketeers backed serious drama, too. A couple of "classy" bootleggers, recalls Joel Schenker, invested in heavy "problem plays." "The plays were awful," he says, "but the bootleggers thought they were literature. It made them feel like professors."

It was also practical in low-tax days for an angel to back a play written by a relative or a play that promoted a pet cause. In 1927 an eccentric Texas oilman named Edwin Davis kept *The Ladder* running to nonpaying audiences for a year at a cost of a million dollars because he believed in the play's theme—immortality. "Vanity" productions were frequent, to the dismay of critics. Mother might pen a costume drama about the court of King Canute and her loving sons would give it a Broadway opening for the sport of it.[5]

A new band of angels now swings high and low over Broad-

[5] In 1970 inflation has driven the "vanity" production to off-Broadway. At least 10 per cent of off-Broadway's annual output is financed by playwrights or their family and friends. Most "vanity" productions have brief lives.

way. These investors are the beneficiaries of a high-tax society geared to high-cost theater. Where once a few wealthy
souls dabbled in theater, now thousands of angels try their
luck each season. In their attitudes, motivations, and backgrounds, they differ sharply from the angels of old. They are
the "new breed" of affluent patrons who have made their
money in the last twenty years, in the postwar boom. The
"old money" is still around, but the "new money" is not just
Texas oil, South African diamond, or Cleveland department-
store money. It is good-natured, high-tax-bracket money
from the new wealth accumulated in high technology, re-
tailing, and manufacturing.

The angels of 1970 are drawn by the glitter of show business, but they are less personally involved with production
than the angels of the 1920's. "I haven't met an investor in
ten years who has asked to get his girl friend into a play,"
says Irving Cooper. "Once it was part of the contract. They
must be doing something else now with their girls, or maybe
the girls don't have the same ambitions."

Most of the new angels are amateur investors for whom a
Broadway show is like a fast hand of poker or a night on the
town, but there is also a hard-headed cadre of professional
angels, serious speculators who play the Broadway market
for profit and only for profit. There are only a few professionals, perhaps a dozen in all, but they are shrewd and ubiquitous and because they know what they're doing one or two
find their way onto the angel roster of every major hit.

Three such high-rollers in the Broadway casino are Max
Brown, an Indiana businessman who maintains an office in
the Sardi Building; Byron Goldman, a New York clothing
manufacturer; and Morton Mitosky, a Philadelphia lawyer who commutes between his law office in the Quaker
City and his investing office in a Central Park South hotel.
These three have placed several million dollars of their own
and their associates' money into Broadway shows over the
past decade. Brown and Goldman were pioneer investors
with David Merrick. Mitosky first struck it rich in 1957 with
a heavy piece of *The Music Man*. He now invests mainly with

Merrick, Prince, and Saint-Subber.

Mitosky, who is almost a full-time angel, speaks for a syndicate of industrialists. Strictly a form player, he bets on "money producers," rarely gambling on unknowns. He tries to keep in touch with and ahead of the theatrical season: he flies to London to check out a New York-bound show, he haunts the tryout towns, he keeps in touch with key producers and managers, lunching with them daily in theater restaurants. He would like to produce plays, but he does too well as an angel to take the step.

Mitosky and other professional angels refute a basic myth of theatrical investing—that it is like throwing money down a rat hole, a myth that goes back to days when unscrupulous promoters fleeced their angels. Such unconscionable abuse of investors led to legislation which is now rigidly enforced for all productions with more than twenty investors. Depending on the size of capitalization, a Broadway show must register either with the New York State Attorney General's office or with the Federal Government's Securities and Exchange Commission. In either case, the producer must issue an approved offering circular or prospectus; he must hold investor money in escrow unless an investor specifically agrees to the contrary; he must execute approved legal agreements before he may legally spend a penny of the funds entrusted to him; and he must disclose to the investor every financial detail of the production. The basic concept of the limited partnership, by which 99 per cent of all plays function, is that the investor's participation is *limited*.

The state and national authorities have done their best to perpetuate the rat-hole myth. As Walter Kerr once pointed out, regulations governing theatrical investment are an open invitation for the theater to commit suicide. (One producer says the laws imply that "in order to be a theatrical investor, you have first to qualify as an idiot.") Every play prospectus must contain explicit warnings of the hazards of investing, much as bottles of poison carry skull-and-crossbones labels. For example, any play which registered with the New York State Attorney General in 1969 was required to include the following material in its offering circular:

> In such a venture, the risk of loss is especially high in contrast with the prospects for any profit. . . .
> These securities should not be purchased unless the investor is prepared for the possibility of total loss. . . .
> While no accurate industry statistics are available, it is claimed that of the plays produced for the New York stage in the 1967–68 season, as high as 80 per cent resulted in loss to investors. . . .
> More than 77 per cent of the plays produced for the New York stage in the 1967–68 season failed to run more than 100 performances. Of those that did, a handful played to capacity audiences.

By comparison, the SEC authorized statement of risk for theatrical investors is euphoric: "There is a high risk of loss to investors in any theatrical production."

How high is the risk, really? The answer lies in something said in jest by Howard Cullman, a tobacco millionaire and sometime investor: "The way to make money as an angel is to invest more money in hits and less money in flops." Professional angels minimize risk by a clinical study of the track records of producers, playwrights, and directors before they put a nickel in. As Mitosky once put it, "A producer with one hit may just be lucky. But a producer with three hits has to have something more."

A recurring exercise for angels is to estimate the total return to investors from backing every play, hit or flop, in a given Broadway season.

Let us once again assume a season of sixty shows, of which fifty open in New York at a total cost of $17.2 million, allowing $200,000 capitalization for each play and $600,000 capitalization for each musical, taking into account that theatrical investors share in subsidiary rights to hit plays for from five to seventeen years after the Broadway opening. In our hypothetical season, we are assuming arbitrarily but reasonably that all plays carry subsidiary rights for ten years and that ten of the fifty shows are hits that return a profit of three dollars for every dollar invested (a very conservative estimate), that twenty are half hits (or half flops) that return half the investment; and that the remaining thirty, including ten flops closing prior to Broadway, are total failures with no returns and no subsidiary rights.

Examine the ten hits. Six are straight plays, four are musicals.[6] Total investment: $3.6 million. Total recoupment: $14.4 million, including return of investment and allowing a three-to-one return of investment and allowing a three-to-one return over ten years.

Next category, *the half hit.* Twenty shows, consisting of seventeen plays and three musicals. Total investment: $5.2 million. Total recoupment over ten years: $2.6 million.

Third and final category, *the catastrophic flop.* We list thirty of these, including the ten that folded out of town. Total investment in nine musicals and twenty-one plays: $5.8 million. Total recoupment: Zero.

Final recapitulation. Investment for the sixty-play season: $17.2 million. Return over ten years: $17 million.

A break-even investment over ten years is certainly not a desirable investment for widows, orphans, or crap shooters, but it is far from unqualified disaster. And as professional angels point out, it would be lunacy to back every play every season. If one is able to invest with only three or four top producers, the return on investment compares favorably with anything on Wall Street.[7]

One theatrical accountant remarks, "Very few industries compare in growth compound percentages with a smash hit.

---

[6] An intriguing aspect of the contemporary theater is that while musicals comprise only 20 per cent of all Broadway productions, they account for 40 per cent of all hits. But this is logical when one considers that musicals appeal to a wider public and that they run longer than straight plays on the average; therefore their incidence of success is higher. On July 7, 1969, the Broadway alphabetical listings in *The New York Times* showed only five straight plays—*Forty Carats, Hadrian VII, Play It Again, Sam, Plaza Suite,* and *The Great White Hope*—to nine musicals—*Cabaret, Fiddler on the Roof, Hair, Hello, Dolly!, Mame, Man of La Mancha, Promises, Promises, 1776,* and *Zorbá.* Of the seven shows that belong to the 1968–69 season and that lasted through July 1969 four were straight plays and three were musicals.

[7] See Chapter 2 for investment data on Harold Prince productions.

Where else will you find a business that earns 10 per cent profit on its investment month after month? A smash hit will pay dividends for years." To a question about flops, the same accountant says, "I have no patience with flops."

Established producers guard their lists of loyal investors. When things go well, a producer-angel relationship may last for decades. Hit producers literally turn money away; the Merrick office, for example, can afford to be selective about its investor list. It is easier for a camel to pass through the needle's eye than for a casual investor to get into a Merrick show.

On the other hand, a producer with a run of bad luck soon finds his investors have fled. "One hit is good for two flops," says producer Morton Gottlieb. In other words, if a producer has one hit, he can hold on to his investors through the next two flops.

Kermit Bloomgarden, who has produced a score of plays in his thirty years in the theater, knows the inconstancy of investors. In the 1950's, with hit after hit (*Death of a Salesman, Diary of Anne Frank, Look Homeward, Angel,* and *The Music Man*), he was swamped with eager investors. On principle he would not allow investors to read scripts, so they had to back him on faith. In recent seasons, after a few flops, scripts became readily available to potential backers.

When letters go unanswered, phone solicitation is rebuffed, and "angel chasers" falter, the backer's audition becomes obligatory. The audition must be produced carefully in a spacious and richly furnished setting; Central Park West or Fifth Avenue apartments are preferred. The audition must be well-paced because angels are impatient. In auditions for a musical show, songs should be performed professionally and narration should be pleasant and brief. "The sure sign of an amateur audition," says manager Richard Seader, "is when more time is spent describing the plot than playing the music." Financial details should be explained crisply and unhesitatingly, and contracts must be available for the investor who is ready to sign.

A backer's audition is an elegant, formalized nite. The

audience looks as though it came out of the first five rows at a Broadway show, and there are many "repeaters." During the drink break, the conversation is peppered with Broadway talk.

"I can't crack the Merrick office. RCA put up all the money."

"You can get dollar-for-dollar from So-and-So. His back is against the wall."

"Stay away from Such-and-Such. The producer is furnishing his apartment with investors' money."

Many shows forego the New York backer's audition to seek angels out of town, where the reception is usually warmer and show business seems more glamorous. Some shows can raise all their money in one or two out-of-town auditions. "Resort towns are the best bet," says one producer. "Take a place like East Hampton on Long Island. In July there's more concentrated wealth there than on Park Avenue. An audition is a great Saturday-night diversion for these people. I've sometimes financed a show there over one weekend."

Auditions can be expensive. Paying for an apartment, liquor, bartender, hors d'oeuvres, folding chairs, performers, and musicians may come to $500 for a musical. Out-of-town auditions are costlier, with air fares, hotel bills, and per diems to consider; $1,500 is not out of line.

There are no statistics on auditions and readings, but they must run into the hundreds each season. Many shows audition for months or years and never raise the money.

When a show has trouble completing its capitalization, the professional angels move in for the kill. The "end money"—the last few percentage points—is often the hardest to raise. When a producer is fighting for time, he is ripe for a deal. The customary limited-partnership arrangement gives investors 50 per cent of the show in exchange for 100 per cent of the money. For example, if a show costs $200,000 to produce, the producer sets up a hundred units, each representing 1 per cent of the show. Keeping 50 per cent, or fifty units, he sells the other fifty units for $4,000 each.

A professional angel always looks for an "edge"—that is,

extra units that come out of the producer's share—in exchange for a substantial investment. Where end money is involved, an edge is easier to get. Sometimes a show will still be looking for money even after it is in rehearsal or has opened out of town. Byron Goldman waited until the last minute to invest in *Man of La Mancha,* for example. The musical had had trouble raising money, and producer Albert W. Selden had invested a great deal in it himself to enable it to open. *La Mancha* played to disappointing houses during its preview weeks, but at that point Goldman decided to invest $20,000. He demanded an edge. After one sparsely attended preview, Selden and Goldman bargained in the box office of the theater, and Goldman got his edge. *Man of La Mancha* has already quadrupled Goldman's investment and his edge will bring him extra dividends for years to come.

Unlike Goldman with *La Mancha,* most angels don't have a chance to see a show on stage before they invest, and even when they do they may guess wrong. One angel remembers his first theatrical investment. "I went to the first backer's audition, and I loved the show. I invested $2,000 of my savings. When I told my wife, she was livid. Let's go to Philadelphia, to the dress rehearsal, I said, you'll see how right I am. We drove down from New York and watched the first run-through. Everything went wrong. The orchestra was off-key, the scenery fell down, the singers were hoarse. My wife was stony-faced. We drove back to New York, and she kept asking me how could I justify wasting $2,000. The next morning I sold off half the investment. That show was *The Music Man* and the $1,000 investment my wife rejected has yielded $6,000 so far. But the experience had a bright side. Now my wife never evaluates a show until after she has read the reviews." [8]

Once financed for production, the play must begin to think of selling tickets, which would seem to be a simple matter. A theater has so many seats; each seat has a cor-

[8] The investment and the wife in question belong to this book's co-author, Arthur Cantor.

responding ticket, numbered to avoid confusion; the seats are priced so that the choicest locations command the highest prices; a ticket office at the entrance sells tickets for cash; hard tickets for hard cash, supply in direct touch with demand. What could be simpler? Yet for centuries the sale of theater tickets has brought on corruption and confusion. When there are more buyers than sellers, a black market results. The so-called "retail" price, the price printed on the ticket, becomes meaningless. Speculation doubles, triples, or quadruples the "real" as opposed to the "legal" asking price. A smash hit on Broadway means "ice"—the difference between the real and legal prices—a well-hidden but substantial cash flow that is divided among shadowy middlemen.

Ticket scandals break out in New York as regularly as the flu. The scenario is familiar. A play opens and becomes a superhit. Tickets become difficult, then impossible, to obtain. There are letters to the newspapers, speeches in the City Council, an inquiry by a public prosecutor. Shocking corruption is discovered. Someone—a broker, a treasurer, a manager—is convicted of overcharging and accepting illegal gratuities. Someone may even go to jail. The black market, valiantly scotched, *never stops for a single moment.*

It is hard to understand how the ticket system works, since no records are kept on Broadway's $60 million gross and how it is collected. Experienced Broadway managers estimate that the ticket revenue breaks down as follows: 15 per cent is sold through theater-party agents and ticket clubs, 30 per cent through ticket brokers, and the remainder at the box office and by mail. When a show is hot, parties and mail may absorb weeks or months of tickets in advance. Except with marginal or waning shows, the "impulse" ticket buyer must take his chances at the box office or with the brokers.

By definition, theater parties are groups of playgoers who band together for an evening to see a show. What could be more rewarding for both play and audience? And if the group decides to raise the price of the ticket and donate the extra money to the group's charity, how much more pleasurable

—art and philanthropy join hands.

Theater parties became popular in the Yiddish theater of the 1920's on the Lower East Side. Later the practice
moved uptown as word spread that large sums of money
could be raised this way, and producers learned they could
accumulate huge advance sales through party bookings.

"We are big business," says Elsa Hoppenfeld, one of today's principal theater-party agents. "They [the producers]
all talk about how they don't like us, but when a show goes
into production they woo us and they need us. The theater
would be nothing without us."

Miss Hoppenfeld, a spirited, motherly, emotional woman,
is one of a dozen theater-party agents, almost all of whom
are women. "This business is too rough for most men," one
theater-party lady recently told a reporter. They derive handsome incomes from commissions ranging from 7.5 to 10 per
cent of their gross sales. By law they are required to be licensed as ticket brokers and yet, unlike ticket brokers, they
deal only with groups and organizations, not with individual
members of the public.[9]

Ticket brokers and party agents are natural enemies. The
Park Avenue banker who pays a hundred dollars for two
tickets (face value thirty dollars), thereby donating seventy
deductible dollars to a charity, is presumably lost to the
broker. Producers now court party agents, leaving the brokers to wait for their allotments.

Theater parties are a mixed blessing to the commercial
theater. Although in a sense they organize an audience for
the theater, they homogenize the same audience in terms of
motivation and composition.

"Put it this way," says a broker. "If someone calls me up
for a show, he wants to see that show on a night when he
wants to see it. If he has to pay something extra, well, it's
still *his* decision. So he's not going to be mad even if the

---

[9] It is one of the anomalies of the theater that under existing law the
broker derives no commission from the producer for the seats he sells, yet
the party agent gets a commission even though she is legally a ticket broker.

show disappoints him.

"But if it's a theater party it's liable to be a show he doesn't want to see on a night he doesn't want to see it at a price he doesn't really want to pay. He gets to the theater and he's mad. Even if the show is good, he carries that mad around with him."

Party audiences are dreaded by most actors because their reactions are always slower than those of other audiences, particularly with serious drama. A sparkling comedy can fall on its face with a theater party out front. One actress says, "A theater party is flat beer. They might be a great audience for a funeral, but not for a live show. You can break your heart out there before they react."

Just as producers subconsciously choose their plays and cast them hoping to please the drama critic of *The New York Times,* so they are conscious of what will bring in parties. Since theater parties charge high prices, the party agents look for big names and escapist themes. In approaching prospective angels, producers often say, "We expect a lot of theater-party interest. We think we have an excellent party show." Parties have been blamed for forcing producers to sacrifice artistic considerations for the "party draw."

"They're all wet," is Elsa Hoppenfeld's reaction. "The regular Broadway audience is exactly the same as the theater-party audience. Very few people want serious theater any more. They all want musicals and comedies—light stuff. And parties can keep weak shows going for weeks and months or longer. Sometimes a show survives only because it has enough parties to tide it over until it catches on. We theater-party agents like good theater, but, after all, we're business people. We have to sell what people want to buy."

The party agents, despite their power, are unknown to the general public. The ticket brokers get all the publicity. During the recurrent ticket scandals they are flayed righteously by legislators as "scalpers" and "specs." "We have a bad image," says a broker, "and we deserve it. When a guy pays through the nose for a ticket we're the only ones he sees. He doesn't know that we're giving him a product at the best price we can get it for and still make a profit. And it's not like bread or milk. Who forces anyone to buy a ticket, anyway?"

There are some sixty active licensed ticket brokers on Broadway (forty years ago there were over a hundred) who sell some three million tickets or $20 million worth a year out of dingy little stalls where telephones ring incessantly and the clerks speak a district patois. By law, brokers may sell only tickets on their premises. English brokers, on the other hand, are permitted to sell recordings, books, and other merchandise and do not extract premiums from their customers but rather receive a commission from the theater. By law, American brokers must not pay "ice" to theater employees for preferential treatment on tickets, nor are theater employees permitted to accept ice for themselves.[10]

But the chaste laws governing theater-ticket sales are wholly unworkable and pharisaical in practice. A handful of brokers abide strictly by ordinance, charging only the currently legal dollar and a half per ticket above box-office prices. (Brokers, through their trade association—New York Ticket Brokers, Inc.—have fought for years to have this maximum repealed, claiming, accurately, that the stipulation is unrealistic.) The overwhelming majority of brokers, however, deal in the black market.

The amount of money involved in ice is fantastically high. A roaring hit easily can dispose of 500 orchestra seats a night through the "ice machine," at an average markup of five dollars per ticket. This can amount to $2,500 a performance, or $20,000 per week, or $1 million a year—on only one show. For an author, whose percentage is 10 per cent of the gross,

[10] Ice is best defined by example, according to attorney John F. Wharton. "Let us suppose," says Wharton, "that the ticket price is ten dollars. A broker in New Jersey knows he can get twenty-one dollars. That's eleven dollars gross profit for him, but in order to get the ticket, he must pay somebody, usually the box-office man. It's a secret system, all in cash. Let's say he pays the treasurer five dollars. That leaves him with six dollars, which represents a short-term unreported capital gain. The five dollars, also usually not reported, is 'ice.'"

this means $100,000 lost. Directors, producers, stars, and investors, who all share in gross or profits, lose money by being cut out of ice.

To see how ice is made, let us examine a typical ticket transaction in the black market. A law-abiding bank president is solicited by a major client to obtain two third-row-center seats to a musical hit priced at fifteen dollars per seat. The client is important to the bank, and the tickets are important to the client ("It's my wife's anniversary"). The bank wouldn't dream of sending someone to the theater to stand in line for tickets, and third-row-center seats on a Saturday night are impossible to get at the box office anyway; for years the bank has done all its business with a ticket broker who can guarantee tickets and delivery. The bank calls the broker. The broker calls the treasurer of the theater, and, the minuet begins. If the treasurer has the seats (and he does) he feels out the "market," evaluating such factors as the night of the week, the time of the year, and the hotness of the ticket. The telephone conversation goes something like this:

Broker to treasurer: "I got a contract coming up for Saturday night. Two very choice. Center stuff down front. A must."

Treasurer to broker: "Call me back at three o'clock. Can't see how I can get them, but call me back."

It is obligatory in this bargaining ritual for the asking party to call back; it heightens the tension and thereby heightens the eventual price. Then the broker calls the bank.

Broker to bank: "I'm working on it, but it looks expensive."

Bank to broker: "Hang the cost!"

Finally, after a few more calls from the broker to the treasurer, the broker will be told: "Okay, I found 'em. Charlie 101 and 102, Tenth Street." [11]

In the meantime, the client will have called the bank to find out what's happening, and the bank will have called

[11] "Charlie 101 and 102" means C101 and 102 (Row C on the aisle); "Tenth Street" means ten dollars over the box-office price.

the broker, who, even though he may have finalized the deal, is likely to say, "I'm still working on it—call me back," playing his own little power game.

Eventually, the minuet plays out, and when the tickets are delivered, the bank gratefully pays forty dollars for the fifteen-dollar ticket and is happy to have treated a favored client so handsomely. The treasurer customarily, but not always, shares his profit with the show's manager, the other treasurers in the box office, the producer, and the theater owner. Payoff percentages vary. At one time, before the last big ticket scandal in 1963, the customary percentage was 20 per cent for the box office, with 80 per cent split up among other echelons of command or procurement.

The procedure we have described is duplicated with minor variations thousands of times with every successful show, and sometimes with even moderate successes on special occasions (the Saturday night of a Thanksgiving football weekend, for example). In 1963, New York Attorney General Louis J. Lefkowitz estimated that ice amounted to about $10 million a year, all in cash, much of it untaxed.

The treasurer is the key man in the operation of the black market. Not every treasurer participates in ice. He may only be a victim of the system, as the system reflects the basic contradictions of human nature, but even if he is a conscientious man, he is often doomed to acquiesce in, if not to initiate, corruption. For years treasurers' salaries were embarrassingly low, but they never bothered to ask for raises, because, like waiters, they made their money from their "tips," and some became wealthy if they worked in a "lucky" house. Treasurers' salaries are higher now. In 1969 a senior box-office man earned $220 for a six-day week, but, as one treasurer points out, "You can make real money in this business only if you have a hit." All treasurers devoutly await the superhit with outstretched palms. They know they will be investigated if the hit is big enough and the ticket tight enough, but there is always the chance that somehow exposure and indictment will be avoided. Most treasurers, incidentally, are scrupulous about declaring their supplementary income from ice on their tax returns.

Eradicating ice is no easier than it was for Prohibition to do away with the liquor traffic. The late Brock Pemberton, producer of *Harvey*, once decided he could eliminate ice from his box office by hiring a Pinkerton man to stand guard outside the ticket window from opening till closing. It didn't work. The trouble, recalls producer Alfred de Liagre, Jr., was that the treasurer could afford to pay the detective more money than Pemberton could.

Treasurers are often accused of rudeness and arrogance, but it is easy for a box-office man to seem rude. For one thing, his quarters are cramped and uncomfortable because theater architects historically display their contempt for the front of the house by making box offices the size of prison cells, an impression that is enhanced by the barred window. The public image of the treasurer is that of a man who withholds tickets from all but the preferred, but, says one treasurer, "The public is no bargain, either. When you can't give them exactly what they want, they become abusive. Would you remain courteous with someone who called you a crook?"

Arrogance in a hit box office is hard to control. It is just as hard to control with hit producers, playwrights, and actors as with treasurers. The ticket represents power—money power, emotional power. The treasurer confers delight and status on others merely by dispensing tickets. He becomes Olympian. As director Arthur Penn once said, "Here's a man who has had nothing, absolutely nothing, to do with the show onstage. He hasn't written, produced, directed, acted, or invested in it. Yet he controls the blood of the show, a show he may never even get to watch."

The black market has its picturesque aspects. The "sidewalk man," a vanishing breed of hustler, is a colorful denizen of the ticket world. He is raffish in the authentic Broadway style. Nobody knows his real name because he uses sidewalk pseudonyms such as "Abie the Punk," "Bronx Willie" (who committed suicide when the "feds" came after him for income tax violation), "Jake the Plumber," "Bugsy," "Alabama," or "Big Fitz." His office is in his hat, and he is rarely seen during the day. He is an entrepreneur to the end of his cigar, pacing the sidewalks along the hits, peddling tickets at changing markups. "Jake the Plumber" was a stutterer. He would stop a prospective customer, offer him seats, and wait for the inevitable, "How much?" to which he would respond, "Th-th-thirty dollars." If the buyer reached immediately into his pocket, indicating no price resistance, Jake would continue, "And-and th-th-three dollars tax, please." [12] Another sidewalk man, when asked for a price, reflexively looks at his watch. If he has a comfortable time margin until curtain, he asks for a higher price. He has to be alert to avoid "eating" his tickets. It is a high-pressure, high-profit game only for born gamblers. One sidewalk man, a Broadway fixture in spring, fall, and winter, takes every summer off to recuperate. He tours Europe in luxury and is especially fond of Venice, where he can sit in the Piazza San Marco in the evening "far away from those cheap sons of bitches who chisel me down when I overbuy. If it rains in Venice at eight o'clock at night, I can say 'What do I care? I don't have any tickets in my fist!' "

The sidewalk men get their tickets through artful dodgers, known as diggers because they "dig" tickets out of the box office. Diggers are obscure, indefatigable ants in the terrain of Times Square. The day after a hit opens, perhaps a third of those on line are diggers—old and young, all ages, all sizes. They are usually paid a dollar for each ticket they dig. Treasurers have a keen eye for diggers—they can tell them by their shoes. "These characters are all out of the automat," says a box-office man. "They may wear a clean tie or shirt, but they have scuffed shoes, every last one of them. They never ask you how much—they always have their money ready to the penny—and they ask for four tickets in the orchestra [the limit treasurers set for a hit], for any performance, and take whatever you give them without a murmur." Mail orders are also used ingeniously by diggers, who will use fake names and letterheads and spurious "mail

[12] This anecdote obviously belong to the days when there was a 10 per cent tax on tickets. As of this writing, there is no tax on theater tickets.

drop" addresses to obtain their tickets.

Once the diggers get the tickets, a remarkably efficient distribution organization goes into action. Many ticket brokers have relocated "overseas"—in New Jersey or Connecticut, where they are immune to prosecution by either New York City or New York State. The unfortunate upshot of the new ticket legislation that grew out of the highly publicized investigations of 1963–64 is that tickets to hit shows are as plentiful as ever for the insistent buyer, but they cost even more than they did when the pipeline was more direct. The "gyp" brokers await the next inquiry, whenever it may be, with equanimity. They can hardly lose.

Many outstanding citizens of the theater—playwrights, producers, actors, and others—actively fight the black market in tickets. They not only feel ticket reform can be made to work, but they lobby vigorously to initiate such reform. Producer Leland Hayward feels the abuses of ticket distribution are "driving away the theater-lover." Hayward has had the uncomfortable experience of calling his own box office, being told there were no seats available, and then that night finding ten rows of empty seats returned by the brokers at the last minute. For decades the Dramatists Guild has campaigned against ice, and for years Actors Equity has officially opposed the campaign by ticket brokers to eliminate a maximum price markup, claiming that this would destroy whatever theatergoing public is left.

The most lucid analyst of all is the redoubtable John F. Wharton, chairman of the Legitimate Theater Industry Exploratory Commission from 1964 through 1967. His official report, "A Fresh Look at Theater Tickets," issued in 1967, is the most penetrating treatise ever written on tickets and their buyers and sellers.

Wharton concentrates his attack on what he calls the "box-office concept" and on the laws affecting the sale and distribution of theater tickets. The theater, Wharton declares, is "a personal-service industry trying to compete in an automated world, with outmoded legislation and regulation keeping it from establishing a sensible ticket price system and from allowing it to make ticket buying more convenient."

Theater tickets, Wharton points out, are priced and sold in exactly the opposite way from almost all other items in the competitive American economy. "Everything else has a retail price and a wholesale price, and in every case the retail price is the highest." A person buying a book at a bookstore expects to pay more than the bookstore owners did, yet in the theater a person who buys a ticket from a broker is amazed at the markup. Theater tickets are a nonexpandable commodity, Wharton observes. "In other industries, when the demand for a non-expandable commodity increases, the price goes up. All theater legislation is directed at the seller; the theatergoing buyer is legally free to offer any price he chooses." Therefore, the public, Wharton sums up, "has *never* been mulcted by a 'black market' in tickets!"

In this manifesto, which deplores the sanctimony surrounding theater tickets, Wharton calls for an end to the present box-office system. He suggests a free-market system in an automated (computerized) environment with a central box office, and advocates only *one* scale of prices at a time with the retail-price scale available at all outlets. Box offices, says Wharton, "should be made into sales outlets for *all* productions. Commissions should be paid by the theater to the salesmen, not by the public." Wharton does not expect easy acceptance of his ideas. "People have lived for a long time under the present insane system," he writes, "and when any system has been in operation for a long time, people begin to regard it as the *only* system—many of them think of it as divinely ordered."

Halting steps are being taken toward these goals. The national computerized-ticket organizations, Ticketron and Computicket, have won ticket allotments from theaters and are running into opposition from old-time treasurers. "A good show don't need the computers," objects one. "A bum show they can't sell." Ticket clubs such as the Play-of-the-Month Guild and Critics Choice provide stable ticketing for theatergoers who can plan ahead. When shows begin to slip, two-for-one discount tickets are distributed through schools, stores, and offices. The audience may be shrinking, the business may be dying, but there is never any quesion of survival in the minds of the men who handle the district's cash. "What's going to happen?" asks a broker, and promptly answers himself, "Nothing's going to happen. The business remains." A treasurer says, "Things go on. Nothing ever really changes. People don't change." And on the street outside a hit, a sidewalk man has the last word before he melts into the crowd. "It's good shows that bring people in and bad shows that keep 'em away. Put on thirty great shows, and the balconies will fill up with youngsters. It might even drive me out of business, because my business is better when there's only one or two good shows so there ain't enough tickets to go around. And when there ain't enough tickets, I get 'em. But you gotta pay for 'em because they cost me more when they're scarce. If you want something, you gotta pay for it."

CHAPTER EIGHT

Critics—The Theater's Severest Friends

Historically, the critic is the enemy of the theater, but we have to define what we mean by the word "enemy." If a critic is to review plays honestly according to a given set of criteria, then obviously he cannot find all plays worthwhile, because all plays are not worthwhile.

But if he is to condemn a play slightly or wholly, then he must bear the brunt, large or small, of the hostility that inevitably rises within people whose egos and pocketbooks are bound up in the play being reviewed.

It is this hostility, traditional in every land and at all times, which is basic to the relationship between theater people and drama critics, and on Broadway, as in Vienna in 1885 or London in 1757 or anywhere that plays are produced, this hostility is behind the inevitable saying, heard today as it doubtless will be in 1984 or 2001, "The critics are killing the theater."

Do critics really kill the theater? Are critics frequently wrong? Is drama criticism today a major reason for the unquestioned decline of the Broadway stage? What should the role of the critic be? The questions pour out in endless panels and debates, in essays and lectures, and they are never satisfactorily answered.

The contradictions and inconsistencies implicit in the relationship between critics and the Broadway theater are part of the larger ambivalences that infect the theater in general and not just in 1969 or in New York.

First, a theater without critics would be inconceivable and probably unbearable. It is not merely the plaudits of audiences or the inflow of cash that drives playwrights to write, producers to produce, and directors to direct. It is the desire for authoritative approval—approval from the judge or father image, approval in which the playmaker can bask, written approval that he can quote or have quoted to others.

It is important to stress that such approval must come from someone who does not invariably approve everything. If all critics praised everything, the value of criticism would vanish immediately. The late Kelcey Allen, drama critic of *Women's Wear Daily,* is thought never to have written a bad review (which may have had something to do with the fact that he also sold ads to producers), and a Kelcey Allen review was worthless not only to the readers of the newspaper, but to the playmakers. The current reviewer for *Women's Wear Daily,* Martin Gottfried, is a particularly savage member of the "new breed" school of critics. He dislikes most plays, but when he approves, Broadwayites will quote him widely, or say triumphantly: "Even Martin Gottfried liked it!"

If it is true that unmitigated approval is disdained by playmakers it follows that a popular critic is not necessarily a good critic. It also follows that the only way in which theater really can be hurt is by undiscriminating critics—critics who invariably condemn everything or critics who invariably praise everything. A critic who shows discrimination in his reviews may use standards with which others differ, but his influence in the long run cannot be construed as "killing the theater."

This brings us to a discussion of "influence." In the American theater of 1969, influence must be interpreted almost completely in terms of how it affects box-office business. This was not always true. Until about a decade ago it was possible for an unfavorable review to stimulate ill feeling among a play's well-wishers but to have relatively little effect on whether a play languished and died at the box office. Unanimously bad reviews invariably killed a play in the old days, as they do now, but a mixed press was not invariably a death sentence. Statistics abound to prove that some plays survived faint praise or critical disagreement to achieve respectable or even triumphant runs.

The *power* of drama critics had changed radically by 1969 because the power of communications had changed drastically, and over a relatively brief span of time.

In 1930 there were fourteen dailies in New York and each one had a drama critic. As attrition hit the newspaper business and the number of newspapers declined, the number of "influential" reviewers simultaneously was reduced.

In 1948, as one theatrical observer puts it, "We had nine major critics in those days. Atkinson (*Times*), Barnes (*Herald Tribune*), and Morehouse (*Sun*) were basically for the carriage trade and the ticket-broker crowd; Chapman (*News*) brought in the mezzanine and balcony; Watts (*Post*), McClain (*Journal*), Coleman (*Mirror*), Hawkins (*Telegram*), and Kronenberger (*PM*) brought up the rear. If you got the *Times* and the *Trib* and the *News,* you were solid. The *Times* was important, but not fatal if you lost it. You could live with three or four of the nine, but you had to have one of the Big Three—*Times, Trib,* or *News*—unless you had a big star, in which case you could live on advance and wait for word-of-mouth to catch up. And there were always the gossip columnists."

In twenty years, the situation has changed—unalterably,

it seems. Concurrent with rising costs and prices, the number of newspapers has declined—at this writing, there are only three in New York—and a new Moloch, the television critic, has emerged to trumpet his disdain or affirmation with electronic speed to millions of watchers.

Gossip columnists have lost their impact. Walter Winchell is credited, almost single-handedly, with keeping *Hellz-apoppin* running for years in the 1940's despite the condemnation of the drama critics. Winchell lost his major New York outlet in 1967, and his influence had diminished widely for years before that; the few other columnists who remain have virtually no power to affect the box office. (Indeed, column-power is losing its impact in most areas of public opinion.)

Of the three newspapers that remain—the *Times,* the *News,* and the *Post*—the *Times* has become, in almost every way, the supreme arbiter of taste and influence on Broadway and off-Broadway. The *News,* despite its enormous circulation, has never seemed to have very much influence at the box office. John Chapman, the straphangers' critic, is always readable and clear; he writes as if for the billboards, and the reader can always tell where he stands. Yet the Chapman rave doesn't succeed in producing a measurable response at the box office. The *Post* is generally assumed to have a greater theatrical following among its readership, and as the only evening newspaper it is valued highly as an advertising medium for off-Broadway, but in recent years Richard Watts, Jr.—his long dedication to theater unchallenged, a critic noted for fairness—apparently has been too easy to please. The hallways of the monolithic *Times* building on West 43rd Street are now, more than ever before, corridors of matchless cultural power.

"It's the *Times* and TV," says one of the playmakers of 1969. "The *Times* makes or breaks. If the *Times* gives the uppercut, it's television that follows through with the rabbit punch." Only shows with enormous box-office advance or big stars who somehow create their own charismatic draws can breast the rip tide of disfavor from *Times* and television combined, and, incidentally, the only two TV stations with power are NBC and CBS.

The *News* and the *Post* and the secondary reviewers can sometimes mute the shock of disapproval from the titans, but in most cases a joint thumbs-down from only three men —Clive Barnes of the *Times,* Edwin Newman of NBC-TV, and Leonard Harris of CBS-TV—means instant trauma.

The rather sudden rise to prominence of the television critics over the past five or six years has been reflected in the changed treatment accorded them in the theatrical community. For years the press agents who control first-night seating plans had been putting newspapermen well down front and relegating radio and television men to the rear. But lately the chief television critics have been treated to a series of giant steps toward the stage, jumping them over once pre-eminent middle-rank newspaper reviewers.

Television reviews have become so important that Vincent Sardi, the proprietor of Sardi's, has made an "opening-night" room out of the second-floor restaurant by installing small television sets near the wall tables. Customers have found that reviews on the eleven o'clock news programs of each of the three principal networks are so timed that by adroit dial-twisting it is possible to catch all three in a five-minute span by starting on Channel 4 to hear Newman and then switching to Channel 2 for Harris. If Harris doesn't appear within forty seconds, they turn to Channel 7 and thereafter go back and forth between the two stations until they have caught both.

CBS's Harris commands the largest audience. According to the early 1969 ratings for the CBS *Eleven O'Clock Report,* the program had 1.3 million listeners, about a quarter of a million more than NBC's *Eleventh Hour News.*

While the impact of television and newspaper reviews is immediate, the influence of weekly magazines is more delayed and academic. Almost no one in the theater thinks they have very much of an effect on the box office, particularly if they are bucking the field. The technical demands of the three different media result in very different reviewing styles, which may be illustrated in the first couple of paragraphs of the reviews of the recent musical, *Promises, Promises.*

Clive Barnes's review in *The New York Times* ran 940 words and its opening paragraphs read as follows:

> Yes, of course, yes! The Neil Simon and Burt Bacharach musical *Promises, Promises* came to the Sam S. Shubert Theatre last night and fulfilled them all without a single breach. In fact it proved to be one of those shows that do not so much open as start to take root, the kind of show where you feel more in the mood to send it a congratulatory telegram than write a review.
>
> Neil Simon has produced one of the wittiest books a musical has possessed in years, the Burt Bacharach music excitingly reflects today rather than the day before yesterday, and the performances, especially from Jerry Orbach as the put-upon and morally diffident hero, contrive, and it's no easy feat, to combine zip with charm.

John Chapman, who was less enthusiastic and whose space allotment is more restricted by the tabloid form of the *Daily News,* expressed himself in 385 words. His opening paragraphs were as follows:

> *Promises, Promises,* the musical which opened at the Shubert Theatre last evening, has some Neil Simon jokes, since Simon wrote the libretto, and an assortment of songs by Burt Bacharach and Hal David which sound like pop records, which they will be, doubtless, in due time.
>
> Simon adapted his story from a movie by Billy Wilder and I. A. L. Diamond, *The Apartment,* which I have managed to miss. The plot is about an ambitious young underling, Jerry Orbach, who begins to work his way up in a big company by lending the keys to his conveniently located one-room apartment to various executives.

A muted enthusiasm and matter-of-fact style for Chapman. Like the tabloids, the news magazines specialize in saying a lot in a little space, and, at *Time,* T. E. Kalem is a master of the packed style. His less-than-ecstatic review of

Promises, Promises ran 507 words. The first two paragraphs accounted for about a third of the review:

> Here is a musical to remember other musicals by. *Promises, Promises* is slick, amiable and derivative. No playgoer will feel gypped if he attends the show, nor will he miss a thing if he skips it.
> Broadway hails fair-to-middling work as genius so long as it succeeds. Along Shubert Alley, the ultimate critic is the box office, and *Promises, Promises* will doubtless satisfy that arbiter of taste. The show follows all the hallowed tactics for promoting mediocrity into success. One does not gamble with $500,000; one invests in the imitation of past successes. That means: Don't create—crib. Thus the plot line of *Promises, Promises* is derived from the Billy Wilder-I. A. L. Diamond film *The Apartment,* which was far sharper in lancing U.S. sexual hypocrisy, and the structure of the show has been borrowed from *How to Succeed in Business Without Really Trying.* The evening is not so much viewed as *deja vu'*d.

It is the television critic, however, who has to get by with the fewest words, since he has about a minute to give his views. The delivery has to be loose and conversational, and this allows Edwin Newman on NBC, for example, between 180 and 200 words. His review for *Promises, Promises* was 164 words long. It is reprinted below in its entirety:

> *Promises, Promises* is a slick and very professional show. It's also a curious mixture. Some of the time it wears a smile. Much of the time it wears a leer. And the effect is not always comfortable. It's based on the movie *The Apartment,* which was about a young man who got ahead in business by lending his apartment to philandering executives. That's where the leer comes in. Jerry Orbach has the lead, and he's extremely winning and humorous. Jill O'Hara is mildly appealing as the girl in his life, though her voice is uncertain. And there's a very funny contribution by Marian Mercer. The book is by Neil Simon, and he's smattered it with jokes from his private assembly line. There are three excellent dance numbers. As for the score by Burt Bacha-

rach, I found it long on beat and short on melody. In a
word, indeterminate. Well, you've heard of shows intended
for tired businessmen. *Promises, Promises* is also about them.

Among all the critics reviewing the Broadway theater today, Brendan Gill of *The New Yorker* is the best stylist, and
he has the space to be as expansive as he likes. His clear liking for *Promises, Promises* comes through in a long opening
paragraph:

> So little need be said in the presence of excellence that
> I am tempted to limit my remarks about *Promises, Promises*
> to the simple statement that it is an absolutely marvellous
> musical and that all two hundred million of my fellow-
> citizens should make plans to go and see it as quickly as
> possible. I sat watching it in a daze of pleasure from start
> to finish, such critical armor as I possess having been pierced
> by my very first glimpse of Jerry Orbach as C. C. Baxter,
> the smallest cog in the vast machine of Consolidated Life.
> Mr. Orbach is a fantastically appealing performer and, if
> he wishes, can go on playing this role until well into the
> twenty-first century. As for Jill O'Hara as his dreamboat
> Fran Kubelik, she has a perky face and a voice that is by
> turns strident and melting, and C. C. is right to be madly
> in love with her. I lost count of the curtain calls on open-
> ing night, but for a while it looked as if the cast would be
> obliged to remain until morning onstage at the Shubert,
> incessantly bowing and smiling; in the nick of time, an
> alert management thought of beginning to turn off the
> lights, and so even the most infatuated and palm-sore
> among us were actually forced to let Mr. Orbach, Miss
> O'Hara and their many colleagues go. It was, you may
> deduce, an occasion.

Drama critics are given free seats, usually in the choicest
locations, for their assignments. The geography and accessibility of these seats are true critic status symbols—they
reflect the importance not so much of the reviewer's opinions as of the impact of the newspaper, magazine, or TV
station for which he is proxy.

On the traditional first night, aisle seats from the third

through the seventh or eighth rows are allocated to first-night critics in the top echelon. Center-aisle seats are uniformly indicative of higher status than side-aisle seats. Aisle seats are considered necessary because at the end of the play the critics customarily leap to beat the crowd to the exits and meet their deadlines.

First-night critics who sit farther back than the eighth row or—poor things!—in the nonaisle locations are generally not equally esteemed, because of the relative secondary importance of their publications. Frequently, keen opening-night observers note that critics in the "A" group generally dress more neatly than critics who rank lower in the pecking order, but it's always mufti on Broadway. In London some critics still don black tie for especially momentous openings. In New York a drama critic who wore a dinner jacket to a first night would be considered exotic, a traitor to his craft, or, at best, a corrupt formalist.

Second-night drama critics are something else again. Although they have committed no crime beyond working on publications whose deadlines are longer or whose circulations are smaller or less select than those of the media permitted to come to openings as feared and honored guests of the management, second-nighters are generally a rumpled, sometimes scruffy group. Incidentally, the percentage of women critics is much larger on second nights; very few first-night reviewers are female.

By the time the second-night press attends, all dice have been cast—the play is either a hit or a flop. If it's a hit, the second night—historically a "let-down" performance for the cast—assumes an unusual glow, and the usual minor-league convocation of writers from suburban dailies and weeklies, trade magazines, denominational monthlies, and dimmer luminaries from the "major" papers and the electronic world of radio-TV react with warmth to the show whose destiny they cannot possibly affect. If the show is a failure, many second-nighters don't bother to attend, or if they do they're conditioned to react coolly. Once in a while an enthusiastic second-night verdict can tip the scales in favor of a show that has been greeted with mixed reaction by the first-night critics. An example of this was the Living Theater's 1959–60 production of *The Connection,* a highly realistic drama of dope addiction by Jack Gelber which most first-nighters found too distasteful to praise. The play was saved by the admiration of the magazine critics who saw it the following night and whose reviews came out a week or two later.

But, in general, second-night critics are just that—pleasant secondary folk whose dress and attitudes reflect the affectionate camaraderie of the also-rans. They are useful to producers when the play is successful, for their reviews round out the impact of the "big boys," but they are treated and behave like pitchers eternally warming up in a sideline bull pen.

The very name that second-nighters have given their formal organization betrays the insecurity of their lives—the Outer Critics Circle, as opposed to the Critics Circle, an easy-going league of first-nighters to which membership is jealously restricted with almost the same pettishness and clannishness with which tony country clubs reject encroaching Jews or Negroes.

The Critics Circle, which meets once a year in August in austere conclave, sprang to modern life in 1935 specifically protesting the awarding of the 1935–36 Pulitzer Prize to *The Old Maid* by Zoë Akins, a wheelhorse drama about the maternal urge. The membership requirements are simple, correctly casual, and sentimental. Only first-nighters may belong, and all the "big boys" are members, although it also includes a number of holdovers. Joseph Shipley, who once reviewed for the *New Leader,* a social-democratic weekly, was a charter member of the Critics Circle, but when he lost his post with his magazine he remained with the Circle —technically on the strength of his reviewer's assignment on the minor radio station WEVD. The first-line establishment has consistently rejected attempts by critics it deems unworthy to muscle into the Circle. For example, Leo Shull, editor and publisher and sometime critic of the trade weekly *Show Business,* has been trying to join the Critics Circle for

years. He has wheedled, cajoled, and threatened legal action, but has repeatedly failed. Some years ago, almost in
desperation, he helped found the Drama Desk, an organization of theater reporters and editors that meets monthly to
hear panel discussions of issues of moment along Broadway.

The annual Critics Circle Awards are of great importance
to the Broadway theater. Currently, awards are given by majority vote to Best Play and Best Musical. These accolades,
which are promptly seized upon and exploited by producers,
generally add at least a month or two to the life expectancy
of shows.

In recent times the Critics Circle Awards have been presented as near to the end of the Broadway season as possible,
but they used to precede the announcement of the Pulitzer
Prizes for the same categories. This was then a deliberate
policy, dating from the presentation of the first Critics Circle Award as a direct expression of New York reviewer hostility to the Pulitzer jury for picking the Zoë Akins play.

Some aspects of the Critics Circle Awards and the voting
procedures are worth noting:

1. It is very unusual for the critics to give a prize to a show
that has already closed. Theoretically, one could argue that
a show that does not run at least until award time does not
deserve a prize. The truth is probably that critics are no less
pragmatic than anyone else on Broadway, and a vote for a
defunct if worthy play would probably be construed by the
critic himself as wasted. Nevertheless, *A Delicate Balance,*
a play which ran only 132 performances during the 1966–67
season, was voted the award even though it had been closed
for three months at the time the prize was given.

2. It is not unusual for a producer who feels his show is
prize material to keep it running until award time in the
hope of gaining the laurels. Generally, as soon as the winners
of the major prizes are announced, a number of artificially
extended losers sag into oblivion.

3. The Outer Critics Circle also has its annual awards, and
its prizes are frequently deliberately bestowed on plays the
(Inner) Circle has not honored. It is to be assumed that this

displays the independence of the second-nighters as opposed to their haughtier opening-night colleagues, but, alas, the garland of the Outer Critics usually gathers no moss for its choices. It must cheerfully be noted that the yearly Outer Critics Circle banquets, usually held upstairs at Sardi's, are always more effusive than the Inner Critics Circle meetings, which are usually held at the Algonquin Hotel. The "big boys" eschew outsiders and lavish dinners—their assemblies are limited to cocktails and hors d'oeuvres—but their austerity is born of strength, snobbishness to the manor born. "It's like the House of Lords and the House of Commons," says one Broadwayite in comparing the two circles, "but in this case, the Lords really run the country."

Visiting foreigners are particularly struck by the power of the press in New York and the fear it spreads among the producing fraternity, resulting sometimes in acrimonious personal contests between the producers and the critics that seem to have nothing to do with the play.

The day after the Irish playwright Brian Friel's *Philadelphia, Here I Come* opened at the Helen Hayes Theatre, Friel was sitting in the lobby at the Algonquin Hotel with some cronies from Ireland who had made the trip across to hold his hand. He was somewhat shaken by the Broadway opening-night convulsions, but the mostly excellent reviews were consoling. Friel had the papers piled on his lap folded neatly open to the theatrical page. The British producer Oscar Lewenstein happened to pass through the lobby and spotted Friel. "It's nice, isn't it, Brian? The reviews even mention your play. Sometimes here you get the impression theater is a contest between the producer and the critic and the play is only some inferior commercial product."

Friel nodded in agreement. "Yes, like 'Philadelphia washes whiter.' "

Strangers in New York might be pardoned for believing that some sort of athletic contest had taken place in which the producers were lined up at one end of the field, the critics at the other, and the newborn play in the middle was the ball that was kicked.

On opening night the producer is an apprehensive host, and the critics are regarded as unwelcome guests. Most first-nighters arrive in a gay, noisy mood, but critics come in stony-faced and businesslike with jobs to do and no time for small talk. David Merrick regards the critic as a dangerous interloper, as potentially destructive as a man with a bomb in his pocket.

The reaction of theater folk to drama criticism is almost defiantly inconsistent. Show people wait for reviews with ill-concealed tension; if the reviews are favorable, they are greeted with transcendent joy and are shamelessly exploited by the producers and press agents. Conversely, if the reviews are unfavorable, it is the rare Broadwayite who will take his licking with equanimity; it is his baby who has been defiled and despoiled, and he will not hear ill of it.

Some years ago Maxwell Anderson wrote, "A new play in our theater is now a sitting duck. When the curtain goes up on it, the critics are posted in a semicircle twenty or thirty feet away, armed with double-barreled shotguns and a supply of whatever food it is that makes ducks lay golden eggs. If they don't like the play they blast it off the stage. If they do like it they toss it their miraculous sustenance and it lives."

The closer to opening time the more apprehensive the producer becomes. Merrick was particularly jumpy bringing in the musical *Subways Are for Sleeping* because he knew the show was bad. Merrick relieves his nerves with ghoulish jokes, and, standing behind the orchestra as the curtain went up on one of the last New York preview performances of *Subways*, when Walter Kerr was still reviewing for the *Herald Tribune* and Howard Taubman for the *Times*, Merrick, grinning, turned to a companion and said, "I had a wonderful dream last night. I dreamed that Walter Kerr dropped dead on his way to Howard Taubman's funeral."

Waiting for the critic, the producer is like the man rehearsing what he will say, and what his neighbor will reply, when he goes next door to borrow the lawnmower. He becomes so worked up over the imaginary conversation on his way over that when the door is opened he punches his neighbor in the nose.

Theater professionals spend hours trying to prejudge and outguess the critics. The appointment of a new critic causes intense speculation as to what he is going to like and what dislike.

Some producers carry their curiosity into the theater. They have been known even to post spies in nearby seats to study the critics' responses, but such surveillance is not likely to be productive. A critic's frown may mean concentration, not distaste; he is too busy to react on a physical level. Within himself he may be responding to the play and the performances to a livelier degree than anyone else in the theater, but he is also watching his own responses and mentally noting them down, even to phrases and sentences, to get a headstart on the review that must be written rapidly at the end of the evening.

Critics practically never join in applause and rarely in laughter, not because they don't share the approval and pleasure of the rest of the audience but because they must remain alert to the meaning of their own reactions. In Harold Clurman's phrase, the critic must have "a double vision." He must not only listen to words but also watch movements to see whether they match meanings. And he must watch himself watching.

The people on the giving and receiving ends of theatrical criticism have wildly different views of the methods and purposes of criticism. Maxwell Anderson, on the receiving end, imagined the critic as climbing into the dentist's chair each night. Only novelty or musicals or light comedy, Anderson thought, were sufficiently diverting to distract him from the torture.

The theater is so small a world that sooner or later everyone comes to know everyone. Producers sometimes cultivate a coolness toward critics as a matter of policy. Producer Leland Hayward, for example, believes it can only hurt to be friends with a critic. "If they know you, they feel they have to lean over not to favor you." One critic Hayward knew well, however, was the late John McClain of the *Journal-American*. On the day Hayward's musical *Gypsy*, with Ethel Merman, was to open, he met McClain on the street outside the theater. They chatted for a moment, steering clear of the sensitive subject of the opening. Hayward saw McClain again that evening arriving at the theater. "I almost played a dirty trick on you," McClain said. "I was going to pretend I was drunk when I saw you this morning so you'd worry about my review all day."

The incident is a wry memory for Hayward. McClain's review, as it happened, was the only one the next day that had anything unfavorable to say about *Gypsy*. The rest were raves.[1]

The converse to the Hayward-McClain relationship is the critic having a personal reason to dislike the producer and therefore feeling obliged to be kind to his play. David Merrick has been accused many times of deliberately castigating a critic in public so that any pan from that critic will look like petty revenge. Clive Barnes disagrees. "I think Merrick's bag is something quite different. He's very conscious of publicity, partly for the good of the show and partly, I think, because he's a very vain man. He likes to see his name in the papers."

Critics in the past may have come up via the sports department or the ship-news desk, as McClain did, and in the old days critics regarded themselves as reporters in a field that, essentially, required no more technical knowledge than baseball or the criminal courts. Theater people regard this as too casual. Edward Albee once said, "I would ask of the critic that he know as much about the theater as the most educated member of the audience and that there be more concern for the health of the theater as an art form than we have now."

As a playwright Albee has been outspoken about critics. After the disappointing notices for his *Tiny Alice*, Albee

[1] It was for this show that Walter Kerr provided the producers with about the best critic quote on record: "Best damn musical I've ever seen."

was ready to take on the critics, even going so far as to call a press conference over which he presided theatrically from center stage of the Billy Rose Theater. Why, Albee asked, should a critic produce superlatives for a slick comedy or musical and save his qualifying words for the serious play of high intentions that has fallen short of perfection? The comedy or musical goes on to become a hit; the serious play dies a slow death. This double standard of criticism— one for light comedies and musicals, another more rigorous standard for serious plays—is a problem that faces every conscientious Broadway critic. Albee expressed the dilemma in mathematical terms. Suppose the play aspires greatly and reaches only 60 on a scale of 100. Is that play then worse than a comedy that aims at 45 on the scale and makes 40? On its own terms the comedy has succeeded more nearly than the play, yet 60 on the scale is higher than 40.

Realistically, Albee doesn't expect such critical discernment. A reporter asked him to name the critic who came closest to describing his intention in *Tiny Alice,* a play that baffled many people. He answered, "I'd rather not. In the theater an author is grateful for good reviews for the wrong reasons. He is enormously fortunate if he gets a good review for the right reasons."

Hard as it is to assess the author's work fairly, it is even harder to assess the director's. Here the critic is on dangerous ground. He risks praising the director wrongly for business devised by the actor or condemning the actor for attitudes imposed on him by the director. "The director is the mystery man," Walter Kerr has said. "You can see the actors and you can at least say how they look and what they wore. The playwright is tangible through his words, but the director has vanished."

Alan Schneider recalls a production of Samuel Beckett's *Endgame* that he directed off-Broadway at the Cherry Lane. All during the first act the radiator pipes clanked because the house manager had turned off the heat half an hour before curtain time. The play had a mixed reception but the radiator got splendid notices. Every critic mentioned the clanking "sound effects" favorably, although one or two criticized the loudness.

Theater people are always suspicious that critics are having fun at the theater's expense and are more interested in being amusing themselves than in giving a fair assessment of the play. In *The Misanthrope,* Molière dissects the showoff critic. Richard Wilbur's translation goes as follows:

> Since he's decided to become a wit
> His taste's so pure that nothing pleases it;
> He scolds at all the latest books and plays,
> Thinking that wit must never stoop to praise,
> That finding fault's a sign of intellect,
> That all appreciation is abject
> And that by damning everything in sight
> One shows oneself in a distinguished light.

More damnable to theater professionals than the show-off critic is the new breed, of whom Kenneth Tynan, in the days he wrote for *The New Yorker,* was the forerunner. The new breed of critic is younger than those he supplants in influence, he is more "modern" in his approach to theater criticism, and he is anti-sentimental. His attitude toward theater is permissive. Tolerant of new methods and techniques, he is more interested in content than form and in stage action and production ideas than speeches and words, and he is opposed almost in principle to the well-made play. Anything resembling the drawing-room comedy or the middle-class "naturalist" drama is anathema to him.

Total involvement of the critic with theater came in the fall of 1968 when editor-critic Richard Schechner attended the first New York performance of the Living Theater's daring *Paradise Now.* Schechner, editor of the quarterly *Drama Review* and an active experimenter in "new theater" techniques, was all ready when the Living Theater actors came down the aisle of the Brooklyn Academy of Music chanting, "We are not allowed to take off our clothes, we are not *allowed* to take off our clothes." Schechner in his aisle seat had already stripped stark naked, and thus became the first critic to practice as well as preach total theater.

There is an intellectual coldness to the new breed. The play that touches invariably is viewed as bland and sentimental. There is a certain joy in nihilism. The new critic is thought, with good reason, to be hostile to the Broadway theater.

The new breed emerged in the late 1950's as the younger generation suffered an influx of doubts about the habits, hang-ups, and hubris of the older generation. When Kenneth Tynan began writing for *The New Yorker* as a guest critic in the early 1960's no critic then writing showed much interest in the social or political content of plays or seemed aware of the possible relationship between the outside world and the simulated life on the stage. While the old breed continued to show a fussy concern for the niceties of construction and accepted dramatic ground rules as they found them, Tynan called into question all the old standards and made *relevance* to what was happening in the political world a criterion of dramatic worth. Social consciousness became the hallmark of the new criticism. Along with Tynan other like-minded critics came into prominence: Robert Brustein, writing in the *New Republic,* Richard Gilman in *Newsweek,* John Simon in the *Hudson Review,* and Elizabeth Hardwicke in the *New York Review of Books.* They were concerned about audience, accessibility, reachability, and pertinence.

The new breed is generally left-wing in politics, permissive of the obscure and avant-garde, uncaring of erstwhile taboos in language. Critics like Tynan and Brustein were activists in the anti-Vietnam War movement. Frequently writing out of anger, the new breed was inclined to be extremely personal in criticism, even to the extent of commenting on an actor's or actress' physical shortcomings. John Simon became a prime offender in *New York* magazine. Years ago this would have been condemned as ungentlemanly. Fair criticism it was, certainly, to judge the actor, however harshly, in the context of the performance or the part; but to cast doubt on an actor's career potential on the basis of a single performance or his physical appearance was considered unprincipled. (In the fall of 1969, Simon was denied membership in the Critics Circle by a 10-7 vote.)

Ideally, the producer would like the critic to understand the limiting conditions of producing. He would like to see the critics show some understanding of economic obstacles, some awareness of the time invested, some sympathy with goals and objectives. And, while they are at it, it wouldn't hurt to show a little love of theater. Let the critic occasionally coax the public into the theater, not continually bar the door.

When a Broadway producer takes considerable financial risk to open what he considers to be an especially fine play, such as David Merrick did in 1960 with *A Taste of Honey,* which anticipated a whole mood of English (and youthful) unrest, he is apt to expect added consideration. "They liked it," Merrick said of the critics on this occasion, "but they didn't say so. Help should have come from the drama critics and reporters."

Producers have the same distrust of critics that the murderer has of the executioner. Producers will always complain of being misunderstood. A need for rationality has never troubled Broadway. Producers suffer freely from the "heads I win, tails you lose" syndrome: between shows David Merrick bedevils the critics, but as soon as a critic gives his show a good review the quotes are spread wide across the front of the theater.

On the receiving end, no criticism is acceptable unless it is outright praise. Theater people don't want to be judged, they want to be appreciated. They want a standing rave. On the day after an opening when the notices have been pans, Shubert Alley is loud with complaint. No group reacts with a keener sense of being unappreciated than the Shubert executives. They are never so together as in adversity, bewailing their helplessness at the hands of an unreasonable group of newspapermen. They walk together in Shubert Alley shaking their heads. Why are the critics such theater-haters? Why so heartless, why such killjoys? Why can't they commend to the public what the public would so clearly enjoy—if only the critics told them to?

CHAPTER NINE

"The Times Will Bury Us"

The New York Times Building, at 229 West 43rd Street, sits stolidly in the middle of the theater district. The rear of the building is on West 44th Street, one of the principal theater streets, and the *Times* loading platforms, which are manned day and night, are only a few steps from the maroon-painted entrance of Sardi's, the theatrical restaurant. Several times a day eastbound traffic on 44th Street is backed up almost to Eighth Avenue while long flatbed trucks turn in the street, jackknife on a red-brick apron, and back into the loading shed to discharge rolls of paper larger than oil drums.

At midevening, when the theater marquees along the street are lit and the curtains are up, outside in the quieted street emerald-green *Times* delivery trucks stand in the same loading berths to receive their bundles of crisp papers, smelling of printer's ink. Day and night, the theater awaits the pleasure of *The New York Times*.

This is the reality that pervades the world of the playmakers. From the high windows of the gray, medieval-looking citadel that is the *Times,* writers through the years have smiled their admiration or frowned their disapproval on their raffish neighbors. At a word from them the artistic traffic of the district can be stalled or moved forward, can be stopped in its tracks or jetted along the path of success.

The first-string critic of *The New York Times* occupies not only a prominent place in the journalistic world but also a unique position in the theatrical establishment, one in which he is alternately honored and vilified but never ignored. When Brooks Atkinson retired as the *Times* drama critic in 1960 after thirty-five years in the job, the theater, in a gesture of unprecedented affection, gave him a party on the second floor of Sardi's. Mary Martin sang verses composed in his honor and Helen Hayes made him a speech. He was presented with a gold lifetime pass to the Shubert theaters. (He once tried to use it but retreated in consternation and embarrassment when the ticket taker stared at it blankly and waved him aside.) After he retired and could no longer fire live ammunition at the stage, Atkinson was adopted by the theatrical establishment as if he were one of the leading citizens of the community, even to having a theater named for him. Actually, in his term, he had shunned the society of theater people religiously. "I made it a rule not to mix with theater people socially. I felt it would be embarrassing to me and embarrassing to them. I never went to parties," Atkinson said. But it was not possible for a man who spent so many years in and around theaters and had to travel so often through the district on his way to and from his office to avoid theater people entirely. "I knew everyone," he confessed.

Out of the same feelings of reticence that Atkinson himself had, theater people seldom sought the critic out while he was top man at the *Times.* Moss Hart, however, was emboldened to do so, and a strong, rather unconventional friendship sprang up between their two families. "After *Once in a Lifetime* opened and was a success and Hart became a millionaire, he asked me to lunch at the Astor,"

Atkinson recalled. "I was shocked but I went. Then my wife and I saw him at a party. She is very funny, and they got along very well. We became friends." But that was the only serious theater friendship Atkinson permitted himself during his days in power.

To arrive at the position of ultimate journalistic authority in the theater world, Brooks Atkinson went through an initiation as a police reporter and served as an assistant to the *Boston Evening Transcript*'s drama critic, H. T. Parker. He joined the *Times* in 1922 as editor of the Book Review section, a mild-mannered, scholarly-looking young man with a Harvard education who spoke in the flat, laconic accents of New England. Bird watcher, forest walker, Thoreauvian, Atkinson was yet to spend most of his professional life within the blinding, fevered theater district. He was to be drama critic from 1925 until his retirement in 1960, with time out for a couple of leaves of absence, one to visit China during the war, from 1942 to 1944, and another to cover Russia as a foreign correspondent during 1945–46.

Al Hirschfeld, the famous theatrical cartoonist whose intricately drawn impressions of costumed actors have appeared for years on the front page of the drama section of the Sunday *Times*, once depicted how a first-night audience appeared to the terrified members of the cast. In a sea of ordinary faces was one enormous protruding head, front and center, that of *Times* critic Brooks Atkinson. Actually, the first-night Atkinson was a small, slight figure slipping inconspicuously into his third-row aisle seat, mildly regarding the stage through steel-rimmed Anglican spectacles with an expression of quizzical amusement and interest.

Retreating quickly up the aisle as the last scene ended and the curtain was about to descend, Atkinson would make his way back to his desk on the *Times*'s third floor. He wrote out his review in longhand on a ruled pad, saw it into type, and proofread it. Meeting the deadline while the presses were humming downstairs, Atkinson felt, put an exciting climax on his day, and he enjoyed it. In tight, neat columns his opening-night report was on the street and being read in another hour.

In the minds of almost everyone in the theater whose destinies have been affected by his words, Atkinson is regarded somehow as an austere judgelike figure, one who not only interpreted law but also wrote it, from review to review. Atkinson considered himself a reporter. Rather than pronouncing judgment in his reviews, he sought to convey some of the excitement of a new theatrical event. Immediacy was important, and day-old news in the theater was stale. There were thirteen daily critics when Atkinson started writing in 1925; there were seven when he stopped. (Only one critic writing in 1925 was still writing in late 1969: Whitney Bolton of the *Morning Telegraph*.) [1] Each critic constituted a kind of public-opinion poll on his own, Atkinson liked to feel. One newspaper would represent one section of the public, another would represent another section with different tastes.

In his years as a critic Atkinson felt the unique pressures of the job—public scrutiny, scornful disapproval, insult (David Merrick once accused him of being senile)—but Atkinson recalls gratefully that a stout management at the *Times* insulated him "100 per cent" from public complaint. Only once in all Atkinson's years did Arthur Hays Sulzberger, the publisher, come to him with a criticism. Atkinson had gone up to Boston for a Theatre Guild production of a new Shaw play in advance of the New York opening because he felt a new Shaw play was news. The Guild's Lawrence Langner, a friend of Sulzberger's, complained to the *Times* publisher. Langner argued that the play should not have been reviewed while it was still trying out and had not yet formally opened. Sulzberger never issued any direct orders to Atkinson, but on this occasion, he quietly told Atkinson he felt Langner had a point.

Atkinson used to concede that a critic had influence. "But it's not clear just what that influence is," he said. "The one clear, cut-and-dried case I can give you of where I did not have influence was the musical *Bye Bye Birdie*. I was the

[1] Bolton died Nov. 4, 1969.

only critic not to give it a good review." The 1959–60 musical about a rock 'n' roll singer became a smash hit and ran for 607 performances. Shortly afterward Atkinson gave a good review to the musical *Greenwillow,* written by Frank Loesser, the composer-lyricist of *Guys and Dolls.* It closed after ninety-six performances. "These are the only times I can remember," Atkinson said, "when I was all alone holding a different opinion from all the other critics." (He has forgotten at least one other play—Irwin Shaw's *The Survivors,* which was panned by everyone except Atkinson and closed in a fortnight.)

Unlike most of the theater people who read him so avidly, Atkinson felt that there was nothing inherently powerful in the critic's position. "By themselves the critics have no power at all," he said. "The only power they have derives from the stage—from the playwright and from the actors. If there is power on the stage the critic can transmit it. But it has to come from there first."

For their part, in 1969 theater people imagine that the power derives almost entirely from the words that are printed in *The New York Times* on the morning after the opening. The power of the *Times* is in direct proportion to the lack of power of the attraction. Producers who recognize the weakness of their productions are ready to entrust the fate of their play to the *Times* critic, knowing that only his strong praise and approval can assure it of any kind of a run. In this situation, the producer is really putting on his play for an audience of one. If what he offers fails to amuse or entertain the *Times* critic, he might as well close the show.

The power of the *Times* is also in inverse proportion to the number of other daily newspapers being published. With the severe fall-off of daily newspapers in New York, from seven in 1960 to three today, the power of the *Times* has become virtually absolute in theatrical matters. The love-hate relationship that was always present between theater people and the paper is stronger than ever today. "The *Times* has total power," according to Edgar Lansbury, the producer of *The Subject Was Roses.* "If you don't have the *Times* you can go home." And according to Theodore Mann, the off-Broadway producer-director who heads Circle in the Square, "The *Times* is the key to the success of a play." This is how practically everyone in the theater feels: success and advancement in the theater, especially for the actor, the playwright, and the producer, depend to an extraordinary degree on what the *Times* says.

It was not quite that serious upon Atkinson's retirement, and Atkinson may have been the last drama critic whose company the theater felt it could actually enjoy. With Atkinson the theater could almost always count on a sympathetic hearing, and a great feeling of trust sprang up between the volatile theater folk and the mild, even-tempered critic. Except perhaps among those who suffered from his critical disapproval—and even, by many of those who once felt themselves wronged—Atkinson is widely remembered and revered for his fairness. He is remembered, too, for his great encouragement to the off-Broadway theater, a recognition he accorded in advance of any of his colleagues.

Like legendary heroes, the two most important journalistic figures in the theater—men whose names were as well known to the theater people as that of any playwright or producer and whose power over the destinies of plays was regarded to be as great as that of any theater owner or union leader—both now belong to the past. Besides Atkinson, the other hero-villain on the *Times* was Sam Zolotow, who, as chief theatrical reporter of the *Times,* for more than forty years had been an insistent voice on the other end of the phone for countless Broadway producers, ferreting out nuggets of production news they wished withheld, details of forthcoming productions before the ink was dry on the contracts. In background and in temperament, no two men could be more different, the one New England and Harvard, the other New York's Lower East Side, where he was born in 1901, and the High School of Commerce. Atkinson was modest and reticent, Zolotow brash, insistent, intimidating.

While still in high school Zolotow worked nights in the *Times* composing room, later becoming office boy in the drama department under Alexander Woollcott when Woollcott was the critic in the 1920's and under George S. Kaufman when the playwright briefly was the *Times* drama editor.

Zolotow is short and squarely built. He wears a pugnacious look that is not contradicted by his personality and has iron-gray hair brushed straight back from a broad forehead. As a reporter asking a question, he had a trick of peering at his subject through steel-rimmed spectacles with round, surprised eyes. At the answer, he would drop the hand holding his cigar to his side, making a low whistlelike sound of disbelief. "Is that so?" he would say softly. "Is *that* so?"

For years the Zolotow manner spread fear and anger through the district's theatrical offices. Everyone dreaded a call from Zolotow, even those hungry for publicity. His demands for "exclusives" alienated press agents and producers alike. Nor did the *Times* help buttress its claims to being a great newspaper when it spitefully played down a story not given to the *Times* exclusively or refused to "recover" on a story a rival had alone. It didn't matter that *Times* readers were left in the dark—the story wasn't important if it wasn't in the *Times.* Zolotow was once asked if he would refuse to run a story the President of the United States released at a news conference simply because it wasn't exclusive. "Not on the theater page," Zolotow replied.

In his later years, (he retired at season's end in 1969 after nearly fifty years of newspapering) Zolotow lost some of his power. During the same period, coincidentally, the *Times* was moving more strongly, and with more sophistication, into the field of arts coverage. By 1969 it had put together an arts staff of thiry-one reporters, critics, and editors, only slightly smaller than the sports staff of forty-one and the business and financial staff of thirty-eight. By column measure the coverage is enormous. In the month of January 1969, for example, the *Times* in its daily editions, exclusive of Sundays, devoted 3,800 column inches to the performing arts in news, pictures, and reviews, coverage of a size and scope not even specialized publications can duplicate.

The *Times* cultural-news department has occasionally been so overcrowded that staff members were reduced to competing not with rival newspapers or magazines but with each other for news and assignments and space. A producer is often left wondering just who on the *Times* he should deal with without making enemies among the others. If he talks to a daily reporter, then Lewis Funke, who conducts the theater-news column, "News of the Rialto," in the Sunday drama section, may be angry. Breaking the story daily may mean forfeiting future space in Funke.

Though it is larger in circulation—1.54 million on Sundays as against a million daily as of the last quarter of 1968 —the Sunday *Times* is not read with quite the same amount of tension or sense of urgency as is the daily, reflecting the general decompression effect of a New York weekend as compared to the hypertension of a weekday. The influence on the theatrical news is to make it seem somehow less crucial, less necessary to survival in a sink-or-swim business.

Most of the Sunday drama section is devoted to features —unblushingly frank interviews by Rex Reed; advance pieces on incoming shows spotted as promising by the section's thoughtful, bearded editor, Seymour Peck; critical reappraisals of playwrights such as Arthur Miller who, like Tennessee Williams, is regularly dragged through the mental observation ward of the Sunday *Times;* and Walter Kerr's second thoughts, the theater's equivalent of a "think" piece.

Reed, contributor to *Esquire,* columnist for *Women's Wear Daily,* and author of *Do You Sleep in the Nude?,* is a curious bird to be found flying so airily through the pages of the weighty Sunday *Times.* He makes no pretense whatsoever to objectivity in his discursive, voyeuristic interviews with famous personalities of the stage and screen. Almost before he arrives for the interview appointment, he is ruffling his feathers and worrying about how he will be received. He injects his own ego measurably into every interview, anticipating resistance, antagonism. He is easily offended, almost purposely so, as he matches self-esteem for self-esteem with his subject.

In the lush garden of opinion and comment that is the Sunday *Times* drama section, Funke's column is the only patch of hard news, and often it relates to pie-in-the-sky theatrical productions many months from realization. Nevertheless, producers have come to regard Funke's Sunday column as an auspicious showcase for future productions, one carefully enough placed to catch the eye of eager investors. On the Monday morning after the first mention of a new production has been made in Funke's column the producer has often happily arrived to a ringing phone and potential investors on the end of the line.

In the field of news coverage the *Times* has not achieved its pre-eminent position without the connivance of the producers themselves, who have favored the *Times* over all other news media as the best outlet for their stories and have complied meekly with the demands of *Times* reporters for exclusives. Even when the *New York Herald Tribune* regularly devoted theater news space equal to that of the *Times*, the producers favored the *Times*. The *Times*, inevitably, pulled out in front: a heftier circulation, a circulation that blanketed the New York theatergoing public, an aura of authority, greater selling punch.

The *Times* as an advertising medium is the overwhelming first choice of the theater industry. In all media, the theater spends about $5 million a year, which is roughly a tenth of what the theater grosses. Of this sum the *Times*, daily and Sunday, gets about half. The bare minimum of advertising a running production must do in the *Times* is to appear daily in the ABC's—a small section of boxes arranged in alphabetical order by show title which gives the times, theater locations, and price scales. The average weekly cost for an ABC listing in the *Times* is $227.

Off-Broadway theater accounts for about half a million of the $5 million annual advertising budget, but has no

ABC listing of its own. As a consequence, each off-Broadway show is obliged to take out ads regularly, some of them microscopic in size, in keeping with off-Broadway budgets. Just before the weekend, when almost every off-Broadway show gives two performances on both Saturday and Sunday, the ads grow modestly.

Particularly in the Sunday drama section, the advertising columns of the *Times* are used to herald the coming of new shows to Broadway, sometimes many months in advance. The favorite season for such display ads, many of them running a full page, is late summer up to Labor Day, when a new theatrical season is about to begin. On late-summer Sundays the *Times* drama section is to the entertainment market what Tiffany's Christmas catalogue in October is to the winter gift-jewelry trade.

These large announcement ads generally feature the logotype of the show—the particular design or device the producer and his advertising artists have chosen to suggest the nature of the show—and give full marquee display to all the names and talents involved in the production. Later, after the show has opened, the theater resorts to its favorite form of publicity, the "quote" ad.

Quote ads—generally sizable in cost and space—are used by producers to solidify the impact of favorable reviews or to soften the blow of unfavorable reviews. Favorable reviews don't have to be all sugar and honey for the quote ad to read compellingly; they are put together with a paste that holds down all solid adjectives and scissors that snip out every qualifying phrase. Both the confident producer who has had excellent notices and the desperate producer who has had generally poor notices often make equally prominent use of the quote ad—the former to snowball his success, the latter to stave off disaster. Only the theater-wise can detect the confident ad from the face-saving appeal.

In days gone by it was customary to prepare a quote ad of modest size, about a fifth of a page, to run in several important New York newspapers immediately after the play had opened. "The sooner the better" was the watchword, and producers strove to have their quote ads in print within twenty-four hours after the opening. Inflation and the reduction in the number of newspapers have seriously affected this procedure.

Nowadays, quote ads for most Broadway shows are at least a half page and usually run only in the daily *Times,* repeated as soon as possible in the Sunday *Times.* Such a policy represents, as of this writing, an expenditure of about $9,000. A full-page program with the same two insertions (once in the daily *Times,* once in the Sunday *Times*) is double this figure, or $18,000. As one old-time manager puts it, "My quote-ad campaign—two ads in one paper—would have financed two Broadway plays in 1936."

This is only the beginning for the lavish musical or the high-powered play. Post-opening advertising campaigns of $50,000 for the musical and $25,000 for the play are now commonplace.

Some theater people believe that in their heavy reliance upon quote ads the producers have succeeded in bringing some of their worst troubles on themselves in that the ads have widened the readership of the critics and helped to confirm their authority. In 1960 one lone producer, Leo Kerz, stood up against the whole system and refused to use quote ads even after the reviews turned out to be largely favorable to his Broadway show, *Rhinoceros,* the Ionesco play that starred Eli Wallach and Zero Mostel. Kerz believed that the producer would pay dearly for the notoriety he gave the critics, and he believed that the public was ill served by a policy of excerpting favorable comment. Instead, Kerz distributed reprints of the full texts of all the reviews to anyone who asked for them. Eric Bentley, the theatrical scholar, celebrated Kerz's stand in verse:

> I love the drama critics so
> I'd even use a quote like "no."
> But since they're saying "yes" to me
> I'm overcome by modesty.

Inevitably it is the *Times* critic who becomes the focal point for the anger that suffuses the theater. In the past decade a succession of gentlemen have borne this onus. Brooks Atkinson was succeeded by Howard Taubman, Taubman gave way to Stanley Kauffmann, Kauffmann to Walter Kerr, and Kerr to Clive Barnes. The critical upheavals at the *Times* were as unsettling to the theatrical community as the imperial convulsions of ancient Rome. Atkinson was remembered for a long, serene, and fruitful reign. If Atkinson was Augustus, then Taubman, his successor, was Tiberius, and Kauffmann, who lasted only eight months, must go down in the imperial succession as the *Times's* Otho, after the Roman emperor whose reign lasted less than a year and was terminated violently.

Howard Taubman succeeded Brooks Atkinson in 1960 and shortly thereafter the *Times* began to develop a new attitude toward theater. "The *Times* is getting culture," theater people began to say jeeringly. In picking Taubman from the music staff, the *Times* was promoting from within, for he had been a member of the staff since 1929, only four years after Atkinson had become drama critic, but no one really knew how he would deal with theater. Those who had to do with musicals were generally apprehensive. Taubman, after all, had been music editor at the *Times* for a long time—from 1935 to 1955—and music critic thereafter.

It soon became clear how he would look on theater. With Taubman, the *Times's* interest in theater as culture began, to the dismay of Broadway's showmen. Informed by this kind of cultural overview, Taubman's style vis-à-vis a Broadway opening adopted a certain coolness and detachment. He was judicious where Atkinson had been enthusiastic. Even in a favorable Taubman notice there was little of the hats-in-the-air jubilation that so delights theater people. Even in writing favorably, Taubman could not, or would not allow himself, to express his enthusiasm enough to affect the box office. David Merrick accused him of being dull.

Merrick lost no time in taking to the war path. He began attacking Taubman publicly at every opportunity. The campaign reached its height in April 1963, when Merrick went on Johnny Carson's *Tonight Show* on NBC. He called Taubman "an incompetent hack" and said he prayed regularly for his removal. The refrain "Taubman must go" began to spread, and, coincidentally, Merrick's liking for the other critics grew.

"I like Walter Kerr," he said. "I think he's hard but he can write and when he likes a show he can stir up some excitement about it. But this Taubman—he can hurt you but he can't help you. Brooks Atkinson was different. People respected him. When he liked a show people went to see it."

Beginning in the reign of Tiberius Taubman, an era of bad feeling commenced between the theater and the *Times*. The long reign of Augustus was over. Now the emperors began to succeed one another with dizzying rapidity. Abetted by Taubman, the *Times* began to regard theater as part of the cultural pattern. The commercially minded Broadway entrepreneurs wanted no such insubstantial glory. Taubman was accused scornfully of having discovered the word "repertory" and, indeed, the *Times* critic now began to stray from Times Square and visit some of the new resident theaters. In its news columns the *Times* began to devote space to theater outside New York. Slowly but perceptibly the emphasis shifted from the commercial to the institutional theater. The *Times* had moved into its *Drang nach Kultur* period..

In Joseph G. Herzberg the *Times* appointed a cultural editor who had little interest in the theater, and even after his appointment he rarely attended a play. The cultural staff was reorganized and an attempt was made to break down the barriers between the arts and allow everyone to become "generalists." Until then each art had been autonomous and self-contained, and the separation was affirmed on the third floor of the *Times* by a series of partitions walling off the different specialties. Under Herzberg the partitions came down and everyone was permitted to cover everything. Reporters who for years had kept to one field found them-

selves mastering the strange terminology of another. Herzberg and the *Times* began to seek out culture, and some of
the niceties and distinctions observed in the trade were
pointedly ignored. The new aggressiveness of the *Times*
was partly traceable to an awareness of the money to be
made out of culture: it had become a significant source of
advertising revenue—the movies and, increasingly, the theater as well as the art sales, gallery openings, and dressy
high-bid auctions at Parke-Bernet. Zolotow escaped the
anti-specialization purge, but he was writing less regularly
than before.

Then, at the end of the 1962–63 season, the *Times* took
a step that turned the theater's displeasure to fury. In a
front-page story under the byline of the then assistant cultural editor Milton Esterow, the *Times* pronounced the
just-past theater season the worst in years. The headlines
carried a startling loss figure of $5.5 million. The placement
and emphasis of the story, the front-page prominence, and
the wording of the headline all suggested that the Broadway theater was fast approaching bankruptcy. The story
listed each of the season's flops with dollar-investment lost.
The measure of the season's failure, according to the *Times*
story, was the total of these losses.

The theater reacted with outrage. The prominent display of bad theater news was insult enough, but by breaking
the story on the front page of the *Times,* Broadway was
now part of the disaster world of domestic tragedy, congres-
sional folly, diplomatic blunders, international wars. The
tone of the story was accusatory, fault-finding, unsympathetic. But what angered the theater most was that the
total impression of Broadway conveyed by the story was one
of blatant inaccuracy. The facts, in themselves substantially
correct, were being used to reach erroneous conclusions. The
arithmetic was right but the equation was faultily set up.
The League of New York Theatres called the story an "unfair, hostile, inaccurate, slanted attack" and a "mass of mis-
information."

Theater economics is a complex subject. Simplifications such as the *Times* story contained are dangerously misleading. A large amount of investment money had indeed gone down the drain, but that happens every year on Broadway. The oil-prospecting industry is not a failure because nine out of ten wells drilled are dry, and the theater has never batted much better than one hit out of every four or five tries.

Applying ordinary accounting methods to the theater is futile if one considers only a fixed time period—the June through May season—and neglects to reduce the losses by the profits. The *Times* story, for example, considered only the shows that opened within the limits of the season under review; it neglected to take into account the profits earned in that season by the still-running shows of previous seasons (*Mary, Mary, How to Succeed in Business Without Really Trying, A Funny Thing Happened on the Way to the Forum*) or give an estimate of the profits the shows that opened in the season under review would earn in future seasons (*Who's Afraid of Virginia Woolf?, Oliver!*). For a fair picture one would have to figure either one or the other; otherwise the balance sheet is blurry. David Merrick, having in mind the season's most successful comedy, asked, "How can you appraise that season without estimating the full run of *Never Too Late?*" In the accounting procedures adopted by the Esterow story, a show that opens at the end of one season and makes its profit in the succeeding season is lost to the balance sheet, an economic nullity. The story further neglected to account for subsidiary rights. Herman Levin, then serving as president of the League of New York Theatres, said, "The theater has never geared its investment to just Broadway box-office receipts." (He certainly hadn't as producer of *My Fair Lady*.) The investors in a Broadway show share in the proceeds of a movie sale, in the profits of tours, and in stock rights—all possible sources of income after the show has closed on Broadway.

On the fifth floor of the old Playhouse Theatre building

on 48th Street, the governors of the League of New York Theatres met a few days after the story appeared to "take action." The League ever since the Taubman era, periodically discusses "what to do" about *The New York Times*.[2] Each of the famous gentlemen who sit around the long table in the League's board room is renowned for some reigning or past Broadway success, but they are all sufferers from the melancholia induced by thoughts of the *Times*. "The *Times*'s policy is to bury us," says the lugubrious David Merrick. Another producer offers a remedy: "Let's get rid of him," referring, of course, to the incumbent critic of the *Times*. Everyone at the table approves of this remedy on principle until a voice of reason says that the only way this can be accomplished is by buying the *Times*. It is very discouraging. On this particular day, the long, angry discussion produced two decisions: the League would prepare its own accurate seasonal profit-and-loss statement utilizing expert economists each year (this was done once and then dropped) and a delegation would seek a meeting with the editors and management of the *Times* to discuss not only the story in question but also the unsympathetic news and critical posture adopted by the paper toward the commercial theater.

The *Times* meeting was held. The producers' delegation, which included David Merrick and Alexander H. Cohen, two of the more vociferous members, met with a *Times* group headed by Turner Catledge and Clifton Daniel, then managing editor and assistant managing editor, respectively, of the *Times*. The theater side aired its objections and asked for specific correction of the distortions of the Esterow story. The *Times* editors defended the story as accurate on

---

[2] At a 1968 meeting of the League, producer David Merrick, during one of the endless and frequent discussions of the power of the *Times*, put his finger squarely on what most producers feel about the good gray monopoly on 43rd Street.

"The *Times* is the enemy," said Merrick.

"And if you get a rave review for one of your shows?" a fellow producer asked.

"Then the *Times* is the friend," said Merrick, feeling not a bit inconsistent.

its own terms but agreed to publish the theater's own accounting report when released—but no correction.

In the continuing era of bad feeling, the next low came over the hiring of Stanley Kauffmann in late 1965 to replace Howard Taubman as drama critic. The theater was happy to see Taubman move upstairs to become a roving cultural reporter (the Shuberts gave him a party in the Belasco Room at Sardi's reminiscent of the one given for Atkinson but different in tone, as soon as he vacated the critic's seat) but no one knew very much about Kauffmann. Kauffmann's intellectual background was not reassuring. He had been sponsored, in fact, by that arch-enemy of the commercial theater, Robert Brustein, critic of the *New Republic*. It did not please theater producers to hear that Kauffmann was the author of some forty unproduced plays; a disappointed playwright with rejections slips, they felt, would not make for a sympathetic critic.

In 1958 Kauffmann became film critic of the *New Republic* and for three years prior to joining the *Times* in 1966 he was drama critic on Channel 13, the educational TV station in New York, where he had come to the attention of the *Times* editors.

Casting about for a replacement for Taubman, the *Times* first contacted the bright, articulate Brustein, but he didn't want the job; in fact, he thought it should be abolished. Pressed for suggestions, Brustein brought up the name of his colleague and friend, Kauffmann.

It was in late August 1965 that the *Times* first approached Kauffmann. Harrison Salisbury, the assistant managing editor, invited him to lunch with other editors under the pretext of "picking his brains" on the cultural coverage of the paper. Kauffmann obliged by informing them that, with some few exceptions, the intellectual community did not hold a high opinion of the quality of *Times* criticism. Kauffmann was not really looking for a job on the *Times*, and was even worried that the *Times* would be "a very considerable step down" from the *New Republic* and that he would be "bartering" some of his "stylistic range" for the "sheer power" of the big, influential newspaper. Some months went by. Then, finally, the *Times* offered, and Kauffmann accepted.

Hobe Morrison wrote in *Variety,* "The appointment of Stanley Kauffmann as the drama critic of *The New York Times* raised the question in Broadway circles as to whether the paper will be able to regain the leadership in theatrical coverage it has lost to the *New York Herald Tribune.*"

Kauffmann made one condition—that the *Times* get the theater to agree to his reviewing the last preview performance instead of the first night. (Actually, as the *New York Post*'s Richard Watts, Jr. recalled, this had been tried many years ago by Gilbert Gabriel of the *Morning American.*) The switch would give him a day of grace, since his review would be published like everyone else's the morning after the opening.

The innocent-seeming request got the Kauffmann reign off to a bad start. The producers of the first two plays Kauffmann was to review were divided on the idea. Richard Barr, Edward Albee, and Clinton Wilder, opening Albee's *Malcolm* during Kauffmann's first week, were for it, already on record as favoring critics reading scripts in advance. But Lyn Austin, the producer of a comedy cryptically named *UTBU,* objected strongly. She pleaded the unreadiness of a production before the preset opening night. Work on her own show, she said, would continue until the last minute, and if she had known in time that Kauffmann wanted to attend the last preview she could have pointed for that night. Clifton Daniel, by then managing editor, had lunch and a number of subsequent telephone conversations with Miss Austin, but she resented the pressure and would not budge. She refused to provide Kauffmann with reviewer's tickets for the preview.

Standing firmly with Miss Austin on the issue was Harold Prince, the president of the League of New York Theatres, who announced that he was "unalterably opposed" to the new *Times* policy. As an example of the harm that could be done, he cited his own production of *A Funny Thing Happened on the Way to the Forum,* which underwent drastic last-minute changes—the brilliant opening number, "Comedy Tonight," wasn't put into the show until after the first preview and wasn't fully ready until opening night. Since then, however, Prince and some other producers have changed their minds about the importance of opening nights. In an attempt to de-emphasize the night of trauma they have been suggesting a series of possible performances to be reviewed but designating one performance as the official opening, after which the reviews could be printed. (Prince did this with his musical *Zorbá.*)

Miss Austin lost out in the end. Mr. Kauffmann bought tickets to a preview of Miss Austin's comedy, saw that performance, and went to the opening night as well, as he had proposed all along.

Kauffmann was regarded skeptically as new boy by the regular critics. Any new *Times* critic had to reckon with Walter Kerr, one of the finest writers under pressure a newspaper has ever produced in any field. Facing the inexorable deadline of the drama critic, Kerr was at his best. When he had more time, as he did with a Saturday-night opening, writing for Monday's paper, he simply used it, and the result was sometimes less good, as he himself admitted. Kerr felt that a producer ought to be given the right to say when he was ready. All the other daily critics also seemed to be content with the system as it was—John Chapman of the *News,* Richard Watts, Jr. of the *Post,* John McClain of the *Journal-American,* Norman Nadel of the *World-Telegram & Sun.*

One after the other the principal theater organizations formally went on record as opposed to reviewing the previews: the League of New York Theatres, the Dramatists Guild, Actors' Equity, the Society of Stage Directors and Choreographers. Sidney Kingsley, president of the Dramatists Guild, said such reviews would contribute "a conclusive judgment on an incomplete work." The critic might be present on a night when the sets weren't working properly, when the scene changes were rough, the lights wavered, and the laughs came in the wrong places.

As for Kauffmann, he was inclined to dismiss the opposition, great as it was, as the pettiness of otherwise decent theater people or as "the elements of show biz uniting against someone who treated theater as an art and only as an art."

Stanley Kauffmann was on the job a month and a half before David Merrick brought in a new show. Up to this point, one way or another, Kauffmann and the *Times* had succeeded in securing preview tickets. Prophetically, Norman Nadel wrote in the *World-Telegram,* "I doubt if any producer would try to stop him by force, though knowing David Merrick, I'm not sure." The Merrick office sent Kauffmann tickets to the last preview performance of Brian Friel's *Philadelphia, Here I Come,* opening Wednesday, February 16, 1966, but attached to the tickets was a cryptic warning, "At your peril." Merrick had a scheme up his sleeve, one of his most elaborate. Shortly before the curtain for the Tuesday preview at the Helen Hayes Theatre, with Kauffmann and the rest of the full-house audience seated, the lights in the theater went out and the performance was canceled. The reason given was "generator trouble" (although the lobby lights were mysteriously unaffected). The baffled audience was offered the option of getting their money back or exchanging their tickets for a later performance at the same low-priced preview rates.

Mr. Kauffmann, of course, was sent home with the rest, with no play to review. Since the formal opening was the following night Kauffmann was forced for the first time to face the same first-night pressures as everyone else. The only explanation the sly Merrick offered for the cancellation of the preview was: "A rat got caught in the generator." To no one's great surprise, power was restored in plenty of time for opening night. Merrick was enormouly pleased with his practical joke. It had cost him $1,750 in ticket refunds and $900 in cast and crew salaries, but the publicity created by the incident ("Broadway Producer Outwits *Times*") more than made up for his loss.[3]

Banning the critic from the theater is a recurrent fantasy of the frustrated producer. Years ago the Shuberts banned Alexander Woollcott, then the *Times* critic, from their theaters in a feud that was dragged through the courts, aroused national interest, and lasted a year. Woollcott had mildly disapproved of a "not vastly amusing" French farce entitled *Taking Chances,* put on by the Shuberts in March 1915. Review tickets for the Shuberts' next opening were pointedly sent not to Woollcott but to Carr Van Anda, the *Times* managing editor, with a request that another critic be assigned. Clearly the *Times* had to stand up for its rights. Woollcott went but was stopped at the door, and the lawyers entered the case. The *Times* won an injunction restraining the Shuberts from barring its critic and threw out all Shubert advertising. Many months later the Shuberts won a reversal of the original decision in the Appellate Division, but it was the loss of the important advertising outlet that eventually persuaded the Shuberts to drop the quarrel. By Christmas of 1916 the Shuberts had mellowed enough to send the *Times* critic a box of cigars. Woollcott's closing line on the incident was, "The whole thing went up in smoke."

There have been few modern incidents of critic banning. Merrick once threatened to bar Walter Kerr but the threat was never carried out, and once Merrick's agents refused NBC's Edwin Newman admittance on the complimentary tickets he was provided but he slipped through on a friend's extra ticket. Not since Woollcott has the theater made any serious attempt to bar the critic of *The New York Times.*

[3] Kauffmann was thrown off stride twice by Merrick's faulty generator. He was also obliged to attend the first night of the season's next play, *Hostile Witness,* whose final preview had fallen on *Philadelphia*'s opening night. And, incidentally, Kauffmann was the only one among his colleagues to give *Philadelphia, Here I Come* a bad notice.

But Merrick kept right after Kauffmann. A couple of months later, during a trip to London, Merrick delightedly spotted a paperback title in the bookstalls—*The Philanderer* by Stanley Kauffmann. Could this be his old friend from New York? It was indeed. Merrick was even more delighted to see a frontispiece note announcing that the book had been prosecuted (unsuccessfully) for obscenity in England. He bought up every copy in sight—eighty-nine—and shipped them back home. In a week, curious editors, reporters, and columnists throughout the city, including ten key editors on *The New York Times,* were opening packages in plain brown wrapping paper. Inside was a copy of *The Philanderer* by Stanley Kauffmann with a card reading, "With the compliments of David Merrickk" (the spelling was a play on the double consonants in Kauffmann's name). All Merrick neglected to do was mark the juicy passages.

A theater executive explains Merrick's critic-baiting proclivities as follows: "One of the great tricks of Merrick's producing is to chew up the critic publicly so that the critic will know how David feels about him and he will hate David and then, having made known his public hatred, he will have to lean over backward in reviewing a Merrick play. It's all preconceived."

Some years after this incident, and after he left the *Times,* Kauffmann could look back on it from a relatively untroubled perspective. "I had no scrap with Mr. Merrick. Mr. Merrick scrapped with me and he did it for his very own shrewd advantage, and he is a very shrewd man. If he thought he could have drawn more attention to himself and his shows by calling me the greatest genius that ever came down the pike, he would have done that. He got more attention by doing this, and the *Times,* in its rather dimwitted way [it had recounted the whole generator incident in a front-page story], played into his hands."

By Broadway standards Kauffmann was a cold, intellectually austere critic. Sometimes he pronounced strong personal judgments on the artistic competence of actors and directors, going beyond the data of the individual performance to appraise whole careers, a practice condemned by unwritten code. Theater professionals returned Kauff-mann's dislike. "Kauffmann?" one of them said. "Lovely man —he just hates the theater. I can understand his hating the theater; he wrote forty-three plays, none of them ever pro-duced. If I'd written forty-three plays and none of them had ever been produced I'd hate the theater right down to my soul."

In short, the theater felt that Stanley Kauffmann was miscast in his role. So, later, did the editors of the *Times,* especially when Walter Kerr became available.

When the *Herald Tribune* was incorporated into the *World Journal Tribune* in the summer of 1966, Walter Kerr, with none of the old claims on his loyalty (a man used to competing against the monolithic *Times* for years does not easily join the opposition), was open to outside offers. The *Times* approached him in Europe, where he was lecturing at the Salzburg Festival. As Kerr thought about it, two mat-ters were uppermost: for one, the years of nightly reviewing were wearing and he was hoping to work himself into a weekly writing schedule. But, more important, he was con-cerned about the reduction of newspapers in New York and the consequent rise in power of the *Times* critic, whoever he might be. In a memorandum to Turner Catledge, then executive editor, Kerr in accepting the job had written:

> The professional theater is in bad shape and the situation is getting tighter all the time. So long as there were six or seven newspapers with contending critical voices, it was al-ways possible for a play to survive on mixed notices. But with the number of newspapers shrinking so, that is no longer going to be possible. . . . It might be very valuable for the *Times* to become the vital center of debate through having at least two separate opinions, one daily, one Sunday.

What Kerr could not himself say, but what everyone else was thinking, was that Kerr's highly respected voice, on the *Tribune,* had acted as an effective counterweight to the power and authority of the *Times.* Now that his voice and the power of the *Times* were to be one, the effect of the

Times's criticism on the fortunes of the theater would be more devastating than ever. One possible way of diluting this power was to move Kerr to Sunday, bring in another critic for the daily review, and let their two opinions contend. In the fall of 1966 managing editor Clifton Daniel conceded, as Kerr began writing daily for the *Times,* that this plan was being considered. In the meantime, critic-watchers suspected that Kerr's style, dipped in the gray columns of the *Times,* had lost some of its color and spontaneity. Or perhaps, conscious of his new power, he was holding back, keeping his exuberance in check and pulling his punches when he wanted to pan a show.

At the end of Kerr's first season at the *Times* the two-critic plan was announced. Kerr moved to Sunday at the beginning of the following season and the *Times*'s dance critic, Clive Barnes, took on the added duty of daily drama critic with seemingly boundless energy.

From the outset, and apparently deliberately, Barnes adopted an informal, personal, almost breezy tone that marked a departure from the wordy and highly descriptive style of Kerr, from the caustic intellectuality of Kauffmann, and from the cultural solemnities of Taubman.

Barnes is a conscious anti-Philistine. Middle-class morality bores and offends him, and he delights in taunting the staid Establishment by pronunciamentos of inflammatory doctrine. Some samples: Pornography has redeeming social value; the playwright has left-wing policies, which is admirable; the nudity in *Hair* is charming. At times Barnes reminds one of the comic saying, "If there's someone in the audience I haven't offended, I apologize."

With the Barnes appointment, the *Times* had returned to its policy of promoting from within, yet Barnes, with his breezy British exuberance, was actually atypical. He was very much the new boy—young, uncowed, precocious. An Oxford graduate, Barnes was dance critic for *The Times* of London. There his bright style caught the eye of *New York Times* editors and they brought him to New York in August

1965 to succeed John Martin. Dance was the field in which Barnes was most at home, although critically he kept abreast of the legitimate theater as well. He remained dance critic. In his first season Barnes popped up all over the paper—in daily reviews of Broadway and off-Broadway, in play reappraisals, in reviews of the major dance openings, in frequent Sunday pieces, and, on the outside, appearing on radio and television, speaking in his unmistakably British, near-Cockney voice, and doing magazine pieces here and there. Of that first Barnes year, Brooks Atkinson, regarding the performance from an amused retirement, remarked, "I felt completely surrounded by Barnes."

Kerr and Barnes would express contrary opinions about the same play at least part of the time and although Kerr would be writing less frequently than Barnes, and with less immediacy, it was hoped that his reputation as the most knowledgeable drama critic of his time would help the paper to establish a strong second critical position and the onus of making or breaking shows would fall less severely on the regular daily critic. But it didn't work out that way—the power swung to the daily review. In half a season the lesser-known Barnes became the deciding critical voice on the *Times,* and the reason for the two-critic experiment was at least partly nullified.

Barnes was as aware of this shift in power as anyone. "People point out that Walter Kerr can have no effect on the success or failure of a play and I think that's true and say good luck to him," said Barnes. "Where he does have an effect is in the overall assessment of the season, in stimulating people to talk about the theater."

From the outset Barnes was accused of being "chatty." In a Sunday piece soon after he took over as drama critic Barnes pleaded guilty. Yes, he was chatty—intentionally so. This un-*Times*like weakness was a part of his approach to drama criticism, designed to counteract the American public's "dangerous tendency to place the newspaper critic upon a pedagogical pedestal." It is all too easy for the critic to pontificate, to pretend to objectivity, to be puffed up with

self-importance. "Believing as I do in the fallibility of critical comment," Barnes wrote, "one of my duties as a critic is
to play down its authority."

Barnes is fascinated with the whole practice of criticism
and has studied it for years. He cannot accept the extreme
view of some producers that mistaken criticism can kill a
worthwhile play outright. In his British experience he can
cite only one good play that was almost universally panned
by critics—Harold Pinter's *The Birthday Party*—and even
then the play survived the initial abortive production and
achieved substantial runs in later productions in both London and New York. In this country Barnes likes to challenge
producers to name one worthy play killed by the critics. No
one, he says, has ever given him a satisfactory answer.

As a critic Barnes gives the impression of being an enormously busy gadfly, yet whenever possible he prepares conscientiously for whatever event he plans to review, even to
reading the script in advance if he can get his hands on it
and if it is a difficult enough play to require preparation. In
this Barnes differs from his colleague Walter Kerr, who has
always refused opportunities to read the script. Kerr prefers
to go to a play cold. In his view, the play has its life and being only as it is being performed on the stage. Barnes would
prefer to take his journeys with a map; he considers it his
duty to get as much information as he can under his belt before the curtain goes up.

Like every critic Barnes is concerned with his credit rating
with the public. He recognizes, as his predecessor Kauffmann
did not, that night after night Broadway cannot be measured only against some purist standard: "Very few things
deserve unqualified raves or unqualified pans. Often in the
worst things there's some very good acting and very often
the best things have faults. It's not Molière and Shakespeare
every night, and it's unrealistic to go into an orgasm of
enthusiasm, because every critic has a credit rating with the
reader and if he's going to cry wolf too many times and the
wolf doesn't come and if he's going to say hit too many times
and the hit isn't there, his credit rating is going to go down

and down and down."

The needs of the producer are quite different. Producers are not interested in critical analysis. They want a triple-A credit rating. With endorsements and testimonials in hand, they can pump in advertising, consolidate their gains, and create a hit, which is their only form of security and success. In the critical spectrum, as most sensible critics are themselves aware, there are not just "money" notices and hits and bad notices and flops; there are also polite notices that denote the merely "artistic" success; there are in-between notices; and there are also what might be called good bad notices and bad good notices.

Clive Barnes offers this example of the good bad notice: "This is disgusting; the women are naked and there was a terrible scene of copulation in the third act."

And this example of a bad good notice: "Mr. Brown's play, which deals with the life of Kierkegaard and takes place during five hours, is intellectually stimulating."

Instead of laying down the law, what Barnes hopes to achieve, by adopting a certain attitude and tone, is a dialogue with the reader. He will be chatty even though some of his readers seem to deplore it. He has introduced the rare use of the first-person singular into his reviews. He seeks a one-to-one relationship with the reader. For there is need to soften the unequal power of the *Times*—the object of such bitter complaint in the theater—as it is brought to bear against the defenseless producer, the vulnerable actors, and the fragile play.

CHAPTER TEN

The Sexual Ethic

Experts disagree on how much theater and show-business sexual standards and customs differ from those of the rest of society. One Broadway veteran maintains that the "casting couch" conception of the producer is fiction. A New York psychoanalyst who is in no sense the victim of stereotyped thinking believes that to this day a Hollywood actress without connections cannot make her way up without distributing sexual favors, and he remains clearly unconvinced that this is not also true of Broadway. Herman Shumlin, producer, director, and playwright, says, "I don't think the sex that goes on in the theater is any different from what goes on in offices everywhere. Yes, it's true that in the theater actors deal directly with their emotions, but just because an actor deals in emotional material does not mean that he is subject to a lack of control. And it is not necessarily true that these emotions are connected with sexual activity."

Shumlin does not differentiate between the sexual mores of the theater and other group endeavors, nor does he believe theater people are more open to temptation than, say, the members of a safari or a scientific expedition. "Doesn't any expedition have the same degree of family intimacy that a touring company does? What about tour groups? The same factors exist in tours as in touring shows—the availability, the attachment of people for one another. In an archeological dig, there is the same kind of intimacy and excitement. I have never seen the theater as a hotbed of sex."

Despite Mr. Shumlin's intimations of normality, there appears to be a definite subculture of theater whose distinguishing characteristic is laissez-faire morality—openness about sexual promiscuity, ease and frequency of sexual encounters, preoccupation with sexual perversion, and toleration of homosexuality. Actors, like writers and other artists, are in a vanguard. Dr. Daniel Casriel, a Manhattan psychiatrist with a group-therapy practice that includes many theater people, says, "Actors are more aware of their feelings than other people. They cater to those feelings. Therefore they are less strict with themselves in their behavior."

The actor and the illusion of promiscuity have been inseparable since theater began. The actor as gypsy and nomad practiced a "Lone Ranger" type of sexuality. Never at home, he traveled about creating and seeking romance and taking his pleasure as he found it. "The fantasy of having sex with a stranger is common among all people," says Dr. Donald Kaplan, a New York psychoanalyst, "but the public expects the actor to take advantage of his peripheral position in society in order to practice sexual liberty."

Actors have never been shy about confirming their sexuality. A seventeenth-century joke from the diary of John Manningham tells how the Shakespearean actor Richard Burbage and Shakespeare himself followed up, with zest, an expression of interest from a member of their audience.

> Upon a time when Burbage played Richard III there was a citizen grew so far in liking with him, that before she went from the play she appointed him to come that night unto her by the name of Richard the Third. Shakespeare, overhearing their conclusion, went before, was entertained

and at his game ere Burbage came. Then, message being brought that Richard III was at the door, Shakespeare caused return to be made that William the Conqueror was before Richard the Third.

Three centuries later, nothing has changed. A young actor in 1969 is frankly bewildered by the abundance of sexual opportunity in his work. "I am thrown into situations you don't usually face in a normal job. When you meet a girl offstage, you know nothing about her, but she knows who you are and everything about you. And you can go to bed with her that night. You don't need to go hunting. It's so easy in my position. It sounds like bragging, but I could have a different girl every night, and I'm not even a 'name.' You bare all your feelings on the stage, and then girls come around backstage afterward goggle-eyed—housewives, college girls, teenagers. It's not a question of my taking their virginity, and it's not as if I was establishing any lasting relationship. It's taken for granted that it's just for one night. If someone throws herself at me, I'm just not disciplined enough yet to say no." [1] For established actors, this fringe benefit can turn into an occupational hazard.

At the very time these casual encounters are most likely to occur—following a performance—the actor is most susceptible to them. A producer describes this phenomenon with understatement: "When the show is over, the actor is highly stimulated. He wants companionship, fun, and activity of a social nature." But an unmarried actress puts it more bluntly. She admits to a state of heightened sexual awareness when she is acting and acting well. "I have what I think is a normal interest in sex," she says, "but when I'm acting, I want to be wild. And the better my acting, the more intense the feeling becomes."

It's almost a truism that onstage romances become off-stage affairs. Often it becomes a test of an actor's skill to approximate, finally to realize, the romantic situation de-

---

[1] At one point in his career, the actor in question, suffering from "a lack of interest in myself," couldn't date a girl unless she had first seen him on the stage.

scribed in the script. It is not unusual for apparently good marriages to be wrecked because the play transforms a fictional relationship between two professional strangers into a liaison. Several times each season two people meet in a stage love affair, fall in love with each other, divorce their respective spouses, and marry each other.

The guilt of infidelity is particularly strong for an actor whose lover appears onstage with him every night. As one actor puts it, "My work suffers. I keep having love affairs, but I kick myself for doing it."

Despite the common-sense prohibitions against intra-company love affairs—and there are compelling circumstances to account for them—the working hours force an actor into the company of other actors ("There is no one else to play with"), and the intensity of the work period—the four-week rehearsal, long hours cooped up in a theater, community living, total concentration on the job at hand—create hothouse relationships. This is particularly true for performers from other media. A folk singer, for example, making her first appearance in a play, exchanges the loneliness of one-night stands for the warmth and companionship of a theatrical community, and personal attachments develop quickly within the new environment.

All actors experience loneliness and insecurity when they are out of town while the show is on tour or when it is trying out for Broadway. One actor regards intracompany love affairs in such circumstances as completely natural and normal. "A love affair within a cast is like a convenience when you're on tour," he says. "I need female companionship. When I'm in a strange town and it comes eleven o'clock, I don't want to go back to my hotel room alone. Out of town, if you have an affair, you have an affair. The company all knows about it. After all, it's impossible to hide it in those circumstances. But they don't tell. And when you get back to New York, each of the partners goes back to his respective home."

Some actresses are inclined to a different view, perhaps

because a woman relinquishes a romantic attachment less easily than a man. There is an old saying in the theater, "She was smart enough not to get involved until she got to New York." This reflects a reluctance to form a serious relationship when the play that has thrown two people together fails and separates them.

A new morality, however, is beginning to assert itself. Arising out of the life style of the youngest echelon of actors, it mirrors the morality of the new generation. Light years removed from the Puritan ethic, these actors have so completely rejected middle-class morality that to speak of them as flouting a moral code is nonsense. They recognize no moral code, at least in the old sense. In their way of life, a sense of community, group action, and commitment to theater are one.

An actress in her thirties who has taught and worked with the new young actors finds them more appealing, more involved, and better informed than members of her own generation. They live together openly without feeling the necessity to marry, she says. "The kids are already a family. Within themselves they form family relationships. They have made a family of each other. They are interested in each other. Four people—two couples interested in each other—make a family unit. These kids are much more group-oriented than we ever were. They have to be. The sheer numbers of them make this necessary. They all feel related to each other. In terms of sexual morality they are part of their generation." And then she adds her own comment: "I find middle-class mores—marrying someone you've been living with because you think it's the thing to do—much more depressing."

Quite apart from the "new morality" of the younger actor, the older actor's defiance of convention, and the ease of sexual encounters in the theater, the sex drive of the actor is also influenced on a psychological level that stems from his primal relationship with the audience. Actors can get recognition and approval only from an audience, and yet the particular approval required by the actor transcends a normal desire for public acceptance.

Dr. Casriel describes the actor's need: "Actors don't trust the approval they get from one significant person. Going before an audience becomes, in effect, an addiction. It doesn't solve their neurosis, it feeds it. It is the one place where their needs can be met. Each time they go before the audience it is like throwing another log on the fire of their anxiety. It fuels their anxiety, it doesn't cure it. Success never makes most actors secure."

Within the theater society, as we have seen, actors are regarded as children—when producers become annoyed with actors, they dismiss them as "childish"; when actors wish to convey a quality of innocence and wonder and make-believe they must bring to their roles they refer to themselves as "childlike." The psychoanalytical term for this is "pregenital," undeveloped sexuality. Dr. Charles Socarides is a psychoanalyst who has treated directors, playwrights, and actors; he is also an authority on homosexuality and the author of *The Overt Homosexual.* He feels that most actors suffer from an exhibitionistic conflict rather than a homosexual conflict. "The actor," says Dr. Socarides, "has a pregenital appetite for applause. He wishes to be fed by the applause of the audience. He has a tendency to exhibitionism, a desire to be loved, a need for showing his body. All this is clearly pregenital. And yet an actor is made of many other things as well: native endowment, genetic characteristics, training, and so forth. Actors have a wish omnipotently to control the audience. This is akin to what is called the 'omnipotence development' in the earliest years of adulthood. Children think they can control things by thought alone, and if something falls to the floor and breaks it is because they will it to happen."

It is through the controlled and disciplined use of such pregenital qualities—what Dr. Socarides calls "the childlike and partial pleasures of looking, seeing, feeling, and touching"—that the actor can amuse and please an audience. The greater the actor's control, the greater his artistry.

The actor's satisfaction comes from the "seduction" of the audience, but he must not overstep the agreed-upon boundaries. The right emotional resonance, a mutual equality of satisfaction, must be preserved between audience and player. It is clear, however, that only the live audience can provide these gratifications to the actor. As Dr. Socarides says, "Only the live audience can produce those 'waves of love' Tennessee Williams spoke about—waves of love coming across the footlights and enveloping the actor. The adulation of a live audience is the only food that feeds his deprived ego."

Another layer of the actor's psychological being must be examined to explain his sexual drives. Dr. Kaplan, a student of the theater, says some form of perversity is always present in the actor's sexual life. (Kaplan has written about homosexuality in the theater and about psychological problems of the stage in the *Tulane Drama Review,* now *The Drama Review.*) In his view, the actor has a "counterphobic personality." Other people hold back in the face of fear, but the actor, says Dr. Kaplan, "has to have the capacity to be counterphobic, to be challenged by fear and to do the very thing he's afraid of." Athletes and daredevils share this characteristic; to them the challenge is physical, while to the actor it is psychological.

All actors refer to their appearance before the audience in terms of "nakedness" (fear of being exposed) and to the performing experience in terms of violence and hostility (fear of punishment). Dr. Kaplan likens the anger the actor feels for the audience to the "pre-emptive first strike" of atomic warfare. Precautionary and self-defensive, it should dissipate itself within the first five minutes of performance, by which time the audience has warmed to the actor and the actor realizes that his expectation of punishment is groundless.

The neurotic basis of the stage personality impinges on

the performer's private life. Dr. Kaplan observes that the counterphobia that underlies performance carries over into the actor's sex life and may cause perversity—group sex, mate swapping, promiscuity, bisexuality, obsessional sexuality, and homosexuality. Dr. Kaplan notes further that the actor has a special feeling for his body as a piece of equipment the way high fashion models do. (The actor constantly refers to himself as "the instrument."[2]) People who use their bodies in their work have a "physical image of themselves and a sexual style of their own—a casual acceptance of sex contacts and a disregard for convention," the "quick sex" that psychiatrists observe in the body-oriented occupations.

Male dancers in Broadway musicals are notorious for homosexuality though by no means is every dancer a homosexual, and it is not only from the dancer that the theater has earned its continuing reputation for perversion. The public has come to regard the theater as "queer," and there is, no doubt, a higher incidence of homosexuality in the theater than in the public at large. The theater is an elite group, a "privileged section of society," as Dr. Kaplan says, and if you sample any privileged section of society you will find a higher incidence of the bizarre. Among the many privileges such a class permits itself, sexual privilege ranks highest.

In recent years there has been an apparent increase in homosexuality in the theater, but it is questionable whether this is a numerical increase or greater visibility. A new openness about all sexual mores has been encouraged by the frank display of homosexual relations on stage. On Broadway, in January 1968, *Staircase,* by the English playwright Charles Dyer, depicted the domestic life of two middle-aged homosexual barbers, and off-Broadway in April of that year *The Boys in the Band,* in which eight out of the nine characters are overtly homosexual, opened as a sensational "inside" look at the queer world. Both plays were revolutionary for handling homosexuality not as a freak

[2] Cf. Chapter 3.

problem requiring social attention but as an unavoidable part of everyday life.[3]

Homosexuality, with no holds barred, is no longer an occasional, shocking theme for plays. Plays dealing with homosexual relationships, but always at arm's length, came along periodically in the old days, and some were successful (*The Green Bay Tree, The Story of Oscar Wilde*), but most of the time homosexuality was peripheral to larger themes (*The Best Man, Tea and Sympathy*). The breakthrough of the new morality has made homosexuality acceptable material for dramatists, as any play reader will tell you, although it is still much easier to get a "homosexual" play produced off-Broadway than on Broadway. *The Boys in the Band* has spawned many imitative studies of the homosexual dilemma, and it is safe to assume that for some time to come there will always be a "queer" play running somewhere in New York.

Homosexuality can be found everywhere in theater, from the producer through the ranks of stage artists and workers to the dancing chorus of the Broadway musical, where it is at its most blatant and obvious. ("There are no queer stagehands, however," says one producer.) Homosexuality is especially prevalent among male costume designers, and indeed many of the people who fashion bits of the fantasy world of the theater—fitters, sewers, tailors, wig makers, mask makers.

It is in musical comedy, according to Dr. Socarides, that homosexuality flourishes and that the feminine identification can be useful. Most homosexuals try to fight their

[3] Initially, some people were doubtful about the audience appeal of an all-homosexual play. In a Sunday drama-section piece in *The New York Times* on May 12, 1968, Rex Reed predicted the play would be a success if only all the homosexuals in America went to see it. This recalls a story S. N. Behrman told on himself when his play *Lord Pengo*, which dealt with the great art collector Duveen, went into rehearsal in 1962. Behrman said the surge of art interest in the country had convinced him the time was right for his play, but he was haunted by a conversation he had overheard between two Hollywood executives discussing *Lust for Life*, which was about Van Gogh. The producer of the film admitted it hadn't turned out well. The other executive consoled him. "Everyone who owns a Van Gogh will go to see it," he said.

homosexuality, and offstage some strike a masculine pose, but in the context of performance, where feminine gestures of dance are appreciated and required, they can express their homosexuality with impunity.

Dr. Kaplan, on the other hand, believes that the homosexuality of dancers has less to do with feminine movements of dance than with the relationship between dancer and choreographer—the submissive lending by the dancer of his body to the choreographer. In all dance, necessarily and purposefully, there is a loss of "gender distinction," Dr. Kaplan asserts. Men who are dancers in musicals are not so much more feminine as they are less masculine.

The dance is only one area of show business in which a homosexual establishment exists.[4] In this not-so-secret society, homosexuality is a passport to employment. Several producing organizations are homosexual in every department, and several large acting companies are ceremoniously homosexual from season to season.

The homosexual establishment tends to embitter "straight" performers who feel excluded from employment or denied full participation, but it is also used as a whipping boy by those of little talent who might not be employed by any kind of establishment. Responsible theater people disclaim and deplore preferential or discriminatory hiring, and first-rate talent in the theater does not have to trade on "social connections" to find work. All things being equal, however, it is only natural for one homosexual to favor another.

There are obvious frustrations for straight people, particularly actresses, in working in a company dominated by homosexuals. One actress says, "There is an incredible amount of promiscuity among them. There's a terrible obsession with sex. Any man, even if he is straight, receives attention from the other boys." One summer she worked in a company of fifty actors and counted only a dozen, male and female, who were unequivocally straight.

---

[4] In England, this establishment is colloquially referred to as "the Homintern."

As a specialist on homosexuality, Dr. Socarides is convinced that most leading actors are not homosexual. One reason, he suggests, is the homosexual's morbid concern for his own body image, a fear that rules out many stage roles. Psychoanalytically, Socarides says, the homosexual suffers from "defective body-ego boundaries." Neurotically preoccupied with the way he presents himself physically to the public, he needs "adornment." But many roles call for a leading actor to dress sloppily or look "unadorned." In rags or old clothes, the homosexual is self-conscious. As a result, homosexuals are found mainly in the more elegant minor parts. There are some homosexual stars, of course, but Dr. Socarides detects in them shared traits—ramrod-stiff precision in performances and a preference for priestly, kingly, or aristocratic roles in which the richness of costume confers physical distinction and superior status and restores defective body-ego boundaries.

Dr. Casriel ascribes homosexuality in the actor to "pansexuality," the ability of the child or adolescent to relate to men and women indiscriminately. The "pansexual" is not the classic homosexual, completely unable to relate to women. Rather, he is unable to relate to anything or anyone seriously on an emotional level.

For many artists, theater may be a means of sublimating pathological sexual drives. A well-known homosexual director suffers from an extreme form of fetishism. As a young man he acted out his aggressions by becoming a puppeteer and creating and manipulating puppets. Repeated acts of creation absolved him of his guilts and aggressions. As a mature man he sublimates the same aggressions through manipulating the live "puppet" figures on the stage.[5]

The theater offers homosexuals a unique degree of acceptance and hospitality. Since it deals in emotional materials

[5] In his *Creativity in the Theater,* Philip Weissman sees the director as the victim of Oedipal wishes. "His wish to be a mother is as useful as his wish to be a father in the artistic function of directing and guiding performers. Maternal or paternal in origin, the identification is transformed and expressed in the sublimated wish to be an artistic parent to his artistic children, the performers."

the theater is more tolerant of human frailty, and since it requires many different talents it welcomes the eccentric. Theater people, prizing self-knowledge, are more understanding of the foibles of others. But the theater's tradition of toleration has been reinforced by the moral openness and sexual frankness of recent years. Among young theater people, homosexuality is no longer taboo in word or practice. Many heterosexual women live with homosexual men and hope for the best ("Joe may never change his sex habits for me, but he says he'll try," says an actress). Such arrangements indicate that the distinction between heterosexuality and homosexuality is being blurred.

Dr. Kaplan, for one, does not believe this distinction is particularly valid to begin with, for even the heterosexuality of the theater is distorted by perversity. Kaplan has written:

> The outcry against a growing infiltration of homosexuals into our theater makes as much sense as the outcry against illiteracy in a child by a parent whose hours at home are exclusively occupied in watching a television screen; such a parent may be able to read, but for all intents and purposes he might just as well be illiterate. And for all the difference it makes, those responsible for the emotional and intellectual climate of current theater might just as well be overtly homosexual. Today, the distinction between heterosexuality and homosexuality in the world of current theater is a thin line of illusion.[6]

One way to paraphrase this might be to say: within an asylum, it is not right to call another mad.

By far the most serious aspect of homosexuality in the theater, if any, is the extent to which the homosexual establishment colors the content of dramatic material. On a winter Sunday in 1966 readers of the drama section of *The New York Times* were surprised to find Stanley Kauffmann, then drama critic, devoting his entire column to "homosexual drama," discussing it in the frankest possible terms

---

[6] *Tulane Drama Review,* Spring 1965.

and all but naming the homosexual dramatists he had in mind. Kauffmann wrote:

> The principal complaint against homosexual dramatists is well known. Because three of the most successful American playwrights of the last twenty years are (reported) homosexuals and because their plays often treat of women and marriage, therefore, it is said, postwar American drama presents a badly distorted picture of American women, marriage, and society in general. Certainly there is substance in the charge; but is it rightly directed?
>
> If he writes of marriage and of other relationships about which he knows or cares little, it is because he has no choice but to masquerade. Both convention and the law demand it. In society the homosexual's life must be discreetly concealed. As material for drama, that life must be even more intensely concealed. If he is to write of his experience, he must invent a two-sex version of the one-sex experience that he really knows. It is we who insist on it, not he.

Kauffmann concluded that the homosexual must be free to write of what he knows best, namely his own homosexual experience, rather than try to disguise it. In this way he might avoid the "viciousness toward women," the "lurid violence," and the "tranvestite sexual exhibitionism" that Kauffmann specifically charged him with when he attempted to deal with heterosexual themes.

Kauffmann's article had strong impact if only because the issues he raised, while often the topic of whispered discussion, had not before been aired so publicly. People at the time gossiped that the quarrelsome marriage Edward Albee pictured in *Who's Afraid of Virginia Woolf?* was really a homosexual ménage. If so, was the public the victim of a hoax or, worse still, a helpless dupe? [7]

[7] John Osborne echoed the familiar *Virginia Woolf* suspicion in his play about homosexuals, *A Patriot for Me,* in the following exchange between the leading character, Redl, and Colonel Oblensky:

> *Oblensky:* It isn't any fun having no clear idea of the future, is it? And you can't re-make your past. And then when one of you writes a book about yourselves, you pretend it's something else, that it's about married people and not two men together. . . . That is not honest, Alfred.
> *Redl:* Don't be maudlin, Colonel.

Psychoanalysts say that it really doesn't matter very much, because homosexual relationships always emulate heterosexual relationships. If a homosexual writes about a relationship between two individuals involving sex, he will, Dr. Kaplan says, cast it in "the paradigm of such relationships," the marriage of a man and woman. The struggle doesn't so much involve gender differences as emotional and intellectual differences, and these battles can be played out just as well by persons of the same sex as by persons of opposite sexes.

The whole dispute means very little to professional theater people, regardless of their sympathies or proclivities. Herman Shumlin, for example, says homosexuality has little or no effect on drama. "Every play is the end result of a number of characteristics possessed by the writer, whether he is homosexual, heterosexual, or asexual," Mr. Shumlin says. "The play is the end product of his make-up. It comes out of his mind, his beliefs, his instincts, and his personality.

"Take a group of playwrights who are all dead now—Moss Hart, Maxwell Anderson, Robert Sherwood—you couldn't think of them in terms of that question. Their plays are the result of what they are. One doesn't look for differences of homosexuality or heterosexuality in their plays. I believe the homosexual playwright can be just as objective as the heterosexual playwright. In fact, because a playwright's homosexuality is an intense problem in his life, he may therefore gain insights that are far more accurate. We know that Plato was a homosexual and Socrates was a homosexual, but what Plato wrote of Socrates' philosophy had little to do with homosexuality. It had to do with truth, beauty, and the humanities."

From the psychoanalytic point of view, one area at least seems closed to the homosexual writer. "I don't think he can contribute any understanding to advanced Oedipal problems involving feelings of guilt, a sense of tragedy, and questions of advanced emotionality," Dr. Kaplan says. "But then many heterosexual writers can't handle them, either.

Genet, who is a homosexual, deals beautifully with illusion and the difference between illusion and reality, with truth and with physical representations. But I don't think Genet could write what it means to sacrifice a piece of your life to a child. I don't think he is capable of understanding that."

Psychoanalytic thinking also rejects the notion that the homosexual is endowed with greater creative sensitivity, a claim vehemently made by homosexuals on behalf of themselves and other homosexuals—the "chosen people" syndrome. Homosexuals, in other words, are neither any better nor any worse in their professional capacities than anyone else.

Marriage in the theater—whether the union is theater-to-theater or theater-to-nontheater—carries a special burden of inconvenience: different hours, job separation, competitiveness, career jealousy, unequal recognition. Yet there are many harmonious and fruitful theater marriages, and the theatrical family, like the circus family in which talent and skill are handed down from one generation to the next, is an attractive, responsible, and cohesive tradition.

There are all kinds of theatrical marriages, and many of them thrive. A producer may marry an actress who works for him, or an actress may marry an agent who then works for her. Husband-and-wife acting teams take their bows together and one doesn't mind if the other gets more applause. Writer marries writer and both continue to write plays, jointly or separately. (One remarkable theatrical marriage unites a successful actress-playwright with an equally successful playwright-novelist-director.) There are also good designer-designer, agent-agent, and producer-producer marriages.

But most lasting theater marriages are those in which one partner defers to the other's career. The very factors that encourage intratheater romance (special working hours, career concentration, stage intimacy) also, perversely, work to negate such relationships. A pretty young actress says, "My acting is already a bone of contention with my boy friends. The actor's first concern, necessarily, is with self. I never want to marry an actor, but I want to be married and have children." The actress already senses that her career, while not precluding happy marriage, makes its attainment more difficult.

Theatrical life not only makes it more difficult for theater people to marry, but also easier for them to separate. Where both parties are working professionals, there is financial independence, and each party therefore has more power to break up the marriage. The same, of course, would be true of marriages in other professions, but the built-in rivalry of the stage sparks the volatility of theatrical marriages.

A successful marriage demands community of interest. If a couple suffers career separation—if he goes to Hollywood to make a film while she remains in New York with a play— an impossible strain may be imposed on the marriage. Similarly, if each achieves a radically different rate of progress in his work, the marriage may be jeopardized. If one partner continually gains more applause, the other may become depressed. Theatrical marriages often waver over the willingness of one partner to sacrifice for the other; usually only a man who is powerful in a noncompetitive area can freely accept the success of a star wife (the Carlo Ponti-Sophia Loren relationship).

A theatrical marriage may start as a union of equals, but the fortunes of show business are such that eventually, perhaps suddenly, the balance can shift. The imbalance is more acute when the wife becomes the star and the husband slips into a subordinate position and roles are reversed. If he stays in the entertainment world, he will have to devote himself increasingly to his wife's career as her manager, overseeing her affairs, handling contractual details, fussing over her grooming, diet, and creature comforts. As a marriage style, this relationship is often characterized by the absence of sexual contact between the partners, as when a lesbian actress is married to homosexual manager. Frankly entered

junct to work and life. Today's young actors do not shrink from the processes of psychoanalysis, unlike many of their parents, for whom the act of asking for help was considered shameful and a confession of failure.

A young actor suffering from a loss of interest in himself, unable to face the humiliations of job hunting, begins to see a psychiatrist. A young actress, an all-around schoolgirl, good at sports, elected a class officer, comes to New York to take up acting and finds herself confused ("Perhaps it's New York, perhaps it's the nature of the business"). She goes to an analyst. Some bizarre sexual practices drive distraught victims to the analyst's couch. Manhattan doctors have treated more than one casualty of encounters with a talented homosexual theatrical designer with severe sado-masochistic tendencies. The damage was more psychic than physical even though it was the designer's particular pleasure to dress up in the uniform of a prison guard, chain his homosexual "guests" to a table, and pretend to beat them.

Analysis requires an "adult ego structure" and therefore a certain kind of actor, identified by psychiatrists as the prototype of the Hollywood star, is regarded as unanalyzable. He is childlike, hysteric, narcissistic, and needs constant approval. Doctors consider him incapable of enduring the necessary regression that goes with "deep analysis." If such actors see psychiatrists, the relationship is usually only a supportive one. The maturity necessary for analysis is found more often in writers, producers, and directors than in actors. Each time a serious actor takes on a new role he puts himself through a rigorous self-examination and motivational self-analysis. In doing so he deals himself cards right out of the Freudian deck. The Actors Studio, founded in 1947 by Elia Kazan, Cheryl Crawford, and Robert Lewis, but bearing the emphatic personal stamp of Lee Strasberg, who has been its artistic director since 1951, has borrowed Freudian techniques in developing the introspective Method approach to acting. Strasberg himself—intent, staring, unsmiling, given to profound pauses and hesitations—seems more like a psychoanalyst than an acting coach. Sessions at the Studio resemble the analytic hour in structure. First the actors do a scene, then Strasberg asks them to explain what they have done and why they did it. Afterwards he launches into his own extensive diagnosis.

Analysis permeates the modern theater. To the generation now in its thirties and forties it may have come late, but it is here. To actors in their twenties analysis came early and is part of their lives. An actress who works with this age group says, "The need for analysis relates to the work. It's such an unbalanced, insecure profession, full of wild people who are involved in dreams. For them, the theater seems a place of salvation. The theater is where you can use your own hang-ups in your work. The 'new theater' acting is much more self-exposure, in an emotional sense. [Nudity is part of this expression, too.] Now the kind of breakthrough that only used to happen in an analyst's office happens in an acting workshop. Using acting exercises, an actor comes into contact with hidden areas of himself and this results in a heightened awareness of self."

Young actors, like young people everywhere, experiment with mind-expanding drugs. All of the kids smoke marijuana, the same actress says, but most of them have learned to use it wisely and would no more think of showing up for work "high" than their elders would show up drunk. Smoking pot has filtered upward; now the young actors are "turning on" the older group, just as the older group turned them on with psychoanalysis.

The new morality that expresses itself in extremes of sexual experimentation and permissiveness reached center stage in the late 1960's, actually as well as figuratively. A series of "entertainments" exploited nudity, homosexuality, and sexual congress in explicit variations.

Nudity in the theater is of course hardly new. In their "Artists and Models" shows of the 1920's the Shuberts posed naked girls—or girls so flimsily clothed as to seem naked—in various reclining, leaning, and kneeling attitudes on multilevel stage settings. At a rehearsal one day in 1923, J. J. Shubert, in a rage at the costuming of his chorus girls, ripped down the blouse of one girl in front of the entire cast. The show opened bare above the waist.

The nudity of the 1960's has been promoted not so much by venally commercial entrepreneurs as by the actors themselves. Except for one startling flash of nudity in the visiting Royal Shakespeare Theatre's production of *Marat/Sade* in 1966—when Marat rose from his tub, his naked backside to the audience—nudity has been used less to make a dramatic point than to expose a new life style and promote the new morality.[10] Certainly this is what Julian Beck and Judith Malina, the co-founders and co-directors of the Living Theater, intended when they returned to New York in 1968 with their production of *Paradise Now,* marching up and down theater aisles shouting, "I am not allowed to take off my clothes!" and performing an incredibly choreographed act of three-way copulation for an intent audience that rose from their seats in the auditorium and gathered onstage to watch. In this sort of expression the actors themselves have actively cooperated; the meek compliance of J. J. Shubert's chorus girls among today's motivated actors would be unthinkable. The performers in *Hair* appear nude because it seems natural to them to do so. Sally Kirkland, a pioneer in the new nudity, appeared nude, tied to a chair, and speechless for nearly fifty minutes in an off-Broadway play called *Sweet Eros* by Terrence McNally in 1968. For Miss Kirkland, a spirited and daring young actress, nudity has more to do with esthetics and a "higher truth" than middle-class concepts of courage. She says, "I came to the theater, as others have, by way of painting and dance. As a painter, I had for my heroes Botticelli and Modigliani; as a dancer, Isadora Duncan, and so the carry-over on the stage of a nude body seemed to me not only stylistically expressive, but a perfectly natural extension of my beliefs." [11]

[10] Marat's nakedness was much less shocking than the visibly erect phallus of another character, Duperret, one of the lunatics in the asylum of Charenton, described in the play as an eroto-maniac.

[11] In a *New York Times* drama section symposium on nudity, June 22, 1969.

Nudity reached its fullest expression in *Oh! Calcutta!*, a revue conceived by English critic Kenneth Tynan and presented in the spring of 1969 in a large off-Broadway theater (allusively named the Eden for the occasion), with the producer charging twenty-five dollars a ticket in the first two rows. In group musical numbers, five actors and five actresses appear totally nude; in the interspersed sketches they appear clothed, partially clothed, or nude and in various sexual postures. The show has occasioned a downpour of public discussion and comment. The cast line is taken by Margo Sappington, a dancer who appears in the show's most erotic dance duet, who says, "In my opinion, nudity's main justification in the theater is context. An actor wears a costume to create an atmosphere of reality and when this atmosphere of reality calls for skin as the costume, any imitation is ludicrous."

At least there is a total absence of euphemism in *Oh! Calcutta!* Miss Sappington justifies nudity solely on artistic grounds, and yet nudity was employed clearly for other purposes in the work—to make social and political points— in a series of sketches elaborating on the sex act. Most critics dismissed the sketches as vulgar and/or inept.

Beyond the voyeurism of *Oh! Calcutta!* lies the sensate theater of off-Broadway in which actual physical contact (groping, feeling, touching) is celebrated between cast and audience. The sensate theater, Dr. Kaplan points out, exists because the surfeit of modern communications (we suffer from an overload of pictures, information, and conveyed experience) has caused "the obliteration of privacy" and established "a new standard for achievement." It is no longer enough simply to want what someone else has; now we must *feel* what the other person feels. This rapacious curiosity, in Dr. Kaplan's judgment, accounts for the eagerness with which drug users compare notes about their "trips" and carries over into sexual experience for the general population.

Compared with this definition, the defense of Jacques Levy, the director of *Oh! Calcutta!*, seems ingenuous. "I think that the effect of *Oh! Calcutta!* is that nudity will be used whenever the script calls for it. I think we've done away with the silliness and hypocrisy. After all, this is what Busby Berkeley would love to have done."

Levy seems to be saying that the expression of sex in the theater should duplicate as nearly as possible the physical conditions of sex in real life. Levy tells the following story: "There's a couple I know who went to see *Oh! Calcutta!* They're straight, middle-class people, and they were shocked and offended by the show, but they liked it. Shortly after they saw it, they went to *Plaza Suite*. Normally, they told me, they would have liked it, but they were bored with it after *Oh! Calcutta!* In the big sex scene in *Plaza Suite* a man puts his hand on the girl's thigh. Normally that would have been quite shocking, but not after *Oh! Calcutta!* They said they nearly fell asleep in the play."

In Jacques Levy's terms, *Oh! Calcutta!* may have priced sex right out of the market. The question most people leave the show asking is what else is left to do on the stage? In his review Walter Kerr was driven to note that no one in *Oh! Calcutta!* becomes "potent even when engaging in the actions of intercourse." Irene Mayer Selznick's two-word critique of the show is "male impotence." Unveiled sex on the stage, made specific, becomes essentially anti-erotic, certainly for performers and usually for audience, which relapses into apathy and surfeit.

Levy adopted his own rehearsal methodology for inducing the actors to behave naturally while performing in the nude before a large, curious audience. At the beginning of rehearsal each actor was given a white bathrobe (the show opens with the actors upstage in half light, back to audience, discarding street clothes and donning bathrobes). Gradually, in rehearsal (the usual four-week rehearsal was extended to seven weeks), the bathrobes were discarded. Levy's purpose was to accustom the actors to being nude before each other. Once adjusted to their own nudity, they were able, in Levy's words, to give each other "strength and support." Appearing in front of their first audience naturally made the cast nervous, but the jump from baring themselves to each other to baring themselves to the public was easy. By the end of the show's opening number, the five male and five female performers discard their robes and stand full-face to the audience on the forestage line, defiantly naked.

Audiences find it difficult to grasp the notion that for the actors themselves nudity is just another level of self-exposure. For actors the primary stage sensation, as we know, is a figurative nudity, a baring of self, an unmasking of personality, an exposure of emotions. As Levy rightly says, "I don't know why it should be braver for an actor to appear in the nude than it is for him to expose his innermost feelings, as he does all the time on the stage. After all, when you're naked you're not showing a lot." Nicol Williamson, the English actor who performed in John Osborne's *Inadmissible Evidence* in a searingly confessional role and brought his unique interpretation of Hamlet to New York, has written, "I am always stripped naked every time I go on a stage. When I did *Diary of a Madman,* for example, I was alone on stage during the entire play and I had to present a man who was repressed and bitter, a confirmed onanist. To perform this kind of humiliating truth is always more painfully naked than the simple act of divesting oneself of one's garments."

When she was a dramatic actress starting voice lessons, Rosemary Murphy was once asked what she would think of appearing in a musical that required her to be nude in one scene. "That doesn't worry me," she replied. "What worries me is the singing."

Onstage nudity is the theater's sometimes clumsily and crudely executed response to a variety of challenges—artistic, social, moral, and commercial. It is the theater's answer to the frankness and physical realism of books and films. It is an assault on the hypocrisy of middle-class morality. It is one answer to the charge that theater is dull and irrelevant. Much of the "new theater," in which nudity has become a central article of faith, is an attempt to experiment with esthetic illusion. Santayana, Dr. Kaplan recalls, said that life is what is lyric in form, comic in execution, and tragic in fate. Dr. Kaplan views an entertainment such as *Oh! Calcutta!* as an experimental comic view in dramatic form of the sexual side of life.

This is the charitable view. A less friendly appraisal is made by Dr. Socarides. Such entertainments as *Oh! Calcutta!*, he feels, particularly in the scenes of explicit sex, are the work of people whose sexual inadequacies lead them to belittle normal sexual response. "If everything goes, then nothing is important," says Dr. Socarides. "This is the dehumanization of sex by men who cannot have normal sexual relations with women."

In any case, the sensate theater necessarily defeats dramatic purpose, for perception must take place at a decent distance from its object; sensation, as direct contact, is the enemy of perception. It has been pointed out that the purpose of theater is not to cause "behavior" in an audience by trying to involve them in the stage action but to stimulate perception. For that it is better for the audience to remain passive and keep its distance from the actors.

Broadway's comprehension of the breakthroughs made by the new theater is limited to exploiting its commercial possibilities. Conservative critics and literate playwrights remain its enemies. But perhaps its most contemptuous rejection has come from the black theater. A black actress, Judyann Elder, has written:

> This preoccupation with nudity under the guise of "sexual liberation" is a white hang-up. Too many white "artists" are constantly making a pretense of coming up with new forms, new ideas, and experiments. This is due to the fact that they are bankrupt when it comes to the tormenting business of artistic creation out of the human condition as it is. This task is much more difficult to confront.[12]

The sensate and participatory theater of nudity and sexual explicitness perhaps was doomed before it started. The theater had issued an impossible invitation to the audience

[12] *The New York Times,* June 22, 1969.

to "participate" with the actors on the stage, to see, feel, and know more than they had ever seen, felt, and known before. But the invitation promised too much, the nature of an essentially private experience—the sex act—was cheapened by overexposure, and the party to which everyone was invited, and many came, was over moments after it began.

CHAPTER ELEVEN

Never a Theater, Always a Theater

Gulliver, as we know, visited four imaginary lands inhabited respectively by the Lilliputians, the Brobdingnagians, Laputans, and Houyhnhnms. In all lands, he found disenchantment, corruption, and disillusion. Of course, he had not yet visited Broadway. If Swift had known of the world of the playmakers, he might have said to his protagonist, "Spend a year with the New York theater. See every play, examine its every aspect, traverse the district, discuss its ways of life with its inhabitants. And after a year of visiting this region, tell me what you think of it and of the larger society which it reflects."

What might Gulliver have written of the commercial American theater in 1970? How might he have judged America itself on the basis of this tiny business that calls itself an art form, practices its crafts in shabby surroundings, sickens perceptibly from year to year, condones laxity and incompetence in its administration, brings distress to its practitioners, operates in an atmosphere of hysteria, avarice, confusion, and decay?

It is easy to be pessimistic about the theater. Its problems are overwhelming. It is beset by an impossible inflation. Its theaters are old. Its costs are mounting alarmingly. Its craft unions, arrogant with power, negotiate crippling contracts with the industry's divided and impotent leaders. Its production costs have multiplied thirty times in half a century. Its audience dwindles steadily. The average Broadway theatergoer is middle-aged—the young people are gone; other forms of entertainment have won them over. And its medieval ticket system groans under the weight of inefficiency and deceit.

The people of the theater work under difficult and archaic conditions. Failure is endemic, the basic ingredient of theater. Most actors cannot find employment in the theater. Most plays are flops. The theater itself fails to hold on to its rare successes. An actor launched on Broadway is almost at once lost to Broadway when the medium that gave him fame makes him highly employable elsewhere. Successful playwrights, directors, and designers find films and television more enduring and higher paying. The mortality rate of production chokes off new producers almost as quickly as they emerge. In short, nothing can be predicted with more certainty for the theater than its continued ill health.

Yet something positive is happening. In England in the 1950's director Joan Littlewood sounded a defiant note. "What is theater?" she demanded. "I want to tear the theater down. There is more life in the street. There is more theater in a bar." She was not alone in Britain. The London theater had become smug, complacent, and rigid. Miss Littlewood and a corps of rebellious young actors, directors, and writers opted for change, and they have altered the fabric of the British theater. On Broadway sometime in the 1960's, in the second half of the decade, whispers turned into shouts. The theater woke up to find itself in a new world. And it will never be the same again.

The "new theater" is companion to the youth rebellion, the generation gap, the failure of the old politics, the loathing for the Vietnam War. It began in the lofts and basements of off-Broadway and it is swiftly moving uptown. The old rules are under attack. Directors and actors are crowding the playwright at one end and the producer at the other. Movement and feeling have become more important than words and characterization. Improvisation, which threatens the written word, has become a major tool of the actor. Subject matter has shifted violently; instead of chronicling psychological interaction among characters, plays now relate more strongly to community and world issues. Plays are becoming less the product of an individual intellect and more the collective work of writers, directors, and actors living and working together on a cooperative basis. Plays are short, vivid, and violent, no longer mannered and leisurely.

Paddy Chayefsky, now "retired" from Broadway, complains that the "noble theater," the theater that as recently as 1961 had allowed him to write *Gideon* in iambic pentameter, is gone. A master craftsman like Arthur Miller wonders what has become of the theater in which his powerful realistic techniques flourished. The writers of the new theater do not find their models in Miller, Chayefsky, Tennessee Williams, William Inge, Robert Anderson—the psychological realists of the old school. They find the old theater lacking in "relevancy" and the old practitioners unskilled in adapting themselves to the impact of new media. The new theater is film-oriented, television-oriented, picture-oriented. The older critics and writers deplore the sketchiness of the one-act form, but the new theater has been watching films and studying the way television shapes its audience to accept the quick story—the Vietnam battle described in two minutes, the thirty-second commercial with its fast sell. Today's audience, the new craftsmen feel, is preconditioned to the one-act play with its quick-thrust message for the medium.

In 1970 the American theater finds itself occupying sev-

eral camps. The Broadway establishment is aging, traditional, tired, insecure, and fearful, like Rome awaiting the
arrival of the Goths. The anti-establishment, the new theater, is radical, fresh, self-assured, defiant, and innovative.
Its facilities are poor, its theaters scattered, its financial
resource limited, but it has the overpowering advantage of
youth—and numbers. But the theater is a place of many
mansions, and can usefully accommodate all comers.

There is still another theater that has attracted attention in the past few years. A decade ago, plays dealing with
blacks in American life were nonexistent. A musical like
No Strings, which described the love affair between a black
girl and a white man, was considered shocking in 1961. Black
attendance at Broadway and off-Broadway shows was negli-
gible. The real breakthrough in the development of black
theater-consciousness oddly enough came with a work by a
white author in 1962, the American premiere off-Broadway
of Jean Genet's *The Blacks.*

Black militancy and the self-assertiveness of black playwrights have created a black theater that disavows both the
old establishment and the new theater, but is nevertheless
much closer in its fundamental spirit of revolt to the new
than to the old.

Where once there were almost no black playwrights, there
now are many, and their number is increasing. Writers such
as Douglas Turner Ward (*Day of Absence*), Ed Bullins (*The
Electronic Nigger*), Charles Gordone (*No Place to Be Some-
Body*), and Lonne Elder III (*Ceremonies in Dark Old Men*)
all write in traditional style, but their content is unique,
they are "hung up" on their blackness and the problems of
the black experience.

The special problem of the black playwright is recognition
and identification, not so much in the white world as in the
black world. The mature black writer shuns the destructive-
ness of black extremism, yet resists the pressures of the white
establishment. Black theater, which has already created a
stunning body of work, promises urgency and controversy

for the American theater of the future. "We black playwrights must explore the conditions that blackness survives under and around," says Lonne Elder. "We must write about the whole American confrontation of terror and violence, excitement and pity. In the face of this we conduct ourselves in a 'normal' fashion."

The theater has its own mythology—myths of bravery, self-reliance, perseverance, victory over odds. The myth of the "fabulous invalid"—always ailing, never dying—is the most persistent. "The show must go on" is another myth that celebrates the theater's ability to keep going no matter what. The myths are sentimental and pietistic, linked with the Judaeo-Christian ethic, itself under violent attack.

Somehow or other, the myths embody an enduring truth. There is an old actor's aphorism: "There is never a job, there is always a job. There is never a play, there is always a play. There is never a theater, there is always a theater."

In 1970 the theater—divided, disordered, and dejected—shows signs of profiting from its own chaos. Plays and playwrights are being turned out in what director Alan Schneider calls a "creative explosion." New theaters are being built, uptown and down, all over New York. Most of them are small playhouses in off-Broadway style, but there will soon be three of them for every Broadway theater. As the old theaters of the district fall to the wrecker, new, larger, more practical theaters are being planned, thanks to an enlightened New York City administration.

A basic talent of the American theater is that it has learned somehow to survive. It may not be recognizable from one generation to another, but it will survive. It may not survive as a piece of geography, but it will survive as a medium of expression. Like the Chinese, the theater absorbs its enemies.

The theater, in another strange way, needs hardship and hunger to survive. When costs become prohibitive, young artists find new ways and places to provide theater. Off-

Broadway expanded because Broadway was feudal and costly. It became rich in achievement in spite, or perhaps because, of its material poverty.

In the decades to come the barriers between the media will break down. Broadway, in John Wharton's phrase, has been the "creative core" where literally all American drama of lasting worth has originated. Great writers and actors have gone forth from Broadway, but the flow has always been one-way. Hollywood is separated from Broadway by 3,000 miles, and no satisfactory recirculation system has been devised to replenish the theater and somehow compensate for its lost talent.

One solution is already on the drawing boards—a New York City film production center adjacent to the theater district. The old despotic system of Hollywood stardom is fading. Film production is moving east. The "ordinary-looking" young actors of the theater are becoming the new stars of films. For all its hardships, the theater overflows with talent. It has brilliant actors, designers, directors, writers, producers. Theater cannot utilize all this talent consistently, and the other media steal it away, but it is in the professional theatrical environment—stimulating, disciplined, principled, and humanistic—that talent flourishes most freely. From a free interchange of talent all media will benefit, and New York is properly the hub of the interchange.

If Gulliver were to visit Broadway in 1970, he might expound on its venality, its pettiness, its corruption, its preoccupation with failure. He might end his travel tale on a note of characteristic Swiftian gloom. And he would be right.

But he would also have to describe its charm, its humor, its hospitality to talent, its attraction for strangers, its power to transmit ideas. He might end the description of his journey on a note of hope. And he would be right.

For, in the end, as Robert Whitehead once put it, "Theater encompasses everything, it is victimized by everything, and, finally, it expresses everything."

Index

311

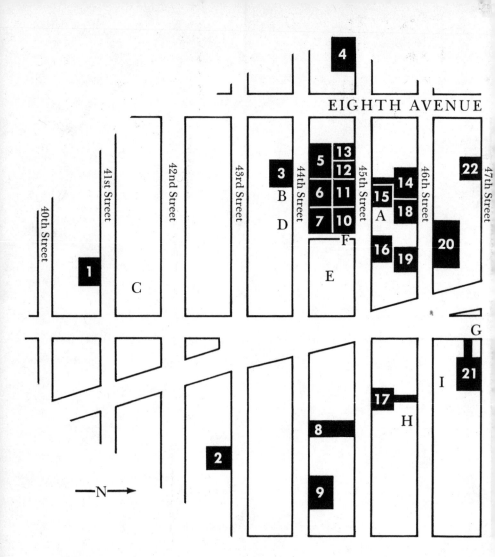

THEATERS

1	Billy Rose	12	Royale	24	Ethel Barrymore
2	Henry Miller's	13	Golden	25	Longacre
3	St. James	14	Imperial	26	Cort
4	Martin Beck	15	Music Box	27	Eugene O'Neill
5	Majestic	16	Morosco	28	Ambassador
6	Broadhurst	17	Lyceum	29	Winter Garden
7	Shubert	18	46th Street	30	Mark Hellinger
8	Hudson	19	Helen Hayes	31	Alvin
9	Belasco	20	Lunt-Fontanne	32	ANTA
10	Booth	21	Palace	33	Broadway
11	Plymouth	22	Brooks Atkinson	34	George Abbott
		23	Biltmore		(54th Street)

Shakespeare on Screen

An International
Filmography and Videography

Kenneth S. Rothwell
and
Annabelle Henkin Melzer

Neal-Schuman Publishers, Inc.
New York   London

WINGATE UNIVERSITY LIBRARY

Cover reproduction: The Granger Collection

Published by Neal-Schuman Publishers, Inc.
23 Leonard Street
New York, NY 10013

Copyright © 1990 by Kenneth S. Rothwell and Annabelle Henkin Melzer

All rights reserved. Reproduction of this book, in whole or in part,
without written permission of the publisher is prohibited.

Printed and bound in the United States of America

This book is printed on acid-free paper which meets the standard
established by the American National Standard Institute Committee for
Information Science—Permanence of Paper for Printed Library
Materials. (Z—39—48, 1984).

Library of Congress Cataloging-in-Publication Data

Rothwell, Kenneth S. (Kenneth Sprague).
   Shakespeare on screen: an international filmography and videography
   / compiled by Kenneth S. Rothwell and Annabelle Henkin Melzer.

   Includes bibliographical references.
   1. Shakespeare, William, 1564-1616—Film and video
adaptations.   I. Melzer, Annabelle Henkin.   II. Title.
PR3093.R68   1990   016.79143'75—dc20   89-13509
ISBN 1-55570-049-7

For Dr. Bernice W. Kliman,
friend and colleague

Table of Contents

Illustrations

Preface

Shakespeare on Screen: An International Filmography and Videography fills a previously unmet need for a reference guide to a growing academic field. The video revolution has combined with emerging concepts in literary theory to give a strong rationale for the study in schools and universities of Shakespearean performance. The idea of a "performance text" as complementary to a printed text has encouraged teachers and scholars to think not only about texts on the page but also about those on stage and screen. At the same time dramatic advances in video technology have transformed what post-modernist critics have called "intertextuality" (the multiple ways that signs and words can interact with one another) from a theory into a reality. Students who have never seen a live Shakespeare production in a theatre can now approximate, though not replicate, the experience with their VCRs. The entire methodology for both teaching and studying Shakespeare will inevitably be reshaped by this relatively inexpensive tool for mechanical reproduction. It is a neo-Gutenberg phenomenon that pays tribute to the prescience of the late Marshall McLuhan.

Shakespeare on Screen grew out of the efforts, at first parallel and then converging, of the editors. The concept underlying the project belongs to Dr. Melzer who saw it as a way of presenting "for the first time . . . to the theatre artist, student, teacher and researcher, data on the collected body of material on theatre, available on film and videotape." Her original plan was to include all dramatic productions, not merely Shakespeare's, in a multi-volume work.

Dr. Melzer envisioned this work as a way to make the teaching of theatre studies more effective through the use of film and video. She hoped that it would ". . . allow the viewer to study theatre-in-performance, in a new way . . . to set up one performance, or performer, alongside another, to investigate aspects of style, form, interpretation, influences, or other resonances." In addition, by directing the viewer to available materials, the guide would help bring screened Shakespeare to areas where live performances were unavailable. Dr Melzer also recognized the utility of such a compilation for the researcher studying the "performance works of a specific theatre artist," as well as its value for a student who could learn from " . . . the finest master teachers, directors, acting coaches, designers, mimes or unique performers whose methods of work defy categories or titles." She believed that the mere existence of this compilation would encourage "new documentation of theatre work on film and video, by presenting very clearly a full compilation of just what does already exist in the field."

Because so ambitious a project required help, in 1985 Dr. Melzer asked me to take primary responsibility for compiling a separate volume on the film and video treatments of the Shakespearean canon. As co-editor and co-founder (with Dr. Bernice W. Kliman) in 1976 of the *Shakespeare on Film Newsletter* and having already been independently engaged by 1985 in the compilation of a Shakespeare-on-screen bibliography and filmography, I was glad to join forces with Dr. Melzer.

Purpose and Scope

While other Shakespeare filmographies and videographies exist (see Bibliography, p. 337), *Shakespeare on Screen* uniquely offers comprehensiveness for researchers and utility for teachers. It is a guide to a major share of films and videos based on Shakespeare's plays that have been produced since 1899—up to and including the 1989 Kenneth Branagh *Henry V*—with the exception of certain silent films that are mostly no longer in existence, as noted at the end of this preface. With more than 750 entries, it covers a wider variety of genres and provides more up-to-date information than any other single reference work in the field. It includes not only the major film adaptations but also modernizations, spinoffs, musical and dance versions, abridgments, travesties and excerpts. It also lists a major share of significant documentary and video films about Shakespeare's life and times, theatre and poetry, as well as documentaries about the actors and directors who have brought his plays to life. In addition, it covers television performances in the United States, Great Britain, Europe, and South America. Each major production receives an entry that gives such information as excerpts of critical commentary, precis of the production, cast and production credits, country of origin and year of production or release, the target audience, supplemental bibliography, and names and locations of distributors and archives. Keys to abbreviations used in the text are set forth preceding the section of entries and include lists for the plays, scholarly books and journals referred to in the text and in the bibliography. A key to abbreviations used for distributors and archives will be found on page 399. By offering information about how to find videos and films, the book becomes useful not only to scholars but also to classroom teachers as a "hands-on" reference. In short, it locates and describes the extensive visual record of Shakespeare's work, facilitating the tasks of teachers and scholars and enriching the student's sources for study.

Every effort has been made to give easy access to the materials described by providing extensive indexes. In addition to the index which locates entries (plays, sonnets and documentaries) by sequence number, there are indexes to entries which are a part of series or genres (such as ballet, opera, An Age of Kings, French silents, Shakespeare in Perspective, etc.), and an index to films and videos by the year of production. Over 6000 names are listed in other indexes to actors, speakers, and panelists; to directors, composers, designers, and other production personnel; and to authors, critics, editors, and compilers. There is also an annotated bibliography.

Method of Compilation

An original ambition to screen every single item in the filmography in a quest for absolute accuracy proved quixotic. In that plan film/video credits were to have been transcribed directly from the screen rather than from printed sources. It soon became apparent, however, that the purist must yield to the pragmatist. Not only do screen credits themselves sometimes err but certainly no human being could live long enough to achieve such a goal. Fortunately, the arrival of the video revolution midway through the project made it possible to screen much that previously had to be tracked down to archives in remote cities. As a result I estimate that more than half of the existing films and videos listed have been personally screened. As for the rest, they have been validated as thoroughly as possible by checking with duly credited reliable publications. Cast credits, when not directly taken from the screen, have been verified against at least two other references whenever possible. In cases where discrepancies were found in the spelling of actors' names— sometimes even on the same press release or program—an attempt has been made to consult a third source. Even so, there will inevitably be some misspellings of actors' names, as well as other varieties of human errors, which the editors, if notified, will gratefully acknowledge and gladly correct in subsequent editions.

Dr. Melzer's contribution to the preparation of this volume included a bibliographical card file, and the results of research at the following European archives: *La videothèque 'Arts du Spectacle' à la maison Jean Vilar,* Avignon, France; *Archivo Storico del Piccolo Teatro di Milano,* Milan; *Archivo Storico, Biennale di Venezia,* Venice; Goethe Institute, New York City; *Institut fur Theaterwissenschaft, Universitat München,* Germany; *Videoteca Centro Teatro Ateneo,* Rome; *Cineteca Nastroteca della Radiotelevisione Italiana* (RAI), Turin; *Katholieke Universiteit Leuven,* Belgium; *Centrum voor Taal-en Literatuurwetanschap Vrije Universiteit Brussel,* Belgium. Dr. Melzer additionally conducted research at the Lincoln Center Library of the Performing Arts, New York City. Through her NEH grant she also provided access to the database software program called MELBASE developed by Dr. James D. Anderson of Rutgers University. It considerably eased the labor.

For my part, I explored the film archives of the Folger Shakespeare Library and the Motion Picture Division of the Library of Congress, Washington D.C.; the Museum of Broadcasting, the Museum of Modern Art, and the Lincoln Center Library of Performing Arts, New York City; and the National Film Archive of the British Film Institute, London. In 1988, with the assistance of a grant from the University of Vermont Graduate College, I also traveled to the BBC Written Archives Centre, Caversham Park, Reading, to compile the record of Shakespeare on British television, which, so far as I know, is published in its entirety in the United States for the first time in this volume. Admittedly the job is never done. Even as I write this I am aware of a new video program about the discovery of the foundations of the Rose and Globe playhouses on London's Bankside, which came too late to be incorporated in this volume. For this and other updates, readers should consult future issues of the *Shakespeare on Film Newsletter* (see Bibliography, p. 337).

A final word. To supplement this reference work, Robert Hamilton Ball's *Shakespeare on Silent Film* (q.v.) remains indispensable. It has been impossible, and indeed would be redundant, to repeat everything in his monumental work. Only silent films of rare historical significance or those that the compiler has been able to screen personally have therefore been included. By the same token, British users will want to refer also to Olwen Terris' *List of Audio/Visual Materials Available in the UK* for additional help. For other useful Shakespeare filmographies, such as the 1964 Weisbaden *Shakespeare Im Film*, see the annotated bibliography.

Kenneth S. Rothwell
Burlington, Vermont
July 26, 1990

Acknowledgments

We are deeply grateful to very many institutions and people for help in completing this volume. For financial assistance, the National Endowment for the Humanities, Rutgers University, and the Graduate College of the University of Vermont belong first on the list. Very special thanks also go to Olwen Terris of the British Universities Film & Video Council for generously sharing the council's data on British film distributors. Contributions by computer specialists such as Dr. James D. Anderson of the School of Communication, Information and Library Studies, Rutgers, The State University of New Jersey, and Mr. Peter Bekker, independent computer consultant, take on a special status in view of the vital role of electronics in developing the manuscript.

Many archivists also cooperated: Joseph Empsucha, Barry Parker, Candace Bothwell, and Betsy Walsh of the Folger Shakespeare Library; Patrick J. Sheehan of the Motion Picture Division of the Library of Congress; Betty Corwin of the Lincoln Center Library of the Performing Arts, New York City; Elias Savada, American Film Institute cataloger; Jacqueline Kavanagh, and Deborah Butler of the BBC Written Archives Centre, Reading; Gillian Hartnoll of the British Film Institute Library; Roger Holman of the National Film Archive, London; Terry Geesken and Mary Corliss of the Museum of Modern Art Film Library, New York City. Public relations people who generously helped were Richard Bornstein of The Samuel Goldwyn Company; Ellen Nesselrode Hoch of Hallmark Cards, Inc., Kansas City; Constance L. Stone and Timothy Hallinan of

TelEd Inc., Los Angeles; and Fernando Meneses of TV Globo Network of Brazil.

Private individuals who offered advice and counsel include Dr. Bernice W. Kliman, co-editor of *The Shakespeare on Film Newsletter*; Dr. H. Philip Bolton; Prof. Jack J. Jorgens and Ms. Christina Egloff, who donated their hundreds of bibliographical cards; Milton Crouch and James Barickman of the Libraries and Martha Day and Martha Patry of the Media Center at the University of Vermont. Students who helped were Richard Whitaker and Sarah Wood. The late Dr. Roger Manvell was an early supporter; Dr. Frank Manchel has also shared his wide knowledge of film; and Mr. Sam Wanamaker of the International Shakespeare Globe Centre in London has been consistently encouraging. Prof. Virginia Clark of the University of Vermont English Department persuaded me to enroll in a computer class, and for that push I am grateful.

Special thanks also go to Susan Holt and Ellen Mangin Ros of Neal-Schuman; Mary Carroll Rothwell, Esq., for tracking *Romeo and Juliet* to Brazil for her father; and to Lyn Gregg Rothwell, for sharing her incomparable knowledge of WORDSTAR 5.5 and providing wifely therapy for jangled nerves.

Acknowledgments for Quotations

The compilers are also grateful to the following individuals and publishers for permission to quote

xiii

from copyrighted materials, as well as to the authors of material quoted from the *Shakespeare on Film Newsletter* who are acknowledged in the appropriate section of the entries:

American Film for excerpt of review by David Kehr.

BBC Written Archives Centre, Caversham Park, Reading, England, for access to *Television Programme as Broadcast, London Station, Radio Times,* and correspondence.

British Universities Film & Video Council for distributor information in the United Kingdom.

Canadian Film Institute, *Institut canadien du film,* 150 rue Rideau St., Ottawa, Ontario K1N5X6 Canada, for quotations from Peter Morris *Shakespeare on Film,* 1972.

CEA Critic, excerpt from Tucker Orbison, "The Stone and the Oak: Olivier's TV Film of King Lear." 47.1.2 (1984): 67-77.

Deeper into Movies by Pauline Kael. © 1971 by Pauline Kael. First appeared in *The New Yorker,* excerpt from "Night of the Living Dead."

Literature/Film Quarterly, excerpts from work by Bernice Kliman (1983), Jack J. Jorgens (1973), Jay Halio (1973), Marsha Kinder (1977), and Samuel Crowl (1983).

Monthly Film Bulletin for excerpts from reviews.

The Nation for James Agee excerpt, which first appeared in *The Nation.* By permission of The Nation Company, Inc.

New York Magazine for the quotation from John Simon.

The New York Review of Books. Excerpt from an essay by Frank Kermode. Reprinted with permission from *The New York Review of Books.* Copyright © 1972 Nyrev, Inc.

The New York Times. "Copyright © 1950/54/56/60/61/67/73/ 78/80/81/82/84/85/87 by The New York Times Company. Reprinted by permission." Excerpts from film, video and theatre reviews.

"Noisy and Nervous: Review of *Romeo and Juliet*" by Marion Armstrong. Copyright 1968. Christian Century Foundation. Reprinted by permission from the March 26, 1969 issue of *The Christian Century.*

Reinhardt Books, London, for the quotation from Paul Dehn.

Shakespeare & The Film by Roger Manvell, Rev. Ed. 1977, A.S. Barnes, San Diego, CA.

The Shakespeare Quarterly for excerpts from copyrighted articles and reviews.

Sight and Sound. The British Film Institute, for excerpts from reviews.

Time. Cinema review of *Romeo and Juliet,* August 24, 1936. Copyright 1936. Time Inc. Reprinted by permission.

Signet Books, excerpt from an essay by David Young.

Soviet Literature, no. 6, 1971, excerpt from an essay by Alexander Anikst

Times Newspapers Limited, London, excerpt from review by Richard Combs in *Times Literary Supplement.*

The Village Voice, excerpts from reviews.

Acknowledgments for Illustrations:

Selected pictures are courtesy of The Shakespeare Plays, a six year series on public television made possible by grants from Exxon Corporation, Metropolitan Life Insurance Company, and Morgan Guaranty Trust Company. A BBC-TV and Time-Life Television co-production, presented for PBS by WNET/New York. (John Stride and Claire Bloom in *Henry the Eighth;* Angela Down and Ian Charleson in *All's Well that Ends Well;* Colin Blakely and Jane Lapotaire as Antony and Cleopatra; Helen Mirren in *Midsummer Night's Dream.*)

British Broadcasting Corporation for 1937 *Henry V.*

The Samuel Goldwyn Company. Kenneth Branagh in *Henry V.* © 1989 Renaissance Films PLC.

Globe Productions/Shakespeare Society of America, R. Thad Taylor, Executive Producer

Hallmark Hall of Fame stills, courtesy of Hallmark Cards, Inc. (Maurice Evans and Judith Anderson in *Macbeth;* Ciaran Madden and Michael Redgrave in *Hamlet.*

Ivy Film for *Men Are Not Gods,* 1936.

Janus Films for Laurence Olivier in *King Richard III,* 1955.

Museum of Modern Art Stills Archive, New York City, for stills from silents. (Sarah Bernhardt as Hamlet; Frederick B. Warde as King Lear; Francis X. Bushman and Beverly Bayne as Romeo and Juliet; Asta Nielsen as Hamlet; Emil Jannings as Othello; Orson Welles as Othello.)

KSR

How to Use This Book

The first route of access is the Table of Contents, which alphabetically lists Shakespeare's plays from *All's Well that Ends Well* to *The Winter's Tale*. Each film/video of an individual title is listed alphabetically by title of the play and chronologically by date of production or release in the Index to Entries, p. 349. Standard abbreviations, as set forth by the style manual of the Modern Language Association, such as *Shr.* for *Taming of the Shrew,* or *Err.* for *The Comedy of Errors,* may sometimes substitute for full titles of the plays (see page xvii for a complete list of abbreviations). Items may be located in the book by looking for the reference number, not the page number. For example, the 1982 *King Lear,* which was a part of the BBC/Time-Life "The Shakespeare Plays" series, may be found listed under *King Lear,* BBC, The Shakespeare Plays, number 267.

Turning to number 267, you will find information about the year of release, history of the production, cast credits, the names of North American and United Kingdom distributors, and the reception by critics. Whenever possible, the opposing viewpoints of various scholars and journalists are juxtaposed to suggest the range of responses to the production. The first entry under each play title defines the genre as comedy, or history, etc., dates the first production, and gives the original performance site. Because some of this information, such as the question of whether or not Shakespeare's *Titus Andronicus* (see #633) played at the Rose Theatre on Bankside is highly problematic, it may be followed with a question mark [?].

Distributors and dealers' names have been coded, so that the distributor in North America for this video is *AVP* (Ambrose Video Publishing) and *possible* rental sources are UIO (University of Iowa) and KSU (Kent State Univ.). The BBC* is the distributor in the United Kingdom (all overseas distributors are tagged with an asterisk [*]). Full addresses and in most instances telephone numbers are listed in the appendices where there is a complete key to distributors' codes (see page 399). With the advent, or onslaught, of the video revolution, however, the quest for the completely stabilized listing of distributors of Shakespeare films and videos is as elusive as Nathaniel Hawthorne's Giant Transcendentalist in "The Celestial Railroad." Distributors add and drop titles with disturbing frequency and prices are as volatile as airline fares. Moreover they may stock only a few copies of a particular title. The lists offered here represent the latest update, however, and they at least offer starting points for inquiries. The prudent consumer will want to shop around. Sometimes he or she may even stumble on a desired title at the corner video store.

Other features include tables that (1) list titles in chronological order of production (page 361); (2) sort out and cross-reference major series (such as *An Age of Kings*—page 357); (3) index authors who have been either quoted or cited (page 396); (4) index technical personnel involved in productions (page 386); and (5) index actors and actresses mentioned in the credits (see 367). A selected and annotated bibliography adds in-depth coverage to the periodical and book references in the body of the text (see page 337). Occasional act, scene and line citations to Shakespeare's plays refer to *The Riverside Shakespeare,* ed. G. Blakemore Evans, *et al.* (Boston: Houghton Mifflin, 1974). Film and video credits do not always spell the names of Shakespeare's characters in the same way (e.g., Calpurnia and Calphurnia in *JC*; Salarino and Salerio in *MV*; Katherine and Katharine in *H5* and *Shr.*). Therefore, based on the evidence of the First Folio (1623), most have been silently regularized, but readers should be prepared to cope with an inconsistency by referring to the textual notes in a standard edition of the play.

Guide to a Typical Entry

Brief description of the film/video discussed.

King Lear. **Video/Teleplay**

Entry number and name of this entry. Each film/video is numbered sequentially beginning with 1.

267. *King Lear.* (Series: The Shakespeare Plays).

Document information. Gives the date, country of origin, year and location of release and/or production.

DOCUMENT INFORMATION: *Country:* GB; *Year of first showing:* 1982; *Location of first showing(s):* BBC, London; PBS stations, USA, 18 Oct. 1982.

Edition, history, contents & evaluation. The main body of each entry gives significant facts about the production and a description including highlights of the action and critical evaluation.

EDITION, HISTORY, CONTENTS, & EVALUATION: *Edition & history:* Shot in London BBC studios with modified attempt to adhere to Folio rather than Quarto text in line with recent critical theory viewing the two texts as different acting versions. *Contents & evaluation:* "Problems in this *Lear* begin with a basic isolation of the actors from the emotional life implied by the words they speak. For example, Shakespeare's actors should weep when they say they are weeping. But when Cordelia bids farewell to her sisters 'with washed eyes,' when the king complains of 'these hot tears' forced from him by Cordelia, and when he tells Cordelia 'mine own tears do scald like molten lead,' the actors' eyes are dry. They don't even pretend to wipe away a tear. Their words are unconnected to what we see happening on the screen" (Urkowitz, Steven, "*King Lear* Without Tears," *SFNL* 7.2. [1983]:2). "While he is not overwhelming, Mr. Hordern is mightily convincing. . . . In the end this *King Lear* . . . works not spectacularly but quite rewardingly" (O'Connor, John J., "TV: A No-Nonsense *King Lear*," *NYT* 18 Oct. 1982: C16). Surely Michael Hordern is the most "down-home" King Lear ever to have played the role. His genius is all the more impressive for its understatement. When he calls for the map, he does not say

xvii

"Give me the map there" but "Give me the map [pause] *there*" and he points to the table on which the map should be placed. In other words put the map *there*. This may seem a simple point but it shows a scrupulous concern for small details. His eschewing of the traditional flowing white beard also comes as a mild surprise. Then again one remembers that Hordern has a special talent for portraying the slightly overwhelmed father, as he did unforgettably in the Zeffirelli *Taming of the Shrew*. There he mediated comically between Kate and Bianca; here he mediates tragically, and even more ineptly, among Goneril, Regan and Cordelia. In this remarkably original reading, Lear was never empowered but already disempowered even before the division of the kingdom. Regan's insight that her father "hath ever but slenderly known himself" (1.1.293) is validated. Hordern gives us Lear not as a tyrant but as a bumbler. The madness that comes later is already foreshadowed here (KSR). *Audience:* College and university; Professional; *Supplementary materials:* Fenwick, Henry. "The Production." *King Lear BSP* (1983): 19-34; Shorter, Eric. "Plays in Performance." *Drama* (Spring 1970): 27-31; Videocasette (25 min.) from "Shakespeare in Perspective" series with Frank Kermode available in U.K. from BBC* (*BUFVC* 19).

Audience and Supplementary materials describe the appropriate audience for the work and where to find more information about it.

MEDIUM INFORMATION: *Medium:* Video; *Sound:* Spoken language; *Color:* Yes; *Condition:* Excellent; *Length:* 180 min.; *Language(s) spoken:* English; *Video type:* B, V, 3/4U.

Medium Information. Describes the medium (film, video, or other), sound, color, running time, etc. B: Beta; V: VHS videocassette; 3/4U: ¾" videocassette; CDV: videodisk; 16mm: 16mm film.

AUTHORSHIP INFORMATION: *Producer(s):* Sutton, Shaun; *Director(s):* Miller, Jonathan; *Adaptor/translator(s):* Snodin, David; Preece, Patricia; *Designer(s):* Lowrey, Colin; *Costume designer(s):* Hughes, Raymond; *Lighting designer(s):* Treays, John; *Other personnel:* Miller-Timmins, Derek (Sound); Wilders, John (Literary consultant), Mair, Eileen (Make-up); *Cast:* Hordern, Michael (King Lear); Shrapnel, John (Kent); Barge, Gillian (Goneril); Wilton, Penelope (Regan); Blethyn, Brenda (Cordelia); Middlemass, Frank (Fool); Bird, John (Albany); Curry, Julian (Cornwall); Kitchen, Michael (Edmund); Lesser, Anton (Edgar); Grillo, John (Oswald).

Authorship Information. Gives the authors of this production and cast credits.

DISTRIBUTION & AVAILABILITY: *Publisher or responsible agency:* BBC-TV/Time Life Inc.; *Distributor:* AVP, UIO, KSU, BBC*, *Copy location:* UVM (Archive only); *Availability:* AVP, all formats, sale $450 (1987); UIO, V (72318H), 3/4U (70318V), rental $25.10; KSU, rental V, 3/4U, 5 days $33.75; BBC*; 16mm or V.

Distribution & Availability. Gives the name/code for the archive and distributor where this film/video may be obtained: AVP is Ambrose Video Publishing in New York City; UIO, University of Iowa Media Library; KSU, Kent State University A/V Service; and BBC*, British Broadcasting Corporation (the asterisk identifies overseas distributors). See page 399 for complete key to distributors and archives.

Key to Abbreviations of Plays

Modern Language Association
Standard Abbreviations
for Shakespeare's Plays

Ado	Much Ado about Nothing		MM	Measure for Measure
Ant.	Antony and Cleopatra		MND	A Midsummer Night's Dream
AWW	All's Well That Ends Well		MV	Merchant of Venice
AYL	As You Like It		Oth.	Othello
Cor.	Coriolanus		Per.	Pericles, Prince of Tyre
Cym.	Cymbeline		R2	Richard II
Err.	Comedy of Errors		R3	Richard III
Ham.	Hamlet		Rom.	Romeo and Juliet
1H4	Henry IV, Part One		Shr.	Taming of the Shrew
2H4	Henry IV, Part Two		Son.	Sonnets
H5	Henry V		TGV	Two Gentlemen of Verona
1H6	Henry VI, Part One		Tim.	Timon of Athens
2H6	Henry VI, Part Two		Tit.	Titus Andronicus
3H6	Henry VI, Part Three		Tmp.	The Tempest
H8	Henry VIII		TN	Twelfth Night
JC	Julius Caesar		TNK	Two Noble Kinsmen
Jn.	King John		Tro.	Troilus and Cressida
LLL	Love's Labor's Lost		Wiv.	Merry Wives of Windsor
Lr.	King Lear		WT	Winter's Tale
Mac.	Macbeth		Ven.	Venus and Adonis

Key to Abbreviations:
Books* and Journals

Code	Publication
AC	American Cinematographer
AF	American Film
AFI	American Film Institute Catalog
AVG	Audio-Visual Guide
BIO	Bioscope
BKL	Booklist
BSP	BBC TV Shakespeare Plays Texts
BUFVC	British Universities Film & Video Council Catalog
CD	Comparative Drama
CDC	Cahiers du Cinema
CEA	CEA Critic
CHM	Chadwick Healey Microfiche
Drama	Drama
EJ	English Journal
ETJ	Educational Theatre Journal
FAF	Films and Filming
FC	Film Criticism
FQ	Film Quarterly
FR	Films in Review

Code	Publication
FSF	[Eckert] Focus on Shakespeare Film
H&M	[Holderness & McCullough] Filmography, ShS, 39
HFTAP	Klimau, Hamlet on Film
HQ	Hollywood Quarterly
HS	Hamlet Studies
JPF	Journal of Popular Film
KMFR	Kinematograph Monthly Film Record
LFQ	Literature/Film Quarterly
Life	Life
MFB	Monthly Film Bulletin
MM	Multi-Media
NCF	New Canadian Film
NY	New Yorker
NYDN	New York Daily News
NYJA	New York Journal-American
NYM	New York Magazine
NYRB	New York Review of Books
NYT	New York Times

Code	Publication
PAJ	Performing Arts Journal
QFRT	Quarterly of Film, Radio and Television
RT	Radio Times
SAB	[McLean] Shakespeare: Annot. Bibliographies and Media Guides
SAF/ SATF	[Manvell] Shakespeare and the Film
SAS	Sight and Sound
SB	Shakespeare Bulletin
SFNL	Shakespeare on Film Newsletter
ShAB	Shakespeare Assoc. Bulletin
ShOF	[Morris] Shakespeare on Film
ShS	Shakespeare Survey
SIF	Shakespeare im Film, Wiesbaden
SIP	Shakespeare in Perspective series for BBC teleplays
SL	Soviet Literature
SN	Shakespeare Newsletter

*For full publication information, see Bibliography, page 337.

Code	Publication	Code	Publication	Code	Publication
SOF	[Jorgens] Shakespeare on Film	TCC	The Christian Century	TRQ	Tri-Quarterly
SOFT	[Loughney] "Sh. on Film at LC," SFNL (April 1988)	TDSP	[Gianakos] TV Drama Series Prog.	TSF	[Parker] Folger Filmography
		TFE	[Katz] The Film Encyclopedia	TSH	The Shakespeare Hour: Companion to PBS-TV Series
SOSF	[Ball] Shakespeare on Silent Film	Time	Time		
		Times	London	TVG	TV Guide
SOT	Shakespeare on Television	TLS	Times Literary Supplement	TVT	TV Times
				VAR	Variety
SQ	Shakespeare Quarterly	TO	Time Out	VV	Village Voice
ST	Sunday Telegraph	TPAB	Television Programme as Broadcast, BBC	WAC	Written Archives Centre, BBC
TA	Theatre Arts				

Shakespeare on Screen

Introduction: An Overview of Shakespeare on Screen

The appearance of Shakespeare's plays on screen coincided with the birth of the film industry at the close of the 19th century. The movie pioneers quickly discovered that Shakespeare could be a rich source for filmmaking. The "Golden Age" of Shakespeare on film, however, came later, after the advent of sound, with brilliant representations of the plays by such directors as Laurence Olivier, Orson Welles, and Roman Polanski. Meanwhile directors also produced numerous filmed spinoffs, modernizations, and musical versions based on the canon. By the late 1930s, television presented new challenges, stimulating notable productions in Great Britain, the United States, and elsewhere. What follows is a chronicle describing these stages in the growth of screened Shakespeare.

I. The Silent Era (1899-1929)

The brave new world of Shakespeare movies was ushered in, according to Robert Hamilton Ball,[1] in 1899 on London's Embankment with the filming of the Magna Charta scene from Sir Herbert Beerbohm Tree's West End theatrical production of *King John* (#238).[2] Although apparently made for his own amusement, Tree's production also verged toward what would be called today an "exploitation film," in the sense that it used the work of William Shakespeare to inflate either the reputation or income of its producer. There is, of course, no Magna Charta scene in Shakespeare's *King John*. By filming it anyway, Tree became the first movie director to make a gratuitous addition to the Shakespearean text. Unwittingly he thus fired the opening shot in the skirmishing between Bardolaters and Cineastes over strategies for representing Shakespearean drama.

For the next several decades, the Bardolaters, the self-appointed centurions of the Shakespeare establishment, were more than eager to denounce Cineastes for their liberties with Shakespeare. They often conveniently overlooked the amiable eccentricities of stage directors, such as Tree himself, who instinctively understood that "pure" Shakespeare, as originally performed at the Globe playhouse in 1600, could never be quite recaptured anyway. Whether on stage or on screen, all Shakespearean representations are acts of mediation. The compromises that film and television directors make are simply different from those made

1

on stage. As Lorne Buchman has argued,[3] film and television are not so much rivals to the stage, or "better" than the stage, as alternative modes of artistic expression. But if the screen is not an artistic threat to the stage, it is certainly an economic one. The gypsy bands of actors who roamed America a century ago have vanished. And therein may lie the root of the turmoil.

At the outset, though, it must be granted that the term "silent Shakespeare movie" is in itself one of history's great oxymorons. How could the master of the English language be represented in silence? Thus the efforts in France of the fabled Sarah Bernhardt to play Hamlet in 1900 on screen at a sideshow during the Paris exhibition (#74), as well as the Shakespeare films of the pioneering Georges Méliès (1861-1938), who produced a 1907 *Hamlet* (#75) and a *Julius Caesar* (#197), remained mere novelties. When the French did take the infant art more seriously, movies emerged in the shadow of theatre. The Film d'Art company was not so much dedicated to making better films as to making records of France's greatest theatre artists at the *Comédie Française*. Paul Mounet acted in a 1910 *Macbeth* (#286), while his more famous brother, Sully-Mounet, appeared in a fragment of *Hamlet* (Ball 108). If the films were no longer regarded as a joke, they were at least safely encapsulated in bourgeois conformity.

To the south, the Italians with an analogous Film d'Arte tradition and an industry in the control of men of educated tastes specialized in making costume dramas from Shakespeare's Roman and Italian Renaissance plays (Katz 604). Director Enrico Guazzoni (1876-1949), who was world famous for his 1912 *Quo Vadis*, brought his flair for costume epic to a 1910 *Brutus* (#201) and 1913 *Marcantonio e Cleopatra* (#10). The latter featured a barge of sufficiently ample proportions to prevent its sinking under the weight of a Giovanna Terribili Gonzales' well fed Cleopatra. And Giovanni Pastrone (1883-1959), the director of the 1914 *Cabiria* that inspired D.W. Griffith's super colossal *Intolerance*, may or may not have had something to do with a 1908 *Julius Caesar* (#200). Through the accident of their love of spectacle in grand opera, the Italians, somewhat like Michelangelo's *Captives*, broke out of the proscenium of theatricality into the spatial/temporal continuum of cinema.

In England, where it had all begun in 1899, filmmakers shared upper-class disdain for anything so vulgar as movies. That Bardolater mentality, which went along with veneration of the Queen, the English Church and the British Navy, was bound to result in an ideologically certified Shakespeare. The way to sanitize the rowdy new art form was to entice London's Shakespearean actors away from the stage and put them in front of

a camera. A paradigm is Cecil M. Hepworth's 1913 *Hamlet* (#82), which transferred the entire cast from the famed Drury Lane theatre to the movie set. None other than Sir Johnston Forbes-Robertson, premiere Shakespearean actor of his time, played Hamlet, even though he was then well into his sixties. That didn't matter—Sir Johnston looked to the public the way that Hamlet should look. And thousands who could never have seen him on stage were allowed an opportunity to view him on screen. As for Sir Johnston apparently he began to enjoy acting before the camera and did everything he could to translate words into actions. A still shows him at Lulworth Cove in Dorset reacting to the appearance of the ghost.

British reluctance to sully Shakespeare on celluloid left a vacuum into which the Americans were not at all reluctant to move. Indeed in 1916 D.W. Griffith imported Sir Herbert Beerbohm Tree to Hollywood to play the title role in *Macbeth* (#289) for what was then considered a staggering salary of $100,000 (Ball 229). Despite the attractions of the great British actor and of Shakespeare, the American public remained unimpressed and the movie of *Macbeth* failed at the box office. Earlier, however, J. Stuart Blackton and William Ranous working at the New York City Vitagraph studios were the leading producers of Shakespeare films. Their one-reelers (ten minutes) included Rose Coghlan in a 1912 *As You Like It* (#32), Tefft Johnson in *Cardinal Wolsey* (#195), William Ranous as Antony in *Julius Caesar* (#199), Julia Gordon as Portia in the *Merchant of Venice* (#354), William Ranous as *Othello* (#436), Florence Turner in *King Richard III* (#496), Florence Lawrence (the "IMP" girl) in *Romeo and Juliet* (#515), and Florence Turner as Viola in *Twelfth Night* (#640).

Typically, the first silent movies were made side by side in a row of stalls on rooftops or in warehouse-like studios with glass roofs. Scenery was likely to have been borrowed from Broadway or hastily put together by a makeshift crew that even included the actors. They were destined to be shown in the Nickelodeons, where, following vaudeville tradition, they shared the bill with an eclectic array of other short movies that might project everything from belly dancing to trained seals. They must be seen, however, to grasp how one can be misled by such generic stereotyping. Some were set on location. Viola apparently comes forth from the water to Illyria on the south shore of Long Island, perhaps near Bay Shore (Ball 315). Others were filmed out of doors in city parks and in their brief one-reel existence do their best to capture the ambiance of the Shakespearean world. Very early on, despite their role as orphans in the storm, these films were beginning to define their own non-theatrical, cinematic codes. The binary of theatre/film still privileged "theatre" but the seeds of subversion had been planted.

By far the most distinguished producer of Shakespearean films in America, however, was Edwin Thanhouser, who combined a passion for theatre with a talent as a cinematic *auteur*. His 1916 *King Lear* (#246), starring the American Shakespearean actor Frederick B. Warde in the title role, retold the Lear story in the idiom of both stage and movie. Warde's nineteenth-century histrionics were supported by battle scenes and horsemen reminiscent of Griffith's epic *Birth of a Nation*. The film struggles to free itself from the constraints of page and stage. It moves from the opening *mise-en-scène* with a man reading in a chair (which is spatial), to the close-up of the *Lear* text (which involves montage), to the Méliès-like stunt of dissolving Warde into Lear, and then to the device of title cards for narrating the play's plot. The director has highlighted the world of the library (the page); used a well-known actor of the time in the title role (the stage); and literally framed his movie (the screen) between the pages of a book. Page, stage and screen, the triad of Shakespearian incarnations, momentarily interface, though the tension generated among the three inevitably favors disconnection of the filmic from page and stage. To accomplish that, the book and the reader are figuratively and literally dissolved, an icon for the usurpation by cinema of the previously uncontested cultural reign of page and stage.

There were other feature length Shakespeare films made in the U.S. during the silent period. In 1916 arch rival movie companies, Metro and Fox, each released a *Romeo and Juliet* (#520, #521). Metro's starred the great Francis X. Bushman as Romeo with Beverly Bayne as Juliet; and the Fox version offered Theda Bara as Juliet with Harry Hilliard as her Romeo. Unfortunately neither print survives, though stills remain to give a hint of the grandeur that was Hollywood Shakespeare (Ball 224, 256).

Despite the efforts of the British and Americans, however, it must be said that the best silent Shakespeare films came from the Germans, whose *avant garde* expressionism made them peculiarly sensitive to the emerging cinematic art. A case in point is the 1920 *Hamlet* directed by Svend Gade (1877-1952), and Heinz Schall. Gade, a stage actor and decorator turned film director, cast an actress, Asta Nielsen, as Hamlet. She had played many classic roles on film including Hedda Gabler and Miss Julie, and also appeared in a 1925 film with Greta Garbo. Her genius was that she thoroughly understood the kind of understatement required for acting in the silents. Indeed Miss Nielsen's career in films ended with the advent of sound in 1929, and she never joined the burgeoning community of European exiles in Hollywood. Her pallid, expressive photogenic face, made many critics speak of her as a kind of precursor to Greta Garbo.

The film, *Hamlet. The Drama of Vengeance* (#86), offers a cinematic version of a pseudo-scholarly theory advanced by the American professor E.P. Vining in 1881 in his *The Mystery of Hamlet. An Attempt to Solve an Old Problem*. Vining reviewed the sources of the play and stressed the differences of Q1, Q2, and *Der bestrafte Brudermord* in the presentation of Hamlet's character which he saw as becoming more feminine in successive versions. Vining concluded that "Hamlet was actually a woman in love with Horatio and jealous of Ophelia." The film's chiaroscuro lighting, its huge studio interiors for the great hall at Elsinore, its close analytical shots, coupled with the curiously prophetic gender theory about Hamlet, set it worlds apart from any previous Shakespeare film. Motifs of intrigue, deception, poisoning, and uncertainty that trace directly back to the play are shrewdly embodied in the film text. An analytical shot of Claudius retrieving a poisonous snake from a pit of vipers, for example, serves as a metaphor for the poisoned kingdom. Hamlet's obsession with Horatio brings to the surface a hidden emotional agenda familiar enough to post-Freudian critics. As its chief student, Dr. J. Lawrence Guntner, has said, it is "arguably the first cinematically successful example of how Shakespeare can and has been re-appropriated for a particular purpose" (*SFNL* 13.1 [Dec. 1988]: 3).

To a lesser degree, many of these same Germanic elements also surface in the Dimitri Buchowetzki 1922 *Othello* (#442), starring Emil Jannings in the title role and Werner Krauss as Iago. Its two stars were prominent in the expressionistic movement in the German film industry, and Jannings subsequently received an Academy Award in Hollywood, where he had joined the many other British and European movie people who had flocked there for sunshine and big money. Krauss, in a long career that included 100 silent films, achieved cinematic immortality as the famous Dr. Caligari. The ostensive acting style of the film, the excessive theatrics, eye-popping, mugging and frantic semaphoring, were nurtured by the Reinhardt school of acting. When Jannings literally chews on Desdemona's handkerchief, he gives one of the most striking examples imaginable of Vsevolod Pudovkin's theory of the "expressive object." That is to say, the human subject and the theatrical object come into contact in an "indefinite realm" where "'no exact limit can be drawn between them'."[4] Jannings' berserk chewing on the handkerchief becomes synecdoche for the spiritual desolation of the brilliant Venetian general duped into disloyalty by a treacherous subordinate.

Luckily for Jannings, however, the general public often interpreted hammy screen acting as High Art and had a tendency to underrate the subtle gestures of the best silent screen actors such as Lillian Gish or Buster Keaton.[5] It was said that Lillian Gish could project the most profound emotions with the flicker of an eyelash.

Subsequently Werner Krauss appeared in another German Shakespeare silent, a grotesquely off-beat 1925 *A Midsummer Night's Dream* (#391) but with the advent of talking pictures fresh challenges confronted the making of Shakespeare films. The wonderful silence yielded to dialogue in the fifth reel of the MGM *Hollywood Revue of 1929* (#525), which was essentially cinematized vaudeville. After a song and dance number by Joan Crawford, a magic show by Laurel and Hardy, and so forth, Norma Shearer and John Gilbert did the balcony scene from *Romeo and Juliet* while Lionel Barrymore directed. Supposedly Gilbert's squeaky voice killed his career, though in this brief excerpt I didn't find it that egregiously bad. His role as Romeo, however, in being the coda to his own career also signalled the end of Shakespeare in the silents. The Hollywood revue closed with the entire cast performing "Singin' in the Rain," which is a talisman of making the best of adversity. And that's in general what the story of Shakespeare on silent film was.

The silent Shakespeare film, however, had made a frontal assault on the dominant cultural icons of the century. With the advent of sound, the capture of Shakespeare on screen for the masses was now inevitable. And paradoxically it had taken a greater rather than a lesser knowledge of Shakespeare's texts to follow the miming of the silent movie actors. Talkies would open up Shakespeare even more to the general public by allowing it to hear as well as to see. With the silents there had been a proleptic fulfillment of John Russell Taylor's belief that often the best filmed Shakespeare is based on the assumption that the audience knows the play. The film "affirms" but does not "record" (*Shakespeare: A Celebration* 113).

II. The Age of Sound

Janus-like, the 1929 Douglas Fairbanks/Mary Pickford *The Taming of the Shrew* (#584) looked backward to the silents and forward to the talkies. Originally a silent, the dialogue and sound effects of this consummate farce were subsequently added. Fairbanks' brash, bravura, bold Petruchio set against a saucy, impish Mary Pickford's Kate, more or less emulated or encouraged a long line of brawling Kates and Petruchios.

In one sequence, they turn into ardent flagellants as each attempts to thrash the other with a wickedly cruel looking whip. And when Mary Pickford faces the camera, looks directly at the audience, and winks to punctuate her controversial pledge of obedience to Petruchio, a statement of prime importance on the rights of American women was made. It may not have been what Shakespeare had in mind, but a beloved actress appropriated his meaning to her own ends.

A 1936 *As You Like It* (#34), directed by Paul Czinner, starred his wife, Elisabeth Bergner (Rosalind), a Polish actress who had made a reputation in German films, and a youthful Laurence Olivier (Orlando). Made in a studio, the film followed the Germanic styles that Czinner had learned from Max Reinhardt and others. Screened today it seems static and stagy, innovative only in the fact that the actors could be heard speaking Shakespeare's language. By coincidence, the movie fits the screwball comedy genre that Frank Capra popularized in Hollywood during the great depression.[6] Orlando as the unwavering idealist in a cruel world resembles the kinds of starry-eyed characters played by Jimmy Stewart in *Mr. Smith Goes to Washington*, or Gary Cooper in *Mr. Deeds Goes to Town* (Poague, "Screwball Comedy"). In the midst of general despair, these films were a ray of hope shining through hopelessness. With the charismatic presence of Olivier and Bergner, the film contributed its own share of gaiety to a troubled world.

Ironically, the German expressionistic movement in Shakespeare film peaked not in Germany but in Hollywood, U.S.A. Max Reinhardt and William Dieterle teamed up in 1935 to produce the Warner Brothers *Midsummer Night's Dream* (#392). With a galaxy of Hollywood stars in the cast, the film was the butt of almost as much condescension as the old silents. The sight of Mickey Rooney (Puck), James Cagney (Bottom), and Joe E. Brown (Quince) as Shakespearean actors enraged some and amused others but won admiration from few. The directors in fact boldly reappropriated Shakespeare's text in a notable effort to make it responsive to contemporary American culture. They committed the heretical act of downloading high to low culture instead of uploading low to high. With a sound track indebted to Mendelssohn's lilting *Overture*, the movie edged toward the Hollywood dance/musical tradition. It offers exquisite black-and-white dance sequences, a baroque forest, and nightmarish little elves who prefigured Jan Kott's vision of the dream as nightmare.

In the next year, Hollywood returned to the box office frays with yet another major production—the multi-million dollar 1936 *Romeo and Juliet* (#526), starring Norma Shearer and Leslie Howard, with the great John Barrymore as an aging Mercutio. Although studded with members of Hollywood's British expatriate cabal (Basil Rathbone as Tybalt, C. Aubrey Smith as Lord Capulet, Reginald Denny as Benvolio, Edna May Oliver as Nurse, and Leslie Howard as Romeo), the production and direction of the film were under the Hollywood control of Irving Thalberg (Norma Shearer's husband), and George Cukor. At enormous expense an approximation of Renaissance Verona, modeled from pictures taken in Italy by a studio photography team, was constructed on a Hollywood lot. (Nowadays of course the entire company, or a second unit, would pack up and travel to Italy instead.) Lavish costumes, a Busby Berkeley-like Capulet ball, theme music from Tchaikovsky—all were thought necessary as adjuncts to Shakespeare's language. At one level these efforts succeeded less in supporting than in smothering the play; at another, however, there was a sacerdotal reverence that endowed Romeo and Juliet with a beatific aura. The close-ups of Norma Shearer verify the passionate sincerity of Shearer's 36-year old Juliet. Probably the filmmakers were driven by a consuming anxiety to please Shakespeareans. They neither subverted nor confronted orthodoxy but instead acquiesced in academic genteelism. Like the couple who commit the terrible Emily Post gaffe of dressing for dinner on the first night out aboard a luxury transatlantic steamer between World Wars I and II, the movie was overdressed for a world that would not welcome it under any circumstances. Despite these shortcomings, the film remains, even if overstuffed, a brilliant and touching example of Shakespeare filtered through the lens of Hollywood's Golden Age.

After the box office problems of its two major Shakespeare films, Hollywood avoided Shakespeare until the post WW II production of the 1953 Houseman/Mankiewicz *Julius Caesar* (#214). With a bold head-on approach to the play, neither too stagy nor too coyly cinematic, and with a superb cast, the film is one of the best Shakespeare films ever made. Marlon Brando as Antony is a triumph. He looks sullen and resentful, mumbles, mutters, and shuffles, but his method-style of naturalistic American acting manages to suggest volumes about the essential character of Shakespeare's playboy of the Mediterranean world. With Brando were also John Gielgud as Brutus, James Mason as Cassius, and Louis Calhern as Caesar. It is Shakespeare without tricks and testifies to the myriad ways in which the plays can be successfully filmed. There are no formulas. A subsequent 1969 *Julius Caesar* (#226), directed by Stuart Burge, despite superb casting that included Charlton Heston as Antony, Jason Robards, Jr., as Brutus, Sir John Gielgud as Caesar, and Diana

Rigg as Portia, regrettably turned out to be a dud. Charlton Heston could be honored with the sobriquet, "Mr. Antony," for having turned up in the role so frequently. As early as 1950 he was Antony in a low budget, undergraduate production of *Julius Caesar* (#211) produced by David Bradley at the University of Chicago. Most recently, however, he was Antony in an epic 1972 *Antony and Cleopatra* (#20) that he himself produced and directed. With his powerful physique and commanding voice, he seems to have been born for the role.

The Golden Age of Shakespeare on Film lasted from about 1944 to 1970 but glittered most brightly with the three Shakespeare films that Lord Laurence Olivier acted and directed in. These were *Henry V* in 1944 (#172), *Hamlet* (#98) in 1948, and *Richard III* (#503) in 1955. Olivier, who had been previously skeptical about the feasibility of making Shakespearean drama into movies, revealed an astonishing talent for visualizing Shakespeare's verbal genius. In *Henry V* Shakespeare's lament for "a Muse of fire" in the prologue was answered by using the camera as a magic carpet to transport the audience from the raucous interior of the Globe playhouse, a rundown Eastcheap, and "the vasty fields of France" to Agincourt, only finally to return to the deflating world of the playhouse. At Agincourt in the spectacular charge of the French cavalry, the "Muse of fire" is again reified in an analytical close-up that actually shows the horses "printing their proud hoofs i' th' receiving earth."

In a 1948 *Hamlet*, the late Laurence Olivier offended scholars by reducing the inner conflict of the Danish prince to a question of his being a "man unable to make up his mind." He also sacrificed Rosencrantz and Guildenstern to the exigencies of time, much to the annoyance of purists who judge productions only by counting the number of lines preserved from Shakespeare's Folio and Quarto. On the other hand, he made the camera a participant in the action. The tracking shots, deep focus sequences, and haunting voice-over soliloquies brought fresh strategies to the rhetoric of Shakespeare on film as well as showing how film can both narrate and interpret a literary work.

In *Richard III*, surrounded by a brilliant cast that included Claire Bloom, Cedric Hardwicke, John Gielgud, and Ralph Richardson, Olivier re-created Richard Duke of Gloucester as a diabolical antichrist. Shriveled, deformed, pasty faced, Olivier's Richard dragged his way through the world cracking sardonic jokes and radiating a miasma of evil. Structurally the film is beautiful in its symbolic arrangement of the crowns at crucial points of the action both prior to Richard's ascendancy and after his horrible death at Bosworth.

Another key metaphor, that of the shadow, also diegetically permeates the film to add a deepened level of consciousness. Later, Olivier was to appear in Shakespeare films directed by others, though the 1965 *Othello* (#464), directed by Stuart Burge, was more of a recording of a National Theatre stage production than it was a full-fledged movie in its own right. The 1983 *King Lear*, which saw Olivier self-referentially play the role of the aging monarch surrounded by courtiers, was technically a television drama not a film at all. Still, to witness the evolution of this brilliant actor from the 1936 Orlando to the 1983 octogenarian King Lear (#271) offers a record of performance not available for great Shakespearean actors until this century.

Ironically because of their brilliance and glitter, the Olivier trilogy left the appetite unsurfeited, as though the true depths of Shakespeare's plays had not yet been plumbed. Thus, turning from the work of Olivier to that of the flamboyant Orson Welles is like abandoning the tidiness of an 18th-century garden for the tangled vines of a South American jungle. For his films, Olivier walked away with all the honors. It is doubtful that Orson Welles, even had he been a British subject, would have been honored with a peerage. And yet the greatest work, flawed though it may have been, on filmed Shakespeare was done by Welles. All occasions informed against him. His life was one financial crisis after another, as his plans for great Shakespeare films ran up against the harsh realities of time and money. But mostly money.[7]

When his 1948 *Macbeth* (#297) appeared, critics fell all over themselves to denounce it. The surrealistic fracturing of surface representation to get at the chaotic, dark forces underlying the tragedy of the Scottish king was either understood and rejected or misunderstood and scorned. There were also technical problems with the sound track that cannot easily be glossed over. Despite these flaws, however, a viewing of the film still leaves audiences with a sense of an artist groping to rediscover the timelessness of a great text. It was not that Welles was at all inexperienced as a Shakespearean. Not only had he produced a modern dress *Julius Caesar* on stage but also a "Voodoo" *Macbeth*. According to Richard Wilson (see #297), he then directed *Macbeth* at a Utah Shakespeare Festival as a preliminary to making the film.

The problems with *Macbeth* were trivial compared to the ordeal of making *Othello* (#453), as fine a Shakespeare film as has ever been made. Financial problems did not stop the director, however, from producing a movie crammed with Wellesian surprises. As usual, Welles was the victim of his own originality. He opened himself up to the familiar litany of charges about being "self-indulgent" and "drawing attention to his cam-

era." Yet the camera work—the high and low angle shots, the trademark deep focus shots, the gloomy shadows and bars, the analytical close-ups of Iago in a cage—actually reflected the paranoia in the mind of Shakespeare's black hero caught in a white world. Welles, who never made any money out of his Shakespeare films, labored like a latter day Michelangelo to incarnate the Bard's work in celluloid. Sadly, rights to the film have been so entangled in litigation that at present it can only be viewed in archives such as the Library of Congress Motion Picture Division.

His tumultuous career inexorably led to the 1965 *Chimes at Midnight* (#161—also released as *Falstaff*), which, though made on a low budget, imaginatively stitched together a collage from the major tetralogy of the English history plays. Playing the role of Falstaff himself, Welles brought a self-referential quality to the tale of an aging humbug that made this poignant film doubly moving. The resourceful use of expressionistic battle scenes, reminiscent of Goya, prefigured the techniques that Jane Howell was to use 17 years later in her triumphant television adaptation of the minor tetralogy (*q. v.*). (Kenneth Branagh's recent *Henry V* (#182.2) also alludes to the Welles battle scenes.) Falstaff, ruined by his own indulgence (Welles) and ruthlessly handled by Hal (the movie moguls), is turned from a comic to a tragic figure. Thereby Welles makes an unforgettable commentary on the horror of the human condition. At another time, though on television not on film, Welles played King Lear in a 1953 "Omnibus" Sunday afternoon production (#250) directed by Andrew McCullough and Peter Brook. As usual his performance was roundly denounced as overblown and sophomoric, though the Kinescope copy in the New York City Museum of Broadcasting reveals him to have been a King Lear whose anguish over the death of Cordelia reaches down into the very depths of human suffering. He drags her like a rag doll across the stage.

In mid-century, the non-English speaking world again felt the need to put Shakespeare's work on film. In 1964 *Coriolanus* (#62) appeared in Italy; in 1935 and 1955 two *Hamlet*s (#91 and #104), in India; in 1950 again a *Hamlet* (#101), this time in Denmark; in 1960 yet another *Hamlet* (#110), in West Germany; in 1964, *Hamlet* (#119) in Ghana; in 1970, again a *Hamlet* in Brazil (#128); in 1965, an Austrian *Merry Wives* (#382); in 1956, a Russian *Much Ado* (#423); in 1942, an Egyptian *Romeo and Juliet* (#530); in 1954, a particularly ambitious Italian *Romeo and Juliet* (#538) directed by Renato Castellani; in 1968, an Italian/Spanish *Romeo and Juliet* (#553); in 1959, a Mexican *Taming of the Shrew* (#595); and in 1947, a Spanish *Twelfth Night* (#644).

The most significant non-English speaking work,

though, came from Japan and Russia. In Japan, Akira Kurosawa (b. 1910), widely acknowledged as the country's leading film director, brought out a modernized *Hamlet* [*The Bad Sleep Well*] (#115) in 1963, an adaptation of *Macbeth* [*The Throne of Blood* and/or *The Castle of the Spider's Web*] (#307) in 1957, and only very recently a version of *King Lear* [*Ran*] (#274) in 1985. *Throne of Blood* has been virtually canonized as the finest possible example of the translation of Shakespeare into the movies on the grounds that the burden of not being hampered by the English language allows the director a freer hand for cinematic invention. The endless circling of the mounted samurai in the primeval forest reflects the embedded references in the play to Duncan's horses making "war with mankind" (2.3.13) and to the labyrinthine fate of Macbeth himself. An inscrutable and enigmatic Lady Macbeth in the best traditions of Noh drama also goads her Lord into the kind of hasty action that brought about the demise of Macbeth. By ferreting out the essence of *Macbeth* and ignoring surface phenomena, Kurosawa has not so much subverted as re-enshrined Shakespeare's play in another medium. The difficulty arises in estimating exactly what that "essence" is. And can it be captured on film without entirely losing its Shakespearean inspiration? In his 1985 *Ran* (#274), Kurosawa ostensibly made an adaptation of *King Lear,* with so many additions, deletions, and transpositions, however, that at times in an uncomfortable sense of *deja vu* the viewer may feel that he is watching *Macbeth,* not *King Lear.* The artistry of Kurosawa's films, however, revitalizes the Shakespearean vision into a universality congenial to all cultures, eastern and western alike.

During this Golden Age of Shakespeare on film and in the midst of the Cold War, the Russians also made important contributions. They may have been thought by cold warriors in the West to have been practicing some sinister brand of cultural imperialism by assimilating Shakespeare into their culture in 1955 with Yan Fried's lavish *Twelfth Night* (#648), and Sergei Yutkevitch's (b. 1904) brooding *Othello* (#456). From another perspective, though, the reaccentuation of Shakespeare with Elizabethan lute songs in Slavic rhythms and gargantuan sets of Eisensteinian dimensions was less an act of cultural imperialism than a tribute to the internationalism of Shakespeare's plays.

It was Grigori Kozintsev (1905-73), a pioneering Soviet filmmaker, who contributed the most to the canon of Soviet Shakespeare films. His 1964 *Hamlet* (#116) and 1970 *King Lear* (#256) grew out of painstaking attention to tiny details and profound respect for the mysteries of the Shakespearean vision. In two book-length meditations, *The Space of Tragedy,* and *Time and Conscience,* Kozintsev showed how every

scrap of his experience as a film maker was focused on translating the decentered worlds of Hamlet and King Lear into the charcoal texture of his films. His *Hamlet* showed how, like the Kurosawa 1957 Japanese version of *Macbeth* (*Throne of Blood*), Shakespeare on film may fare at the hands of a non-English speaking director. When the phonetics of a particular language no longer govern, film is free to enter into the realm of pure ideograph that is theoretically its special milieu. Kozintsev's dark, brooding, black-and-white images of sea, stone and castle once again showed film's capacity to probe the Shakespearean subtext. Ophelia's iron farthingale, for example, served as a visual metaphor for her encasement in the prison house of patriarchal hegemony. Similarly the remarkable use of Dreyer-like faces, of stone fortresses, of burning villages and of a pathetic Fool and a haggard old king made this *King Lear* a film that not just renewed but revalorised the epic scale of Shakespeare's play.

Although less experienced as a film director than Kozintsev, Peter Brook with his 1971 *King Lear* also displayed genius. An Englishman, Brook (b. 1925), with Lord Michael Birkett as producer, released his film shortly after the premiere of Kozintsev's version. The times apparently were ripe for *King Lear,* which, as so many have said, perfectly embodied the doomsday, post-Holocaust atmosphere of the Vietnam era. Brook's film also captured in charcoal hues and *Verfremdung* cinematic effects (freeze frames, accelerated motion, silent movie title cards, and so forth), the existential despair of Jan Kott's influential *Shakespeare Our Contemporary.* If as Jan Kott wrote, Shakespeare was "our contemporary," then in Brook's vision (and he made it plain in the credits that this was "Peter Brook's film about Shakespeare's *King Lear,*" not the thing itself), *King Lear* was indeed about the end of the world that Hiroshima foreshadowed. He even managed to bring in overtones of Beckett's apocalyptic *Waiting for Godot* in the sequence between King Lear and Gloucester at Dover. There were also bone chilling panoramas of the northern wasteland near Jutland that provided the film's *mise en scène* for exterior shots. The atmosphere of the film was so bleak and forbidding, so curiously less redemptive than the "Marxist" Kozintsev *King Lear,* that many found the film not just a subversion but a grotesque distortion of the Shakespeare text. *King Lear* is, however, a play that stubbornly mirrors each successive age. During the depressing years of the Vietnam war, no one was likely to find anything very optimistic about anything, let alone a play so dark as *King Lear.* In this sense, Peter Brook was simply re-appropriating Shakespeare for a new generation.

Among directors of Shakespeare films in those miraculous years before television nearly conquered all, Franco Zeffirelli must be rated at the very top. His Shakespeare films are perhaps not so urbanely contrived as Olivier's, nor so wickedly subversive as Welles's but they surpass both in their lush seductiveness. True enough, his 1966 *The Taming of the Shrew* (#598) did privilege the rough-and-tumble antics of Elizabeth Taylor and Richard Burton over the Shakespearean text. On the other hand, as an experienced Shakespeare director with credits from the Royal Shakespeare Company, Zeffirelli had an uncanny ability to visualize Shakespeare's verbal genius. Portions of the Sly and Bartholomew episode in the Induction scene get transposed to Petruchio's activities, and Sly himself appears briefly suspended from a cage at the city gates of Padua as Kate and Petruchio exit for the groom's country house. Of course Burton and Taylor, who were then the uncrowned king and queen of the film world, play the roles broadly because this play is a farce about the ancient Battle of the Sexes, not a seminar on feminist issues.

Zeffirelli also revelled in the Italian Renaissance opulence of Baptista Minola's magnificent residence. Minola, as played by veteran Shakespearean actor Michael Hordern, achieved a crescendo of helplessness in his despair over Kate and Bianca. Other highlights were an opening saturnalian street procession reminiscent of the carnival scene in Marcel Carne's 1944 *Les Enfants du Paradis;* a remarkably zestful and lively musical score by Nino Rota that reminds one of Zeffirelli's operatic background; and an especially winning performance by Michael York as Lucentio.

A smash box office hit, the 1968 *Romeo and Juliet*, starred a teen-age Romeo and Juliet, Olivia Hussey and Leonard Whiting, who were ideally suited to Zeffirelli's palimpsest. He had filtered Shakespeare through Leonard Bernstein's 1961 *West Side Story* (#544). Filmed in a hilltop town in Italy, the movie's neo-realism also emulated Renato Castellani's 1954 *Romeo and Juliet* (#538). Its cultish popularity was by no means undeserved. Its swirling patterns of images, the ball at the Capulets, the duel between Romeo and Tybalt, effectively envision the friar's belief that "they stumble who run too fast." The impassioned scenes between Romeo and Juliet at the balcony, during their marriage, in the *aubade* scene, and at the tomb, make crafty use of youthful actors because of film's ability to permit generous re-taking and editing. And Nino Rota's score, with its recurring theme of a pop hit, "What is a Youth?," skillfully faked an Elizabethan idiom while keeping audiences almost as emotionally spent as the lovers themselves. This combination of music, spectacle and words was further embellished with superb performances from a threatening Michael

York as Tybalt, a manic/depressive John McEnery as Mercutio, and a sturdy Pat Heywood as Nurse.

Astounded audiences not knowing quite how to react also saw released in 1971 the Playboy production of *Macbeth* directed by Roman Polanski and starring Jon Finch and Francesca Annis. If Zeffirelli's *Romeo and Juliet* drew crowds because of its baroque sentimentality, Polanski's *Macbeth* packed the movie houses with voyeurs. Polanski's text, co-adapted with Kenneth Tynan, included not only about one-half of Shakespeare's text but also traces of the notorious Manson murders in an egregiously violent on-screen stabbing of Duncan. The imagery of blood and Golgotha in Shakespeare's tragedy became a lens for a vision of a world gone mad. The opening shot, a long take that took in sweeping panoramas of deserted beach before closing in on the three hags, served as a prologue to a disturbing cinematic experience. Embedded in the framework of this daring and trendy film (the music was provided by 'The Third Ear Band') was a silent film that privileged Ross (John Stride) in such a way as to make him not only the third murderer but also the butcher of Macduff's family, a major architect of Macbeth's ultimate defeat, and in many respects a mirror image to Macbeth himself. The story of Ross is indeed a silent film nested in the deep structure of Polanski's film. Polanski and Kenneth Tynan apparently borrowed the whole idea for magnifying Ross's importance to the action from a Victorian schoolmaster, M.F. Libby of Toronto, who published a version of this interpretation in 1893. Grafted on to this was a youthful, slender Lady Macbeth who appeared nude in the sleepwalking scene. The film thus conflated Victorian character criticism with Playboy porn in a bizarre but unforgettable treatment of the Scottish play (Rothwell, #324 below).

There have of course also been full-scale pornographic versions of Shakespeare's plays, one of the most recent being a 1986 Cinderella Productions version of *Twelfth Night* transmitted on the Playboy channel in December 1988 (Coursen). And punk/gay has appeared on the scene with Derek Jarman's 1980 *Tempest* and Celestino Coronado's 1984 *Midsummer Night's Dream* (#416). In the latter Hermia and Helena and Lysander and Demetrius wind up pairing off not with their lovers of the opposite sex but with each other. Although both the Jarman and Coronado movies are serious re-appropriations of Shakespeare's text for modern times, there is a line, difficult to draw, at which these free-swinging adaptations pass over into travesties. Robert Hamilton Ball's fine book on the silent Shakespeare film lists dozens. They also are a sub-species of yet another category, Shakespeare derivatives, which are discussed below.

While these big budget cinematic realizations of the Shakespearean text offered the rich texture of film on a large screen, in the sixties and seventies television production methods began to influence the ways of putting Shakespearean drama on screen. Actually as early as 1960 George Schaefer had filmed *Macbeth* (#309) in Scotland prior to showing it as both a Hallmark television and a theatrical release. This, along with a gangster show called *The Scarface Mob*, was thus one of the first made-for-television movies, a genre now all too familiar to the public. Of similar origins was a 1960 West German *Hamlet* (#110) with dubbed-in English starring Maximilian Schell as a teutonic prince. Its expressionistic sets and bare stage hinted at the thriftiness that would soon replace the lavish multi-million dollar films. By far the most successful of the made-for-television Shakespeare films, however, was Lord Birkett and Peter Hall's 1968 *A Midsummer Night's Dream* (#405), which combined the realism of a hand-held camera in the *cinema verité* tradition with the expressionism of fragmentary editing. Costumes suggested the then voguish Carnaby street mini-skirts and Nehru jackets, and the dazed young lovers were lost in a real English wood in a real Warwickshire forest far from Athens. At the same time, they stumbled through an expressionistic fairy land of twinkling lights and jump cuts. With Diana Rigg as Helena, Helen Mirren as Hermia, Ian Richardson as Oberon, and Judi Dench as Titania, this film remains a sparkling but unpretentious gem.

Also in the category of "made-for-television" was Tony Richardson's 1969 *Hamlet* (#123), starring the tumultuous and unpredictable Nicol Williamson. A three-way compromise among film, TV, and theatre, it records a stage production at the Roundhouse Theatre in London. Filmed almost entirely in close and midshots, the production cuts off the actors' legs but magnifies the raw intensity of Williamson's angry Hamlet. Williamson, who had enjoyed a success with the role on stage in New York and London, dug out a subtext that had eluded the sonorities of a John Gielgud and the panache of a Laurence Olivier. While not a Hamlet for all seasons, he was indubitably a Hamlet for that troubled time, who, as a *Time* critic wrote, carried with him "the smell of smoldering cordite."[8]

Another made-for-television film, starring Laurence Harvey as Leontes, which recorded a 1966 stage production of *The Winter's Tale* (#672) at the Edinburgh Festival, offered a then rare opportunity to see this play on screen, though without critical or box office success.

In the 1960's, before the development of cable television and home VCR's made the practice anachronistic, the recording of stage performances for subsequent screening in neighborhood movie houses, was briefly attempted. Upscale audiences in the provinces would assemble to watch a recording of a London or Broadway production. A famous one was the 1964 *Hamlet* (#117), directed by Sir John Gielgud and starring Richard Burton. Recorded on Electronovision by several cameras in a New York theatre, and performed in rehearsal clothes, the tape has since vanished from general circulation. Archival copies unveil, however, a fiery and explosive but unpredictable, indeed stormy, Hamlet surrounded by a stellar cast including Hume Cronyn as Polonius, Alfred Drake as Claudius, and John Gielgud as the Ghost. Burton's inner reserves gave him the psychological strength to portray Hamlet as an angry young man without sinking, as Williamson had done, to unprincely fits of histrionics. Another recording of a stage production was the already cited 1965 Stuart Burge *Othello* (#464), starring Laurence Olivier as the Moor and Frank Finlay as an unforgettable Iago. For the most part a record of a National Theatre stage play, cinematically it is no match for the lavish 1955 USSR Yutkevich *Othello* (#456). It was, even so, an actor's triumph for an Olivier whose blackface reminded one critic of the "end man in a minstrel show." In a bold celebration of the miscegenation in the text, a lily-white Maggie Smith was cast as Desdemona to contrast with Olivier's blackness. Finlay's Iago, by playing on every weakness of the Moor, exemplified the view of British critic F.R. Leavis that Othello's ruin lies in his own frailties.

III. Spinoffs and Modernizations

Shakespeare's plays also inspired dozens of films that stubbornly resist classification because of their many overlappings and protean shapes. Testimony to the pervasive influence of Shakespeare as a cultural symbol, they may variously be labeled "derivatives," "offshoots," "travesties," "spinoffs," "modernizations," and "musical/operatic/dance versions." In the silent era, movie makers found the Shakespearean canon a happy hunting ground for titles even when the scenario may have had virtually nothing to do with the Bard's work, as, for example, a 1909 *Much Ado* (#420) and 1913 Italian film, *Measure for Measure* (#347).

Other movies, often without Shakespearean titles, borrowed bits and scraps from the bard: a 1922 *Day Dreams* (#87) in which Buster Keaton imagines himself as Prince Hamlet; a 1933 *Morning Glory* (#90) in which Katharine Hepburn as an aspiring actress livens up a dull party with a recitation of the "To be or not to be" soliloquy; and a 1946 *My Darling Clementine* (#96) in which traveling thespians perform Shakespeare in a frontier saloon. Another type vaguely weaves Shakespearean plot elements into their own design: for example, Maurice Elvey's 1916 *Love in a Wood* (#33) with overtones from *As You Like It;* the 1910 *Romeo Turns Bandit* (#517) with its garbling of Shakespeare's plot; the 1956 *Jubal* (#458) starring Ernest Borgnine whose fit of sexual jealousy may or may not echo Othello's; and the 1954 *Broken Lance* (#251) starring Spencer Tracy whose scenario includes a Cordelia-type figure and mirrors the Gloucester plot in *King Lear.* The difficulty in making these assessments is that Shakespeare and the Hollywood scenarists were often drawing on a common source—the universal human condition.

Links between Shakespeare and the living film are on firmer ground with the sub-genre of backstage films about Shakespearean actors who in one way or another confuse their stage and real identities. For some reason *Othello* has stimulated three major examples: the 1936 *Men Are Not Gods* (#444) in which an actor playing Othello (Sebastian Shaw) develops an unhealthy need to smother Desdemona (Gertrude Lawrence) for real on stage; the classic 1947 *film noir A Double Life* (#446) in which an actor playing Othello (Ronald Colman) transfers his smothering activities from an on-stage Desdemona to an unsuspecting offstage victim; and the 1962 *All Night Long* (#461) in which jazz musicians in a London luxury flat incongruously housed in the East End restage the Othello story in the fierce jealousy between a white drummer and a black band leader over the affections of a vocalist. A non-*Othello* type variation on this kind of plot is Ernst Lubitsch's 1942 *To Be or Not to Be* (#93) in which the movie action is entangled with Jack Benny's delivering of Hamlet's soliloquy on stage. In 1983, Mel Brooks did a re-make of the same story (#147).

More challenging to evaluate are adaptations that re-represent Shakespeare's text in a contemporary and sometimes even in a post-modernist idiom. The beautifully photographed 1949 French film, *Les amants de Verona* (#534), based on *Romeo and Juliet,* carries the young lovers in and out of a glass factory and into a complicated meta-cinematic love affair. The 1945 *film noir Strange Illusion* (#94) rediscovers Freud's Oedipal theory and puts the Hamlet story in the context of American upper middle class family life. Henry Cass's 1955 *Joe Macbeth* (#306) with Paul Douglas in the title role as a Chicago gangster masks debts to Shakespeare's tragedy behind the facade of a commercial film. Paul Mazursky adopted that same strategy with his 1974 *Harry and Tonto* (#260) and 1982 *The Tempest* (#626), which betray thoughtful connections with *King*

Lear and *The Tempest.* Surely one of the most *recherché* modernizations, however, is Claude Chabrol's 1962 *Ophelia* (#111) whose camera work re-appropriates the fractured world of *Hamlet* into a post-modernist vision of a village in France. And in a slot by itself is Fred Wilcox's 1956 *Forbidden Planet* (#611), a wonderful science fiction reworking of *The Tempest* starring Walter Pidgeon.

Everybody's favorite Shakespeare "spinoff" film may well be the 1965 James Ivory *Shakespeare Wallah* (#696), which in narrating the poignant tale of a down-at-the-heels British acting company in India also crams in some superb Shakespearean acting.

Problems in classification become even more thorny as one moves into the genre of musical/operatic versions of Shakespeare. Most are really films of Shakespeare adaptations previously mounted on stage but still they appear on screen or television and invite consideration in this treatise. Such outstanding popular hits as the 1940 *Boys from Syracuse* (#48) based on *Comedy of Errors,* the 1953 *Kiss Me Kate* (#591) based on *Taming of the Shrew* (but also with a backstage plot), and the 1961 *West Side Story* (#544) offer obvious examples. Lesser known is the 1973 *Catch My Soul* (#466), a rock opera version of *Othello* that began its life as a stage production in London and became a film in the American Southwest. These kinds of musicals then segue into operatic and dance treatments that with rare exceptions represent recordings of stage productions. One such exception is Franco Zeffirelli's recent 1986 film of Verdi's *Otello* (#478), which was planned and made as a movie. For the most part, however, recordings of staged operatic and dance versions exist on the periphery of this book's principal concerns. They cannot be entirely ignored if one is to have a full overview of the entire field but they also require the attention of music and dance critics.

Finally, before moving on from film to television, a word needs to be said about a huge category of Shakespeare movie—the educational film. The Shakespeare film primarily made for classroom exhibition is often non-narrative, a "talking head," as it were, in the style of Dr. Frank Baxter, learned host of the 1960's "Fair Adventure Series," speaking with the aid of a few stage props on the topic of "Shakespeare's London" (#688) . A more up-to-date series constructed along these lines and called "Shakespeare in Perspective" brings a galaxy of first-rate intellects, such as Dr. Frank Kermode on *King Lear* (#269), to analyze the BBC Shakespeare plays. Another species, such as Hugh Richmond's 1982 "Shakespeare and the Globe" (#736), may stitch together film clips and stills to give a first-hand sense of the atmosphere of Shakespeare's Britain. Still another variety features repertory actors both acting and explaining their craft in a workshop format, as in the highly successful 1984 series, called "Playing Shakespeare," distributed in the U.S. by Films for the Humanities and hosted by John Barton. Finally, some educational films offer condensed versions of the plays, or individual scenes for study. The best of the former to my knowledge are the National Geographic series (see, for example, the Walsh *Romeo and Juliet* at #564 and #565), and of the latter the series produced by the Stratford, Canada, Shakespeare Festival (see, for example, the 1985 *Taming of the Shrew*, #606). In 1985 there emerged yet another sub-species—a film made for the student who wants animated crib notes (#151.1). Indeed there are many options for the interested teacher to select or to reject from and they are best found by browsing through the alternatives offered in the following pages.[9]

IV. The Television Revolution

Shakespeare on television began inauspiciously in the winter of 1937 with a series of abbreviated BBC programs aimed at the handful of Londoners who owned home receivers. As with Sir Herbert Tree's 1899 *King John* movie, the fledgling television industry instinctively grasped at Shakespeare programming as a tactic for wooing the British cultural establishment. A flurry of articles in the late 1930's on Shakespearean topics in *The Listener*, a BBC house organ, by such luminaries as J. Dover Wilson, G.B. Harrison, and Tyrone Guthrie, all signaled a literary and theatrical bias. Moreover television's natural roots were in radio, not movies, so that cinematic art was by no means the dominant model for the pioneers of television. As had similarly been the case with the early silent films, stage actors were imported to parade before the crude television cameras of the day located in Alexandra Palace. On Friday afternoon, February 6, 1937, at 3:55 p.m., the new era began with the transmission of an 11-minute scene from *As You Like It* (#35). It was directed by Robert Atkins with Margaretta Scott (b. 1912), a West End actress, as Rosalind and Ion Swinlay (or Swinley) as Orlando. Later that same day, there was also a transmission of a segment from *Henry V* (#171), directed by George More O'Ferrall.[10]

As BBC producers both Atkins and O'Ferrall were to play key roles in the subsequent expansion of Shakespeare programming on British television.

From 1937 to 1939, the BBC scheduled some 20 Shakespeare programs. Varying in length from a few minutes to nearly two hours, they were most frequently transmitted from the BBC studios at Broadcasting House but very soon the technology was in place for live recordings from London's West End playhouses. Representative titles include studio scenes based on an Embassy Theatre production of *Cymbeline* (#69); an abridged (100-minute) version of Orson Welles' modern dress New York Mercury Theatre *Julius Caesar* (#207); an abridged (60 minute) studio *Othello* (#445) with Celia Johnson as Desdemona and Anthony Quayle as Cassio; and a recording of a live performance in the Open Air Theatre, Regents Park, of *A Midsummer Night's Dream* (#397). By 1939 Dallas Bower's *The Tempest* (#610) was allowed one hour and forty minutes of air time for a virtually full-scale production. There was some dismay expressed by the BBC production staff about technical problems such as wandering stagehands,[11] but with Peggy Ashcroft as Miranda, Shakespeare on television seemed to be growing to maturity. World War II intervened, however, and on September 1, 1939 at the end of a Mickey Mouse film,[12] with the "lights going out all over Europe," the BBC also switched off its lights for the duration.

In the postwar period, BBC energetically continued to transmit Shakespeare to the public, sometimes without much success but always persistently. Doubtless profiting from their pre-war experiences, producers Ian and Robert Atkins and George More O'Ferrall along with Michael Barry continued to be closely associated with the BBC's Shakespeare productions. For three decades beginning in 1947, British television averaged nearly three Shakespeare programs a year. In 1978, however, the great geyser of the BBC Shakespeare Plays series began to saturate the market with six plays a year. Prior to the BBC series, however, the BBC and independent television drama producers, despite such competing events as boxing and football matches, managed to squeeze out of stingy budgets some admirable and some less than admirable results. Some nominees for the "admirable" would include George More O'Ferrall's full-length two-part, meticulously planned 1947 BBC *Hamlet* (#98) with Sebastian Shaw as Claudius, for which the British Television Society awarded O'Ferrall its Silver Medal; Jonathan Miller's and John Sichel's 1969 Precision Video re-recording of the National Theatre production of *The Merchant of Venice* (#367) starring Laurence Olivier as Shylock; and Trevor Nunn's 1979 Thames Television *Macbeth* (#332) with Ian McKellen and Judi Dench. All are milestones in the history of televised Shakespeare. For example, as Michael Barry has shown, the tracking camera in O'Ferrall's 1947 *Hamlet* even influenced the fascinating cinematography for the 1948 Olivier filmed *Hamlet*.[13]

In fact Great Britain's most extraordinary Shakespeare on television emerged in the form of three major series based on the English and Roman history plays. The first and most ambitious of these, the 1960 *An Age of Kings* (*R2*, #485-6; *1H4* and *2H4*, #156-9; *H5*, 178-9; *1-3 H6*, 185, 188, 190-2; *R3*, 505-6) represented the minor and major tetralogies of the English history plays in a 15-week cycle that compressed the eight plays into segments of 60 to 90 minutes each. Cinematic resources were limited (a reviewer thought the results were essentially "filmed plays"), but the talents of such RSC actors as Frank Pettingell (Falstaff), Robert Hardy (Prince Hal), and Paul Daneman (Richard III) made the series one of the best received Shakespeare programs ever transmitted on television. Three years later in the 1963 nine-part *Spread of the Eagle*, Director Peter Dews used the same formula with somewhat less success to present a mini-series drawn from *Julius Caesar* (#221-3), *Antony and Cleopatra* (#14-16), and *Coriolanus* (#59-61). Finally in 1964 Peter Hall and John Barton adapted the minor tetralogy of the three parts of *Henry the Sixth* (#183-4) and *Richard III* (#509) into yet another sprawling historical epic of English kings and queens. All three leaned heavily on theatrical rather than video techniques and all suffered from under-funding but the high quality foreshadowed the future cultural hegemony of British over U.S. programming for the educated audiences of North American public television.

In the United States, where free market philosophies made financing more difficult, television prior to World War II lagged behind Britain's. In the postwar era, though, U.S. television in general and Shakespeare on television in particular began to surpass the entire world in quantity and sometimes even in quality. Thus, so far as I know, the first U.S. transmission of a Shakespeare "event" was not a ten-minute snippet but a full-blown live broadcast of a 1948 performance of Verdi's *Otello* (#448) from the stage of New York's old Metropolitan Opera House. During the next decade or so, Shakespeare on television benefited from the generosity that commercial networks and sponsors accorded to live television drama in the halcyon years of the industry. Philco Playhouse, Studio One, Kraft Theatre, Omnibus, and the Hallmark Hall of Fame all offered Shakespeare to the masses. By basking in the reflected glory of Shakespeare, companies achieved an enviable image of public service. The rich rewards from lobotomizing the American public with mindless entertainment had not yet been discovered by the advertising industry.

From 1953 to 1970 the Hallmark greeting card company underwrote George Schaefer's remarkable series of televised Shakespeare plays. Maurice Evans, fresh from his triumphs in the wartime "GI" *Hamlet*, played the title role with Sarah Churchill as Ophelia in a 1953

Hamlet (#102). He appeared again in the leading role in a 1954 *Richard II* (#484) that also featured Sarah Churchill, this time as the unhappy little queen; and in 1954 a *Macbeth* (#305) in a pioneering color transmission with Judith Anderson as Lady Macbeth. In 1956 there was a *Taming of the Shrew* (#593), with Evans miscast as a not very convincing Petruchio and Lilli Palmer as Katharine Minola; in 1957, a *Twelfth Night* (#649) with Evans as Malvolio and Rosemary Harris as Viola; and in 1960 a truly wonderful *Tempest* (#613) with Evans as Prospero, Lee Remick as Miranda and Richard Burton as Caliban. In 1960 Hallmark restaged *Macbeth* (#309) and in 1970 the company sponsored a British *Hamlet* (#126), directed by Peter Wood and with a cluster of big name actors, including Richard Chamberlain as the Prince, John Gielgud as the Ghost, and Michael Redgrave as Polonius. In turning to England, however, for theatrical talent, Hallmark foreshadowed the impending collapse of serious drama on American television. From now on the television audience would be split between two cultures: the plain folk of Middle America who enjoyed sitcoms and beer-sponsored ball games, and the minority of quiche-and-white-wine connoisseurs who preferred Masterpiece Theatre on public television. It was a replay in North America on a massive scale of the division in Elizabethan London between the public audience at the Globe and the "private" audience at Blackfriars playhouse.

Hallmark did not, however, own a monopoly on televised Shakespeare in North America, though it may have seemed that way. In the 30 years between 1949 and 1979 (when the BBC Shakespeare Plays series began to dominate the genre), there were nearly 50 major televised Shakespeare programs broadcast in the United States. As early as 1949 NBC made a pilot scene from *Henry V* featuring Sam Wanamaker. At CBS in 1949 Worthington Miner produced for Studio One, a *Julius Caesar* (#210) starring Robert Keith, and in 1951 a *Macbeth* (#301) starring Charlton Heston and *Coriolanus* (#58) starring Richard Greene. In 1956 an audience estimated, perhaps with some exaggeration, at 25,000,000 watched a colorized Olivier *Richard III* (#503) on television at the same time that the movie was being theatrically released. Importing British Shakespeare on television continued to be a national habit, as, for example, with the 1959 CBS showpiece, the Old Vic *Hamlet* (#107), starring John Neville. Three made-in-the-USA Shakespeare productions, all of them simply recordings of stage performances, did manage to make a heavy splash on the national scene. Two of them emanated from the workshops of Joseph Papp's New York Shakespeare Festival: a 1977 *King Lear* (#263) starring James Earl Jones, and an "Americanized"

1973 *Much Ado* (#428), directed by A.J. Antoon with Sam Waterston as Benedick and Kathleen Widdoes as Beatrice. By shifting the time frame for the play to Teddy Roosevelt's America and by employing such cinematic devices as slow and accelerated motion and Keystone Kop antics, Antoon re-appropriated Shakespeare's text for American audiences. The third memorable production was the American Conservatory Theatre's 1976 *Taming of the Shrew* (#602) in which William Ball's San Francisco company displaced traditional *Commedia* tropes into a cinematic farce of slapstick routines and Mickey Mouse sound effects. The presentation was, however, frankly theatrical, not telegenic, in the sense that even the offstage audience was made a part of the *mise en scène*. By the close of the seventies, then, television remained a passive recorder of theatrical productions rather than a dynamic innovator of fresh ways to put Shakespeare on screen. Moreover the sponsorship of major corporations insured that no director would commit any creatively irresponsible acts likely to upset the community norms. It was Shakespeare made safe for the millions.

The plan begun in 1978 by BBC and Time/Life Inc. to put the 36 Folio plays in a six-year series called "The Shakespeare Plays," marked a watershed in the history of Shakespeare on screen. In hindsight it can be seen that the plan was flawed. The logistics of recruiting actors, designing sets and costumes, and finding creative directors, all within the constraints of a six-year timetable, inevitably put the BBC production staff under fearful pressure. To expect total success under those circumstances would be unreasonable. Moreover in the United States the ancient inferiority complex over things British was revived with the decision to include only British actors in the casting. If there were defeats, however, there were also victories. And certainly the series revolutionized the teaching of Shakespeare. Great numbers of skeptical classroom teachers began exploring the dynamics of screening a scene on the classroom television monitor as a supplement to a reading of the text. The death knell was at hand for the days when dear old Professor Chips hogged the limelight by reading all the parts aloud himself, while his hapless students squirmed and silently abjured Shakespeare for life.

The series got off to a slow start with a lackluster *Julius Caesar* (#233), whose studio Rome and bedsheet costuming indicated a decision to play it safe at all costs. There was estimable acting in Richard Pasco's Brutus, Keith Michell's Antony, and especially Elizabeth Spriggs's Calphurnia but the rhetorical paralysis that often afflicts this play could not be overcome even on television.

In quick succession there followed a spritely out-of-doors *As You Like It* (#42), filmed at Glamis Castle, Scotland, with Helen Mirren as Rosalind; a dismal *Romeo and Juliet* (#563) that, try as it might, could not get out from under the shadow of the Zeffirelli film; a king-centered *Richard II* (#492) that became a rostrum for the sinewy talents of Derek Jacobi as the unhappiest of monarchs; a highly successful *Measure for Measure* (#350); and a surprisingly appealing *Henry VIII* (#196). Director Desmond Davis' *Measure for Measure* was the season's hit. Kate Nelligan's Isabella and Tim Piggott-Smith's Angelo, with strong support from John McEnery (Mercutio in the Zeffirelli *Romeo and Juliet*) and Kenneth Colley as the godlike Duke Vincentio, offered a familiar tale of sexual harassment well suited to a medium so congenial to soap opera. John Stride, who was the ubiquitous Ross in the Polanski film version of *Macbeth*, also brought the infrequently performed *King Henry VIII* to life.

The second season (1980) began with John Gorrie's *Twelfth Night* (#659.1). A repeat performance of *Richard II* then served as prologue to the *First and Second Parts of Henry IV* (#166, #167) and *Henry V* (#182). The season ended with an inert *Tempest* (#620), starring Michael Hordern and directed by John Gorrie again. It was a plastic island dead even to the cry of seagulls. Trevor Peacock's Feste was the star of *Twelfth Night*, and, while the sets could not match the extravagant 1955 Lenfilm version directed by Yakov Fried, sensitive performances by Sinead Cusack as Olivia and Felicity Kendal as Viola, re-created some of the magic of Illyria.

The subsequent televising of the major tetralogy of the English history plays gave viewers a rare opportunity, as with *An Age of Kings*, to see the four plays virtually uncut. Jon Finch as Henry Bolingbroke portrayed the various stages of his unjust exile by Richard II, his usurpation of the crown from Richard II (Derek Jacobi), his ascension to power, and finally his deathbed repentance before the final journey to Westminster's Jerusalem Chamber. The mysterious skin disease that plagued Bolingbroke, and almost homeopathically begins to make the audience itch, serves as a metaphor for the diseased body of king and state. As the "guilt" beneath the "gilt" of the crown surfaces, tension between father and son (Prince Hal is played by David Gwillim) escalates. The great reconciliation scene toward the close of *Henry IV Part Two* allows each actor a full opportunity for catharsis. In the rejection scene during the coronation procession, Anthony Quayle as Falstaff divulges the inner pathos of the fat warrior, and the tavern sequences, so reminiscent of the domestic tableaux of the seventeenth-century Dutch painters, introduce a garrulous Brenda Bruse as Mrs. Quickly and a blowsy Frances Cuka as Doll Tearsheet (in contrast with the youthful Jeanne Moreau in Orson Welles's *Chimes at Midnight*). A drawback was that the commitment to realism throughout the tetralogy even when the scenes were obviously unrealistic, as in the lists at Coventry, alienated the audience. The tiny television screen also tended to shrink the epical Henriad down in scale so that David Gwillim as the "mirror of Christian princes" seemed to be wearing the borrowed robes of Laurence Olivier. His best efforts could not authenticate the soldierly rhetoric of King Henry V (#182).

Nothing revolutionary happened in the beginning of the third season in 1981 with a *Hamlet* (#140), starring Derek Jacobi, which suffered from the same demon that had haunted nearly all the previous productions. Unable to decide whether it was theatrical or telegenic, the representation succeeded in being neither. Few concessions were made to a camera, though the bare *mise en scène* either acknowledged the impossibility of realistic strategies or betrayed the strains on the budget. Derek Jacobi gave his usual brilliant readings but for those who had only recently seen his *Richard II* it was sometimes hard to tell whether he was Hamlet or the self-pitying Richard II. The characters acted but did not interact. It was a Hamlet without *Hamlet,* so to speak, but Claire Bloom was a memorable Gertrude and Richard Emrys a fine first player. An interesting metatheatrical touch was to have Hamlet directly enter into the performance of the mouse trap as a foil to Lucianus, the nephew of the player king. More such resourcefulness would have colored the scene.

The producer of the series in the first two years had been Cedric Messina, a veteran BBC professional, who at the outset guided it through perilous and uncharted seas. In the third year he was replaced by Jonathan Miller who had the advantage of profiting from his predecessor's mistakes. The most notable change was an explicit policy that each production should reflect the practices of Shakespeare's own time by costuming the players in contemporary rather than in period costumes. Shakespeare's players, as is testified to by the Longleat sketch of *Titus Andronicus,* except for the principals, mainly wore Elizabethan dress on stage. The way to reconstruct those dress codes and the *mise en scène* of Shakespeare's time was to emulate the style of painters contemporaneous with Shakespeare. This same idea had already been explored in the first season with Desmond Davis' *Measure for Measure,* when the designer (Odette Barrow) drew on 17th-century Dutch painters for the costumes. Now, however, it was to be promulgated as official doctrine.

Thus in *Antony and Cleopatra* (#23), the work of Veronese provided the inspiration for costumes and sets, while Colin Blakely and Jane Lapotaire in the principal roles reduced the sprawling drama to the size of a geriatric love duet for the television screen. In *All's Well that Ends Well* (#3), when Helena is seated at the clavichord with a mirror on the wall above her, she closely resembles the lady in Emanuel de Witte's "Interior with a Woman at a Clavichord." Beyond that, director Elijah Moshinsky and lighting designer John Summers figured out how to light the set so as to enrich the really spooky performance of Angela Down as Helena. An acerbic Ian Charleson as a grumpy Bertram and the ubiquitous Michael Hordern, who magically seemed to pop up in so many BBC plays, made the production as successful as the first season's problem play, *Measure for Measure.*

Director Jack Gold's *Merchant of Venice* (#370) drew on Titian as a backdrop for a stony-faced Portia (Gemma Jones), who in true post-structuralist style subverts her own speech on mercy at the trial of Shylock (Warren Mitchell). Gold's camera also nicely pinpoints the spiritual desolation of both Jessica and Antonio, who at the end are left apart from the other, far happier, more integrated, citizens of a Wasp-ish Belmont.

One does not need great expertise in art history, though, to appreciate all of Dr. Miller's innovations. Considerable leeway remained for the genius of individual directors such as Jane Howell, whose *Winter's Tale* (#673) used minimalist, expressionistic sets and symbolic costumes (a bearskin hat and cloak for Leontes as a prefiguration of the famous bear in the third act). And Dr. Miller himself created a truly offbeat *Taming of the Shrew* (#603) when he cast John Cleese of Monty Python notoriety as a puritanical and deadly serious Petruchio. Cleese's prune-faced Petruchio contrasts so vividly with the farcicality of Richard Burton's in the Zeffirelli film as to make the two versions ideally suited for classroom analysis and comparison.

The pace slowed somewhat in the fourth season (1981-82) with only four plays: *Othello* (#472), *Timon of Athens* (#632), *A Midsummer Night's Dream* (#412), and *Troilus and Cressida* (#638). The two satirical plays, *Timon of Athens* and *Troilus,* brought Elizabethan esoterica within the range of mass audiences. Jonathan Pryce as the curmudgeonish and indubitably crazy Timon progressed from the excesses of generosity to the deficiencies of misanthropism. In *Troilus,* Charles Gray, a workhorse BBC actor, who in 1979 had played the title role in *Julius Caesar* and the Duke of York in *Richard II,* was cast as Pandarus, while the Incredible Orlando [*sic*] was the spiteful Thersites. Director Elijah Moshinsky, an emerging video *auteur,* in his *Midsummer Night's Dream,* followed the tactics of his earlier *All's Well* by borrowing design ideas from the Dutch masters. One shot of the "rude mechanicals" perched on a bench inside a tavern mirrored Hans Bols's "Members of the Wine Merchants' Guild," while a touch of whimsy made Cherith Mellor as Helena with her granny glasses and stick figure a triumph of adolescent misery. The season's most ambitious but not most rewarding production was *Othello* (#472). With Anthony Hopkins as the Moor, Bob Hoskins as Iago and Penelope Wilton as Desdemona, Director Miller brought his usual bundle of surprises to the production. Low-keyed, almost humdrum, at the beginning, Hopkins' Moor erupts in a Vesuvian blast when Hoskins' demonic, insinuating, cackling Iago finally unhinges him in the third act. Even if a mere coincidence, the linkage of the names, "Ho*p*kins" and "Ho*s*kins," hints at the production's stress on the *Doppelganger* relationship between hero and villain.

In the fifth season (1982-83), six more plays rolled off the BBC assembly line. An understated *King Lear* (#267) marked the third time, no less, that Director Jonathan Miller, and actors Michael Hordern (King Lear) and Frank Middlemass (Fool) had worked together on Shakespeare's supreme tragedy. The grizzled, somewhat dyspeptic, grumpy old man who emerged as the king was then hardly a casual product. Miller and Hordern de-mythologized King Lear by showing how his wicked daughters, with entire logic, might indeed have found the old man a pain in the neck. Instead of the flamboyant, ranting King Lear of a Frederick B. Warde (#246) or a "Sir" in *The Dresser* (#273), this king looked more like almost anybody's father on the verge of Alzheimer's disease. This undermining of the conventional image of the king as Jove-figure made the father-daughter bond notably more poignant. Since Hordern appeared as King Lear at virtually the same time as the Granada TV Olivier *King Lear* (#271), the two treatments make fine visual texts for comparison. Competing with Lord Olivier is hardly anyone's desire, but Hordern's rather cynical old man compares favorably with the more romantic image projected by Olivier. Both actors were self-referentially playing an aged star at the end of lengthy stage and film careers. The way that they chose to do Lear was the way that they had lived out their professional lives: Hordern as a skilled and reliable journeyman actor, and Olivier as a mercurial and spectacular superstar. Needless to say, following BBC institutional policy of catering to the schools, of the two versions the Hordern/Miller remains more faithful to Shakespeare's Quarto and Folio texts.

The *Cymbeline* (#73) that followed allowed the highly successful Elijah Moshinsky to demonstrate afresh his talent as an *auteur* of TV Shakespeare. It also brought the distinguished Shakespearean actress, Claire Bloom, back on the screen as the malevolent queen, while Robert Lindsay as Iachimo played out his erotic desires for Helen Mirren as Imogen. The following month saw Ben Kingsley as a paranoid Mr. Ford and Richard Griffiths as the scapegoated Falstaff in a *Merry Wives of Windsor* (#385). The season's triumph, however, was the sleeper of the entire Shakespeare series—Jane Howell's wonderful production of the minor tetralogy of the English history plays, *1-3 Henry VI* (#186, #187, #193) and *Richard III* (#513). The BBC plays got better as the directors began to discover the best strategies for presenting them, but Jane Howell completely abandoned the stodgy realism that had put audiences to yawning in favor of a visually exciting expressionism. With mirrors and with the aid of a children's play set inspired by, of all things, an "adventure playground" in Fulham, Howell's illusory battles became gorier than the real thing. Ron Cook as Richard Duke of Gloucester and Julia Foster as the "She-wolf of France," outdid each other in their portrayals of nasty royal personages. At the same time, as a person of the twentieth century, Howell managed to rearrange matters so that this saga of division and rebellion implicitly condemned warfare while portraying it.

The sixth season (1983-84), which was to have marked the coda, was not quite the end as four plays still had yet to be released. Shaun Sutton had by then replaced Jonathan Miller as producer and each year the series seemed more capable of solving the insoluble problems of putting Shakespeare on the small screen. With sponsorship from Exxon Corporation, Morgan Guaranty Trust Company, and the Metropolitan Life Insurance Company, as well as public broadcasting stations, the season in North America included *Coriolanus* (#67), *The Comedy of Errors* (#55), *Two Gentlemen of Verona* (#667), *Pericles* (#482), and *Macbeth* (#336).

The way that Alan Howard played Coriolanus opposite Mike Gwilym's Aufidius hinted at an erotic emotional bond between them, while veteran Shakespearean actress, Irene Worth, was Volumnia, mother of the "boy of tears." Both *Comedy of Errors* and *Two Gentlemen of Verona* delivered the farce and romance expected of them, though the sets for *Errors* with a huge built-in map of the Mediterranean right out of Ortelius' atlas, seemed the more brilliantly adapted to the medium. Pop singer Roger Daltrey, doubling as the Dromios, in *Errors* made a big hit with American students, because they could more readily identify with him than with actors from the Royal Shakespeare Company. Starring Mike Gwilym in the title role, director David Jones's *Pericles* with its soft Mediterranean lighting and rapid reversals in fortune captured the flavor of the Greek romance tradition. Trevor Peacock as Boult and Amanda Redman as Marina in the brothel scenes, and an unusually high frequency of dissolves to support Gower's narrative commentary, added visual bite to this strange and exotic tale. Again it was the tragedy that dominated the season. Nicol Williamson and Jane Lapotaire as Macbeth and his Lady thoroughly mined the subtext for imaginative readings. Lapotaire's handling of the "unsex me here" soliloquy will surely go down in acting history as anything but unsexed. Nicol Williamson, as in the Tony Richardson *Hamlet*, again brutally assaulted the text until it confessed its innermost secrets. No actor could be more energetic in the quest for truth.

The final group of four plays from the BBC series was released in the U.S.A. in 1984: Elijah Moshinsky's *Love's Labor's Lost* (#283), Stuart Burge's *Much Ado about Nothing* (#432), David Giles's *King John* (#240), and Jane Howell's *Titus Andronicus* (#633). The first, *Love's Labor's Lost*, broke with the BBC house style when Director Moshinsky put his cast in 18th-century instead of Elizabethan or Jacobean dress. The *Much Ado about Nothing* gave pioneering television director Stuart Burge, who had directed Maurice Evans in the Hallmark Shakespeare of the fifties, a chance to put Shakespeare on television once again. David Giles did something unusual with *King John* in casting a British comic actor, Leonard Rossiter, in the title role, though the anomaly was lost on American audiences. By rediscovering the possibilities for gothic chills in Shakespeare's strange Senecan tragedy, *Titus Andronicus*, Jane Howell marched off with the season's honors. It is a Rocky Horror Picture Show and yet more than that. It manages to lend a great deal of credibility to the incredibility of the Ovidian/Senecan rhetoric in Shakespeare's weird but compelling Roman history play.

Even as the BBC series marked a watershed in the history of Shakespeare on screen, other scenarios began to be written. For one thing the possibilities for easy video recording of Shakespeare on stage began to be exploited more and more, and organizations such as the New York City Lincoln Center Library TOFT (Theatre on Film and Tape) collection, the Folger Library, and the embryonic Globe Bankside Centre in London, began collecting videotapes for their archives. Indeed the concept of "video as archive" as opposed to "video as creation" has created a new category of screened Shakespeare. Presumably one day researchers will be able to study the history of Shakespeare in production on a video screen, though the stringent rules of actors and musicians' unions often make the taping of a commercial theatrical production so restrictive as to be impracticable.

Commercial groups have also begun to market full-scale video productions, which had never or rarely been transmitted on public television, directly to the schools. These include, for example, R. Thad Taylor's 1979 videotape of a lively *Merry Wives* (#383) starring Gloria Grahame as Mistress Page at the Los Angeles Globe playhouse. Another video series has been prepared for release through Encyclopedia Britannica by Bard Productions, Ltd., with the intention of allowing students to see popular American actors from the soaps in Shakespeare. So far the titles include *Macbeth* (#340), *Richard II* (#494), *Antony and Cleopatra* (#27), and *The Tempest* (#627). Certainly the *Richard II*, starring a well known television star, David Birney, is impressive. When Bolingbroke interrogates Bushy and Green, the "caterpillars of the commonwealth," the scene is more of a good old fashioned American police third degree than a lecture by the stern headmaster. There is also a *Macbeth* (#333) directed by Sarah Caldwell available on videocassette from Films for the Humanities, which has also been shown locally on television. In fact the best of this new VCR genre is the 1987 Cambridgeshire post-modernist *Hamlet* (#154) that, with only four actors, deconstructs and then reconstructs Shakespeare's text in the idiom of a pyschodelic rock/video. Its re-envisionment of the text springs from an honest drive to use the camera not just for recording a play but for artistry in its own right.

Still another thriving sub-species of the Shakespeare on screen genre lies in the appropriation of bits, pieces, and segments of Shakespeare by the scenarists for popular television shows. Difficult to track down because they are not listed separately in the television guides, and therefore not fully covered in this volume, are Shakespearean episodes in such commercial programs as *Cheers* and *Star Trek*. These kinds of flash appearances stem partly, no doubt, from the fact that Shakespeare is in the public domain and therefore a cheap source for material. They also validate, however, how deeply he is embedded in the general culture.

The grand agenda for putting Shakespeare on screen that began modestly at the end of the last century continues to expand and grow at the end of this century. In this past decade when the full-scale Shakespeare film had been thought eclipsed by the television industry, the counter-culture filmmaker, Derek Jarman, has brought out his punk *Tempest* (#622), which unfortunately received a hostile reception at the New York Film Festival. Jean-Luc Godard's 1987 Shakespeare-based *King Lear* (#277) has also been released, though to unfavorable reviews. And most recently there has appeared a brilliant multi-million dollar cinema, not television, version of *King Henry V* starring Kenneth Branagh (see #182.2). There is also word of a forthcoming *Hamlet* to be filmed by Franco

Zeffirelli. In the age of Walter Benjamin's "mechanical reproduction," movies and television, which technologically grow closer and closer together, assert their cultural roles in the transmission of the Shakespeare text to successive generations. Surely in the 21st century this new art form, aptly labelled "electronic literature" by Prof. H. Philip Bolton, will play a greater and greater role in the preservation and transmission of the Shakespearean canon.

K.S.R.

Endnotes

1. For works cited parenthetically, see bibliography at the end of this book. All others will be cited in footnotes.
2. Numbers following film titles indicate the location of the full entry in the main filmography.
3. See dissertation abstract, "From the Globe to the Screen: An Interpretive Study of Shakespeare through Film," Stanford 1984, in *SFNL* 11.1 (Dec. 1986): 11.
4. James Naremore, *Acting in the Cinema* (Berkeley: U of California P, 1988): 85.
5. Blake Lucas, "Acting Styles in Silent Films," in *Magill's Survey of Cinema*, I, ed. Frank N. Magill. (Englewood Cliffs: Salem Press, 1981): 1-11.
6. See Leland A. Poague, "*As You Like It* and *It Happened One Night:* The Generic Pattern of Comedy," *LFQ* 5.4 (Fall 1974): 346-50; and, Robert F. Willson, Jr., "'Ill Met by Moonlight': Reinhardt's *A Midsummer Night's Dream* and Musical Screwball Comedy," *Journal of Popular Film* 5 (1976): 185-97.
7. For a recent biography, see Charles Higham, *Orson Welles: The Rise and Fall of an American Genius* (New York: St. Martins Press, 1985).
8. *Time* 93 (28 Feb. 1969): 74.
9. Educational films about a particular play are included under the title of the play; topics of a more general nature, such as "acting," or "verse," are listed in chronological order at the end of the book under the heading "Documentaries."
10. Transmission data from mimeographed *Programme as Broadcast*, 1937. BBC Written Archives Centre, Reading.
11. "Floor Mistakes," Internal Circulating Memo, BBC WAC TS/508 6 Feb. 1939.
12. Gordon Ross, *Television Jubilee: The Story of 25 Years of BBC Television* (London: Allen, 1961): 59.
13. "Shakespeare on Television," *BBC Quarterly* 9.3 (Autumn 1954): 146.

The Plays

All's Well That Ends Well

ORIGINAL WORK AND PRODUCTION: Dark comedy. *Year written:* 1604; *Site of first production:* Whitehall Palace [?].

All's Well that Ends Well. **Video/Teleplay**

1. *All's Well that Ends Well.*

DOCUMENT INFORMATION: *Country:* GB; *Year of first showing:* 1968; *Location of first showing:* BBC-2, Transmitted 9:00 to 11:00 P.M., Monday, 3 June 1968.

EDITION, HISTORY, CONTENTS, & EVALUATION: *Edition & history:* A Royal Shakespeare Company production adapted to television. Despite its excellent cast, no copy of it seems to exist. Ian Hogg, who plays Lavatch, turned up in the Polanski *Macbeth* as the vicious murderer of Macduff's son, and Ian Richardson played an unforgettable Oberon in the Peter Hall film version of *MND. Supplementary materials:* "Program." *RT* 30 May 1968: 17.

MEDIUM INFORMATION: *Length:* 120 min.

AUTHORSHIP INFORMATION: *Producer(s):* Travers, Ronald; *Director(s):* Barton, John (RSC); Whatham, Claude (BBC); *Composer(s):* Oldfield, Derek; *Designer(s):* O'Brien, Timothy; Spence, Susan (BBC); *Costume designer(s):* Firth, Tazeena; *Lighting designer(s):* Wright, Robert; *Other role(s):* Mackie, Gordon (Sound); Musgrove, Janet (Make-up); *Cast:* Lacey, Catherine (Countess of Rousillion); Richardson, Ian (Bertram); Mason,

Brewster (LaFeu); Fairleigh, Lynn (Helena); Swift, Clive (Parolles); Shaw, Sebastian (King of France); Hogg, Ian (Lavatch); Moynihan, Daniel (Lord Dumain); Ashford, David (Duke of Florence); Bailie, David (Morgan); Spriggs, Elizabeth (Widow); Kent, Natalie (Mariana); Hunt, Caroline (Diana); + Soldiers, Attendants, and Musicians.

DISTRIBUTION & AVAILABILITY: *Copy location:* Unavailable.

All's Well that Ends Well. **Video/Recording**

2. *All's Well that Ends Well.*

DOCUMENT INFORMATION: *Country:* USA; *Year of first showing:* 5 July 1978; *Location of first showing:* Delacorte Theatre, New York City.

EDITION, HISTORY, CONTENTS, & EVALUATION: *Edition & history:* A recording of a 1978 New York Shakespeare Festival performance in the Delacorte Theatre, Central Park. For other New York Shakespeare Festival recorded productions, see numbers 66, 120, 152, 235, 263, 329, 413, 428, 469. *Contents & evaluation:* "All the shapes [of this production] are changed. The play's large features are made to dwindle and its details are absurdly magnified. What is essential is toyed with, often ingeniously, and what is secondary is sometimes expounded and expanded for no better reason, apparently, than that it offers the possibility of doing something showy with it. . . . Wilford Leach has both designed and directed, and his fertile and playful imagination is stamped all over the production. The design is quite marvelous: a tiny Paris, Florence and Rousillon nestle side by side into Central Park's gentle hills. . . ." Mark Linn Baker [Bertram] "looks a bit like Woody Allen and a bit like Chaplin. [Baker's performance] . . . is well done, and Mr. Baker has great promise, but it is totally inadequate to sustain the role." Pamela Reed gives "a performance that is original, witty and touching as Helena. She bursts with brains, quivers with passion, and carries these charges with a stiff girlishness. But she is not allowed sufficient force or continuity; each time she begins to develop her character the music comes in or some distracting bit of comic staging shunts her aside" (Eder, Richard, "Stage: 'All's Well' Comes to Park," *NYT* 7 July 1978, sec.3, 3). *Audience:* College and university; General use; *Supplementary materials:* Berkvist, Robert. "All's Well with Shakespeare in the Park." *NYT* 30 June 1978: C3.

MEDIUM INFORMATION: *Medium:* Video; *Sound:* Spoken language; *Color:* Yes; *Length:* 160 min.; *Language(s) spoken:* English; *Video type:* 3/4U.

AUTHORSHIP INFORMATION: *Producer(s):* Papp, Joseph; *Director(s):* Leach, Wilford; *Composer(s):* Weinstock, Richard; *Designer(s):* Leach, Wilford; *Cast:* Baker, Marc Linn (Bertram); Reed, Pamela (Helena); Wilson, Elizabeth (Countess of Rossillion); Pine, Larry (Parolles); Conroy, Frances (Diana); Williams, Barbara (Widow); Ferraro, John (Lavatch).

DISTRIBUTION & AVAILABILITY: *Publisher or responsible agency:* New York Shakespeare Festival; *Copy location:* LCL TOFT Collection; *Call or copy number:* NCOV 82; *Availability:* By appt.(Call Mrs. Betty Corwin, 212-870-1641).

All's Well that Ends Well. Video/Teleplay

3. *All's Well that Ends Well.* (Series: The Shakespeare Plays (USA); The BBC Shakespeare Plays (GB).

DOCUMENT INFORMATION: *Country:* GB/USA; *Year of first showing:* 1980; *Location of first showing(s):* BBC, London; PBS stations, USA, 18 May 1981.

EDITION, HISTORY, CONTENTS, & EVALUATION: *Edition & history:* Script based on Peter Alexander text, as adapted by David Snodin for TV. *Contents & evaluation:* "Elijah Moshinsky's *All's Well* impresses us as one of the best BBC productions because of fine casting, and extremely intelligent and sensitive performing and editing. One admires this director's close attention to the lines and feels that, despite the extensive cutting, he faces rather than evades the basic problems of the play. Angela Down, cool, troubled, flexible, and restrained, complements particularly well

the exceptional pictorial settings that skilfully evoke the lighting, the casements, mirrors, and drapery of Vermeer. Ian Charleson surpasses his other roles in the series, preparing us for his deceit by saying the right things in a tight, cold, quiet way, and Pippa Guard suggests lively playfulness. . . . Even those pleased with this production could hardly have expected its brilliant consummation in the notorious conclusion. . . . With a technique impossible on stage but finely suited to the screen, the camera very slowly pans from right to left . . . finding first Parolles, then the smiling Diana, then Lafeu, the King, the Countess, and finally Bertram. We see their eyes and mouths express their wonder as they see Helena—before we finally see her. The scene is strikingly effective. . . ." (Weil, Herbert J., Jr., "*All's Well that Ends Well,*" *SFNL* 7.1 [1982]:2). *Audience:* College and university; General use; *Supplementary materials:* Willis, Susan. "Taping *All's Well.*" *SFNL* 6.1 (1982): 3; Videocassette (25 min.) from "Shakespeare in Perspective" series with Barry Took as lecturer available in U.K. from BBC* (*BUFVC* 1).

MEDIUM INFORMATION: *Medium:* Video; *Sound:* Spoken language; *Color:* Yes; *Condition:* Excellent; *Length:* 160 min.; *Language(s) spoken:* English; *Video type:* B, V, 3/4U.

AUTHORSHIP INFORMATION: *Producer(s):* Miller, Jonathan; *Director(s):* Moshinsky, Elijah; *Adaptor/translator(s):* Snodin, David; *Composer(s):* Oliver, Stephen; *Choreographer(s):* Fazan, Eleanor; *Designer(s):* Myerscough-Jones, David; *Costume designer(s):* Lavers, Colin; *Lighting designer(s):* Summers, John; *Other personnel:* Wilders, John (Literary consultant); Broad, Suzan (Make-up); Miller-Timmins, Derek (Sound); *Cast:* Johnson, Celia (Countess of Rousillion); Charleson, Ian (Bertram); Hordern, Michael (Lafeu); Down, Angela (Helena); Jeffrey, Peter (Parolles); Sinden, Donald (King of France); Lindsay, Robert; (French Lord); Jephcott, Dominic (French Lord); Brooke, Paul (Lavatch); Stoney, Kevin (Steward); Leach, Rosemary (Widow); Guard, Pippa (Diana).

DISTRIBUTION & AVAILABILITY: *Distributor:* AVP, UIO, BBC*, *Copy location:* CTL*, UVM (Archive); *Availability:* AVP, all formats $450 (1987), sale; IOA, V (72030H), 3/4U (7013OV), $23.00; BBC* 16mm or V, apply .

All's Well that Ends Well. Video/Recording

4. *All's Well that Ends Well.*

DOCUMENT INFORMATION: *Country:* USA; *Year of first showing:* 1982.

EDITION, HISTORY, CONTENTS, & EVALUATION: *Edition & history:* A videotaping of scenes from a 1982 stage production of *All's Well that Ends Well* performed by the Berkeley Shakespeare Festival. A copy is housed in the TOFT collection (Theatre on Film and Tape) at the Billy Rose Theatre Collection of the Library of Performing Arts, Lincoln Center, New York Public Library. It may be viewed by appointment (see below). *Contents & evaluation:* Not seen. *Audience:* College and university; General use.

MEDIUM INFORMATION: *Medium:* Video; *Sound:* Spoken language; *Color:* Yes; *Length:* 38 min.; *Language(s) spoken:* English; *Video type:* 3/4U.

AUTHORSHIP INFORMATION: *Producer(s):* Berkeley Shakespeare Festival; *Director(s):* Not known.

DISTRIBUTION & AVAILABILITY: *Publisher or responsible agency:* Berkeley Shakespeare Festival; *Copy location:* LCL TOFT Collection; *Call or copy number:* NCOV 308; *Availability:* By appt. (Call Mrs. Betty Corwin, 212-870-1641).

All's Well that Ends Well. Video/Scenes

5. *The Shakespeare Hour.*

DOCUMENT INFORMATION: *Country:* GB/USA; *Year of release:* 1985.

EDITION, HISTORY, CONTENTS, & EVALUATION: *Edition & history:* The series, "The Shakespeare Hour," was shown on national educational television beginning on January 5, 1985. It was funded by the National Endowment for the Humanities and produced by Station WNET/THIRTEEN, New York City. For further references to and commentary on this series, see numbers 276, 352, 417, 663. *Contents & evaluation:* The 1985 season was the first and last for this ambitious series. The original concept seemed promising enough: the teleplays in the BBC/Time-Life "The Shakespeare Plays" series were to be "recycled" by being subdivided into one-hour segments. Scripts were written by Kenneth Cavendar of WNET for opening and closing

"wraparounds," and famed screen star Walter Matthau was signed on as host and commentator. It was hoped by these strategies to attract a larger audience than the original BBC productions had drawn. Having been made in England, the original programs were produced without much thought to the needs of American television, on which everything must be fitted to 15 or 30-minute station breaks for commercials. In England TV programs have traditionally begun at almost any moment in an hour—ten past, twelve of, whatever—and go on cheerily until they end, whatever the minute of the hour. As a result some of the BBC teleplays are inordinately lengthy, running three and four hours even. Each year, the WNET/Thirteen program was to have had a different theme. In the first year, which featured five plays—*MND, TN, AWW, MM,* and *Lr.*—the choice was "Love." The themes of "Power" and "Revenge" were scheduled for the next two years, but those programs never materialized. The first season became the last, the victim of low ratings. The abrupt demise was not entirely the fault of the producers, who put together some excellent material. In addition, a book of essays by distinguished scholars to accompany the series was compiled and edited by Prof. Edward Quinn. *Supplementary materials:* Quinn, Edward, ed. TSH.

MEDIUM INFORMATION: *Medium:* Video; *Sound:* Spoken language; *Color:* Yes; *Length:* 180 min.; *Language(s) spoken:* English; *Video type:* V.

AUTHORSHIP INFORMATION: *Producer(s):* BBC-WNET/THIRTEEN; *Director(s):* Moshinsky, Elijah; Johnson, Donald; Kieffer, Tom; Bellin, Harvey (WNET); *Screenplay writer(s):* Cavendar, Kenneth; *Other role(s):* Squerciati, Marie Therese (Project director); *Cast:* Matthau, Walter; Cast of BBC/Time Life *All's Well that Ends Well.* (q.v.).

DISTRIBUTION & AVAILABILITY: *Publisher or responsible agency:* WNET/THIRTEEN; *Distributor:* ALS.

Antony and Cleopatra

ORIGINAL WORK AND PRODUCTION: Tragedy of Mature Love. *Year written:* 1606-7; *Site of first production:* Globe Playhouse [?].

Antony and Cleopatra. **Motion Picture/Scene**

6. *Cleopatra.*

DOCUMENT INFORMATION: *Country:* France; *Year of release:* 1899.

EDITION, HISTORY, CONTENTS, & EVALUATION: *Edition & history:* This lost film of Cleopatra's death scene is of great interest because it was produced by the pioneering French filmmaker, Georges Méliès. The infatuation of early movie directors with the Bard stemmed from several considerations, not all of them equally praiseworthy. There was a human tendency for the fledgling industry to overcome some of its disreputability by borrowing from the works of the great masters of English literature. In that sense these early silents were often the first examples of the so-called "exploitation film." With Shakespeare's prestige as high then as it is now among the general public, filmmakers hoped to bask in the reflected glory (KSR). *Supplementary materials:* Ball, *SOSF* 307.

MEDIUM INFORMATION: *Length:* 5 min.

AUTHORSHIP INFORMATION: *Director(s):* Méliès, Georges.

Antony and Cleopatra. **Motion Picture/Abbreviated**

7. *Antony and Cleopatra.*

DOCUMENT INFORMATION: *Country:* USA; *Year of release:* 1903.

EDITION, HISTORY, CONTENTS, & EVALUATION: *Edition & history:* Another in a series of one-reel (ten-minute) Vitagraph silent movies made in New York City at the turn of the century. The Vitagraph series is described in greater detail elsewhere (See *TN,* below #640). *Supplementary materials:* Ball, *SOSF* 47.

MEDIUM INFORMATION: *Length:* 10 min.

AUTHORSHIP INFORMATION: *Director(s):* Kent, Charles.

DISTRIBUTION & AVAILABILITY: *Distributor:* JEF.

Antony and Cleopatra. **Motion Picture/Derivative**

8. *Cleopatra.*

DOCUMENT INFORMATION: *Country:* France; *Year of release:* 1910.

EDITION, HISTORY, CONTENTS, & EVALUATION: *Edition & history:* A Film d'Art production by Pathé, which with elaborate costuming, tinting, and actors from the Comédie Francaise sought to bring artistic respectability to cinema. French filmmakers felt a responsibility to record theatrical performances of great actors. *Supplementary materials:* Ball, *SOSF* 112.

MEDIUM INFORMATION: *Length:* 18 min.

AUTHORSHIP INFORMATION: *Director(s):* Zecca, Ferdinand.

9. *Cleopatra.*

DOCUMENT INFORMATION: *Country:* USA; *Year of release:* 1912.

EDITION, HISTORY, CONTENTS, & EVALUATION: *Edition & history:* A blockbuster of extraordinary length for its time (six reels) but apparently not very closely related to Shakespeare's play. *Supplementary materials:* Ball, *SOSF* 147; *SIF* 113.

MEDIUM INFORMATION: *Length:* 60 min.

AUTHORSHIP INFORMATION: *Director(s):* Gaskill, Charles; *Cast:* Gardner, Helen (Cleopatra).

10. *Marcantonio e Cleopatra.*

DOCUMENT INFORMATION: *Country:* Italy; *Year of release:* 1913; *Country of first showing:* Italy.

EDITION, HISTORY, CONTENTS, & EVALUATION: *Edition & history:* Made in Italy in 1913, this film resembles Shakespeare's play in title only. Only the spirit of Shakespeare's play lingers on, and that barely alive. *Contents & evaluation:* Although remote from its alleged source, the film (and the film industry) benefited from being identified with the Bard at a time when movies were struggling for artistic recognition. This early silent film, vaguely based on *Antony*, offers a prefiguration of the Cecil B. DeMille superextravaganza with a cast of thousands. At eight reels, it was, according to R.H. Ball, the longest "Shakespeare" film yet produced. Unfairly removed from its 1913 historical position and re-viewed in 1990, the film may seem ludicrous. For one thing the pre-WWI Italian actresses did not feel compelled to starve themselves to the point of anorexia. A well fed Cleopatra has arms ample enough to squeeze the life out of the hardiest Antony. Despite such anachronisms, the film dazzles with its callow exuberance. Rooted in the Italianate operatic tradition, the movie's lavish costumes compete for the eye with a gigantic replica of Cleopatra's barge that fills the whole screen. This is a far cry from the puny efforts of the Vitagraph people in New York. A sample of the action: when Cleopatra catches Antony ogling Charmian, she has the poor girl whipped and then thrown to the crocodiles. The spectacle of such pain and suffering fills Cleopatra with joy. This bit of dialogue from one card best epitomizes the production's flavor: "Methinks the sternness of thy brow be but a mask to cover the tenderness of thy conqueror's heart" (KSR). *Audience:* General use; *Supplementary materials:* Ball, *SOSF* 166-68.

MEDIUM INFORMATION: *Medium:* Motion Picture;

Sound: Silent; *Color:* No (black & white); *Condition:* Good; *Length:* 63 min.; *Language of subtitles:* English, French, Italian; *Film type:* 16mm.

AUTHORSHIP INFORMATION: *Producer(s):* Kleine, George; Guazzoni, Enrico; *Director(s):* Guazzoni, Enrico; *Cast:* Gonzales, Giovanna Terribili (Cleopatra); Novelli, Antony (Antony); Lupi, Ignazio (Augustus Caesar); Lenard, Elsa (Octavia); Marzio, Matilde di (Charmian).

DISTRIBUTION & AVAILABILITY: *Copy location:* FOL; *Call or copy number:* MP 6; *Availability:* By appointment.

Antony and Cleopatra. **Motion Picture/ Abbreviated**

11. *Antony and Cleopatra.*

DOCUMENT INFORMATION: *Country:* Italy; *Year of release:* 1913.

EDITION, HISTORY, CONTENTS, & EVALUATION: *Edition & history:* See Professor Ball's discussion of the tangled history behind this film. *Supplementary materials:* Ball, *SOSF* 165.

AUTHORSHIP INFORMATION: *Director(s):* Cines Italy.

Antony and Cleopatra. **Motion Picture/Derivative**

12. *Cleopatra.*

DOCUMENT INFORMATION: *Country:* USA; *Year of release:* 1917.

EDITION, HISTORY, CONTENTS, & EVALUATION: *Edition & history:* Simply because Theda Bara (b. Theodosia Goodman), a Hollywood legend, played Cleopatra, this lost film is worth recording here. Professor Ball establishes that the film was "concocted out of Plutarch, Sardou, Shakespeare, and a lot of Adrian Johnson, who wrote the script" (*SOSF* 253). *Supplementary materials:* *SIF* 113.

MEDIUM INFORMATION: *Length:* 110 min.

AUTHORSHIP INFORMATION: *Director(s):* Edwards, J. Gordon; *Adaptor/translator(s):* Johnson, Adrian; *Cast:* Bara, Theda (Cleopatra); Leiber, Fritz (Caesar).

Antony and Cleopatra. **Motion Picture/ Abridgment**

13. *Antony and Cleopatra.*

DOCUMENT INFORMATION: *Country:* GB; *Year of release:* 1951.

EDITION, HISTORY, CONTENTS, & EVALUATION:

Contents & evaluation: Not seen. Morris gives it low grades. He describes it as a "condensation" in terms that suggest its textual amputations are too casual to make it a well planned "abridgment." In any event this is all academic, since there does not seem to be a current distributor or archivist. Its inaccessibility is all the more regrettable in view of the acting talent of Robert Speaight, a committed Shakespearean. *Supplementary materials:* Morris ShOF 15; H&M 15.

MEDIUM INFORMATION: *Color:* No (black & white); *Length:* 33 min.

AUTHORSHIP INFORMATION: *Producer:* Parthian Productions; *Cast:* Speaight, Robert; Letts, Pauline.

Antony and Cleopatra, 1-2. Video/Teledrama

14. *Serpent, The.* (Series: The Spread of the Eagle [VII]).

DOCUMENT INFORMATION: *Country:* GB; *Year of first showing:* 1963; *Location of first showing:* BBC TV. Transmitted 9:25 to 10:15 P.M., Friday, 14 June 1963.

EDITION, HISTORY, CONTENTS, & EVALUATION: *Edition & history:* The title for the series, "The Spread of the Eagle," came from the Roman eagle, "aloof, golden, and cruel," according to Producer/Director Peter Dews. The nine-part series drew on three of the Roman history plays—*Coriolanus, Julius Caesar* and *Antony and Cleopatra.* The dominant theme was identical to that of *An Age of Kings*: the Tudor passion for order and strong government. This Tillyardian view reflected the ideology of the mid-Sixties, whose bland acceptance of bourgeois values had not yet been challenged by the disarray of the Vietnam era. Coriolanus becomes the "ex-soldier who tries to run post-war politics on wartime principles," without the slightest success. The production involved a huge cast of some 76 actors and expenses in excess of £9,000. For other segments in the series, see also numbers 15, 16, 59-61, 221-23. *Contents & evaluation:* The London *Times* critic felt that the episodes lacked continuity since the only character who appears in more than one of the three plays is Antony. It was apparently a recorded stage reading more than a full-scale teleplay ("Continuity Problem of New B.B.C. Shakespeare Series," *Times* 4 May 1963: 5d). *Audience:* General use; *Supplementary materials:* Dews, Peter. "The Spread of the Eagle." *RT* 25 Apr. 1963: 49; "Program." *RT* 6 June 1963: 47.

MEDIUM INFORMATION: *Medium:* Video; *Sound:* Spoken language; *Color:* No (black & white); *Length:* 51 min.; *Language(s) spoken:* English; *Video type:* Video, Kinescope.

AUTHORSHIP INFORMATION: *Producer(s):* Dews, Peter; *Director(s):* Dews, Peter; *Composer(s):* Whelen, Christopher; *Designer(s):* Hatts, Clifford; *Costume de-signer(s):* Agombar, Elizabeth; *Other personnel:* Manderson, Tommy (Make-up); *Cast:* Michell, Keith (Antony); Morris, Mary (Cleopatra); Selway, George (Enobarbus); William, David (Octavius Caesar); Laurence, Charles (Philo); Weston, David (Demetrius); Dixon, Jill (Charmian); Barcroft, John (Alexas); Bailey, Paul (Soothsayer); Young, Lucy (Iras); Greenwood, John (Messenger); Oulton, Brian (Lepidus); Cracknell, Leonard (Messenger); King, David (Mardian); Willis, Jerome (Pompey); Jackson, Barry (Menecrates); Hinsliff, Geoffrey (Menas); Harte, Ben (Varrius); Gay, John (Maecenas); Rowe, Alan (Agrippa); Dickson, Hugh (Messenger); Wale, Terry (Eros); Croucher, Roger (Dolabella); Lloyd, Bernard (Scarus); + Clarke, Raymond; Craig, Pamela; Desmond, Marion; Finch, Bernard; Harris, Paul; Herrick, Roy; Stephens, Caroline; Varnals, Wendy; Webster, Paul; Wright, Hilary.

DISTRIBUTION & AVAILABILITY: *Publisher or responsible agency*: BBC; *Copy location:* BBC archive (6 of 9 parts).

Antony and Cleopatra, 2-4. Video/Teledrama

15. *Alliance, The.* (Series: The Spread of the Eagle [VIII]).

DOCUMENT INFORMATION: *Country:* GB; *Year of first showing:* 1963; *Location of first showing:* BBC TV. Transmitted 9:25 to 10:15 P.M., Friday, 21 June 1963.

EDITION, HISTORY, CONTENTS, & EVALUATION: *Edition & history:* For background, see the account of the first episode in the series, number #14 above. *Audience:* General use; *Supplementary materials:* Dews, Peter. "The Spread of the Eagle." *RT* 25 Apr. 1963: 49; "Program." *RT* 13 June 1963: 47.

MEDIUM INFORMATION: *Medium:* Video; *Sound:* Spoken language; *Color:* No (black & white); *Length:* 51 min.; *Language(s) spoken:* English; *Video type:* Video, Kinescope.

AUTHORSHIP INFORMATION: *Producer(s):* Dews, Peter; *Director(s):* Dews, Peter; *Composer(s):* Whelen, Christopher; *Choreographer(s):* Stevenson, Geraldine; *Designer(s):* Hatts, Clifford; *Costume designer(s):* Agombar, Elizabeth; *Other personnel:* Manderson, Tommy (Make-up); *Cast:* Michell, Keith (Antony); Morris, Mary (Cleopatra); Selway, George (Enobarbus); William, David (Octavius Caesar); Laurence, Charles (Thidias); Weston, David (Canidius); Dixon, Jill (Charmian); Barcroft, John (Alexas); Young, Lucy (Iras); Greenwood, John (Servant); Oulton, Brian (Lepidus); King, David (Ambassador); Willis, Jerome (Pompey); Hinsliff, Geoffrey (Menas); Gay, John (Maecenas); Rowe, Alan (Agrippa); Dickson, Hugh (Messenger); Wale, Terry (Eros); Croucher, Roger (Dolabella); Lloyd, Bernard (Scarus); Jackson, Nancie (Octavia); Harris, Paul (Taurus); + Bailey, Paul; Cracknell, Leonard;

Craig, Pamela; Desmond, Marion; Finch, Bernard; Herrick, Roy; Jackson, Barry; Stephens, Caroline; Varnals, Wendy; Webster, Paul; Wright, Hilary.

DISTRIBUTION & AVAILABILITY: *Publisher or responsible agency:* BBC; *Copy location:* BBC (6 of 9 parts).

Antony and Cleopatra, 4-5. Video/Teledrama

16. *Monument, The.* (Series: The Spread of the Eagle [IX]).

DOCUMENT INFORMATION: *Country:* GB; *Year of first showing:* 1963; *Location of first showing:* BBC TV. Transmitted 9:25 to 10:20 P.M., Friday, 28 June 1963.

EDITION, HISTORY, CONTENTS, & EVALUATION: *Edition & history:* This final installment used a cast of 31 principals and 10 extras. The budget came close to £6,000. For additional background information, see first episode of *Antony and Cleopatra,* number #14 above. *Audience:* General use; *Supplementary materials:* Dews, Peter. "The Spread of the Eagle." *RT* 25 Apr. 1963: 49; "Program." *RT* 20 June 1963: 47.

MEDIUM INFORMATION: *Medium:* Video; *Sound:* Spoken language; *Color:* No (black & white); *Length:* 55 min.; *Language(s) spoken:* English; *Video type:* Video, Kinescope.

AUTHORSHIP INFORMATION: *Producer(s):* Dews, Peter; *Director(s):* Dews, Peter; *Composer(s):* Whelen, Christopher; The Philip Jones Ensemble; *Designer(s):* Hatts, Clifford; *Costume designer(s):* Agombar, Elizabeth; *Lighting designer(s):* Whitmore, Wally; *Other personnel:* Hutchings, Sam (Technical Manager); Mackie, Gordon (Sound); Barclay, Richard; Perfitt, Richard (Editors); Dudley, Philip (Prod. Asst.); Manderson, Tommy (Make-up); Greenwood, John; Ware, Derek (Fight coordinators); *Cast:* Michell, Keith (Antony); Morris, Mary (Cleopatra); Selway, George (Enobarbus); William, David (Octavius Caesar); Wale, Terry (Eros); Hinsliff, Geoffrey (Soldier); Dixon, Jill (Charmian); Young, Lucy (Iras); Rowe, Alan (Agrippa); Harte, Ben (Messenger); Jackson, Barry (Soldier); Lloyd, Bernard (Scarus); Greenwood, John (A Centurion); Webster, Paul; Herrick, Roy (Sentries); King, David (Mardian); Laurence, Charles (Dercetas); Cracknell, Leonard; Barcroft, John; Finch, Bernard; Harris, Paul (Guardsmen); Weston, David (Diomedes); Dickson, Hugh (An Egyptian); Croucher, Roger (Dolabella); Gay, John (Maecenas); Bailey, Paul (A Clown); + Craig, Pamela; Desmond, Marion; Stephens, Caroline; Varnals, Wendy; Wright, Hilary.

DISTRIBUTION & AVAILABILITY: *Publisher or responsible agency:* BBC; *Copy location:* BBC archive (6 of 9 parts).

Antony and Cleopatra. Motion Picture/Derivative

17. *Carry on Cleo.*

DOCUMENT INFORMATION: *Country:* GB; *Year of release:* 1964; *Year of first showing:* London, Dec. 1964; New York, 22 Oct. 1965.

EDITION, HISTORY, CONTENTS, & EVALUATION: *Edition & history:* In a way *Carry on Cleo* is to *Julius Caesar* and *Antony and Cleopatra* what *Boys from Syracuse* is to *Comedy of Errors.* On the other hand *Carry on Cleo* is more of a travesty than a farce because it transmogrifies tragic materials into a farcical context. It thereby crudely violates its Shakespearean source, though not very much of Shakespeare is left in the script. *Contents & evaluation:* This is a ridiculous farce at the level of *Bromo and Juliet* but wittier. Actually the gift of English scenarists for inspired silliness of the Monty Python variety rescues the film from total oblivion. The level of the dialogue can be judged from the following exchange between Caesar and Calphurnia: Caesar says, "I have stones from Gaul." Calphurnia's father replies, "She already has gallstones." Again, when Julius Caesar says "Draw near and lend me your ear," Calphurnia's father warns, "Don't dear. You'll never get it back!" The scenario is also crammed with British in-jokes, such as a reference to "Marcus et Spencius," a famous London department store in Oxford Street. In *Carry on Cleo*, Britons are auctioned off there by the Romans. The absurd plot blithers wildly afield from any connection with the Bard. Recommended for people who are in a thoroughly carnivalesque mood (KSR). *Audience:* General use.

MEDIUM INFORMATION: *Medium:* Motion Picture; *Sound:* Spoken language; *Color:* Yes; *Length:* 92 min.; *Language(s) spoken:* English; *Film type:* 16mm.

AUTHORSHIP INFORMATION: *Producer(s):* Rogers, Peter; Bevis, Frank; *Director(s):* Thomas, Gerald; Bolton, Peter; *Screenplay writer(s):* Rothwell, Talbot; *Adaptor/translator(s):* Rothwell, Talbot ("from an original idea by William Shakespeare"); *Composer(s):* Rogers, Eric; *Designer(s):* Davey, Bert; *Costume designer(s):* Harris, Julie; Rodway, Geoff (Makeup); Fordyce, Ann (Hair); *Lighting designer(s):* Hume, Alan; *Other personnel:* Ludski, Archie (Editor); Godar, Godfrey (Camera); Toms, Donald (Unit manager); Lancaster, Christopher (Sound editor); Daniel, Bill; McCallum, Gordon R. (Sound recordists); Brook, Olga (Continuity); *Cast:* James, Sidney (Mark Anthony); Williams, Kenneth (Julius Caesar); Connor, Kenneth (Hengist Pod); Hawtrey, Charles (Seneca); Sims, Joan (Calphurnia); Dale, Jim (Horsa); Barrie, Amanda (Cleopatra); Madden, Victor (Sgt. Major); Hancock, Sheila (Seneca Pod); DeWolff, Francis (Agrippa); Oulton, Brian (Brutus); Stevens, Julie (Gloria); Pertwee, Jon (Soothsayer); Ward, Michael (Archimedes); Clegg, Tom (Sosages); Bunning, Tanya (Virginia); Davenport, David (Bilius); Wilson, Ian (Messenger); Klauber, Gertan (Marcus); Gilmore, Peter (Galley master); Rawlinson, Brian (Driver); Mitchell, Warren (Spencius); Emmett, E.V.H. (Narrator); + Nightingale, Michael; Jesson, Peter.

DISTRIBUTION & AVAILABILITY: *Publisher or responsible agency:* Anglo-Amalgamated/Peter Rogers Production; *Distributor:* FCM, *Copy location:* NFA*; *Availability:* FCM, sale, V, $39.95.

Antony and Cleopatra. **Motion Picture/ Documentary**

18. *Antony and Cleopatra: The World Well Lost.* (Series: Explorations in Shakespeare I).

DOCUMENT INFORMATION: *Country:* Canada; *Year of release:* 1969.

EDITION, HISTORY, CONTENTS, & EVALUATION: *Edition & history:* Part one in a series of twelve 23-minute films made in 1969 by the Ontario Educational Communications Authority. For other segments, see numbers 40, 65, 124, 162, 257, 322, 465, 488, 555, 617, and 637. The overriding goal was to relate "Shakespeare's timeless ideas and understanding of human motivations to contemporary society." The lively hermeneutics of the series sought to re-interpret Shakespeare's work from the historical perspective of the 1960s rather than of the 1560s. A background collage of striking photographs depicting modern social turmoil implicitly comments on the stage action in the foreground. The programs reflect the passion for "relevance" that so obsessed university students in the Vietnam era and that made Jan Kott's *Shakespeare Our Contemporary* a cult book. An extensive telephone survey revealed that only five segments in this interesting series, of which unhappily this part is not included, are still readily available for rental (apply CNU). *Contents & evaluation:* Not seen. According to the 1969 publicity blurb issued by NBC Educational Enterprises, the film is "an examination of the conflict between Antony's major roles: his public duty as a statesman and his private obligation as Cleopatra's lover. While critics have called this play a 'tragedy of mature love,' the question arises as to exactly how 'mature' Antony and Cleopatra were in privileging personal inclination over public responsibility." *Audience:* College and university.

MEDIUM INFORMATION: *Medium:* Motion Picture; *Sound:* Spoken language; *Color:* Yes; *Length:* 23 min.; *Language(s) spoken:* English; *Film type:* 16mm.

AUTHORSHIP INFORMATION: *Producer(s):* Reis, Kurt; Moser, Ed; *Screenplay writer(s):* Webster, Hugh; *Composer(s):* Yanovsky, Zal; *Set designer(s):* Adeney, Chris; *Lighting designer(s):* Galbraith, Howard; *Perform-*

ance group(s): Ontario Educational Communications/ NBC Educational Enterprises.

DISTRIBUTION & AVAILABILITY: *Distributor:* [CNU]?.

Antony and Cleopatra. **Motion Picture/ Documentary**

19. *Caesar and Cleopatra.* (Series: Shaw Versus Shakespeare, III).

DOCUMENT INFORMATION: *Country:* USA; *Year of release:* 1970.

EDITION, HISTORY, CONTENTS, & EVALUATION: *Edition & history:* Comparison of Shaw's play about Cleopatra with Shakespeare's treatment of her in *Antony*. This entry is also repeated at number 231, where it overlaps with *Julius Caesar*. The other parts of the series are listed at numbers 229 and 230. *Supplementary materials:* Loughney, Katharine. "Shakespeare on Film and Tape at Library of Congress." *SFNL* 12.2 (Apr. 1988): 7.

MEDIUM INFORMATION: *Sound:* Spoken language; *Color:* Yes; *Length:* 31 min.

DISTRIBUTION & AVAILABILITY: *Distributor:* EBE, *Copy location:* LCM; *Call or copy number:* FCA 6930.

Antony and Cleopatra. **Motion Picture/ Adaptation**

20. *Antony and Cleopatra.*

DOCUMENT INFORMATION: *Country:* GB/Spain; *Nationality:* GB/Spain/U.S.; *Year of release:* 1972; *Country of first showing:* GB.

EDITION, HISTORY, CONTENTS, & EVALUATION: *Edition & history:* Rehearsed in London and filmed in Spain, this version of Shakespeare's *Antony and Cleopatra*, while never widely exhibited in theatres, is now available on videocassette. Charlton Heston tells something of its genesis: "Not all the films of Shakespeare's plays have been directed by actors playing the parts in them . . . but most of them have. When I found myself undertaking this daunting assignment in *Antony and Cleopatra*, I was heartened to recall that Laurence Olivier and Orson Welles had provided examples and models for me in the three films each has made from the plays and illuminated with his performances. . . . Each man [Olivier and Welles] . . . gave me identical advice . . . : 'You must rehearse the whole play for as many weeks as you can before you start shooting, and you must have a good actor to play Antony for you while you are setting up the shots [Heston describes the intense pre-location readings at a 'dingy rehearsal hall near Covent Garden']." There he learned the value of advance rehearsal for a film adaptation heavily dependent on acting skills (Heston, Charlton, "Heston Directs Heston," Publicity Release, 1972) *Contents & evaluation:* "There is no need to waste much time on Charlton Heston's *Antony and Cleopatra,* a work of no imagination. During the negotiations for Antony's marriage to Octavia two gladiators thump one another in the arena below. As one impales the other with his trident the negotiations conclude, and Octavia gives a thumbs-up sign at the words 'the power of Caesar.' This bright idea is so tediously executed, cutting back and forth from the arena to the politicians, that one dreads the bright ideas to follow. However, there are very few. The disastrous Cleopatra of Hildegarde Neil has neither presence (when she speaks of her majesty, as she often does, we take it as a kind of in-joke) nor sexuality" (Kermode, Frank, "Shakespeare in the Movies," *NYRB* 4 May 1972: 18); This version of *Antony* is to *Ben Hur* as Zeffirelli's *Romeo and Juliet* is to *West Side Story.* In effect a re-representation run through the alembic of a prior re-representation. That derivative quality colors the whole production. The sea battles are fine, with many chained galley slaves under the lash as they frantically tug at their gigantic oars and the sea water gushes through hulls ripped open by enemy battering rams. All is splendid blood and thunder. But little of Shakespeare's haunting language comes through either in verbalized or visualized form. Heston's film has its high points, but Cleopatra seems to have been bitten by the asp even before the establishing shot of the messenger travelling by ship and horse from Rome to Egypt. For those who have come to care about electronic Shakespeare, this fumbling is disappointing. An expensive movie is stillborn, when it might have at least rivalled the rather stodgy BBC television version (KSR). *Audience:* College and university; General use.

MEDIUM INFORMATION: *Medium:* Motion Picture; *Sound:* Spoken language; *Color:* Yes; *Length:* 160 min.; *Language(s) spoken:* English; *Film type:* 35 mm, Todd-AO; *Video type:* V.

AUTHORSHIP INFORMATION: *Producer(s):* Snell, Peter; *Director(s):* Heston, Charlton; *Adaptor/translator(s):* Davis, Pamela; *Composer(s):* Scott, John; Algero, Augusto (Additional music); *Designer(s):* Pelling, Maurice; *Set designer(s):* Alguero, Jose (Exteriors); Ma Alarcon, Jose (Interiors); *Costume designer(s):* Dickson, Wendy; *Lighting designer(s):* Pacheco, Rafael; *Other personnel:* Criado, Cristobal (Make-up); Boyd-Perkins, Eric (Editor); Messenger, Vernon (Sound editor); Stephenson, George (Sound mixer); *Cast:* Heston, Charlton (Antony); Neil, Hildegarde (Cleopatra); Porter, Eric (Enobarbus); Castle, John (Octavius); Rey, Fernando (Lepidus); Galiardo, Juan Luis (Alexas); Sevilla, Carmen (Octavia); Jones, Freddie (Pompey); Alba [n.i.] (Schoolmaster); Arne, Peter (Menas); Boo, Luis Bar (Varrius); Bilbao, Fernando (Menecrates); Clarke, Warren (Scarus); Delgado, Roger (Soothsayer); Glover, Julian; (Proculeius); Gracia,

Sancho (Canidius); Hagan, Garrick (Eros); Hallam, John (Thidias); Lapotaire, Jane (Charmian); Melia, Joe (1st Messenger); Peterson, Monica (Iras); Redondo, Emiliano; (Mardian); Sambrel, Aldo (Ventidius); Solano, Felipe (Soldier); Wilmer, Doug (Agrippa).

DISTRIBUTION & AVAILABILITY: *Publisher or responsible agency:* Folio Films, London, England; *Distributor:* DCV, EMB, ERS, FCM, *Copy location:* UCL; *Availability:* Available sale, B,V (Apply); DCV, V $58.

Antony and Cleopatra. Video/Teledrama

21. *Antony and Cleopatra:* RSC in Trevor Nunn's Production of.

DOCUMENT INFORMATION: *Country:* GB; *Year of release:* 1974; USA, 1975; *Country of first showing:* GB.

EDITION, HISTORY, CONTENTS, & EVALUATION: *Edition & history:* A television recording of a 1972 RSC production of *Antony,* which was subsequently restaged at London's Aldwych theatre in 1973. It was transmitted in England on July 8, 1974, and in the USA on ABC Network on Jan. 4, 1975. UK package distributed by TSO* includes teaching notes prepared by Ina Calvey, Principal Lecturer in Education at Oxford Polytechnic. *Contents & evaluation:* From the first spectacular opening shot of a Greek vase in rich color with the credits superimposed and the lively music up, this memorable production of *Antony and Cleopatra* sets a standard for what televised Shakespeare should be. Alert, compelling, Janet Suzman brings a sparkle to the role of Cleopatra that makes the mercurial Egyptian queen at once both human and divine. The opening sequence neatly dovetails Enobarbus' description of Antony as "the triple pillars of the world" with a montage of vivid shots of orgies, soldiers, faces, etc. to remind us of the sweeping emotional and physical landscape. Then there is an effective cut to the principals themselves, Antony and Cleopatra. Unlike some of the virtually "silent" TV productions of Shakespeare, this one is full of sea sounds: gulls, waves, and so forth. The lessons of radio with its marvelous sound effects have not been forgotten by the producers. Moreover the acting is at such a high level that the director did not even need to rely solely on cinematic devices. An example is Patrick Stewart's marvelous rendition of the speech about Cleopatra's barge. Although entirely in close-up, there is none of the tedium of the "talking head" syndrome that so often infects television drama. Stewart's face is full of expression as though he is really describing what he saw to other actors not just mechanically grinding out words. Few will soon forget Suzman's Cleopatra when she utters the haunting words, "I have immortal longings in me," and "I am fire and air." At the end she stands as a mummy, an Egyptian icon, who has entered into history. These and other performances in this extraordinary production, which I had difficulty tearing myself away from, show again how success on TV ultimately depends more on acting talent than on any other consideration (KSR). *Audience:* General use; *Supplementary materials:* See *TVT,* 8 July 1974: 39.

MEDIUM INFORMATION: *Medium:* Video; *Sound:* Spoken language; *Color:* Yes; *Length:* 162 min.; *Language(s) spoken:* English; *Video type:* V.

AUTHORSHIP INFORMATION: *Producer(s):* Clarke, Cecil (TV); Mason, Lorna; *Director(s):* Nunn, Trevor (RSC); Scoffield, Jon (ATV Network); *Composer(s):* Woolfenden, Guy; *Designer(s):* Morley, Christopher; Curtis, Ann (RSC); Bailey, Michael (ATV); *Costume designer(s):* Gurrell, Stuart; *Lighting designer(s):* Boyers, Jim; *Other personnel:* Barry, B.H. (Fight arranger); Hawkins, John (Tape editor); Bird, Henry (Audio); Reeves, Jim (Engineer); Bartlett, Dennis (Camera); Muslim, Shirley (Makeup); Maton, Felicity (Vision mixer); *Cast:* With Antony: Johnson, Richard (Antony); Stewart, Patrick (Enobarbus); Marcell, Joe (Eros); De Goguel, Constantin (Ventidius); Holt, Jonathan (Decretas); Bott, John (Soothsayer); with Cleopatra: Suzman, Janet (Cleopatra); McHale, Rosemary (Charmian); Blake, Mavis Taylor (Iras); Angadi, Darien (Alexas); Livingstone, Sidney (Mardian); Hutchings, Geoffrey (Fig seller); Burton, Loftus (Diomedes); Pierce, Leonard (Schoolteacher); with Octavius: Redgrave, Corin (Octavius); Rutherford, Mary (Octavia); Westwell, Raymond (Lepidus); Locke, Philip (Agrippa); Godfrey, Patrick (Mecaenas); Kingsley, Ben (Thidias); Milman, Martin (Dolabella); Pigott-Smith, Tim (Proculeius); and many eunuchs, kings, servants, watchmen, soldiers, etc. *Performance group(s):* Royal Shakespeare Company.

DISTRIBUTION & AVAILABILITY: *Copy location:* FOL, MOB, TSO*; *Call or copy number:* Pts. 1-3. T79:0426/428 (MOB); VCR (FOL); *Restrictions:* Archive viewing by appointment in USA.

Antony and Cleopatra. **Motion Picture/Scenes**

22. *Antony and Cleopatra,* 2.2.; 5.2. (Series: The Shakespeare Series [IFB], I).

DOCUMENT INFORMATION: *Country:* Great Britain; *Year of release:* 1974.

EDITION, HISTORY, CONTENTS, & EVALUATION: *Edition & history:* Part of a series of twelve British educational films showing scenes intended "to serve as an introduction to each play's theme or atmosphere." (See also numbers 131, 164, 232, 326, 430, 467, 490, 510, 556, 601, 619.) In this part there are episodes from *Antony and Cleopatra:* Enobarbus's description of his stay in Egypt and his description of her barge (2.2); and Cleopatra's suicide by means of the asps in a

basket of figs (5.2). The films were also designed to reproduce the conditions of acting in Elizabethan times. For example by having the same actors play several roles, the students are to glean some idea of how the plays were originally written "for a specific company of actors" (P.R. blurb, IFB). A word of caution: this series, the "IFB," can easily be confused with "The Shakespeare Series" (BHE/BFA), which is comprised of six abbreviated versions of the plays (see numbers 41, 228, 258, 323, 406, and 656). *Contents & evaluation:* If you like *Antony and Cleopatra* without Antony, then this excerpt should be appealing. Paul Chapman does Enobarbus' great description of Cleopatra's barge pretty much as a talking head and without great passion. The costumes lack clout, the acting is definitely stagy, but Cleopatra (Linda Renwick) manages to perform memorably in the scene when she takes the asp from the clown. *Audience:* High school (grades 10-12).

MEDIUM INFORMATION: *Medium:* Motion Picture; *Sound:* Spoken language; *Color:* Yes; *Length:* 11 min.; *Language(s) spoken:* English; *Film type:* 16mm; *Video type:* V, 3/4U (4 cassettes).

AUTHORSHIP INFORMATION: *Producer(s):* Seabourne, John; *Director(s):* Seabourne, Peter; *Cast:* Chapman, Paul (Enobarbus); Fennell, David (Maecenas); Gilbert, Derrick (Agrippa); Renwick, Linda (Cleopatra); Jameson, Susan (Iras); Hall, Elizabeth (Charmian); Farrell, Colin (Clown).

DISTRIBUTION & AVAILABILITY: *Publisher or responsible agency:* Realist Film Unit; *Distributor:* IFB (USA), *Copy location:* FOL; *Call or copy number:* FOL, MP 90; *Availability:* IFB, rental 16mm $12.50, sale 16mm, V $175.

Antony and Cleopatra. **Video/Teleplay**

23. *Antony and Cleopatra.* (Series: The Shakespeare Plays).

DOCUMENT INFORMATION: *Country:* GB; *Year of filming:* 5-10 March 1980; *Year of first showing:* 1980; *Location of first showing(s):* BBC, London; PBS stations, USA, 20 April 1981.

EDITION, HISTORY, CONTENTS, & EVALUATION: *Edition & history:* Although director Jonathan Miller sought to present the play as set down in the 1951 Peter Alexander edition of Shakespeare's plays, he did not hesitate to make alterations that he considered useful for pleasing the audience. As with his *Taming of the Shrew,* Miller also made bold casting decisions that in effect drastically revised traditional interpretations of the play. Colin Blakely and Jane Lapotaire in their middle-aged world weariness sharply contrast with the more glamorized, jet-set, Antony and Cleopatra portrayed, for example, by Elizabeth Taylor and Richard Burton in an earlier film (that owed as much or more to its scenarist than to Shakespeare and was only vaguely indebted to Shakespeare's play). Blakely himself was quoted as saying that by the time Antony met Cleopatra he was already "over the hill" and "physically past his prime" from the soft life at court. Director Miller embellished the image by presenting Antony then as a kind of "middle-aged psychological failure." (P.R. release). *Contents & evaluation:* "[Director Miller's] . . . casting of [Jane] Lapotaire as Cleopatra, ostensibly to assure stripping the role of its 'myths about sexual prowess and sensuality' does little justice to the achievements of both her acting and this production. Although neither voluptuous nor beautiful, this Cleopatra was nevertheless sexually alluring. Moreover the chemistry set up between Lapotaire and Blakely's Antony made them plausible as middle-aged lovers. . . . But was the production as a consequence smallish, almost domestic? No doubt cutting the early reference to Pompey damages the significance of his first appearance. The larger cuts of 3.1 (the Ventidius scene immediately following the shipboard revelries), 4.3. (the music said to be 'the god Hercules' leaving Antony prior to his battlefield triumph), and the Seleucus portion of the final scene further reduce the ironies, the unsynchronized sequences, the complexities of the dramatic action somewhat" (Lower, Charles B., "Antony and Cleopatra," *SFNL* 6.2 [1982.: 2]. *Audience:* College and university; General use; *Supplementary materials:* Fenwick, Henry. *Antony and Cleopatra* in *BSP* 17-27; Videotape (25 min.) from "Shakespeare in Perspective" series with Anna Raeburn as lecturer available in U.K. from BBC* (*BUFVC* 1).

MEDIUM INFORMATION: *Medium:* Video; *Sound:* Spoken language; *Color:* Yes; *Length:* 177 min.; *Language(s) spoken:* English; *Video type:* B, V, 3/4U.

AUTHORSHIP INFORMATION: *Producer(s):* Miller, Jonathan; *Director(s):* Miller, Jonathan; *Adaptor/translator(s):* Snodin, David; *Composer(s):* Oliver, Stephen; *Choreographer(s):* Gilpin, Sally; *Designer(s):* Lowrey, Colin; *Costume designer(s):* Hughes, Alun; *Lighting designer(s):* Channon, Dennis; *Other personnel:* Stenning, Peter (Prod. asst.); Preece, Patricia (Director's asst.); Lowden, Fraser (Prod. unit manager); Wilders, John (Literary consultant); Mair, Eileen (Make-up); Angel, Ray (Sound); *Cast:* Blakely, Colin (Antony); Lapotaire, Jane (Cleopatra); Charleson, Ian (Caesar); James, Emrys (Enobarbus); Knight, Esmond (Lepidus); Sumpter, Donald (Pompeius); Chandler, Simon (Eros); Pedley, Anthony (Agrippa); Collins, Geoffrey (Dolabella); Waters, Harry (Thyreas); Innes, George (Menas); Stokes, Desmond (Menecrates); Paul, John (Canidius); Clifford, Richard (Silius); Howe, George (Euphrenius); Angadi, Darien (Alexas); Shamsi, Mohammad (Mardian); Adams, Jonathan (Ventidius); Ettridge, Chris (Scarus); Sabin, Alec (Decertas); Neal, David (Proculeius); Farleigh, Lynn (Octavia); Key, Janet (Charmian); McFarlane, Cassie (Iras); Kincaid, David (Messenger); Goorney, Howard (Soothsayer); Gardner, Jimmy

(Clown); Huckstep, Kevin (Messenger One); Anthony, Michael (Messenger); Connell, Pat (Soldier); Rattray, Iain (Soldier); Warder, Frederick (Soldier); Egan, Michael (Soldier); Eastham, John; Rumney, Jon; Lund, Hugh (Servants).

DISTRIBUTION & AVAILABILITY: *Publisher or responsible agency:* BBC/TLF; *Distributor:* AVP, UIO, BBC*, *Copy location:* CTL*, UVM (Archive); *Availability:* AVP, B, V, 3/4U $450 (1987), sale; UIO, V (72031H), 3/4U (70131V), rental, $24.50; BBC* 16mm or V, apply (*BUFVC* 1).

Antony and Cleopatra. Video/Recording

24. *Antony and Cleopatra.*

DOCUMENT INFORMATION: *Country:* USA; *Year of first showing:* 1981.

EDITION, HISTORY, CONTENTS, & EVALUATION: *Edition & history:* A videotaping of a 1981 stage production of *Antony and Cleopatra* performed by the Berkeley Shakespeare Festival. A copy is housed in the Theatre on Film and Tape Collection at the Billy Rose Theatre Collection of the Library of Performing Arts, Lincoln Center, New York Public Library. It may be viewed by appointment (see below). *Contents & evaluation:* Not seen. *Audience:* College and university; General use.

MEDIUM INFORMATION: *Medium:* Video; *Sound:* Spoken language; *Color:* Yes; *Length:* 152 min.; *Language(s) spoken:* English; *Video type:* 3/4U.

AUTHORSHIP INFORMATION: *Producer(s):* Berkeley Shakespeare Festival; *Director(s):* Not known.

DISTRIBUTION & AVAILABILITY: *Publisher or responsible agency:* Berkeley Shakespeare Festival; *Copy location:* LCL TOFT Collection; *Call or copy number:* NCOV 307; *Availability:* By appt.

Antony and Cleopatra. Video/Documentary

25. *Jonathan Miller Directs: The Making of* Antony and Cleopatra.

DOCUMENT INFORMATION: *Country:* GB; *Year of release:* 1982.

EDITION, HISTORY, CONTENTS, & EVALUATION: *Supplementary materials:* BUFVC 2.

MEDIUM INFORMATION: *Length:* 50 min.

AUTHORSHIP INFORMATION: *Producer(s):* Nordin, Esther; *Other role(s):* Armstrong, Ronald (Editor); *Cast:* Miller, Jonathan.

DISTRIBUTION & AVAILABILITY: *Distributor:* BBC.

26. *Acting Cleopatra.*

DOCUMENT INFORMATION: *Country:* GB; *Year of release:* 1983.

EDITION, HISTORY, CONTENTS, & EVALUATION: *Edition & history:* "An interview with Glenda Jackson, who played Cleopatra in Peter Brook's production for the RSC in 1978-79" (*BUFVC* 1).

MEDIUM INFORMATION: *Length:* 18 min.

AUTHORSHIP INFORMATION: *Cast:* Havely, Cicely Palser (Interviewer); Jackson, Glenda.

DISTRIBUTION & AVAILABILITY: *Publisher or responsible agency:* BBC; *Distributor:* OPU*.

Antony and Cleopatra. **Video/Interpretation**

27. *Antony and Cleopatra.* (Series: The Bard Series).

CURRENT PRODUCTION: *Year:* 1985. DOCUMENT INFORMATION: *Country:* USA; *Year of release:* 1985.

EDITION, HISTORY, CONTENTS, & EVALUATION: *Edition & history:* A videotaping with a cast of well known American actors in a Bard Productions series that has been seen on the Arts & Entertainment cable tv channel. Lynn Redgrave of *Georgy Girl* (1966) plays Cleopatra; Tony Geary of *General Hospital*, Octavius Caesar; and veteran actor, John Carradine, the Soothsayer. For others in this series, see numbers 340, 477, 494, and 627. *Contents & evaluation:* Not seen. *Audience:* High school (grades 10-12); College and university; *Supplementary materials:* Stevenson, M. George. "Et Tu, Shakespeare?: The Bard's Greatest Hits on Tape and Disc." *Video* (Aug. 1986): 66+.

MEDIUM INFORMATION: *Medium:* Video; *Sound:* Spoken language; *Color:* Yes; *Length:* 183 min.; *Language(s) spoken:* English; *Video type:* B, V.

AUTHORSHIP INFORMATION: *Producer(s):* Campbell, Ken; *Director(s):* Carra, Lawrence; *Composer(s):* Serry, John; *Cast:* Dalton, Timothy (Anthony); Redgrave, Lynn (Cleopatra); Nichols, Nichelle (Charmian); Carradine, John (Soothsayer); Ingham, Barrie (Enobarbus); Geary, Anthony (Octavius Caesar); Koenig, Walter (Pompey); Kerwin, Brian (Eros); Gwillam, Jack (Rustic); Billington, Michael (Ventidius); Woolman, Claude (Silius); Miyori, Kim (Iras); Holland, Anthony (Alexas); Avery, James (Mardian); Boen, Earl (Lepidus); Sicari, Joseph R. (Messenger); Sorel, Ted (Menas); Robinson, Earl (Maecenas); Rosqui, Tom (Agrippa); Stanley, Alvah (Thidias); Barr, Sharon (Octavia); Devlin, John (Dolabella); Mason, Dan (Euphronius); Sutton, Henry (Proculeius); Drischell, Ralph (Seleucus); Bowman, Paul; Everett, Tom; Keyes-Hall, Michael; O'Neill, Grey; Wright, Alex (Soldiers); Brady, Randall; Graves, Jason; Larson, Stuart; Minklein, John; Peters, Larry; Thomas, Patrick (Extras).

DISTRIBUTION & AVAILABILITY: *Publisher or responsible agency:* Bard Productions Ltd.; *Distributor:* ILL, FCM, TWC, DCV, INM *Availability:* ILL, sale, V (S 01592) $89.95; FCM, sale, V $89.95; TWC, sale, apply; DCV, sale, V $95 (1988); INM, sale, V $99.00.

Antony and Cleopatra. **Video/Documentary**

28. *Shakespeare: Antony and Cleopatra: Workshop.* (Series: Open University Film Library).

DOCUMENT INFORMATION: *Country:* GB; *Year of release:* 1985.

EDITION, HISTORY, CONTENTS, & EVALUATION: *Edition & history:* One of several programs prepared for the Open University television programs in Great Britain. Not seen in the U.S. According to the *BUFVC* catalog, each program features a director leading one of the actors through his/her role. In this program, director John Russell Brown shows James Laurenson (Antony) and Gillian Barge (Cleopatra) how to make donning a suit of armour into a dramatic asset rather than a distraction. *Audience:* College and university; *Supplementary materials:* BUFVC 1.

MEDIUM INFORMATION: *Medium:* Video; *Sound:* Spoken language; *Color:* Yes; *Length:* 24 min.; *Language(s) spoken:* English; *Video type:* V,B.

AUTHORSHIP INFORMATION: *Producer(s):* Hoyle, David; *Cast:* Brown, John Russell (Dir.); Laurenson, James (Antony); Barge, Gillian (Cleopatra).

DISTRIBUTION & AVAILABILITY: *Publisher or responsible agency:* BBC Open University; *Distributor:* GSV*, *Copy location:* BBC; *Availability:* Available in U.K. only.

Antony and Cleopatra. **Motion Picture/Documentary**

29. *Antony and Cleopatra.*

DOCUMENT INFORMATION: *Country:* GB; *Year of release:* 1985.

EDITION, HISTORY, CONTENTS, & EVALUATION: *Edition & history:* This is a special "teaching" package available only in the U.K. and based on the 1972 RSC production starring Janet Suzman. *Supplementary materials:* BUFVC 1.

MEDIUM INFORMATION: *Length:* 162 min.

AUTHORSHIP INFORMATION: *Director(s):* Scoffield, Jon; *Cast:* Same as Scoffield/Nunn 1972 stage production (See Record #21, above).

DISTRIBUTION & AVAILABILITY: *Distributor:* TSO*.

As You Like It

ORIGINAL WORK AND PRODUCTION: Romantic comedy. *Year of first production:* 1599; *Site of first production:* Globe Playhouse.

As You Like It. Motion Picture/Scenes

30. *Seven Ages of Man.*

DOCUMENT INFORMATION: *Country:* USA; *Year of release:* 1903.

EDITION, HISTORY, CONTENTS, & EVALUATION: *Edition & history:* Worth mentioning because it was a very early experiment by the famed inventor, Thomas Edison. Based on Jaques' speech in *AYL,* the film was probably an attempt to synchronize sight and sound with a phonograph. *Supplementary materials:* Ball, *SOSF* 32, 307.

AUTHORSHIP INFORMATION: *Director(s):* Edison, Thomas.

As You Like It. Motion Picture/Abbreviated

31. *As You Like It.*

DOCUMENT INFORMATION: *Country:* USA; *Year of release:* 1908.

EDITION, HISTORY, CONTENTS, & EVALUATION:

Edition & history: The producers (the Kalem Company) of this lost movie did some unusual exterior shooting (for the times) at Cos Cob, Conn. Despite its visual effects and an accompanying lecture on the play, the production was not widely acclaimed. "Kalem" was an acronym for the New York City movie company's partners: George Kleine, Samuel Long, and Frank Marion. *Supplementary materials:* Ball, *SOSF* 61.

MEDIUM INFORMATION: *Length:* 10 min.

DISTRIBUTION & AVAILABILITY: *Publisher or responsible agency:* Kalem

As You Like It. Motion Picture/Abridgment

32. *As You Like It.*

DOCUMENT INFORMATION: *Country:* USA; *Year of release:* 1912.

EDITION, HISTORY, CONTENTS, & EVALUATION: *Edition & history:* One of a dozen or so silent Shakespeare films made by the Vitagraph company in its Brooklyn studios in the early years of cinema. This film was a second generation effort in that its three reels marked a distinct advance in length over the earlier ten-minute one-reelers. It also starred a famous British actress, Rose Coghlan, in the female lead, though at sixty she was surely the world's oldest living Rosalind. Some filmographies list two 1912 *As You Like Its* starring Rose Coghlan. I suspect they are actually

33

the same film. Certainly Ball makes no reference to two versions. For other Vitagraph movies, see 7, 32, 47, 195, 199, 242, 354, 387, 436, 496, 515, and 640. *Contents & evaluation:* Despite criticism that Rose Coghlan, a well known British actress, was too old for the role of Rosalind, she was so charismatic in personality that even that late in her career her youthful charms had not yet deserted her. Other characters are equally well delineated, as with the very effective Old Adam. Surprisingly advanced camera and editing work and stylish exterior shots move the action away from the staginess of the earlier silents. Interior sequences also reveal subtle advances in technique; for example, a shot with a character standing by the open window is free of shadows. On the other hand, in one exterior shot the harsh sunlight in a Brooklyn wood casts deep shadows across the actors' faces. Title cards provide a clear narrative bridge, as in, for example: "Rosalind begs to accompany her banished father but is detained by her uncle, Duke Frederick, as a companion for his daughter, Celia." The cinematic peak occurs with the use of cross-cutting to illustrate Jaques' Seven Ages speech. As Jaques refers to the "mewling and puking" infant, a baby appears, and then in succession a schoolboy, young man, soldier and so forth. Audiences 75 years ago must have been delighted with such tricks, and doubtless thought of them as enhancements rather than as desecrations. *Audience:* General use; *Supplementary materials:* Ball, *SOSF* 139-45.

MEDIUM INFORMATION: *Medium:* Motion Picture; *Sound:* Silent; *Color:* No (black & white); *Length:* 30 min.; *Language(s) spoken:* English; *Film type:* 16mm.

AUTHORSHIP INFORMATION: *Producer(s):* Blackton, J. Stuart; *Director(s):* Kent, Charles and/or Young, James; *Adaptor/translator(s):* Birch, Margaret; *Cast:* Coghlan, Rose (Rosalind); Costello, Maurice (Orlando); Theby, Rosemary (Celia); Gaillard, Robert (Oliver); Kent, Charles (Jaques); Johnson, Tefft (Duke Senior); McWade, Robert, Sr. (Touchstone); Morey, Harry (Duke Frederick); Tapley, Rose (Phoebe); Price, Kate (Audrey); Ober, George (Adam); Randolph George C. (Charles); Eldridge, Charles (Corin); Morrison, James (Silvius); Mason, Frank; (Amiens); McGowan, Hugh (William); Delaney, Leo (Jaques de Bois; Young, James (Le Beau or Sir Roland de Bois)—Credits from Ball, 140.; *Performance group(s):* Vitagraph Players with Rose Coghlan.

DISTRIBUTION & AVAILABILITY: *Distributor:* JEF, *Copy location:* FOL; *Call or copy number:* MP 5; *Availability:* Apply JEF.

As You Like It. Motion Picture/Derivative

33. *Love in a Wood.*

DOCUMENT INFORMATION: *Country:* GB; *Year of release:* 1916.

EDITION, HISTORY, CONTENTS, & EVALUATION:

Edition & history: One of many silent adaptations with a vague connection to the Shakespearean canon, discussed in detail by Professor Ball. If all of these types of silent derivations were included in a Shakespeare filmography, the list would be overwhelming. A few, such as this one, need to be mentioned here to suggest the wide range of possibilities. For full details, see Ball. *Supplementary materials:* Ball, *SOSF* 221-22.

AUTHORSHIP INFORMATION: *Director(s):* Elvey, Maurice; *Cast:* Risdon, Elizabeth (Rosalind); O'Neill, Edward (Duke); Groves, Fred (Frederick); Foss, Kenelm (Oliver); Ames, Gerald (Orlando); Stanmore, Frank (Touchstone); Cunningham, Vera (Celia).

DISTRIBUTION & AVAILABILITY: *Publisher or responsible agency:* London Film Company.

As You Like It. Motion Picture/Interpretation

34. *As You Like It.*

DOCUMENT INFORMATION: *Country:* GB; *Year of release:* 1936.

EDITION, HISTORY, CONTENTS, & EVALUATION: *Contents & evaluation:* "Finally, there was Paul Czinner's million-dollar *As You Like It,* a film which made little mark, even though Laurence Olivier appeared as Orlando. The production was once again the victim of the star system. Paul Czinner's wife, Elisabeth Bergner, whatever her merits as an actress in modern plays and films, had a screen personality diametrically opposed to that of Rosalind. Rosalind is a forthright woman, capable, provocative and determined beneath her surface diffidence and charm. Elisabeth Bergner's screen character was exactly the opposite—she derived her charm from depicting an ageless, kittenish quality in women, a kind of self-destructive femininity, half innocent, half knowing, which inevitably led to frustrated infatuations with a tragic outcome. She had the habit of turning somersaults and did so as Rosalind" (Manvell, *SATF* 30-31). *Audience:* General use.

MEDIUM INFORMATION: *Medium:* Motion Picture; *Sound:* Spoken language; *Color:* No (black & white); *Length:* 97 min.; *Film type:* 16 mm.; *Video type:* V.

AUTHORSHIP INFORMATION: *Producer(s):* Schenck, Joseph M.; Czinner, Paul; *Director(s):* Czinner, Paul; Baird, Teddy; Bower, Dallas; *Adaptor/translator(s):* Cullen, R.J.; Barrie, J.M.; *Composer(s):* Walton, William; Kurtz, Efrem conducting London Philharmonic Orchestra; *Designer(s):* Meerson, Lazare; *Costume designer(s):* Armstrong, John; Strassner, Joe; *Lighting designer(s):* Rosson, Hal; *Other personnel:* Cardiff, Jack (Camera); Lean, David (Editing); Overton, R.E. and Stevens, C.C. (Recording); Quartermaine, Leon (Dialogue); *Cast:* Ainley, Henry (Exiled Duke); Aylmer, Felix (Duke Frederick); Robertson, Stuart (Amiens); Quartermaine, Leon (Jaques); Trevor, Austin (Le Beau);

Braham, Lionel (Charles); Laurie, John (Oliver); Olivier, Laurence (Orlando); White, J. Fisher; (Adam); Ward, MacKenzie (Touchstone); Mather, Aubrey (Corin); Ainley, Richard (Sylvius); Bull, Peter (William); Bergner, Elisabeth (Rosalind); Stewart, Sophie (Celia); White, Joan (Phebe); Fordred, Durice (Audrey).

DISTRIBUTION & AVAILABILITY: *Publisher or responsible agency:* 20th Century British Fox; *Distributor:* FNC, DCV, FCM, VID, TWC, ERS, *Copy location:* FOL; *Call or copy number:* MP 5; *Availability:* Rental 16mm: FNC, apply, KIT $75; Sale V, B: DCV, FCM, VID, TWC, ERS, INM—apply as prices fluctuate from $29 to $69.

As You Like It. Video/Scenes

35. *As You Like It* 3.2. (Series: Scenes from Shakespeare).

DOCUMENT INFORMATION: *Country:* GB; *Year of first showing:* 1937; *Location of first showing:* BBC, London. Transmitted 3:55 to 4:06 P.M., Friday, 6 Feb. 1937.

EDITION, HISTORY, CONTENTS, & EVALUATION: *Edition & history:* The handful of people in the greater London area who owned television sets and who happened to have them tuned in witnessed an historic event on this cold February afternoon in 1937—the first transmission ever of scenes from a Shakespearean play. The huge Shakespeare on television industry can be said to have sprung from this decidedly inauspicious, and widely ignored, event. As with the beginnings of Shakespeare on film in Britain, the beginnings of Shakespeare on television drew heavily on theatrical talent from the London stage. The program based on *As You Like It*, Act Three, scene two, was then immediately followed by a second Shakespeare program featuring scenes from *Henry V*. *Supplementary materials:* "Program." *TPAB* 6 Feb. 1937: n.p.

MEDIUM INFORMATION: *Length:* 11 min.

AUTHORSHIP INFORMATION: *Producer(s):* Atkins, Robert; *Director(s):* Thomas, Stephen; *Cast:* Scott, Margaretta (Rosalind); Swinley, Ion (Orlando).

DISTRIBUTION & AVAILABILITY: *Publisher or responsible agency:* BBC; *Copy location:* Unavailable.

As You Like It. Video/Recording

36. *As You Like It.*

DOCUMENT INFORMATION: *Country:* GB; *Year of first showing:* Transmitted 8:31 to 10:21 P.M., Sunday, 14 July 1946; *Location of first showing:* BBC, London Station.

EDITION, HISTORY, CONTENTS, & EVALUATION:

Edition & history: The talents of father and son made this early post-WWII Shakespeare performance possible. Robert Atkins was the director of the Bankside Players, a Regent's Park Open Air Theatre Company, which provided the actors. Ian Atkins, his son, was a trained cameraman, who could bridge the gap between stage and screen. As the first Shakespeare program to be broadcast after the suspension of television transmission during World War II, this production also deserves a special niche in the history of screened Shakespeare. Shakespeare had not been seen on British television since the 22 April 1939 transmission of *Katherine and Petruchio*, a spinoff from *Shrew*. One wonders what became of all these bright young actors who participated in this historic occasion. Their names are today something less than well known, at least in North America. In 1946 of course the BBC lacked a feasible technology for preserving the program. *Supplementary materials:* "Program." *TPAB* 14 July 1946: 1.

MEDIUM INFORMATION: *Length:* 110 min.

AUTHORSHIP INFORMATION: *Producer(s):* Atkins, Ian; *Director(s):* Atkins, Robert; *Composer(s):* Watson, Rosabel; *Cast:* Bennett, Vivienne; Honer, Mary; Hicks, Patricia; Shafto, Angela; Staff, Ivan; Vere, John; Llewelyn, Desmond; Byron, John; Littledale, Richard; Read, David; Thorndike, Georgia; Wilson, Diana; Marshall, Elizabeth; Woodroofe, Ronald; Humphrey, John; Quitak, Oscar; Enders, David; Hamelin, Clement; Dance, Thomas; Hayes, Reginald; Bell, Peter; March, David; + Regent's Park Orchestra.

DISTRIBUTION & AVAILABILITY: *Publisher or responsible agency:* BBC; *Copy location:* Not preserved.

As You Like It. Video/Teleplay

37. *As You Like It.*

DOCUMENT INFORMATION: *Country:* GB; *Year of first showing:* 1953; *Location of first showing:* BBC. Transmitted 8:45 to 9:33 P.M., Sunday, 15 March 1953.

EDITION, HISTORY, CONTENTS, & EVALUATION: *Edition & history:* A major difference between this program and the earlier BBC 1946 *As You Like It* is the presence in the cast of major actors such as Margaret Leighton, Michael Hordern and Laurence Harvey. The program notes for the music are especially revealing in their scholarly concern to bring the authentic music from Shakespeare's own day into the production. The BBC also used 125 feet of film to support the televised script. The cast included 24 principals plus extras, and the cost came to £2,343. *Supplementary materials:* "Program and Notes." *TPAB* 15 March 1953: n.p.

MEDIUM INFORMATION: *Length:* 48 min.

AUTHORSHIP INFORMATION: *Producer(s):* Logan, Campbell; Ebert, Peter; *Designer(s):* Bundy, Stephen; *Cast:* Hudd, Walter (Duke Senior); Oscar, Henry (Duke Frederick); Holme, Stanford (Le Beau and William); Brennan, Michael (Charles); Connor, Kenneth (Touchstone); Leighton, Margaret (Rosalind); Dean, Isabel (Celia); Lovell, Roderick (Oliver); Verney, Guy (Jaques de Boys); Harvey, Laurence (Orlando); Sequeira, Horace (Adam); Malnick, Michael (Dennis); Schlesinger, John (Amiens); Hordern, Michael (Jaques); Makeham, Eliot (Corin); Wyngarde, Peter (Sylvius); Latham, Stuart (Sir Oliver Martext); Alan, Pamela (Phebe); Hope, Vida (Audrey); + Lords, Attendants, Foresters, Musicians.

DISTRIBUTION & AVAILABILITY: *Copy location:* Unavailable.

As You Like It. Motion Picture/Documentary

38. *Ages of Man.*

DOCUMENT INFORMATION: *Country:* USA; *Year of release:* 1953.

EDITION, HISTORY, CONTENTS, & EVALUATION: *Edition & history:* A reading of the melancholy Jaques' famous seven ages of man speech from *As You Like It*. *Supplementary materials:* Loughney, Katharine. "Shakespeare on Film and Tape at Library of Congress." *SFNL* 12.2 (Apr. 1988): 7+.

MEDIUM INFORMATION: *Length:* 15 min.

AUTHORSHIP INFORMATION: *Cast:* Laughton, Charles (Reader).

DISTRIBUTION & AVAILABILITY: *Copy location:* LCM; *Call or copy number:* FAB 2604.

As You Like It. Video/Teleplay

39. *As You Like It.*

DOCUMENT INFORMATION: *Country:* GB; *Year of first showing:* 1963; *Location of first showing:* BBC TV. Transmitted 8:20 to 10:45 P.M., Friday, 22 March 1963.

EDITION, HISTORY, CONTENTS, & EVALUATION: *Edition & history:* "The production was originally staged by the Royal Shakespeare Company, first in Stratford-upon-Avon and then at the Company's London theatre, the Aldwych" (*RT*). Costs were £10,279 and the cast included 37 principals. *Supplementary materials:* "Program." *RT* 14 March 1963: n.p.

MEDIUM INFORMATION: *Length:* 138 min.

AUTHORSHIP INFORMATION: *Director(s):* Elliott, Michael (RSC); Eyre, Ronald (BBC); *Composer(s):* Hall, George; *Designer(s):* Negri, Richard (RSC); Welstead,

Andree (BBC); *Lighting designer(s):* Channon, Dennis; *Other personnel:* Alexis, Charles (Wrestling); Collison, David (Sound effects); Pisk, Litz (Movement); *Cast:* Redgrave, Vanessa (Rosalind); Allen, Patrick (Orlando); Buck, David (Oliver); Rose, Clifford (Adam); Breaks, Sebastian (Charles); Knight, Rosalind (Celia); Wymark, Patrick (Touchstone); Richardson, Ian (Le Beau); Church, Tony (Duke Frederick); Hardwick, Paul (Duke Senior); Flynn, Eric (Amiens); Hunter, Russell (Corin); Gill, Peter (Silvius); Adrian, Max (Jaques); Byrne, Patsy (Audrey); Wallis, William (Sir Oliver Martext); Hepple, Jeanne (Phebe); Gostelow, Gordon (William); Normington, John (Jaques De Boys); + thirteen Forest Lords and Court Ladies.

DISTRIBUTION & AVAILABILITY: *Publisher or responsible agency:* RSC/BBC; *Copy location:* BBC archive.

As You Like It. Motion Picture/Documentary

40. *As You Like It: Doing Your Own Thing.* (Series: Explorations in Shakespeare II).

DOCUMENT INFORMATION: *Country:* Canada; *Year of release:* 1969.

EDITION, HISTORY, CONTENTS, & EVALUATION: *Edition & history:* Part two in a series of twelve 23-minute films made in 1969 by the Ontario Educational Communications Authority. For fuller information, see number 18, above. Description of other segments will also be found at numbers 65, 124, 162, 257, 322, 465, 488, 555, 617, and 637. *Contents & evaluation:* Not seen. According to the publicity release issued by NBC Educational Enterprises, this episode "explores the superficiality of relationships and the romanticism of 'dropping out' of society. The film begins with a montage of changing seasons juxtaposed with the voice of a woman reading a love poem. The interplay of Orlando, Rosalind and Jaques in the Forest of Arden follows." *Audience:* College and university.

MEDIUM INFORMATION: *Medium:* Motion Picture; *Sound:* Spoken language; *Color:* Yes; *Length:* 23 min.; *Language(s) spoken:* English; *Film type:* 16mm.

AUTHORSHIP INFORMATION: *Producer(s):* Reis, Kurt; Moser, Ed; *Screenplay writer(s):* Webster, Hugh; *Composer(s):* Yanovsky, Zal; *Set designer(s):* Adeney, Chris; *Lighting designer(s):* Galbraith, Howard; *Performance group(s):* Ontario Educational Communications/ NBC Educational Enterprises.

DISTRIBUTION & AVAILABILITY: *Distributor:* CNU.

As You Like It. Motion Picture/Abridgment

41. *As You Like It: An Introduction.* (Series: Shakespeare Series [BHE/BFA], V).

DOCUMENT INFORMATION: *Country:* GB; *Year of first showing:* 1969.

EDITION, HISTORY, CONTENTS, & EVALUATION: *Edition & history:* The fifth in a series of six abridged versions of the plays. According to the distributor's flyer, "the plays of Shakespeare are introduced in the abbreviated versions performed by a talented English company. Brief narrative bridges connect the performances of key scenes, forming a compact and dramatic introduction to the play. Each adaptation is structured to preserve the continuity and drama of the play and offers the first-time reader an opportunity to grasp the main theme and threads of action—an awareness that will enrich his understanding and appreciation of the play as he reads it." This series of six films (see also numbers 228, 258, 323, 406, 656) should not be confused with "The Shakespeare Series (IFB)" [see numbers 22, 131, 164, 232, 326, 430, 467, 490, 510, 556, 601, and 619], twelve films offering even briefer excerpts, originally distributed by the International Film Bureau. *Audience:* High school (grades 10-12); College and university.

MEDIUM INFORMATION: *Medium:* Motion Picture; *Sound:* Spoken language; *Color:* Yes; *Length:* 24 min.; *Language(s) spoken:* English; *Film type:* 16mm.

AUTHORSHIP INFORMATION: *Producer(s):* BHE/Seabourne Enterprises; *Cast:* Goosens, Jennie (Rosalind); Spink, Brian (Orlando); Kidd, Delinda (Celia), Gwillim, Jack (Duke Frederick); Burke, Alfred (Jaques); Jones, Dudley (Touchstone).

DISTRIBUTION & AVAILABILITY: *Publisher or responsible agency:* BHE/Seabourne; *Distributor:* BFA.

As You Like It. Video/Teleplay

42. *As You Like It.* (Series: The Shakespeare Plays).

DOCUMENT INFORMATION: *Country:* GB; *Year of filming:* 30 May-16 June 1978; *Year of first showing:* 1978; *Location of first showing(s):* BBC, London; PBS stations, USA, 28 Feb. 1979.

EDITION, HISTORY, CONTENTS, & EVALUATION: *Edition & history:* Along with *King Henry VIII,* this production was one of two in the first year of "The Shakespeare Plays" series made outdoors on location away from from the London BBC studios. The site chosen, Glamis Castle, is of course better known to Americans through its association with *Macbeth.* The exterior shots also gave the Forest of Arden a naturalistic look that better correlated with its status as a place for "adversity." According to script editor Alan

Shallcross very little of the the text was cut to accommodate the needs of television. *Contents & evaluation:* "Apart from the considerable triumphs of Helen Mirren's Ganymede-Rosalynde, the acting interest in this *As You Like It* is generated by Richard Pasco (*Julius Caesar*'s Brutus) as Jaques. Pasco's alienating facial features—heavy eyelids, bulging eyes, pronounced bags under those eyes, and minimal change in expression—work as well for this cynical Jaques as they did for the priggish Brutus. Pasco effectively demands attention yet does not command assent. He strikes a balance as right for the malcontent (whom Shakespeare here gives the most famous lines but yet excludes from the ending comic celebration) as it is for the humorless 'noble' ideologue, Brutus. Coleman's blocking efficiently signals Jaques' separation from the band of exiles the first time we see him. . . . Ambivalence—or even ambiguity—informs the entire play. And since *As You Like It* lacks a narrative plot that will sustain interest and give momentum, the drama has to come from the subtle interplay of contrasting attitudes (toward love, toward marriage, toward the socio-political order; the list admits of enormous extension). Most of that subtlety escapes this production, despite the judicious cutting of text to speed things along and, one would think, highlight the contrasts by accelerating the juxtapositioning. Perhaps such subtlety is best captured by the reader and we have here one of those plays least susceptible to effective close-range visualization, particularly when the camera work is so utterly conventional" (Kimbrough, R. Alan, "*As You Like It,*" *SFNL* 3.2.[1979]: 5+). *Audience:* High school (grades 10-12); General use; *Supplementary materials:* Fenwick, Henry. *As You Like It* in *BSP* 20-26; Videotape (25 min.) from "Shakespeare in Perspective" series with Brigid Brophy as lecturer available in U.K. from BBC*; in USA, from FNC (see number 44).

MEDIUM INFORMATION: *Medium:* Video; *Sound:* Spoken language; *Color:* Yes; *Length:* 150 min.; *Language(s) spoken:* English; *Video type:* B, V, 3/4U.

AUTHORSHIP INFORMATION: *Producer(s):* Messina, Cedric; *Director(s):* Coleman, Basil; *Adaptor/translator(s):* Shallcross, Alan; *Composer(s):* Burgon, Geoffrey; Lloyd-Jones, David; *Choreographer(s):* Stephenson, Geraldine; *Designer(s):* Taylor, Don; *Costume designer(s):* Fraser-Paye, Robin; *Lighting designer(s):* Potter, Clive; *Other personnel:* Morgan, Brian; Banks, Terence (Prod. assts.); Lowden, Fraser (Prod. unit manager); Wright, Terry (Fight arranger); Bowman, Ron (Videotape editor); de Winne, Kezia (Make-up); Luxford, Robin (Sound); Wilders, John (Literary consultant); *Cast:* Mirren, Helen (Rosalind); Stirner, Brian (Orlando); Pasco, Richard (Jaques); Rees, Angharad (Celia); Bolam, James (Touchstone); Francis, Clive (Oliver); Easton, Richard (Duke Frederick); Church, Tony (Banished Duke); Quentin, John (Le Beau); Williams, Maynard (Silvius); Plucknett, Victoria (Phebe); Le Conte, Marilyn (Audrey); McDonnell, Tom (Amiens); Meredith,

David L. (Corin); Hewlett, Arthur (Adam); Holland, Jeffrey (William); Bateson, Timothy (Sir Oliver Martext); Prowse, Dave (Charles); Moulder-Brown, John (Hymen); Bentall, Paul (Jaques de Boys); Tullo, Peter; Lewin, Mike (Palace Lords); Forgione, Carl; Harvey, Max (Banished Duke's Lords); Sullivan, Chris (Dennis); Phoenix, Paul; Holden, Barry (Pages); London Pro Musica (Musicians).

DISTRIBUTION & AVAILABILITY: *Publisher or responsible agency:* BBC/TLF; *Distributor:* AVP, UIO, KSU, BBC* *Copy location:* UVM (Archive); *Availability:* AVP, B, V, 3/4U $450, sale; UIO, V (72032H), 3/4U (70132V), rental, $26.30; KSU, V, 3/4U, rental, (1-5 days) $33.75; BBC* 16mm or V, apply (*BUFVC* 29).

As You Like It. Video/Teleplay

42.1 *Comme il vous plaire*

DOCUMENT INFORMATION: *Country:* GB/France.

EDITION, HISTORY, CONTENTS, & EVALUATION: *Edition & history:* Identical to entry #42 above except that it has French subtitles. Available in Paris archive, see below.

MEDIUM INFORMATION: *Language of subtitles:* French.

DISTRIBUTION & AVAILABILITY: *Copy location:* VAA; *Call or copy number:* THE 1.7.

As You Like It. Video/Documentary

43. *A Contemporary Look at Shakespeare.*

DOCUMENT INFORMATION: *Country:* USA; *Year of first showing:* 1980.

EDITION, HISTORY, CONTENTS, & EVALUATION: *Edition & history:* Keith Keating interviews the distinguished scholar/critic, G. Wilson Knight. Interview also includes mention of *King Lear,* and *Timon.* A copy is housed in the Theatre on Film and Tape (TOFT) Collection at the Billy Rose Theatre Collection of the Library of Performing Arts, Lincoln Center, New York Public Library. It may be viewed by apppointment (see below). *Audience:* College and university; Professional.

MEDIUM INFORMATION: *Medium:* Video; *Sound:* Spoken language; *Color:* Yes; *Length:* 50 min.; *Language(s) spoken:* English; *Video type:* 3/4U.

AUTHORSHIP INFORMATION: *Cast:* Knight, G. Wilson (Interviewee); Keating, Keith (Interviewer).

DISTRIBUTION & AVAILABILITY: *Publisher or responsible agency:* Lincoln Center; *Copy location:* LCL TOFT Collection; *Call or copy number:* NCOX 152; *Availability:* By appt.(Call Mrs. Betty Corwin, 212-870-1641).

As You Like It. Video/Documentary

44. *As You Like It.* (Series: Shakespeare in Perspective).

DOCUMENT INFORMATION: *Country:* GB; *Year of release:* 1984.

EDITION, HISTORY, CONTENTS, & EVALUATION: *Edition & history:* The "Shakespeare in Perspective" series was made to accompany the BBC/Time Life Inc. "The Shakespeare Plays" series. Each 25-minute tape features a well known British writer, critic, or theatre director. The distributor's blurb says that these are "brisk, unpretentious and enthusiastic guided tours . . . of William Shakespeare's most loved works." We are told that "noted critics, journalists and broadcasters take viewers from any sophistication level on a unique and highly subjective journey into Shakespeare's mind and time and explore the relevance of his works today." The seven in the series that are currently available in the United States are individually reviewed in this volume as follows: *Ham.* (142), *JC* (234), *Lr.*(269), *Mac.*(335), *MND* (411), *Rom.*(566) and *Tmp.* (624). The rest are in distribution in the British isles. Although Americans may be put off by their condescending tones of voice, the speakers nevertheless maintain a very high standard of discourse. *Contents & evaluation:* As has already been suggested, not all viewers on this side of the Atlantic will agree with the producers that the commentaries are "unpretentious and enthusiastic." At their worst they conjure up images of the news commentators in the Monty Python show. At their best, however, they show good minds at work with large problems. Novelist and essayist Brigid Brophy manages to be minimally condescending while giving a very good talk on the literary background of *AYL.* Placing heavy stress on Shakespeare's debt to Thomas Lodge's romance, *Rosalynde,* she reads aloud from Lodge to demonstrate how closely Shakespeare stuck to his sources. Her stress on the narrative background of the play indeed explains why this comedy often seems not so much dramatic as narrative. She traces the title of the play to Lodge's "If you like it" in the opening of his romance. There are also helpful insights on pastoral conventions (she sees modern cowboy westerns as "debased" offshoots of the tradition), and on what Brophy calls the "drag act." That is to say, the motifs of sexual ambiguity that mark so much of the disguising and cross dressing. And, as her publicists say, she sums up the play's effect in the belief that it is a "A social comedy which deals with adultery, foolishness and lust . . . but opts for the gamble of marriage." She delivers all of this from a desk in a pleasant study that looks as though it too belonged in the Forest of Arden. And the unfolding of a lively but not heavily academic mind coming to grips with a Shakespearean play makes for an interesting interlude (KSR).

MEDIUM INFORMATION: *Medium:* Video; *Sound:*

Spoken language; *Color:* Yes; *Length:* 25 min.; *Language(s) spoken:* English; *Video type:* V, B.

AUTHORSHIP INFORMATION: *Producer(s):* Poole, Victor; *Director(s):* Denkow, Barbara; *Other personnel:* Waters, Joe (Camera); Friedman, Liz (Graphics); Gabell, Steve (Editor); Lovelock, Chris (Sound); *Cast:* Brophy, Brigid (Commentator).

DISTRIBUTION & AVAILABILITY: *Publisher or responsible agency:* BBC; *Distributor:* BBC*; FNC, *Availability:* Double cassette (w.*MND*), Rental $50; Quad cassette (w.*MND, Lr., Tmp.*), Rental $75.

As You Like It. Video/Documentary/Scenes

45. *As You Like It.* (Series: From Page to Stage).

DOCUMENT INFORMATION: *Country:* Canada; *Year of release:* 1985; *Location of first showing:* Stratford Shakespeare Festival, Ontario, Canada.

EDITION, HISTORY, CONTENTS, & EVALUATION: *Edition & history:* One of a series of educational cassettes issued by the Stratford Shakespeare Festival, Ontario, Canada. (See also numbers 572, 606, 628, and 661.) As of this writing excerpts from five plays (*AYL, Rom.* [572], *Shr.* [606], *Tmp.* [628], and *TN* [661]) have been made available. Each play comes in a kit that includes a videotape for classroom viewing, a study guide and the Stratford Festival edition of the play. The study guide and cassette are keyed to specific parts of the play for handy reference. *Contents & evaluation:* Rosemary Dunsmore, Celia in the summer 1983 Stratford *AYL*, which is the basis for this program, is the charming hostess. She has some interesting things to say about the contrast between the urban and pastoral, which is so central to this play. Roberta Maxwell in the excerpts from the play is a wonderful Rosalind with a refreshing North American voice, a mix of brashness, boyishness and femininity. The standout performance from the Stratford production is Nicholas Pennell's marvelous rendering of Jaques' Seven Ages speech. It's as though he had for months of rehearsals polished each syllable until it glittered, and then had rearranged all this shining language into a single, apparently effortless utterance. "Magnificent" is the only word to describe a performance, which exemplifies what we often hear piously said but rarely see practiced: that the crowning glory of Shakespeare is the spoken language itself. *Audience:* General use; *Supplementary materials:* Hayes, Elliott, ed. [Teachers' Committee] *From Page to Stage: Study Guide.* Stratford Shakespeare Festival, 1985.

MEDIUM INFORMATION: *Medium:* Video; *Sound:* Spoken language; *Color:* Yes; *Length:* 30 min.; *Language(s) spoken:* English; *Video type:* B, V, 3/4U.

AUTHORSHIP INFORMATION: *Producer(s):* Levene,

Sam; *Director(s):* Hirsch, John (Stage); Roland, Herb (CBC); *Composer(s):* Whitefield, Raymond; *Choreographer(s):* Broome, John; *Designer(s):* Heeley, Desmond; *Cast:* Maxwell, Roberta (Rosalind); Gillies, Andrew (Orlando); Dunsmore, Rosemary (Celia/Narrator); Pennell, Nicholas (Jaques); with, Abbey, Graham; Blake, Mervyn (Adam); Bradbury, Simon; Campanaro, Paddy; Campbell, Graeme (Duke Frederick); Colicos, Nicolas; Cook, Christopher; Dennison, Holly; Dinicol, Keith; Evans, Maurice E.; Gibson, Christopher; Gordon, Lewis (Touchstone); Haney, Mary (Phebe); Hazel, Deryck; Jarvis, John (Silvius); Lachance, Robert; Lawson, Gregg; Leich-Milne, Elizabeth; Linehan, Hardee T.; Mappin, Jefferson; McKeever, Michael; McKenna, Seana; Needles, William; Novak, John; Ruckavina, Elizabeth; Russell, Stephen (Oliver); Sarabia, Ric; Shafer, John; Shepherd, Michael; Smith, David; Stillin, Marie; Tierney, Patrick; Vallancourt, Christiane; Waren, E. Joan; Whelan, Tim.

DISTRIBUTION & AVAILABILITY: *Publisher or responsible agency:* CBC Enterprises; *Distributor:* BEA, *Availability:* B (1-181-8) V (1-182-6) $120, schools $96; 3/4U (1-183-4) $135, schools $108).

As You Like It. Video/Documentary

45.1. *As You Like It.*

DOCUMENT INFORMATION: *Country:* Canada; *Year of release:* 1985[?]; *Location of first showing:* Stratford Shakespeare Festival, Ontario, Canada.

EDITION, HISTORY, CONTENTS, & EVALUATION: *Edition & history:* A recorded performance of the summer 1983 production at the Stratford, Canada, Shakespeare Festival. For more details and credits, see entry 45 above, which deals with a program of excerpts taken from this same production. This full-length version has only recently become available from video outlets.

MEDIUM INFORMATION: *Medium:* Video; *Sound:* Spoken language; *Color:* Yes, *Length:* 158 min.; *Video type:* V

DISTRIBUTION & AVAILABILITY: Publisher or responsible agency: Stratford, Canada, Shakespeare Festival; *Distributor:* INM (#DB25) V, $109.

As You Like It. Video/Documentary

46. *Love: As You Like It.*

DOCUMENT INFORMATION: *Country:* GB; *Year of release:* 1986.

EDITION, HISTORY, CONTENTS, & EVALUATION: *Edition & history:* "The theme of love and friendship is discussed by sixth formers (high school seniors) from a school in Tunbridge Wells, Kent'' (*BUFVC* 2). *Supplementary materials: BUFVC* 2.

MEDIUM INFORMATION: *Length:* 20 min.

DISTRIBUTION & AVAILABILITY: *Publisher or responsible agency:* Kent Educational TV Centre; *Distributor:* KTV*.

The Comedy of Errors

ORIGINAL WORK AND PRODUCTION: Comedy/ Plautine Farce. *Year written:* 1592; *Site of first production:* Inns of Court [?].

The Comedy of Errors. **Motion Picture/ Abbreviated**

47. *The Comedy of Errors.*

DOCUMENT INFORMATION: *Country:* USA; *Year of release:* 1908.

EDITION, HISTORY, CONTENTS, & EVALUATION: *Edition & history:* An early Vitagraph production chronicled by Professor Ball in his *SOSF.* This film actually only borrowed Shakespeare's title. *Supplementary materials:* Ball, *SOSF* 40, 310.

MEDIUM INFORMATION: *Length:* 10 min.

AUTHORSHIP INFORMATION: *Director(s):* Blackton, J. Stuart.

DISTRIBUTION & AVAILABILITY: *Publisher or responsible agency:* Vitagraph.

The Comedy of Errors. **Motion Picture/Derivative**

48. *The Boys from Syracuse.*

DOCUMENT INFORMATION: *Country:* USA; *Year of release:* 1940; *Country of first showing:* USA.

EDITION, HISTORY, CONTENTS, & EVALUATION: *Edition & history:* Based on the Broadway musical, *Boys from Syracuse* with book by George Abbott and music by Richard Rodgers and Lorenz Hart. Abbott's play was in turn based on Shakespeare's *The Comedy of Errors. Contents & evaluation:* Persons expecting a literal adaptation on screen from Shakespeare's stage play, *The Comedy of Errors,* will be sorely disappointed in this frivolous treatment, or mis-treatment, of the adventures of the two boys from Syracuse, Antipholus and Dromio, respectively played by Allan Jones and Joe Penner. Those expecting a light-hearted, free-swinging take-off of Shakespeare's play will, however, be uproariously entertained. The surface touches of absurdity (a metered chariot that functions as a Checker Cab, for example, and takes you to the "Wooden Horse Inn"), may intrude a bit but the underlying plot is clearly Shakespeare's familiar comedy of mistakings about the two pairs of twins. Shakespeare himself imitated the work of the Roman playwright Plautus. The film is also one of those relics of a past when the Hollywood star system catered to the whims of the public for stereotyped reigning favorites. Few among today's audience will get the point of old-fashioned "show business" jokes, such as this one: "Antipholus to the taxi driver, 'Take me to the Palace.' Taxi Driver: 'Who's playing there this week?'" The newspaper headlines in Ephesus that read "Ephesus Blitzkriegs Syracuse" employ a topically relevant but now virtually forgotten buzzword from World War II, "Blitzkrieg." Despite these anachronisms, nearly everyone will be tolerably amused by the impertinence of George Abbott and his colleagues in re-appropriating a Shakespearean play for a broad, mass audience. Shakespeare was himself not without concern for the groundlings. And after all *Errors* ranks as Shakespeare's campiest farce, not a solemn tragedy by any means, though a scholar can point out epistemological dilemmas about the nature of reality even in it (KSR). *Audience:* General use.

MEDIUM INFORMATION: *Medium:* Motion Picture; *Sound:* Spoken language; *Color:* No (black & white); *Length:* 73 min.; *Language(s) spoken:* English; *Film type:* 35 mm; 16 mm.

AUTHORSHIP INFORMATION: *Producer(s):* Levey, Jules; *Director(s):* Sutherland, A. Edward; *Adaptor/translator(s):* Spiegelgass, Leonard; Grayson, Charles; Smith, Paul Gerard; *Composer(s):* Rogers, Richard; Hart, Lorenz; Previn, Charles; *Lighting designer(s):* Valentine, Joseph; *Other personnel:* Carruth, Milton (Editor); *Cast:* Jones, Allan (Antipholus of Ephesus and of Syracuse); Raye, Martha (Luce); Penner, Joe (Dromio of Ephesus and of Syracuse); Lane, Rosemary (Phyllis); Butterworth, Charles (Duke); Hervey, Irene (Adriana); Mowbray, Alan (Angelo); Blore, Eric (Pinch); Hinds, Samuel S. (Aegeon); Acuff, Eddie (Taxi Driver); Dugan, Tom (Octavius); Charters, Spencer (Turnkey); Waite, Malcolm (Captain of the Guard); Desmond, William (Driver); Lloyd, Doris (Woman); Oliver, Dave (Messenger).

DISTRIBUTION & AVAILABILITY: *Publisher or responsible agency:* Universal Pictures; *Distributor:* SWA; *Copy location:* FOL; *Call or copy number:* MP 1; *Availability:* 16mm rental, Apply.

The Comedy of Errors. Video/Abridgment

49. *The Comedy of Errors*

DOCUMENT INFORMATION: *Country:* USA; *Year of first showing:* 1949; *Location of first showing:* Kraft Television Theatre, 9 to 10:00 P.M., Wednesday, 7 Dec. 1949.

EDITION, HISTORY, CONTENTS, & EVALUATION: *Supplementary materials:* "Program." *NYT* 7 Dec. 1949: 62.

MEDIUM INFORMATION: *Sound:* Spoken language; *Color:* No (black & white); *Length:* 60 min.

CAST INFORMATION: Stewart, Bradley; Daly, James; Townes, Harry; Richards, Kurt.

DISTRIBUTION & AVAILABILITY: *Publisher or responsible agency:* Kraft Television Theatre.

The Comedy of Errors. Video/Teleplay

50. *The Comedy of Errors.*

DOCUMENT INFORMATION: *Country:* GB; *Year of first showing:* 1954; *Location of first showing:* BBC. Transmitted 9:02 to 10:26 P.M., Sunday, 16 May 1954.

EDITION, HISTORY, CONTENTS, & EVALUATION: *Edition & history:* An "operatic" production with music especially composed for this production by Julian Slade and James Turner. In the manner of *The Beggar's Opera* there was an alternation of speech, recitative and song. Examples of the verse set to music include "When women weep" (Luciana), "Music for Aegeon's speech," "Teach me, dear creature" (Ant./S. and Luciana), and "Go get thee from the door" (Dromio). The cast included twenty, and the cost was £1,943. Accompanying all this with "live" music was Eric Robinson and his 12-member orchestra. Joan Plowright took the role of Adriana. *Contents & evaluation:* The *Times* critic found Mr. Slade's music "delightful" with an "eighteenth-century tunefulness about it." The costumes, he wrote, "seemed to take us still farther forward, to the period of Jane Austen." But the settings were more appropriate for the lengthier vistas of the stage than for the close range of the tv studio. And overall "the imagination in this production lay rather in the original conception than the performance" ("Television Performances," *Times* 18 May 1954: 10b). *Supplementary materials:* "Program." *TPAB* 16 May 1954: n.p.

MEDIUM INFORMATION: *Length:* 84 min.

AUTHORSHIP INFORMATION: *Producer(s):* Harris, Lionel; *Adaptor/translator(s):* Harris, Lionel; McNab, Robert; *Composer(s):* Slade, Julian; Turner, James; *Designer(s):* Bould, James; *Other personnel:* Young, Marguerite (Stage manager); *Cast:* Cross, Gerald (Duke of Ephesus, Dr. Pinch); Vernon, Richard (Egeon); Pool, David (Antipholus/E.); Cairncross, James (Dromio/E. and S.); Hansard, Paul (Antipholus/S.); Bird, David (Angelo); Bowers, Lally (Aemilia); Plowright, Joan (Adriana); Wenham, Jane (Luciana); Lawrence, Esther (Luce/Harlot/Nun); Humphrey, Christie (Courtesan).

DISTRIBUTION & AVAILABILITY: *Publisher or responsible agency:* BBC; *Copy location:* Unavailable.

The Comedy of Errors. Video/Adaptation

51. *Komödie Der Irrungen.*

DOCUMENT INFORMATION: *Country:* West Germany; *Year of release:* 1964.

EDITION, HISTORY, CONTENTS, & EVALUATION: *Edition & history:* Made for West German television *Contents & evaluation:* Not seen *Audience:* College and university; *Supplementary materials:* SIF 74.

MEDIUM INFORMATION: *Medium:* Video; *Sound:* Spoken language; *Length:* 98 min.; *Language(s) spoken:* German; *Video type:* Not available.

AUTHORSHIP INFORMATION: *Producer(s):* May, Alexander; *Director(s):* Schwarze, Hans Dieter; *Adaptor/translator(s):* Rothe, Hans; *Composer(s):* Ferstl, Erich; *Designer(s):* Kleber, Hans; *Set designer(s):* Blokesch, Walter; *Costume designer(s):* Von Winterfield, Hannelore; *Other personnel:* Holzapfel, Gisella (Sound); *Cast:* Schumann, Erik (Antipholus of Ephesus); Biederstaedt, Claus (Antipholus of Syracuse); Schwartzkopf, Klaus (Dromio of Ephesus); Lichenfeld, Manfred (Dromio of Syracuse); Weisemann, Edgar (Angelo); Jäger, Hanns Ernst (Captain); Kähler, Ruth; (Aemilia); Marhold, Irene (Adriana); Schmahl, Hildegard (Luciana); Brasch, Helmut (Police Officer); Mehring, Wolfram (Police Officer); Martin, Hans, (Captain); Ferstl, Erich (Guitarist); Carl, Margaret (Julia).

DISTRIBUTION & AVAILABILITY: *Publisher or responsible agency:* Bavaria Atelier GmbH

The Comedy of Errors. Video/Recording

52. *The Comedy of Errors.*

DOCUMENT INFORMATION: *Country:* GB; *Year of first showing:* 1964; *Location of first showing:* BBC. Transmitted 9:25 to 10:55 P.M., Wed., 1 Jan. 1964.

EDITION, HISTORY, CONTENTS, & EVALUATION: *Edition & history:* A part of the quatercentenary celebration of Shakespeare's birth, this RSC production was adapted for television as a New Year's day treat for British audiences during an engagement at the Aldwych Theatre in London. *Supplementary materials:* "Program." RT 26 Dec. 1963: 35.

MEDIUM INFORMATION: *Length:* 92 min.

AUTHORSHIP INFORMATION: *Producer(s):* Luke, Peter (BBC); Williams, Clifford (RSC); *Director(s):* Duguid, Peter; *Composer(s):* Wishart, Peter; *Designer(s):* Wyckham, John; Williams, Clifford; *Costume designer(s):* Powell, Anthony; *Cast:* Sinden, Donald (Solinus); Welsh, John (Aegeon); Richardson, Ian (Antipholus of Ephesus); McCowen, Alec (Antipholus of Syracuse); Rose, Clifford (Dromio of Ephesus); MacGregor, Barry (Dromio of Syracuse); Murray, Michael (Balthazar); Wynne, Ken (Angelo); Black, Philip (First Merchant); Hussey, John (Second Merchant); Smith, Derek (Pinch); Corvin, John (An Officer); Falk, Ronald (A Messenger); Jenkins, Martin (A Gaoler); Thomas, Madoline (Aemilia); Rigg, Diana (Adriana); Suzman, Janet (Luciana); Maud, Caroline (Luce); Engel, Suzan (Courtesan); + Barnett, Barbara; Curry, Shaun; Cutts, Valerie; Falkland, James; Geddis, Peter; Harrison, Brian; Jones, Marshall; Jennings, Robert; Urquhart, Philippa; Wylton, Tim.

DISTRIBUTION & AVAILABILITY: *Publisher or responsible agency:* BBC; *Copy location:* BBC, archive.

The Comedy of Errors. Video/Rebroadcast

53. *The Comedy of Errors.* (Series: Festival Series).

DOCUMENT INFORMATION: *Country:* GB; *Year of first showing:* 1964; *Location of first showing(s):* BBC. Transmitted 9:25 to 10:55 P.M., 1 Jan. 1964; NET Playhouse, USA, 8 to 10 P.M., 13 Jan. 1967.

EDITION, HISTORY, CONTENTS, & EVALUATION: *Edition & history:* This is the identical Royal Shakespeare Company production listed above under entry #52. It was televised for U.S. audiences by WNET. An astonishing number of high quality U.S. television broadcasts, not only including Shakespeare but also other dramatists, have had their origins in the British television industry. So far commercial television in the United States has been unable to match the British in quality, though the toppling of the BBC user tax, which has been threatened by the Thatcher government, may well also force British programmers to compete for the lowest common denominator of viewer taste. *Supplementary materials:* "Program." NYT 13 Jan. 1967: 83.

MEDIUM INFORMATION: See above, #52.

DISTRIBUTION & AVAILABILITY: *Publisher or responsible agency:* WNET; *Copy location:* BBC (Archive).

The Comedy of Errors. Video/Recording

54. *The Comedy of Errors.*

DOCUMENT INFORMATION: *Country:* GB; *Year of release:* 1974.

EDITION, HISTORY, CONTENTS, & EVALUATION: *Edition & history:* Based on an RSC stage production, the recording was done by British commercial television. Hence, it is available on videocassette in the British isles. *Supplementary materials:* BUFVC 3.

MEDIUM INFORMATION: *Color:* Yes; *Length:* 130 min.; *Video type:* VHS.

AUTHORSHIP INFORMATION: *Director(s):* Nunn, Trevor (RSC); Casson, Philip (Video); *Composer(s):* Woolfenden, Guy; *Cast:* Dench, Judi (Adriana); Annis, Francesca (Luciana); Rees, Roger (Antipholus S.); Gwilym, Mike (Antipholus E.).

DISTRIBUTION & AVAILABILITY: *Publisher or responsible agency:* Precision Video for Royal Shakespeare Company; *Distributor:* RSC*.

The Comedy of Errors. Video/Interpretation

55. *The Comedy of Errors.* (Series: The Shakespeare Plays).

DOCUMENT INFORMATION: *Country:* GB; *Year of filming:* 1983; *Year of first showing:* 1984; *Location of first showing(s):* BBC, London; PBS stations, USA, 1984.

EDITION, HISTORY, CONTENTS, & EVALUATION: *Edition & history:* As with all the BBC television productions, the text is based on the Peter Alexander edition with cuts and alterations made by the BBC's own editor, in this case Mr. David Snodin. A main feature is the "doubling" of the principal characters, the Antipholuses and the Dromios, the latter being portrayed by rock star, Roger Daltrey. The director felt that doubling was called for not just in the context of trick photography but also because of internal textual evidence suggesting the same actor played both roles even in Shakespeare's time. The *commedia dell arte* style allows integration of mimes and street players into the plot and *mise en scène.* Equally attention-getting is the huge map of the eastern Mediterranean that makes up the market floor and the marvelous lighting that gives the illusion of a sun-drenched Mediterranean seaport town. Subtly underscoring the play's adherence to the neoclassical doctrine of the unities of time and place is the lighting on the set's small houses that shifts with the sun's movements. *Contents & evaluation:* "The aura of romance was greatly enhanced from the start by the superb performance of Cyril Cusack as Aegeon. He quickly persuaded us of the genuine pathos of his loss of family and the desolation of his futile search. He was aged, fragile, vulnerable, and yet stoically brave. His long recitation of his misfortunes was artfully and illuminatingly mimed, as he spoke, by the troupe of performers. Even though it flirted openly with self-parody by adding sentimental violin music to the sad story, the scene brought audiences on and off the screen closer to tears than to laughter. . . . Farcical realism was not banished, however. Rock star Roger Daltrey played the two Dromios with engaging vacuity, nicely emphasizing this quality in the Ephesian and giving his brother a small edge of dignity. . . . Most striking of all was the success with which this production conveyed through stylization of performance and slight over-acting the sense that the action in progress was not real life. With remarkable consistency Aegeon, Adriana, Luciana, the Courtesan, the Duke, and the Abbess overdid their parts to emphasize their roles. Susan Bertish's Adriana became a commanding figure, not just a jealous shrew, but a justly aggrieved wife, quietly chastened by the Abbess, but with no loss of dignity—a very personification of Wife. As Luciana, Joanne Pearce recited her lines on female duty with appealing, if naive, fervor, emerging as the type of an innocent virgin. Ingrid Pitt's Courtesan was a model of wittily-knowing sensuality. Charles Gray as the Duke presided like an inscrutable Super-ego while Dame Wendy Hiller as Abbess overrode him with her 'supernatural' invention. . . . Confused by his certainty that he was threatened by witchcraft, Antipholus of Syracuse ignored or discounted visual hints in the background of the solution to his dilemma. Twin mimes passed unnoticed, and I believe at one moment Antipholus actually saw 'himself' entering the Portentine and shrugged his vision off. . . . Openly acknowledging his strange oblivion served to point up the irrational blindness of the pysche in search of itself. . . . Every word was crystal clear; the delights of eye and ear were superbly harmonized" (Roberts, Jeanne Addison, "*The Comedy of Errors,*" *SFNL* 9.1 [1984]:4). *Audience:* General use; *Supplementary materials:* Willis, Susan. "*Errors* in Production." *SFNL* 8.2 [1984]:8; Videocassette (25 min.) from "Shakespeare in Perspective" series with Roy Hudd as lecturer available in U.K. from BBC* (BUFVC 39).

MEDIUM INFORMATION: *Medium:* Video; *Sound:* Spoken language; *Color:* Yes; *Length:* 110 min.; *Language(s) spoken:* English; *Video type:* B, V, 3/4U.

AUTHORSHIP INFORMATION: *Producer(s):* Sutton, Shaun; *Director(s):* Cellan-Jones, James; *Adaptor/translator(s):* Snodin, David; *Composer(s):* Holmes, Richard; *Designer(s):* Homfray, Don; *Costume designer(s):* Hudson, June; *Lighting designer(s):* Sydenham, Dave; *Other personnel:* Hay-Arthur, Cecile (Make-up); Hider, Peter (Prod. manager); Ebbutt, Raquel (Director's asst.); Lowden, Fraser (Prod. assoc.); Bird, John (Tech. coordinator); Mann, Julie (Vision mixer); Field, Geoff (Camera); Raason, Peter (Videotape Editor), Olenda, Magda (Buyer); Chick, Anthony (Sound); Wilders, John Dr. (Literary Consultant); *Cast:* Gray, Charles (Solinus); Cusack, Cyril (Aegeon); Kitchen, Michael (Antipholus's); Daltrey, Roger (Dromios); Kelly, David (Balthazar); Dastor, Sam (Angelo); Johnson, Noel (First Merchant); Hoffman, Alfred (Second Merchant); Rose, Geoffrey (Pinch); Hiller, Wendy (Aemilia); Bertish, Suzanne (Adriana); Pearce, Joanne (Luciana); Fitzalan, Marsha (Luce); Pitt, Ingrid (Courtezan); Reed, Bunny (Gaoler); Williams, Frank (Officer); MacKriel, Peter (Messenger); Chagrin, Nicholas (Master Mime); Burnell, Nick; Christopher, Grahm; Davidson, Ross; Lee, Howard; Rouvai, Daniel; Springer, Paul; Weston, Jenny (Mime Troupe).

DISTRIBUTION & AVAILABILITY: *Publisher or responsible agency:* BBC/TLF; *Distributor:* AVP, UIO, BBC*, *Copy location:* UVM; *Availability:* AVP, sale, all formats, $450 (1987); UIO rental, V (72007H), 3/4U (70122V) $22.70; BBC* 16mm or V, apply.

The Comedy of Errors. Video/Recordings

56. *The Comedy of Errors.*

DOCUMENT INFORMATION: *Country:* USA; *Year of release:* 1986.

EDITION, HISTORY, CONTENTS, & EVALUATION: *Edition & history:* A videotaping of the production by Company Commedia, Ltd., at the Washington Square church in New York City on February 28, 1986. *Audience:* General use.

MEDIUM INFORMATION: *Medium:* Video; *Sound:* Spoken language; *Color:* Yes; *Length:* 100 min.; *Language(s) spoken:* English; *Video type:* V.

AUTHORSHIP INFORMATION: *Producer(s):* Company Commedia, Ltd.; *Director(s):* Shampain, Robert. DISTRIBUTION & AVAILABILITY: *Publisher or responsible agency:* Company Commedia, Ltd.; *Copy location:* LCL; *Call or copy number:* NCOV 484; *Availability:* Archive.

57. *The Comedy of Errors.*

DOCUMENT INFORMATION: *Country:* USA; *Year of filming:* 1987; *Year of first showing:* 24 June 1987; *Location of first showing:* PBS stations. EDITION, HISTORY, CONTENTS, & EVALUATION: *Edition & history:* A recording of the "circus" production of *Comedy of Errors* as performed "live" at the Vivian Beaumont theatre, Lincoln Center, New York City, in June 1987. The play was originally produced at Chicago's Goodman theatre in 1984. *Contents & evaluation:* A zany, slapstick, treatment of Shakespeare's play about the boys from Syracuse. Circus acts such as The Flying Karamazov Brothers and the Kamikaze Ground Crew escalate the carnivalesque even beyond Shakespeare's farcical instincts. Despite all the non-verbal gesturing, the words of Shakespeare remain intact most of the time. There are amusing intrusions when the actors inadvertently recite lines from the wrong play. An ironic distancing effect has an actor gotten up to look like Will Shakespeare appear occasionally to behold sadly the acts of desecration that have been committed against his play. The doubling of the cast emulates theatrical practices in the playhouses of Shakespeare's own day. Karla Burns, who plays an outrageously gross Luce, also doubles in the unlikely role of the Duke of Ephesus (she wears a goatee). Avna Eisenberg plays both the Janitor and Dr. Pinch, while Ethyl Eichelberger validates the Elizabethan jokes about nunneries by being both the abbess (Emilia) and the courtesan. Nearly everyone will enjoy this witty adaptation of Shakespeare's text. It privileges farce over comedy, no doubt. Those looking for the more profound subtext—feminist issues, Marxist overtones, etc.—will be sorely disappointed. Happily for them, however, they may be able to ferret out a hidden Freudian agenda in the fact that the same actress doubles as both Emilia and the courtesan (KSR). *Audience:* General use; *Supplementary materials:* Oliver, Edith. "Some Boys from Syracuse." *NY* 15 June 1987: 72.

MEDIUM INFORMATION: *Medium:* Video; *Sound:* Spoken language; *Color:* Yes; *Length:* 120 min.; *Language(s) spoken:* English; *Video type:* Not known.

AUTHORSHIP INFORMATION: *Producer(s):* Gersten, Bernard; *Director(s):* Mosher, Gregory; Woodruff, Robert; *Composer(s):* Wieselman, Douglas; Spae, Thaddeus; *Set designer(s):* Gropman, David; *Costume designer(s):* Hilferty, Susan; *Lighting designer(s):* Gallo, Paul; Dumas, Debra; *Other personnel:* Kilgore, John (Sound); *Cast:* Magid, Paul (Antipholus of Syracuse); Patterson, Howard Jay (Antipholus of Ephesus); Williams, Sam (Dromio of Syracuse); Nelson, Randy (Dromio of Ephesus); Leishman, Gina (Luciana); Hayden, Sophie (Adriana); Burns, Karla (Luce and Duke); Mankin, Daniel (Egeon); Eichelberger, Ethyl (Courtesan/Emilia); Eisenberg, Avna (Dr. Pinch/Janitor); "The Flying Karamazov Brothers"; "The Kamikaze Ground Crew"; "Vaudeville Nouveau".

DISTRIBUTION & AVAILABILITY: *Publisher or responsible agency:* Lincoln Center Vivian Beaumont Theatre/PBS; *Copy location:* Vivian Beaumont.

Coriolanus

ORIGINAL WORK AND PRODUCTION: Roman History/Tragedy. *Year of first production:* 1611-12; *Site of first production:* Globe on Bankside.

Coriolanus. Video/Recording

58. *Coriolanus.*

DOCUMENT INFORMATION: *Country:* USA; *Year of first showing:* 1951; *Location of first showing:* Westinghouse Studio One. Transmitted 10 P.M., Monday, 11 June 1951.

EDITION, HISTORY, CONTENTS, & EVALUATION: *Edition & history:* A modern dress update, reminiscent of the famous Orson Welles Mercury Theatre *Julius Caesar*, that moves the action to Mussolini's Italy. Nowadays few directors can stage *Coriolanus* without remaking Shakespeare's hero into some modern prototype such as General of the Army Douglas MacArthur. (Could the patrician MacArthur ever have stooped to being packaged for the hoi polloi as "Mac" in the way that his fellow West Pointer, Eisenhower, allowed himself to be marketed as "Ike"?) Unlike so many other televised Shakespearean productions from the past, this production is now available on commercial videocassette. In a flurry of nostalgia, it even includes Betty Furness doing her fabled Westinghouse commercials. The producer, perhaps optimistically, estimated that the Studio One program caught an audience of ten million. *Contents & evaluation:* The program received a mixed review from *The New York Times* critic who praised the producer for his "courage" in bucking commercialism. Nevertheless the play "faltered," perhaps almost as much because of the inherent weaknesses of the play itself more than because of any particular problem with television. The modern dress costumes also raised some reservations. The military uniforms "begged for the score of *The Student Prince*." And the ladies were "done up by couturieres from Fifth and Madison Avenues rather than from the Appian Way." *Supplementary materials:* Gould, Jack. "Studio One Introduces *Cor*." *NYT* 17 June 1951: X 11; Schumach, Murray. "Video's Mr. Miner." *NYT* 11 Feb. 1951: X 9.

MEDIUM INFORMATION: *Length:* 60 min.

AUTHORSHIP INFORMATION: *Producer(s):* Miner, Worthington; *Director* Nickell, Paul; *Adaptor:* Nickell, Paul; *Cast:* Greene, Richard (Coriolanus); Evelyn, Judith (Volumnia); Purdy, Richard; Worlock, Frederic; Chamberlin, Sally; Poston, Tom.

DISTRIBUTION & AVAILABILITY: *Distributor:* FCM, *Availability:* V, $24.95.

Coriolanus, 1. Video/Teleplay

59. *Hero, The.* (Series: The Spread of the Eagle [I]).

DOCUMENT INFORMATION: *Country:* GB; *Year of first showing:* 1963; *Location of first showing:* BBC TV. Transmitted 9:25 to 10:15 P.M., Friday, 3 May 1963.

EDITION, HISTORY, CONTENTS, & EVALUATION: *Edition & history:* For background on this series, see number #14, above. The eight other episodes from the Roman history plays in *The Spread of the Eagle* series can be located at numbers 14-16, 60-61, and 221-23. *Contents & evaluation:* The London *Times* critic felt that the episodes lacked continuity since the only character who appears in more than one of the three plays is Antony. It was apparently a recorded stage reading more than a full-scale teleplay ("Continuity Problem of New B.B.C. Shakespeare Series," *Times* 4 May 1963: 5d). *Audience:* General use; *Supplementary materials:* Dews, Peter. "The Spread of the Eagle." *RT* 25 Apr. 1963: 49.; Williams, Michael. "Robert Hardy in 'The Voices.'" *RT* 2 May 1963: 45.

MEDIUM INFORMATION: *Medium:* Video; *Sound:* Spoken language; *Color:* No (black & white); *Length:* 51 min.; *Language(s) spoken:* English; *Video type:* Video, Kinescope.

AUTHORSHIP INFORMATION: *Producer(s):* Dews, Peter; *Director(s):* Dews, Peter; *Composer(s):* Whelen, Christopher; *Designer(s):* Hatts, Clifford; *Costume designer(s):* Agombar, Elizabeth; *Other personnel:* Manderson, Tommy (Make-up); Greenwood, John; Ware, Derek (Fight coordinators); *Cast:* Hardy, Robert (Coriolanus); Lehmann, Beatrix (Volumnia); Culver, Roland (Menenius Agrippa); Colbourne, Maurice (Senator); Johnson, Noel (Cominius); Croucher, Roger (Titus Lartius); Jeffrey, Peter (Sicinius Velutus); Pettingell, Frank (Junius Brutus); Willis, Jerome (Aufidius); Daniel, Jennifer (Virgilia); Wright, Hilary (Gentlewoman); Steele, Mary (Valeria); Greenwood, John (Messenger); Laurence, Charles (Roman Lieutenant); Barcroft, John (Lieutenant to Aufidius); Dickson, Hugh (The Aedile); Lloyd, Bernard; Wale, Terry; Cox, Michael; Bailey, Paul (Citizens); Herrick, Roy (Messenger); King, David; Harris, Paul (Volsce Senators); Clarke, Raymond; Weston, David; Cracknell, Leonard; Harte, Ben; Hinsliff, Geoffrey (Soldiers); + Craig, Pamela; Desmond, Marion; Finch, Bernard; Gay, John; Jackson, Barry; Stephens, Caroline; Varnais, Wendy; Webster, Paul.

DISTRIBUTION & AVAILABILITY: *Publisher or responsible agency:* BBC; *Copy location:* BBC (6 of 9 parts in archive).

Coriolanus, 2-4. Video/Teleplay

60. *Voices, The.* (Series: The Spread of the Eagle [II]).

DOCUMENT INFORMATION: *Country:* GB; *Year of first showing:* 1963; *Location of first showing:* BBC TV. Transmitted 9:25 to 10:15 P.M., Friday, 10 May 1963.

EDITION, HISTORY, CONTENTS, & EVALUATION: *Edition & history:* For fuller information, see above, numbers 14 and 59. *Audience:* General use; *Supplementary materials:* Dews, Peter. "The Spread of the Eagle." *RT* 25 Apr. 1963: 49; "Program." *RT* 2 May 1963: 45.

MEDIUM INFORMATION: *Medium:* Video; *Sound:* Spoken language; *Color:* No (black & white); *Length:* 49 min.; *Language(s) spoken:* English; *Video type:* Video, Kinescope.

AUTHORSHIP INFORMATION: *Producer(s):* Dews, Peter; *Director(s):* Dews, Peter; *Composer(s):* Whelen, Christopher; *Designer(s):* Hatts, Clifford; *Costume designer(s):* Agombar, Elizabeth; *Other personnel:* Manderson, Tommy (Make-up); Greenwood, John; Ware, Derek (Fight coordinators); *Cast:* Hardy, Robert (Coriolanus); Lehmann, Beatrix (Volumnia); Culver, Roland (Menenius Agrippa); Colbourne, Maurice; Gay, John (Senators); Johnson, Noel (Cominius); Croucher, Roger (Titus Lartius); Jeffrey, Peter (Sicinius Velutus); Pettingell, Frank (Junius Brutus); Daniel, Jennifer (Virgilia); Webster, Paul; King, David (Officers); Lloyd, Bernard; Wale, Terry; Cox, Michael; Bailey, Paul; Clarke, Raymond; Finch, Bernard; Jackson, Barry (Officers); Dickson, Hugh; Harte, Ben (The Aediles); + Barcroft, John; Herrick, Roy; Harris, Paul; Weston, David; Cracknell, Leonard; Hinsliff, Geoffrey; Craig, Pamela; Desmond, Marion; Stephens, Caroline; Varnais, Wendy; Wright, Hilary.

DISTRIBUTION & AVAILABILITY: *Publisher or responsible agency:* BBC; *Copy location:* BBC (6 of 9 parts).

Coriolanus, 5. Video/Teleplay

61. *Outcast, The.* (Series: The Spread of the Eagle [III]).

DOCUMENT INFORMATION: *Country:* GB; *Year of first showing:* 1963; *Location of first showing:* BBC TV. Transmitted 9:25 to 10:15 P.M., Friday, 17 May 1963.

EDITION, HISTORY, CONTENTS, & EVALUATION: *Edition & history:* For commentary, see numbers 14 and 59, above. *Audience:* General use; *Supplementary materials:* Dews, Peter. "The Spread of the Eagle." *RT* 25 Apr. 1963: 49; "Program." *RT* 9 May 1963: 51.

MEDIUM INFORMATION: *Medium:* Video; *Sound:* Spoken language; *Color:* No (black & white); *Length:* 49 min.; *Language(s) spoken:* English; *Video type:* Video, Kinescope.

AUTHORSHIP INFORMATION: *Producer(s):* Dews,

Peter; *Director(s):* Dews, Peter; *Composer(s):* Whelen, Christopher; *Designer(s):* Hatts, Clifford; *Costume designer(s):* Agombar, Elizabeth; *Other personnel:* Manderson, Tommy (Make-up); Greenwood, John; Ware, Derek (Fight coordinators); *Cast:* Hardy, Robert (Coriolanus); Lehmann, Beatrix (Volumnia); Culver, Roland (Menenius Agrippa); Clarke, Raymond (Volsce Citizen); Bailey, Paul; Laurence, Charles; Weston, David (Serving Men); Willis, Jerome (Aufidius); Pettingell, Frank (Junius Brutus); Jeffrey, Peter (Sicinius Velutus); Lloyd, Bernard; Wale, Terry; Cox, Michael (Citizens); Dickson, Hugh; Harte, Ben (Aediles); Greenwood, John; Herrick, Roy (Messengers); Johnson, Noel (Cominius); Barcroft, John (Lieutenant to Aufidius); Jackson, Barry; Harris, Paul (Volsce Sentries); Daniel, Jennifer (Virgilia); Steele, Mary (Valeria); Martin, Kirk (Young Martius); Hinsliff, Geoffrey; Croucher, Roger (Messengers); Colbourne, Maurice (Roman Senator); Cracknell, Leonard; Weston, David; Laurence, Charles (Conspirators); King, David; Gay, John; Finch, Bernard (Volsce Lords); + Craig, Pamela; Desmond, Marion; Stephens, Caroline; Varnals, Wendy; Webster, Paul; Wright, Hilary.

DISTRIBUTION & AVAILABILITY: *Publisher or responsible agency:* BBC; *Copy location:* BBC (6 of 9 parts).

Coriolanus. **Motion Picture/Derivative**

62. *Coriolano, eroe senza patria.* [*Thunder of Battle*].

DOCUMENT INFORMATION: *Country:* Italy/France; *Year of release:* 1964.

EDITION, HISTORY, CONTENTS, & EVALUATION: *Edition & history:* Based on Plutarch and Shakespeare. *Contents & evaluation:* The *MFB* reviewer was unenthusiastic: "The treatment is, in general, as colorless as the construction is unexciting" ("Review," *MFB* 32, nos. 372-83 [1965]: 149). *Supplementary materials:* SIF 113.

MEDIUM INFORMATION: *Color:* Yes; *Length:* 88 min.; *Language(s) spoken:* Dubbed English.

AUTHORSHIP INFORMATION: *Director(s):* Ferroni, Giorgi; *Adaptor/translator(s):* Del Grosso, Remigio; *Lighting designer(s):* Tiezzi, Augusto; *Cast:* Scott, Gordon (Coriolanus); Brignone, Lilla (Volumnia); Hersent, Philippe (Cominius); Minervini, Angela (Livia); Lupo, Alberto (Sicinius); Neri, Rosalba (Virgilia).

DISTRIBUTION & AVAILABILITY: *Publisher or responsible agency:* Dorica Films/Explorer Films; *Distributor:* Eagle Films.

Coriolanus. **Video/Teleplay**

63. *Coriolanus.*

DOCUMENT INFORMATION: *Country:* GB; *Year of first showing:* Transmitted 7:25 to 9:55 P.M., Sunday, 23 May 1965; *Location of first showing:* BBC-2.

EDITION, HISTORY, CONTENTS, & EVALUATION: *Edition & history:* The production was first staged in the proscenium setting of the Queen's Theatre in summer 1964 and was recorded for television at the Chichester Festival Theatre in April 1965. The National Youth Theatre was a company of young people from 15 to 21 who performed plays for the fun of it more than from any desire to be professionals. The main goal was to get young people to enjoy the theatre. *Supplementary materials:* Croft, Michael. "Coriolanus." *RT* 20 May 1965: 15; Morris, *SHOF* 30.

MEDIUM INFORMATION: *Length:* 146 min.

AUTHORSHIP INFORMATION: *Producer(s):* Croft, Michael (NYT); Hepton, Bernard (BBC); *Director(s):* Jenkins, Roger (BBC); *Designer(s):* Lawrence, Christopher; Newberry, Barry; *Other personnel:* Henderson, Ann (Make-up); *Cast:* Nightingale, John (Coriolanus); Block, Timothy (Cominius); Stockton, David (Meninius); Seaton, Derek (Sicinius); Robarts, Leslie (Brutus); Powell, Mark (Young Marcus); Davies, Robert (Aufidius); Grimes, Mary (Volumnia); Womersley, Charlotte (Virgilia); Holmes, Elizabeth (Valeria); Meats, Timothy (Lartius).

DISTRIBUTION & AVAILABILITY: *Publisher or responsible agency:* NYT/BBC; *Copy location:* Unavailable.

Coriolanus. **Video/Scenes**

64. *Coriolanus.*

DOCUMENT INFORMATION: *Country:* USA; *Year of first showing:* 1965; *Location of first showing:* Esso Repertory Theatre. Transmitted 9:00 P.M., Wed. and Sunday, 5 and 12 May 1965.

EDITION, HISTORY, CONTENTS, & EVALUATION: *Edition & history:* Scenes recorded live at the American Shakespeare Festival, Stratford, Conn., from several plays. In addition to *Coriolanus* there were sequences from *Romeo and Juliet, King Lear,* and *The Taming of the Shrew. Supplementary materials:* "Advertisement." *NYT* 16 May 1965: 4 X.

MEDIUM INFORMATION: *Length:* 90 min. [?].

DISTRIBUTION & AVAILABILITY: *Publisher or responsible agency:* American Shakespeare Festival.

Coriolanus. **Motion Picture/Documentary**

65. *Coriolanus: The People's Choice.* (Series: Explorations in Shakespeare III).

DOCUMENT INFORMATION: *Country:* Canada; *Year of release:* 1969.

EDITION, HISTORY, CONTENTS, & EVALUATION: *Edition & history:* Part three in a series of twelve 23-minute films made in 1969 by the Ontario Educational Communications Authority. For fuller information about it, see number #18, above. Descriptions of other parts of the series will be found at 40, 124, 162, 257, 322, 465, 488, 555, 617, and 637. *Contents & evaluation:* Not seen. According to the publicity release issued by NBC Educational Enterprises, this segment examines "the dynamics of the relationship between the politician and his electorate. It demonstrates a politician to be a successful popular leader, must be an actor even at the cost of his own self respect. Here we have the dilemma of Coriolanus, the autocratic soldier-politican, who is unable to simulate gratitude in order to win the votes of the common people who demand his emotional capitulation." *Audience:* College and university.

MEDIUM INFORMATION: *Medium:* Motion Picture; *Sound:* Spoken language; *Color:* Yes; *Length:* 23 min.; *Language(s) spoken:* English; *Film type:* 16mm.

AUTHORSHIP INFORMATION: *Producer(s):* Reis, Kurt; Moser, Ed; *Screenplay writer(s):* Webster, Hugh; *Composer(s):* Yanovsky, Zal; *Set designer(s):* Adeney, Chris; *Lighting designer(s):* Galbraith, Howard; *Performance group(s):* Ontario Educational Communications/ NBC Educational Enterprises.

DISTRIBUTION & AVAILABILITY: *Distributor:* CNU [?].

Coriolanus. **Video/Recording**

66. *Coriolanus.*

DOCUMENT INFORMATION: *Country:* USA; *Year of first showing:* 1979; *Location of first showing:* Delacorte Theatre, New York City.

EDITION, HISTORY, CONTENTS, & EVALUATION: *Edition & history:* A video recording of a New York Shakespeare Festival 1979 stage production of *Coriolanus* with an all-black and Hispanic cast. Producer Joseph Papp intended to provide professional opportunities for actors of minority ethnic backgrounds. *Contents & evaluation: The New York Times* drama critic was brutally frank. He thought that the actors confused "vehemence" with "conviction," that the cast was often "ragged," and "aimless," and that Earle Hyman as Cominius seemed to think that "acting a Shakespearean Roman means standing with statuesque stiffness and making violent facial contortions." Redeeming

performances were found, however, in the work of Michele Shay as Virgilia, Morgan Freeman as Coriolanus, and Robert Christian as Aufidius. Fortunately a record has been preserved on videotape so that anyone can now independently assess the production's merits and demerits (Eder, Richard, "Stage: 'Coriolanus'," *NYT* 29 June 1979: C 3). *Audience:* College and university; General use; *Supplementary materials:* Blau, Eleanor. "Papp Starts Repertory Troupe." *NYT* 21 Jan. 1979: n.p. (Discusses Papp's visionary plan to organize a troupe of black and Hispanic actors.)

MEDIUM INFORMATION: *Medium:* Video; *Sound:* Spoken language; *Color:* Yes; *Length:* 160 min.; *Language(s) spoken:* English; *Video type:* 3/4U.

AUTHORSHIP INFORMATION: *Producer(s):* Papp, Joseph; *Director(s):* Leach, Wilford; *Composer(s):* Silverman, Stanley; *Costume designer(s):* McCourty, Patricia; *Lighting designer(s):* Tipton, Jennifer; *Other personnel:* Fredricksen, Erik (Fight Arranger); *Cast:* Woods, Maurice (Agrippa); Hyman, Earle (Cominius); Freeman, Morgan (Coriolanus); Fernandez, Jay (Officer); Foster, Gloria (Volumnia); Shay, Michele (Virgilia).

DISTRIBUTION & AVAILABILITY: *Publisher or responsible agency:* New York Shakespeare Festival; *Copy location:* LCL TOFT Collection; *Call or copy number:* NCOV 104; *Availability:* By appt.

Coriolanus. **Video/Teleplay**

67. *Coriolanus.* (Series: The Shakespeare Plays).

DOCUMENT INFORMATION: *Country:* GB; *Year of filming:* 18-26 April 1983; *Year of first showing:* 1983; *Location of first showing(s):* BBC, London; PBS stations, USA, 26 March 1984.

EDITION, HISTORY, CONTENTS, & EVALUATION: *Edition & history:* Yet another of the BBC Shakespeare plays, based on the 1951 Peter Alexander text. Modest cuts and alterations focus attention on the main rather than on the subordinate characters. Other changes underscore Coriolanus' emotional struggle with Volumnia and enhance the drama of his ultimate capitulation (5.3). To further highlight 5.3, the scene at 5.4 has been transposed to precede it. *Contents & evaluation:* "Elijah Moshinsky's *Coriolanus* is strikingly painterly and static. In this version it is a play from Shakespeare's Blue Period, and the classical world is luminous and Mediterranean. There is a lot of talk and surprisingly little action. The aristocratic values of the patricians are assumed, so that plebeian aspirations, as expressed through the Tribunes, are seen to be intrusive and presumptuous. Although the Tribunes are represented as a couple of old-style Marxist scholars, the class war is heavily weighted against the revolutionary party. . . . There are some wonderful individual performances in this production, yet the overall conception doesn't make good critical sense of Shakespeare's play. We are, however, happily distracted from total meanings by vibrant and appealing details. Alan Howard is a very energetic and self-assured Coriolanus, who has no doubts about his own integrity and the baseness and vulgarity of the commoners. He appears so often on horseback in the early scenes that we think of him as an equestrian statue, grand and towering and commanding. He is obviously much too old for Shakespeare's Martius, who can be stung by the accusation of 'Boy' and whose attachment to his mother is still deeply oedipal. A Coriolanus of 35 disrupts the logic of the play. Alan Howard is splendidly dismissive. All of his speeches to the plebeians are virtually asides because he doesn't believe them worth speaking to. . . . *Coriolanus* has thankfully dispensed with the 'talking heads' close-ups that marred earlier plays in this series, although it does have a penchant for profiles. The battle scenes are beautifully stylized, with surprising aesthetic effects created by music and dance. The mob, however, is wooden and cannot play the crucial political role laid out for it in Shakespeare. I [also] had some trouble with the use of voice-overs to represent thought. Since there's not much speculation or meditation in the play, [they] didn't seem to have the essential function they might have, for example, in *Hamlet*" (Charney, Maurice, "Moshinksy's *Coriolanus*," *SFNL* 9.1 (Dec. 1984]: 1+). *Audience:* College and university; *Supplementary materials:* Fenwick, Henry. *Coriolanus* in *BSP* 18-28; Videotape (25 min.) from "Shakespeare in Perspective" series with General Sir John Hackett as lecturer available in U.K. from BBC* (*BUFVC* 3).

MEDIUM INFORMATION: *Medium:* Video; *Sound:* Spoken language; *Color:* Yes; *Length:* 150 min.; *Language(s) spoken:* English; *Video type:* B, V, 3/4U.

AUTHORSHIP INFORMATION: *Producer(s):* Sutton, Shaun; *Director(s):* Moshinsky, Elijah; *Adaptor/translator(s):* Snodin, David; *Composer(s):* Oliver, Stephen; *Choreographer(s):* Fazan, Eleanor; *Designer(s):* Coles, Dick; *Costume designer(s):* Burdle, Michael; *Lighting designer(s):* Summers, John; *Other personnel:* Busby, Sarah (Prod. manager); Pool, Ros (Director's asst.); Lowden, Fraser (Prod. assoc.); Ranson, Malcolm (Fight arranger); Wilders, John (Literary consultant); de Winne, Kezia (Make-up); Miller-Timmins, Derek (Sound); *Cast:* Howard, Alan (Caius Marcius Coriolanus); Sands, Peter (Titus Lartius); Godfrey, Patrick (Cominius); Ackland, Joss (Menenius Agrippa); Burgess, John (Sicinius); Pedley, Anthony (Brutus); Franklin, Damien (Young Marcius); Gwilym, Mike (Aufidius); Dyall, Valentine (Adrian); Worth, Irene (Volumnia); McCallum, Joanna (Virgilia); Canning, Heather (Valeria); Smart, Patsy (Gentlewoman); Jesson, Paul; Roberts, Ray; Lissek, Leon; Rumney, Jon; Kilmister, Russell (Citizens); Rowe, John (Roman Senator); Poyser, Brian; Jessup, Reginald (Volscian Senators); Ruparelia, Jay (Soldier); Amer, Nicholas (Aedile); Kempner, Teddy (Nicanor); Finlay, S. (Citizen of Antium).

DISTRIBUTION & AVAILABILITY: *Publisher or responsible agency:* BBC/TLF; *Distributor:* AVP, UIO, BBC* *Copy location:* UVM (Archive); *Availability:* AVP, B, V, 3/4U $450 (1987), sale; UIO, V (72053H), 3/4U (70153V), rental, $25.50; BBC* 16mm or V, apply (*BUFVC* 3).

Cymbeline

ORIGINAL WORK AND PRODUCTION: Tragi-Comedy. *Year of first production:* 1608; *Site of first production:* Blackfriars

Cymbeline. Motion Picture/Abbreviation

68. *Cymbeline.*

DOCUMENT INFORMATION: *Country:* USA; *Year of release:* 1913.

EDITION, HISTORY, CONTENTS, & EVALUATION: *Edition & history:* One of the silent Shakespeare films made by Edwin Thanhouser. Because the Library of Congress print lacks credits, I've relied here on R.H. Ball's reconstruction of them. His comment that he could not even "guess" William Russell's role because of the "abundant whiskers" on the male actors sums up the difficulties of identification. *Contents & evaluation:* This truncated version of *Cymbeline* remains one of the best of the early Shakespeare silents. The print at the Library of Congress abruptly begins without any clear establishing shot. The first title card simply reads, "The King's sons are reared as woodsmen by the former courtier who stole them." The film then cuts to the court and a series of inter-titles bridge the narra-tive: "Imogen is secretly wed to Leonatus"; "At Rome the banished man [Leonatus] boasts of his royal wife's devotion." The Roman orgy scene with its dancing girls and two dozen or so sharply etched faces packed into the frame helps to explain how Leonatus came to make such a regrettable wager about his wife's chasti-ty. The voyeurism of the evil Iachimo as he watches the unsuspecting Imogen is deftly handled, so that the subsequent title card, "Imogen searches in vain for her lost bracelet," makes good sense. It is impossible here to match Professor Ball's painstaking description of the film's narrative (*SOSF* 151-55), but Thanhouser's great achievement, it seems to me, was in becoming the supreme *auteur* of the silent Shakespeare film in America. His signature is unmistakable in the crowd scenes at court (reminiscent of the division-of-the-kingdom sequence in his 1916 *King Lear*—see #246). He managed to use his theatrical flair to make effective cinema, especially in his talent for arranging actors in an effective *mise en scène*. He also relished more cinematically based exterior action shots, where, like D.W. Griffith in *Birth of a Nation*, he favored thunder-ing troops of mounted cavalry. And the sharp, even lighting he managed to achieve with his primitive equipment is also notable. Positioned as Thanhouser was in history, he made a serious effort to bring middle class culture to the masses without denigrating his source material. *Audience:* General use; *Supplemen-tary materials:* Ball, *SOSF* 151-55.

MEDIUM INFORMATION: *Medium:* Video; *Sound:* Silent; *Color:* No (black & white); *Length:* 41 min.; *Film type:* 16mm.

AUTHORSHIP INFORMATION: *Producer(s):* Than-houser, Edwin; *Director(s):* Sullivan, Frederick; *Cast:*

LaBadie, Florence (Imogen); Garwood, William (Iachimo); Darnell, Jean (Queen); Russell, William [Credits: Ball].

DISTRIBUTION & AVAILABILITY: *Publisher or responsible agency:* Thanhouser; *Distributor:* EMG, JEF (?); *Copy location:* LCM; *Availability:* Archive.

Cymbeline. Video/Scenes

69. *Cymbeline.* (Series: Scenes from Shakespeare).

DOCUMENT INFORMATION: *Country:* GB; *Year of first showing:* 1937; *Location of first showing:* BBC. Transmitted from 3:39 to 4:24 P.M., 29 Nov. 1937.

EDITION, HISTORY, CONTENTS, & EVALUATION: *Edition & history:* One of the very earliest transmissions of Shakespeare on television when the industry was still in its infancy. By special arrangement, the scenes were taken from Andre Van Gysegham's Embassy Theatre production. *Supplementary materials: TPAB* 29 Nov. 1937.

MEDIUM INFORMATION: *Sound:* Spoken language; *Color:* No (black & white); *Length:* 45 min.

AUTHORSHIP INFORMATION: *Producer(s):* Morley, J. Royston; *Cast:* Bland, Joyce (Imogen); Toone, Geoffrey (Posthumus); Lindo, Olga (The Queen); Hayes, George (Iachimo); Woodbridge, George (Cymbeline); Devlin, William (Pisanio); Francelli, Mario (Philario); Paddick, Hugh (The Frenchman); Hignett, Mary (Helen).

DISTRIBUTION & AVAILABILITY: *Publisher or responsible agency:* BBC; *Copy location:* Unavailable.

70. *Cymbeline.*

DOCUMENT INFORMATION: *Country:* GB; *Year of first showing*: 1956; *Location of first showing:* BBC. Transmitted 10:15 P.M., 30 Oct. 1956.

EDITION, HISTORY, CONTENTS, & EVALUATION: *Edition & history:* Scenes from the production of *Cymbeline* at London's Old Vic Theatre with an introduction by Dame Sybil Thorndike. *Supplementary materials:* "Program." *RT* 26 Oct. 1956: 26-27.

MEDIUM INFORMATION: *Length:* [?] min.

AUTHORSHIP INFORMATION: *Producer(s):* Elliott, Michael; *Director(s):* Benthall, Michael (Stage); *Designer(s):* Cruddas, Audrey; *Cast:* Jefford, Barbara (Imogen); Godfrey, Derek (Iachimo); Whiting, Margaret (Helen).

DISTRIBUTION & AVAILABILITY: *Publisher or responsible agency:* BBC; *Copy location:* Unavailable.

Cymbeline. Video/Recordings

71. *Cymbeline.*

DOCUMENT INFORMATION: *Country:* USA; *Year of first showing:* 1981.

EDITION, HISTORY, CONTENTS, & EVALUATION: *Edition & history:* A videotaping of a 1981 stage production of *Cymbeline* performed by the Berkeley Shakespeare Festival. A copy is housed in the Theatre on Film and Tape Collection at the Billy Rose Theatre Collection of the Library of Performing Arts, Lincoln Center, New York Public Library. It may be viewed by appointment (see below). *Contents & evaluation:* Since I have not personally screened this video, I cannot speak to its visual qualities, but Laurence H. Jacobs' review of the stage performance is helpful: "The most experimental of BSF's 1981 offerings was *Cymbeline*. Patrick Tucker's production sought to open up the play by emphasizing the likeness between its action and the fantasy fictions that move contemporary audiences. Cymbeline's queen wore the costume of the wicked stepmother in Disney's *Snow White*, and her performance was dominated by the cartoon strip gestures of a Disney villainess. In the best imperial tradition Cymbeline punctuated his pronouncements by popping jelly beans." Professor Jacobs goes on to note that "Ms. Engle's Imogen displayed a gusty self-assurance and energy that were comically reassuring" (Jacobs, Laurence H., "Shakespeare in the San Francisco Bay Area," *SQ* 33.3 [Autumn 1982]: 397-98). *Audience:* College and university; General use.

MEDIUM INFORMATION: *Medium:* Video; *Sound:* Spoken language; *Color:* Yes; *Length:* 152 min.; *Language(s) spoken:* English; *Video type:* 3/4U.

AUTHORSHIP INFORMATION: *Producer(s):* Berkeley Shakespeare Festival; *Director(s):* Tucker, Patrick; *Composer(s):* Nin-Culmell, Joaquin; Madsen, Gunnar; *Choreographer(s):* Berges, Sarah; *Set designer(s):* Travis, Warren; *Lighting designer(s):* Duarte, Derek; *Cast:* Sicilia, Michael (Arviragus); Henry, Steve (Belarius); López-Morillas, Julian (Cloten/Posthumus); Chugg, Gail (Cymbeline); Parr, David (Guiderius); Sicular, Robert (Iachimo); Engle, Rebecca (Imogen); Henriques, Philip (Philario); Orozepa, Luiz (Pisanio); Conklin, Katherine (Queen).

DISTRIBUTION & AVAILABILITY: *Publisher or responsible agency:* Berkeley Shakespeare Festival; *Copy location:* LCL TOFT Collection; *Call or copy number:* NCOV 306; *Availability:* By appt.(Call Mrs. Betty Corwin, 212-870-1641); *Restrictions:* Archive.

72. *Cymbeline.*

DOCUMENT INFORMATION: *Country:* Belgium; *Year of release:* 1981.

EDITION, HISTORY, CONTENTS, & EVALUATION: *Edition & history:* Produced at Koninklijk Conservatory, Brussels *Audience:* General use.

MEDIUM INFORMATION: *Medium:* V; *Sound:* Spoken language; *Color:* Yes; *Length:* 311 min.; *Language(s) spoken:* Flemish (?); *Video type:* V.

AUTHORSHIP INFORMATION: *Producer(s):* Koninlijk Conservatory; *Director(s):* Decorte, Jan; *Cast:* Thomas, Willy; Verdin, M.; Rouffart, B.

DISTRIBUTION & AVAILABILITY: *Publisher or responsible agency:* A.V. Dienst Katholieke Universiteit; *Distributor:* Koninlijk, *Copy location:* Archive, NTI, Amsterdam; *Call or copy number:* 700140201 BDA.

Cymbeline. Video/Teleplay

73. *Cymbeline.* (Series: The Shakespeare Plays).

DOCUMENT INFORMATION: *Country:* GB; *Year of filming:* 29 July-5 Aug. 1982; *Year of first showing:* 1982; *Location of first showing(s):* BBC, London; PBS stations, USA, 20 Dec. 1982.

EDITION, HISTORY, CONTENTS, & EVALUATION: *Edition & history:* As with all the plays in this BBC series, the chosen text is the 1951 Peter Alexander edition. Probably more alterations than usual took place in making this adaptation of Shakespeare's play because of the extreme complexity of the plot. An effort was made to iron out difficulties for the audience. *Contents & evaluation:* "The confusing fragmentation of the play was handled with judicious cutting and extremely rapid pacing. For the most part, Moshinsky showed a great deal of care for Shakespeare's text, cutting so as to maintain the flow and focus of *Cymbeline* without damaging the fabric of the play. . . . There was, however, one glaring exception to this careful treatment of the text. The tape cut (whether by Moshinsky or by PBS editors) the fight between Posthumus and Iachimo and Iachimo's subsequent paroxysm of contrition (5.2.s.d. + 1-10). This 'unkindest cut' resulted in two serious problems later in the catastrophe. When Posthumus says to Iachimo, 'I had you down, and might Have made you finish,' we have no idea what he is talking about. More seriously, the omission of the fight and Iachimo's contrition leave his apparent change of heart at the close of the play unclear and unmotivated. . . . The great strength of this production may be found in Moshinsky's treatment of the characters and the superb performances that he elicited from most of the actors. Richard Johnson's Cymbeline was a man whose judgment and moods were controlled by his own changeability and his wife's manipulations rather than by age or sickness. Indeed, this Cymbeline never does change very much; he is as mercurial in the catastrophe as he was at the play's opening. . . . Claire Bloom's portrayal of the Queen was a model of subtle and cold malevolence. Moshinsky avoided the excess of turning the Queen into an archetypal witch/stepmother. Michael Pennington's Posthumus similarly avoided excesses while Paul Fesson's Cloten was an interesting if eccentric mixture of fop, oaf, braggart (Jacobs, Henry E., "Cymbeline," *SFNL* 7.2. [1983]: 6). *Audience:* College and university; General use; *Supplementary materials:* Fenwick, Henry. *Cymbeline* in *BSP* 16-26; Videotape (25 min.) from "Shakespeare in Perspective" series with Dennis Potter as lecturer available in U.K. from BBC* (*BUFVC* 3).

MEDIUM INFORMATION: *Medium:* Video; *Sound:* Spoken language; *Color:* Yes; *Length:* 175 min.; *Language(s) spoken:* English; *Video type:* B, V, 3/4U.

AUTHORSHIP INFORMATION: *Producer(s):* Sutton, Shaun; *Director(s):* Moshinsky, Elijah; *Adaptor/translator(s):* Snodin, David; *Designer(s):* Gosnold, Barbara; *Costume designer(s):* Collin, Dinah; *Lighting designer(s):* Summers, John; *Other personnel:* Fewings, Michael (Prod. manager); Plowright, Wendy (Prod. asst); Lowden, Fraser (Prod. assoc.); Wilders, John (Literary consultant); Smith, Elaine (Make-up); Miller-Timmins, Derek (Sound); *Cast:* Johnson, Richard (Cymbeline); Bloom, Claire (Queen); Mirren, Helen (Imogen); Pennington, Michael (Posthumus); Lindsay, Robert (Iachimo); Gough, Michael (Belarius); Thomas, Hugh (Cornelius); Kane, John (Pisanio); Smart, Patsy (Helen); Creedon, David (Arviragus); Burridge, Geoffrey (Guiderius); Jesson, Paul (Cloten); Hordern, Michael (Jupiter); Young, Nicholas (Lord); Crowden, Graham (Caius Lucius); Hayes, Patricia (Soothsayer); Mort, Ray (Gaoler); Delamain, Aimee (Gentlewoman); Lumsden, Geoffrey (Philario); Goring, Marius (Leonatus); Ryan, Madge (Mother); Hendrick, Allen (Frenchman); McGinity, Terence; Aldwyn, Peter (British Captains); Robson, Nigel (Singer); Pickett, Philip; Beznosiuk, Pavlo; Pleeth, Anthony; Finucane, Tom (Musicians).

DISTRIBUTION & AVAILABILITY: *Publisher or responsible agency:* BBC/TLF; *Distributor:* AVP, UIO, BBC* *Copy location:* UVM (Archive); *Availability:* AVP, B, V, 3/4U $450 (1987), sale; UIO, V (72053H), 3/4U (70153V), rental, $25.50; BBC*, 16mm or V, apply (*BUFVC* 3).

Hamlet

ORIGINAL WORK AND PRODUCTION: Tragedy/ Problem Play. *Year produced:* 1600; *Site of first production:* Globe Playhouse [?]

Hamlet. Motion Picture/Scenes

74. *Hamlet.*

DOCUMENT INFORMATION: *Country:* France; *Year of release:* 1900.

EDITION, HISTORY, CONTENTS, & EVALUATION: *Edition & history:* The legendary pioneering film of Sarah Bernhardt performing the duel scene from *Hamlet* in the theatre of Mme. Marguerite Chenu at the 1900 Paris Exposition. To create an illusion of the sound of the duel, assistants clacked kitchen knives together from somewhere off or behind the screen. According to Professor Ball, the film was actually screened at the 1964 UNESCO Shakespeare celebration in Paris; hence it may still exist. *Supplementary materials:* Ball, *SOSF* 304; *SIF,* 96; For all *Hamlet* entries, see also Bernice W. Kliman *HFTAP.*

MEDIUM INFORMATION: *Length:* 5 min.

AUTHORSHIP INFORMATION: *Director(s):* Maurice, Clement; *Cast:* Bernhardt, Sarah (Hamlet); Magnier, Pierre (Laertes).

75. *Hamlet.*

DOCUMENT INFORMATION: *Country:* France; *Year of release:* 1907.

EDITION, HISTORY, CONTENTS, & EVALUATION: *Edition & history:* The celebrated Georges Méliès, pioneering French movie maker, put himself in this film as Hamlet in the graveyard scene. The film is lost but a summary of it by Gaston Méliès, Georges' brother and U.S. agent, happily survives in Ball's splendid book (34). *Supplementary materials:* Ball, *SOSF* 34, 307.

MEDIUM INFORMATION: *Sound:* Silent; *Color:* No (black & white); *Length:* 10 min.

AUTHORSHIP INFORMATION: *Director(s):* Méliès, Georges; *Cast:* Méliès, Georges (Hamlet).

Hamlet. Motion Picture/Abbreviated

76. *Amleto.*

DOCUMENT INFORMATION: *Country:* Italy; *Year of release:* 1908.

EDITION, HISTORY, CONTENTS, & EVALUATION: *Edition & history:* An Italian *Hamlet* made in 1908, which could be the same as number 77, below. *Supplementary materials:* Ball, *SOSF* 98; *SIF,* 96; Kliman, *HFTAP* 229-36.

MEDIUM INFORMATION: *Length:* 10 min.

AUTHORSHIP INFORMATION: *Director(s):* Comerio, Luca.

77. *Amleto.*

DOCUMENT INFORMATION: *Country:* Italy; *Year of release:* 1908.

EDITION, HISTORY, CONTENTS, & EVALUATION: *Edition & history:* A second Italian 1908 *Hamlet*, this one made by Cines which was "the principal cinema company in Italy" and "the chief rival of Pathe and Gaumont for the European film market" (Ball 96). The Weisbaden filmography (*SIF* 96) gives Guiseppe de Liguoro as the film's director but R.H. Ball, citing Maria Prolo's history of Italian film, disputes the attribution (Ball, *SOSF* 326). *Supplementary materials:* Kliman, *HFTAP* 229-36; *SIF* 96.

MEDIUM INFORMATION: *Length:* 9 min.

AUTHORSHIP INFORMATION: *Director(s):* Caserini, Mario [?].

78. *Hamlet.*

DOCUMENT INFORMATION: *Country:* GB; *Year of filming:* 1910 [?]; *Year of release:* 1910.

EDITION, HISTORY, CONTENTS, & EVALUATION: *Edition & history:* W.G. Barker was an important pioneer in the British film industry who, among other things, made the first British film version of *Hamlet*, which is now lost. According to Professor Ball, who spared no pains in tracing its history, the film was shot on a budget of £180 in a kind of greenhouse located on Barker's suburban estate. Except for a shot of Ophelia floating down the Thames on a raft of flowers, the entire film was made in fewer than six sunlit hours (Ball, 77-8). *Supplementary materials:* Ball, *SOSF* 77-8, 318-20.

MEDIUM INFORMATION: *Medium:* Motion Picture; *Sound:* Silent; *Color:* No (black & white); *Length:* 20 min.

AUTHORSHIP INFORMATION: *Producer(s):* Barker, William George; *Director(s):* Barker, William George; *Cast:* Raymond, Charles (Hamlet); Foster, Dorothy (Ophelia); Backner, Constance (Gertrude).

DISTRIBUTION & AVAILABILITY: *Publisher or responsible agency:* Autoscope Company; *Availability:* Apparently lost.

79. *Hamlet.*

DOCUMENT INFORMATION: *Country:* France; *Year of release:* 1910.

EDITION, HISTORY, CONTENTS, & EVALUATION: *Edition & history:* Fragments of this *Hamlet*, made by Lux, survive in the Museum of Modern Art, New York City. *Supplementary materials:* Kliman, *HFTAP* 236-45; Ball, *SOSF* 105-7.

MEDIUM INFORMATION: *Length:* 10 min.

AUTHORSHIP INFORMATION: *Director(s):* Bourgeois, Gerard (?).

DISTRIBUTION & AVAILABILITY: *Copy location:* MMA.

80. *Hamlet.*

DOCUMENT INFORMATION: *Country:* France; *Year of release:* 1910.

EDITION, HISTORY, CONTENTS, & EVALUATION: *Edition & history:* A silent that was probably made in France by the Éclipse company. *Supplementary materials:* Ball, *SOSF* 197; *SIF* 96.

MEDIUM INFORMATION: *Length:* 10 min.

AUTHORSHIP INFORMATION: *Director(s):* Desfontaines, Henri; *Cast:* Grétillat, Jacques (Hamlet); Romano, Colonna (Gertrude).

81. *Hamlet.*

DOCUMENT INFORMATION: *Country:* Denmark; *Year of release:* 1910.

EDITION, HISTORY, CONTENTS, & EVALUATION: *Edition & history:* Made at the actual castle of Hamlet in Kronborg, Denmark, the film may be thought of as an early example of *cinéma vérité*. In its style it emulated the realism of the Lumière brothers ("Train Arriving at the Station") rather than the expressionism of Georges Méliès ("A Trip to the Moon"). *Supplementary materials:* Ball, *SOSF* 108; *SIF* 96.

MEDIUM INFORMATION: *Length:* 12 min.

AUTHORSHIP INFORMATION: *Director(s):* Blom, August; *Cast:* Neuss, Alwin (Hamlet); Hertel, Aage (Claudius); Zengenberg, Einar (Laertes); La Cour, Ella (Gertrude); Sannom, Emilie (Ophelia).

Hamlet. Motion Picture/Interpretation

82. *Hamlet*

DOCUMENT INFORMATION: *Country:* GB; *Year of release:* 1913; *Location of first showing:* New Gallery Kinema, Regent St., London.

EDITION, HISTORY, CONTENTS, & EVALUATION: *Edition & history:* In a 1913 interview, Cecil M. Hepworth, the producer, said that this *Hamlet* was ". . . the most notable event up to the present in the history of British cinema." Even allowing for PR-hype, which even then was escalating into a major industry, the film deserves a niche in history as a unique record of the performance of a major 19th-century Shakespearean actor, Sir Johnston Forbes-Robertson. Sir Johnston's electrifying portrayal of Hamlet, along with the Frederic B. Warde *King Lear*, provides a time capsule for viewing the acting techniques of eminent Victorians. Moreover, since Forbes-Robertson and his colleagues were actually speaking the lines as they declaimed them on the stage of London's famous Drury Lane theatre, those familiar with the text can follow the play almost word for word. To appreciate this film, you need to know not less but more about Shakespeare's play. No danger whatsoever exists, as seems to have been the case with the Barker silent *Hamlet*, that an audience of mutes might decode vile oaths from the actors' lip movements ("Interview with C. Hepworth," *Bioscope* 24 July 1913:275). *Contents & evaluation:* Despite the lack of spoken verse, there is high seriousness, even gravity, about the actors' performances. Forbes-Robertson, though much too old for the part, nevertheless with his cadaverous and melancholy face captured the essential tone of Hamlet. Modern audiences, sated on post-Freudian readings, will find such decorous restraint as Hamlet *not* putting his head on Ophelia's lap at the play scene somewhat novel and refreshing. There is skilful intercutting between shots of Ophelia walking by a stream ("There is a willow grows") and of Claudius and Laertes conspiring to poison Hamlet. The latter shot, one among many exterior locales, was made in a garden at Halliford-on-Thames. Some fine cinematic touches include a close-up of the point of Laertes' sword dripping venom; of poison being dropped by Claudius into the cup; of the ghost appearing superimposed on the bedchamber frames and then dissolving again, after the fashion of Georges Méliès' trick photography. To me, the duel scene offers a model for contemporary directors. In this version, the Queen drinks off the poisoned cup while Claudius is deeply engaged in conversation with Laertes. Claudius does not actually see Gertrude drink from the cup, and he never should! By the time Claudius turns away from Laertes and sees her drinking, it is too late. It defies common sense that a man of his resourcefulness would permit a beloved wife to destroy herself without attempting to rescue her. He might have had the wit to strike the offending goblet from her hand and cry out "It's corky, Gertrude. I'll send it back!" In another deft touch, Claudius then attacks Hamlet, and is slain. He doesn't, as in so many modern productions, sit like Humpty Dumpty patiently waiting for Hamlet to attack him. For its time, the film was generously conceived. Much was made of the construction of a replica of Elsinore Castle at Lulworth Cove in Dorset, though an American might well wonder why that was necessary in a country so full of marvelous old castles (KSR, "Notes from National Film Archive Screening, 1985"). *Audience:* Professional; General use; *Supplementary materials:* Ball, *SOSF* 186-92; *KMFR* 2. 17 (1913): 189; Kliman, *HFTAP* 247-74.

MEDIUM INFORMATION: *Medium:* Motion Picture; *Sound:* Silent; *Color:* No (black & white); *Length:* 22 min.; *Language of subtitles:* English; *Film type:* 16mm.

AUTHORSHIP INFORMATION: *Producer(s):* Hepworth, Cecil M.; *Director(s):* Plumb, Hay; *Adaptor/translator(s):* Craven, Hawes; *Cast:* Forbes-Robertson, Johnston (Hamlet); Elliott, Gertrude (Ophelia); Cookson, S.A. (Horatio); Barnes, J.H. (Polonius); Scott-Gatty, Alex (Laertes); Atkins, Robert (Marcellus/ 1st Player); Rhodes, Percy (Ghost); Bentley, Grendon (Fortinbras); Rutherford, Montague (Rosencrantz); Ross, E.A.

(Guildenstern); Hayes, George (Osric); Richards, G. [a.k.a., Andean, Richard] (Barnardo); Ericson, E. [a.k.a. Adeney, Eric] (Francisco); Atkins, Robert (Player); Andean, Richard (Player); Ryley, J.H. (Gravedigger); Pearce, S.T. (Gravedigger); Montague, R.[a.k.a. Rutherford, Montague] (Priest); Bourne, Adeline (Queen); Richardson, Olive (Player Queen); *Performance group(s):* The Drury Lane Company.

DISTRIBUTION & AVAILABILITY: *Publisher or responsible agency:* Gaumont; *Distributor:* BFI*; *Copy location:* NFA, FOL; *Call or copy number:* MP 75 (FOL); *Availability:* BFI* Rental 16mm, Apply; *Restrictions:* Archival viewing by appointment.

Hamlet. Video/Scenes

83. *Hamlet.*

DOCUMENT INFORMATION: *Country:* USA; *Year of first showing:* 1913 [?]

EDITION, HISTORY, CONTENTS, & EVALUATION: *Edition & history:* Silent film clips from *Hamlet*, as yet undated, shown at Center Stage, Baltimore. The film is housed in the Theatre on Film and Tape Collection at the Billy Rose Theatre Collection of the Library of Performing Arts, Lincoln Center, New York Public Library. It may be viewed by appointment (see below). *Contents & evaluation:* Not seen. *Audience:* College and university; General use.

MEDIUM INFORMATION: *Medium:* Motion picture; *Sound:* Silent; *Color:* No (black & white); *Length:* 11 min.; *Language of subtitles:* English; *Video type:* 16mm.

DISTRIBUTION & AVAILABILITY: *Copy location:* LCL TOFT Collection; *Call or copy number:* NCOV 60; *Availability:* By appt.

Hamlet. Motion Picture/Abridgment

84. *Amleto.* [*Hamlet*].

DOCUMENT INFORMATION: *Country:* Italy; *Year of release:* 1917.

EDITION, HISTORY, CONTENTS, & EVALUATION: *Edition & history:* Professor Ball sees this film as marking a breakthrough in the severing of film from stage conventions. Hamlet was played by Ruggero Ruggeri, an actor who was as well known as the great Tommaso Salvini and Ernesto Rossi. Although by then a paunchy 46, Ruggeri still managed to create a memorable prince (Ball 262). *Supplementary materials:* Ball, *SOSF* 254-62; *SIF*, 97.

MEDIUM INFORMATION: *Length:* 30 min.

AUTHORSHIP INFORMATION: *Director(s):* Rodolfi,

Eleuterio; *Adaptor/translator(s):* Chiaves, Carlo; *Cast:* Ruggeri, Ruggero (Hamlet); Makowska, Elena (Ophelia).

DISTRIBUTION & AVAILABILITY: *Copy location:* NFA*.

Hamlet. Film/Excerpt

85. *One Night Only.*

DOCUMENT INFORMATION: *Country:* USA; *Year of release:* 1919.

EDITION, HISTORY, CONTENTS, & EVALUATION: *Edition & history:* A traveling Shakespeare company plays *Hamlet. Supplementary materials:* Loughney, Katharine. "Shakespeare on Film and Tape at Library of Congress." *SFNL* 13.2 (Apr. 1989): 2.

MEDIUM INFORMATION: *Length:* 6 min.

AUTHORSHIP INFORMATION: *Director(s):* Parrott, Charles; *Cast:* White, Leo; Banks, Monte; Dorety, Charles.

DISTRIBUTION & AVAILABILITY: *Copy location:* LCM; *Call or copy number:* FEA 3732.

Hamlet. Motion Picture/Adaptation

86. *Hamlet: The Drama of Vengeance.*

DOCUMENT INFORMATION: *Country:* Germany; *Year of release:* 1920.

EDITION, HISTORY, CONTENTS, & EVALUATION: *Awards:* "Ten best films of year," *The New York Times; Edition & history:* One of the very best silent Shakespeare films, this *Hamlet* yet plays havoc with the common understanding of the Prince of Denmark's story. Based on Edward P. Vining's eccentric book, *The Mystery of Hamlet* (Philadelphia, 1881), it features a prince who, though actually a woman, for reasons of state has been raised by Gertrude as a young man. Burdened with this secret, Hamlet at Wittenberg falls in love with Horatio. Naturally Hamlet rejects Ophelia but still feels pangs of jealousy when Horatio falls in love with Ophelia. Only at Hamlet's death when Horatio holds her in his arms is the prince's true gender revealed. *Contents & evaluation:* Cinematically speaking the movie displays the visual excitement so characteristic of the German filmmakers of that period. Beginning with a battle scene involving hundreds of extras, the action goes on to show the Queen, who mistakenly thinks the King has been killed in combat, deliberately falsifying her baby daughter's sex in order to save the line of succession in Denmark. Much of the action draws on the old Saxo Grammaticus story that underlay Shakespeare's own play. When Hamlet sets fire to the castle, the King suffocates. His mother then joins with Laertes in a plot to kill Hamlet. Vining's

interpretation of Hamlet as a man disguised as a woman "explains" Hamlet's lack of the kind of macho qualities exhibited by, for example, Laertes, who never hesitates to avenge the death of his father. It would also account for Hamlet's rejection of Ophelia and other hints of repressed homosexuality that Victorians were reluctant to bring out of the closet.

Setting all that aside, the film's cinematic achievements are noteworthy—some memorable shots: The Great Hall at Elsinore; Horatio discovering Claudius' dagger by a snakepit that has furnished the poison for murdering the King; an impressive exterior shot when the players are erecting a scaffold for their evening performance. It is a lovely, spacious picture with lots of rooms, extras, stylish sets, sybaritic orgies. Hamlet's death in the arms of Horatio twists the story around into a variation on Romeo and Juliet. The subtitles on the screen dramatically signal Horatio's amazement and wonder: "Death reveals thy tragic secret! Now I understand what bound me to that matchless form and feature." One of many famous actresses who has performed the role of Hamlet, Asta Nielsen, with her brooding, photogenic face, singlehandedly transforms the production from mediocrity into art. As Hamlet's body is borne out of the Great Hall under an umbrella of pikes, the filmgoer discovers a plausibility amidst implausibility. And in the grand style of the old silents, an iris-out terminates the action (KSR). *Audience:* College and university; *Supplementary materials:* Ball, *SOSF* 272-78; Duffy, Robert A. "Gade, Olivier, Richardson: Visual Strategy in *Hamlet* Adaptation." *LFQ* 4.2 (1976): 141-52; Guntner, J. Lawrence. "Was Hamlet a Woman?" *SFNL* 13.1 (Dec. 1988): 3. [Dr. Guntner is the leading student of this film.]

MEDIUM INFORMATION: *Sound:* Silent; *Color:* No (black & white); *Length:* 78 min.; *Film type:* 16mm.

AUTHORSHIP INFORMATION: *Producer(s):* Art-Film; *Director(s):* Gade, Svend; Schall, Heinz; *Costume designer(s):* Baruch, Hugo and Verch, L.; *Other personnel:* Courant, Curt and Graatkajer, Axel (Photography); *Cast:* Nielsen, Asta (Hamlet); Winterstein, Eduard von (Claudius); Brandt, Mathilde (Gertrude); Verdier, Anton de (Laertes); Jacobssen, Lilly (Ophelia); Junkermann, Hans (Polonius); Stieda, Heinz (Horatio); Conradi, Paul (Ghost); Achterberg, Fritz (Fortinbras).

DISTRIBUTION & AVAILABILITY: *Publisher or responsible agency:* Art Film; *Copy location:* NFA, FOL; *Call or copy number:* MP 70 (FOL); *Availability:* By appointment.

Hamlet. Film/Excerpt

87. *Day Dreams.*

DOCUMENT INFORMATION: *Country:* USA; *Year of release:* 1922.

EDITION, HISTORY, CONTENTS, & EVALUATION: *Edition & history:* Included here only because of the existence of a fabulous still (see Ball 289) of Keaton, a Walter Mitty figure, as he fantasizes being a great actor playing Hamlet. The power of the Shakespeare myth reaches out to ensnare virtually every member of the acting profession. *Supplementary materials:* Ball, *SOSF* 374.

MEDIUM INFORMATION: *Length:* 30 min.

AUTHORSHIP INFORMATION: *Cast:* Keaton, Buster; Adorée, Renée.

DISTRIBUTION & AVAILABILITY: *Distributor:* Probably lost.

Hamlet. **Motion Picture/Excerpt**

88. *The Royal Box.*

DOCUMENT INFORMATION: *Country:* USA; *Year of release:* 1930.

EDITION, HISTORY, CONTENTS, & EVALUATION: *Edition & history:* Alexander Moissi as Edmund Kean plays a scene from *Hamlet* with Camilla Horn as Ophelia. The film is based on a play by Charles Coghlan that opened in New York on November 20, 1928. *Supplementary materials:* Eckert, *FSF* 168.

MEDIUM INFORMATION: *Sound:* Spoken language; *Color:* No (black & white); *Length:* 89 min.

AUTHORSHIP INFORMATION: *Director(s):* Foy, Bryan; *Adaptor/translator(s):* Roth, Murray; *Composer(s):* Levy, Harold; *Designer(s):* Namczy, Frank; *Cast:* Moissi, Alexander (Edmund Kean); Horn, Camilla (Alice Doren).

DISTRIBUTION & AVAILABILITY: *Publisher or responsible agency:* Warner Bros.

Hamlet. **Motion Picture/Scenes**

89. *Hamlet: Test Shots.*

DOCUMENT INFORMATION: *Country:* USA; *Year of release:* 1933.

EDITION, HISTORY, CONTENTS, & EVALUATION: *Edition & history:* Test shots of the great John Barrymore made for a film that never materialized. Includes the "rogue and peasant slave" soliloquy (2.2), and the ghost scene (1.5). Apparently the brilliant but somewhat unreliable Barrymore had trouble remembering his lines, which resulted in cancellation of the picture. There may also have been the dread of box office catastrophe. A test one year later for a Shakespeare film with Alexander Korda's organization had the same unhappy results. *Contents & evaluation:* A rare glimpse of a great Shakespearean actor at work. On stage he was one of the finest Hamlets of this century. In film he can also be seen as an over-aged and overacted Mercutio in the 1936 MGM *Romeo and Juliet,* starring Norma Shearer and Leslie Howard in the title roles, and as Richard duke of Gloucester in a brief excerpt from the 1928 *Show of Shows.* As a screen actor, Barrymore was a great theatrical presence. He tended to chew the scenery and generally show off his talents at the expense of production values. *Audience:* Professional.

MEDIUM INFORMATION: *Medium:* Motion Picture; *Sound:* Spoken language; *Color:* Yes; *Length:* 10 min.; *Language(s) spoken:* English; *Film type:* 16mm.

AUTHORSHIP INFORMATION: *Director(s):* Jones, Robert Edmond; Carrington, Margaret; *Cast:* Barrymore, John; Pichel, Irving; Denny, Reginald; Crisp, Donald.

DISTRIBUTION & AVAILABILITY: *Publisher or responsible agency:* RKO Studios; *Distributor:* MMA, FGF*, *Copy location:* LCM, FOL; *Call or copy number:* FOL MP 102.

Hamlet. **Motion Picture/Excerpt**

90. *Morning Glory.*

DOCUMENT INFORMATION: *Country:* USA; *Year of release:* 1933.

EDITION, HISTORY, CONTENTS, & EVALUATION: *Edition & history:* Contains a famous scene in which Katharine Hepburn as an ambitious young actress makes something of a spectacle of herself reciting the "To be or not to be" soliloquy at a party attended mainly by stuffed shirts. Needless to say she is the only interesting thing at the party and her rendition of Hamlet's soliloquy is superb. It's too bad that she could not have joined the ranks of other distinguished women Hamlets, such as Asta Nielsen, Sarah Bernhardt and Judith Anderson. *Supplementary materials:* Kliman, Bernice. "Katharine Hepburn as Hamlet and Juliet." *SFNL* 13.2 (April 1989): 6.

MEDIUM INFORMATION: *Length:* 72 min.

AUTHORSHIP INFORMATION: *Director(s):* Sherman, Lowell; *Cast:* Hepburn, Katharine; Fairbanks, Douglas, Jr.

DISTRIBUTION & AVAILABILITY: *Publisher or responsible agency:* RKO Pictures; *Distributor:* GLB*, FCM, *Availability:* FCM, V, sale, $19.95.

Hamlet. **Motion Picture/Recording**

91. *Khoon ka khoon.*

DOCUMENT INFORMATION: *Country:* India; *Year of release:* 1935.

EDITION, HISTORY, CONTENTS, & EVALUATION: *Edition & history:* Reported by Peter Morris (q.v.), as a recording of a stage production, this Indian film was one of the earliest Shakespeare talkies. I assume that it is the same 1935 *Hamlet* listed in *Indian Film Index: 1912-67*, comp. Rangoonwalla, Firoze (Bombay: Vishwanath Das, 1968). *Supplementary materials:* Morris, *SHOF* 8; H&M 18.

MEDIUM INFORMATION: *Length:* 90 min.; *Language(s) spoken:* Hindi.

AUTHORSHIP INFORMATION: *Director(s):* Modi, Sohrab; *Cast:* Modi, Sohrab (Hamlet).

Hamlet. **Motion Picture/Derivative**

92. *Hamlet and Eggs.*

DOCUMENT INFORMATION: *Country:* USA; *Year of release:* 1937.

EDITION, HISTORY, CONTENTS, & EVALUATION: *Edition & history:* Comedy about a Shakespearean actor on vacation in Arizona. *Supplementary materials:* Loughney, Katharine. "Shakespeare on Film and Tape at Library of Congress." *SFNL* 12.2 (Apr. 1988): 7+.

MEDIUM INFORMATION: *Length:* 18 min.

AUTHORSHIP INFORMATION: *Director(s):* Watson, William; *Cast:* Ryan, Tim; Ryan, Noblette Irene; Pat Petterson's Cowboy Trio.

DISTRIBUTION & AVAILABILITY: *Copy location:* LCM; *Call or copy number:* FGE 5139.

Hamlet. **Motion Picture/Derivative**

93. *To Be Or Not To Be.*

DOCUMENT INFORMATION: *Country:* USA; *Year of filming:* 1942.

EDITION, HISTORY, CONTENTS, & EVALUATION: *Edition & history:* Ernst Lubitsch's clever exploitation of portions of *Hamlet* in which Hamlet's famous soliloquy becomes the key device for signalling a member of the audience that the way is clear for a backstage assignation with the performer's wife. Made during WWII, the film also served as anti-Nazi propaganda. *Contents & evaluation:* Highly acclaimed for its "wit, surprise, drama and suspense throughout" (*MFB* 9:101 [May 1942]: 63). "Jack Benny as Hamlet—funny in itself—is standing alone on a theatre stage. He closes the little book he has been reading, folds his arms, composes himself, and asks wistfully: 'To be, or not to be.' Suddenly, Robert Stack in the role of a Polish flyer— also funny in itself—rises from his seat in the second row and moves noisily toward the exit. Benny, a ham actor, is outraged at this affront to his reputation. Yet Stack has left at this crucial moment not because of a poor performance but to visit Benny's wife (played by Carole Lombard), who has designated the first words of this soliloquy as a code telling the flyer when to visit her dressing room. . . . The director, Ernst Lubitsch, transforms this burlesque gag into one of the funniest pieces of business in film comedy. . . . But he gets his laugh at the cost of Shakespeare's text. Not that anyone should care too much (even purists like myself don't), but the manipulation of this scene from *Hamlet* is instructive of what happens when the Bard is used by Hollywood as a backdrop for comic or romantic situations. . . . In Lubitsch's case, he is required to mangle the *text* for the sake of the joke. Readers of *Hamlet* will recall that the hero is not, as Benny is, entirely alone when he delivers his famous soliloquy (3.1.56). . . . Ophelia is sometimes kneeling at prayer in a room intended to represent a study. . . . Following the text would not have been possible, however, since Carole Lombard is cast as Ophelia, and she must be back in her dressing room to receive the amorous Stack. Moreover, it is clear from their conversation that she expects Benny as Hamlet to be on stage for some time, allowing precious moments with her admirer. To accept the dressing room scene we must completely ignore the demands of *Hamlet*, which require Lombard as Ophelia to be fielding the insults of a distracted hero" (Willson, Robert Jr., "Lubitsch's *To Be Or Not To Be*," *SFNL* 1.1. [Dec. 1976]: 2+). *Audience:* General use.

MEDIUM INFORMATION: *Medium:* Motion Picture; *Sound:* Spoken language; *Color:* No (black & white); *Length:* 99 min.; *Language(s) spoken:* English; *Film type:* 16mm.

AUTHORSHIP INFORMATION: *Producer(s):* Lubitsch, Ernst; *Director(s):* Lubitsch, Ernst; *Screenplay writer(s):* Mayer, Edwin Justus; Lengyel, Melchior; Lubitsch, Ernst; *Composer(s):* Heyman, Werner; *Designer(s):* Korda, Vincent; *Lighting designer(s):* Mate, Rudolph; *Other personnel:* Spencer, Dorothy (Editor); *Cast:* Lombard, Carole (Maria Tura); Benny, Jack (Joseph Tura); Stack, Robert (Lt. Stanislav Sobinski); Bressart, Felix (Greenberg); Atwill, Lionel (Rawitch); Ridges, Stanley (Prof. Alexander Siletsky); Rumann, Sig (Col. Ehrhardt); Dugan, Tom (Bronski); Halton, Charles (Dobosh); Lynn, George (Actor); Victor, Henry (Captain Schulz); Eburne, Maude (Anna); Wright, Armand (Makeup man); Verebes, Arno (Stage manager); Hobbes, Halliwell (General); Mander, Miles (Major Cunningham); Caldwell, Peter (Wilhelm).

DISTRIBUTION & AVAILABILITY: *Publisher or re-*

sponsible agency: United Artists; *Distributor:* FNC, FCM, BFI*, *Copy location:* FOL; *Call or copy number:* MP 100; *Availability:* FNC, 16mm, rental; FCM, V, sale, $59.95.

94. *Strange Illusion.*

DOCUMENT INFORMATION: *Country:* USA; *Year of release:* 1945.

EDITION, HISTORY, CONTENTS, & EVALUATION: *Edition & history:* This "B" (low-budget) movie, actually an offshoot from *Hamlet*, like Chabrol's *Ophelia* retells the Hamlet legend in modern guise. The principal actors were all highly professional but shared a common fate of spending most of their careers in Hollywood playing in B movies. For a time, James Lydon made a career out of playing Henry Aldrich. The film, just made available on videocassette, was shown in 1986 at the Library of Congress as a part of a special program devoted to Shakespeare on film and television at the Mary Pickford Theater. *Contents & evaluation:* The movie opens with Paul Cartwright's nightmare about the strange death of his father. Paul's mother has since found Brett Curtis, who corresponds of course to the uncle Claudius. Paul is a sullen young man with a taste for wide-lapeled double-breasted suits who mopes about in the splendor of the baronial family mansion. Thought to be quite mad by his stepfather and mother, he is shunted away into a psychiatric hospital run by the evil Dr. Vincent. A posthumous letter from Paul's late father warns the young man that he must protect his mother. Paul also loves a young lady by the name of Lydia who corresponds to Ophelia. About midway through the film turns into a conventional murder mystery but the overtones from the Shakespearean influence remain. Paul's experiments with real and pretended madness as a way of delaying his mother's re-marriage to Brett especially link the film to *Hamlet*. *Audience:* General use; *Supplementary materials:* Simmon, Scott. "New Print" in program for "Acting It in Many Ways: Shakespeare on Film and Television." Mary Pickford Theater, Library of Congress, January 1986.

MEDIUM INFORMATION: *Medium:* Motion Picture; *Sound:* Spoken language; *Color:* No (black & white); *Length:* 80 min.; *Language(s) spoken:* English; *Film type:* 35mm.

AUTHORSHIP INFORMATION: *Producer(s):* Fromkess, Leon; *Director(s):* Ulmer, Edgar G.; Kadish, Ben; *Screenplay writer(s):* Comandini, Adele; Rotter, Fritz; *Composer(s):* Erdody; *Set designer(s):* Reif, E.H.; *Costume designer(s):* Bradow, Harold; *Lighting designer(s):* Tannura, Philip; *Other personnel:* Rotsten, Herman (Dialogue director); Palmentola, Paul (Art); Stevens, Charles (Props); McWhorter, Frank (Sound); Pierson, Carl (Film editor); *Cast:* Lydon, James (Paul Cartwright—Hamlet); William, Warren (Brett Curtis—Claudius); Eilers, Sally (Virginia Cartwright—Gertrude); Toomey, Regis (Dr. Vincent—Polonius [?]); Arut, Charles (Professor Muhlbach); Reed, George H. (Benjamin); Hazard, Jayne

(Dorothy Cartwright); Clark, Jimmy (George—Horatio); McLeod, Mary (Lydia—Ophelia); Watkin, Pierre (Armstrong); Sorel, Sonia (Miss Farber); Potel, Vic (Game warden); Sherwood, George (Langdon); Stutenroth, Gene; Hamilton, John (Mr. Allen).

DISTRIBUTION & AVAILABILITY: *Publisher or responsible agency:* A PRC Picture; *Copy location:* LCM (AFI/Tayler collection); *Call or copy number:* FGE 5145; *Availability:* FCM, V (S10692), $29.95.

Hamlet. Motion Picture/Excerpts

95. *Diary for Timothy, A.*

DOCUMENT INFORMATION: *Country:* GB; *Year of release:* 1946.

EDITION, HISTORY, CONTENTS, & EVALUATION: *Edition & history:* Wartime film about England in 1944. It includes gravedigger scene with John Gielgud. *Supplementary materials:* BUFVC 4.

MEDIUM INFORMATION: *Color:* No (black & white); *Length:* 39 min.; *Film type:* 16mm.

AUTHORSHIP INFORMATION: *Producer(s):* Wright, Basil; *Adaptor/translator(s):* Jennings, Humphrey; *Cast:* Gielgud, John.

DISTRIBUTION & AVAILABILITY: *Distributor:* BFI*.

96. *My Darling Clementine.*

DOCUMENT INFORMATION: *Country:* USA ; *Year of release:* 1946.

EDITION, HISTORY, CONTENTS, & EVALUATION: *Edition & history:* A rough western barroom becomes the site for a performance of *Hamlet* by a troupe of Shakespearean actors. (Thanks to Dr. Frank Manchel for pointing this one out to us.)

MEDIUM INFORMATION: *Sound:* Spoken language; *Color:* No (black & white); *Length:* 97 min.; *Film type:* 16mm.

AUTHORSHIP INFORMATION: *Director(s):* Ford, John; *Cast:* Fonda, Henry; Darnell, Linda; Mature, Victor.

DISTRIBUTION & AVAILABILITY: *Publisher or responsible agency:* Fox; *Distributor:* FNC, *Availability:* Apply.

Hamlet. Video/Teleplay

97. *Hamlet.*

DOCUMENT INFORMATION: *Country:* GB; *Year of first showing:* 1947; *Location of first showing:* BBC, Alexandra Palace, London. Transmitted in two parts:

8:30 to 10:10 P.M., Sunday, 7 and 14 Dec. 1947 (Repeated on Tuesdays).

EDITION, HISTORY, CONTENTS, & EVALUATION: *Awards:* Silver Medal, British Television Society, 1948; *Edition & history:* Producer George More O'Ferrall began work on this major production in the summer of 1947. Some 70 persons were approached to fill 48 roles (with some doubling). Special recordings had to be made for Ophelia's songs and the noise of the ghost. Fittings for costumes at Foxes ate up considerable time, and Hamlet's customary suits of solemn black had to be made dark green because of the technical requirements of early television. During the five weeks of rehearsals in bare rooms, the cast was provided with scale models of the proposed sets to orient them to the actual conditions of the live broadcast. The scenery itself was not completed until December 4th, three days before the broadcast. From this timetable, one can imagine the anxiety attacks that must have wracked the producer and his associates (WAC TS/220 4.3.48). If, as Michael Barry suggests ("Shakespeare on TV," *BBC Quarterly* 9.3 [Autumn 1954]: 146), the tracking shots in O'Ferrall's production influenced Olivier's 1948 filmed version of *Hamlet,* the performance takes on even greater importance in the history of screened Shakespeare and was worth all the pain of creation. For its merits, in 1948 Producer O'Ferrall won the first television award for artistic achievement from the British Television Society. Drew Middleton's *New York Times* story may also well be the first review in North America of a televised Shakespeare performance. *Contents & evaluation:* Mr. Drew Middleton thought that John Byron played the Prince "for all that it was worth," and that he did not commit the error of overplaying to the camera. The play's "whole pathetic, bitter story with all its blood and thunder elements [gripped] the audience without interruption." *Supplementary materials:* Middleton, Drew. "Televised *Hamlet.*" *NYT* 14 Dec. 1947: X 11; "Television Trophies." *Daily Herald* 3 Apr. 1948: n.p.

MEDIUM INFORMATION: *Length:* 180 min.

AUTHORSHIP INFORMATION: *Producer(s):* O'Ferrall, George More; Adams, Basil; *Designer(s):* Bax, Peter; *Other personnel:* Loraine, Denis (Fights); *Cast:* Byron, John (Hamlet); Shaw, Sebastian (Claudius); Wontner, Arthur (Polonius); Troughton, Patrick (Horatio); Macnee, Patrick (Horatio); Dexter, Aubrey (Voltemand); Williams, Dudley (Cornelius); Rietty, Robert (Rosencrantz); Warner, Richard (Guildenstern); Devlin, William (Marcellus); Somers, Julian (Barnardo); Lemin, Stanley (Francisco); Dean, Roy; Duncan, David; Caborn, Michael; Ainsworth, John (Players); Rawlings, Margaret (Gertrude); Pavlow, Muriel (Ophelia); Holloway, W.E. (Ghost); + Lords, Ladies, Attendants.

DISTRIBUTION & AVAILABILITY: *Publisher or responsible agency:* BBC; *Copy location:* Unavailable.

Hamlet. Motion Picture/Interpretation

98. *Hamlet.*

DOCUMENT INFORMATION: *Country:* GB; *Year of filming:* 1947; *Year of release:* 1948; *Country of first showing:* GB.

EDITION, HISTORY, CONTENTS, & EVALUATION: *Awards:* "Best Picture" of the Year (1948), MPAAS; Olivier, Academy Award for "Best Actor"; *Edition & history:* This famous version of *Hamlet* grew out of long meditation by the producer, director and star player, Laurence Olivier. As early as 1937, when he played Orlando against Elisabeth Bergner's Rosalind in the 1936 film of *As You Like It,* he had been thinking of making a film of *Hamlet.* The success of his 1944 *Henry V* encouraged the J. Arthur Rank organization to grant Olivier complete artistic control over the production of this film. Transforming a four-and-a-half hour play into a two-and-a-half hour movie required drastic cutting of the Quarto and Folio texts. To the dismay of many purists, Rosencrantz and Guildenstern entirely disappeared, and other major textual alterations and amputations occurred. Perhaps most controversial (resulting in Peter Alexander's book, *Hamlet, Father and Son*) were the words in the film's prologue that seemed to reduce the play to a tale of a "man who could not make up his mind." Visually, however, Olivier boldly moved toward a black-and-white film. To him *Hamlet* was an 'engraving' not an 'oil painting.' And the prying and moving camera, with the deep focus, also became integral in this famous movie. *Contents & evaluation:* "[Olivier] relies upon [Dr. Ernest] Jones to approach the cause of the delay: the oedipal conflict. As Olivier says in an interview: 'Hamlet could safely be a man of action under the auspices of that particular idea.' (Obviously, then, indecisiveness does not have much to do with Olivier's concept of Hamlet). The question is, aside from the debatable worth of the thesis, can a film express such deeply unconscious feelings as Jones describes? The best Olivier can do is present a set loaded with Freudian symbolism and a Gertrude who leans sensuously toward Claudius, whose gowns reveal fully her sumptuously curved body, who kisses Hamlet with an ardor which we in our post-Freudian age consider too intense to be merely maternal. Olivier does not convey the subconscious identification with Claudius or the rigidly suppressed sexual identification to his mother. To 'know' these things about Hamlet the audience must bring the Freudian structure to the play. It defies staging or screening precisely because it does lie buried in the subconscious" (Kliman, Bernice, "The Spiral of Influence: 'One Defect' in *Hamlet,*" *LFQ* 11.3 [1983]: 162). "The black-and-white photographic treatment of *Hamlet* has been criticized for the over-use of travelling shots, the camera tracking, panning and circling around the sets and the actors. Hamlet is seen for the first time sitting apart in the Court when a movement by Laertes is followed through with the traveling camera until the whole Court group is included in the frame; this is completed when the Queen and later the King, move over to Hamlet's side to create a new grouping in the manner of the theatre. The close-up of the film, when Hamlet's body is being carried to lie in state in the tower on the ramparts, brings a prolonged survey of the whole castle, place after place associating with earlier scenes in the film. Crane shots, moving high up or low down emphasize the nature of the action; for example, the camera glides from the roof of the great hall down to the seated figure of Hamlet, deep in thought. . . ." (Manvell, *SATF* 41). *Audience:* General use; *Supplementary materials:* Cross, Brenda. *The Film* Hamlet: *A Record of Its Production.* London: Saturn Press, 1948; Dent, Alan, ed. *Hamlet, the Film and the Play.* London: World, 1948 [Important essays by film's makers].

MEDIUM INFORMATION: *Medium:* Motion Picture; *Sound:* Spoken language; *Color:* No (black & white); *Length:* 152 min.; *Language(s) spoken:* English; *Film type:* 16mm, 35mm; *Video type:* CDV, V, 3/4U.

AUTHORSHIP INFORMATION: *Producer(s):* Olivier, Laurence; Beck, Reginald; *Director(s):* Olivier, Laurence; *Adaptor/translator(s):* Dent, Alan; *Composer(s):* Walton, William; Mathieson, Muir [and] Hollingsworth, John (w. The Philharmonia Orchestra); *Designer(s):* Furse, Roger; Dillon, Carmen; *Set designer(s):* Lindegarde, E.; Sheriff, Paul; Harris, Henry; Whitehead, Jack (Special Effects); *Costume designer(s):* Hennings, Elizabeth; *Lighting designer(s):* Dickinson, Desmond; Hamilton, James; *Other personnel:* Samuel, P.C. (Prod. Sup.); Bushell, A. (Asst. Prod.); Cranston, Helga (Editor); Gossage, John (Prod. Manager); Sturgess, Ray (Camera Operator); Miller, H. (Sound Editor); Bolton, Peter (Asst. Director); Paltenghi, David (Mime play); Loraine, Denis (Fencing); Sforzini, Tony (Make-up); Walker, Vivienne (Hairdressing); Everson, Elizabeth (Continuity); *Cast:* Olivier, Laurence (Hamlet); Herlie, Eileen (Gertrude); Sydney, Basil (Claudius); Simmons, Jean (Ophelia); Aylmer, Felix (Polonius); Wooland, Norman (Horatio); Morgan, Terence (Laertes); Holloway, Stanley (Gravedigger); Peter Cushing (Osric); Knight, Esmond (Barnardo); Quayle, Anthony (Marcellus); Williams, Harcourt (Chief Player); Laurie, John (Francisco); MacGinnis, Niall (Sea Captain); Thorndike, Russell (Priest); Troughton, Patrick (Player King); Tarver, Tony (Player Queen).

DISTRIBUTION & AVAILABILITY: *Publisher or responsible agency:* A J. Arthur Rank Enterprise/A Universal-International Release/A Two Cities Film under the Management of Filippo Del Guidice; *Distributor:* FNC, CWF, BLK, FFH, RCA, DCV, FMB*, *Copy location:* FOL, CTL*; *Call or copy number:* MP 11; *Availability:* FNC, rental, 16mm, $100 + ; ROA, Apply; HAR*; Apply; Sale, BLK $34.98; RCA (CED) $29.95; FFH (958F),

B,V, $249, 3/4U $349, rental $125; DCV, V, $38; INM, V (DS05), $39.95; FCM, V, $19.95.

Hamlet. **Motion Picture/Documentaries**

99. *Sets and Costumes for* Hamlet.

DOCUMENT INFORMATION: *Country:* GB; *Year of release:* 1948.

EDITION, HISTORY, CONTENTS, & EVALUATION: *Edition & history:* Documentary about the making of sets and costumes for the Olivier film version of *Hamlet.* Scene from Olivier film at end. *Supplementary materials:* BUFVC 36.

MEDIUM INFORMATION: *Sound:* Spoken language; *Color:* No (black & white); *Length:* 6 min.

AUTHORSHIP INFORMATION: *Director(s):* Olivier, Laurence.

DISTRIBUTION & AVAILABILITY: *Distributor:* BFI* (Out of circulation).

100. *Elsinore: Room of State.*

DOCUMENT INFORMATION: *Country:* GB; *Year of release:* 1950.

EDITION, HISTORY, CONTENTS, & EVALUATION: *Edition & history:* A documentary made in conjunction with the Olivier *Hamlet* that describes how the sets and costumes were designed for the film. It seems to overlap, or perhaps even duplicate, number 99 above.

DISTRIBUTION & AVAILABILITY: *Distributor:* MMA, *Copy location:* MMA; *Call or copy number:* 004932.

101. *Shakespeare og Kronborg.*

DOCUMENT INFORMATION: *Country:* Denmark; *Year of release:* 1950.

EDITION, HISTORY, CONTENTS, & EVALUATION: A look at the historic setting for *Hamlet.* *Supplementary materials:* SIF 121.

MEDIUM INFORMATION: *Length:* 10 min.

AUTHORSHIP INFORMATION: *Director(s):* Roos, Jorgen.

Hamlet. **Video/Abridgment**

102. *Hamlet.* (Series: Hallmark Hall of Fame).

DOCUMENT INFORMATION: *Country:* USA; *Year of first showing:* 1953; *Location of first showing:* NBC/TV. Transmitted 3:30 to 5:30 P.M., Sunday 26 Apr. 1953.

EDITION, HISTORY, CONTENTS, & EVALUATION: *Edition & history:* One of ten Hallmark Hall of Fame productions devoted to Shakespeare (see also numbers 126, 305, 309, 484, 593, 594, 613, and 649). Joyce

Hall, the Kansas City greeting card tycoon, generously supported these unique contributions to American culture. According to Alice Griffin this "two-hour" production of *Hamlet*, which appropriately appeared on the anniversary of Shakespeare's christening, was "the longest drama ever done on American television." Playing time was, however, more like 90 minutes, so that one infers the commercials must have been especially intrusive. Maurice Evans brought impressive credentials to this television version. Throughout WWII as a commissioned officer in the U.S. Army, his assignment had been to bring his "GI Hamlet" to the troops. He had also played Hamlet on Broadway. *Contents & evaluation:* "As he has played it on the stage, Evans' Hamlet is a vigorous young man, an interpretation not unfamiliar to modern scholars and stagers. Evans says of his portrayal: 'too often Hamlet has been played as a study in dyspepsia rather than as the inner conflict of a man who was a very normal human being caught up in a web of circumstance which sets him to questioning the values and standards by which he has lived. Hamlet has been called a psychopath. I think he just has a universal reaction to a pretty staggering problem.' . . . Evans and Barry Jones as Polonius were much the best performers on the show, with Jones adding a touch of sympathy and humor to the old statesman, but not playing him as a comic character. . . . On the distaff side, Sarah Churchill as Ophelia and Ruth Chatterton as Gertrude were so inadequate in their roles that the viewer might well have wondered whether they did not appear on this program by mistake, having actually been destined for some other television production, like a mystery thriller. In addition to her acting Ophelia like a debutante just out of finishing school, Miss Churchill's costume and coiffure were quite modern and completely out of key with the rest of the production" (Griffin, Alice, "Shakespeare Through the Camera's Eye," *SQ* 4.3 (1953); 33-4). *Audience:* General use; *Supplementary materials:* Kliman, Bernice. "The Setting in Early TV." *Shakespeare and the Arts,* ed. C.W. Cary and H.S. Limouze. Washington, D.C.: UPA, 1982. 135-53; Evans, Maurice. "An Actor." *NYT* 26 Apr. 1955: X 11; Simon, Ronald. "Interview: George Schaefer." in *Hallmark Hall of Fame: A Tradition of Excellence.* New York: Museum of Broadcasting, 1985. 23-30.

MEDIUM INFORMATION: *Medium:* Video; *Sound:* Spoken language; *Color:* No (black & white); *Length:* 98 minutes (?); *Language(s) spoken:* English; *Film type:* Kinescope [?].

AUTHORSHIP INFORMATION: *Producer(s):* Schaefer, George; *Director(s):* Schaefer, George; McCleery, Albert; *Adaptor/translator(s):* Alberg, Mildred Freed; Sand, Tom; *Designer(s):* Sylbert, Richard; *Cast:* Evans, Maurice (Hamlet); Jones, Barry (Polonius); Churchill, Sarah (Ophelia); Chatterton, Ruth (Gertrude); Schildkraut, Joseph (Claudius); Addy, Wesley (Horatio); Keen, Malcolm (Ghost); Smithers, William (Laertes).

DISTRIBUTION & AVAILABILITY: *Publisher or responsible agency:* National Broadcasting Company; *Copy location:* UCL, MOB [?].

Hamlet/Richard the Third. Motion Picture/Excerpts

103. *Prince of Players.*

DOCUMENT INFORMATION: *Country:* USA; *Year of release:* 1954.

EDITION, HISTORY, CONTENTS, & EVALUATION: *Edition & history:* Richard Burton in portraying the theatrical career of Edwin Booth superbly performs scenes from *Hamlet, King Lear, Romeo and Juliet* and *Richard III.* The fabled actress, Eva LeGallienne, acted as a special consultant on the scenes involving Shakespearean acting, which is surely one of the reasons that they are done so well. *Contents & evaluation:* The truism that some of the finest Shakespearean acting on screen often occurs when a film actor is portraying an actor in a stage production embedded in a film is amply validated by this remarkable film. As Edwin Booth, the storied nineteenth-century American actor, Burton displays a dazzling talent as a Hamlet, Romeo, or Richard III. The plot line is merely an excuse for stringing together these exciting moments of theatre. Burton's skills, especially as Richard duke of Gloucester (King Richard III) serve as a reminder that often there is nothing intrinsically wrong with the cinematic medium for Shakespeare production; it is simply that so few first-rate actors are in supply to exploit the medium. The film also offers an absorbing insight into U.S. history. Edwin Booth's mad brother, John Wilkes, is portrayed as President Lincoln's assassin. This film should have a special appeal for high school students who are hesitant about approaching Shakespeare's work directly, though there is much here for all ages (KSR).

MEDIUM INFORMATION: *Medium:* Motion Picture; Cinemascope; *Sound:* Spoken language; *Color:* Yes; *Length:* 105 min.; *Language(s) spoken:* English; *Film type:* 16mm.

AUTHORSHIP INFORMATION: *Producer(s):* Dunne, Philip; *Director(s):* Dunne, Philip; Dunn, Eli; *Screenplay writer(s):* Hart, Moss; Ruggles, Eleanor (Book author); *Composer(s):* Herrman, Bernard; *Designer(s):* Wheeler, Lyle; Kirk, Mark Lee; *Set designer(s):* Scott, Walter M.; Fox, Paul S.; *Costume designer(s):* Wills, Mary; LeMaire, Charles; *Other personnel:* Clarke, Charles G. (Dir. photog.); Kellogg, Ray (Special effects); Spencer, Dorothy (Film editor); Nye, Ben (Make-up); Turpin, Helen (Hair); Bruzlin, Alfred; Leonard, Harry M. (Sound); LeGallienne, Eva (Special consultant); *Cast:* Burton, Richard (Edwin Booth); McNamara, Maggie (Devlin, Mary); Derek, John (John Wilkes Booth); Massey, Raymond (Junius Brutus Booth); Bickford, Charles

(Dave Prescott); Sellars, Elizabeth (Asia); LeGallienne, Eva (Gertrude); Cook, Christopher (Edwin Booth—age 10); Lummis, Dayton (English doctor); Keith, Ian (Claudius); Stader, Paul (Laertes); Alexander, Louis (John Booth—; age 12); Wright, Ben (Horatio); Walker, William (Old Ben); Raine, Jack (Theatre manager).

DISTRIBUTION & AVAILABILITY: *Publisher or responsible agency:* Twentieth-Century Fox; *Distributor:* FNC, *Copy location:* FOL; *Call or copy number:* MP 25; *Availability:* Apply FNC.

Hamlet. Motion Picture/Interpretation

104. *Hamlet.*

DOCUMENT INFORMATION: *Country:* India; *Year of release:* 7 Jan. 1955; *Location of first showing:* Metro Theatre, Bombay.

EDITION, HISTORY, CONTENTS, & EVALUATION: *Edition & history:* Unfortunately I have been unable to locate a distributor for this film in the United States, as it offers an example of how the large and prolific Indian film industry would handle a Shakespeare movie. Not only as a result of British cultural imperialism but also, one hopes, because of his intrinsic merit, Shakespeare has long been a major literary figure in India. The journal, *Hamlet Studies*, for example, with a distinguished board of editors, is published in New Delhi. *Contents & evaluation:* A review in *Film India* reads as though some personal vendetta was involved. Its flavor can be inferred from the headline: "Sahu's *Hamlet* Flops at the Metro." Not only does the film "slander" Shakespeare's memory but also "Hiralal who plays the King was made a drunken clown." Laertes, we are told, had "a callow and silly face," and the picture is "at once stupid and selfish." Not stopping at that, the critic adds that the movie is "stinking selfishness." After this diatribe, one can't help wondering what the hidden agenda was. An accompanying photograph shows Dame Sybil Thorndike on the opening night posing with the proud theatre manager, Mr. Butani. *Audience:* General use; *Supplementary materials:* "Hamlet Flops." *Film India* (Feb. 1955): 71-75.

MEDIUM INFORMATION: *Medium:* Motion Picture; *Sound:* Spoken language; *Color:* No (black & white); *Length:* ? min.; *Language(s) spoken:* Urdu; *Film type:* 35mm.

AUTHORSHIP INFORMATION: *Producer(s):* Sahu, Kishore; *Director(s):* Sahu, Kishore; *Screenplay writer(s):* Sahu, Kishore; *Adaptor/translator(s):* Hilal, Amanot; Verma, E.D. Prof.; *Composer(s):* Jaipuri, Hasrat; Nardu, Ramesh; *Lighting designer(s):* Kapadia, K.H.; *Other personnel:* Pandya, Chandrakani (Sound); *Cast:* Sahu, Kishore; Sinha, Mala; Bannerjee, Venus; Nazir, Hiralai S.; Jir, Kamal.

DISTRIBUTION & AVAILABILITY: *Publisher or responsible agency:* Hindustan Chitra; *Copy location:* Unknown.

Hamlet. Video/Documentary

105. "To Be or Not To Be": *Some Views of Shakespeare's* Hamlet.

DOCUMENT INFORMATION: *Country:* USA; *Year of release:* 1955.

EDITION, HISTORY, CONTENTS, & EVALUATION: *Edition & history:* Presented as a part of the Omnibus series on CBS-TV. Examines Hamlet's soliloquy. *Supplementary materials:* Loughney, Katharine. "Shakespeare on Film and Tape at Library of Congress." *SFNL* 12.2 (Apr. 1988): 7.

MEDIUM INFORMATION: *Medium:* Video; *Sound:* Spoken language; *Color:* No (black & white); *Length:* 40 min.

AUTHORSHIP INFORMATION: *Producer(s):* Saudek, Robert; *Director(s):* Robbie, Seymour; *Cast:* Stratford (Ontario) Shakespeare company.

DISTRIBUTION & AVAILABILITY: *Copy location:* LCM; *Call or copy number:* VDB 7056-7057.

Hamlet. Motion Picture/Documentary

106. *Baylor Theatre's* Hamlet.

DOCUMENT INFORMATION: *Country:* USA; *Year of release:* 1958.

EDITION, HISTORY, CONTENTS, & EVALUATION: *Edition & history:* Film exploring technical problems of production. *Supplementary materials:* SIF 117.

MEDIUM INFORMATION: *Length:* 20 min.

AUTHORSHIP INFORMATION: *Director(s):* McKinney, Gene.

DISTRIBUTION & AVAILABILITY: *Distributor:* Baylor Univ.[?]

Hamlet. Video/Teleplay

107. *Hamlet.* (Series: DuPont Show of the Month).

DOCUMENT INFORMATION: *Country:* GB; *Year of first showing:* 1959; *Location of first showing:* CBS. Transmitted 9:30 to 11:00 P.M., 24 Feb. 1959.

EDITION, HISTORY, CONTENTS, & EVALUATION: *Edition & history:* Essentially a record of the touring Old Vic Company's *Hamlet.* To cut the Old Vic stage version to 90 minutes for television, TV director Ralph

Nelson went to the "pirated" 1601 Quarto for guidance. That much shortened version, though often spoken of as a "bad" quarto, actually makes for an effective stage performance. As a part of the event, CBS published the television script for *Hamlet* in a handsomely printed volume on rag paper with original sketches. A foreword by the CBS president, Louis G. Cowan, testifies to the heroic efforts being made in those early days of commercial television to put worthwhile drama on the air. Besides the Dupont Show of the Month, which sponsored the Old Vic *Hamlet*, there were also Playhouse 90, the Armstrong Circle Theatre, United States Steel Hour, and others. Television lacked the technical sophistication of a modern program such as *Miami Vice* but it paid more than lip service to quality theatre. Perhaps the idea that mass audiences could be won over to Shakespeare was inherently quixotic anyway. *Contents & evaluation:* After Frederic March introduces the members of the Old Vic company in a theatre lobby, the play *Hamlet* actually begins as credits roll over a background of the parapets at Elsinore. Rapidly the camera moves to 'The Room of State' where the enthroned king and queen are shown seated in splendor as the title *Hamlet* dissolves on the screen. A fade in to Hamlet follows who is shown brooding in close-up. With startling rapidity, Claudius polishes off his opening speech in 1.2 and Hamlet abruptly has launched on the 'O that this too too solid flesh' soliloquy. That rapidity of action runs against the grain of a play about "delay" but nicely fits the demands of video. The ideologies implicit in John Neville's Hamlet curiously mirror the Eisenhower era's last ditch defense of Victorianism. He might almost be the ideal Hamlet for 1888, a Forbes-Robertson, or perhaps even a 1936 Leslie Howard—thin, anxiety-ridden, neurasthenic but even so vibrant and alive. The Regency period costumes reinforce rather than undercut that image. In his meeting with the players, Neville is so plausible that we barely realize that Hamlet's advice to them has been drastically cut, and that Rosencrantz and Guildenstern are nowhere to be found about the palace. Also vanished, or perhaps "banished," is the bawdy innuendo surrounding Hamlet's relationship with Ophelia. Unhappily commercial breaks did ruthlessly intrude when the sponsors felt that marketing deserved a higher priority than art. When left alone, though, the production offers magical moments. I'm thinking of when Claudius calls for "Lights" after Lucianus pours the poison in the player king's ear. The disorder in the court becomes choreographed confusion: many camera angles, close-ups, bits of business by harried actors, much rushing to and fro, make the scene an emblem for the chaotic state of Denmark following the unmasking of Claudius. In voice-over soliloquies Neville as Hamlet also manages to connect inner thoughts with facial expressions. All of him is acting. He is not merely a talking head or a photographed bust. With the improved technology of television by 1959, the *mise en scène* for this excellent

production remains sharply textured in black and white. It is still well worth viewing. *Audience:* Professional; General use; *Supplementary materials:* Hamlet:*A Television Script,* ed. Benthall, Michael and Nelson, Ralph. New York: CBS, 1959; Shanley, John P. "Tailored *Hamlet." NYT* 22 Feb. 1959: X 15.

MEDIUM INFORMATION: *Medium:* Video; *Sound:* Spoken language; *Color:* No (black & white); *Length:* 90 min.; *Language(s) spoken:* English; *Video type:* V.

AUTHORSHIP INFORMATION: *Producer(s):* Nelson, Ralph; Orr, Paul; *Director(s):* Nelson, Ralph; Benthall, Michael (for Old Vic); *Adaptor/translator(s):* Nelson, Ralph; *Designer(s):* Kransgill, Ken; *Costume designer(s):* Renfield, Leslie; *Lighting designer(s):* Barry, Bob; *Other personnel:* Vance, Rowland (Assoc. Director); Miller, Ted (Tech. Director); Bunce, Bull (Graphic Artist); *Cast:* Neville, John (Hamlet); Jefford, Barbara (Ophelia); Neville, Oliver (Claudius); Courtenay, Margaret (Gertrude); O'Conor, Joseph (Polonius); Wordsworth, Richard (Ghost); Humphrey, John (Laertes); Dodimead, David (Horatio); Stewart, Job (Osric); Jones, Dudley (Gravedigger); Ackland, Joss (Marcellus); Patrick, Roy (Barnardo); Wordsworth, Richard (Player King); Leigh-Hunt, Barbara (Player Queen); Culliford, James (Clown); Algar, Robert (Clown); March, Frederic (Host); *Performance group(s):* The Old Vic; by arrangement with S. Hurok.

DISTRIBUTION & AVAILABILITY: *Publisher or responsible agency:* Old Vic/Dupont Show of the Month/ CBS; *Copy location:* MOB; *Call or copy number:* Pts. 1-3 T77:0290/291; *Restrictions:* Archive use by appointment.

Hamlet. Motion Picture/Documentary

108. *Hamlet: The Age of Elizabeth.* (Series: The Humanities Series).

DOCUMENT INFORMATION: *Country:* USA; *Year of release:* 1959; Possibly 1962 [?]

EDITION, HISTORY, CONTENTS, & EVALUATION: *Edition & history:* This is Part One of a four-part series on *Hamlet* (see also numbers 112, 113, and 114). Using portraits (e.g., Sir Francis Drake), maps (Visscher's View), and models (Globe playhouse), Prof. Maynard Mack of Yale University discusses the relationship between the age of Elizabeth and *Hamlet.* Included also are excerpts from *King Henry VIII, Titus,* and *Hamlet* by actors from the Stratford, Canada, Shakespearean Festival. *Contents & evaluation:* Essentially this is an excellent slide show lecture with Mack as the "talking head," though the intervals of acting by the Stratford players are well done. The commentary, as one might expect, is astute and informative, and while aimed at the high school population never condescends to the audience as the British "Shakespeare in Perspective" series sometimes does. The film was made under the auspices of the remarkable Floyd Rinker and the Massachusetts Council for the Humanities when after the Sputnik scare the United States government was being especially generous in support of educational programs. Even though a pioneering effort, this film still remains valuable. *Audience:* High school (grades 10-12); College and university.

MEDIUM INFORMATION: *Medium:* Motion Picture; *Sound:* Spoken language; *Color:* Yes; *Length:* 30 min.; *Language(s) spoken:* English; *Film type:* 16mm.

AUTHORSHIP INFORMATION: *Producer(s):* Encyclopaedia Britannica Educational Corporation; *Director(s):* Langham, Michael; Barnes, John; Rinker, Floyd; McDermott, Angelo; *Designer(s):* Brown, Tom; Hodges, C. Walter; *Costume designer(s):* Heeley, Desmond; *Other personnel:* Livesey, Michael (Photography); Johnson, Robert; Lasse, Fred (Editors); Johnson, Brian (Properties); Boehmer, Michael (Director for film); Davis, Curtis (Production manager); Hall, William (Operations); *Cast:* Donat, Peter (Hamlet); Van Bridge, Tony; Davis, Donald; Campbell, Douglas; Needles, William; Mack, Maynard (Lecturer).

DISTRIBUTION & AVAILABILITY: *Distributor:* UVM, EBE, SYR, KSU, SFL*, *Call or copy number:* EBF #47521.

Hamlet. Motion Picture/Derivative

109. *Der Rest Ist Schweigen.* [*The Rest Is Silence*].

DOCUMENT INFORMATION: *Country:* GFR; *Year of first showing:* 1959.

EDITION, HISTORY, CONTENTS, & EVALUATION: *Edition & history:* A *Hamlet* derivative updating the tale into modern postwar Germany. A young intellectual feels grief over his father's death and remorse for his family's implication in WWII profiteering (Parker, *TSF* 25). *Supplementary materials:* See also *SIF* 100.

MEDIUM INFORMATION: *Sound:* Spoken language; *Color:* No (black & white); *Length:* 106 min.; *Language(s) spoken:* German; *Language of subtitles:* English; *Film type:* 35mm.

AUTHORSHIP INFORMATION: *Producer(s):* Käutner, Helmut; *Director(s):* Käutner, Helmut; *Composer(s):* Eichhorn, Bernhard; *Lighting designer(s):* Oberberg, Igor; *Cast:* Van Eyck, Peter (Claudius); Kruger, Hardy (Hamlet); Forster, Rudolf (Polonius); Penkert, Rainer (Horatio); Drache, Heinz (Laertes); Seeck, Adelheid (Gertrude); Andree, Ingrid (Ophelia).

DISTRIBUTION & AVAILABILITY: *Publisher or responsible agency:* Frele Film Production.

Hamlet. Video/Interpretation

110. *Hamlet: Prinz von Danemark.*

DOCUMENT INFORMATION: *Country:* West Germany; *Year of release:* 1960; *Country of first showing:* West German TV.

EDITION, HISTORY, CONTENTS, & EVALUATION: *Awards:* San Francisco Film Festival, 1962; *Edition & history:* Made originally to be shown on television, the production achieved such success that Hollywood Director, Edward Dmytryk, bought it and arranged to dub in English dialogue. Unfortunately many viewers have objected to the dubbing, which inevitably makes the actors appear to be "out of sync." The staging is bare, almost minimalist, one might say, with sets of cubes, blocks and risers to demarcate the different areas of the castle. As the late Lillian Wilds wrote, the set becomes "unremittingly claustrophobic" and there is "perhaps no daylight, no world outside. Hamlet's world is completely circumscribed by blackness" (Wilds 139). *Contents & evaluation:* This film is mainly a triumph for Maximilian Schell whose Teutonic Hamlet, clipped, direct, terse, almost decisive, sharply contrasts with the bevy of neurotic, frenzied young men who normally portray the role. Sparse in sets, the production mainly survives on the basis of the energy and intelligence of the extremely alert and sensitive actors (KSR); "Rolf Unkel's music for this *Hamlet* is all of a piece, consisting of variations on rough, jarring, discordant sounds. As stylized in its way as the set and cinematography, it is also a corroboration of Hamlet's anguished evaluation that the 'time is out of joint' and a projection of the 'jangled bells' of his inner state. Thus it forms a bridge between the artifice of the set and cinematography, and the realism of Schell's performance. Here is no general harmony, no music of the spheres to tell us all is not rotten in Denmark" (Wilds, Lillian, "On Film: Maximilian Schell's Most Royal *Hamlet*," *LFQ* 4.2 [1976]: 134-40). *Audience:* High school (grades 10-12); College and university; General use.

MEDIUM INFORMATION: *Medium:* Motion Picture; *Sound:* Spoken language; *Color:* No (black & white); *Length:* 127 min.; *Language(s) spoken:* German; *Dubbed language:* English; *Film type:* 16 mm.

AUTHORSHIP INFORMATION: *Producer(s):* Gottschalk, Hans; *Director(s):* Wirth, Franz Peter; *Adaptor/translator(s):* Schlegel, A.W.W.; Dmytryk, Edward (English dubbing); *Composer(s):* Unkel, Rolf; *Designer(s):* Richter, Gird; *Other personnel:* Scheyssleder, Adolf (Film Editor); Moller, Rudolf (Sound); Brown, Fred (English Sound Editor); Gewissen, Kurt/Gruber, Herman/Jakob, Rudolf H./Goriup, Boris (Camera); Guthke, Frank (Asst.Dir.); Hengst, Lutz; Ringelmann, Helmut (Production Managers); *Cast:* Schell, Maximilian (Hamlet);

Caninenberg, Hans (Claudius); Rotha, Wanda (Queen); Movar, Dunja (Ophelia); Schafheitlin, Franz (Polonius); Kirchlechner, Dieter (Laertes); Vogler, Karl Michael (Horatio); Dux, Eckard (Rosenkranz); Bötticher, Herbert (Guildenstern); Lieffen, Karl (Osric); Boysen, Rolf (Bernardo); Paryla, Michael (Francisco); Engel, Alex (Ghost); Gerstung, Adolf (1st Player); Verhoeven, Paul (Gravedigger).

DISTRIBUTION & AVAILABILITY: *Publisher or responsible agency:* Bavaria Attelier, Gmbh, Munchen-Geiselgasteig; *Distributor:* SYR, UNF, ROA, WCF; *Copy location:* FOL; *Call or copy number:* MP 42 (FOL); AFI-F6.2020; *Availability:* Rental, Apply (c. $50).

Hamlet. Motion Picture/Derivative

111. *Ophelia.*

DOCUMENT INFORMATION: *Country:* France; *Year of release:* 1962.

EDITION, HISTORY, CONTENTS, & EVALUATION: *Edition & history:* The director of this film, Claude Chabrol (1930—), is well known as a *Nouvelle Vague* filmmaker and critic, one of the coteries whose serious interest in film as art was inscribed in the pages of *Cahiers du Cinéma*, the celebrated film journal. An admirer of Alfred Hitchcock, Chabrol shows that influence in the suspenseful sequences in *Ophelia*, as in the opening episode that so portentously depicts the funeral of Yvan's father. Chabrol's dislike of the French petty bourgeois also surfaces in the tavern scenes where the locals taunt the neurotic Yvan. The film was shot on location in rural France. The village name, "Erneles," is of course an attempt to link it to "Elsinore." *Contents & evaluation:* Chabrol's *Ophelia* is the perfect post-modernist film, in many ways ahead of its time. Certainly the commercial critics of the Sixties did not seem to understand it. Offering at least three planes of reality—the world of the village, the world of Yvan, and the world of a fabled Hamlet—there are multiple perspectives within each of these categories. For example, the LeSurfs (Claudius and Gertrude) and LaGrange (Polonius) are all inscribing reality into their own subtexts in protean ways.

The film ultimately deals with the impenetrability of the text that each person brings to "Erneles." As a disciple of Derrida might say, "there is no outside" to their texts. One of the more astute reviews of this brilliant film is worth quoting here: "Chabrol's *Ophelia* is of interest to Shakespeareans [because] it is about the process of adaptation and interpretation. The film depends more on versions and adaptations of the original tragedy [than] on *Hamlet* itself. . . . The se-

quence in which Yvan comes to identify his circumstances with those of Hamlet is a paradigm for those processes of identification between spectator and film which Christian Metz and other film theoreticians have described and analysed. Yvan identifies with the character of Hamlet and with Olivier in his role as Hamlet, an identification Chabrol emphasizes by focusing on the poster portrait of Olivier and by using the film rather than the literary text to motivate Yvan. . . . What interests us and Chabrol is not the compulsion to repeat by returning to the repressed castration complex and by subsequently fixing on the father, but the sheer process of substitution or exchange expressed in the compulsion to repeat fictions and stories, a compulsion Yvan enacts in the film and Chabrol in making *Ophelia*. Chabrol's film is a whimsical and half-heartedly frightening parody of the entire enterprise of adaptation, for Shakespeare himself repeated his *Hamlet* from some unknown ur-*Hamlet* which formed part of the large body of legends and stories about the Danish royal line; Olivier repeated Shakespeare's text as read by Freud; Chabrol repeats Shakespeare's, Freud's and Olivier's texts" (Newman, Karen, "Chabrol's *Ophelia*," *SFNL* 6.2 [March 1982]: 1+). *Audience:* General use; *Supplementary materials:* Kliman, Bernice. "Chabrol's *Ophelia*: Mirror for *Hamlet*." *SFNL* 3.1.1+; Moskowitz, Gene. "Review." *VAR* 30 May 1962.

MEDIUM INFORMATION: *Medium:* Motion Picture; *Sound:* Spoken language; *Color:* No (black & white); *Length:* 105 min.; *Language(s) spoken:* English; *Film type:* 35mm.

AUTHORSHIP INFORMATION: *Producer(s): Lux Compagne Cinématographique de France*/Boreal; *Director(s):* Chabrol, Claude; *Screenplay writer(s):* Matthieu, Martial; *Composer(s):* Jansen, Pierre; Girard, Andre (Conductor); *Set designer(s):* Ollier, Clément; *Costume designer(s):* Léonard; *Lighting designer(s):* Rabier, Jean; *Other personnel:* Marchetti, Jean-Claude (Sound); Gaillard, Jacques; Gaillard, Monique; Vitsoris, Catherine (Montage); Levent, Alain (Cameraman); Begon, Maude (Hair); Adam, Cécile; Capitolis, Luce (Secretaries of production); Louvet, Maurice (Administrator); Bernard, Constance (Direction Generale); Lavie, Jean (Director of production); *Cast:* Valli, Alida (Claudia Lesurf—Gertrude); Cerval, Claude (Adrien Lesurf—Claudius); Jocelyn, André (Yvan—Hamlet); Mayniel, Juliette (Lucie—Ophelia); Burnier, Robert (Andre Lagrange—Polonius); Briquet, Sacha (Gravedigger); Bento, Serge (Francois—Horatio); Vernier, Pierre (Paul); Carel, Roger (Worker); David, Litiane (Ginette); Maury, Jean-Louis (Sparkos).

DISTRIBUTION & AVAILABILITY: *Publisher or responsible agency:* Boreal Pictures; *Distributor:* NLC, *Copy location:* FOL; *Call or copy number:* MP 66.

Hamlet. **Motion Picture/Documentaries**

112. *What Happens in* Hamlet. II (Series: The Humanities Series).

DOCUMENT INFORMATION: *Country:* US; *Year of release:* 1962.

EDITION, HISTORY, CONTENTS, & EVALUATION: *Edition & history:* Part two in the Encyclopaedia Britannica series on *Hamlet* (see also numbers 108, 113, and 114). Prof. Maynard Mack finds that the play divides into three sections: a ghost story, a detective story, and a revenge story. His observations are illustrated with scenes from the play acted by topnotch talent from Canada's Stratford Festival. *Contents & evaluation:* A plausible and workable account of *Hamlet*, which I found thoroughly enjoyable. Later on students may want to discard this seductive but somewhat reductive account in favor of admitting the unspeakable truth that *Hamlet* is too complex ever to be reduced to the common understanding. In the meanwhile, however, Professor Mack has performed a great service in bringing the weight of his intellect and personality to the task of attracting students to, rather than repelling them from, that most mysterious of all plays, *Hamlet*. *Audience:* High school (grades 10-12); College and university.

MEDIUM INFORMATION: *Medium:* Motion Picture; *Sound:* Spoken language; *Color:* Yes; *Length:* 30 min.; *Language(s) spoken:* English; *Film type:* 16mm.

AUTHORSHIP INFORMATION: *Producer(s):* Encyclopaedia Britannica Educational Corporation; *Director(s):* Langham, Michael; Barnes, John; Campbell, Douglas; Rinker, Floyd; McDermott, Angelo; *Designer(s):* Brown, Tom; Hodges, C. Walter; *Costume designer(s):* Heeley, Desmond; *Other personnel:* Livesey, Michael (Photography); Johnson, Robert; Lasse, Fred (Editors); Johnson, Brian (Properties); Boehmer, Michael (Director for film); Davis, Curtis (Production manager); Hall, William (Operations); *Cast:* Mack, Maynard (Lecturer); Donat, Peter (Hamlet); Van Bridge, Tony (Ghost); King, Charmion (Gertrude); Helpmann, Max (Claudius); Peddie, Frank (Polonius); Gardiner, John (Laertes); Needles, William (Horatio).

DISTRIBUTION & AVAILABILITY: *Distributor:* EBE, SYR, KSU, SFL*, *Copy location:* UVM, EBF #47522.

113. *Hamlet: The Poisoned Kingdom*. III (Series: The Humanities Series).

DOCUMENT INFORMATION: *Country:* US; *Year of release:* 1962.

EDITION, HISTORY, CONTENTS, & EVALUATION: *Edition & history:* Part three of the Encyclopaedia Britannica four-part series on *Hamlet* (see also numbers 108, 112, and 114). Prof. Maynard Mack explores some of the play's thematic concerns, using players from the Stratford Festival to illustrate his points. *Contents & evaluation:* In this lecture, stress falls on the Elizabe-than idea of the King's body as metaphor for the state. The diseased, poisoned, kingdom, becomes a reflection of the disorders of the usurped crown. Especially valuable is his analysis of Polonius as a man who through abuse of language warps truth. Polonius becomes the type of modern Orwellian politician, more concerned with "image" than with substance. *Audience:* High school (grades 10-12); College and university.

MEDIUM INFORMATION: *Medium:* Motion Picture; *Sound:* Spoken language; *Color:* Yes; *Length:* 30 min.; *Language(s) spoken:* English; *Film type:* 16mm.

AUTHORSHIP INFORMATION: *Producer(s):* Encyclopaedia Britannica Educational Corporation; *Director(s):* Langham, Michael; Barnes, John; Campbell, Douglas; Rinker, Floyd; McDermott, Angelo; *Designer(s):* Brown, Tom; Hodges, C. Walter; *Costume designer(s):* Heeley, Desmond; *Other personnel:* Livesey, Michael (Photography); Johnson, Robert; Lasse, Fred (Editors); Johnson, Brian (Properties); Boehmer, Michael (Director for film); Davis, Curtis (Production manager); Hall, William (Operations); *Cast:* Mack, Maynard (Lecturer); Donat, Peter (Hamlet); Van Bridge, Tony (Ghost); King, Charmion (Gertrude); Helpmann, Max (Claudius); Peddie, Frank (Polonius); Gardiner, John (Laertes); Needles, William (Horatio).

DISTRIBUTION & AVAILABILITY: *Distributor:* UVM, EBE, SYR, KSU, SFL*; *Call or copy number:* EBF #47523.

114. *Hamlet IV: The Readiness Is All*. (Series: The Humanities Series).

DOCUMENT INFORMATION: *Country:* US; *Year of release:* 1962.

EDITION, HISTORY, CONTENTS, & EVALUATION: *Edition & history:* The fourth film in the *Hamlet* series (see also numbers 108, 112, and 113) takes a look at Hamlet as a young man, a person suffering from the shock of his father's death and mother's re-marriage. The prince is shown as the type of the alienated youth. *Contents & evaluation:* Again the lecture by Professor Mack is sensitive and informative, and the acting by the Stratford players, first-class. I can think of no better introduction to *Hamlet*. This film of two decades ago has aged well. *Audience:* High school (grades 10-12); College and university.

MEDIUM INFORMATION: *Medium:* Motion Picture; *Sound:* Spoken language; *Color:* Yes; *Length:* 30 min.; *Language(s) spoken:* English; *Film type:* 16mm.

AUTHORSHIP INFORMATION: *Producer(s):* Encyclopaedia Britannica Educational Corporation; *Director(s):* Langham, Michael; Barnes, John; Campbell, Douglas; Rinker, Floyd; McDermott, Angelo; *Designer(s):* Brown, Tom; Hodges, C. Walter; *Costume designer (s):* Heeley, Desmond; *Other personnel:* Livesey, Michael (Photography); Johnson, Robert; Lasse, Fred (Editors); Johnson, Brian (Properties); Boehmer, Michael (Director for film); Davis, Curtis (Production manager); Hall, William (Operations); *Cast:* Mack, Maynard (Lecturer); Donat, Peter (Hamlet); Van Bridge, Tony (Ghost); King, Charmion (Gertrude); Helpmann, Max (Claudius); Peddie, Frank (Polonius); Gardiner, John (Laertes); Needles, William (Horatio).

DISTRIBUTION AND AVAILABILITY: *Distributor:* UVM, SFL*, *Call or copy number:* EBF #47524

Hamlet. **Motion Picture/Derivative**

115. *The Bad Sleep Well.*

DOCUMENT INFORMATION: *Country:* Japan; *Year of first showing:* 1963.

EDITION, HISTORY, CONTENTS, & EVALUATION: *Edition & history:* Another updated *Hamlet* story in which the setting becomes corporate life in modern day Japan. The director is of course also the maker of the important Shakespeare films, *Throne of Blood* (307) and *Ran* (274). (The credits here are taken from Parker's Folger filmography, which is especially valuable for spinoffs and derivatives from the Shakespeare canon.) *Supplementary materials:* Parker, *TSF*, 26.

MEDIUM INFORMATION: *Sound:* Spoken language; *Color:* No (black & white); *Length:* 135 min.; *Film type:* 35mm. Tohoscope.

AUTHORSHIP INFORMATION: *Producer(s):* Tanaka, Tomiyuku; *Director(s):* Kurosawa, Akira; *Composer(s):* Sato, Masaru; *Designer(s):* Muraki, Yoshiro; *Lighting designer(s):* Aizawa, Yuzura; *Cast:* Mifune, Toshiro; Kato, Tokashi; Mori, Mosayuki; Shimura, Tokashi.

DISTRIBUTION & AVAILABILITY: *Publisher or responsible agency:* Toho; *Distributor:* Not known.

Hamlet. **Motion Picture/Adaptation**

116. *Gamlet.* [*Hamlet*].

DOCUMENT INFORMATION: *Country:* USSR; *Year of filming:* 1963; *Year of release:* 1964.

EDITION, HISTORY, CONTENTS, & EVALUATION: *Edition & history: Awards:* Lenin Prize, 1964; The director of this film (and of an equally impressive *King Lear* [256]), Grigori Kozintsev, has written two extraordinarily valuable books about his experiences as a director of Shakespeare films, both of which have been translated into English. Kozintsev's own words best describe his intentions: "My film will use a wide screen format and black-and-white photography. In *Don Quixote* I used colour because I wanted to capture the quality, the ambience of the warm South; but for *Hamlet* I want the cool greys of the North. . . . Pushkin said: 'Let Shakespeare be your teacher.' He was aware that the general theme of Shakespeare is the fate of

humanity in the condition of society based on inhuman conditions. . . . *Hamlet* for me shows the relationship of people in many circles: government, education of children, war, problems of morality and so on. It is a restatement of the true relationships of men" (from *FAF* [Sept. 1962], quoted in Manvell, 80). *Contents & evaluation:* "To avoid the heavy, self-conscious straining after significance which mars so many Shakespeare films, the director occasionally cuts across these chains of associations with random naturalistic detail. Unlike the 'classical' Olivier film, which abstracts the tragic action from everyday reality and creates a solipsistic/neurotic feel, Kozintsev litters his wide screen with things. This, of course, is more in keeping with Hamlet's mode of perception, since he sees life in terms of concrete images—an unweeded garden, a mildewed ear, a nutshell. But there is more to it than that. By showing chickens scratching for bugs and a woman leading a horse by as Hamlet sits on the players' wagon, [he] implies other patterns than the one in this play, a larger world which like the ploughman or the ship in Brueghel's painting "Icarus" is oblivious to the tragedy. In addition, he heightens the sense of impending disaster: 'The sense of approaching catastrophe is not only seen in the darkness of the clouds moving over the land, but is perceptible in the accumulation of life's numberless trivia, rendering that life senseless and draining it of spiritual meaning'[quoted from Kozintsev]. Hamlet confronts not only incest and murder, but a whole social order drowning in irrelevancies, ciphers, and dead-ends; a world summed up in the sublimely comic images of Hamlet's stopping (to the endless consternation of his guards) to remove a stone from his shoe before going to answer for the death of Polonius, and the crass, oblivious gravedigger who eats, drinks, and jokes even as he is waist deep in Ophelia's grave" (Jorgens, Jack J., "Image and Meaning in the Kozintsev *Hamlet*," *LFQ* 1.4 [1973]: 309). No filmmaker ever more obsessively ransacked a subtext than has this Russian cineaste. Veteran filmmaker Kozintsev brings a spiritual fervor to his Shakespeare films. In this *Hamlet*, the elemental forces of nature—earth, stone, fire—counterpoint the supernatural realm in which the prince gropes for elusive truths. Ophelia's imprisonment, for example, in an iron corset and farthingale is emblematic of the brute forces constraining any impulse toward freedom. The politics of the court almost begin to rival the inner perturbations of the prince (KSR). *Audience:* General use; *Supplementary materials:* "Review." *MFB* 32 [1964]: 20; Kozintsev, Grigori. *Shakespeare: Time and Conscience.* New York: Hill & Wang, 1966.

MEDIUM INFORMATION: *Medium:* Motion Picture; *Sound:* Spoken language; *Color:* No (black & white); *Length:* 148 min.; *Language(s) spoken:* Russian; *Language of subtitles:* English; *Film type:* 16 mm, Cinemascope.

AUTHORSHIP INFORMATION: *Producer(s):* Lenfilm; *Director(s):* Kozintsev, Grigori; Shapiro, I.; *Adaptor/*

translator(s): Kozintsev, Grigori; Pasternak, Boris; *Composer(s):* Shostakovich, Dmitri; Rabinovich, N. (w. Leningrad State Orch.); *Designer(s):* Ene, E.; Kropachev, G.; *Costume designer(s):* Virsaladze, S.; *Other personnel:* Gritsyus, I. (Photography); Makhankova, E. (Editor); Khutoryanski, B. (Sound); *Cast:* Smoktunovsky, Innokenti (Hamlet); Nazwanov, Michail (Claudius); Vertinskaya, Anastasia (Ophelia); Radzin-Szolkonis, Elza (Gertrude); Tolubyev, Yuri (Polonius); Erenberg, V. (Horatio); Oleksenko, S. (Laertes); Medvediev, V. (Guildenstern); Dmitriev, I. (Rosencrantz); Krevald, A. (Fortinbras); Kolpakov, V. (Gravedigger); Chekaeriskii, A. (Actor); Aren, R. (Actor); Berkun, Y. (Actor); Lauter, A. (Priest).

DISTRIBUTION & AVAILABILITY: *Publisher or responsible agency:* Lenfilm; British Lion; *Distributor:* COR, FNC, GLB*, *Copy location:* FOL; *Call or copy number:* MP 47; *Availability:* COR, Rental Standard $150, High School $100; FNC, Rental $100 + ; GLB* Apply.

Hamlet. Motion Picture/Recording

117. *Hamlet.*

DOCUMENT INFORMATION: *Country:* USA; *Year of release:* 1964; *Location of first showing:* Theatres throughout USA.

EDITION, HISTORY, CONTENTS, & EVALUATION: *Edition & history:* This famous but elusive version of *Hamlet* was recorded at the Lunt-Fontanne Theatre, New York City, on June 30 and July 1, 1964 during a regularly scheduled performance of the play. Directed by John Gielgud, the play came to New York City after a stormy interval in Toronto. The recording of the play was done by a technological system called "Electronovision," which involved several strategically deployed hidden cameras that transmitted impulses to a master camera. The production was then at once relayed to theatre audiences throughout America. This method, which allowed audiences to view New York theatre on home-town movie screens, where people had gathered especially for the occasion, was a kind of hybrid of live theatre and movie-going. It brought a glimpse of the ritual and glory of great theatre into middle America, but was doomed by encroaching technological advances that would make it harder and harder to entice audiences away from electronic home entertainment centers. *Contents & evaluation:* The trouble with an actor like Richard Burton is that he can never be totally bad. The unevenness of his performance is more than compensated for by its breathtaking power. This is not the introspective Hamlet of the romantics but a vigorous, brawling man with the gusto and appetite of a dock laborer. Thus, even with the poor quality of the recording, this production offers something special and unique. The insouciance, the devil-may-care swaggering, of Richard Burton

stands out even when he is surrounded by an excellent cast of supporting players. Dressed in rehearsal clothes (noting the presence of a costume designer in the credits, one realizes that there is casual chic attached to even these simple outfits), the actors tear into a virtually uncut conflation of Quarto and Folio versions. Hume Cronyn makes an unforgettable Polonius because of his intensity and utter concentration, while one has a rare chance to see Eileen Herlie as Gertrude again some sixteen years after her performance of that role in the Olivier *Hamlet*. But the driving force, like some wildly gyrating particle in space, remains Richard Burton. No actor in this century could so powerfully dominate the stage or screen. The gift of his resonant Welsh voice and uncanny charisma bring out a side of Hamlet deeply buried in the subtext—the irascible, wilful, petulant, yes, even dangerous, Hamlet that too easily eludes the grasp of lesser actors (KSR). *Audience:* Professional; *Supplementary materials:* Danziger, Marlies K. "Shakespeare in N.Y." *SQ* 15 (Fall 1964): 420; Davies, Brenda. "*Hamlet* USA 1964." *MFB* 39 [Aug. 1972]): 163-4; Sterne, Richard L. *John Gielgud Directs Richard Burton in* Hamlet: *A Journal of Rehearsals.* New York: Random House, 1967.

MEDIUM INFORMATION: *Medium:* 16 mm; 35 mm; *Sound:* Spoken language; *Color:* No (black & white); *Length:* 199 min.; *Language(s) spoken:* English; *Film type:* Electronovision.

AUTHORSHIP INFORMATION: *Producer(s):* Sargent, William, Jr.; Crown, Alfred W.; Cohen, Alexander H.; *Director(s):* Gielgud, John (Stage); Colleran, Bill (Filming); *Adaptor/translator(s):* Gielgud, John; *Designer(s):* Edwards, Ben; *Costume designer(s):* Greenwood, Jane; *Lighting designer(s):* Rosenthal, Jean (for Lunt-Fontanne Theatre); *Other personnel:* Pierce, Bruce (Editor); Fritch, James (Sound); Houseman, Carl (Video); LaForce, Charles (Technical Director); Glickman, Joel; Smith, Dan (Asst. Directors); Kilgore, J.E. (Prod. Supervisor); *Cast:* Burton, Richard (Hamlet); Cronyn, Hume (Polonius); Drake, Alfred (Claudius); Herlie, Eileen (Gertrude); Redfield, William (Guildenstern); Rose, George (1st Gravedigger); Voskovec, George (Player King); Coolidge, Philip (Voltemand); Gielgud, John (Ghost); Cullum, John (Laertes); Ebert, Michael (Francisco); Evans, Dillon (Osric/Reynaldo); Fowler, Clement (Rosencrantz); Garland, Geoff (Lucianus); Hughes, Barnard (Marcellus/Priest); Marsh, Linda (Ophelia); Milli, Robert (Horatio); Young, Frederick (Bernardo); Alexander, Hugh (Cornelius/Gravedigger/English Ambassador); Hetherington, John (Player Prologue); Culkin, Christopher (Player Queen); Sterne, Richard (A Gentleman); Giannini, Alex (A Messenger); Harz, Claude; Ragin, Gerome; Seff, Linda; Teitel, Carol (Supernumeraries).

DISTRIBUTION & AVAILABILITY: *Publisher or responsible agency:* Classic Cinemas; *Copy location:* LCM, FOL, LIN; *Call or copy number:* VCR 5 (FOL); TOFT,

NCOV86 (LIN); *Restrictions:* Archival use (restrictions may apply).

Hamlet. Video/Teleplay

118. *Hamlet at Elsinore.*

DOCUMENT INFORMATION: *Country:* GB; *Year of first showing:* 1964; *Location of first showing:* BBC TV. Transmitted 8:05 to 9:25 P.M., Sunday, 19 April 1964; USA, WNEW/TV, 8 to 11 P.M., Sunday, 15 Nov. 1964.

EDITION, HISTORY, CONTENTS, & EVALUATION: *Edition & history:* The main feature of this *Hamlet*, besides the excellent cast, is the setting, which is the actual castle in Elsinore, where the events depicted in Shakespeare's play may or may not have occurred in the tenth century. The play has been necessarily cut to under three hours time and the order of events is that set forth in the 1603 First Quarto. The production was done in cooperation with Danish television in a kind of semi-documentary form. For an excellent summary of the technical details, see Morris (q.v., below). Following some difficulties in finding a corporate sponsor, it was televised in the U.S.A. on both commercial (CBS) and PBS channels on 17 June 1964 and 15 November 1964 as a part of the Shakespeare Quatercentenary celebration. *Contents & evaluation:* The London *Times* critic (q.v., below) was highly favorable. Jo Maxwell Muller's Ophelia was "nastily" crazy; Alec Clunes's Polonius, the master of "a smoke screen of verbiage"; and Christopher Plummer's prince, the "Hamlet of Goethe and Coleridge, the gentle spirit broken by a burden too heavy for him to bear." The presence in the cast also of Michael Caine as Horatio, Robert Shaw as Claudius, Donald Sutherland as Fortinbras, all destined for fame in Hollywood (e.g., *The Eagle Has Landed*, *The Deep*, *M.A.S.H.*), plus stage actor Christopher Plummer and mime Lindsay Kemp (Player Queen) further embellishes the production. *Audience:* General use; *Supplementary materials:* "Gentle Spirit of Hamlet in Its Native Setting." *Times* 20 April 1964: 16f.; Gardner, Paul. "The Bard's Play." *NYT* 15 Nov. 1964: X 17 ("inventive TV theatre").

MEDIUM INFORMATION: *Medium:* Video; *Sound:* Spoken language; *Color:* No (black & white); *Length:* 80 min.; *Language(s) spoken:* English; *Video type:* BBC, 35mm.

AUTHORSHIP INFORMATION: *Producer(s):* Luke, Peter; *Director(s):* Saville, Philip; *Composer(s):* Bennett, Richard Rodney; Hollingsworth, John (Conductor); *Designer(s):* Thomsen, Poul Arnt; *Costume designer(s):* Harris, Olive; *Lighting designer(s):* Wright, Robert; *Other personnel:* Hillcoat, Christine (Make-up); Hobbs, William (Fights); Drerer, Ole (Technical Director); *Cast:* Caine, Michael (Horatio); Prowse, Peter (Marcellus); Goldie, Michael (Barnardo); Shaw, Robert (Claudius); Lovell, Dyson (Laertes); Clunes, Alec (Polonius); Tobin, June (Gertrude); Plummer, Christopher (Hamlet); Muller, Jo Maxwell (Ophelia); Calderisi, David (Rosencrantz); Wallis, Bill (Guildenstern); Swift, David (Player King); Kemp, Lindsay (Player Queen); Hobbs, William (Prologue); Berkoff, Steven (Lucianus); Sutherland, Donald (Fortinbras); Blanshard, Joby (Captain); Kinnear, Roy (Gravedigger); Carson, Charles (Priest); Locke, Philip (Osric).

DISTRIBUTION & AVAILABILITY: *Publisher or responsible agency:* BBC/Danmarks Radio; *Distributor:* BBC, *Copy location:* BBC; WNEW/TV.

Hamlet. Motion Picture/Derivative

119. *Hamile: The Tongo Hamlet.* [*Hamlet*].

DOCUMENT INFORMATION: *Country:* Ghana; *Year of release:* 1964; *Location of first showing:* Commonwealth Film Festival, 23 Sept. 1965 [?], National Film Theatre, London.

EDITION, HISTORY, CONTENTS, & EVALUATION: *Edition & history:* "The action of the play takes place in Tongo, the home of the Frafra People, who live in the far north of Ghana. The text is unaltered, except where it would not make sense in a Frafra community, or where an archaic word obscures the meaning. Based on the stage production as performed by the students of the University of Ghana School of Music and Drama" (P.R. handout). *Supplementary materials:* "Review." *VAR* 20.10 (1965).

MEDIUM INFORMATION: *Length:* 120 min.

AUTHORSHIP INFORMATION: *Producer(s):* De Graft, Joe (Theatre); Aryeetey, Sam (Film); *Director(s):* Bishop, Terry; *Composer(s):* Nketia, J.N.; *Lighting designer(s):* Fenuku, R.O.; *Other personnel:* Awoonor-Williams, George (Prod. Advisor); Adjeso, Egbert (Film Editor); Ampah, Steve (Dubbing Mixer); Wordie, Anson (Camera Operator); *Cast:* Akornor, Joe (Claudius); Kofi, Middleton-Mends (Hamlet); Abbequaye, Ernest (Ibrahim/Polonius); Sey, Frances (Gertrude); Yirenkyi, Mary (Habiba/Ophelia); Owusu, Martin (Horatio); Gadugan, Gad (Abdulai/Rosencrantz and Guildenstern); Akuffo-Lartey, Fred (Osric); Gharbin, Jacob (Marcellus); Okuampa, Ahuofe (1st Gravedigger); Arkhurst, Sandy (Ghost).

DISTRIBUTION & AVAILABILITY: *Publisher or responsible agency:* Ghana Film Industry Corp.

Hamlet. Video/Recording

120. *Hamlet.*

DOCUMENT INFORMATION: *Country:* USA; *Year of first showing:* 1964; *Location of first showing:* Delacorte Theatre, New York/CBS. Transmitted 8 to 11 P.M., Sunday 17 June 1964.

EDITION, HISTORY, CONTENTS, & EVALUATION: *Edition & history:* An ambitious recording of a stage performance at the New York City Shakespeare Festival outdoor theatre in Central Park. The exceptionally lengthy broadcast also coincided with the 400th anniversary of the year of Shakespeare's birth, an event marked by many commemorative activities. A full-page ad in the *Times* attested to the seriousness of the occasion. *Supplementary materials:* "Program." *NYT* 17 June 1964: 86.

MEDIUM INFORMATION: *Length:* 180 min.

AUTHORSHIP INFORMATION: *Producer(s):* Papp, Joseph; *Cast:* Ryder, Alfred (Hamlet); Harris, Julie (Ophelia); Da Silva, Howard (Claudius); Martin, Nan (Gertrude); Cotsworth, Staats; David, Clifford; Randolph, John; Klunis, Tom.

DISTRIBUTION & AVAILABILITY: *Publisher or responsible agency:* New York Shakespeare Festival.

Hamlet. Motion Picture/Cartoon

121. *Enter Hamlet.*

DOCUMENT INFORMATION: *Country:* USA; *Year of first showing:* 1965 [?]; 1967 [?]

EDITION, HISTORY, CONTENTS, & EVALUATION: *Edition & history:* An animated cartoon based on *Hamlet* and narrated by Maurice Evans. *Contents & evaluation:* "'Enter *Hamlet*' is a 10-minute animated sequence, the creation of Fred Mogubgub, based on 'To be or not to be.' The title refers to the stage direction . . . before Hamlet speaks. . . . Mogubgub deconstructs 'to be or not to be' by layering the familiar words with images often irrelevant to the sense of the lines but in puns parallel to Shakespeare's own art. Because each frame lasts only as long as each word, we perceive just how Evans holds a word or speeds over several. This is, in fact, an excellent means to observe sound. A demythifier, a bringer down of this famous speech to pop-culture level, wholly irreverent, 'Enter *Hamlet*' makes it possible to talk about 'to be' in ways different from any other" (Kliman, Bernice, "A Demythifying Approach to *Hamlet*," [Forthcoming in] *SFNL* 15.1 [Fall 1990]: n.p.). *Audience:* High school (grades 10-12); College and university; General use.

MEDIUM INFORMATION: *Medium:* Motion Picture; *Sound:* Spoken language; *Color:* Yes; *Length:* 4 min.; *Language(s) spoken:* English; *Film type:* 16mm.

AUTHORSHIP INFORMATION: *Producer(s):* Mogubgub, Fred; *Cast:* Evans, Maurice (Narrator).

DISTRIBUTION & AVAILABILITY: *Publisher or responsible agency:* Janus New Cinema; *Copy location:* FOL; *Call or copy number:* MP 12; *Distributor:* PYR.

Hamlet. Motion Picture/Scenes

122. *Opus.*

DOCUMENT INFORMATION: *Country:* GB; *Year of first showing:* 1967.

EDITION, HISTORY, CONTENTS, & EVALUATION: *Edition & history:* Of interest because this overview of the state of the arts in Great Britain in the 1960's includes a scene from the Royal Shakespeare Company production of *Hamlet* starring David Warner. *Supplementary materials:* BUFVC 4.

MEDIUM INFORMATION: *Sound:* Spoken language; *Color:* Yes; *Length:* 28 min.; *Film type:* 16mm.

AUTHORSHIP INFORMATION: *Director(s):* Hall, Peter; *Cast:* Warner, David.

DISTRIBUTION & AVAILABILITY: *Distributor:* CFL*.

Hamlet. Motion Picture/Recording

123. *Hamlet.*

DOCUMENT INFORMATION: *Country:* GB; *Year of release:* 1969.

EDITION, HISTORY, CONTENTS, & EVALUATION: *Edition & history:* This 1969 *Hamlet* originally was a stage production that received wide acclaim both in London and New York as well as on subsequent road shows in lesser cities. The film version, actually made for television, was produced at London's Roundhouse Theatre, a recycled railway locomotive shop. The damp walls, flickering candles, and dark ambience curiously capture the essence of Elsinore. *Contents & evaluation:* Few who saw Nicol Williamson act this *Hamlet* on stage will ever forget his riveting performance. Fearlessly committed to following his innermost intuitions about a character, regardless of stage conventions, Williamson, whether enacting a choleric Macbeth or a frenetic Hamlet, always brings dozens of surprises to the audience. He is the most physical of actors. Tall and even ungainly, awkward looking, he will more than any other actor, throw his entire body into a strenuous effort to capture thoughts in gestures and gestures in thoughts. He turns the 'To be or not to be' soliloquy into a gymnastics exercise. He is also very much the angry young Hamlet, after the vogue of the late Sixties when the fashion in London decreed rebellion against middle-class stuffiness. Signifying that corrupt and obsolete older generation that Hamlet rebelled against (and that today have become the targets for the Angry Young Men of the Sixties and Punks of the Eighties) were the totally sensuous and depraved Claudius (Anthony Hopkins) and Gertrude (Judy Parfitt) swinishly eating sticky things in bed while dogs snuggle up to them. More than most *Hamlet*s, this one managed to capture the flavor of its times. Done almost entirely in mid-shot and close-up, the film's technique even reinforces the concept of an era impatient with anything but the most closely examined truths of the human experience (KSR). *Audience:* College and university; General use; *Supplementary materials:* Litton, Glen. "Diseased Beauty in Tony Richardson's *Hamlet*." *LFQ* 4.2. [1976]:108-23; Mullin, Michael. "Tony Richardson's *Hamlet*: Script and Screen." *LFQ* 4.2. [1976]: 123-33.

MEDIUM INFORMATION: *Medium:* Motion Picture; *Sound:* Spoken language; *Color:* Yes; *Length:* 117 min.; *Film type:* 16mm.

AUTHORSHIP INFORMATION: *Producer(s):* Linder, Leslie; Rausahoff, Martin; *Director(s):* Richardson, Tony; *Composer(s):* Gowers, Patrick; *Designer(s):* Herbert, Jocelyn; *Other personnel:* Fisher, Gerry (Camera); Rees, Charles (Editing); *Cast:* Williamson, Nicol (Hamlet); Hopkins, Anthony (Claudius); Parfitt, Judy (Gertrude); Dignam, Mark (Polonius); Faithfull, Marianne (Ophelia); Pennington, Michael (Laertes); Jackson, G. (Horatio); Aris, Ben (Rosencrantz); Graham, Clive (Guildenstern); Gale, Peter (Osric); Livesey, Roger (Lucianus/ Gravedigger); Carney, John (Marcellus); Trenaman, John (Barnardo/Player/2nd Sailor); Chadwick, Robin (Francisco/Courtier/Sailor); Everett, Richard (Player Queen/ Courtier); Pack, Roger Lloyd (Reynaldo/Courtier/Player); Epphick (Captain/Courtier); Jarvis, Bill (Courtier); Collier, Ian (Priest); Tudor, Jennifer (Court Lady); Huston, Anjelica (Court Lady); Griffith, Mark (Messenger/Courtier).

DISTRIBUTION & AVAILABILITY: *Publisher or responsible agency:* A Woodfall Production/Columbia Pictures; *Distributor:* BUD, FMB*, KIT, WFC, FCM. *Copy location:* FOL (MP 46); *Call or copy number:* AFI-F6.2021; *Availability:* Rental 16mm, KIT, $60; INM, V, $79.95; FCM, V, $69.95.

Hamlet. Motion Picture/Documentaries

124. *Hamlet: The Trouble with Hamlet.* (Series: Explorations in Shakespeare, IV).

DOCUMENT INFORMATION: *Country:* Canada; *Year of release:* 1969.

EDITION, HISTORY, CONTENTS, & EVALUATION: *Edition & history:* Part four in a series of twelve 23-minute films made in 1969 by the Ontario Educational Communications Authority (see also numbers 18, 40,

65, 162, 257, 322, 465, 488, 555, 617 and 637). For full discussion of background, see number 18, above.

Contents & evaluation: A screening of this program and the one for *The Tempest* (see 617) has provided the basis for evaluating the entire series, which is now extremely difficult to locate in its entirety. The program opens with a background collage of photographs of war and death in the back ground, while in the foreground two artisans in work clothes discuss the life of Hamlet. The musical score is compelling and it soon becomes clear that the actors correspond to Horatio and the gravedigger, though at first the contemporaneity of it all makes the viewer wonder if the distributor has not sent the wrong print. Horatio is still telling the tale of Hamlet, as he was pledged to do by Hamlet's dying words. Creating a Horatio to tell Hamlet's story in contemporary dress is similar to Hyam Plutzik's 1961 narrative poem, *Horatio*. Meanwhile the actors play scenes from *Hamlet* in the foreground on a bare platform. Act three, scene one, which includes the "To be or not to be" soliloquy and Hamlet's confrontation with Ophelia is the centerpiece. In general the program stresses Camus' dictum: 'There is but one truly philosophical problem, and that is suicide.' The emphasis falls on Hamlet's existentialist dilemma. All of this is very stimulating, and even though the playing of the scenes suffers somewhat from miscasting, the overall imaginativeness puts the program in a class by itself when measured against other "educational" films. Script writer Hugh Webster deserves praise for turning out intellectually challenging material (KSR). *Audience:* College and university.

MEDIUM INFORMATION: *Medium:* Motion Picture; *Sound:* Spoken language; *Color:* Yes; *Length:* 23 min.; *Language(s) spoken:* English; *Film type:* 16mm.

AUTHORSHIP INFORMATION: *Producer(s):* Reis, Kurt; Moser, Ed; *Screenplay writer(s):* Webster, Hugh; *Composer(s):* Yanovsky, Zal; *Set designer(s):* Adeney, Chris; *Lighting designer(s):* Galbraith, Howard; *Cast:* Petchey, Briain (Hamlet); Webster, Hugh (Horatio); Burroughs, Jackie (Ophelia); Greenhalgh, Dawn (Gertrude); Dainard, Neil (Gravedigger [?]); Behrens, Bernard (Claudius); *Performance group(s):* Ontario Educational Communications/NBC Educational Enterprises.

DISTRIBUTION & AVAILABILITY: *Distributor:* CNU.

125. *Repetition chez Jean Louis Barrault.*

DOCUMENT INFORMATION: *Country:* France; *Year of release:* 196?.

EDITION, HISTORY, CONTENTS, & EVALUATION: *Edition & history:* A rehearsal of *Hamlet* on the stage of the Théâtre de France. *Supplementary materials:* BUFVC 5.

MEDIUM INFORMATION: *Sound:* Spoken language; *Length:* 19 min.; *Language(s) spoken:* French/English; *Film type:* 16mm.

AUTHORSHIP INFORMATION: *Director(s):* Hessens, Robert; *Cast:* Barrault, Jean Louis; Gilabert, Mme. Daste.

DISTRIBUTION & AVAILABILITY: *Distributor:* IFR*.

Hamlet. Video/Teleplay

126. *Hamlet.*

DOCUMENT INFORMATION: *Country:* GB; *Year of first showing:* 1970; *Country of first showing:* USA; *Location of first showing:* Hallmark Hall of Fame/NBC, Tuesday, 9 to 11 P.M., 17 Nov. 1970.

EDITION, HISTORY, CONTENTS, & EVALUATION: *Edition & history:* A drastically cut made-for-TV version, costumed in the Regency period. The program was prepared in London and on location at Raby Castle. Richard Chamberlain had also starred in *Hamlet* on the London stage prior to the making of this teleplay. *Contents & evaluation:* "Both Olivier and Chamberlain simplify Shakespeare's *Hamlet* a good deal, but both attempt, at the same time, to develop a new and integral pattern from the abundant richness of the original. Olivier tries to emphasize the tortured soul of Hamlet anguished as much by sexual revulsion, compounded by suppressed oedipal feelings, as by the terrible duty of revenge. Rosencrantz and Guildenstern, who help develop the political dimension of the play and the theme of ambition, could then be disposed of, although with them (as with Reynaldo) much of the spying motif is necessarily sacrificed, too. Chamberlain's passionate, idealistic Hamlet gains from the contrast with the toadying 'fellow students' and, by retaining them, the great 'What a piece of work is man' speech, which Olivier cuts is preserved. [. . .] One effect used by Chamberlain in I.v, where the ghost tells Hamlet the story of his murder, strongly suggests a major aspect of interpretation and is quite filmic in style. The Ghost leads Hamlet not along the ramparts of a castle, as in Olivier's version, but through the churchyard near the palace and stops at last in a gothic archway of what is apparently an old church. Between the figure of the Ghost and Hamlet can be seen an iron gate or railing, surmounted by a clearly delineated cross. As the Ghost eventually fades altogether from our view, the cross that stands between the two figures comes still more clearly and brilliantly into focus for a few moments. In the Nunnery Scene as Hamlet goes through the 'To be or not to be' soliloquy, Ophelia can be seen from time to time kneeling at a small altar to the right side of the screen (behind Hamlet's left shoulder). . . . Again, in the Prayer Scene, as Hamlet leaves Claudius to go to his mother's closet, the camera picks out in close-up a statue of the Madonna and Child. The Christian context thus seems far more important to Chamberlain's *Hamlet* than to

[the Olivier and Burton *Hamlet*s]" (Halio, Jay, "Three Filmed *Hamlet*s," *LFQ* 1.4 [1973]:317-18). *Audience:* General use; *Supplementary materials:* "TV Today [with still]." *NYT* 17 Nov. 1970: 70 [advertisement], 71.

MEDIUM INFORMATION: *Medium:* Video; *Sound:* Spoken language; *Color:* Yes; *Length:* 115 min.

AUTHORSHIP INFORMATION: *Producer(s):* Lemaire, George; Clarke, Cecil; *Director(s):* Wood, Peter; *Adaptor/translator(s):* Barton, John; *Composer(s):* Addison, John; *Designer(s):* Roden, Peter; *Cast:* Chamberlain, Richard (Hamlet); Redgrave, Michael (Polonius); Leighton, Margaret (Gertrude); Johnson, Richard (Claudius); Gielgud, John (Ghost); Madden, Ciaran (Ophelia); Stock, Nigel (Player); Bossington, Norman (Gravedigger); Bennett, Alan (Osric); Shaw, Martin (Horatio); Jones, Nicholas (Laertes); Laurenson, James (Rosencrantz); James, Godfrey (Marcellus); Brack, Philip (Barnardo); Oates, Robert (Francisco); Coleby, Robert (Fortinbras); Layne, Donald (Priest); Bourne, Helen; Belcher, David; Adams, Alan; Williams, Stephen; Barclay, D. (Players).

DISTRIBUTION & AVAILABILITY: *Publisher or responsible agency:* NBC Hallmark Hall of Fame; *Distributor:* FNC; *Availability:* Rental, 16mm, $100+.

Hamlet. Video/Documentary

127. *Hamlet* Revisited: *Approaches to* Hamlet.

DOCUMENT INFORMATION: *Country:* USA; *Year of first showing:* 1970; *Location of first showing:* N.E.T., Channel 13. Transmitted 14 Jan. 1970.

EDITION, HISTORY, CONTENTS, & EVALUATION: *Edition & history:* Sir John Gielgud shares his experiences as an actor by surveying the history of performances of *Hamlet*. *Contents & evaluation:* According to a reviewer, John Gielgud sat alone in an empty theatre and reviewed past history of *Hamlet* productions with actors Tom Courtenay, Brian Bedford, and Richard Chamberlain. Film clips of performances by Nicol Williamson, Maximilian Schell, Innokenti Smoktunovsky, and John Barrymore were also shown. *Audience:* General use; *Supplementary materials:* Gould, Jack. "TV: Appeal and Relevance of 'Hamlet'." *NYT* 15 Jan. 1970: 91.1).

MEDIUM INFORMATION: *Medium:* Video; *Sound:* Spoken language; *Color:* Yes; *Length:* 45 [?] min.; *Language(s) spoken:* English; *Video type:* Video.

AUTHORSHIP INFORMATION: *Producer(s):* Hobin, Ron; *Cast:* Gielgud, Sir John; Courtenay, Tom; Chamberlain, Richard; *Shown on film:* Williamson, Nicol; Schell, Maximilian; Smoktunovsky, Innokenti; Barrymore, John.

DISTRIBUTION & AVAILABILITY: *Publisher or responsible agency:* WNET, Channel 13; *Distributor:* Unknown.

Hamlet. Motion Picture/Derivative

128. *Heranca.*

DOCUMENT INFORMATION: *Country:* Brazil; *Year of release:* 1970.

EDITION, HISTORY, CONTENTS, & EVALUATION: *Edition & history:* "Based on the Shakespearean play." *Supplementary materials:* "Review." *Guia de Filmes,* 34 (July-Aug. 1971): 152; H&M 19.

MEDIUM INFORMATION: *Color* Yes; *Length:* 87 min.

AUTHORSHIP INFORMATION: *Director(s):* Candelas, Ozualdo R.; *Music:* Lona, Fernando; *Cast:* Cardoso, David (Omeleto); Fázio, Barbara (Mae de Omelete); Caçador, Rosalvo (Tio); Taricano, Américo (Polonio); Gouveia, Deoclides (Laerte); Maria, Zuleika (Otelia); Rayol, Agnaldo (Fortinbras).

DISTRIBUTION & AVAILABILITY: *Publisher or responsible agency:* Longfilm Produtora Cinematografica.

Hamlet. Video/Teleplay

129. *Hamlet.*

DOCUMENT INFORMATION: *Country:* GB; *Year of first showing:* 1972; *Location of first showing:* BBC-2. Transmitted 9:05 to 11:00 P.M., Saturday, 23 Sept. 1972.

EDITION, HISTORY, CONTENTS, & EVALUATION: *Edition & history:* The Prospect Theatre Company *Hamlet* adapted to television with superstar Ian McKellen in the title role. The PR blurb announced that "the special production for television retains the excitement of the stage production which was warmly received by audiences both at home and in five countries abroad" (*RT*). *Supplementary materials:* "Program." *RT* 23 Sept. 1972: 17.

MEDIUM INFORMATION: *Length:* 115 min.

AUTHORSHIP INFORMATION: Producer(s): Kulukundis, Eddie;*Director(s):* Giles, David; Chetwyn, Robert (Prospect Theatre); *Cast:* McKellen, Ian (Hamlet); Woodvine, John (Claudius); Brook, Faith (Gertrude); Fleetwood, Susan (Ophelia); Cairncross, James (Polonius); Pigott-Smith, Tim (Laertes/First Player); Wilton, Terence (Rosencrantz); Prebble, Simon (Guildenstern); Ashton, David (Francisco); Curry, Julian (Horatio); Preston, Duncan (Reynaldo); Pigot, Ian (Player Queen); O'Rourke, Stephen (Lucianus); Morley, Christopher (Fourth Player); Dougherty, Terence (Fifth Player).

DISTRIBUTION & AVAILABILITY: *Publisher or responsible agency:* BBC/Prospect Theatre; *Copy location:* Unavailable.

Hamlet. Motion Picture/Recording

130. *Hamlet.*

DOCUMENT INFORMATION: *Country:* Canada; *Year of release:* 1973.

EDITION, HISTORY, CONTENTS, & EVALUATION: *Edition & history:* "A complete version of Shakespeare's play adapted by a Toronto theatre group. The film was shot entirely with one camera during several different presentations. Certain parts of the text were transformed into song by George Taros and sung by the performers. Steven Bush, the director, initiated the modern adaptation of the great playwright's work" (*NCF*). *Audience:* General use; *Supplementary materials:* "Review," *NCF,* 21, vol 5. no.1 (Aug. 1973): 22.

MEDIUM INFORMATION: *Medium:* Motion Picture; *Sound:* Spoken language; *Color:* Yes; *Length:* 170 min.; *Language(s) spoken:* English; *Film type:* 16mm.

AUTHORSHIP INFORMATION: *Producer(s):* Crawley, F.R.; *Director(s):* Bush, Stephen; Bonniere, René; *Other personnel:* Leiterman, Douglas (Camera); McMillan, David (Sound); Crawley, Leonore (Manager).

DISTRIBUTION & AVAILABILITY: *Publisher or responsible agency:* Crawley Films, Ottawa, Canada; *Distributor:* CRW, *Copy location:* Not known; *Call or copy number:* LC #[PR 2807] 74-700810.

Hamlet. Motion Picture/Scenes

131. *Hamlet* 1.4; 5.1. (Series: The Shakespeare Series [IFB], II).

DOCUMENT INFORMATION: *Country:* Great Britain; *Year of release:* 1974.

EDITION, HISTORY, CONTENTS, & EVALUATION: *Edition & history:* The second in "The Shakespeare Series," films designed to introduce students to the general theme and atmosphere of a play (see also numbers 22, 164, 232, 326, 430, 467, 490, 510, 556, 601 and 619). This one includes excerpts from *Hamlet:* Hamlet's meeting with his father's ghost (1.4); and the gravedigger unearthing the skull of Yorick with Hamlet's celebrated meditation on death (5.1). This series, the "IFB," can easily be confused with "The Shakespeare Series" (BHE/BFA), which is a series of six abbreviated versions of the plays (see numbers 41, 228, 258, 323, 406, and 656). *Contents & evaluation:* Not seen. *Audience:* High school (grades 10-12);.

MEDIUM INFORMATION: *Medium:* Motion Picture; *Sound:* Spoken language; *Color:* Yes; *Length:* 10 min.; *Language(s) spoken:* English; *Film type:* 16mm; *Video type:* V, 3/4U (4 per cassette).

AUTHORSHIP INFORMATION: *Producer(s):* Seabourne, John; *Director(s):* Seabourne, Peter; *Cast:* Pennington, Michael; Suchet, David; Russell, William; Marsden, Roy.

DISTRIBUTION & AVAILABILITY: *Publisher or responsible agency:* Anvil film and recording group; *Distributor:* IFB, CNU, *Copy location:* FOL; *Call or copy number:* ISBN 0-8354-1576-7; FOL, MP 88; *Availability:* CNU, rental 16mm $8; IFB sale, 16mm, V, $175.

Hamlet. Video/Documentary

131.1 *Approaches to Hamlet.* (Series: History of Drama).

DOCUMENT INFORMATION: *Country:* USA; *Year of release:* 1975

EDITION, HISTORY, CONTENTS, & EVALUATION: *Edition & history: Contents & evaluation:* A highly praised documentary that features Prof. Daniel Seltzer, a distinguished actor and Shakespearean. It provides a brief history of Elizabethan and Jacobean drama as well as glimpses of different scenes and versions of *Hamlet.* Film clips of John Barrymore, Nicol Williamson and Laurence Olivier with an accompanying narrative by John Gielgud serve as a background for Seltzer's instructions to a young actor, played by Stephen Tate. *Supplementary materials:* Rev.: McLean, Andrew M. "Review." *SFNL* 4.2 (April 1980): 6. *Audience:* High school (grades 10-12); College and university.

MEDIUM INFORMATION: *Medium:* Video; *Sound:* Spoken language; *Color:* Yes; *Length:* 45 min.; *Language(s) spoken:* English; *Video type:* FFH (1987) b, v, $199; 3/4U $299; 16mm $695; Rental $75.

AUTHORSHIP INFORMATION: *Producer(s):* Mantell, Harold; *Cast:* Seltzer, Daniel; Tate, Stephen; Gielgud, John.

DISTRIBUTION & AVAILABILITY: *Distributor:* FFH, *Availability:* B, V, $149, 3.4U $249, rental $75.

Hamlet. Motion Picture/Interpretation

132. *Hamlet.*

DOCUMENT INFORMATION: *Country:* GB; *Year of release:* 1976.

EDITION, HISTORY, CONTENTS, & EVALUATION: *Edition & history:* Another of the Shakespeare films emanating from the group centering around Lindsay Kemp and his all-purpose band of theatre and cinema actors. Coronado later directed Kemp's 1984 *A Midsummer Night's Dream.* The chief innovative feature seems to be that Hamlet is played by a pair of twin actors to underscore the Prince's split personality (*BUFVC* 4). *Contents & evaluation:* Not seen. *Audience:* College and university.

MEDIUM INFORMATION: *Medium:* Motion Picture; *Sound:* Spoken language; *Color:* Yes; *Length:* 67 min.; *Language(s) spoken:* English; *Film type:* 16mm.

AUTHORSHIP INFORMATION: *Producer(s):* Royal College of Art, Dept. of Film and Television; *Director(s):* Coronado, Celestino; *Designer(s):* Coronado, Celestino; *Cast:* Crisp, Quentin; Mirren, Helen (Gertrude and Ophelia); Stanton, Barry; Sheybal, Vladek; Mayer, Anthony (Hamlet); Mayer, David (Hamlet).

DISTRIBUTION & AVAILABILITY: *Publisher or responsible agency:* Royal College of Art, Dept. of Film and Television; *Distributor:* CVF*, *Availability:* CVF*, rental (no known U.S. dist. in 1988).

Hamlet. Video/Documentaries

133. Hamlet *at the Guthrie: Costumes.*

DOCUMENT INFORMATION: *Country:* USA; *Year of release:* 1977.

EDITION, HISTORY, CONTENTS, & EVALUATION: *Edition & history:* Actress Pat Fraser describes the creation of costumes for the Guthrie production of *Hamlet.* Costume designer Carrie Robbins comments. *Audience:* Professional.

MEDIUM INFORMATION: *Medium:* Video; *Sound:* Spoken language; *Color:* Yes; *Length:* 20 min.; *Language(s) spoken:* English; *Video type:* 3/4U.

AUTHORSHIP INFORMATION: *Producer(s):* Guthrie Theatre; *Cast:* Fraser, Pat; Robbins, Carrie.

DISTRIBUTION & AVAILABILITY: *Publisher or responsible agency:* Guthrie Theatre; *Copy location:* LCL; *Call or copy number:* NCOX75-TOFT; *Availability:* Archive.

134. Hamlet *at the Guthrie: Properties.*

DOCUMENT INFORMATION: *Country:* USA; *Year of release:* 1977.

EDITION, HISTORY, CONTENTS, & EVALUATION: *Edition & history:* William Macey describes the creation of properties. Propmaster Michael Beery comments. *Audience:* Professional.

MEDIUM INFORMATION: *Medium:* Video; *Sound:* Spoken language; *Color:* Yes; *Length:* 17 min.; *Language(s) spoken:* English; *Video type:* 3/4U.

AUTHORSHIP INFORMATION: *Producer(s):* Guthrie Theatre; *Cast:* Macey, William; Beery, Michael.

DISTRIBUTION & AVAILABILITY: *Publisher or responsible agency:* Guthrie Theatre; *Copy location:* LCL; *Call or copy number:* NCOX75-TOF; *Availability:* Archive.

Hamlet. Video/Recording

135. *Hamlet.*

DOCUMENT INFORMATION: *Country:* Japan; *Year of release:* 1977.

EDITION, HISTORY, CONTENTS, & EVALUATION: *Edition & history:* A recording of what appears to be a Japanese version of *Hamlet* housed on videotape in the Netherlands Theatre Collection (NTI).

MEDIUM INFORMATION: *Length:* 185 min.

AUTHORSHIP INFORMATION: *Producer(s):* Toho productions.

DISTRIBUTION & AVAILABILITY: *Distributor:* NTI, *Copy location:* NTI; *Call or copy number:* 70014301 BDA.

Hamlet. Motion Picture/Recording

136. *Dogg's Troupe Hamlet.*

DOCUMENT INFORMATION: *Country:* GB; *Year of release:* 1977.

EDITION, HISTORY, CONTENTS, & EVALUATION: *Edition & history:* A recorded performance of Tom Stoppard's condensed version of *Hamlet. Supplementary materials:* BUFVC 4.

MEDIUM INFORMATION: *Color:* Yes; *Length:* 15 min.; *Film type:* 16mm.

AUTHORSHIP INFORMATION: *Director(s):* Berman, Ed; *Cast:* Gambia, Jane; Noble, Katina; Perry, John.

DISTRIBUTION & AVAILABILITY: *Distributor:* CVF*.

Hamlet. Motion Picture/Abridgment

137. *Hamlet.* (Series: The World of William Shakespeare).

DOCUMENT INFORMATION: *Country:* USA; *Year of release:* 1978.

EDITION, HISTORY, CONTENTS, & EVALUATION: *Edition & history:* One of seven educational films cooperatively made by Station WQED Pittsburgh, Carnegie-Mellon University and The Shakespeare Birthplace Trust, Stratford-upon-Avon (see also numbers 138, 330-1, 564-5, and 715). A companion film (138 below) to this one, ''The Time Is Out of Joint,'' offers a commentary on the play. Dr. Louis B. Wright, then director of the Folger Shakespeare Library, Washington, D.C., acted as consultant and script writer. Dr. Levi Fox, Director of the Shakespeare Birthplace Trust, Stratford-upon-Avon, England, also served as a special consultant. Jeffery Dench of the Royal Shakespeare Company is narrator, though curiously the films give no credits for the other actors. *Contents & evaluation:* Scenes from *Hamlet* appear on screen with a voiceover commentary making bridges. The production is first class in every way with excellent sets, costumes and impressive acting from an anonymous cast. The camera work is creative enough to allow for a traveling shot that closes in on Claudius at prayer to convey the sense of discovery and pursuit that drives Hamlet at that point in the action. Typically, in order to squeeze the play into so brief a period, whole chunks of speeches get cut. For example, very little is left of the ghost's lengthy first speech to Hamlet. On the other hand, this being an educational film, evidently the producers thought that those lacunae could be discussed in class. The color is muted but rich and the musical score exceptionally good. This series is in many ways more dramatically powerful and visually attractive than the BBC ''Shakespeare Plays.'' Highly recommended. *Audience:* High school (grades 10-12); *Supplementary materials: The World of William Shakespeare:* Hamlet: *The Time Is Out of Joint* (Teachers' Guide). Washington [D.C.]: NGS, 1978; McLean, Andrew. ''Educational Films.'' *SQ* 30 (Summer 1979): 416.

MEDIUM INFORMATION: *Medium:* Motion Picture; *Sound:* Spoken language; *Color:* Yes; *Length:* 35 min.; *Language(s) spoken:* English; *Film type:* 16mm; *Video type:* V, 3/4U.

AUTHORSHIP INFORMATION: *Producer(s):* Von Brauchitsch, M.; Cantini, Lisa; *Director(s):* Walsh, Bob; Clinton, Zilla; Hitch, Geoffrey; *Adaptor/translator(s):* Wright, Louis B.; Fowler, Elaine W.; *Designer(s):* Anderson, Cletus; *Set designer(s):* Matthews, William F.; *Costume designer(s):* Anderson, Barbara; *Lighting designer(s):* Brennecke, Alan; *Other personnel:* Stanton, David (Cameraman); Alper, Gary (Sound recordist); Buba, Pasquale (Film editor); Feil, Gerald (Special consultant).

DISTRIBUTION & AVAILABILITY: *Publisher or responsible agency:* National Geographic; *Distributor:* KAR, NGS; *Copy location:* FOL; *Call or copy number:* MP 94, FOL; LC PN1997. 78-700749; *Availability:* NGS, sale, 16mm, $353.50 (50268); V, $69.95 (51088); KAR, rental, $42+.

Hamlet. Motion Picture/Documentary

138. *The Time Is Out of Joint.* (Series: The World of William Shakespeare).

DOCUMENT INFORMATION: *Country:* USA; *Year of release:* 1978.

EDITION, HISTORY, CONTENTS, & EVALUATION: *Edition & history:* Companion film to *Hamlet* (see 137 above). For commentary, see 137. *Contents & evaluation:* Not seen. According to blurbs, the film offers a gloss on *Hamlet* that explores the medieval setting and the political context for Hamlet's misfortunes. If it has the same excellence as the other NGS films, it is well worth watching. *Audience:* High school (grades 10-12); *Supplementary materials:* McLean, Andrew. ''Educational Films.'' *SQ* 30 (Summer 1979): 416. (Summarizes film's action.).

MEDIUM INFORMATION: *Medium:* Motion Picture; *Sound:* Spoken language; *Color:* Yes; *Length:* 20 min.; *Language(s) spoken:* English; *Film type:* 16mm; *Video type:* V, 3/4U.

AUTHORSHIP INFORMATION: *Producer(s):* Walsh, Bob; Clinton, Zilla; *Director(s):* Walsh, Bob; *Screenplay writer(s):* Wright, Louis B.; Fowler, Elaine W.; *Designer(s):* Anderson, Cletus; *Costume designer(s):* Anderson, Barbara; *Lighting designer(s):* King, Greg; *Other personnel:* Newbury, Sam; Seamans, Joe (Cameramen); Butler, John (Sound recordist); Stanton, David (Film editor).

DISTRIBUTION & AVAILABILITY: *Publisher or responsible agency:* National Geographic; *Distributor:* KAR, NGS, *Copy location:* FOL; *Call or copy number:* MP 93, FOL; LC PR2807. 78-700753; *Availability:* NGS, sale, 16mm, $220.50 (50327); V, $59.95 (51223); KAR, rental, $32+.

Hamlet **Video/Adaptation**

138.1 *Amleto.*

DOCUMENT INFORMATION: *Country:* Italy; *Year of first showing:* 1978; *Location of first showing:* RAI/Radio Television Italy.

EDITION, HISTORY, CONTENTS, & EVALUATION: *Edition & history:* Filmed in and transmitted from RAI studios, 22 April 1978. The original production was performed in September 1975 at the Teatro Metastasio di Prato.

MEDIUM INFORMATION: *Sound:* Spoken language; *Color:* No (black & white); *Length:* 63 min.

AUTHORSHIP INFORMATION: *Producer(s):* Carlotto, R.; *Director(s):* Bene, Carmelo; *Composer(s):* Zito, L.; *Cast:* Vincenti, Alfiero; Bene, Carmelo; Boucher, Jean Paul; Lero, Franco; Baroni, Paolo; Mazzanote, Daniela Silverio; Javicoli, Susanna; Bosisio, Luca; Nobecourt, M. Agnes; Morante, Laura; Mancinelli, Lydia; Cinieri, Cosimo.

DISTRIBUTION & AVAILABILITY: *Publisher or responsible agency:* RAI (Radio Television Italy); *Copy location:* RAI.

Hamlet. **Video/Documentary**

139. *Cleavon Little as Hamlet on Joseph Papp and the Public.*

DOCUMENT INFORMATION: *Country:* USA; *Year of first showing:* 1979.

EDITION, HISTORY, CONTENTS, & EVALUATION: *Edition & history:* Excerpts from *Hamlet* appear as a part of this program about Joseph Papp's New York Shakespeare theatre. *Audience:* General use.

MEDIUM INFORMATION: *Medium:* Video; *Sound:* Spoken language; *Color:* Yes; *Length:* 30 min.; *Language(s) spoken:* English; *Video type:* 3/4U.

AUTHORSHIP INFORMATION: *Producer(s):* WNET/13; *Cast:* Little, Cleavon; Papp, Joseph.

DISTRIBUTION & AVAILABILITY: *Publisher or responsible agency:* WNET/13; *Distributor:* WNET/13, *Copy location:* LCL; *Call or copy number:* NCOX 129; *Availability:* Archive.

Hamlet. **Video/Teleplay**

140. *Hamlet.* (Series: The Shakespeare Plays).

DOCUMENT INFORMATION: *Year of first showing*: 1980; *Location of first showing(s):* BBC, London; PBS Stations, USA, 10 Nov. 1980.

EDITION, HISTORY, CONTENTS, & EVALUATION: *Edition & history:* The production was shot at the BBC Studio 1 in one week from 31 January to 8 February 1980. According to the BBC account, Director Rodney Bennett, primarily a television director not a Shakespearean, teamed up with designer Don Homfray to make the sets as ambiguously defined as Hamlet's own perception of the nature of reality. Quite deliberately they avoided the naturalism that is so often identified with television by enclosing the huge sound stage with a circular ramp that made distances almost impossible to judge. Walls and even floors became equally amorphous. Moreover since *Hamlet* is itself a dark play, there was an effort to re-create visually a sense of that darkness. The star of the cast, Derek Jacobi, brought a refreshing note to the rehearsals by confessing that he had no theory about how to interpret the role of the prince. Instead Jacobi wanted to feel his way through the role to bring out those aspects of Hamlet that he felt within himself. Thus the face of Hamlet is ever changing (See Fenwick, Henry, *Hamlet*, BSP 17-29). *Contents & evaluation:* ''The BBC-TV *Hamlet* was one of the better productions of this series. While we have been subjected to a *Romeo and Juliet* that fares badly beside Zeffirelli's film and a *Tempest* that was too obviously a low-budget job, these productions have been relatively straightforward and usually well acted. Those who object to their lack of innovation tend to forget the bizarre fiascos of Stratford, Connecticut's Civil War *Troilus*, Barton's *Richard II*, and Brustein's Spaceship *Macbeth*—the garbage unloaded upon us in the 60's and early 70's when Shakespeare was too much 'our contemporary.' BBC-TV remains a vehicle for acting, as U.S. TV is not. BBC-TV's *Hamlet* brought the spoken verse to our ears, as Papp's productions seldom do. And, BBC-TV's *Hamlet* brought some questions with it. A *Hamlet* that did not would not be *Hamlet*. . . . The major problem with this production, as with many of the other BBC-TV versions of the plays, was that this was obviously a studio production. . . . Were shooting schedule and budget so tight that BBC-TV could not go on location to the churchyard at Holy Trinity Church in Stratford? As it was, we got a cut-down scene, sixty lines and one gravedigger excised in the American broadcast version" (Coursen, H.R., "*Hamlet*," *SFNL* 5.2 [1981]: 5+). "Derek Jacobi, whose resourcefulness cannot be overstated, pours energy into a hyped-up Hamlet who sometimes resembles John McEnery's manic-depressive Mercutio in the Zeffirelli *Romeo and Juliet*. After a splurge of crude Hamlets, hippie Hamlets, and rebellious Hamlets, Jacobi returns to the old-fashioned neurotic Hamlet of the nineteenth century. The neuroticism, however, includes a tinge of feline hostility not always pleasant to contemplate. His sardonic applause for the King and Queen in I. ii., his effeminate curtsy to the players at Elsinore, his scathing verbal aggression to Ophelia—these may make the audience wonder what happened to the 'sweet' Prince Horatio bids farewell to. Is it that Jacobi's Hamlet comes too close on the heels of his Richard II? It's hard not to see a petulant Richard II struggling to emerge from inside a Hamlet, who is, of course, a far more complex figure" (KSR, "*Hamlet* and the Five Plays of Season Three," *SQ* 32.3 [1981]: 396). *Audience:* General use; *Supplementary materials:* Kliman, Bernice. "The BBC *Hamlet*." *HS* 4.1-2 (1982) 99-105; Videocassette (25 min.) from "Shakespeare in Perspective" series with Clive James as lecturer available from BBC* and FNC (see 142 for description).

MEDIUM INFORMATION: *Medium:* Video; *Sound:* Spoken language; *Color:* Yes; *Length:* 210 min.; *Language(s) spoken:* English; *Video type:* B, V, 3/4U.

AUTHORSHIP INFORMATION: *Producer(s):* Messina, Cedric; *Director(s):* Bennett, Rodney; *Adaptor/translator(s):* Shallcross, Alan; *Composer(s):* Simpson, Dudley; Lloyd-Jones, David; *Designer(s):* Homfray, Don; *Costume designer(s):* Kronig, Barbara; *Lighting designer(s):* Barclay, Sam; *Other personnel:* Barry, B.H. (Fight Arranger); Ancock, Jeremy (Prod. Asst.); Reeves, Jill (Director's Asst.); Lowden, Fraser (Unit Manager); Tyler, James (Mime Music); Wilders, John (Literary Consultant); Meager, Pam (Make-up); Anthony, Chick (Sound); Atkinson, Jim (Camera); Coward, Shirley (Vision Mixer); Hillier, David (Editing); *Cast:* Jacobi, Derek (Hamlet); Bloom, Claire (Gertrude); Porter, Eric (Polonius); Stewart, Patrick (Claudius); Allen, Patrick (Ghost); James, Emrys (Player); Ward, Lalla (Ophelia); Swann, Robert (Horatio); Robb, David (Laertes); Baines, Christopher (Francisco); Padden, Niall (Bernardo); Humpoletz, Paul (Marcellus); Humphry, John (Voltemand); Sterland, John (Cornelius); Mason, Raymond (Reynaldo); Hyde, Jonathan (Rosencrantz); Bateman, Geoffrey (Guildenstern); Kemp, Jason (Player Queen); Beevers, Geoffrey (Lucianus); Homewood, Bill (Mime

King); Richards, Peter (Mime Queen); McGinity, Terence (Mime Murderer); Burroughs, Peter; Fell, Styart (Players); Charleson, Ian (Fortinbras); Meaden, Dan (Captain); Blair, Iain (Sailor); Jessup, Reginald (Messenger); Wylton, Tim (First Gravedigger); Benson, Peter (Second Gravedigger); Poole, Michael (Priest); Gale, Peter (Osric); Henry, David (English Ambassador).

DISTRIBUTION & AVAILABILITY: *Publisher or responsible agency:* BBC/TLF; *Distributor:* AVP, UIO, KSU, BBC*, *Copy location:* UVM; *Availability:* AVP, sale, all formats $450 (1987); Rental UIO V (72317H), 3/4U (70317V) $27.00; KSU (1-5 days) $33.75; BBC*, 16mm or V, apply.

Hamlet. Video/Teleplay

140.1. *Hamlet.*

DOCUMENT INFORMATION: *Country:* GB/France.

EDITION, HISTORY, CONTENTS, & EVALUATION: *Edition & history:* Identical to entry #140 above except that it has been given French subtitles. Available in archives, see below.

MEDIUM INFORMATION: *Language of subtitles:* French.

DISTRIBUTION & AVAILABILITY: *Copy location:* VAA; *Call or copy number:* THE 1.18.

Hamlet. Video/Recording

141. *Hamlet.*

DOCUMENT INFORMATION: *Country:* Netherlands; *Year of release:* 1980.

EDITION, HISTORY, CONTENTS, & EVALUATION: *Edition & history:* A video recording of a *Hamlet* production at the Footsbarn Theatre, Amsterdam, Netherlands made as a part of the "Festival of Fools," in June 1980. Stored at the Nederlands Theatre Instituut, Amsterdam. *Contents & evaluation:* Not seen.

MEDIUM INFORMATION: *Medium:* Video; *Sound:* *Color:* Yes; *Length:* 120 min. [?]); *Language of subtitles:* Dutch [?].

AUTHORSHIP INFORMATION: *Producer(s):* Footsbarn Theatre.

DISTRIBUTION & AVAILABILITY: *Publisher or responsible agency:* Footsbarn; *Copy location:* NTI; *Call or copy number:* 700107101 BDA; *Restrictions:* NTI Archive.

Hamlet. **Video/Documentary**

142. *Hamlet.* (Series: Shakespeare in Perspective).

DOCUMENT INFORMATION: *Country:* GB; *Year of release:* 1980.

EDITION, HISTORY, CONTENTS, & EVALUATION: *Edition & history:* The "Shakespeare in Perspective" series was made to accompany the BBC/Time Life Inc. "The Shakespeare Plays" series. For an overview and description of the series, see number 44, above. *Contents & evaluation:* In this unit, journalist Clive James gives what is in my view the best lecture of the eight in the series. Perhaps it is not so much what he says as how he says it that impresses the viewer. Speaking at first from a cloistered courtyard of Pembroke College, Cambridge, James highlights the university background to *Hamlet* and compares his own love for Cambridge to Hamlet's devotion to Wittenberg. To James, Horatio is the Don who never left Wittenberg; and Hamlet, the reluctant alumnus who wishes that he could have stayed on in the university rather than being turned out into the world. In this way Mr. James strongly identifies with Hamlet. He believes that all of Shakespeare's characters are "aspects of himself." In a side swipe at the anti-Stratfordians who think Shakespeare too ignorant to have written the plays, James claims that Shakespeare's university was the theatre. (One is reminded of Melville's Ishmael for whom the whale ship was a Harvard and Yale.) There are shots of Berkeley castle, which might have made a good model for Elsinore. At Elsinore, Hamlet's imagination brings about a kind of impotence. "He loses his mirth and the world with it." The program gradually shifts into the history of *Hamlet* in performance. There are stills of the great Hamlets from Betteron and Garrick to Forbes-Robertson and Olivier. There is an interior shot of the Theatre Royal in Drury Lane, and of James's office in London's Fleet street, in which he poses the question that he thinks *Hamlet* raises so profoundly: "Is life worth living?" He of course answers affirmatively. Along the way one has listened to an energetic, straightforward, "man to man," believable commentary devoid of affectation or pretentiousness. Mr. James has not only read *Hamlet* but lived it. And that has made all the difference (KSR).

MEDIUM INFORMATION: *Medium:* Video; *Sound:* Spoken language; *Color:* Yes; *Length:* 25 min.; *Language(s) spoken:* English; *Video type:* 3/4U, V.

AUTHORSHIP INFORMATION: *Producer(s):* Poole, Victor; *Director(s):* Wilson, David; *Other personnel:* Wyatt, John (Camera); Boyd, Michel (Editor); Hore, John; Bond, Rodney (Sound); Bird, Peter (Videotape editor); Friedman, Liz (Graphics); Bright, Barbara (Prod. asst.); *Cast:* James, Clive (Commentator).

DISTRIBUTION & AVAILABILITY: *Publisher or responsible agency:* BBC; *Distributor:* BBC*, FNC; *Availability:* Double cassette (w. *Rom.*), Rental $50; Quad cassette (w. *Rom., JC, Mac.*), Rental $75.

Hamlet. **Film/Excerpt**

143. *Theatre in Poland.*

DOCUMENT INFORMATION: *Country:* Poland; *Year of release:* 1981.

EDITION, HISTORY, CONTENTS, & EVALUATION: *Edition & history:* A program of Polish theatre that includes an excerpt from a mime theatre production of *Hamlet. Supplementary materials:* BUFVC 5.

MEDIUM INFORMATION: *Sound:* Spoken language; *Color:* Yes; *Length:* 23 min.; *Film type:* 16mm.

AUTHORSHIP INFORMATION: *Producer(s):* Waller, Albert; *Director(s):* Moszczuk, Stanislaw; *Cast:* Wroclaw Mime Theatre.

DISTRIBUTION & AVAILABILITY: *Distributor:* PCI*.

Hamlet. **Motion Picture/Documentary**

144. *Hamlet Act.*

DOCUMENT INFORMATION: *Country:* USA; *Year of filming:* 1982; *Year of release:* 1982.

EDITION, HISTORY, CONTENTS, & EVALUATION: *Edition & history:* Made as an experimental *avant-garde,* post-modernist, film at the University of Wisconsin-Milwaukee. Its visual exploration of epistemological puzzles in *Hamlet* is analogous to verbal explorations in Tom Stoppard's *Rosencrantz and Guildenstern Are Dead. Contents & evaluation:* "The title of Robert Nelson's new film, based on Joseph Chang's remarkable screen-'play,' is ambiguous; the work itself is ambitious, indeed a considerable challenge to our thinking about the powerful filmic impression of reality which is in fact not real but constructed. Nelson develops Chang's scripted reflections on the film process and shows us the construction of an 'act' based on a theatre text which is structured as performances-within-performances-within-a-performance. . . . As a manifestation of the post-structuralist era, Nelson's film is designed to explore its own process by allegorizing the most self-consciously metadramatic scene in Shakespeare's play—Hamlet's encounter with the Players. The film opens with the film crew in a hallway of the University of Wisconsin-Milwaukee film department getting ready for the first take; the subtitle reads: 'Elsinore. Enter the Players.' The players enter into a kind of rehearsal space, Elsinore's Actors' Studio, and it reminds me of those ugly factories in which German film directors in the late '70s staged their revisionary Shakespeare productions (e.g., Peter Zadek's 1977

Hamlet in Bochum). . . . Nelson's film experiment goes several steps further, since it involves the spectator in a series of dialectical games acted out between seemingly incompatible forms of mediation: theatre rehearsal/film, body/screen, film image/'live' video. But the question of mediation, or representation itself, is what is at stake, and the production of images is here directly related to the problematics of the positionality of the actors in the film as well as of the producers of the film. What fascinates me is the circuitous struggle of the performers/producers with the 'editing' of their actions, with the technology of film-making and the various disruptions, the cuts, and re-takes that become part of the film's discourse . . . we see [Hamlet] shout his angry words not at the imagery of murder, but at his own video-image, at the pale face that is his own shadow. . . . The play is the thing by which we are deceived" (Birringer, Johannes, "Rehearsing the Mousetrap: Robert Nelson's *Hamlet Act*," *SFNL* 9.1 [1984]: 1 +). *Audience:* College and university; Professional.

MEDIUM INFORMATION: *Medium:* Motion Picture; *Sound:* Silent; *Color:* No (black & white); *Length:* 21 min.; *Film type:* 16 mm.

AUTHORSHIP INFORMATION: *Director(s):* Nelson, Robert; *Adaptor/translator(s):* Chang, Joseph; *Cast:* Blau, Dick (Hamlet); Fischer, Dave (Player); Whitney, Bob (Polonius); *Performance group(s):* Univ. of Wisconsin-Milwaukee Film Department.

DISTRIBUTION & AVAILABILITY: *Publisher or responsible agency:* Univ. of Wisconsin-Milwaukee Film Department; *Distributor:* FMC, *Copy location:* FOL; *Availability:* Rental $50, 16mm.

Hamlet. Video/Documentary

145. *Hamlet: Rehearsing Hamlet.*

DOCUMENT INFORMATION: *Country:* USA; *Year of first showing:* 1982; *Location of first showing:* ABC television.

EDITION, HISTORY, CONTENTS, & EVALUATION: *Edition & history:* An ABC News closeup documentary on the New York Shakespeare Festival production of *Hamlet. Contents & evaluation:* Fascinating commentary as Joseph Papp coaches Diane Venora for her role as Hamlet in the New York production. There is a great deal of close-in analysis of the actress' hopes, fears and aspirations as she, a woman, undertakes the daunting task of playing Hamlet. Papp supports her every inch of the way. Interesting comments as well by other members of the company, such as costumer Theoni V. Aldredge. *Audience:* Professional; General use; *Supplementary materials:* Kerr, Walter. "This Boyish Princeling Is an Unpersuasive Hamlet." *NYT* 12 Dec. 1982: H3.

MEDIUM INFORMATION: *Medium:* Video; *Sound:* Spoken language; *Color:* Yes; *Length:* 54 min.; *Language(s) spoken:* English; *Video type:* V.

AUTHORSHIP INFORMATION: *Producer(s):* ABC Video Enterprises; *Director(s):* Charlson, Carl (ABC); *Composer(s):* Shawn, Alan; *Lighting designer(s):* Clifton, Chuck; *Cast:* Papp, Joseph; Venora, Diane (Hamlet); Sheridan, Jamey (Bernardo); Cromwell, James (Horatio); Pearthree, Pippa (Ophelia); Gunton, Bob (Claudius); Widdoes, Kathleen (Gertrude); Westenberg, Robert (Laertes); Sisto, Rocco (Osric); Walsh, J.T. (Marcellus); McNaughton, Stephen (Francisco); Hamlin, George (Ghost/Player King); Hall, Joseph (Polonius).

DISTRIBUTION & AVAILABILITY: *Publisher or responsible agency:* ABC Video Enterprises; *Copy location:* LCL, FOL; *Call or copy number:* NCOX 319 (LCL); VCR (FOL); *Availability:* Archive.

Hamlet. Video/Documentary

146. *The Tortured Mind.* (Series: Shakespeare Video Workshop Series).

DOCUMENT INFORMATION: *Country:* GB; *Year of release:* 1982.

EDITION, HISTORY, CONTENTS, & EVALUATION: *Edition & history:* According to *BUFVC* catalog this is "an examination of the mind under stress in four tragedies based on the New Shakespeare company workshops performed at the Roundhouse [a London theatre]." *Audience:* High school (grades 10-12); College and university; *Supplementary materials:* BUFVC 30.

MEDIUM INFORMATION: *Medium:* Video; *Sound:* Spoken language; *Color:* Yes; *Length:* 60 min.; *Language(s) spoken:* English; *Video type:* V, B.

AUTHORSHIP INFORMATION: *Producer(s):* Hardy, Noel; *Director(s):* Hardy, Noel.

DISTRIBUTION & AVAILABILITY: *Publisher or responsible agency:* Lloyds Bank; *Distributor:* TWC, CFL*; *Availability:* TWC, B (MML106B-K4), V (MML106V-K4), $80 .

Hamlet. Motion Picture/Excerpt

147. *To Be or Not To Be.*

DOCUMENT INFORMATION: *Country:* USA; *Year of release:* 1983.

EDITION, HISTORY, CONTENTS, & EVALUATION: *Edition & history:* A remake of the Ernst Lubitsch 1942 film of the same title. *Supplementary materials:* Even the great Mel Brooks cannot quite recreate the sparkle of the Jack Benny original, though this is an amusing film, well worth viewing.

MEDIUM INFORMATION: *Length:* 108 min.

AUTHORSHIP INFORMATION: *Producer(s):* Brooks, Mel; *Director(s):* Johnson, Alan; *Cast:* Brooks, Mel; Bancroft, Anne; Matheson, Tim.

DISTRIBUTION & AVAILABILITY: *Distributor:* FNC, CWF, *Copy location:* LCM; *Call or copy number:* VBC 7786-7787; *Availability:* CWF, 16mm, rental $80; FNC, apply.

Hamlet. Video/Interpretation

148. *Den Tragiska Historien om Hamlet, Priz av Danmark.* [*Hamlet, Prince of Denmark*].

DOCUMENT INFORMATION: *Country:* Sweden; *Year of first showing:* 1984; *Country of first showing:* Swedish TV.

EDITION, HISTORY, CONTENTS, & EVALUATION: *Edition & history:* Made for Swedish television, broadcast on SVT 1 in 1984 and aired in the United States on February 7, 1987 by WYNC-TV. Filmed in 16mm for television. *Contents & evaluation:* "[The film] carves out its own well deserved place in the select company of artists who interpret Shakespeare through visual media" (Kliman, *SFNL*, 11.2 [1987]:1 +); Kliman, *HFTAP* 202-24. *Audience:* College and university; General use.

MEDIUM INFORMATION: *Medium:* Video; *Sound:* Spoken language; *Color:* Yes; *Length:* 160 min.; *Language(s) spoken:* Swedish; *Language of subtitles:* English; *Film type:* 16mm; *Video type:* V.

AUTHORSHIP INFORMATION: *Producer(s):* Swedish Television; *Director(s):* Lyth, Ragnar; *Adaptor/translator(s):* Mark, Jan; *Other personnel:* Olsson, John (Photography); *Cast:* Skarsgaard, Stellan (Hamlet); Malm, Mona (Gertrude); Lindquist, Frej (Claudius); Wallgren, Pernella (Ofelia); Lindberg, Sven (Polonius); Ekborg, Dan (Laertes); Eggers, Per (Oratio); Bolme, Tomas (Rosencrantz); Brost, Johannes (Gyldenstern); Norgaard, Dag (Fortinbras); Rundquist, Mikael (Osric).

DISTRIBUTION & AVAILABILITY: *Publisher or responsible agency:* NET; *Distributor:* NET.

149. *Understanding Shakespeare: Hamlet.*

DOCUMENT INFORMATION: *Country:* GB; *Year of release:* 1984.

EDITION, HISTORY, CONTENTS, & EVALUATION: *Edition & history:* An educational film designed for secondary students. A shortened version (100 min.) of *Hamlet* is accompanied by a workshop run by RSC director Ron Daniels. A 42-page booklet also is furnished with the video. (See *BUFVC* 14). *Audience:* High school (grades 10-12), college; *Supplementary materials:*

Booklet with critical assessment by Mike Afford accompanies program.

MEDIUM INFORMATION: *Medium:* Video; *Sound:* Spoken language; *Color:* Yes; *Length:* 140 min.; *Language(s) spoken:* English; *Video type:* V,B.

AUTHORSHIP INFORMATION: *Producer(s):* Schofield & Sims; *Cast:* Jarvis, Martin (Presenter); Culwick, Marc; Parker, Nat.

DISTRIBUTION & AVAILABILITY: *Publisher or responsible agency:* SSV*, EAV (1VH 8844 VHS) $70.

Hamlet. Video/Derivative

150. *Englishman Abroad.*

DOCUMENT INFORMATION: *Country:* GB; *Year of release:* 1984.

EDITION, HISTORY, CONTENTS, & EVALUATION: *Edition & history:* Only tangentially related to *Hamlet* in that the acting troupe in Moscow is playing *Hamlet* when Guy Burgess, the celebrated English spy, appears in the star's dressing room. Transmitted in 1985 on U.S. public television. *Supplementary materials:* BUFVC 4.

MEDIUM INFORMATION: *Color:* Yes; *Length:* 60 min.; *Video type:* Not known.

AUTHORSHIP INFORMATION: *Director(s):* Schlesinger, John; *Cast:* Bates, Alan; Browne, Coral.

DISTRIBUTION & AVAILABILITY: *Distributor:* BBC*.

Hamlet. Video/Documentary

151. *Shakespeare: Hamlet: Workshops I and II.* (Series: Open University Film Library).

DOCUMENT INFORMATION: *Country:* GB; *Year of release:* 1985.

EDITION, HISTORY, CONTENTS, & EVALUATION: *Edition & history:* One of several programs prepared for the Open University television programs in Great Britain. Not seen in the U.S. According to the *BUFVC* catalog, each program features a director leading one of the actors through his/her role. In this program, director John Russell Brown works with actor David Yelland as Hamlet. *Audience:* College and university; Professional; *Supplementary materials:* BUFVC 6.

MEDIUM INFORMATION: *Medium:* Video; *Sound:* Spoken language; *Color:* Yes; *Length:* 24 min. (each workshop); *Language(s) spoken:* English; *Video type:* V,B.

AUTHORSHIP INFORMATION: *Producer(s):* Hoyle, David; *Cast:* Brown, John Russell (Dir.); Yelland, David (Hamlet).

DISTRIBUTION & AVAILABILITY: *Publisher or responsible agency:* BBC Open University; *Distributor:* GSV*; *Copy location:* BBC; *Availability:* Available in U.K. only.

Hamlet. **Video/Abridgment**

151.1. *Hamlet by William Shakespeare* (Series: Classics on Video).

DOCUMENT INFORMATION: *Country:* USA; *Year of release:* 1985.

EDITION, HISTORY, CONTENTS, & EVALUATION: *Edition & history:* This could be called the "Condo" *Hamlet* since it seems to have been filmed on the grounds of the Valeria Condominiums in White Plains, New York. Essentially it is a video-ized set of crib notes for students who find *Cliff's Notes* too challenging. It pauses every few minutes to ask inane questions about the play, and assaults the text not only with interpolated commentary but also with amazing distortions of Shakespeare's language. *Evaluation:* Anyone who knows Shakespeare's tragedy will find this production either awfully funny, or just awful, depending on the mood he/she is in. It would be difficult to say who are the worst actors. They are all sublimely and spectacularly incompetent, almost beyond belief, except possibly for Claudius who stands out like a searchlight at night in this ocean of malfeasance. Hamlet saws the air, Ophelia speaks with a nasal whine, and Laertes looks terrified. To watch it is to risk brain damage (KSR).

MEDIUM INFORMATION: *Sound:* Spoken language; *Color:* Yes; *Length:* 40 min.; *Video type:* V.

AUTHORSHIP INFORMATION: *Producer(s):* Cronin, James; *Director:* Fisher, Douglas; *Screenplay:* Hamma, Robert; *Costumes:* Wiodarski, Sandra Scenario; *Cast:* Riley, Wardjames (Hamlet); Gallagher, Daniel (Horatio); Pizzuro, Lauren (Ophelia); Gordon, John (Claudius); Garcia-Reynart, Prudence (Gertrude); Blais, Frederick (Polonius); Benner, Timothy (Laertes); Reisman, Mark; Ribreau, Daniel (Gravediggers)

DISTRIBUTION & AVAILABILITY: *Publisher or responsible agency:* Best Films and Video; made with facilities of Station CVE, North White Plains, New York; *Distributor:* BFV (#410), apply.

Hamlet. **Video/Recording**

152. *Hamlet.* (Series: Theatre on Film).

DOCUMENT INFORMATION: *Country:* USA; *Year of first showing:* 7 March 1986.

EDITION, HISTORY, CONTENTS, & EVALUATION: *Contents & evaluation:* A tape of the New York Shakespeare Festival production of *Hamlet* at the Public/Newman Theatre in 1986. *Audience:* Professional. *Supplementary materials:* Gussow, Mel. "Theatre: Kevin Kline as Hamlet at Public." *NYT* 10 March 1986: C13.

MEDIUM INFORMATION: *Medium:* Video; *Sound:* Spoken language; *Color:* Yes; *Length:* 214 min.; *Language(s) spoken:* English; *Video type:* V.

AUTHORSHIP INFORMATION: *Producer(s):* Papp, Joseph; *Director(s):* Ciulei, Liviu; *Design:* Shaw, Bob *Costumes:* Ivey, William; *Lighting:* Tipton, Jennifer; *Cast:* Kline, Kevin (Hamlet); Frank, Richard (Horatio); Weiss, Jeff (Ghost/Player); Yulin, Harris (Claudius); Pierce, David (Laertes); Cimino, Leonardo (Polonius); Smith, Priscilla (Gertrude); Harris, Harriet (Ophelia)

DISTRIBUTION & AVAILABILITY: *Publisher or responsible agency:* New York Shakespeare Festival; *Copy location:* LCL; *Call or copy number:* NCOV 511; *Availability:* Viewing restricted until May 7, 1988.

Hamlet. **Video/Documentary**

153. *Introducing Hamlet.*

DOCUMENT INFORMATION: *Country:* GB; *Year of release:* 1986.

EDITION, HISTORY, CONTENTS, & EVALUATION: *Edition & history:* A pedagogical film in which Geoff Hemstedt of the Univ. of Sussex discusses the difficulties of teaching *Hamlet* to high school students. Ways are suggested for overcoming these problems. *Supplementary materials:* BUFVC 6.

MEDIUM INFORMATION: *Sound:* Spoken language; *Color:* Yes; *Length:* 20 min.; *Video type:* V, 3/4U.

AUTHORSHIP INFORMATION: *Producer(s):* Kent Educational TV Centre; *Cast:* Hemstedt, Geoff (Discussant).

DISTRIBUTION & AVAILABILITY: *Publisher or responsible agency:* Univ. of Kent; *Distributor:* KTV*.

Hamlet. **Motion Picture/Derivative**

153.1 *Blue City.*

DOCUMENT INFORMATION: *Country:* USA; *Year of release:* 1986.

EDITION, HISTORY, CONTENTS, & EVALUATION: *Edition & history:* A modernized *Hamlet* in which Hamlet becomes a young man who returns home to discover that his father was murdered nine months previously. *Contents & evaluation:* Not seen. When Billy Turner sets out to avenge the death of his father, prime targets are his young stepmother (Malvina) and her business associate (Perry Kerch), who obviously resemble Gertrude and Claudius. Annie, his best friend's sister, would seem to be Ophelia, and Blue City itself displaces Elsinore. Vincent Canby describes it as "a witless, primitively composed little movie" that appears to have been edited by "someone wearing earplugs and a blindfold." Judging from the reviewer's comments about the deplorable language, it also seems to be another would-be Shakespeare film that belongs to the "F-word" genre. *Audience:* Professional; *Supplementary materials:* Canby, Vincent. "Film: 'Blue City'." *NYT* 2 May 1986: C9.

MEDIUM INFORMATION: *Medium:* Motion picture/ Video; *Sound:* Spoken language; *Color:* Yes; *Length:* 95 min. [?].

AUTHORSHIP INFORMATION: *Producer(s):* Hayward, William; Hill, Walter; *Director(s):* Manning, Michelle; *Screenplay writer(s):* Heller, Lukas; Hill, Walter; St. John, Nicholas; Based on a novel by Ross MacDonald; *Composer(s):* Cooder, Ry; *Lighting designer(s):* Poster, Steven; *Cast:* Nelson, Judd (Billy Turner); Sheedy, Ally (Annie Rayford); Caruso, David (Joey Rayford); Winfield, Paul (Luther Reynolds); Wilson, Scott (Perry Kerch); Morris, Anita (Malvina Turner).

DISTRIBUTION & AVAILABILITY: *Publisher or responsible agency:* Paramount Pictures; *Distributor:* Unknown. Local video rentals [?].

Hamlet. Video/Teleplay

154. *Hamlet.*

DOCUMENT INFORMATION: *Country:* GB; *Year of release:* 1987.

EDITION, HISTORY, CONTENTS, & EVALUATION: *Edition & history:* According to the *BUFVC Newsletter*, "this production, which disturbed and fascinated audiences throughout Britain and Europe during its 1985 tour, is presented here in a version conceived for video, which uses the medium to extend and heighten the discontinuities and ambiguities which are located at the centre of the production" (quoted in *SFNL* 12.1 [1987]: 10). The company is the Cambridge Experimental Theatre. *Contents & evaluation:* No video production of *Hamlet* makes fuller use of the medium than this funky exploration of the inner tensions within *Hamlet*. The cast of four turn themselves and their material inside out to capture the fragmented self that is the melancholy prince. All voices speak separately, together, and contrapuntally to create a sonic equivalent to the split self that Shakespeare created in Hamlet. Alternately raucous, irreverent, and deadly serious, the production is not afraid to visualize as well as to vocalize the *Hamlet* text. The bodies of the actors writhe and twist in rhythmical but nevertheless strictly choreographed patterns reminiscent of Oriental theatre. Faces are stylized masks of white with orange bands around the eyes, and costumes seem to be little

more than L.L. Bean long johns. Rock video fans will discover familiar motifs in this exciting production; others will have much to learn from it (KSR). *Supplementary materials:* Crowl, Samuel. "Fragments." *SFNL* 13.1 (Dec. 1988): 7; Spaul, Richard; Ritchie, Charlie; Wheale, Nigel. *Hamlet: A Guide.* Cambridge: CCAT, 1988.

MEDIUM INFORMATION: *Medium:* Video; *Sound:* Spoken language; *Color:* Yes; *Length:* 96 min.; *Language(s) spoken:* English; *Video type:* NTSC format.

AUTHORSHIP INFORMATION: *Producer(s):* Cambridge Experimental Theatre; *Director(s):* Kenyon, Roland (Stage); MacDonald, Rod (Video); *Adaptor/translator(s):* Kenyon, Roland; *Other personnel:* Spaul, Richard; MacDonald, Rod (Editors); McCarthy, Justine; Couch, Nikki; Simpson, Becky; Young, Neal; Austen, John; Gallick, John (Cameras); *Cast:* Hitchcock, Tricia (Ophelia); Revill, Melanie (Gertrude); Spaul, Richard (Claudius); Wilson, Alan (Polonius); Entire Cast (Hamlet).

DISTRIBUTION & AVAILABILITY: *Publisher or responsible agency:* A-V Unit, CCAT; *Distributor:* CCA, *Availability:* "Standard formats (NTSC)"; £49; US $195.

Hamlet Video/Documentary

154.1 *Hamlet.*

DOCUMENT INFORMATION: *Country:* GB; *Year of first showing:* 1989; *Location of first showing:* The South Bank Show, London Television. Transmitted 2 April 1989.

EDITION, HISTORY, CONTENTS, & EVALUATION: *Edition & history:* A documentary that explores the popularity and appeal of *Hamlet*. "After introductory remarks, [Producer] Melvin Bragg summarizes the plot using illustrative clips, exploring the question of Hamlet's possible madness and the Oedipus complex. The film juxtaposes actors' interpretations of soliloquies and directors' views of the play. . . . Highlights are [Pryce's] internalized ghost and Rylance's Hamlet, whose head is submerged in a basin by Claudius as he asks where Polonius' body is" (Tatspaugh, Patricia. "Notes from London." *SFNL* 14.1 [Dec. 1989]: 7).

MEDIUM INFORMATION: *Sound:* Spoken language; *Color:* Yes; *Length:* 60 min. [?]; *Video type:* V.

AUTHORSHIP INFORMATION: *Producer(s):* Hunt, Chris; *Director(s):* Bragg, Melvyn; *Other personnel:* Bragg, Melvyn (Editor); *Cast:* Bragg, Melvyn; Pennington, Michael; Rylance, Mark; Eyre, Richard; Barton, John; Daniels, Ron; Welles, Orson; Guthrie, Tyrone; Marowitz, Charles; Lyubimov, Yuri.

DISTRIBUTION & AVAILABILITY: *Publisher or responsible agency:* Iambic Productions, Ltd., 24 Scala St., London W1P ILU; *Copy location:* Iambic Productions.

King Henry the Fourth,
The First and Second Parts

ORIGINAL WORK AND PRODUCTION: English History Play. *Year written:* 1596-99; *Site of first production:* The Curtain [?] (as Shakespeare's *1H4* and *2H4*)

Henry the Fourth, Parts One and Two. **Video/Teleplay**

155. *The Life and Death of Sir John Falstaff: The Gadshill Job.*

DOCUMENT INFORMATION: *Country:* GB; *Year of first showing:* 1959; *Location of first showing:* BBC. Transmitted in seven parts beginning 2:05 to 2:35 P.M., Tuesday, 20 Jan. 1959.

EDITION, HISTORY, CONTENTS, & EVALUATION: *Edition & history:* In British terminology "a schools broadcast," which means that it was made especially for young students with all the perils and virtues thereto attached. The subtitle of "The Gadshill Job" obviously is an attempt by the makers to ingratiate themselves with the young. Still, an opportunity to hear Roger Livesey's unique, husky voice uttering Falstaff's words would be well worth anyone's time. This was presented as a mini-series in seven 30-minute segments, only the first of which is recorded here. *Supplementary materials:* "Program." *RT* 16 Jan. 1959: 11.

MEDIUM INFORMATION: *Length:* 210 min. [?—total all 7 parts].

AUTHORSHIP INFORMATION: *Producer(s):* Eyre, Ronald; *Composer(s):* Leighton, Kenneth; Salter, Lionel (Conductor); *Designer(s):* Roland, Gordon; *Costume designer(s):* Muggeridge, Maureen; *Other personnel:* Speight, Shirley (Make-up); *Cast:* Harris, Robert (King Henry IV); Hudd, Walter (Lord Chief Justice); Livesey, Roger (Falstaff); Jeavons, Colin (Prince Henry); Thompson, Eric (Poins); White, Meadows (First Carrier); Webb, David (Second Carrier); Shaw, Maxwell (Gadshill); Blackwell, Patrick (Chamberlain); Benson, George (Bardolph); Cook, Roderick (Nym); Wilson, Ian (A Traveler); Noble, Audrey (Mistress Quickly); + Forbes-Robertson, Peggy; Hunn, Meriel; Gordon, Martin; Moorehead, Brian.

DISTRIBUTION & AVAILABILITY: *Publisher or responsible agency:* BBC; *Copy location:* Unavailable.

Henry the Fourth Part One, 1-2. **Video/Teleplay (Part 3 in 15-part series)**

156. *Rebellion from the North.* (Series: *An Age of Kings,* III).

DOCUMENT INFORMATION: *Country:* GB; *Year of*

first showing: 1960; *Location of first showing:* BBC TV. Transmitted 9 to 10:15 P.M., Thursday, 26 May 1960; subsequently shown in the United States on selected public television stations.

EDITION, HISTORY, CONTENTS, & EVALUATION: *Awards:* Dews, Peter: Excellence in directing (British Guild of Directors); *Edition & history:* Based on Acts 1-2 of *King Henry IV, Part 1).* The third installment in an ambitious 15-part series, *An Age of Kings* (see also numbers 157-9, 178-9, 185, 188, 190-2, 485-6, and 505-6). For background, see *The Hollow Crown* (485), which is based on *Richard II* and which is therefore the first episode in the series. *Contents & evaluation:* "The new king is faced with seemingly insuperable problems. Reckless 'Hotspur' and his family revolt in the North, while his son, Prince Hal, prefers the environment of London's disreputable Eastcheap Tavern. The London *Times* reviewer was less happy with the televised *Henry IV, pt.1* than with *Richard II.* The small screen is better equipped to handle the private woes in soliloquy of the tormented Richard than the grand movements from court to battlefield to tavern of the Henriad. Neither Frank Pettingell as Falstaff nor Robert Hardy as Hal received high praise, though Hardy is credited with a "thoughtful, even melancholy" reading. Tom Fleming was a "shifty" Henry IV and Sean Connery (later James Bond) was Hotspur. Angela Baddeley (known in the States as the cook in the *Upstairs/Downstairs* imported British series), made a "ripe and bawdy" Mistress Quickly ("Cast of *Henry IV* None Too Happy," *Times* 27 May 1960: 18g). *Audience:* General use; *Supplementary materials:* Campbell, O.J. Introduction. *An Age of Kings* [The 15 parts as they appeared on television]. New York: Pyramid, 1961; Weiner, Albert. *An Age of Kings Study Guide.* New York: NET, 1960.

MEDIUM INFORMATION: *Medium:* Video; *Sound:* Spoken language; *Color:* No (black & white); *Length:* 75 min.; *Language(s) spoken:* English; *Video type:* 16mm, Kinescope.

AUTHORSHIP INFORMATION: *Producer(s):* Dews, Peter; *Director(s):* Hayes, Michael; *Adaptor/translator(s):* Crozier, Eric; *Composer(s):* Whelen, Christopher/Bliss, Arthur; Salter, Lionel (Conducting Royal Philharmonic Orchestra); *Designer(s):* Morris, Stanley; *Cast:* Fleming, Tom (King Henry); Connery, Sean (Hotspur); Hardy, Robert (Prince Hal); Pettingell, Frank (Falstaff); Baddeley, Angela (Hostess Quickly); Glover, Julian (Westmoreland); Windsor, Frank (Sir Walter Blunt); Garland, Patrick (Lancaster); Smith, Brian (Poins); Bayldon, Geoffrey (Worcester); Cooper, George A. (Northumberland); Willis, Jerome; Cox, Michael (Carriers); Farrington, Kenneth (Gadshill); Gostelow, Gordon (Bardolph); Lodge, Terence (Peto); Heneghan, Patricia (Lady Percy); Ware, Derek (Servant); Harley, Timothy (Francis); Ringham, John (Vintner); Lang, Robert (Sheriff); + Andrews, David; Rowe, Alan;

Bisley, Jeremy; Scully, Terry; Greenwood, John; Shepperdson, Leon; Wreford, Edgar; Valentine, Anthony.

DISTRIBUTION & AVAILABILITY: *Publisher or responsible agency:* BBC; *Copy location:* BBC*, SCL*, Apply.

Henry the Fourth Part One, 3-5. Video/Teleplay (Part 4 in 15-part series)

157. *Road to Shrewsbury, The.* (Series: *An Age of Kings,* IV).

DOCUMENT INFORMATION: *Country:* GB; *Year of first showing:* 1960; *Location of first showing:* BBC TV. Transmitted 8:45 to 10 P.M., Thursday, 9 June 1960.

EDITION, HISTORY, CONTENTS, & EVALUATION: *Awards:* Dews, Peter: Excellence in directing (British Directors Guild); *Edition & history:* Based on Acts 3-5 of *King Henry IV Part 1.* The fourth installment in an ambitious 15-part series, *An Age of Kings* (see also numbers 156, 158-9, 178-9, 185, 188, 190-2, 485-6, and 505-6). For background, see 156 above, and *The Hollow Crown* (485), which is based on *Richard II.* Both as the first play in Shakespeare's tetralogy and from the standpoint of historical chronology, *Richard II* belongs first in the series. *Contents & evaluation:* "The conspiracy against Henry comes to a head in open battle. Prince Hal and Falstaff fight valiantly [Falstaff too?] on the side of the King" (PR blurb). The London *Times* reviewer found this segment unsatisfactory because of the confusing nature of the plot lines at this stage of the dramatic epic's development. The overall design of turning the individual plays into a grand saga also made it inevitable that Falstaff's appearances would be somewhat overshadowed by the court intrigues. At times Falstaff seemed "a tiresome interruption to the flow of historical events" ("Conflict in *An Age of Kings,*" *Times* 24 June 1960: 4c). American reviewer, Milton Crane, in contrast, thought that Mr. Pettingell's Falstaff "began well, and then rose steadily through the ten acts of *Henry IV.* Mr. Pettingell conveyed not only the wickedness of Falstaff, which we have all come to accept as essential if Hal's progress toward heroic kingship is to be properly understood, but the sheer intelligence of the man. Pathos he had too, even to excess. The great scenes—at the Boar's Head Tavern in each of the two parts; with Justice Shallow; with the Lord Chief Justice; the incomparable monologues on honor and on sack; and the rejection scene—went from strength to strength" ("Shakespeare on Television," *SQ* 12.3 [Summer 1961]: 326). *Audience:* General use; *Supplementary materials:* Campbell, O.J. Introduction. *An Age of Kings* [The 15 parts as they appeared on television]. New York: Pyramid, 1961; Weiner, Albert. *An Age of Kings Study Guide.* New York: NET, 1960.

MEDIUM INFORMATION: *Medium:* Video; *Sound:*

Spoken language; *Color:* No (black & white); *Length:* 71 min.; *Language(s) spoken:* English; *Video type:* 16mm, Kinescope.

AUTHORSHIP INFORMATION: *Producer(s):* Dews, Peter; *Director(s):* Hayes, Michael; *Adaptor/translator(s):* Crozier, Eric; *Composer(s):* Whelen, Christopher/Bliss, Arthur; Salter, Lionel (Conducting Royal Philharmonic Orchestra); *Designer(s):* Morris, Stanley; *Cast:* Fleming, Tom (Bolingbroke); Hardy, Robert (Prince Hal); Baddeley, Angela (Hostess Quickly); Connery, Sean (Hotspur); Andrews, David (Mortimer); Squire, William (Glendower); Bayldon, Geoffrey (Worcester); Gearon, Valerie (Lady Mortimer); Heneghan, Patricia (Lady Percy); Windsor, Frank (Sir Walter Blunt); Pettingell, Frank (Falstaff); Gostelow, Gordon (Bardolph); Faulds, Andrew (Douglas); Valentine, Anthony (Messenger); Rowe, Alan (Vernon); Glover, Julian (Westmoreland); Wreford, Edgar (Scroop); Farrington, Kenneth (Sir Michael); Garland, Patrick (John of Lancaster); + Bisley, Jeremy; Scully, Terry; Cox, Michael; Shepperdson, Leon; Greenwood, John; Smith, Brian; Harley, Timothy; Wale, Terry; Lodge, Terence; Ware, Derek; Scott, John; Willis, Jerome.

DISTRIBUTION & AVAILABILITY: *Publisher or responsible agency:* BBC; *Copy location:* BBC*, SCL*, Apply.

Henry the Fourth Part Two, 1-2. Video/Teleplay (Part 5 in 15-part series)

158. *New Conspiracy, The.* (Series: *An Age of Kings,* V).

DOCUMENT INFORMATION: *Country:* GB; *Year of first showing:* 1960; *Location of first showing:* BBC TV. Transmitted 8:45 to 10 P.M., Thursday, 23 June 1960.

EDITION, HISTORY, CONTENTS, & EVALUATION: *Awards:* Dews, Peter: Excellence in directing (British Directors Guild); *Edition & history:* Based on Acts 1-2 of *King Henry IV Pt. 2.* The fifth installment in an ambitious 15-part series, *An Age of Kings* (see also numbers 156, 157, 159, 178-9, 185, 188, 190-2, 485-6, and 505-6). For background, see *The Hollow Crown* (485), which is based on *Richard II* and which is therefore the first episode in the series. This segment, "The New Conspiracy," was by itself budgeted at over £3,000 with a cast of forty eight. *Contents & evaluation:* "The spark of rebellion is set off again. Falstaff, now a 'hero' of the war, and Prince Hal return enthusiastically to their madcap life at the Boar's Head" (PR blurb). Professor Crane had special praise for Robert Hardy: "[He] grew visibly through *Henry IV* toward the magnificence of *Henry V.* Mr. Hardy's comic vein was as excellent as his heroic, and his scenes with Mr. Fleming were especially moving, hinting at a far more complex and intimate father-son relationship than is often shown in productions of *Henry IV*" ("Shakespeare on Television," *SQ* 12.3 [Summer 1961]: 326). It should be

mentioned that Professor Crane felt that the lines were spoken throughout the series so rapidly that American viewers had great difficulty in following the sense (Crane 324-5). British regional dialects can sound like a foreign language to American ears. If it is indeed true that the first production of the BBC "The Shakespeare Plays" was scrapped because the diction was unintelligible to Americans, then in the 25 years since *An Age of Kings* there has been a significant increase in sensitivity by British producers toward the needs of the American market. *Audience:* General use; *Supplementary materials:* Campbell, O.J. Introduction. *An Age of Kings* [The 15 parts as they appeared on television]. New York: Pyramid, 1961; Weiner, Albert. *An Age of Kings Study Guide.* New York: NET, 1960.

MEDIUM INFORMATION: *Medium:* Video; *Sound:* Spoken language; *Color:* No (black & white); *Length:* 59 min.; *Language(s) spoken:* English; *Video type:* 16mm, Kinescope.

AUTHORSHIP INFORMATION: *Producer(s):* Dews, Peter; *Director(s):* Hayes, Michael; *Adaptor/translator(s):* Crozier, Eric; *Composer(s):* Whelen, Christopher/Bliss, Arthur; Salter, Lionel (Conducting Royal Philharmonic Orchestra); *Designer(s):* Morris, Stanley; *Cast:* Hardy, Robert (Prince Hal); Baddeley, Angela (Hostess Quickly); Baddeley, Hermione (Doll Tearsheet); Pettingell, Frank (Falstaff); Andrews, David (Lord Bardolph); Ringham, John (Porter); Cooper, George (Northumberland); Bayldon, Geoffrey (Chief Justice); Howell, Dane (Page); Greenwood, John (Servant); Wreford, Edgar (York); Johnson, Noel (Mowbray); Lang, Robert (Hastings); Ringham, John (Fang); Rowe, Alan (Snare); Bisley, Jeremy (Gower); Courtenay, Margaret (Wife of Northumberland); Heneghan, Patricia (Lady Percy); Smith, Brian (Poins); Gostelow, Gordon (Bardolph); Harley, Timothy; Cox, Michael (Drawers); Cooper, George A. (Pistol); Lodge, Terence (Peto); + Farrington, Kenneth; Brine, Adrian; Scott, John Murray; Wale, Terry.

DISTRIBUTION & AVAILABILITY: *Publisher or responsible agency:* BBC; *Copy location:* BBC*, SCL*, Apply.

Henry the Fourth, Part Two, 3-5. Video/Teleplay (Part 6 of 15 parts)

159. *Uneasy Lies the Head.* (Series: *An Age of Kings,* VI).

DOCUMENT INFORMATION: *Country:* GB; *Year of first showing:* 1960; *Location of first showing:* BBC TV. Transmitted 9 to 10 P.M., Thursday, 7 July 1960.

EDITION, HISTORY, CONTENTS, & EVALUATION: *Awards:* Dews, Peter: Excellence in Directing (British Guild of Directors); *Edition & history:* Based on Acts 3-5 of *King Henry the Fourth, Pt. 2.* The sixth installment in *An Age of Kings* (see also numbers 156-8, 178-9, 185, 188, 190-2, 485-6, and 505-6). For background, see *The*

Hollow Crown (485), which is based on *Richard II* and which is therefore the first episode in the series. *Contents & evaluation:* "King Henry is near death, when his son Prince John of Lancaster, by an evil ruse exterminates his enemies. Soon after, Prince Hal leaves the Boar's Head forever, for the throne of England" (PR blurb). The London *Times* critic continued to think that Pettingell's Falstaff was marginal. This time "he was too easy to reject and [was] almost killed by rejection." Robert Hardy continued to be praised for his Henry V. His rejection of Falstaff was soft spoken and regretful rather than a public humiliation. This king, it was thought, would not turn out to be a Machiavellian ("Uneasy Lies the Head," *Times* 8 July 1960: 4g). *Audience:* General use; *Supplementary materials:* Campbell, O.J. Introduction. *An Age of Kings* [The 15 parts as they appeared on television]. New York: Pyramid, 1961; "Program." *RT* 1 July 1960:19.

MEDIUM INFORMATION: *Medium:* Video; *Sound:* Spoken language; *Color:* No (black & white); *Length:* 60 min.; *Language(s) spoken:* English; *Video type:* 16mm, Kinescope.

AUTHORSHIP INFORMATION: *Producer(s):* Dews, Peter; *Director(s):* Hayes, Michael; *Adaptor/translator(s):* Crozier, Eric; *Composer(s):* Whelen, Christopher/Bliss, Arthur; Salter, Lionel (Conducting Royal Philharmonic Orchestra); *Designer(s):* Morris, Stanley; *Cast:* Fleming, Tom (Henry IV); Hardy, Robert (Hal and H5); Pettingell, Frank (Falstaff); Farrington, Kenneth (Warwick); Squire, William (Shallow); Warner, John (Silence); Gostelow, Gordon (Bardolph); Howell, Dane (Page); Lodge, Terence (Mouldy); Shepperdson, Leon (Shadow); Wale, Terry (Wart); Smith, Brian (Feeble); Windsor, Frank (Bullcalf); Garland, Patrick (Prince John); Glover, Julian (Westmoreland); Wreford, Edgar (York); Johnson, Noel (Mowbray); Lang, Robert (Hastings); Ringham, John (Humphrey of Gloucester); Greenwood, John (Thomas of Clarence); Rowe, Alan (Harcourt); Bayldon, Geoffrey (Chief Justice); Cox, Michael (David); Cooper, George A. (Pistol); Ware, Derek; Valentine, Anthony (Grooms); Squire, William (Epilogue); + Brine, Adrian; Harley, Timothy; Garnett, Tony; Scott, John Murray.

DISTRIBUTION & AVAILABILITY: *Publisher or responsible agency:* BBC; *Copy location:* BBC*, SCL*.

Henry the Fourth, Part One. Video/Teleplay

160. *Henry the Fourth, Part One.*

DOCUMENT INFORMATION: *Country:* USA; *Year of first showing:* 1960; *Location of first showing:* TV Play of the Week. Transmitted 8:30 to 10:30 P.M., 26 Sept. 1960.

EDITION, HISTORY, CONTENTS, & EVALUATION: *Edition & history:* A Phoenix theatre production adapt-

ed to television. Surely, however, no troupe of Shakespearean actors ever ran into heavier competition for an audience. That same evening the celebrated Nixon/Kennedy debate was transmitted from 9:30 to 10:30 P.M. Most likely at 9:30 most of the audience deserted Shakespeare in favor of watching this historic confrontation in which Kennedy played an upstart Hal to Nixon's lugubrious Henry Bolingbroke. *Supplementary materials:* "Program." *NYT* 26 Sept. 1960: n.p.

MEDIUM INFORMATION: *Length:* 120 min.

AUTHORSHIP INFORMATION: *Cast:* Berry, Eric (Falstaff); Madden, Donald (Hotspur); Joyce, Stephen (Prince Hal); Davis, Donald (King Henry IV).

Henry the Fourth and *Henry the Fifth.* Motion Picture/Adaptation. History play

161. *Campanadas a media noche/Falstaff/Chimes at Midnight.*

DOCUMENT INFORMATION: *Country:* Spain/Switzerland; *Year of release:* 1966; *Year of first showing:* 1967 (USA).

EDITION, HISTORY, CONTENTS, & EVALUATION: *Awards:* 20th Anniversary "Grand Prix," Cannes Film Festival; *Edition & history:* "This film is a Spanish-Swiss venture from Internacional Films Espanola, S.A.-Alpine productions. The exteriors were filmed in Spain at Calatanazor, Lecumberri, Lesaca, Cardona, Soria, Casas de Campo, Colmenar Viejo, Avila, Mostoles and the Monastery of Santa Maria de Huerta" (Bothwell, Candace); Manvell also notes that Welles "in addition to producing, scripting, directing and playing, designed the sets and costumes. Emiliano Piedra and Angel Escolano were respectively a film producer and lawyer, who as friends of Welles made the filming possible in Spain" (Manvell, 71). Although a great film artist, Mr. Welles enjoyed less success with bankers and often had to go outside of normal channels to obtain financing for his movies. The film draws for its scenario on elements taken from the major tetralogy (*R2, 1* and *2H4, H5*) as well as *Merry Wives* and Holinshed's *Chronicles. Contents & evaluation:* The title, *Chimes at Midnight,* is from Falstaff's lament to Shallow for the lost days of their youth ("We have heard the chimes at midnight, Master Shallow" [*2H4* 3.2.214]). The film's central theme is nostalgia for a golden age before England, the home of generous souls, in the words of old John of Gaunt, had been leased out like "a pelting farm" (*R2* 2.1.60). In this new world neither Falstaff nor Orson Welles can flourish (KSR). "The Shrewsbury battle scene is one of the film's most justly celebrated achievements, and Pauline Kael is right to see it as belonging with sequences from Eisenstein, D.W. Griffith, Kurosawa, and John Ford. From a Shakespearean's viewpoint, it corresponds directly with Jan Kott's chilling, middle-European reading of the history plays as dramas re-enacting not the sanctity of hierarchy but the brutality of armed aggression: The Grand Mechanism. . . . [Welles] meant to endow his Shrewsbury with a very different tone and atmosphere from the romantic and stirring version of Agincourt Olivier achieved in his justly-admired film of *Henry V*. Shakespeare presents multiple perspectives on Shrewsbury's significance: Worcester's cold Machiavellianism, Henry IV's shrewd military strategy, Hotspur's heady intemperance, Douglas' exasperated professionalism, Falstaff's knowing cynicism, and Hal's practical assurance that this is his day to seize. Abandoning Shakespeare's multiplicity, Welles concentrates on a modern extension of Falstaff's understanding that war's appetite is fed by 'mortal men,' that war can make all of us 'food for powder.' Welles attempts to capture what war is like for the men in the trenches rather than for those mounted on dashing chargers gliding athletically toward their opponents. If Olivier's film version of Agincourt was a patriotic evocation of Hal's unsullied triumph (all lines revealing his darker side having been cut, including 'Kill all the prisoners'), shot in a manner to highlight his vitality and pluck, Welles's treatment of Shrewsbury is a slow, painful, exhausting depiction of mud-laden soldiers enacting some primal destructive rite" (Crowl, Samuel, "The Long Goodbye: Welles and Falstaff," *SQ* 31.3 [1980]: 377-8). *Audience:* College and university; General use; *Supplementary materials:* T.M. "Campanadas a media noche." *MFB* 34.400 [1967]: 70; Jorgens, Jack J. "Orson Welles's *Chimes at Midnight (Falstaff)*." *SOF* 106-21; McLean, Andrew M. "Orson Welles and Shakespeare." *LFQ* 11.3 [1983]: 197-202.

MEDIUM INFORMATION: *Medium:* Motion Picture; *Sound:* Spoken language; *Color:* No (black & white); *Length:* 119 min.; *Language(s) spoken:* English; *Film type:* 16mm, 35mm.

AUTHORSHIP INFORMATION: *Producer(s):* Piedra, Emiliano; Escolano, Angel; Tasca, Alessandro (Exec. prod.); *Director(s):* Welles, Orson; Fuentes, Tony; *Adaptor/translator(s):* Welles, Orson; *Composer(s):* Lavignino, Angelo Francesco; Urbini, Pierluigi; *Designer(s):* Guerra, José Antonio de la; *Costume designer(s):* Madrid, Cornejo; *Other personnel:* Richmond, Edmond (Photography); Mueller, Fritz (Editing); Quintana, Gustavo (Prod. Manager); Cobos, Juan (Asst. to Dir.); Alejandroullos [n.i.] (Cameraman); Chalet, Adolph (Camera Operator); Herrero, Jose (Second Unit Operator); Jaumandreu, Elena (Asst.Editor); Parasheles, Peter (Sound Editor); *Cast:* Welles, Orson (Falstaff); Baxter, Keith (Prince Hal); Gielgud, John (King Henry IV); Rutherford, Margaret (Hostess Quickly); Moreau, Jeanne (Doll Tearsheet); Rodway, Norman (Henry Percy); Vlady, Marina (Kate Percy); Rey, Fernando (Worcester); Webb, Alan (Justice Shallow); Chiari, Walter (Silence); Aldridge, Michael (Pistol); Beckley, Tony (Poins); Welles, Beatrice (The Child); Faulds, Andrew (Westmoreland); Nieto, Jose (Northumberland); Richardson, Ralph (Nar-

rator); Rowe, Jeremy; Bedford, Paddy; Pena, Julio; Hilbert, Fernando; Mejuto, Andres; Pyott, Keith; Farrell, Charles (Supernumeraries).

DISTRIBUTION & AVAILABILITY: *Publisher or responsible agency:* Internacional Films Espanola, S.A./ Peppercorn Wormser Film Enterprises; *Distributor:* JAN, FCM, *Copy location:* FOL (MP 54); *Availability:* JAN, 16mm, rental, apply; FCM, sale, V, $79.95 (1988); No U.K. dist. in 1988 (see *BUFVC* 35).

Henry the Fourth. Motion Picture/Documentary

162. *Henry the Fourth, Parts One and Two: The Making of the Ideal King.* (Series: Explorations in Shakespeare V).

DOCUMENT INFORMATION: *Country:* Canada; *Year of release:* 1969.

EDITION, HISTORY, CONTENTS, & EVALUATION: *Edition & history:* Part five in a series of twelve 23-minute films made in 1969 by the Ontario Educational Communications Authority (see also 18, 40, 65, 124, 257, 322, 465, 488, 555, 617 and 637). For more details see the entry at number 18, above. Luckily this is one of the five in the series that is available for rental. *Contents & evaluation:* Not seen. According to the publicity release issued by NBC Educational Enterprises, this program shows "Prince Hal's transformation from libertine to responsible leader." It opens with posters depicting famous political figures while student voices are overheard responding to questions about leadership. Then a series of passages from *Henry IV*, which focus on the development of the ideal king, are quoted. The action moves from the Boar's Head Tavern where Falstaff is king, to Westminster Abbey where Hal becomes king." The descriptions suggest that this series was anything but timid about being intellectually stimulating. Shakespeare's Henriad in fact offers a rich supply of political advice for any age. *Audience:* College and university.

MEDIUM INFORMATION: *Medium:* Motion Picture; *Sound:* Spoken language; *Color:* Yes; *Length:* 23 min.; *Language(s) spoken:* English; *Film type:* 16mm.

AUTHORSHIP INFORMATION: *Producer(s):* Reis, Kurt; Moser, Ed; *Screenplay writer(s):* Webster, Hugh; *Composer(s):* Yanovsky, Zal; *Set designer(s):* Adeney, Chris; *Lighting designer(s):* Galbraith, Howard; *Performance group(s):* Ontario Educational Communications/ NBC Educational Enterprises.

DISTRIBUTION & AVAILABILITY: *Distributor:* CNU.

Henry the Fourth, Part One. **Motion Picture/ Scenes**

163. *Henry the Fourth, Part One: An Introduction.*

DOCUMENT INFORMATION: *Country:* GB; *Year of release:* 1971.

EDITION, HISTORY, CONTENTS, & EVALUATION: *Edition & history:* Extracts from 2.4 and 5.4. Handbook accompanies film. *Supplementary materials:* BUFVC 7.

MEDIUM INFORMATION: *Color:* Yes; *Length:* 17 min.

AUTHORSHIP INFORMATION: *Director(s):* Seabourne Enterprises and Anvil Films.

DISTRIBUTION & AVAILABILITY: *Distributor:* Formerly EFV*, *Availability:* 16mm, V.

Henry the Fourth, Part Two. **Motion Picture/ Scenes**

164. *Henry the Fourth, Part Two,* 2.2. (Series: The Shakespeare Series [IFB], III).

DOCUMENT INFORMATION: *Country:* Great Britain; *Year of release:* 1974.

EDITION, HISTORY, CONTENTS, & EVALUATION: *Edition & history:* The third in a series of twelve British educational films showing scenes intended "to serve as an introduction to each play's theme or atmosphere" (see also numbers 22, 131, 232, 326, 430, 467, 490, 510, 556, 601 and 619). This part shows the fun-loving Hal in the tavern with Poins rehearsing for another of his nasty little practical jokes on Falstaff (2.2). This series, the "IFB," should not be confused with "The Shakespeare Series" (BHE/BFA), a series of abridged plays (see 41, 228, 258, 323, 406, 656). The *BUFVC* catalog (8) lists a *Henry IV Part 2: An Introduction,* which includes II.ii as well as V.v, and seems to be an expanded version of this film. The U.K. distributor (EFV), however, no longer seems to be in existence. *Contents & evaluation:* Not seen. *Audience:* High school (grades 10-12); *Supplementary materials:* Notes in *New Shakespeare* issued by Seabourne Enterprises in Great Britain in 1974 and distributed by EFVA.

MEDIUM INFORMATION: *Medium:* Motion Picture; *Sound:* Spoken language; *Color:* Yes; *Length:* 5½ min.; *Language(s) spoken:* English; *Film type:* 16mm; *Video type:* V, 3/4U (4 per cassette).

AUTHORSHIP INFORMATION: *Producer(s):* Seabourne, John; *Director(s):* Seabourne, Peter; *Cast:* Pennington, Michael; Suchet, David; Pyne, Natasha.

DISTRIBUTION & AVAILABILITY: *Publisher or responsible agency:* Seabourne Enterprises, Ltd.; *Distributor:* IFB; CNU, *Copy location:* FOL; *Call or copy number:* ISBN 0-8354—1598-8; FOL, MP 82; *Availability:* CNU, 16mm, rental $7.00; IFB, sale 16mm or V $110.

Henry the Fourth. **Video/Opera**

165. *Falstaff.*

DOCUMENT INFORMATION: *Country:* GB; *Year of release:* 1976.

EDITION, HISTORY, CONTENTS, & EVALUATION: *Edition & history:* Verdi's *Falstaff* taped at a performance of the Glyndebourne Festival Opera with the London Philharmonic Orchestra. *Supplementary materials:* Novacom Video Inc. catalog.

MEDIUM INFORMATION: *Length:* 123 min.

AUTHORSHIP INFORMATION: *Producer(s):* Heather, Dave; *Director(s):* Ponnelle, Jean Pierre; Pritchard, John (Conductor); *Composer(s):* Verdi, Guiseppi; *Cast:* Penkova, Reni; Griffel, Kay; Gale, Elizabeth; Gramm, Donald; Dickerson, Bernard; Trama, Ugo; Condo, Nucci.

DISTRIBUTION & AVAILABILITY: *Distributor:* NOV, FCM, *Availability:* NOV, B, V $68; FCM, sale, V, $69.95.

Henry the Fourth, Part One. **Video/Teleplay**

166. *Henry the Fourth, Part One.* (Series: The Shakespeare Plays).

DOCUMENT INFORMATION: *Year of first showing:* 1979; *Location of first showing(s):* BBC, London; PBS stations, USA, transmitted 26 March 1980.

EDITION, HISTORY, CONTENTS, & EVALUATION: *Edition & history:* The production was recorded at the BBC studios between 7 and 12 March 1979. *Contents & evaluation:* "Henry IV, Part One represents Shakespeare at his most dazzling: epic in sweep; ironic in structure; festive in spirit. The small screen just can't contain or capture its massive energies. Director David Giles employs several of the strategies which worked well for him in last season's claustrophobic *Richard II*, but *1H4* can't be squeezed into a series of medium close-ups. Such an approach places a premium on the control and command of the actor's face, and unfortunately Jon Finch's range of expression appears to extend from dread to dead. . . . To compensate, Finch gives his king an embarrassing and irritating series of hand gestures as his sole means of displaying Henry's care, concern, guilt and insecurity. Finch cannot refrain, in his every scene, from indulging in the most amateurish sign language: he rubs his hands together, strokes the left with the right, plays nervously with his gloves and his signet ring, massages his forehead, and goes through an elaborate ritual cleansing of those busy hands in the scene (III.3) where ironically he accuses his son of misbehavior [for an opposing view of this stage business, see Peter Saccio's review of *2H4* below]. The stain of Henry's usurpation becomes such an over-powering image that it subverts Shakespeare's certain intention to create in *1H4* not an embryonic *Macbeth*, but a far more generous and optimistic work about the rewards and risks of power politics" (Crowl, Samuel, "*Henry IV, Part One*" *SFNL* 5.1 [1980]: 3 +). No script is better arranged for cinematic editing than *1H4* with its rapid alternating between court and tavern. Unfortunately the editing in this production fails to counterpoint between the outwardly different but inwardly similar values of each world. It's as though the actors had indeed been imprisoned inside a studio and held to a rigid production schedule. As might be expected, however, these RSC and BBC actors are too professional to allow the enterprise to fail. There are splendid performances. Anthony Quayle's Falstaff is a genuine achievement and David Gwillim often endows Prince Hal with subtleties that are notably lacking in the Olivier film version. Tim Pigott-Smith makes a believable Hotspur and Jon Finch as Bolingbroke reveals more than traces of the guilt beneath the gilt of the crown (KSR). *Audience:* General use; *Supplementary materials:* Fenwick, Henry. "The Production." *Henry IV Part I* in *BSP,* 1980: 19-27; Videocassette (25 min.) from "Shakespeare in Perspective" series with George Melly as lecturer available in U.K. from BBC* (*BUFVC* 7).

MEDIUM INFORMATION: *Medium:* Video; *Sound:* Spoken language; *Color:* Yes; *Length:* 155 min.; *Video type:* B, V, 3/4U.

AUTHORSHIP INFORMATION: *Producer(s):* Messina, Cedric; *Director(s):* Giles, David; *Adaptor/translator(s):* Shallcross, Alan; *Composer(s):* Lloyd-Jones, David; *Designer(s):* Homfray, Don; *Costume designer(s):* Barrow, Odette; *Lighting designer(s):* Channon, Dennis; *Other personnel:* Walsh, Terry (Fight Arranger); Macarthur, Jenny (Prod. Asst.); Watts, Beryl (Director's Asst.); Lowden, Fraser (Prod. Unit Manager); Wilders, John (Literary Consultant); Moss, Elizabeth; (Make-up); *Cast:* Finch, Jon (Henry IV); Gwillim, David (Prince of Wales); Edwards, Rob (Lancaster); Buck, David (Westmoreland); Brown, Robert (Sir Walter); Swift, Clive (Worcester); Purchase, Bruce (Northumberland); Pigott-Smith, Tim (Hotspur); Morris, Robert (Earl of March); Cairney, John (Earl of Douglas); Neal, David (Scroop); Rutherford, Norman (Sir Michael); Owens, Richard (Owen Glendower); Wilton, Terence (Sir Richard Vernon); Quayle, Anthony (Sir John Falstaff); Galloway, Jack (Poins); Gostelow, Gordon (Bardolph); Beard, Steven (Peto); Dotrice, Michele (Lady Percy); Morgan, Sharon (Lady Mortimer); Bruce, Brenda (Mistress Quickly); Lewin, Mike (First Carrier); Bailie, David (Second Carrier); Milvain, Douglas (Chamberlain); Barber, Neville (Sheriff); Winter, George (Servant to Hotspur); Heath, Michael (First Messenger).

DISTRIBUTION & AVAILABILITY: *Publisher or responsible agency:* BBC/TLF; *Distributor:* AVP, UIO, BBC*; *Copy location:* UVM; *Availability:* AVP, sale, all formats,

$450 (1987); UIO, rental V (72034H), 3/4U (70134V0) $23.30; BBC*, 16mm or V, apply.

Henry the Fourth, Part Two. Video/Teleplay

167. *Henry the Fourth, Part Two.* (Series: The Shakespeare Plays).

DOCUMENT INFORMATION: *Country:* GB; *Year of first showing:* 1979; *Location of first showing(s):* BBC, London; Transmitted on PBS stations, USA, 9 Apr. 1980.

EDITION, HISTORY, CONTENTS, & EVALUATION: *Edition & history:* By using the same principal actors that appeared in *1H4,* this production offers a rare opportunity to witness on screen the ongoing fortunes of Prince Hal, Falstaff and company. In *1H4,* as has been noted by others, Hal wins his spurs as a warrior at Shrewsbury; here in *2H4* he demonstrates his statesmanship at Westminster. He thus becomes the epitome of the renaissance prince skilled in the talents of both the lion and the fox. Set designer Homfray also noted that the opening up of the social scene in the second part of *Henry IV* created difficult problems. He had to include not only tavern but also countryside; not only court but battlefield. *Contents & evaluation:* "In the BBC Lancastrian trilogy, the small screen has diminished some important things: the pageantry of *R2,* the range of bustling life in *1H4,* the battles and public oratory of *H5.* Despite a 25% cut in the text, *2H4* has lost least, and emerges for me as the most absorbing of the four productions. For politics takes place not only in public display, oratory, battles, and crowds, but also in tense private conversations, and these are the heart of *2H4.* What happens in this play occurs largely in the personal struggle of two or three individuals. The small camera can catch that superbly in the juxtaposition of faces. . . . The production offers a fine gallery of old faces. Falstaff and the Lord Chief Justice strongly establish the motif: Anthony Quayle, flushed, puffy, bearded, hoarse, clad in rough browns, confronting Ralph Michael, a distinguished gent, clean-shaven, clear-voiced, robed in green damasked silk. The Archbishop has a sharp asceticism, verging on the fanatical in his prominent facial bones and deeply incised facial lines. Shallow, with a pursed, twitchy, blinking face and wispy beard, contrasts with the placid idiocy of a nightcapped Silence. Mowbray has been changed from a youngster into a stout greybeard. With the King, a long-suspended obscurity is at last clarified. Jon Finch's obsessive hand-rubbing in *1H4* was emphasized but ambiguous [see Crowl review above]: Was it nervousness? Calculation? Pilate-like guilt? The leprosy legend? All are appropriate of course. In *2H4,* the leprosy takes over, scarring his handsome face. The lesions, together with his restless eyes and disordered hair, give us a hagridden king epitomizing his sick realm" (Saccio, Peter, "*Henry the Fourth, Part Two*," *SFNL* 6.1 [1981]: 2). *Audience*: General use; *Supplementary materials*: *Henry IV Part 2, BSP*; Videocassette (25 min.) from "Shakespeare in Perspective" series with Fred Emery as lecturer available in U.K. from BBC* (*BUFVC* 8).

MEDIUM INFORMATION: *Medium*: Video; *Sound*: Spoken language; *Color*: Yes; *Length*: 155 min.; *Video type*: B, V, 3/4".

AUTHORSHIP INFORMATION: *Producer(s)*: Messina, Cedric; *Director(s)*: Giles, David; *Adaptor/translator(s)*: Shallcross, Alan; *Composer(s)*: Lloyd-Jones, David; *Designer(s)*: Homfray, Don; *Costume designer(s)*: Barrow, Odette; *Lighting designer(s)*: Channon, Dennis; *Other personnel*: Macarthur, Jenny (Prod. Asst.); Watts, Beryl (Director's Asst.); Lowden, Fraser (Prod. Unit Manager); Wilders, John (Literary Consultant); Moss, Elizabeth (Make-up); *Cast*: Finch, Jon (King Henry IV); Gwillim, David (Prince of Wales); Edwards, Rob (Lancaster); Neil, Martin (Gloucester); Davenport, Roger (Clarence); Purchase, Bruce (Northumberland); Neal, David (Scroop); Miller, Michael (Mowbray); Bebb, Richard (Hastings); Humphry, John (Bardolph); Stewart, Salvin (Colville); Strong, David (Travers); Oatley, Carl (Morton); Beacham, Rod (Warwick); Buck, David (Westmoreland); Poyser, Brian (Gower); Michael, Ralph (Justice); Quayle, Anthony (Falstaff); Galloway, Jack (Poins); Gostelow, Gordon (Bardolph); Pringle, B. (Pistol); Beard, Steven (Peto); Fowler, John (Page); Eddison, Robert (Shallow); French, Leslie (Silence); Platt, Raymond (Davy); Proud, Frederick (Fang); Battersby, Julian (Mouldy); Herrick, Roy (Shadow); Tordoff, John (Feeble); Laird, Jenny (Lady Northumberland); Dotrice, Michele (Lady Percy); Bruce, Brenda (Mistress Quickly); Cuka, Frances (Doll).

DISTRIBUTION & AVAILABILITY: *Publisher or responsible agency*: BBC/TLF; *Distributor*: AVP, UIO, BBC*, *Copy location*: UVM; *Availability*: AVP, sale, all formats $450 (1987); IOA, V (72035H), 3/4U (70135V) rental $23.50; BBC*, 16 mm or V, apply.

Henry the Fourth. Video/Opera

168. *Falstaff.*

DOCUMENT INFORMATION: *Country*: GB; *Year of release*: 1983.

EDITION, HISTORY, CONTENTS, & EVALUATION: *Edition & history*: Verdi's *Falstaff* taped at a performance at The Royal Opera House. *Supplementary materials*: Novacom Video Inc. catalog.

MEDIUM INFORMATION: *Length*: 140 min.

AUTHORSHIP INFORMATION: *Producer(s)*: Eyre, Ronald; *Director(s)*: Giulini, Carlo Maria (Conductor);

Composer(s): Verdi, Guiseppi; *Cast*: Ricciarelli, Katia; Hendricks, Barbara; Valentini-Terrani, Lucia; Bruson, Renato; Gonzalez, Dalmacio.

DISTRIBUTION & AVAILABILITY: *Distributor*: NOV, FCM, *Availability*: NOV, B, V $40; FCM V, $39.95.

Henry Fourth, Parts One and Two. Video/Documentary

169. *Shakespeare: Henry the Fourth, Parts One and Two: Workshops I and II.* (Series: Open University Film Library).

DOCUMENT INFORMATION: *Country*: GB; *Year of release*: 1985.

EDITION, HISTORY, CONTENTS, & EVALUATION: *Edition & history*: One of several programs prepared for the Open University television programs in Great Britain. Not seen in the U.S. According to the *BUFVC* catalog, each program features a director leading one of the actors through his/her role. In this program, director John Russell Brown explores the father-son bond between Prince Hal and King Henry IV. *Contents & evaluation*: Not seen. *Audience*: College and university; Professional; *Supplementary materials*: BUFVC 8.

MEDIUM INFORMATION: *Medium*: Video; *Sound*: Spoken language; *Color*: Yes; *Length*: 24 min. (each workshop); *Language(s) spoken*: English; *Video type*: V,B.

AUTHORSHIP INFORMATION: *Producer(s)*: Hoyle, David; *Cast*: Brown, John Russell (Dir.); West, Timothy (Falstaff); Thomas, Michael (Prince Hal); Jeffrey, Peter (King Henry IV).

DISTRIBUTION & AVAILABILITY: *Publisher or responsible agency*: BBC Open University; *Distributor*: GSV*, *Copy location*: BBC; *Availability*: Available in U.K. only.

Henry the Fourth. Video/Opera

170. *Falstaff.*

DOCUMENT INFORMATION: *Country*: Austria/USA; *Year of release*: 1985.

EDITION, HISTORY, CONTENTS, & EVALUATION: *Edition & history*: A recorded performance of Verdi's opera shown on PBS stations, USA, in 1985. *Supplementary materials*: Loughney, Katharine. "Shakespeare on Film and Tape at Library of Congress." *SFNL* 14.1 (Dec. 1989): 4.

MEDIUM INFORMATION: *Length*: 150 min.

AUTHORSHIP INFORMATION: *Director(s)*: Solti, Sir George; *Cast*: Bacquier, Gabriel (Falstaff).

DISTRIBUTION & AVAILABILITY: *Copy location*: LCM; *Call or copy number*: VAA 5214.

King Henry the Fifth

ORIGINAL WORK AND PRODUCTION: English History Play. *Year written:* 1599; *Site of first production:* Globe, Bankside.

Henry the Fifth. Video/Scenes

171. *Henry the Fifth.*

DOCUMENT INFORMATION: *Country:* GB; *Year of first showing:* 1937; *Location of first showing:* BBC. Transmitted 9:01 to 9:18 P.M., Friday, 6 Feb. 1937.

EDITION, HISTORY, CONTENTS, & EVALUATION: *Edition & history:* The program has the distinction, along with *As You Like It,* transmitted immediately before it on the same day (see 35), of having been a part of the inauguration of televised Shakespearean drama. The scene selected seems to have been the wooing of Princess Katherine by King Henry after the defeat of the French at Agincourt. The BBC has a still from the production in its archives. For lack of technology, no recording is preserved, though at the time no one would have thought it worth saving for the archives anyway. The BBC's function was to transmit not to preserve. *Supplementary materials:* TPAB 6 Feb. 1937.

MEDIUM INFORMATION: *Length:* 16 min.

AUTHORSHIP INFORMATION: *Producer(s):* O'Ferrall, George More; *Cast:* Arnaud, Yvonne (Katherine); Os-car, Henry (Henry V); Marvin, Mary [also "Marie"] (Alice).

DISTRIBUTION & AVAILABILITY: *Publisher or responsible agency:* BBC; *Copy location:* Not preserved.

Henry the Fifth. Motion Picture/Interpretation. History play

172. *Henry the Fifth.*

DOCUMENT INFORMATION: *Country:* GB; *Year of filming:* 1943-44; *Year of release:* 1944; *Year of first showing:* Nov. 22, 1944; *Country of first showing:* GB; *Location of first showing(s):* Carlton Theatre, London; 6 Apr. 1946, Boston, USA.

EDITION, HISTORY, CONTENTS, & EVALUATION: *Awards:* Special Oscar for Olivier; New York Critics' Award (Best Actor); *Edition & history:* Dedicated to the British Paratroops who were preparing then for the WW II D-day landings in Normandy, this film was designed to bolster the morale of an embattled nation. It bears close comparison therefore with the differently oriented Kenneth Branagh 1989 film of *Henry V* (182.2). The exploits of England's fifteenth-century Henry V in France were to be emulated by the soldiers of the mid-twentieth century. The colorful battle scenes, which required the construction of a half-mile-long track for the camera to record the famous French cavalry charge, were shot at Enniskerry, Ireland, with extras recruited from among the Home Guard. The rest of the film was made at the Denham and Pinewood studios, England. The replica of medieval London, modeled after Visscher's famous view, was especially constructed for the establishing shot that tracks a fluttering handbill down to the site of the Globe. In a crane shot, the camera glances over the city, momentarily pauses at the adjacent Bear Garden and then closes in on the Globe playhouse. The lively realism of the Elizabethan playhouse is contrasted with the subsequent artifice of the sequences in France, modeled after an illuminated manuscript, *Les très riches heures du Duc de Berry*. Olivier thus offers the audience "a Muse of fire" (KSR). *Contents & evaluation:* No critic was more eloquent in describing Olivier's achievement than the late James Agee, reviewer for the *The Nation:* "Some people, using I wonder what kind of dry ice for comfort, like to insist that *Henry V* is relatively uninteresting Shakespeare. This uninteresting poetry is such that after hearing it, in this production, I find it as hard to judge fairly even the best writing since Shakespeare as it is to see the objects in a room after looking into the sun. . . . The one great glory of the film is this language. The greatest credit I can assign to those who made the film is that they have loved and served the language so well. I don't feel that much of the delivery is inspired; it is merely so good, so right, that the words set loose in the graciously designed world of the screen . . . take care of themselves. Neither of the grimmest Shakespearian vices, ancient or modern, is indulged; that is to say, none of the text is read in that human, down-to-earth, poetry-is-only-hopped-up-prose manner which is doubtless only proper when a charter subscriber to *PM* reads the Lerner editorial to his shop-wise fellow traveler; nor is any of it intoned in the nobler manner, as if by a spoiled deacon celebrating the Black Mass down a section of sewerpipe. Most of it is merely spoken by people who know and love poetry as poetry and have spent a lifetime learning how to speak it accordingly. Their voices, faces, and bodies are all in charge of a man who has selected them . . . as a good conductor conducts an orchestral piece. It is, in fact, no surprise to learn that Mr. Olivier is fond of music; charming as it is to look at, the film is essentially less visual than musical" ("Review," *The Nation* 163.5 [3 Aug. 1946]: 136-8). "Musical" as the film may be, it remains a blend also of memorable sights and sounds. Its unforgettable episodes range from the brawling interior of the Globe playhouse to the delicate *mise en scène* for the French court to the rousing French cavalry charge at Agincourt. That feast of color, however, is accompanied by richness of sound: the coarse voices of the swaggering Nym and Pistol (2.1); Mistress Quickly's moving description of Falstaff's death throes that contains Theobald's memorable 18th-century emendation ". . . and 'a [babbl'd] of green fields" (2.3.17—on the sound track is William Walton's dirge-like musical score based on the slow

movements of the *passacaglia*); and Michael Williams' devastating commentary on the monarch's responsibilities for sending men to battlefield slaughter (4.1.134). To this montage of vignettes must be added the sparkling conversations in French between Princess Katherine of France and her lady-in-waiting, Alice (3.4), and the dazzling performance of Leslie Banks as Chorus, especially with the opening "O for a Muse of fire." Finally, there are the great "locker-room" speeches of Olivier himself that would stir the blood of even Falstaff's wretched draftees (KSR).

Not everyone would agree with these favorable assessments. Another reviewer thought almost the exact opposite, that indeed the film ". . . distracts from spoken language." He disliked "the poor slapstick fooling between Felix Aylmer as the Archbishop of Canterbury and Robert Helpman as the Bishop of Ely. Too great an accent is thus placed on what is in effect a very minor scene." He also believed that "the filmic value of Agincourt causes it to be overstated" and that "the courtship scene is similarly dragged out." It was "an unwise decision," as well, to put the opening scene in the Globe. Finally, though, he says that "the film is a notable achievement of purely British cinema" (O.B., "Henry V," *MFB* 11.132 [Dec. 1944]: 139). *Audience:* General use; *Supplementary materials:* Geduld, H. M. *Filmguide to* Henry V. Bloomington: Indiana UP, 1973; Phillips, James E. "Adapted from a Play by W. Shakespeare." *HQ* 2 (Oct. 1944): 82-90; Jorgens, *SOF* 122-35.

MEDIUM INFORMATION: *Medium:* Motion Picture; *Sound:* Spoken language; *Color:* Yes; *Length:* 137 min.; *Film type:* 35 mm; 16mm; Technicolor; *Video type:* B, V, CED.

AUTHORSHIP INFORMATION: *Producer(s):* Olivier, Laurence; *Director(s):* Olivier, Laurence; Beck, Reginald; *Adaptor/translator(s):* Dent, Alan; *Composer(s):* Walton, William; Mathieson, Muir (c. London Symphony); *Designer(s):* Sheriff, Paul; Dillon, Carmen; *Costume designer(s):* Furse, Roger; Furse, Margaret; *Lighting designer(s):* Wall, W.; *Other personnel:* Bower, Dallas (Assoc. Prod.); Permane, Vincent (Asst. Dir.); Krasker, Robert (Photography); Hildyard, Jack (Camera Op.); Lindegaard, E. (Scenic Artist); Day, Percy (Special Effects); Sforzini, Tony (Make-up); Walker, Vivienne (Hairdressing); Barry, Joan (Continuity); White, John (Master of Horse); Dennis, John/Dew, D. (Sound); Newton, W. (Stills); Samuel, Phill (Prod. Super.); *Cast:* Olivier, Laurence (Henry V); Newton, Robert (Ancient Pistol); Banks, Leslie (Chorus); Asherson, Renée (Princess Katherine); Knight, Esmond (Fluellen); Helpmann, Robert (Bishop of Ely); Aylmer, Felix (Canterbury); Genn, Leo (Constable of France); St. Helier, Ivy (Lady-in-Waiting); Jackson, Freda (Mistress Quickly); Thesiger, Ernest (French Ambassador); Hanley, Jimmy (Williams); Adrian, Max (Dauphin); Laurie, John (Jamy); Dyall, Valentine (Burgundy); Robey, George (Falstaff); Lister,

Francis (Orleans); MacGinnis, Niall (MacMorris); Thorndike, Russell (Bourbon); Emmerton, Roy (Bardolph); Shepley, Michael (Gower); Jones, Griffith (Salisbury); Graham, Morland (Sir Thos. Erpingham); Hambling, Arthur (Bates); Nissen, Brian (Court); Cooper, Frederick (Nym); Case, Gerald (Westmoreland); Warre, Michael (Gloucester); Burnell, Janet (Isabel); Tickle, F. (Gov. Harfleur); Cole, G.(Boy); Field, J. (Mess.); Hare, E. (Priest); Greeves, V.(Herald).

DISTRIBUTION & AVAILABILITY: *Publisher or responsible agency:* Twin Cities Film; *Distributor:* WRF, FNC, FFH, FMB* (16 mm), *Second distributor:* DCV, SHE, TAM (CED), RVL*, INM, ILL, FCM; *Copy location:* FOL; *Call or copy number:* MP 13; *Availability:* WRF, rental, 16mm, apply; FNC $115+ (1974); Sale, CED (01003), $29.95; TAM, B,V, ($69.00); FFH B,V, $249, 3/4U $349, Rental $125; RVL*, V, apply; DCV, V, $38; INM, V, $39.95; ILL $19.95; FCM, V, $19.95.

Henry the Fifth. Motion Picture/Scenes

173. *Henry the Fifth.*

DOCUMENT INFORMATION: *Country:* GB; *Year of release:* 1944.

EDITION, HISTORY, CONTENTS, & EVALUATION: *Edition & history:* Study extracts from Olivier's film: The Globe Playhouse, Prologue, 1.1 and 2; IV (Agincourt) *Supplementary materials:* BUFVC 9.

MEDIUM INFORMATION: *Color:* Yes; *Length:* 30 min.; *Film type:* 16 mm.

DISTRIBUTION & AVAILABILITY: *Publisher or responsible agency:* Two Cities Films; *Distributor:* FMB*.

Henry the Fifth. Video/Teleplay

174. *The Life of Henry the Fifth.*

DOCUMENT INFORMATION: *Country:* GB; *Year of first showing:* 1951; *Location of first showing:* BBC. Transmitted 8:33 to 10:49 P.M., Sunday, 22 Apr. 1951.

EDITION, HISTORY, CONTENTS, & EVALUATION: *Edition & history:* For its time an ambitious and elaborate production into which much time and energy were poured by BBC Producer Royston Morley and a large cast. *TPAB* lists an impressive array of musical selections to accompany the action, including part 18 of Bruckner's Symphony #5. Props and sets were designed and arranged with equal care.

MEDIUM INFORMATION: *Length:* 135 min.

AUTHORSHIP INFORMATION: *Producer(s):* Morley, Royston; Brett, Leonard; *Designer(s):* Learoyd, Barry; *Other personnel:* Crean, Patrick (Fights); Bell, Joan;

Nesbit, Prudence (Stage managers); *Cast:* McCallin, Clement (Henry V); Pitoeff, Varvara (Katherine); Goring, Marius (Chorus); Pooley, Olaf (Dauphin); Claridge, Norman (King); Jones, John Glyn (Fluellen); Keen, Geoffrey (Gower); Duncan, Archie (Jamy); Lexy, Edward (Macmorris); Gray, Willoughby (Pistol); Woodbridge, George (Bardolph); Hall, Cameron (Nym); Brown, Robert (Williams); Tickle, Frank (Bates); Ross, Frederick (Erpingham); Winter, Virginia (Hostess); Clement, Michele (Alice); + Others and Extras.

DISTRIBUTION & AVAILABILITY: *Publisher or responsible agency:* BBC; *Copy location:* Unavailable.

175. *Henry the Fifth.*

DOCUMENT INFORMATION: *Country:* GB; *Year of first showing:* 1953; *Location of first showing:* BBC. Transmitted 8:46 to 10:23 P.M., Tuesday, 19 May 1953.

EDITION, HISTORY, CONTENTS, & EVALUATION: *Edition & history:* A less ambitious production than the 1951 Royston Morley *Life of Henry V* and indeed it was received by audiences less favorably. The BBC Research Report for that week showed that 36% of the adult viewing public watched it, but their responses added up to a "Reaction Index" of only 52, as compared with 71 for Morley's 1951 *Life of H5* (WAC T5/232/2, 8 June 1953). One reason for its lukewarm reception may have been the highbrow posturings of the players, mostly British university students led by John Barton, who believed in doing the plays "as they had been done in Shakespeare's own day" without scenery or costumes, to speak of. In a flyer, the "Elizabethan Theatre Company," as they called themselves, described how they took Shakespeare's Chorus literally when he urged "into a thousand parts divide one man." With that mandate in mind, they undertook the most rigorous doubling and tripling of roles imaginable. For example, Jocelyn Page took on the unlikely combination of Hostess Quickly and Queen Isabel, while Clifford Rose tried his hand at being French Ambassador, Governor of Harfleur, Salisbury and good Sir Thomas Erpingham. *Supplementary materials:* "Program." *TPAB* 19 May 1953: n.p.

MEDIUM INFORMATION: *Length:* 90 min.

AUTHORSHIP INFORMATION: *Producer(s):* MacOwan, Michael (BBC); Barton, John (ETC); *Designer(s):* Pemberton, Reece; *Other personnel:* Petty, Cecil (Stage Manager); *Cast:* George, Colin (Henry V); Robertson, Toby (Ely, Gower, York); David, Michael (Canterbury, Dauphin, Warwick); Selou, Reginald (Nym, Rambures); Page, Jocelyne (Hostess, Queen Isabel); Jeffrey, Peter (Constable); Gostelow, Gordon (Westmoreland, Fluellen); Milner, Roger (Bates, Soldier, Herald); Rose, Clifford (Ambassador, Gov. of Harfleur, Salisbury, Erpingham); Faulkner, Keith (Boy); Stanley, Trenor (Grandpre); Roughead, James (Exeter); Bonnamy, Yvonne (Alice); Southworth, John (King Charles VI, Montjoy); Lawford,

William (Bardolph, Orleans, Gloucester); Windsor, Frank (Pistol, Williams); Sorel, Bernadette (Katherine). DISTRIBUTION & AVAILABILITY: *Publisher or responsible agency:* Elizabethan Theatre Co./BBC; *Copy location:* Unavailable.

Henry the Fifth. Video/Scenes

176. *Henry the Fifth.*

DOCUMENT INFORMATION: *Country:* USA; *Year of first showing:* 1953; *Location of first showing:* Omnibus. Transmitted 4:30 to 6:00 P.M., Sunday, 11 Jan. 1953.

EDITION, HISTORY, CONTENTS, & EVALUATION: *Edition & history:* The Ford Foundation sponsored Omnibus, a Sunday afternoon program of remarkably high quality. In fact during that period, the programming on commercial television was so excellent on Sunday afternoons that one was tempted to drop everything else to watch it. Even so, in a prophetic article, Jack Gould warned against the peril of the show's becoming too "arty," for fear that loss of a wide audience could undermine support. Unhappily events proved Gould right ("Momentary Lapse," *NYT* 25 Jan. 1953: X 13). *Supplementary materials:* "Program." *NYT* 11 Jan. 1953: X 12.

MEDIUM INFORMATION: *Length:* 15 min. [?]; *Video type:* V.

AUTHORSHIP INFORMATION: *Cast:* Aherne, Brian; Lindfors, Viveca.

DISTRIBUTION & AVAILABILITY: *Publisher or responsible agency:* TV/Radio Workshop of the Ford Foundation.

Henry the Fifth. Video/Teledrama

177. *The Life of Henry the Fifth.* (Series: Television World Theatre).

DOCUMENT INFORMATION: *Country:* GB; *Year of first showing:* 1957; *Location of first showing:* BBC TV. Transmitted 8:30 to 10:30 P.M. on Sunday, 29 Dec. 1957.

EDITION, HISTORY, CONTENTS, & EVALUATION: *Edition & history:* The first in a new series called "Television World Theatre," produced at a cost of £4,069 with a cast of 44. *Contents & evaluation:* According to the *Times* reviewer, the play began with none other than "William Shakespeare" appearing and doubling as a kind of chorus in search of his "muse of fire," an interesting throwback to a favorite trope of the silent film era—the screen actor reading from Shakespeare's text. It was a device that directors had hit on for

assuaging their guilt over wrenching Shakespeare from page and stage to screen. This use of a presentational rather than a representational mode also anticipates the style of the chorus in the 1979 BBC David Giles production, and again in Kenneth Branagh's 1989 film. The reviewer also felt that the 36 characters were admirably crammed into the small television screen and that John Neville as Henry V performed well, often revealing some new facet of the king's character when "a turn of the action required it" ("BBC Television," *Times* 30 Dec. 1957: 10c). *Audience:* General use; *Supplementary materials:* "Around and About." *RT* 27 Dec. 1957: 4.

MEDIUM INFORMATION: *Medium:* Video; *Sound:* Spoken language; *Color:* No (black & white); *Length:* 120 min.; *Language(s) spoken:* English; *Video type:* Not known.

AUTHORSHIP INFORMATION: *Producer(s):* Dews, Peter; *Director(s):* Dews, Peter; *Designer(s):* Sheppard, Guy; *Cast:* Neville, John (Henry V); Hepton, Bernard (Chorus); Church, Tony (Canterbury); Jones, Dudley (Fluellen); Bayldon, Geoffrey (Pistol); Wood, John (Dauphin); Palmer, Richard (Gloucester); Coe, Richard (Bedford); Somers, Julian (Exeter); Hines, Ronald (Salisbury); Selway, George (Westmoreland); Lambert, Peter (Cambridge); Billingsley, Peter (Scroop); Hickson, Hugh (Grey); Skillan, George (Erpingham); Morant, Philip (Gower); McClelland, Allan (Macmorris); Blanshard, Joby (Bates); Batchelor, Della (Hostess); Milner, Roger (Nym); Bates, Michael (Bardolph/Williams); Hudd, Walter (Charles VI); Dunning, Jessica (Isabel); Creb, Patricia (Katherine); Jackson, Nancie (Alice); Johnson, Noel (Constable of France); Wreford, Edgar (Mountjoy).

DISTRIBUTION & AVAILABILITY: *Publisher or responsible agency:* BBC; *Copy location:* BBC*.

Henry the Fifth, 1-3. Video/Teleplay (Part 7 of 15 parts)

178. *Signs of War.* (Series: *An Age of Kings,* VII).

DOCUMENT INFORMATION: *Country:* GB; *Year of first showing:* 1960; *Location of first showing:* BBC TV. Transmitted 9 to 10 P.M., Thursday, 21 July 1960.

EDITION, HISTORY, CONTENTS, & EVALUATION: *Awards:* Dews, Peter: Excellence in Directing (British Guild of Directors); *Edition & history:* Based on Acts 1-3 of *King Henry the Fifth.* The seventh installment in *An Age of Kings* (see also numbers 156-9, 179, 185, 188, 190-2, 485-6, and 505-6). This was one of the more expensive segments with total costs amounting to £3,993 and a huge cast of 46 actors. For more background on the series, see *The Hollow Crown* (485), which is based on *Richard II* and which is therefore the first episode in the series. *Contents & evaluation:* "The new king's claim to the French throne is rejected. Henry barely escapes assassination and sails for France. Near Agincourt he prepares for battle against a confident French army" (PR blurb). The London *Times* critic noted the special problem posed by so sprawling a play as *Henry V* for a small television screen. "Savage cutting" took care of some of the problems, but also Robert Hardy, who continues on as Henry V, was costumed in such a way that he stood out unmistakably in the crowd scenes. For example, the cowardice of Bardolph and Pistol at Harfleur did not appear. William Squire's Chorus comes in for special praise. An interesting addition to the cast is Judi Dench as Princess Katherine of France, a "model of empty headed prettiness" ("Good Acting in *Henry V*," *Times* 22 July 1960: 16g). (Miss Dench was to become a major figure with the Royal Shakespeare Company. Shakespeare filmgoers will particularly remember her as Titania in the 1968 Peter Hall *MND*. And most recently as Hostess Quickly in the 1989 Branagh *Henry V* she showed an acting talent in middle age that is remote from "empty-headed.") *Audience:* General use; *Supplementary materials:* Campbell, O.J. Introduction. *An Age of Kings* [The 15 parts as they appeared on television]. New York: Pyramid, 1961; "Program." *RT* 15 July 1960: 16.

MEDIUM INFORMATION: *Medium:* Video; *Sound:* Spoken language; *Color:* No (black & white); *Length:* 61 min.; *Language(s) spoken:* English; *Video type:* 16mm, Kinescope.

AUTHORSHIP INFORMATION: *Producer(s):* Dews, Peter; *Director(s):* Hayes, Michael; *Adaptor/translator(s):* Crozier, Eric; *Composer(s):* Whelen, Christopher/Bliss, Arthur; Salter, Lionel (Conducting Royal Philharmonic Orchestra); *Designer(s):* Morris, Stanley; *Cast:* Hardy, Robert (Henry V); Squire, William (Chorus); Dench, Judi (Princess Katherine); Johnson, Noel (Exeter); Glover, Julian (Westmoreland); Luckham, Cyril (Canterbury); Shepperdson, Leon (Rambures); Windsor, Frank (Cambridge); Smith, Brian (Scroop); Garnett, Tony (Gray); Valentine, Anthony (Herald); Gostelow, Gordon (Bardolph); Andrews, David (Nym); Cooper, George A. (Pistol); Baddeley, Angela (Hostess Quickly); Harley, Timothy (Boy); Garland, Patrick (Bedford); Ringham, John (Humphrey); Rowe, Alan (Charles VI); Warner, John (Dauphin); Selway, George (Constable of France); Lodge, Terence (Messenger); Willis, Jerome (Orleans); Brine, Adrian (Bourbon); Bidmead, Stephanie (Isabel); Coulette, Yvonne (Alice); Farrington, Kenneth (Fluellen); Bisley, Jeremy (Gower); Blanshard, Joby (Jamy); Cox, Michael (Macmorris); Lang, Robert (Montjoy); + Howell, Dane; Wale, Terry; Scott, John; Ware, Derek.

DISTRIBUTION & AVAILABILITY: *Publisher or responsible agency:* BBC; *Copy location:* BBC*, SCL*.

Henry the Fifth, 4–5. Video/(Teleplay (Part 8 of 15 parts)

179. *Band of Brothers, The.* (Series: *An Age of Kings*, VIII).DOCUMENT INFORMATION: *Country:* GB; *Year of first showing:* 1960; *Location of first showing:* Transmitted 9 to 10 P.M., Thursday, 4 August 1960.

EDITION, HISTORY, CONTENTS, & EVALUATION: *Awards:* Dews, Peter: Excellence in Directing (British Guild of Directors); *Edition & history:* Based on Acts 4-5 of *King Henry the Fifth*. The eighth installment in *An Age of Kings* (see also numbers 156-9, 178, 185, 188, 190-2, 485-6, and 505-6). This segment cost £3,950 and required the services of 28 male actors, 3 women and 16 extras. For additional background information on the series, see *The Hollow Crown* (485), which is based on *Richard II* and which is therefore the first episode in the series. *Contents & evaluation:* "On the eve of battle, the King searches his soul. The battle brings vindication and victory. Peace is sealed when Henry woos and wins the attractive Katherine in marriage" (PR blurb). The London *Times* critic blamed the play as much as the producer for the lack of centrality in the Agincourt sequence. Since the defeat and death of Hotspur, Henry has had no single antagonist to stand as symbol of the enemies of his monarchy. The crucial St. Crispin speech was, however, well handled. Hardy's failure to make the wooing of Katherine believable is mentioned but then again the reviewer felt that the scene is in itself an "unfortunate" one ("Agincourt on Television," *Times* 5 Aug. 1960: 11d). *Audience:* General use; *Supplementary materials:* Campbell, O.J. Introduction. *An Age of Kings* [The 15 parts as they appeared on television]. New York: Pyramid, 1961; Weiner, Albert. *An Age of Kings Study Guide.* New York: NET, 1960.

MEDIUM INFORMATION: *Medium:* Video; *Sound:* Spoken language; *Color:* No (black & white); *Length:* 57 min.; *Language(s) spoken:* English; *Video type:* 16mm, Kinescope.

AUTHORSHIP INFORMATION: *Producer(s):* Dews, Peter; *Director(s):* Hayes, Michael; *Adaptor/translator(s):* Crozier, Eric; *Composer(s):* Whelen, Christopher/Bliss, Arthur; Salter, Lionel (Conducting Royal Philharmonic Orchestra); *Designer(s):* Morris, Stanley; *Cast:* Hardy, Robert (Henry V); Squire, William (Chorus); Dench, Judi (Princess Katherine); Ringham, John (Humphrey); Garland, Patrick (Bedford); Gostelow, Gordon (Sir Thomas Erpingham); Cooper, George A. (Pistol); Bisley, Jeremy (Gower); Farrington, Kenneth (Fluellen); Wale, Terry (Court); Garnett, Tony (Bates); Windsor, Frank (Williams); Blanshard, Joby (Capt. Jamy); Cox, Michael (Macmorris); Willis, Jerome (Orleans); Warner, John (Dauphin); Selway, George (Constable of France); Shepperdson, Leon (Constable of France); Lodge, Terence (Le Fer); Brine, Adrian (Bourbon); Glover, Julian (Westmoreland); Johnson, Noel (Exeter); Andrews, David (Salisbury); Lane, Robert (Montjoy); Greenwood, John (York); Harley, Timothy (Boy); Valentine, Anthony (Herald); Rowe, Alan (Charles VI); Bidmead, Stephanie (Isabel); Wreford, Edgar (Burgundy); Coulette, Yvonne (Alice); + Howell, Dane; Scott, John Murray; Ware, Derek.

DISTRIBUTION & AVAILABILITY: *Publisher or responsible agency:* BBC; *Copy location:* BBC*, SCL*.

Henry the Fifth. **Documentary/Abridgment**

180. *Henry the Fifth.* (Series: Fair Adventure Series).

DOCUMENT INFORMATION: *Country:* USA; *Year of release:* 1964.

EDITION, HISTORY, CONTENTS, & EVALUATION: *Edition & history:* A three-part abridgment of the play with commentary by Dr. Frank Baxter. *Contents & evaluation:* Not seen. *Audience:* Junior High (grades 7-9); High school (grades 10-12);.

MEDIUM INFORMATION: *Medium:* Motion Picture; *Sound:* Spoken language; *Color:* No (black & white); *Length:* 84 min.; *Language(s) spoken:* English; *Film type:* 16mm.

DISTRIBUTION & AVAILABILITY: *Publisher or responsible agency:* Westinghouse Broadcast Corporation; *Distributor:* Not known.

Henry the Fifth. **Video/Recording**

181. *Henry the Fifth.*

DOCUMENT INFORMATION: *Country:* Canada; *Year of first showing:* 1967; *Location of first showing:* CBC. Transmitted 29 Jan. 1967.

EDITION, HISTORY, CONTENTS, & EVALUATION: *Edition & history:* A television adaptation of the 1966 Stratford Festival of Canada production, this was also the first Shakespeare play transmitted in color on the Canadian airwaves. Reaction of reviewers was mixed. Despite their acknowledged excellence, few Stratford, Canada, productions have ever been telecast, apparently owing to legal complications about ownership rights. That is also probably why Mary Jane Miller's recent *Turn Up the Contrast: CBC Television Drama Since 1952* (Vancouver: UBC P, 1987) says virtually nothing about Shakespeare on Canadian television. *Contents & evaluation:* A review of the stage production (not the televised version) was on the whole favorable. Douglas Rain "looked more like a commoner than a king" and the "comic relief was lustily done" with Behrens as Fluellen coming in for particular praise. The idea of having French Canadians play the French roles, however, did not work out too well because no one could

understand their broken English. As far as the reviewer was concerned, clear diction was a greater virtue than deference to Canadian bi-lingualism (Edinborough, Arnold, "The Canadian Shakespeare Festival." *SQ* 17 [Autumn 1966]: 399-402). *Supplementary materials:* Morris, *SHOF* 31.; H&M, 20.

MEDIUM INFORMATION: *Color:* Yes; *Length:* 120 min.

AUTHORSHIP INFORMATION: *Director(s):* Langham, Michael (Stage); Freed, Lorne (TV); *Designer(s):* Heeley, Desmond; *Cast:* Rain, Douglas (Henry V); Behrens, Bernard (Fluellen); Thomas, Powys (Pistol); Christmas, Eric (Bardolph); Hall, Aemilia (Mistress Quickly); Hutt, William (Chorus); Gascon, Jean (Charles VI); LeBlanc, Diana (Katherine).

DISTRIBUTION & AVAILABILITY: *Publisher or responsible agency:* CFTO/TV, Toronto.

Henry the Fifth. **Video/Teleplay**

182. *Henry the Fifth.* (Series: The Shakespeare Plays).

DOCUMENT INFORMATION: *Year of filming:* 18-25 June 1979; *Year of first showing:* 1979; *Location of first showing(s):* BBC, London; PBS stations, USA, 23 Apr. 1980.

EDITION, HISTORY, CONTENTS, & EVALUATION: *Edition & history:* Even Director David Giles was haunted by the shadow, or overpowering image, of the earlier Olivier film version of *Henry V*. His solution was an attempt to see the play with fresh eyes again, as though Olivier had never made his unforgettable film. Textually he and script editor Alan Shallcrosss sought to reduce the length to about two and a half hours not by cutting major speeches but by 'filleting,' that is to say, cutting a line here and a line there. Even so, a great swatch from Canterbury's lecture on the law 'Salic,' which Olivier made into a farce, disappeared. Audiences find it incomprehensible anyway, unless they have been fortunate enough to hear it made comprehensible in Kenneth Branagh's brilliant 1989 *Henry V* (181.2). In costuming, Odette Barrow color coded the English in beige, brown and gold; the French, in blue, green and gold. The audience in this way can the more easily keep the protagonists sorted out. *Contents & evaluation:* "David Giles, the distinguished director of the Second Tetralogy, skillfully engages the problem of the unreliable Chorus to move as a bridge between the loose episodic scenes of the play. The Chorus plays an Alistair Cooke smugly providing exposition as though we couldn't enjoy the play without his presumably indispensable commentary. At the outset he stresses we are at a play as he walks through the set of immobile figures to address us and then turns his back to activate the performance. He can appear with little intrusion at the Southhampton docks or at the French court that dissolves into the English encampment. When at the end he tells us there isn't simply time enough and that his story must 'brook abridgment,' we understand as a television audience that cuts must be made in Shakespeare's text. . . . Giles is never intimidated by the Olivier movie, his monumental predecessor. He succeeds as Olivier did by making the medium express in its best mode what is available to each in Shakespeare's text. There is no army here with crossbows whirring across the screen, yet entrances from various angles skillfully create the sense of larger spaces. The one stunning, silently focused close-up of Boy, the play's delightful and perceptive junior chorus, bleeding at the mouth and lying dead, says more about the victory of Agincourt and its 'spotless cause' and 'spotted men' than all the absurd exaggeration of the French body count. The fine performances by the members of the French court like the comic counterperspectives of Fluellen, MacMorris and Pistol create the ironic balances that prevent Henry's jingoistic rhetoric and strenuous exhortations from undermining themselves. . . . *Henry V* is perhaps Shakespeare's most perplexing history play because it is seemingly filled with little but static characters, formal set speeches, ambiguous contradictions, undramatic conflicts and dubious continuity. Yet this splendid production makes it a handsome and stylish conclusion to Shakespeare's Second Tetralogy" (Cubeta, Paul M., "The Shakespeare Plays on TV," *SFNL* 5.1. [1980]: 4 +). *Audience:* General use; *Supplementary materials: Henry V BSP;* Gaertner, J. "Notes on Costume Design." *SFNL* 5.1 (1980): 4; Videocassette (25 min.) from "Shakespeare in Perspective" series with Lord Chalfont available from BBC* (*BUFVC* 9).

MEDIUM INFORMATION: *Medium:* Video; *Sound:* Spoken language; *Color:* Yes; *Length:* 170 min.; *Video type:* B, V, 3/4" U.

AUTHORSHIP INFORMATION: *Producer(s):* Messina, Cedric; *Director(s):* Giles, David; *Composer(s):* Lloyd-Jones, David; *Designer(s):* Homfray, Don; *Costume designer(s):* Barrow, Odette; *Lighting designer(s):* Channon, Dennis; *Other personnel:* Walsh, Terry (Fight Arranger); Macarthur, Jenny (Prod. Asst.); Watts, Beryl (Director's Asst.); Lowden, Fraser (Unit Manager); Dixon, Colin (Sound); Rowell, Elizabeth (Make-up); Wilders, John (Literary Consultant); *Cast:* McCowen, Alec (Chorus); Gwillim, David (Henry V); Smith, M. (Gloucester); Edwards, R. (Bedford); Davenport, Roger (Clarence); Parrish, Clifford (Exeter); Hollis, Derek (York); Ashby, Robert (Salisbury); Buck, David (Westmoreland); Beacham, Rod (Warwick); Baxter, Trevor (Archbishop); Abineri, John (Bishop); Whymper, William (Cambridge); Price, Ian (Scroop); Howe, George (Erpingham); Rowlands, David (Grey); Poyser, Brian (Gower); Wylton, Tim (Fluellen); Ward, Paddy (MacMorris); McKevitt, Michael (Jamy); Forfar, Ronald (Bates); Ritchie, Joe (Court); Pinner, David (Williams); Holland, Jeffrey (Nym); Gostelow, Gordon (Bardolph); Pringle, Bryan (Pistol); Fowler, John (Boy); Broad, Simon (Herald); Walters, Thorley (Charles VI); Drinkel, Keith (Lewis); Harris, Robert (Burgundy); Saunders, John (Orleans); Bryans, John (Bourbon); Glover, Julian (Constable); Forgione, Carl (Rambures); Brown, Alan (Governor); Hagon, Garrick (Montjoy); Ruddock, Pamela (Queen); Boisseau, Jocelyne (Katherine); Quayle, Anna (Alice); Bruce, Brenda (Hostess).

DISTRIBUTION AND AVAILABILITY: *Publisher or responsible agency:* BBC/TLF; *Distributor:* AVP, UIO, BBC*, *Copy location:* UVM, ITM*; *Availability:* AVP, sale, all formats $450 (1987); UIO, V, (72036H), 3/4U (70136V), rental $24.10; BBC* 16mm or V, apply.

Henry the Fifth. Video/Recording

182.1 *Held Henry.* [*Heroic Henry*].

DOCUMENT INFORMATION: *Country:* Belgium; *Year of first showing:* 1984.

EDITION, HISTORY, CONTENTS, & EVALUATION: *Edition & history:* Recording of a play, apparently based on the life of Henry V, at Theatre der Freien Hansestadt Bremen.

MEDIUM INFORMATION: *Medium:* V; *Video type:* B.

AUTHORSHIP INFORMATION: *Director(s):* Zadek, Peter.

DISTRIBUTION & AVAILABILITY: *Copy location:* CTL; *Call or copy number:* B L500/MT: KUL.

Henry the Fifth. Motion Picture/Adaptation

182.2 *Henry the Fifth.*

DOCUMENT INFORMATION: *Country:* GB; *Year of release:* 1989.

EDITION, HISTORY, CONTENTS, & EVALUATION: *Edition & history:*

Premiered in New York City on November 8, 1989, Kenneth Branagh's *Henry V* is one of the best Shakespeare movies ever made because it strikes a nearly perfect balance between the demands of Shakespeare's language and the aesthetics of filmmaking. Director and star, Kenneth Branagh, who has been active with London's Renaissance Theatre group, saw his movie not so much as a challenge to Laurence Olivier's famous 1944 production as an attempt to reinterpret *Henry V* for our own time. At mid-century when Britain was under siege from Nazi Germany, Olivier stressed nationalism and the values of the heroic warrior. In Branagh's contemporary production, the emphasis falls on the personal struggle and maturation of the young prince as he comes to power. In preparation, Branagh interviewed Prince Charles of England, to get a feeling for how a real life prince might feel when walking in mufti among the populace. A distinguished cast supports Branagh, including Dame Judi Dench, Derek Jacobi, Ian Holm, Paul Scofield, and Alec McCowen. *Contents & evaluation:* To an astonishing degree, Branagh's film of *Henry V* displays both literary and cinematic integrity. Bardolaters will be pleased by the ways in which Shakespeare's text and subtext are not only mined but sifted for every possible nuance. The establishment, for example, of the heartrending context for Bardolph's gruesome hanging enlarges a few lines into a mini-essay on the grave responsibilites of kingly duties. Cineastes will rediscover the power of the close and mid-shot. Unlike Olivier's movie of *H5*, which was epic in scale, oratorical in utterance, and long in shot, Branagh's film, without diminishment in effect, is personal, introspective, and in close and medium shot. Moreover when Derek Jacobi as a Brechtian chorus (he intervenes in the action at Harfleur) first appears to switch on the lights of a film studio, notice seems to have been given that Shakespeare in the movies is at last overtly to become the "Muse of fire." The camera does not merely record but participates in the action and becomes a silent partner with the actors—but differently from the Olivier film. There the big speeches, such as the St. Crispin's day oration, begin in close and end in long shots; here they begin at, say, midshot and end in close-ups. The expressive faces of the talented actors convey an ocean of thoughts: Jacobi's chorus, intently; Judi Dench's Hostess, pathetically; and Branagh's Kennedy-esque young king, with a kind of heroic vulnerability.

Moreover the film is not just a movie about Shakespeare's play but a movie about making movies about Shakespeare's play. The obvious allusions to other Shakespeare films, not only Olivier's but also Polanski's, Kurosawa's and Welles's, imply a wry alertness by the director to the meta-cinematic and guarantee a shock of recognition for the perceptive viewer.

There is no competition with Olivier's film, only a brilliant, innovative reworking of Shakespeare's play. When it emerges on videocassette, teachers will find it an indispensable ally (KSR). *Supplementary materials:* Johnston, Sheila. "A Kingdom for a Stage." *Elle* (Oct. 1989): 118-9; Billington, M. "A 'New Olivier'." *NYT* 8 Jan. 1989: H18; Nightingale, B. "Henry V Returns" *NYT* 5 Nov. 1989: H17 +; Canby, Vincent. "A Down to Earth *H5*." *NYT* 8 Nov. 1989: C19; Kliman, Bernice. "Branagh's *Henry V*: Allusion and Illusion." *SFNL* 14.1 [Dec. 1989]: 1 +.

MEDIUM INFORMATION: *Length:* 138 min.

AUTHORSHIP INFORMATION: *Producer(s):* Evans, Stephen; Sharman, Bruce; Parfitt, David; *Director(s):* Branagh, Kenneth; *Composer(s):* Doyle, Pat; Rattle, Simon; *Designer(s):* Cruttwell, Hugh; Dorme, Norman; Harvey, Tim; *Costume designer(s):* Dalton, Phyllis; *Director of Photography:* MacMillan, Kenneth; *Other personnel:* Bradsell, Mike (Editor); Frampton, Peter (Makeup); Jackson, Russell (Text Advisor); *Cast:* Branagh, Kenneth (Henry V); Jacobi, Derek (Chorus); Shepherd, Simon (Gloucester); Larkin, James (Bedford); Blessed, Brian (Exeter); Simmons, James (York); Gregory, Paul (Westmoreland); McCowen, Alec (Ely); Kay, Charles (Canterbury); Cartwright, Fabian (Cambridge); Simms, Stephen (Scroop); Villiers, Jay (Grey); Jewesbury, Edward (Erpingham); Holm, Ian (Fluellen); Webb, Daniel (Gower); Yuill, Jimmy (Jamy); Sessions, John (MacMorris); Prendergast, Shaun (Bates); Doyle, Pat (Court); Williams, Michael (Williams); Briers, Richard (Bardolph); Stephens, Robert (Pistol); Coltrane, Robbie (Falstaff); Bale, Christian (Boy); Dench, Judi (Mistress Quickly); Scofield, Paul (French King); Maloney, Michael (Dauphin); Inman, Mark (Soldier); Easton, Richard (Constable); Thompson, Emma (Katherine); McEwan, Geraldine (Alice); Parfitt, David (Messenger); Ferguson, Nicholas (Warwick); Whitehouse, Tom (Talbot); Yuill, Calum (Child).

DISTRIBUTION & AVAILABILITY: *Publisher or responsible agency:* The Samuel Goldwyn Company; *Distributor:* Available commercially only at present time.

King Henry the Sixth, Parts One through Three

Please note: Entries listed under the *Three Parts of King Henry the Sixth* are not in strict chronological order because of the complicated overlappings growing out of different strategies for adapting parts of, or the entirety of, a three-part drama.

ORIGINAL WORK AND PRODUCTION: English History Plays. *Year of first production:* 1592; *Country of first production:* GB; *Site of first production:* The Theatre, Shoreditch, or Rose playhouse, Bankside [?].

Henry the Sixth, Parts One and Two. **Video/Recording**

183. *Henry the Sixth.* (Series: *Wars of the Roses*, I).

DOCUMENT INFORMATION: *Country:* GB; *Year of first showing:* 1965; *Location of first showing:* Royal Shakespeare Theatre/BBC. Transmitted 8 to 10:55 P.M., with one news break, Thursday, 8 April 1965.

EDITION, HISTORY, CONTENTS, & EVALUATION: *Edition & history:* Originally conceived and directed for the Stratford RSC stage by John Barton and Peter Hall, this series of programs adapts the minor tetralogy (three parts of *Henry VI* and *Richard III*) to three plays, called *Henry VI, Edward IV* and *Richard III* (See also 184 and 509). Each segment in turn was three hours in

length. The production is something more than a mere recording of a stage play. Twelve cameras taped the performers who acted on a stage that had been extended 40 feet by boarding over orchestra seats. The effect was to achieve a sense of space for the battle scenes that was lacking in the original RSC stage production. Rehearsal and recording took eight weeks. By working closely with the RSC and taping in their own theatre, the producer got a sense of continuity and unity that might otherwise have been lacking in so sprawling a venture. *Contents & evaluation:* "A second seeing of the British Broadcasting Company's television films of the Royal Shakespeare Company's *Henry VI, Edward IV,* and *Richard III* convinced the writer (who had seen both the stage productions and the television films previously in England) that these are the best television productions of Shakespeare's plays in the history of television . . . greatly to the credit of the television directors, Robin Midgley and Michael Hayes, that truth to the script was their first consideration and that the techniques of the medium were employed in the best interests of the play, never as an end in themselves" (Griffin, Alice, "Shakespeare Through the Camera's Eye," *SQ* 17.4 [1966]: 385). *Audience:* General use; *Supplementary materials:* "A Shakespearian Experience on TV." *Times* 21 April 1965: 13d.; Williams, Michael. "*Wars of the Roses.*" *RT* 1 Apr. 1965: 43.

MEDIUM INFORMATION: *Medium:* Video; *Sound:* Spoken language; *Color:* No (black & white); *Length:* 175 min.; *Language(s) spoken:* English; *Video type:* Kinescope, 16mm.

AUTHORSHIP INFORMATION: *Producer(s):* Hall, Peter (Stage); Barry, Michael (TV); *Director(s):* Hayes, Michael; Midgeley, Robin (TV); Hall, Peter (Stage); *Adaptor/translator(s):* Barton, John; *Composer(s):* Woolfenden, Guy; Bennett, Gordon; and others; *Designer(s):* Bury, John; *Lighting designer(s):* Wright, Robert; *Other personnel:* Henderson, Ann (Make-up); Clarke, Roy (Editor); *Cast:* Warner, David (Henry VI); Ashcroft, Peggy (Margaret); Suzman, Janet (Joan); Morton, Clive (Talbot); Selby, Nicholas (Winchester); Normington, John (Bedford); Hardwick, Paul (Gloucester); Burton, Donald (Exeter); Sinden, Donald (Plantagenet); Squire, William (Suffolk); Brack, Philip (Somerset); Mason, Brewster (Warwick); McConnochie, Rhys (Vernon); Forbes-Robertson, Peter (Lawyer); Hancock, Stephen (Bassett); Thomas, Charles (Mortimer); Gale, Peter (John Talbot); O'Neil, Colette (Eleanor); Kay, Charles (Sir John Hume); Morgan, Gareth (Bolingbroke); Thomas, Madoline (Margery Jourdain); Normington, John (Simpcox); Grant, Sheila (Simpcox's wife); Kay, Charles (Dauphin); Layne-Smith, Donald (Reignier); Geddis, Peter (Alencon); Morgan, Gareth (Orleans); Sullivan, Hugh (Burgundy); Hales, John (Papal Legate); + Soldiers, Servants, Messengers.

DISTRIBUTION & AVAILABILITY: *Publisher or responsible agency:* BBC/RSC; *Distributor:* BBC, *Copy location:* BBC*, archive.

Henry the Sixth, Parts Two and Three. **Video/Recording**

184. *Edward the Fourth.* (Series: *Wars of the Roses,* II)

DOCUMENT INFORMATION: *Country:* GB; *Year of first showing:* 1965; *Location of first showing:* Royal Shakespeare Theatre/BBC TV. Transmitted 8 to 11:05 P.M. with one news break, Friday, 15 Apr. 1965.

EDITION, HISTORY, CONTENTS, & EVALUATION: *Edition & history:* Originally conceived and directed for the Stratford RSC stage by John Barton and Peter Hall, this series of programs adapts the minor tetralogy (three parts of *Henry VI* and *Richard III*) to three plays, called *Henry VI, Edward IV* and *Richard III* (see also 183, above, for description and 509). *Contents & evaluation:* This second installment was also well received. Alice Griffin, a pioneering critic of Shakespeare on screen, had this to say: "Although all of the parts were well played, it was a boon for the viewer to see in close-up the faces of the principals, with all of the subtleties revealed which these actors brought to their parts: Peggy Ashcroft as Margaret, David Warner as Henry VI, and Ian Holm as Richard III. Dame Peggy is indisputably the finest Shakespearian actress on the English-speaking stage, and it is an unforgettable experience to witness at such close range her portrayal of Margaret from the coquettish French princess in the first play to the vengeful crone of the third" (Griffin, Alice, "Shakespeare Through the Camera's Eye," *SQ* 17.4 [1966]: 386). *Audience:* General use; *Supplementary materials:* "A Shakespearian Experience on TV." *Times* 21 April 1965: 13d.; "Program." *RT* 8 Apr. 1965: 3.

MEDIUM INFORMATION: *Medium:* Video; *Sound:* Spoken language; *Color:* No (black & white); *Length:* 180 min.; *Language(s) spoken:* English; *Video type:* Kinescope, 16mm.

AUTHORSHIP INFORMATION: *Producer(s):* Hall, Peter (Stage); Barry, Michael (TV); *Director(s):* Hayes, Michael; Midgeley, Robin (TV); Hall, Peter (Stage); *Adaptor/translator(s):* Barton, John; *Composer(s):* Woolfenden, Guy; Bennett, Gordon; and others; *Designer(s):* Bury, John; *Lighting designer(s):* Wright, Robert; *Other personnel:* Henderson, Ann (Make-up); Clarke, Roy (Editor); *Cast:* Warner, David (Henry VI); Ashcroft, Peggy (Margaret); Sinden, Donald (York); Morton, Clive (Talbot); Selby, Nicholas (Winchester); Holm, Ian (Gloucester); Dotrice, Roy (Jack Cade); Tucker, Alan (Prince Edward); Burton, Donald (Exeter); Layne-Smith, Donald (Lord Say); Corvin, John (Lord Clifford); Normington, John (Young Clifford); Dench, Jeffery (Stafford); Brack, Philip (Somerset); Jones, Maurice (Oxford); Geddis, Peter (Son That Killed Father); Menzies, Lee (Richmond); Mason, Brewster (Warwick); Dotrice, Roy (Edward IV); Kay, Charles (Clarence); McClelland, Fergus (Rutland); Thomas, Madoline (Duchess of York); Waller, David (Father That Killed Son); Engel, Susan (Lady Elizabeth); Sullivan, Hugh (Hastings); Waring, Derek (Rivers); Squire, William (Buckingham); Webster, Malcolm (Iden); Hussey, John (Lewis XI); O'Neil, Colette (Lady Bona); Sullivan, Hugh (Burgundy).

DISTRIBUTION & AVAILABILITY: *Publisher or responsible agency:* BBC/RSC; *Distributor:* BBC, *Copy location:* BBC*, archive.

Henry the Sixth, Part One. **Video/Teleplay (Part 9 of 15 parts)**

185. *Red Rose and the White, The.* (Series: *An Age of Kings,* IX).

DOCUMENT INFORMATION: *Country:* GB; *Year of first showing:* 1960; *Location of first showing(s):* BBC TV; Transmitted 9 to 10 P.M., Thursday, 25 Aug. 1960.

EDITION, HISTORY, CONTENTS, & EVALUATION: *Awards:* Dews, Peter: Excellence in Directing (British Guild of Directors); *Edition & history:* Based on the entirety of *King Henry the Sixth.* The ninth installment in *An Age of Kings* (see also numbers 156-9, 178-9, 188,

190-2, 485-6, and 505-6). Producing the sprawling minor tetralogy obviously created horrendous casting problems, which were solved by ingenious allocation of personnel. This segment was managed with a total of 39 actors. A new face was Jack May, who played Richard duke of York, father to Richard duke of Gloucester who was to become the notorious King Richard III. Cost for this section was only £2,598 but when the expense of producing the next two parts of *Henry VI* is added, the total adds up to over £9,000. For additional background information, see *The Hollow Crown* (485), which is based on *Richard II* and which is therefore the first episode in the series. *Contents & evaluation:* "On Henry V's death, his baby son becomes Henry VI of England. The infant's two protectors, one of the House of Lancaster and the other of York, are politically divided. The long-festering enmity between their two houses finally erupts into the famous War [s] of the Roses" (PR blurb). The London *Times* critic noted the abrupt shift in style that must accompany a change from the mature verse of the major tetralogy to the youthful verse of the minor tetralogy. He seemed to feel, however, that the actors adroitly exploited the "thundering pentameters" of the play's verse. Compressed into but one hour, much had to be cut. But there was room for Joan la Pucelle (played by Eileen Atkins)—"Shakespeare Serial Changes Style," *Times* 26 August 1960: 5b. *Audience:* General use; *Supplementary materials:* Campbell, O.J. Introduction. *An Age of Kings* [The 15 parts as they appeared on television]; "Program." *RT* 10 Aug. 1960: 19.

MEDIUM INFORMATION: *Medium:* Video; *Sound:* Spoken language; *Color:* No (black & white); *Length:* 59 min.; *Language(s) spoken:* English; *Video type:* 16mm, Kinescope.

AUTHORSHIP INFORMATION: *Producer(s):* Dews, Peter; *Director(s):* Hayes, Michael; *Adaptor/translator(s):* Crozier, Eric; *Composer(s):* Whelen, Christopher/Bliss, Arthur; Salter, Lionel (Conducting Royal Philharmonic Orchestra); *Designer(s):* Morris, Stanley; *Cast:* Scully, Terry (King Henry VI); May, Jack (Duke of York); Atkins, Eileen (Joan la Pucelle); Garland, Patrick (Bedord); Ringham, John (Humphrey); Johnson, Noel (Exeter); Lang, Robert (Beaufort); Willis, Jerome (Dauphin); Valentine, Anthony (Alanson); Warner, John (Regnier); Andrews, David (Bastard); Shepperdson, Leon (Woodville); Cox, Michael (Lord Mayor); Morris, Mary (Margaret); Wreford, Edgar (Suffolk); Rowe, Alan (Somerset); Windsor, Frank (Warwick); Garnett, Tony (Vernon); Greenwood, John (Lawyer and messenger); Cox, Michael (Shepherd); Scott, John; Wale, Terry (Messengers); Glover, Julian; Bisley, Jeremy (Warders); Harley, Timothy; Ware, Derek; Farrington, Kenneth (Serving men).

DISTRIBUTION & AVAILABILITY: *Publisher or responsible agency:* BBC; *Copy location:* BBC*, SCL*.

Henry the Sixth, Part One. **Video/Teleplay. History**

186. *Henry the Sixth, Part One.* (Series: The Shakespeare Plays).

DOCUMENT INFORMATION: *Year of filming:* 13-19 Oct. 1981; *Year of first showing:* 1982; *Location of first showing(s):* BBC, London; PBS, USA, 27 March 1983.

EDITION, HISTORY, CONTENTS, & EVALUATION: *Edition & history:* Not content with televising the entire major tetralogy (*R2* through the two parts of *H4* and then *H5*), the BBC producers then took on the immensely complicated minor tetralogy, which is comprised of the three parts of *H6* plus *King Richard III* (see 187, 193 and 513). The inability to fit the entire cast credits into the number of bytes allocated by the MELBASE software program, which has easily handled nearly every other play in the canon, suggests the enormous size and scope of this production. Director Jane Howell, after much thought, solved the problem of sets for this epical tale, in many respects more narrative than dramatic, by borrowing from a schoolyard 'adventure playground' set as a basis for the *mise en scène.* The results are quite astonishing. Somehow the well-disciplined soldiers, the rhythmic martial flourishes, and this raggle-taggle collection of entrances and exits endow the performance with more heart-stopping realism than realism itself (KSR). *Contents & evaluation:* "[This] . . . production of the *Henry VI-Richard III* tetralogy, a sequence of plays, which despite its large number of events and personalities, is a fascinating, fast-paced, and surprisingly tight-knit study in political and national deterioration. . . . Covering nearly sixty years in England's tumultuous fifteenth century, the plays trace quite closely the progression of what later came to be called the 'Wars of the Roses.' . . . The chief credit for the success of these productions must go, of course, to Jane Howell, who directed the entire tetralogy, and whose sense of their purpose strikes me as clear and accurate throughout. She sees the role of King Henry and of the emerging Richard of Gloucester as set apart from the many other important characters in the plays. . . . Her Henry is a non-political man in an era dominated by political men. (As which era has not been?) Henry, who has aptly been called Henry the 'Wimp,' comes gradually to be, in this production, which bears his name, an image of King Henry the Wise. He is here seen as an incipient pacifist living among power brokers who consider no means of resolving political differences other than violent ones. He withdraws from the others, both because they want him to withdraw, and because he has a different perspective on political and (human) affairs—a perspective which in his age was seen as *heavenly,* and in our time might also be called sane" (Manheim, Michael, "The *Henry VI-Richard III* Tetralogy," *SFNL* 8.2. [1984]:2). *Audience:* General use; *Supplementary materials: Henry VI Part One, BSP;*

Videocassette (25 min.) from "Shakespeare in Perspective" series with Michael Wood as lecturer available in U.K. from BBC* (*BUFVC* 9).

MEDIUM INFORMATION: *Medium:* Video; *Sound:* Spoken language; *Color:* Yes; *Length:* 185 min.; *Video type:* B, V, 3/4U.

AUTHORSHIP INFORMATION: *Producer(s):* Miller, Jonathan; *Director(s):* Howell, Jane; *Adaptor/translator(s):* Snodin, David; *Composer(s):* Simpson, Dudley; *Designer(s):* Bayldon, Oliver; *Costume designer(s):* Peacock, John; *Lighting designer(s):* Barclay, Sam; *Other personnel:* Campbell-Hill, Corin (Prod. Manager); Ranson, Malcolm (Fight Arranger); Alston, Cherry (Make-up); Edmonds, Alan (Sound); Dowdall, Jim/Musetti, Val/Potter, Mike (Stunt Men); *Cast:* Benson, Peter (Henry VI/Singer); Burke, David (Gloucester); Evans, Tenniel (Bedford/Mortimer/General); O'Conor, Joseph (Exeter/Shepherd); Middlemass, Frank (Bishop); Deacon, B. (Somerset); Hill, B. (York +); Wing-Davey, Mark (Warwick); Chapman, Paul (Suffolk/Glansdale); Farr, Derek (Salisbury/William Lucy/First Keeper); Peacock, Trevor (Lord Talbot); Guard, A. (Talbot); Cox, Arthur (Fastolfe, Mayor +); Wyatt, Peter (Woodville + four); Benfield, John (Basset/Keeper/Sergeant); Daker, David (Vernon/Reignier); Saynor, Ian (Charles); Brown, Antony (Burgundy); Byrne, Michael (Alencon); Protheroe, Brian (Bastard/First Messenger); Pugh, David (Officer + two); Fuke, Derek (Captain/First Servant); Jesson, Paul (Second Messenger); Cook, Ron (Third Messenger/Porter); MacNamara, Oengus (Messenger); + Blethyn, Brenda (Joan); Foster, Julia (Margaret); McCallum, Joanna (Countess); Alford, John (Boy); Musicians and Soldiers.

DISTRIBUTION & AVAILABILITY: *Publisher or responsible agency:* BBC/TLF; *Distributor:* AVP, UIO, KSU, BBC* *Copy location:* UVM; *Availability:* AVP, sale all formats $450 (1987); UIO V (72321H), 3/4U (70321V) rental, $24.90; KSU, rental V, 3/4U 5 days, $33.75; BBC*, 16mm or V, apply.

Henry the Sixth, Part Two. Video/Teleplay. History

187. *Henry the Sixth, Part Two.* (Series: The Shakespeare Plays).

DOCUMENT INFORMATION: *Year of filming:* 17-23 Dec. 1981; *Year of first showing:* 1982; *Location of first showing(s):* BBC, London; PBS, USA, 2 April 1983.

EDITION, HISTORY, CONTENTS, & EVALUATION: *Edition & history:* Increasingly noticeable to the viewer who has the leisure to study the four different BBC plays (see also 186, 193 and 513) in the minor tetralogy is the way in which director Jane Howell handles them as though the actors were a part of a repertory company. The doubling of roles is so pervasive that there is

insufficient space in this report to list all the different roles a single actor may play (thus a ' + ' must suffice to indicate an actor's performing more than one role). David Burke is both the Bishop of Winchester and Dick the Butcher; Arthur Cox, not only Sir John Falstofe but also Mayor of London and Papal Legate. And so it goes. Meanwhile actors with major roles in one production may be mere attendant lords or flunkies in another: witness Ron Cook as "Third Messenger" in *1H6* and as Richard Plantagenet, en route to becoming King Richard III, in *2H6*; or, to go the other way, there is Peter Benson as King Henry VI in *2H6* reduced to a spectral monk in *R3*. It's fun for the audience to watch out for these marvelous transformations but also stimulating for the actors to work in such a context of give-and-take and cheerful professionalism. *Contents & evaluation:* "Howell's staging of the many battle scenes supports the inherent pacifism she sees as central to the plays. In part one, rapid reversals are conveyed by the simple device of swinging doors. At one instant, the English pursue the French through these doors with great cheers and flourishes; at another, they are themselves pursued back with the physical evidence of defeat suddenly plastered on their countenances. . . . While such devices enhance the sense of the pointlessness of the battle in part one, they also contribute to the somewhat comic quality of the early battles in these plays. But as the true Wars of the Roses begin late in parts two and three, there is little comedy. What we now see are montages of the false glory of battle (represented by trumpets and drums), followed by the very graphic examples of hand-to-hand combat which are quite free from any kind of glory). . . . Howell individualizes these battles, seemingly so similar to one another as one reads them on the printed page. Each has its own noteworthy feature. For example, there is Tewkesbury, which, before it concludes with the brutal on-stage murder of the foolish Prince Edward, is preceded by marvelous, balletic montages of bloody winter battle which perhaps better than anything else in these productions suggests the cold absurdity of men killing each other for vaguely conceived ambition and senseless revenge" (Manheim, Michael, "The *Henry VI-Richard III* Tetralogy," *SFNL* 8.2 [1984]: 4). *Audience:* General use; *Supplementary materials: Henry VI Part 2 BSP*; Videocassette (25 min.) from "Shakespeare in Perspective" series with Michael Wood as lecturer available in U.K. from BBC* (*BUFVC* 9).

MEDIUM INFORMATION: *Medium:* video; *Sound:* Spoken language; *Color:* Yes; *Length:* 201 min.; *Video type:* B, V, 3/4U.

AUTHORSHIP INFORMATION: *Producer(s):* Miller, Jonathan; *Director(s):* Howell, Jane; *Adaptor/translator(s):* Snodin, David; *Composer(s):* Oliver, Stephen/Simpson, Dudley; *Designer(s):* Bayldon, Oliver; *Costume designer(s):* Peacock, John; *Lighting designer(s):* Barclay, Sam; *Other personnel:* Campbell-Hill, Corin

(Prod. Manager); Ranson, Malcolm (Fight Arranger); Alston, Cherry (Make-up); Edmonds, Alan (Sound); Chuntz, Alan (Stunt Man); Stephenson, Geraldine (Movement Coordinator); *Cast:* Benson, Peter (Henry VI); Burke, David (Gloucester/Butcher); Middlemass, Frank (Winchester); Hill, Bernard (York); Protheroe, Brian (E. Plantagenet); Cook, Ron (R. Plantagenet/ 'One'); Jesson, Paul (George Plantagenet + two); Deacon, Brian (Somerset/Smith); Chapman, Paul (Suffolk); Daker, David (Buckingham); Wing-Davey, Mark (Warwick); Evans, Tenniel (Salisbury/Clerk); Cox, A. (Clifford); Farr, Derek (Say + two); Wyatt, Peter (Stafford + three); Peacock, Trevor (Cade/Sheriff); Byrne, Michael (Hume/Lieutenant); Brown, Antony (Stanley + two); Pugh, David (Stafford + three); Fuke, Derek (First Petitioner + four); MacNamara, Oengus (Clifford + six); Benfield, Peter (Beadle + four); Guard, Alex (Second Prentice + two); Foster, Julia (Margaret); Carroll, Anne (Duchess); Keen, Pat (Margery Jourdain); Lloyd, Gabrielle (Wife); Wright, Joseph (Edward); Alford, John (Richard); Breeze, Timothy (George); Musicians.

DISTRIBUTION & AVAILABILITY: *Publisher or responsible agency:* BBC/TLF; *Distributor:* AVP, UIO, KSU, BBC*, *Copy location:* UVM; *Availability:* AVP, sale, all formats, $450 (1987); UIO, V (72322H), 3/4U (70322V), $26.20; KSU, V, 3/4U, 5 days, rental $33.75; BBC*, 16mm and V, apply.

Henry the Sixth, Part Two. Video/Teleplay (Part 10 of 15 parts)

188. *Fall of a Protector, The.* (Series: *An Age of Kings*, X).

DOCUMENT INFORMATION: *Country:* GB; *Year of first showing:* 1960; *Location of first showing:* BBC TV. Transmitted 9 to 10 P.M., Thursday, 8 Sept. 1960.

EDITION, HISTORY, CONTENTS, & EVALUATION: *Awards:* Dews, Peter: Excellence in Directing (British Guild of Directors); *Edition & history:* Based on Acts 1-3 of *King Henry the Sixth, pt. 2.* The tenth installment in *An Age of Kings* (see also numbers 156-9, 178-9, 185, 190-2, 485-6, and 505-6). For background, see *The Hollow Crown* (485), which is based on *Richard II* and which is therefore the first episode in the series. *Contents & evaluation:* "Suffolk's conspiracy comes to a head. Henry VI's marriage to Margaret of Anjou leads to Richard, Duke of York's ascendancy to power. Humphrey, Duke of Gloucester, falls victim to Suffolk's ambition" (PR blurb). The London *Times* critic felt that the way to handle the broadness and simplicity of *Henry VI* was to find a simple and straightforward style for presenting the play's tangled events. Producer Peter Dews on the whole succeeded in doing this,

even though his "camera style in general remains unobtrusive and academic." Actress Mary Morris as Margaret of Anjou also came in for high praise ("Extravert Acting in *An Age of Kings*," *Times* 10 Sept. 1960: 4g); Prof. Milton Crane had special praise for Terry Scully as "the pitiful King Henry VI, [who] even convinced one from time to time that the King has some useful function in the plays that bear his name" ("Shakespeare on Television," *SQ* 12.3 [Summer 1961]: 326). *Audience:* General use; *Supplementary materials:* Campbell, O.J. Introduction. *An Age of Kings* [The 15 parts as they appeared on television]. New York: Pyramid, 1961; Weiner, Albert. *An Age of Kings Study Guide.* New York: NET, 1960.

MEDIUM INFORMATION: *Medium:* Video; *Sound:* Spoken language; *Color:* No (black & white); *Length:* 60 min.; *Language(s) spoken:* English; *Video type:* 16mm, Kinescope.

AUTHORSHIP INFORMATION: *Producer(s):* Dews, Peter; *Director(s):* Hayes, Michael; *Adaptor/translator(s):* Crozier, Eric; *Composer(s):* Whelen, Christopher/Bliss, Arthur; Salter, Lionel (Conducting Royal Philharmonic Orchestra); *Designer(s):* Morris, Stanley; *Cast:* Scully, Terry (King Henry VI); May, Jack (Duke of York); Morris, Mary (Margaret of Anjou); Jackson, Nancie (Duchess of Gloucester); Wreford, Edgar (Suffolk); Ringham, John (Humphrey); Lang, Robert (Beaufort); Gostelow, Gordon (Salisbury); Windsor, Frank (Warwick); Farrington, Kenneth (Buckingham); Rowe, Alan (Somerset); Greenwood, John (Messenger, Prentice); Garland, Patrick (Priest); Valentine, Anthony; Andrews, David (Petitioners); Ware, Derek (Peter); Glover, Julian (Thomas Horner); Lodge, Terence (Conjuror); Bisley, Jeremy (Southwell); Watson, Nan (Mother Jordan); Scott, John (Spirit); Harley, Timothy (Citizen); Warner, John (Simpcox); Noble, Audrey (Wife to Simpcox); Willis, Jerome (Mayor); Shepperdson, Leon (Beadle); Wickham, Jeffry (Sheriff); Willis, Jerome (Sir John Stanley); Garnett, Tony; Valentine, Anthony; Wale, Terry (Neighbors); Harley, Timothy (Prentice).

DISTRIBUTION & AVAILABILITY: *Publisher or responsible agency:* BBC; *Copy location:* BBC*, SCL*.

Henry the Sixth. Motion Picture/Scenes

189. *Gloucester's Soliloquy.*

DOCUMENT INFORMATION: *Country:* USA; *Year of release:* 1928.

EDITION, HISTORY, CONTENTS, & EVALUATION: *Edition & history:* A ten-minute sequence in one of Hollywood's first talking pictures, *Show of Shows*, in which John Barrymore recites lines from the minor tetralogy that belong to Richard duke of Gloucester.

This would make the film probably the first Shakespeare talking picture. Al Jolson's 1927 *The Jazz Singer*, generally regarded as the earliest "talkie," had appeared only a year or so before. In the pre-television era, this film snippet allowed millions in the hinterlands to gawk at the fabled Broadway stage star, John Barrymore. *Contents & evaluation:* No one can mug the way John Barrymore could when he put his mind to it. In most respects he was a dreadful movie actor, though his reputation as a stage actor remains secure. Set against an impressive, hellish backdrop, the grinning, leering figure of Richard duke of Gloucester impresses the audience with his unparalleled villainy. Horribly misshapen, as is the stage tradition for his character, Barrymore's evil is accentuated by the harsh lighting that casts deep shadows over his face. Gulls on the soundtrack and distant booming cannon add further atmosphere. The idea must have been to offer the American public a smattering of culture mixed in with the low and middlebrow material elsewhere in the film. *Audience:* General use.

MEDIUM INFORMATION: *Medium:* Motion Picture; *Sound:* Spoken language; *Color:* No (black & white); *Length:* 10 min.; *Language(s) spoken:* English; *Film type:* 16mm.

AUTHORSHIP INFORMATION: *Producer(s):* Warner Brothers; *Director(s):* Adolfi, John; *Other personnel:* McGill, Bernard (Editor); *Cast:* Barrymore, John (Richard duke of Gloucester).

DISTRIBUTION & AVAILABILITY: *Publisher or responsible agency:* Warner Brothers; *Copy location:* FOL, NFA*; *Call or copy number:* MP 103.

Henry the Sixth, Part Two, 3-5. **Video/Teleplay (Part 11 of 15 parts)**

190. *Rabble from Kent, The.* (Series: *An Age of Kings*, XI).

DOCUMENT INFORMATION: *Country:* GB; *Year of first showing:* 1960; *Location of first showing:* BBC TV. Transmitted 9 to 10 P.M., Thursday, 22 Sept. 1960.

EDITION, HISTORY, CONTENTS, & EVALUATION: *Awards:* Dews, Peter: Excellence in Directing (British Guild of Directors); *Edition & history:* Based on Acts 3-5 of *King Henry VI, pt. 2.* The eleventh installment in *An Age of Kings* (see also numbers 156-9, 178-9, 185, 188, 191-2, 485-6, and 505-6). For background, see *The Hollow Crown* (485), which is based on *Richard II* and which is therefore the first episode in the series. *Contents & evaluation:* "Suffolk is banished. The Duke of York incites an unruly mob to attack the capital and stir up trouble. At St.Albans, the White Rose of York gains a momentary victory" (PR blurb). The London *Times* critic continued to praise the series, even though the plot is declared to be "packed with penny-dreadful batterings and blood." Treatment of the material

was understated rather than flamboyant. The critic wonders if a flashier style might not have been more suited to the mercurial nature of this installment. Esmond Knight's Jack Cade is praised ("Nothing but Bonfires," *Times* 23 Sept. 1960: 18g). *Audience:* General use; *Supplementary materials:* Campbell, O.J. Introduction. *An Age of Kings* [The 15 parts as they appeared on television]. New York: Pyramid, 1961; "Program." *RT* 16 Sept. 1960: 23.

MEDIUM INFORMATION: *Medium:* Video; *Sound:* Spoken language; *Color:* No (black & white); *Length:* 58 min.; *Language(s) spoken:* English; *Video type:* 16mm, Kinescope.

AUTHORSHIP INFORMATION: *Producer(s):* Dews, Peter; *Director(s):* Hayes, Michael; *Adaptor/translator(s):* Crozier, Eric; *Composer(s):* Whelen, Christopher/Bliss, Arthur; Salter, Lionel (Conducting Royal Philharmonic Orchestra); *Designer(s):* Morris, Stanley; *Cast:* Scully, Terry (King Henry VI); May, Jack (Duke of York); Morris, Mary (Margaret of Anjou); Knight, Esmond, (Jack Cade); Ringham, John (Humphrey, Master); Wreford, Edgar (Suffolk); Lang, Robert (Beaufort); Rowe, Alan (Somerset); Windsor, Frank (Warwick); Gostelow, Gordon (Salisbury); Scott, John (Vaux); Andrews, David (Sea Captain); Ware, Derek (Master's Mate, Soldier); Brine, Adrian (Whitmore, Murderer); Harley, Timothy (Bevis); Garnett, Tony (John Holland); Valentine, Anthony (Dick the Butcher); Lodge, Terence (Weaver, Murderer); Wale, Terry (Clerk); Jackson, Barry (Michael); Shepperdson, Leon (Humphrey); Scott, John (Stafford's Brother); Farrington, Kenneth (Buckingham); Warner, John (Lord Say); Barcroft, John (Clifford); Willis, Jerome (Young Clifford); Glover, Julian (Edward); Garland, Patrick (George, Murderer); Daneman, Paul (Richard).

DISTRIBUTION & AVAILABILITY: *Publisher or responsible agency:* BBC; *Copy location:* BBC*, SCL*.

Henry the Sixth, Part Three, 1-3. **Video/Teleplay (Part 12 of 15 parts)**

191. *Morning's War, The.* (Series: *An Age of Kings*, XII).

DOCUMENT INFORMATION: *Country:* GB; *Year of first showing:* 1960; *Location of first showing:* BBC TV. Transmitted 9:45 to 10:45 P.M., Thursday, 6 Oct. 1960.

EDITION, HISTORY, CONTENTS, & EVALUATION: *Awards:* Dews, Peter: Excellence in Directing (British Guild of Directors); *Edition & history:* Based on Acts 1-3 of *King Henry VI, Part Three.* The twelfth installment in *An Age of Kings* (see also numbers 156-9, 178-9, 185, 188, 190, 192, 485-6, and 505-6). It looks as though the usual 9 P.M. time slot for this series was usurped on Oct. 6, 1960 by professional boxing. At 8:30 the fight between middleweights, Ron Redrup of Ham and Gert van Heerden of South Africa, engaged the attention of the masses. By 9:45 P.M., following a news break, Britons were once again ready for Shakespeare. For additional background, see *The Hollow Crown* (485), which is based on *Richard II* and which is therefore the first episode in the series. *Contents & evaluation:* "Margaret's vengeance is swift, if fleeting. York is captured and beheaded. But the White Rose soon gains an important victory, and York's oldest son becomes Edward IV" (PR blurb); Prof. Milton Crane had special praise for Terry Scully as "the pitiful King Henry VI, [who] even convinced one from time to time that the King has some useful function in the plays that bear his name" ("Shakespeare on Television," *SQ* 12.3 [Summer 1961]: 326). *Audience:* General use; *Supplementary materials:* Campbell, O.J. Introduction. *An Age of Kings* [The 15 parts as they appeared on television]. New York: Pyramid, 1961; "Program." *RT* 30 Sept. 1960: 19.

MEDIUM INFORMATION: *Medium:* Video; *Sound:* Spoken language; *Color:* No (black & white); *Length:* 60 min.; *Language(s) spoken:* English; *Video type:* 16mm, Kinescope.

AUTHORSHIP INFORMATION: *Producer(s):* Dews, Peter; *Director(s):* Hayes, Michael; *Adaptor/translator(s):* Crozier, Eric; *Composer(s):* Whelen, Christopher; Bliss, Arthur; Salter, Lionel (Conducting Royal Philharmonic Orchestra); *Designer(s):* Morris, Stanley; *Cast:* Scully, Terry (King Henry VI); May, Jack (Duke of York); Morris, Mary (Margaret of Anjou); Windsor, Frank (Warwick); Glover, Julian (Edward); Garland, Patrick (Clarence); Daneman, Paul (Richard Duke of Gloucester); Brine, Adrian (Montague); Wickham, Jeffry (Norfolk); Farrington, Kenneth (Northumberland); Willis, Jerome (Clifford); Shepperdson, Leon (Westmoreland); Lodge, Terence (Exeter); Greenwood, John (Edward Prince of Wales); Ware, Derek (Servant); Valentine, Anthony (Mortimer); Wale, Terry (Rutland); Garnett, Tony; Scott, John (Messengers); Andrews, David (Son that Killed Father); Ringham, John (Father that Killed son); Harley, Timothy (Sinklo); Warner, John (Humphrey); Wenham, Jane (Elizabeth); Bisley, Jeremy (Nobleman); + Lang, Robert; Wreford, Edgar.

DISTRIBUTION & AVAILABILITY: *Publisher or responsible agency:* BBC; *Copy location:* BBC*, SCL*.

Henry the Sixth, Part Three, 4-5. Video/Teleplay (Part 13 of 15 parts)

192. *Sun in Splendour, The.* (Series: *An Age of Kings,* XIII).

DOCUMENT INFORMATION: *Country:* GB; *Year of first showing:* 1960; *Location of first showing:* BBC TV. Transmitted 9:30 to 10:30 P.M., Thursday, 20 Oct. 1960.

EDITION, HISTORY, CONTENTS, & EVALUATION:

Awards: Dews, Peter: Excellence in Directing (British Guild of Directors); *Edition & history:* Based on Acts 4-5 of *King Henry VI, pt. 3.* The thirteenth installment in *An Age of Kings* (see also numbers 157-9, 178-9, 185, 188, 190-1, 485-6, and 505-6). For background, see *The Hollow Crown* (485), which is based on *Richard II* and which is therefore the first episode in the series. *Contents & evaluation:* "Again, intrigue and murder mark the scene, as Warwick and the Duke of Clarence change sides in the bloody War[s] of the Roses. . . . Henry VI's heir, the young Prince of Wales, is brutally murdered before his mother's eyes at Tewkesbury, and in a gloomy chamber of the Tower of London, the pathetic Henry VI is stabbed to death by the wicked Richard, Duke of Gloucester. This leads to the crowning of Edward IV in London amidst great rejoicing" (PR blurb). *Audience:* General use; *Supplementary materials:* Campbell, O.J. Introduction. *An Age of Kings* [The 15 parts as they appeared on television]. New York: Pyramid, 1961; "Program." *RT* 13 Oct. 1960: 49.

MEDIUM INFORMATION: *Medium:* Video; *Sound:* Spoken language; *Color:* No (black & white); *Length:* 60 min.; *Language(s) spoken:* English; *Video type:* 16mm, Kinescope.

AUTHORSHIP INFORMATION: *Producer(s):* Dews, Peter; *Director(s):* Hayes, Michael; *Adaptor/translator(s):* Crozier, Eric; *Composer(s):* Whelen, Christopher/Bliss, Arthur; Salter, Lionel (Conducting Royal Philharmonic Orchestra); *Designer(s):* Morris, Stanley; *Cast:* Scully, Terry (King Henry VI); Morris, Mary (Margaret of Anjou); Glover, Julian (King Edward IV); Warner, John (King of France); Hinchco, Tamara (Lady Bona); Greenwood, John (Prince of Wales); Lang, Robert (Oxford); Windsor, Frank (Warwick); Valentine, Anthony (Post); Daneman, Paul (Richard of Gloucester); Garland, Patrick (Clarence); Rowe, Alan (Somerset); Wenham, Jane (Elizabeth); Farrington, Kenneth (Rivers); Andrews, David (Hastings); Ware, Derek (Huntsman); Scott, Hennie (Henry Tudor); Scott, John (Messenger); Wickham, Jeffry (Mayor of York); Willis, Jerome (Sir John Montgomery); Wale, Terry (Soldier); Lodge, Terence (Exeter); Harley, Timothy; Bisley, Jeremy (Messengers); Garnett, Tony (Somerville); Brine, Adrian (Montague); Shepperdson, Leon (Messenger); Ringham, John; Harley, Timothy (Watchmen).

DISTRIBUTION & AVAILABILITY: *Publisher or responsible agency:* BBC; *Copy location:* BBC*, SCL*.

Henry the Sixth, Part Three. Video/Teleplay. History

193. *Henry the Sixth, Part Three.* (Series: The Shakespeare Plays).

DOCUMENT INFORMATION: *Year of filming:* 10-17 Feb. 1982; *Year of first showing:* 1982 [?]; *Location of first showings:* BBC, London; PBS stations, USA, 24 Apr. 1983.

EDITION, HISTORY, CONTENTS, & EVALUATION: *Edition & history:* The third segment of the BBC minor tetralogy (see also 186, 187 and 513). Henry Fenwick gives a fascinating account of problems faced by the lighting personnel and pays high tribute to Sam Barclay, the lighting designer, who was "perhaps the most crucial figure in the look of the production." In charge of the lighting of all four plays of the sequence, Barclay cleverly "rung changes" to give the impression of a much greater variety of *mise en scène* than was actually the case. His task, says Fenwick, then became one of answering the challenge of each scene moment by moment. Whether it was a little cell or great palace, it remained the same set with only the ingenuity of the lighting to keep it unique (Fenwick, *Henry VI, Part Three BSP* 23). *Contents & evaluation:* "Since the three parts of *H6* cover such a long sequence of years, one naturally needs actors who can show us something of the maturation, over the years, of the characters they play. The actor who does this most successfully is Bernard Hill as the Duke of York, whom we first see as the debonair youth involved in what seems a trivial argument over a minor point of law in part one (which is of course the beginning of the rivalry of the Roses). . . . Hill develops quite convincingly into the tough, middle-aged baron who almost achieves his kingly ambition, and he leaves us with a strong sense of the lingering 'medieval' honor which underlies some of York's actions and the raw ambition which competes successfully with that honor. . . . That his sons lack the honor—and that their ambition is a cruder thing than their father's—is successfully realized in this production. . . . Hill also suggests—and I think this is important to the interpretation of the role—that York is not quite the marvelous candidate for kingship he thinks he is. He does not quite have the stature that he has awarded himself, and there are moments when he seems really a small man who has convinced himself

of his greatness" (Manheim, Michael, "Review," *SFNL* 8.2 [1984]: 4). *Supplementary materials:* Videocassette (25 min.) from "Shakespeare in Perspective" series with Michael Wood as lecturer available in U.K. from BBC* (*BUFVC* 9).

MEDIUM INFORMATION: *Medium:* Video; *Sound:* Spoken language; *Color:* Yes; *Length:* 200 min.; *Video type:* B, V, 3/4U.

AUTHORSHIP INFORMATION: *Producer(s):* Sutton, Shaun; *Director(s):* Howell, Jane; *Adaptor/translator(s):* Snodin, David; *Composer(s):* Oliver, Stephen; Simpson, Dudley; *Designer(s):* Bayldon, Oliver; *Costume designer(s):* Peacock, John; *Lighting designer(s):* Barclay, Sam; *Other personnel:* Campbell-Hill, Corin (Prod. Manager); Ranson, Malcolm (Fight Arranger); Hay-Arthur, Cecile (Make-up); Edmonds, Alan (Sound); Stephenson, Geraldine (Movement Coordinator); *Cast:* Benson, Peter (Henry VI); Reding, Nick (Edward); Hill, Bernard (York); Protheroe, Brian (Edward IV); David, M. (Rutland) Jesson, P. (Clarence); Cook, Ron (Richard, Duke of Gloucester); Cox, Arthur (Somerset/Mortimer); Farr, Derek (Exeter + four); Wyatt, Peter (Norfolk/ Second Keeper); Wing-Davey, Mark (Warwick); Benfield, John (Northumberland + three); Deacon, Brian (Oxford); Fuke, Derek (Westmoreland + three); Byrne, Michael (Montague/Father); Chapman, Paul (Rivers); Guard, Alex (Dorset/Son); Daker, David (Hastings); Evans, Tenniel (Stanley + four); Brown, Antony (Louis XI + two); MacNamara, Oengus (Clifford + two); Foster, Julia (Queen Margaret); Cooper, Rowena (Lady Grey); Kendal, Merelina (Lady Bona); Fuke, Tim (Richmond); Gomm, Nigel; Walsh, Frank; Little, Brian; Paine, Steven; Broadley, Gerald; Dempster, John (Musicians); plus, "Second Company" w. 26 actors.

DISTRIBUTION & AVAILABILITY: *Publisher or responsible agency:* BBC-Time/Life Inc.; *Distributor:* AVP, UIO, KSU, BBC*, *Copy location:* UVM; *Availability:* AVP, sale, all formats, $450 (1987); UIO V (72323H), 3/ 4U (70323V), rental $25.60; KSU, V, 3/4U rental 5 days, $33.75; BBC*, 16mm or V, apply.

King Henry the Eighth

ORIGINAL WORK AND PRODUCTION: English History Play. *Year of first production:* 1612-13; *Site of first production:* Globe Playhouse, Bankside.

Henry the Eighth. Motion Picture/Abbreviated

194. *King Henry the Eighth.*

DOCUMENT INFORMATION: *Year of filming:* 9 Feb. 1911; *Year of release:* 1911; *Year of first showing:* 27 Feb. 1911; *Location of first showing:* London.

EDITION, HISTORY, CONTENTS, & EVALUATION: *Edition & history:* An early PR blurb announced that this film was "an epoch-making picture of *Henry VIII*, as given by Sir Herbert Tree at His Majesty's Haymarket Theatre." Proximity to London's West End theatres was an accidental but major force in the shaping of the British film industry, not all to its benefit. By comparison in North America the fledgling movie industry soon left New York and its theatres in favor of Hollywood. The clean break with the New York theatres allowed film in Hollywood to concentrate on innovations in cinema instead of being straitjacketed by stage traditions. *Contents & evaluation:* For a full account, see Ball, *SOSF* 80-83 *Audience:* General use; *Supplementary materials: Bioscope* 2 March 1911: 21.

MEDIUM INFORMATION: *Medium:* Motion Picture; *Sound:* Silent; *Color:* No (black & white); *Length:* Unknown; *Availability:* Lost.

AUTHORSHIP INFORMATION: *Producer(s):* Barker, Will; *Director(s):* Barker, Will; *Cast:* Bourchier, Arthur (King Henry VIII); Tree, Herbert (Wolsey); Cookson, S.A. (Campeius); Fuller, Charles (Cranmer); George, A.E. (Norfolk); Gill, Basil (Buckingham); O'Neill, Edward (Suffolk); Lawrence, Gerald (Surrey); Sass, Edward (Lord Chamberlain); Vanbrugh, Violet (Catherine); Cowie, Laura (Anne Bullen); Calvert, Mrs. Charles (Old Lady); Barclay, Lila (Patience).

DISTRIBUTION & AVAILABILITY: *Copy location:* Not known.

Henry the Eighth. Motion Picture/Derivative

195. *Cardinal Wolsey.*

DOCUMENT INFORMATION: *Country:* USA; *Year of release:* 1912.

EDITION, HISTORY, CONTENTS, & EVALUATION: *Edition & history:* One of the silent Shakespeare films made in the Brooklyn studios of the Vitagraph Company at the dawn of the motion picture era. Mostly one-reelers, about ten-minutes in length, the films often showed a good grasp of film grammar, though at other times the actors were photographed pretty much as though the camera were nailed to a tenth-row orchestra seat in a theatre. J. Stuart Blackton developed a keen interest in the advancement of motion picture techniques. Vitagraph's interest in Shakespeare may also have stemmed from the fact that the Bard's works were in the public domain. There was no fear of copyright suits from irate heirs of authors, such as Lew Wallace, who sued the Kalem film company over the rights to *Ben Hur*. *Contents & evaluation:* The establishing credits show Julia Swayne Gordon as Queen Catherine, a regal looking lady with slightly bulging eyes; Clara Kimball Young as Ann Boleyn, an apprehensive looking, tallish, dark lady; and Tefft Johnson as Henry VIII. Johnson mainly specializes in leering at Ann Boleyn. The opening title card tells us that "Henry VIII sees Ann Boleyn, the new lady-in-waiting," and from there on the outcome is inevitable. The next title card says that "Henry VIII becomes more infatuated with Ann." It is followed by a ballroom scene that in its visual appeal comes close to deep focus photography. Indeed, the crowds in the ballroom and court are particularly impressive. Space is expanded through the use of *trompe l'oeil* scenery painting in the *mise en scène*. The film also has its high moments: for example when Wolsey holds up a cross to the King and Henry VIII slinks back like a vampire. The processionals, apparently managed with an overhead camera, are handled well, as is the sequence showing the crowning of Ann Boleyn. The high (or low) point of the film, as in the play, is the fall of Wolsey. The actor who plays Wolsey is fine—tall, severe, authoritative. He makes the words on his title card believable: "Had I but served my God with half the zeal I served my King, He would not in my old age, have left me naked to mine enemies." A good and absorbing film. The Cardinal is so charismatic, however, that he steals the show from a bumbling Tefft Johnson as Henry VIII. But perhaps that is the way it was, or should be, intended (KSR). *Audience:* General use; *Supplementary materials:* Ball, *SOSF* 136-39.

MEDIUM INFORMATION: *Medium:* Motion Picture; *Sound:* Silent; *Color:* No (black & white); *Length:* 10 min.; *Language of subtitles:* English; *Film type:* 35mm.

AUTHORSHIP INFORMATION: *Producer(s):* Vitagraph; *Director(s):* Trimble, Laurence; *Adaptor/translator(s):* Reid, Hal; *Cast:* Gordon, Julia Swayne (Catherine); Young, Clara Kimball (Anne Boleyn); Johnson, Tefft (Henry VIII); Paul, Logan (Canterbury); Gaillard, Robert (Secretary); Wilson, Harold (Courtier); Reid, Hal (Wolsey ?).

DISTRIBUTION & AVAILABILITY: *Publisher or responsible agency:* Vitagraph; *Copy location:* FOL, NFA*; *Call or copy number:* MP 71; *Restrictions:* Archive viewing only.

Henry the Eighth. **Video/Teleplay. History**

196. Henry the Eighth. (Series: The Shakespeare Plays).
DOCUMENT INFORMATION: *Year of filming:* 1978-79; *Year of first showing:* 1979; *Location of first showing(s):* BBC, London; PBS stations, USA, 25 Apr. 1979.

EDITION, HISTORY, CONTENTS, & EVALUATION: *Edition & history:* Two of the BBC plays of the first season, *Henry VIII* and *AYL* were made outdoors on location. *Henry VIII* was produced on location at Leeds Castle, near Maidstone, Kent; Penshurst Place, Penshurst, Kent; and Hever Castle, Edenbridge, Kent between 27 Nov. 1978 and 7 Jan. 1979. *Contents & evaluation:* "My heart sank when I first heard that *Henry VIII* was being shot at Leeds Castle, Haver Castle *and* at Penshurst Place. I feared some crossbreeding of Shakespeare and *Beautiful Britain*. But the settings remain what they are, and the camera generally stays with the significant characters. No one would necessarily realize that the setting shifts from ancient pile to ancient pile. Nor do processions and ceremonial scenes interrupt the rhythm of the production. Billington rejected Shakespeare's apparent open invitation to make the play a spectacle with appended speeches. (He even cuts a procession at the opening of II.iv in which the court assembles to hear the case against Henry's marriage to Katherine.) Katherine's vision in IV. ii is less a masque than a troubled dream. The camera concentrates upon the important players, and 500-year-old rooms and ostentatious courtliness remain as the background to the dramatic action. . . . Shakespeare's *Henry VIII* pretties up some nasty business. Billington and Stride decide to pretty up Shakespeare. The only hint of the Henry most of us remember is that old figure who slumps on the throne during the prologue. The production itself is a kind of nationalistic romance in which time stops at a moment of birth and reconciliation. It is good melodrama and excellent television" (Colley, Scott, "The Shakespeare Plays on TV: Season One," *SFNL* 4.1 [1979]: 4). *Audience:* General use; *Supplementary materials:* *Henry VIII BSP*; Videocasette (25 min.) from "Shakespeare in Perspective" series with Anthony Burgess as lecturer available in U.K. from BBC* (*BUFVC* 10).

MEDIUM INFORMATION: *Medium:* Video; *Sound:* Spoken language; *Color:* Yes; *Length:* 145 min.; *Video type:* B, V, 3/4U.

AUTHORSHIP INFORMATION: *Producer(s):* Messina, Cedric; *Director(s):* Billington, Kevin; *Adaptor/translator(s):* Shallcross, Alan; *Composer(s):* Tyler, James; Lloyd-Jones, David; *Choreographer(s):* Stephenson, Geraldine; *Designer(s):* Taylor, Don; *Costume designer(s):* Hughes, Alun; *Lighting designer(s):* Cartwright, Hugh; *Other personnel:* Alcock, Dawn (Make-up); Lieper, Ian (Sound); *Cast:* Stride, John (King Henry VIII); West, Timothy (Wolsey); Bloom, Claire (Queen); Pickup, Ronald (Cranmer); Vaughan, Peter (Gardiner); Glover, Julian (Buckingham); Kemp, Jeremy (Norfolk); Kellermann, Barbara (Anne Bullen); Rowe, John (Cromwell); Poole, Michael (Campeius); Dodimead, David (Bishop); Pack, Charles Lloyd (Sandys); Nettleton, John (Chamberlain); Fiander, Lewis (Suffolk); Cotton, Oliver (Surrey); Rintoul, David (Abergavenny); May, Jack (Chancellor); Bareham, Adam (Guildford); Lambert, Nigel (Lovell); McKenzie, Jack (Vaux); Rogan, John (Butts); Bailey, John (Griffith); Home, Sally (Patience); Coleridge, Sylvia (Old Lady); Kirkby, Emma (Girl); Rhys-Davies, John (Capuchius); Cater, John (Gentleman); Pack, Roger Lloyd (Gentleman); Troughton, David (Surveyor); Leith, Alan (Sergeant); Osborne, Brian (Door-Keeper); Barker, Tim (Page); Gaunt, Michael (Crier); Walker, M. (Messenger); Daunton, J. (Scribe); Church, Tony (Speaker).

DISTRIBUTION & AVAILABILITY: *Publisher or responsible agency:* BBC/TLF; *Distributor:* AVP, UIO, BBC* *Copy location:* UVM; *Availability:* AVP, sale, $450 (1987); UIO 3/4U (70137V), rental $24.20; BBC*, 16mm, or V, apply.

Henry the Eighth. Video/Educational

196.1 *Parables of Power: Shakespeare's* Henry VIII.

DOCUMENT INFORMATION: *Country:* USA; *Year of first showing:* 1987.

EDITION, HISTORY, CONTENTS, & EVALUATION: *Edition & history:* "Appropriately introduced by Niccolo Machiavelli, scenes from Shakespeare's *Henry VIII* depict the king's struggle to consolidate power as absolute monarch. By highlighting the play's subtext, the film reveals how Cardinal Wolsey, Queen Catherine of Aragon, and Anne Boleyn, each played their own game of power. A rich spectrum of location shots provides a tapestry of background for Shakespeare's 'parable of power'" (IAS Catalog). *Contents & evaluation:* Not seen.

MEDIUM INFORMATION: *Sound:* Spoken language; *Color:* Yes; *Length:* 38 min.; *Video type:* V. *Producer(s):* IASTA.

DISTRIBUTION & AVAILABILITY: *Publisher or responsible agency:* IAS; *Distributor:* IAS, sale $350; rental, $50 + shipping.

Julius Caesar

ORIGINAL WORK AND PRODUCTION: Roman History Play. *Year written:* 1599; *Site of first production:* Globe.

Julius Caesar. **Motion Picture/Derivative**

197. *Shakespeare Writing Julius Caesar.*

DOCUMENT INFORMATION: *Country:* France; *Year of release:* 1907.

EDITION, HISTORY, CONTENTS, & EVALUATION: *Edition & history:* Another "Shakespeare" film by the innovative movie genius, Georges Méliès (1861-1938). In this one he portrays Shakespeare penning *Julius Caesar,* a self-referential gesture that perhaps revealed an unconscious deference to the spoken and written word. From the beginning, movie makers have exhibited this uneasiness about visualizing the Bard's works. *Supplementary materials:* Ball, *SOSF* 308.

MEDIUM INFORMATION: *Length:* 5 min.

AUTHORSHIP INFORMATION: *Director(s):* Méliès, Georges; *Cast:* Méliès, Georges (Shakespeare).

Julius Caesar. **Motion Picture/Abbreviations**

198. *Julius Caesar.*

DOCUMENT INFORMATION: *Country:* USA; *Year of release:* 1908.

EDITION, HISTORY, CONTENTS, & EVALUATION: *Edition & history:* Shakespeare seems a little recherché for Sigmund "Pop" Lubin (1851-1923), who was more likely to go in for such popular material as a faked re-creation of the Corbett-Fitzsimmons prizefight, in which he did not hesitate to use stand-ins for the two pugilists. Lubin competed with Thomas Edison for a foothold in the fledgling movie industry. *Supplementary materials:* Ball, *SOSF* 61.

MEDIUM INFORMATION: *Sound:* Silent; *Color:* No (black & white); *Length:* 10 min.

AUTHORSHIP INFORMATION: *Director(s):* Lubin, Sigmund.

DISTRIBUTION & AVAILABILITY: *Distributor:* Lost.

199. *Julius Caesar.*

DOCUMENT INFORMATION: *Country:* USA; *Year of release:* 1908.

EDITION, HISTORY, CONTENTS, & EVALUATION: *Edition & history:* A one-reel Vitagraph film produced by J. Stuart Blackton when pioneering filmmakers were seeking ways to translate Shakespeare into the idiom of popular culture. The gap between modern technology and subject matter remained wide enough to allow Shakespeare in. Professor Ball reports that fragments of the film remain in the Library of Congress in paper film-strips. *Supplementary materials:* Ball, *SOSF* 48.

MEDIUM INFORMATION: *Length:* 10 min.

AUTHORSHIP INFORMATION: *Director(s):* Ranous, William; *Cast:* Ranous, William (Antony).

DISTRIBUTION & AVAILABILITY: *Copy location:* LCM.

Julius Caesar. Motion Picture/Derivative

200. *Julius Caesar.*

DOCUMENT INFORMATION: *Country:* Italy; *Year of release:* 1908.

EDITION, HISTORY, CONTENTS, & EVALUATION: *Edition & history:* According to Robert Hamilton Ball, the film may have been either produced or directed by Giovanni Pastrone, who was to achieve fame with his spectacular *Cabiria* (1914), a landmark movie that influenced D.W. Griffith's *Intolerance* (1916). *Supplementary materials:* Ball, *SOSF* 98.

MEDIUM INFORMATION: *Length:* 10 min.

AUTHORSHIP INFORMATION: *Director(s):* Pastrone, Giovanni.

DISTRIBUTION & AVAILABILITY: *Copy location:* Not known.

201. *Brutus.*

DOCUMENT INFORMATION: *Country:* Italy; *Year of release:* 1910.

EDITION, HISTORY, CONTENTS, & EVALUATION: *Edition & history:* Originally of some length, but what remains is merely an 8-minute fragment. A spinoff from *Julius Caesar, Brutus* is important in the history of filmed Shakespeare as an example of the Italian taste for operatic spectacle even in cinema. *Contents & evaluation:* This film really has not very much to do with Shakespeare's Roman history plays, but nevertheless memorable are the grandiose shots of triumphal processions through the streets, while hundreds of extras gawk and swirl. Well handled are the scenes where Calphurnia begs Caesar not to go to the forum and Brutus' tent before Philippi. Guazzoni's love of camera work shows through in such touches as the superimposing on the frame of Calphurnia's dream and the ghost of Caesar at Philippi. The wild fighting on the battlefield is also shown from the perspective of the interior of Brutus' tent in a technique that seems in an early silent a remarkable prefiguration of the Wellesian "deep focus" shot. The explanatory titles are barely visible in the Folger print, but here is one that conveys the general flavor: "Calphurnia warns Caesar against going to the forum." Whatever else, the film shows that Guazzoni was a clever and dedicated filmmaker. R. H. Ball in his authoritative book on Shakespeare and the silent film gives the film a very high rating. *Audience:* General use; *Supplementary materials:* Ball, *SOSF* 118-20.

MEDIUM INFORMATION: *Medium:* Motion Picture; *Sound:* Silent; *Color:* No (black & white); *Length:* 8 min.; *Language of subtitles:* English; *Film type:* 16mm.

AUTHORSHIP INFORMATION: *Producer(s):* Cines; *Director(s):* Guazzoni, Enrico.

DISTRIBUTION & AVAILABILITY: *Publisher or responsible agency:* Cines; *Copy location:* FOL, NFA*; *Call or copy number:* MP 65; *Restrictions:* Archive viewing.

202. *Bruto I and II.*

DOCUMENT INFORMATION: *Country:* Italy; *Year of release:* 1910.

EDITION, HISTORY, CONTENTS, & EVALUATION: *Edition & history:* Presumably this film also followed the Italianate tradition of appropriating the spectacular trappings of opera for cinema. *Supplementary materials:* Ball, *SOSF* 115; *SIF* 92.

MEDIUM INFORMATION: *Length:* 20 min.

AUTHORSHIP INFORMATION: *Director(s):* De Liguoro, Guiseppe; *Cast:* De Liguoro, Guiseppe.

Julius Caesar. Motion Picture/Abbreviated

203. *Julius Caesar.*

DOCUMENT INFORMATION: *Country:* GB/France; *Year of release:* 1911.

EDITION, HISTORY, CONTENTS, & EVALUATION: *Edition & history:* Although the film was apparently made in Nice, France, the producer, Charles Urban (1871-1942), an early developer of color film, was a U.S. citizen who emigrated to England to work in the film industry. *Supplementary materials:* Ball, *SOSF* 115.

MEDIUM INFORMATION: *Length:* 10 min.

AUTHORSHIP INFORMATION: *Director(s):* Urban, Charles; *Cast:* Frenkel, Theo (Julius Caesar).

DISTRIBUTION & AVAILABILITY: *Copy location:* Not known.

204. *Julius Caesar.*

DOCUMENT INFORMATION: *Country:* GB; *Year of release:* 1911.

EDITION, HISTORY, CONTENTS, & EVALUATION: *Edition & history:* This film is one of three recordings of stage productions at the Stratford Memorial Theatre performed by the F.R. Benson acting company. Actual photography and film production seem to have been the work of the Co-Operative Cinematograph Company of Sir William ("Will") G. Barker (1867-1951), an important figure in the early British film industry. Barker is the man who paid Sir Herbert B. Tree the unheard of sum of £1,000 for a single day's work on *Henry VIII*. The movie also illustrates again the close ties between British film and theatre in its infancy. *Supplementary materials:* Ball, *SOSF* 83.

MEDIUM INFORMATION: *Length:* 10 min.

AUTHORSHIP INFORMATION: *Director(s):* Benson, Frank (Stage); Jones, G.W. (Film); *Cast:* Benson, Frank (Mark Antony); Benson, Lady Constance (Portia); Rathbone, Guy (Caesar); Carrington, Murray (Brutus); Maxim, Eric (Cassius); Lancaster, Nora (Calphurnia).

Julius Caesar. **Motion Picture/Derivative**

205. *Giulio Cesare.*

DOCUMENT INFORMATION: *Country:* Italy; *Year of filming:* 1911-14; *Year of release:* 1914.

EDITION, HISTORY, CONTENTS, & EVALUATION: *Edition & history:* Except for part five, which depicts the assassination of Caesar, this film is more indebted to Plutarch's *Lives* than it is to Shakespeare. It remains important, however, as an example of the highly influential Italian art film. Director Enrico Guazzoni's interest in film spectacle, which peaked with his 1912 *Quo Vadis*, attracted world wide attention. He was especially interested in literary adaptations. *Contents & evaluation:* The chief delight in this film is its spectacular shots of marching Roman soldiers, of unruly crowds in the Roman streets, and of Caesar's army crossing the Rubicon. The lighting is often erratic, as when the whiteness of dozens of togas in the Roman forum reflects off the camera lens, and sometimes there seem to be very few camera setups for a complicated action, as when Caesar crosses the Rubicon (we see cavalry in the stream, horses hooves, and a high angle shot of infantry). Against those technical flaws, however, are colossal scenes of thousands marching through Rome, of galleys fighting at sea, and of warfare with catapults and arrows against the Goths. Even Shakespeare's play manages to appear briefly when the dialogue card before the assassination of Caesar warns: "Beware, O Caesar, of the Ides of March." Another dialogue card at Caesar's death says "and thou too, Brutus," while at the funeral oration, yet another reads: "Friends, Romans, countrymen." While very tenuously connected to Shakespeare, the film yet attracts by its courageous energy, which seeks to capture all of the ancient world on celluloid. The freshness and exuberance of these silent films should never be underestimated. There is magnetism in the actors' faces that can be emulated by few contemporary actors (KSR). *Audience:* Professional; *Supplementary materials:* Ball, *SOSF* 208-10.

MEDIUM INFORMATION: *Medium:* Motion Picture; *Sound:* Silent; *Color:* No (black & white); *Condition:* Good; *Length:* 62 min. (FOL); Originally about 104 min.

AUTHORSHIP INFORMATION: *Producer(s):* Kleine,

George; *Director(s):* Guazzoni, Enrico; *Cast:* Novelli, Amleto (Julius Caesar); Gonzales-Terribili, Gianna.

DISTRIBUTION & AVAILABILITY: *Distributor:* EMG, JEF, *Copy location:* FOL, MOM; *Call or copy number:* MP 40; *Availability:* Scholarly use.

Julius Caesar. **Video/Teleplay**

206. *Julius Caesar.* (Series: Scenes from Shakespeare).

DOCUMENT INFORMATION: *Country:* GB; *Year of first showing:* 1937; *Location of first showing:* BBC. Transmitted 11 Feb. 1937.

EDITION, HISTORY, CONTENTS, & EVALUATION: *Edition & history:* Coming less than a week after the BBC's inaugural 1937 transmission of scenes from Shakespeare, this performance ranks among the very earliest. The ten-minute program was composed of Mark Antony's funeral oration over Caesar's body in the Forum. *Supplementary materials:* TPAB 11 Feb. 1937.

MEDIUM INFORMATION: *Length:* 10 min.

AUTHORSHIP INFORMATION: *Producer(s):* O'Ferrall, George More; *Cast:* Oscar, Henry (Antony).

DISTRIBUTION & AVAILABILITY: *Publisher or responsible agency:* BBC; *Copy location:* Not preserved.

207. *Julius Caesar.*

DOCUMENT INFORMATION: *Country:* GB; *Year of first showing:* 1938; *Location of first showing:* BBC. Transmitted from 9:05 to 10:46 P.M. on Sunday, July 24, 1938.

EDITION, HISTORY, CONTENTS, & EVALUATION: *Edition & history:* For its time an ambitious "modern dress" version of *Julius Caesar* with special scenic effects from stock news footage and incidental music. The use of stock news footage had the effect of pushing the drama "backwards in depth and outwards in space." A contrasting school of theorists believed that the TV camera should instead concentrate on "closing in" to achieve an effect of intimacy. According to BBC producer Michael Barry, the production was influenced by Orson Welles's famous Mercury theatre production in New York City, which pioneered in re-appropriating Shakespearean drama for contemporary times. As Barry suggests, the political turmoil in Europe in the ominous years before the outbreak of WW II made this use of *Julius Caesar* particularly meaningful (Barry, Michael, "Shakespeare on Television," *BBC Quarterly* 9.3 [Autumn 1954]: 145). *Supplementary materials:* TPAB 24 July 1938.

MEDIUM INFORMATION: *Length:* 101 min.

AUTHORSHIP INFORMATION: *Director(s):* Bower, Dallas; *Composer(s):* Hartley, James; *Other personnel:* Baker-Smith, Malcolm (Special scenic effects); *Cast:* Shaw, Sebastian (Brutus); Milton, Ernest (Julius Caesar); Clarke-Smith, D.A. (Antony); Matthews, Douglas (Octavius C.); Keir, David (Lepidus); Steerman, A.H. (Publius); Stewart, Douglas (Popilius); Ireland, Anthony (Cassius); Hanray, Lawrence (Casca); Price, Dennis (Trebonius/Volumnius); Turnbull, John (Decius Brutus/Messala); Latham, Stuart (Metullus Cimber); Chitty, Erik (Cinna); Gent, Colin (Soothsayer); Ludlow, Patrick (Cinna, a poet); Wood, J.I. (Lucilius); Wheatley, Alan (Titinius); Paton, Charles (Varro/Commoner); Wentworth, Robin (Clitius); Thomas, Phil H. (Claudius/Commoner); Vyvyan, Jack (Strato/Citizen); Maule, Robin (Lucius); Eaves, Kenneth (Dardanus); Ludlow, Patrick (Pindarus); Courtland, Van (Ligarius); Cowie, Laura (Calphurnia); Goodner, Carol (Portia); Leighton, Will (Servant); Aldridge, Alan (Waiter).

DISTRIBUTION & AVAILABILITY: *Publisher or responsible agency:* BBC*; *Copy location:* Unavailable.

Julius Caesar. Motion Picture/Scenes

208. *Julius Caesar*, 3.2. (Series: Famous Scenes from Shakespeare, No. #1).

DOCUMENT INFORMATION: *Country:* GB; *Year of release:* 1945.

EDITION, HISTORY, CONTENTS, & EVALUATION: *Edition & history:* The Forum scene (3.2) from *Julius Caesar* designed to be shown in classrooms. In black and white, the technology seems outdated after four decades. *Contents & evaluation:* Of interest is Felix Aylmer in the role of Brutus, though unhappily most Shakespeare film buffs have Aylmer permanently typecast as either the comical archbishop in the Olivier *Henry V*, or the windbag of a Polonius in *Hamlet*. For these two no doubt unfair reasons, he seems miscast as Brutus. An apprehensive ectomorph, this Brutus hardly seems capable of plotting the assassination of great Caesar. There are some bold but mainly inept attempts to manipulate the *grex* in the forum scenes. The *sotto voce* ad-libbing from the crowd never really seems plausible, and the costumes look as though they had seen better days, perhaps because this was post-WW II Britain. But then again, I've rarely seem costumes for the Roman history plays that were very inspired. The bedsheet as toga predictably appears. The musical score played by the London Symphony adds fine support (KSR). *Audience:* High school (grades 10-12).

MEDIUM INFORMATION: *Medium:* Motion Picture; *Sound:* Spoken language; *Color:* No (black & white); *Length:* 20 min.; *Language(s) spoken:* English; *Film type:* 16mm.

AUTHORSHIP INFORMATION: *Producer(s):* Box, Sydney; Laing, Knox; *Director(s):* Cass, Henry; *Composer(s):* Frankel, Ben; Mathieson, Muir (and London Symphony); *Designer(s):* Bennett, Compton; Carter,

James; *Costume designer(s):* Sinclair, Dorothy; *Lighting designer(s):* Palmer, Ernest; *Other personnel:* Wintle, Julian (Editor); Burgess, George; Clark, L. (Recording); Taylor, Nell (Makeup); *Cast:* Aylmer, Felix (Brutus); Genn, Leo (Antony); Slater, John; Jones, Emrys; Cooper, Frederick; Williams, Ben; Allarydyce, Grace; Hambling, Arthur; Monckton, Sydney (Crowd).

DISTRIBUTION & AVAILABILITY: *Publisher or responsible agency:* Theatrecraft Ltd.; *Copy location:* FOL, NFA*; *Call or copy number:* MP 79.

Julius Caesar. Video/Recording

209. *Julius Caesar.*

DOCUMENT INFORMATION: *Country:* USA; *Year of first showing:* 1949; *Location of first showing:* NBC/TV. Transmitted 3:30 to 5:15 P.M., Sunday, 3 April 1949.

EDITION, HISTORY, CONTENTS, & EVALUATION: *Edition & history:* Documentation of a 1949 performance of *Julius Caesar*, the first play ever presented on the stage of the Folger theatre in Washington, D.C. Transmitted nationally on NBC television, the event was sponsored by Socony Vacuum Oil, whose winged horse logo appears prominently in the wraparounds. The Folger videocassette represents a copy of a blurry Kinescope, of such poor quality that often the picture more resembles a negative than a print. (A "Kinescope" was a recording device widely used before the invention of magnetic tape to record studio televison productions, apparently more for legal than archival purposes.) Fortunately, though, the sound track remains intact. The players are from the Amherst College drama department, under the direction of Prof. Curtis Canfield. A still in the *The New York Times* shows Arch Taylor as Brutus and George T. Bliss as Julius Caesar (both looking terribly youthful) costumed in Elizabethan dress. *Contents & evaluation:* The movement from page to screen is indicated by the opening sequence that shows a close-up of the Folio page of *Julius Caesar*. A voiceover describes the Folger Shakespeare Library against an exterior shot, and then the camera moves inside to show the Folger's imitation Elizabethan playhouse. What follows is a video recording of the stage play. James Maxwell makes an impressive Brutus with his excellent voice; and Donald Roberts, an effective Cassius. In truth, most of the actors are vaguely outlined, shadowy figures in what resemble Elizabethan costumes. There are some overhead shots during the crowd scenes but in general the camera merely records, does not comment on, a conventional stage production. As a sample of live broadcast television in the golden early years of television, however, the performance has historical value. At the end, as the camera plays over the faces of the live audience at the Folger and a voiceover narrator bids the national audience "a pleasant Sunday evening," there is a a sense of nostalgia for a lost television era. Those were the last days of the lost dream of high culture for the masses (KSR); "Lost dream" or not, the *New York Times*'s astute critic, Mr. Jack Gould, thought at the time that the production was "amateurish" and "ill-advised." There was more "posturing than playing" and the stage of the Folger theatre was woefully unsuitable for a televised play ("Programs in Review." *NYT* 10 April 1949: X 9); From another perspective, Wallace A. Bacon liked the performance on stage but seemed to blame television for having "lost" most of it in transmission ("*Julius Caesar* at Folger," *SHAB* 24 (1949): 112-16). *Audience:* General use; *Supplementary materials:* "Still." *NYT* 3 April 1949: X 9.

MEDIUM INFORMATION: *Medium:* Video; *Sound:* Spoken language; *Length:* 90 min.; *Language(s) spoken:* English; *Video type:* V.

AUTHORSHIP INFORMATION: *Producer(s):* Davis, Owen; *Director(s):* Simpson, Garry; *Cast:* Bliss, George (Julius Caesar); Taylor, Arch (Brutus); Roberts, Donald (Cassius); McDonnell, Raymond (Antony); Maxwell, James [many credits illegible]; *Performance group(s):* Amherst College Masquers.

DISTRIBUTION & AVAILABILITY: *Publisher or responsible agency:* NBC/Folger Library; *Copy location:* FOL; *Call or copy number:* VCR; *Availability:* Archive.

Julius Caesar. Video/Abridgment

210. *Julius Caesar.* (Series: Studio One).

DOCUMENT INFORMATION: *Country:* USA; *Year of first showing:* 1949; *Location of first showing:* CBS/TV, Studio One. Transmitted 7:30 to 8:30 P.M., Sunday, 6 March 1949. Restaged and repeated 1 May 1949.

EDITION, HISTORY, CONTENTS, & EVALUATION: *Edition & history:* Shakespeare's *JC* in modern dress. A still in the *New York Times* shows the actors outfitted in the bulky business suits with padded shoulders and wide lapels that were the fashion during what history should rightly stigmatize as one of the tackiest eras in American history. The production was restaged and shown again on Studio One on 1 May 1949 with Richard Hart replacing Philip Bourneuf as Antony. That same evening also saw a transmission of the Philco theatre *Macbeth*, which must have made it a busy evening for Shakespeare buffs. *Contents & evaluation:* The television critic for the *NYT* enthusiastically reviewed the production for its imaginative camera work and for the overall quality of the performance. He even went so far as to say that it "was the most exciting television yet seen on the home screen—a magnificently bold, imaginative achievement. He also wrote (in a well-turned phrase) that Miner went to the heart of video's needs, "which is to make a picture and

not take one" (Gould, Jack, "Worthington Miner's Version in Modern Dress Proves Spectacular," *NYT* 13 March 1949: X 13). Whenever we think of early TV drama, we must re-position ourselves in history and remember that these productions were broadcast "live," with all the perils appertaining thereto. They were closer to live theatre than modern television, which is almost always taped prior to transmission. Because the medium was still finding its way, the reaction of the TV critic to this early production is especially interesting. *Audience:* General use; *Supplementary materials:* "Still." *NYT* 6 March 1949: X 11.

MEDIUM INFORMATION: *Medium:* Video; *Sound:* Spoken language; *Color:* No (black & white); *Length:* 60 min.; *Language(s) spoken:* English; *Video type:* V.

AUTHORSHIP INFORMATION: *Producer(s):* Miner, Worthington; *Director(s):* Nickell, Paul; *Designer(s):* Rychtarick, Richard; *Lighting designer(s):* Stoetzel, George; *Cast:* Keith, Robert (Brutus); Bourneuf, Philip; Hart, Richard (Antony); O'Shaughnessy, John (Cassius); Post, William (Julius Caesar); Taylor, Vaughan (Casca); Silver, Joseph (Decius); Rogers, Emmett (Metellus); *Performance group(s):* Studio One.

DISTRIBUTION & AVAILABILITY: *Publisher or responsible agency:* CBS TV; *Copy location:* MOB; *Call or copy number:* T76:0020; *Availability:* Archive fee.

Julius Caesar. **Motion Picture/Interpretation**

211. *Julius Caesar.*

DOCUMENT INFORMATION: *Country:* USA; *Year of filming:* 1949; *Year of release:* 1950.

EDITION, HISTORY, CONTENTS, & EVALUATION: *Awards:* Best Film, 1953 Locarno Film Festival; *Edition & history:* Filmed in and around the environs of Northwestern University and cleverly exploiting the abandoned University of Chicago football stadium (which also produced the atom bomb), the film was made on a tiny budget of $15,000. That investment paid handsome dividends for some of the principals, however. Charlton Heston, who in this film first played a Roman hero, went on to fame and glory in Hollywood and the producer, David Bradley, was also favored with a Hollywood contract. For what was essentially an amateur production, the film was a remarkable achievement. *Contents & evaluation:* Although amateurish in technique, the film has some highly credible moments and provides a unique oportunity to see the emerging talent of a great film star, Charlton Heston, who plays Antony. For students of Shakespeare, the text, though shortened, remains quite faithful to the 1623 Folio version. *Audience:* General use.

MEDIUM INFORMATION: *Medium:* Motion Picture; *Sound:* Spoken language; *Color:* No (black & white);

Length: 90 min.; *Language(s) spoken:* English; *Film type:* 16mm.

AUTHORSHIP INFORMATION: *Producer(s):* Bradley, David; *Director(s):* Bradley, David; *Adaptor/translator(s):* Bradley, David; *Composer(s):* Becker, John; Fletcher, Grant (w. Chicago Symphony); *Lighting designer(s):* McMahon, Louis; *Other personnel:* Keigher, Robert (Production Manager); Foy, Art (Sound); *Cast:* Heston, Charlton (Mark Antony); Tasker, Harold (Julius Caesar); Bradley, David (Brutus); Glenn, Grosvenor (Cassius); Ross, Helen (Calphurnia); Darr, Molly (Portia); Russell, William (Casca).

DISTRIBUTION & AVAILABILITY: *Distributor:* SYR, KIT, *Copy location:* FOL; *Availability:* SYR, rental, 16mm $27.00, KIT $95.

Julius Caesar. Film/Abbreviated

212. *Julius Caesar.*

DOCUMENT INFORMATION: *Country:* GB; *Year of release:* 1951.

EDITION, HISTORY, CONTENTS, & EVALUATION: The great Robert Speaight plays a leading role in this otherwise obscure "schools" production. *Supplementary materials:* H&M 22; Morris, *SOF* 15.

MEDIUM INFORMATION: *Length:* 33 min.

AUTHORSHIP INFORMATION: *Director(s):* Parthian productions; *Cast:* Speaight, Robert; Trouncer, Cecil.

Julius Caesar. Video/Teleplay

213. *Julius Caesar.*

DOCUMENT INFORMATION: *Country:* GB; *Year of first showing:* 1951; *Location of first showing:* BBC, London Station. Transmitted 8:15 to 10:22 P.M., Sunday, 25 Feb. 1951.

EDITION, HISTORY, CONTENTS, & EVALUATION: *Edition & history:* Another ambitious televised version of *Julius Caesar* on which the producers lavished nearly £2,000 and for which they enlisted the services of some 63 actors, principals and extras. By 1951 television audiences were sufficiently large so that Mr. Harrison expected to receive "shoals of letters from clever viewers pointing out the anachonisms" in his production, which he of course deliberately employed (WAC [TS/272] Feb. 28, 1951). After all one of the most often cited anachronisms in the canon appears in this play—the clock that strikes long before clocks were invented. *Supplementary materials: TPAB* 25 Feb. 1951.

MEDIUM INFORMATION: *Length:* 127 min.

AUTHORSHIP INFORMATION: *Producer(s):* Harrison, Stephen; *Director(s):* Brett, Leonard; *Cast:* Hudd, Walter (Julius Caesar); Hawtrey, Anthony (Mark Antony); Bebb, Richard (Octavius); Berry, Eric (Lepidus); Barr, Patrick (Brutus); McCallin, Clement (Cassius); Brennan, Michael (Casca); Colmer, Tom (Cinna/Lucilius); Bathurst, Peter (Trebonius/Volumnius); Gatrell, John (Decius Brutus/Clitus); Purdom, Edmund (Cimber/Timinius); Bathurst, Peter (Flavius/Volumnius); Berry, Eric (Marullus); Dunbar, John (Popilius/Plebeian); Reid, Alan (Artemidorus/Pindarus); Vere, John (Soothsayer); Greenidge, Terence (Cinna, a poet/Dardanius); Oliver, Anthony (Messala/Servant); Arnold, John (Strato/Servant); Hinton, Mary (Calphurnia); Diamond, Margaret (Portia); + many more citizens, plebians, and soldiers.

DISTRIBUTION & AVAILABILITY: *Publisher or responsible agency:* BBC; *Copy location:* Unavailable.

Julius Caesar. Motion Picture/Interpretation

214. *Julius Caesar.*

DOCUMENT INFORMATION: *Country:* USA; *Year of release:* 1953.

EDITION, HISTORY, CONTENTS, & EVALUATION: *Edition & history:* The producer and director decided to recreate the contemporaneous effect of the newsreels, which then enjoyed a great vogue among moviegoers. It was their intention to exploit the huge sets of cinema without in any way diminishing the stature of the actors. Although not quite so lavish as D.W. Griffith's epic *Intolerance* or the Cecil B. DeMille extravaganzas in Technicolor with a cast of thousands, the sets are nevertheless impressively crammed with the icons and bric-a-brac of ancient Rome. Swarms of hoi polloi jam the streets and statues of the Roman great are lavishly sprinkled about among the moving, living actors in togas. Fortunately the film may soon become available on videocassette so that its really fine qualities will again be readily available. For an informative account of production details, see Pasinetti, P.M., "Julius Caesar: The Role of the Technical Advisor," *QFRT,* 8.2 [1953]: 131-38. Producer John Houseman also had these comments to make about the film: "For years we have all been admiring Gordon Craig's magnificent theatrical conceptions while regretfully realising that their proportions could never be satisfactorily contained within the restricted framework of our modern proscenium arches. In the motion picture, *Julius Caesar,* however, we have to a great extent been able to satisfy our hunger for heroic setting. And through the magic power of lens and microphone, registering every syllable and facial expression, no matter how whispered the voice or how intimate the secret thought, the actors and their conflicts are never dwarfed by their surroundings. Rather they gain from the set's great size and their own changing and controlled dramatic relation to it" ("Filming *Julius Caesar*," *SAS*, 23 [1953]: 24-27). *Contents & evaluation:* Indubitably this is one of the most remarkable films based on a Shakespearean play that has ever been produced. Perhaps its inaccessibility in recent years has made us overlook Marlon Brando's performance as a surly but electrifying Mark Antony. As usual, Brando acts with his whole body as well as with words but even so the eloquence of Antony's funeral oration comes alive anyway. Amazingly the mumbling and virtually incoherent Stanley Kowalski of Tennessee Williams' *A Streetcar Named Desire* is metamorphosed in a stunning *tour de force* into Shakespeare's celebrated hero of ancient Rome. He absolutely demands attention at every moment as though to underscore that the "method" works even when spoken rhetoric and body language seem to be at odds. The rest of the cast also rivals the recent Olivier *King Lear* in acting talent. Caught at the height of their careers are such superstars as Louis Calhern (Caesar), James Mason (Brutus), John Gielgud (Cassius), Greer Garson (Calphurnia) and Deborah Kerr (Portia). This absorbing movie successfully mediates between the Shakespearean text on page and on screen. Its sheer energy must ultimately conquer the audience (KSR). *Audience:* General use; *Supplementary materials:* Lewin, William. *A Guide to the Discussion of the MGM Screen Version of* Julius Caesar. Maplewood [NJ]: Educational Guides, 1953 ["Photoplay Studies," rpt. from *Audio Visual Guide* (May 1953)].

MEDIUM INFORMATION: *Medium:* Motion Picture; *Sound:* Spoken language; *Color:* No (black & white); *Length:* 121 min.; *Language(s) spoken:* English; *Film type:* 16mm; 35 mm.

AUTHORSHIP INFORMATION: *Producer(s):* Houseman, John; *Director(s):* Mankiewicz, Joseph L.; *Adaptor/translator(s):* Mankiewicz, Joseph L.; *Composer(s):* Rozsa, Miklos; *Designer(s):* Gibbons, Cedric; Carfagno, Edward; *Set designer(s):* Willis, Edwin B.; Hunt, Hugh; *Costume designer(s):* McCoy, Herschel; *Lighting designer(s):* Rittenberg, Joseph; *Other personnel:* Dunning, John (Film Editor); Shearer, Douglas (Recording Supervisor); Newcombe, Warren (Special Effects); Guilaroff, Sydney (Hair Styles); Tuttle, William (Make-up); Pasinetti, P.M. (Technical Adviser); *Cast:* Brando, Marlon (Mark Antony); Mason, James (Brutus); Gielgud, John (Cassius); Calhern, Louis (Julius Caesar); O'Brien, Edmond (Casca); Garson, Greer (Calphurnia); Kerr, Deborah (Portia); Doucette, John (Carpenter); Macready, George (Marullus); Pate, Michael (Flavius); Hale, Richard (Soothsayer); Napier, Alan (Cicero); Cottrell, William (Cinna); Hardy, John (Lucius); Hoyt, John (Decius Brutus); Powers, Tom (Metellus Cimber); Raine, Jack (Trebonius); Wolfe, Ian (Ligarius); Stratton, Chester (Servant to Caesar); Hare, Lumsden (Publius); Farley, Morgan (Artemidorus); Perry, Victor (Popilius Lena); Phipps, Bill (Servant to Antony); Tolan, Mi-

chael (Officer to Octavius); Watson, Douglas (Octavius Caesar); Dumbrille, Douglas; (Lepidus); Williams, Rhys (Lucilius); Ansara, Michael (Pindarus); Lummis, Dayton (Messala); Purdom, Edmund (Strato); Guilfoyle, Paul (1st Citizen); and a dozen more citizens.

DISTRIBUTION & AVAILABILITY: *Publisher or responsible agency:* MGM; *Distributor:* FMB*, FNC, DCV [?], FCM *Copy location:* FOL (MP32); *Availability:* FNC, rental, 16mm ($175 + 50%); DCV, call; FCM, V, $19.95.

Julius Caesar. Video/Scenes

215. *Julius Caesar.*

DOCUMENT INFORMATION: *Country:* GB; *Year of first showing:* 1955; *Location of first showing:* BBC. Transmitted 5 Sept. 1955.

EDITION, HISTORY, CONTENTS, & EVALUATION: *Edition & history:* Three members of the London Old Vic appear in scenes from Michael Benthall's production. The program was also a backstage tribute to the Old Vic as it commenced the third year in a five-year plan to mount the entire Shakespearean canon. *Supplementary materials:* "Program." *RT* 4 Sept. 1955: n.p.

MEDIUM INFORMATION: *Length:* 26 min.

AUTHORSHIP INFORMATION: *Producer(s):* Burton, Hal; *Cast:* Wordsworth, Richard (Cassius); Rogers, Paul (Brutus); Neville, John (Marc Antony).

DISTRIBUTION & AVAILABILITY: *Publisher or responsible agency:* BBC; *Copy location:* Unavailable

Julius Caesar. Video/Teleplay

216. *Julius Caesar.*

DOCUMENT INFORMATION: *Country:* USA; *Year of first showing:* 1955; *Location of first showing:* Studio One Summer Theater. Transmitted 1 August 1955.

EDITION, HISTORY, CONTENTS, & EVALUATION: *Edition & history:* One notable feature of this production was the presence of Shepperd Strudwick, who enjoyed considerable success both as a New York actor and in Hollywood. *Supplementary materials:* "Program." *NYT* 1 Aug. 1955: 39; Gianokos, *TDSP* 158.

MEDIUM INFORMATION: *Color:* No (black & white); *Length:* 90 min. [?].

AUTHORSHIP INFORMATION: *Producer(s):* Penn, Leon; *Cast:* Bikel, Theodore; Strudwick, Shepperd; Ryder, Alfred; Brit-Neva, Maria; Bourneuf, Philip.

DISTRIBUTION & AVAILABILITY: *Publisher or responsible agency:* Studio One.

Julius Caesar. Motion Picture/Scenes

217. *Julius Caesar.* (Series: Great Plays in Rehearsal).

DOCUMENT INFORMATION: *Country:* USA; *Year of release:* 1958.

EDITION, HISTORY, CONTENTS, & EVALUATION: *Edition & history:* Rehearsal scenes from *Julius Caesar* *Supplementary materials:* Loughney, Katharine. "Shakespeare on Film and Tape at Library of Congress." *SFNL* 13.2 (Apr. 1989): 2.

MEDIUM INFORMATION: *Length:* 60 min.

AUTHORSHIP INFORMATION: *Director(s):* Salmon, Eric.

DISTRIBUTION & AVAILABILITY: *Copy location:* LCM; *Call or copy number:* FCA 4064-4065.

Julius Caesar. Video/Teledrama

218. *Julius Caesar.*

DOCUMENT INFORMATION: *Country:* GB; *Year of first showing:* 1959; *Location of first showing:* BBC TV. Transmitted 5 May 1959.

EDITION, HISTORY, CONTENTS, & EVALUATION: *Edition & history:* Director Stuart Burge was able to use this television production as preparation for his 1969 film version with Jason Robards, Jr. and Charlton Heston. If this video could be screened at the BBC Archive, it would be interesting to compare it with the subsequent film. According to Peter Morris the extensive battle scenes were designed to wipe out the image of "staginess" so often associated with television drama. At a price tag of £8,152 and with a cast of 99, it was a generous undertaking. *Contents & evaluation:* The *Times* reviewer was quite enthusiastic, noting particularly the use of closeups during the assassination scene to give individuality to each of the conspirators. For him/her, however, the performance never quite "took fire." Caesar was faulted as looking like a "business tycoon" and Michael Gough as Cassius did not seem to have the voice for the role. Only Eric Porter as Brutus got unqualified praise ("*Julius Caesar* on Television," *Times* 6 May 1959: 15r). *Audience:* General use.

MEDIUM INFORMATION: *Medium:* Video; *Sound:* Spoken language; *Color:* No (black & white); *Length:* 115 min.; *Language(s) spoken:* English; *Video type:* 16mm Kinescope.

AUTHORSHIP INFORMATION: *Producer(s):* Burge, Stuart; *Director(s):* Burge, Stuart; *Designer(s):* Learoyd, Barry; *Cast:* Perceval, Robert (Caesar); Moffatt, John (Casca); Kidd, John (Decius Brutus); Gough, Michael (Cassius); Sylvester, William (Antony); Porter, Eric (Brutus); Slater, Daphne (Portia); Gage, Roger (Flavius); Warner, Richard (Marullus); Ball, Ralph (Commoner); Rea, Charles (Cobbler); White, Valerie (Calpurnia); Burnham, Jeremy (Octavius Caesar); Stoney, Kevin (Lepidus); Brambell, Wilfrid (Soothsayer); Ringham, John (Trebonius); Grahame, David (Ligarius); Wentworth, John (Metellus Cimber); Lee, Paul (Cinna); Hitchman, Michael (Cicero); Leaman, Graham (Popilius Lena); Malone, Cavane; Carpenter, Richard (Servants); Goolden, Richard (Cinna the Poet); Woodward, Edward (Titinius); Hare, Ernest (Messala); Spink, Brian (Volumnius); Cracknell, Leonard (Lucius); Brown, William Lyon (Varro); Dodd, Ronald Scott (Claudius); Lynch, Sean (Strato); Becker, Neville (Pindarus); + 6 Citizens.

DISTRIBUTION & AVAILABILITY: *Publisher or responsible agency:* BBC; *Copy location:* BBC*.

Julius Caesar. Video/Teleplay

219. *Julius Caesar.*

DOCUMENT INFORMATION: *Country:* GB; *Year of first showing:* 1960; *Location of first showing:* BBC. Part one was transmitted 2:05 to 2:35 P.M., Tuesday, Nov. 8, 1960.

EDITION, HISTORY, CONTENTS, & EVALUATION: *Edition & history:* The first part of a four-part production of *Julius Caesar* designed mainly for the schools. *Supplementary materials:* "Program." *RT* Nov. 3, 1960.

MEDIUM INFORMATION: *Length:* 120 min. (Total 4 parts).

AUTHORSHIP INFORMATION: *Producer(s):* Eyre, Ronald; *Designer(s):* Spriggs, Austen; *Cast:* Michael, Ralph (Caesar); Maxwell, James (Antony); Goodliffe, Michael (Brutus); Schroder, Hilda (Calphurnia); Grout, James (Flavius); Abineri, John (Marullus); Bolam, James (Carpenter); Gillespie, Robert (Cobbler); Brambell, Wilfrid (Soothsayer); Foster, Dudley (Casca); Laurie, John (Cassius); McClelland, Allan (Cinna); Brooks, Ray (Lucius); Southworth, John (Decius); Lewis, Duncan (Metellus); Harrison, Brian (Trebonius).

DISTRIBUTION & AVAILABILITY: *Publisher or responsible agency:* BBC; *Copy location:* Unavailable.

Julius Caesar. Motion Picture/Scenes

220. *Julius Caesar: The Forum Scene.*

DOCUMENT INFORMATION: *Country:* USA; *Year of release:* 1961.

EDITION, HISTORY, CONTENTS, & EVALUATION: *Edition & history:* The forum scene from *Julius Caesar,* which has apparently been taken from the David Bradley 1950 feature length film starring Charlton Heston. *Contents & evaluation:* Not seen, but for an evaluation of the Bradley *Julius Caesar* from which this scene is excerpted, see number 211. *Audience:* High school (grades 10-12); College and university; *Supplementary materials:* See Bradley *JC* entry.

MEDIUM INFORMATION: *Medium:* Motion Picture; *Sound:* Spoken language; *Color:* No (black & white); *Length:* 17 min.; *Language(s) spoken:* English; *Film type:* 16mm.

AUTHORSHIP INFORMATION: *Producer(s):* Bradley, David; *Director(s):* Bradley, David; *Cast:* Heston, Charlton (For full credits, see the entry under Bradley *JC*).

DISTRIBUTION & AVAILABILITY: *Distributor:* SYR.

Julius Caesar, 1-2. Video/Teledrama

221. *Colossus, The.* (Series: *The Spread of the Eagle* IV).

DOCUMENT INFORMATION: *Country:* GB; *Year of first showing:* 1963; *Location of first showing:* BBC TV. Transmitted 9:25 to 10:15 P.M., Friday, 24 May 1963.

EDITION, HISTORY, CONTENTS, & EVALUATION: *Edition & history:* The title for the series, "The Spread of the Eagle," came from the Roman eagle, "aloof, golden, and cruel," according to Producer/Director Peter Dews. The nine-part series included three of the Roman history plays—*Coriolanus* (59-61), *Julius Caesar* (221-23) and *Antony and Cleopatra* (14-16). For background and discussion, see number 14, above. *Contents & evaluation:* See 14, above. *Audience:* General use; *Supplementary materials:* Dews, Peter. "The Spread of the Eagle." *RT* 16 May 1963: 51.

MEDIUM INFORMATION: *Medium:* Video; *Sound:* Spoken language; *Color:* No (black & white); *Length:* 49 min.; *Language(s) spoken:* English; *Video type:* Video, Kinescope.

AUTHORSHIP INFORMATION: *Producer(s):* Dews, Peter; *Director(s):* Dews, Peter; *Composer(s):* Whelen, Christopher; *Designer(s):* Hatts, Clifford; *Costume designer(s):* Agombar, Elizabeth; *Other personnel:* Manderson, Tommy (Make-up); *Cast:* Jones, Barry (Julius Caesar); Michell, Keith (Antony); Cushing, Peter (Cassius); Eddington, Paul (Brutus); Dickson, Hugh (Flavius); Weston, David (Carpenter); King, David (Marullus); Wale, Terry (Cobbler); May, Jack (Casca); Bonnamy, Yvonne (Calphurnia); Webster, Paul (Soothsayer); Gay, John (Cicero); Herrick, Roy (Lucius); Barcroft, John (Trebonius); Willis, Jerome (Decius Brutus); Croucher, Roger (Cinna); Cracknell, Leonard (Metellus Cimber); Wenham, Jane (Portia); Finch, Bernard (Caius Ligarius); + Bailey, Paul; Clarke, Raymond; Craig, Pamela; Desmond, Marion; Greenwood, John; Harris, Paul; Hinsliff, Geoffrey; Jackson, Barry; Harte, Ben; Laurence, Charles; Lloyd, Bernard; Stephens, Caroline; Varnals, Wendy; Wright, Hilary.

DISTRIBUTION & AVAILABILITY: *Publisher or re-*sponsible agency: BBC; *Copy location:* BBC archive (6 of 9 parts).

Julius Caesar, 2-4

222. *Fifteenth, The.* (Series: *The Spread of the Eagle* V).

DOCUMENT INFORMATION: *Country:* GB; *Year of first showing:* 1963; *Location of first showing:* BBC TV. Transmitted 9:25 to 10:15 P.M., Friday, 31 May 1963.

EDITION, HISTORY, CONTENTS, & EVALUATION: *Edition & history:* For description, see 14, 221 above. *Audience:* General use; *Supplementary materials:* Dews, Peter. "The Spread of the Eagle." *RT* 23 May 1963: 51.

MEDIUM INFORMATION: *Medium:* Video; *Sound:* Spoken language; *Color:* No (black & white); *Length:* 52 min.; *Language(s) spoken:* English; *Video type:* Video, Kinescope.

AUTHORSHIP INFORMATION: *Producer(s):* Dews, Peter; *Director(s):* Dews, Peter; *Composer(s):* Whelen, Christopher; *Designer(s):* Hatts, Clifford; *Costume designer(s):* Agombar, Elizabeth; *Other personnel:* Manderson, Tommy (Make-up); Greenwood, John; Ware, Derek (Fight coordinators); *Cast:* Jones, Barry (Julius Caesar); Michell, Keith (Antony); Cushing, Peter (Cassius); Eddington, Paul (Brutus); May, Jack (Casca); Bonnamy, Yvonne (Calphurnia); Webster, Paul (Soothsayer); Herrick, Roy (Lucius); Barcroft, John (Trebonius); Willis, Jerome (Decius Brutus); Croucher, Roger (Cinna); Cracknell, Leonard (Metellus Cimber); Wenham, Jane (Portia); Greenwood, John (Servant); Harris, Paul (Popiliius); Finch, Bernard (Caius Ligarius); Bailey, Paul (Artemidorus); Hinsliff, Geoffrey; Jackson, Barry; Harte, Ben; Weston, David (Plebeians); Laurence, Charles (Servant); + Clarke, Raymond; Craig, Pamela; Desmond, Marion; Gay, John; King, David; Lloyd, Bernard; Stephens, Caroline; Varnals, Wendy.

DISTRIBUTION & AVAILABILITY: *Publisher or responsible agency:* BBC; *Copy location:* BBC archive (6 of 9 parts).

Julius Caesar, 4-5

223. *Revenge, The.* (Series: *The Spread of the Eagle* VI).

DOCUMENT INFORMATION: *Country:* GB; *Year of first showing:* 1963; *Location of first showing:* BBC TV. Transmitted 9:25 to 10:15 P.M., Friday, 7 June 1963.

EDITION, HISTORY, CONTENTS, & EVALUATION: *Edition & history:* For description, see *Ant.*, 14, and *Julius Caesar*, Part One, 221, above. *Audience:* General use; *Supplementary materials:* Dews, Peter. "The Spread of the Eagle." *RT* 25 Apr. 1963: 49; "Program." *RT* 30 May 1963: 47.

MEDIUM INFORMATION: *Medium:* Video; *Sound:* Spoken language; *Color:* No (black & white); *Length:* 51 min.; *Language(s) spoken:* English; *Video type:* Video, Kinescope.

AUTHORSHIP INFORMATION: *Producer(s):* Dews, Peter; *Director(s):* Dews, Peter; *Composer(s):* Whelen, Christopher; *Designer(s):* Hatts, Clifford; *Costume designer(s):* Agombar, Elizabeth; *Other personnel:* Manderson, Tommy (Make-up); Greenwood, John; Ware, Derek (Fight coordinators); *Cast:* Michell, Keith (Antony); Cushing, Peter (Cassius); Eddington, Paul (Brutus); Herrick, Roy (Lucius); Barcroft, John (Messala); Croucher, Roger (Lucilius); Greenwood, John (Dardanius); Hinsliff, Geoffrey (Clitus); Harte, Ben (Claudius); Harris, Paul (Varro); Weston, David (Cato); Laurence, Charles (Pindarus); Webster, Paul; Bailey, Paul; Clarke, Raymond; Jackson, Barry (Soldiers); Gay, John (A Poet); King, David (Volumnius); Lloyd, Bernard (Strato); Jones, Barry (Ghost of Caesar); William, David (Octavius Caesar); Dickson, Hugh (Titinius); + Cracknell, Leonard; Finch, Bernard.

DISTRIBUTION & AVAILABILITY: *Publisher or responsible agency:* BBC; *Copy location:* BBC archive (6 of 9 parts).

Julius Caesar. Motion Picture/Documentary

224. *Four Views of Caesar.*

DOCUMENT INFORMATION: *Country:* GB; *Year of release:* 1964.

EDITION, HISTORY, CONTENTS, & EVALUATION: *Edition & history:* According to the distributor's description, this program is comprised of "four excellently staged playlets" in which there are seen "four profiles of Caesar as he was seen by four great men. The first is Caesar himself, and Caesar saw himself as a just and humane man. The second is the biographer, Plutarch, who saw Caesar as a great soldier and wily politician attempting to make himself king. The third is William Shakespeare, who saw Caesar as a pompous tyrant. The fourth is George Bernard Shaw, who saw Caesar as a wise and disenchanted old man. But which is the real Caesar? The film will provide students with an informative and provocative experience, one that will motivate them towards a greater appreciation and understanding of the literary art" (BFA Educational Media). *Audience:* High school (grades 10-12); College and university.

MEDIUM INFORMATION: *Medium:* Motion picture; *Sound:* Spoken language; *Color:* No (black & white); *Length:* 23 min.; *Language(s) spoken:* English; *Film type:* 16mm.

AUTHORSHIP INFORMATION: *Producer(s):* CBS/TV.

DISTRIBUTION & AVAILABILITY: *Publisher or responsible agency:* BFA Educational Media; *Distributor:* BFA, SYR.

Julius Caesar. Video/Teleplay

225. *Julius Caesar.*

DOCUMENT INFORMATION: *Country:* GB; *Year of release:* 1964; *Location of first showing:* BBC. Transmitted on April 23, 1964.

EDITION, HISTORY, CONTENTS, & EVALUATION: *Edition & history:* A recording of a modern dress performance by the National Youth Theatre. The production first opened at the Queen's Theatre in 1960, was revived at Sadler's Wells, and was then taken on an extensive European tour. In its relentless efforts to make Shakespeare's play relevant to contemporary politics, it became known as the "Teddy Bear Caesar," a reference to a certain type of aimless thug then fashionable in London, early "Punk," one might say. *Supplementary materials:* Hill, Paul. "Julius Caesar." *RT* 16 April 1954: 51; Morris, *SHOF* 29; H&M, 22.

MEDIUM INFORMATION: *Length:* 80 min.

AUTHORSHIP INFORMATION: *Producer(s):* Vernon, John; *Director(s):* Croft, Michael; *Cast:* Stacy, Neil; Block, Giles.

DISTRIBUTION & AVAILABILITY: *Publisher or responsible agency:* NYT, BBC; *Copy location:* Not known.

Julius Caesar. Motion Picture/Interpretation

226. *Julius Caesar.*

DOCUMENT INFORMATION: *Country:* GB; *Year of release:* 1969.

EDITION, HISTORY, CONTENTS, & EVALUATION: *Edition & history:* This was a film that grew out of Stuart Burge's experience in directing a BBC television *Julius Caesar* that was transmitted on May 5, 1959 (see 218), as well as with a subsequent London stage production. *Contents & evaluation:* Reviewers withheld praise. "The new picture is as flat and juiceless as a dead haddock," wrote Howard Thompson ("Jason Robards *et al,*" *NYT* 4 Feb. 1971: 30); Tom Castner in the *Village Voice* shared those feelings: "Acting buffs who like to watch pros at work will find much to enjoy . . . [but] Robards appears to be receiving his lines by concealed radio transmitter, and delivering them as part of the responsive reading in a Sunday sermon" ("Et tu, Charlton?" *VV* 25 Feb. 1971: 57). To me, however, the film remains something of a mystery since everyone connected with it from director Burge to actor Jason Robards had enjoyed previous successes on stage and film. Yet it is undeniably stillborn. This despite great performances from John Gielgud, Charlton Heston and Diana Rigg. Perhaps it is time to acknowledge that far from being one of Shakespeare's most accessible plays, *Julius Caesar* remains as remote and aloof as the statue of Pompey before which great Caesar fell. Seduced by the ease of costuming an entire cast in togas constructed from bedsheets, countless directors have rushed in who might otherwise have avoided its complexities. Testimony to the play's innate pitfalls comes from the 1988 RSC Barbican production, which was certifiably wooden. This film version is neither better nor worse than many other attempts to perform this tricky play (KSR). *Audience:* General use.

MEDIUM INFORMATION: *Medium:* Motion Picture; *Sound:* Spoken language; *Color:* Yes; *Length:* 117 min.; *Language(s) spoken:* English; *Film type:* 16 mm; Technicolor, Cinemascope; *Video type:* V.

AUTHORSHIP INFORMATION: *Producer(s):* Snell, Peter; *Director(s):* Burge, Stuart; *Adaptor/translator(s):* Furnival, Robert; *Composer(s):* Lewis, Michael; *Designer(s):* Oman, Julia Trevelyan; Pelling, Maurice; *Other personnel:* Higgins, Ken (Camera); Perkins, Eric Boyd (Editor); *Cast:* Heston, Charlton (Antony); Robards, Jason (Brutus); Gielgud, John (Julius Caesar); Johnson, Richard (Cassius); Vaughn, Robert (Casca); Chamberlain, Richard (Octavius Caesar); Rigg, Diana (Portia); Bennett, Jill (Calphurnia); Lee, Christopher; (Artemidorus); Browning, Alan (Marullus); Bowler, Norman (Titinius); Crawford, Andrew (Volumnius); Dodimead, David (Lepidus); Eyre, Peter (Cinna the Poet); Neal, David (Cinna); Finn, Edward (Publius); Godfrey, Derek (Decius Brutus); Gough, Michael (Metellus Cimber); Hardwick, Paul (Messala); Harrington, Laurence (Carpenter); Heathcote, Thomas (Flavius); Hooper, Ewan (Strato); Keegan, Robert (Lucillius); Lockwood, Preston (Trebonius); Moffatt, John (Popilius Lena); Morell, Andre (Cicero); Pacey, Steven (Lucius); Pember, Ron (Cobbler); Tate, John (Clitus); Thomas, Damien (Pindarus); Hutchinson, Ken; Keating, Michael; Hardwicke, Derek; Wynne, Michael.

DISTRIBUTION & AVAILABILITY: *Publisher or responsible agency:* A Commonwealth United Production; *Distributor:* FNC, DCV, ERS, KIT, FCM, FMB*, ILL *Availability:* Rental BUD $57.50 (1976), KIT $95 (1989), FNC apply, FMB* apply, Sale, V, DCV (B) $58, FCM $59.95, ERS apply, INM (DSO7) $39.95, ILL (S00694) $24.95

Julius Caesar. Video/Interpretation

227. *Julius Caesar.*

DOCUMENT INFORMATION: *Country:* GB; *Year of first showing:* 1969; *Location of first showing:* BBC1 TV. Transmitted 10 April 1969.

EDITION, HISTORY, CONTENTS, & EVALUATION: *Edition & history:* Another in the series of eight Shakespeare plays, produced on British television by Cedric Messina, as a prelude to the subsequent lengthier and more ambitious BBC series known as "The Shakespeare Plays." Transmitted in the United States on NET Playhouse from 8:30 to 10:30 P.M., 17 June 1971, under the title of "Biographies: *Julius Caesar.*" The principal cast members listed for the NET production are the same as those listed here for the BBC version. *Audience:* General use; *Supplementary materials:* "Program." *RT* 10 April 1969: 13.

MEDIUM INFORMATION: *Medium:* Video; *Sound:* Spoken language; *Color:* No (black & white); *Length:* 120 min.; *Language(s) spoken:* English; *Video type:* Video/Teleplay.

AUTHORSHIP INFORMATION: *Producer(s):* Messina, Cedric; *Director(s):* Bridges, Alan; *Designer(s):* Chapman, Spencer; *Cast:* Stephens, Robert (Mark Antony); Finlay, Frank (Brutus); Denham, Maurice (Julius Caesar); Woodward, Edward (Cassius); Bate, Anthony (Casca); Rowe, Alan (Decius Brutus); Mason, Raymond (Cinna); Rollason, Jon (Metellus Cimber); Kelland, John (Trebonius); Burrell, Richard (Ligarius); Alderton, John (Octavius Caesar); James, Godfrey (Lepidus); Rix, Colin (Flavius); Moore, John (Titinius); Abineri, John (Marullus); D'Albie, Julian (Cicero); Steele, Christopher (Pablius); De Marney, Terence (Popilius Lena); Castle, Ann (Portia); Cherrell, Gwen (Calphurnia); Jesson, Peter (Pindarus); Scott, Jonathan (Soothsayer); Guard, Christopher (Lucius); Timothy, Christopher (Cinna the Poet); Martin, Trevor (Artemidorus); Vaughan, Brian (Carpenter); Benjamin, Christopher (Cobbler); Leyshon, Emrys (Lucilius); Denham, Christopher (Young Cato); Gordon, Graham (Clius); Sadgrove, David (Dardanius); Sheppard, Stephen (Varro); Simmonds, Nikolas (Claudius); Wright, Tony (Messala).

DISTRIBUTION & AVAILABILITY: *Publisher or responsible agency:* BBC; *Copy location:* BBC*, archive.

Julius Caesar. Motion Picture/Abridgment

228. *Julius Caesar: An Introduction.* (Series: Shakespeare Series [BHE], III).

DOCUMENT INFORMATION: *Country:* GB; *Year of first showing:* 1969.

EDITION, HISTORY, CONTENTS, & EVALUATION: *Edition & history:* The third in a series of six abridged versions of the plays (see 41, 258, 323, 406, 656). For commentary see 41, above. *Contents & evaluation:* Not seen. *Audience:* High school (grades 10-12); College and university.

MEDIUM INFORMATION: *Medium:* Motion Picture; *Sound:* Spoken language; *Color:* Yes; *Length:* 28 min.; *Language(s) spoken:* English; *Film type:* 16mm.

AUTHORSHIP INFORMATION: *Producer(s):* BHE/ Seabourne Enterprises; *Cast:* [BUFVC, 20, credits] Innocent, Harold (Julius Caesar); Humphrey, John (Brutus); Flemying, Robert (Cassius); Spink, Brian (Mark Antony).

DISTRIBUTION & AVAILABILITY: *Publisher or responsible agency:* BHE/Seabourne; *Distributor:* BFA.

Julius Caesar. Motion Picture/Documentary

229. *Shaw vs. Shakespeare: The Character of Caesar*, Part One. (Series: The Humanities Series).

DOCUMENT INFORMATION: *Country:* US; *Year of release:* 1970.

EDITION, HISTORY, CONTENTS, & EVALUATION: *Edition & history:* Part one in three of a series on *Julius Caesar.* The purpose is to throw light on Shakespeare's play by comparing its treatment of persons and events with that of George Bernard Shaw in his *Caesar and Cleopatra.* Donald Moffat portrays the opinionated G.B. Shaw. *Audience:* High school (grades 10-12); College and university.

MEDIUM INFORMATION: *Medium:* Motion Picture; *Sound:* Spoken language; *Color:* Yes; *Length:* 35 min.; *Language(s) spoken:* English; *Film type:* 16mm; *Video type:* 3/4U, B, V.

AUTHORSHIP INFORMATION: *Cast:* Moffat, Donald (G.B. Shaw).

DISTRIBUTION & AVAILABILITY: *Publisher or responsible agency:* Encyclopaedia Britannica Educational Corporation; *Distributor:* UIO; *Copy location:* LCM; *Availability:* UIO (50172F), 16mm, rental, $25.80.

230. *Shaw vs. Shakespeare: The Tragedy of Julius Caesar*, Part Two. (Series: The Humanities Series).

DOCUMENT INFORMATION: *Country:* US; *Year of release:* 1970.

EDITION, HISTORY, CONTENTS, & EVALUATION: *Edition & history:* Part two in three of a series on *Julius Caesar.* For description, see 229 above. *Audience:* High school (grades 10-12); College and university.

MEDIUM INFORMATION: *Medium:* Motion Picture; *Sound:* Spoken language; *Color:* Yes; *Length:* 35 min.; *Language(s) spoken:* English; *Film type:* 16mm; *Video type:* 3/4U, B, V.

AUTHORSHIP INFORMATION: *Cast:* Moffat, Donald (G.B. Shaw).

DISTRIBUTION & AVAILABILITY: *Publisher or responsible agency:* Encyclopaedia Britannica Educational Corporation; *Distributor:* UIO, *Copy location:* LCM; *Availability:* UIO (60149F), 16mm, rental, $27.10.

231. *Shaw vs. Shakespeare: Caesar and Cleopatra* Part Three. (Series: The Humanities Series).

DOCUMENT INFORMATION: *Country:* US; *Year of release:* 1970.

EDITION, HISTORY, CONTENTS, & EVALUATION: *Edition & history:* The third and final part in a series on *Julius Caesar.* For description see 229, above. *Audience:* High school (grades 10-12); College and university.

MEDIUM INFORMATION: *Medium:* Motion Picture; *Sound:* Spoken language; *Color:* Yes; *Length:* 33 min.; *Language(s) spoken:* English; *Film type:* 16mm; *Video type:* 3/4U, B, V.

AUTHORSHIP INFORMATION: *Cast:* Moffat, Donald (G.B. Shaw).

DISTRIBUTION & AVAILABILITY: *Publisher or responsible agency:* Encyclopaedia Britannica Educational Corporation; *Distributor:* UIO, *Copy location:* LCM; *Availability:* UIO (50806F), 16mm, rental, $25.80.

Julius Caesar. Motion Picture/Scenes

232. *Julius Caesar*, 2.2; 4.3. (Series: The Shakespeare Series [IFB], IV).

DOCUMENT INFORMATION: *Country:* GB; *Year of release:* 1974.

EDITION, HISTORY, CONTENTS, & EVALUATION: *Edition & history:* The fourth in a series of twelve British educational films showing scenes intended "to serve as an introduction to each play's theme or atmosphere" (see also numbers 22, 131, 164, 326, 430, 467, 490, 510, 556, 601 and 619). For description, see 22, above. In this unit, Caesar, despite Calphurnia's misgivings, is flattered by Decius Brutus into going to the forum (2.2); Cassius and Brutus quarrel in the "tent scene" and news comes of Portia's weird death (4.3). *Contents & evaluation:* A youthful Calphurnia and Julius Caesar reenact the anxious moments when Decius Brutus fatally persuades Caesar to come to the forum. The blocking of the scene is excellent, very similar to the way it is handled in the 1978 BBC version with Elizabeth Spriggs and Charles Gray. Calphurnia maintains an eloquent silence as her husband's ego conquers his sensitivity to his wife's feelings. The other scene, the quarrel in the tent between Cassius and Brutus, seems less effective, precisely because silence rather than rant often works best on screen. When stage actors appear this way on screen, one begins to understand why film critics insist that the stony-faced Buster Keaton was the greatest of screen actors. *Audience:* High school (grades 10-12).

MEDIUM INFORMATION: *Medium:* Motion Picture; *Sound:* Spoken language; *Color:* Yes; *Length:* 14 min.; *Language(s) spoken:* English; *Film type:* 16mm; *Video type:* V, 3/4U (4 per cassette).

AUTHORSHIP INFORMATION: *Producer(s):* Realist Film Unit; *Director(s):* Seabourne, Peter; *Cast:* Kingston,

Mark (Julius Caesar); Jameson, Susan (Calphurnia); Fennell, David (Decius Brutus); Ferrell, Colin (Cassius); Gilbert, Derrick (Brutus).

DISTRIBUTION & AVAILABILITY: *Publisher or responsible agency:* Realist film unit; *Distributor:* IFB (USA); CNU, *Copy location:* FOL; *Call or copy number:* ISBN 0 8354-180-5; FOL, MP 86; *Availability:* CNU, rental 16mm, $9; IFB, sale 16mm, $225, V, $195.

Julius Caesar. Video/Teleplay

233. *Julius Caesar.* (Series: The Shakespeare Plays).

DOCUMENT INFORMATION: *Country:* GB; *Year of first showing:* 1978; *Location of first showing(s):* BBC, London; PBS stations, USA, 14 Feb. 1979.

EDITION, HISTORY, CONTENTS, & EVALUATION: *Edition & history:* As the inaugural performance in the USA of the unprecedented series known as "The Shakespeare Plays," the North American televising of this production had special interest for Shakespeareans. Director Herbert Wise's previous success with *I, Claudius,* which had captured a wide following among public television viewers, seemed to make him particularly well suited for taking on yet more Roman history. Mr. Wise himself, however, saw little connection. To him Shakespeare's play was not really about Rome at all but a tale of Elizabethan England disguised as a Roman history play. *Contents & evaluation:* "The BBC production of *Julius Caesar* is notable for a number of reasons. First, the quality of the acting is uniformly high. One is not likely to see a more subtle Cassius than David Collings, a slower-witted Brutus than Richard Pasco, or a more eloquent Antony than Keith Michell. . . . The Caesar of Charles Gray is fully realized if less forceful, less dangerous, than some readers of the play find the character to be. If Caesar is only a Mussolini windbag, then the fears of Republican Romans are undercut and the issue diminished. Still, one must credit Gray for achieving admirably what he set out to do. He is a very accomplished actor, as we can see when we compare his Caesar to his York of *Richard II.* . . . The production is interesting for additional reasons. We are not likely ever to see a better *television* version of this play. Constantly the cameras give us close-ups of the conspirators, and we look into their eyes with an intimacy not possible on the stage or in the cinema" (Knoll, Robert, "The Shakespeare Plays," *SFNL* 3.2 [1979]: 1+). *Audience:* High school (grades 10-12); General use; *Supplementary materials:* Andrews, John F. "Messina Discusses 'The Shakespeare Plays'." *SQ* 30 [1979]: 134-7; Videotape from "Shakespeare in Perspective" series with Jonathan Dimbleby reviewed elsewhere (see 234).

MEDIUM INFORMATION: *Medium:* Video; *Sound:*

Spoken language; *Color:* Yes; *Length:* 180 min.; *Video type:* B, V, 3/4"U.

AUTHORSHIP INFORMATION: *Producer(s):* Messina, Cedric; *Director(s):* Wise, Herbert; *Composer(s):* Steer, Mike; *Designer(s):* Abbott, Tony; *Costume designer(s):* Barrow, Odette; *Lighting designer(s):* King, Howard; *Other personnel:* Hobbs, William (Fight director); Steward, Jean (Make-up); *Cast:* Pasco, Richard (Brutus); Gray, Charles (Caesar); Michell, Keith (Antonius); Collings, David (Cassius); McKenna, Virginia (Portia); Spriggs, Elizabeth (Calphurnia); Dastor, Sam (Casca); Laurimore, John (Flavius); Sterland, John (Marullus); Hagon, Garrick (Octavius); Coburn, Brian (Messala); Preston, Leonard (Titinius); Davion, Alex (Decius); Angadi, Darien (Cinna); Hilton, A. (Lucilius); Dawes, Anthony (Ligarius); Bizley, Roger (Metellus); Wilson, Manning (Cicero); Forfar, Ronald (Soothsayer); Marley, Patrick (Artemidorus); Simons, William (Trebonius); Tordoff, John (Cinna the Poet); York, Philip (Cato); Good, Christopher (Clitus); Oates, Robert (Pindarus); Thompson, Alan; Dolan, Leo; Wade, Johnny; Henry, David (Plebeians/Soldiers); Scott-Taylor, Jonathan (Lucius); Kelly, Tom; Elliott, Jack; Cogan, Michael (Servants); Jessup, R. (Poet); Thorogood, Maurice (Strato); Greatorex, Michael (Varro); + five more.

DISTRIBUTION & AVAILABILITY: *Publisher or responsible agency:* BBC/TLF; *Distributor:* AVP, BBC*, *Copy location:* UVM, CTL*; *Availability:* AVP, sale, $450 all formats (1987); not listed by UIO, KSU; BBC*, 16mm or V, apply.

Julius Caesar. Video/Documentary

234. *Julius Caesar.* (Series: Shakespeare in Perspective).

DOCUMENT INFORMATION: *Country:* GB; *Year of release:* 1978.

EDITION, HISTORY, CONTENTS, & EVALUATION: *Edition & history:* The "Shakespeare in Perspective" series was made to accompany the BBC/Time Life Inc. "The Shakespeare Plays" series. See description at 44. *Contents & evaluation:* Jonathan Dimbleby gives a brilliant analysis of the uses and abuses of power in Shakespeare's *Julius Caesar.* People in power, he says, survive by secrecy and salesmanship. Brutus, happily for himself, decides that what he wants to do is what he ought to do—murder Caesar. He furnishes some excellent news clips from political speeches on modern British TV to point up the relevance of the manipulative speech acts in Shakespeare's play. "The more devious the more open you should appear to be," says Dimbleby, as he stands in front of the Westminster Houses of Parliament. The orations that Brutus and Antony delivered over the body of Caesar in the forum are only precursors to the modern need that politicians have to manipulate the *grex.* The contest between

Brutus and Antony is essentially one of salesmanship. Nowadays politicans can no longer peddle rhetoric but instead they package images. The upshot of the power struggle for Brutus is that he becomes as much a victim of it as Caesar himself. Dimbleby is a precise, articulate speaker whose keen analysis is well worth listening to (KSR).

MEDIUM INFORMATION: *Medium:* Video; *Sound:* Spoken language; *Color:* Yes; *Length:* 25 min.; *Language(s) spoken:* English; *Video type:* 3/4U, V.

AUTHORSHIP INFORMATION: *Producer(s):* Poole, Victor; *Director(s):* Denkow, Barbara; *Other personnel:* Gabell, Steve (Editor); Waters, Joe (Camera); Friedman, Liz (Graphics); *Cast:* Dimbleby, Jonathan (Commentator).

DISTRIBUTION & AVAILABILITY: *Publisher or responsible agency:* BBC; *Distributor:* BBC*; FNC, *Availability:* Double cassette (w. *Mac.*), Rental $50; Quad cassette (w. *Ham., Mac., Rom.*), Rental $75.

Julius Caesar. Video/Recording

235. *Julius Caesar.*

DOCUMENT INFORMATION: *Country:* USA; *Year of first showing:* 1979; *Location of first showing:* Delacorte Theatre, New York City.

EDITION, HISTORY, CONTENTS, & EVALUATION: *Edition & history:* A videotaping of a New York Shakespeare Festival production with an all black and Hispanic cast from which white actors had been entirely excluded. *Contents & evaluation:* The all-black/Hispanic *Julius Caesar* fared somewhat better at the hands of *The New York Times* critic than did the subsequent *Coriolanus* by the same company. Chief flaw was the inconsistency in spoken dialects between black and Hispanic actors, and a general inability to summon up enunciations suitable to Shakespearean rhetoric. On the whole, he felt, the production was a mix of "strengths and weaknesses" (Eder, Richard, "Julius Caesar at Public," *NYT* 20 Jan. 1979: n.p.). *Audience:* College and university; General use; *Supplementary materials:* Kerr, Walter. "A Mostly Muddled Caesar." *NYT* 4 Feb. 1979: n.p. (Mr. Kerr was also unhappy about the actors' speaking voices, which he found obtrusively accented.)

MEDIUM INFORMATION: *Medium:* Video; *Sound:* Spoken language; *Color:* Yes; *Length:* 150 min.; *Language(s) spoken:* English; *Video type:* 3/4U.

AUTHORSHIP INFORMATION: *Producer(s):* Papp, Joseph; *Director(s):* Langham, Michael; *Composer(s):* Silverman, Stanley; *Lighting designer(s):* Tipton, Jennifer; *Other personnel:* Fredricksen, Erik (Fight Arranger); *Cast:* Hyman, Earle (Cicero); Sanchez, Jaime (Antony); Freeman, Morgan (Casca); Gaines, Sonny Jim (Caesar); Christian, Robert.

DISTRIBUTION & AVAILABILITY: *Copy location:* LCL TOFT Collection; *Call or copy number:* NCOV 103; *Availability:* By appt.

Julius Caesar. Video/Recording

235.1 *Julius Caesar.*

DOCUMENT INFORMATION: *Country:* Belgium; *Year of first showing:* 1985.

EDITION, HISTORY, CONTENTS, & EVALUATION: *Edition & history:* Recording of a production of *Julius Caesar* under auspices of Katholieke Universiteit, Leuven, Belgium.

MEDIUM INFORMATION: *Sound:* Spoken language; *Color:* Yes; *Length:* 107 min.; *Language(s) spoken:* Dutch; *Video type:* V.

AUTHORSHIP INFORMATION: *Producer(s):* Audiovisuele Dienst, K.U., Leuven, Belgium; *Director(s):* Peyskens, P.

DISTRIBUTION & AVAILABILITY: *Copy location:* KAL; *Availability:* An agreement with the Department of Literature, Katholieke Univ., Leuven, and the director is necessary.

Julius Caesar. Video/Excerpts

236. *Julius Caesar: The Cosby Show.*

DOCUMENT INFORMATION: *Country:* USA; *Year of first showing:* 22 Oct. 1987; *Location of first showing:* NBC.

EDITION, HISTORY, CONTENTS, & EVALUATION: *Edition & history:* In this episode of the popular situation comedy, "The Cosby Show," the children are studying Shakespeare's *Julius Caesar.* The father brings two professors home, who, with the grandfather (Earle Hyman) do a brilliant reading from *Julius Caesar.* The children are sufficiently impressed so that they come up with a "rap" travesty of the play. There should be more such entries in this book recording episodes from Shakespeare that appear in commercial television entertainment. They are elusive and difficult to catch, unless one happens to be watching. Moreover, they do not appear in the television programs with any degree of regularity. I relied on a colleague, Dolores S. Sandoval, for this account. *Contents & evaluation:* From all accounts an amusing and informative episode that could be useful in enticing children into paying attention to Shakespeare. *Audience:* High school (grades 10-12); General use.

MEDIUM INFORMATION: *Medium:* Video; *Sound:* Spoken language; *Color:* Yes; *Length:* 6 min.; *Language(s) spoken:* English.

AUTHORSHIP INFORMATION: *Producer(s):* NBC/The Cosby Show; *Cast:* Plummer, Christopher (The Columbia professor); Brown, Roscoe Lee (Professor from Hillman); Hyman, Earle (Cosby's father).

DISTRIBUTION & AVAILABILITY: *Publisher or responsible agency:* NBC; *Distributor:* Apply NBC.

Julius Caesar. Video/Teleplay

237. *Giulio Cesare.*

DOCUMENT INFORMATION: *Country:* Italy; *Year of release:* 19[?].

EDITION, HISTORY, CONTENTS, & EVALUATION: *Edition & history:* An Italian language performance of *Julius Caesar* by *Il Teatro Populare di Roma. Supplementary materials:* BUFVC 10.

MEDIUM INFORMATION: *Sound:* Spoken language; *Color:* No (black & white); *Length:* 120 min.; *Language(s) spoken:* Italian.

AUTHORSHIP INFORMATION: *Director(s):* Scaparro, Maurizo; *Adaptor/translator(s):* Dallagiacoma, Angelo; *Composer(s):* Chiaramello, Giancarlo; *Costume designer(s):* Rossi, Vittoria; *Cast:* Giouampietro, Reizo (Julius Caesar); Micol, Pino (Mark Antony); Diberi, Luigi (Brutus); Pannuno, Fernando (Cassius); Negroni, Leda (Portia); De Marchi, Laura (Calphurnia).

DISTRIBUTION & AVAILABILITY: *Publisher or responsible agency:* RAI; *Distributor:* ITI*; *Availability:* Free loan in Great Britain.

King John

ORIGINAL WORK AND PRODUCTION: English History Play. *Year written:* 1594-96; *Site of first production:* The Theatre in Shoreditch [?].

King John. Motion Picture/Scene

238. *King John.*

DOCUMENT INFORMATION: *Country:* GB; *Year of release:* 1899.

EDITION, HISTORY, CONTENTS, & EVALUATION: *Edition & history:* Of prime importance to historians of Shakespeare on film as the first Shakespeare movie ever made. As Professor Ball argues, this recording of a scene from Sir Herbert Beerbohm Tree's spectacular production of *King John* at Her Majesty's Theatre showed the signing of the Magna Charta, which scene is of course not in Shakespeare's play at all. Hence the inaugural attempt to put Shakespeare on screen embodied the unending dialectical struggle between film directors and the Shakespeare text. It therefore might be said that Tree was the first director to attempt to impose his own signature as *auteur* on a Shakespeare film. He was also the creator of the first "exploitation" movie in the sense that the film was made for his own entertainment, but also conveniently publicized his stage production of the play. *Supplementary materials:* Ball, *SOSF* 21-23.

MEDIUM INFORMATION: *Length:* 4 min. [?].

AUTHORSHIP INFORMATION: *Director(s):* Tree, Sir Herbert Beerbohm; *Cast:* Tree, Sir Herbert (King John); Neilson, Julia (Constance); Waller, Lewis (Faulconbridge).

DISTRIBUTION & AVAILABILITY: *Distributor:* Lost.

King John. Video/Teleplay

239. *King John.*

DOCUMENT INFORMATION: *Country:* GB; *Year of first showing:* 1952; *Location of first showing:* BBC. Transmitted 9:02 to 11:12 P.M. on Sunday, 20 Jan. 1952.

EDITION, HISTORY, CONTENTS, & EVALUATION: *Edition & history:* Only the second time that *King John* had been placed on screen, following the lost 1899 Sir Herbert Tree film. The BBC employed 36 actors in this live performance and expanded its spatial horizons by inserting some filmed sequences. There was also generous use of canned music. Unfortunately the scripts have been destroyed. *Supplementary materials: TPAB* 20 Jan. 1952.

MEDIUM INFORMATION: *Length:* 118 min.

AUTHORSHIP INFORMATION: *Producer(s):* Harrison, Stephen; *Other personnel:* Bedford, Denis; Brenton, Guy; Mullins, Peter (Stage Managers); *Cast:* Wolfit, Donald (King John); Venning, Una (Queen Elinor); Stott, Judith (Blanch of Spain); Malone, Cavan (Prince

127

Henry); Croudson, Michael (Prince Arthur); Dresdel, Sonia (Constance); Southworth, John (Faulconbridge); O'Conor, Joseph (Philip); Latimer, Megan (Lady Faulconbridge); Devlin, William (Robert de Burgh); Colbourne, Maurice (Salisbury); Lovell, Roderick (Pembroke); Dale, James (King Philip); Bebb, Richard (Dauphin); Lucas, Victor (Duke of Austria); Brook-Jones, Elwyn (Cardinal Pandulph); Sansom, Robert (Chatillion); Raghan, Michael (Peter of Pomfret); Arnold, John (French Herald); Woodman, David (English Herald); + 14 Lords, Citizens, Soldiers and Attendants.

DISTRIBUTION & AVAILABILITY: *Publisher or responsible agency:* BBC; *Copy location:* Unavailable.

King John. Video/Interpretation

240. *King John: The Life and Death of.* (Series: The Shakespeare Plays).

DOCUMENT INFORMATION: *Country:* GB; *Year of filming:* 1984; *Year of first showing:* 1984; *Location of first showing(s):* BBC, London; PBS stations, USA, 11 Jan. 1985.

EDITION, HISTORY, CONTENTS, & EVALUATION: *Edition & history:* The rarely filmed *King John* returned to the screen for the third time in this production that made use of the celebrated Claire Bloom as Constance and the comic actor, Leonard Rossiter, as King John. Many will remember Rossiter's performance as the pusillanimous British officer in Stanley Kubrick's widely acclaimed film of the Thackeray novel, *Barry Lyndon.* Rossiter is superb at looking frightened, confused, cunning, sinister and terrified all at once. He is ideal for the role of that unhappy and careworn monarch, whose most memorable achievement, or non-achievement, the signing of Magna Charta, was generated by pressure from his enemies. Shakespeare's play makes no mention of Magna Charta, of course. *Contents & evaluation:* "David Giles's production of *King John* could strike some viewers as a brave effort in an ambiguous cause. Indeed, Giles might have recognized how Lewis of France felt when it became clear to him that victory was impossible. With supplies lost at sea and allies slipping away on all sides, Lewis settled for a truce. As it was, he lost heart too soon: the English forces were no match for him. We will never know if David Giles lost heart when victory was within his grasp. But through much of the production, Giles seems to have been trying simply to avoid a rout. . . .

True Shakespeareans surely appreciate the opportunity to see *King John* enacted, but less hardy souls will emulate Salisbury, Pembroke, and Bigot in deserting the campaign before it is done. In my living room, first one family member, then another, and eventually even the dog abandoned King John well before Salisbury and his crew did. This version will strike many of us as one which fills a gap in the series rather than one which alerts us to new dimensions of the canon. . . . It is too bad that the production is sometimes lifeless, for there are bright moments and some skillful acting. The late Leonard Rossiter, a quirky, mannered comic actor, surprisingly brings both menace and desperation to the role of King John. . . . Rossiter makes John seem a king even true patriots would desert" (Colley, Scott, "BBC-TV *King John,*" *SFNL* 10.1 [1985]: 10). *Audience:* College and university; General use; *Supplementary materials:* Videotape (25 min.) from "Shakespeare in Perspective" series with Sir Peter Parker as lecturer available in U.K. from BBC* (*BUFVC* 11).

MEDIUM INFORMATION: *Medium;* Video; *Sound:* Spoken language; *Color:* Yes; *Length:* 155 min.; *Language(s) spoken:* English; *Video type:* B,V, 3/4"U.

AUTHORSHIP INFORMATION: *Producer(s):* Sutton, Shaun; *Director(s):* Giles, David; *Composer(s):* Sell, Colin; *Designer(s):* Pensel, Chris; *Costume designer(s):* Waterson, Juanita; *Lighting designer(s):* King, Howard; *Other personnel:* Macarthur, Jenny (Prod. manager); Lowden, Fraser (Prod. assoc.); Coward, Shirley (Vision mixer); Pow, Stan (Videotape editor); Rowell, Elizabeth (Make-up); Anthony, Chick (Sound); Field, Geoff (Camera); Mapson, Colin (Visual effects); Wood, Roger (Properties); Wilders, John (Literary consultant); *Cast:* Rossiter, Leonard (King John); Whymper, William (Chatillion); Morris, Mary (Queen Elinor); Brown, Robert (Pembroke); Castle, John (Salisbury); Flint, John (Bigot); Thaw, John (Hubert); Costigan, George (Philip the Bastard); Hibbert, Edward (Faulconbridge); Law, Phillida (Lady Faulconbridge); Lewin, Mike (Gurney); Kay, Charles (Philip of France); Coy, Jonathan (Dauphin); Owen, Luc (Arthur); Kaye, Gordon (Lymoges); Bloom, Claire (Constance); Moreno, John (Melune); Barrett, Ian (Herald); Maw, Janet (Blanch); Oately, Carl (Herald); Parrish, Clifford (Citizen); Wordsworth, Richard (Pandulph); Brimble, Ian (Executioner); Chenery, Ronald (Messenger); Collins, Alan (Peter); Brown, Tom (Mesenger); Livingstone, Rusty (Prince Henry).

DISTRIBUTION & AVAILABILITY: *Publisher or responsible agency:* BBC/TLF; *Distributor:* AVP, UIO, BBC*. *Availability:* AVP, B, V, 3/4U $450 (1987), sale; UIO, V (72008H).

King Lear

ORIGINAL WORK & PRODUCTION: Tragedy of Old Age. *Year written:* 1605; *Site of first production:* Whitehall Palace [?]

King Lear. **Motion Picture/Abbreviated**

241. *King Lear.*

DOCUMENT INFORMATION: *Country:* Germany; *Year of release:* 1905.

EDITION, HISTORY, CONTENTS, & EVALUATION: *Edition & history:* Professor Ball cites Ernst Stahl (*Shakespeare und Das Deutsche Theatre* [Stuttgart, 1947]: 682) as the source for this film title. The film is now lost. *Supplementary materials:* Ball, *SOSF* 305.

MEDIUM INFORMATION: *Length:* 10 min.

King Lear. **Motion Picture/Abridgment**

242. *King Lear.*

DOCUMENT INFORMATION: *Country:* USA; *Year of release:* 1909.

EDITION, HISTORY, CONTENTS, & EVALUATION: *Edition & history:* Another of the famous Vitagraph one-reelers, made in New York City under the general supervision of J. Stuart Blackton. The print entitled *Koenig Lear* at the NFA may possibly be this film. Its German title cards notwithstanding, it seems to fit Professor Ball's description, based on his examination of the paper film strips in the Library of Congress. For one thing, it contains the Gloucester subplot, which is egregiously missing in the 1910 Italian Film d'Arte *King Lear* directed by De Liguoro. *Contents & evaluation:* A remarkable job of compressing elements from the main and subplot into a short film. The rapid editing, after an opening shot showing the old King and a plump clown, takes the viewer through a breathtaking sequence of episodes. The *mise en scène* seems to be mostly painted backdrops, so that even the heath and cliff at Dover have a lamentable inauthenticity. Most of the play's major events are there: Kent disguising himself; Lear visiting Goneril; Kent's stocking; Edmund looking villainous; Edgar as mad Tom; the wounding of Cornwall and blinding of Gloucester; the cliff scene at Dover; the duel between Edmund and Edgar; the death of Cordelia, and so forth. The film abruptly ends with the death of the old King. A genuine attempt has been made at abridgment rather than mere abbreviation. What makes coherent what otherwise might be incoherent are the title cards. In the NFA 35mm print, they are in German, a cause for some uneasiness in positively attributing the film to Vitagraph, but the foreign language dialogue cards may have been spliced in when the film was exported to Europe, a common practice then (KSR). *Supplementary materials:* Ball, *SOSF* 51-52; 313.

MEDIUM INFORMATION: *Length:* 10 min.

AUTHORSHIP INFORMATION: *Director(s):* Ranous, William; *Cast:* Ranous, William (King Lear); Auer, Florence; Turner, Florence (Goneril or Regan); Gordon, Julia Swayne (Cordelia).

DISTRIBUTION & AVAILABILITY: *Publisher or responsible agency:* Vitagraph; *Copy location:* NFA [?].

King Lear. **Motion Picture/Adaptation**

243. *Re Lear.* [*King Lear*].

DOCUMENT INFORMATION: *Country:* Italy; *Year of release:* 1910.

EDITION, HISTORY, CONTENTS, & EVALUATION: *Edition & history:* A Film d'Arte production made in Italy in 1910. *Contents & evaluation:* The print begins abruptly with a title card that is somewhat askew. Something is said about the King being displeased with Cordelia. The lavish exterior shots and the plump actresses quickly identify the film as early Italian cinema. In a motif that perhaps influenced the later (1916) American-made, Thanhouser/Warde *King Lear*, the Fool is shown sprawled at the king's feet during the opening scene. As with most silents there is exaggerated pantomiming to convey feelings. An explanatory card follows: "Goneril shamefully drives her father from her home. He leaves to seek refuge with Regan." Next, Lear is shown striking Oswald, petting a dog, and being scolded by Regan. Another explanatory card: "King Lear goes mad from excess of grief." Then, Kent is shown being stocked, but he is almost immediately released. Another card reads, "Cordelia and her father are made prisoners. Cordelia is killed by her captors' orders and King Lear expires in despair." The film ends as abruptly as it begins with the King expiring over Cordelia's lifeless body. A stiff breeze that ruffles the actors' hair and garments adds a touch of realism. Obviously this is not one of the better Italian silents, but by omitting the complications of the Gloucester plot, it does concentrate effectively on the story of Lear, Kent, and the three sisters. The excessive employment of explanatory title cards nearly always signals a failure in silent movie making. F.W. Murnau entirely avoided title cards in his famous *The Last Laugh* (1924) starring Emil Jannings, which showed how in movies the visual could independently exist without the verbal (KSR). *Audience:* Professional; *Supplementary materials:* Ball, *SOSF* 120-22; "Review." *Bioscope.* 8 Dec. 1912: 25.

MEDIUM INFORMATION: *Medium:* Motion Picture; *Sound:* Silent; *Color:* No (black & white); *Condition:* Poor; *Length:* 17 min.; *Language of subtitles:* English [?]; *Film type:* 35 mm.

AUTHORSHIP INFORMATION: *Producer(s):* Filme d'Arte Italiana (F.A.I.); *Director(s):* Lo Savio, Gerolamo;

Cast: Novelli, Ermete (King Lear); Bertini, Francesca (Cordelia); Chiantoni, Giannina (Goneril or Regan?).

DISTRIBUTION & AVAILABILITY: *Distributor:* Pathe Freres, *Copy location:* NFA; *Availability:* Archive, apply.

King Lear. **Motion Picture/Abbreviation**

244. *King Lear.*

DOCUMENT INFORMATION: *Country:* Italy; *Year of release:* 1910.

EDITION, HISTORY, CONTENTS, & EVALUATION: *Edition & history:* Possibly directed by the Italian actor, Guiseppe De Liguoro. The absence of the Gloucester subplot differentiates this film from the 1909 *King Lear* made by Vitagraph. *Supplementary materials:* Ball, *SOSF* 120.

MEDIUM INFORMATION: *Length:* 5 min.

AUTHORSHIP INFORMATION: *Director(s):* De Liguoro, Guiseppe; *Cast:* De Liguoro, Guiseppe (King Lear [?]).

DISTRIBUTION & AVAILABILITY: *Publisher or responsible agency:* Film d'arte.

King Lear. **Motion Picture/Derivative**

245. *Le roi Lear au village.*

DOCUMENT INFORMATION: *Country:* France; *Year of release:* 1911.

EDITION, HISTORY, CONTENTS, & EVALUATION: *Edition & history:* See Ball for an excellent account of this film. He shows how the film broke fresh ground by reworking a Shakespearean play into a contemporary framework. *Supplementary materials:* Ball, *SOSF* 131-32.

MEDIUM INFORMATION: *Length:* 12 min.

AUTHORSHIP INFORMATION: *Director(s):* Feuillade, Louis.

King Lear. **Motion Picture/Abbreviated**

246. *King Lear.*

DOCUMENT INFORMATION: *Country:* USA; *Year of release:* 1916.

EDITION, HISTORY, CONTENTS, & EVALUATION: *Contents & evaluation:* Warde's *King Lear* did not offer anything quite so spectacular as, for example, the celebrated 1927 Abel Gance *Napoléon* with its triple screens and thunderous musical accompaniment, but freed from the 'unworthy scaffold' and 'wooden O,' the film boasts a great battle scene, which was shot in and around the environs of a 'castle' located in New Rochelle, N.Y. For that time, when heavy equipment made cameras immobile, the results are impressive. A series of reaction shots depict a gloating Goneril and Regan ecstatic over the carnage spread out before them; dozens of extras outfitted in costume armor carry out a rousing cavalry charge while foot soldiers hack away with menacing looking swords or hurl boulders on the helpless wounded. Intercut are reaction shots of an angelic and anguished Cordelia. And even as the film attempts to sever the ancient bond with the theatre, the veteran actor, Warde, as did the more celebrated Forbes-Robertson in his *Hamlet,* offers a documentary of how a nineteenth-century actor approached a major Shakespearean role (KSR). *Audience:* College and university; General use; *Supplementary materials:* Ball, SOSF 241-44.

MEDIUM INFORMATION: *Medium:* Motion Picture; *Sound:* Silent; *Color:* No (black & white); *Condition:* Good; *Length:* 43 min.; *Language of subtitles:* English subtitles; *Film type:* 16mm.

AUTHORSHIP INFORMATION: *Producer(s):* Thanhouser, Edwin; *Director(s):* Warde, Ernest; *Adaptor/translator(s):* Lonergan, Philip; *Cast:* Warde, Frederick B. (King Lear); Huling, Lorraine (Cordelia); Warde, Ernest (Fool); Hammer, Ian (Goneril); Arey, Wayne (Albany); Diestal, Edith (Regan); Brooks, Charles (Cornwall); Gilmour, J.H. (Kent); Marshall, Boyd (France); Stanley, Edwin (Edgar); Whittier, Robert (Oswald).

DISTRIBUTION & AVAILABILITY: *Distributor:* JEF, *Copy location:* FOL; *Call or copy number:* MP 15; *Availability:* Rental, 16mm, $125 (1987); *Restrictions:* Archive, FOL.

King Lear. Motion Picture/Excerpt

247. *Success.*

DOCUMENT INFORMATION: *Country:* USA; *Year of release:* 1923.

EDITION, HISTORY, CONTENTS, & EVALUATION: *Edition & history:* Professor Eckert lists this film as a spinoff from *King Lear* in his filmography. Apparently it contains an excerpt from Shakespeare's play. *Supplementary materials:* Eckert, FSF 169.

MEDIUM INFORMATION: *Length:* 68 min.

AUTHORSHIP INFORMATION: *Director(s):* Ince, Ralph; *Cast:* Astor, Mary; Tynan, Brandon.

King Lear. Motion Picture/Derivative

248. *Yiddish King Lear.*

DOCUMENT INFORMATION: *Country:* USA; *Year of release:* 1935.

EDITION, HISTORY, CONTENTS, & EVALUATION: *Edition & history:* The Weisbaden filmography cites this as "a modern version." The title may seem to remove it far afield from Shakespeare but on second thought, one realizes that this Yiddish adaptation gives yet more evidence of Shakespeare's universality. This is one reason why today he still remains such a powerful cultural symbol. *Supplementary materials:* SIF 108.

MEDIUM INFORMATION: *Length:* 86 min.

AUTHORSHIP INFORMATION: *Director(s):* Thomashefsky, Harry; *Cast:* Krohner, Maurice; Paskewitsch, Jeanette; Levenstein, Fannie; Adler, Esther.

King Lear. Video/Teleplay

249. *King Lear.*

DOCUMENT INFORMATION: *Country:* GB; *Year of first showing:* 1948; *Location of first showing:* BBC. Transmitted in two parts on Sunday, Aug. 22 and Sunday, Aug. 29, 1948.

EDITION, HISTORY, CONTENTS, & EVALUATION: *Edition & history:* Royston Morley, the BBC drama producer, poured energy and enthusiasm into this postwar *King Lear* that was the most ambitious Shakespeare production in many years. His attempts to persuade John Gielgud to play the title role failed because the star was in Mexico at the time, but the cast was made up of well known stage actors. By today's standards, the budget was tiny (somewhat over £2,000) but the fan mail was nevertheless abundant (WAC T5/247, 22 Aug. 1948).

MEDIUM INFORMATION: *Length:* 200 min.

AUTHORSHIP INFORMATION: *Producer(s):* Morley, Royston; Allen, Douglas; *Designer(s):* Learoyd, Barry; *Cast:* Sansom, Robert (Kent); Oscar, Henry (Gloucester); Troughton, Patrick (Edmund); Devlin, William (King Lear); Crutchley, Rosalie (Goneril); Howells, Ursula (Cordelia); Bernard, Nicolette (Regan); Claridge, Norman (Albany); Tate, Reginald (Cornwall); Conway, Cyril (Burgundy); Ashwin, Michael (France); Harris, Robert (Edgar); Chandos, John (Oswald); Wheatley, Alan (The Fool); Vere, John (Gentleman); Jackson, Maxwell; Hardingham, Cyril; Baker, John; Ross, Frederick (Knights, Courtiers, Attendants and Servants).

DISTRIBUTION & AVAILABILITY: *Publisher or responsible agency:* BBC; *Copy location:* Unavailable.

King Lear. Video/Abridgment

250. *King Lear.* (Series: The TV-Radio Workshop of the Ford Foundation).

DOCUMENT INFORMATION: *Country:* USA; *Year of first showing:* 1953; *Location of first showing:* Omnibus, 18 Oct. 1953.

EDITION, HISTORY, CONTENTS, & EVALUATION: *Contents & evaluation:* As was so often the case with any production that Orson Welles was involved in, critics tended to disagree over its merits. A widely respected scholar, Prof. Marvin Rosenberg, writing at the time, found the action "difficult to keep in focus" and thought that Peter Brook, despite his indisputable theatrical talents, had failed as a television director. Rosenberg's feelings are encapsulated in one acute observation about ". . . the fool, a restless acrobat who tried ineffectively to talk as he bounced" ("Shakespeare on TV," *FQ* 9 [1954-55]:171). Thirty years later, Robert Hetherington also had reservations: "The Omnibus broadcast on Sunday night, October 18, 1953, presented American audiences with the first broadcast uninterrupted by sponsors, the television debut of Orson Welles in a starring role, and an extremely abridged *Lear.* The entire performance lasted all of 73 minutes. 'Peter Brook has simply taken the sub-plot and thrown it out the window,' explained Alistair Cooke in his prefatory remarks. 'But everything that bears on the tragedy of Lear is in this version.' One wonders [how] given the enormity of the deletions, if . . . the audience could follow the story at all" ("The *Lears* of Peter Brook," *SFNL* 6.1 [1982]: 7). Although the director was blamed for whatever went wrong in this production, what went right was that it preserved a record for posterity of Orson Welles playing King Lear. At the time of his death at age 70, he was planning a film version of *King Lear* to be made in France. It can be said of Orson Welles's career as a Shakespearean that never has an actor with so much talent earned so little praise from the critics. There was a tendency on the part of some to excoriate his Shakespeare films almost ritualistically. Besides including Welles in the cast, this production of *King Lear* also has intrinsic interest simply as a document from the early years of television when the medium went on the air 'live,' sometimes with surprising results. Despite the Wellesian flaws, he was generous and vulnerable as an actor, director and a Shakespearean. He deserved a better press than he got in his lifetime (KSR). *Supplementary materials:* Rothwell, Kenneth S. "Representing *King Lear* on Screen." *ShS* 39 (1987): 82-3.

MEDIUM INFORMATION: *Medium:* Video; *Sound:* Spoken language; *Color:* No (black & white); *Condition:* Good; *Length:* 73 min.; *Language(s) spoken:* English; *Video type:* V.

AUTHORSHIP INFORMATION: *Producer(s):* Rickey, Fred; Feigay, Paul; *Director(s):* McCullough, Andrew;

Brook, Peter; *Composer(s):* Thomson, Virgil; *Designer(s):* Callahan, Gene; May, Henry; Wakhevitch, Georges; *Cast:* Welles, Orson (King Lear); Parry, Natasha (Cordelia); Moss, Arnold (Albany); Fletcher, Bramwell (Kent); Stewart, David J. (Oswald); Phillips, Margaret (Regan); Straight, Beatrice (Goneril); Badel, Alan (Fool); MacLiammoir, Michael (Poor Tom); Worlock, Frederic (Gloucester); Forbes, Scott (Cornwall); Addy, Wesley (France); Bochner, Lloyd (First Gent.); Gampel, Chris (First Servant); Operti, Le Roi (Doctor).

DISTRIBUTION & AVAILABILITY: *Publisher or responsible agency:* Omnibus, TV/Radio Workshop of the Ford Foundation; *Copy location:* MOB, FOL; *Call or copy number:* MOB (Omnibus, II, 3, pts. 1-3: *King Lear* T77:0369/370); FOL (MP 105); *Availability:* Archive, MOB, FOL by appointment; FCM, V, $39.95.

King Lear. Motion Picture/Derivative

251. *Broken Lance.*

DOCUMENT INFORMATION: *Country:* USA; *Year of filming:* 1954.

EDITION, HISTORY, CONTENTS, & EVALUATION: *Edition & history:* Frequently cited as a Shakespeare film, *Broken Lance* actually has but thin connections with *King Lear.* One could argue that traces of the Gloucester plot linger on in the relationship between Matt Devereux (Spencer Tracy) and his sons, three of whom are disloyal (Ben, Mike and Denny) and one loyal (Joe). There is also a kind of Cordelia figure in Judge Horace's daughter, Barbara (Jean Peters). But beyond that it's difficult to see much else of *King Lear.* *Contents & evaluation:* Shakespeare aside, *Broken Lance* is a fine movie with a strong theme in which the Old West of rugged individualism is pitted against the New West of law and order. Spencer Tracy loves to carry a whip in the hope of using it on fellow human beings. In the new world, however, that sort of thing is frowned upon. The title, *Broken Lance,* derives from the "old Comanche custom" of striking a lance into the earth over the grave of a fallen brave. When Joe, the half-breed son of Matt by an Indian squaw, breaks the lance over his father's grave, the symbolism suggests a clean break with patriarchal hegemony. As a film, it is visually exciting, with rich exterior shots and a stirring musical score by Leigh Harline. *Audience:* General use; *Supplementary materials:* Kliman, Bernice. "*Broken Lance* Is Not *Lear.*" *SFNL* 2.1 (Dec. 1977): 3.

MEDIUM INFORMATION: *Medium:* Motion Picture; *Sound:* Spoken language; *Color:* Yes; *Length:* 96 min.; *Language(s) spoken:* English; *Film type:* 16mm.

AUTHORSHIP INFORMATION: *Producer(s):* Siegel, Sol C.; *Director(s):* Dmytryk, Edward; Weinberger, Henry; *Screenplay writer(s):* Yordan, Philip; *Adaptor/translator(s):* Murphy, Richard; *Composer(s):* Harline,

Leigh; Newman, Lionel; Powell, Edward B.; *Designer(s):* Wheeler, Lyle; Ransford, Maurice; *Set designer(s):* Scott, Walter M.; Reiss, Stuart; *Costume designer(s):* Travilla; Le Maine, Charles; *Other personnel:* MacDonald, Joe (Photography); Kellogg, Ray (Special effects); Spencer, Dorothy (Film editor); Nye, Ben (Makeup); Turpin, Helen (Hair); Rick, W.D.; Heman, Roger (Sound); *Cast:* Tracy, Spencer (Matt Devereux); Wagner, Robert (Joe Devereux); Peters, Jean (Barbara); Widmark, Richard (Ben Devereux); Jurado, Katy (Senora Devereux); O'Brian, Hugh (Mike Devereux); Franz, Eduard (Two Moons); Holliman, Earl (Denny); Marshall, E.G. (Governor Horace); Reid, Carl (Clem Lawton); Ober, Philip (Van Cleve); Burton, Robert (MacAndrews).

DISTRIBUTION & AVAILABILITY: *Publisher or responsible agency:* Twentieth Century-Fox; *Distributor:* FNC; *Copy location:* FOL; *Call or copy number:* MP 23; *Availability:* Apply FNC.

King Lear. Motion Picture/Scenes

252. *King Lear.* (Series: On Stage Series).

DOCUMENT INFORMATION: *Country:* USA; *Year of release:* 1954.

EDITION, HISTORY, CONTENTS, & EVALUATION: *Edition & history:* An Audio-Brandon catalog describes this as a scene in which "King Lear is rejected by both his daughters." Monty Woolley stars.

MEDIUM INFORMATION: *Medium:* Motion Picture; *Sound:* Spoken language; *Color:* No (black & white); *Length:* 15 min.

AUTHORSHIP INFORMATION: *Cast:* Woolley, Monty (King Lear).

DISTRIBUTION & AVAILABILITY: *Distributor:* FNC [?].

King Lear. Motion Picture/Derivative

253. *The Big Show.*

DOCUMENT INFORMATION: *Country:* USA/Germany; *Year of release:* 1961.

EDITION, HISTORY, CONTENTS, & EVALUATION: *Edition & history:* Another "spinoff" from *King Lear* with much closer links to the Gloucester subplot than to the main plot. As with *Broken Lance* there is a tale of loyal and disloyal sons and a betrayed father, only this time the setting is not the Wild West but a circus. *Contents & evaluation:* The only resemblance to Shakespeare's play is that a father, who could be stretched into a Gloucester-figure, is betrayed by his sons and through suffering learns to feel as wretches feel. For

the rest there are some spectacular circus acts—trapeze artists, wild animal routines, and so forth. When a turnbuckle snaps, resulting in manslaughter charges against the circus owners, good Joe, an Edgar/Cordelia figure, takes the blame and goes to jail. At the end of the film, Bruno, the father, discovers that his other sons have stolen the circus from him. A dwarf seems to correspond to the Fool in Shakespeare's play. *Audience:* General use; *Supplementary materials:* Thompson, Howard. "Review," *NYT* 11 May 1961: 42:4.

MEDIUM INFORMATION: *Medium:* Motion Picture; *Sound:* Spoken language; *Color:* Yes; *Length:* 113 min.; *Language(s) spoken:* English; *Film type:* 35mm Cinemascope.

AUTHORSHIP INFORMATION: *Producer(s):* Sherdeman, Ted; Clark, James B.; *Director(s):* Clark, James B.; Goebal, Herman; *Screenplay writer(s):* Sherdeman, Ted; *Composer(s):* Sawtell, Paul; Shefter, Bert; *Choreographer(s):* Circus Krone, Munich; *Designer(s):* Rieber, Ludwig; *Costume designer(s):* Turai-Rossi, Teddy; Birger Christensen (Furs); Cossfield, Josef; Kraft, Klara (Makeup); *Lighting designer(s):* Heller, Otto; *Other personnel:* Eurist, Clarence (Production manager); Laird, Benjamin (Film editor); Ruhland, Walter; McKay, Don (Sound); *Cast:* Williams, Esther (Hillary); Robertson, Cliff (Josef); Persoff, Nehemiah (Bruno); Vaughn, Robert (Klaus); Dean, Margia (Carlotta); Nelson, David (Eric); Christensen, Carol (Garda); Pecher, Kurt (Hans); Mannhardt, Renata (Teresa); Andrei, Franco (Frederick); Capell, Peter (Vizzini); Schnabel, Stephen; Young, Carleton; Hanser, Philo; Tomic, Mariza; Vesperman, Gerd; Members of Circus Krone, Munich: Alizee, Pierre; Nicolet, Jacques; Tanz, Marlies; Stapper, Gerhard; The Rudolph Stey High Wire Troupe; Doris Arndt and the Ice Bears; the Wandruscka Family and Animals of Circus Krone.

DISTRIBUTION & AVAILABILITY: *Publisher or responsible agency:* Twentieth-Century Fox; *Copy location:* LCM.

King Lear. Motion Picture/Abridgment

254. *King Lear.* (Series: Fair Adventure Series).

DOCUMENT INFORMATION: *Country:* USA; *Year of release:* 1964.

EDITION, HISTORY, CONTENTS, & EVALUATION: *Edition & history:* A five-part abridgment of the play with commentary by Dr. Frank Baxter. For other films in this series, see 180, 311, 426, 463, 487, 508, 546, 614 and 653. *Contents & evaluation:* Not seen. The series has not been actively marketed in recent years. *Audience:* Junior High (grades 7-9); High school (grades 10-12).

MEDIUM INFORMATION: *Medium:* Motion Picture; *Sound:* Spoken language; *Color:* No (black & white); *Length:* 140 min.; *Language(s) spoken:* English; *Film type:* 16mm.

DISTRIBUTION & AVAILABILITY: *Publisher or responsible agency:* Westinghouse Broadcasting Corp.; *Distributor:* Not known.

King Lear. Video/Documentary

255. *Albert van Dalsum, man van het toneel.*

DOCUMENT INFORMATION: *Country:* Netherlands; *Year of release:* 1964.

EDITION, HISTORY, CONTENTS, & EVALUATION: *Edition & history:* Interview with Albert van Dalsum and discussion about producing *King Lear.*

MEDIUM INFORMATION: *Length:* 97 min.

AUTHORSHIP INFORMATION: *Director(s):* Vondel, Jvd; *Cast:* Shaffy, R.; Koning, D.; Bouman, M.

DISTRIBUTION & AVAILABILITY: *Distributor:* NTI, *Copy location:* NTI, Amsterdam; *Call or copy number:* 700164201 BDA.

King Lear. Motion Picture/Adaptation

256. *Karol Lear:* [*King Lear*].

DOCUMENT INFORMATION: *Country:* USSR; *Year of filming:* 1967-69; *Year of release:* 1970, 1972 in the West; *Location of first showing:* USSR.

EDITION, HISTORY, CONTENTS, & EVALUATION: *Awards:* Grand Prix, Teheran Film Festival, 1972; *Contents & evaluation:* "Among all modern directors making screen versions of Shakespeare's plays, Grigori Kozintsev is especially impressive with his serious, deeply thoughtful, I should say, philosophical approach . . . there are no attempts at sensationalism, no efforts to 'modernize' Shakespeare by introducing Freudian themes, Existentialist ideas, eroticism, or sexual perversion. He has simply made a film of Shakespeare's tragedy. . . . In losing everything he [Lear] is lowered to the level of all the poor and downtrodden. It is at this moment that his personal tragedy merges with the tragedy of all the unfortunate. Pushkin, the great national Russian poet, held that the basis of true tragedy is 'the fate of man, the fate of the people.' The merging of the catastrophe of one man with the suffering of the whole people is the central point of Shakespeare's tragedy" (Anikst, Alexander, *SL* 6 [1971]:176+). When just prior to his ill-conceived division of the kingdom among his three daughters, the crotchety old King Lear cries out "Give me the map there" (1.1.37), Shakespeare, the actor and director, is signaling the entry of an important object. The test of a director's cinematic instincts might be said to rest on how that map is handled or mis-handled. Kozintsev never flinches. The map, first glimpsed through the flames of the hearth, is privileged to underscore its powerful potential. It then becomes the locus for all of the king's movements and gestures during the division of two-thirds of the kingdom to Goneril and Regan. At the end of the sequence, however, Kozintsev shows how to use the map most effectively. The king punctuates his denunciation of Cordelia (1.1.108 ff.) by waving it, ripping it, tearing it. The map becomes what V.I. Pudovkin calls an "expressive object," which in tandem with the actor, can create a "filmic monologue without words" (*Film Technique and Film Acting* [1929. London: Vision, 1968. 143]). Kozintsev does not squander this cinematic opportunity (KSR). *Audience:* College and university; Professional; General use; *Supplementary materials:* Hodgdon, Barbara. "Kozintsev's *King Lear:* Filming a Tragic Poem." *LFQ* 5.4 (1977): 291-98; Jorgens, Jack J. *SOF* 236+; Mackintosh, Mary, trans. "Introduction." Grigori Kozintsev, *The Space of Tragedy;* Millar, Sylvia. "*King Lear.*" *MFB* 39 [1972]: 165-66.

MEDIUM INFORMATION: *Medium:* Motion picture; *Sound:* Spoken language; *Color:* No (black & white); *Length:* 140 min.; *Language(s) spoken:* Russian; *Language of subtitles:* English; *Film type:* 16 mm; 35 mm Sovscope; *Video type:* B, V.

AUTHORSHIP INFORMATION: *Producer(s):* Lenfilm; *Director(s):* Kozintsev, Grigori; *Adaptor/translator(s):* Pasternak, Boris; *Composer(s):* Shostakovich, Dmitri; *Designer(s):* Enei, Y.; Ulitko, V.; *Costume designer(s):* Virsaladze, Simon; *Other personnel:* Gricius, Jonas (Photography); Vanunts, E. (Sound); *Cast:* Yarvet, Yuri (King Lear); Radzins, E. (Goneril); Volchek, G. (Regan); Shendrikova, V. (Cordelia); Dal, O. (Fool); Sebris, K. (Gloucester); Merzin, L. (Edgar); Adomaitis, R. (Edmund); Emelyanov, V. (Kent); Vokach, A. (Cornwall); Banionis, D. (Albany); Petrenko, A. (Oswald); Budraitis, I. (France).

DISTRIBUTION & AVAILABILITY: *Distributor:* COR, GLB*, FCM, TAM, INM *Availability* Rental (COR, GLB*) 16mm; Sale, TAM, FCM, B, V, (Apply); INM, V (DS#20) $89.95.

King Lear. Motion Picture/Documentary

257. *King Lear: Who Is It Who Can Tell Me Who I Am?*. (Series: Explorations in Shakespeare, VI).

DOCUMENT INFORMATION: *Country:* Canada; *Year of release:* 1969.

EDITION, HISTORY, CONTENTS, & EVALUATION: *Edition & history:* Part six in a series of twelve 23-minute films made in 1969 by the Ontario Educational Communications Authority (see also 18, 40, 65, 124, 162, 322, 465, 488, 555, 617 and 637). *Contents & evaluation:* Not seen. According to the publicity release issued by NBC Educational Enterprises, this unit explores two major areas: "the absurd world of folly, madness, despair and human destruction which the King himself appears to unleash; and the growth of a man in self-knowledge and awareness. Standing in front of a poster which uses a phrase from *Waiting for Godot*: 'We are all born mad. Some remain so,' the Fool comments on the folly of Lear's actions: the division of his kingdom, his banishment of Cordelia, his madness and final excruciating loss. The film deliberately ends with the unresolved question of Lear's regeneration and growth in self-knowledge." From the descriptions, it seems that these films were not timid about being intellectually stimulating. *Audience:* College and university.

MEDIUM INFORMATION: *Medium:* Motion Picture; *Sound:* Spoken language; *Color:* Yes; *Length:* 23 min.; *Language(s) spoken:* English; *Film type:* 16mm.

AUTHORSHIP INFORMATION: *Producer(s):* Reis, Kurt; Moser, Ed; *Screenplay writer(s):* Webster, Hugh; *Composer(s):* Yanovsky, Zal; *Set designer(s):* Adeney, Chris; *Lighting designer(s):* Galbraith, Howard; *Performance group(s):* Ontario Educational Communications/NBC Educational Enterprises.

DISTRIBUTION & AVAILABILITY: *Distributor:* CNU [?].

King Lear. Motion Picture/Abridgment

258. *King Lear: An Introduction.* (Series: The Shakespeare Series (BHE/BFA), VI).

DOCUMENT INFORMATION: *Country:* GB; *Year of release:* 1969.

EDITION, HISTORY, CONTENTS, & EVALUATION: *Edition & history:* The sixth in a series of six abridged versions of the plays (see also 41, 228, 323, 406, 656). See *AYL*, 41, for overview. *Contents & evaluation:* Not seen. *Audience:* High school (grades 10-12); College and university.

MEDIUM INFORMATION: *Medium:* Motion Picture; *Sound:* Spoken language; *Color:* Yes; *Length:* 27 min.; *Language(s) spoken:* English; *Film type:* 16mm.

AUTHORSHIP INFORMATION: *Producer(s):* BHE/Seabourne Enterprises; *Cast:* Not known.

DISTRIBUTION & AVAILABILITY: *Publisher or responsible agency:* BHE/Seabourne; *Distributor:* BFA.

King Lear. Motion Picture/Interpretation

259. *King Lear:* Peter Brook's Film of William Shakespeare's *King Lear.*

DOCUMENT INFORMATION: *Country:* GB/Denmark; *Year of filming:* 1969/70; *Year of first showing:* 1971; *Location of first showing:* Great Britain.

EDITION, HISTORY, CONTENTS, & EVALUATION: *Contents & evaluation:* "In a two hour film, it would be hard, and absurd, to try to include all the elements that make up a five hour *Lear* in the theatre. So we tried to evolve an impressionistic movie technique, cutting language and incident to the bone, so that the total effect of all the things heard and seen could capture in different terms Shakespeare's rough, uneven, jagged and disconcerting vision" (Brook, Peter, "Peter Brook on *King Lear*," P.R. release, Paris, 1971: 1); "Peter Brook's *Lear* had a bad press in England; it disappeared very quickly and is now hard to find. It wouldn't be difficult to say why it displeased people who think they know about movies, and why it displeased others who thought they knew about Shakespeare. . . . In fact the really difficult thing is to explain why it *is* very good . . . and why the common judgment, that Brook is a genius in the theatre but a bad movie director is wrong. A genius, certainly; but he has also made the best of all Shakespeare movies" (Kermode, Frank, "Shakespeare in the Movies," *NYRB* 4 May 1972: 19); "Peter Brook's "King Lear" is gray and cold, and the actors have dead eyes. I didn't just dislike this production; I hated it. . . . The conception is resolutely joyless and unbeautiful—a "Lear" without passion, "Lear" set in a glacial desert" (Kael, Pauline, "The Night of the Living Dead," *The New Yorker* 11 Dec. 1971: 135. Rpt. *Deeper Into Movies* [Boston: Little Brown, 1973]). In his film version of *King Lear*, director Peter Brook forces the audience to share in the last bitter dregs of the geriatric experience. Old age demands recognition of the essentially tragic nature of the human experience, which is something that few of us want to confront. Like Macbeth we would hope in old age for "honor, love, obedience, troops of friends," which are things denied to both him and Lear. Instead, each encounters the corrosive truth of the Seventh Age of Man: "Sans teeth, sans eyes, sans taste, sans everything." True enough, Shakespeare often celebrates the joy of life, but not especially in *King Lear*. In refusing to sentimentalize the unsentimental, Peter Brook makes artistic integrity the first consideration (KSR). *Audience:* General use. *Supplementary materials:* Millar, Sylvia. "King Lear." *MFB* 38 (1971): 182-3.

MEDIUM INFORMATION: *Medium:* Motion picture; *Sound:* Spoken language; *Color:* No (black & white); *Length:* 137 min.; *Language(s) spoken:* English; *Film type:* 16 mm, 35mm, B, V.

AUTHORSHIP INFORMATION: *Producer(s):* Filmways (London); Athene/Laterna Films (Copenhagen); Birkett, Lord Michael; *Director(s):* Brook, Peter; *Designer(s):* Wakhevitch, Georges; *Costume designer(s):* Angard, Adele; *Lighting designer(s):* Kristiansen, Henning; *Other personnel:* Lintott, Ken; Mahler, Ruth (Make-up);

Schyberg, Kasper (Editor); *Cast:* Scofield, Paul (King Lear); Worth, Irene (Goneril); MacGowran, Jack (Fool); Webb, Alan (Gloucester); Cusack, Cyril (Albany); Magee, Patrick (Cornwall); Lloyd, Robert (Edgar); Fleming, Tom (Kent); Engel, Susan (Regan); Gabold Annelise (Cordelia); Hogg, Ian (Edmund); Stanton, Barry (Oswald); Elung-Jensen, Soren (Burgundy).

DISTRIBUTION & AVAILABILITY: *Distributor:* FNC, FMB*, DCV, FCM, *Availability:* Rental (FNC, FMB*), 16mm, apply; Sale, DCV, V, $38; FCM, B,V (apply).

King Lear. Video/Recording

259.1 *King Lear.*

DOCUMENT INFORMATION: *Country:* GB; *Year of first showing:* 1971.

EDITION, HISTORY, CONTENTS, & EVALUATION: *Edition & history:* Apparently a recording of a theatrical production by London's Prospect Theatre Company in September 1971. Housed in a Venetian archive.

AUTHORSHIP INFORMATION: *Director(s):* Robertson, Toby.

DISTRIBUTION & AVAILABILITY: *Copy location:* ASV; *Call or copy number:* A 5.100.105-6.

King Lear. Video/Adaptation

259.2 *Re Lear, de un'idea di gran teatro di William Shakespeare.*

DOCUMENT INFORMATION: *Country:* Italy; *Year of first showing:* 1972.

EDITION, HISTORY, CONTENTS, & EVALUATION: *Edition & history:* An adaptation for television filmed in the RAI Studios. Transmitted 19 Feb. 1972.

MEDIUM INFORMATION: *Medium:* Video; *Language(s) spoken:* Italian.

AUTHORSHIP INFORMATION: *Director:* Ricci, Mario.

DISTRIBUTION & AVAILABILITY: *Publisher or responsible agency:* RAI Productions/Videoteca RAI; *Copy location:* Cineteca nastroteca.

King Lear. Motion Picture/Derivative

260. *Harry and Tonto.*

DOCUMENT INFORMATION: *Country:* USA; *Year of first showing:* 1974.

EDITION, HISTORY, CONTENTS, & EVALUATION: *Awards:* Academy Award, Art Carney, acting; *Edition & history:* As he also did with his 1982 *The Tempest,* Paul Mazursky appropriates a Shakespearean theme for a tale of modern life. A retired 72-year old teacher, who quotes from *King Lear* as he is being evicted from his apartment, journeys across the country to visit with his children. Like King Lear he discovers that the disempowered old person receives scant respect from the world. The film was included in the Jan.-March 1986 Library of Congress film series, "Acting it Many Ways: Shakespeare on Film and Television," at the Pickford Theatre. It was introduced by Prof. S. Schoenbaum, who is generally acknowledged to be the world's most eminent authority in the field of Shakespeare biography. *Contents & evaluation:* As a version of the Lear story displaced into modern America, this film is a triumph. When Harry, a retired English teacher, is evicted from his upper West Side apartment in New York City, he protests his mistreatment in the grand style of King Lear. The shots of life along upper Broadway in New York achieve memorable levels of realism. The dreary wasteland of upper Broadway with its demented street people and welfare winos replaces the stark northern European landscape of the Brook film version. The heart of the film, however, shows Harry's misery as he tries living with his own children, who are about as easy to get along with as Goneril and Regan. Tonto, his cat, with whom he travels across the continent, corresponds in loyalty to Cordelia and in proximity to the Fool. The film offers another example of how Shakespeare has been embedded in modern culture. Director Mazursky deserves special praise for his willingness to undertake these kinds of ventures (KSR). *Audience:* General use; *Supplementary materials:* Schoenbaum, S. "Looking for Shakespeare," in *Shakespeare's Craft,* ed. P. Highfill (Carbondale: SIUP, 1982): 156-77.

MEDIUM INFORMATION: *Medium:* Motion Picture; *Sound:* Spoken language; *Color:* Yes; *Length:* 115 min.; *Language(s) spoken:* English; *Film type:* 16mm; *Video type:* V.

AUTHORSHIP INFORMATION: *Producer(s):* Mazursky, Paul; Ray, Tony; *Director(s):* Mazursky, Paul; *Screenplay writer(s):* Mazursky, Paul; Greenfield, Josh; *Composer(s):* Conti, Bill; *Designer(s):* Haworth, Ted; *Costume designer(s):* Wolsky, Albert; *Lighting designer(s):* Butler, Michael; *Other personnel:* Halsey, Richard (Editor); O'Bradovich, Bob (Makeup); *Cast:* Carney, Art (Harry); Burstyn, Ellen (Shirley); George, Chief Dan (Sam Two Feathers); Fitzgerald, Geraldine (Jessie); Hagman, Larry (Eddie); Bruns, Phil (Burt); Berghof, Herbert (Rivetowski); Mostel, Joshua (Norman); Mayron, Melanie (Ginger); Long, Avon (Leroy); Hunnicut, Arthur (Wade); Rhoades, Barbara (Hooker); Jonah, Dolly (Elaine); De Young, Cliff (Burt, Jr.); Bowan, Sybil (Old Lady); Mart, Sally K. (Cat lady); Enriquez, Rene (Grocery clerk); Norton, Cliff (Salesman); Roth, Phil (Vegas gambler); Guss, Louis (Dominic); McCleery, Michael (Mugger).

DISTRIBUTION & AVAILABILITY: *Publisher or responsible agency:* Twentieth-Century Fox; *Distributor:* HAR*, FNC, FCM, *Copy location:* LOC; *Availability:* FCM, V, $59.98.

King Lear. Video/Interpretation

261. *King Lear.*

DOCUMENT INFORMATION: *Country:* GB; *Year of first showing:* 1975; *Location of first showing:* BBC TV. Transmitted 23 March 1975.

EDITION, HISTORY, CONTENTS, & EVALUATION: *Edition & history:* Another in the series of eight Shakespeare plays, produced on British television by Cedric Messina, as a prelude to the later, more ambitious BBC series, "The Shakespeare Plays." This production is Jonathan Miller's second *King Lear* starring Michael Hordern; the first was a 1970 Nottingham Playhouse stage production. J.W. Lambert in reviewing it found Hordern's 'grizzled style' and the 'grey sets' faithful to the Shakespearian intention ("Plays in Performance," *Drama* [Summer 1970]:24). Miller's third *King Lear* with Hordern in the title role was the 1982 BBC version in "The Shakespeare Plays" series. Michael Hordern, a celebrated British film actor, also appeared in that same series as Prospero in *The Tempest* and as Capulet in *Romeo and Juliet*. His Baptista Minola in the Zeffirelli *Taming of the Shrew* was also endearing for its display of paternal vulnerability. *Contents & evaluation:* Not seen. From all accounts, however, this televised version must have been in conception close to the stage performance described above and to the third version made in 1982 for "The Shakespeare Plays" series. Indeed many of the same actors appear in both versions. Presenting Hordern as anything but the traditional King Lear, as embodied by Ernest Warde in his 1916 film or the character of "Sir" in *The Dresser*, Miller's king has been demythologized, so to speak. He is less grand than grumpy, which is the way his daughters saw him. It is a sobering performance. *Audience:* General use.

MEDIUM INFORMATION: *Medium:* Video; *Sound:* Spoken language; *Color:* Yes; *Length:* 120 min. [?]; *Language(s) spoken:* English; *Video type:* Video.

AUTHORSHIP INFORMATION: *Producer(s):* Miller, Jonathan; *Director(s):* Miller, Jonathan; *Designer(s):* Symonds, Vic; *Cast:* Hordern, Michael (King Lear); Down, Angela (Cordelia); Middlemass, Frank (Fool); Badel, Sarah (Goneril); Wilton, Penelope (Regan); Pickup, Ronald (Edgar); Jayston, Michael (Edmund).

DISTRIBUTION & AVAILABILITY: *Publisher or responsible agency:* BBC; *Copy location:* BBC*, archive, probably unavailable.

262. *King Lear.*

DOCUMENT INFORMATION: *Country:* GB; *Year of release:* 1976.

EDITION, HISTORY, CONTENTS, & EVALUATION: *Edition & history:* A reworking of a 1973 stage version by the Triple Action Theatre Group. Filmed entirely on location "bare to the elements." *Supplementary materials:* BUFVC 11.

MEDIUM INFORMATION: *Color:* No (black & white); *Length:* 48 min.; *Film type:* 16mm.

AUTHORSHIP INFORMATION: *Director(s):* Rumbelow, Steve; *Cast:* Auvache, Chris; Saner, Gengiz; Buferd, Monia; Paul, Helena.

DISTRIBUTION & AVAILABILITY: *Distributor:* BFI*.

King Lear. Video/Teleplay

263. *King Lear.*

DOCUMENT INFORMATION: *Country:* USA; *Year of release:* 1973; *Year of first showing:* 1977; *Country of first showing:* USA; *Location of first showing:* Theatre in America series.

EDITION, HISTORY, CONTENTS, & EVALUATION: *Edition & history:* A record of a 1973 New York Shakespeare Festival production at the Delacorte Theatre in Central Park, this unusual version of *King Lear* starred leading black American actor, James Earl Jones, as the old king. Shakespeare in the park, as probably everyone knows, offers free Shakespeare to citizens willing to stand in line and wait for tickets. Reviews of the original stage production were a mixture of favorable and unfavorable, though most found Jones's performance intriguing. Currently it is not in distribution. *Contents & evaluation:* "James Earl Jones starring in the title role, like Morris Carnovsky but differently, teaches us about the range of Shakespeare's most dynamic character. Carnovsky projected a once powerful king, now old and fragile; Jones reveals a king newly conscious of senescence. Weary but strong, with the slow movement of old age, Jones still displays an astonishing array of emotions. His acting makes the production memorable. [While generally successful], the speedy transitions of the neo-Elizabethan Delacorte stage are not adequately translated into video conventions. On the stage with one group exiting as another enters, scene succeeds scene without noticeable delay; on video, the dissolves and fades implying the passage of time, make the pace excruciatingly slow. . . . Performances by the women were disappointingly wooden, though in the first act this defect becomes a virtue for Cordelia by suggesting a girl unendowed with her sisters' rhetorical gifts" (Kliman, B.W., "Shakespeare and the People: Elizabethan Drama on Video," *SFNL* 1.2. [1977]: 4). Other critics had mixed opinions. John Simon felt that ". . . the New York Shakespeare Festival has now changed the Bard's greatest tragedy, *King Lear*, into a lackluster farce. . . . Edwin Sherin's staging, which is one part Peter Brook (whose *Lear*, which Sherin copies, was also offensive but at least it was Brook's own), one part weird excogitations, and one part letting the actors do whatever they can come up with, which, in this case, is not much" ("Review [of stage production]," *NYM* 20 Aug. 1973: n.p.). The *Village Voice* drama critic was a little more enthusiastic: "The *King Lear* in Central Park is like baseball in wartime, mixing seasoned players with people who have yet to develop into major league Shakespearians. As for James Earl Jones's Lear, I couldn't get enough of him" (Brukenfeld, Dick "Review [of stage production]," *VV* 9 Aug. 1973: n.p.). The *Times* drama (not TV) critic expressed similar thoughts: "*Lear* is one of Shakespeare's greatest roles, and in it Jones is giving one of his finest performances. . . . There is, however, an unevenness about this production. . . . Much of the difficulty is in the casting. . . . Raul Julia, so disarming in romantic roles in musicals, tries to use some of the same humor in playing the bastard Edmund. Never for a moment do we believe in his villainy or in his seductiveness" (Gussow, Mel, "Review [stage prod.]," *NYT* 2 Aug. 1973: 28). *Audience:* General use.

MEDIUM INFORMATION: *Medium:* Video; *Sound:* Spoken language; *Color:* Yes; *Length:* 120 min.; *Language(s) spoken:* English.

AUTHORSHIP INFORMATION: *Producer(s):* Papp, Joseph; Gersten, Bernard; *Director(s):* Sherin, Edwin; *Composer(s):* Gross, Charles; *Set designer(s):* Loquasto, Santo; *Costume designer(s):* Aldridge, Theoni V.; *Lighting designer(s):* Aaronson, Martin; *Other personnel:* Cohen, Jason Steven (Stage manager); *Cast:* Jones, James Earl (King Lear); Watson, Douglas (Kent); Sorvino, Paul (Gloucester); Julia, Raul (Edmund); Auberjonois, Rene (Edgar); Cash, Rosalind (Goneril); Holly, Ellen (Regan); Chamberlin, Lee (Cordelia); Aldredge, Tom (Fool); Lanchester, Robert (Cornwall); Quinones, Louis (Burgundy); Coffin, Frederick (Oswald); Stewart, Jean-Pierre (France); Stattel, Robert (Albany); *Performance group(s):* New York Shakespeare Festival.

DISTRIBUTION & AVAILABILITY: *Publisher or responsible agency:* New York Shakespeare Festival; *Distributor:* NYS; *Availability:* Inquire at Festival.

King Lear. Video/Recording

263.1 *Re Lear.* [*King Lear*].

DOCUMENT INFORMATION: *Country:* Italy; *Year of first showing:* 1979; *Location of first showing:* Transmitted October 5 and 6, 1979, on Radiotelevisione Italiana.

EDITION, HISTORY, CONTENTS, & EVALUATION: *Edition & history:* A television adaptation of the production directed by Giorgio Strehle.

MEDIUM INFORMATION: *Length:* 195 min.

AUTHORSHIP INFORMATION: *Producer(s):* RAI Productions; *Director(s):* Battistoni, Carlo; *Cast:* Carraro, Tino; De Carmine, Renato.

DISTRIBUTION & AVAILABILITY: *Publisher or responsible agency:* Videoteca RAI; *Copy location:* ASP.

264. *King Lear.*

DOCUMENT INFORMATION: *Country:* USA; *Year of first showing:* 1980.

EDITION, HISTORY, CONTENTS, & EVALUATION: *Edition & history:* A videotaping of a stage production performed by the Berkeley Shakespeare Festival in 1980. A copy is housed in the Theatre on Film and Tape Collection at the Billy Rose Theatre Collection of the Library of Performing Arts, Lincoln Center, New York Public Library. It may be viewed by appointment (see below). *Contents & evaluation:* A partial viewing revealed that the camera work is reasonably good, and the main features of the production decently preserved on tape. According to critic Laurence H. Jacobs, the production "grew" as the season unfolded. King Lear was played by Jack Shearer as "a tired, somewhat confused old man, desperate for the loving support of his daughters in his old age." The test-of-love scene was turned into a rhetorical contest between Goneril and Regan as each sought to outdo the other in flattering the old king. *Audience:* College and university; General use; *Supplementary materials:* Jacobs, Laurence H. "Shakespeare in the San Francisco Bay Area." *SQ* 32.2 (Summer 1981): 264-65.

MEDIUM INFORMATION: *Medium:* Video; *Sound:* Spoken language; *Color:* Yes; *Length:* 188 min.; *Language(s) spoken:* English; *Video type:* 3/4U.

AUTHORSHIP INFORMATION: *Producer(s):* Berkeley Shakespeare Festival; *Director(s):* Lopez-Morillas, Julian; *Composer(s):* Thewlis, Stephen; Lopez-Morillas, Julian; *Set designer(s):* Angell, Dean; Pratt, Ron; *Costume designer(s):* Stone, Diana; *Lighting designer(s):* Stocker, Tom; *Cast:* Yeuell, Paul D. (Albany); Mayock, Molly (Cordelia); Henry, Steve (Cornwall); Vickery, John (Edgar); Sicular, Robert (Edmund); Prusky, Mike (Fool); Brady, Lance (Gloucester); Hoy, Linda (Goneril); Durrant, Regan (Kent); Shearer, Jack (Lear); Renner, Mike (Oswald); Scott, Robin (Regan).

DISTRIBUTION & AVAILABILITY: *Publisher or responsible agency:* Berkeley Shakespeare Festival; *Copy location:* LCL TOFT Collection; *Call or copy number:* NCOV 303; *Availability:* By appt. (Call 212-870-1641); *Restrictions:* Archive.

King Lear. Video/Recording

265. *King Lear.*

DOCUMENT INFORMATION: *Country:* GB; *Year of release:* 1980.

EDITION, HISTORY, CONTENTS, & EVALUATION: *Edition & history:* Production in six 20-minute parts made especially for schools in England. Stresses themes of family relationships and youth vs. age. *Supplementary materials:* BUFVC 11.

MEDIUM INFORMATION: *Color:* Yes; *Length:* 120 min.; *Video type:* V.

AUTHORSHIP INFORMATION: *Director(s):* Thames TV.

DISTRIBUTION & AVAILABILITY: *Distributor:* TTI*.

King Lear. Video/Documentary

266. *Stages: Houseman Directs* Lear.

DOCUMENT INFORMATION: *Country:* USA; *Year of release:* 1981.

EDITION, HISTORY, CONTENTS, & EVALUATION: *Edition & history:* The program "explores the actors' and directors' creative process by following John Houseman, Academy Award winning actor, eminent director and producer as he rehearses The Acting Company, the repertory company he founded, in a new production of Shakespeare's *King Lear.* Jason Robards is on-camera host. Filmed segments of the final production allow the audience to judge for themselves the outcome of the endeavor" (*SFNL* 6.2 (March 1982): 6). *Contents & evaluation:* Not seen. *Audience:* College and university.

MEDIUM INFORMATION: *Medium:* Video; *Sound:* Spoken language; *Color:* Yes; *Length:* 54 min.; *Language(s) spoken:* English; *Film type:* 16mm; *Video type:* V, 3/4U.

AUTHORSHIP INFORMATION: *Producer(s):* Pope, Amanda C.; *Cast:* Houseman, John; Robards, Jason; The Acting Company; *Performance group(s):* The Acting Company.

DISTRIBUTION & AVAILABILITY: *Publisher or responsible agency:* Amanda C. Pope; *Distributor:* FNC, *Availability:* Rental, $95; Sale 16mm $785; 3/4U $1298; V, $198.

King Lear. Video/Teleplay

267. *King Lear.* (Series: The Shakespeare Plays).

DOCUMENT INFORMATION: *Country:* GB; *Year of*

first showing: 1982; *Location of first showing(s):* BBC, London; PBS stations, USA, 18 Oct. 1982.

EDITION, HISTORY, CONTENTS, & EVALUATION: *Edition & history:* Shot in London BBC studios with modified attempt to adhere to Folio rather than Quarto text in line with recent critical theory viewing the two texts as different acting versions. *Contents & evaluation:* "Problems in this *Lear* begin with a basic isolation of the actors from the emotional life implied by the words they speak. For example, Shakespeare's actors should weep when they say they are weeping. But when Cordelia bids farewell to her sisters 'with washed eyes,' when the king complains of 'these hot tears,' forced from him by Cordelia, and when he tells Cordelia "mine own tears do scald like molten lead,' the actors' eyes are dry. They don't even pretend to wipe away a tear. Their words are unconnected to what we see happening on the screen" (Urkowitz, Steven, "*King Lear* Without Tears," *SFNL* 7.2. [1983]:2). "While he is not overwhelming, Mr. Hordern is mightily convincing. . . . In the end this *King Lear . . .* works not spectacularly but quite rewardingly" (O'Connor, John J., "TV: A No-Nonsense *King Lear,*" *NYT* 18 Oct. 1982: C16). Surely Michael Hordern is the most "down-home" King Lear ever to have played the role. His genius is all the more impressive for its understatement. When he calls for the map, he does not say "Give me the map there" but "Give me the map [pause] *there*" and he points to the table on which the map should be placed. In other words put the map *there*. This may seem a simple point but it shows a scrupulous concern for small details. His eschewing of the traditional flowing white beard also comes as a mild surprise. Then again one remembers that Hordern has a special talent for portraying the slightly overwhelmed father, as he did unforgettably in the Zeffirelli *Taming of the Shrew.* There he mediated comically between Kate and Bianca; here he mediates tragically, and even more ineptly, among Goneril, Regan and Cordelia. In this remarkably original reading, Lear was never empowered but already disempowered even before the division of the kingdom. Regan's insight that her father "hath ever but slenderly known himself" (1.1.293) is validated. Hordern gives us Lear not as a tyrant but as a bumbler. The madness that comes later is already foreshadowed here (KSR). *Audience:* College and university; Professional; *Supplementary materials:* Fenwick, Henry. "The Production." *King Lear BSP* (1983): 19-34; Shorter, Eric. "Plays in Performance." *Drama* (Spring 1970): 27-31; Videocassette (25 min.) from "Shakespeare in Perspective" series with Frank Kermode available in U.K. from BBC* (*BUFVC* 19).

MEDIUM INFORMATION: *Medium:* Video; *Sound:* Spoken language; *Color:* Yes; *Condition:* Excellent; *Length:* 180 min.; *Language(s) spoken:* English; *Video type:* B, V, 3/4U.

AUTHORSHIP INFORMATION: *Producer(s):* Sutton, Shaun; *Director(s):* Miller, Jonathan; *Adaptor/translator(s):* Snodin, David; Preece, Patricia; *Designer(s):* Lowrey, Colin; *Costume designer(s):* Hughes, Raymond; *Lighting designer(s):* Treays, John; *Other personnel:* Miller-Timmins, Derek (Sound); Wilders, John (Literary consultant); Mair, Eileen (Make-up); *Cast:* Hordern, Michael (King Lear); Shrapnel, John (Kent); Barge, Gillian (Goneril); Wilton, Penelope (Regan); Blethyn, Brenda (Cordelia); Middlemass, Frank (Fool); Bird, John (Albany); Curry, Julian (Cornwall); Kitchen, Michael (Edmund); Lesser, Anton (Edgar); Grillo, John (Oswald).

DISTRIBUTION & AVAILABILITY: *Publisher or responsible agency:* BBC-TV/Time Life Inc.; *Distributor:* AVP, UIO, KSU, BBC*, *Copy location:* UVM (Archive only); *Availability:* AVP, all formats, sale $450 (1987); UIO, V (72318H), 3/4U (70318V), rental $25.10; KSU, rental V, 3/4U, 5 days $33.75; BBC*, 16mm or V.

King Lear. Video/Documentary

268. *Morris Carnovsky Performs Shakespeare.*

DOCUMENT INFORMATION: *Country:* USA. *Year of release:* 1982 [?]

EDITION, HISTORY, CONTENTS, & EVALUATION: *Edition & history:* A videotape from the Max Waldman archives featuring Morris Carnovsky performing scenes from *The Tempest*, *King Lear*, and *The Merchant of Venice*. *Audience:* General use.

MEDIUM INFORMATION: *Medium:* Video; *Sound:* Spoken language; *Color:* Yes; *Length:* 45 min.; *Language(s) spoken:* English; *Video type:* V.

AUTHORSHIP INFORMATION: *Cast:* Carnovsky, Morris.

DISTRIBUTION & AVAILABILITY: *Publisher or responsible agency:* Max Waldman archives; *Copy location:* LCL; *Call or copy number:* NCOV 423; *Availability:* Archive.

King Lear. Video/Documentary

269. *King Lear.* (Series: Shakespeare in Perspective).

DOCUMENT INFORMATION: *Country:* GB; *Year of release:* 1982.

EDITION, HISTORY, CONTENTS, & EVALUATION: *Edition & history:* The "Shakespeare in Perspective" series was made to accompany the BBC/Time Life Inc. "The Shakespeare Plays" series (see also 44, 142, 234, 335, 411, 566 and 624). For overview, see 44, above. *Contents & evaluation:* The important British Shakespeare critic, Dr. Frank Kermode, hosts this program

on *King Lear*. As he strolls casually across the landscape near Dover, he reveals his thoughts about *King Lear* as one of the most pessimistic of representations of the human condition. Excerpts from the BBC *King Lear* starring Michael Hordern support and illustrate Dr. Kermode's commentary (KSR).

MEDIUM INFORMATION: *Medium:* Video; *Sound:* Spoken language; *Color:* Yes; *Length:* 25 min.; *Language(s) spoken:* English; *Video type:* 3/4U, V.

AUTHORSHIP INFORMATION: *Producer(s):* Poole, Victor; *Director(s):* Kirkwood, Sally; *Other personnel:* Munn, Colin (Camera); Crump, Martin (Editor); Webberley, Malcolm (Sound); Friedman, Liz (Graphics); *Cast:* Kermode, Frank (Commentator).

DISTRIBUTION & AVAILABILITY: *Publisher or responsible agency:* BBC; *Distributor:* BBC*, FNC; *Availability:* Double cassette (w. *Tmp.*), Rental $50; Quad cassette (w. *AYL, MND, Tmp.*), Rental $75.

King Lear. Video/Recording

270. *Koning Lear.*

DOCUMENT INFORMATION: *Country:* Netherlands; *Year of release:* 1982.

EDITION, HISTORY, CONTENTS, & EVALUATION: *Edition & history:* A video recording of a performance of *King Lear* at Kijkhuis Conservatory, Den Haag, in 1982.

MEDIUM INFORMATION: *Length:* 189 min.

AUTHORSHIP INFORMATION: *Producer(s):* Straat, Evert; Horst, Hent van der; *Director(s):* Vos, Erik; *Composer(s):* Hamel, Neils; *Cast:* Linden, P.; Orager, R.; Maerten, H.; Greidanus, A.; Edzard, R.; Voetl, H.; Pancras, N.; Gillis, H.; Radier, R.; Roofthooft, D.; Wagter, W.; Mass, H.; Kaul, P.

DISTRIBUTION & AVAILABILITY: *Publisher or responsible agency:* Toneelgroep de Appel; *Distributor:* NTI, *Copy location:* NTI; *Call or copy number:* 700154601 BDA.

King Lear. Video/Interpretation

271. *King Lear.*

DOCUMENT INFORMATION: *Country:* GB; *Year of release:* 1983; *Country of first showing:* GB.

EDITION, HISTORY, CONTENTS, & EVALUATION: *Edition & history:* The production, taped in three weeks at the Manchester TV Centre, is set in ninth-century Britain. The set required twenty-four huge stones of polystyrene in imitation of the mysterious druidic ruin at Stonehenge in Salisbury Plain, an oak tree, hundreds of clumps of heather, and twelve butterflies, among other things. Olivier had played the title role in *King Lear* (with Alec Guinness as the Fool) at London's Old Vic in 1946. The U.S. premiere of this television production took place on May 4, 1983 at the New York City Museum of Broadcasting as a part of the celebration marking the "Britain Salutes New York" Festival. *Contents & evaluation:* Director Michael Elliott's vision of *King Lear* can be compared to a symphonic poem, structured along the lines of Franz Liszt's *Dante* with movements for the Inferno, Purgatorio, and Paradiso. In *King Lear* they should perhaps be redesignated as "Limbo: A Prelude" (when the old king thinks that he can "unburthen'd crawl toward death"), ending with the expulsion of Cordelia; "Inferno" (Lear's rage against the people who betrayed him), ending with the meeting with Gloucester; "Purgatorio," King Lear's recognition of his own vulnerability; and "Paradiso," or crypto-Paradiso, with the imprisonment of the king and his daughter. In Elliott's production each phase is punctuated with some striking emblem: in the Prelude it is the King's crown and gigantic map; in the "Inferno," his de-crowning on the heath; in the Purgatorio, his crown of flowers; and in the fourth and final phase, his status as the old man in the Seventh Age, "sans teeth, sans taste" etc. With Cordelia he is a lamb ready for sacrifice on the altars of a polystyrene Stonehenge (KSR); ". . . [after many favorable comments about the production these qualifications appear]: There are some problems. Shakespeare designed the great storm scene of Act three as a dialogue between the king and the thunder—the sky talks and Lear answers. But extravagant rain and swelling background music temporarily submerge Shakespeare's words under too much orchestrated sound. For technical verisimilitude to a real-life storm we pay the price of understanding what Lear says. For viewers familiar with the text, too many intrusive changes appear in the screenplay . . . [e.g.,] in the last scene, Goneril will 'ne'er trust *poison* rather than *medicine*'" (Urkowitz, Steven, "Olivier's *Lear*," *SFNL*, 8.1 [1983]:1+). "In Brook's film Paul Scofield was a Lear 'more sinning than sinn'd against,' as Richard Proudfoot puts the matter (p.165), and in Miller's television film, 'The real interest throughout the play,' one reviewer wrote, 'seems to be not in Lear's suffering, but in the character of his enemies.' Elliott and Olivier reverse these tendencies. The blinding of Gloucester does receive emphasis, it is true, but the film focuses on the pathos of Lear's suffering and subsequent change in attitude and understanding" (Orbison, Tucker, "The Stone and the Oak: Olivier's TV Film of *King Lear*," *CEA*, 47. i and ii (1984): 67-77). *Audience:* High school (grades 10-12); College and university; General use; *Supplementary materials:* Occhiogrosso, Frank. "Manual Gesture in the Elliott-Olivier *King Lear*." *SB*, 2.9 (1984): 16-19; Wells, Stanley. "Shakespeare: *King Lear* Channel 4." *TLS* (8 Apr.1983): 352.

MEDIUM INFORMATION: *Medium:* Video; *Sound:* Spoken language; *Color:* Yes; *Length:* 158 min.; *Language(s) spoken:* English; *Video type:* B, V, 3/4"U.

AUTHORSHIP INFORMATION: *Producer(s):* Plowright, David; *Director(s):* Eliott, Michael; *Composer(s):* Crosse, Gordon; *Designer(s):* Stonehouse, Roy; *Costume designer(s):* Moiseiwitsch, Tanya; *Cast:* Olivier, Laurence (King Lear); Tutin, Dorothy (Goneril); Rigg, Diana (Regan); Blakely, Colin (Kent); Calder-Marshall, Anna (Cordelia); Hurt, John (Fool); Kemp, Jeremy, (Cornwall); Lang, Robert (Albany); Lindsay, Robert (Edmund); McKern, Leo (Gloucester); Threlfal, David (Edgar); Petherbridge, Edward (France); Cox, Brian (Burgundy); Bateman, Geoffrey (Oswald); Cording, John (Knight); Knight, Esmond (Old Man); Curran, Paul (Doctor).

DISTRIBUTION & AVAILABILITY: *Responsible agency:* Granada Television; *Distributor:* FFH, ILL, GRN*, GTI* (Sale); *Copy location:* FOL; *Call or copy number:* VCR; *Availability:* FFH (272F), B, V, $249, 3/4U $349, Rental $125 (Prices given 1987); ILL (S02821), V, $29.95 (1990).

King Lear. Motion Picture/Burlesque

272. *King Real and the Hoodlums.*

DOCUMENT INFORMATION: *Country:* GB; *Year of release:* 1983.

EDITION, HISTORY, CONTENTS, & EVALUATION: *Edition & history:* Described by Olwen Terris as a "musical grotesquerie" based on *King Lear. Supplementary materials:* BUFVC 11.

MEDIUM INFORMATION: *Length:* 50 min.

AUTHORSHIP INFORMATION: *Director(s):* Fox, John.

DISTRIBUTION & AVAILABILITY: *Distributor:* CVF*.

King Lear. Motion Picture/Derivative

273. *The Dresser.*

DOCUMENT INFORMATION: *Country:* GB; *Year of release:* 1985.

EDITION, HISTORY, CONTENTS, & EVALUATION: *Edition & history:* Originally a stage play, *The Dresser* was turned by Peter Yates into an engrossing film. The story is a backstage look at a troupe of travelling Shakespearean actors in Great Britain during World War II. The scenes performed from *King Lear* by Albert Finney are first-rate. *Contents & evaluation:* Albert Finney as "Sir," the curmudgeonly and dying old Shakespearean actor and Tom Courtenay as Norman, his "dresser," give inspired performances. Sir is really King Lear, and Norman his Fool, while the faithful manager functions as a kind of Cordelia figure. Despite Sir's bombastic acting style, Finney manages to suggest a deep sense of what heavy spiritual freight goes with being called to the vocation of a Shakespearean actor. Indeed when Finney as Sir orders a train to stop, it stops—in sign of the awesome authority the man brings to his life, however tinselly and shabby it may seem at other times. A highly recommended film. *Audience:* General use.

MEDIUM INFORMATION: *Medium:* Motion Picture; *Sound:* Spoken language; *Color:* Yes; *Length:* 110 min. [?]; *Language(s) spoken:* English; *Film type:* 16mm.

AUTHORSHIP INFORMATION: *Producer(s):* Yates, Peter; Woole, Nigel; *Director(s):* Yates, Peter; Armstrong, Andy; *Screenplay writer(s):* Harwood, Ronald; *Composer(s):* Horner, James; *Designer(s):* Grimes, Stephen; *Set designer(s):* McAvin, Josie; *Costume designer(s):* Burrows, Rosemary; *Other personnel:* Lovejoy, Ray (Editor); Pike, Kelvin (Photography); John, David (Sound mixer); Quentin, Jill (Property); Boyle, Alan (Make-up); Ritchie, Barbara (Hair style); Humphreys, D. (Camera op.); Sax, Caroline (Continuity); Robinson, P. (Camera focus); Langley, Geoff (Construction); Neale, Rachel (Prod. asst.); Peake, B. (Stills); White, Joan (Hairdresser); Webster, F. (Gaffer); + more; *Cast:* Finney, Albert (Sir); Courtenay, Tom (Norman); Fox, Edward (Oxenby); Walker, Zena (Her Ladyship); Atkins, Eileen (Madge); Gough, Michael (Carrington); Harrison, Cathryn (Irene); Marsden, Betty (Violet); Reid, Sheila (Lydia); West, Lockwood (Geoffrey); Eccles, Donald (Mr. Gadstone); Rees, Llewellyn (Horace Brown); Manning, Guy (Benton); Mannion, Ann (Beryl); Stoney, Kevin (C. Rivers Lane); Way, Ann (Miss White); Sharp, John (Mr. Bottomley); Staff, Kathy (Bombazino Woman); Avon, Roger (Charles); Irvin, Christopher (Evelyn); Richman, Stuart (Evelyn's friend); Gough, Sandra (Actress); Belcher, Joe (Arthur); Manfield, Johnny (Electrician); Luty, Paul (Stallkeeper); Wells, Lori (Barmaid); Starkey, Alan (Train Guard).

DISTRIBUTION & AVAILABILITY: *Publisher or responsible agency:* World Film Services and Goldcrest/Columbia Pictures; *Distributor:* FCM, FMB*, *Copy location:* FOL; *Call or copy number:* MP; *Availability:* FCM, V, $79.95.

King Lear. Motion Picture/Adaptation

274. *Ran.* ["Chaos"].

DOCUMENT INFORMATION: *Country:* Japan; *Year of filming:* 1984; *Year of release:* 1985; *Location of first showing:* New York Film Festival, 1985.

EDITION, HISTORY, CONTENTS, & EVALUATION: *Edition & history:* Free adaptation of William Shakespeare's *King Lear* in which the sisters have been transformed into the sons of Hidetora, a medieval Japanese warlord. While there are major differences between Kurosawa's script and Shakespeare's play, there are enough similarities to make comparison inevitable. *Contents & evaluation:* "Though big in physical scope and of a beauty that suggests a kind of drunken, barbaric lyricism, *Ran* has the terrible logic and clarity of a morality tale seen in tight close-up, of a myth that, while being utterly specific and particular in its time and place, remains ageless, infinitely adaptable" (Canby, Vincent, "Power and Pathos," *NYT* 27 Sept. 1985: C14). "Like *Throne of Blood*, Akira Kurosawa's *Ran* is a reworking of Shakespeare set in feudal Japan, which with its hierarchical clans, samurai codes (bushido), and system of duty (giri) resembles the medieval feudal system in Europe. The aging head of the Ichimonji clan, Hidetora (Tatsuya Nakadai), has brutally united his land with fifty years of war. But his hold is weakening. Neighboring lords threaten. His family is in turmoil. His mind and emotions are slipping toward the "ran" ("chaos" of the title). In place of Lear's three daughters, Kurosawa gives us three sons: Taro (Akira Terao), Jiro (Jinpachi Nezu), and Saburo (Daisuke Ryu). When Hidetora turns over leadership (but not the title of Lord) to his eldest son Taro, the second son Jiro becomes jealous, and the youngest, Saburo, begs his father to take back his power before disaster strikes. For his honesty, the Cordelia-like Saburo is banished along with a Kent-like retainer Tango (Masayuki Yui). Taro's wife, Lady Kaede (Mieko Harada), absorbs the evil and lust of Goneril and Regan and injects much needed conflict. She is a sinister, powerful figure, a combination as Vincent Canby says of 'Goneril, Regan, and Lady Macbeth, with a little bit of Barbara Stanwyck's Phyllis Dietrichson from *Double Indemnity*'[*NYT*, 27 Sept. 1985]" (Jorgens, Jack, *SFNL*, 10.2 [Apr. 1986]:1,4). "It is possible that Kurosawa too has become more Japanese as he has grown older. Though *Ran* treats the grand universal themes that have always occupied Kurosawa—the horror of war, the folly of mankind—the family context serves to place them within the dense, complicated network of interpersonal obligations that the Japanese call *giri*: the duty owed by a child to his parents, by a younger brother to an older brother, by a wife to a husband, by a samurai to his lord" (Kehr, Dave, "Samurai *Lear*," *AF* 10 [1985]:21-26) *Audience:* College and university; General use; *Supplementary materials:* Kott, Jan. "The Edo *Lear*. *Ran:* A Film Written and Directed by Akira Kurosawa." *NYRB* 2 May 1986: 13-15.

MEDIUM INFORMATION: *Medium:* Motion Picture; *Sound:* Spoken language; *Color:* Yes; *Length:* 160 min.; *Language(s) spoken:* Japanese; *Language of subtitles:* English; *Film type:* 35 mm.

AUTHORSHIP INFORMATION: *Producer(s):* Silberman, Serge; Hara, Masato; *Director(s):* Kurosawa, Akira; *Adaptor/translator(s):* Kurosawa, Akira; Oguni, Hideo; Ide, Masato; *Composer(s):* Takemitsu, Toru; *Designer(s):* Muraki, Yoshiro; *Lighting designer(s):* Saito, Takao; Ueda, Masaharu; *Other personnel:* Furukawa, Katsumi (Exec.

producer); Pickardt, Lilly (Prod. manager); *Cast:* Nakadai, Tatsuya (Hidetora Ichimonji [King Lear]); Terao, Akira (Taro); Nezu, Jinpachi (Jiro); Ryu, Daisuke (Saburo); Harada, Mieko (Lady Kaede); Kato, Kazuo (Ikoma); Yui, Masayuki (Tango); Peter (Kyoami); Ueki, Hitoshi (Fujimaki); Ikawa, Hisashi (Kurogane); Nomura, Takeshi (Tsurumaru); Miyazaki, Yoshiko (Lady Sue).

DISTRIBUTION & AVAILABILITY: *Publisher or responsible agency:* Orion Classics; *Availability:* INM, V (DS21) $89.95.

King Lear. Video/Documentary

275. *Shakespeare: King Lear: Workshops I and II.* (Series: Open University Film Library).

DOCUMENT INFORMATION: *Country:* GB; *Year of release:* 1985.

EDITION, HISTORY, CONTENTS, & EVALUATION: *Edition & history:* One of several programs prepared for the Open University television programs in Great Britain. Not seen in the U.S. According to the *BUFVC* catalog, each program features a director leading one of the actors through his/her role. In this program, director John Russell Brown explores ways of coping with the "reason in madness" theme in the play and examines the reunion of Gloucester and Lear. *Audience:* College and university; Professional; *Supplementary materials: BUFVC* 12.

MEDIUM INFORMATION: *Medium:* Video; *Sound:* Spoken language; *Color:* Yes; *Length:* 24 min. (each workshop); *Language(s) spoken:* English; *Video type:* V,B.

AUTHORSHIP INFORMATION: *Producer(s):* Hoyle, David; *Cast:* Brown, John Russell (Dir.); Glover, Julian (King Lear).

DISTRIBUTION & AVAILABILITY: *Publisher or responsible agency:* BBC Open University; *Distributor:* GSV*, *Copy location:* BBC; *Availability:* Sale or rental in Great Britain only.

King Lear. Video/Scenes

276. *The Shakespeare Hour.*

DOCUMENT INFORMATION: *Country:* GB/USA; *Year of release:* 1985.

EDITION, HISTORY, CONTENTS, & EVALUATION: *Edition & history:* The series, "The Shakespeare Hour," was shown on national educational television beginning on January 5, 1985 (see also 5, 352, 417, and 663). For an overview, see number 5, above. *Audience:* High school (grades 10-12); College and university; General use; *Supplementary materials:* Quinn, *TSH*.

MEDIUM INFORMATION: *Medium:* Video; *Sound:* Spoken language; *Color:* Yes; *Length:* 180 min.; *Language(s) spoken:* English; *Video type:* V.

AUTHORSHIP INFORMATION: *Producer(s):* BBC-WNET/THIRTEEN; *Director(s):* Miller, Jonathan; Johnson, Donald; Kieffer, Tom; Bellin, Harvey (WNET); *Screenplay writer(s):* Cavendar, Kenneth; *Other personnel:* Squerciati, Marie Therese (Project director); *Cast:* Matthau, Walter; Cast of BBC/Time Life *King Lear,* directed by Jonathan Miller (q.v.).

DISTRIBUTION & AVAILABILITY: *Publisher or responsible agency:* WNET/THIRTEEN; *Distributor:* ALS.

King Lear. Video/Educational

276.1 *Shakespeare's King Lear and the Middle Ages.*

DOCUMENT INFORMATION: *Country:* USA; *Year of first showing:* 1985.

EDITION, HISTORY, CONTENTS, & EVALUATION: *Edition & history:* "The film holds, 'as t'were the mirror' up to the Middle Ages, for the Medieval image of the world survived into the Elizabethan Age. The king-father symbolizing the authority of the past, primogeniture, astrology and the dowry are all representative of the Medieval culture as reflected in Shakespeare's *King Lear.* In this film, Robert Stattel recreates his role of Shakespeare's tragic monarch" (IAS Catalog). *Contents & evaluation:* Not seen.

MEDIUM INFORMATION: *Sound:* Spoken language; *Color:* Yes; *Length:* 31 min.; *Video type:* V.

AUTHORSHIP INFORMATION: *Producer(s):* IAS; *Cast:* Stattel, Robert (King Lear).

DISTRIBUTION & AVAILABILITY: *Publisher or responsible agency:* IAS; *Distributor:* IAS, V, sale $350; rental, $50 + shipping.

King Lear. Motion Picture/Derivative

277. *King Lear.*

DOCUMENT INFORMATION: *Country:* France; *Year of release:* 22 Jan. 1987; *Location of first showing:* Golden Quad Cinema, New York City.

EDITION, HISTORY, CONTENTS, & EVALUATION: *Edition & history:* The most recent modernization of *King Lear,* this Godard production was screened at the Montreal Film Festival in August 1987. The celebrity cast makes it of special interest. *Contents & evaluation:* Predictably, early reviews of this avant-garde adaptation ranged from hostile to abusive, as post-modernist deconstructions of Shakespeare's text often backfire with the journalistic critics (one thinks of Derek Jarman's

Tempest). What seems especially interesting is the hermeneutics of the film—the way, from all accounts, that Godard translates Shakespeare into the iconology of the contemporary world. Although Shakespeare as cultural symbol on a T-shirt offends many persons, it is possible that the film's post-modernist discontinuities may yet win an audience. There are implications perhaps even Ben Jonson never dreamed of when he said that Shakespeare was "not of an age but for all time" (KSR). *Supplementary materials:* Nokes, David. "Echoes of Godard." *TLS* 29 Jan. 1988: 112. [Unsympathetic review that begins by announcing "This is a sad film. . . ."].

MEDIUM INFORMATION: *Medium:* Motion Picture; *Color:* Yes; *Length:* 91 min.; *Film type:* 35 mm.

AUTHORSHIP INFORMATION: *Producer(s):* Golan, Menahan; Globus, Yoran; *Director(s):* Godard, Jean-Luc; *Adaptor/translator(s):* Godard, Jean-Luc; *Cast:* Sellars, Peter (Will Shakespeare, Jr.the Fifth); Meredith, Burgess (Don Learo); Ringwald, Molly (Cordelia); Mailer, Norman (Himself); Mailer, Kate (Herself); Godard, Jean-Luc (The Professor); Allen, Woody (Film Editor).

DISTRIBUTION & AVAILABILITY: *Publisher or responsible agency:* Cannon Releasing Corp.; *Distributor:* Cannon [?].

King Lear (Ran). Motion Picture/Documentary

278. *A.K.: The Making of* Ran.

DOCUMENT INFORMATION: *Country:* Japan; *Year of release:* 1988.

EDITION, HISTORY, CONTENTS, & EVALUATION: *Edition & history:* Not seen. This was listed in *The New York Times* entertainment section as a program to be aired on March 7, 1988, in the New York City metropolitan area by Cable Station BRV.

MEDIUM INFORMATION: *Length:* 90 min.

AUTHORSHIP INFORMATION: *Director(s):* Kurosawa, Akira.

King Lear. Video/Derivative

279. *King Lear Reflections.*

DOCUMENT INFORMATION: *Country:* GB; *Year of release:* [198?].

EDITION, HISTORY, CONTENTS, & EVALUATION: *Edition & history:* Four separate programs (20 min. each) that place themes from *King Lear* in a modern context. *Supplementary materials:* BUFVC 12.

MEDIUM INFORMATION: *Length:* 80 min.

AUTHORSHIP INFORMATION: *Director(s):* Thames TV.

DISTRIBUTION & AVAILABILITY: *Distributor:* TTI*.

King Lear. Motion Picture/Documentary

280. *Shakespeare.*

DOCUMENT INFORMATION: *Country:* GB; *Year of release:* [19??].

EDITION, HISTORY, CONTENTS, & EVALUATION: *Edition & history:* Critic C.L.R. James interprets *King Lear.* *Supplementary materials:* BUFVC 12.

MEDIUM INFORMATION: *Length:* 26 min.

AUTHORSHIP INFORMATION: *Director(s):* Penumbra Prod.; *Cast:* James, C.L.R.

DISTRIBUTION & AVAILABILITY: *Distributor:* ICA*.

Love's Labor's Lost

ORIGINAL WORK AND PRODUCTION: Comedy of Manners. *Year of first production:* 1593; *Site of first production:* Inns of Court [?].

Love's Labor's Lost. Video/Recording

281. *Love's Labor's Lost.*

DOCUMENT INFORMATION: *Country:* GB; *Year of filming:* 1964; *Year of first showing:* 1965; *Location of first showing:* BBC-2 TV. Transmitted 7:55 P.M. to 9:50 P.M. (with 5-minute news break), Sunday, 6 June 1965.

EDITION, HISTORY, CONTENTS, & EVALUATION: *Edition & history:* Produced as a part of the celebration of the 400th anniversary of Shakespeare's birth in 1564. A recording of an earlier stage production by the Bristol Old Vic company in the Theatre Royal, Bristol. The Bristol Old Vic, a spinoff from the better known Old Vic in London, has a distinguished history. Among the more famous names who have been connected with it are Peter O'Toole, Dorothy Tutin, and Richard Pasco. This performance of Shakespeare's comedy went on tour in 45 cities and 16 countries before being recorded in Bristol in the fall of 1964. (See *RT* 3 June 1965: 12). The cast included 22 men and 5 women. *Contents & evaluation:* The London *Times* reviewer was quite pleased with the production, though he/she noted that the actors seemed to be speaking to the theatre audience rather than to one another. The technique of simply recording a stage play for television when done properly, as was apparently the case here, does not necessarily result in a product inferior to a full-scale teleplay. There was, however, some feeling that the clowns became too intrusive for the intimacy of television. *Audience:* General use; *Supplementary materials:* "New TV Approach to Shakespeare." *Times* 7 June 1965: 4d; Speaight, Robert. "Shakespeare in Britain." *SQ* 15.4 (1964): 389; Adams, Bernard. "The Bristol Old Vic." *RT* 23 June 1965: 12.

MEDIUM INFORMATION: *Medium:* Video; *Sound:* Spoken language; *Color:* No (black & white); *Length:* 110 min.; *Language(s) spoken:* English.

AUTHORSHIP INFORMATION: *Producer(s):* Foa, George; *Director(s):* Jenkins, Roger (TV); May, Val (Theatre); *Composer(s):* Spencer, Robert; *Designer(s):* Annais, Michael; *Cast:* Pasco, Richard (Berowne); Leigh-Hunt, Barbara (Rosaline); Dunne, Eithne (Princess of France); Hunter, Russell (Costard); Dodimead, David (King of Navarre); Jayston, Michael (Longaville); Baldwin, Peter (Dumaine); Curry, Julian (Dull); Benjamin, Christopher (Armado); Bates, Stanley (Moth); Woodford, Jennie (Jaquenetta); Hardiman, Terrence (Boyet); Cooper, Rowena (Katherine); Hurren, Bonnie (Maria); Fleming, Michael (Lord); Battersby, Julian; Quinto, Michael (Foresters); Middlemass, Frank (Nathaniel); Cossins, James (Holofernes); Hawkins, Leader (Chamberlain); Knight, Alan; Vogel, Antony (Lords); Collins, Alan (Clerk); Wreford, Edgar (Mercade); Pemberton, Charles; Quinto, Michael; Thorpe-Tracey, Noel (Vilagers).

DISTRIBUTION & AVAILABILITY: *Publisher or re-*

sponsible agency: BBC/Bristol Old Vic; *Copy location:* BBC*, archive [?].

Love's Labor's Lost. Video/Scene

282. *Love's Labor's Lost.*

DOCUMENT INFORMATION: *Country:* USA; *Year of first showing:* 1980.

EDITION, HISTORY, CONTENTS, & EVALUATION: *Edition & history:* A scene from the play performed on 20 September 1980 by The Acting Company on television for *New Actors for the Classics.* A copy is housed in the Theatre on Film and Tape Collection at the Billy Rose Theatre Collection of the Library of Performing Arts, Lincoln Center, New York Public Library. It may be viewed by appointment (see below). *Contents & evaluation:* Not seen. *Audience:* College and university; General use.

MEDIUM INFORMATION: *Medium:* Video; *Sound:* Spoken language; *Color:* Yes; *Length:* 59 min.; *Language(s) spoken:* English; *Video type:* V.

DISTRIBUTION & AVAILABILITY: *Copy location:* LCL TOFT Collection; *Call or copy number:* NCOX 253; *Availability:* By appt.(Call Mrs. Betty Corwin, 212-870-1641).

Love's Labor's Lost. Video/Teleplay

283. *Love's Labor's Lost.* (Series: The Shakespeare Plays).

DOCUMENT INFORMATION: *Year of first showing:* 1984; *Location of first showing(s):* BBC, London; PBS stations, USA, 31 May 1985.

EDITION, HISTORY, CONTENTS, & EVALUATION: *Edition & history:* Another in the BBC series based on the 1951 Peter Alexander one-volume edition of Shakespeare's plays. The most striking visual feature of the production is the use of 18th-century costumes, a departure from the series' earlier habits, with rare exceptions (e.g., *Julius Caesar*), of dressing the actors in the clothing of Shakespeare's own time, or at least close to Shakespeare's own time (!). *Contents & evaluation:* ". . . the play moved slowly. The performances, which ought to sparkle, seemed heavy and drained of energy. One reason was characterization: Rosaline (Jenny Agutter) was sullen, Berowne surly, and Holofernes (John Wells) nasty and arrogant. Most startling of all, Moth (John Kane) was full-grown, so that all the jokes about his size fell flat and he had to play the infant Hercules on his knees. . . . If Moshinsky

felt that something was amiss, he did not try to change the tone of the bittersweet melancholy, but instead changed the pace of the play, speeding it along with heavy cuts and rearranged speeches. Despite some imaginative cross-cutting, many changes were annoying. Immediately after the king's description of Armado in 1.1, the scene moved to Armado's musings on love in 1.2. Then it was back to 1.1. for the rest of that scene, followed by the end of 1.2. Was there some fear that in 150 lines of blank verse the audience might forget who Armado was? . . . Because the tone of the performance was at odds with the setting, the production was handicapped. Visually and aurally the production was so serene and careful that one lost sight of Shakespeare's quicksilver comedy. An air of melancholy, with an occasional flash of mean-spiritedness, obscured the play's charming, farcical wit. And without wit, *Love's Labor's Lost* is lifeless. In short, the production ignored what the 18th-century artist Blake knew: tastefulness is an enemy of art" (Teague, Frances, "*Love's Labor's Lost,*" *SFNL* 10.1 [Dec. 1985]: 1+). *Audience:* College and university; General use; *Supplementary materials:* Maher, M.Z. "*Love's Labor's Lost.*" *SFNL* 10.1 [1985]: 2; Videotape (25 min.) from "Shakespeare in Perspective" series with Emma Tennant as lecturer available in U.K. from BBC* (*BUFVC* 13).

MEDIUM INFORMATION: *Medium:* Video; *Sound:* Spoken language; *Color:* Yes; *Length:* 120 min.; *Language(s) spoken:* English; *Film type:* B, V, 3/4U.

AUTHORSHIP INFORMATION: *Producer(s):* Sutton, Shaun; *Director(s):* Moshinsky, Elijah; *Composer(s):* Oliver, Stephen; Rabinowitz, Harry; *Designer(s):* Gosnold, Barbara; *Costume designer(s):* Lavers, Colin; *Lighting designer(s):* Summers, John; *Other personnel:* Stenning, Peter (Prod. manager); Lowden, Fraser (Prod. assoc.); Pow, Stan (Editor); de Winne, Kezia (Make-up); Miller-Timmins, Derek (Sound); Wilders, John (Literary consultant); *Cast:* Gwilym, Mike (Berowne); Warner, David (Armado); Markham, Petra (Katherine); Burridge, Geoffrey (Dumain); Jesson, Paul (Costard); Kent, Jonathan (King of Navarre); Blake, Christopher (Longaville); Kane, John (Moth); Williams, Frank (Dull); Navin, Paddy (Jacquenetta); Rose, Clifford (Boyet); Lipman, Maureen (Princess of France); Behean, Katy (Maria); Agutter, Jenny (Rosaline); Ruparelia, Jay (Adrian); Burgess, John (Nathaniel); Wells, John (Holofernes); Dyall, Valentine (Marcade); Kitchen, Linda (Spring); Ross, Susanna (Winter).

DISTRIBUTION & AVAILABILITY: *Publisher or responsible agency:* BBC/TLF; *Distributor:* AVP, UIO, BBC* *Copy location:* UVM (Archive); *Availability:* AVP, B, V, 3/4U $450 (1987), sale; UIO, V (72009H), 3/4U (70124V), rental, $23.30; BBC*, 16mm or V, apply (*BUFVC* 13).

Macbeth

ORIGINAL WORK AND PRODUCTION: Tragedy. *Year written:* 1606; *Site of first production:* Whitehall palace [?]

Macbeth. **Motion Picture/Scenes**

284. *Duel Scene from* Macbeth.

DOCUMENT INFORMATION: *Country:* USA; *Year of release:* 1905.

EDITION, HISTORY, CONTENTS, & EVALUATION: *Edition & history:* Of historical interest because of its status as one of the earliest attempts in the United States to put Shakespeare into moving images. This clip was a part of a series called "Fights of Nations," which was evidently designed to document various styles of combat. The cameraman was the famous Billy Bitzer (1872-1944), a longtime associate of D.W. Griffith. Bitzer is credited with the technical achievements in such classics as *Birth of a Nation* and *Broken Blossoms.* Somehow Shakespeare's play got entangled in the Fights of the Nations series. But in those wonderful days all kinds of things surfaced in the movies. *Contents & evaluation:* The film in the Library of Congress is a brief (21 ft.) bit of helter-skelter action based on *Mac.* (5.7-8) as three men (presumably Young Siward, Macduff and Macbeth) wildly duel against a painted theatrical backdrop. For the time, the images are surprisingly sharp and clear. The kilted actors put on the best show they can. Siward falls dead, and then presumably Macbeth and Macduff continue the fight. It ends as abruptly as it begins (KSR). *Audience:* Professional; *Supplementary materials:* Ball, SOSF 30.

MEDIUM INFORMATION: *Medium:* Motion picture; *Sound:* Silent; *Color:* No (black & white); *Length:* -1 min.; *Film type:* 16mm.

AUTHORSHIP INFORMATION: *Producer(s):* American Mutoscope and Biograph Company.

DISTRIBUTION & AVAILABILITY: *Publisher or responsible agency:* Unknown; *Copy location:* LCM; *Call or copy number:* LC #1577; *Availability:* Archive.

Macbeth. **Motion Picture/Abridgment**

285. *Macbeth.*

DOCUMENT INFORMATION: *Country:* Italy; *Year of release:* 1909.

EDITION, HISTORY, CONTENTS, & EVALUATION: *Awards:* Milan prize, 1909 [?]; *Edition & history:* This early silent made by Cines of Rome and directed by the pioneering Mario Caserini (1874-1920) offers another example of the Italian operatic taste for lavish spectacle. Italian films ultimately influenced the kind of spectacle that D.W. Griffith brought to an apotheosis in his 1916 *Intolerance.* Caserini's wife, Maria, plays Lady Macbeth in this film. *Contents & evaluation:* Interesting as an example of very early Italian filmmaking before the era of Guazzoni and the great spectacle. Indeed the Italians seemed to do better with the Roman history plays anyway. Scotland comes through in this film as looking remarkably like Italy (this film indeed could be called one of the first of the "Spaghetti Westerns"). Costumes are not so much Scottish kilts as remnants of togas from a film about Julius Caesar. The witches and a sleepwalking Lady Macbeth both appear in the glaring Italian sun, and an overweight Lady Macbeth is either falling over and fainting on the floor, or dragging her husband around as though he were a sack of flour. While both seem afflicted with St. Vitus dance, in fact it is only the exaggerated, stagy acting that gives this impression. There is one trick shot that has the ghost of Banquo abruptly vanish, and there are certainly tendencies to move toward the spectacular dimensions of the later Italian silents. In the version I saw the title cards are in Russian, a reminder of the *international* status of these Shakespeare silent films. Audiences depended mainly on the actors' gifts for pantomime but dialogue cards in many different languages could easily be spliced in and out of the film. The movie is early, primitive art, but a step beyond the Lumières' *Train Arriving at the Station*. It furnishes a glimpse into the genesis of the Italian film industry (KSR). *Audience:* General use; *Supplementary materials:* Kliman, B. "1909 Lady Macbeth on Film." *SFNL* 12.2 (Apr. 1988): 3 + ; Ball, *SOSF* 101-2; 327-8.

MEDIUM INFORMATION: *Medium:* Motion Picture; *Sound:* Silent; *Color:* No (black & white); *Length:* 16 min.; *Language of subtitles:* Russian; *Film type:* 16mm.

AUTHORSHIP INFORMATION: *Producer(s):* Cines of Rome; *Director(s):* Caserini, Mario; *Cast:* Capelli, Dante (Macbeth); Gasperini, Maria Caserini (Lady Macbeth).

DISTRIBUTION & AVAILABILITY: *Publisher or responsible agency:* The film Import and Trading Company; *Copy location:* FOL, LCM; *Call or copy number:* MP 24; AFI FEO7137.

Macbeth. Film/Abbreviated

286. *Macbeth.*

DOCUMENT INFORMATION: *Country:* France; *Year of release:* 1910.

EDITION, HISTORY, CONTENTS, & EVALUATION: *Edition & history:* One of the first Film d'Art Shakespeare productions, starring Paul Mounet, younger brother of the more famous Jean-Sully Mounet (Mounet-Sully) in the title role. Film d'Art was a French company founded in 1908 that was devoted to bringing stage classics to the mass cinema audience. It generally employed famous actors from the Comèdie Française. Unfortunately most of the films were more

stagy than cinematic, but the movement aided in bringing respectability to the fledgling movie industry. *Supplementary materials:* Ball, *SOSF* 91-96.

MEDIUM INFORMATION: *Length:* 10 min.

AUTHORSHIP INFORMATION: *Director(s):* Calmettes, André; *Cast:* Mounet, Paul (Macbeth); Delvair, Jeanne (Lady Macbeth).

DISTRIBUTION & AVAILABILITY: *Copy location:* Unknown.

287. *Macbeth.*

DOCUMENT INFORMATION: *Country:* GB; *Year of release:* 1911.

EDITION, HISTORY, CONTENTS, & EVALUATION: *Edition & history:* The F.R. Benson theatrical company at the Stratford Memorial Theatre in collaboration with the Barker film company made several Shakespeare movies, mostly theatrical recordings. I doubt that a print survives, since the NFA does not list it among its holdings. *Supplementary materials:* Ball, *SOSF* 84.

MEDIUM INFORMATION: *Length:* 14 min.

AUTHORSHIP INFORMATION: *Director(s):* Benson, F.R.; *Cast:* Benson, F.R. (Macbeth); Benson, Constance (Lady Macbeth).

DISTRIBUTION & AVAILABILITY: *Copy location:* Unknown.

Macbeth. Motion Picture/Abridgment

288. *Macbeth*

DOCUMENT INFORMATION: *Country:* Germany; *Year of release:* 1913.

EDITION, HISTORY, CONTENTS, & EVALUATION: *Edition & history:* R.H. Ball's book has a full discussion of this lost film, which was unusual for the time in its ambitious scope, a footage of over 4000 feet. *Supplementary materials:* Ball, *SOSF* 183-88; *SIF* 110 [Gives "Bourchie" as director].

MEDIUM INFORMATION: *Length:* 47 min.

AUTHORSHIP INFORMATION: *Director(s):* Landmann, Ludwig; *Cast:* Bourchie, Arthur (Macbeth); Vanbrugh, Violet (Lady Macbeth).

DISTRIBUTION & AVAILABILITY: *Copy location:* Unknown.

Macbeth. Motion Picture/Abbreviated

289. *Macbeth.*

DOCUMENT INFORMATION: *Country:* USA; *Year of release:* 1916.

EDITION, HISTORY, CONTENTS, & EVALUATION:

Edition & history: Under the general supervision of D.W. Griffith, the British actor, Sir Herbert Beerbohm Tree, was hired at enormous expense to play Macbeth. For a full account of this ambitious production, see *SOSF. Supplementary materials:* Ball, *SOSF* 229-35.

MEDIUM INFORMATION: *Length:* [?] min.

AUTHORSHIP INFORMATION: *Director(s):* Emerson, John; *Cast:* Tree, Sir Herbert (Macbeth).

DISTRIBUTION & AVAILABILITY: *Copy location:* Unknown.

Macbeth. Motion Picture/Abridgment

290. *Macbeth.*

DOCUMENT INFORMATION: *Country:* France; *Year of release:* 1916.

EDITION, HISTORY, CONTENTS, & EVALUATION: *Edition & history:* R.H. Ball describes the picture as a "series of illustrative scenes." Since the star was a famous diva, one might speculate that the production offers an example of opera into film as much as Shakespeare into film. In any event, the film has disappeared. *Supplementary materials:* Ball, *SOSF* 244-45.

MEDIUM INFORMATION: *Length:* [?] min.

AUTHORSHIP INFORMATION: *Producer(s):* Eclair; *Cast:* Leblanc-Maeterlinck, Georgette (Lady Macbeth).

DISTRIBUTION & AVAILABILITY: *Copy location:* Unknown.

Macbeth. Motion Picture/Parody

291. *The Real Thing at Last.*

DOCUMENT INFORMATION: *Country:* GB; *Year of release:* 1916.

EDITION, HISTORY, CONTENTS, & EVALUATION: *Edition & history:* For an amusing account of this clever spoof on *Macbeth,* originally composed by J.M. Barrie, see Ball. *Supplementary materials:* Ball, *SOSF* 223-26.

MEDIUM INFORMATION: *Length:* [?] min.

AUTHORSHIP INFORMATION: *Director(s):* Matthews, A.E.; MacBean, L.C.; *Screenplay writer(s):* Barrie, J.M.; *Cast:* Gwenn, Edmund (Macbeth); Keys, Nelson (Lady Macbeth).

DISTRIBUTION & AVAILABILITY: *Copy location:* Unknown.

Macbeth. Motion Picture/Derivative

292. *Lady Macbeth.*

DOCUMENT INFORMATION: *Country:* Italy; *Year of release:* 1917.

EDITION, HISTORY, CONTENTS, & EVALUATION: *Edition & history:* A modernized version based on Nikolay Leskov's novel, *Lady Macbeth of Minsk* (1865). *Supplementary materials:* Ball, *SOSF* 228; *SIF* 112.

MEDIUM INFORMATION: *Length:* [?] min.

AUTHORSHIP INFORMATION: *Director(s):* Guazzoni, Enrico.

DISTRIBUTION & AVAILABILITY: *Copy location:* Unknown.

Macbeth. Motion Picture/Abbreviated

293. *Macbeth.*

DOCUMENT INFORMATION: *Country:* Germany; *Year of release:* 1922.

EDITION, HISTORY, CONTENTS, & EVALUATION: *Supplementary materials:* SIF 110.

MEDIUM INFORMATION: *Length:* 30 min.

AUTHORSHIP INFORMATION: *Director(s):* Schall, Heinz.

DISTRIBUTION & AVAILABILITY: *Copy location:* Unknown.

Macbeth. Video/Scenes

294. *Macbeth.* (Series: Scenes from Shakespeare).

DOCUMENT INFORMATION: *Country:* GB; *Year of first showing:* 1937; *Location of first showing:* BBC. Transmitted 25 March 1937.

EDITION, HISTORY, CONTENTS, & EVALUATION: *Edition & history:* A pioneering BBC transmission of Shakespeare on television when the industry was still in its infancy. Judging from the cast list, one might infer that the scene selected was Lady Macbeth's disastrous dinner party when the ghost of Banquo appears to ruin the evening for everybody. *Supplementary materials:* TPAB 25 March 1937.

MEDIUM INFORMATION: *Length:* 25 min.

AUTHORSHIP INFORMATION: *Producer(s):* O'Ferrall, George More; *Cast:* Oscar, Henry (Macbeth); Rawlings, Margaret (Lady Macbeth); Logan, George Campbell (Messenger)/Witch/Murderer; Emery, Polly (Witch/Guest); Clayton, Harold (Witch/Ross); Burne, Arthur (Banquo).

DISTRIBUTION & AVAILABILITY: *Publisher or responsible agency:* BBC; *Copy location:* Unavailable.

Macbeth. Motion Picture/Scenes

295. *Macbeth, 2.2.; 5.1.* (Series: Famous Scenes from Shakespeare).

DOCUMENT INFORMATION: *Country:* GB; *Year of release:* 1945.

EDITION, HISTORY, CONTENTS, & EVALUATION: *Edition & history:* Another in a British series of scenes from Shakespeare designed for classroom use. *Contents & evaluation:* Of special interest is veteran actor, Felix Aylmer, this time in the role of the Doctor who cannot help Lady Macbeth's emotional disorder. He seems far more plausible as a doctor than as Brutus in the first production of this series (see 208). There is good, solid professional level acting throughout, though the dark and murky print that I screened made the experience perilously akin to watching a shadow play. Again, the sound track from the London Symphony, conducted by Muir Mathieson, adds sonic embellishment. *Audience:* High school (grades 10-12);.

MEDIUM INFORMATION: *Medium:* Motion Picture; *Sound:* Spoken language; *Color:* No (black & white); *Length:* 17 min.; *Language(s) spoken:* English; *Film type:* 16mm.

AUTHORSHIP INFORMATION: *Producer(s):* Box, Sydney; Laing, Knox; *Director(s):* Cass, Henry; *Composer(s):* Frankel, Ben; Mathieson, Muir (and London Symphony); *Designer(s):* Bennett, Compton; Carter, James; *Costume designer(s):* Sinclair, Dorothy; *Lighting designer(s):* Palmer, Ernest; *Other personnel:* Wintle, Julian (Editor); Burgess, George; Clark, L. (Recording); Taylor, Nell (Makeup); *Cast:* Aylmer, Felix (Doctor); Lawson, Wilfred (Macbeth); Nesbitt, Catherine (Lady Macbeth); Lacey, Catherine (Gentlewoman).

DISTRIBUTION & AVAILABILITY: *Publisher or responsible agency:* Theatrecraft Ltd.; *Copy location:* FOL, NFA*; *Call or copy number:* MP 78.

Macbeth. Motion Picture/Interpretation

296. *Macbeth.*

DOCUMENT INFORMATION: *Country:* USA; *Year of release:* 1947.

EDITION, HISTORY, CONTENTS, & EVALUATION: *Edition & history:* Another of David Bradley's low budget, amateur Shakespeare films. As with his *Julius Caesar,* Bradley produced the movie on an incredibly slim budget, this time spending about $5000. The film was produced in and around the environs of North-western University near Chicago and made considerable use of student talent and home-made costumes, which, according to Peter Morris, were designed by Charlton Heston. Ironically the film career of this most promising young producer did not flourish when in later life he turned to making commercial films. Katz records Bradley's last film, *The Madmen of Mandoras,* as having been made in 1963. *Contents & evaluation:* Not seen, but favorably reviewed in contemporary press. Moreover, Peter Morris praises the film as "an interesting test run for Welles's version two years later" (Morris, *SOF:* 11). *Audience:* General use; *Supplementary materials:* Lightman, H.A. "Out-Orsoning Orson." *AC* (Sept. 1947); Bradley, David. "Shakespeare on a Shoestring." *Movie Makers* (Apr. 1947): 146 + ; See also, "Review." *NYT,* Jan. 5, 1947: x5.

MEDIUM INFORMATION: *Medium:* Motion Picture; *Sound:* Spoken language; *Color:* No (black & white); *Length:* 73 min.; *Language(s) spoken:* English; *Film type:* 16mm.

AUTHORSHIP INFORMATION: *Producer(s):* Bradley, David; *Director(s):* Blair, Thomas A.; *Screenplay writer(s):* Bradley, David; *Adaptor/translator(s):* Bradley, David; *Designer(s):* Bradley, David; *Costume designer(s):* Heston, Charlton; *Lighting designer(s):* Bradley, David; *Cast:* Bradley, David (Macbeth); Thompson, Ann; Elster, Irene; Winter, Alexander (Three Witches); Wilimovsky, Jain (Lady Macbeth); Bartholomay, William (Macduff); Nelson, Virginia (Lady Macduff); Northrop, Louis; (Duncan); Sweeney, William (Doctor/Porter); Mills, J. Royal (Malcolm); Dunn, J. Norton (Seyton).

DISTRIBUTION & AVAILABILITY: *Publisher or responsible agency:* Willow Productions; *Copy location:* Not known.

Macbeth. Motion Picture/Adaptation

297. *Macbeth.*

DOCUMENT INFORMATION: *Country:* USA; *Year of release:* 1948.

EDITION, HISTORY, CONTENTS, & EVALUATION: *Edition & history:* Since the sound track for this film, originally made in 23 days shooting time on a low budget, was re-recorded over a period of three years, the exact date of release depends on whether one is speaking of the original or revised version. The running time of the revised version is generally given as 86 min., though the initial cut supposedly ran 105 minutes. Welles himself described this hastily made film as 'a violently sketched charcoal drawing of a great play' (Manvell, *SATF* 59) and, as one might expect, the result was fair game for the critics who seemed to take a special joy in attacking this talented but vulnerable filmmaker. A major departure from the Shakespearean text, which brought in obtrusively Christian elements to suggest a mighty struggle between forces of Good and Evil, aroused much scorn. His famous "Voodoo" *Macbeth*, produced in Harlem on stage antecedent to the film, should have prepared audiences for something so typically Wellesian. Moreover, as Richard Wilson has shown, Welles's *Macbeth* at the Utah Centennial Festival as a rehearsal for his "surreal" film somewhat compensated for the brief shooting schedule. *Contents & evaluation:* "In the established Welles tradition, which has been building for a number of years, the theatrical mechanics of the medium are permitted to dominate the play and Shakespeare is forced to lower billing than either the director, the star or the cameraman. On weird sets, concocted by Fred Ritter, which cause the castle of Dunsinane to look less like a Scottish castle than like some sort of chasm or cave and the blasted heath of witches to look like a bath of live steam, Mr. Welles deploys himself and his actors so that they move and strike the attitudes of tortured grotesques and half-mad zealots in a Black Mass or an ancient ritual" (Crowther, Bosley, "*Macbeth*," *NYT* 28 Dec. 1950: 22). Welles's *Macbeth*, like so many of his other efforts, has aroused almost as much hostility as admiration, despite his talents as an *auteur*. In defence of this *Macbeth*, which does have many drawbacks, it must be noted that he operated on a tiny budget, that he was pressed for time, and that he chose to dive into the play's subtext rather than tread water on the surface. Quite contrary to what most people think, the outcome was not narrowly cinematic at all but deeply obliged to his experience in radio and on stage. No one knew better than Welles how to make use of human voices and no one had a better theatrical sense. His genius lay in his ability to point a camera at a subject in odd but thoroughly significant ways (KSR). *Audience:* College and university; *Supplementary materials:* Johnson, Ian. "Merely Players." *FAF* 10.7 (1964): 46; Manvell, *SATF* 55-61; G.L. "*Macbeth* USA 1948." *MFB* 209.18 (1951): 275-6; Nouryeh, Andrea. "Understanding Xanadu." *SFNL* 14.1 (Dec. 1989): 3; Wilson, Richard. *Macbeth* on Film." *TA* 33 (June 1949): 53-55.

MEDIUM INFORMATION: *Medium:* Motion Picture; *Sound:* Spoken language; *Color:* No (black & white); *Length:* 89 min.; *Film type:* 16mm.; *Video type:* V, B.

AUTHORSHIP INFORMATION: *Producer(s):* Welles, Orson; *Director(s):* Welles, Orson; *Adaptor/translator(s):* Welles, Orson; *Composer(s):* Ibert, Jacques; Kurtz, Efrem; *Designer(s):* Ritter, Fred; McCarthy Jr., John; Redd, James; *Costume designer(s):* Palmer, Adele; *Other personnel:* Russell, John L. (Photography); Lydecker, Howard and Theodore (Special Effects); *Cast:* Welles, Orson (Macbeth); Nolan, Jeanette (Lady Macbeth); O'Herlihy, Dan (Macduff); McDowall, Roddy (Malcolm); Barrier, Edgar (Banquo); Napier, Alan (A Holy Father); Sanford, Erskine (Duncan); Dierkes, John (Ross); Curtis, Keene (Lennox); Webber, Peggy (Lady Macduff, Witch); Braham, Lionel (Siward); Heugly, Archie (Young

Siward); Farber, Jerry (Fleance); Welles, Christopher (Macduff Child); Farley, Morgan (Doctor); Tuttle, Lurene (Gentlewoman/Witch); Duffield, Brainerd (First Murderer/Witch); Alland, William (Second Murderer); Chirello, George (Seyton).

DISTRIBUTION & AVAILABILITY: *Publisher or responsible agency:* Republic Pictures and Mercury Films; *Distributor:* FNC, GLB*, TWC, REP, ERS, FCM, DCV, *Copy location:* FOL; *Call or copy number:* MP 107 (Original Scottish-British soundtrack—105 min.); *Availability:* Rental 16mm FNC, GLB*, KIT ($95 and $125 "Restored"); TWC, B,V, $60.95; REP, V, $59.95; ERS, V, $74.95; FCM, V, $39.95; DCV, V, $58; INM $29.95

Macbeth. Video/Teleplay

298. *Macbeth.*

DOCUMENT INFORMATION: *Country:* USA; *Year of first showing:* 1949; *Location of first showing:* NBC TV, USA. Transmitted from 9 to 10 P.M., Sunday, 1 May 1949.

EDITION, HISTORY, CONTENTS, & EVALUATION: *Edition & history:* A "Kinescope" (legal record) of the original live TV performance of the New York City Players Club production of *Macbeth* is in the Folger Library. Astonishingly this production was scheduled on the same evening as the restaged *Julius Caesar* (see 210). Nowadays two Shakespeare performances competing for an audience on major network prime time would be unthinkable. *Contents & evaluation:* If these "shadows do offend," it is through no fault of the actors who are superb, including the presence of such veterans as Walter Hampden, Leo G. Carroll, Ralph Bellamy and John Carradine. The problem is mainly technological, as the blurry images on the screen take on the look of berserk *film noir*, or perhaps a negative of a film. While the production may remain of interest to historians of the theatre, all the same it is a little sad to see these great names from the past coming to us, as it were, like shadowy ghosts desperately seeking our remembrance of them as Shakespearean actors. *Audience:* General use; *Supplementary materials:* "The Players Club Presents [Still]." *NYT*, 1 May 1949: X 11.

MEDIUM INFORMATION: *Medium:* Video; *Sound:* Spoken language; *Color:* No (black & white); *Length:* 120 min. [Folger copy]; *Language(s) spoken:* English; *Video type:* Kinescope [on Video].

AUTHORSHIP INFORMATION: *Producer(s):* McGee, Harold; *Director(s):* Brown, Anthony; Davis, Owen; Simpson, Garry (for NBC); *Cast:* Hampden, Walter (Macbeth); Redman, Joyce (Lady Macbeth); Abel, Walter (Macduff); Carroll, Leo G. (Duncan); Blackmer, Sidney (Ross); Bellamy, Ralph (Porter); Carradine, John (First murderer); Clark, Alexander (Lennox).

DISTRIBUTION & AVAILABILITY: *Publisher or responsible agency:* NBC/Players Club, New York City/ Philco Repertory Theatre; *Copy location:* FOL; *Call or copy number:* VCR 11.

299. *Macbeth.*

DOCUMENT INFORMATION: *Country:* GB; *Year of first showing:* 1949; *Location of first showing:* BBC. Transmitted from 8:30 to 10:45 P.M., Sunday, 20 Feb. 1949.

EDITION, HISTORY, CONTENTS, & EVALUATION: *Edition & history:* A 1949 publicity blurb pointed out that all available space at Alexandra Palace (the BBC headquarters) would be needed for George More O'Ferrall's production. Some 27 separate sets of scenery had to be constructed in the Alexandra Palace workshops, and several of the actors were equipped with masks that could change expressions, an innovation in the eyes of the producers. Peter Bax, the designer, copied illuminations from the ninth-century Book of Kells for the Celtic and Scandinavian designs in scenery and dresses. Obviously great excitement surrounded this enterprise in the early days of television. For George More O'Ferrall, the producer, who had produced snippets of *Macbeth* in 1937 on BBC, this opportunity to do the entire play on the relatively generous budget of £2,260 must have been welcome indeed (KSR). *Contents & evaluation:* Almost as soon as this play had been performed for television, the critics began to worry over the special needs of television as compared with the stage. An internal BBC memorandum pointed out that the facial expressions in close-ups often did not mesh with the words, that Macbeth looked more like a saint than a villain, that the "knocking at the gate" failed because there was no sense of any space around Macbeth and his Lady, who were isolated in two-shot. Indeed when Macbeth should have looked dwarfed by his surroundings in his "borrowed robes," instead the close-up gave the illusion that he was dominating his world. Other critics simply thought that the actors didn't understand their lines well enough to give them the proper emphasis, but that can be a hazard as much on stage as on screen (KSR—WAC T5/356 22 Feb. 1949). *Supplementary materials:* TPAB 20 Feb. 1949.

MEDIUM INFORMATION: *Length:* 120 min.

AUTHORSHIP INFORMATION: *Producer(s):* O'Ferrall, George More; *Other personnel:* Petty, Cecil; Angus, Archie (Stage Managers); Jones, Maurice (Fight Arranger); *Cast:* Murray, Stephen (Macbeth); Lodge, Ruth (Lady Macbeth); Dignam, Mark (Macduff); Vines, Margaret (Lady Macduff); Malone, Cavan (Macduff's son); Knight, Esmond (Banquo); Stebbings, Alan (Fleance); More, Kenneth (Ross); Brooking, John (Caithness); Walter, Richard (Monteith); Lemin, Stanley (Angus); Ainsworth, John (Malcolm); Doran, Charles (Siward); Connell, Paul (Young Siward); Mullins, Peter (Donalbain); Wontner, Arthur (Duncan); Mills, James (Doctor); Troughton, Patrick (Seton); Somers, Julian (Sergeant);

Crier, Gordon (Porter); Leahy, Eugene; Jones, Maurice (Murderers); Thesinger, Ernest; Harvey, Michael Martin; Greenwood, Rosamund (Witches); + 14 soldiers and ladies in waiting.

DISTRIBUTION & AVAILABILITY: *Publisher or responsible agency:* BBC; *Copy location:* Unavailable.

Macbeth. Video/Abbreviated

300. *Macbeth.*

DOCUMENT INFORMATION: *Country:* USA; *Year of first showing:* 1950; *Location of first showing:* NBC TV Kraft Theatre. Transmitted 9 to 10 P.M., Wed., 10 May 1950.

EDITION, HISTORY, CONTENTS, & EVALUATION: *Edition & history:* One of the earlier U.S. Shakespeare productions on network television in the golden age of TV drama. This one competed for an audience with "What's My Line?" and trotting races in Yonkers, which were transmitted at the same time. *Supplementary materials:* "On TV." NYT 10 May 1950: 62.

MEDIUM INFORMATION: *Length:* 60 min.

AUTHORSHIP INFORMATION: *Cast:* Marshall, E.G. (Macbeth); Hagen, Uta (Lady Macbeth).

DISTRIBUTION & AVAILABILITY: *Copy location:* LCM; *Call or copy number:* VBE 6513.

301. *Macbeth.*

DOCUMENT INFORMATION: *Country:* USA; *Year of first showing:* 1951; *Location of first showing:* Westinghouse Studio One/CBS. Transmitted 10 to 11:00 P.M., Monday, 22 Oct. 1951.

EDITION, HISTORY, CONTENTS, & EVALUATION: *Edition & history:* Wrapped around by Betty Furness' primitive but cogent commercials ("You can be sure if it's Westinghouse") and an appeal to contribute to the "Crusade for Freedom" in the cold war against communism, this flickering, black-and-white Kinescope reflects not only the history of *Macbeth* in performance but the cultural development of the nation itself. That a corporation such as Westinghouse would willingly underwrite *Macbeth* for the masses again underscores the magnetism of the Shakespearean aura, even to corporate sponsors. If, however, this dreary, lackluster event had anyone's name but Shakespeare's attached to it, the scenarists would have been stripped of their expense accounts and swimming pools. It does, however, provide a fascinating memento of what the "live" television drama of grandfather's day was like. It is anything but polished and slick. The opening sequence that shows the news from the battle being transmitted in lightning flashes has the actors' faces flashing on and off like strobe lights, and one has the sense of looking at a negative rather than a positive print (KSR). *Contents & evaluation:* Despite the inadvertent gloom of this Kinescope, the rich, mellifluous voice of Charlton Heston conveys the reassuring tones of a great star. Although barely visible, Heston does the "two truths" soliloquy with commendable flair. The deletions to compress the action into sixty minutes are of course horrendous so that the arrival of Duncan at the castle occurs with incredible speed. Since most of Heston's speeches are in voiceover, he has no need to make his facial expressions display any emotion whatsoever. The tracking shots down the castle corridors (reminiscent of the Olivier *Hamlet*) must have been a daunting challenge to the technical staff in the era of "live" studio transmission. The creaking iron gate as the Porter opens the portcullis for Banquo stands as a hackneyed but dependable visual and aural portent of evil. All of Heston's great talent, however, is needed to compensate for the incompetence of other cast members. For Judith Evelyn as Lady Macbeth there is no apparent connection between words and body so that her speeches may as well be issuing from a cassette. She brings to the role all the energy of a woman ordering groceries over a telephone, though when interacting with Heston she finally begins to sparkle and glitter. Rivalling Lady Macbeth in inadequacy is the Porter who seems in an effeminate way to carry not an iota of conviction in his voice. Banquo's 'most sacriligious murder' announcement becomes a kind of Thurberesque travesty of itself. If this were not enough, there are also the abrasive commercial breaks as Betty Furness demonstrates a TV set with 'no streaks, no flutter, no flopover,' a state of grace one yearns for in this *Macbeth*. On the other hand, as live performance it comes closer to the excitement and defects of the stage than the air-brushed slickness of modern television. Even the actors' only human fluffs and slips turn out to be more endearing than disturbing. Perhaps an index to the whole production is the portrayal of Ross as a kind of doddering, mendicant friar. John Stride's smirking Ross of Polanski's 1971 film would hardly seem to be the same character. One will move in two decades from innocence to experience (KSR). *Audience:* Professional; *Supplementary materials:* Gould, Jack. "Worthington Miner's Production." *NYT* 24 Oct. 1951: 34 ["A provocative 60 minutes but not always Shakespeare's hour."].

MEDIUM INFORMATION: *Medium:* Video (Kinescope); *Sound:* Spoken language; *Color:* No (black & white); *Length:* 60 min.; *Film type:* Kinescope.

AUTHORSHIP INFORMATION: *Producer(s):* Miner, Worthington; *Director(s):* Schaffner, Franklin; *Adaptor/translator(s):* Miner, Worthington; *Designer(s):* Levitas, Willard; *Cast:* Heston, Charlton (Macbeth); Evelyn, Judith (Lady Macbeth); McGavin, Darren (Macduff); Boyne, Peter (Banquo); Brown, Josephine (First Witch); Romer, Tomi (Second Witch); Melish, Vera Fuller (Third Witch); Seldes, Marian (Gentlewoman); Dickinson, Don (Doctor); Devitt, Alan (Angus); Shayne, Alan (Ross); Brandon, Peter (Malcolm).

DISTRIBUTION & AVAILABILITY: *Publisher or responsible agency:* Westinghouse Studio One/CBS; *Copy location:* MOB; *Call or copy number:* T77:0092; *Availability:* Archive viewing by appt.

Macbeth. Motion Picture/Abbreviated

302. *Macbeth.*

DOCUMENT INFORMATION: *Country:* USA; *Year of release:* 1951.

EDITION, HISTORY, CONTENTS, & EVALUATION: *Edition & history:* An abbreviated but nevertheless ambitious production of *Macbeth* made by the faculty and students of Bob Jones University. *Contents & evaluation:* Shakespeare's study of evil corrupting a Scottish king becomes in the hands of this bible belt producer a kind of morality play. Traces of the old, late medieval tradition behind Shakespeare's account of the two overreaching lovers are privileged over the metaphysical dimension. Even so this is quite a lavish production. To be sure, the play has been somewhat sanitized for the occasion. None of the bizarre but heady twists and turns of Polanski's film will be found here. Even the poor old Porter is missing, and one waits in vain for such beloved phrases as "multitudinous seas incarnadine, / Making the green one red." Lady Macbeth's "unsex me here" speech has vanished, presumably another victim to piety (and time). There are some thoughtful editing and camera angles (the knight dismounting from a high angle shot in front of the castle and a special effects routine in the dagger scene). Both Lady Macbeth and Macbeth turn in credible performances, though Bob Jones, Jr. as Macbeth remains somewhat wooden. As is sometimes the theatrical practice, three young men in drag play the witches. The artistic rationale for this touch, which is also reminiscent of Hitchcock's *Psycho*, is not clear. The down-home South Carolina voices may also be a distraction, but only to Yankees. The color is lavish but a little harsh and unmodulated, a bold move nevertheless in 1951 for an amateur production. Other details of the *mise en scène*, such as interior castle sets, costumes and music, have also been generously provided. High school students will find much about this innocent *Macbeth* that is enjoyable and teachers can rest assured that it does indeed "murder sleep." *Audience:* High school (grades 10-12);.

MEDIUM INFORMATION: *Medium:* Motion Picture; *Sound:* Spoken language; *Color:* Yes; *Length:* 80 min.; *Language(s) spoken:* English; *Film type:* 16mm.

AUTHORSHIP INFORMATION: *Producer(s):* Bob Jones Univ.; *Director(s):* Stenholm, Katherine; *Composer(s):* Girvin, Richard; Keefer, Karl; *Designer(s):* Stratton,

Melvin; *Set designer(s):* Stratton, Lyle; Sowers, J.W.; *Costume designer(s):* Livingston, Thais; Jensen, Marilyn; *Lighting designer(s):* Craig, Bob; *Other personnel:* Nichols, Ralph (Editing); Reece, Leonard; Cook, William (Production engineers); Jensen, George (Electrician); Holbrooke, Jo; Nichterlein, Lois; Kelly, Wayne (Makeup); Tuttle, Eileen (Hair); Roth, Sherman; Clarke, James (Properties); Johnson, Edwin; Lindsay, Jack (Sound); Havens, Murray; Ingbretsen, David (Titling); *Cast:* Sowers, Barbara Hudson (Lady Macbeth); Jones, Bob Jr. (Macbeth); Yearick, David (Macduff); Vanaman, Paul (Duncan); Peters, Gordon (Banquo); Pratt, Robert (Ross); Jackson, Dale (Lennox); Galstad, George (Malcom); Myers, Kenneth (Donalbain); Kelly, Wayne (Seyton); Jones, Bob III (Fleance); Yost, Jack (First Murderer); Evans, John (Second Murderer); Noe, Herbert (Doctor); Barnes, Geraldine (Lady in Waiting); Mercer, Theodore; Gustafson, Dwight; Osterberg, Bob (Witches).

DISTRIBUTION & AVAILABILITY: *Publisher or responsible agency:* Bob Jones University; *Distributor:* UNU, *Copy location:* FOL; *Call or copy number:* MP 57.

Macbeth. Video/Derivative

303. *Macbeth.*

DOCUMENT INFORMATION: *Country:* USA; *Year of first showing:* 1951; *Location of first showing:* CBS/TV. Transmitted 8 to 9:00 P.M., Tuesday, 9 Jan. 1951.

EDITION, HISTORY, CONTENTS, & EVALUATION: *Edition & history:* It is easier to find out about Desi Arnaz and *Counter-Spy* than to dig out solid information about this *Macbeth.* Certainly it was abridged and apparently it was a modern-dress version with a subtitle of *Sure as Fate.*

MEDIUM INFORMATION: *Color:* No (black & white); *Length:* 60 min.; *Video type:* V.

AUTHORSHIP INFORMATION: *Cast:* Carradine, John; Evelyn, Judith.

DISTRIBUTION & AVAILABILITY: *Publisher or responsible agency:* CBS.

Macbeth. Motion Picture/Derivative

304. *Le rideau rouge: Ce soir, on joue Macbeth.*

DOCUMENT INFORMATION: *Country:* France; *Year of release:* 1952.

EDITION, HISTORY, CONTENTS, & EVALUATION: *Edition & history:* Modern version of *Macbeth* with scenario by Jean Anouilh. *Supplementary materials:* SIF 112.

MEDIUM INFORMATION: *Length:* 81 min.

AUTHORSHIP INFORMATION: *Director(s):* Barsacq, André; *Cast:* Simon, Michel; Brasseur, Pierre.

DISTRIBUTION & AVAILABILITY: *Distributor:* Cinephone [?].

Macbeth. Video/Teleplay

305. *Macbeth.* (Series: Hallmark Hall of Fame).

DOCUMENT INFORMATION: *Country:* USA; *Year of first showing:* 1954; *Location of first showing:* NBC. Transmitted 4 to 6 P.M., 28 Nov. 1954.

EDITION, HISTORY, CONTENTS, & EVALUATION: *Edition & history:* In a historic first, the production was transmitted in color for the benefit of the relatively few Americans who then owned color television sets. Maurice Evans, who played the title role, and George Schaefer, with the enlightened sponsorship of Kansas City's Joyce Hall, were key figures in bringing televised Shakespeare to North Americans. For other Shakespeare programs in the Hallmark series, see 102, 126, 309, 484, 593, 594, 613, and 649. *Contents & evaluation:* "The realistic approach in the direction turned the tragedy into a domestic rather than cosmic one. The weird sisters, suggesting Wyrd or fate, were portrayed as three meddling old women, with little of the supernatural about them except their green faces, and the important first scene in Act IV, when Macbeth again goes to consult them, was changed into a dream of Macbeth's while he is lying in bed, so that his future actions lost motivation and impact. Omitted completely from this scene with the witches was all mention of Banquo's 'line of kings.' After the first shot, from below, looking up into the faces of the witches there was little imagination either in the use of the camera or in the 'stage business.' In the banquet scene the depiction of Banquo's presence by a disembodied head, shining with red blood and bouncing about like a tennis ball was just short of ludicrous. This was one in a series of literal and somewhat repulsive shots on the colorcast accentuating blood—the wounded sergeant was covered with it; there was a closeup of the bloody hands of Macbeth and Lady Macbeth after the murder. . . . Except for Miss Anderson, there was no grandeur and little poetry in this production. Her interpretation moved steadily to a climax, from the reading of the letter and the realization of what it could mean; then her steeling herself, in a magnificently rendered delivery of the soliloquy 'The raven himself is hoarse'; and later her concern for her husband and mounting apprehensions about their deed; until finally the truly terrifying sleepwalking scene. . . . Mr. Evans' Macbeth was less successful, because in the close range of television he did not seem to convey the stature or the complexity of this character. And again as in the *Richard II,* a number of his passages seemed recited rather than acted. . . . The color did not seem to be used for any particular theatrical effect, although the costumes in their off tones and tartans were pleasing to the eye, and the scenes of splendor such as the banquet at which Macbeth and Lady Macbeth first appear as king and and queen, were considerably enhanced by the use of color" (Griffin, Alice, "Shakespeare Through the Camera Eye, 1953-54," *SQ* 6.1 [1955]:65-6). *Audience:* Professional; *Supplementary materials:* Jones, Claude E. "The Imperial Theme: *Macbeth* on TV." *QFRT* 9 (1955): 292-98; "*Macbeth* in Color." *Time* (13 Dec. 1954): 64; "TV." *NYT* 28 Nov. 1954: X 13; Coursen, H.R. "The Schaefer 1954 *Mac.* Revisited." *SFNL* (Dec. 1989): 12 + .

MEDIUM INFORMATION: *Medium:* Video; *Sound:* Spoken language; *Color:* Yes; *Length:* 103 min.; *Language(s) spoken:* English; *Video type:* V.

AUTHORSHIP INFORMATION: *Producer(s):* Schaefer, George; *Director(s):* Schaefer, George; *Composer:* Engel, Lehman; *Designer:* Riggs, Otis; *Costumes:* Taylor, Noel *Cast:* Evans, Maurice (Macbeth); Anderson, Judith (Lady Macbeth); Cotsworth, Staats (Banquo); Waring, Richard (Macduff); Fernandez, Peter (Donalbain); Hamilton, Roger (Malcolm); Jameson, House (Duncan); Reese, John (Fleance); Stevenson, Margot (Lady Macduff).

DISTRIBUTION & AVAILABILITY: *Publisher or responsible agency:* NBC, Hallmark Hall of Fame; *Distributor:* VID, FCM, *Copy location:* FOL, Video of Kinescope (VCR); *Availability:* VID, B,V $24.95; FCM, $19.95 [states 1954 version].

Macbeth. Motion Picture/Derivative

306. *Joe Macbeth.*

DOCUMENT INFORMATION: *Country:* GB; *Year of release:* 1955.

EDITION, HISTORY, CONTENTS, & EVALUATION: *Edition & history:* This film is an "offshoot" from Shakespeare's *Macbeth*, influenced by it, obviously shaped by it but with no pretensions whatsoever to representing Shakespeare's text on screen. Instead it creates another text from Shakespeare's text. Indeed it borrows extensively from the plot of Shakespeare's play to displace the Scottish tragedy into the underworld of Chicago's gangland. Its mere existence, however, along with so many other films of this category, powerfully testifies to the way that Shakespeare's plays still act as universal metaphors for the human condition. *Contents & evaluation:* After credits superimposed upon an urban skyline (probably Chicago) come Macduff's lines about Macbeth: 'Not in the legions of horrid hell / Can come a devil more damn'd / In evils to top Macbeth.' That shot having established the Shakespearean link, the next sequence inscribes the film's identity as a species of the gangster movie genre by showing a joint

called "Tommy's Cafe." The parallels with Shakespeare's play are pervasive. Joe Macbeth, for example, after "rubbing out" the Mob Boss's Lieutenant (Macbeth conquering Cawdor for Duncan?), learns from "Rosie," a fortune teller, who addresses him as "Noble Macbeth," that he is destined to be "Lord of Lakeview Drive." Macbeth is puzzled because Tommy was the "Lord of Lakeview Drive." Moreover he is to be "Macbeth King of the City." The plot parallels continue both in the dialogue and in the visuals. For example, a hackneyed cops-and-robbers chase yields to a quick cut to a bawling baby ("Pity like a new-born babe"); Lili, Joe's wife, becomes increasingly ambitious for her husband's rise in power, and arranges a dinner party. The Duke (Duncan) arrives to spend the night with Lenny and Banky (obviously Lennox and Banquo). Lenny and Banky, however, are to be set up as the murderers of the Duke, so that they correspond in some tangled way to the "sleepy grooms" in *Macbeth*. Shakespearean inspiration shines through the script of this vulgarization when Lili offers a knife to Joe. The moment is authentic *film noir* as the darkness of the deed is reflected in the texture of the lighting and *mise-en-scène*. Joe's anguish over his betrayal of Banky shows in his tortured eyes. Across the lake a bell tolls, reminiscent of the bell in *Macbeth*. When the Duke's insomnia thwarts the stabbing plot, Joe elects to drown him in the lake. The shot of fowl swirling overhead alludes to the play's many bird images and when Joe has completed the horrible deed he says, like Macbeth, "It's done." Lili has to go get the knife. Joe can't. A Porter even appears: the servant, Angus, who answers to the knocking at the door. Like Shakespeare's hero, Joe kills himself when he kills the boss. One remark to Joe sums up the mystery of the witches' prophecies in *Macbeth*: "Maybe it didn't happen because Rosie said it would but because you did what she said" (KSR). *Audience:* General use.

MEDIUM INFORMATION: *Medium:* Motion picture; *Sound:* Spoken language; *Color:* No (black & white); *Length:* 91 min.; *Language(s) spoken:* English; *Film type:* 35mm.

AUTHORSHIP INFORMATION: *Producer(s):* Frankovich, M.J.; Maynard, George; *Director(s):* Hughes, Ken; Shipway, Philip; *Adaptor/translator(s):* Yordan, Philip; *Composer(s):* Duncan, Trevor; Taylor, Richard; *Designer(s):* Harris, Alan; *Costume designer(s):* Fairlie, Jean; *Lighting designer(s):* Emmot, Basil; *Other personnel:* Johnson, Peter Rolfe (Editor); Lindorf, W.; Cameron, K. (Sound); Cox, Alfred (Sound editor); Deason, Splinters (Continuity); Bonnor-Moris, R.; Torrington, Terry (Makeup); Broe, Nina (Hair); Jympson, John (Art editor); Pearson, Freddie (Prod. manager); *Cast:* Douglas, Paul (Joe Macbeth);Roman, Ruth (Lili); Colleano, Bonar (Lennie); Aslan, Gregoire (Duncan the Duke); James, Sidney (Banky); Green, Harry ("Big Dutch"); + Grisham, Walter; Gallard, Kay; Arden, Robert;

Marco, George; Pious, Minerva (Rosie); Vickers, Philip; Baker, Mark; Nagy, Bill; Mulock, Alfred.

DISTRIBUTION & AVAILABILITY: *Publisher or responsible agency:* Columbia Pictures; *Distributor:* KIT, *Copy location:* FOL MP45; *Availability:* Rental 16mm, Apply.

Macbeth. Motion Picture/Adaptation

307. *Kumonosu-Djo (The Castle of the Spider's Web).* [*Throne of Blood*].

DOCUMENT INFORMATION: *Country:* Japan; *Year of filming:* 1957; *Year of release:* 1957; *Country of first showing:* Japan.

EDITION, HISTORY, CONTENTS, & EVALUATION: *Edition & history:* Not shown in the United States until 1961, the film has been critically acclaimed as one of the finest "translations" of Shakespeare's language into filmic art. In re-creating Shakespeare's play in the idiom of Japanese theatre, Kurosawa makes a visual text of his own, embedded in but not completely indebted to Shakespeare's text. *Contents & evaluation:* "We label it amusing because lightly is the only way to take this serio-comic rendering of an ambitious Scot into a form that combines characteristics of the Japanese Noh theatre and the American western film. Probably Mr. Kurosawa, who directed the classic "Rashomon," did not intend it to be amusing for his formalistic countrymen, but its odd amalgamation of cultural contrasts hits the occidental funnybone. . . . He has simply purloined the thread of the drama and used it as the plot of a film that splatters the screen with a wild horse-opera set in medieval Japan . . . the action in this drama is grotesquely brutish and barbaric, reminiscent of the horse-opera business in Kurosawa's *The Magnificent Seven* with Toshiro Mifune as the warrior grunting and bellowing monstrously and making elaborately wild gestures to convey his passion and greed, while other of the warriors behave accordingly. To our western eyes, it looks fantastic and funny . . . and the final scene, in which the hero is shot so full of arrows that he looks like a porcupine, is a pictorial extravagance that provides a conclusive howl" (Crowther, Bosley, "*Throne of Blood,*" *NYT* 23 Nov. 1961: 50). "In the final sequence, Washiju moves between his dual roles as performer and observer. As he energetically struts on a platform above his men, he observes the movements of his approaching enemies and commands the attention of his followers, making a final attempt to unify his forces. In his first speech, he moves smoothly from observation to performance; he is the confident leader, who successfully draws approving laughter and raised banners from his admiring audience. But later when he is informed that the forest is moving and watches his men panic, he is forced into the weaker role of foolish observer. Although he tries to regain control, his men seize the power and become the performers; they unleash their arrows like a jeering audience stopping a bad performance. . . . Washizu's final *danse macabre* is the last powerful demonstration of his superhuman energy, which defines his character; it takes hundreds of arrows to make him halt" (Kinder, Marsha, "*Throne of Blood*: A Morality Dance," *LFQ* 5.4 [1977]:345). *Audience:* College and university; General use; *Supplementary materials:* Jorgens, *SOF* 153-9.

MEDIUM INFORMATION: *Medium:* Motion Picture; *Sound:* Spoken language; *Color:* No (black & white); *Length:* 105 min.; *Language(s) spoken:* Japanese; *Language of subtitles:* English; *Film type:* 16mm.

AUTHORSHIP INFORMATION: *Producer(s):* Kurosawa, Akira; *Director(s):* Kurosawa, Akira; *Adaptor/translator(s):* Kurosawa, Akira; Oguni, Hideo; Hashimoto, Shinbuo; Kikushima, Ryuzo; Richie, Donald; *Composer(s):* Sato, Masaru; *Designer(s):* Murai, Yoshiro; *Other personnel:* Nakai, Asaichi; Kurosawa, Akira (Editing); *Cast:* Mifune, Toshiro (Taketoi Washizu/Macbeth); Yamada, Isuzu (Asaji/Lady Macbeth); Shimura, Takashi (Noriyasu Odagura); Chiaki, Minoru (Yoshiaki Miki/Banquo); Kubo, Akira (Yoshiteru/Fleance); Sasaki, Takamaru (Kuniharu Tsuzuki/Duncan); Tachikawa, Yoichi (Kunimaru/Malcolm); Naniwa, Chieko (Weird Woman).

DISTRIBUTION & AVAILABILITY: *Distributor:* FNC, FCM, GLB*, BFI*, INM *Availability:* FNC, GLB* rental 16mm, apply; FCM, V, $59.95; INM, V, (SU128) $69.95; 10 min. study extract at BFI*.

Macbeth. Motion Picture/Scene

308. *Throne of Blood.*

DOCUMENT INFORMATION: *Country:* Japan; *Year of release:* 1957.

EDITION, HISTORY, CONTENTS, & EVALUATION: *Edition & history:* Individual scene for classroom study from the 1957 Kurosawa *Throne of Blood.* The scene begins "where Washizu's wife, Asaji, tries to persuade him to take over Cobweb Castle" (*BUFVC*). *Supplementary materials:* BUFVC 13.

MEDIUM INFORMATION: *Length:* 10 min.

AUTHORSHIP INFORMATION: *Director(s):* Kurosawa, Akira.

DISTRIBUTION & AVAILABILITY: *Distributor:* BFI*.

Macbeth. Video/Recording

308.1 *Macbeth.*

DOCUMENT INFORMATION: *Country:* France; *Year of first showing:* 1959.

EDITION, HISTORY, CONTENTS, & EVALUATION: *Edition & history:* A recording of a 1959 production in Paris.

MEDIUM INFORMATION: *Sound:* Spoken language; *Color:* No (black & white); *Length:* 105 min.; *Video type:* 3/4"U.

AUTHORSHIP INFORMATION: *Producer(s):* O.R.T.F.; *Director(s):* Barma, Claude; *Adaptor/translator(s):* Curtis, Jean (Translator); *Composer(s):* Delerue, Georges; *Cast:* Casares, Maria (Lady Macbeth); Sorano, Daniel (Macbeth); Topart, Jean; Paris, Andre Oumansky.

DISTRIBUTION & AVAILABILITY: *Publisher or responsible agency:* O.R.T.F.; *Distributor:* INA, *Copy location:* VAA*; *Call or copy number:* THE 1.22.

Macbeth. Motion Picture/Interpretation

309. *Macbeth.* (Series: Hallmark Hall of Fame).

DOCUMENT INFORMATION: *Country:* USA; *Year of first showing:* 1960; *Location of first showing:* NBC, 6 to 8:00 P.M., Sunday, 20 Nov. 1960.

EDITION, HISTORY, CONTENTS, & EVALUATION: *Edition & history:* In 1960, Maurice Evans joined forces with George Schaefer to redo the 1954 *Macbeth* for television. This time, however, the production was first made as a movie in color. Most of it was filmed on location in Scotland at considerable expense. The decision to make a film for television marked a major breakthrough in television practice. Indeed this *Macbeth* and a gangster show called *The Scarface Mob* (from *The Untouchables*) compete for the honor of being the first to innovate the now common practice of combining a theatrical film with a television production. The expanded theatrical version was released in 1963 and made widely available on 16mm film for schools. Because the film was originally made for TV, close-ups and mid-shots tend to prevail and give it a kind of claustrophobic atmosphere, though ironically the exterior shots made on location in Scotland have been thought incongruously sunny and cheerful for a play so steeped in evil. For other Shakespeare programs in the Hallmark series, see 102, 126, 305, 484, 593, 594, 613, and 649. *Contents & evaluation:* Despite the star quality cast, Maurice Evans and Judith Anderson in the leading roles, this production of *Macbeth* never quite captures the imagination. The anxiety to make a faithful copy of the Shakespearean text works against the need to re-create the play in the exciting new medium of film. Oftentimes Evans seems to be orat-

ing, or playing an actor playing Macbeth, rather than projecting a sense of the appalling state of Macbeth's mind. This is a man, like Dr. Faustus, who is damned to eternal torment but we get little sense of that urgency. Judith Anderson generates slightly more plausibility as Lady Macbeth, though even she is somewhat handicapped by an acting style that values elocution above illocution. By comparison the Welles *Macbeth*, though teetering on the absurd, nevertheless fearlessly plunges into the depths of the human soul for codes to represent the inner agony of the Scottish king. *Audience:* High school (grades 10-12); College and university; General use; *Supplementary materials:* Hutton, Clayton. Macbeth: *The Making of a Film.* London: Parrish, 1960; "TV." *NYT* 20 Nov. 1960: X 20.

MEDIUM INFORMATION: *Medium:* Motion Picture; *Sound:* Spoken language; *Color:* Yes; *Length:* 107 min.; *Language(s) spoken:* English; *Film type:* 16mm.

AUTHORSHIP INFORMATION: *Producer(s):* Samuel, Phil C.; Kaufman, Sidney; Schaefer, George *Director(s):* Schaefer, George; *Adaptor/translator(s):* Schaefer, George; Squire, Anthony; *Composer(s):* Addinsell, Richard; Mathieson, Muir (w. Sinfonia of London); *Designer(s):* Corrick, Edward; *Costume designer(s):* Dawson, Beatrice; *Other personnel:* Young, Fred A. (Camera); Kemplen, Ralph (Editor); *Cast:* Evans, Maurice (Macbeth); Anderson, Judith (Lady Macbeth); Keen, Malcolm (Duncan); Brett, Jeremy (Malcolm); Warren, Berry (Donalbain); Hordern, Michael (Banquo); Banner, Ian (Macduff); Hutt, William (Ross); Lack, Simon (Menteith); Mason, Brewster (Angus); Carson, Charles (Caithness); Finch, Scot (Fleance); Faulkner, Trader (Seyton); Aylmer, Felix (Physician); Rose, George (Porter).

DISTRIBUTION & AVAILABILITY: *Publisher or responsible agency:* A Grand Prize Films Production; *Distributor:* IOA, *Copy location:* MMA (#006006); *Availability:* IOA (68022F), 16mm, rental, $13.90 (1988); INM, V (DS22) $49.95.

Macbeth. Motion Picture/Derivative

310. *Siberian Lady Macbeth.*

DOCUMENT INFORMATION: *Country:* Yugoslavia; *Year of release:* 1961.

EDITION, HISTORY, CONTENTS, & EVALUATION: *Edition & history:* A film adaptation from the 19th-century novel by Nikolay Leskov, *Lady Macbeth of Minsk* (1865), which was also made into a movie by Enrico Guazzoni in 1917 (see 292). According to the *BUFVC* catalog, in this version there is "a fusion of Leskov's psychological naturalism and the broader, more poetic sweep of Shakespeare's play." *Supplementary materials:* BUFVC 13.

MEDIUM INFORMATION: *Sound:* Spoken language; *Color:* Yes; *Length:* 92 min.; *Film type:* 16mm.

AUTHORSHIP INFORMATION: *Director(s):* Wajda, Andrzej; *Cast:* Markovic, Olivera; Tadic, Ljuba; Lazarevic, Miodrag.

DISTRIBUTION & AVAILABILITY: *Distributor:* BFI*.

Macbeth. Motion Picture/Abridgment

311. *Macbeth.* (Series: Fair Adventure Series).

DOCUMENT INFORMATION: *Country:* USA; *Year of release:* 1964.

EDITION, HISTORY, CONTENTS, & EVALUATION: *Edition & history:* A five-part abridgment of the play with commentary by Dr. Frank Baxter. For other films in this series, see 180, 254, 426, 463, 487, 508, 546, 614 and 653. *Contents & evaluation:* Not seen. *Audience:* Junior High (grades 7-9); High school (grades 10-12);.

MEDIUM INFORMATION: *Medium:* Motion Picture; *Sound:* Spoken language; *Color:* No (black & white); *Length:* 140 min.; *Language(s) spoken:* English; *Film type:* 16mm.

DISTRIBUTION & AVAILABILITY: *Publisher or responsible agency:* Westinghouse Broadcasting Corp.; *Distributor:* Not known.

Macbeth. Video/Teleplay

312. *Macbeth.*

DOCUMENT INFORMATION: *Country:* GB; *Year of first showing:*1966; *Location of first showing:* BBC-1, Transmitted 2:05 to 4:15 P.M., Tuesday, Oct. 11, 1964.

EDITION, HISTORY, CONTENTS, & EVALUATION: *Edition & history:* Advertised in *RT* as "for schools and colleges." Kenneth Colley, who was fourteen years later to play the "duke of dark corners" as Vincentio in the 1978 BBC *Measure for Measure* is here in the minor role of a servant. *Supplementary materials:* "Program." *RT* 6 Oct. 1964: 35.

MEDIUM INFORMATION: *Length:* 130 min.

AUTHORSHIP INFORMATION: *Producer(s):* Simpson, Michael; *Designer(s):* Lawrence, Charles; *Other personnel:* Diamond, Peter (Fight Arranger); *Cast:* Keir, Andrew (Macbeth); Meyers, Ruth (Lady Macbeth); Wagstaff, Elsie (First Witch); Duncan, Brenda (Second Witch); Heard, Daphne (Third Witch); Eccles, Donald (Duncan); Tucker, Alan (Malcolm); Lambert, Nigel (Donalbain); Beint, Michael (Bleeding Captain); Godfrey, Patrick (Lennox); Matthews, Martin (Ross); Tierney, Malcolm (Angus); Grout, James (Banquo); Bate, Anthony (Macduff); Murray, Michael (Mentieth);

Colley, Kenneth (Macbeth's Servant); Grout, Paul (Fleance); Diamond, Peter (Macdonald).

DISTRIBUTION & AVAILABILITY: *Publisher or responsible agency:* BBC; *Copy location:* Unavailable.

Macbeth. Motion Picture/Documentary

313. *Macbeth I: The Politics of Power.* (Series: The Humanities Series).

DOCUMENT INFORMATION: *Country:* US; *Year of release:* 1964.

EDITION, HISTORY, CONTENTS, & EVALUATION: *Edition & history:* The purpose of this series of three films on *Macbeth* (see also 314, 315) is to show how the meaning of the play will change in the hands of a director. Director Douglas Campbell has firm convictions about *Macbeth* (among other things that parts of the play have been lost), which he forcefully avers with the help of some skilled actors. Students might be alerted to the fact that not all textual scholars agree that parts of *Macbeth* have been lost. These losses rarely seem apparent to an audience. Nevertheless this is well done. *Contents & evaluation:* The loss of the authoritative voice of Professor Mack in this *Macbeth* series is compensated for by the advances in filmic technique that make the *Macbeth* series even more attractive than the EBF *Hamlet* films. The scenes are superbly acted and Campbell's exploration of the political dimensions of the play is highly plausible. *Audience:* High school (grades 10-12); College and university; *Supplementary materials:* A filmstrip, "Shakespeare's *Macbeth*" (173 G37), makes connections between the films and the text.

MEDIUM INFORMATION: *Medium:* Motion Picture; *Sound:* Spoken language; *Color:* Yes; *Length:* 28 min.; *Language(s) spoken:* English; *Film type:* 16mm; *Video type:* 3/4U, B, V.

AUTHORSHIP INFORMATION: *Director(s):* Barnes, John; Campbell, Douglas; *Designer(s):* Creme, Benjamin; *Other personnel:* Ambor, Josef; Hasse, Charles; Barnes, John (Editing); *Cast:* Squire, William (Macbeth); Ure, Gudrun (Lady Macbeth); Lamont, Duncan (Macduff); Ragan, George (Banquo); Gwynn, Michael (Duncan); Campbell, Douglas (Presenter).

DISTRIBUTION & AVAILABILITY: *Publisher or responsible agency:* Encyclopaedia Britannica Educational Corporation; *Distributor:* UVM, SFL*, *Copy location:* LCM; *Call or copy number:* EBF #47571.

314. *Macbeth II: The Themes of* Macbeth. (Series: The Humanities Series).

DOCUMENT INFORMATION: *Country:* US; *Year of release:* 1966.

EDITION, HISTORY, CONTENTS, & EVALUATION:

Edition & history: In this segment, director Campbell argues that the theme of *Macbeth* is not only that "absolute power corrupts" but also that appearances cannot be trusted. He has no time to stress that the ambiguity of appearance vs. reality is also one of the most pervasive motifs in the entire canon. To make his point he employs some effective actors from the Canada Festival. *Contents & evaluation:* Campbell offers high level discourse for a "beginner's film", though never beyond comprehension. For example, his comparison of Macduff's silence at the news of his Lady's death and Macbeth's eloquence offers an eye-opening insight. *Audience:* High school (grades 10-12); College and university; *Supplementary materials:* A filmstrip, "Shakespeare's *Macbeth*" (173 G37), makes connections between the films and the text.

MEDIUM INFORMATION: *Medium:* Motion Picture; *Sound:* Spoken language; *Color:* Yes; *Length:* 28 min.; *Language(s) spoken:* English; *Film type:* 16mm; *Video type:* 3/4U, B, V.

AUTHORSHIP INFORMATION: Same as 313, above.

DISTRIBUTION & AVAILABILITY: Same as 313 above, except that the EBF call or copy number is #47572.

315. *Macbeth III: The Secret'st Man.* (Series: The Humanities Series).

DOCUMENT INFORMATION: *Country:* US; *Year of release:* 1966.

EDITION, HISTORY, CONTENTS, & EVALUATION: *Edition & history:* In this third part of the EBF *Macbeth* series, Douglas Campbell looks at the inner torment of Macbeth and his Lady, as the full horror of their situation becomes apparent to them. *Contents & evaluation:* Through an analytical method of isolating key scenes, Campbell shows how they fit together to make up a network of thematic statements. Shakespeare's Gothic imagery is underscored. Extremely well done. *Audience:* High school (grades 10-12); College and university; *Supplementary materials:* A filmstrip, "Shakespeare's *Macbeth*" (173 G37), makes connections between the films and the text.

MEDIUM INFORMATION: *Medium:* Motion Picture; *Sound:* Spoken language; *Color:* Yes; *Length:* 33 min.; *Language(s) spoken:* English; *Film type:* 16mm; *Video type:* 3/4U, B, V.

AUTHORSHIP INFORMATION: Same as 313, above.

DISTRIBUTION & AVAILABILITY: Same as 313, above, except that the EBF number is #47573.

Macbeth. **Motion Picture/Documentary**

316. *Macbeth: Patterns of Sound.* (Series: The Art of Shakespeare in *Macbeth*).

DOCUMENT INFORMATION: *Country:* USA; *Year of release:* 1967.

EDITION, HISTORY, CONTENTS, & EVALUATION: *Edition & history:* The first in a series of six short films dealing with the art of Shakespeare in *Macbeth* (see 316-21). A booklet accompanies each program. In this initial program, "Patterns of sound," the producers proposed to show that "Shakespeare uses not only the meanings of words to express his ideas, but also the sounds of words. Scenes from *Macbeth* are presented by Shakespearean actors. Commentary on these scenes is reinforced with animated portions of the text." *Contents & evaluation:* Not seen. *Audience:* High school (grades 10-12); College and university.

MEDIUM INFORMATION: *Medium:* Motion picture; *Sound:* Spoken language; *Color:* Yes; *Length:* 15 min.; *Language(s) spoken:* English; *Film type:* 16mm.

AUTHORSHIP INFORMATION: *Producer(s):* Univ. of Washington [?]; *Cast:* Joseph, Bertram (Narrator); Shepherd, Elizabeth; Duncan, Ross.

DISTRIBUTION & AVAILABILITY: *Copy location:* KSC

317. *Macbeth: Imagery.* (Series: The Art of Shakespeare in *Macbeth*).

DOCUMENT INFORMATION: *Country:* USA; *Year of release:* 1967.

EDITION, HISTORY, CONTENTS, & EVALUATION: *Edition & history:* The second in a series of six short films dealing with the art of Shakespeare in *Macbeth* (See 316, 318-21). In this program, "Imagery," the producers proposed to show that "Shakespeare excelled at using words to evoke images and moods. Moving from the simple example of 'Light thickens and the crow makes wing to the rooky wood,' the film progresses to more complex imagery, showing how Shakespeare uses imagery in describing, in making implications, and in stating the theme." *Contents & evaluation:* Not seen. *Audience:* High school (grades 10-12); College and university.

MEDIUM INFORMATION: *Medium:* Motion Picture; *Sound:* Spoken language; *Color:* Yes; *Length:* 16 min.; *Language(s) spoken:* English; *Film type:* 16mm.

AUTHORSHIP INFORMATION: *Producer(s):* Univ. of Washington [?]; *Cast:* Joseph, Bertram (Narrator); Shepherd, Elizabeth; Duncan, Ross.

DISTRIBUTION & AVAILABILITY: *Copy location:* KSC.

318. *Macbeth: Character.* (Series: The Art of Shakespeare in *Macbeth*).

DOCUMENT INFORMATION: *Country:* USA; *Year of release:* 1967.

EDITION, HISTORY, CONTENTS, & EVALUATION: *Edition & history:* The third in a series of six short films dealing with the art of Shakespeare in *Macbeth* (see 316-17, 319-21). In this program, "Character," the producers proposed to examine "two crucial relationships . . . as examples of how Shakespeare sets forth the qualities of his characters and how they act upon each other. The relationships between Macbeth and Lady Macbeth and between Macbeth and Banquo serve as models showing how Shakespeare makes his characters come to life." *Audience:* High school (grades 10-12); College and university.

MEDIUM INFORMATION: *Medium:* Motion Picture; *Sound:* Spoken language; *Color:* Yes; *Length:* 19 1/2 min.; *Language(s) spoken:* English; *Film type:* 16mm.

AUTHORSHIP INFORMATION: *Producer(s):* Univ. of Washington [?]; *Cast:* Joseph, Bertram (Narrator); Shepherd, Elizabeth; Duncan, Ross.

DISTRIBUTION & AVAILABILITY: *Copy location:* KSC.

319. *Macbeth: Turning points.* (Series: The Art of Shakespeare in *Macbeth*).

DOCUMENT INFORMATION: *Country:* USA; *Year of release:* 1967.

EDITION, HISTORY, CONTENTS, & EVALUATION: *Edition & history:* The fourth in a series of six short films dealing with the art of Shakespeare in *Macbeth* (see 316-18, 320-21). In this program, "Turning points," the producers proposed to examine *Macbeth* as "a skillfully structured dramatic work. In this film no definition of 'structure' is given. But by illuminating Macbeth's progress from indecision and rejection to acceptance of Lady Macbeth's plan to murder Duncan, Professor Joseph shows how to find the structure of a play." *Contents & evaluation:* Not seen. *Audience:* High school (grades 10-12); College and university.

MEDIUM INFORMATION: *Medium:* Motion Picture; *Sound:* Spoken language; *Color:* Yes; *Length:* 18 1/2 min.; *Language(s) spoken:* English; *Film type:* 16mm.

AUTHORSHIP INFORMATION: *Producer(s):* Univ. of Washington [?]; *Cast:* Joseph, Bertram (Narrator); Shepherd, Elizabeth; Duncan, Ross.

DISTRIBUTION & AVAILABILITY: *Copy location:* KSC.

320. *Macbeth: Tragedy.* (Series: The Art of Shakespeare in *Macbeth*).

DOCUMENT INFORMATION: *Country:* USA; *Year of release:* 1967.

EDITION, HISTORY, CONTENTS, & EVALUATION: *Edition & history:* The fifth in a series of six short films dealing with the art of Shakespeare in *Macbeth* (see 316-19, 321). In this program, "Tragedy," the producers sought to show how the play "affects us as a tragedy. We see clearly how Macbeth, in the circumstances in which he lives and because of the decisions he has made, is led inevitably by a chain of cause and effect to suffering and death. By his art, Shakespeare makes us grieve the death of a great man who became a traitor and a murderer." *Audience:* High school (grades 10-12); College and university.

MEDIUM INFORMATION: *Medium:* Motion Picture;

Sound: Spoken language; *Color:* Yes; *Length:* 14 min.; *Language(s) spoken:* English; *Film type:* 16mm.

AUTHORSHIP INFORMATION: *Producer(s):* Univ. of Washington [?]; *Cast:* Joseph, Bertram (Narrator); Shepherd, Elizabeth; Ross, Duncan.

DISTRIBUTION & AVAILABILITY: *Copy location:* KSC.

321. *Macbeth: A Creative Rehearsal.* (Series: The Art of Shakespeare in *Macbeth*).

DOCUMENT INFORMATION: *Country:* USA; *Year of release:* 1967.

EDITION, HISTORY, CONTENTS, & EVALUATION: *Edition & history:* The last in a series of six short films dealing with the art of Shakespeare in *Macbeth* (see 316-20). A booklet accompanies each program. This program, "A Creative Rehearsal," offers, in the words of the producers, "an actual rehearsal of *Macbeth* in which Dr. Joseph directs Barry Boys, Elizabeth Shepherd, and Duncan Ross. . . . This is a revealing look into the way director and actors come to understand what Shakespeare intended, just as the reader of Shakespeare can do for himself when the language of the play is fully understood." *Audience:* High school (grades 10-12); College and university.

MEDIUM INFORMATION: *Medium:* Motion Picture; *Sound:* Spoken language; *Color:* Yes; *Length:* 15 min.; *Language(s) spoken:* English; *Film type:* 16mm.

AUTHORSHIP INFORMATION: *Producer(s):* Univ. of Washington [?]; *Cast:* Joseph, Bertram (Narrator); Boys, Barry; Shepherd, Elizabeth; Ross, Duncan.

DISTRIBUTION & AVAILABILITY: *Copy location:* KSC.

Macbeth. **Motion Picture/Documentary**

322. *Macbeth: Nothing Is But What Is Not.* (Series: Explorations in Shakespeare, VII).

DOCUMENT INFORMATION: *Country:* Canada; *Year of release:* 1969.

EDITION, HISTORY, CONTENTS, & EVALUATION: *Edition & history:* Part seven in a series of twelve 23-minute films made in 1969 by the Ontario Educational Communications Authority (see also 18, 40, 65, 124, 162, 257, 465, 488, 555, 617 and 637). For an overview, see 18, above. *Contents & evaluation:* Not seen. According to the publicity release issued by NBC Educational Enterprises, the film takes the position that Macbeth is a man who "lives in a world of fantasy. In terms of the psychiatric approach to Macbeth and Lady Macbeth which the film takes, the title also suggests that Macbeth is a man who has not yet found his identity. He must 'do a deed' in order to become. This hypothesis, that Macbeth has to kill Duncan to assert his identity forms the basis for an examination of murder, aggression and repression as seen in the workings of Shakespeare's characters." If on the same level with the *Hamlet* and *Tempest* programs described elsewhere (see 124 and 617), then this program is well worth viewing for its intellectual excitement. *Audience:* College and university.

MEDIUM INFORMATION: *Medium:* Motion Picture; *Sound:* Spoken language; *Color:* Yes; *Length:* 23 min.; *Language(s) spoken:* English; *Film type:* 16mm.

AUTHORSHIP INFORMATION: *Producer(s):* Reis, Kurt; Moser, Ed; *Screenplay writer(s):* Webster, Hugh; *Composer(s):* Yanovsky, Zal; *Set designer(s):* Adeney, Chris; *Lighting designer(s):* Galbraith, Howard; *Performance group(s):* Ontario Educational Communications/ NBC Educational Enterprises.

DISTRIBUTION & AVAILABILITY: *Distributor:* CNU [?].

Macbeth. Motion Picture/Abridgment

323. *Macbeth: An Introduction.* (Series: Shakespeare Series [BHE] IV).

DOCUMENT INFORMATION: *Country:* GB; *Year of first showing:* 1969.

EDITION, HISTORY, CONTENTS, & EVALUATION: *Edition & history:* The fourth in a series of six abridged versions of the plays (see also 41, 228, 258, 406, 656). For overview, see 41, above. *Contents & evaluation:* Not seen. *Audience:* High school (grades 10-12); College and university.

MEDIUM INFORMATION: *Medium:* Motion Picture; *Sound:* Spoken language; *Color:* Yes; *Length:* 26 min.; *Language(s) spoken:* English; *Film type:* 16mm.

AUTHORSHIP INFORMATION: *Producer(s):* BHE/ Seabourne Enterprises; *Cast:* [BUFVC, 26, credits]: Leech, Richard (Macbeth); Goosens, Jennie (Lady Macbeth); Spink, Brian (Macduff); Barcroft, John (Banquo); Harvey, Edward (Duncan).

DISTRIBUTION & AVAILABILITY: *Publisher or responsible agency:* BHE/Seabourne; *Distributor:* BFA.

Macbeth. Motion Picture/Adaptation

324. *Macbeth: Roman Polanski's Film of.*

DOCUMENT INFORMATION: *Country:* GB; *Year of release:* 1971.

EDITION, HISTORY, CONTENTS, & EVALUATION: *Edition & history:* Financed by Hugh Hefner of Playboy Productions, scripted by Kenneth Tynan with Roman Polanski himself, and shot on location in Wales, this film emerged with more sensational publicity than any other Shakespeare film. *Contents & evaluation:* I am inclined, to agree with Jack Jorgens that the sensational comparisons between Polanski's life and art (the Manson murders and stabbing of Duncan, the *Playboy* centerfold models and a nude Lady Macbeth, the ugly crones in *Rosemary's Baby* and witches in *Macbeth*), tended to obscure the film's very real virtues. If Polanski is obsessed with blood (the stabbing of Duncan is too horrible to watch), so is Shakespeare's play in which the dominant image is that of "blood." More importantly, though, the surface violence detracts from some of the film's great artistic achievements. The *mise en scène* is filled with the kinds of "expressive objects" (dogs, bears, straw pallets, chickens, washing) that serve as icons for the play's themes. This embedding of domestic squalor into the imperial theme becomes a visual metaphor for the soul of Macbeth himself. The film is actually controlled *cinema verité*, organized dissonance (KSR). Critic Nigel Andrews saw the film as another example of Polanski's "cinema of obsession." In all his films, says Andrews, Polanski "has established a central claustrophobic theatre of action, stressed its isolation by running counterpoint with glimpses of the world outside, and used his characters' imprisonment as a catalysing force to bring their obsessions to a climax." He goes on to distinguish between Polanski's black comedies (*Cul de sac, Dance of the Vampires*) and "psychological shockers" (*Repulsion, Rosemary's Baby*). The castle or apartment settings of these films support either surrealistic comedy or psychological drama. Then in an interesting argument too complex for adequate summary here, Andrews concludes that Polanski's film, notable for its castle setting, "locates the mental torment of its characters not in an indulgent novelistic limbo, but in a credible historically detailed social context" "*Macbeth,*" *SAS* 41 [Spring 1972]: 108). Critic Herbert Coursen actively disliked the film: "Roman Polanski's *Macbeth* is a multi-million dollar disaster mitigated occasionally by the things films can do that the stage cannot duplicate. . . . For all Polanski's sweep of landscape and spectacle, the cosmic dimensions of the drama are lost. Macbeth's crime brushes the ultimate reaches of the universe; Polanski reduces it to a nasty storm. Macbeth's 'eternal jewel' is given to 'the common enemy of man.' Polanski . . . suggests that he sees no 'deep damnation,' but merely an unsuccessful career whose archetypes are Mussolini and his mistress, Clara Petracci" (Coursen, H.R., "Polanski's *Macbeth,*" *SFNL* 3.1 [1978]: 2 +). *Audience:* College and university; Professional; *Supplementary materials:* Rothwell, K.S. "Polanski's *Macbeth,* Ross and the Third Murderer." *CEA* 46 [1983-84]: 50-55; Berlin, Normand. "*Macbeth,* Polanski and Shakespeare." *LFQ* 1.4 [1973]: 291-8.

MEDIUM INFORMATION: *Medium:* Motion Picture; *Sound:* Spoken language; *Color:* Yes; *Length:* 140 min.; *Language(s) spoken:* English; *Film type:* Todd-AO 35mm; 16mm; *Video type:* V.

AUTHORSHIP INFORMATION: *Producer(s):* Braunsberg,

Andrew; Polanski, Roman; Hefner, Hugh M.; *Director(s):* Polanski, Roman; *Adaptor/translator(s):* Tynan, Kenneth; *Composer(s):* Third Ear Band; *Designer(s):* Shingleton, Wilfred; Carter, Fred; *Costume designer(s):* Mendleson, Anthony; *Other personnel:* Taylor, Gilbert (Camera); McIntrye, Alastair (Editing); *Cast:* Finch, Jon (Macbeth); Annis, Francesca (Lady Macbeth); Shaw, Martin (Banquo); Selby, Nicholas (Duncan); Stride, John (Ross); Chase, Stephan (Malcolm); Shelley, Paul (Donalbain); Bayler, Terence (Macduff); Laurence, Andrew (Lennox); Wylie, Frank (Mentieth); Archard, Bernard (Angus); Purchase, Bruce (Caithness); Chegwin, Keith (Fleance); Davis, Noel (Seyton); Rimmington, Noelle (Young Witch); MacFarquhar, Maisie (Blind Witch); Taylor, Elsie (First Witch); Abbott, Victor (Cawdor); Drysdale, Bill; Jones, Roy (King's Grooms); Mason, Patricia (Gentlewoman); Hogg, Ian; Reed, Geoffrey; Ashton, Nigel (Minor Thanes); Dightam, Mark (Macduff's Son); Fletcher, Diane (Lady Macduff); Pearson, Richard (Doctor); Bromley, Sydney (Porter); Hobbs, William (Young Seyward); Joint, Alf (Old Seyward); Balfour, Michael/McCullough, Andrew (First and Second Murderers); Lang, H.; Mountain, T. (Soldiers).

DISTRIBUTION & AVAILABILITY: *Publisher or responsible agency:* Columbia Pictures; Playboy Productions/Caliban Films; *Distributor:* SWA, RCC, DCV, FCM, FMB*; *Copy location:* FOL; *Call or copy number:* MP 61; *Availability:* SWA, rental 16mm, apply; FMB*, 16 mm, hire; FCM, sale, V, $59.95; RCC, V, $59.95; RSC*, V, apply; DCV, V (#71140), $58; INM, V (DS15) $69.95.

Macbeth. Video/Opera

325. *Macbeth.*

DOCUMENT INFORMATION: *Country:* GB; *Year of release:* 1972.

EDITION, HISTORY, CONTENTS, & EVALUATION: *Edition & history:* Verdi's *Macbeth* taped at a performance of the Glyndebourne Festival Opera with the London Philharmonic Orchestra. *Supplementary materials:* Novacom Video Inc. catalog.

MEDIUM INFORMATION: *Length:* 148 min.

AUTHORSHIP INFORMATION: *Producer(s):* Burton, Humphrey; *Director(s):* Pritchard, John (Conductor); *Composer(s):* Verdi, Guiseppi; *Cast:* Barstow, Josephine; Paskalis, Kostas; Morris, James; Ewen, Keith; Caley, Ian.

DISTRIBUTION & AVAILABILITY: *Distributor:* NOV, FCM, VAI *Availability:* NOV, B, V (2 cass.) $78; VAI (69007), V $59.95; FCM, V (SO2466) $59.95.

Macbeth. Motion Picture/Scenes

326. *Macbeth,* 1.1; 1.3. (Series: The Shakespeare Series [IFB], V).

DOCUMENT INFORMATION: *Country:* Great Britain; *Year of release:* 1974.

EDITION, HISTORY, CONTENTS, & EVALUATION: *Edition & history:* In this fifth unit in "The Shakespeare Series" (see also numbers 22, 131, 164, 232, 430, 467, 490, 510, 556, 601 and 619) excerpts from *Macbeth* show the witches' prophecies of Macbeth's political future (1.1.; 1.3), and a sequence in which Macbeth beholds the spectral dagger and contemplates the murder of Duncan (2.1). For overview, see 22. *Contents & evaluation:* The cast is not at the professional level of one of Cass's productions but it shows a clinical mastery of the text. Unfortunately the brief excerpts seem a little out of context, though of potential value for classroom discussion, especially with the accompanying notes. *Audience:* High school (grades 10-12);.

MEDIUM INFORMATION: *Medium:* Motion Picture; *Sound:* Spoken language; *Color:* Yes; *Length:* 11 min.; *Language(s) spoken:* English; *Film type:* 16mm; *Video type:* V, 3/4U (4 per cassette).

AUTHORSHIP INFORMATION: *Producer(s):* Realist Film Unit; *Director(s):* Seabourne, Peter; *Cast:* Kingston, Mark (Macbeth); Hall, Elizabeth; Key, Alison; Renwick, Linda (Three Witches).

DISTRIBUTION & AVAILABILITY: *Publisher or responsible agency:* Realist Film Unit; *Distributor:* IFB, CNU, *Copy location:* FOL; *Call or copy number:* FOL, MP 87; LCM [PR2823.A3] 73-714376 ; *Availability:* CNU, rental 16mm $8; IFB, sale 16mm, V, $175.

Macbeth. Video/Teleplay

327. *Macbeth.* (Series: Play of the Month).

DOCUMENT INFORMATION: *Country:* GB; *Year of first showing:* 1970; *Location of first showing(s):* BBC1. Transmitted 8:15 to 10:25 P.M., Sunday, 20 Sept. 1970; USA, PBS, 27 Sept. 1975.

EDITION, HISTORY, CONTENTS, & EVALUATION: *Edition & history:* Made for television by the BBC. In the U.S.A., under the sponsorship of the NEH and Mobil Corporation, it was shown on PBS stations as a segment in the 13-part great plays series of Classic Theatre: Humanities in the Drama, at 9:00 P.M. on Saturday, 27 Sept. 1975. Both the producer and the director (Cedric Messina and John Gorrie) were to play a heavy role subsequently in the BBC Shakespeare series, shown in the United States as "The Shakespeare Plays." The Humanities series was produced by Joan Sullivan of Station WGBH-Boston for public television. *Contents & evaluation:* "In outward beauty and inner degradation Eric Porter's Macbeth and Janet Suzman's Lady Macbeth suggest the fairness of the foul and the foulness of the fair. That equivocal condition, deeply embedded in the play's language, gets visual support from camera angles forcing the audience to look down, not up, at these two gorgeous but treacherous creatures. . . . Especially subtle is Janet Suzman's portrayal of Lady Macbeth's disastrous misreading of her husband's character. Despite these virtues, it is also a production that does not quite seem to have found its own vision of the play's 'metaphysical core'" ("Shakespeare and the People: Elizabethan Drama on Television,"*SFNL* 1.2 [1977]:4). Although the level of acting remans quite high, the use of camera work and dramaturgical strategies seem relatively uninspiring. A high frequency of "talking heads" suggests a record of a filmed stage play more than an independent cinematic realization of Shakespeare's play. Janet Suzman gives a dynamic reading, however, of Lady Macbeth's lines. She favors voice over gesture. Compare, for example, the way that she vocalizes the "Unsex me here" soliloquy with the way in which Jane Lapotaire calls upon nonverbal gesture to highlight the speech. Being neither film nor stageplay but televised drama, however, the results are predictably uneven. Some shots such as the empty throne at the beginning are inspired; while others, such as having Duncan walk into the castle on foot, suggest either a low-budget or a paralysis of imagination (KSR). *Audience:* High school (grades 10-12); College and university; General use; *Supplementary materials:* Kane, John, ed. *Classic Theatre: The Humanities in Drama.* Boston: WGBH, 1977; Nkosi, Lewis. "Janet Suzman . . . in *Macbeth.*" *RT,* 188 (17 Sept. 1970): 6-7; "TV." *NYT* 27 Sept. 1975: 60 [Ad.], 61.

MEDIUM INFORMATION: *Medium:* Video; *Sound:* Spoken language; *Color:* Yes; *Length:* 137 min.; *Language(s) spoken:* English; *Video type:* 3/4U.

AUTHORSHIP INFORMATION: *Producer(s):* Messina, Cedric; *Director(s):* Gorrie, John; *Composer(s):* Whelen, Christopher; *Designer(s):* Kroll, Natasha; *Costume designer(s):* Bloomfield, John; *Cast:* Porter, Eric (Macbeth); Suzman, Janet (Lady Macbeth); Alderton, John (Malcolm); Goodliffe, Michael (Duncan); Thaw, John (Banquo); Woodvine, John (Macduff); Browne, Robin (Donalbain); Beint, Michael (Sergeant); Douglas, Donald (Lennox); Rowe, Alan (Ross); Palmer, Geoffrey (Menteith); Fisher, Colin (Caithness); Kelland, John (Messenger); McFee, Malcolm (Fleance); Spenser, David (Seyton); Morris, Wolfe (Porter); Merritt, George (Old Man); Eagles, Leon; Caunter, Tony (Murderers); Davis, Ray (Servant); Cooper, Rowena (Lady Macduff); Dashwood, Nicholas (Boy); Bailey, John (Doctor); Burne, Rosamund (Gentlewoman); Greenhalgh, Paul (Servant); Tyrrell, Norman (Siward); Sadgrove, David (Young Siward); Heard, Daphne; Coleridge, Sylvia; Mason, Hilary (Witches); *Performance group(s):* BBC

Play of the Month; Classic Theatre, the Humanities in Drama.

DISTRIBUTION & AVAILABILITY: *Publisher or responsible agency:* BBC; *Distributor:* TLF, *Copy location:* FOL; *Call or copy number:* VCR 1.

Macbeth. Motion Picture/Documentary

328. *A Sense of the Other.*

DOCUMENT INFORMATION: *Country:* USA; *Year of release:* 1977.

EDITION, HISTORY, CONTENTS, & EVALUATION: *Edition & history:* Filmed at Northwestern University, the film shows Prof. Wallace A. Bacon working with students by teaching literature through performance. *Contents & evaluation:* "Through the performance of students in the class, interviews with them, conversations with Professor Wallace A. Bacon, and a class discussion of *Macbeth,* the film demonstrates that the student is led out from himself and the world he knows into the experience embodied in the plays of Shakespeare—'A sense of the other'. Professor Bacon's technique explores character motivation, use of language, and dramatic structure. One of his major concerns, however, is getting a student to believe in the characters of a play. In his experiential approach the feel of literature is not apart from, but congruent with meaning. Literature is to be experienced, not simply analyzed. 'How does a literary work feel when it speaks?' Bacon asks." (P.R. flyer from producers); Professor Andrew McLean concludes that the film provides "a good model for an enjoyable and valuable classroom experience" ("Educational Films," *SQ* 30 [Summer 1979]: 415-16). *Audience*: High school (grades 10-12); College and university; *Supplementary materials:* "Review." *SN* 28 (Feb. 1978): 5.

MEDIUM INFORMATION: *Medium:* Motion Picture; *Sound:* Spoken language; *Color:* Yes; *Length:* 33 min.; *Language(s) spoken:* English; *Film type:* 16mm.

AUTHORSHIP INFORMATION: *Producer(s):* Galati, Frank; *Cast:* Bacon, Wallace A. (Discussion leader).

DISTRIBUTION & AVAILABILITY: *Publisher or responsible agency:* Northwestern Univ.; *Distributor:* NWU, *Copy location:* Northwestern.

Macbeth. Video/Documentary

329. *Macbeth.*

DOCUMENT INFORMATION: *Country:* USA; *Year of first showing:* 1977.

EDITION, HISTORY, CONTENTS, & EVALUATION: *Edition & history:* A videotape of Ian Richardson coaching a scene from *Macbeth*. There is an archive copy in the TOFT collection (Theatre on Film and Tape) at the Library of Performing Arts, Lincoln Center, New York Public Library. It may be viewed by appointment (see below). *Contents & evaluation:* Not seen. *Audience:* College and university; General use.

MEDIUM INFORMATION: *Medium:* Video; *Sound:* Spoken language; *Color:* No (black & white); *Length:* 55 min.; *Language(s) spoken:* English; *Video type:* V, 3/4U.

DISTRIBUTION & AVAILABILITY: *Copy location:* LCL TOFT Collection; *Call or copy number:* NCOW 27; *Availability:* By appt.

Macbeth. Motion Picture/Abridgment

330. *Macbeth.* (Series: The World of William Shakespeare).

DOCUMENT INFORMATION: *Country:* USA; *Year of release:* 1978.

EDITION, HISTORY, CONTENTS, & EVALUATION: *Edition & history:* One of a series made in cooperation with Station WQED Pittsburgh, Carnegie-Mellon University and The Shakespeare Birthplace Trust, Stratford-upon-Avon (see also 137-8, 331, 564-5, and 715). A companion film, *Fair Is Foul, and Foul Is Fair* (331), offers interesting historical background. *Contents & evaluation:* An abbreviated but nevertheless highly successful screen version of the play. The excellent young actors turn in a splendid performance. In the sleepwalking scene, for example, Lady Macbeth delivers the line, "Who would have thought the old man was so full of blood," with a shattering effect. Inevitably much is missing. There is no scene showing the murder of Banquo. On the other hand, the witches are superb. It is an ambitious, well executed production. Settings, costumes, camera work, color, music, and lighting are all at a three or four star level. The banquet scene is especially effective, as the camera tracks in to reveal Banquo's head at the table, while the non-diegetic score on the sound track provides sonic atmosphere. Indeed the tropes and rhythms of the banquet scene favorably compare with the brilliance of this same scene in the Polanski *Macbeth*. *Audience:* High school (grades 10-12); *Supplementary materials: National Geographic Film Studies Series. Teachers' Guides.* Washington: NGS, 1978; McLean, Andrew. "Educational Films." *SQ* 30 (Summer 1979): 416.

MEDIUM INFORMATION: *Medium:* Motion Picture; *Sound:* Spoken language; *Color:* Yes; *Length:* 36 min.; *Language(s) spoken:* English; *Film type:* 16mm; *Video type:* V, 3/4U.

AUTHORSHIP INFORMATION: *Director(s):* Walsh, Bob; *Cast:* Cast credits not given in print that I saw (KSR).

DISTRIBUTION & AVAILABILITY: *Publisher or re-*sponsible agency: National Geographic; *Distributor:* KAR, NGS, *Copy location:* FOL; *Call or copy number:* MP 96; *Availability:* NGS, sale, 16mm, $353.50 (50290); V, $69.95 (51136); KAR, rental, $42 + .

Macbeth. Motion Picture/Documentary

331. *Fair Is Foul, and Foul Is Fair.* (Series: The World of William Shakespeare).

DOCUMENT INFORMATION: *Country:* USA; *Year of release:* 1978.

EDITION, HISTORY, CONTENTS, & EVALUATION: *Edition & history:* One of a series made in cooperation with Station WQED Pittsburgh, Carnegie-Mellon University and The Shakespeare Birthplace Trust, Stratford-upon-Avon (see also 137-8, 330, 564-5, and 715). A companion film, *Macbeth* (330), provides an abbreviated version of the play. *Contents & evaluation:* Excellent presentation of historical background for *Macbeth*. It opens with an actor speaking the lines from Macbeth's soliloquy, "If it were done," and then by narrative bridges in voiceover moves on to such historical matters as King James's preoccupation with witches, the preaching of homilies on the doctrine of passive obedience, and the twists and turns of the Gunpowder plot, all of which help in full understanding of the play. "Like Faustus, Macbeth sells good for evil," intones the narrator, whose script stresses the powerful presence of evil in the play. It's a handsomely mounted production, a worthy addition to this National Geographic educational series, "The World of William Shakespeare." *Audience:* High school (grades 10-12); *Supplementary materials: National Geographic Film Studies Series. Teachers' Guides.* Washington: NGS, 1978; McLean, Andrew. "Educational Films." *SQ* 30 (Summer 1979): 417.

MEDIUM INFORMATION: *Medium:* Motion Picture; *Sound:* Spoken language; *Color:* Yes; *Length:* 20 min.; *Language(s) spoken:* English; *Film type:* 16mm; *Video type:* V, 3/4U.

AUTHORSHIP INFORMATION: *Director(s):* Walsh, Bob; *Cast:* Cast credits not given in print that I saw (KSR).

DISTRIBUTION & AVAILABILITY: *Publisher or responsible agency:* National Geographic; *Distributor:* KAR, NGS, *Copy location:* FOL; *Call or copy number:* MP 95, Folger; LC #PR2823. 78-700752; *Availability:* NGS, sale, 16mm, $220.50 (50257); V, $59.95 (51064); KAR, rental, $32 + .

Macbeth. Video/Educational

331.1 *Shakespeare's Theatre and Macbeth.*

DOCUMENT INFORMATION: *Country:* USA; *Year of first showing:* 1978.

EDITION, HISTORY, CONTENTS, & EVALUATION: *Edition & history:* An educational film with footage from *Macbeth* distributed by The Institute for Advanced Studies in the Theatre Arts. Features John Blatchley of the RSC directing scenes and analyzing aspects of Shakespearean style. *Contents & evaluation:* Not seen. Information here is from the IAS Catalog. *Supplementary materials:* Companion volume: *Macbeth Unjinxed*, $25 (c), $17.50 (p).

MEDIUM INFORMATION: *Sound:* Spoken language; *Color:* Yes; *Length:* 16 min.; *Video type:* V.

AUTHORSHIP INFORMATION: *Cast:* Blatchley, John, director w. cast.

DISTRIBUTION & AVAILABILITY: *Publisher or responsible agency:* IAS; *Distributor:* IAS, sale $250; rental $40 + shipping.

Macbeth. Video/Interpretation

332. *Macbeth.*

DOCUMENT INFORMATION: *Country:* GB; *Year of filming:* 1978; *Year of release:* 1979; *Country of first showing:* GB; *Location of first showing:* Thames Television International.

EDITION, HISTORY, CONTENTS, & EVALUATION: *Edition & history:* Originally staged in 1976 by Trevor Nunn for the Royal Shakespeare Company, the production was remade by Britain's Thames television in 1978, and aired on 4 Jan. 1979. The TV director was Philip Casson. *Contents & evaluation:* For sound reasons, many critics regard this production as the finest made-for-TV Shakespeare ever done, though it is not so innovative as the 1987 Cambridge *Hamlet.* Through the meta-theatricality of putting the actors in a circle so that they are themselves both actors and audience, the spectators may also imagine themselves to be encircled with them. Adroit camera angles and close-ups enhance the illusion that the screen is a mirror for ourselves rather than a frame for defining the actors. The excessive realism on a tight budget that has proved the iceberg to so many TV Titanics among Shakespeare plays is also avoided. Ritual replaces realism. Costumes are eclectic. They run the gamut from turtle neck sweaters on the Scots lords to a black-leather-and-boots Nazi outfit on Macbeth, and from a tent-like garment and black skullcap on Lady Macbeth, to

an Edwardian business suit for Ross. The result of these alienating costumes is to focus attention back on the emotional riptides generated by the brilliant cast. Ian McKellen's punk-like hairdo, slicked down and greased, gives him a villainous face that is shockingly at odds with the A.C. Bradley concept of a romantic/tragic hero. And Judi Dench as Lady Macbeth, despite the vast folds of her black robes, exudes a sensuality that makes Macbeth's infatuation with his lady plausible. In one close-up, she and Macbeth virtually melt into each other as their fervor vanquishes decorum. By contrast, Griffith Jones as Duncan seems frail and saintly, as though to underscore the evil that drives the Macbeths to crazy excesses. Unlike most *Macbeths*, this one disdains to conceal the uglier side of the ambitious couple. In Ian McKellen's hands, the tragedy of Macbeth becomes the unmasking of Macbeth, the exposure of the man's inner sordidness. Surrounding him with toadies such as a wimpish Ross, who comes across as an effete Osric-like creature, adds even more macabre overtones. Brilliantly, the same actor (Ian McDiarmid) who plays Ross then turns around and doubles as an astonishing Porter, which surely must be one of the most virtuoso performances ever recorded on television. As Prof. Michael Mullin, an expert on the stage history of *Macbeth* has pointed out, the arrangement of actors and audience resulted in the sense that this had more to do with ritual exorcism than with theatre, a "quasi-religious ceremony," as it were (KSR). *Audience:* College and university; General use; *Supplementary materials:* Mullin, Michael. "Stage and Screen: the Trevor Nunn *Macbeth*." *SQ* 38.3 (1987): 350-59.

MEDIUM INFORMATION: *Medium:* Video; *Sound:* Spoken language; *Color:* Yes; *Length:* 120 min.; *Language(s) spoken:* English; *Video type:* V, B, 3/4U.

AUTHORSHIP INFORMATION: *Producer(s):* Nunn, Trevor; Lambert, Verity; *Director(s):* Casson, Philip; *Composer(s):* Woolfenden, Guy; *Designer(s):* Napier, John; Hall, Mike (TV); *Costume designer(s):* Harvey, Lyn; *Lighting designer(s):* Bottone, Luigi; *Cast:* Turner, Fred (Editor); Ford, Julian (Sound); Coombs, Peter (Camera); Thorpe, Sally (Makeup); Woodward, Peter (Fight director); McKellen, Ian (Macbeth); Dench, Judi (Lady Macbeth); Bowen, John (Lennox); Drury, Susan (Third witch/Lady Macduff); Harte, Judith (Second witch/Gentlewoman); Hicks, Greg (Donalbain/Seyton); Howey, David (Sergeant/First Murderer/Doctor); Jones, Griffith (Duncan); Kean, Marie (First Witch); McDiarmid, Ian (Ross/Porter); Peck, Bob (Macduff); Preston, Duncan (Angus); Rees, Roger (Malcolm); Taylor, Zak (Fleance/Messenger); Warner, Stephen (Young Macduff); Woodvine, John (Banquo) [*TVT* 21 Dec. 1978: 69].

DISTRIBUTION & AVAILABILITY: *Publisher or responsible agency:* Thames Television; *Distributor:* FFH, TTI*, *Availability:* B,V ($249); 3/4U ($349); Rental, $125.

Macbeth. **Video/Recording**

333. *Macbeth.*

DOCUMENT INFORMATION: *Country:* USA; *Year of [televison] release:* 1982.

EDITION, HISTORY, CONTENTS, & EVALUATION: *Edition & history:* A recording of a stage play, which ran from 23 January to 8 March, 1981, at Lincoln Center for the Performing Arts, New York City. According to Gianakos' *Television Drama,* it was transmitted on cable television (ARTS) on 3 March 1982. *Contents & evaluation:* "The role of Macbeth is traditionally cast with a 'heroic' actor of imposing stature and weighty vocal character. Philip Anglin, best known for his creation of the deformed Elephant Man in Bernard Pomerance's play, is slender, youthful, handsome, a natural Hamlet (which role he has in fact played). But instead of using his presence to illuminate a fresh theatrical truth, that Macbeth is in large part a lyrical role, and emphasizing the character's brooding, inward torments and flights of poetic vision, he opted for thick, monotonous vocalizing and for the conventional heavy military man, which he did neither very badly nor very well. We were deprived of both the monster and the poet in the role" (Charney, Maurice, "Shakespeare in NYC," *SQ* 33 [Summer 1982]: 222). *Audience:* High school (grades 10-12); College and university; *Supplementary materials:* Coursen, H.R. "*Macbeth.*" SOT 274-75.

MEDIUM INFORMATION: *Medium:* Video; *Sound:* Spoken language; *Color:* Yes; *Length:* 148 min.; *Language(s) spoken:* English; *Video type:* B, V, 3/4U.

AUTHORSHIP INFORMATION: *Producer(s):* Crinkley, Richmond; *Director(s):* Caldwell, Sarah; Browning, Kirk; *Composer(s):* Barnes, Edward; *Designer(s):* Senn, Herbert; Pond, Helen; *Costume designer(s):* Robins, Carrie; *Lighting designer(s):* Gleason, John; *Other personnel:* Barry, B.H. (Stage Combat); *Cast:* Anglim, Philip (Macbeth); Anderman, Maureen (Lady Macbeth); Campbell, J. Kenneth (Macduff); Sperberg, Fritz (Banquo); Vipond, Neil (Duncan); Lee, Kaiulani (Lady Macduff); Vickery, John (Malcolm); Dash, Michael; Gould, Ellen; Cordis, Heard; Ivey, Dana (Witches).

DISTRIBUTION & AVAILABILITY: *Publisher or responsible agency:* Lincoln Center for the Performing Arts; *Distributor:* FFH *Availability:* FFH, B, V, $249; 3/4" U, $349; Rental $65.

Macbeth. **Video/Adaptation**

334. *Toil and Trouble.*

CURRENT PRODUCTION: *Year:* 1982 [?].

DOCUMENT INFORMATION: *Country:* Canada.

EDITION, HISTORY, CONTENTS, & EVALUATION:

Edition & history: Examines what has been called a "controversial" production of *Macbeth* at Winnipeg's Warehouse theatre under the direction of Richard Ouzounian. It follows the production schedule, discussing set and prop designs, the influence of period painting in costume construction, and the work of the actor. *Audience:* General use.

MEDIUM INFORMATION: *Medium:* Motion picture; *Sound:* Spoken language; *Color:* Yes; *Length:* 27 min.; *Language(s) spoken:* English; *Film type:* 16mm.

AUTHORSHIP INFORMATION: *Producer(s):* Manitoba, Dept. of Education Productions and School Broadcasts; *Director(s):* Harris, Neil; *Cast:* Ball, Michael; Innes, John; Willoughby, Leneen.

DISTRIBUTION & AVAILABILITY: *Publisher or responsibie agency:* Manitoba Dept. of Education; *Distributor:* WFG.

Macbeth. **Video/Documentary**

335. *Macbeth.* (Series: Shakespeare in Perspective).

DOCUMENT INFORMATION: *Country:* GB; *Year of release:* 1982.

EDITION, HISTORY, CONTENTS, & EVALUATION: *Edition & history:* The "Shakespeare in Perspective" series was made to accompany the BBC/Time Life Inc. "The Shakespeare Plays" series (see also 44, 142, 234, 269, 411, 566 and 624). For overview, see 44, above. *Contents & evaluation:* Julian Symons, mystery writer, opens his analysis of *Macbeth* with the challenging statement that "I always find the witches in *Macbeth* a problem." From there he goes on to offer some interesting ideas on the resemblance between some notorious modern couples who have committed murders and the Macbeths. There is a delusional condition called "folie a deux" that makes two people setting each other off more lethal than they could ever be acting independently. Some such mental condition triggers the mad behavior of Lady Macbeth and her husband. It is Lady Macbeth who "puts the machine of murder into motion." Curiously all the witches' prophecies turn out to be tricks, as Macbeth discovers to his dismay. The play's greatness lies in its poetry and in its intensity. It is about ambition and greed, and its towering obsessions remind us of Dostoyevsky. Despite the moral collapse of Macbeth and his Lady, though, we still feel sympathy for them. To paraphrase Symons, however, is to do him a disservice. He develops his ideas engagingly against the backdrop of fabled Cawdor and with the help of splendid clips from the extraordinary BBC production starring Nicol Williamson and Jane Lapotaire (KSR).

MEDIUM INFORMATION: *Medium:* Video; *Sound:*

Spoken language; *Color:* Yes; *Length:* 25 min.; *Language(s) spoken:* English; *Video type:* 3/4U, V.

AUTHORSHIP INFORMATION: *Producer(s):* Poole, Victor; *Director(s):* Kirkwood, Sally; *Other personnel:* Crump, Martin (Editor); Tharby, Barrie (Sound); Hooper, John (Camera); Friedman, Liz (Graphics); Bright, Barbara (Prod. asst.); *Cast:* Symons, Julian (Commentator).

DISTRIBUTION & AVAILABILITY: *Publisher or responsible agency:* BBC; *Distributor:* BBC*; FNC, *Availability:* Double cassette (w. *JC*), Rental $50; Quad cassette (w. *Ham., JC, Rom.*), Rental $75.

Macbeth. Video/Teleplay

336. *Macbeth.* (Series: The Shakespeare Plays).

DOCUMENT INFORMATION: *Country:* GB; *Year of filming:* 22-28 June 1982; *Year of first showing:* 1982; *Location of first showing(s):* BBC, London; PBS stations, USA, 17 Oct. 1983.

EDITION, HISTORY, CONTENTS, & EVALUATION: *Edition & history:* The production follows the Peter Alexander edition, with some further alterations by script editor David Snodin. As he explains, the play is already one of Shakespeare's briefest anyway, though for the sake of compression Hecate's two appearances (in 3.5. and 4.1) have been eliminated along with the English Doctor's report on the King's 'evil' (4.3). In addition 3.6. takes place after rather than before 4.1 in order to achieve greater tension (*BSP* 31]). *Contents & evaluation:* Surely no two actors playing Macbeth and his Lady have ever exceeded Nicol Williamson and Jane Lapotaire in sheer dynamism and energy. Next to Williamson's performance, Maurice Evans seems wooden and even Orson Welles somehow wide of the mark. And Jane Lapotaire's rendering of the 'unsex me here' speech defiantly links Lady Macbeth's words with hidden sexual agendas that have traditionally been taboo. Many will misunderstand and dislike the production because of its flouting of stage tradition. Few, however, would deny the extraordinary efforts of the principal actors (KSR). "In this superbly acted production the BBC Shakespeare has fulfilled much of the promise so sadly lacking in its earlier work. Central to its interpretation are several basic production choices. The setting blends a quasi-realistic heath (large boulders and swirling mists and fogs) with a starkly expressionistic castle of angular stone slabs that create an acting space for all the interior scenes. A change of light, a different camera angle, some furniture, and the unit set is transformed from the battlements, where Lady Macbeth reads the letter, to the Macbeths' bedroom, the banqueting hall, the palace courtyard, even into sunny England. . . . The producer and director have obviously thought through the play to offer not just a fresh reading, but a clear cut reimagining . . . the camera's ability to bring us close to Nicol Williamson's perfervid acting makes possible an intensity difficult to imagine in any but the smallest theatre. . . . The staging itself keeps alive a play so familiar on stage and on films that it carries the double jeopardy of outright failure or failure through boring repetition" (Mullin, Michael, "The BBC *Macbeth*," *SFNL* 9.1.[1984]: 2). *Audience:* College and university; *Supplementary materials:* Fenwick, H. *Macbeth. BSP* 19-28; Videotape (25 min.) from "Shakespeare in Perspective" series with Julian Symons as lecturer available in U.K. from BBC*, and in USA from FNC (see 335, above).

MEDIUM INFORMATION: *Medium:* Video; *Sound:* Spoken language; *Color:* Yes; *Length:* 150 min.; *Language(s) spoken:* English; *Video type:* B, V, 3/4U.

AUTHORSHIP INFORMATION: *Producer(s):* Sutton, Shaun; *Director(s):* Gold, Jack; *Adaptor/translator(s):* Snodin, David; *Composer(s):* Davis, Carl; *Designer(s):* Scott, Gerry; *Costume designer(s):* Burdle, Michael; *Lighting designer(s):* Channon, Dennis; *Other personnel:* Stenning, Peter (Prod. manager); Hurdle, Beryl (Director's asst.); Lowden, Fraser (Prod. assoc.); Ranson, Malcolm (Fight arranger); Wilders, John (Literary consultant); Shircore, Jenny (Make-up); Angel, Ray (Sound); *Cast:* Williamson, Nicol (Macbeth); Hogg, Ian (Banquo); Dignam, Mark (Duncan); Hazeldine, James (Malcolm); Bowles, Tom (Donalbain); Doyle, Tony (Macduff); Rowe, John (Lennox); Grainger, Gawn (Ross); Long, Matthew (Menteith); Lyon, David (Angus); Porteous, Peter (Caithness); Henderson, Alistair (Fleance); Abney, William (Siward); Coppin, Nicholas (Young Siward); Boland, Eamon (Seyton); Woodnutt, John (Scottish Doctor); Ellison, Christopher (Captain); Bolam, James (Porter); Leighton, Will (Old Man); Kane, Gordon (First Messenger/Servant); Fulford, Christopher (Second Messenger); Lowe, Barry (First Murderer); Reich, Christopher (Second Murderer); Dunbar, Philip (Third Murderer); Cardiff, Rodney (Fourth Murderer); Lindsay, Mark (Fifth Murderer); Mair, C. (Macduff's Son); Lapotaire, Jane (Lady Macbeth); Baker, Jill (Lady Macduff); Alexander, Denyse (Gentlewoman); Bruce, Brenda (First Witch); Way, Eileen (Second Witch); Dyson, Anne (Third Witch).

DISTRIBUTION & AVAILABILITY: *Publisher or responsible agency:* BBC/TLF; *Distributor:* AVP, UIO, KSU, BBC*, *Copy location:* UVM (Archive), ITM*; *Availability:* AVP, B, V, 3/4U $450 (1987), sale; UIO, V (72058H), 3/4U (70158V), rental, $24.20; KSU, rental, V, 3/4U (1-5 days), $33.75; BBC* 16mm or V, apply (*BUFVC* 13).

Macbeth. Video/Musical

337. *Macbeth.*

DOCUMENT INFORMATION: *Country:* USA; *Year of release:* 1982.

EDITION, HISTORY, CONTENTS, & EVALUATION: *Edition & history:* A rock operatic adaptation of *Macbeth* with considerable fidelity to the original Shakespearean text. *Contents & evaluation:* Essentially this is a recording of a stage production at Howard University with an Afro-American cast. It is vibrant and robust with heavy use of percussion effects. *Audience:* General use.

MEDIUM INFORMATION: *Medium:* Video; *Sound:* Spoken language; *Color:* Yes; *Length:* 120 min.; *Language(s) spoken:* English; *Video type:* V.

AUTHORSHIP INFORMATION: *Producer(s):* Howard University; *Director(s):* Butcher, James W.; *Cast:* Marshall, William; Sidney, Carol Foster; Walker, Joseph A.; Perkins, Anton.

DISTRIBUTION & AVAILABILITY: *Publisher or responsible agency:* Howard University and WHMM TV, Washington, DC; *Copy location:* FOL; *Call or copy number:* VCR.

Macbeth. Video/Recording

337.1 *Play Macbeth.*

DOCUMENT INFORMATION: *Country:* Belgium; *Year of first showing:* 1982.

EDITION, HISTORY, CONTENTS, & EVALUATION: *Edition & history:* Recording of a production at the Raam Theatre, Antwerp.

MEDIUM INFORMATION: *Sound:* Spoken language; *Color:* Yes; *Length:* 120 min.; *Language(s) spoken:* Dutch; *Video type:* V.

AUTHORSHIP INFORMATION: *Producer(s):* Audiovisuele dienst, Katholieke Universiteit, Leuven; *Director(s):* Tillemans, W.; *Adaptor/translator(s):* Kohout, P.; Claus, H.

DISTRIBUTION & AVAILABILITY: *Copy location:* KAL; *Availability:* An agreement with the Department of Literature Sciene, K.U., Leuven and the director is necessary.

Macbeth. Video/Documentary

337.2 *Macbeth.*

DOCUMENT INFORMATION: *Country:* Italy; *Year of first showing:* 1982.

EDITION, HISTORY, CONTENTS, & EVALUATION: *Edition & history:* Video documentary of the rehearsal process of Carmelo Bene's production of *Macbeth* including the first part of the dress rehearsal. Recorded from 22 Oct. to 23 Nov. 1982.

MEDIUM INFORMATION: *Sound:* Spoken language; *Color:* Yes; *Length:* 35 Hours; *Video type:* V.

AUTHORSHIP INFORMATION: *Producer(s):* Videoteca Centro Teatro Ateneo, Rome; *Director(s):* Bene, Carmelo; Muschietti, A. (Video); *Designer(s):* Bene, Carmelo; *Other personnel:* Chessari, R.; Burroni, G. (Sound); Carletti, M. (Lights); Contini, M. (Stage manager); Cabiddu, G. (Video sound); Casaluci, S. (Video technician); *Cast:* Bene, Carmelo; Javicoli, Susanna.

DISTRIBUTION & AVAILABILITY: *Publisher or responsible agency:* Teatro Ateneo, Rome; *Copy location:* VCT*.

Macbeth. Video/Scenes

338. *Macbeth.*

DOCUMENT INFORMATION: *Country:* Netherlands; *Year of release:* 1983.

EDITION, HISTORY, CONTENTS, & EVALUATION: *Edition & history:* A video recording of excerpts from an outdoor performance of *Macbeth* in Holland.

AUTHORSHIP INFORMATION: *Producer(s):* Theatre La Luna; *Director(s):* Geraedts, Canci; *Composer(s):* Lakier, Ward; *Set designer(s):* Bo, Jago; *Cast:* Buddingh, C.; Berenos, Paul; Hermsen, A.

DISTRIBUTION & AVAILABILITY: *Publisher or responsible agency:* Theatre La Luna; *Distributor:* NTI; *Copy location:* NTI; *Call or copy number:* 700140101 BDA.

Macbeth. Motion Picture/Documentary

339. *Macbeth: A Tragedy.*

DOCUMENT INFORMATION: *Country:* GB; *Year of release:* 1983.

EDITION, HISTORY, CONTENTS, & EVALUATION: *Edition & history:* "A comparison of text from the *Oxford Companion to English Literature* with the 'Tomorrow' speech from *Macbeth.* An art school exercise" (*BUFVC*). *Supplementary materials:* BUFVC 15.

MEDIUM INFORMATION: *Sound:* Spoken language; *Color:* Yes; *Length:* 4 min.; *Film type:* 16mm.

AUTHORSHIP INFORMATION: *Producer(s):* Rees-Mogg, Anne.

DISTRIBUTION & AVAILABILITY: *Distributor:* LFM*.

Macbeth. Video/Documentary

339.1 *Macbeth.*

DOCUMENT INFORMATION: *Country:* Italy; *Year of first showing:* 1983.

EDITION, HISTORY, CONTENTS, & EVALUATION: *Edition & history:* Video documentary of the rehearsal process of *Macbeth* directed by Vittorio Gassman of Teatro Ateneo, Verona, Italy, made in March 1983.

MEDIUM INFORMATION: *Sound:* Spoken language; *Color:* Yes; *Length:* 48 hrs.; *Language(s) spoken:* Italian; *Video type:* V, 3/4U.

AUTHORSHIP INFORMATION: *Producer(s):* Videoteca Centro Teatro Ateneo; *Director(s):* Muschietti, A. (Video); *Other personnel:* Casaluci, S. (Sound and filming); *Cast:* Gassman, Vittorio; Guarnieri, Anna Maria; Virgilio, Luciano; Montagna, Carlo; Esposito, Alessandro; De Sandro, Stefano; Ciulli, Sergio; Nisivoccia, Alessandro; Carcasci, Giovanna; Medina, Rodolfo.

DISTRIBUTION & AVAILABILITY: *Copy location:* VCT*.

339.2 *Macbeth.*

DOCUMENT INFORMATION: *Country:* Italy; *Year of first showing:* 1983.

EDITION, HISTORY, CONTENTS, & EVALUATION: *Edition & history:* Video documentary of the dress rehearsal and premiere of *Macbeth*, September 1983, at Teatro Ateneo, Verona, Italy. Presented also at Bottega Teatrale di Firenze; Tietro Manzoni di Milano; Estate Teatrale Veronese Compagnia Teatro Manzon.

MEDIUM INFORMATION: *Sound:* Spoken language; *Color:* Yes; *Length:* 12 hrs.; *Language(s) spoken:* Italian; *Video type:* V, 3/4U.

AUTHORSHIP INFORMATION: *Producer(s):* Centro Teatro Ateneo Productions; *Director(s):* Gassman, Vittorio; *Composer(s):* Gazzola, G.; Esposito, Toni (Percussion); *Designer(s):* Tommasi, P.; *Lighting designer(s):* Saleri, G.; *Other personnel:* Czarnote, L. (Acrobatics); Saura, G. (Sound); *Cast:* Gassman, Vittorio; Guarnieri, Anna Maria; Virgilio, Luciano; Montagna, Carlo; Esposito, Alessandro; De Sandro, Stefano; Ciulli, Sergio; Nisivoccia, Alessandro; Carcasci, Giovanna; Medina, Rodolfo; Gioielli, Lorenzo; Meograossi, Sergio; Grassi, Guiseppe; Lazzareschi, Luca; Bussotti, Fabio; Basile, Sergio; De Girolamo, Danilo; Chiani, Garriella; Tardella, Francesca.

DISTRIBUTION & AVAILABILITY: *Publisher or responsible agency:* Centro Teatro Atenio, Verona; *Copy location:* VCT*.

Macbeth. Video/Interpretation

340. *Macbeth.* (Series: The Bard Series).

DOCUMENT INFORMATION: *Country:* USA; *Year of release:* 1981.

EDITION, HISTORY, CONTENTS, & EVALUATION: *Edition & history:* This production of *Macbeth* in the Bard Productions series features the well known film and TV star, Piper Laurie, as Lady Macbeth. She along with the other members of the cast has been cast to create a Shakespeare production made up of American rather than British actors. *Contents & evaluation:* H.R. Coursen's review was highly unfavorable. His conclusion follows: "At the end, the Weird sisters, who had popped up inconveniently at odd moments throughout this descent into hell, wove their way among the victors, pursued by a fan-blown trail of dry ice. I mention this detail only to prove that I did not cry 'Hold—enough!' sooner. If this is the best that America can do, I understand why the BBC-TV version has been so highly praised. Against the Shakespeare Video Society [Bard] production, the BBC-TV version looks no worse than mediocre" ("Not Fit to Live," *SFNL* 13.1 [Dec. 1988]: 4). *Audience:* High school (grades 10-12); College and university.

MEDIUM INFORMATION: *Medium:* Video; *Sound:* Spoken language; *Color:* Yes; *Length:* 150 min.; *Language(s) spoken:* English; *Video type:* B, V.

AUTHORSHIP INFORMATION: *Producer(s):* Bard Productions; *Director(s):* Seidelman, Arthur Alan; *Cast:* Brett, Jeremy (Macbeth); Laurie, Piper (Lady Macbeth); MacCorkindale, Simon (Macduff); Alfieri, Richard (Malcolm); Perkins, Millie (Lady Macduff); Primus, Barry (Banquo); Oppenheimer, Alan (Duncan); Seales, Franklyn (Lennox); Robinson, Jay (Porter); Stockton, Brad David (Ross); Mitty, Nomi; Mayenzet, Maria; Wright, Eugenia (Witches); Waxman, Stanley (Siward); Crawford, Johnny (Seyton); Augenstein, Michael (Donalbain); Kaback, Douglas (Fleance); Persons, Philips (Menteith); Cook, Fredric (Caithness); Aberdeen, Robert (Young Siward); Papais, John (Angus); Prager, Tim (Sergeant); Mandell, Alan (Doctor); Bozian, James; Lieber, Shawn; Hirokane, David (Apparitions); Piper, Jim; Asner, Roy (Messengers); Bisig, Gary; Fortus, Daniel (Murderers); Jaffe, Elliot (Macduff's son); Burger, Julie (Gentlewoman).

DISTRIBUTION & AVAILABILITY: *Publisher or responsible agency:* Bard Productions Ltd.; *Distributor:* ILL, FCM, TWC, DCV, *Availability:* ILL, sale, V (S 00551) $89.95; FCM, sale, V $89.95; TWC, sale, apply; DCV, sale, V (#84151) $95 (1987); INM, V, $99.

Macbeth. Motion Picture/Documentary

341. *Power and Corruption.*

DOCUMENT INFORMATION: *Country:* GB; *Year of release:* 1984.

EDITION, HISTORY, CONTENTS, & EVALUATION: *Edition & history:* An edited version of Polanki's 1971 *Macbeth* with commentary by Orson Welles. Relates

Shakespeare's "treatment of power and corruption to that of other writers including William Golding in *Lord of the Flies* and Marlowe in *Dr. Faustus*" (*BUFVC*). *Supplementary materials:* BUFVC 15.

MEDIUM INFORMATION: *Length:* 34 min.

AUTHORSHIP INFORMATION: *Director(s):* Polanski, Roman; *Cast:* Welles, Orson (Narrator); and cast of Polanski film.

DISTRIBUTION & AVAILABILITY: *Distributor:* EFV*.

Macbeth. **Video/Documentary**

342. *The Scottish Tragedy.*

DOCUMENT INFORMATION: *Country:* GB; *Year of release:* 1984.

EDITION, HISTORY, CONTENTS, & EVALUATION: *Edition & history:* Shows the hazards of going out on location with a film, presumably exacerbated when the film is *Macbeth.* Among theatre people *Macbeth* is often superstitiously regarded as a notoriously unlucky show. Theatre legend is full of horror stories about assorted disasters accompanying its production. Most recently the Glenda Jackson/Christopher Plummer 1988 *Macbeth,* though a commercial success on the Broadway stage, endured more than its share of misfortunes, according to press accounts. An absorbing murder mystery by Marvin Kaye, *Bullets for Macbeth* (New York: Dutton, 1976) capitalizes on this tradition of hard luck. *Supplementary materials:* BUFVC 15.

MEDIUM INFORMATION: *Length:* 30 min.

AUTHORSHIP INFORMATION: *Director(s):* Crisp, Mike.

DISTRIBUTION & AVAILABILITY: *Distributor:* BBC*.

Macbeth. **Video/Ballet**

343. *Macbeth.*

DOCUMENT INFORMATION: *Country:* USSR; *Year of release:* 1984.

EDITION, HISTORY, CONTENTS, & EVALUATION: *Edition & history:* A videotaping of a "free dance interpretation of the Shakespearean tragedy" by The Bolshoi Ballet. *Supplementary materials:* Novacom Video Inc. catalog.

MEDIUM INFORMATION: *Length:* 105 min.

AUTHORSHIP INFORMATION: *Director(s):* Mansurov, Fuat (Conductor); *Choreographer(s):* Vasiliev, Vladimir.

DISTRIBUTION & AVAILABILITY: *Distributor:* NOV, FCM, *Availability:* NOV, B, V $58.

Macbeth. **Video/Documentary**

343.1 *Il Macbeth nascosto*

DOCUMENT INFORMATION: *Country:* Italy; *Year of first showing:* 1984.

EDITION, HISTORY, CONTENTS, & EVALUATION: *Edition & history:* Two tapes that represent an edited version of the rehearsal process, using the video documentation made during the rehearsal of Vittorio Gassman's *Macbeth* with Compagnia Teatro Manzoni, Rome. See 339.1 and 339.2, above. Part One: Author and Director.; Part Two: Lady Macbeth: Rehearsal and Performance.

MEDIUM INFORMATION: *Sound:* Spoken language; *Color:* Yes; *Length:* 60 min. (Part One); 60 min. (Part Two); *Language(s) spoken:* Italian; *Video type:* V, 3/4U.

AUTHORSHIP INFORMATION: *Producer(s):* Marotti, Ferruccio; Valentini, Valentin (Curator); *Director(s):* Muschietti, A.; Marotti, F.; *Other personnel:* Casaluci, S. (Audio); Muschietti, A. (Editing); *Cast:* Gassman, Vittorio; Guarnieri, Anna Maria (See also credits in 339.1, 339.2, above).

DISTRIBUTION & AVAILABILITY: *Publisher or responsible agency:* Videoteca Centro Teatre Ateneo, Rome; *Copy location:* VCT*.

Macbeth. **Video/Documentary**

343.2 *The Macbeth of Carmelo Bene*

DOCUMENT INFORMATION: *Country:* Italy; *Year of first showing:* 1985.

EDITION, HISTORY, CONTENTS, & EVALUATION: *Edition & history:* A video documentary in two parts of the rehearsal process of Carmelo Bene's *Macbeth.* Part One: Concerto for a Solo Author; Part Two: The Performance Process.

MEDIUM INFORMATION: *Sound:* Spoken language; *Color:* Yes; *Length:* 79 min. (Part One); 70 min. (Part Two); *Language(s) spoken:* Italian; *Video type:* V, 3/4U.

AUTHORSHIP INFORMATION: *Producer(s):* Marotti, Ferruccio; Grande, Maurizio (Curator); *Director(s):* Muschietti, A.; *Other personnel:* Cabbidu, G. (Sound); Casaluci, S. (Audio); Conforti, A. (Editing); *Cast:* Bene, Carmelo; Javicoli, Susanna.

DISTRIBUTION & AVAILABILITY: *Publisher or responsible agency:* Centro Teatro Ateneo, Rome; *Copy location:* VCT*.

Macbeth. **Video/Recording**

344. *Shogun Macbeth.*

DOCUMENT INFORMATION: *Country:* USA; *Year of first showing:* 1986.

EDITION, HISTORY, CONTENTS, & EVALUATION: *Edition & history:* A Japanese adaptation by John R. Briggs. It was videotaped at Playhouse 46 on December 5, 1986. A copy is housed in the TOFT (Theatre on Film and Tape) Collection at the Library of Performing Arts, Lincoln Center, New York Public Library. It may be viewed by appointment (see below). *Contents & evaluation:* Not seen. *Audience:* College and university; General use.

MEDIUM INFORMATION: *Medium:* Video; *Sound:* Spoken language; *Color:* Yes; *Length:* 125 min.; *Language(s) spoken:* English; *Video type:* V.

AUTHORSHIP INFORMATION: *Producer(s):* Pan Asian Repertory; *Director(s):* Briggs, John R.

DISTRIBUTION & AVAILABILITY: *Copy location:* LCL TOFT Collection; *Call or copy number:* Not known; *Availability:* By appt.

Macbeth. **Video/Documentary**

345. *Macbeth: Reflections.*

DOCUMENT INFORMATION: *Country:* GB; *Year of release:* 198[?].

EDITION, HISTORY, CONTENTS, & EVALUATION: *Edition & history:* A five-part (25 min. each) production that "relates some of the themes of *Macbeth* to the realities of the twentieth century" (*BUFVC*). *Supplementary materials: BUFVC* 14.

MEDIUM INFORMATION: *Sound:* Spoken language; *Color:* Yes; *Length:* 125 min.

AUTHORSHIP INFORMATION: *Director(s):* Thames TV.

DISTRIBUTION & AVAILABILITY: *Distributor:* TTI*.

Macbeth. **Motion Picture/Documentary**

346. *Art of Persuasion: A Different Approach to English Literature.*

DOCUMENT INFORMATION: *Country:* GB; *Year of release:* 19[?].

EDITION, HISTORY, CONTENTS, & EVALUATION: *Edition & history:* A pedagogical film in which four actor/teachers discuss ways of teaching *Macbeth* to school children. *Supplementary materials: BUFVC* 14.

MEDIUM INFORMATION: *Sound:* Spoken language; *Color:* Yes; *Length:* 37 min.; *Film type:* 16mm.

DISTRIBUTION & AVAILABILITY: *Publisher or responsible agency:* Scottish Central Film Library; *Distributor:* SFL*.

Macbeth. **Video/Opera**

346.1 *Macbeth.*

DOCUMENT INFORMATION: *Country:* Italy/Germany; *Year of first showing:* 19 ?.

EDITION, HISTORY, CONTENTS, & EVALUATION: *Edition & history:* A recording of a performance at Deutsche Opera of Verdi's *Macbeth*, available from FNC.

MEDIUM INFORMATION: *Length:* 150 min.

AUTHORSHIP INFORMATION: *Director(s):* Sinopoli, Guiseppe; *Composer(s):* Verdi, Guiseppe; *Designer(s):* Camiani, Luciano; *Cast:* Bruson, Renata; Zampieri, Mara.

DISTRIBUTION & AVAILABILITY: *Publisher or responsible agency:* RM Arts; *Distributor:* FNC, FCM, V, $49.95.

Measure for Measure

ORIGINAL WORK AND PRODUCTION: Dark Comedy. *Year of first production:* 1604; *Site of first production:* Whitehall Palace.

Measure for Measure. Film/Abbreviated

347. *Dente per dente.*

DOCUMENT INFORMATION: *Country:* Italy; *Year of release:* 1913.

EDITION, HISTORY, CONTENTS, & EVALUATION: *Edition & history:* Professor Ball thinks that this film may be connected to Shakespeare's play only by its title. The Weisbaden filmography offers the information without comment. *Supplementary materials:* SIF 102; Ball, *SOSF* 164.

MEDIUM INFORMATION: *Length:* 31 min.

AUTHORSHIP INFORMATION: *Director(s):* Latium film; *Cast:* Vassallo, Mignon; Gauthier, Lidia.

DISTRIBUTION & AVAILABILITY: *Distributor:* Lost.

Measure for Measure. Motion Picture/Interpretation

348. *Dente per dente.* [*Measure for Measure*].

DOCUMENT INFORMATION: *Country:* Italy; *Year of release:* 1942.

EDITION, HISTORY, CONTENTS, & EVALUATION: *Edition & history:* No one except Professor Ball seems to know very much about this Italian film, which Peter Morris categorizes as "lost." It was screened courtesy of the US distributor (Jack Hoffberg) by Professor Ball in New York City on Sept. 8, 1948. The credits given here are taken from the notes in the Ball Collection at the Folger Library. *Contents & evaluation:* Not seen. Professor Ball saw the film as a loose adaptation of Shakespeare's play retaining the broad outline of the plot but not a great deal of the dialogue. *Audience:* General use.

MEDIUM INFORMATION: *Medium:* Motion Picture; *Sound:* Spoken language; *Color:* No (black & white); *Length:* 90 min.; *Language(s) spoken:* English; *Film type:* 35mm.

AUTHORSHIP INFORMATION: *Producer(s):* F.E.R.T. Studios, Turin, Italy; Della Monia, U.; Gentile, Y. *Director(s):* Della Monia, U.; *Screenplay writer(s):* Usellini, Gugliemi; Ribulsi, Errico; *Composer(s):* D'Archiardi, Franco; *Designer(s):* Filippone, P.; *Costume designer(s):* Senzani, Prof. G.; *Lighting designer(s):* Marzari, E. A.; Villa, G.; *Other personnel:* Paliero, E. M.; Sable, U. (Sound); Sansoni, M. (Editor); *Cast:* Boratto, Caterina; Tamberlani, Carlo; Varelli, Alfredo; Corradi, Nelly; Silvani, Aldo; Chellini, Amelia; Baseggio, Cesco; Bragaglia, Arturo; Nazzoni, J.; Benossi, Meno; Picasso, Lamberto; Cellino, Fredrico; Ermelli, Claudio.

DISTRIBUTION & AVAILABILITY: *Publisher or re-*

sponsible agency: Artists Assoc./Atlas Film/S.E.F.M. Rome.

Measure for Measure. Video/Teleplay

349. *Zweierlei mass*

DOCUMENT INFORMATION: *Country:* German Fed. Republic; *Year of release:* 1963.

EDITION, HISTORY, CONTENTS, & EVALUATION: *Supplementary materials: SIF* 103; Morris, *SHOF* 24.

MEDIUM INFORMATION: *Length:* 145 min.

AUTHORSHIP INFORMATION: *Director(s):* Verhoeven, Paul; *Cast:* Caninenberg, Hans (Vincentio); Blumhagen, Lothar (Angelo); Berliner, Martin (Escalus); Schumann, Erik (Claudio); Weis, Heidelinde (Isabella).

Measure for Measure. Video/Teleplay

350. *Measure for Measure.* (Series: The Shakespeare Plays).

DOCUMENT INFORMATION: *Country:* GB; *Year of first showing:* 1978; *Location of first showing(s):* BBC, London; PBS stations, USA, 4 Nov. 1979.

EDITION, HISTORY, CONTENTS, & EVALUATION: *Edition & history:* Desmond Davis' *Measure for Measure* proved to be the runaway favorite of the audience for the first year of "The Shakespeare Plays" series on North American PBS stations. In view of the play's relative obscurity that was surprising in one way but totally predictable in another. The director was not working in the shadow of past cinematic behemoths, such as Olivier's *Henry V* or Zeffirelli's *Romeo and Juliet.* Davis also grabbed every chance to make the production fit the small screen of television. His *Measure for Measure* identifies with, though in more subtle and complex ways, the ethical dilemmas and emotional roller coasters of the daytime soaps. Add to that, brilliant lighting, superbly designed sets, fine acting by Kate Nelligan and Tim Pigott-Smith, and success was inevitable. *Contents & evaluation:* "Of the three principal roles, the Duke's is the most difficult. Unfortunately, Kenneth Colley's interpretation does little to clarify the part, making its inconsistencies all the more glaring. This Vincentio has no ducal presence. He appears uncomfortable on his throne and his eyes shift nervously as he delivers his opening lines, thus weakening the formality of the play's opening speech. Accordingly (and also because of Angelo's youth), the Duke's withdrawal from power seems even less reasonable than it does in the text. . . . Colley's Duke certainly does not fit G. Wilson Knight's conception of the role as a figure of divine providence, nor does he

seem especially a 'duke of dark corners.' The Duke instead seems incongruously insecure. He appears stunned by Angelo's decision to execute Claudio despite the bed trick, and his conversations with Lucio and Escalus reveal a man who most wants to hear good things about himself. Listening to Lucio's slanders, Colley seems to crave Escalus' compensating praise. His pithy sayings are hastily delivered, as he puzzles over his experiences, seeking some formula to explain them. Colley is most convincing as the Friar; when he returns to the princely role at the play's conclusion, he still looks uncomfortable with power. His offhand proposal to Isabella gives no assurance that Vienna will now have a better regime" (Carr, Virginia, "The Shakespeare Plays," *SFNL* 4.1 [1979]: 4). *Audience:* College and university; General use; *Supplementary materials:* Andrews, John F. "*Measure for Measure.*" *TSH* 105-24; Videotape (25 min.) from "Shakespeare in Perspective" series with John Mortimer as lecturer available in U.K. from BBC* (*BUFVC* 15).

MEDIUM INFORMATION: *Medium:* Video; *Sound:* Spoken language; *Color:* Yes; *Length:* 150 min.; *Video type:* B;V, 3/4U.

AUTHORSHIP INFORMATION: *Producer(s):* Messina, Cedric; *Director(s):* Davis, Desmond; *Adaptor/translator(s):* Shallcross, Alan; *Composer(s):* Lloyd-Jones, David; Tyler, James (w. London Early Music Group); *Designer(s):* Walker, Stuart; *Costume designer(s):* Barrow, Odette; *Lighting designer(s):* Barclay, Sam; *Cast:* Colley, Kenneth (Duke); Nelligan, Kate (Isabella); Pigott-Smith, Tim (Angelo); Strauli, Christopher (Claudio); McEnery, John (Lucio); Pearce, Jacqueline (Mariana); Middlemass, Frank (Pompey); Armstrong, Alun (Provost); Corri, Adrienne (Overdone); Jones, Ellis (Elbow); Clegg, John (Froth); Sleigh, William (Barnardine); McCarthy, Neil (Abhorson); Palfrey, Yolande (Juliet); Page, Eileen (Francisca); Stoney, Kevin (Escalus); Jackman, Godfrey (Friar Thomas); Tucker, Alan (First Gentleman); Abbott, John (Second Gentleman); Browning, David (Justice); Cousins, Geoffrey (Servant); Lassman, David; Friel, Tony; Jones, Harry; Sarbutt, John; Tudor, Nicholas (Pageboys).

DISTRIBUTION & AVAILABILITY: *Publisher or responsible agency:* BBC/TLF; *Distributor:* AVP, UIO, KSU, BBC*, *Copy location:* UVM; *Availability:* AVP, sale, $450 all formats (1987); UIO, V (72040H), 3/4U (70140V), rental $23.20; KSU, rental, 5 days, $33.75; BBC* 16mm or V, apply.

Measure for Measure. Video/Documentary

351. *Shakespeare: Measure for Measure: Workshops I and II.* (Series: Open University Film Library).

DOCUMENT INFORMATION: *Country:* GB; *Year of release:* 1985.

EDITION, HISTORY, CONTENTS, & EVALUATION: *Edition & history:* One of several programs prepared for the Open University television programs in Great Britain. Not seen in the U.S. According to the *BUFVC* catalog, each program features a director leading one of the actors through his/her role. In this program, director John Russell Brown shows that Isabella is far more complicated than the priggish moralist that she is usually thought to be. The focus is on Act II, scene ii when Isabella comes to plead with Angelo for Claudio's life. In the second workshop, the scene shifts to III, i, when she informs her brother, Claudio, to his discomfiture, that she considers her maidenhead more precious than his head. *Audience:* College and university; Professional; *Supplementary materials: BUFVC* 16.

MEDIUM INFORMATION: *Medium:* Video; *Sound:* Spoken language; *Color:* Yes; *Length:* 24 min. (each workshop); *Language(s) spoken:* English; *Video type:* V,B.

AUTHORSHIP INFORMATION: *Producer(s):* Hoyle, David; *Cast:* Brown, John Russell (Dir.); Agutter, Jenny (Isabella); Thomas, Michael (Angelo); Yelland, David (Claudio).

DISTRIBUTION & AVAILABILITY: *Publisher or responsible agency:* BBC Open University; *Distributor:* GSV*, *Copy location:* BBC; *Availability:* Sale or rental in Great Britain only.

Measure for Measure. Video/Scenes

352. *The Shakespeare Hour.*

DOCUMENT INFORMATION: *Country:* GB/USA; *Year of release:* 1985.

EDITION, HISTORY, CONTENTS, & EVALUATION: *Edition & history:* The series, "The Shakespeare Hour," was shown on national educational television beginning on January 5, 1985 (see also 5, 276, 417, 663). For further commentary, see *Measure for Measure,* directed by Desmond Davis, 1978 (350), and *All's Well* (5). *Audience:* High school (grades 10-12); College and university; General use; *Supplementary materials:* Quinn, *TSH.*

MEDIUM INFORMATION: *Medium:* Video; *Sound:* Spoken language; *Color:* Yes; *Length:* 180 min.; *Language(s) spoken:* English; *Video type:* V.

AUTHORSHIP INFORMATION: *Producer(s):* BBC-WNET/THIRTEEN; *Director(s):* Moshinsky, Elijah; Johnson, Donald; Kieffer, Tom; Bellin, Harvey (WNET); *Screenplay writer(s):* Cavendar, Kenneth; *Other personnel:* Squerciati, Marie Therese (Project director); *Cast:* Matthau, Walter; Cast of BBC/Time Life *Measure for Measure,* directed by Desmond Davis (q.v.).

DISTRIBUTION & AVAILABILITY: *Publisher or responsible agency:* WNET/THIRTEEN; *Distributor:* ALS.

The Merchant of Venice

ORIGINAL WORK AND PRODUCTION: Social Comedy. *Year of first production:* [c.] 1594; *Site of first production:* The Theatre in Shoreditch.

The Merchant of Venice. **Motion Picture/Title Only**

353. *Le miroir de Venise : Une mesaventure de Shylock.*
DOCUMENT INFORMATION: *Country:* France; *Year of release:* 1902.

EDITION, HISTORY, CONTENTS, & EVALUATION: *Edition & history:* Worth recording simply because this lost film is yet another "Shakespeare" production by Georges Méliès, the pioneer filmmaker. R.H. Ball thinks, however, that the film may have had very little to do with Shakespeare's play. Possibly Méliès was only borrowing the title. *Supplementary materials:* SIF 88; Ball, *SOSF* 34.

MEDIUM INFORMATION: *Length:* 2 min. [?].

AUTHORSHIP INFORMATION: *Director(s):* Méliès, Georges; *Cast:* Méliès, Georges.

The Merchant of Venice. **Motion Picture/Abridged**

354. *The Merchant of Venice.*
DOCUMENT INFORMATION: *Country:* USA; *Year of release:* 1908.

EDITION, HISTORY, CONTENTS, & EVALUATION: *Edition & history:* One of several Vitagraph one-reel Shakespeare films made in New York City and its environs at the dawn of the motion picture industry. Producer J. Stuart Blackton recruited William V. Ranous, a New York Shakespearean actor, to direct Shakespeare films. As R.H. Ball points out (*SOSF* 41), after Ranous' departure for the new Carle Laemmle IMP company, production of Shakespeare films at Vitagraph precipitously dropped (KSR). *Supplementary materials:* Ball, *SOSF* 50-51.

MEDIUM INFORMATION: *Sound:* Silent; *Color:* No (black & white); *Length:* 10 min.

AUTHORSHIP INFORMATION: *Director(s):* Ranous, William; *Cast:* Gordon, Julia (Portia).

355. *Il mercante di Venezia.*

DOCUMENT INFORMATION: *Country:* Italy; *Year of release:* 1910.

EDITION, HISTORY, CONTENTS, & EVALUATION: *Edition & history:* A film made in Italy by Film d'Arte Italiana, which was a kind of rival to the French Film d'Art. As with the French movie makers, the object of the Italians was to make films based on major literary works featuring well known actors. *Contents & evaluation:* The first title card of this beautifully tinted film somewhat skews the thrust of the drama from Shakespeare's original intention: "Lorenzo who is in love with Jessica, daughter of Shylock, the Jew, arranges to come for her." From there on to the end, the movie should rightly be re-titled, "Daughter of Shylock," as the emphasis falls more on Jessica and Lorenzo and less on the central bond plot. Even so this is a vivid, well acted Shylock with a long beard and a dark gown, who is visibly distraught over the loss of his daughter. An important innovation is the use of exterior, location shots. The streets and canals of Venice seem to be the real thing. A rather plump Portia is shown at an ornate domicile in Belmont, and shortly afterward an explanatory title card reads "Portia disguised as a lawyer saves Antonio." And indeed she does, in a trial scene that faithfully reproduces the stage convention of an intensely cruel and obsessed Shylock, who gloatingly whets his knife in the foreground during the trial's preliminaries (almost exactly as it was staged nearly 80 years later in 1988 at the Barbican RSC production and in the 1990 Dustin Hoffman production in New York). When Portia reads the bond, the camera cuts to a page from the Venetian statutes, in an interesting bit of analytical editing, to show the penalty for shedding Christian blood. Shylock, thus condemned through both image and word, laments the bitterness of his fate as the film abruptly ends. This in most respects is an excellent film with good editing, clear lighting, and exciting exterior shots, though of course severely truncated. What it lacks in subtlety, it attempts to compensate for with visual energy. Available for archival screening at the NFA in London (KSR). *Supplementary materials:* Ball, *SOSF* 122-4; *SIF,* 88.

MEDIUM INFORMATION: *Sound:* Silent; *Color:* Yes; *Length:* 8 min.; *Film type:* 35mm.

AUTHORSHIP INFORMATION: *Director(s):* Lo Savio, Gerolamo [?]; *Cast:* Novelli, Ermete (Shylock); Bertini, Francesca (Portia).

DISTRIBUTION & AVAILABILITY: *Copy location:* NFA*.

356. *The Merchant of Venice.*

DOCUMENT INFORMATION: *Country:* USA; *Year of release:* 1912.

EDITION, HISTORY, CONTENTS, & EVALUATION: *Edition & history:* One of the Thanhouser films that were the most distinguished examples of the silent Shakespeare film in North America. Edwin and Gertrude Thanhouser were committed Shakespeareans whose goal was to transfer the text to the screen with as much integrity as possible. Unfortunately most of their films seem to have been lost (KSR). *Supplementary materials:* Ball, *SOSF* 146; *SIF* 88.

MEDIUM INFORMATION: *Length:* 30 min.

AUTHORSHIP INFORMATION: *Director(s):* O'Neil, Barry; *Cast:* Bowman, William J. (Shylock); La Badie, Florence (Portia).

357. *Shylock, ou le more de Venise.* [*The Merchant of Venice*].

DOCUMENT INFORMATION: *Country:* France; *Year of release:* 1913.

EDITION, HISTORY, CONTENTS, & EVALUATION: *Edition & history:* This French, 1913 silent version of *Merchant of Venice* was one of the last of the so-called Film d'Art movies, in which an attempt was made to transfer stage classics to the screen. Unfortunately they were often too stagy and static to make good films. On the other hand, they nudged Americans into making films longer than one reel and they polished the tarnished image of movies with a cultural sheen. *Contents & evaluation:* This adaptation of *Merchant* is an abbreviated but intelligent film that re-represents the play in an effective cinematic text. Unlike the Fellner version, it does not privilege the Jessica plot at all, but simply drops her from the narrative altogether. Exterior shots of Venice take on the atmosphere of a sketch for a Canaletto painting. The film's strongest Shakespearean echoes are in the casket sequences, which are carried out within the solid confines (no painted sets here) of Portia's lavish Belmont villa. The title cards suggest how the play's thematic values remain embedded in the film text. With a kind of Bradley-ian majesty an explanatory foreword sets the tone: "Who among us has not in imagination lived with the characters of Shakespeare's immortal drama—portraying as they do, the great elemental qualities of life itself?" (no anxiety here that the text may not represent anything but itself). Then again, as the faces of the key players appear on screen, further information is released: "The friendship of Bassanio and Antonio—one of the finest tributes on the loyalty of man to man that has ever been written. According to Venetian law a bond cannot be altered without danger to the state" (no anxiety here that their relationship might be in some way perverse). And of course Shylock emerges as "the crafty money lender who for centuries has stood forth as a living symbol of cunning and greed" (no anxiety here in this age of innocence about the anti-Semitism that led to Hitler's death camps). It is ironic that Harry Baur (1880-1943), the distinguished French actor who played Shylock, should himself have been tortured by the Gestapo in a French prison. He died a few days after his release (Katz, 90). The film, in other words, allows glimpses of the ideology of its makers as much as into the systems of discourse for appropriating Shakespeare's text for the silver screen. A powerful theatrical influence residually persists in the opening credits of the NFA copy, where much is made of Harry Baur's association with the Athenian Theatre, Jean Hervé's with the Odeon, and Mlle. Pépa Bonafé's with the Apollo (KSR). *Audience:* General use; *Supplementary materials:* Ball, *SOSF* 177-83; 348.

MEDIUM INFORMATION: *Medium:* Motion Picture; *Sound:* Silent; *Color:* No (black & white); *Length:* 33 min.; *Language of subtitles:* English; *Film type:* 16mm.

AUTHORSHIP INFORMATION: *Producer(s):* Eclipse; *Director(s):* Desfontaines, Henri; *Cast:* Baur, Harry (Shylock); Hervé, Jean (Bassanio); Bonafé, Pépa (Portia); Joubé, Romuald (Antonio).

DISTRIBUTION & AVAILABILITY: *Publisher or responsible agency:* Eclipse/George Kleine; *Copy location:* FOL, NFA; *Call or copy number:* FOL MP 29.

The Merchant of Venice. Motion Picture/Adaptation

358. *The Merchant of Venice.*

DOCUMENT INFORMATION: *Country:* USA; *Year of release:* 1914.

EDITION, HISTORY, CONTENTS, & EVALUATION: *Edition & history:* An ambitious silent film produced by the Carl Laemmle organization as a Universal Special Feature. *Supplementary materials:* Ball, *SOSF* 206-7; *SIF* 88; H&M, 26.

MEDIUM INFORMATION: *Length:* 40 min.

AUTHORSHIP INFORMATION: *Director(s):* Weber, Lois; Smalley, Phillips; *Cast:* Smalley, Phillips (Shylock); Weber, Lois (Portia).

The Merchant of Venice. Motion Picture/Abridgment

359. *The Merchant of Venice.*

DOCUMENT INFORMATION: *Country:* GB; *Year of release:* 1916.

EDITION, HISTORY, CONTENTS, & EVALUATION: *Edition & history:* "Typical" of British silent film in the sense that it leaned heavily on the London theatre. The entire cast of the St. James Theatre production was persuaded by the Broadwest Film Company to allow the production to be photographed pretty much "as is." The print at the Folger is incomplete (there may not be a complete print anywhere). It abuptly ends as the trial scene begins with Portia's query: "Is your name Shylock?" It further shows the vogue for putting the *Merchant of Venice* on screen in an era that was still innocent of the virulent anti-Semitism of Hitler's Europe. *Contents & evaluation:* The *Merchant of Venice* is a play of so many subtexts that it should come as no surprise that an abridged silent film version can represent only a part of the whole. Jessica and Shylock get the lion's share of attention, perhaps because of the timelessness of the ungrateful child motif (brought to a peak in *King Lear*). The director thoroughly understood the significance of the ring that Jessica sold for a

monkey and how her father, unlike the young Christian merchants, would not have traded off so sacred an icon for the whole world. Shylock, despite his surface unpleasantness, possesses integrity made out of granite. That trope is brilliantly expressed with a cutaway from a grieving Shylock to a roistering Jessica. Shylock comes into his own with his famous speech, "Hath not a Jew?," which is given in full in the dialogue cards. In its increasing concern about the mistreatment of Shylock, the film edges toward current liberal humanitarianism, but then Shylock undercuts that mood with his harsh rejection of any compromise at the beginning of the trial scene (KSR). *Audience:* General use; *Supplementary materials:* Ball, *SOSF* 245-52; 366-7.

MEDIUM INFORMATION: *Medium:* Motion Picture; *Sound:* Silent; *Color:* No (black & white); *Length:* 21 min.; *Language of subtitles:* English; *Film type:* 16mm.

AUTHORSHIP INFORMATION: *Producer(s):* Broadwest; *Director(s):* West, Walter; *Cast:* Lang, Matheson (Shylock); Britton, Hutin (Portia); O'Brien, Terence (Tubal); Jones, Kathleen Hazel (Jessica); Morgan, George (Launcelot); Caselli, Ernest (Lorenzo); Tozer, J.R. (Bassanio).

DISTRIBUTION & AVAILABILITY: *Publisher or responsible agency:* Broadwest; *Copy location:* FOL; *Call or copy number:* MP 77.

The Merchant of Venice. Motion Picture/Scene

360. *Trial Scene.*

DOCUMENT INFORMATION: *Country:* GB; *Year of release:* 1922.

EDITION, HISTORY, CONTENTS, & EVALUATION: *Edition & history:* Uniquely appears in the Eckert filmography. *Supplementary materials:* Eckert, *FSF* 171.

MEDIUM INFORMATION: *Length:* 10 min.

AUTHORSHIP INFORMATION: *Director(s):* Masters Films; *Cast:* Thorndike, Sybil; Berlyn, Ivan.

The Merchant of Venice. Motion Picture/Derivative

361. *Der Kaufmann von Venedig: The Jew of Mestri.* [*The Merchant of Venice*].

DOCUMENT INFORMATION: *Country:* Germany; *Year of first showing:* 1923; re-edited and released abroad, 1926.

EDITION, HISTORY, CONTENTS, & EVALUATION: *Edition & history:* This is a rather free adaptation of Shakespeare's play, with debts to the source, *Il Pecorone*. There is a complicated history behind this 1923 film which was re-edited and released to the English-speaking world as *The Jew of Mestri* in 1926. Produced in Germany during the height of the film renaissance following WW I, it featured superstars Werner Krauss (Iago with Emil Jannings in the Buchowetzki *Othello*) and Henny Porten (leading German actress) as Portia. Cast credits as given here are from the German Film Institute but R.H. Ball's account should be consulted also, as the German and English versions contain bewildering variants. In general, the narrative focuses more directly on the woes of Jessica ("Rachela" in this version) than on Portia ("the Lady of Belmont"). *Contents & evaluation:* It may not be, as R.H. Ball suggests, "good Shakespeare" but it is certainly a good film, one of the best Shakespeare silents. Paradoxically no Shakespeare film can be true to its source if it does not recreate Shakespeare's text within the configurations of its own system of visual discourse. If forced to choose between servility and independence, a director may well prefer the latter. Ambitious location shots of Venice with analytical closeups of feeding pigeons, city clocks, market stalls, and canals establish an authentic atmosphere. The German expressionistic delight in vast interior shots also surfaces in the great hall in Belmont and in the mammoth trial scene. These ambitious settings, with the complicated lighting patterns, echo the influence of Max Reinhardt, who was in turn under the spell of Arthur Gordon Craig, the English theatrical genius. The editing is sophisticated, with skilful intercutting between the barren world of the moneylender and the carefree world of the young merchants. Henny Porten's Russian wolfhounds suggest a Portia with grace, power, and elegance. A wonderful sequence has a grieving Shylock searching his bleak house for Rachela with crosscutting to the jubilant mob caught up in the carnivalesque spirit of Venice. As he reels outside, the maskers swirl around him, depart, and leave him to stagger toward the entrance to his house, where he collapses in the street, a lonely discarded bundle of rags. Nothing could better visualize his alienation from the life around him. The great trial scene is also dextrously managed, with analytical closeups of a gloating Shylock whetting his knife and with Gianetti (Antonio) fainting with fright. The quintessentially Freudian ring plot remains, as a cute Portia and Nerissa wrangle their rings away from their not-too-acute boy friends. At the end, the film reverts to Shakespeare's tale by cutting back to the smart young set at Belmont. The abrupt switch from the horror and desolation on Shylock's face to the careless indifference of the young revellers is wrenching. Comedy swallows tragedy. In that way the film emulates Shakespeare's play (KSR). *Audience:* General use; *Supplementary materials:* Ball, *SOSF* 287-97.

MEDIUM INFORMATION: *Medium:* Motion Picture; *Sound:* Silent; *Color:* No (black & white); *Length:* 64 min.; *Language of subtitles:* English; *Film type:* 16mm.

AUTHORSHIP INFORMATION: *Producer(s):* Felner, Peter Paul; *Director(s):* Felner, Peter Paul; *Screenplay writer(s):* Felner, Peter Paul; *Adaptor/translator(s):* Aretine, Peter; Fiorentino, Giovanni; Massucio, Guardati Tommaso; *Set designer(s):* Warm, Hermann; *Other personnel:* Graatkjaer, Axel; Mayer, Rudolf (Camera); *Cast:* Schreck, Max (Doge of Venice); Ebert, Carl (Antonio); Liedtke, Harry (Bassanio); May, Gustav (Solanio); Münz, Heinz-Rolf (Salario); Grünberg, Max (Graziano); Krauss, Werner (Shylock); Steinrück, Albert (Tubal); Brausewetter, Hans (Launcelot Gobbo); Porten, Henny (Portia); Rommer, Clare (Nerissa); Eibenschütz, Lia (Jessica); Helfer, Emil (Marco); Richard, Frida (Shylock's mother); Lobe, Friedrich (Elias); Tiedtke, Jakob (Beppo); Geppert, Carl (Reppo); Allen, Willi (Ali).

DISTRIBUTION & AVAILABILITY: *Publisher or responsible agency:* Peter Paul Felner-Film Co.; *Copy location:* FOL, NFA*; *Call or copy number:* MP 73.

The Merchant of Venice. Motion Picture/Modernization

361.1 *Gentleman's Agreement.*

DOCUMENT INFORMATION: *Country:* USA; *Year of release:* 1946.

EDITION, HISTORY, CONTENTS, & EVALUATION: *Awards:* Best picture, director, supporting actress (Holm), 1947; *Edition & history:* A film that pioneered in breaking Hollywood's code of silence about anti-Semitism in America. Gregory Peck as a magazine writer pretending to be Jewish has an occasion to deliver to his secretary, who cannot believe that he is not Jewish, a speech that strongly echoes Shylock's famous speech beginning "Hath not a Jew eyes?" (3.1.59). *Audience:* General use; *Supplementary materials:* Willson, Robert. "Gentleman's Agreement." *SFNL* 13.2 (April 1989): 1+.

MEDIUM INFORMATION: *Medium:* Motion Picture; *Sound:* Spoken language; *Color:* No (black & white); *Length:* 118 min.

AUTHORSHIP INFORMATION: *Producer(s):* Zanuck, Darryl F.; *Director(s):* Kazan, Elia; *Adaptor/translator(s):* Hart, Moss; Hobson, Laura Z. (Based on her novel); *Cast:* Peck, Gregory; McGuire, Dorothy; Garfield, John; Revere, Anne; Holm, Celeste.

DISTRIBUTION & AVAILABILITY: *Publisher or responsible agency:* 20th Century Fox; *Distributor:* FNC, *Availability:* 16mm, apply.

The Merchant of Venice. Video/Teleplay

362. *The Merchant of Venice.*

DOCUMENT INFORMATION: *Country:* GB; *Year of first showing:* 1947; *Location of first showing:* BBC. Transmitted 8:31 to 10:07 P.M., Tuesday, 1 July 1947.

EDITION, HISTORY, CONTENTS, & EVALUATION: *Edition & history:* The music was especially composed for this production by Anthony Bernard. The reappearance of Margaretta Scott as Portia marks her return to Shakespeare on television. She had played Rosalind in the inaugural BBC television Shakespeare program, *As You Like It,* in 1937 (see 35). *Supplementary materials:* "Program." *TPAB* 1 July 1947.

MEDIUM INFORMATION: *Length:* 90 min.

AUTHORSHIP INFORMATION: *Producer(s):* O'Ferrall, George More; *Composer(s):* Bernard, Anthony (and London Chamber Players); *Cast:* Sofaer, Abraham (Shylock); Scott, Margaretta (Portia); Martlew, Mary (Nerissa); Morrell, André (Bassanio); Trevor, Austin (Antonio); Balcon, Jill (Jessica); Wontner, Arthur (Duke of Venice); Hurn, Douglas (Salanio); Warner, Richard (Salarino); Gatrell, John (Gratiano); Ingham, Michael (Lorenzo); Bannister, Maurice (Tubal); Martin, John (Leonardo and Servant); Adams, Robert (Morocco); Benson, George (Launcelot Gobbo); Sheldon, Kevin (Stephano); Angus, Archie (Balthazar); Regan, Gerald (Boy Singer).

DISTRIBUTION & AVAILABILITY: *Publisher or responsible agency:* BBC; *Copy location:* Probably not preserved.

The Merchant of Venice. Video/Scene

363. *Trial Scene from* Merchant of Venice.

DOCUMENT INFORMATION: *Country:* GB; *Year of first showing:* 1949; *Location of first showing:* BBC. Transmitted 9:39 to 4:29 P.M., 24 Jan. 1949.

EDITION, HISTORY, CONTENTS, & EVALUATION: *Edition & history:* A post WW II production showing only the trial scene with Rosalind Iden as Portia and Donald Wolfit as Shylock. *Supplementary materials: TPAB* 24 Jan, 1949.

MEDIUM INFORMATION: *Length:* 37 min.

AUTHORSHIP INFORMATION: *Producer(s):* Davis, Desmond; *Cast:* Bretherton, Martin (The Duke); Cullen, Anthony (Antonio); Wynyard, John (Bassanio); Nunn, Alan (Solanio); Ryder, Clive (Salarino); O'Conor, Joseph (Gratiano); Grierson, Ronald (Tubal); Wolfit, Donald (Shylock); Iden, Rosalind (Portia); Chalkley, Ann (Nerissa); Killner, John (Clerk); Sanders, Brian (Gaoler); Raye, Pat (Page); Humphrey, Heathcote; Parr, Earnest (Spectators).

DISTRIBUTION & AVAILABILITY: *Publisher or responsible agency:* BBC; *Copy location:* Unavailable.

The Merchant of Venice. Motion Picture/Derivative

364. *Il mercante di Venezia: Le marchand de Venise.*

DOCUMENT INFORMATION: *Country:* Italy/France; *Year of release:* 1952.

EDITION, HISTORY, CONTENTS, & EVALUATION: *Edition & history:* A joint Italian/French production with location shots made in Venice itself. Nighttime scenes were actuallly recorded on the Rialto. The remainder of the film was shot indoors at the Turin studios in seven weeks. (P.R. handout at BFI). *Supplementary materials: SIF* 89.

MEDIUM INFORMATION: *Length:* 92 min.

AUTHORSHIP INFORMATION: *Director(s):* Billon, Pierre; *Screen play writer(s):* Marchand, Leopold; Decreux, Louis *Cast:* Simon, Michel (Shylock); Debar, Andrée (Portia); Serato, Massimo (Antonio); Tellini, Liliana (Jessica); Francioli, Armando (Bassanio); Solbelli, Olga (Bianca).

The Merchant of Venice. Video/Teleplay

365. *The Merchant of Venice.* (Series: Stage by Stage).

DOCUMENT INFORMATION: *Country:* GB; *Year of first showing:* 1955; *Location of first showing:* BBC. Transmitted 8:30 P.M. to 10:30 P.M., Sunday, 13 March 1955

EDITION, HISTORY, CONTENTS, & EVALUATION: *Edition & history:* The appearance of a major actor, Michael Hordern, in the role of Shylock suggests the weightiness of this production, which is now [apparently] lost. *Contents & evaluation:* In an internal memorandum, one BBC executive stoutly defended the program against its critics, though he admitted that there were certain technical problems such as a series of dissolves that masked the actors' exits and entrances from the audience (WAC TS/328 16 March 1955). The *Times* critic was so hostile toward the idea of Shakespeare on television that his review turns into a diatribe. He disliked the pretence that the audience was being allowed to watch a performance at the Globe; he denounced the "uniform greyness of the settings," and "the dreary sort of bored superciliousness" of Antony's melancholy. Actor Michael Hordern as Shylock, however, nearly 'scaped whipping. The anonymous critic thought he did a good job of being unsympathetic and "base" ("*The Merchant of Venice,*" *Times* 14 March 1955: 4 C). *Supplementary materials:* Barry, Michael. "The Heart of the Theatre." *RT* 11 March 1955: 14.

MEDIUM INFORMATION: *Length:* 105 min.

AUTHORSHIP INFORMATION: *Producer(s):* Burton, Hal; *Composer(s):* Arnold, Cecily; Johnson, Marshall; *Designer(s):* Burton, Hal; *Cast:* Westwell, Raymond (Antonio); Hayter, John (Salerio); Taylor, Geoffrey (Solanio); Quilley, Denis (Bassanio); Breslin, John (Lorenzo); Payne, Laurence (Gratiano); Gurney, Rachel (Portia); Wenham, Jane (Nerissa); Davies, Leonard (Balthasar); Hordern, Michael (Shylock); Westbrook, John (Prince of Morocco); Dench, Jeffery (Launcelot Gobbo); Garley, John (Old Gobbo); Holmes, Derek (Leonardo); Wells, Veronica (Jessica); Jones, Dudley (Stephano); Mullins, Ian (Prince of Arragon); Stone, Hartnoll (Servant); Garley, John (Tubal); Stainton, Michael (Gaoler); Westbrook, John (Duke of Venice).

DISTRIBUTION & AVAILABILITY: *Publisher or responsible agency:* BBC; *Copy location:* Probably not preserved.

The Merchant of Venice. Motion Picture/Scenes

366. *The Merchant of Venice.* (Series: Great Plays in Rehearsal).

DOCUMENT INFORMATION: *Country:* USA; *Year of release:* 1958.

EDITION, HISTORY, CONTENTS, & EVALUATION: *Edition & history:* Rehearsal scenes from *The Merchant of Venice. Supplementary materials:* Loughney, Katharine. "Shakespeare on Film and Tape at Library of Congress." *SFNL* 14.1 (Dec. 1989): 4.

MEDIUM INFORMATION: *Length:* 60 min.; *Film type:* 16mm.

AUTHORSHIP INFORMATION: *Director(s):* Salmon, Eric.

DISTRIBUTION & AVAILABILITY: *Publisher or responsible agency:* WHA-TV, Madison, WI; *Copy location:* LCM; *Call or copy number:* FCA 4070-4071.

The Merchant of Venice. Video/Teleplay

367. *The Merchant of Venice.*

DOCUMENT INFORMATION: *Country:* GB; *Year of first showing:* 1969; *Location of first showing:* ABC Theatre, USA, 8:30 to 11 P.M., 16 March 1974.

EDITION, HISTORY, CONTENTS, & EVALUATION: *Edition & history:* Originally presented at the National Theatre in London, the production was subsequently recorded for television. It is available on videocassette in Great Britain but presently not in the United States. The high quality of the season's television entertainment put Olivier and company in the position of competing for the prime time audience against Ernest Borgnine in *Twice in a Lifetime* at 8 P.M. that same evening. *Contents & evaluation:* Directed by the brilliant Jonathan Miller, this *Merchant* will be difficult to surpass. Laurence Olivier as Shylock is masterful and the supporting cast worthy of the star's presence. In Edwardian costumes, the merchants of Venice, Antonio and Bassanio and their cronies, are envisioned as smooth, young entrepreneurs without a care in the world. As Shylock, Lord Olivier explores the heights and depths of the role. Shylock moreover is well dressed, outfitted in a frock coat and wing collar, and he occupies a comfortably furnished office, though his skullcap rests firmly on his head. This is not the stereotypical Shylock as a grubby miser. Peering always, apparently near-sighted, Olivier's Shylock is both infuriating and heartrending. At the end of the trial scene, with a trapped and desperate look in his eyes, he shrieks "I am content." Later, as the scene fades from somewhere off screen comes the pitiful wailing and howling of the broken money lender. By abruptly cutting from a close-up of the three caskets to a mid-shot of Shylock meditating over his "3000 ducats," the editing also reenforces the narrative line. The juxtaposition of these two shots clearly underscores the contrast between frivolous Belmont and solemn Venice. An astonishing *tour de force* (one might say a typical Jonathan Miller touch) suddenly brings two spinsterish looking ladies (Clare Walmesley and Laura Sarti) on screen to erupt into the most unexpected but magnificent rendition imaginable of "Tell me where is fancy bred?" The contrast between their appearance and their singing is delicious. At the end in Belmont after the ring episode is brought to closure, Jessica is left standing all alone, while on the sound track there is the sound of the Jewish requiem, the "Kaddish" (sung by Heinz Danziger). The indictment of Jessica for the betrayal of her father is thus accomplished without words. The interior scenes are handsomely mounted and the exteriors at Belmont attractive. Costuming Portia in an Edwardian riding habit and furnishing her with a riding whip slyly comments on the aggressive character of this lady of "mercy." Miller and company have captured the subtleties of this complicated play with admirable skill (KSR). *Audience:* General use; *Supplementary materials:* O'Connor, John J. "TV: Olivier as the Controversial Shylock, in 1880's." *NYT* 15 March 1974: 67.

MEDIUM INFORMATION: *Medium:* Video; *Sound:* Spoken language; *Color:* Yes; *Length:* 120 min.; *Language(s) spoken:* English; *Video type:* VHS/B.

AUTHORSHIP INFORMATION: *Producer(s):* Clarke, Cecil (TV); *Director(s):* Miller, Jonathan (Stage); Sichel, John (TV); *Composer(s):* Davis, Carl; *Set designer(s):* Oman, Julia Trevelyan; Roden, Peter; *Costume designer(s):* Sproul, Keith; Dawson, Beatrice; *Lighting designer(s):* Hudspith, Tony; *Other personnel:* Simper, Roy (Camera); Pigden, Al (Editor); Mann, Sheila (Make-up); Bird, Henry (Audio); Reeves, Jim (Video engineer); *Cast:* Olivier, Laurence (Shylock); Plowright, Joan (Portia); Jayston, Michael (Gratiano); Carteret, Anna (Nerissa); James, Barry (Salerio); Nicholls, Anthony (Antonio); Reid, Malcolm (Lorenzo); Kay, Charles (Arragon); Whitrow, Benjamin (Duke); Greif, Stephen (Morocco); Mackintosh, Kenneth (Tubal); Barnes, Michael Tudor (Solanio); Lawson, Denis (Gobbo); Rocca, Peter (Stephano); Joyce, John (Balthazar); Walmesley, Clare; Sarti, Laura (Singers).

DISTRIBUTION & AVAILABILITY: *Publisher or responsible agency:* Precision Video; *Distributor:* TSO*, *Copy location:* FOL; *Call or copy number:* VCR; *Availability:* Sale or rental in UK only; FOL, archive.

The Merchant of Venice. Motion Picture/Scenes

368. *The Merchant of Venice: An Introduction.*

DOCUMENT INFORMATION: *Country:* GB; *Year of release:* 1971.

EDITION, HISTORY, CONTENTS, & EVALUATION: *Edition & history:* A Seabourne Enterprises and Anvil Film production that has been distributed in the U.K. but not in the United States. Produced for the school market. *Contents & evaluation:* Not seen. *Supplementary materials:* BUFVC 16.

MEDIUM INFORMATION: *Length:* 21 min.

AUTHORSHIP INFORMATION: *Director(s):* Seabourne, Peter.

DISTRIBUTION & AVAILABILITY: *Distributor:* EFV* [Formerly].

The Merchant of Venice. Video/Interpretation

369. *The Merchant of Venice.*

DOCUMENT INFORMATION: *Country:* GB; *Year of first showing:* 1972; *Location of first showing:* BBC. Transmitted 8:15 to 10:25 P.M., Sunday, 16 April 1972.

EDITION, HISTORY, CONTENTS, & EVALUATION: *Edition & history:* The program notes in *Radio Times* observe that "the Venice of Titian and the Belmont of Botticelli are the visual inspiration behind . . . [this] lavish production." Subsequently this policy of designing sets and costumes by emulating the works of painters more or less contemporary with Shakespeare became virtually standard practice in the later years of the BBC Shakespeare Plays series. This production shows that the idea was already well developed in the prior work of Cedric Messina and his colleagues. *Contents & evaluation:* Writing in the London *Times* (17 April 1972: 9d), critic Stanley Reynolds praised it for a visual excellence, which "is as easy on the eye as a set

of visual transparencies." On the other hand he felt somewhat uncomfortable with the play itself, which in the post-Holocaust era has undergone a sea change in public perception of it. As Shylock, however, Frank Finlay in the courtroom scene resembled a "blue-eyed Karl Marx," which apparently gave the scene an undertone at least of comedy. (Probably thought of in Shakespeare's day as a farcical scapegoat, Shylock, to modern eyes, often emerges as a tragic figure. History has imposed a new set of guidelines for interpreting his character. The post-holocaust *Merchant of Venice* has been virtually re-written by stage and screen directors.) *Audience:* General use; *Supplementary materials:* "Cover Story." RT 16 Apr. 1972: 56-58.

MEDIUM INFORMATION: *Medium:* Video; *Sound:* Spoken language; *Color:* Yes; *Length:* 132 min.; *Language(s) spoken:* English; *Video type:* Video.

AUTHORSHIP INFORMATION: *Producer(s):* Savory, Gerald; *Director(s):* Messina, Cedric; *Adaptor/translator(s):* Hill, Rosemary; *Composer(s):* Rooley, Anthony; Tyler, James (Consort of Musicke); *Designer(s):* Abbott, Tony; *Costume designer(s):* Waterson, Juanita; *Lighting designer(s):* Wright, Robert; *Cast:* Smith, Maggie (Portia); Gray, Charles (Antonio); Gable, Christopher (Bassanio); Finlay, Frank (Shylock); Harris, Robert (Duke of Venice); Stoddard, Malcolm (Gratiano); Hughes, Nerys (Nerissa); Marson, Ania (Jessica); Petherbridge, Edward (Lorenzo); Spenser, David (Morocco); Moffatt, John (Arragon); Graham, Clive (Salerio); Morant, Richard (Solanio); May, Bunny (Launcelot Gobbo) ; Parry, Ken (Old Gobbo); Leno, Charles (Tubal); Hug, John (Leonardo); Lefebvre, Rolf (Balthazar); Tucker, Alan (Stephano); Hill, Martyn (Soloist).

AVAILABILITY: *Responsible agency:* BBC; *Copy location:* BBC*.

The Merchant of Venice. Video/Teleplay

370. *The Merchant of Venice.* (Series: The Shakespeare Plays).

DOCUMENT INFORMATION: *Country:* GB; *Year of filming:* 15-20 May 1980; *Year of first showing:* 1980; *Location of first showing(s):* BBC, London; PBS stations, USA 23 Feb. 1981.

EDITION, HISTORY, CONTENTS, & EVALUATION: *Edition & history:* Visually the production continues the BBC practice of emulating the master artists of Shakespeare's own lifetime in the *mise en scène.* Belmont, the seat of Portia's ancestral home, swirls in a gauzy mist of airy color. Venice is earthier in texture, as it should be. For Belmont, the model was Titian; for Venice, Canaletto or Watteau. Thus the director played off the idealism of the rural retreat against the crassness of the commercial city, though ironically neither locale is invulnerable to folly or evil. He also accented the play's artistry, which relies on the tension between Portia's surface moralizing and a subterranean current of moral ambiguity. *Contents & evaluation:* Producer Jonathan Miller saw the play's central theme as "the conflict between the world of the Old Testament and the world of the New Testament. It's not about Jews versus Christians in the racial sense. It's about . . . the world of legislation versus the world of mercy. And Shakespeare, as he always does with a complicated issue, instead of just presenting a cut-and-dried case of mercy being better than law, shows us that those who are the exponents of mercy act unmercifully when given the opportunity to use the law against the Jew." Miller went on in this interview to say that the "play, again, is about the conflict between two worlds under which Europe has always lived. It's the world represented on the fronts of the great cathedrals in France, where on the great west doors of Chartres or of Amiens you will see on the left-hand side the prophets of the Old Testament, and on the right side the apostles and the disciples of the New Testament" (Hallinan, Tim. "Miller on 'The Shakespeare Plays'." *SQ* 32.2 [Summer 1981]: 141-42). In director Jack Gold's *The Merchant of Venice*, the camera pauses often enough on the three caskets of lead, silver and gold to suggest that they are somehow emblematic. This is a Venice in which 'all that glisters' is most certainly not gold. Behind the amiable facade—the 'shallow foppery,' as Shylock calls it, of the old-boy network around Antonio and Bassanio lies savagery in the hearts of Jews and Christians alike. Arragon's vicious striking of his dwarf after the defeat in the casket competition exposes the inner cruelty behind the veneer of manners. Even Portia herself, so often thought of as a paragon of virtue, is the archetypal rich girl who thinks money can buy anything—even a bond. Shylock, who by his own cloddishness brings this dirty little Venetian secret to the surface, must be banished to save the city for good manners. . . . Shylock, so this version seems to suggest, is the lead casket; the Christian cronies, the gold casket. Outwardly in no way affable, congenial, agreeable, or sociable, Shylock is yet inwardly the man of integrity. As Mitchell implies, this Shylock would never have dreamt of giving away Leah's ring at the request of two young strangers, something that the wily Portia and Nerissa goad Bassanio and Gratiano into doing. A man of business, this Shylock is without small talk, without banter, without irony" (KSR, "The Shakespeare Plays," *SQ* 32.3 [1981]: 398). *Supplementary materials:* Manheim, Michael. "The Merchant of Venice." *SFNL* 5.2 [1981]: 11; Videotape (25 min.) from "Shakespeare in Perspective" series with Wolf Mankowitz as lecturer available in U.K. from BBC* (*BUFVC* 16).

MEDIUM INFORMATION: *Medium:* Video; *Sound:* Spoken language; *Color:* Yes; *Length:* 160 min.; *Video type:* B, V, 3/4U.

AUTHORSHIP INFORMATION: *Producer(s):* Miller, Jonathan; *Director(s):* Gold, Jack; *Adaptor/translator(s):* Snodin, David; *Composer(s):* Davis, Carl; *Designer(s):* Bayldon, Oliver; *Costume designer(s):* Hughes, Raymond; *Lighting designer(s):* Channon, Dennis; *Other personnel:* Anthony, Chick (Sound); Richards, Marion (Make-up); Barclay, John (Mixer); Field, Geoffrey (Camera); Banthorpe, Malcolm (Editor); *Cast:* Mitchell, Warren (Shylock); Jones, Gemma (Portia); Jameson, Susan (Nerissa); Franklyn-Robbins, John (Antonio); Nettles, John (Bassanio); Cranham, Kenneth (Gratiano); Rhys-Davies, John (Salerio); David, Alan (Solanio); Morant, Richard (Lorenzo); Udwin, Leslee (Jessica); Diamond, Arnold (Tubal); Reitel, Enn (Launcelot Gobbo); Gladwin, Joe (Old Gobbo); Wilmer, Douglas (Duke of Venice); Zuber, Marc (Prince of Morocco); Gale, Peter (Prince of Arragon); Martin, Roger (Leonardo); Mitchell, Daniel (Balthasar); Scott, Shaun (Stephano); Austin, Richard (Antonio's Servant).

DISTRIBUTION & AVAILABILITY: *Publisher or responsible agency:* BBC/TLF; *Distributor:* AVP, UIO, BBC* *Copy location:* UVM, CTL*; *Availability:* AVP B, V, 3/4U $450 (1987), sale; UIO, V (72041H), 3/4U (7014V), rental $23.80; BBC*, 16mm or V, apply.

Merchant of Venice, The. **Video/Documentary**

371. *Shylock.*

DOCUMENT INFORMATION: *Country:* GB; *Year of release:* 1986.

EDITION, HISTORY, CONTENTS, & EVALUATION: *Edition & history:* A teaching package in four parts that explores such topics as the play's stage history; the problem of anti-Semitism; direction (with Jonathan Miller); and acting (with RSC players). *Contents & evaluation:* Every participant in this program makes valuable contributions. It is the most intelligent discussion that one could hope for of *The Merchant of Venice*, a play whose real virtues are often obscured in a fog of controversy. *Supplementary materials:* BUFVC 17.

MEDIUM INFORMATION: *Length:* 75 min.

AUTHORSHIP INFORMATION: *Director(s):* Dorset Inst.; *Cast:* Matheson, Tom; Frankel, William; Miller, Jonathan (Participants); MacDiarmid, Ian; Stewart, Patrick (Actors).

DISTRIBUTION & AVAILABILITY: *Distributor:* DIH*.

The Merry Wives of Windsor

ORIGINAL WORK AND PRODUCTION: Comedy/
Farce. *Year of first production:* 1597; *Site of first production:* Windsor Castle [?].

***The Merry Wives of Windsor.* Motion Picture/
Abbreviated**

372. *Merry Wives of Windsor, The.*

DOCUMENT INFORMATION: *Country:* USA; *Year of release:* 1910.

EDITION, HISTORY, CONTENTS, & EVALUATION:
Edition & history: Early silent adaptation by William Selig (1864-1948), pioneering filmmaker, who made many technical and artistic contributions to the fledgling film industry. Besides developing the Selig Standard Camera he also invented the faked newsreel shot with his spurious pictures of Teddy Roosevelt shooting a lion in Africa. This same man who made a Shakespeare film also brought Tom Mix into the movies. One might say that he was versatile in every way. *Supplementary materials:* Ball, *SOSF* 67; *SIF* 101; Katz, *TFE.*

MEDIUM INFORMATION: *Sound:* Silent; *Color:* No (black & white); *Length:* 11 min.

AUTHORSHIP INFORMATION: *Director(s):* Selig, William.

DISTRIBUTION & AVAILABILITY: Archive, LCM

***The Merry Wives of Windsor.* Motion Picture/
Abbreviated**

373. *Falstaff.*

DOCUMENT INFORMATION: *Country:* France; *Year of release:* 1911.

EDITION, HISTORY, CONTENTS, & EVALUATION:
Edition & history: An adaptation of *Wiv.* with well known French stage actors released both in Europe and in the U.S. For a full account, see Ball. *Supplementary materials:* Ball, *SOSF* 127-8.

MEDIUM INFORMATION: *Length:* 10 min.

AUTHORSHIP INFORMATION: *Director(s):* Desfontaines, Henri; *Cast:* DeGeorge, M. (Falstaff).

***The Merry Wives of Windsor.* Motion Picture/
Musical**

374. *Die lustigen Weiber von Windsor.*

DOCUMENT INFORMATION: *Country:* Germany; *Year of release:* 1917.

EDITION, HISTORY, CONTENTS, & EVALUATION:
Edition & history: It may sound oxymoronic to speak of a "silent film/musical" but this *Wives* seems to have been more an adaptation of Otto Nicolai's operatic version of Shakespeare's play than of Shakespeare's

play itself. It should also be remembered that silent filmmakers were as fond of adapting operas to the screen as of using Shakespeare's plays. Live pianists, organists and even full orchestras filled in the silences. *Supplementary materials: SIF* 101.

MEDIUM INFORMATION: *Length:* [?] min.

AUTHORSHIP INFORMATION: *Director(s):* Wauer, William.

DISTRIBUTION & AVAILABILITY: *Distributor:* Beck-film.

The Merry Wives of Windsor. Motion Picture/ Feature

375. *Die lustigen Weiber.*

DOCUMENT INFORMATION: *Country:* Germany; *Year of release:* 1935.

EDITION, HISTORY, CONTENTS, & EVALUATION: *Edition & history:* Early foreign language sound adaptation of a Shakespearean play. For some reason, the Germans took special pleasure in making films out of *Wives. Supplementary materials: SIF* 101; Morris, *SHOF* 8.

MEDIUM INFORMATION: *Length:* 90 min.

AUTHORSHIP INFORMATION: *Director(s):* Hoffmann, Carl; *Cast:* Slezak, Leo (Falstaff).

The Merry Wives of Windsor. Video/Teleplay

376. *The Merry Wives of Windsor.* (Series: Scenes from Shakespeare series).

DOCUMENT INFORMATION: *Country:* GB; *Year of first showing:* 1937; *Location of first showing:* BBC. Transmitted 12 March 1937.

EDITION, HISTORY, CONTENTS, & EVALUATION: *Edition & history:* A part of the "Scenes from Shakespeare" series transmitted in the second year of the BBC's television operation. In this segment Robert Atkins' Bankside Players performed the letter scene. *Supplementary materials:* "Program." *TPAB* 12 March 1937.

MEDIUM INFORMATION: *Length:* 15 [?] min.

AUTHORSHIP INFORMATION: *Producer(s):* Thomas, Stephen; *Cast:* Vanbrugh, Violet (Mistress Ford); Vanbrugh, Irene (Mistress Page).

DISTRIBUTION & AVAILABILITY: *Publisher or responsible agency:* BBC; *Copy location:* Unavailable.

The Merry Wives of Windsor. Motion Picture/ Opera

377. *Falstaff in Wien.*

DOCUMENT INFORMATION: *Country:* Germany; *Year of release:* 1940.

EDITION, HISTORY, CONTENTS, & EVALUATION: *Edition & history:* A musical adaptation in part based on the 1848 Otto Nicolai opera. *Supplementary materials: SIF,* 102.

MEDIUM INFORMATION: *Length:* 86 min.

AUTHORSHIP INFORMATION: *Director(s):* Hainisch, Leopold; *Cast:* Berndsen, Hellmuth (Falstaff).

DISTRIBUTION & AVAILABILITY: Archive, LCM

378. *Die lustigen Weiber von Windsor.*

DOCUMENT INFORMATION: *Country:* German Dem. Republic; *Year of release:* 1950.

EDITION, HISTORY, CONTENTS, & EVALUATION: *Edition & history:* One of three German/Austrian film adaptations of Otto Nicolai's popular 1848 opera based on Shakespeare's comedy. *Supplementary materials: SIF,* 102.

MEDIUM INFORMATION: *Length:* 94 min.

AUTHORSHIP INFORMATION: *Producer(s):* Lehmann, Walter; *Director(s):* Wildhagen, George; *Cast:* Esser, Paul (Falstaff); Dux, Eckart (Fenton).

The Merry Wives of Windsor. Video/Teleplay

379. *The Merry Wives of Windsor.*

DOCUMENT INFORMATION: *Country:* GB; *Year of first showing:* 1952; *Location of first showing:* BBC, London Station. Transmitted 8:42 P.M. to 10:29 P.M. on Sunday, Nov. 16, 1952.

EDITION, HISTORY, CONTENTS, & EVALUATION: *Edition & history:* This carefully planned production eventually cost well over £2,000. Sets, props and costumes were all meticulously assembled, everything from "casement windows in Dr. Caius' house" that needed to open inwardly, to tankards for ale and six wine goblets. A host of technical details had to be managed, to include the assembling of three booms, two microphones, and two crane dollies. Panic set in at the last minute when the set builder almost failed to meet his deadline. A peek at the backstage activity for this production suggests the huge expenditure of raw energy that went into a "live" studio production in the early days of TV (KSR—WAC T5/330 16 Nov. 1952). *Supplementary materials: TPAB* 16 Nov. 1952.

MEDIUM INFORMATION: *Length:* 110 min.

AUTHORSHIP INFORMATION: *Producer(s):* Atkins, Ian; *Director(s):* Amyes, Julian; *Composer(s):* Saunders, Max; *Designer(s):* Bould, James; *Cast:* Atkins, Robert (Falstaff); Beaumont, Robert (Slender); Chitty, Erik (Justice Shallow); Pryse, Hugh (Sir Hugh Evans); White, Meadows (Host of Garter Inn); Davies, Rupert (Mr. Page); Bennett, Peter (Bardolph); Hamelin, Clement (Pistol); Bass, Alfie (Nym); Regan, Elizabeth (Ann Page); Kerridge, Mary (Mistress Page); Huntley-Wright, Betty (Mistress Ford); Bromley, Sidney (Simple); Rendall, Peter (Fenton); Burle, Helene (Mistress Quickly); Sperber, Milo (Dr. Caius); Mander, Charles (Rugby); Moore, Thomas (Robin); Franklyn, Peter; Glover, William (Servants); + several others.

DISTRIBUTION & AVAILABILITY: *Publisher or responsible agency:* BBC; *Copy location:* Unavailable.

The Merry Wives of Windsor. Video/Scenes

380. *The Merry Wives of Windsor.*

DOCUMENT INFORMATION: *Country:* USA; *Year of first showing:* 1954; *Location of first showing:* Omnibus. Transmitted 5 to 6:30 P.M., Sunday, 21 Feb. 1954.

EDITION, HISTORY, CONTENTS, & EVALUATION: *Edition & history:* A story in *The New York Times* indicated that the original plan was for Omnibus to pick up this show "live" in New Haven, Conn., where it was to be performed by the Yale University Drama Department. There was also talk of the student actors' using the London dialect of Shakespeare's own time, which to most people today sounds something like a thick Irish brogue. If that indeed happened, then television has rarely again offered programming so exquisitely high brow. On the same bill that afternoon were rarified Southern African songs by Marais and Miranda. Not fare for the Sunday afternoon football crowd. *Supplementary materials:* "Prospect." *NYT* 31 Jan. 1954: X 13; Gianokos, *TDSP* 327.

MEDIUM INFORMATION: *Color:* No (black & white); *Length:* 30 min. [?]; *Video type:* V.

DISTRIBUTION & AVAILABILITY: *Publisher or responsible agency:* Omnibus/Yale Univ. School of Drama.

The Merry Wives of Windsor. Video/Recording

381. *The Merry Wives of Windsor.* (Series: Sunday-Night Theatre).

DOCUMENT INFORMATION: *Country:* GB; *Year of first showing:* 1955; *Location of first showing:* BBC. Transmitted 9:00 to 10:00 P.M., Sunday, Oct. 2, 1955.

EDITION, HISTORY, CONTENTS, & EVALUATION: *Edition & history:* A special "telerecording" made at the Shakespeare Memorial Theatre at Stratford-upon-Avon of the second part only of Glen Byam Shaw's *Wives.* Anthony Quayle who was later to play Falstaff in the BBC Henriad appears here in that same role (or as much as it can be called "that same role" given the difference in character between the Falstaff of this play and of the Henriad), and Keith Michell who plays Antony in the BBC *Julius Caesar* is also included as Master Ford. As Michael Mullin, author of *Macbeth Onstage*, has shown, Glen Byam Shaw with the assistance of the "Motley" design team was responsible for several memorable productions at Stratford. The BBC went to great pains to arrange this broadcast, which was the very first to be transmitted from the Stratford theatre. *Contents & evaluation:* Many difficulties lay behind this production. The Actors Equity complicated matters by demanding extra pay for a Sunday night performance. At the special performance in Stratford, the entirety of the play was performed for the audience of distinguished guests but only Act II was transmitted over the air. BBC took responsibility for the make-up which in the early days of television was a particular problem. A minor flap occurred when the name of Keith Michell was misspelled as "Mitchell" on the credits, which is only another illustration of the difficulty of getting actors' names straight. With good reason the Hollywood moguls demanded that their stars' professional names be readily spellable, e.g., Tom Mix, Gary Cooper, Clara Bow (KSR—WAC T/5 330 Oct 2, 1955). *Supplementary materials:* "Program." *RT* 2 Oct. 1955: [n.p.].

MEDIUM INFORMATION: *Length:* 60 min.

AUTHORSHIP INFORMATION: *Producer(s):* Harrison, Stephen; Edgar, Barrie; *Director(s):* Shaw, Glen Byam (Stage); *Composer(s):* Bridgewater, Leslie; Ingram, Harold (Orchestra); *Designer(s):* Design Team Motley; *Costume designer(s):* Motley; *Cast:* Quayle, Anthony (Falstaff); Denison, Michael (Dr. Caius); Southworth, John (Rugby); Wymark, Patrick (Host of Garter Inn); Atienza, Edward (Justice Shallow); Bayldon, Geoffrey (Slender); Michael, Ralph (Master Page); Devlin, William (Sir Hugh Evans); Sasse, Geoffrey (Simple); Baddeley, Angela (Mistress Page); Rogers, John (Robin); Michell, Keith (Master Ford); Redman, Joyce (Mistress Ford); Robinson, Rex; Haywood, Alan (Servants); Dixon, Jill (Ann Page); Faulkner, Trader (Fenton); Atkinson, Rosalind (Mistress Quickly); Hunter, Robert (Bardolph); Thomas, Philip (William Page).

DISTRIBUTION & AVAILABILITY: *Publisher or responsible agency:* BBC/RSC; *Copy location:* RSC* [?].

The Merry Wives of Windsor. **Motion Picture/ Opera**

382. *Die lustigen Weiber von Windsor.*

DOCUMENT INFORMATION: *Country*: Austria; *Year of release*: 1965.

EDITION, HISTORY, CONTENTS, & EVALUATION: *Edition & history:* One of three German and Austrian operatic film adaptations of Otto Nicolai's popular 1848 *Merry Wives of Windsor.*

MEDIUM INFORMATION: *Medium:* Motion Picture; *Sound:* Spoken language; *Color:* Yes; *Length:* 97 min.; *Language(s) spoken:* English.

AUTHORSHIP INFORMATION: *Producer(s):* Foster, Norman; *Director(s):* Tressler, Georg; *Adaptor/translator(s):* Foster, Norman; *Composer(s):* Nicolai, Otto; Zagreb Symphony Orchestra; *Designer(s):* Halbig, Hugo; *Costume designer(s):* Pinnow, Helga; *Other personnel:* Hofer, Robert; Riff, Sepp; *Cast:* Foster, Norman (Falstaff); Boky, Colette (Mistress Ford); Miller, Mildred (Mistress Page); Popp, Lucia (Anna Page); Schutz, Ernest (Fenton); Gorin, Igor (Mr. Ford).

DISTRIBUTION & AVAILABILITY: *Publisher or responsible agency:* Norman Foster Productions; *Distributor:* FNC.

The Merry Wives of Windsor. **Video/Recording**

383. *The Merry Wives of Windsor.*

DOCUMENT INFORMATION: *Country:* USA; *Year of release:* 1979.

EDITION, HISTORY, CONTENTS, & EVALUATION: *Edition & history:* A recording of a stage production done at the Globe playhouse of the Shakespeare Society of America, Los Angeles, California in December 1979. *Contents & evaluation:* ''The production . . . is marked by fine performances by key characters. Leon Charles is a Falstaff of convincing corpulency, with strongly marked features and a forceful presence which makes him genuinely reminiscent of the Falstaff of the Boar's Head Tavern. When he says in the last scene, 'I was three or four times in thought that they were not fairies,' one fancies for a breathless second that he may recover from deception as miraculously as he did at Gad's Hill. Gloria Grahame's Mistress Page is also unusually effective. Her resonant voice and beautiful articulation work splendidly to signal a sudden shift from realism to myth as she intones her key speech in IV. iv about the old tale of Herne the Hunter, while her cohorts line up ritualistically to recite their parts, and a mysterious black-cloaked figure emerges to dance about them.

Fenton also takes on unusual stature in this production. He actually emerges as one capable of writing

verses, speaking holiday, and smelling of April and May. . . . The set, in spite of the vaunted Elizabethan authenticity of the stage, seems in the filming rigid and confining. . . . Shakespeare's text is treated with extreme freedom. Throughout, many of the more difficult lines are simply dropped. . . . The Latin lesson and most of the horse-stealing plot are gone and little missed; but the omission of Ford's soliloquy in III.ii diminishes our sense of the violence of his jealousy and flattens his character. . . . The treatment of the whole work, while certainly not reverential is, for the most part, responsible and intelligent'' (Roberts, Jeanne Addison, ''Review,'' *SFNL* 6.2 (March 1982): 8 +). *Audience:* General use; *Supplementary materials:* ''Shakespeare on Video at the Globe.'' *SFNL* 4.2 (April 1980): 1 +.

MEDIUM INFORMATION: *Medium:* Video; *Sound:* Spoken language; *Color:* Yes; *Length:* 120 min.[?]; *Language(s) spoken:* English; *Video type:* V.

AUTHORSHIP INFORMATION: *Producer(s):* Taylor, R. Thad; Ashley, Jay; *Director(s):* Manning, Jack; Wilds, Lillian; *Adaptor/translator(s):* Booth, Stephen (Consultant); *Cast:* Houseman, John (Introd.); Grahame, Gloria (Mistress Page); Charles, Leon (Falstaff); Seelie-Snyder, Valerie (Mistress Ford); Tymitz, Dixie (Mistress Quickly); Asher, Joel (Dr. Caius).

DISTRIBUTION & AVAILABILITY: *Publisher or responsible agency:* Globe Playhouse of Shakespeare Society of America, Los Angeles; *Distributor:* SSA; *Availability:* Rental.

The Merry Wives of Windsor. **Video/Recording**

384. *The Merry Wives of Windsor.*

DOCUMENT INFORMATION: *Country:* USA; *Year of first showing:* 1980.

EDITION, HISTORY, CONTENTS, & EVALUATION: *Edition & history:* A videotaping of a 1980 stage production of *The Merry Wives* performed by the Berkeley Shakespeare Festival. A copy is housed in the TOFT (Theatre on Film and Tape) Collection at the Library of Performing Arts, Lincoln Center, New York Public Library. It may be viewed by appointment (see below). *Contents & evaluation:* Since I have not personally screened this video, I cannot speak to its visual qualities. But a review of the stage performance by Laurence H. Jacobs is helpful: ''[Richard E.T. White] presented this play as a tableau of Elizabethan town life. The keynote was a realistic detail in costume, setting, and acting. The great moments were triumphs of characterization. Linda Hoy's reading of Falstaff's love letter to Mistress Page moved wondrously and hilariously back and forth between her flattered vanity and housewifely indignation. Gail Chugg brought to his Falstaff an enlivening ability to shift moods and emotions within a single speech. . . . His Falstaff was at once melancholic, vain, conscious of his decay, and indomitable in his schemes to avoid it" ("Shakespeare in the San Francisco Bay Area," *SQ* 32.2 [Summer 1981]: 264). *Audience:* College and university; General use.

MEDIUM INFORMATION: *Medium:* Video; *Sound:* Spoken language; *Color:* Yes; *Length:* 147 min.; *Language(s) spoken:* English; *Video type:* 3/4U.

AUTHORSHIP INFORMATION: *Producer(s):* Berkeley Shakespeare Festival; *Director(s):* White, Richard E.T.; *Composer(s):* Thewlis, Stephen; *Set designer(s):* Angell, Jean; Pratt, Ron; *Costume designer(s):* Chugg, Eliza; *Lighting designer(s):* Ulnic, George; *Cast:* Jensen, Steven (Bardolph); Vickery, John (Dr. Caius); Chugg, Gail (Falstaff); Sicular, Robert (Ford); Sweeney, Beth (Mistress Ford); Phillips, J.P. (Nym); Brady, Lance (Page); Dixon, Lisa Ann (Ann Page); Hoy, Linda (Mistress Page); Carr, Kevin (Pistol); Afterman, Jean (Quickly); Dean, Charles (Shallow); Taylor, Scott (Slender).

DISTRIBUTION & AVAILABILITY: *Publisher or responsible agency:* Berkeley Shakespeare Festival; *Copy location:* LCL TOFT Collection; *Call or copy number:* NCOV 304; *Availability:* By appt. *Restrictions:* Archive.

The Merry Wives of Windsor. Video/Teleplay

385. *The Merry Wives of Windsor.* (Series: The Shakespeare Plays).

DOCUMENT INFORMATION: *Country:* GB; *Year of filming:* 1-8 Nov. 1982; *Year of first showing:* 1982; *Location of first showing(s):* BBC. London; PBS stations, USA, 31 Jan. 1983.

EDITION, HISTORY, CONTENTS, & EVALUATION: *Edition & history:* The richness of the Shakespearean acting tradition behind these BBC plays is illustrated by the cast for this play. Elizabeth Spriggs, who plays Mistress Quickly, took the role of Mistress Alice Ford in an RSC production at London's Aldwych theatre in 1968. Many will also remember Miss Spriggs as an unforgettable Calphurnia in the BBC *Julius Caesar.* Ben Kingsley, the star of this production, shortly afterwards became internationally celebrated for his movie role as Gandhi. British audiences also have an advantage not available to North Americans in that they may recognize many of these actors from their roles in domestic popular TV shows. *Contents & evaluation:* "Rather reluctantly we must add *The Merry Wives* to the debit side of the ledger in accounting for the plays produced so far by the BBC. In spite of a few inspired moments, intelligent editing, and some creditable acting, the production simply never cohered into an exciting whole.

Unfortunately the very first scene was enough to send

most viewers back to the rerun of *Shogun,* where unintelligibility could be clearly accounted for by foreign land and language. . . . The two characters who ought to be the stars of the show, Falstaff and Ford, were strangely mismatched. Richard Griffiths as Falstaff was subdued, with an undertone of melancholy which turned his second love scene with Mistress Ford into a pensive, romantic interlude reminiscent of *Chimes at Midnight.* By contrast, Ben Kingsley, fresh in the minds of American audiences from his performance as Gandhi, clearly thought he was playing in a farce. His Ford was not only choleric but frequently hysterical; he was a short man frantically insecure in his marital role. Either style might have been the basis for a consistent interpretation, but together they worked at cross purposes. Similarly the lower-class accent, affected determinedly by Mistress Page but much less reliably by Mistress Ford and the husbands, proved distracting, perhaps even confusing, since Mistress Page sounded like a downstairs character from *Upstairs Downstairs* rather than a prosperous village landowner. . . . After so much complaint, it is pleasant to be able to end on a note of almost unqualified praise. The final scenes were extremely well done. . . . If the whole videotape had been carried out with the unity of vision and imaginative detail of the conclusion, it would have been a notable success instead of a mediocre near-failure" (Roberts, Jean Addison, "*The Merry Wives of Windsor,*" *SFNL* 7.2 [1983]: 5). *Audience:* College and university; General use; *Supplementary materials:* Fenwick, Henry. *The Merry Wives of Windsor.* BSP 17-28; Videotape (25 min.) from "Shakespeare in Perspective" series with Jilly Cooper as lecturer available in U.K. from BBC* (*BUFVC* 17).

MEDIUM INFORMATION: *Medium:* Video; *Sound:* Spoken language; *Color:* Yes; *Length:* 150 min.; *Video type:* B, V, 3/4U.

AUTHORSHIP INFORMATION: *Producer(s):* Sutton, Shaun; *Director(s):* Jones, David; *Adaptor/translator(s):* Snodin, David; *Composer(s):* Muldowney, Dominic; *Choreographer(s):* Stephenson, Geraldine; *Designer(s):* Homfray, Don; *Costume designer(s):* Rawlins, Christine; *Lighting designer(s):* Treays, John; *Other personnel:* Ford, Marianne (Make-up); Chubb, Richard (Sound); Garrick, Anthony (Prod. manager); Wilders, John (Literary consultant); *Cast:* Griffiths, Richard (Falstaff); Chandler, Simon (Fenton); Bennett, Alan (Shallow); O'Callaghan, Richard (Slender); Kingsley, Ben (Ford); Marshall, Bryan (Page); Mair, Crispin (William Page); Evans, Tenniel (Sir Hugh Evans); Bryant, Michael (Dr. Caius); Cox, Michael Graham (Host); Gostelow, Gordon (Bardolph); Terry, Nigel (Pistol); Robbins, Michael (Nym); Whitlock, Lee (Robin); Cook, Ron (Simple); Joyce, John (Rugby); Brown, Ralph (John); Gordon, Peter (Robert); Davis, Judy (Mistress Ford); Scales, Prunella (Mistress Page); Foster, Miranda (Anne Page); Spriggs, Elizabeth (Mistress Quickly); Brown, Harvey;

A Midsummer Night's Dream

ORIGINAL WORK AND PRODUCTION: Festive Comedy. *Year written:* 1595-96; *Site of first production:* Greenwich Palace [?].

A Midsummer Night's Dream. Motion Picture/ Abridgment

387. *A Midsummer Night's Dream.*

DOCUMENT INFORMATION: *Country:* USA; *Year of release:* 1909.

EDITION, HISTORY, CONTENTS, & EVALUATION: *Edition & history:* One of the Vitagraph Shakespeare films that were made in Brooklyn at the dawn of the motion picture industry (see 640 for discussion). Although early American movie-making tended to be dominated more by movie than by theatrical people, Vitagraph did hire a man of the theatre, William V. Ranous, to supervise its Shakespeare films. In making this one, the director eschewed the mercury-vapour lamps of the studios in favor of going outdoors in search of realistic exterior locations. *Contents & evaluation:* A compact, squeezed in, little movie that one way or another manages to cram just about everything into eight minutes (like the trick of the man who recites all of *Hamlet* in five minutes). The price paid of course is a breathless, narrative pace that also drains the film of context and depth. From the opening with an incredibly lengthy title card explaining the plight of the young lovers, to such exteriors as the Bethesda fountain in New York's Central Park (recently restored after falling victim for decades to vandals), the film moves at an accelerated pace. There are, however, referrals to the "new" film grammar with a Puck who miraculously flies through the air (Puck is made to order for Méliès-like cinematographers anyway). In its refreshing naivete, the movie is reminiscent of the rude mechanicals' "Pyramus and Thisby" sequence in the play itself (KSR). *Audience:* General use; *Supplementary materials:* Ball, *SOSF* 52-6; 313-4.

MEDIUM INFORMATION: *Medium:* Motion Picture; *Sound:* Silent; *Color:* No (black & white); *Length:* 8 min.; *Language of subtitles:* English; *Film type:* 16mm.

AUTHORSHIP INFORMATION: *Producer(s):* Vitagraph; *Director(s):* Kent, Charles; *Cast:* Costello, Maurice (Lysander); Costello, Dolores and Helene (Fairies); Hulette, Gladys (Puck); Ranous, William (Bottom); Chapman, Charles (Quince); Ackerman, Walter (Demetrius); Gordon, Julia Swayne (Helena); Tapley, Rose (Hermia [?]); Turner, Florence (Titania [?]); Shea, Will (Mechanical) [Credits: Ball].

DISTRIBUTION & AVAILABILITY: *Publisher or responsible agency:* Vitagraph Company; *Copy location:* FOL, LCM; *Call or copy number:* MP 68.

A Midsummer Night's Dream. **Motion Picture/Derivative**

388. *Le song d'une nuit d'éte, d'après Shakespeare.*

DOCUMENT INFORMATION: *Country:* France; *Year of release:* 1909.

EDITION, HISTORY, CONTENTS, & EVALUATION: *Edition & history:* From the title it sounds like a very loose adaptation. *Supplementary materials:* Ball, *SOSF* 105; *SIF* 85.

MEDIUM INFORMATION: *Length:* 17 min.

AUTHORSHIP INFORMATION: *Director(s):* Le Lion films; *Cast:* "Footit" (Hall, Tudor); Napierkowska, Stacia.

A Midsummer Night's Dream. **Motion Picture/Abridgment**

389. *A Midsummer Night's Dream.*

DOCUMENT INFORMATION: *Country:* Italy; *Year of release:* 1913.

EDITION, HISTORY, CONTENTS, & EVALUATION: *Edition & history:* Advanced cinematic techniques such as iris-outs, dissolves and cross-cutting fill this movie, which was also made out of doors on location, another radical step. Unhappily only remnants of it have survived. *Contents & evaluation:* Four years of technological advancement in filmmaking technique may account for the superiority of this Italian *Midsummer Night* to the 1909 Vitagraph version. There is also a finer artistic sensibility at work. Puck is an absolute doll, seated, laughing in a tree when first glimpsed. The outdoor lighting gives a wonderful chiaroscuro effect to the faces of the actors, and there is even a fairly successful attempt to represent the wood at night through a darkening of the background. True, there are probably too many title cards (the bane of silent Shakespeare) but on the other hand the film's production values are decidedly ambitious. One is left at the end with the sight of the fairies happily skipping across a field before the picture dissolves. R.H. Ball's description of the film as "refreshing" is surely merited (KSR). *Audience:* General use; *Supplementary materials:* Ball, *SOSF* 168-9; 346.

MEDIUM INFORMATION: *Medium:* Motion Picture; *Sound:* Silent; *Color:* No (black & white); *Length:* 22 min.; *Language of subtitles:* English; *Film type:* 16mm.

AUTHORSHIP INFORMATION: *Producer(s):* Warner Features (for USA); *Director(s):* Azzuri, Paulo [?]; *Cast:* Tommasi, Socrate (Lysander); Hübner, Bianca Maria (Helena).

DISTRIBUTION & AVAILABILITY: *Publisher or responsible agency:* Artistic Cinema Negatives of San Remo (?); *Copy location:* FOL; *Call or copy number:* MP 58.

A Midsummer Night's Dream. **Motion Picture/Derivative**

390. *Ein Sommernachtstraum.*

DOCUMENT INFORMATION: *Country:* Germany; *Year of release:* 1913.

EDITION, HISTORY, CONTENTS, & EVALUATION: *Edition & history:* Ball, *SOSF*, gives an interesting account of this film, which was apparently somewhat risque, indeed a "gross and nasty distortion" (177). A product of the Reinhardt school, it sounds like a precursor to such post-modernist films as Celestino Coronado's punk/gay 1984 *Dream. Supplementary materials:* SIF 85; Ball, *SOSF* 176-77.

MEDIUM INFORMATION: *Length:* [?] min.

AUTHORSHIP INFORMATION: *Director(s):* Rye, Stellan; *Cast:* Berger, Grete (Puck).

391. *Ein Sommernachtstraum: En heiteres Fastnachtsspiel.*

DOCUMENT INFORMATION: *Country:* Germany; *Year of release:* 1925.

EDITION, HISTORY, CONTENTS, & EVALUATION: *Edition & history:* The Berlin censors forbade children to see this one. The German filmmakers were way ahead of their times in their eagerness to deconstruct the Shakespearean text. Werner Krauss, famous for his role as Dr. Caligari as well as for his Iago with Emil Jannings in *Othello*, appears as Bottom. *Supplementary materials:* Ball, *SOSF* 297-99; *SIF* 86.

MEDIUM INFORMATION: *Sound:* Silent; *Color:* No (black & white); *Length:* 50 min.

AUTHORSHIP INFORMATION: *Director(s):* Neumann, Hans; *Cast:* Krauss, Werner (Bottom); Becker, Theodor (Theseus); Weyher, Ruth (Hippolyta).

A Midsummer Night's Dream. **Motion Picture/Interpretation**

392. *A Midsummer Night's Dream.*

DOCUMENT INFORMATION: *Country:* USA; *Year of release:* 1935.

EDITION, HISTORY, CONTENTS, & EVALUATION: *Edition & history:* An ambitious Hollywood production that is almost a paradigm for the large-studio production methods of the Golden Years prior to WW II. The star-studded cast includes the biggest names in Hollywood, such as Mickey Rooney, James Cagney and Joe E. Brown. The combination of the director's German expressionism (particularly apparent in the unforgettable ballet sequence when Nini Theilade portrays the coming of night) with Hollywood realism (gangster types like Cagney cast as one of the rude mechanicals) resulted in a curious hybrid that baffled the critics. Fifty years ago none had a vocabulary for coping with such a radical re-representation of a Shakespearean play. At one level the film seemed to be a Hollywood vulgarization, and at another a gigantic tribute to Shakespeare's timeless charm. Hence in its own day the production was alternately damned and praised. Although the film boldly and creatively adapted the play, it was neither quite a critical nor a commercial success. Its poor showing at the box office contributed to Hollywood's growing apprehension about Shakespeare's plays being "box office poison." *Contents & evaluation:* "If, in a *Midsummer Night's Dream*, Shakespeare is, in C.L. Barber's fine phrase, 'making up fresh things in Ovid's manner,' then Reinhardt and Dieterle, in their film of the play, are making up some stale cliches in Hollywood's fashion. In the midst of a bold attempt to create on film a visual metaphor for Shakespeare's green world, Reinhardt and Dieterle are foiled by trying to impose literal narrative on the suggestive reaches of Shakespeare's imagination. The dark and erotic possibilities of the visual landscape they create fall victim to the light and recognizable tale they ask it to contain. The possibilities they seize upon, and which Jack Jorgens celebrates, for film's ability to envelop us in Shakespeare's rich twilight world evaporate in their inability to imagine narrative metaphors as powerful as its scenic equivalents. As much as we enjoy and delight in the exuberance of their achievement, we must still be prepared to assess their failures to transcend early sound film's tendency to grind its material into the grist of domestic melodrama" (Crowl, Samuel, "Babes in the Woods, or 'The Lost Boys'," *LFQ* 11.3 [1983]:186-7). Many British critics were driven almost to apoplexy by the spectacle of Shakespeare's world so Americanized that such types as Cagney and Rooney could appear in the cast. Yet the "Americanization" of Shakespeare by way of German Expressionism was what this film was all about. It was a cultural Declaration of Independence against the widely held prejudice that only British actors can play Shakespeare. Hollywood was saying Shakespeare is for the entire English-speaking world, not just for the English. After all, the language spoken by the actors at the Globe playhouse in Queen Elizabeth's day would have been equally incomprehensible to either a modern British or North American audience (KSR). *Audience:* High school (grades 10-12); General use; *Supplementary materials:* Jorgens, *SOF* 36-58; Manvell, *SATF* 25-7; Willson, Robert F., Jr. "Ill Met by Moonlight: Reinhardt's *A Midsummer Night's Dream* and Musical Screwball Comedy." *JPF* 5 [1976]: 185-97.

MEDIUM INFORMATION: *Medium:* Motion picture; *Sound:* Spoken language; *Color:* Yes; *Length:* 132 min.; *Language(s) spoken:* English; *Film type:* 16mm, 35mm; *Video type:* V.

AUTHORSHIP INFORMATION: *Producer(s):* Reinhardt, Max; *Director(s):* Reinhardt, Max; Dieterle, William; *Adaptor/translator(s):* Kenyon, Charles; McCall, Mary; *Composer(s):* Mendelssohn, Felix; Korngold, Erich Wolf-

gang; Forbstein, Leo F.; *Choreographer(s):* Nijinska, Bronislawa; Theilade, Nini; *Designer(s):* Grot, Anton; *Costume designer(s):* Ree, Max; *Other personnel:* Dawson, Ralph (Editor); Mohr, Hal Haskin, Byron Jackman, Fred Konekamp, Hans (Photography); Westmore, Perc (Cosmetician); *Cast:* Cagney, James (Bottom); Brown, Joe E. (Flute); Havilland, Olivia de (Hermia); Jory, Victor (Oberon); Rooney, Mickey (Puck); Powell, Dick (Lysander); Muir, Jean (Helena); Louise, Anita (Titania); Alexander, Ross (Demetrius); McHugh, Frank (Quince); Robinson, Dewey (Snug); Herbert, Hugh (Snout); Harlan, Otis (Starveling); Teasdale, Verree (Hippolyta); Barty, Billy (Mustardseed); Treacher, Arthur (Ninny's Tomb); Hunter, Ian (Theseus); Mitchell, Grant (Egeus); Theilade, Nini (First Fairy).

DISTRIBUTION & AVAILABILITY: *Publisher or responsible agency:* Warner Brothers; *Distributor:* UAC, ERS, TWC, DCV, FCM, ITM*, FMB*, BFI*, *Availability:* UAC Rental 16mm, Apply; Sale KEY, B,V, $59.95; TWC,B,V, $68.50; ERS, B,V, $79.98; DCV (#35117), V, $58.00; FCM, V, $19.98; FMB* apply; BFI* 10-min. study extract only.

A Midsummer Night's Dream. Video/Scenes

393. *A Midsummer Night's Dream.* (Series: Scenes from Shakespeare).

DOCUMENT INFORMATION: *Country:* GB; *Year of first showing:* 1937; *Location of first showing:* BBC. Transmitted 18 Feb. 1937.

EDITION, HISTORY, CONTENTS, & EVALUATION: *Edition & history:* A part of the BBC pioneering "Scenes from Shakespeare" series, the earliest transmissions of Shakespeare on television. The program called for Mendelssohn's music during the intervals. *Supplementary materials:* TPAB 18 Feb. 1937.

MEDIUM INFORMATION: *Length:* 25 min.

AUTHORSHIP INFORMATION: *Producer(s):* Bower, Dallas; *Cast:* Hilliard, Patricia (Titania); Petrie, D. Hay (Bottom).

DISTRIBUTION & AVAILABILITY: *Publisher or responsible agency:* BBC; *Copy location:* Unavailable.

A Midsummer Night's Dream. Video/Ballet

394. *A Midsummer Night's Dream.*

DOCUMENT INFORMATION: *Country:* GB; *Year of first showing:* 1937; *Location of first showing:* BBC. Transmitted from 3:38 to 4:10 P.M., 23 Apr. 1937.

EDITION, HISTORY, CONTENTS, & EVALUATION: *Edition & history:* One of the very earliest transmissions of Shakespeare on television when the industry was still in its infancy. A "Mask" arranged from the fairy scenes of the play, this performance was the most ambitious up until then. *Supplementary materials: TPAB* 23 Apr. 1937.

MEDIUM INFORMATION: *Length:* 32 min.

AUTHORSHIP INFORMATION: *Producer(s):* Thomas, Stephen; *Composer(s):* Mendelssohn, Felix; Packer, Boris (Leader); Greenbaum, Hyam (Conductor); *Choreographer(s):* Howard, Andree; *Cast:* Hayes, Patricia (Puck); Moon, Eva (Fairy); Holme, Thea (Titania); Knox, Alexander (Oberon); Howard, Andree; Schooling, Elizabeth; Braithwaite, Margaret; Gore, Walter; Laying, Hugh; Tod, Quentin (Dancers); Cohen, Marie; Green, Dorothy (Singers).

DISTRIBUTION & AVAILABILITY: *Publisher or responsible agency:* BBC; *Copy location:* Unavailable.

A Midsummer Night's Dream. Video/Scenes

395. *Pyramus and Thisby.* (Series: Scenes from Shakespeare).

DOCUMENT INFORMATION: *Country:* GB; *Year of first showing:* 1937; *Location of first showing:* BBC. Transmitted 3:01 to 3:20 P.M., 14 July 1937; repeat 23 July 1937.

EDITION, HISTORY, CONTENTS, & EVALUATION: *Edition & history:* The episodes transmitted on this early BBC television program were the "Fools scenes," featuring Bottom and Company. Repeated 28 Jan. 1938 but with a somewhat different cast. The fact that Mr. Wilfrid Walter received £15 15 s. ($75 [?]) to play the role of Bottom furnishes some insight into the spartan economics of television production in those days. *Supplementary materials: TPAB* 14 July 1937.

MEDIUM INFORMATION: *Length:* 19 min.

AUTHORSHIP INFORMATION: *Producer(s):* Bussell, Jan; *Cast:* Walter, Wilfrid, (Bottom); Lefeaux, Charles (Quince); Gemmell, Don (Flute); Chitty, Erik (Snout); Lees, Herbert (Snug); Leslie, Hubert (Starveling); Villiers, Kenneth (Philostate); Rudling, John (Theseus).

DISTRIBUTION & AVAILABILITY: *Publisher or responsible agency:* BBC; *Copy location:* Unavailable.

396. *Pyramus and Thisby.*

DOCUMENT INFORMATION: *Country:* GB; *Year of first showing:* 1938; *Location of first showing:* BBC. Transmitted 9:39 to 10:07 P.M., 1 Jan. 1938.

EDITION, HISTORY, CONTENTS, & EVALUATION: *Edition & history:* One of the earlier transmissions of Shakespeare on television when the industry was still in its infancy. This seems to be a reworking of the 1937 *Pyramus and Thisby* directed by Jan Bussell (see 395). Frank Birch replaced Wilfrid Walter as Bottom. *Supplementary materials: TPAB* 28 Jan. 1938.

MEDIUM INFORMATION: *Length:* 26 min.

AUTHORSHIP INFORMATION: *Producer(s):* Bussell, Jan; *Cast:* Birch, Frank (Bottom); Lefeaux, Charles (Quince); Gemmell, Don (Flute); Chitty, Erik (Snout); Lees, Herbert (Snug); Leslie, Hubert (Starveling); Rudling, John (Theseus); Sandilands, Jillian (Hippolyta); Villiers, Kenneth (Demetrius/Philostrate).

DISTRIBUTION & AVAILABILITY: *Publisher or responsible agency:* BBC; *Copy location:* Unavailable.

A Midsummer Night's Dream. Video/Recording

397. *A Midsummer Night's Dream.*

DOCUMENT INFORMATION: *Country:* GB; *Year of first showing:* 1946; *Location of first showing:* Regents Park. BBC transmission 2:30 to 5:00 P.M., Wed., 24 July 1946.

EDITION, HISTORY, CONTENTS, & EVALUATION: *Edition & history:* A recording of a post WW II performance by the Bankside players at the famous Open Air Theatre in London's Regents Park. The program notes show that Felix Mendelssohn's romantic music supported the players. The production was fairly successful since one year later another *MND* in Regents Park was transmitted, with Robert Atkins co-producing with I. Orr-Ewing. The elaborate provisions for music and dance raised great technical challenges in those inaugural years of broadcast television. *Supplementary materials: TPAB* 24 July 1946.

MEDIUM INFORMATION: *Length:* 150 min.

AUTHORSHIP INFORMATION: *Producer(s):* Atkins, Robert; *Composer(s):* Mendelssohn, Felix; Watson, Rosabel (Orchestra); *Choreographer(s):* Honer, Mary; *Cast:* Llewelyn, Desmond (Theseus); Dance, Thomas (Egeus); Faulds, Andrew (Lysander); Bell, Peter (Demetrius); March, David (Philostrate); Thorndike, Russell (Quince); Marning, Hugh (Bottom); Lynn, Jack (Snout); Staff, Ivan (Flute); Hamelin, Clement (Starveling); Stocks, Ronald (Snug); Shafto, Angela (Hippolyta); Baker, Iris (Helena); Hicks, Patricia (Hermia); Byron, John (Oberon); Bennett, Vivienne (Titania); Honer, Mary (Puck); Wilson, Diana (First Fairy); Harting, Bridget; Stuart, Wendy; Bussell, Mary; Spencer-Levis [?], Diana; Gampels, Zoe; Newman, Ann; Jory, Ann; Bessell, Dinette; Burgess, Lorna (Fairy Ballet).

DISTRIBUTION & AVAILABILITY: *Publisher or responsible agency:* BBC; *Copy location:* Unavailable.

398. *A Midsummer Night's Dream.*

DOCUMENT INFORMATION: *Country:* GB; *Year of first showing:* 1947; *Location of first showing:* BBC. Transmitted in Two Parts: 7:30 P.M., Monday and Wednesday, July 28, 29, 1947.

EDITION, HISTORY, CONTENTS, & EVALUATION:

Edition & history: The Open Air Theatre, contiguous with the fabulous Queen Mary's Rose Garden in Regents Park, London, was once again the setting for this *Midsummer Night's Dream*, which repeated the 1946 television show (see 397) but with many new faces in cast and production crews. Mary Honer stayed on as Puck and as choreographer and Rosabel Watson again conducted the orchestra. Lysander and Demetrius were new, however, and the Fairy Ballet was entirely different from the 1946 corps. The recording of a live performance would make the performance available to thousands who might otherwise never have bothered to visit the Open Air Theatre, though the virtues of this goal are balanced by the defects—only a trip to the Open Air Theatre on a summer evening could capture the full magic of the experience. Ironically in 1947 perhaps the same persons who could afford television were also the ones who could afford to go to the Open Air Theatre. *Supplementary materials: TPAB* 28 July 1947.

MEDIUM INFORMATION: *Length:* 120 min. [60 min. each part].

AUTHORSHIP INFORMATION: *Producer(s):* Atkins, Robert; Orr-Ewing, I.; *Composer(s):* Mendelssohn, Felix; Watson, Rosabel (Conductor); *Choreographer(s):* Honer, Mary; *Other personnel:* Blyth, Eric (General Manager); Burney, David (Stage Director); Noel-Smith, Monica (Stage Manager); Carew, John (Asst. Stage Manager); *Cast:* Manning, Hugh (Theseus); Bale, Ernest (Egeus); Hutchinson, William (Lysander); Solon, Ewen (Demetrius); Meacham, Michael (Philostrate); Dance, Thomas (Quince); Atkins, Robert (Bottom); Wright, Leslie (Snout); March, David (Flute); Hamelin, Clement (Starveling); Woodroofe, Ronald (Snug); Dante, Gwendolyn (Hippolyta); Brooke, Anne (Helena); Forster, Yvonne (Hermia); Hansard, Paul (Oberon); Kneale, Patricia (Titania); Honer, Mary (Puck); Wilson, Diana (First Fairy); Fox, Sheila (Singing Fairy); Grant, Joan; Banyard, Joan; Harvey, Joy; Lineham, Joyce; Portsmouth, Bernice; Heritage, Roma; Warren, Constance; Boyd, Joan; Harris, Patricia; Ross, Kate; Karnivola, Kristile (Fairy ballet).

DISTRIBUTION & AVAILABILITY: *Publisher or responsible agency:* BBC; *Copy location:* Unavailable.

A Midsummer Night's Dream. Motion Picture/Scenes

399. *A Midsummer Night's Dream.*

DOCUMENT INFORMATION: *Country:* USA; *Year of release:* 1954.

EDITION, HISTORY, CONTENTS, & EVALUATION: *Edition & history:* Intended as an introduction for school children. *Supplementary materials:* Loughney, Katharine.

"Shakespeare on Film and Tape at Library of Congress." *SFNL* 14.1 (Dec. 1989): 4.

MEDIUM INFORMATION: *Length:* 15 min.

AUTHORSHIP INFORMATION: *Cast:* Krutch, Joseph Wood (Consultant).

DISTRIBUTION & AVAILABILITY: *Copy location:* LCM; *Call or copy number:* FBA 1087.

A Midsummer Night's Dream. Video/Scenes

400. *Summer in Dubrovnik Festival.*

DOCUMENT INFORMATION: *Country:* GB; *Year of first showing:* 1957; *Location of first showing:* BBC. Transmitted [c.] 12 April 1957.

EDITION, HISTORY, CONTENTS, & EVALUATION: *Edition & history:* The 1956 festival in Dubrovnik, Yugoslavia, included scenes from *A Midsummer Night's Dream* and *Hamlet* that were recorded for BBC. *Supplementary materials:* "Program." *RT* 12 April 1957: 15.

MEDIUM INFORMATION: *Length:* [?] min.

AUTHORSHIP INFORMATION: *Cast:* Wright, Kenneth (Englishman); Mvmak, Sava (Robert); Mircik, Voja (Jean-Jacques).

DISTRIBUTION & AVAILABILITY: *Publisher or responsible agency:* BBC; *Copy location:* Unavailable.

401. *A Midsummer Night's Dream.* (Series: Theatre Flash).

DOCUMENT INFORMATION: *Country:* GB; *Year of first showing:* 1957; *Location of first showing:* BBC. Transmitted 8:15 to 8:30 P.M. 31 Jan. 1957.

EDITION, HISTORY, CONTENTS, & EVALUATION: *Edition & history:* Transmitted directly from the stage of London's Old Vic Theatre as a New Year's eve glimpse at the West End theatre scene. Dame Judi Dench, then plain Judi Dench, could have been glimpsed in the obscure role of a fairy. *Supplementary materials:* "Program." *RT* 27 Dec. 1957: 10.

MEDIUM INFORMATION: *Length:* 15 min.

AUTHORSHIP INFORMATION: *Producer(s):* Burrell-Davis, Derek; *Director(s):* Benthall, Michael; *Cast:* Howerd, Frankie (Bottom); Daneman, Paul (Quince); Culliford, James (Snug); Francis, Derek (Snout); Fraser, Ronald (Flute); Thorndike, Daniel (Starveling); Redman, Joyce (Titania); Taylor, Keith (Puck); Bosworth, Gillian (Cobweb); Gibson, Valerie (Mustardseed); Orton, Stella (Moth); Wood, Bridget (Peaseblossom); Dench, Judi; Cooke, Juliet; Kwan, Nancy; Atkinson, Jean (Fairies).

DISTRIBUTION & AVAILABILITY: *Publisher or responsible agency:* BBC; *Copy location:* Unavailable.

A Midsummer Night's Dream. Video/Teleplay

402. *A Midsummer Night's Dream.* (Series: Sunday Night Theatre Series).

DOCUMENT INFORMATION: *Country:* GB; *Year of release:* 1958; *Year of first showing:* 1958; *Location of first showing:* BBC TV, Transmitted 9 Nov. 1958.

EDITION, HISTORY, CONTENTS, & EVALUATION: *Edition & history*: This was the first full-length TV studio production of *MND* in England. Previously, however, there had been excerpts transmitted on television, twice in 1937 (on Feb. 18 and April 23), and then again July 24, 1946 and July 28 and 29, 1947, from the Open Air Theatre in Regents Park, as well as in January 1957 directly from the Old Vic (see 401). This production was originally budgeted at £4,500, then considered an enormous sum of money. Despite grumblings from studio executives, the final cost soared to over £6,000. A cast of 12 men and 10 women, plus a Corps de Ballet of 28 contributed to the escalating costs (WAC TS/232 Nov. 1958). *Contents & evaluation:* Not seen. Peter Morris comments, however, that this was a "16mm Kinescope recording of a production for BBC television" and that "for television of that period, this was a surprisingly lavish production, well designed, staged and costumed and presented with full musical accompaniment and ballet" (ShOF 21). *Audience:* General use; *Supplementary materials:* Barry, Michael. "*A Midsummer Night's Dream*." RT 7 Nov. 1958: 4+.

MEDIUM INFORMATION: *Medium:* Video; *Sound:* Spoken language; *Color:* No (black & white); *Length:* 105 min.; *Language(s) spoken:* English; *Video type:* Kinescope.

AUTHORSHIP INFORMATION: *Producer(s):* Cartier, Rudolph; *Director(s):* Cartier, Rudolph; *Composer(s):* Mendelssohn, Felix; Bridgewater, Leslie; *Choreographer(s):* Rodrigues, Alfred; *Designer(s):* Hatts, Clifford; *Costume designer(s):* Glanville, Pamela; *Other personnel*: Crozier, Eric (TV editor); Ross, Rosemary (Make-up); *Cast:* Rogers, Paul (Bottom); Parry, Natasha (Titania); Justin, John (Oberon); Lynne, Gillian (Puck); Westbrook, John (Theseus); Whiting, Margaret (Hippolyta); Finn, Christine (Hermia); Drummond, Vivienne (Helena); Lander, Eric (Demetrius); Oxley, David (Lysander); Longden, John (Egeus); Malleson, Miles (Quince); Fraser, Ronald (Flute); Sallis, Peter (Snug); Warner, John (Snout); Bates, Michael (Starveling); Daniel, Jennifer (First Fairy); Shore, Jane (Peaseblossom); MacSweenie, Gaynie (Mustardseed); Ruthven, Vernie (Cobweb); Merry, Hazel (Moth); *Performance group(s):* BBC.

DISTRIBUTION & AVAILABILITY: *Publisher or responsible agency:* British Broadcasting Co.; *Copy location:* NFA* *Restrictions:* NFA* print not available in 1988.

A Midsummer Night's Dream. Motion Picture/ Derivative

403. *Sen Noci Svatojanske.* [*Midsummer Night's Dream*].

DOCUMENT INFORMATION: *Country:* Czechoslovakia; *Year of release:* 1959.

EDITION, HISTORY, CONTENTS, & EVALUATION: *Awards:* Cannes Film Festival, 1959; *Edition & history:* Although many people tend to back away when they hear that this film is a puppet version of Shakespeare's play, boredom turns into enthusiasm when they learn that the dubbed-in voices belong to some of the theatre's most distinguished actors and actresses. Richard Burton acts as the Narrator; Alec McCowen as Nick Bottom, and so forth. It was first shown in the English dialogue version in New York City at the Guild Theatre on 18 Dec. 1961. *Contents & evaluation:* Not seen, but the reviews were favorable. Gene Moskowitz wrote in *Variety* of "uncannily animated puppets who gave it all a dreamlike quality" *Audience:* General use; *Supplementary materials:* Moskowitz, Gene. "Review." *VAR* 13 (1959):7.

MEDIUM INFORMATION: *Medium:* Motion Picture; *Sound:* Spoken language; *Color:* Yes; *Length:* 74 min.; *Language(s) spoken:* English; *Film type:* 35mm Eastman Cinemascope.

AUTHORSHIP INFORMATION: *Producer(s):* Trnka, Jiři; *Director(s):* Trnka, Jiři; *Screenplay writer(s):* Trnka, Jiři; *Adaptor/translator(s):* Sackler, Howard (English version); Appelsen, Len (English dialogue supervisor); *Composer(s):* Trojan, Václav; *Designer(s):* Trnka, Jiři; *Lighting designer(s):* Vojta, Jiři; *Other personnel:* Karpas, Jan; Latál, Stanislav; Jurajdova, Vlasta; Pojar, Bretislav; Adam, Jan; Sramek, Bohuslav (Animators); Formanek, Emanuel; Vleek, Josef; Polednik, Emil (Sound); Walachova, Hana (Editor); *Cast:* Burton, Richard (Narrator); Criddle, Tom (Lysander); Bell, Ann (Hermia); Meacham, Michael (Demetrius); McCowen, Alec (Nick Bottom); Gwillim, Jack (Oberon); Leigh, Barbara (Helena).

DISTRIBUTION & AVAILABILITY: *Publisher or responsible agency:* Ceskoslovensky Film.

A Midsummer Night's Dream. Video/Interpretation

404. *A Midsummer Night's Dream.*

DOCUMENT INFORMATION: *Country:* GB; *Year of first showing:* 1964; *Location of first showing:* Rediffusion Network Television. Transmitted 9:10 P.M., 24 June 1964.

EDITION, HISTORY, CONTENTS, & EVALUATION: *Edition & history:* A studio television production made by one of Britain's independent (non-BBC) television companies. Now suddenly this once rare production is widely available for a nominal cost on videocassette. "George Rylands of Cambridge University was brought in to advise and edit the script, and Michael Yates was appointed to design the sets. [The production] eschewed any attempt at the modern approach." It was made at Wembley Studio 5, with 200 stagehands, 400 lamps, and 40 lighting changes." And was declared to be "the most imaginative TV production of a Shakespeare play during the quarter-centenary year" (Blyth, Alan, "*A Midsummer Night's Dream*," *TV Times* 19 June 1964: 10 +). *Contents & evaluation:* A copy of this production is still available at the NFA in black and white on 16mm film. This is a very lovely, romantic, beautiful, virtually uncut, adaptation of Shakespeare's play, done theatrically with Mendelssohn's music and supplementary ballet. The expressionistic influences of the Reinhardt school swim just below the surface. The verse is spoken in a spritely fashion. John Fraser as Lysander makes notable use of gesture and expression to get across his speech to Helena about meeting her in the wood near Athens. He looks directly at her and makes plain that she means more to him than the words coming out of his mouth. The Pyramus and Thisby play is wittily performed by a talented group while the young people sit around and sneer at the pathetic attempts of the yokels to act. The woodland *mise en scène* is truly amazing, considering the severe limitations of the studio. Shrieking animals, a ubiquitous Puck, and a formidable Oberon with a pre-Punk haircut, add further excitement. The choreography supports the high standard of performance, especially with the stately closing number. Curiously anachronistic, though, are the actors' trim, short haircuts, but they only serve to remind us that Shakespearean performance inevitably mirrors current fashions (KSR). *Audience:* General use.

MEDIUM INFORMATION: *Medium:* Video; *Sound:* Spoken language; *Color:* Yes; *Length:* 111 min.; *Language(s) spoken:* English; *Film type:* 16mm.

AUTHORSHIP INFORMATION: *Producer(s):* Rediffusion; *Director(s):* Kemp-Welch, Joan; *Adaptor/translator(s):* Rylands, George; *Composer(s):* Mendelssohn, Felix; Woolfenden, Guy (w. Philharmonia Orchestra); *Choreographer(s):* Corelli, Juan; *Designer(s):* Yates, Michael; *Costume designer(s):* Jackson, Sheila; *Lighting designer(s):* Lee, Bill; *Cast: The Lovers:* Bennett, Jill (Helena); Beck, Maureen (Hermia); Fraser, John (Lysander); Elkin, Clifford (Demetrius); *The Court:* Allen, Patrick (Theseus); Heath, Eira (Hippolyta); Luckham, Cyril (Egeus); Bateman, Tony (Philostrate); *The Fairies:* Massey, Anna (Titania); Wyngarde, Peter (Oberon); Tanner, Tony (Puck); Frazer, Kay (Fairy); Church, Peter (Peaseblossom); Newport, Michael (Mustardseed); Thomas, Stanley (Moth); Simpson, Diana (Cobweb); *The Mechanicals:* Hill, Benny (Bottom); Malleson, Miles (Quince); Bass, Alfie (Flute); Hewlett, Arthur (Snug); Shine, Bill (Starveling); Bresslaw, Bernard (Snout); *The Dancers:* Aston, Natasha; Chele, Dianne;

Grant, Carole; Jones, Lynda; Joseph, Yvonne; King, Annabel; Kinson, Janet; Magner, Helen; Curran, Ronnie; Gilbert, Terry; Ruffell, Priscilla; Toombs, Rosemary; *Performance group(s):* Royal Shakespeare Company.

DISTRIBUTION & AVAILABILITY: *Publisher or responsible agency:* Rediffusion Network Production; *Distributor:* VID, FCM, DCV, *Copy location:* NFA*; *Availability:* VID, V (#212), B $29.95; DCV, V (#65111), $48; FCM, V, $29.95; INM, V, $59.95.

A Midsummer Night's Dream. Motion Picture/ Interpretation

405. *A Midsummer Night's Dream.*

DOCUMENT INFORMATION: *Country:* GB; *Year of filming:* 1968; *Year of release:* 1969; *Year of first showing:* 9 Feb. 1969; *Country of first showing:* USA; *Location of first showing:* Television.

EDITION, HISTORY, CONTENTS, & EVALUATION: *Edition & history:* Originally made for TV and nationally broadcast in the USA in 1969, this film combines the expressionism of a Reinhardt with the realism of the Italian movie makers. Shot outdoors in Warwickshire at Compton Verney, emphasis falls on the down-to-earth problems of the young lovers (their faces are even daubed with mud). At the same time, however, the peculiar color of the terrain, the whippings about of Puck, the bizarre nature of the fairy world speak to an expressionistic, or even surrealistic, vision at odds with the mundane and prosaic. The costumes reflect also the swinging new London of the late Sixties when mini-skirts and Carnaby Street dominated the scene. (A film that perfectly captures the essence of this last gasp of Victorian culture is *Georgy Girl* [1966], starring Lyn Redgrave and Alan Bates.) *Contents & evaluation:* "The film abounds with so many good things, from conceptual setting to graceful subtleties of visual composition, that I am puzzled by the poor reviews. These point to a special difficulty the film encounters with a general audience, a difficulty minimized for us as teachers and critics of Shakespeare's plays by our interest in the verse and in the interpretation of the play. Hall's documentary camera techniques call into play realistic cinematic conventions which may distort a true response to the film as a film. Because we associate close-ups and handheld cameras with documentary, especially with television news reporting, the film is in constant danger of merely seeming to be a film of actors acting. If this convention prevails, as it did for about one third of the British reviewers, the film fails. The modern clothes and setting then seem a cute attempt to be up-to-date, 'rather as if,' Hall had assembled a house party of brilliant people and said, 'Let's make a movie!' The interplay between posing and ironic reality collapses. The special effects, devoid of magic, only irritate. To argue that Shakespeare films are a genre unto themselves, while true, substitutes a lesser truth for a greater. For a play itself, as its stage history attests, is of a strange, mixed genre, constantly calling attention to its actors as actors, playing with our suspended disbelief at every turn, and tempting us to dismiss it, with Pepys, as merely 'insipid.' Perhaps more than Hall guessed when he said it 'it may not be a film at all,' the film is a true rendering of Shakespeare's *Midsummer Night's Dream*. Like the play itself, it challenges its audience to set their notions of conventional film aside, to believe with Hippolyta that this rare vision does indeed grow to something of great constancy" (Mullin, Michael, "Peter Hall's *Midsummer Night's Dream* on Film," *ETJ* 27 [1975]: 529-34). *Audience:* High school (grades 10-12); General use; *Supplementary materials:* Jorgens, *SOF* 51-65; Manvell, *SATF* 119-27.

MEDIUM INFORMATION: *Medium:* Motion Picture; *Sound:* Spoken language; *Color:* Yes; *Length:* 124 min.; *Language(s) spoken:* English; *Film type:* 16mm; Eastman Color.

AUTHORSHIP INFORMATION: *Producer(s):* Birkett, Michael; *Director(s):* Hall, Peter; *Composer(s):* Woolfenden, Guy; *Designer(s):* Bury, John; *Costume designer(s):* Curtis, Ann; *Other personnel:* Suschitzky, Peter (Camera); Harris, Jack (Editing); *Cast:* Godfrey, Derek (Theseus); Jefford, Barbara (Hippolyta); Sullivan, Hugh (Philostrate); Selby, Nicholas (Egeus); Warner, David (Lysander); Jayston, Michael (Demetrius); Rigg, Diana (Helena); Mirren, Helen (Hermia); Richardson, Ian (Oberon); Dench, Judi (Titania); Holm, Ian (Puck); Rogers, Paul (Bottom); Shaw, Sebastian (Quince); Travers, Bill (Snout); Normington, John (Flute); Swift, Clive (Snug); Eccles, Donald (Starveling); *Performance group(s):* Royal Shakespeare Company.

DISTRIBUTION & AVAILABILITY: *Publisher or responsible agency:* Royal Shakespeare Company Enterprise/Alan Clore/Filmways; *Distributor:* FNC, FCM, DCV, DAR*, *Availability:* FNC, rental 16mm, apply; FCM, V, $19.95 (1988); DCV, V, $38.

A Midsummer Night's Dream. Motion Picture/Abridgment

406. *Midsummer Night's Dream: An Introduction.* (Series: Shakespeare Series [BHE], II).

DOCUMENT INFORMATION: *Country:* GB; *Year of first showing:* 1969.

EDITION, HISTORY, CONTENTS, & EVALUATION: *Edition & history:* The second in a series of six abridged versions of the plays (see 41, 228, 258, 323, 656). For further information, see *AYL*, 41. *Contents & evaluation:* Not seen. *Audience:* High school (grades 10-12); College and university.

MEDIUM INFORMATION: *Medium:* Motion Picture; *Sound:* Spoken language; *Color:* Yes; *Length:* 25 min.; *Language(s) spoken:* English; *Film type:* 16mm.

AUTHORSHIP INFORMATION: *Producer(s):* BHE/Seabourne Enterprises; *Cast:* Not known.

DISTRIBUTION & AVAILABILITY: *Publisher or responsible agency:* BHE/Seabourne; *Distributor:* BFA.

A Midsummer Night's Dream. Video/Recording

407. *A Midsummer Night's Dream.*

DOCUMENT INFORMATION: *Country:* GB; *Year of release:* 197[?].

EDITION, HISTORY, CONTENTS, & EVALUATION: *Edition & history:* A recording of a performance, which may no longer be available, by an Experimental Theatre Group at Cambridge University. *Supplementary materials:* BUFVC [lst edition, 1986 only] 33.

MEDIUM INFORMATION: *Length:* 135 min.

AUTHORSHIP INFORMATION: *Director(s):* Cambridge Players.

DISTRIBUTION & AVAILABILITY: *Distributor:* EVI*, inquire.

A Midsummer Night's Dream. Video/Teleplay

408. *A Midsummer Night's Dream.* (Series: Play of the Month).

DOCUMENT INFORMATION: *Country:* GB; *Year of first showing:* 1971; *Location of first showing:* BBC1 TV. Transmitted 8:10 to 10:10 P.M., Sunday, 26 Sept. 1971.

EDITION, HISTORY, CONTENTS, & EVALUATION: *Edition & history:* As the BBC program notes point out, compared to the production of Peter Brook's radical staging of *Dream*, then a smash hit in the London West End, this production was very traditional, despite its being performed in Edwardian costume and set in 1865. Filming was entirely on location in and around Scotney Castle, Kent. *Contents & evaluation:* The London *Times* critic was generally pleased with this effort to bring Shakespeare to the non-theatre-going public. He felt that the production "told a complicated story with admirable clarity" and that the result was "consistent, charming." Only the rude mechanicals were sufficiently funny, though, for the rest of the cast seemed to be bent on an inappropriately solemn manner (Raynor, Henry, "The Dream as Fantasy." *Times* 27 Sept. 1971: 10a). *Audience:* General use; *Supplementary materials:* Burn, Gordon. "Ronnie Barker's Bottom." *RT* 25 Sept. 1971: 8.

MEDIUM INFORMATION: *Medium:* Video; *Sound:*

Spoken language; *Color:* Yes; *Length:* 120 min.; *Language(s) spoken:* English; *Video type:* Video.

AUTHORSHIP INFORMATION: *Producer(s):* Messina, Cedric; *Director(s):* Jones, James Cellan; *Composer(s):* Chappell, Herbert; *Choreographer(s):* Stephenson, Geraldine; *Designer(s):* Andrews, Roger; *Costume designer(s):* Alley, Ian; *Lighting designer(s):* Thomas, Harry; *Cast:* Stephens, Robert (Oberon); Gambon, Michael (Theseus); Bron, Eleanor (Hippolyta); Glyn-Jones, John (Egeus); May, Bunny (Puck); Barrie, Amanda (Hermia); Redgrave, Lynn (Helena); Atkins, Eileen (Titania); Fox, Edward (Lysander); Clyde, Jeremy (Demetrius); Laurie, John (Quince); Barker, Ronnie (Bottom); Henry, Paul (Flute); Orchard, Julian (Snug); Parry, Ken (Snout); Rose, Clifford (Starveling); Taunton, Sarah (The Fairy).

DISTRIBUTION & AVAILABILITY: *Publisher or responsible agency:* BBC; *Copy location:* BBC*, archive; ITM* (1a Sha 3a).

A Midsummer Night's Dream. Video/Recording

408.1 *A Midsummer Night's Dream.*

DOCUMENT INFORMATION: *Country:* GB; *Year of first showing:* 1972.

EDITION, HISTORY, CONTENTS, & EVALUATION: *Edition & history:* Apparently a recording housed in Italy of the Peter Brook RSC production of *A Midsummer Night's Dream* at Stratford-upon-Avon in September 1972. If so, this is a rare opportunity to catch a glimpse of this famous production but best inquire before boarding a jet to Venice.

AUTHORSHIP INFORMATION: *Producer(s):* RSC; *Director(s):* Brook, Peter.

DISTRIBUTION & AVAILABILITY: *Copy location:* ASV; *Call or copy number:* A 5.101.206-3-4.

A Midsummer Night's Dream. Video/Documentary

409. *Magic in the Web of Art.*

DOCUMENT INFORMATION: *Country:* GB; *Year of release:* 1979.

EDITION, HISTORY, CONTENTS, & EVALUATION: *Edition & history:* An Open University lecture on *MND* by the celebrated American scholar, C.L. Barber. Regrettably the present location of the videotape is unknown to this compiler (KSR). *Supplementary materials: BUFVC* [1st Edition, 1986 only] 34.

MEDIUM INFORMATION: *Length:* 25 min.

AUTHORSHIP INFORMATION: *Director(s):* Kafno, Paul; *Cast:* Barber, C.L. (Speaker).

DISTRIBUTION & AVAILABILITY: *Distributor:* GSV*, inquire.

410. *Mendelssohn's Dream.*

DOCUMENT INFORMATION: *Country:* GB; *Year of release:* 1979.

EDITION, HISTORY, CONTENTS, & EVALUATION: *Edition & history:* An Open University program that relates Mendelssohn's music to the play. Ends with a scene from the play first without and then with the music to show its importance to the mood. *BUFVC*, 2nd edition, reports that it is no longer in distribution. *Supplementary materials: BUFVC*, 1st Edition, 35.

MEDIUM INFORMATION: *Sound:* Spoken language; *Color:* Yes; *Length:* 25 min.

AUTHORSHIP INFORMATION: *Director(s):* Philip, R.

DISTRIBUTION & AVAILABILITY: *Distributor:* GSV*, BBC*, inquire.

411. *A Midsummer Night's Dream.* (Series: Shakespeare in Perspective).

DOCUMENT INFORMATION: *Country:* GB; *Year of release:* 1981.

EDITION, HISTORY, CONTENTS, & EVALUATION: *Edition & history:* The "Shakespeare in Perspective" series was made to accompany the BBC/Time Life Inc. "The Shakespeare Plays" series (see also 44, 142, 234, 269, 335, 566 and 624). For overview, see 44, above. *Contents & evaluation:* Despite a certain uneasiness in front of the camera, Dr. Roy Strong succeeds in throwing considerable light on the kinds of celebrations in Shakespeare's day that would have called for a production of *A Midsummer Night's Dream.* Shots of Hatfield house and its great hall give a clear picture of the milieu in which upper tier Elizabethans celebrated nuptials. Through an analysis of the richly adorned gown in a portrait of Elizabeth, Strong shows how much Shakespeare's audience depended on secret symbols such as the moon, eyes, and flowers through which "layers of hidden meanings" were unfolded. Extracts from the BBC Moshinsky version support Dr. Strong's commentary. American students will benefit the most from the visual display of Britain's architectural treasures, and least probably from the gap between the joyousness of the play and the solemnity of Dr. Strong's manner (KSR).

MEDIUM INFORMATION: *Medium:* Video; *Sound:* Spoken language; *Color:* Yes; *Length:* 25 min.; *Language(s) spoken:* English; *Video type:* 3/4U, V.

AUTHORSHIP INFORMATION: *Producer(s):* Poole, Victor; *Director(s):* Wilson, David; *Other personnel:*

Whitson, David (Camera); Crump, Martin (Editor); Chesterman, Arthur (Sound); Friedman, Liz (Graphics); *Cast:* Strong, Roy (Commentator).

DISTRIBUTION & AVAILABILITY: *Publisher or responsible agency:* BBC; *Distributor:* BBC*; FNC; *Availability:* Double cassette (w. *AYL*), Rental $50; Quad cassette (w. *AYL, Lr., Tmp.*), Rental $75.

A Midsummer Night's Dream. Video/Teleplay

412. *A Midsummer Night's Dream.* (Series: The Shakespeare Plays).

DOCUMENT INFORMATION: *Country:* GB; *Year of filming:* 19-25 May 1981; *Year of first showing:* 1981; *Location of first showing(s):* BBC, London; PBS, USA, 19 April 1982.

EDITION, HISTORY, CONTENTS, & EVALUATION: *Edition & history:* After 1980, with Jonathan Miller as the new producer replacing Cedric Messina, the BBC Shakespeare Plays increasingly stressed the contemporaneousness of Shakespeare's plays. That is to say, an effort was made to copy the life styles of Shakespeare's own period as portrayed in the works of the great masters of the Italian and Northern Renaisssance. The theory was that in Shakespeare's playhouses only the principals were likely to wear authentic costumes anyway no matter what the time period. A famous engraving actually shows a performance of *Titus Andronicus* in which the major actors wear Roman dress but the lesser persons are garbed as Elizabethans. In this *Midsummer Night's Dream* the influence of Rembrandt is particularly apparent with special reference to *Danae's Bower*. The results, as also with director Moshinksy's very baroque *All's Well*, are not merely visually striking but also historically appropriate. *Contents & evaluation:* "If the Reinhardt/Dieterle film recalls Inigo Jones, and the Hall the exotic flora and fauna of Richard Dadd, then Moshinsky's *MND* comes straight out of the seventeenth-century Dutch school of de Hooch, Hals, and Rembrandt. He learns well from his Dutch models even down to the chiaroscuro of many interior shots. . . . His problem is that moving images require spatial arrangements different from those of the Dutch masters. Once Bols arranges his 'Members of the Wine Merchants Guild,' he can sustain that grouping forever. A TV camera, however, demands movement and a tight frame can become a noose that chokes the actors. . . . Even the forest seems cramped: few characters can find their way through the woods without falling into a giant mud puddle, giving the impression that there is only one damp path to follow. . . . Dogberry tells us that comparisons are odorous and yet the scent of comparison cannot be resisted. Moshinsky's *MND* places third in the sweepstakes after the Reinhardt and Hall films. This version seems too dark (in a metaphorical as well as in the sense of set lighting and design), too given to menace for its own good" (Colley, Scott, "A Midsummer Night's Dream," *SFNL* 8.1.[1983]: 5 +). "All that has to happen for this [*Pyramus and Thisby* play] to work in production is for the clowns to be funny and real. Their subplot and their activities, climaxing in *Pyramus and Thisby*, take care of the aesthetic issues effortlessly. . . . In this respect, the Moshinsky version is more than a little puzzling. The clowns are not as much fun as one would expect them to be, and their performance of *Pyramus and Thisby*, when it comes, simply isn't very funny. That may well be a deliberate production choice, but it is unlikely to win approval from anyone who has seen a really hilarious performance of the clowns' play. Perhaps the most charitable conclusion is that live performance is needed to bring the great fun of *Pyramus and Thisby* out" (Young, David, "A Midsummer Night's Dream," *TSH* 45-46). *Audience:* Junior High (grades 7-9); High school (grades 10-12); General use; *Supplementary materials:* Fenwick, Henry. "The Production," *BSP*, 1981:18-21; Videotape (25 min.) from "Shakespeare in Perspective" series with Roy Strong as lecturer discussed elsewhere (see 411, above).

MEDIUM INFORMATION: *Medium:* Video; *Sound:* Spoken language; *Color:* Yes; *Length:* 120 min.; *Video type:* B, V, 3/4U.

AUTHORSHIP INFORMATION: *Producer(s):* Miller, Jonathan; *Director(s):* Moshinsky, Elijah; *Adaptor/translator(s):* Snodin, David; *Composer(s):* Oliver, Stephen; *Choreographer(s):* Fazan, Eleanor; *Designer(s):* Myerscough-Jones, David; *Costume designer(s):* Roberts, Amy; Samuel, Reg; *Lighting designer(s):* Summers, John; *Other personnel:* Jackley, Mike (Prod. Manager); Shircore, Jenny (Make-up); Miller-Timmins, Derek (Sound); *Cast:* Davenport, Nigel (Theseus); Lumsden, Geoffrey (Egeus); Lindsay, Robert (Lysander); Henson, Nicky (Demetrius); Quarshie, Hugh (Philostrate); Palmer, Geoffrey (Quince); Mort, Ray (Snug); Glover, Brian (Bottom); Fowler, John (Flute); Jackley, Nat (Snout); Estelle, Don (Starveling); Kohler, Estelle (Hippolyta); Guard, Pippa (Hermia); Mellor, Cherith (Helena); McEnery, Peter (Oberon); Mirren, Helen (Titania); Daniels, Phil (Puck); Savage, Bruce (Peaseblossom); Mezzofanti, Massimo (Cobweb); Martelli, Dominic (Moth); Cross, Timothy (Mustardseed); Bennett, Tania; Segal, Alexandra; Mason, Louise (First Fairies); Macdonald, Lee (Second Fairy).

DISTRIBUTION & AVAILABILITY: *Publisher or responsible agency:* BBC/TLF; *Distributor:* AVP, UIO, BBC*, *Copy location:* UVM, CTL*, ITM* (1a Sha 3c); *Availability:* AVP, B, V, 3/4U $450, sale; UIO, V (72013H), 3/4U (70297V), rental, $21.30; BBC*, 16mm or V, apply.

A Midsummer Night's Dream. Video/Recording

413. *A Midsummer Night's Dream.*

DOCUMENT INFORMATION: *Country:* USA; *Year of release:* 1982; *Location of first showing:* Delacorte Theatre, Central Park, NY.

EDITION, HISTORY, CONTENTS, & EVALUATION: *Edition & history:* A recording of a 1982 stage play in New York City's Central Park, though it must be said that the resourceful camera work almost qualifies it for the more exalted status of a film made for television. It is also a good example of the innovative Shakespeare presented by the New York Shakespeare Festival outdoors in Central Park, under the leadership of Joseph Papp, producer. *Contents & evaluation:* Like the 1935 Reinhardt *MND*, this is also an aggressively "Americanized" production with a variety of regionalisms heard in the actors' voices. Hermia has a strident, piercing Midwestern voice, while Philostrate sounds very New York; the "rude mechanicals" (as Puck calls them) resemble "hard-hat" blue-collar workers; and Bottom looks like a reincarnation of Jimmy Durante. Highly stylized, the production captures the mood of the play in movement almost as much as with voices. When Lysander begins tearing at Helena's clothes, though, or when an astonished Oberon glances quizzically at Helena's kinky desire to have Demetrius treat her as a spaniel, these modernized touches decode Shakespeare into an idiom for modern discourse. Nor as should be expected is the production devoid of the "darker" elements that have been so widely detected in the play since the appearance of Jan Kott's famous study, *Shakespeare Our Contemporary.* The dream always threatens to become nightmare. Especially notable performances come from Marcel Rosenblatt as a distinctly eccentric Puck and from the versatile Jeffrey DeMunn as Bottom (KSR). *Audience:* High school (grades 10-12); General use; *Supplementary materials:* Gussow, Mel. "Review." *NYT* 16 Aug. 1982: III.5; Dunning, Jennifer. "The 'Dream' Comes to Park." *NYT* 8 Aug. 1982: III.1.

MEDIUM INFORMATION: *Medium:* Video; *Sound:* Spoken language; *Color:* Yes; *Length:* 165 min.; *Video type:* B, V, 3/4U.

AUTHORSHIP INFORMATION: *Producer(s):* Papp, Joseph; Cohen, Jason Steven; *Director(s):* Lapine, James; Ardolino, Emile; *Composer(s):* Shawn, Allen; *Choreographer(s):* Daniele, Graciela; *Designer(s):* Landesman, Heidi; *Costume designer(s):* Barcelo, Randy; *Lighting designer(s):* Aronson, Frances; Holmes, Ralph; *Other personnel:* Jay, Ricky (Magic effects); Balmori, Diana (Landscape consultant); Milland, Jay (Asst. director); Auggliaro, Rizz (Technical director); Steiner, Nina (Production manager); Naier, Andrea; (Stage manager); Gerson, Norma (Make-up); Marino, Bill; Moroff, Sandi (Audio); Tichler, Rosemarie; Novack, Ellen (Casting); Koehler, D.W.; Murray, Johnna (Delacorte Theatre Stage Managers); *Cast:* Venora, Diane (Hippolyta); Hurdle, James (Theseus); Jay, Ricky (Philostrate); Drischell, Ralph (Egeus); Rush, Deborah (Hermia); Lieberman, Rick (Demetrius); Conroy, Kevin (Lysander); Baranski, Christine (Helena); Vinovich, Steve (Quince); De Munn, Jeffrey (Bottom); Bates, Paul (Flute); O'Brien, J. Patrick (Starveling); Katsulas, Andreas (Snout); Crook, Peter (Snug); Rosenblatt, Marcel (Puck); Hurt, William (Oberon); Shay, Michele (Titania); Capodice, Tessa; Flavin, Tim; Gordone, Leah Carla; Handwerger, Roshi; Kreshka, Paul; Lewis, Emmanuel; McFadden, Cheryl; Paraiso, Nicky; Paul, Tina; Pietropinto, Angela; Richert, Rosemary (Fairies); McGee, Caroline; Logan, David; Shaw, Marcie (Attendants).

DISTRIBUTION & AVAILABILITY: *Publisher or responsible agency:* ABC Video Enterprises Inc.; *Distributor:* FFH, *Copy location:* FOL; *Call or copy number:* VCR; *Availability:* Sale: B, V $249, 3/4 U $349, Rental $75.

A Midsummer Night's Dream. Motion Picture/ Derivative

414. *A Midsummer Night's Sex Comedy.*

DOCUMENT INFORMATION: *Country:* USA; *Year of release:* 1982.

EDITION, HISTORY, CONTENTS, & EVALUATION: *Edition & history:* Modernization of elements from Shakespeare's comedy. *Contents & evaluation:* The three paramount connections to Shakespeare's play are the exchange of partners during a single hectic period, the spirits and fairies, and Mendelssohn's famous score for Shakespeare's play on the sound track. Otherwise this is an urbane comedy about sophisticated New Yorkers on a summer romp. *Supplementary materials:* Maslin, Janet. "Film: A New Woody Allen." *NYT* 16 July 1982: C4.

MEDIUM INFORMATION: *Length:* 88 min.

AUTHORSHIP INFORMATION: *Producer(s):* Greenhut, Robert; *Director(s):* Allen, Woody; *Composer(s):* Mendelssohn, Felix; *Lighting designer(s):* Willis, Gordon; *Other personnel:* Morse, Susan E. (Editor); *Cast:* Allen, Woody (Andrew); Farrow, Mia (Ariel); Ferrer, Jose (Leopold); Hagerty, Julie (Dulcy).

DISTRIBUTION & AVAILABILITY: *Distributor:* FCM, *Copy location:* LCM; *Call or copy number:* VAA 0606.

A Midsummer Night's Dream. Video/Opera

415. *A Midsummer Night's Dream.*

DOCUMENT INFORMATION: *Country:* GB; *Year of*

first showing: 1982; *Location of first showing:* Glyndenbourne Festival.

EDITION, HISTORY, CONTENTS, & EVALUATION: *Edition & history:* A recording of Benjamin Britten's operatic version of *Midsummer Night's Dream. Supplementary materials:* FCM Catalog, 116.

MEDIUM INFORMATION: *Length:* 194 min.

AUTHORSHIP INFORMATION: *Director(s)* Hall, Peter; Heather, Dave (TV) *Composer(s):* Britten, Benjamin; Haitink, Bernard (Conductor w. London Symphony); Glover, Jane (Chorus Director); *Designer:* Bury, John; *Lighting:* Bryan, Robert; Burgess, Bill; *Cast:* Cotrubas, Ileana (Titania); Bowman, James (Oberon); Appelgren, Curt (Bottom); Lott, Felicity (Helena); Nash, Damien (Puck); Davies, Ryland (Lysander); Duesing, Dale (Demetrius); Buchan, Cynthia (Hermia); Visser, Lieuwe (Theseus); Buchan, Cynthia (Hermia); Powell, Claire (Hippolyta)

DISTRIBUTION & AVAILABILITY: *Distributor:* FCM, FNC; *Availability:* V, $59.95.

A Midsummer Night's Dream. Motion Picture/ Adaptation

416. *A Midsummer Night's Dream: After William Shakespeare.*

DOCUMENT INFORMATION: *Country:* Spain/GB; *Year of release:* 1984.

EDITION, HISTORY, CONTENTS, & EVALUATION: *Edition & history:* Originally a London stage production by the Lindsay Kemp company, which specializes in outrageous and shocking performances, this film version was co-produced in Spain for television audiences. *Contents & evaluation:* "As a creator of sheer spectacle and inventive theatricality Lindsay Kemp is an acknowledged master, and his enchanting adaptation of *A Midsummer Night's Dream* ("Screen on the Hill") . . . is proof positive of his legendary genius. The hugely successful stage version has been reverently transferred to the screen by Celestino Coronado with few departures from the original Lindsay Kemp/ David Haughton production, although this transfer has enabled a more detailed and broader scope of vision and particularly with regard to the imaginative settings, stunning costumes, and clever visual effects. The disparate elements of high camp and low burlesque, aesthetic courtliness and bawdy vaudeville, are interlaced with snatches from Shakespeare's text and bound together by Carlos Miranda's haunting original musical score. Although ensemble is the key word to Kemp's work some individual performances are outstanding—The Incredible Orlando creates a magnificent and imposing Titania. Francois Testory's Changeling (El Pajo) is an androgynous creature with a remarkable voice, and Kemp himself as the definitive

Puck is a chimerical mixture of magic and mischief, exploiting with delight the impotence of man against the power of natural forces and appointing himself chief puppet-master to ably demonstrate 'Lord, what fools these mortals be.' This visual delight should not be missed. (Griffiths, Michael, "Review Gay-Music," *TO* London, 1984 n.p.). Despite Griffiths' enthusiasm, some will find the film perverse and even mischievous. The Gay/Punk school of filmmakers excels at ferreting out of the subtext the most recondite and recherche, even twisted, of meanings. In this cinematic text for *Dream* the crossed lovers awaken from their enchantment in the wood not to fall in love as Hermia with Lysander or Helena with Demetrius, but as Hermia with Helena and Lysander with Demetrius, though all show versatility by sorting out their sexual proclivities in time to return to orthodox heterosexuality. Love in this *Dream* transcends gender to include all creatures willy nilly (Rothwell, K.S., "Shakespeare on Film All Over the World," *SFNL* 10.2 [1986]: 5+). *Audience:* College and university; Professional.

MEDIUM INFORMATION: *Medium:* Motion picture; *Sound:* Spoken language; *Color:* Yes; *Length:* 72 minutes; *Language(s) spoken:* English; *Film type:* 35mm.

AUTHORSHIP INFORMATION: *Producer(s):* Kemp, Lindsay; Haughton, David; *Director(s):* Coronado, Celestino; *Adaptor/translator(s):* Kemp, Lindsay; *Composer(s):* Miranda, Carlos; *Designer(s):* Kemp, Lindsay; *Costume designer(s):* Lolita (Madrid); *Other personnel:* Middleton, Peter (Photography); *Cast*:* The Incredible Orlando (Hippolyta/Titania); Testory, Francois (Changeling); Kemp, Lindsay (Puck); Matou, Michael (Theseus/ Oberon); Heazelwood, Cheryl (Hermia); Lopez, Atilio (Lysander); Owen, Sally (Helena/Lion); Michaelson, Christian (Demetrius/Thisbe); Sanz, Javier (Moon); Caplan, Neil (Pyramus) [*Credits partially from London stage production.] *Performance group(s):* Lindsay Kemp & Company.

DISTRIBUTION & AVAILABILITY: *Publisher or responsible agency:* Lindsay Kemp Co.; *Distributor:* GLB*, *Availability:* GLB*, apply.

A Midsummer Night's Dream. Video/Adaptation

416.1 *Droom Van een Zomernacht.* [*A Midsummer Night's Dream*].

DOCUMENT INFORMATION: *Country:* Belgium; *Year of first showing:* 1984.

EDITION, HISTORY, CONTENTS, & EVALUATION: *Edition & history:* A recording of an adaptation of *MND* presented in Dutch.

MEDIUM INFORMATION: *Sound:* Spoken language; *Color:* Yes; *Length:* 140 min.; *Language(s) spoken:* Dutch; *Video type:* V.

AUTHORSHIP INFORMATION: *Producer(s):* Audiovisuele dienst Katholieke Univ., Leuven, Belgium; *Director(s):* Tillemans, W.; *Adaptor/translator(s):* Kohout, P.; Claus, H. (Translator).

DISTRIBUTION & AVAILABILITY: *Publisher or responsible agency:* Katholieke Univ., Leuven; *Copy location:* KAL; *Availability:* An agreement with the Department of Literature Sciene, K.U. Leuven, and the director is necessary.

A Midsummer Night's Dream. Video/Recording

416.2 *Midzomernachtsdroom.* [*A Midsummer Night's Dream*].

DOCUMENT INFORMATION: *Country:* West German Republic; *Year of first showing:* 1984.

EDITION, HISTORY, CONTENTS, & EVALUATION: *Edition & history:* Recording of a production at Kammerspiele, Munich, Germany.

MEDIUM INFORMATION: *Sound:* Spoken language; *Color:* Yes; *Video type:* B.

AUTHORSHIP INFORMATION: *Director(s):* Dorn, Dieter.

DISTRIBUTION & AVAILABILITY: *Publisher or responsible agency:* Kammerspiele München; *Copy location:* CTL*, ITM*; *Call or copy number:* Betamax L750 (CTL*); 1a Sha 3b (ITM*).

A Midsummer Night's Dream. Video/Scenes

417. *The Shakespeare Hour.*

DOCUMENT INFORMATION: *Country:* GB/USA; *Year of release:* 1985.

EDITION, HISTORY, CONTENTS, & EVALUATION: *Edition & history:* The series, "The Shakespeare Hour," was shown on public television beginning on January 5, 1985 (see also 5, 276, 352 and 663). It was funded by the National Endowment for the Humanities and produced by Station WNET/THIRTEEN, New York City. *Contents & evaluation:* For background, see 5, above. See also entry 412, *A Midsummer Night's Dream,* directed by Elijah Moshinsky, 1981. *Audience:* High school (grades 10-12); College and university; General use; *Supplementary materials:* Quinn, Edward, ed. *TSH.*

MEDIUM INFORMATION: *Medium:* Video; *Sound:* Spoken language; *Color:* Yes; *Length:* 120 min.; *Language(s) spoken:* English; *Video type:* V.

AUTHORSHIP INFORMATION: *Producer(s):* BBC-WNET/THIRTEEN; *Director(s):* Moshinsky, Elijah; Johnson, Donald; Kieffer, Tom; Bellin, Harvey (WNET); *Screenplay writer(s):* Cavendar, Kenneth; *Other personnel:* Squerciati, Marie Therese (Project director); *Cast:* Matthau, Walter; Cast of BBC/Time Life *A Midsummer Night's Dream* (q.v.).

DISTRIBUTION & AVAILABILITY: *Publisher or responsible agency:* WNET/THIRTEEN; *Distributor:* ALS

A Midsummer Night's Dream. Video/Ballet

418. *A Midsummer Night's Dream.*

DOCUMENT INFORMATION: *Country:* USA; *Year of release:* 1986.

EDITION, HISTORY, CONTENTS, & EVALUATION: *Edition & history:* Great Performances, PBS stations, 1986 *Supplementary materials:* Loughney, Katharine. "Shakespeare on Film and Tape at Library of Congress." *SFNL* 14.1 (Dec. 1989): 4.

MEDIUM INFORMATION: *Length:* 120 min.

AUTHORSHIP INFORMATION: *Director(s):* Martins, Peter; *Choreographer(s):* Balanchine, George; *Cast:* Calegari, Maria; Andersen, Ib; Frohlich, Jean-Pierre; Hall, Victoria.

DISTRIBUTION & AVAILABILITY: *Copy location:* LCM; *Call or copy number:* VBE 0375-0376.

A Midsummer Night's Dream. Video/Recording

419. *A Midsummer Night's Dream.*

DOCUMENT INFORMATION: *Country:* USA; *Year of first showing:* 1986.

EDITION, HISTORY, CONTENTS, & EVALUATION: *Edition & history:* A videotape of a production at the "Pepsico Summerfare" at SUNY-Purchase, New York on 16 July 1986. A copy is housed in the TOFT collection (Theatre on Film and Tape) in the Library of Performing Arts, New York City Public Library. *Contents & evaluation:* Not seen. *Audience:* College and university; General use.

MEDIUM INFORMATION: *Medium:* Video; *Sound:* Spoken language; *Color:* Yes; *Length:* 162 min.; *Language(s) spoken:* English; *Video type:* 3/4U.

AUTHORSHIP INFORMATION: *Producer(s):* Pepsico Summerfare; *Director(s):* Ciulei, Liviu; *Composer(s):* Glass, Philip.

DISTRIBUTION & AVAILABILITY: *Copy location:* LCL TOFT Collection; *Call or copy number:* NCOV 543; *Availability:* By appt.

Midsummer Night's Dream, A. **Motion Picture/ Excerpt**

419.1 *Dead Poets Society.*

DOCUMENT INFORMATION: *Country:* USA; *Year of first showing:* 1989.

EDITION, HISTORY, CONTENTS, & EVALUATION: *Edition & history:* Popularly acclaimed film in which the students at a New England prep school put on a performance of *A Midsummer Night's Dream,* excerpts of which are shown in the film. Filmed at the St. Andrews School, Middletown, Delaware. *Contents & evaluation:* Defying his stuffy father (Kurtwood Smith), and encouraged by his maverick teacher (Robin Williams), Neil Perry (Robert Leonard), plays Puck in a school production of Shakespeare's comedy. *Supplementary materials:* Brain, Richard. "Subversive Forces." *TLS* 29 Sept.-5 Oct. 1989: 1063.

MEDIUM INFORMATION: *Sound:* Spoken language; *Color:* Yes.

AUTHORSHIP INFORMATION: *Producer(s):* Haft, Steven; Witt, Paul Junger; Thomas, Tony; *Director(s):* Weir, Peter; *Screenplay writer(s):* Schulman, Tom; *Composer(s):* Jarre, Maurice; *Lighting designer(s):* Seale, John; *Cast:* Williams, Robin (John Keating); Leonard, Robert Sean (Neil Perry); Hawke, Ethan (Todd Anderson); Waterston, James (Gerard Pitts); Lloyd, Norman (Mr. Nolan); Burrell, Pamela (Directing Teacher); Hedges, Allison (Actor/Fairy); D'Ercole, Christine (Titania).

DISTRIBUTION & AVAILABILITY: *Publisher or responsible agency:* Touchstone Pictures; *Distributor:* Commercial distribution only at time of this entry.

Much Ado about Nothing

ORIGINAL WORK AND PRODUCTION: Comedy of Manners. *Year written:* c.1599; *Site of first production:* Globe [?].

Much Ado about Nothing. **Motion Picture/Title Only**

420. *Much Ado about Nothing.*

DOCUMENT INFORMATION: *Country:* USA; *Year of release:* 1909.

EDITION, HISTORY, CONTENTS, & EVALUATION: *Edition & history:* According to Professor Ball, this film merely exploited Shakespeare's title. *Supplementary materials:* Ball, *SOSF* 66.

AUTHORSHIP INFORMATION: *Director(s):* Lubin, Sigmund.

Much Ado about Nothing. **Motion Picture/ Derivative**

421. *Wet Paint.*

DOCUMENT INFORMATION: *Country:* USA; *Year of release:* 1926.

EDITION, HISTORY, CONTENTS, & EVALUATION: *Edition & history:* A highly derivative treatment (Ball, *SOSF* 267). A Hollywood slapstick farce with a plot line that vaguely parallels the motif of endangered romance through slander in Shakespeare's play. *Supplementary materials: SIF* 90.

MEDIUM INFORMATION: *Length:* 57 min.

AUTHORSHIP INFORMATION: *Director(s):* Rosson, Arthur; *Cast:* Griffith, Raymond; Washburn, Bryant; Costello, Helene.

DISTRIBUTION & AVAILABILITY: *Publisher or responsible agency:* Famous Players Lasky Corporation.

Much Ado about Nothing. **Video/Teleplay**

422. *Much Ado about Nothing.* (Series: Scenes from Shakespeare).

DOCUMENT INFORMATION: *Country:* GB; *Year of first showing:* 1937; *Location of first showing:* BBC. Transmitted 11 Feb., 1937.

EDITION, HISTORY, CONTENTS, & EVALUATION: *Edition & history:* One of the earliest BBC Shakespeare programs in a series featuring scenes from the plays. *Supplementary materials: TPAB* 11 Feb. 1937.

MEDIUM INFORMATION: *Length:* 10 min.

AUTHORSHIP INFORMATION: *Producer(s):* O'Ferrall, George More; *Cast:* Scott, Margaretta (Beatrice); Oscar, Henry (Benedick); Oldacre, Max (Singer).

DISTRIBUTION & AVAILABILITY: *Publisher or responsible agency:* BBC; *Copy location:* Unavailable.

Much Ado about Nothing. **Motion Picture/ Recording**

423. *Mnogo shuma iz nichevo.*

DOCUMENT INFORMATION: *Country:* USSR; *Year of release:* 1956.

EDITION, HISTORY, CONTENTS, & EVALUATION: *Edition & history:* Recording of stage performance at the Evgeni Vachtangov theatre. *Supplementary materials:* Morris, ShOF 20.

MEDIUM INFORMATION: *Length:* 96 min.

AUTHORSHIP INFORMATION: *Director(s):* Zamkovoi, L.

Much Ado about Nothing. **Video/Teleplay**

424. *Much Ado about Nothing.*

DOCUMENT INFORMATION: *Country:* USA; *Year of first showing:* 1958; *Location of first showing:* Matinee Theatre. Transmitted in two parts: 3 to 4:00 P M Tuesday and Wednesday, 20-21 May 1958.

EDITION, HISTORY, CONTENTS, & EVALUATION: *Supplementary materials:* "Program." *NYT* 20 May 1958: 67; Gianakos, *TDSP* 467.

MEDIUM INFORMATION: *Sound:* Spoken language; *Color:* Yes; *Length:* 120 min.

AUTHORSHIP INFORMATION: *Cast:* Foch, Nina (Beatrice); Norton, Robert (Benedick); Bernardi, Herschel; Hutton, Robert.

DISTRIBUTION & AVAILABILITY: *Publisher or responsible agency:* Matinee Theatre.

425. *Viel Larm um Nichts.*

DOCUMENT INFORMATION: *Country:* German Dem. Republic; *Year of release:* 1963.

EDITION, HISTORY, CONTENTS, & EVALUATION: *Supplementary materials:* Morris, ShOF 24.

MEDIUM INFORMATION: *Length:* 103 min.; *Language(s) spoken:* German.

AUTHORSHIP INFORMATION: *Director(s):* Hellberg, Martin.

Much Ado about Nothing. **Motion Picture/ Abridgment**

426. *Much Ado about Nothing.* (Series: Fair Adventure Series).

DOCUMENT INFORMATION: *Country:* USA; *Year of release:* 1964.

EDITION, HISTORY, CONTENTS, & EVALUATION: *Edition & history:* A three-part abridgment of the play with commentary by Dr. Frank Baxter. *Contents & evaluation:* Not seen. *Audience:* Junior High (grades 7-9); High school (grades 10-12);

MEDIUM INFORMATION: *Medium:* Motion Picture; *Sound:* Spoken language; *Color:* No (black & white); *Length:* 84 min.; *Language(s) spoken:* English; *Film type:* 16mm.

AUTHORSHIP INFORMATION: *Producer(s):* Hubbard, Ray [?].

DISTRIBUTION & AVAILABILITY: *Publisher or responsible agency:* Westinghouse Broadcasting Company (Group W); *Distributor:* ASF [?].

Much Ado about Nothing. **Video/Teleplay**

427. *Much Ado about Nothing.*

DOCUMENT INFORMATION: *Country:* GB; *Year of release:* Transmitted 7:25 to 9:35 P.M., Sunday, Feb. 5, 1967; in USA, NET Playhouse, 8:30 P.M., 11, 18 March 1971; *Location of first showing:* BBC-1.

EDITION, HISTORY, CONTENTS, & EVALUATION: *Edition & history:* A version of the 1967 National Theatre Company production of *Much Ado*, edited for television. The play, originally directed for the stage by Franco Zeffirelli, was pre-recorded in the studio on January 11, 1967. The cast of 43 actors spent three weeks in rehearsal for the TV performance. Hence the production passes over the line from being a mere "recording" of a stage play to the status of a full-scale television drama. The team of Zeffirelli and Rota, who were subsequently to act as director and composer of the fabulously successful 1968 film of *Romeo and Juliet*, brought their special gifts to the production. With such luminaries as Maggie Smith (Beatrice), Derek Jacobi (Don Pedro), Frank Finlay (Dogberry), John McEnery (Gentleman), it glittered with talent. Unfortunately (and improbably) no copy seems to have been preserved. *Supplementary materials:* Adams, Bernard. "Much Ado." *RT* 2 Feb. 1967: 11; "Program." *NYT* 11 March 1971: 79.

MEDIUM INFORMATION: *Length:* 123 min.

AUTHORSHIP INFORMATION: *Producer(s):* Messina, Cedric; Stephens, Robert; *Director(s):* Zeffirelli, Franco (Stage); Cooke, Alan (BBC); *Adaptor/translator(s):*

Graves, Robert; *Composer(s):* Rota, Nino; *Choreographer(s):* Grigorova, Romayne; *Designer(s):* Cornish, Mel; *Cast:* Jacobi, Derek (Don Pedro); Pickup, Ronald (Don John); Byrne, Michael (Claudio); Stephens, Robert (Benedick); De Marne, Denis (A Lord); James, Gerald (Leonato); Lomax, Harry (Antonio); John, Caroline (Hero); Smith, Maggie (Beatrice); Clark, Wynne (Ursula); Johns, Carolyn (Margaret); Petherbridge, Edward (Conrade); Hargreaves, David (Borachio); Fitzpatrick, Neil (Balthazar); McEnery, John (Gentleman); Finlay, Frank (Dogberry); Crowden, Graham (Verges); Ryall, David (Sexton); Curran, Paul (Friar Francis); The Town Band; The Inanimates.

DISTRIBUTION & AVAILABILITY: *Publisher or responsible agency:* BBC.

Much Ado about Nothing. **Video/Teleplay**

428. *Much Ado about Nothing.*

DOCUMENT INFORMATION: *Country:* USA; *Year of first showing:* 1973; *Location of first showing:* New York Shakespeare Festival/CBS. Transmitted 8 to 11 P.M., Friday, 2 Feb. 1973.

EDITION, HISTORY, CONTENTS, & EVALUATION: *Edition & history:* A recording on 16mm film of Joseph Papp's and A.J. Antoon's "American ragtime" adaptation of *Much Ado about Nothing.* Originally produced for the New York Shakespeare Festival Delacorte Theatre in Central Park, it then enjoyed a commercial success at the Winter Garden on Broadway. For rights to the national television program, CBS gave the Festival Theatre $775,000. This apparent bonanza backfired badly though when the cost of the television production soared to $810,100, and, even worse, hurt box office sales for the live show. The show was then forced to close down on February 11, 1973, only nine days after the national television transmission on February 2, 1973 (see "*Much Ado* of TV Dooms Stage Version," *NYT* 7 Feb. 1973: 30). Ironically IBM, the sponsor, had taken out a full page ad in *The New York Times* on February 2nd that pointed out how much cheaper it was to watch the play on television than to see it live in the theatre for $9.50 [*sic*] (Broadway ticket prices now range from $25 to $60 and up!). In any event this struggle between television and live theatre for an audience is paradigmatic of the gradual withering away of theatre audiences even in such traditional bastions of the stage as New York City. *Contents & evaluation:* This is an "Americanized" *Ado* transplanted from Messina, Sicily, to small town USA, circa 1910. The soldiers are returning from some kind of vague war waged against Spanish speaking troublemakers in central America, or perhaps the Philippines. It doesn't really matter where the soldiers were coming from because the director, who was denounced by some

critics for doing so, was attempting to capture the play's timeless concerns with the battle of the sexes. At the time this modernization seemed quite daring, though the technique has been industriously copied ever since. The play has been done in WWI costumes (Regents Park, London), or aboard ship on a luxury liner (Folger company). Antoon's production sparkled with Kathleen Widdoes as Beatrice and veteran actor Douglas Watson as Don Pedro. To make Shakespeare "our contemporary," Dogberry's constables became Keystone Kops, an innovative idea that was widely decried and just as widely imitated by directors who knew a good idea when they saw one. In fact the use of cinematic techniques in general, not just Keystone Kops but freeze frames, accelerated motion, Mickey Mouse sound effects, etc., were movie technologies. Antoon and Papp did not pioneer in this tendency, as Bertolt Brecht's "epic" theatre had already previously borrowed from cinema. But it does seem that after this production, directors of Shakespearean plays increasingly used cinematic devices on stage (KSR). Not everyone agreed that the production was wonderful. Harris Green deplored the whole approach as one of simply "dragging [Shakespeare] down to our level" and as "overflowing with incidentals and barren of essentials" ("All's Well that Kills Well?" *NYT* 14 Jan. 1973: 1:5). On the other side, John J. O'Connor called the production "A brilliant Americanization" of Shakespeare's play, which is precisely what has always been Joseph Papp's goal ("Ragtime *Much Ado.*" *NYT* 2 Feb. 1973: 62). *Audience:* General use; *Supplementary materials:* Jones, Edward T. "Another Noting of the Papp/ Antoon *Much Ado about Nothing.*" *SFNL* 3.1. (Dec. 1978): 5.

MEDIUM INFORMATION: *Medium:* Motion picture; *Sound:* Spoken language; *Color:* Yes; *Length:* 120 min.; *Language(s) spoken:* English; *Film type:* 16mm.

AUTHORSHIP INFORMATION: *Producer(s):* Papp, Joseph (Stage); Hitzig, Rupert (TV); *Director(s):* Antoon, A.J.; *Composer(s):* Link, Peter; *Choreographer(s):* Saddler, Donald; *Designer(s):* John, Tom; *Costume designer(s):* Aldredge, Theoni; *Cast:* Waterston, Sam (Benedick); Widdoes, Kathleen (Beatrice); Watson, Douglas (Don Pedro); Hughes, Barnard (Dogberry); Walken, Glenn; Shawhan, April (Hero); Mayo, Jerry (Don John).

DISTRIBUTION & AVAILABILITY: *Publisher or responsible agency:* New York Shakespeare Festival; *Distributor:* NYS, *Copy location:* NYS, LCL (NCOX4); *Availability:* Apply NYS rental, 16mm, special restrictions.

Much Ado about Nothing. **Motion Picture/ Adaptation**

429. *Beaucoup de bruit pour rien.*

DOCUMENT INFORMATION: *Country:* USSR; *Year of release:* 1973.

EDITION, HISTORY, CONTENTS, & EVALUATION: *Supplementary materials:* H&M 29.

AUTHORSHIP INFORMATION: *Director(s):* Samsonov, Samson; *Cast:* Loguinova, Galina (Beatrice); Raikine, Constantin (Benedick).

Much Ado about Nothing. **Motion Picture/Scenes**

430. *Much Ado about Nothing,* 4.1; 5.2. (Series: The Shakespeare Series [IFB], VI).

DOCUMENT INFORMATION: *Country:* Great Britain; *Year of release:* 1974.

EDITION, HISTORY, CONTENTS, & EVALUATION: *Edition & history:* In this sixth unit of "The Shakespeare Series," there are scenes (see also numbers 22, 131, 164, 232, 326, 467, 490, 510, 556, 601 and 619) from *Much Ado about Nothing* in which the indomitable Beatrice urges Benedick to "kill Claudio," (4.1), and in which the witty lovers become reconciled (5.2). For background, see 22. *Contents & evaluation:* Useful as a sample of the witty exchanges between Beatrice and Benedick. Beatrice tells Benedick to "Kill Claudio!" but without the fire and conviction that one expects from her. The "gay couple" (a term that has been appropriated by others in modern times) have a tendency to orate rather than directly relate to each other. Most of the action is in close-up or midshot with a definite trend toward stage acting on screen. The color is good, however; the *mise en scène,* quite rich; and the acting, tolerable. *Audience:* High school (grades 10-12);.

MEDIUM INFORMATION: *Medium:* Motion Picture; *Sound:* Spoken language; *Color:* Yes; *Length:* 11 1/2 min.; *Language(s) spoken:* English; *Film type:* 16mm; *Video type:* V, 3/4U (4 per cassette).

AUTHORSHIP INFORMATION: *Producer(s):* Realist Film Unit; *Director(s):* Seabourne, Peter; *Cast:* Gilbert, Derrick (Benedick); Key, Alison (Beatrice); Renwick, Linda (Margaret); Jameson, Susan (Ursula).

DISTRIBUTION & AVAILABILITY: *Publisher or responsible agency:* Realist Film Unit; *Distributor:* IFB, CNU, *Copy location:* FOL; *Call or copy number:* ISBN 0-8354-1594-5; FOL, MP 84; *Availability:* CNU, rental 16mm $8; IFB, sale 16mm, V, $195.

Much Ado about Nothing. **Video/Teleplay. Comedy**

431. *Much Ado about Nothing.*

DOCUMENT INFORMATION: *Country:* GB; *Year of filming:* 1978.

EDITION, HISTORY, CONTENTS, & EVALUATION: *Edition & history:* Originally scheduled to be shown in the opening season of the BBC "Shakespeare Plays" series, this was the first production completed for the ambitious six-year project (actually more like seven years). It never found its way to the television screens of the United States. Conjecture had it that the dialects of the lower-class characters in the play were too richly British to be understood by Americans. Whatever the reason, North American audiences lost an opportunity to see Michael York as Benedick. According to the Holderness and McCullough filmography (q.v.), the videocassette is available for "hire or sale" in the United Kingdom from the BBC. For the time being, Americans must content themselves with the publicity still in *SFNL* 2.1. (April 1978):1. *Contents & evaluation:* Not seen; *Audience:* High school (grades 10-12); *Supplementary materials:* H&M, 29.

MEDIUM INFORMATION: *Medium:* Video; *Sound:* Spoken language.

AUTHORSHIP INFORMATION: *Producer(s):* Messina, Cedric; *Director(s):* McWhinnie, Donald; *Designer(s):* Taylor, Don; *Cast:* York, Michael (Benedick); Keith, Penelope (Beatrice); Richardson, Ian (Don John); Davenport, Nigel (Don Pedro).

DISTRIBUTION & AVAILABILITY: *Publisher or responsible agency:* BBC* (See H&M, 29); *Copy location:* BBC* (Archive[?]).

Much Ado about Nothing. **Video/Intepretation**

432. *Much Ado about Nothing.* (Series: The Shakespeare Plays).

DOCUMENT INFORMATION: *Country:* GB; *Year of filming:* 1984; *Year of first showing:* 1984; *Location of first showing(s):* BBC, London; PBS stations, USA, 30 Nov. 1984.

EDITION, HISTORY, CONTENTS, & EVALUATION: *Edition & history:*

This production replaced an earlier *Much Ado,* starring Michael York and Penelope Keith as Benedick and Beatrice (see 431), that was to have been the inaugural play in The Shakespeare Plays series. *Contents & evaluation:* "The new version of *Much Ado* is not that bad [i.e., as bad as the 1977 version that was shelved] but, again unfortunately, not very good either. As it happens, the Royal Shakespeare Company's interpretation of the play is currently on Broadway at the Gershwin Theatre and the inevitable comparison is not very flattering for television. . . . The television production by Shaun Sutton . . . is almost relentlessly pedestrian. Directed by Stuart Burge . . . [it] keeps sinking into the kind of lifelessness that sometimes afflicts repertory companies in the hinterlands. One suspects that the actors didn't have much time to get to know each other, not to mention their parts. . . . There are some bright spots. Robert Lindsay and Cherie Lunghi are spirited enough as Benedick and Beatrice engaged in their ongoing 'wit skirmishings.' . . . Perhaps the most puzzling aspect . . . is the uninspired level of much of the acting, an area in which British television has consistently excelled. . . . What should be crisp and lively, then, turns out to be too frequently dull and awkward" (O'Connor, John J., "Tonight, *Much Ado about Nothing*," *NYT* 30 Nov. 1984, C30). "This *Much Ado* opens in the courtyard of Leonato's splendid residence, where the massive statue of a lion sits atop a fountain. At the end of the scene, one quick cut takes us from the courtyard's brilliant light to the deep gloom of Don John's apartment, where the villain sits atop his dark-curtained bed, wishing for mischief. The set designer, Ian Spocznyski, and the lighting director, Derek Slee, understood *Much Ado* well. This is precisely the contrast on which the play turns: between the sunlit comedy of Beatrice and Benedick's courtship and the potentially tragic darkening of Claudio's love for Hero. . . . This is also, unfortunately, the contrast much of this production would obscure. The problem of harmonizing the play's comic and tragic elements is central to *Much Ado's* stage history. The solution does not lie in splitting the difference between them, as Burge's production does" (McCloskey, Susan, "*Much Ado about Nothing*," *SFNL* 9.2 [1985]:5). *Audience:* College and university; *Supplementary materials:* Videotape (25 min.) from "Shakespeare in Perspective" series with Eleanor Bron as lecturer available in U.K. from BBC* (*BUFVC* 18).

MEDIUM INFORMATION: *Medium:* Video; *Sound:* Spoken language; *Color:* Yes; *Length:* 150 min.; *Language(s) spoken:* English; *Video type:* B, V, 3/4" U.

AUTHORSHIP INFORMATION: *Producer(s):* Sutton, Shaun; *Director(s):* Burge, Stuart; *Composer(s):* Rogers, Simon; *Designer(s):* Spoczynski, Ian; *Costume designer(s):* Hudson, June; *Lighting designer(s):* Slee, Derek; *Other personnel:* Davies, Sally; Dias, Fiona (Asst. floor managers); Watts, Beryl (Prod. asst.); Garrick, Anthony (Prod. manager); Lowden, Fraser (Prod. assoc.); Granger, Peter (Technical co-ordinator); Barclay, John (Vision mixer); Vincent, John (Camera); Williams, Ian (Editor); Olender, Magda (Properties); Ailes-Stevenson, Ann (Make-up); Angel, Raymond (Sound); Wilders, John (Consultant); *Cast:* Montague, Lee (Leonato); Faulkner, Tim (Messenger); Lunghi, Cherie (Beatrice); Levy, Katharine (Hero); Finch, Jon (Don Pedro); Lindsay, Robert (Benedick); Reynolds, Robert (Claudio); Whiting, Gordon (Antonio); Dobtcheff, Vernon (Don John); Gwilym, Robert (Conrade); Rohr, Tony (Borachio); Moisciwitsch, Pamela (Margaret); Bennison, Ishia (Ursula); Clarke, Oz (Balthasar); Losch, Ben (Boy); Elphick, Michael (Dogberry); Dunn, Clive (Verges); Kaye, Gordon (First Watch); Benson, Perry (Second Watch); Frost, Roger; Mulholland, Declan; Wale, Stephen (Watch); Crowden, Graham (Friar Francis); Kidd, John (Sexton); Dancers, Musicians, and The Faye Consort of Viols.

DISTRIBUTION & AVAILABILITY: *Publisher or responsible agency:* BBC/TLF; *Distributor:* AVP, UIO, BBC* *Copy location:* UVM (Archive); *Availability:* AVP, B, V, 3/4U $450 (1987), sale; UIO, V (72010H), 3/4U (70125V), rental, $25.80; BBC*, 16mm or V, apply (*BUFVC* 18).

Othello

ORIGINAL WORK & PRODUCTION: Tragedy of Jealous Love. *Year written:* 1604; *Site of first production:* Palace at Whitehall [?]

Othello. **Motion Picture/Abbreviated**

433. *Othello.*

DOCUMENT INFORMATION: *Country:* Italy; *Released:* 1907.

EDITION, HISTORY, CONTENTS, & EVALUATION: *Supplementary materials:* SIF 104; Ball, *SOSF* 29.

MEDIUM INFORMATION: *Length:* 5 min.

AUTHORSHIP INFORMATION: *Director(s):* Caserini, Mario.

DISTRIBUTION & AVAILABILITY: *Distributor:* Lost.

Othello. **Motion Picture/Scene**

434. *Othello.*

DOCUMENT INFORMATION: *Country:* Germany; *Year of release:* 1907.

EDITION, HISTORY, CONTENTS, & EVALUATION: *Edition & history:* According to R.H. Ball, this film marked a primitive attempt at sound, as Henny Porten, the German film star, mimed for the camera "The

Death of Othello" from Verdi's opera. Meanwhile, backstage a phonograph record supplied the sound. *Supplementary materials:* Ball, *SOSF* 32; H&M 29.

MEDIUM INFORMATION: *Length:* [?] min.

AUTHORSHIP INFORMATION: *Director(s):* Messter, Oskar; *Cast:* Porten, Franz (Othello); Porten, Henny (Desdemona).

DISTRIBUTION & AVAILABILITY: *Distributor:* Lost.

Othello. **Motion Picture/Abridgment**

435. *Othello.*

DOCUMENT INFORMATION: *Country:* Austria; *Year of release:* 1908.

EDITION, HISTORY, CONTENTS, & EVALUATION: *Edition & history:* Made in Austria by Pathé Freres, this film, which is listed in the Wiesbaden filmography (104), was apparently equipped with some kind of sound accompaniment. The Russian title cards show the *international* flavor of silent films, which were recycled for export simply by splicing in title cards in the appropriate language. Originally the titles of this film were in German. Often rare prints such as this one show up in remote places and find their way back to the archives of other countries. *Contents & evaluation:* The craving for location shots of Venice characteristic of filmed versions of *Othello* and the *Merchant of Venice* surfaces here also. By comparison, the interior shots seem somewhat campy, painted flats for the most part. The truncated narrrative follows the Shakespearean plot, however. For a film made so early in the century (1908), the cinematic values are noteworthy: an exterior shot of a ship arriving at Cyprus, for example, which was way beyond the resources of the Vitagraph company in Brooklyn. There is no background for the ship, only a bleak whiteness, but the mere attempt at realism deserves mention. In the marshaling of Othello's troops, there is a commendable rhythm and pace in the editing. The acting offers one drawback. Othello has an unfortunate tendency to simper, though Iago, a fat little fellow, carries within him the hint of malevolence needed for the role. The handkerchief scene, when Othello spots Cassio with his mother's gift, is especially overdone. Actually silent film acting as an art was technologically displaced just about the time it began to be understood. Few could match the genius of Lillian Gish or Buster Keaton in conveying emotion without disrupting all other production values. The ending of the film moves spasmodically but powerfully as, following Othello's slapping of Desdemona, the general (who is represented here as very light skinned by the way) writhes on the floor, while Iago maliciously cackles, or rather *mimes* cackling. Quickly Desdemona is dispatched. She awakens once and then Othello slashes his own throat and dies. Iago seems to evaporate in a blur of hate (KSR). *Audience:* General use; *Supplementary materials:* Ball, SOSF 98.

MEDIUM INFORMATION: *Medium:* Motion Picture; *Sound:* Silent; *Color:* No (black & white); *Length:* 29 min.; *Language of subtitles:* Russian, German; *Film type:* 16mm.

AUTHORSHIP INFORMATION: *Cast:* Not known.

DISTRIBUTION & AVAILABILITY: *Publisher or responsible agency:* Pathés Freres; *Copy location:* FOL; *Call or copy number:* MP 43.

Othello. Motion Picture/Abbreviated

436. *Othello.*

DOCUMENT INFORMATION: *Country:* USA; *Year of release:* 1908.

EDITION, HISTORY, CONTENTS, & EVALUATION: *Edition & history:* Another in the Vitagraph series of silent Shakespeare films under the general supervision of J. Stuart Blackton of the Vitagraph company. William Ranous, an itinerant Shakespearean actor, played Othello and may also have directed the film. (For more about the Vitagraph silents, see numbers 7, 32, 47, 195, 199, 242, 354, 387, 496, 515, and 640.) *Supplementary materials:* SIF 104; Ball, *SOSF* 45. MEDIUM INFORMATION: *Length:* 10 min. AUTHORSHIP

INFORMATION: *Director(s):* Ranous, William V.; *Cast:* Ranous, William (Othello); Dion, Hector (Iago); Gordon, Julia Swayne (Desdemona).

DISTRIBUTION & AVAILABILITY: *Distributor:* Lost.

437. *Othello.*

DOCUMENT INFORMATION: *Country:* Italy; *Year of release:* 1909.

EDITION, HISTORY, CONTENTS, & EVALUATION: *Edition & history:* Another production of Film d'Arte Italiana, set up to record performances of famous stage actors in classic theatrical presentations, to include Shakespeare. *Supplementary materials:* SIF, 104; Ball, *SOSF* 102-5.

MEDIUM INFORMATION: *Length:* 11 min.

AUTHORSHIP INFORMATION: *Director(s):* Lo Savio, Gerolamo; *Cast:* Garavaglia, Ferruccio (Othello); Dondini, Cesare (Iago); Lepanto, Vittoria (Desdemona).

DISTRIBUTION & AVAILABILITY: *Copy location:* Lost.

Othello. Motion Picture/Derivative

438. *Desdemona.*

DOCUMENT INFORMATION: *Country:* Denmark; *Year of release:* 1911.

EDITION, HISTORY, CONTENTS, & EVALUATION: *Edition & history:* Professor Ball remarks that its innovative idea of modernizing the Othello story into a "scandal" film marked the end of the Film d'Art movement, which in the early silent days had insisted on sticking more or less faithfully to theatrical and literary representations of the Shakespearean text. The film in its concern with the collapse of firm demarcations between illusion and reality also prefigures such later re-inscriptions of *Othello* as George Cukor's 1947 *A Double Life* (446) starring Ronald Colman. *Supplementary materials:* Ball, *SOSF* 132-34, 337; Eckert, *SOF* 173; Hodgdon, Barbara. "Kiss Me Deadly, or The Des/Demonized Spectacle." unp. ms. paper.

MEDIUM INFORMATION: *Length:* 18 min.

AUTHORSHIP INFORMATION: *Producer(s):* Olsen, Ole; *Director(s):* Blom, August; *Cast:* Psilander, Valdemar (Ejnar Lowe—Othello); Reimann, Thyra (Maria Lowe—Desdemona); Pontopiddian, Clara; Frohlich, Else.

DISTRIBUTION & AVAILABILITY: *Copy location:* LCM; *Call or copy number:* FLA 5858.

Othello. Motion Picture/Abbreviated

439. *Othello.*

DOCUMENT INFORMATION: *Country:* Italy; *Year of release:* 1914.

EDITION, HISTORY, CONTENTS, & EVALUATION: *Edition & history:* An Italian silent film based on *Othello.* Unfortunately the surviving print in the Library of Congress is, to use R. H. Ball's understated description, "badly disorganized" (214). It is in fact a shambles. It's as though the film had been sliced up and re-edited by a mad man. With the titles missing as well, the viewer has great difficulty in following the action. For example, in the third reel, well before the "willow" scene, Othello is suddenly discovered strangling Desdemona. The original length of the film (4215 feet) also seems to have been nearly four times lengthier than what now remains (1194 feet). *Contents & evaluation:* Enough of the film remains to establish that it was cinematically sophisticated. The opening exterior shots of Venice are excellent, showing Venetians emerging through a heavy iron door and setting forth on the canals in a gondola. Othello is a heavy man who resembles an Italian tenor in black face. An analytical shot reveals a flower falling from a window as a gift to Othello. The lavish interior shots actually have real doors instead of curtains. The level of camera work shows how advanced the Italian film industry had become by the eve of WW I. Lamentably the war disrupted and delayed development of the film industry everywhere, just as a generation later the first blossoming of British television was also delayed by the outbreak of WW II. *Audience:* College and university; Professional; *Supplementary materials:* Ball, *SOSF* 211-215.

MEDIUM INFORMATION: *Medium:* Motion Picture; *Sound:* Silent; *Color:* No (black & white); *Length:* 32 min.; *Other language information:* Title cards missing.; *Film type:* 16mm.

AUTHORSHIP INFORMATION: *Producer(s):* Ambrosio-Photodrama; *Director(s):* Ambrosio, Arturo; *Lighting designer(s):* Beccaria; *Cast:* Colaci, Paolo (Othello); Tolentino, Riccardo (Iago); Stefani, Ubaldo (Cassio); Lenard, Léna (Desdemona) [Credits from Ball, 213].

DISTRIBUTION & AVAILABILITY: *Publisher or responsible agency:* George Kleine; *Copy location:* LCM; *Call or copy number:* FLA 1705-10 (Kleine coll.); *Availability:* Archive.

Othello. Motion Picture/Derivative

440. *Othello.*

DOCUMENT INFORMATION: *Country:* Germany; *Year of release:* 1918.

EDITION, HISTORY, CONTENTS, & EVALUATION: *Edition & history:* Although listed in two Shakespeare filmographies, this film does not seem to have been viewed by any living human being. As usual Professor Ball gives the most thorough account of its history. It is included here as a reminder of the activity in Shakespeare films during the silent era. *Supplementary materials:* H&M 29; *SIF* 106; Ball, *SOSF* 228, 361.

MEDIUM INFORMATION: *Length:* [?] min.

AUTHORSHIP INFORMATION: *Director(s):* Mack, Max; *Cast:* Montano, Beni (Othello); Korth, Ellen (Desdemona).

DISTRIBUTION & AVAILABILITY: *Copy location:* Lost.

Othello. Motion Picture/Derivative

441. *Carnival.*

DOCUMENT INFORMATION: *Country:* GB/Italy; *Year of release:* 1921.

EDITION, HISTORY, CONTENTS, & EVALUATION: *Edition & history:* A prefiguration from the silent era of *Men Are Not Gods* and *A Double Life.* Essentially a backstage plot in which real life actors playing *Othello* on stage find the *Othello* story mirrored in their own lives, with a potential for disastrous consequences. The film was made partly in London and partly in Venice and grew out of an earlier stage version presented at London's New Theatre. *Contents & evaluation:* "The neglected wife of an Italian actor amuses herself with his best friend and as a consequence is nearly strangled by her husband during a performance of *Othello.* Silvia Steno, a great Italian Shakespeare actor, lives in Venice with his actress wife, Simonetta. Silvio, engrossed with his forthcoming production of *Othello,* neglects his wife who amuses herself with Count Andreone Scipione, his best friend. Ottavia, Silvia's sister, warns him that he is allowing Simonetta too much freedom. Lelio, Simonetta's 'scapegrace' brother, plays a kind of Iago figure. . . . Silvio at last suspects the truth and during the last act, mad with jealousy, he almost strangles his wife, who is playing Desdemona. When Simonetta recovers she explains in a flashback how she repulsed Andrea's passionate advances on the way home from the ball in a gondola and a reconciliation takes place between husband and wife" (NFA Catalog, typescript). *Audience:* General use; *Supplementary materials:* Ball, *SOSF* 267; "Review." *Bioscope* 66:749 (17 Feb. 1921): 72.

MEDIUM INFORMATION: *Medium:* Motion Picture; *Sound:* Silent; *Color:* No (black & white); *Length:* 48 min.; *Language of subtitles:* English; *Film type:* 16mm.

AUTHORSHIP INFORMATION: *Producer(s):* Knoles, Harley; *Director(s):* Knoles, Harley; *Screenplay writer(s):* Hardinge, H.C.M.; Lang, Matheson; *Adaptor/transla-*

tor(s): Johnson, Adrian; Henley, Rosina; *Lighting designer(s):* Hatkin, Philip; *Cast:* Lang, Matheson (Silvio Steno); Bayley, Hilda (Simonetta); Novello, Ivor (Count Andrea Scipione); De Bernaldo, Maria (Ottavia); Gray, Clifford (Lelio).

DISTRIBUTION & AVAILABILITY: *Publisher or responsible agency:* Alliance Films; *Distributor:* JEF [?], *Copy location:* NFA*.

Othello. Motion Picture/Abridgment

442. *Othello.*

DOCUMENT INFORMATION: *Country:* Germany; *Year of release:* 1922.

EDITION, HISTORY, CONTENTS, & EVALUATION: *Edition & history:* Until recently this silent *Othello* was buried in archives, but it has now become available on the video market. An outgrowth of German expressionism, it shows the flamboyant acting styles of the period. *Contents & evaluation:* Two stalwarts of the silent era, Werner Krauss (Iago), and Emil Jannings (Othello) provide the mainstays of this curiously uneven filming of *Othello.* Krauss's grotesque but compelling Iago will remain etched into the memory of the viewer long after other Iagos have been forgotten. Pudgy, pasty-faced, curiously evocative of Adolph Hitler, a thoroughly repulsive person, Krauss's Iago projects the man's inner malevolence. As the star of the landmark expressionistic film, *The Cabinet of Dr. Caligari,* Krauss carries that same certificate of evil into his relationship with Othello. The Othello that Krauss as Iago seduces, and "seduces" is probably the right word, is large, flamboyant, and literally guilty of scenery chewing when he tries to eat the handkerchief in a disastrously overacted but nevertheless intense and unforgettable moment. Between the two of them, Krauss and Jannings do convey through moving images the strange chemistry that has always made this most implausible of stories plausible. While Director Buchowetzki never became a major figure in Hollywood as did some of the other German expatriates of the Twenties, his work offers an interesting example of how Shakespeare was adapted to the idiom of German theatrical expressionism. The Reinhardt influence lingers on in this *Othello* in such indulgences as the great steps outside of the ducal palace, the chiaroscuro lighting effects, and the exaggerated acting style of costume drama. Moreover, by reason of its availability on videocassette, it is now one of the most accessible Shakespeare silents (KSR). *Audience:* College and university; General use; *Supplementary materials:* Swift, D.C. "Summary and Notes." NFA; Ball, *SOSF* 279-84; Stevenson, M. George. "Et Tu, Shakespeare? : The Bard's Greatest Hits on Tape and Disc." *Video* (Aug. 1986): 66 + .

MEDIUM INFORMATION: *Medium:* Motion picture; *Sound:* Silent; *Color:* No (black & white); *Length:* 93 min.; *Language of subtitles:* English; *Film type:* 16mm; *Video type:* V.

AUTHORSHIP INFORMATION: *Producer(s):* Worner Film; Blumenthal, Paul; Howells, David P. (American version); *Director(s):* Buchowetzki, Dimitri; *Designer(s):* Kraencke, Fritz; Machus, Karl; *Other personnel:* Hasselman, Karl; Paulmann, Friedrich (Camera); Bartlett, Don (Editor, American version); *Cast:* Jannings, Emil (Othello); Krauss, Werner (Iago); Lenkeffy, Ica (Desdemona); de Putti, Lya (Emilia); Von Alten, Ferdinand (Roderigo); Loos, Theodor (Cassio); Kühne, Friedrich (Brabantio); Stifter, Magnus (Montano).

DISTRIBUTION & AVAILABILITY: *Publisher or responsible agency:* Worner Film; *Distributor:* EMG, COR, KIT, FCM, DCV, BFI* (26 min. See *BUFVC*), *Copy location:* FOL; NFL; *Call or copy number:* MP 72 (Folger); *Availability:* EMG rental 16mm $35; COR, rental, 16mm, apply; KIT $22.50; VID, V, $29.95; FMC, V, sale, $29.95; DCV, V (#2281), sale, $38; BFI*, 16mm, apply (*BUFVC* 19).

Othello. Motion Picture/Derivative

443. *Carnival: Venetian Nights* (USA).

DOCUMENT INFORMATION: *Country:* GB; *Year of release:* 1931.

EDITION, HISTORY, CONTENTS, & EVALUATION: *Edition & history:* This is a sound version of the 1921 *Carnival* (see 441) released in the United States as *Venetian Nights.* Director Herbert Wilcox became one of the titans of the British film industry. *Contents & evaluation:* Not seen but listed in the NFA catalog with cast credits. Matheson Lang again plays the leading role of the jealous actor. *Audience:* General use; *Supplementary materials:* "Review." *MFB* 5:208.

MEDIUM INFORMATION: *Medium:* Motion Picture; *Sound:* Spoken language; *Color:* No (black & white); *Length:* 80 min.; *Language(s) spoken:* English; *Film type:* 35mm.

AUTHORSHIP INFORMATION: *Producer(s):* Wilcox, Herbert; *Director(s):* Wilcox, Herbert; *Cast:* Lang, Matheson; Schildkraut, Joseph; Bouchier, Dorothy; Braithwaite, Lilian; Hammond, Kay; Buchel, Brian; Edwards, Dickie; Wills, Bromber; Alfred Rode and His Tzigane Band.

DISTRIBUTION & AVAILABILITY: *Publisher or responsible agency:* British & Dominions; *Copy location:* NFA*.

Othello. **Motion Picture/Derivative**

444. *Men Are Not Gods.*

DOCUMENT INFORMATION: *Country:* GB; *Year of release:* 1936.

EDITION, HISTORY, CONTENTS, & EVALUATION: *Edition & history:* Another Shakespeare derivative in which the *Othello* story is reworked around the earnest efforts of a London newspaper employee to protect the reputation of a Shakespearean actor. *Contents & evaluation:* This is a delightful film that shares with *Othello* mainly its title line (it comes from Desdemona's explanation to Emilia [3.4.148] of Othello's misbehavior). The picture is neatly framed at beginning and ending by a London theatre audience rising to sing *God Save the Queen* in a jingoistic but endearing ritual that fizzled out sometime after the end of WW II. As in *A Double Life*, there is a frame around the onstage activities of Edmond Davey, an actor playing the role of Othello. When Davey flops on opening night, Barbara Halford, his leading lady (played by Gertrude Lawrence), persuades little Ann Williams (Miriam Hopkins), secretary to the waspish drama critic, to lose the review. From then on, Ann, as the sacked secretary who is smitten with the actor, attends performance after performance of *Othello* to watch the man that she sacrificed her job for. In the end, she just manages to prevent Othello from smothering Desdemona for real on stage. Meanwhile she is courted by a newspaperman, Tommy Stapleton, played by a youthful Rex Harrison. Miriam Hopkins is superb in this role and the film never falters for a moment. The movie also offers some impressive intercalations of *Othello* being acted on stage by Gertrude Lawrence and Sebastian Shaw. Often the best Shakespeare on screen takes place in these representations of a theatrical performance in the film text (KSR). *Audience:* General use.

MEDIUM INFORMATION: *Medium:* Motion Picture; *Sound:* Spoken language; *Color:* No (black & white); *Length:* 110 [?] min.; *Language(s) spoken:* English; *Film type:* 16mm.

AUTHORSHIP INFORMATION: *Producer(s):* Korda, Alexander; *Director(s):* Reisch, Walter; *Screenplay writer(s):* Stern G.B.; Wright, Iris; *Composer(s):* Mathieson, Muir; Coleridge-Taylor, Samuel "Othello Suite"; *Designer(s):* Korda, Vincent; *Costume designer(s):* Hubert, Rene; *Lighting designer(s):* Roscher, Charles; *Other personnel:* Mann, Ned (Special effects); Cunynghame, David B. (Production manager); Hornbeck, William (Editor); Cornelius, Henry (Editor); *Cast:* Hopkins, Miriam (Ann Williams); Lawrence, Gertrude (Barbara); Shaw, Sebastian (Edmond Davey); Harrison, Rex (Tommy Stapleton); Matthews, A.E. (Skeates); Gielgud, Val (Producer); Smithson, Laura (Katherine); Grossmith, Lawrence (Stanley); Grove, Sybil (Painter); Patch, Wally (Attendant); Willard, Winifred (Mrs. Williams).

DISTRIBUTION & AVAILABILITY: *Publisher or responsible agency:* United Artists; *Distributor:* FNC, IVY, LFP*, *Copy location:* NFA*.

Othello. **Video/Scenes**

445. *Othello.* (Series: Scenes from Shakespeare).

DOCUMENT INFORMATION: *Country:* GB; *Year of first showing:* 1937; *Location of first showing:* BBC. Transmitted 3:22 to 4:29 P.M., 14 Dec. 1937.

EDITION, HISTORY, CONTENTS, & EVALUATION: *Edition & history:* One of the very earliest transmissions of Shakespeare on television when the industry was still in its infancy. Jessica Tandy and Ralph Richardson were originally approached to play Desdemona and Othello but the substitutes proved to be just about as well known. Total cost of this production was under £300 nevertheless (*CHM*). *Contents & evaluation:* "The watching of televised dramas, especially of Shakespearian drama, is an astonishing experience to the spectator who is completely new to the medium . . . there are [times] when the tiny screen seems magnified to the proportions of the theatre and Othello is the great man, spiritually and physically, that he was. Mr. Baliol Holloway treats certain of Othello's speeches as though they were recitations, but in the final scenes he is moving and impresssive, and he had in Miss Celia Johnson a Desdemona who made one forget the marvels of science and remember only the beauty of the English language as it should be spoken . . . at the end of this constricted but fluid adaptation of *Othello*, the impression is left that a great play, and not merely a conjuring trick, has been performed" ("Televised Drama," *Times* 15 Dec. 1937: n.p.). *Supplementary materials:* TPAB 14 Dec. 1937.

MEDIUM INFORMATION: *Length:* 37 min.

AUTHORSHIP INFORMATION: *Producer(s):* O'Ferrall, George More; *Cast:* Johnson, Celia (Desdemona); Holloway, Baliol (Othello); Clarke-Smith, D.A. (Iago); Lindo, Olga (Bianca); Quayle, Anthony (Cassio); Black, Dorothy (Emilia); Desborough, Philip (Gratiano/Herald); Dodsworth, John (Roderigo); Logan, Campbell (Montano); Wilson, Marion; Langfield, Therese; Vincent, Mayura; Dignam, Basil; Endle, Jock (Dancers); Clarke, Cyril; Robinson, Eric; Webster, Gilbert (Musicians).

DISTRIBUTION & AVAILABILITY: *Publisher or responsible agency:* BBC; *Copy location:* Unavailable.

Othello. **Motion Picture/Derivative**

446. *A Double Life.*

DOCUMENT INFORMATION: *Country:* USA; *Year of release:* 1947.

EDITION, HISTORY, CONTENTS, & EVALUATION: *Awards:* Academy Award, Best Actor, Ronald Colman, 1947; *Edition & history:* A spinoff from *Othello* in which an actor who plays the role of Othello on stage begins to confuse the events in the play with his off-stage life. This interesting exercise in "metatheatricality," or the interplay between reality and illusion, was scripted by Ruth Gordon and Garson Kanin and directed by George Cukor. With those kinds of talents, little wonder that Ronald Colman won the 1947 Academy Award as best actor. *Contents & evaluation:* "As Anthony John, a British matinee idol performing on Broadway, Ronald Colman finds himself besieged by his agent to undertake a major, 'worthy' project—*Othello*—as a way of reviving his flagging energies. Tempted to make the effort yet strangely apprehensive about the role, the actor decides to pass for the moment. His personal life seems adrift, now that his acting partner and wife Brita (Signe Hasso) has left him. ('We love each other too much to get married again,' he announces to his agent.) Yet the *Othello* project might prove the vehicle for their reuniting" (Willson, see below). Later when he meets a waitress played by Shelley Winters the interplay between his stage persona and real life persona begins to blur, until finally in a fit of passion he smothers the poor waitress, thinking she is an unfaithful Desdemona. Intercut are many wonderful episodes from *Othello* taking place on stage. Indeed some of the finest Shakespearean acting ever screened appears in the context of this quite remarkable film. Ultimately the film speaks self-referentially about the agonies and doubts of being an actor and how much that profession demands from the emotional storehouse of an actor (KSR). *Audience:* College and university; General use; *Supplementary materials:* Willson, Robert F., Jr. "A Double Life: Othello as *Film Noir* Thriller." *SFNL* 11.1 (Dec. 1986): 3+.

MEDIUM INFORMATION: *Medium:* Motion Picture; *Sound:* Spoken language; *Color:* No (black & white); *Length:* 103 min.; *Language(s) spoken:* English; *Film type:* 16 mm.

AUTHORSHIP INFORMATION: *Producer(s):* Kanin, Michael; *Director(s):* Cukor, George; Shaw, Frank; *Screenplay writer(s):* Gordon, Ruth; Kanin, Garson; *Composer(s):* Rozsa, Miklas; *Designer(s):* Horner, Harry; Herzbrun, Bernard; Gillett, Harvey; *Set designer(s):* Gausman, Russel A.; Austin, John; *Costume designer(s):* Wood, Yvonne; Banton, Travis; *Other personnel:* Krasner, Milton (Photography); Parrish, Robert (Editor); Carey, Leslie; Lopes, Joe (Sound); Horsley, David S. (Special photography); Hampden, Walter (Advisor); Dirigo, Carmen (Hair stylist); Westmore, Bud (Make-up); Yohalem, George; Murton, Jack (Prod. assistants); *Cast:* Colman, Ronald (Anthony John); Hasso, Signe (Brita); O'Brien, Edmond (Bill Friend); Winters, Shelley (Pat Kroll); Collins, Ray (Victor Donlan); Loeb, Philip (Max Lasker); Mitchell, Millard (Al Cooley); Sawyer, Joe (Ray Bonner); La Torre, Charles (Stellini); Bissell, Whit (Dr. Stauffer); Colt, John Drew (Stage manager); Thompson, Peter (Asst. stage manager); Dunne, Elizabeth (Gladys); Edmiston, Alan (Rex); Smith, Art; Tomack, Sid (Wigmakers); Graff, Wilton (Dr. Mervin); Briggs, Harlan (Oscar Bernard); Carleton, Claire (Waitress); Blair, Betsy; Warren, Janet; Woodworth, Marjory (Girls in Wig Shop); Conway, Curt (Reporter); Chayevsky, Paddy (Photographer); Cast for on-screen *Othello:* Post, Guy Bates; Bond, David; Denison, Leslie; Patton, Virginia; Roberts, Thayer; Kanin, Fay; Gould-Porter, Arthur; Worlock, Frederick; Irwin, Boyd; Vivian, Percival; Cast *A Gentlemen's Agreement:* Reed, Elliott; Caine, Georgia; Young, Mary; Vivian, Percival.

DISTRIBUTION & AVAILABILITY: *Publisher or responsible agency:* Universal International/Kanin Productions; *Distributor:* IVY, FCM, *Copy location:* FOL; *Call or copy number:* MP 92; *Availability:* IVY, 16mm, apply; FCM, V, $24.95.

Othello. **Motion Picture/Abridgment**

447. *Othello.*

DOCUMENT INFORMATION: *Country:* USA; *Year of release:* 1947.

EDITION, HISTORY, CONTENTS, & EVALUATION: *Edition & history:* My information about this abridgment of *Othello*, which is supposed to have been presented with "simple settings," is derivative. Its current availability is in doubt. A Shakespeare film with Sebastian Cabot does sound interesting, simply because he was so memorable as Father Capulet in the Renato Castellani *Romeo and Juliet* (see 538). *Audience:* College and university; *Supplementary materials:* Morris, *SHOF* 12; McClean dismisses it as "not worth the effort" (*SAB* 240).

MEDIUM INFORMATION: *Medium:* Motion Picture; *Sound:* Spoken language; *Color:* No (black & white); *Length:* 44 min.; *Language(s) spoken:* English; *Film type:* 16mm.

AUTHORSHIP INFORMATION: *Producer(s):* Halsted, H.G.; *Cast:* Slater, John; Cabot, Sebastian; Shaw, Luanna.

Othello. Video/Recording/Opera

448. *Otello.*

DOCUMENT INFORMATION: *Country:* USA; *Year of first showing:* 1948; *Location of first showing:* Metropolitan Opera House, New York City. Transmitted 29 Nov. 1948.

EDITION, HISTORY, CONTENTS, & EVALUATION: *Edition & history:* Of prime interest because this may well have been the first televised performance of any Shakespearean drama, derivative or otherwise, in North America. The British had already begun transmitting Shakespearean drama as early as 1937 but television programming in the United States without direct government support had lagged somewhat. True enough, this was Verdi's opera not the play itself but televising it live from the Metropolitan Opera House presented the same difficulties as transmitting any stage presentation live from a theatre. The ABC television network needed to light the *mise en scène* without destroying the illusion of darkness called for by the action on stage. The technicians solved the problem with an infra-red lamp invisible to the naked eye. For the sound they simply hooked up the equipment for the regular Saturday afternoon radio broadcast from the Metropolitan. Four cameras, two at stage level and two in the grand tier, plus the expenditure of $35,000 completed the arrangements ("TV Goes to the Met," *Newsweek* 32 [13 Dec. 1948]: 55-57). *Contents & evaluation:* Leo Lerman complained that what he saw on the television screen made him think "he was peering through a thick sleet storm." He also felt that the great Licia Albanese as Desdemona looked "pretty awful." But none of that bothered him. He was aware the whole time that he was taking part in a historic event. Some two million Americans saw a performance at the Met of an adaptation from a Shakespearean play. One man apparently was punched in the eye in a barroom when he insisted on watching the opera instead of a boxing match. The performance itself was "spirited" and "exciting" (Lerman, Leo, "New Notes in Music," *TA* 33 [Jan. 1949]: 28-9).

MEDIUM INFORMATION: *Length:* 240 min. [Including intervals].

AUTHORSHIP INFORMATION: *Producer(s):* Texaco/ABC/Metropolitan Opera; *Director(s):* Crotty, Burke; *Composer(s):* Verdi, Guiseppe; Busch, Fritz (Conductor); *Cast:* Albanese, Licia (Desdemona); Vinay, Ramon (Othello); Warren, Leonard (Iago).

DISTRIBUTION & AVAILABILITY: *Publisher or responsible agency:* ABC Television.

Othello. Video/Teleplay

449. *Othello.*

DOCUMENT INFORMATION: *Country:* USA; *Year of first showing:* 1950; *Location of first showing:* Masterpiece Theatre, 9 to 10 P.M., Sunday, 27 Aug. 1950.

EDITION, HISTORY, CONTENTS, & EVALUATION: *Supplementary materials:* "On TV." *NYT* 27 Aug. 1950: X 9.

MEDIUM INFORMATION: *Medium:* 16mm, Kinescope; *Sound:* Spoken language; *Length:* 60 min.

AUTHORSHIP INFORMATION: *Producer(s):* Coe, Fred; *Director(s):* Mann, Delbert; *Cast:* Thatcher, Torin; Ryder, Alfred; Deering, Olive; Reane, George; Seymour, John D.; Shayne, Alan; Hutchinson, Muriel; Cullen, Edward.

DISTRIBUTION & AVAILABILITY: *Copy location:* UCL.

Othello. Video/Teleplay

450. *Tragedy of Othello.*

DOCUMENT INFORMATION: *Country:* GB; *Year of first showing:* 1950; *Location of first showing:* BBC. Transmitted 8:31 to 10:51 P.M., Sunday, 23 April 1950.

EDITION, HISTORY, CONTENTS, & EVALUATION: *Edition & history:* What better way to celebrate Shakespeare's birthday than with a Sunday evening performance of *Othello*? Perhaps *As You Like It* might have been more appropriate for the occasion but nevertheless the BBC must be credited for having remembered England's national poet. A relatively generous budget of £1,652 must also have cheered up the producers (*CHM*). The presence of Margaretta Scott as Emilia glanced backward to the very first 1937 BBC Shakespeare production, and of Laurence Harvey as Cassio, forward to his glamorous screen career. The program lists a gaggle of special effects from the BBC sound and vision archives, to include a cheering crowd, sea sounds, weather, a bell, and a gun. *Supplementary materials:* "Program." *TPAB* 23 Apr. 1950.

MEDIUM INFORMATION: *Length:* 135 min.

AUTHORSHIP INFORMATION: *Producer(s):* O'Ferrall, George More; Sheldon, Kevin; *Screenplay writer(s):* Skillan, George; *Designer(s):* Learoyd, Barry; *Other personnel:* Philips, Michael; Calder, Gil (Studio Managers); Askey, David (Stage Manager); Jones, Maurice (Fights Arranger); *Cast:* Morell, Andre (Othello); Scott, Margaretta (Emilia); Murray, Stephen (Iago); Hopkins, Joan (Desdemona); Harvey, Laurence (Cassio); Wheatley, Alan (Roderigo); Arliss, Pamela (Bianca); Birch, Frank (Brabantio); Skillan, George (Gratiano); Wontner, Arthur (Duke); Coleman, Brian (Montano); Macnee, Patrick (Lodovico); Doran, Charles (Senator); Harkin, Dennis; Benson, John; Askey, David; McLeod,

Kenneth (Gentlemen); [B]iggerstaff, John (Messenger); Winter, Donovan (Sailor); Bodington, Lisa (Attendant).

DISTRIBUTION & AVAILABILITY: *Publisher or responsible agency:* BBC; *Copy location:* Unavailable.

Othello. Video/Scenes

451. *Othello.*

DOCUMENT INFORMATION: *Country:* GB; *Year of first showing:* 1950; *Location of first showing:* BBC. Transmitted 8:31 to 9:00 P.M., 8 March 1950.

EDITION, HISTORY, CONTENTS, & EVALUATION: *Edition & history:* At considerable expense of time (two days of special rehearsals) and of money (£800), the Old Vic *Othello* by the Comédie Francaise was reworked for television. The program was introduced by Michel St. Denis. The BBC viewer research report laconically noted that the "language barrier proved a serious deterrent to enjoyment" (WAC TS/March 1950). *Supplementary materials:* TPAB 8 March 1950.

MEDIUM INFORMATION: *Length:* 30 min.; *Language(s) spoken:* French.

AUTHORSHIP INFORMATION: *Producer(s):* Fawcett, Eric; *Director(s):* Meyer, Jean (Stage); *Adaptor/translator(s):* Neveux, Georges; *Composer(s):* Beydts, Louis; *Designer(s):* Bould, James; *Cast:* Clariond, Aime (Othello); Debucourt, Jean (Iago); Chevrier, Jean (Cassio); Eymond, Louis (Montano); Vibert, Francois (Ludovico); Faure, Renée (Desdemona); Noro, L [?] ine (Emilia); + Gontier, J; Galopin, M.; Cuaz, B.; Belle, A.

DISTRIBUTION & AVAILABILITY: *Publisher or responsible agency:* BBC; *Copy location:* Unavailable.

Othello. Video/Recording

452. *The Moor's Pavane.*

DOCUMENT INFORMATION: *Country:* USA; *Year of first showing:* 1953; *Location of first showing:* Omnibus. Transmitted 5 to 6:30 P.M., Sunday, 15 Nov. 1953.

EDITION, HISTORY, CONTENTS, & EVALUATION: *Edition & history:* Originally this modern dance sequence based on *Othello* was transmitted on Omnibus, the intellectual's television show of the Fifties. Since then it has been transferred to 16mm film and made widely available by distributors. On the day that it was broadcast, the *Times* reported that as of Oct, 1, 1953, there were 25,690,000 TV sets in American homes, or 56% of them. Clearly television was booming and able to find an audience for even such esoterica as modern dance. *Contents & evaluation:* In a review article, critic Marie Nesthus declares this film to be "a disaster well worth seeing." She adds that the "film is a complicated melange of successful and unsuccessful adaptation; its grave flaws granted, however, a valuable trace of a magnificent original can still be found in this twice removed *Othello*" ("*Othello* Twice Removed," *SFNL* 2.1 (Dec. 1977): 1).

MEDIUM INFORMATION: *Sound:* Spoken language; *Color:* Yes; *Length:* 16 min.; *Film type:* 16mm.

AUTHORSHIP INFORMATION: *Producer(s):* Jose Limon Troupe; *Director(s):* Limon, Jose; *Cast:* Limon, Jose; Humphrey, Doris.

DISTRIBUTION & AVAILABILITY: *Publisher or responsible agency:* Joffrey Ballet; *Distributor:* CNU, FNC, *Availability:* CNU, 16mm, rental $8.

Othello. Motion Picture/Interpretation

453. *The Tragedy of Othello, The Moor of Venice: A Motion Picture Adaptation of the Play by William Shakespeare.*

DOCUMENT INFORMATION: *Country:* Morocco/Italy; *Year of release:* 1952.

EDITION, HISTORY, CONTENTS, & EVALUATION: *Awards:* Grand Prix, Cannes Film Festival, 1952; *Edition & history:* As with all of the late Orson Welles's films, this one proved no exception in subjecting everyone involved to what sounds like a fictional Hollywood backstage drama. Orson Welles, America's greatest film director, did not impress bankers as much as cineastes, perhaps because he never hesitated to make films based on Shakespearean plays, even though the box office rewards were less than promising. Micheál MacLiammóir, who played Iago, wrote a book about the making of *Othello* that is a mine of amusing anecdotes. Welles, for example, saw Iago's impotence as the key to his character. That made MacLiammóir worry over whether or not Welles thought MacLiammóir looked impotent! (See MacLiammóir, Micheál, *Put Money in Thy Purse: A Diary of the Film of* Othello. London: Methuen, 1952.) *Contents & evaluation:* "For the liberties Orson Welles has taken with *Macbeth* and *Othello* there is even less excuse [author has just expressed reservations about the Castellani *Romeo and Juliet* which she sees as '. . . wrenching Shakespeare's proportions all awry']. Mr. Welles really does know something about Shakespeare and has done him good service on the stage, yet, when he makes a film, he thinks, apparently, only of Orson Welles and his reputation for originality. He does not hesitate to begin *Othello* with a funeral procession and to set *Macbeth* in an early Gaelic cave" (Thorp, Margaret F., "Shakespeare and the Movies," *SQ* 9.3 [1958]: 359-60). Writing in the influential *Cahiers du Cinéma* (13 June 1952: 18-19), the celebrated critic, André Bazin, commented how "profoundly faithful" (*une conformité profonde*) Orson Welles was to Shakespeare's *Othello*. That may seem surprising to those who quantify the value of a Shakespeare film into a textual balance sheet: if the number of lines in the movie equals the number of lines in the Shakespeare text, then the books balance; if any lines are missing, the hunt for the embezzler is on. From the vantage point of looking back at the total *oeuvre* of Welles's career, it seems that he earned the right to reshape the text. Welles is faithful to *Othello* by being faithful to his own art. His eloquence lies in his uncanny talent for pointing a camera. The opening shot of Iago suspended in a cage high above the city remains embedded in the mind years after seeing it. The way in which Welles uses iron bars and stone vaults to suggest the inexorable forces that surround and ultimately destroy the Moorish general goes far to express in pictures what Shakespeare represented in words. *Othello* as tragedy is about agony, and the Wellesian technique of skewed angles, funhouse mirror effects, surrealistic visions, captures those kinds of emotional destabilizations (KSR). *Audience:* College and university; General use; *Supplementary materials:* Kozelka, Paul. "A Guide to the Screen Version of Shakespeare's *Othello*." *AVG* 22 (1955): 31-40; Hatch, Robert. "Films." *Nation* 290 (1955): 290 + .

MEDIUM INFORMATION: *Medium:* Motion picture; *Sound:* Spoken language; *Color:* No (black & white); *Length:* 91 min.; *Language(s) spoken:* English; *Film type:* 16mm; 35mm.

AUTHORSHIP INFORMATION: *Producer(s):* Welles, Orson; *Director(s):* Welles, Orson; *Adaptor/translator(s):* Welles, Orson; Sacha, Jean; *Composer(s):* Lavagnino, Francesco; Barberis, Alberto; *Designer(s):* Trauner, Alexander; Schiaccianoce, Luigi; de Matteis, Maria; *Other personnel:* Ferrero, Willy (Conductor); Derode, Julien (Production Assoc.); Shepridge, John; Sacha, Jean; Lucidi, Renzo; Morton, William (Film Editors); Brizzi, Anchisi; Aldo, G. R.; Fanto, George; Troani, O.; Fusi, R. (Photography); de Matteis, Maria (Costumes); *Cast:* MacLiammóir, Micheál (Iago); Coote, Robert (Roderigo); Welles, Orson (Othello); Cloutier, Suzanne (Desdemona); Edwards, Hilton (Brabantio); Bruce, Nicholas (Lodovico); Lawrence, Michael (Cassio); Compton, Fay (Emilia); Dowling, Doris (Bianca); Davis, Jean (Montano); Cotten, Joseph (Senator); Fontaine, Joan (Page).

DISTRIBUTION & AVAILABILITY: *Publisher or responsible agency:* Mogador Films/Mercury Productions; *Distributor:* No USA Dist. in 1988; BFI* (see *BUFVC BFI**), *Copy location:* FOL; LCM (35mm); *Call or copy number:* MP 63 (FOL).

Othello. Video/Abridgment

454. *Othello.*

DOCUMENT INFORMATION: *Country:* USA; *Year of first showing:* 1953; *Location of first showing:* The Philco Television Playhouse/NBC. Transmitted 9:00 P.M., 6 Sept. 1953.

EDITION, HISTORY, CONTENTS, & EVALUATION: *Edition & history:* Billed as "a streamlined version" of Shakespeare's tragedy. *Supplementary materials:* "Othello on TV." *NYT* 6 Sept. 1953: X 9; Gianokos, *TDSP* 134.

MEDIUM INFORMATION: *Color:* No (black & white); *Length:* 60 min. [?].

AUTHORSHIP INFORMATION: *Producer(s):* Coe, Fred; *Cast:* Thatcher, Torin (Othello); Deering, Olive (Desdemona); Matthau, Walter (Iago); Lyons, Gene (Cassio); Manning, Jack (Roderigo).

DISTRIBUTION & AVAILABILITY: *Publisher or responsible agency:* NBC.

Othello. Video/Teleplay

455. *Othello.*

DOCUMENT INFORMATION: *Country:* Canada; *Year of first showing:* 1953; *Location of first showing:* Canadian Broadcasting Company.

EDITION, HISTORY, CONTENTS, & EVALUATION: *Edition & history:* A full scale televised version of *Othello* that placed a high value on making effective use of the camera. Background music was from Bartok. *Contents & evaluation:* Alice Griffin, who wrote about Shakespeare on screen and television regularly for the prestigious *Shakespeare Quarterly*, had nothing but praise for this Canadian production. It was "marked by imagination, dramatic unity, and ensemble acting." As Othello, Lorne Greene was dark-skinned but not "negroid" so that the plain references to Othello's blackness were eliminated. In the style of the peering, roving, tracking camera in the Olivier *Hamlet*, the camera followed Othello down a long gallery on his way to Desdemona's bedchamber. A close-up then showed Othello's anguish. The close-up lens, Dr. Griffin also reports, was particularly advantageous in underscoring the significance of the handkerchief as a key symbol in the play's design. *Supplementary materials:* Griffin, Alice V. "Shakespeare Through the Camera's Eye." *SQ* 4 (July 1953): 330-36.

MEDIUM INFORMATION: *Color:* Black & white; *Length:* 84 min. AUTHORSHIP INFORMATION: *Director(s):* Greene, David; *Adaptor/translator(s):* Greene, David; *Composer(s):* Bartok, Bela; *Designer(s):* Soloviov, Nicolai; *Lighting designer(s):* Nutt, Tom; *Cast:* Greene, Lorne (Othello); Loder, Peggi (Desdemona); Furst, Josef (Iago); McNee, Patrick (Cassio); Blake, Katherine (Emilia); Easton, Richard (Roderigo).

DISTRIBUTION & AVAILABILITY: *Publisher or responsible agency:* Canadian Broadcasting Company.

Othello. Motion Picture/Interpretation

456. *Othello.*

DOCUMENT INFORMATION: *Country:* USSR; *Year of filming:* 1955; *Year of release:* 1956.

EDITION, HISTORY, CONTENTS, & EVALUATION: *Awards:* Best direction, Cannes Film Festival, 1956; *Edition & history:* Originally the film was made with a Russian-speaking cast, using Boris Pasternak's translation. Subsequently a version with dubbed-in English, spoken by British actors, was completed. Director Yutkevich's commitment to filmed Shakespeare may best be indicated by the existence of his book, *Shekspir i Kino [Shakespeare and Film]* (Moscow, 1973). Reviewer Mark Pomar wrote that Yutkevich thought of film as the heir to Shakespeare's theatre because of its ability to "encompass different events, entertain the public, and at the same time, probe the serious questions of life" (Pomar, Mark, "Books in Review," *SFNL* 4.1. [1979]: 10 +). *Contents & evaluation:* "In transporting *Othello* to the screen both the Russian producers and the American distributors have epitomized the historic indecision of Hamlet's classic query, 'To be or not to be?' The import, unveiled last night at the Fifty-fifth Street Playhouse as the latest offering in the United States-Soviet Union cultural-exchange program, is, beyond a doubt, a most beautiful, literally colorful and motion-filled version of the tragedy that dwarfs any *Othello* constricted by the confines of stage and proscenium arch. Simultaneously it presents a nagging and persistent distraction in the dubbed-in English dialogue. . . . The English thespians whose voices are heard, strangely enough, are excellent" (Weiler, A.H., "Review," *NYT* 16 May 1960: 39). To western eyes this Russianized *Othello* resembles an operatic spectacle, more emulative of Verdi's *Otello* than of Shakespeare's *Othello.* The impressive crowd scenes reflect an economy that could hire extras on the extravagant scale of a D.W. Griffith. The lavish color also lulls the senses. The greatest fascination, as is always the case with Shakespeare films from non-English speaking nations, comes in watching the appropriation of British cultural codes by a Russian sensibility. What remains of the "original" text is the underlying grammatical structure but not the semiotics of a unique national character. Othello's smothering of Desdemona, reminiscent of Emil Jannings in the old 1922 Butchowetzki silent (see 442), reaches new heights in ostensive acting. Even so, audiences will find much to admire in this movie (KSR). *Audience:* College and university; General use; *Supplementary materials:* Prouse, Derek. "Review." *SAS* 26 (1956): 30; Yutkevich, Sergei. "My Way with Shakespeare." *FAF* 41 (1957): 8 +.

MEDIUM INFORMATION: *Medium:* Motion picture; *Sound:* Spoken language; *Color:* Yes; *Length:* 108 min.; *Language(s) spoken:* Russian; *Dubbed language:* English; *Film type:* 16mm.

AUTHORSHIP INFORMATION: *Producer(s):* Mosfilm; *Director(s):* Yutkevich, Sergei; Lea, William de Lane (English version); *Adaptor/translator(s):* Pasternak, Boris; Radlova, Anna; *Composer(s):* Khatchaturian, Aram; *Designer(s):* Vaisfield, A.; Dorrer, V.; *Costume designer(s):* Kariakin, M.; Krochinina, O.; *Other personnel:* Volsky, B (Sound); *Cast:* Bondarchuk, Sergei (Othello); Skobtseva, Irina (Desdemona); Popov, Andrei (Iago); Soshalsky, Vladimir (Cassio); Vesnik, E. (Roderigo); Maximova, A. (Emilia); Teterin, E. (Brabantio); Troyanovsky, M. (The Doge); Kelberer, A. (Montano); Brilling, N. (Lodovico); English Version: Crawford, Howard Marion (Othello); Diamond, Arnold (Iago); Byron, Katherine (Desdemona); Warner, Richard (Roderigo); Westwood, Patrick (Cassio), Nevinson, Nancy (Emilia); Snowdon, Roger (Lodovico); Churchman, Ybanne (Bianca); Moore, Michael (Brabantio); Burt, Oliver (The Doge).

DISTRIBUTION & AVAILABILITY: *Publisher or responsible agency:* Mosfilm; Universal International; *Distributor:* COR; *Availability:* Rental 16mm $175 (Standard); $115 (High School).

Othello. Video/Teledrama

457. *Othello.*

DOCUMENT INFORMATION: *Country:* GB; *Year of first showing:* 1955; *Location of first showing:* BBC, London station. Transmitted 7:30 to 9:30 P.M., Thursday, 15 Dec. 1955.

EDITION, HISTORY, CONTENTS, & EVALUATION: *Edition & history:* Another relatively lavish Shakespeare production by the BBC, produced at a cost of £1,246 with a cast of 22 principals and 29 extras (CHM). *Contents & evaluation:* Not seen. *Audience:* General use; *Supplementary materials:* "Program." *RT* 9 Dec. 1955: 38.

MEDIUM INFORMATION: *Medium:* Video; *Sound:* Spoken language; *Color:* No (black & white); *Length:* 120 min.; *Language(s) spoken:* English; *Video type:* Not known.

AUTHORSHIP INFORMATION: *Producer(s):* Richardson, Tony; *Director(s):* Richardson, Tony; *Composer(s):* Chase, Leonard; *Designer(s):* Pemberton, Reece; *Cast:* Maxwell, James (Roderigo); Rogers, Paul (Iago); Willard, Edmund (Brabantio); Heath, Gordon (Othello); Hardy, Robert (Cassio); Welch, Peter (First Officer); Skillan, George (Duke); Royde, Frank; Clifford, Jefferson (Senators); Dartnell, Stephen (Sailor); Grant, Kim (Messenger); Davenport, Nigel (Lodovico); Harris, Rosemary (Desdemona); Wymark, Patrick (Montano); Miles, Kevin; Horgan, Patrick; Blanshard, Joby (Gentlemen); Anderson, Daphne (Emilia); Whitelaw, Billie (Bianca); Rosmer, Milton (Gratiano); + Soldiers, Citizens, Sailors, etc.

DISTRIBUTION & AVAILABILITY: *Publisher or responsible agency:* BBC; *Copy location:* BBC*.

Othello. Motion Picture/Derivative

458. *Jubal.*

DOCUMENT INFORMATION: *Country:* USA; *Year of release:* 1956.

EDITION, HISTORY, CONTENTS, & EVALUATION: *Edition & history:* On the surface the movie is a western. Actually, however, it is an adaptation of *Othello* based on a novel by Paul I. Wellman, which is in turn based on *Othello*. *Contents & evaluation:* A lonely ranch hand, Jubal, is taken up by a generous rancher, "Shep" (Ernest Borgnine), who promotes him over the head of Pinky (Rod Steiger). Worse yet, Shep's voluptuous wife casts flirtatious glances in Jubal's direction. The embittered Pinky (Rod Steiger) begins to plant the seeds of suspicion in the mind of Shep, who, like Othello, becomes insanely jealous of his wife. A visually exciting film that illustrates the timelessness of Shakespeare's theme. *Audience:* General use.

MEDIUM INFORMATION: *Medium:* Motion Picture; *Sound:* Spoken language; *Color:* Yes; *Length:* 101 min.; *Language(s) spoken:* English; *Film type:* 16mm; Cinemascope.

AUTHORSHIP INFORMATION: *Producer(s):* Fadiman, William; *Director(s):* Daves, Delmer; Saeta, Eddie; *Screenplay writer(s):* Hughes, Russell S.; Daves, Delmer; *Composer(s):* Raksin, David; Morton, Arthur; Stoloff, Morris; *Designer(s):* Anderson, Carl; *Set designer(s):* Diage, Louis; *Costume designer(s):* Louis, Jean; *Other personnel:* Lawton, Charles, Jr. (Photography); Jaffa, Henri (Technicolor consultant); Clark, Al (Film editor); Corky, Ray (Second Unit Photog.); Campbell, Clay (Make-up); Hunt, Helen (Hair styles); Livadary, John (Recording); Smith, Harry (Sound); *Cast:* Ford, Glenn (Jubal); Borgnine, Ernest (Shep); Steiger, Rod (Pinky); Farr, Felicia (Naomi); French, Valerie (Maie); Ruysdael, Basil (Shem); Berry, Noah, Jr. (Sam); Bronson, Charles (Reb Haislipp); Dierkes, John (Carson); Elam, Jack (McCoy); Burton, Robert (Dr. Grant).

DISTRIBUTION & AVAILABILITY: *Publisher or responsible agency:* Columbia Pictures; *Distributor:* FNC, *Copy location:* FOL; *Call or copy number:* MP 48.

Othello. Motion Picture/Excerpts

459. *Kean.*

DOCUMENT INFORMATION: *Country:* Italy; *Year of release:* 1956.

EDITION, HISTORY, CONTENTS, & EVALUATION: *Edition & history:* The great Edmund Kean is portrayed playing scenes on stage from *Othello* and *Hamlet*. *Supplementary materials:* SIF 107.

MEDIUM INFORMATION: *Length:* 75 min.

AUTHORSHIP INFORMATION: *Director(s):* Gassman, Vittorio; *Cast:* Gassman, Vittorio (Kean).

Othello. Motion Picture/Ballet

460. *Ballet of* Othello.

DOCUMENT INFORMATION: *Country:* USSR; *Year of first showing:* 1960.

EDITION, HISTORY, CONTENTS, & EVALUATION: *Edition & history:* A recording of a ballet performance of *Othello* by the Paliashvili Opera Theatre and Ballet of Tbilisi. Not easily available at present but listed by Parker. *Supplementary materials:* Parker, *TSF* 42.

MEDIUM INFORMATION: *Sound:* Spoken language; *Color:* Yes; *Length:* 95 min.; *Film type:* 35mm.

AUTHORSHIP INFORMATION: *Director(s):* Chabukiani, Vakhtang; *Composer(s):* Machavariani, Aleksey; *Choreographer(s):* Chabukiani, Vakhtang; *Cast:* Chabukiani, Vakhtang (Othello); Tsignadze, Vera (Desdemona); Kikaleyshvili, Zurab (Iago); Chabukiani, Eteri (Bianca).

DISTRIBUTION & AVAILABILITY: *Publisher or responsible agency:* Gruziya-Film/Artkino Pictures; *Distributor:* Unknown.

Othello. Motion Picture/Derivative

461. *All Night Long.*

DOCUMENT INFORMATION: *Country:* GB; *Year of release:* 1962.

EDITION, HISTORY, CONTENTS, & EVALUATION: *Edition & history:* The *Othello* story modernized and grafted onto a typical back-stage show business plot. Iago is played by Patrick McGoohan, who later directed the 1973 *Catch My Soul* (#466), which appropriated *Othello* into the world of rock just as *All Night Long* put it in the context of jazz. The cast was a mix of jazz musicians and well known actors such as Keith Michell. *Contents & evaluation:* The *mise en scène* is a luxuriously renovated flat in an abandoned warehouse in London's East End that resembles one of the old buildings on Clink Street near the original site of the Globe (at least before the bulldozers began "yuppifying" the neighborhood in the Seventies). Johnny Cousin (Iago) is motivated to steal Delia (Desdemona) from Aurelius Rex (Othello) because he needs her as a vocalist in his own band. The principals are assembled at the expensive flat of Rod Hamilton for an evening of jazz played by such big names as Johnny Dankworth and David

Brubeck. (With their Fifties-type short hair, narrow ties, dark suits and breast-pocket handkerchiefs, the musicians resemble J. Edgar Hoover style FBI agents.) Othello's handkerchief turns into an expensive cigarette case, Iago uses a tape recorder to entrap people, and Cassio falls victim to pot, not booze. While Cassio (Cass) is high on pot he succeeds in alienating Berger, a big producer. At the same time, Johnny (Iago) takes the opportunity to slip Delia's cigarette case (a gift from Rex) into Cass's pocket. Fortunately at the end Cass's perfidy is discovered in time to save Delia from Desdemona's fate and while Rex and Delia are reconciled, the insufferable Johnny is left alone at the end beating on his drums. Along the way there is much jamming of jazz and reaction shots of people ecstatically listening to it, the latter being a bit embarrassing to watch (KSR). *Audience:* General use; *Supplementary materials:* Haun, Harry. "Touch Up Your Shakespeare." *FR* (Nov. 1982): 529-30.

MEDIUM INFORMATION: *Medium:* Motion Picture; *Sound:* Spoken language; *Color:* No (black & white); *Length:* 82 min.; *Language(s) spoken:* English; *Language of subtitles:* French, German; *Film type:* 35mm.

AUTHORSHIP INFORMATION: *Producer(s):* Roberts, Bob; Relph, Michael; *Director(s):* Dearden, Basil; Hosgood, Stanley; *Screenplay writer(s):* King, Nel; Achilles, Peter; *Composer(s):* Green, Philip; Hayes, Tubby; Napper, Kenny; Scott, Johnny; Brubeck, David; Dankworth, Johnny; Mingus, Charles; *Designer(s):* Relph, Michael; *Set designer(s):* Simm, Ray; *Costume designer(s):* Harris, Julie; Rodway, Geoffrey (Makeup); Rivers, Stella (Hair); *Lighting designer(s):* Scaife, Ted; *Other personnel:* Hill, Bill (Prod. manager); Guthridge, John D. (Editor); Thomson, H.A.R. (Camera operator); Dyson, Sue (Continuity); Daniels, Bill (Sound recorder); MacPhee, Robert T. (Music recorder); Lancaster, Christopher (Sound ed.); *Cast:* McGoohan, Patrick (Johnny Cousin); Michell, Keith (Cass); Harris, Paul (Aurelius Rex); Blair, Betsy (Emily); Stevens, Marti (Delia); Attenborough, Richard (Rod Hamilton); Braden, Bernard (Berger); Tomb, Harry (Phales); Velasco, Maria (Benny); w. Courtley, Bert; Christie, Keith; Dempsey, Ray; Ganley, Alan; Morgan, Barry; Purbrook, Colin (Musicians).

DISTRIBUTION & AVAILABILITY: *Publisher or responsible agency:* J. Arthur Rank; *Distributor:* IVY, SWA, *Copy location:* NFA*, LC.

Othello. Video/Recording

462. *Othello.*

DOCUMENT INFORMATION: *Country:* France; *Year of first showing:* 1962; *Location of first showing:* Paris O.R.T.F. dist. I.N.A.

EDITION, HISTORY, CONTENTS, & EVALUATION:

Edition & history: Recording of a 1962 performance in Paris.

MEDIUM INFORMATION: *Sound:* Spoken language; *Color:* No (black & white); *Length:* 126 min.; *Video type:* 3/4"U.

AUTHORSHIP INFORMATION: *Director(s):* Barma, Claude; *Adaptor/translator(s):* Neveux, Georges; *Composer(s):* Jarre, Maurice; *Designer(s):* Dieulot, Marcel-Louis; *Costume designer(s):* Coste, Christiane; *Cast:* Bergé, Francine (Desdemona); Sorano, Daneil (Othello); Topart, Jean (Iago); Le Royer, Michel.

DISTRIBUTION & AVAILABILITY: *Publisher or responsible agency:* O.R.T.F.; *Copy location:* VAA; *Call or copy number:* THE 1.29.

Othello. Motion Picture/Abridgment

463. *Othello.* (Series: Fair Adventure Series).

DOCUMENT INFORMATION: *Country:* USA; *Year of release:* 1964.

EDITION, HISTORY, CONTENTS, & EVALUATION: *Edition & history:* A five-part abridgment of the play with commentary by Dr. Frank Baxter. *Contents & evaluation:* Not seen. *Audience:* Junior High (grades 7-9); High school (grades 10-12);.

MEDIUM INFORMATION: *Medium:* Motion Picture; *Sound:* Spoken language; *Color:* No (black & white); *Length:* 140 min.; *Language(s) spoken:* English; *Film type:* 16mm.

DISTRIBUTION & AVAILABILITY: *Publisher or responsible agency:* Westinghouse Broadcasting Corp.; *Distributor:* Not known.

Othello. Motion Picture/Recording

464. *Othello: The Moor of Venice.*

DOCUMENT INFORMATION: *Country:* GB; *Year of release:* 1965.

EDITION, HISTORY, CONTENTS, & EVALUATION: *Edition & history:* A recording of John Dexter's National Theatre production, which, though restyled somewhat for film, retains the "staginess" of its source. *Contents & evaluation:* In creating his role, Olivier apparently elected to follow the F.R. Leavis theory that makes Othello as much or more than Iago responsible for his own tragic downfall. In other words, the seeds of his own destruction already inhabit Othello's consciousness. Practice, however, does not seem to follow theory, for many critics have found an intrinsic dignity in Olivier's performance that belies the theory. In general the production was well received for the brilliance of both Olivier's Othello and Finlay's remarkable Iago. Maggie Smith as Desdemona gave one of the great performances of a distinguished career. The stark contrast between the whiteness of her flesh and the made-up blackness of Othello graphically underscores the play's subtext about miscegenation. Although the *New York Times* critic complained that Olivier was got up in blackface to "look like the end man in a minstrel show," most viewers have found his interpretation of the role quite overwhelming. His remarkable voice carries him through any number of implausibilities into plausibilies. Finlay's Iago is a sinister, leering, foul-minded lower class East London type, whose pervasive control of the situation is underscored by camera work that consistently foregrounds him in profile to give the impression of the master puppeteer at work. Filmed mostly in close and midshot, the effect is often less cinematic than videomatic, though one memorable crane shot punctuates the high moment of Iago's demonic seduction of Othello. He becomes a Mephistopheles to Othello's Faustus. The visual effect makes this single act a microcosm for the macrocosm of the human experience. For those familiar with his later career as a Shakespearean actor (Richard II and Hamlet in the BBC television plays, and most recently Chorus in the 1989 Branagh *Henry V*), the presence of a youthful Derek Jacobi in the role of Cassio will have special interest (KSR). *Audience:* General use; *Supplementary materials:* Jorgens, *SOF* 191-206; Manvell, *SAF* 117-9; Brown, Constance. "Olivier's Othello." *FQ*, 19.4 (Summer 1966): 48-50; "One Man's Moor." *Time* (4 Feb. 1966): 103.

MEDIUM INFORMATION: *Medium:* Motion Picture; *Sound:* Spoken language; *Color:* Yes; *Length:* 166 min.; *Language(s) spoken:* English; *Film type:* 16mm Panavision and Technicolor.

AUTHORSHIP INFORMATION: *Producer(s):* Havelock-Allan, Anthony; Brabourne, John; *Director(s):* Burge, Stuart; *Designer(s):* Herbert, Jocelyn; Kellner, William; *Other personnel:* Unsworth, Geoffrey (Camera); Marden, Richard (Editing); *Cast:* Olivier, Laurence (Othello); Finlay, Frank (Iago); Smith, Maggie (Desdemona); Redman, Joyce (Emilia); Jacobi, Derek (Cassio); Lang, Robert (Roderigo); Mackintosh, Kenneth (Lodovico); Nicholls, Anthony (Brabantio); Reid, Sheila (Bianca); Turner, Michael (Gratiano); Hardwicke, Edward (Montano); Lomax, Harry (Doge); Holder, Roy (Clown).

DISTRIBUTION & AVAILABILITY: *Publisher or responsible agency:* BHE Production through Eagle Films Ltd.; *Distributor:* CWF, GLB*, *Copy location:* FOL, MMA (004824); *Call or copy number:* MP 39; *Availability:* Apply CWF ($70 16mm rental in 1988).

Othello. Motion Picture/Documentary

465. *Othello: An Anatomy of a Marriage.* (Series: Explorations in Shakespeare, VIII).

DOCUMENT INFORMATION: *Country:* Canada; *Year of release:* 1969.

EDITION, HISTORY, CONTENTS, & EVALUATION: *Edition & history:* Part eight in a series of twelve 23-minute films made in 1969 by the Ontario Educational Communications Authority (see also 18, 40, 65, 124, 162, 257, 322, 488, 555, 617 and 637). *Contents & evaluation:* Not seen. According to the publicity release issued by NBC Educational Enterprises, the film studies Othello as "a character of mighty opposites; he is as extravagant in his love as in his hatred. Like the man, his marriage pivots between these two extremes. The film concentrates on those scenes in which Othello's torment begins and ends. It emphasizes the poisonous nature of jealousy and its appalling consequences. A young married couple discuss mechanisms of marriage and jealousy with respect to both Othello and Desdemona and to themselves. They raise the major question of whether or not marriage is archaic in its present form." From this description, it seems that this program, like the others in the series, was unafraid to explore some controversial ideas. *Audience:* College and university.

MEDIUM INFORMATION: *Medium:* Motion Picture; *Sound:* Spoken language; *Color:* Yes; *Length:* 23 min.; *Language(s) spoken:* English; *Film type:* 16mm.

AUTHORSHIP INFORMATION: *Producer(s):* Reis, Kurt; Moser, Ed; *Screenplay writer(s):* Webster, Hugh; *Composer(s):* Yanovsky, Zal; *Set designer(s):* Adeney, Chris; *Lighting designer(s):* Galbraith, Howard; *Performance group(s):* Ontario Educational Communications/ NBC Educational Enterprises.

DISTRIBUTION & AVAILABILITY: *Distributor:* CNU.

Othello. Motion Picture/Derivative/Musical

466. *Catch My Soul: Santa Fe Satan.*

DOCUMENT INFORMATION: *Country:* USA; *Year of release:* 1973.

EDITION, HISTORY, CONTENTS, & EVALUATION: *Edition & history:* A "rock operatic" version of *Othello*, in the tradition of *Hair* or *Jesus Christ Superstar*, a genre that was fashionable in the late Sixties and early Seventies. Originally produced on stage in London, but later revised for filming in Santa Fe, New Mexico. Director Patrick McGoohan had appeared in the 1962 *All Night Long* (461), a film also based on *Othello* but about London jazz musicians. This film and *All Night Long* re-appropriate *Othello* for the eras of jazz and rock. *Contents & evaluation:* The setting of *Othello* has been transmogrified from Venice and Cyprus to a hippie religious cult in the New Mexico desert. The black evangelical cult leader (Richie Havens) is analogous to Othello, while Desdemona (Season Hubley) is a round-faced white girl with granny glasses. Susan Tyrell as Emilia plays a raffish looking hippie woman, and Iago (Launce Le Gault) fits all negative stereotypes for hippies with his bearded, scruffy look. The plot closely follows Shakespeare's. For example, the scene in which Cassio becomes drunk is transformed into an episode where the camp church building burns down while Cassio (Tony Joe White) is in a drunken stupor, and Iago tortures Othello with innuendoes about Desdemona's relationship with Cassio. Iago's great line, "Ha, I like not that," is even left intact in the film. The Santa Fe Satan turns out to be of course Iago, who laughs demonically while literally riding Othello into a pit. Othello smothers Desdemona while his "Put out the light" speech pulsates in electronic rock rhythms. The color is spectacular; the long shots of the New Mexico desert, memorable; the acting, believable; and the rock music, frenetic (KSR). *Audience:* General use.

MEDIUM INFORMATION: *Medium:* Motion Picture; *Sound:* Spoken language; *Color:* Yes; *Length:* 100 min.; *Language(s) spoken:* English; *Film type:* 16mm.

AUTHORSHIP INFORMATION: *Producer(s):* Rosenbloom, Richard; Good, Jack; Davies, Huw; Fries, Charles; *Director(s):* McGoohan, Patrick; Neumann, Kurt Jr.; *Screenplay writer(s):* Good, Jack; Atterbury, Mal; *Composer(s):* Bramlett, Delaney; White, Tony Joe; Glass, Paul; Whitfield, Ted; O'Keefe, Jim; *Designer(s):* Reed, Tex; *Costume designer(s):* Lipin, Arnold M.; Norrin, John (Makeup); *Lighting designer(s):* Hall, Conrad; *Other personnel:* Stolnitz, Art (Production exec.); Harris, Richard A. (Editor); Warder, Joe (Prod. manager); Gerlich, Gary (Post-production sup.); Briggs, Richard (Location adm.); Wineman, Jerry (Coordinator); Campbell, Charles (Sound); Litt, Robert (Recording sup.); Post, Bob (Sound mixer); Davies, Jack (Asst. ed.); Loughridge, Tom (Camera op.); Maehl, Ross (Electrician); *Cast:* Havens, Richie (Othello); Le Gault, Launce (Iago); Hubley, Season (Desdemona); White, Tony Joe (Cassio); Tyrrell, Susan (Emilia); w. Bramlett, Delaney; Bramlett, Bonnie; Gardenhire, Raleigh; Waterhouse, Wayne "Eagle"; Family Lotus.

DISTRIBUTION & AVAILABILITY: *Publisher or responsible agency:* Metromedia Productions; *Copy location:* FOL; *Call or copy number:* MP 56.

Othello. Motion Picture/Scenes

467. *Othello,* 2.1; 5.2. (Series: The Shakespeare Series [IFB], VII).

DOCUMENT INFORMATION: *Country:* GB; *Year of release:* 1974.

EDITION, HISTORY, CONTENTS, & EVALUATION: *Edition & history:* The seventh unit in "The Shakespeare Series," designed to emulate the conditions of playing in the Elizabethan theatre (see also numbers 22, 127, 164, 232, 326, 430, 490, 510, 556, 601 and 619). For background, see also 22. In this segment, there are vignettes from *Othello* showing Iago uttering his paranoid hatred of the Moor (2.1); and the devastating episode in which Othello in a fit of jealous self-righteousness smothers and then chokes poor Desdemona (5.2). *Contents & evaluation:* A miscast Colin Farrell makes a much better King Richard II (in this same series) than a scheming Iago. He just doesn't have the sinister edge underneath the congeniality that the role calls for. Mark Kingston as Othello is much more convincing, while Susan Jameson makes a believable Desdemona. Despite some cinematic touches (over the shoulder shot of Othello kissing Desdemona, for example) there is the usual tendency toward staginess typical of this series. The problem is to represent an Elizabethan stage on screen without making it look artificial. The dilemma was solved in the opening sequence of the Olivier *Henry V,* but it takes both money and people who know how to point a camera to do it. *Audience:* High school (grades 10-12); *Supplementary materials:* Notes in *New Shakespeare* issued by Seabourne Enterprises in Great Britain in 1974 and distributed by EFVA.

MEDIUM INFORMATION: *Medium:* Motion Picture; *Sound:* Spoken language; *Color:* Yes; *Length:* 9 1/2 min.; *Language(s) spoken:* English; *Film type:* 16mm; *Video type:* V, 3/4U (4 per cassette).

AUTHORSHIP INFORMATION: *Producer(s):* Realist Film Unit; *Director(s):* Seabourne, Peter; *Cast:* Kingston, Mark (Othello); Jameson, Susan (Desdemona); Farrell, Colin (Iago).

DISTRIBUTION & AVAILABILITY: *Publisher or responsible agency:* Realist Film Unit; *Distributor:* IFB, CNU, *Copy location:* FOL; *Call or copy number:* ISBN 0-8354-1584-8; FOL, MP 89; *Availability:* CNU, rental 16mm $8; IFB, sale 16mm, V, $175.

Othello. Video/Recording

467.1 *Otello.*

DOCUMENT INFORMATION: *Country:* Italy; *Year of first showing:* 1974; *Location of first showing:* Rome, Nov. 1974.

EDITION, HISTORY, CONTENTS, & EVALUATION: *Edition & history:* A recording of a performance of *Othello* by the Gruppe La Maschera, Rome.

AUTHORSHIP INFORMATION: *Director(s):* Perlini, Mémé.

DISTRIBUTION & AVAILABILITY: *Publisher or re-*

sponsible agency: Gruppo La Meschera; *Copy location:* ASV; *Call or copy number:* A5.100.206-07.

Othello. **Video/Opera**

468. *Otello.*

DOCUMENT INFORMATION: *Country:* USA; *Year of release:* 1978.

EDITION, HISTORY, CONTENTS, & EVALUATION: *Edition & history:* A broadcast of Verdi's *Otello,* "Live from the Met," on WNET-TV in 1978. *Supplementary materials:* Loughney, Katharine. "Shakespeare on Film and Tape at Library of Congress." *SFNL* 14.1 (Dec.1989): 6.

MEDIUM INFORMATION: *Length:* 210 min.

AUTHORSHIP INFORMATION: *Producer(s):* Zeffirelli, Franco; Sarson, Christopher; *Director(s):* Browning, Kirk; *Composer(s):* Verdi, Guiseppe; Levine, James (Conductor); *Cast:* Milnes, Sherrill; Domingo, Placido; Cruz-Romo, Gilda.

DISTRIBUTION & AVAILABILITY: *Copy location:* LCM; *Call or copy number:* VBB 3304-3307.

Othello. **Video/Recording**

469. *Othello.*

DOCUMENT INFORMATION: *Country:* USA; *Year of first showing:* 1979; *Location of first showing:* Delacorte Theatre, New York City.

EDITION, HISTORY, CONTENTS, & EVALUATION: *Edition & history:* A videotape of a production at the 1979 New York Shakespeare Festival. *Contents & evaluation:* Quite a remarkable performance by Raul Julia as Othello, and Richard Dreyfuss as Iago. *The New York Times* drama critic found Raul Julia's handling of the role of Othello "a step forward in his career," and Mr. Dreyfuss' Iago "a crafty manipulator" capable of "pouring pestilence into Othello's ear" (Gussow, Mel, "Raul Julia Plays *Othello*," *NYT* 9 Aug. 1979: n.p.). *Audience:* College and university; General use; *Supplementary materials:* Oliver, Edith. "The Theatre: Off Broadway." *NY,* 27 (1979): 85.

MEDIUM INFORMATION: *Medium:* Video; *Sound:* Spoken language; *Color:* Yes; *Length:* 190 min.; *Language(s) spoken:* English; *Video type:* 3/4U.

AUTHORSHIP INFORMATION: *Producer(s):* Papp, Joseph; *Cast:* Dreyfuss, Richard (Iago); Julia, Raul (Othello); Kalulani, Lee (Emilia); Heard, John (Cassio); Conroy, Frances (Desdemona); McGill, Bruce (Lodovico).

DISTRIBUTION & AVAILABILITY: *Copy location:* LCL, TOFT Collection.

Othello. **Video/Adaptation**

469.1 *Otello.*

DOCUMENT INFORMATION: *Country:* Italy; *Year of first showing:* 1979; *Location of first showing:* Transmitted Radiotelevisione Italiana 1979.

EDITION, HISTORY, CONTENTS, & EVALUATION: *Edition & history:* Filmed in the RAI studios at Tornio from Oct. 10 to Nov. 11, 1979. The original production was performed in January 1979 at the Teatro Quirino di Rome with the same cast and director as the televised performance.

AUTHORSHIP INFORMATION: *Director(s):* Bene, Carmelo; *Composer(s):* Zito, L.; *Cast:* Bene, Carmelo (Othello); Cinieri, Cosimo (Iago); Bosisio, Luca (Cassio); Javicoli, Susanna (Bianca); Dotti, Licia (Emilia); Boucher, Jean Paul (Roderigo); Dell'Aguzzo, Cesare (Jolly); Martini, Michèle.

DISTRIBUTION & AVAILABILITY: *Publisher or responsible agency:* RAI (Radio Television Italy); *Copy location:* RAI.

Othello. **Motion Picture/Interpretation**

470. *Othello.*

DOCUMENT INFORMATION: *Year of release:* 1980; *Location of first showing:* May 1980, Howard University, Washington, DC.

EDITION, HISTORY, CONTENTS, & EVALUATION: *Edition & history:* Filmed on the island of Martha's Vineyard, Mass., and Cobbleclose Farm, New Jersey. For an in-depth analysis of the film, see Peter Donaldson's article, below. *Contents & evaluation:* Not seen. Publicity release in Museum of Modern Art Film Library reads as follows: "Liz White, veteran producer-director has mounted a stunning film . . . an unusual and provocative treatment of Shakespeare's Othello developed in an innovative and creative way . . . a visual treat with a brilliant score of Afro-American Jazz and an all-black cast. . . . The first of its kind." *Audience:* General use; *Supplementary materials:* Donaldson, Peter. "Liz White's *Othello.*" *SQ,* 38 (Winter 1987): 482-95.

MEDIUM INFORMATION: *Medium:* Motion picture; *Sound:* Spoken language; *Color:* Yes; *Length:* 115 min.; *Language(s) spoken:* English; *Film type:* 16mm; Eastman color.

AUTHORSHIP INFORMATION: *Producer(s):* White, Liz; *Director(s):* White, Liz; *Adaptor/translator(s):* White, Liz; *Composer(s):* Gwangwa, Jonas; *Costume designer(s):* Bowles, Olive; James, Christy; *Other personnel:* Dorkins, Charles (Photography); *Cast:* Kotto, Yaphet (Othello); Dixon, Richard (Iago); Dixon, Audrey (Desdemona); Chisholm, Louis (Cassio); Bowles, Olive (Emilia); Gray,

Douglas (Roderigo); Williams, Jim (Brabantio); Ashburn, Benjamin (Montano); White, Liz (Bianca); Pope, Lincoln (Duke of Venice).

DISTRIBUTION & AVAILABILITY: *Publisher or responsible agency:* Cultural Committee, Howard University; *Distributor:* Howard University, Washington, DC; *Availability:* Apply to Howard University.

Othello. Video/Documentary

471. *In the Making: Theatre Design.*

DOCUMENT INFORMATION: *Country:* GB; *Year of release:* 1980.

EDITION, HISTORY, CONTENTS, & EVALUATION: *Edition & history:* Discusses set and costume design for 1979 RSC *Othello. Supplementary materials:* BUFVC 19.

MEDIUM INFORMATION: *Length:* 20 min.

AUTHORSHIP INFORMATION: *Director(s):* Read, John; *Cast:* Howard, Pamela (Interviewee).

DISTRIBUTION & AVAILABILITY: *Distributor:* BBC*.

Othello. Video/Teleplay

472. *Othello.* (Series: The Shakespeare Plays).

DOCUMENT INFORMATION: *Country:* GB; *Year of filming:* 9-17 March 1981; *Year of first showing:* 1981; *Location of first showings:* BBC; PBS, USA, 12 Oct. 1981.

EDITION, HISTORY, CONTENTS, & EVALUATION: *Edition & history:* The most surprising feature of this *Othello* is the downgrading of Othello's blackness in favor of portraying the Moor as a light-skinned Arab. The director, Jonathan Miller, felt that over-concern with the complexion of the Venetian general had often obscured the play's deeper meanings. As Miller would have it, fundamentally the play is about jealousy, a condition not confined to members of the black community. Even so, Othello's blackness is a stage tradition that dies hard, especially in light of the classic performances by such actors as Paul Robeson and James Earl Jones. For the settings, Miller and his designer, Colin Lowrey, emulated the Renaissance paintings of De La Tour and Tintoretto, while a palace in Urbino inspired the antechamber of the Cyprian palace in which so much of the action transpires. *Contents & evaluation:* "Mr. Miller works incessantly against what is perhaps the most familiar interpretation of the play: the Noble Savage booming out his lines sonorously, the scheming aide worming his way into total confidence[,] and the victimized wife, delicate and helpless. Mr. Miller offers an Othello who is almost conversational within the cramped confines of a television screen. Mr. Hoskins, complete with a

cockney accent, turns Iago into a hysterically giggling, cackling psychopath. And Miss Wilton's Desdemona, anything but passive, is an outgoing woman incensed at being wrongfully accused. . ... The performances in this production are, at the very least, distinctive, if not distinguished. Mr. Hopkins' speech mannerisms seem to have settled into a pattern of delivering the lines in somewhat punchy phrases and momentary pauses. This can often produce a remarkable clarity of meaning but occasionally it comes dangerously close to the experimental Shakespeare readings of a comic character in the current stage version of 'The Life & Adventures of Nicholas Nickleby,' a character who declaims, 'To be or not/To be is the question.' And when Mr. Hopkins explodes emotionally, he seems to slide incomprehensibly into the accents of his native Wales" (O'Connor, John J., "Miller Directs 'Othello'," *NYT* 12 Oct. 1981: C24). "The BBC *Othello* shows flashes of brilliance, particularly in the acting of Bob Hoskins and in the support of Penelope Wilton and Rosemary Leach [as Emilia]. Anthony Hopkins' portrayal and Jonathan Miller's confining of Othello, however, limit the achievement of the production. A valid debate about the relative weight and worth of the two main figures continues, but Miller so prejudices the argument that the dialectic of the play is lost. The largeness of the character of Othello is thrown away like the pearl 'richer than all his tribe.' We may well sympathize with Othello's cry: 'every puny whipster gets my sword'" (Simone, R. Thomas, "Jonathan Miller's Iago," *SFNL* 6.2 [1982]: 4+). *Audience:* College and university; General use; *Supplementary materials:* Fenwick, Henry. *Othello.* BSP 18-28; Videotape (25 min.) from "Shakespeare in Perspective" series with Susan Hill as lecturer available in U.K. from BBC* (*BUFVC* 19).

MEDIUM INFORMATION: *Medium:* Video; *Sound:* Spoken language; *Color:* Yes; *Length:* 210 min.; *Video type:* B, V, 3/4" U.

AUTHORSHIP INFORMATION: *Producer(s):* Miller, Jonathan; *Director(s):* Miller, Jonathan; *Composer(s):* Oliver, Stephen; *Designer(s):* Lowrey, Colin; *Costume designer(s):* Hughes, Ray; *Lighting designer(s):* Treays, John; *Cast:* Hopkins, Anthony (Othello); Hoskins, Bob (Iago); Wilton, Penelope (Desdemona); Leach, Rosemary (Emilia); Chater, Geoffrey (Brabantio); Pedley, Anthony (Roderigo); Yelland, David (Cassio); Barron, John (Duke); Steedman, Tony (Montano); Davion, Alexander (Gratiano); O'Conor, Joseph (Lodovico); Morgan, Wendy (Bianca); Green, Seymour (First Senator); Goorney, Howard (Second Senator); Harvey, Max (First Gentleman); McGinity, Terence (Second Gentleman); Nobes, Nigel (Third Gentleman); Walmsley, Peter (Officer).

DISTRIBUTION & AVAILABILITY: *Publisher or responsible agency:* BBC/TLF; *Distributor:* AVP, UIO, BBC*, *Copy location:* UVM; *Availability:* AVP, B, V, 3/4U $450

(1987), sale; UIO, V (72324H), 3/4U (70324V), rental, $26.30; BBC* V only, apply (BUFVC 19).

Othello. Motion Picture/Derivative

473. *Othello: Black Commando.*

DOCUMENT INFORMATION: *Year of release:* 1982; *Location of first showing:* Cine Roxy A, Madrid, Spain.

EDITION, HISTORY, CONTENTS, & EVALUATION: *Edition & history:* The film "updates" the Bard's Moor of Venice by making him over into an American mercenary in Africa who falls in love with the daughter of a U.S. senator. Beethoven symphonic scores are on the sound track. *Contents & evaluation:* Not seen. The only available review calls the film a "travesty," which "pompously claims to be based on the work of William Shakespeare." Also "disastrously" the name "'Shakespeare' is misspelled 'Sheakespeare' in the credits." The reviewer goes on to say that "there is enough brainless shooting going on to appeal to unsophistocated audiences, who won't be concerned about niceties or non-sequiturs" (Besa, "Othello," *VAR* 22 Dec.1972: 14). *Audience:* General use.

MEDIUM INFORMATION: *Medium:* Motion picture; *Sound:* Spoken language; *Color:* Yes; *Length:* 103 min.; *Language(s) spoken:* Spanish; *Film type:* 35mm. Eastmancolor.

AUTHORSHIP INFORMATION: *Producer(s):* Gonzalez, Maria J.; *Director(s):* Boulois, Max H.; *Adaptor/translator(s):* Boulois, Max H.; *Composer(s):* Beethoven, Ludwig Von; *Other personnel:* Gimeno, Antonio (Editor); Solano, Domingo (Camera); *Cast:* Boulois, Max H. (Othello); Curtis, Tony (Iago); Oliveros, Ramiro (Cassio), Pettet, Joanna (Desdemona).

DISTRIBUTION & AVAILABILITY: *Publisher or responsible agency:* M.B. Diffusion, S.A. (Madrid, Spain), and Eurocine (Paris, France); *Distributor:* Not known.

Othello. Video/Opera

474. *Otello.*

DOCUMENT INFORMATION: *Country:* Italy; *Year of release:* 1982.

EDITION, HISTORY, CONTENTS, & EVALUATION: *Edition & history:* A taped performance of Verdi's *Otello* in Verona. *Supplementary materials:* Novacom Video Inc. catalog.

MEDIUM INFORMATION: *Length:* 145 min.

AUTHORSHIP INFORMATION: *Producer(s):* De Bosio, Gianfranco; *Director(s):* Montell, Preben; Pesko, Zoltan (Conductor); *Composer(s):* Verdi, Guiseppe; *Cast:* Kanawa,

Kiri Te; Atlantov, Vladimir; Capucili, Piero; Bevacqua, Antonio; Manganotti, Gianfranco.

DISTRIBUTION & AVAILABILITY: *Distributor:* NOV, FCM, *Availability:* NOV, B, V $40; FCM, V (SO2449) $39.95.

Othello. Video/Recording

475. *Otello.*

DOCUMENT INFORMATION: *Country:* Italy; *Year of release:* 12 June 1984.

EDITION, HISTORY, CONTENTS, & EVALUATION: *Edition & history:* Video production of the performance by Falso Movimento.

MEDIUM INFORMATION: *Sound:* Spoken language; *Color:* Yes; *Length:* 30 min.; *Video type:* 3/4U.

AUTHORSHIP INFORMATION: *Producer(s):* Radiotelevisione Italiana (RAI); *Director(s):* Martone, Mario; *Designer(s):* Fiorito, L.; *Lighting designer(s):* Corcione, M.; *Other personnel:* Doccos, G. (Editing); Bigliardo, D. (Graphics); Corti, A. (Video director); Rondanini, D. (Sound); *Cast:* Arana, Tomàs; Maglietta, Licia; Renzi, Andrea.

DISTRIBUTION & AVAILABILITY: *Publisher or responsible agency:* Theatre Co: Falso Movimento; *Copy location:* NTI, Amsterdam; SOV, Rome; *Call or copy number:* 700148001 BDA (NTI).

Othello. Video/Derivative

476. *Otelo de Oliveira: Recriaca de Otelo, O Mouro de Venezia de William Shakespeare.* [*Othello*].

DOCUMENT INFORMATION: *Year of release:* 1984; *Country of first showing:* Globo TV, Brazil.

EDITION, HISTORY, CONTENTS, & EVALUATION: *Edition & history:* This *Othello* along with the Brazilian *Romeo and Juliet* are offshoots from Shakespeare's plays, directed and adapted by Aguinaldo Silva. It has received a warm welcome from Latin American audiences, though it has never appeared on U.S. television. *Contents & evaluation:* In this Portuguese version of *Othello*, the Moor of Venice and Desdemona are transmogrified into Otelo and Denise, residents of a shanty town in Rio de Janeiro. Otelo is the leader of a samba band that is shot through with poisonous rivalries. He is a convincingly handsome, light-skinned man, married to a very fair Desdemona [Denise]. Emilia is an agreeable black woman, and Cassio is a white man, a guitar player, who is the victim of Iago's machinations. Iago is played by a magnetically forceful black man with a deceptively soft face capable of twisting into convincing malevolence upon demand.

The most celebrated stage prop in theatrical history, Othello's handkerchief, is replaced by a mysterious ring that Otelo is inordinately fond of. The entire play has been "Latinized"; for example, the "magic in the web" of Othello's handkerchief, which Shakespeare's play tells us was woven by a "sybil," in this version gets displaced into a series of weird rites on a voodoo altar. The photography and ambiance of the film are extraordinarily attractive, though many will not appreciate how far it drifts away from a literal representation of Shakespeare's tragedy (KSR). *Audience:* Professional; Special audiences (see Contents & evaluation, above); *Supplementary materials:* Rothwell, K.S. "Shakespeare All Around the World." *SFNL* 10.2 (1986): 5+.

MEDIUM INFORMATION: *Medium:* Video; *Sound:* Spoken language; *Color:* Yes; *Length:* 120 min. (?); *Language(s) spoken:* Portuguese (Brazilian dialect); *Other language information:* To date no English version available; *Video type:* V.

AUTHORSHIP INFORMATION: *Producer(s):* Grisolli, Paulo Afonso; *Director(s):* Grisolli, Paulo Afonso; *Adaptor/translator(s):* Silva, Aguinaldo; *Cast:* Bonfim, Roberto (Otelo); Lemmertz, Julia (Denise [Desdemona]); Concalves, Milton; Dourado, Regina; Lureiro, Oswaldo; Conde, Eduarde; Coutinho, Jorge; Dantas, Daniel; Bottelo, Wellington; D'Angelo, J.; Ferraz, Buza; Costa, Claudia; Fayad, Marcos; Mayer, Jose; Crassi, Antonio; Sampaio, Sergio; Augusto, Sergio; Ferreira, Helvecio; de Oliveira, Maria Jose; Katani, Ana Lucia.

DISTRIBUTION & AVAILABILITY: *Publisher or responsible agency:* Globo TV/Network Brazil; *Distributor:* GTV, *Availability:* Inquire GTV.

Othello. Video/Interpretation

477. *Othello: The Moor of Venice.* (Series: The Bard Series).

CURRENT PRODUCTION: *Year:* 1985.

DOCUMENT INFORMATION: *Country:* USA; *Year of release:* 1985.

EDITION, HISTORY, CONTENTS, & EVALUATION: *Edition & history:* A major purpose of this series of video productions (for others see 27, 340, 494 and 627) seems to have been to offer Shakespeare on screen with North American actors, many of whom would be recognizable to students familiar with commercial TV drama. That way Shakespeare might seem less remote and formidable to American high school and college students. A rival to the BBC series, which notoriously excluded American actors, some titles have been transmitted on the Arts & Entertainment cable network in the U.S. *Contents & evaluation:* "Good, readily available videos and films of *Othello* are in such short supply that the fairly recent offering from Bard Productions,

Ltd., is bound to spark a certain amount of interest. In some ways the director, Frank Melton, has moved toward a successful interpretation, most notably by casting William Marshall as Othello and Jenny Agutter as Desdemona. Visually and aurally both actors instantly meld with their roles. . . . Unfortunately too many other aspects spoil the viewer's pleasure . . . both Ron Moody as Iago and Leslie Paxton as Emilia are extraordinarily poor choices for these critical roles. . . . [Moody] is too old, too odd, too bald to be the Moor's nemesis. . . . For Paxton I could find no extenuation. In a production where everyone speaks with a different native accent, she adds shrillness or shouting or both to her pedestrian reading of Emilia's lines. . . . Beyond the casting, problems of staging, costuming and pacing plague this *Othello.* . . . Before the action ends, most audiences may wish all the playing areas were carpeted, because the noise of every footfall on the bare wooden portions of the stage adds an oral distraction worse than the clumsy sound effects. . . . Despite an extraordinarily lucid rendering of the literal meaning of the text, this production mars the subtlety, the intensity, the beauty of *Othello.* Marshall and Agutter sometimes break through to a more profound experience—but not often enough. A pity, too, because the public needs a better version of the play than Bard or the BBC has offered. Clearly, however, the segments with Marshall and Agutter will be useful in the classroom, even when something better comes along for the whole play" (Cook, Ann Jennalie, "Othello," *SFNL* 12.1 [Dec. 1987]: 1+). *Audience:* High school (grades 10-12); College and university; *Supplementary materials:* Stevenson, M. George. "Et Tu, Shakespeare: The Bard's Greatest Hits on Tape and Disc." *Video* (Aug. 1986): 66+.

MEDIUM INFORMATION: *Medium:* Video; *Sound:* Spoken language; *Color:* Yes; *Length:* 195 min.; *Language(s) spoken:* English; *Video type:* B, V.

AUTHORSHIP INFORMATION: *Producer(s):* Nakano, Jack; Manning, Jack; *Director(s):* Melton, Franklin; *Composer(s):* Cohen, Gerard Bernard; *Designer(s):* Manning, Jack; *Cast:* Marshall, William (Othello); Moody, Ron (Iago); Agutter, Jenny (Desdemona); Bookwalter, DeVeren (Cassio); MacLean, Peter (Brabantio); Robinson, Jay (Duke of Venice); Paxton, Leslie (Emilia); Asher, Joel (Roderigo); Wright, Eugenia (Bianca); Dresdon, Anna (Courtesan); Persons, Phil (Ludovico); Hayward, Mike (Montano); Markussen, Arnold (Gratiano); Steininger, Dan (Messenger); Nye, Will (Soldier); Broyles, Lanny (First Senator); Bliss, John (Second Senator).

DISTRIBUTION & AVAILABILITY: *Publisher or responsible agency:* Bard Productions, Ltd.; *Distributor:* ILL, FCM, DCV, *Availability:* ILL, sale, V (S 01594) $89.95; FCM, sale, V $89.95; DCV, sale, V (84195) $95; INM, V (DS10) $99.00.

Othello. Motion Picture/Opera

478. *Otello.*

DOCUMENT INFORMATION: *Country:* USA/Italy; *Year of release:* 1986.

EDITION, HISTORY, CONTENTS, & EVALUATION: *Edition & history:* An outstanding film version of Guiseppe Verdi's *Otello* made in Milan, Italy, at the famed La Scala opera house and on location.

MEDIUM INFORMATION: *Medium:* Motion picture; *Sound:* Spoken language; *Color:* Yes; *Length:* 123 min.

AUTHORSHIP INFORMATION: *Producer(s):* Golan, Menaham; Globus, Yoram; *Director(s):* Zeffirelli, Franco; *Composer(s):* Verdi, Guiseppe; Maazel, Lorin (Conductor, Orchestra Teatro Alla Scala); *Designer(s):* Quaranta, Gianni; *Costume designer(s):* Anni, Anna; *Lighting designer(s):* Guarnieri, Ennio; *Cast:* Domingo, Placido (Othello); Ricciarelli, Katia (Desdemona); Diaz, Justino (Iago); Di Cesare, Ezio (Cassio); Zaharia, Constantin (Roderigo); MacCurdy, John (Lodovico); Toumajian, Edward (Montano); Pigliucci, Giannicola (Herald); Malakova, Petra (Emilia).

DISTRIBUTION & AVAILABILITY: *Publisher or responsible agency:* The Cannon Group; *Distributor:* FCM, *Availability:* FCM, V, $79.95.

Othello. Video/Documentary

479. *Filming Othello.*

DOCUMENT INFORMATION: *Country:* West Germany; *Year of filming:* 1978; *Year of release:* 1987 (USA); *Year of first showing:* 1978; *Country of first showing:* Germany; *Location of first showing:* West German Television.

EDITION, HISTORY, CONTENTS, & EVALUATION: *Edition & history:* Made for West German television in 1978, *Filming Othello* was released for theatrical viewing in the United States in February 1987 with a premiere at Film Forum I, 57 Watts St., New York City, for a limited run. See also *Shakespeare et Orson Welles* (710.1) for a similar documentary about Welles's work. *Contents & evaluation:* "[*Filming Othello*] is a fascinating collage made up of various things, including some re-edited footage from the magnificent opening sequence of *Othello*. More or less at the center of the memoir is a luncheon reunion at which Welles, a sometimes brilliantly funny Mr. MacLiammóir and a patiently funny Hilton Edwards, who played Brabantio in *Othello*, discuss the play, Coleridge, the film, Dostoyevsky, Lord Olivier, Dante, and envy as opposed to jealousy, which Welles, ever ready with an aphorism, calls the 'seasickness of passion'" (Canby, Vincent, "Welles in 'Filming Othello'," *NYT*, Feb. 4, 1987: C24). It should also be mentioned that the film features Micheál MacLiammóir and Hilton Edwards, who respectively played Iago and Brabantio in Welles's *Othello. Audience:* General use; *Supplementary materials:* Kliman, Bernice. "Review." *SFNL* 11.2 (April 1987): 2.

MEDIUM INFORMATION: *Medium:* Motion Picture; *Sound:* Spoken language; *Color:* Yes; *Length:* 90 min.; *Language(s) spoken:* English; *Film type:* 35mm.

AUTHORSHIP INFORMATION: *Producer(s):* Hellwig, Klaus; Hellwig, Juergen; *Director(s):* Welles, Orson; *Composer(s):* Lavagnino, Francesco; *Other personnel:* Graver, Gary (Camera); Roth, Marty (Editor); *Cast:* Welles, Orson; MacLiammóir, Micheál; Edwards, Hilton.

DISTRIBUTION & AVAILABILITY: *Publisher or responsible agency:* West German TV; *Distributor:* JAG.

Othello. Video/Documentary

480. *Making Shakespeare.*

DOCUMENT INFORMATION: *Country:* GB; *Year of first showing:* 1987 [?].

EDITION, HISTORY, CONTENTS, & EVALUATION: *Edition & history:* Explores the idea of Shakespeare as the British "National Poet" and the ideological assumptions growing out of that status. The film investigates the many contexts in which the image of Shakespeare is constructed—theatre, film, classroom, college and public life. It then attempts to relate this wide range of influences to the ways in which Shakespeare is "taught" in the English educational system. Focus of the discussion is *Othello* because it introduces issues of importance to a newly emerging multi-cultural society in Britain. The panelists include such British "cultural materialists" as Jonathan Dollimore and Raymond Williams and well known actors and directors as Sam Wanamaker and Jonathan Miller. Although aimed at a British audience, there is much here that would seem to be of interest to Americans concerned with a critique of "National Totemism." *Supplementary materials:* Not seen. *BUFVC Newsletter* 26 (Feb. 1988): 5.

MEDIUM INFORMATION: *Length:* 50 min.; *Video type:* B,V, 3/4U.

AUTHORSHIP INFORMATION: *Producer(s):* Alternative Video Group; *Director(s):* Ritchie, Charlie; Musgrove, Brian; *Cast:* Williams, Raymond; Greer, Germaine; Jardine, Lisa; Sinfield, Alan; Dollimore, Jonathan; Holland, Peter; Wanamaker, Sam; Miller, Jonathan; Jowett, Jill (Speakers).

DISTRIBUTION & AVAILABILITY: *Publisher or responsible agency:* Alternative Video Group; *Distributor:* AVG.

Othello. **Video/Opera**

481. *Otello.*

DOCUMENT INFORMATION: *Country:* Germany; *Year of release:* 19[?].

EDITION, HISTORY, CONTENTS, & EVALUATION: *Edition & history:* Verdi's opera performed by the Berlin "Komischen Opera" with an operatic cast of hundreds. *Supplementary materials:* FCM catalog.

MEDIUM INFORMATION: *Length:* 123 min.

AUTHORSHIP INFORMATION: *Cast:* Knocker, Hanns; Van Kamptz, Christa Noack.

DISTRIBUTION & AVAILABILITY: *Distributor:* FCM; *Availability:* FCM, V, sale, $39.95.

Pericles

ORIGINAL WORK AND PRODUCTION: Tragi-Comedy/Romance. *Year of first production:* 1607-8; *Site of first production:* Whitehall palace [?].

Pericles. Video/Teleplay

482. *Pericles: Prince of Tyre.* (Series: The Shakespeare Plays).

DOCUMENT INFORMATION: *Country:* GB; *Year of first showing:* 1983; *Location of first showing:* BBC, London; PBS stations, USA, 4 June 1984.

EDITION, HISTORY, CONTENTS, & EVALUATION: *Edition & history:* The textual authority for the play is the 1951 Peter Alexander edition of Shakespeare's plays, as modified by the director. This production of a rarely staged play displays the same resourcefulness in invoking the ambiance of the eastern Mediterranean that made the 1984 *Comedy of Errors* so visually attractive. The sounds of the sea are everywhere on the sound track to remind the audience that this narrative drama of the peregrinations of Pericles is every bit as sea-drenched as *Midsummer Night's Dream* is moon-drenched. *Contents & evaluation:* "The insistent realism of this 1983 production often is at odds with the remoteness and fairy-tale world that Shakespeare created in the play. Shades of ambiguity fall to morality's good versus evil in the portrayal of this legendary hero and his restored-from-ashes narrator,

Gower. . . . Trying to make things seem natural, to explain cause for effect often defeats the rareness of Shakespeare's tragi-comic vision. Consider the restoration scene between Marina and Pericles as an example of what happens when realism gets in the way of theatre. Pericles repeatedly strikes out at Marina (once is called for in the text), his nose drips from his shedding of tears as he comes out of what seems more like a drug-withdrawal than a self-imposed mourning. Marina, sensitively and attractively played by Amanda Redman, valiantly withstands the repeated assaults from Pericles until he finally hears the music of the spheres after recognizing that his daughter is not dead. But Pericles stumbles about, embracing everyone, and generally destroys the delicacy of the merging of two different worlds—his ability to hear what no one else does comes across as a delusion of madness. Only the dream-shrouded descent of Diana offers evidence that Pericles is in tune with divine harmony. . . . The final effect of this production is that there is more tragedy and somberness here than comedy and a sense of hope; that joy is a 'flat' state of mind rather than an elevating one; that 'wonder' is a state we cannot know here and now, unless we mightily strain for it" (Hartwig, Joan, "*Pericles:* An Unclaimed World," *SFNL* 9.2 [1985]: 1+). *Audience:* College and university; *Supplementary materials: Pericles* in *BSP,* 1984; Videotape (25 min.) from "Shakespeare in Perspective" series with P.J. Kavanagh as lecturer available in U.K. from BBC* (*BUFVC* 20).

MEDIUM INFORMATION: *Medium:* Video; *Sound:* Spoken language; *Color:* Yes; *Length:* 180 min.; *Language(s) spoken:* English; *Video type:* B, V, 3/4U.

AUTHORSHIP INFORMATION: *Producer(s):* Sutton, Shaun; *Director(s):* Jones, David; *Adaptor/translator(s):* Snodin, David; *Composer(s):* Best, Martin; *Choreographer(s):* Stephenson, Geraldine; *Designer(s):* Taylor, Don; *Costume designer(s):* Lavers, Colin; *Lighting designer(s):* Barclay, Sam; *Other personnel:* Green, Ron (Camera); Alcock, Dawn (Make-up); Charlesworth, Alan (Prod. manager); Lowden, Fraser (Prod. assoc.); Hambelton, Dave (Editor); Chick, Anthony (Sound); Wilders, John (Advisor); *Cast:* Petherbridge, Edward (Gower); Woodvine, John (Antiochus); Brychia, Edita (Antiochus' daughter); Gwilym, Mike (Pericles); Ashby, Robert (Thaliard); Patrick, Godfrey (Helicanus); Salaman, Toby (Escanes/Pander); Rodway, Norman (Cleon); Crosbie, Annette (Dionyza); Allen, Patrick (Simonides); Redman, Amanda (Marina); Peacock, Trevor (Boult); Kaye, Lila (Bawd); Ryecart, Patrick (Lysimachus); Sharling, Elayne (Goddess Diana); Stevenson, Juliet (Thaisa); Lush, Valerie (Lychorida); Swift, Clive (Cerimon); Clayton, Edward (Philemon); Brumble, Nick (Leonine); Ravenscroft, Christopher; Kaye, Malcolm; Kurakin, Adam; Saul, Christopher; Ashby, Robert; Clayton, Edward; Oxley, Stephen; Bardon, John; Derrington, Richard; Bizley, Roger; Gordon, Peter; Mitchell Iain; Kelly, Frances; + several others (Knights, Lords, Ladies, Servants, Attendants, Musicians, Dancers, Fishermen, Base Knaves, etc.).

DISTRIBUTION & AVAILABILITY: *Publisher or responsible agency:* BBC/TLF; *Distributor:* AVP, UIO, BBC* *Copy location:* UVM (Archive); *Availability:* AVP, B, V, 3/4U $450 (1987), sale; UIO, V (72320H), 3/4U (70320V), rental, $27.40; BBC*, 16mm or V, apply (*BUFVC* 21).

King Richard the Second

ORIGINAL WORK AND PRODUCTION: English History Play. *Year of first production:* 1595; *Site of first production:* The Theatre in Shoreditch [?].

Richard the Second. Video/Teleplay

483. Richard the Second.

DOCUMENT INFORMATION: *Country:* GB; *Year of first showing:* 1950; *Location of first showing:* BBC. Transmitted 8:00 to 10:45 P.M., Sunday, 29 Oct. 1950.

EDITION, HISTORY, CONTENTS, & EVALUATION: *Edition & history:* Royston Morley's *Richard II* is the first full-length television treatment of an English history play, a kind of precursor to subsequent extravaganzas such as *An Age of Kings*. To that end the BBC committed over £2,000, elaborate sets, and a cast of 36. At one point a professional boxing match threatened to usurp the 8:00 o'clock time slot but apparently that menace evaporated for the production is listed as starting at 8:00 P.M (WAC T5/430 2 Nov. 1950). *Supplementary materials:* "Program." *TPAB* 20 Oct. 1950.

MEDIUM INFORMATION: *Length:* 145 [with intervals] min.

AUTHORSHIP INFORMATION: *Producer(s):* Morley, Royston; Muir, Graeme; *Designer(s):* Learoyd, Barry; *Other personnel:* Bell, Joan; Barnard, Pamela (Stage Managers); *Cast:* Wheatley, Alan (Richard); McCallin,

Clement (Bolingbroke); Oscar, Henry (Gaunt); Wontner, Arthur (York); Barr, Patrick (Northumberland); Shelton, Joy (Queen); Sachs, Leonard (Mowbray); Nissen, Brian (Aumerle); Skillan, George (Carlisle); Hinton, Mary (Duchess of York); Thorndike, Eileen (Duchess of Gloucester); Bebb, Richard (Henry Percy); Dale, Philip (Bagot/Exton); Holmes, Denis (Green); Gilbert, Richard (Bushy); Burt, Oliver (Marshal); Woodbridge, George (Gardener); Wellman, James (Servant); Sequeira, Horace (Salisbury); Witty, John (Ross/Herald); Wearing, Geoffrey (Willoughby/Herald); Burt, Oliver (Scroop); Brock, Cecil (Fitzwater); Sachs, Leonard (Surrey); Holmes, Denis (Lord); Johnstone, Viola (Lady); Gilder, Patricia (Lady); Brock, Cecil (Berkeley); Munro, Hugh (Servant/Groom); Baker, John (Gaoler); Wellman, James (Welsh Captain); + Pages, Soldiers, Lords.

DISTRIBUTION & AVAILABILITY: *Publisher or responsible agency:* BBC; *Copy location:* Unavailable.

Richard the Second. Video/Teleplay

484. Richard the Second. (Series: Hallmark Hall of Fame).

DOCUMENT INFORMATION: *Country:* USA; *Year of first showing:* 1954; *Location of first showing:* NBC TV. Transmitted, 4:00 to 6:00 P.M., Sunday, 24 Jan. 1954.

EDITION, HISTORY, CONTENTS, & EVALUATION: *Edition & history:* One of the several Hallmark greeting cards productions of Shakespeare (for other Shakespeare programs in the Hallmark series, see 102, 126, 305, 309, 593, 594, 613, and 649). This one was broadcast "live" on television to 55 cities. The risks and perils of going "live" before a TV camera added to the charms of that genre by making it almost as much a theatrical as a cinematic event. The entire production cost $175,000 of which a major share went into 2500 hours needed for construction of the sets. The copy that remains in the Folger is a videotape of a Kinescope recording. ("Kinescope" recordings, crude black-and-white records of productions, were made largely for legal purposes.) The Folger copy is listed as having "audio problems." In an interview, Mr. Evans revealed that the face of King Richard's corpse in the coffin at the end of the play was actually a bronze bust of Mr. Evans as Hamlet, a bizarre touch ("Maurice Evans Stars [w. still]." *NYT* 24 Jan. 1954: X 13). *Contents & evaluation:* "The main impression of *Richard II* was that it was too cluttered, and like the *Macbeth* it substituted the literal for the imaginative. The setting consisted of an over-abundance of towers and turrets, massive but unconvincing, while the garden set was so filled with flowers and leaves that one had trouble distinguishing the actors. . . . Richard II is Maurice Evans' best role, and he was especially effective in the first half of the play, though the total character lacked the electricity and depth which Michael Redgrave brought to it at Stratford-on-Avon in 1951. Mr. Evans conveyed well the self-indulgent, sentimental side of Richard; the passage "What must the King do now?" (III.iii) was very well spoken, as is true of all Mr. Evans' lines. But sometimes he seems to "speechify" rather than act, and at other times seems to employ the facile and obvious in his interpretation. . . . The trimming of the script was well done, and the chief merit of this presentation was its clarity, being far more easy to follow for the new viewer of Shakespeare than was the *King Lear.* The conclusion of the play was in questionable taste, sacrificing the dignity of the funeral procession for a closeup of the dead Richard. The supporting characters were not particularly impressive, although Aumerle was well played. Kent Smith's Bolingbroke was sturdy if somewhat lacking in humanity. As has been true of all television productions of Shakespeare so far, the supporting actors have yet to learn to wear their costumes, instead of looking as if the costumes were wearing them" (Griffin, Alice V., "Shakespeare Through the Camera's Eye," *SQ* 6 [1955]: 64). *Audience:* General use; *Supplementary materials:* Gould, Jack. "Scenery and Props." *NYT* 31 Jan. 1954: X 13 ("Better a bare stage than all this [scenery]"); "Horses, Ships & Kings." *Time* (1 Feb. 1954): 59.

MEDIUM INFORMATION: *Medium:* Video; *Sound:* Spoken language; *Color:* No (black & white); *Length:* 120 min.; *Language(s) spoken:* English; *Video type:* Video/Kinescope.

AUTHORSHIP INFORMATION: *Producer(s):* Maurice Evans Productions; McCleery, Albert (for NBC); *Director(s):* Schaefer, George; *Composer(s):* Menges, Herbert; Brooks, William (Conductor); *Designer(S):* Sylbert, Richard; *Costumes:* Taylor, Noel. *Cast:* Evans, Maurice (King Richard); Churchill, Sarah (Queen); Smith, Kent (Bolingbroke); Gordon, Bruce (Mowbray); Purdy, Richard (York); Da Costa, Morton (Aumerle); Hector, Louis (Northumberland); Harris, Jonathan (Exton); Worlock, Fredric (John of Gaunt).

DISTRIBUTION & AVAILABILITY: *Publisher or responsible agency:* NBC Television/Hallmark Hall of Fame; *Copy location:* FOL; *Call or copy number:* VCR.

Richard the Second, 1-3. Video/Teleplay (Part 1 in 15-part series)

485. **Hollow Crown, The.** (Series: *An Age of Kings* [I]).

DOCUMENT INFORMATION: *Country:* GB; *Year of first showing:* 1960; *Location of first showing:* BBC TV. Transmitted 9 to 10 P.M., Thursday, 28 April 1960.

EDITION, HISTORY, CONTENTS, & EVALUATION: *Awards:* Dews, Peter: Excellence in directing (British Guild of Directors); *Edition & history:* Based on Acts 1-3 of *King Richard II. An Age of Kings* was an ambitious and expensive undertaking that set out to do something on TV that could not be done on stage or film. Its 15 parts covered the events in Shakespeare's "major" tetralogy (*R2, 1&2 H4, H5*) and minor tetralogy (*1-3H6* and *R3*). For other segments in this series, see also numbers 156-9, 178-9, 185, 188, 190-2, 486, and 505-6. In the United States the series played for 15 weeks on some 61 TV stations, including WNEW/NY. Producer Peter Dews grappled with casting some 600 parts for the sprawling, epical dramas. Actual rehearsals and filming took 30 weeks. In electing to present the plays in the order of their historical chronology rather than in the order in which Shakespeare wrote them, the director gained clarity. To do otherwise would be analogous to first dramatizing the American Civil War and then subsequently the American Revolution. The drawback, however, was that many persons felt let down when the apprentice minor tetralogy, spanning the years 1422 to 1485, followed the artistically mature major tetralogy, covering the period from 1390 to 1422. Milton Crane aptly remarked that it was a little bit like seeing *Titus* after *Hamlet* ("Shakespeare on Television." *SQ* 12.3 [Summer 1961]: 323-7). Standard Oil of N.J. sponsored it. *Contents & evaluation:* "Murder, banishment and rebellion mark the violent action of this opening play. The scene [when it opens] is London in 1399—King Richard's palace—a day of decision" (PR blurb). The London *Times* reviewer expressed considerable enthusiasm for both segments of the *Richard II* production. He felt that the director had done a fine job, that the camera work was "clean and unaffected," and that the acting was well suited to an ensemble. David William was praised for his King Richard II, Tom Fleming for his Bolingbroke, and Sean Connery for Hotspur ("Television Cycle of Shakespeare." *Times* 29 March 1960: 16a). *Audience:* General use; *Supplementary materials:* Campbell, O.J. Introduction. *An Age of Kings* [The 15 parts as they appeared on television]. New York: Pyramid, 1961; Barry, Michael. "An Age of Kings." *RT* 22 April 1960: 3.

MEDIUM INFORMATION: *Medium:* Video; *Sound:* Spoken language; *Color:* No (black & white); *Length:* 60 min.; *Language(s) spoken:* English; *Video type:* 16mm, Kinescope.

AUTHORSHIP INFORMATION: *Producer(s):* Dews, Peter; *Director(s):* Hayes, Michael; *Adaptor/translator(s):* Crozier, Eric; *Composer(s):* Whelen, Christopher; Bliss, Arthur; Salter, Lionel (Conducting Royal Philharmonic Orchestra); *Designer(s):* Morris, Stanley; *Cast:* William, David (Richard II); Fleming, Tom (Bolingbroke); Connery, Sean (Hotspur); Wreford, Edgar (Gaunt); Johnson, Noel (Mowbray); Andrews, David (Bushy); Lodge, Terence (Bagot); Willis, Jerome (Green); Glover, Julian (Marshal); Greenwood, John (Aumerle); Bayldon, Geoffrey (Edmund); Cooke, Juliet (Queen); Cooper, George (Northumberland); Rowe, Alan (Ross); Gostelow, Gordon (Willoughby); Smith, Brian (Servant); Ringham, John (Berkeley); Windsor, Frank (Carlisle); Shepperdson, Leon (Salisbury); Garland, Patrick (Scroop); + Atkins, Eileen; Barton, Maggie; Valentine, Anthony; and a dozen others.

DISTRIBUTION & AVAILABILITY: *Publisher or responsible agency:* BBC; *Copy location:* BBC*, SCL*.

Richard the Second, 3-5. **Video/Teleplay (Part 2 in 15-part series)**

486. *Deposing of a King, The.* (Series: *An Age of Kings* [II]).

DOCUMENT INFORMATION: *Country:* GB; *Year of first showing:* 1960; *Location of first showing:* BBC TV. Transmitted 9 to 10 P.M., Thursday, May 12, 1960.

EDITION, HISTORY, CONTENTS, & EVALUATION: *Awards:* Dews, Peter: Excellence in directing (British Guild of Directors); *Edition & history:* Based on Acts 3-5 of *King Richard II.* Second installment in *An Age of Kings.* For background, see *The Hollow Crown* (485). For other programs in the series, see also numbers 156-9, 178-9, 185, 188, 190-2, 485, and 505-6. *Contents & evaluation:* "The rebels are successful, and the king is taken prisoner. Bolingbroke becomes Henry IV and Richard is slain" PR blurb. For commentary, see 485 above.

MEDIUM INFORMATION: *Medium:* Video; *Sound:* Spoken language; *Color:* No (black & white); *Length:* 58

min.; *Language(s) spoken:* English; *Video type:* 16mm, Kinescope.

AUTHORSHIP INFORMATION: *Producer(s):* Dews, Peter; *Director(s):* Hayes, Michael; *Adaptor/translator(s):* Crozier, Eric; *Composer(s):* Whelen, Christopher; Bliss, Arthur; Salter, Lionel (Conducting Royal Philharmonic Orchestra); *Designer(s):* Morris, Stanley; *Cast:* William, David (Richard II); Fleming, Tom (Bolingbroke); Connery, Sean (Hotspur); Cooper, George A. (Northumberland); Bayldon, Geoffrey (York); Greenwood, John (Aumerle); Cooke, Juliet (Queen); Barton, Maggie; Atkins, Eileen (Attendant ladies); Gostelow, Gordon (Gardener); Lodge, Terence (Servant); Windsor, Frank (Carlisle); Cox, Michael (Abbot); Law, Mary (Duchess of York); Lang, Robert (Exton); Glover, Julian (Groom); Cox, Michael (Keeper); + two dozen others.

DISTRIBUTION & AVAILABILITY: *Publisher or responsible agency:* BBC; *Copy location:* BBC*, SCL*, Apply.

Richard the Second. **Documentary/Abridgment**

487. *Richard the Second.* (Series: Fair Adventure Series).

DOCUMENT INFORMATION: *Country:* USA; *Year of release:* 1964.

EDITION, HISTORY, CONTENTS, & EVALUATION: *Edition & history:* A four-part abridgment of the play with commentary by Dr. Frank Baxter. For other films in this series, see 180, 254, 311, 426, 463, 508, 546, 614 and 653. *Contents & evaluation:* Not seen. *Audience:* Junior High (grades 7-9); High school (grades 10-12);.

MEDIUM INFORMATION: *Medium:* Motion Picture; *Sound:* Spoken language; *Color:* No (black & white); *Length:* 112 min.; *Language(s) spoken:* English; *Film type:* 16mm.

DISTRIBUTION & AVAILABILITY: *Publisher or responsible agency:* Westinghouse Broadcast Corporation; *Distributor:* Not known.

Richard the Second. **Motion Picture/Documentary**

488. *Richard the Second: How to Kill a King.* (Series: Explorations in Shakespeare, IX).

DOCUMENT INFORMATION: *Country:* Canada; *Year of release:* 1969.

EDITION, HISTORY, CONTENTS, & EVALUATION: *Edition & history:* Part nine in a series of twelve 23-minute films made in 1969 by the Ontario Educational

1. Kenneth Branagh stars as the young king in the 1989 *Henry V* (see 182.2).

© 1989 Renaissance Films PLC

2. Sarah Bernhardt as Hamlet takes on Pierre Magnier as Laertes in a 1900 movie (see #74).

The Museum of Modern Art Stills Archive.

3. Emil Jannings in *Othello*, Germany, 1922 (see #442).

The Museum of Modern Art Stills Archive.

4. Francis X. Bushman and Beverly Bayne as Romeo and Juliet, USA, 1916 (see #520).

The Museum of Modern Art Stills Archive.

The Museum of Modern Art Stills Archive.

5. Asta Nielsen as Hamlet, Germany, 1920 (see #86).

The Museum of Modern Art Stills Archive.

6. Frederick B. Warde as King Lear in the 1916
Thanhouser production. (see #246).

Courtesy, Ivy Film.

7. Sebastian Shaw as the great Shakespearean actor, Edmond Davey, and Rex Harrison as the brash young newspaperman, Tommy Stapleton, in the 1936 modernization of *Othello*, *Men Are Not Gods* (see #444).

© BBC Copyright Photograph.

8. The dawn of televised Shakespeare on the BBC in 1937. Yvonne Arnaud as Katherine and Mary Marvin as Alice in a scene from *Henry V* (see #171).

9. Orson Welles as Othello in the award-winning 1952 production (see #453).

The Museum of Modern Art Stills Archive.

10. Laurence Olivier as the malevolent Richard duke of Gloucester in the 1955 *King Richard III* (see #503).

Photo Courtesy of Janus Films.

Courtesy of Hallmark Cards, Inc.

11. Ophelia, played by Ciaran Madden, seeks the advice of Polonius (Michael Redgrave) in a scene from the 1970 Hallmark Hall of Fame *Hamlet* televised on NBC-TV (see #126).

Courtesy of Hallmark Cards, Inc.

12. Maurice Evans and Judith Anderson in the leading roles of the televised 1954 Hallmark Hall of Fame *Macbeth* (see #305).

The GLOBE PLAYHOUSE PRODUCTIONS/SHAKESPEARE SOCIETY OF AMERICA.
R. Thad Taylor, Executive Producer.

13. Valerie Seelie-Snyder as Mistress Ford, Leon Charles as Falstaff and Gloria Grahame as Mistress Page in a video recording of a 1979 stage performance of *The Merry Wives of Windsor* at the Globe Playhouse, Los Angeles, California (see #383).

14. Helen Mirren with her fairy retinue in the 1981 *Midsummer Night's Dream* in the televised "The Shakespeare Plays" series (see #412).

Courtesy of "The Shakespeare Plays."

Courtesy of "The Shakespeare Plays."

15. Helena (Angela Down) is embraced by Bertram (Ian Charleson) in the 1980 television production of *All's Well that Ends Well* (see #3).

Courtesy of "The Shakespeare Plays."

16. Colin Blakely and Jane Lapotaire are Antony and Cleopatra in a 1980 production of "The Shakespeare Plays" series (see #23).

Courtesy of "The Shakespeare Plays."

17. John Stride and Claire Bloom as King Henry VIII and the unhappy Queen Katherine in a 1979 television production (see #196).

Communications Authority. (See also 18, 40, 65, 124, 162, 257, 322, 465, 555, 617 and 637.) For background, see 18, above. *Contents & evaluation:* Not seen. According to the publicity release issued by NBC Educational Enterprises, the film "illustrates a recurring historical situation: the position of the mighty is always precarious; rebellion and assassination are constant threats to the statesman. The reasons for Richard's fall from power and Bolingbroke's success are examined by the commentator. He emphasizes the clash between two political orders represented by the principal characters: the old world of Richard based on the false security of divine sanction and the more realistic world of Bolingbroke in which personal merit and strength are the dominant factors. Contemporary parallels to this confrontation of authority and rebellion are provided by stage effects such as graphics of recent riots and popular music. From the description, this program apparently follows the rest of the series in an effort to re-position Shakespeare's plays in the modern world. *Audience:* College and university.

MEDIUM INFORMATION: *Medium:* Motion Picture; *Sound:* Spoken language; *Color:* Yes; *Length:* 23 min.; *Language(s) spoken:* English; *Film type:* 16mm.

AUTHORSHIP INFORMATION: *Producer(s):* Reis, Kurt; Moser, Ed; *Screenplay writer(s):* Webster, Hugh; *Composer(s):* Yanovsky, Zal; *Set designer(s):* Adeney, Chris; *Lighting designer(s):* Galbraith, Howard; *Performance group(s):* Ontario Educational Communications/ NBC Educational Enterprises.

DISTRIBUTION & AVAILABILITY: *Distributor:* CNU [?].

Richard the Second. **Video/Teleplay**

489. *Richard the Second.*

DOCUMENT INFORMATION: *Country:* GB; *Year of first showing:* 1970; *Location of first showing:* BBC. Transmitted 30 July 1970.

EDITION, HISTORY, CONTENTS, & EVALUATION: *Edition & history:* An adaptation of the 1969 Prospect Theatre production at the Edinburgh Festival. *Audience:* General use.

MEDIUM INFORMATION: *Medium:* Video; *Sound:* Spoken language; *Color:* Yes; *Length:* 120 min.; *Language(s) spoken:* English; *Video type:* V.

AUTHORSHIP INFORMATION: *Producer(s):* Shivas, Mark; Cottrell, Richard; Robertson, Toby; *Designer(s):* Abbott, Tony; *Cast:* McKellen, Ian (Richard II); West, Timothy (Bolingbroke); Hardwick, Paul (John of Gaunt); Fleming, Lucy (Queen).

DISTRIBUTION & AVAILABILITY: *Publisher or responsible agency:* BBC; *Copy location:* BBC*, archive.

Richard the Second. **Motion Picture/Scenes**

490. *Richard the Second* 2.1.; 5.5. (Series: The Shakespeare Series [IFB], VIII).

DOCUMENT INFORMATION: *Country:* Great Britain; *Year of release:* 1974.

EDITION, HISTORY, CONTENTS, & EVALUATION: *Edition & history:* In this eighth unit of The Shakespeare Series, there are sequences from *Richard II* featuring old John of Gaunt's celebrated deathbed speech (2.1.), and King Richard's melancholy soliloquy in the dungeon at Pomfret (5.5.). (For others in this series, see numbers 22, 131, 164, 232, 326, 430, 467, 510, 556, 601 and 619.) For background, see 22, above. *Contents & evaluation:* Mark Kingston as old John of Gaunt delivers the famous "this sceptred isle" speech competently but in a curiously lifeless way. He and Colin Farrell, who plays Richard II, seem burdened by the knowledge that they are recording for a camera. Very much of the action is in close-up, not so much talking head as talking mouth. The costumes are rich, not stingy. And Farrell as Richard does deliver the long soliloquy at Pomfret with conviction. Certainly he is more convincing in this role than as Iago in the *Othello* of this same series. The problem is an old one: marriages of stage actors with cameras that merely record often produce a stillborn child (KSR). *Audience:* High school (grades 10-12).

MEDIUM INFORMATION: *Medium:* Motion Picture; *Sound:* Spoken language; *Color:* Yes; *Length:* 12 min.; *Language(s) spoken:* English; *Film type:* 16mm; *Video type:* V, 3/4U (4 per cassette).

AUTHORSHIP INFORMATION: *Director(s):* Seabourne, Peter; *Cast:* Farrell, Colin (Richard II); Kingston, Mark (John of Gaunt); Chapman, Paul (Duke of York).

DISTRIBUTION & AVAILABILITY: *Publisher or responsible agency:* Realist film unit; *Distributor:* IFB; CNU, *Copy location:* FOL; *Call or copy number:* ISBN 0-699-38675-6; FOL, MP 91; *Availability:* CNU, rental 16mm, $8; IFB, sale 16mm, V, $175.

Richard the Second. **Video/Documentary**

491. *Richard and Bolingbroke.*

DOCUMENT INFORMATION: *Country:* GB; *Year of release:* 1975.

EDITION, HISTORY, CONTENTS, & EVALUATION: *Edition & history:* Dr. Anne Barton interviews actors Ian Richardson and Richard Pasco about their alternating of the roles of Richard and Bolingbroke in a RSC production. *Supplementary materials:* BUFVC 20.

MEDIUM INFORMATION: *Length:* 56 min.

AUTHORSHIP INFORMATION: *Director(s):* Clark, David; *Cast:* Richardson, Ian; Pasco, Richard; Barton, Anne.

DISTRIBUTION & AVAILABILITY: *Distributor:* ULA*.

Richard the Second. Video/Teleplay

492. *Richard the Second.* (Series: The Shakespeare Plays).

DOCUMENT INFORMATION: *Country:* GB; *Year of filming:* 12-17 April 1978; *Year of first showing:* 1978; *Location of first showing:* BBC, London; PBS stations, USA, 28 March 1979.

EDITION, HISTORY, CONTENTS, & EVALUATION: *Edition & history:* The production was recorded at the BBC studios from 12 to 17 April 1978. *Contents & evaluation:* "That Derek Jacobi is for me the best Richard witnessed in over thirty years of seeing productions of this play in no way renders those who support him less memorable. One would expect a superlative John of Gaunt from Gielgud, and one gets it, his 'sceptred isle' speech being the very essence of the patriotic component of these plays. But others of less repute fare just as well. Jon Finch's Bolingbroke shows that this 'thief in the night' is indeed father to the forthcoming hero of Agincourt. It is too bad that his sole reference to Hal in this play is cut. Finch's Bolingbroke is a full embodiment of the new Machiavellian ideal in Shakespeare's time—that ideal by which savvy, competent leaders were expected to devise attractive images of themselves in order to win the masses of followers their medieval predecessors felt no compulsion to defer to" (Manheim, Michael, "*Richard II*," *SFNL* 4.1 [1979]: 5). Despite all the virtues of Jacobi's performance, this production shows again that *Richard II* is better as poetry than as drama. Subsequently, as in *Macbeth*, Shakespeare was able to fuse poetry and drama; at this stage in his career he could write drama without poetry (*The Taming of the Shrew*) or poetry without drama (*Richard II*) but he had not yet hit on the formula for merging the two. As a result a recurring complaint about this and other productions of *Richard II* is that it is just plain too long. That may be, but Jacobi's lengthy speeches, particularly in the prison cell at the end when at last the camera is allowed to intervene, achieve dazzling eloquence. Perhaps one should behave as an Elizabethan at the Globe and just allow the richly textured language to flow like a great waterfall and not be terribly concerned about getting the exact meaning of every word. And there are some special moments: Bolingbroke's exile speech; the "Armada" rhetoric of Gaunt's unforgettable deathbed oration; the emblem-like gardeners' scene; and the serio-comical pleading of the Duchess of York before King Henry IV for the life of her son, Aumerle. Too long? Unlike Dr. Samuel Johnson's famous quip about *Paradise Lost* ("no man ever wished it longer"), one might wish Shakespeare's

Richard II were longer (KSR). *Audience:* College and university; General use; *Supplementary materials:* Fenwick, Henry. "The Production." *Richard II BSP* 19-26; Videotape (25 min.) from "Shakespeare in Perspective" series with Paul Johnson as lecturer available in U.K. from BBC* (*BUFVC* 20).

MEDIUM INFORMATION: *Medium:* Video; *Sound:* Spoken language; *Color:* Yes; *Length:* 180 min.; *Video type:* B, V, 3/4U.

AUTHORSHIP INFORMATION: *Producer(s):* Messina, Cedric; *Director(s):* Giles, David; *Adaptor/translator(s):* Shallcross, Alan; *Composer(s):* Lloyd-Jones, David; *Designer(s):* Abbott, Tony; *Costume designer(s):* Fraser-Paye, Robin; *Lighting designer(s):* Summers, John; *Other personnel:* Wright, Terry (Fight arranger); Banks, Terence (Prod. asst.); Rayment, Ann (Make-up); Wilders, John (Literary consultant); *Cast:* Jacobi, Derek (Richard II); Gielgud, John (John of Gaunt); Finch, Jon (Bolingbroke); Hiller, Wendy (Duchess of York); Gray, Charles (Duke of York); Morris, Mary (Duchess of Gloucester); Swift, David (Northumberland); Rose, Clifford (Bishop); Keating, Charles (Aumerle); Owens, Richard (Mowbray); Maw, Janet (Queen); Holland, Jeffrey (Surrey); Bulloch, Jeremy (Henry Percy); Sachs, Robin (Bushy); Thomas, Damien (Bagot); Dalton, Alan (Green); Dodimead, David (Ross); Flint, John (Willoughby); Oatley, Carl (Berkeley); Whymper, William (Scroop); Barcroft, John (Salisbury); Garfield, David (Welsh Captain); Adams, Desmond (Exton); Ritchie, Joe (Groom); Ward, Paddy (Keeper); Barnabé, Bruno (Abbot); Adams, Jonathan (Gardener); Collins, Alan (Gardener's Man); Curless, John (Lord Fitzwater); Wright, Terry (Murderer); Fernee, Ronald (Servant); Brown, T.; Lewin, M. (Heralds); Sewell, P.; Frieze, S. (Queen's Ladies).

DISTRIBUTION & AVAILABILITY: *Publisher or responsible agency:* BBC/TLF; *Distributor:* AVP, UIO, BBC* *Copy location:* UVM; *Availability:* AVP, B, V, 3/4U $450 (1987), sale; UIO, V (72044H), 3/4U (70144V), rental, $23.80; BBC* V only, apply (*BUFVC* 19).

492.1 *King Richard the Second.*

DOCUMENT INFORMATION: *Country:* GB/France; *Year of first showing:* 1978; *Location of first showing:* Paris. Dist. F.R.3.

EDITION, HISTORY, CONTENTS, & EVALUATION: *Edition & history:* Identical to entry #492 above except that it has French subtitles. Available in archives, see below.

MEDIUM INFORMATION: *Video type:* 3/4U.

DISTRIBUTION & AVAILABILITY: *Copy location:* VAA; *Call or copy number:* THE 1.33.

Richard the Second. **Video/Documentary**

493. *A Dream in Progress.*

DOCUMENT INFORMATION: *Country:* USA; *Year of first showing:* 1980; *Location of first showing:* Ashland, Oregon.

EDITION, HISTORY, CONTENTS, & EVALUATION: *Edition & history:* Documentary about backstage life at the Ashland Oregon Festival, with most of the attention focused on a production of *Richard II. Contents & evaluation:* Jerry Turner, director of the Ashland Festival, talks about the history of the company. There are shots of Turner directing (sounding very professional with his "Let's take it from the top"), of the makeup room, of the costuming shop, of the dancers, and of the acting onstage of *Richard II.* It's a montage of activities at the festival with Turner insisting that "It's only the performance that counts." The program will interest students of theatre. *Audience:* High school (grades 10-12); College and university.

MEDIUM INFORMATION: *Medium:* Video; *Sound:* Spoken language; *Color:* Yes; *Length:* 55 min.; *Language(s) spoken:* English; *Video type:* V.

AUTHORSHIP INFORMATION: *Producer(s):* Bowmer, Angus; *Director(s):* Bryson, Terria; *Other personnel:* Boettcher, Ken (Editor); *Cast:* Turner, Jerry; Rubin, Margaret; Edmondson, James; Dryden, Deborah.

DISTRIBUTION & AVAILABILITY: *Publisher or responsible agency:* Oregon Shakespeare Festival; *Distributor:* OSF, *Copy location:* FOL; *Call or copy number:* VCR 12; *Availability:* Archive.

Richard the Second. **Video/Interpretation**

494. *Richard the Second.* (Series: The Bard Series).

CURRENT PRODUCTION: *Year:* 1982.

DOCUMENT INFORMATION: *Country:* USA; *Year of release:* 1982.

EDITION, HISTORY, CONTENTS, & EVALUATION: *Edition & history:* One of the Bard Productions of Shakespeare performed on a bare stage by American actors, some of which have been seen on the cable TV channel, "Arts & Entertainment." (For others, see 27, 340, 477, and 627.) King Richard II, for example, is played by David Birney, well known from his role in *Bridget Loves Bernie. Contents & evaluation:* Neither quite a record of a stage play and certainly not a film, this production falls into the category of television drama. Its success stems from a notable respect for Shakespeare's language. The cast's mastery of the lines compensates for a bare stage with minimum props. Moreover the subtext is deeply explored for hints about stage business, as when Bushy and Bagot are physically abused while Paul Shenar as Bolingbroke

pronounces their death sentences. Because Mary-Joan Negro as Anne is a grown woman, not the child-queen that history and stage tradition usually call for, her king and husband grows in stature and manliness. David Birney makes a highly convincing King Richard II, despite the unfortunate costume in the first scene that makes him look as though he is wearing a white mini-skirt. He is a playboy who surrounds himself with yuppie flatterers. While the staging is sparse and the costumes often at thrift shop level, the overall commitment to the play shows how stingy budgets and generous art can often co-exist. North American students in particular will be attracted to the reassuring, "down-home," voices and mannerisms of this cast, after so much exposure to British dialects in the BBC series. *Audience:* High school (grades 10-12); College and university; *Supplementary materials:* Stevenson, M. George. "Et Tu, Shakespeare? The Bard's Greatest Hits on Tape and Disc." *Video* 66 (1986): 66 + .

MEDIUM INFORMATION: *Medium:* Video; *Sound:* Spoken language; *Color:* Yes; *Length:* 172 min.; *Language(s) spoken:* English; *Video type:* V.

AUTHORSHIP INFORMATION: *Producer(s):* Nakano, Jack; Manning, Jack; *Director(s):* Woodman, William; *Cast:* Birney, David (Richard II); Shenar, Paul (Bolingbroke); MacLean, Peter (York); Negro, Mary-Joan (Anne); Devlin, John (Northumberland); Pomerantz, Jeff (Mowbray); McLiam, John (Gaunt); Ramsey, Logan (Carlisle); Martin, Nan (Duchess of York); Bookwalter, DeVeren (Aumerle); Robinson, Jay (Gardener); Hammond, Nicholas (Hotspur); Bassett, William H. (Surrey); Berendt, Charles (Gardener); Stanley, Alvah (Exton); Conley, Matt (Willoughby); Mason, Dan (Scroop); Loudenback, Jay T. (Bushy); Cumming, Michael (Bagot); Gamble, William (Green); Fitzmaurice, Kate (Lady); Snyder, Drew (Groom); Broyles, Lanny (Keeper); Dusich, Larry; Kenedy, Patrick M.; Steininger, Daniel W. (Soldiers); Allen, Randy; Anderson, Enoch; Buttenheim, Curtis; Didlake, Tim; Fisher, Noel; Huffman, Linus; Owen, Mack; Rivald, Matt; Ruddock, Phill; Thomas, David A. (Members of the Court).

DISTRIBUTION & AVAILABILITY: *Publisher or responsible agency:* Bard Productions Ltd.; *Distributor:* INM, ILL, FCM, TWC, DCV, *Availability:* ILL, sale, V (S 00550) $89.95; FCM, sale, V $89.95; TWC, sale, apply; DCV, sale, V $95 (1987); INM, V, $99.

Richard II. **Video/Recording**

495. *Richard II.*

DOCUMENT INFORMATION: *Country:* USA; *Year of first showing:* 1986.

EDITION, HISTORY, CONTENTS, & EVALUATION:

Edition & history: A videotape of a production at the San Diego, California, Old Globe theatre made on August 24, 1986. A copy is housed in the TOFT collection (Theatre on Film and Tape) of the Library of Performing Arts, New York Public Library. It may be viewed by appointment (see below). *Audience:* College and university; General use.

MEDIUM INFORMATION: *Medium:* Video; *Sound:* Spoken language; *Color:* Yes; *Length:* 142 min.; *Language(s) spoken:* English; *Video type:* 3/4U.

AUTHORSHIP INFORMATION: *Director(s):* Hardy, Joseph.

DISTRIBUTION & AVAILABILITY: *Copy location:* LCL TOFT Collection; *Call or copy number:* NCOV 550; *Availability:* By appt.

King Richard the Third

ORIGINAL WORK AND PRODUCTION: English History Play. *Year written:* c.1592; *Site of first production:* The Theatre in Shoreditch [?]

Richard the Third. Motion Picture/Abbreviated (See also, *Prince of Players*, 103)

496. *Richard the Third.*

DOCUMENT INFORMATION: *Country:* USA; *Year of release:* 1908.

EDITION, HISTORY, CONTENTS, & EVALUATION: *Edition & history:* Another Vitagraph one-reel Shakespeare film produced under the general supervision of J. Stuart Blackton, but probably directed by the Shakespearean actor William Ranous. For further discussion of Vitagraph Shakespeare movies, see entry at 640. *Supplementary materials:* Ball, *SOSF* 45-47, 312.

MEDIUM INFORMATION: *Length:* 10 min.

AUTHORSHIP INFORMATION: *Producer(s):* Blackton, J. Stuart; *Director(s):* Ranous, William V.; *Cast:* Ranous, William (Richard Duke of Gloucester); Turner, Florence; Gordon, Julia Swayne.

Richard the Third. Motion Picture/Derivative

497. *Les enfants d'Edouard.*

DOCUMENT INFORMATION: *Country:* France; *Year of release:* 1910.

EDITION, HISTORY, CONTENTS, & EVALUATION: *Edition & history:* A filming of Casimir Delavigne's adaptation of *Richard III* in the Film d'Art tradition that was designed to put famous actors into famous plays. As Professor Ball's commentary shows, there is an immense amount of doubt surrounding the cast credits for this film. The Weisbaden credits differ markedly from Ball's for the reason that Professor Ball could not verify them to his satisfaction. Moreover the film often has been confused with a 1914 film of the same title. *Supplementary materials:* Ball, *SOSF* 96, 325; *SIF* 72.

MEDIUM INFORMATION: *Length:* [?] min.

AUTHORSHIP INFORMATION: *Director(s):* Calmettes, André [?].

Richard the Third. Motion Picture/Abridgment

498. *Richard the Third.*

DOCUMENT INFORMATION: *Country:* GB; *Year of release:* 1911.

EDITION, HISTORY, CONTENTS, & EVALUATION:

Edition & history: A silent movie probably produced under the auspices of the British entrepreneur and film pioneer, William George Barker. The first two scenes were taken from *King Henry the Sixth, Part Three,* a common stage tradition since Colly Cibber's eighteenth-century production. Olivier's famous *King Richard III* uses the same tactic (see 503). Cast credits given below are from the performance of the F.R. Benson company at the Shakespeare Memorial Theatre on April 21, 1911. Not all of these actors necessarily appeared in the screen version. *Contents & evaluation:* R.H. Ball condemns the film as being "neither film nor stage," and there is justice to his observation. Mostly the film is an arrangement of uninspired title cards (in America the title card began to develop into an art form of its own) intercut with tableaux from Shakespeare's play. There is a sequence from the Battle of Tewkesbury (which is really in *Henry the Sixth, Part Three* but conflations from different parts of the minor tetralogy have always been popular). Painted street scenes and tower walls contribute to the theatricality of the film (a camera exposes visual phoniness pitilessly). The actors exit and entrance as though they were on a stage, the director having apparently forgotten about cinematic transitions. There are no analytical shots, only long shots that suggest a camera nailed to the floor in the fourth row orchestra. The battle scenes are done as stage battles, not film sequences. Even the dream sequence at Bosworth when the ghosts appear to Richard on the eve of battle fails to take advantage of the obvious opportunity for cinematic illusion. For a theatre historian, the production may have value in showing how a theatrical production looked in the early part of the century. For those unfamiliar with Shakespeare, however, there will be great difficulty in figuring out what is going on (KSR). *Audience:* Professional; *Supplementary materials:* "Review." *BIO* 9 March 1911: 57; Ball, *SOSF* 84-88.

MEDIUM INFORMATION: *Medium:* Motion Picture; *Sound:* Silent; *Color:* No (black & white); *Length:* 27 min.; *Language of subtitles:* English; *Film type:* 16mm.

AUTHORSHIP INFORMATION: *Producer(s):* Barker, W.G.; Jones, G.W.; *Director(s):* Benson, F.R.; *Cast:* Benson, F. R. (Richard III); Maxon, Eric (Henry Earl of Richmond); Carrington, Murray (George duke of Clarence); Johnston, Moffat (Duke of Buckingham); Caine, Harry (Lord Hastings); Farebrother, Violet (Elizabeth, Queen of Edward IV); Aickin, Elinor (Duchess of York, Mother to King Edward IV); Benson, Mrs. (Lady Anne); Berry, James (King Henry VI); Brydone, Alfred (King Edward IV); Yorke, Kathleen (Edward Prince of Wales); Kenyon, Betty (Richard duke of York); Maclean, James (Duke of Norfolk); McClure, Victor (Earl of Surrey); Conrick, R. L. (Earl Rivers); Manship, George (Earl of Oxford); Caithness, Wilfred (Lord Stanley); Rupert, L. (Sir Richard Ratcliff); James, H. (Sir James Tyrrell); Wild, Alfred (Catesby); Dighton, Cecil (Sir James Blount); Howell, John (Brackenbury); Victor, J.

(Lord Mayor of London); Nicholson, H. O. (First Murderer); Wild, A. (Second Murderer).

DISTRIBUTION & AVAILABILITY: *Publisher or responsible agency:* Co-operative; *Distributor:* JEF, *Copy location:* FOL, NFA*; *Call or copy number:* MP 74; *Availability:* Apply JEF.

Richard the Third. Motion Picture/Abbreviated

499. *Richard the Third.*

DOCUMENT INFORMATION: *Country:* USA; *Year of release:* 1913.

EDITION, HISTORY, CONTENTS, & EVALUATION: *Edition & history:* R.H. Ball's description remains the definitive account and must be read for an appreciation of this film's elaborate effects. The movie starred the great tragedian, Frederick B. Warde, who subsequently played King Lear in the 1916 Thanhouser film. Apparently the performance was a combination of film, lecture and recital, with Warde on hand in person. In the days of transition from theatre to movies personal appearances by actors on stage, along with vaudeville performers, were common practices. *Supplementary materials:* Ball, *SOSF* 155-62.

MEDIUM INFORMATION: *Length:* 50+ min.

AUTHORSHIP INFORMATION: *Director(s):* Dudley, M.B.; *Cast:* Warde, Frederick B. (Richard duke of Gloucester).

DISTRIBUTION & AVAILABILITY: *Publisher or responsible agency:* Thanhouser, Edwin; *Copy location:* Lost.

Richard the Third. Video/Scenes

500. *Richard the Third.* (Series: Scenes from Shakespeare).

DOCUMENT INFORMATION: *Country:* GB; *Year of first showing:* 1937; *Location of first showing:* BBC. Transmitted 9 Apr. 1937.

EDITION, HISTORY, CONTENTS, & EVALUATION: *Edition & history:* One of the very earliest transmissions of Shakespeare on television when the industry was still in its infancy. The scene selected was the wooing of Lady Anne by Richard duke of Gloucester over her father-in-law's bier. *Supplementary materials: TPAB* 9 Apr. 1937.

MEDIUM INFORMATION: *Length:* 18 min.

AUTHORSHIP INFORMATION: *Producer(s):* Thomas, Stephen; *Cast:* Milton, Ernest (Richard duke of Gloucester); Lehmann, Beatrix (Lady Anne); Glyn, R.; Fleming, W. (Men-at-arms); Hamilton, A. (Corpse of King Henry VI [!]).

DISTRIBUTION & AVAILABILITY: *Publisher or responsible agency:* BBC; *Copy location:* Unavailable.

Richard the Third. Motion Picture/Derivative

501. *Tower of London [1939].*

DOCUMENT INFORMATION: *Country:* USA; *Year of release:* 1939.

EDITION, HISTORY, CONTENTS, & EVALUATION: *Edition & history:* Although only vaguely indebted to Shakespeare, the movie does touch on the historical background for Shakespeare's *Three Parts of Henry VI* and *King Richard III*, which include the bloody battles between the houses of York and Lancaster in the Wars of the Roses. *Contents & evaluation:* What happens in the Tower of London in the 14th century is here filtered through the wonderful lens of Hollywood's Golden Age on the eve of WW II. That archetypal villain, Basil Rathbone, makes a splendidly appropriate Richard duke of Gloucester, while his executioner is none other than the most sinister figure of all, Boris Karloff (as Mord). The opening title card (the silent influence was still powerful in the thirties) sets the right tone: "No age is without its ruthless men—who in their search for power, leave dark stains upon the pages of history. During the Middle Ages—to seize the Tower of London was to seize the Throne of England. . . . A web of intrigue veils the lives of all who know only too well that today's friends might be tomorrow's enemies." *Audience:* General use; *Supplementary materials:* "Review." *MFB* 7.77 (May 31, 1940): 76.

MEDIUM INFORMATION: *Medium:* Motion Picture; *Sound:* Spoken language; *Color:* No (black & white); *Length:* 92 min.; *Language(s) spoken:* English; *Film type:* 16mm.

AUTHORSHIP INFORMATION: *Producer(s):* Lee, Rowland V.; *Director(s):* Lee, Rowland V.; Frank, Fred; *Screenplay writer(s):* Lee, Robert N.; *Composer(s):* Previn, Charles; Skinner, Frank; *Designer(s):* Otterson, Jack; Riedel, Richard; *Set designer(s):* Garsman, R.A.; *Costume designer(s):* West, Vera; *Lighting designer(s):* Robinson, George; *Other personnel:* Curtiss, Edward (Editor); Brown, Bernard B. (Sound); Bagley, G.O.T. and Grove, Sir Gerald (Technical advisors); *Cast:* Rathbone, Basil (Richard duke of Gloucester); Karloff, Boris (Mord); O'Neil, Barbara (Queen Elyzabeth [*sic*]; Hunter, Ian (King Edward IV); Price, Vincent (Clarence); Grey, Nan; (Lady Alice Barton); Gossart, Ernest (Tom Clink); Sutton, John (John Wyatt); Carroll, Leo G. (Lord Hastings); Mander, Miles (King Henry VI); Belmore, Lionel (Beacon); Hobart, Rose (Anne Neville); Sinclair, Ronald (Boy King Edward); Herbert-Bond, John (Young Prince Richard); Forbes, Ralph (Henry Tudor); Robinson, Frances (Duchess Isobel); Huntley, G.P. (Wales);

Rodion, John (Lord DeVere); Tetley, Walter (Chimney sweep); Dunagan, Donnie (Baby prince).

DISTRIBUTION & AVAILABILITY: *Publisher or responsible agency:* Universal Pictures; *Copy location:* FOL; *Call or copy number:* MP 3.

Richard the Third. Video/Abridgment

502. *Richard the Third.*

DOCUMENT INFORMATION: *Country:* USA; *Year of first showing:* 1950; *Location of first showing:* Masterpiece Playhouse/WNBT. Transmitted 9 to 10:00 P.M., 30 July 1950.

EDITION, HISTORY, CONTENTS, & EVALUATION: *Edition & history:* To give some idea of the degree of interest in Shakespeare that the media then exhibited, it is worth noting that in this same week a radio, not TV, program featured John Barrymore reading from *Hamlet, Macbeth, Richard III,* and *Twelfth Night* on NBC at 8 P.M. on Thursdays. The week before this presentation of *Richard III,* Masterpiece Playhouse had offered Ibsen's *Hedda Gabler* with Jessica Tandy in the title role. In the halcyon early days of television, obviously there was still faith in the reality of a mass audience for great drama. *Supplementary materials:* "On TV." *NYT* 30 July 1950: X 7.

MEDIUM INFORMATION: *Color:* No (black & white); *Length:* 60 min.; *Video type:* V.

AUTHORSHIP INFORMATION: *Cast:* Windom, William; Williams, Hugh; Yurka, Blanche.

DISTRIBUTION & AVAILABILITY: *Publisher or responsible agency:* Masterpiece Playhouse/WNBT.

Richard the Third. Motion Picture

503. *Richard the Third: by William Shakespeare with Some Interpolations by David Garrick, Colly Cibber, etc..*

DOCUMENT INFORMATION: *Country:* GB; *Year of release:* 1955.

EDITION, HISTORY, CONTENTS, & EVALUATION: *Edition & history:* As the subtitle suggests, the script for Olivier's film drew heavily on the stage tradition set by Colly Cibber when he grafted the last part of *3H6* on to *Richard III* to make the narrative more comprehensible to an average audience. Designer Roger Furse needed special care with the details of the 15th-century settings because the new technique of VistaVision photography could pick out the most distant background scene with pinpoint clarity. Carmen Dillon completed the job of transferring the settings to the three large stages at Shepperton Studios, London. The film was premiered in the USA simultaneously on screen and television, being televised nationally from 2:30 to 5:30 PM, 11 March 1956, by NBC to 146 stations in 45 states. America's then most visible Shakespeare expert, Dr. Frank Baxter, offered an intermission talk on the gap between Shakespeare's Richard III and the historical Richard III. The viewers, estimated at 25 million, exceeded the combined audiences for all Shakespeare productions throughout history. Since only 25,000 American homes then had color TV, most people viewed the production in a depressing black and white. *Contents & evaluation:* "Sir Laurence's Richard is tremendous—a weird, poisonous portrait of a super-rogue whose dark designs are candidly acknowledged with lick-lip relish and sardonic wit. Heavily made-up with one dead eyelid, a hatchet nose, a withered hand, a humped back, a drooping shoulder and a twisted limping leg, he is a freakish-looking figure that Sir Laurence so articulates that he has an electric vitality and a fascinatingly grotesque grace. A grating voice, too, is a feature of his physical oddity. More important to the character, however, is the studiousness and subtlety with which Sir Laurence builds up tension within him as his mischiefs and crimes accumulate. From a glib and egotistical conniver at the outset of the play, when he confides his clever purpose to the audience and hypocritically woos Lady Anne, he becomes a cold and desperate tyrant after he has ordered Clarence and Hastings dispatched and faces up to the horror of slaying the little princes in the Tower" (Crowther, Bosley, "Review," *NYT* 12 March 1956: III.1). *Audience:* College and university; General use; *Supplementary materials:* Brown, Constance. "Olivier's R3." *FQ* 20 (1967): 23-32; Thorp, M. F. "Shakespeare in Movies." *SQ* 9 (1958): 357-66; "Olivier." *NYT* 16 Jan. 1955: M14+; "Richard's Rating." *NYT* 18 March 1956 X11.

MEDIUM INFORMATION: *Medium:* Motion picture; *Sound:* Spoken language; *Color:* Yes (Vistavision by Technicolor); *Length:* 138 min.; *Language(s) spoken:* English; *Film type:* 16mm; 35mm; *Video type:* V.

AUTHORSHIP INFORMATION: *Producer(s):* Olivier, Laurence; *Director(s):* Olivier, Laurence; *Adaptor/translator(s):* Dent, Alan; *Composer(s):* Walton, Sir William; Mathieson, Muir (w. Royal Philharmonic); *Designer(s):* Furse, Roger; Dillon, Carmen; *Costume designer(s):* Nathan, L & H., Ltd.; *Other personnel:* Bushnell, Anthony (Assoc. director); Heller, Otto (Photography); Gossage, John (Prod. supervisor); Cranston, Helga (Editor); Veevers, Wally (Special effects); Sforzini, Tony (Make-up); Coop, Denys (Camera); Martin, Jack (Prod. mgr.); O'Hara, Gerry (Asst. dir.); Davis, Pamela (Continuity); Rule, Bert (Sound); *Cast:* Hardwicke, Cedric (King Edward IV); Gielgud, John (Clarence); Olivier, Laurence (Richard); Huson, Paul (Prince of Wales); Shine, Andy (Duke of York); Haye, Helen (Duchess of York); Brown, Pamela (Jane Shore); Richardson, Ralph (Duke of Buckingham); Clunes, Alec (Lord Hastings); Naismith, Laurence (Lord Stanley); Kerridge, Mary (Queen Eliza-

beth); Morton, Clive (Lord Rivers); Cunningham, Dan (Lord Grey); Wilmer, Douglas (Lord Dorset); Bloom, Claire (Lady Anne); Baker, Stanley (Richmond); Cruickshank, Andrew (Brackenbury); Greenidge, Terence (Scrivener); Wooland, Norman (Catesby); Woodbridge, George (Mayor of London); Knight, Esmond (Ratcliffe); Laurie, John (Lovel); Phillips, John (Norfolk); Thorndike, Russell (Priest); Williams, Peter (Messenger); Wilton, Anne (Scrubwoman); Prentice, Derek; Wells, Deering (Clergymen); Bennett, Richard (Stanley); Russell, Roy (Abbott); + Messengers.

DISTRIBUTION & AVAILABILITY: *Publisher or responsible agency:* London Film Productions; *Distributor:* FNC, DCV, TWC, ILL, INM,EMB, FMB*, TSO*, *Availability:* FNC, Rental 16mm $200+; DCV, V, $38; FCM, V, $19.95; TWC, B, V, $45.95; EMB, B, V, $112.95; FMB*, 16mm, apply; TSO*, V; ILL, V $19.95; INM, V $29.95.

Richard the Third. Motion Picture/Excerpts

504. *Richard the Third.*

DOCUMENT INFORMATION: *Country:* GB; *Year of release:* 1955.

EDITION, HISTORY, CONTENTS, & EVALUATION: *Edition & history:* Study extracts of episodes from the 1955 Olivier film. *Supplementary materials:* BUFVC 21.

MEDIUM INFORMATION: *Sound:* Spoken language; *Length:* 22 min.; *Film type:* 16mm.

AUTHORSHIP INFORMATION: *Director(s):* Olivier, Laurence.

DISTRIBUTION & AVAILABILITY: *Distributor:* FMB*.

Richard the Third, 1-3. Video/Teleplay (Part 14 of 15 parts)

505. *Dangerous Brother, The.* (Series: *An Age of Kings* [XIV]).

DOCUMENT INFORMATION: *Country:* GB; *Year of first showing:* 1960; *Location of first showing:* BBC TV. Transmitted 9 to 10 P.M., Thursday, 3 Nov. 1960.

EDITION, HISTORY, CONTENTS, & EVALUATION: *Awards:* Dews, Peter: Excellence in Directing (British Guild of Directors); *Edition & history:* Based on Acts 1-3 of *King Richard III.* The fourteenth installment in *An Age of Kings.* (See also numbers 156-9, 178-9, 185, 188, 190-2, 485-6, and 506.) Paul Daneman, who first appears in the cast credits in episode #11 ("The Rabble-from Kent"—190), now moves center stage in assuming the role of the villainous Richard Duke of Gloucester, soon to be King Richard III. For additional background, see *The Hollow Crown* (485). *Contents &*

evaluation: "The deadly struggle for the throne continues with evil Richard plotting to overthrow the boy King" (PR blurb). "Richard III was well played by Paul Daneman, who endeavored to distinguish between the character's Machiavellian cunning in *Henry VI* and his diabolism in *Richard III.* Inevitably the grotesque villainy of the latter play swallowed up any subtleties attempted in the earlier ones. And it insistently recalled—as if one could forget!—how preposterous a farce *Richard III* is despite its occasional excellences. Richard's wooing of Anne, for example, was perhaps as good as one could expect" (Crane, Milton, "Shakespeare on Television," *SQ* 12.3 [Summer 1961]: 326). *Audience:* General use; *Supplementary materials:* Campbell, O.J. Introduction. *An Age of Kings* [The 15 parts as they appeared on television]. New York: Pyramid, 1961; "Program." *RT* 27 Oct. 1960: 49.

MEDIUM INFORMATION: *Medium:* Video; *Sound:* Spoken language; *Color:* No (black & white); *Length:* 60 min.; *Language(s) spoken:* English; *Video type:* 16mm, Kinescope.

AUTHORSHIP INFORMATION: *Producer(s):* Dews, Peter; *Director(s):* Hayes, Michael; *Adaptor/translator(s):* Crozier, Eric; *Composer(s):* Whelen, Christopher; Bliss, Arthur; Salter, Lionel (Conducting Royal Philharmonic Orchestra); *Designer(s):* Morris, Stanley; *Cast:* Daneman, Paul (Richard Duke of Gloucester); Morris, Mary (Queen Margaret); Glover, Julian (Edward IV); Janes, Hugh (Edward V); Garland, Patrick (Clarence); Windsor, Frank (Brackenbury); Andrews, David (Hastings); Dixon, Jill (Lady Anne); Greenwood, John (Gentleman); Scully, Terry (King Henry VI); Farrington, Kenneth (Rivers); Shepperdson, Leon (Lord Grey); Wenham, Jane (Queen Elizabeth); Wreford, Edgar (Buckingham); May, Jack (Lord Stanley); Ringham, John (Catesby); Lang, Robert; Wale, Terry (Murderers); Valentine, Anthony (Dorset); Carson, Violet (Duchess of York); Lodge, Terence (Messenger); Sharp, John (Lord Mayor); Willis, Jerome (Cardinal Bourchier).

DISTRIBUTION & AVAILABILITY: *Publisher or responsible agency:* BBC; *Copy location:* BBC*, SCL*.

Richard the Third, 3–5. Video/Teleplay (Part 15 in 15-part series)

506. *Boar Hunt, The.* (Series: *An Age of Kings* [XV]).

DOCUMENT INFORMATION: *Country:* GB; *Year of first showing:* 1960; *Location of first showing:* BBC TV. Transmitted 8:45 to 10 P.M., Thursday, 17 Nov. 1960.

EDITION, HISTORY, CONTENTS, & EVALUATION: *Awards:* Dews, Peter: Excellence in Directing (British Guild of Directors); *Edition & history:* Based on Acts 3–5 of *King Richard III.* The fifteenth and final episode in *An Age of Kings.* (See also numbers 156-9, 178-9, 185, 188, 190-2, 485-6, and 505). This last program involved a cast of 57 actors and a budget of £4,020 which made it the most expensive in the series. Not surprisingly Shakespeare's longest play required an extra 15 minutes in viewing time. Of special interest is the sudden re-emergence of Frank Pettingell, Falstaff earlier in the series, as Bishop of Ely. For additional background, see *The Hollow Crown* (485). *Contents & evaluation:* "Richard is King at last. One of his first bloody deeds is to murder the two little princes in the Tower. Vengeance appears in the person of Henry Tudor who slays Richard in battle at Bosworth" (PR blurb). For review by Milton Crane, see 505, above. *Audience:* General use; *Supplementary materials:* Campbell, O.J. Introduction. *An Age of Kings* [The 15 parts as they appeared on television]. New York: Pyramid, 1961; "Program." *RT* 10 Nov. 1960: 49.

MEDIUM INFORMATION: *Medium:* Video; *Sound:* Spoken language; *Color:* No (black & white); *Length:* 75 min.; *Language(s) spoken:* English; *Video type:* 16mm, Kinescope.

AUTHORSHIP INFORMATION: *Producer(s):* Dews, Peter; *Director(s):* Hayes, Michael; *Adaptor/translator(s):* Crozier, Eric; *Composer(s):* Whelen, Christopher; Bliss, Arthur; Salter, Lionel (Conducting Royal Philharmonic Orchestra); *Designer(s):* Morris, Stanley; *Costume designer(s):* Harris, Olive; *Lighting designer(s):* Whitmore, Walter; *Other personnel:* Greenwood, John (Fight Arranger); Manderson, Tommy (Make-up); Summers, George (Technical Supervisor); *Cast:* Daneman, Paul (King Richard III); Willis, Jerome (Henry Tudor); Andrews, David (Hastings); Ringham, John (Catesby); May, Jack (Stanley); Bisley, Jeremy (Sir John); Wreford, Edgar (Buckingham); Rowe, Alan (Ratcliff); Farrington, Kenneth (Rivers); Shepperdson, Leon (Grey); Lang, Robert (Sir Thomas Vaughan); Pettingell, Frank (Bishop of Ely); Brine, Adrian (Lovel); Sharp, John (Lord Mayor); Carson, Violet (Duchess of York); Dixon, Jill (Anne); Wenham, Jane (Queen Elizabeth); Valentine, Anthony (Dorset); Windsor, Frank (Brackenbury); Wale, Terry (Urswick); Harley, Timothy (Page, Messenger); Ware, Derek; Scott, John (Messengers); Glover, Julian (Oxford); Wells, Michael (Sir Walter Herbert); Wickham, Jeffry (Sir James Blunt); Johnson, Noel (Norfolk); Jackson, Barry (Surrey); Greenwood, John (Messenger, Ghost of Prince Edward); Scully, Terry (Ghost); Garland, Patrick (Ghost); Janes, Hugh (Ghost); Lewis, Michael (Ghost).

DISTRIBUTION & AVAILABILITY: *Publisher or responsible agency:* BBC; *Copy location:* BBC*, SCL*.

Richard the Third. Motion Picture/Derivative

507. *Tower of London.*

DOCUMENT INFORMATION: *Country:* USA; *Year of release:* 1962; *Year of first showing:* Oct. 24, 1962; *Country* of first showing: USA; *Location of first showing:* Washington, DC.

EDITION, HISTORY, CONTENTS, & EVALUATION: *Edition & history:* A "remake" of the 1939 Universal *Tower of London.* If the 1939 version had little to do with Shakespeare then this one has even fewer connections. It is included here, though, because it is a Roger Corman "cult" movie, one of a series of exploitation films in the sixties. Corman's disciples included such subsequently famous screen directors and actors as Francis Ford Coppola (*The Godfather*), Martin Scorsese (*Taxi Driver*), and Jack Nicholson. Francis Ford Coppola served as the dialogue director for this film, which I have not screened (KSR). *Contents & evaluation:* Not seen. *Audience:* General use.

MEDIUM INFORMATION: *Medium:* Motion Picture; *Sound:* Spoken language; *Color:* No (black & white); *Length:* 79 min.; *Language(s) spoken:* English; *Film type:* 35mm.

AUTHORSHIP INFORMATION: *Producer(s):* Corman, Gene; *Director(s):* Corman, Roger; Bohrer, Jack; *Screenplay writer(s):* Gordon, Leo V.; Powell, Amos; Gordon, James B.; Andersen, Michael; *Designer(s):* Haller, Daniel; *Lighting designer(s):* Dalzell, Arch R.; *Other personnel:* Sinclair, Ronald (Editor); Mitchell, Philip (Sound); Coppola, Francis (Dialogue director); *Cast:* Price, Vincent (Richard duke of Gloucester); Pate, Michael (Sir Ratcliffe); Freeman, Joan (Lady Margaret); Brown, Robert (Sir Justin); Watson, Justice (Edward IV); Selby, Sarah (Queen); McCauly, Richard (Clarence); Martin, Eugene, (Edward IV); Knight, Sandra (Mistress Shore); Hale, Richard (Tyrus); Losby, Donald (Prince Richard); Gordon, Bruce (Buckingham); Camden, Joan (Anne);Taft, Sara (Queen Elizabeth).

DISTRIBUTION & AVAILABILITY: *Publisher or responsible agency:* United Artists.

Richard the Third. Motion Picture/Abridgment

508. *Richard the Third.* (Series: Fair Adventure Series).

DOCUMENT INFORMATION: *Country:* USA; *Year of release:* 1964.

EDITION, HISTORY, CONTENTS, & EVALUATION: *Edition & history:* A four-part abridgment of the play with commentary by Dr. Frank Baxter. For others in this series, see 180, 254, 311, 426, 463, 487, 546, 614 and 653. *Contents & evaluation:* Not seen. *Audience:* Junior High (grades 7-9); High school (grades 10-12).

MEDIUM INFORMATION: *Medium:* Motion Picture; *Sound:* Spoken language; *Color:* No (black & white); *Length:* 112 min.; *Language(s) spoken:* English; *Film type:* 16mm.

DISTRIBUTION & AVAILABILITY: *Publisher or re-*

sponsible agency: Westinghouse Broadcasting Corp.; *Distributor:* Not known.

Richard the Third. Video/Recording

509. *Richard the Third.* (Series: *Wars of the Roses,* III)

DOCUMENT INFORMATION: *Country:* GB; *Year of first showing:* 1965; *Location of first showing:* Royal Shakespeare Theatre/BBC TV. Transmitted 8 to 10:35 P.M., Thursday, 22 April 1965.

EDITION, HISTORY, CONTENTS, & EVALUATION: *Edition & history:* Originally conceived and directed for the Stratford RSC stage by John Barton and Peter Hall, this series of programs rearranges the minor tetralogy (three parts of *Henry VI* and *Richard III*) into three plays, called *Henry VI, Edward IV* and *Richard III.* Each segment in turn was three hours in length (see also 183-4). The result is something more than a mere recording of a stage play. Twelve cameras taped the performers who acted on a stage that had been extended 40 feet by boarding over orchestra seats. The effect was to achieve a sense of space for the battle scenes that was lacking in the original stage production. Rehearsal and recording took eight weeks. By working closely with the RSC and taping in their own theatre, the producer got a sense of continuity and unity that might otherwise have been lacking in so sprawling a venture. *Contents & evaluation:* This third part was well received by the critics. The London *Times* critic found special virtue in David Warner's portrayal of King Henry, Peggy Ashcroft's Margaret, and Donald Sinden's York. There was objection to some textual changes as showing a "patronizing attitude" or as a "semi-Brechtian machinery" at odds with Shakespeare's medievalism. The objections, however, seem to be registered in a minor key. *Audience:* General use; *Supplementary materials:* "A Shakespearian Experience on TV." *Times* 21 April 1965: 13d.; "Program." *RT* 15 Apr. 1965: 48.

MEDIUM INFORMATION: *Medium:* Video; *Sound:* Spoken language; *Color:* No (black & white); *Length:* 135 min.; *Language(s) spoken:* English; *Video type:* Kinescope, 16mm.

AUTHORSHIP INFORMATION: *Producer(s):* Hall, Peter (Stage); Barry, Michael (TV); *Director(s):* Hayes, Michael; Midgeley, Robin (TV); Hall, Peter (Stage); *Adaptor/translator(s):* Barton, John; *Composer(s):* Woolfenden, Guy; Bennett, Gordon; and others; *Designer(s):* Bury, John; *Costume designer(s):* Curtis, Ann; *Lighting designer(s):* Wright, Robert; *Other personnel:* Henderson, Ann (Make-up); Clarke, Roy (Editor); *Cast:* Dotrice, Roy (Edward IV); Engel, Susan (Queen Elizabeth); McClelland, Fergus (Prince Edward); Martin, Paul (Richard); Barker, Katharine (Princess Elizabeth); Kay, Charles (Clarence); Holm, Ian (Gloucester); Thomas, Madoline (Duchess of York); Sullivan, Hugh (Hastings); Waring, Derek (Rivers); Squire, William (Buckingham); Thomas, Charles (Catesby); Corvin, John (Ratcliff); Hargreaves, David (Norfolk); Knowles, Henry (Tyrrel); Warner, David (King Henry VI); Ashcroft, Peggy (Margaret); Tucker, Alan (Prince Edward); Suzman, Janet (Lady Anne); Porter, Eric (Richmond); Jones, Maurice (Oxford); Hussey, John (Derby); Rose, Michael (Bishop of Ely); Valentine, Ted (Lt. of Tower); Burton, Donald; Brack, Philip (Murderers); Webster, Malcolm (Lord Mayor); Jones, Marshall; Greenidge, Terence; Dench, Jeffery (Citizens); Ellison, David; Brown, Murray; Boden, Anthony; Morton, David (Messengers).

DISTRIBUTION & AVAILABILITY: *Publisher or responsible agency:* BBC/RSC; *Distributor:* BBC, *Copy location:* BBC*, archive.

Richard the Third. **Motion Picture/Scenes**

510. *Richard the Third,* 1.1.; 1.2. (Series: The Shakespeare Series [IFB], IX).

DOCUMENT INFORMATION: *Country:* Great Britain; *Year of release:* 1974.

EDITION, HISTORY, CONTENTS, & EVALUATION: *Edition & history:* Excerpts from *Richard III,* Act one, scenes one and two, performed on a reconstruction of an Elizabethan stage to give the impression of rapid movement characteristic (in all likelihood) of the original performances. (For others in the series, see numbers 22, 131, 164, 232, 326, 430, 467, 490, 556, 601 and 619.) *Contents & evaluation:* Shows the malevolent Richard duke of Gloucester's famed opening soliloqy beginning, "Now is the winter of our discontent" (2.1.), and Richard's outrageous wooing of the widowed Lady Anne (2.2), whose father-in-law and husband Richard has himself slain at the end of *The Third Part of Henry VI.* Unhappily Paul Chapman as Richard duke of Gloucester simply lacks the malevolent clout, the reserves of power, that the role calls for. All too often he is acting the role of Richard rather than being Richard, which is a fatal flaw under the pitiless eye of the camera. He makes a much better Ferdinand in the Seabourne *Tempest.* Alison Key also lacks the passion needed to spit convincingly in Richard's face. There is some editing of the shot/reverse shot type, but close-ups of talking heads with dental problems set up barriers between the viewer and Shakespeare's language (KSR). *Audience:* High school (grades 10-12).

MEDIUM INFORMATION: *Medium:* Motion Picture; *Sound:* Spoken language; *Color:* Yes; *Length:* 11 1/2 min.; *Language(s) spoken:* English; *Film type:* 16mm; *Video type:* V, 3/4U (4 per cassette).

AUTHORSHIP INFORMATION: *Producer(s):* Realist Film Unit; *Director(s):* Seabourne, Peter; *Cast:* Chapman, Paul (Richard III); Key, Alison (Lady Anne).

DISTRIBUTION & AVAILABILITY: *Publisher or responsible agency:* United Kingdom, Realist Film Unit/ Seabourne Enterprises, Ltd.; *Distributor:* IFB, CNU, *Copy location:* FOL; *Call or copy number:* ISBN 0-8354-1590-2; FOL, MP 80; *Availability:* CNU rental 16mm, $8; IFB sale 16mm, V, $195.

Richard the Third. **Motion Picture/Excerpts**

511. *The Goodbye Girl.*

DOCUMENT INFORMATION: *Country:* USA; *Year of release:* 1977.

EDITION, HISTORY, CONTENTS, & EVALUATION: *Edition & history:* The movie sets up a play-within-a-play situation as scenes from *Richard III* are acted in the film. *Contents & evaluation:* An amusing film adaptation of a Neil Simon script that sets up complicated parallels between the amorous concerns of a budding young actor (played by Richard Dreyfuss) and Shakespeare's villain hero. A ludicrous interpretation of Richard duke of Gloucester as a homosexual cripple in lavendar provides the center of the hilarity. But there is also an undercurrent of barbed wit in this satirical putdown of stage directors who take themselves too seriously (KSR). *Supplementary materials:* Willson, Robert Jr. "Shakespeare in *The Goodbye Girl." SFNL* 2.2. (April 1978): 1+).

MEDIUM INFORMATION: *Length:* 110 min.

AUTHORSHIP INFORMATION: *Director(s):* Ross, Herbert; *Screenplay writer(s):* Simon, Neil; *Cast:* Dreyfuss, Richard.

Richard III. **Video/Interpretation**

512. *Richard III.*

DOCUMENT INFORMATION: *Country:* USSR; *Year of first showing:* 1980.

EDITION, HISTORY, CONTENTS, & EVALUATION: *Edition & history:* This adaptation of *King Richard III* was originally produced at the Rustaveli theatre, Tbilisi [Georgia], USSR, on March 10, 1980, and later at the 1980 Edinburgh Festival. Subsequently a videotaping was shown to delegates to the International World Shakespeare Congress, Stratford upon Avon, England, 1981. *Contents & evaluation:* One does not need to know Georgian [a language entirely different from Russian], to follow this play. One only needs to know Shakespeare's play. The production amply demonstrates that Richard duke of Gloucester speaks an international language recognizable everywhere. Ramaz

Chkhikvadze is an actor of such powerful talents that language barriers melt away. *Audience*: Professional; *Supplementary materials:* Kiasashvili, Nico. "A Georgian *Richard III*." *SQ* 31.3 (Autumn 1980): 438-39.

MEDIUM INFORMATION: *Medium:* Video; *Sound:* Spoken language; *Color:* Yes; *Length:* [?] min.; *Language(s) spoken:* Georgian; *Video type:* Unknown.

AUTHORSHIP INFORMATION: *Director(s):* Sturua, Robert; *Screenplay writer(s):* Kichadze, Zurab; *Composer(s):* Concheli, Gorgi; *Designer(s):* Shveldeze, Mikhail; *Costume designer(s):* Shveldeze, Mikhail; *Cast:* Gegechkori, Giorgi (Buckingham); Kan_cheli, Salome (Elizabeth); Chkhikvadze, Ramaz (Richard III).

DISTRIBUTION & AVAILABILITY: *Publisher or responsible agency:* Rustaveli Theatre; *Copy location:* Rustaveli Theatre, USSR

512.1 *Riccardo III.*

DOCUMENT INFORMATION: *Country:* Italy; *Year of first showing:* 1981; *Location of first showing:* Transmitted 7 Dec. 1981.

EDITION, HISTORY, CONTENTS, & EVALUATION: *Edition & history:* Filmed in the RAI (Radio Television Italy) studios. The original production was performed in January 1978 at the Teatro Quirino di Rome with the same cast as the television production.

AUTHORSHIP INFORMATION: *Producer(s):* Carlotto, R.; *Director(s):* Bene, Carmelo; *Composer(s):* Zito, L.; *Cast:* Bene, Carmelo; Mancinelli, Lydia; Silverio, Daniel; Grassini, Maria Grazia; Javicoli, Susanna; Morante, Laura; Boccuni, Maria.

DISTRIBUTION & AVAILABILITY: *Publisher or responsible agency:* RAI (Radiotelevisione Italiana); *Copy location:* RAI.

Richard the Third. Video/Teleplay

513. *Richard the Third.* (Series: The Shakespeare Plays).

DOCUMENT INFORMATION: *Year of first showing:* 1983; *Location of first showing:* BBC, London; PBS stations, USA, 2 May 1983.

EDITION, HISTORY, CONTENTS, & EVALUATION: *Edition & history:* As the grand finale for the minor tetralogy, this production follows the stylistic policies already established by director Jane Howell for the three parts of *Henry VI* (see 186-7, 193). Again ingenious use of extremely simple settings (based on a children's playground), along with the judicous use of mirrors for battle scenes, creates an illusion of calamitous violence and turmoil. The text is based on the 1951 Peter Alexander edition. *Contents & evaluation:* "For more than two centuries, actors have built reputations by playing Richard of Gloucester. Few, however, have been able to portray that figure's emergence as the greatest of all villains. Hence, Ron Cook has a magnificent opportunity to show the more boyish Richard, one of three rowdy brothers who seize power in England following their father's murder. Cook is unfailingly at his best whenever Richard's 'alacrity of spirit' and the essential toughness of his soldierly determination are called for. Quite surprising, then, is the flatness of Cook's treatment of Richard's famous soliloquies in *3H6* and *R3*. He recites these speeches as though he wants to get through them with the least amount of passion possible. . . . Of course, the major woman's role in these plays is that of Queen Margaret, and Julia Foster is quite sufficient in that role. Her savagery is blood-curdling, and she gives Margaret's curses and prophecies in the last play a Hecate-like dimension. Howell makes her a kind of death-goddess at the conclusion of the tetralogy, as she sits atop the mound of corpses which have been steadily piling up at the end of each play" (Manheim, Michael, "The H6-R3 Tetralogy," *SFNL* 8.2. [1984.: 2+). *Audience:* College and university; *Supplementary materials:* Videotape (25 min.) from "Shakespeare in Perspective" series with Rosemary Anne Sisson as lecturer available in U.K. from BBC* (*BUFVC* 21).

MEDIUM INFORMATION: *Medium:* Video; *Sound:* Spoken language; *Color:* Yes; *Length:* 230 min.; *Language(s) spoken:* English; *Video type:* B, V, 3/4U.

AUTHORSHIP INFORMATION: *Producer(s):* Sutton, Shaun; *Director(s):* Howell, Jane; *Adaptor/translator(s):* Snodin, David; *Cast:* Cook, Ron (Richard duke of Gloucester); Foster, Julia (Queen Margaret); Byrne, Michael (Buckingham); Daker, David (Hastings); Cooper, Rowena (Queen Elizabeth); Wanamaker, Zoë (Lady Anne); Crosbie, Annette (Duchess of York).

DISTRIBUTION & AVAILABILITY: *Publisher or responsible agency:* BBC/TLF; *Distributor:* AVP, UIO, BBC* *Copy location:* UVM (Archive); *Availability:* AVP, B, V, 3/4U $450 (1987), sale; UIO, V (72320H), 3/4U (70320V), rental, $27.40; BBC*, 16mm or V, apply (*BUFVC* 21).

Romeo and Juliet

ORIGINAL WORK AND PRODUCTION: Tragedy of Young Love. *Year written:* 1594-96; *Site of first production:* The Curtain in Shoreditch [?]

Romeo and Juliet. Motion Picture/Burlesque

514. *Burlesque on Romeo and Juliet.*

DOCUMENT INFORMATION: *Country:* USA; *Year of release:* 1902.

EDITION, HISTORY, CONTENTS, & EVALUATION: *Edition & history:* Professor Ball thinks that this early effort was "derived" by the Thomas Edison company from an earlier film by Georges Méliès. It is mentioned here only because it involves the names of two celebrated early filmmakers. *Supplementary materials:* Ball, SOSF 306.

MEDIUM INFORMATION: *Length:* 5 min. [?].

AUTHORSHIP INFORMATION: *Director(s):* Méliès, Georges [?].

Romeo and Juliet. Motion Picture/Abridgment

515. *Romeo and Juliet.*

DOCUMENT INFORMATION: *Country:* USA; *Year of release:* 1908.

EDITION, HISTORY, CONTENTS, & EVALUATION: *Edition & history:* Another of the early Vitagraph films hastily made and sold to Nickelodeon owners for a few pennies a foot. They were likely to share the bill with an odd assortment of other films to include weight lifters and acrobats, all in the spirit of vaudeville. The film's major distinction may be the presence in the cast of Florence Lawrence, who subsequently became famous under Carl Laemmle's grooming as the first movie actress to be identified to audiences by name. That precedent paved the way for the star system that was ultimately to revolutionize the economics of the film industry by giving actors greater leverage than anyone else in negotiating salaries. An interesting historical touch is the presence of the Vitagraph "V" trademark hidden away in many of the sets (as over the bed in Juliet's bedchamber) as a way of warding off film pirates. Then as now the pirating of material was an obsession in the film industry, which doesn't so much sell films as give limited "rights" to them. *Contents & evaluation:* Florence Lawrence makes an attractive Juliet and Paul Panzer, who subsequently became the villain in the *Perils of Pauline* series, makes a believable Romeo. Mostly these are crude interior shots with painted cardboard sets. It has been said that the cast members themselves, who were not paid terribly well, could be found in their Elizabethan costumes helping to paint the sets. The apothecary shop is the most convincing *mise en scène*, while the tomb scene, because it is implausibly but probably necessarily lit from above, the least realistic. Film grammar, though rudimentary in modern eyes, nevertheless reflected the then advanced techniques of J. Stuart Blackton, the supervising producer, whose innovations, such as discovery of the close shot, were remarkable in their day. In fact if it had not been for Blackton and his interest in putting literature on screen, these Vitagraph films may never have come into existence (KSR). *Audience:* Professional; *Supplementary materials:* Ball, *SOSF* 43-5.

MEDIUM INFORMATION: *Medium:* Motion Picture; *Sound:* Silent; *Color:* No (black & white); *Length:* 11 min.; *Language of subtitles:* English; *Film type:* 16mm.

AUTHORSHIP INFORMATION: *Producer(s):* Blackton, J. Stuart; *Director(s):* Ranous, William V. [?]; *Cast:* Lawrence, Florence (Juliet); Panzer, Paul (Romeo); Adolfi, John G. (Tybalt); Kent, Charles (Capulet); Chapman, Charles (Montague); Shea, William (Peter); Carver, Miss [Louise ?] (Nurse); [Credits: Ball].

DISTRIBUTION & AVAILABILITY: *Publisher or responsible agency:* Vitagraph; *Distributor:* JEF, GLB*, *Copy location:* FOL; *Call or copy number:* MP 27; *Availability:* Apply JEF; GLB*, V, "Flicker Flashbacks #18".

Romeo and Juliet. Motion Picture/Abbreviated

516. *Romeo and Juliet.*

DOCUMENT INFORMATION: *Country:* Italy; *Year of release:* 1908.

EDITION, HISTORY, CONTENTS, & EVALUATION: *Supplementary materials:* SIF 78; Ball, *SOSF* 101.

MEDIUM INFORMATION: *Length:* 7 [?] min.

AUTHORSHIP INFORMATION: *Director(s):* Caserini, Mario; *Cast:* Bertini, Francesca [?].

Romeo and Juliet. Motion Picture/Derivative

517. *Romeo Turns Bandit.*

DOCUMENT INFORMATION: *Country:* France; *Year of release:* 1910.

EDITION, HISTORY, CONTENTS, & EVALUATION: *Edition & history:* A brief adaptation of the play by the Pathé company, France's largest and most ambitous producer of films in the early days of cinema. *Contents & evaluation:* Delightfully Gallic in spirit, the movie merrily uproots Shakespeare's play, and puts the actors in contemporary dress. The scholarship is at best questionable, especially when Juliet is declared in a dialogue title to be a "Montague." On the other hand, from a cinematic point of view, the movie shows a rudimentary film grammar, especially in the shots of

Romeo climbing around the wall of the Capulet (Montague [?]) mansion. Both amusing and of historic interest, it will please film buffs and interest film scholars but not necessarily send Shakespeareans into ecstasy (KSR). *Audience:* Professional; General use; *Supplementary materials:* Ball, *SOSF* 115.

MEDIUM INFORMATION: *Medium:* Motion Picture; *Sound:* Silent; *Color:* No (black & white); *Length:* 6 min.; *Language of subtitles:* English; *Film type:* 16mm.

AUTHORSHIP INFORMATION: *Producer(s):* Pathé Freres; *Director(s):* Not known; *Cast:* Not known.

DISTRIBUTION & AVAILABILITY: *Publisher or responsible agency:* Pathé Freres; *Distributor:* JEF [?], *Copy location:* FOL; *Call or copy number:* MP 33.

Romeo and Juliet. Motion Picture/Abridgment

518. *Giulietta e Romeo.* [*Romeo and Juliet*].

DOCUMENT INFORMATION: *Country:* Italy; *Year of release:* 1911.

EDITION, HISTORY, CONTENTS, & EVALUATION: *Edition & history:* A Film d'Arte Italiana production made in Verona that in its unusual length for the time marked an ambitious attempt to represent the play on screen as something more than a fragment. By using the actual streets of Verona for settings, the film offers another example of the Italian flair for spectacle that was the hallmark of the industry. Indeed this Italian proclivity for making Renaissance Italy a setting for Shakespeare's language prefigures modern Italian movies of *Romeo and Juliet* such as the 1954 Castellani and the 1968 Zeffirelli versions. The Russian language title cards suggest that this copy had been recovered from exile abroad. The title cards of silent films could be spliced in and out at will to accommodate the nationality of the audience. *Contents & evaluation:* Of all the silent screen actresses who played Juliet, Francesca Bertini stands out not merely because she was an unusually attractive young lady but also because she seemed to grasp instinctively the elusive art of silent screen acting. Although capable of being radiant with her Romeo, in one sequence with Father Capulet and Paris, when she hears that she is to be married, she exudes a sullen, moody expression that would match the inchoate resentments of any modern teen-ager. To do so, she does not need to semaphore, writhe, or somersault about. With the same kind of gift for subtle facial expression that made D.W. Griffith's Gish sisters so successful, she conveys the nuances of her inner state of mind. True to the Italian operatic tradition, there is lavish spectacle: the Capulet ball, rousing sword fights, the funeral cortege for Juliet. Indeed the latter almost matches the opulence of the Zeffirelli *Romeo and Juliet* with the procession of knights, monks, lackeys, nuns, children strewing flowers, begowned ladies, idlers, and so forth. When Romeo spots Juliet on her bier, the effect is devastating. In a baroque tomb, Romeo and Juliet depart a bit from Shakespeare's narrative. Juliet awakens to find Romeo still alive, not yet dead but slowly dying. After he succumbs, Juliet stabs herself (KSR). *Audience:* General use; *Supplementary materials:* Ball, *SOSF* 125-7.

MEDIUM INFORMATION: *Medium:* Motion Picture; *Sound:* Silent; *Color:* No (black & white); *Length:* 25 min.; *Language of subtitles:* Russian; *Film type:* 16mm.

AUTHORSHIP INFORMATION: *Producer(s):* Film d'Arte Italiana; *Director(s):* Lo Savio, Gerolamo; *Cast:* Bertini, Francesca (Juliet); Serena, Gustavo (Romeo).

DISTRIBUTION & AVAILABILITY: *Publisher or responsible agency:* Film d'Arte Italiana; *Distributor:* JEF, *Copy location:* FOL; *Call or copy number:* MP 31; *Availability:* Apply JEF.

519. *Romeo and Juliet.*

DOCUMENT INFORMATION: *Country:* USA; *Year of release:* 1911.

EDITION, HISTORY, CONTENTS, & EVALUATION: *Edition & history:* One of a distinguished group of silent films produced by Edwin and Gertrude Thanhouser, who were genuine lovers of Shakespeare and sought to bring a higher standard to the production of Shakespeare on screen than previously had been the case. Unfortunately most of this film is lost but if the Thanhouser *King Lear* and the stills of this film that remain are any evidence, then it was probably at a fairly high level of competence. *Contents & evaluation:* Although only a fragment of the original film, this production obviously had many features of artistic merit for its time. The exterior shots are well lit and manage to convey richness and opulence, while the interior shots feature genuine paneling, not painted flats. Titles seem to have been held to a minimum. The film begins, however, virtually *in medias res* with this title: "Romeo breaks edict against dueling." Thanhouser has the same problem everyone else had in lighting the tomb scene (how to make the *mise en scène* dark when a camera lens needs light), which was not going to be solved for a number of years. The photography throughout is clear and sharp. It is a shame so much of this film has been lost to posterity. Old films, as is well known, were subject to all kinds of hazards, from deterioration in the can to warehouse fires to simple indifference (KSR). *Audience:* General use; *Supplementary materials:* Ball, *SOSF* 72-72.

MEDIUM INFORMATION: *Medium:* Motion Picture; *Sound:* Silent; *Length:* 27 min.; *Language of subtitles:* English; *Film type:* 16mm.

AUTHORSHIP INFORMATION: *Producer(s):* Thanhouser, Edwin; *Director(s):* O'Neil, Barry; *Adaptor/translator(s):* Thanhouser, Gertrude; Lonergan, Lloyd; *Cast:* Taylor, Julia M. (Juliet); Lessey, George A. (Romeo); Walton, George W. Mrs. (Nurse).

DISTRIBUTION & AVAILABILITY: *Publisher or responsible agency:* Thanhouser, Edwin; *Distributor:* JEF [?], *Copy location:* FOL; *Call or copy number:* MP 62.

Romeo and Juliet. Motion Picture/Adaptation

520. *Romeo and Juliet.*

DOCUMENT INFORMATION: *Country:* USA; *Year of release:* 1916.

EDITION, HISTORY, CONTENTS, & EVALUATION: *Edition & history:* It is sad that this ambitious Metro *Romeo and Juliet* starring the great Francis X. Bushman has been lost. In the same year Fox released a rival *Romeo and Juliet* starring Theda Bara, which has also been lost. Prior to 1950 films were made with a cellulose nitrate base, which self-destructed over time. In other instances, films were consumed by warehouse fires, or simply junked as rubbish. *Supplementary materials:* Ball, *SOSF* 235-9, 363-4; *SIF* 79; Eckert, *FSF* 175.

MEDIUM INFORMATION: *Length:* 80 min.

AUTHORSHIP INFORMATION: *Director(s):* Noble, John W.; *Cast:* Bushman, Francis X. (Romeo); Bayne, Beverly (Juliet).

DISTRIBUTION & AVAILABILITY: *Distributor:* Lost.

521. *Romeo and Juliet.*

DOCUMENT INFORMATION: *Country:* USA; *Year of release:* 1916.

EDITION, HISTORY, CONTENTS, & EVALUATION: *Edition & history:* The "rival" *Romeo* produced by Fox in the same year that Metro brought out its own version starring Francis X. Bushman. Both films are lost. *Supplementary materials:* Ball, *SOSF* 239-41, 364-5; *SIF*, 79; Eckert, *FSF* 175.

MEDIUM INFORMATION: *Length:* 50 min.

AUTHORSHIP INFORMATION: *Director(s):* Edwards, J. Gordon; *Cast:* Bara, Theda (Juliet); Hilliard, Harry (Romeo).

DISTRIBUTION & AVAILABILITY: *Distributor:* Lost.

Romeo and Juliet. Motion Picture/Excerpt

522. *Doubling for Romeo.*

DOCUMENT INFORMATION: *Country:* USA; *Year of release:* 1921.

EDITION, HISTORY, CONTENTS, & EVALUATION: *Edition & history:* Worth mentioning in this filmography because Will Rogers played Romeo in a burlesque balcony scene. Professor Ball describes the film as a "joyous charade." *Supplementary materials:* *SIF* 82; Ball, *SOSF* 267-8.

MEDIUM INFORMATION: *Length:* 50 min.

AUTHORSHIP INFORMATION: *Director(s):* Badger, Clarence; *Cast:* Rogers, Will; Breamer, Sylvia.

DISTRIBUTION & AVAILABILITY: *Copy location:* MMA.

523. *Triumph.*

DOCUMENT INFORMATION: *Country:* USA; *Year of release:* 1924.

EDITION, HISTORY, CONTENTS, & EVALUATION: *Edition & history:* Balcony scene appears in this film. From about 1917 to end of the silent era, there were many films with connections of varying strength to Shakespeare. Some such as this one contained only brief scenes, while others were travesties or burlesques, or simply borrowed only their titles. Since it is impossible to cover this vast subject adequately here, I refer the interested reader to R.H. Ball's book, especially Chapters VII and VIII. *Supplementary materials: SIF* 82; Ball, *SOSF* 270.

MEDIUM INFORMATION: *Length:* 80 min.; *Film type:* 35mm.

AUTHORSHIP INFORMATION: *Director(s):* DeMille, Cecil B.; *Cast:* La Rocque, Rod (Romeo); Joy, Leatrice (Juliet).

Romeo and Juliet. Motion Picture/Travesty

524. *Bromo and Juliet.*

DOCUMENT INFORMATION: *Country:* USA; *Year of release:* 1926.

EDITION, HISTORY, CONTENTS, & EVALUATION: *Edition & history:* In this travesty of *Romeo and Juliet,* a young lady attempts to put on an amateur performance of *Romeo and Juliet* with her reluctant boy friend as Romeo. It has little or nothing to do with Shakespeare's play in any other sense. The casting of Oliver Hardy as a chauffeur is interesting. Typical Hal Roach comedy style of the Twenties. *Contents & evaluation:* Harmless spoof with theatre shots of an actor playing Romeo under the influence. Heavy sight gags predominate such as Romeo traveling on a two tier bus with his hosiery stuffed with sponges to make his calves look bulkier (actually Elizabethan men did stuff their hosiery, usually with sawdust, though). Through a hole in the stockings, the water squirts out and leaks on to the head of a passenger seated one deck below. When the drenched man, apoplectic with rage, struggles up the stairs to locate the cause of his problem, he discovers "Romeo" holding an infant that had just been handed to him by another passenger. He comes to a logical but wrong conclusion about the cause of the flood. The light-hearted tone can be inferred from the following title card: "I'm gonna shake Shakespeare as he's never been shook." Those who prefer their

Shakespeare unshook should probably avoid *Bromo and Juliet. Audience:* General use.

MEDIUM INFORMATION: *Medium:* Motion Picture; *Sound:* Silent; *Color:* No (black & white); *Length:* 20 min.; *Language of subtitles:* English; *Film type:* 16mm.

AUTHORSHIP INFORMATION: *Producer(s):* Roach, Hal; *Director(s):* McCarey, Leo; *Cast:* Chase, Charley; Hardy, Oliver; Orlamond, William (Father); Palmer, Corliss (Girl).

DISTRIBUTION & AVAILABILITY: *Publisher or responsible agency:* USA Pathé; *Copy location:* FOL; *Call or copy number:* MP 104.

Romeo and Juliet. Motion Picture/Scene

525. *The Hollywood Revue.*

DOCUMENT INFORMATION: *Country:* US; *Year of first showing:* 1929.

EDITION, HISTORY, CONTENTS, & EVALUATION: *Edition & history:* Very much a variety show like Warner Brothers' *Show of Shows,* in this extravaganza there is a balcony scene from *Romeo and Juliet. Contents & evaluation:* Of historical interest because it represents the transition from silent to talking pictures. John Gilbert as Romeo is heard speaking. The legend then emerged that Gilbert's movie career was ruined because of an inadequate speaking voice. To my ears, his voice in this scene with Norma Shearer was not all that egregiously bad. Despite its being plunked down in the midst of vaudeville routines, the sequence generates some plausibility and even conviction. Those film historians who have said that Gilbert's demise occurred not because of an inadequate voice but because his style of romantic heroes went out of fashion are probably right. Lionel Barrymore poses as the director of this little vignette. Even though the whole enterprise looks suspiciously like another Hollywood guilt trip in which a smattering of edification amidst banalities is thought sufficient to bring culture to the masses, the performance is satisfying enough to make tracking the film down worthwhile (KSR). *Supplementary materials:* Parker, *TSF* 32.

MEDIUM INFORMATION: *Sound:* Spoken language; *Color:* Yes; *Length:* 113 min.; *Film type:* 35mm.

AUTHORSHIP INFORMATION: *Director(s):* Reisner, Charles; *Composer(s):* Lang, Arthur; *Choreographer(s):* Lee, Sammy; *Cast:* Gilbert, John (Romeo); Shearer, Norma (Juliet); Barrymore, Lionel (Director).

DISTRIBUTION & AVAILABILITY: *Publisher or responsible agency:* Metro-Goldwyn-Mayer; *Copy location:* NFA*.

Romeo and Juliet. **Motion Picture/Interpretation**

526. *Romeo and Juliet.*

DOCUMENT INFORMATION: *Country:* USA; *Year of release:* 1936.

EDITION, HISTORY, CONTENTS, & EVALUATION: *Edition & history:* Despite the care and attention that went into its production, this film has never been highly regarded. At enormous expense an entire replica, based on first-hand photographs, of an Italian Renaissance city was constructed on a Hollywood back lot. No expense was spared to achieve historical accuracy. Professor Strunk was brought from Cornell University to insure academic respectability and the greatest stars of the day were cast in major roles: Norma Shearer as Juliet, Leslie Howard as Romeo, John Barrymore as Mercutio, Basil Rathbone as Tybalt, and so forth. The Capulet ballroom scene rivalled a Busby Berkeley musical extravaganza. Yet for all these good intentions, the film did poorly both at the box office and at the hands of critics. The leading players, it was said, were too old for the teenage lovers, and yet decades later Zeffirelli would be denounced for having cast actors who were too inexperienced for the roles. I believe the film should be cherished as a masterwork from antiquity: a bit archaic, a little rigid, slightly overdone, but, yes, still withal warm and good (KSR). *Contents & evaluation:* "In the avowed effort to make the production what Shakespeare would have wanted had he possessed the facilities of cinema, it apparently occurred to no one that, could he really have gone to Hollywood to work on the script, Shakespeare would simply have thrown away *Romeo and Juliet* and written a new play, as was his inflexible habit with the classics of his own day. Instead, Professor Strunk and Adapter Talbot Jennings . . . scrupulously arranged a script without a line of dialog not written by the Bard" ("Review," *Time* 24 Aug. 1936: 30-32). "Mr. Howard, at this time, had reached the peak of his powers. He was old enough to understand Romeo, and the camera made him look young enough to play him. Miss Shearer, on the other hand, had somewhat dropped from her zenith. She gives the impression of being no longer young enough to remember how Juliet must have felt, and a little too old to be able to simulate (even with the camera's help) what she must have looked like. For me (Mr. Howard's Romeo apart), the picture is chiefly memorable for the best Mercutio and the best Tybalt I ever saw. Tybalt is played by Mr. Basil Rathbone with a white-hot, whipping elegance of diction that matches his sword-play in the duel scene; Mercutio, by Mr. John Barrymore in what we may call 'old-style' Shakespearean fashion at its finest and most enthusiastic. 'Ham' possibly—but how exquisitely cured!" (Dehn, Paul, *Talking of Shakespeare,* ed. John Garrett [London: Hodder & Stoughton, 1954]: 59). *Audience:* High school (grades 10-12); College and university; General use; *Supplementary materials:* Romeo and Juliet *by William Shakespeare,* ed. William Strunk *et al.* New York: Random House, 1936.

MEDIUM INFORMATION: *Medium:* Motion picture; *Sound:* Spoken language; *Color:* No (black & white); *Length:* 126 min.; *Language(s) spoken:* English; *Film type:* 16 mm; *Video type:* V,B.

AUTHORSHIP INFORMATION: *Producer(s):* Thalberg, Irving; *Director(s):* Cukor, George; *Screenplay writer(s):* Jennings, Talbot; *Composer(s):* Stothart, Herbert; *Choreographer(s):* de Mille, Agnes; *Designer(s):* Gibbons, Cedric; *Set designer(s):* Messel, Oliver; *Costume designer(s):* Messel, Oliver; Messel, Adrian; *Other personnel:* Daniels, William (Camera); Booth, Margaret (Editor); Strunk, William (Literary consultant); *Cast:* Howard, Leslie (Romeo); Shearer, Norma (Juliet); Tearle, Conway (Escalus); Barrymore, John (Mercutio); Forbes, Ralph (Paris); Kolker, Henry (Friar Laurence); Warwick, Robert (Montague); Hammond, Virginia (Lady Montague); Denny, Reginald (Benvolio); Smith, C. Aubrey (Lord Capulet); Cooper, Violet (Lady Capulet); Rathbone, Basil (Tybalt); Oliver, Edna (Nurse); Devine, Andy (Peter).

DISTRIBUTION & AVAILABILITY: *Publisher or responsible agency:* MGM; *Distributor:* FNC, DCV, BLK, *Copy location:* FOL; *Call or copy number:* MP 38; *Availability:* FNC, 16mm, $175 vs. 50%, rental; DCV, V (#36126), sale (apply); BLK, V, $49.95, sale; FCM, V, sale, $19.95 (1988).

Romeo and Juliet. **Video/Scenes**

527. *Romeo and Juliet.* (Series: Scenes from Shakespeare).

DOCUMENT INFORMATION: *Country:* GB; *Year of first showing:* 1937; *Location of first showing:* BBC. Transmitted 3:44 to 4:10 P.M., 16 Aug. 1937.

EDITION, HISTORY, CONTENTS, & EVALUATION: *Edition & history:* One of the very earliest transmissions of Shakespeare on television when the industry was still in its infancy. *Supplementary materials:* TPAB 16 Aug. 1937.

MEDIUM INFORMATION: *Length:* 26 min.

AUTHORSHIP INFORMATION: *Producer(s):* Morley, Royston; *Cast:* Forbes-Robertson, Jean (Juliet); Redgrave, Michael (Romeo); Wyse, John (Friar Laurence); Francelli, Mario (Balthasar).

DISTRIBUTION & AVAILABILITY: *Publisher or responsible agency:* BBC; *Copy location:* Unavailable.

Romeo and Juliet. Motion Picture

528. *Julieta Y Romeo.*

DOCUMENT INFORMATION: *Country:* Spain; *Year of release:* 1940.

EDITION, HISTORY, CONTENTS, & EVALUATION: *Edition & history:* Spanish language version of *Romeo and Juliet* made in 1940, about which little is known. *Audience:* General use; *Supplementary materials:* Credits, SIF 80.

MEDIUM INFORMATION: *Medium:* Motion Picture; *Sound:* Spoken language; *Color:* No (black & white); *Length:* 93 min.; *Language(s) spoken:* English; *Film type:* 35mm.

AUTHORSHIP INFORMATION: *Producer(s):* Cinedia; *Director(s):* Castellvi, Jose Marie; *Screenplay writer(s):* Castellvi, Jose Marie; Pemán, Jose Maria; *Lighting designer(s):* Izzarelli, Francesco; *Cast:* Flores, Marta; Guitart, Enrique; Medina, Candelaria; Hernandez, Francisco; Idel, Teresa.

DISTRIBUTION & AVAILABILITY: *Publisher or responsible agency:* Cinedia.

Romeo and Juliet. Motion Picture/Cartoon

529. *Shakespearean Spinach.*

DOCUMENT INFORMATION: *Country:* USA; *Year of release:* 1940.

EDITION, HISTORY, CONTENTS, & EVALUATION: *Edition & history:* Popeye the Sailor cartoon taking off from Shakespeare's play. *Supplementary materials:* Loughney, Katharine. "Shakespeare on Film and Tape at Library of Congress." *SFNL* 14.1 (Dec. 1989): 6.

MEDIUM INFORMATION: *Length:* 7 min.

AUTHORSHIP INFORMATION: *Director(s):* Fleischer, Dave.

DISTRIBUTION & AVAILABILITY: *Copy location:* LCM; *Call or copy number:* FEB 7280.

Romeo and Juliet. Motion Picture/Derivative

530. *Shuhaddaa el gharam.*

DOCUMENT INFORMATION: *Country:* Egypt; *Year of release:* 1942.

EDITION, HISTORY, CONTENTS, & EVALUATION: Egyptian language film. *Supplementary materials:* Morris, *SHOF* 10; H&M, 32.

MEDIUM INFORMATION: *Length:* 90 min.

AUTHORSHIP INFORMATION: *Director(s):* Selim, Kamal; *Cast:* Mourad, Leila; Hamouda, Ibrahim.

531. *Romeo y Julieta.*

DOCUMENT INFORMATION: *Country:* Mexico; *Year of release:* 1943.

EDITION, HISTORY, CONTENTS, & EVALUATION: *Edition & history:* A burlesque of *Romeo and Juliet* starring the great Mexican actor, Cantinflas (Mario Moreno Reyes), best known for his role as Passepartout in Mike Todd's *Around the World in Eighty Days* (1960). *Contents & evaluation:* The reviews suggest that the screen story featured a plot within a plot. A taxi driver (Cantinflas) is persuaded by a drunken fare to play Romeo in a production. His burlesque performance as the great lover emerges in a series of flashbacks as he tries to explain in court how he came to be brought there for disturbing the peace. Episodes inspired by Shakespeare's play include a street brawl modeled along that of the Capulets and Montagues and a comic duel with Tybalt. Apparently the hilarity peaks when Cantinflas' girl friend beholds him putting his arms around the dead Juliet in the tomb scene. She indignantly charges up on stage to put things right. *Audience:* General use; *Supplementary materials:* Masters, Dorothy, "Review," *NYDN* 17 June 1944 [Clippings file, LCL]; Parsons, Louella, "In Hollywood," *NYJA* 15 Oct. 1944 [Clippings file, LCL].

MEDIUM INFORMATION: *Medium:* Motion Picture; *Sound:* Spoken language; *Color:* Yes; *Length:* 110 min. [?]; *Language(s) spoken:* English; *Film type:* 35mm.

AUTHORSHIP INFORMATION: *Producer(s):* Delgado, Miguel; *Director(s):* Delgado, Miguel; *Screenplay writer(s):* Salvador, Jaime; *Composer(s):* Esperon, Manuel; *Designer(s):* Alvarez, Fernando Martinez; *Lighting designer(s):* Draper, Jack; *Other personnel:* Randall, Howard; Esparza, Rafael (Sound); *Cast:* Cantinflas [Mario Moreno Reyes] (Romeo); Marques, Maria Elena (Juliet); Soler, Andres (Capulet); Garasa, Angel (Brother Lorenzo); Roldán, Ema (Lady Capulet); Baviera, Jose (Paris); Barret, Carolina (Luchita); Junco, Tito (Theobald); Zarate, Ortiz de (Duke).

DISTRIBUTION & AVAILABILITY: *Publisher or responsible agency:* Aztec/Posa Films; *Copy location:* Not known.

Romeo and Juliet. Video/Teleplay

532. *Romeo and Juliet.*

DOCUMENT INFORMATION: *Country:* GB; *Year of first showing:* 1947; *Location of first showing:* BBC. Transmitted 8:30 to 10:30 P.M., Sunday, 5 Oct. 1947.

EDITION, HISTORY, CONTENTS, & EVALUATION: *Edition & history:* The scant internal correspondence surrounding this production makes it sound as though the program was not an unqualified success. There were complaints about that bane of live television drama, the dreaded "boom shadow" from the intruding microphones on the sound stage. There were also scheduling difficulties (WAC 5 Oct. 1947) *Supplementary materials:* "Program." *RT* 5 Oct. 1947: n.p.

MEDIUM INFORMATION: *Length:* 120 min.

AUTHORSHIP INFORMATION: *Producer(s):* Barry, Michael; *Composer(s):* Hartley, James; *Designer(s):* Bundy, Stephen; *Cast:* Osborn, Andrew (Chorus); Maitland, Marne; Rudling, John (Servants); Platt, Victor (Abraham); Firth, Kenneth (Balthasar); Gatrell, John (Benvolio); Goodliffe, Michael (Tybalt); Byrne, Stafford (Montague); Belfrage, Bruce (Capulet); Young, Marguerite (Lady Montague); Venning, Una (Lady Capulet); Sansom, Robert (Escalus); Bailey, John (Romeo); Dawson, Basil (Paris); Ottoway, James (Peter); Crutchley, Rosalie (Juliet); Lauchlan, Agnes (Nurse); Van Gyseghem, Andre (Mercutio); Boiteaux, Jacqueline (Page); Rudling, John (Old Man); Howe, George (Friar Laurence); Platt, Victor (Apothecary); Rudling, John (Friar John); Hope, Margaret; Arden, Jane; Forrest, Norma; Rodney, Jack; Hurn, Douglas; Raggett, John; Laurent, John; Bacon, Anthony; Hillyard, Eric (Citizens of Verona, Kinfolk, Maskers, Guards, Pages and Attendants).

DISTRIBUTION & AVAILABILITY: *Publisher or responsible agency:* BBC; *Copy location:* Unavailable.

Romeo and Juliet. Motion Picture/Derivative

533. *Anjuman.*

DOCUMENT INFORMATION: *Country:* India; *Year of release:* 1948.

EDITION, HISTORY, CONTENTS, & EVALUATION: *Edition & history:* A Hindi language film with debts to Shakespeare's play. *Supplementary materials:* Morris, *SHOF* 13; *SIF* 80.

MEDIUM INFORMATION: *Length:* 140 min.

AUTHORSHIP INFORMATION: *Director(s):* Hussain, Akhtar; *Cast:* Nargis (Juliet); Jaraj (Romeo).

534. *Les amants de Verone.* [*The Lovers of Verona*].

DOCUMENT INFORMATION: *Country:* France; *Year of release:* 1949.

EDITION, HISTORY, CONTENTS, & EVALUATION: *Edition & history:* This film was made in the Paris-Studios-Cinema at Brillancourt and in the glass factory of Pauly & Co., Venice, Italy. *Contents & evaluation:* Another film-within-a-film, like Chabrol's *Ophelia*, this modernized version of *Romeo and Juliet* also is reminiscent of *West Side Story* and the 1982 Brazilian *Romeo and Juliet*. The story begins in a Venetian glass factory where some members of a film company about to make *Romeo and Juliet* visit the premises. Angelo, a handsome young glassblower, makes a heart-shaped piece of glass for the voluptuous actress, Bettina. A foreshadowing mirror shot puts Bettina and Angelo in the same glass. The director explains to a friend, Maglia, that he will film only interior shots in Venice; the rest of the film will be made in Verona on location. "Poor Shakespeare," says Maglia. Increasingly then the film becomes self-referential in a concern with movie making and with the aesthetics of Shakespeare adaptation. On the movie set the sissy actor hired to play Romeo is too "giddy" to climb the balcony. Angelo, hired as an extra, is pulled out of the ranks to stand in for Romeo, while the stand-in for Juliet is Georgia Maglia, a daughter of the proud and haughty Maglia family, who disdain simple glassblowers. From then on the plot thickens and curdles as it is revealed that Maglia is an ex-fascist judge with underworld connections, and in a wild shootout, Angelo is fatally wounded. The lovers act out their tomb scene then on the movie set, while Shakespeare's lines are spoken in voiceover and a stagehand closes the door to leave the tomb in darkness. A dark, *film noir*, movie in black and white, *Les amants* offers a brooding, atmospheric montage of Venice and Verona. This is Romeo and Juliet displaced to a movie set, as though their myth could only be inscribed in the celluloid epic of film. There are splendid closeups—one thinks of Carl Dreyer's *Passion of Joan of Arc*—as well as an interesting commentary on "decay" in an ancient European city that corrupts youthful love and innocence (KSR). *Audience:* General use; *Supplementary materials: Les amants de Verone. Un filme d'André Cayatte. Scenario original d'André Cayatte. Adaptation et dialogues de Jacques Prevert.*[*Classiques du Cinema Francais*]. Paris: La Nouvelle Edition, 1949.

MEDIUM INFORMATION: *Medium:* Motion picture; *Sound:* Spoken language; *Color:* No (black & white); *Length:* 110 min.; *Language(s) spoken:* French; *Language of subtitles*: English; *Film type:* 16mm.

AUTHORSHIP INFORMATION: *Producer(s):* Raymond-Borderie Production; *Director(s):* Cayatte, Andre; Léand, Pierre; *Screenplay writer(s):* Cayatte, Andre; *Adaptor/translator(s):* Prévert, Jacques; *Composer(s):* Kosma, Joseph; *Designer(s):* Moulaert, Rene; Schmitt, Henri; Demangeat, Camille; Petit, Rene; *Costume designer(s):* Delamare, Rosine; Dean, Paul (Makeup); *Lighting designer(s):* Alekan, Henri; *Other personnel:* Tiquet, Henri (Cameraman); Borderie, Charles (Adm. super.); Michaud, Andre (Unit manager); Volper, Albert (Properties); Latouzet, R.; Menvielle, R. (Camera assts.); Pease, Mildred (Continuity); Capelier, Margot (Prod. sec.); Seitz, Guy (Technical advisor); Gaudin, Christian (Editor); Stengel, Christiane (Asst. Ed.); Clerc, Jean (Prod. Manager); Canel, Leon (Prod. asst.); *Cast:* Brasseur, Pierre (Raffaele); Dalio, Marcel (Amedeo Maglia); Reggiani, Serge (Angelo); Salou, Louis (Ettore Maglia); Carol, Martine (Bettina Verdi); Armontel (Bianchini); de Champs, Charles (Sandrini); Genin,

René (The Keeper); Aimée, Anouk (Georgia Maglia); Denaud, Yves (Ricardo); Oswald, Marianne (Laetitia); Sicard, Solange (Luccia Maglia); Carter, Claudye (Clio); w. Peres, Marcel; Favieres, Guy; Dalbau, Max; Le Maire, Philippe; Nicot, Claude.

DISTRIBUTION & AVAILABILITY: *Publisher or responsible agency:* Films de France, Ltd.; *Copy location:* NFA*.

Romeo and Juliet. **Video/Abbreviated**

535. *Romeo and Juliet.*

DOCUMENT INFORMATION: *Country:* USA; *Year of first showing:* 1949; *Location of first showing:* Philco Arena Theatre, NBC/TV. Transmitted 9 to 10:00 P.M. 15 May 1949.

EDITION, HISTORY, CONTENTS, & EVALUATION: *Edition & history:* There was a stir of excitement in the advance publicity over the fact that the play was to be televised in an "arena theater" setting. The plan was to have four cameras, two looking down and two at eye level, with the possibility of switching to a back view. *Contents & evaluation:* Unhappily the critic did not think that the arena theatre arrangement had indeed solved all the problems of televising drama. The production was declared to be "static," the camera too prone to look at the "backs of the actors," and the costumes "too ornate" for television. Only Kevin McCarthy as Romeo escaped the impression of being an actor "at loose ends" (Gould, Jack, "Review," *NYT* 22 May 1949: X 9). *Supplementary materials:* Lohmann, Sidney. "*Rom.* with Arena Theater Techniques." *NYT* 15 May 1949: X 9.

MEDIUM INFORMATION: *Length:* 60 min.

AUTHORSHIP INFORMATION: *Producer(s):* Wade, Warren; *Designer(s):* McCleery, Albert; *Cast:* McCarthy, Kevin (Romeo); Breslin, Patricia (Juliet); Evers, Herbert (Paris); Bolger, Bob (Montague); Post, William (Capulet); Gerringer, Robert (Mercutio); Andrews, Todd (Benvolio).

DISTRIBUTION & AVAILABILITY: *Publisher or responsible agency:* Philco Theatre/NBC; *Copy location:* Not known.

Romeo and Juliet. **Motion Picture/Documentary**

536. *Romeo Land.*

DOCUMENT INFORMATION: *Country:* USA; *Year of release:* 1951.

EDITION, HISTORY, CONTENTS, & EVALUATION: *Edition & history:* A brief tour of the Italian "sites" for *Romeo and Juliet. Supplementary materials:* Loughney,

Katharine. "Shakespeare on Film and Tape at Library of Congress." *SFNL* 14.1 (Dec. 1989): 6.

MEDIUM INFORMATION: *Length:* 7 min.

AUTHORSHIP INFORMATION: *Director(s):* Wright, Hamilton, Jr.

DISTRIBUTION & AVAILABILITY: *Copy location:* LCM; *Call or copy number:* FEA 1716.

Romeo and Juliet. **Video/Scenes**

537. *Romeo and Juliet.*

DOCUMENT INFORMATION: *Country:* USA; *Year of first showing:* 1951; *Location of first showing:* Showtime USA. Transmitted 7:30 P.M. to 8:00 P.M., 8 April 1951.

EDITION, HISTORY, CONTENTS, & EVALUATION: *Edition & history:* A glimpse of Olivia De Havilland as Juliet, a role she performed on the Broadway stage when she was in her thirties. *Supplementary materials:* "Leading Events." *NYT* 8 April 1951: X 10.

MEDIUM INFORMATION: *Length:* 30 min.; *Video type:* V.

AUTHORSHIP INFORMATION: *Cast:* De Havilland, Olivia; Sarnoff, Dorothy.

DISTRIBUTION & AVAILABILITY: *Publisher or responsible agency:* Showtime USA.

Romeo and Juliet. **Motion Picture/Interpretation**

538. *Giulietta e Romeo.* [*Romeo and Juliet*].

DOCUMENT INFORMATION: *Country:* GB/Italy; *Year of release:* 1954.

EDITION, HISTORY, CONTENTS, & EVALUATION: *Awards:* Venice Film Festival, 1954; *Edition & history:* An innovative movie that dazzled moviegoers of the fifties by using a hilltop town in northern Italy as an authentic backdrop. There were the inevitable outcries against its cavalier use or misuse of Shakespeare's text. And unfortunately the principal actors, Laurence Harvey and Susan Shentall, came through as more wooden than passionate. Yet the film paved the way for the later more successful 1968 *Romeo and Juliet* of Franco Zeffirelli. *Contents & evaluation:* "Obviously, Director Castellani was not interested in putting on the screen a routine transcript of the Shakespearean drama, cramped with the usual fidelity to scenes and lines. He set out to make a motion picture of a murderous and meaningless feud between two proud and powerful families in fifteenth-century Italy. . . . The lyrical language of Shakespeare, generally spoken by mature performers on the stage, was plainly secondary to his concept of a vivid visual build-up of his theme. His notion quite clearly was a film drama in the violent, smashing, uncompromising style of the Italian neo-realist school. . . . And so the most striking feature of this beautiful Anglo-Italian film . . . is the dramatic realism and sensuousness of its Renaissance *mise-en-scène* and the headlong impulsiveness and passion with which it is artfully played" (Crowther, Bosley, "Review," *NYT* 22 Dec. 1954: 28). The ideal film of *Romeo and Juliet* would combine the splendid photography of this one, the acting of the 1936 Cukor version, and the passion of the Zeffirelli movie (KSR). *Audience:* High school (grades 10-12); College and university.

MEDIUM INFORMATION: *Medium:* Motion Picture; *Sound:* Spoken language; *Color:* Yes; *Length:* 138 min.; *Language(s) spoken:* English; *Film type:* 16mm; *Video type:* B, V.

AUTHORSHIP INFORMATION: *Producer(s):* Ghenzi, Sandro; Janni, Joseph; *Director(s):* Castellani, Renato; *Composer(s):* Vlad, Roman; *Costume designer(s):* Fini, Leonor; *Cast:* Harvey, Laurence (Romeo); Shentall, Susan (Juliet); Robson, Flora (Nurse); Johns, Mervyn (Friar Laurence); Wooland, Norman (Paris); Travers, Bill (Benvolio); Fiermonte, Enzo (Tybalt); Zollo, Aldo (Mercutio); Rota, Giovanni (Prince of Verona); Cabot, Sebastian (Capulet); Sherwood, Lydia (Lady Capulet); Garbinetti, Guilio (Montague); Zocchi, Nietta (Lady Montague); Josipovich, Dagmar (Rosaline); Bodi, Luciano (Abraham); Nicholls, Thomas (Friar John); Gielgud, John (Chorus).

DISTRIBUTION & AVAILABILITY: *Publisher or responsible agency:* Verona Productions; *Distributor:* FNC, TWC, DCV, TAM, FFH, FMB* , *Copy location:* LCM; *Availability:* FNC, rental, 16mm; TWC, V (SV260V-K4), B (SV260B-K4), $69.95; TAM, B,V $59; FFH (1235F), B. V, $249, 3/4U $349, rental, $75; FMB*, rental, 16mm (*BUFVC* 22); DCV, V (#54138), sale, apply.

Romeo and Juliet. Video/Ballet

539. *Romeo and Juliet.*

DOCUMENT INFORMATION: *Country:* USSR; *Year of release:* 1954.

EDITION, HISTORY, CONTENTS, & EVALUATION: *Edition & history:* A videotaping of a performance of the Bolshoi Ballet. *Supplementary materials:* Novacom Video Inc. catalog.

MEDIUM INFORMATION: *Length:* 95 min.

AUTHORSHIP INFORMATION: *Cast:* Ulanova, Galina.

DISTRIBUTION & AVAILABILITY: *Distributor:* NOV, FCM, *Availability:* NOV, B, V $63; FCM, V, $64.95.

Romeo and Juliet. Video/Abridgment

540. *Romeo and Juliet.*

DOCUMENT INFORMATION: *Country:* USA; *Year of first showing:* 1954; *Location of first showing:* Kraft Television Theater. Transmitted 9 to 10:00 P.M., 9 June 1954.

EDITION, HISTORY, CONTENTS, & EVALUATION: *Edition & history:* A sixteen-year-old Susan Strasberg starred in this vehicle, which was a scaled down version of Shakespeare's play. *Supplementary materials:* "Program." *NYT* 9 June 1954: 45; Gianokos, *TDSP* 185.

MEDIUM INFORMATION: *Color:* No (black & white); *Length:* 60 min.

AUTHORSHIP INFORMATION: *Cast:* Strasberg, Susan (Juliet); Sullivan, Liam; McComas, Carroll; Leslie, Noel; Deebank, Felix.

DISTRIBUTION & AVAILABILITY: *Publisher or responsible agency:* Kraft TV Theater.

Romeo and Juliet. Video/Teledrama

541. *Romeo and Juliet.*

ORIGINAL WORK AND PRODUCTION: *Site of first production:* BBC TV.

DOCUMENT INFORMATION: *Country:* GB; *Year of first showing:* 1955; *Location of first showing:* BBC TV. Transmitted 8:30 to 10:45 P.M., Sunday, 22 May 1955.

EDITION, HISTORY, CONTENTS, & EVALUATION: *Edition & history:* The London *Times* critic thought that this production definitely showed that a Shakespearean play could be put on television after all. In fact, he wrote, "the limitations of television" may "actually [be] turned to advantage." Apparently there was considerable camera work, with a very realistic vault for the tomb scene and a peering camera that moved in on Juliet's bedchamber. In what was then a rather lavish expenditure of resources, the BBC invested some £3,334 and included 59 actors in the cast (CHM). *Contents & evaluation:* Virginia McKenna as Juliet received praise for her "range of subtle expressions perfectly suited to television acting." Tony Britton's Romeo, Flora Robson's Nurse and Harcourt Williams' Friar all got high grades. The reviewer thought that Laurence Payne's Mercutio was "too broadly comical" but that all the rest were "in character" ("Shakespeare on Television," *Times* 23 May 1955: 3e). *Audience:* General use; *Supplementary materials:* "Two Lovers of Verona." *RT* 20 May 1955: 15.

MEDIUM INFORMATION: *Medium:* Video; *Sound:* Spoken language; *Color:* No (black & white); *Length:* 120 [?] min.; *Language(s) spoken:* English; *Video type:* Video.

AUTHORSHIP INFORMATION: *Producer(s):* Clayton,

Harold; *Director(s):* Bower, Dallas; *Cast:* Phillips, John (Chorus and Prince of Verona); Lander, Eric (Benvolio); Wordsworth, Richard (Tybalt); Horne, David (Capulet); Esmond, Jill (Lady Capulet); Raglan, James (Montague); Hood, Noel (Lady Montague); Britton, Tony (Romeo); Holder, Owen (Paris); Robson, Flora (Nurse); McKenna, Virginia (Juliet); Payne, Laurence (Mercutio); Williams, Harcourt (Friar Laurence); Frith, J. Leslie (Apothecary); Douglas, Colin (Sampson); Moorehead, Brian (Gregory); Gage, Roger (Abraham); Davies, Henry (Balthasar); Henchie, Peter (Officer); Phillips, John (Escalus); Scroggins, Robert (Page); Brennan, Michael (Peter); Garth, David (Friar John); and 26 extras.

DISTRIBUTION & AVAILABILITY: *Publisher or responsible agency:* BBC; *Copy location:* BBC*.

Romeo and Juliet. Motion Picture/Derivative

542. *Romeo, Julie a tma.* [*Romeo, Juliet and Darkness; Sweet Light in a Dark Room* (USA)].

DOCUMENT INFORMATION: *Country:* Czechoslovakia; *Year of release:* 1959.

EDITION, HISTORY, CONTENTS, & EVALUATION: *Edition & history:* Shown at 5th Stratford (Ont.) Shakespeare Festival; San Francisco 4th International Film Festival, 1960. *Contents & evaluation:* Review unavailable. *Audience:* General use; *Supplementary materials:* SIF 84.

MEDIUM INFORMATION: *Medium:* Motion Picture; *Sound:* Spoken language; *Length:* 93 min.; *Language(s) spoken:* Czech; *Film type:* 35mm.

AUTHORSHIP INFORMATION: *Producer(s):* Weiss, Jiři; *Director(s):* Weiss, Jiři; *Screenplay writer(s):* Weiss, Jiři; Otcenasek, Jan; *Composer(s):* Srnka, Jiři; *Designer(s):* Škvor, Karel; *Costume designer(s):* Hajek, Miloslav; *Lighting designer(s):* Hanuš, Vaclav; *Other personnel:* Polednik, Emil (Sound); *Cast:* Mistrik, Ivan (Pavel); Smutná, Daniela (Hanka); Šejbalová, Jiřina (Pavel's mother); Smolik, František (Pavel's grandfather); Bohdanová, Blanka (Kubiasova); Mrázova, Eva (Alena); Svoboda, Dr. Miroslav (Wurm).

DISTRIBUTION & AVAILABILITY: *Publisher or responsible agency:* Staatsfilm Studio Barrandov.

543. *Romanoff and Juliet.*

DOCUMENT INFORMATION: *Country:* USA; *Year of release:* 1961.

EDITION, HISTORY, CONTENTS, & EVALUATION: *Edition & history:* A loose adaptation of *Romeo and Juliet* that puts the ancient tale of the Capulet-Montague feud in the context of recent Cold War politics. Originally a 1957 Broadway stage play. Location shots filmed in Italy. *Contents & evaluation:* Romanoff falls in love with the daughter of the U.S. ambassador to Concordia, a country so obscure even the UN has difficulty in locating it. Juliet's ex-boy friend from the States becomes a Paris figure, favored by her parents, who are of course surrogates for the Capulets. Tybalt emerges as a sinister KGB agent. The President of Concordia in mediating between the factions corresponds to Prince Escalus. Unlike Shakespeare's tragedy, however, all ends happily with the wedding of Lt. and Mrs. Igor Romanoff. The optimistic film shows the power of young love to triumph over an older generation. The surface lightness of the film, however, only conceals an inner satire on the tragic ways of great powers in conducting their foreign relations. Peter Ustinov's brilliant performance accounts for much of the film's charm (KSR). *Audience:* General use.

MEDIUM INFORMATION: *Medium:* Motion Picture; *Sound:* Spoken language; *Color:* Yes; *Length:* 112 min.; *Language(s) spoken:* English; *Film type:* 16mm Technicolor.

AUTHORSHIP INFORMATION: *Producer(s):* Ustinov, Peter; *Director(s):* Ustinov, Peter; *Screenplay writer(s):* Ustinov, Peter; *Composer(s):* Naicimbene, Mario; *Designer(s):* Trauner, Alexander; *Other personnel:* Krasker, Robert (Photography); Lucidi, Renzo (Editor); Fisher, Sash (Sound); *Cast:* Ustinov, Peter (The General); Dee, Sandra (Juliet Moulsworth); Gavin, John (Igor Romanoff); Tamiroff, Akim (Vadim Romanoff); Talton, Alix (Beulah Moulsworth); Von Nutter, Rik (Freddie van der Stuyt); Phillips, John (Hooper Moulsworth); Jones, Peter (Otto); Shayne, Tamara (Evdokia Romanoff); Cloutier, Suzanne (Maria Zlotochienko); Atienza, Edward (Patriarch); Alderton, John (Randle Wix); Chalmers, Thomas (Chief Executive); Don, Carl (Spy); Selwart, Tonio (President); Chiantoni, Renato (Joseph); Colman, Booth (Customs man); Budberg, Moura (Cook); Maffei, Ginpaolo; Brown, Strelsa (Credits: Folger Filmography).

DISTRIBUTION & AVAILABILITY: *Publisher or responsible agency:* Pavor, S.A. and Universal/International; *Distributor:* SWA, *Copy location:* FOL; *Call or copy number:* MP 4.

Romeo and Juliet. Motion Picture/Musical

544. *West Side Story.*

DOCUMENT INFORMATION: *Country:* USA; *Year of first showing:* 1961.

EDITION, HISTORY, CONTENTS, & EVALUATION: *Awards:* Academy award, 1961; *Edition & history:* Award winning musical adaptation of *Romeo and Juliet* in which the tale of the two lovers in Renaissance Verona has been made over into a tale of feuding street gangs in New York City. The film is now available on videocassette but, according to Scott Simmon of the Library of Congress, the spectacular choreography is considerably diminished on the television screen. *Contents & evaluation:* This motion picture version of one of the great Broadway musicals of all times was in general warmly received by the critics. The Capulets and Montagues are replaced by warring street gangs in a New York City slum neighborhood, while Maria and Tony correspond to Juliet and Romeo. The choreography by Jerome Robbins is spectacular and the musical score, memorable. So powerful was the musical that when Franco Zeffirelli made his filmed *Romeo and Juliet* he seemed to be almost as much influenced by *West Side Story* as by Shakespeare's play. *Audience:* General use; *Supplementary materials:* "Whit." "Smash Picturization." *VAR* 27 Sept. 1961.

MEDIUM INFORMATION: *Medium:* Motion picture; *Sound:* Spoken language; *Color:* Yes; *Length:* 155 min.; *Language(s) spoken:* English; *Film type:* 35mm; *Video type:* V.

AUTHORSHIP INFORMATION: *Producer(s):* Wise, Robert; *Director(s):* Wise, Robert; Robbins, Jerome; *Screenplay writer(s):* Lehman, Ernest (from play by Arthur Laurents); *Composer(s):* Bernstein, Leonard; Sondheim, Stephen (Lyrics); Green, Johnny (Conductor); Chaplin, Saul; Ramin, Sid; Kostal, Irwin; *Choreographer(s):* Robbins, Jerome; *Designer(s):* Leven, Boris; Gangelini, Victor; *Costume designer(s):* Sharaff, Irene; *Lighting designer(s):* Fapp, Daniel; *Other personnel:* Stanford, Thomas (Editor); *Cast:* Wood, Natalie (Maria); Beymer, Richard (Tony); Moreno, Rita (Anita); Tamblyn, Russ (Riff); Chakiris, George (Bernardo); Oakland, Simon (Lt. Shrank); Bramley, William (Officer Krupke); Glass, Ned (Doc).

DISTRIBUTION & AVAILABILITY: *Publisher or responsible agency:* United Artists; *Distributor:* TWC, CBF, FMB*, FCM, *Availability:* TWC, B (SV-165B-K4), $92.50; V (SV165V-K4), $92.50; FMB*, 16mm; FCM, V, $29.98.

Romeo and Juliet. Motion Picture/Derivative

545. *Los tarantos.*

DOCUMENT INFORMATION: *Country:* Spain; *Year of release:* 1963.

EDITION, HISTORY, CONTENTS, & EVALUATION: *Edition & history:* A dance/musical adaptation of *Romeo and Juliet* transferred to an impoverished quarter of Barcelona. Haunting guitar music and stacatto flamenco dancing re-appropriate the timeless story of the two young lovers into a torrid love affair in contemporary Spain. (Audio Brandon Films Catalog, 1976). *Contents & evaluation:* Not seen but from all accounts it sounds very much like a Spanish *West Side Story.* *Supplementary materials:* Parker, *FSF* 44.

MEDIUM INFORMATION: *Sound:* Spoken language; *Color:* Yes; *Length:* 81; *Language(s) spoken:* Spanish; *Language of subtitles:* English; *Film type:* 16mm.

AUTHORSHIP INFORMATION: *Director(s):* Rovira-Beleta; *Screenplay writer(s):* Manas, Alfredo; Rovira-Beleta; *Composer(s):* Pujol, Emilio; Morcillo, Fernando Garcia; *Designer(s):* Soler, Juan Alberto; *Lighting designer(s):* Dallamano, Massimo; *Cast:* Amaya, Carmen; Lezana, Sara; Martin, Daniel; Gades, Antonio; Carmen Amaya Company (Flamenco Dancers).

DISTRIBUTION & AVAILABILITY: *Distributor:* FNC, *Availability:* Apply.

Romeo and Juliet. Documentary/Abridgment

546. *Romeo and Juliet.* (Series: Fair Adventure Series).

DOCUMENT INFORMATION: *Country:* USA; *Year of release:* 1964.

EDITION, HISTORY, CONTENTS, & EVALUATION: *Edition & history:* A five-part abridgment of the play with commentary by Dr. Frank Baxter. For others in this series, see 180, 254, 311, 426, 463, 487, 508, 614 and 653. *Contents & evaluation:* Not seen. *Audience:* Junior High (grades 7-9); High school (grades 10-12);.

MEDIUM INFORMATION: *Medium:* Motion Picture; *Sound:* Spoken language; *Color:* No (black & white); *Length:* 140 min.; *Language(s) spoken:* English; *Film type:* 16mm.

DISTRIBUTION & AVAILABILITY: *Publisher or responsible agency:* Westinghouse Broadcasting Corp.; *Distributor:* Not known.

Romeo and Juliet. Motion Picture/Recording

547. *Romeo and Juliet.*

DOCUMENT INFORMATION: *Country:* GB; *Year of release:* 1966.

EDITION, HISTORY, CONTENTS, & EVALUATION: *Edition & history:* Based on a stage production by Hugh Morrison, this movie is actually a record of a stage performance of *Romeo and Juliet* produced by faculty and students of the Royal Academy of Dramatic Arts and London Polytechnic Institute. *Contents & evaluation:* The positive side is the well meant effort to replicate the staging methods and costumes of an Elizabethan playhouse. Students have an opportunity to see an approximation of a sixteenth-century performance. The negative side is that all cinematic values are sacrificed to merely recording a stage performance. The result is embalmed theatre, though the principals manage to break through and make an appealing enough pair of young lovers (KSR). *Audience:* General use.

MEDIUM INFORMATION: *Medium:* Motion Picture; *Sound:* Spoken language; *Color:* No (black & white);

Length: 107 min.; *Language(s) spoken:* English; *Film type:* 16mm.

AUTHORSHIP INFORMATION: *Producer(s):* John, Paul; Fernald, John; *Director(s):* Drumm, Val; Lee, Paul; *Composer(s):* Hewson, Richard; *Cast:* Francis, Clive (Romeo); Scoular, Angela (Juliet); Court-Thomas, Damien (Tybalt); Clifford, Veronica (Nurse); Morse, Hayward (Mercutio).

DISTRIBUTION & AVAILABILITY: *Publisher or responsible agency:* Royal Academy of Dramatic Arts and Regent Polytechnic Institute, London; *Distributor:* SYR, MCG, *Call or copy number:* LC #Fi68-231.

Romeo and Juliet. **Video/Ballet**

548. *Romeo and Juliet.*

DOCUMENT INFORMATION: *Country:* GB; *Year of release:* 1966.

EDITION, HISTORY, CONTENTS, & EVALUATION: *Edition & history:* A videotaping of a dance interpretation of *Romeo and Juliet* by The Royal Ballet. *Contents & evaluation:* The incredible grace of movement displayed by the principals in this dance adaptation transcends the severe limitations of the human body. Fonteyn even looks wonderful walking backwards, and Nureyev is a marvel as Romeo. The narrative line of the action closely follows Shakespeare's text so that all the familiar scenes from the play appear: the Capulet ball, the duel between Romeo and Tybalt, the tomb scene, and so forth. The difference is that words have been choreographed into movement and gesture to capture the ecstasy of the young lovers. For example in the aubade scene, Romeo and Juliet act out their love by dancing a duet suggestive of both hope and despair. Lighting, sets (the tomb scene is really bizarre), costumes—all contribute to a performance of sustained magnificence (KSR). *Supplementary materials:* "Review." *MFB* 33.394 (Nov. 1966): 165-66.

MEDIUM INFORMATION: *Sound:* Spoken language; *Color:* Yes; *Length:* 124 min.; *Video type:* B,V.

AUTHORSHIP INFORMATION: *Director(s):* Czinner, Paul; *Composer(s):* Prokofiev, Serge; Lanchbery, John (Conductor); *Choreographer(s):* MacMillan, Kenneth; *Designer(s):* Georgiadis, Nicholas; *Lighting designer(s):* Onions, S.D.; *Other personnel:* Vetter, Edgar (Sound); Claff, George (Make-up); Angelinetta, Olga (Hairdresser); *Cast:* Fonteyn, Margot (Juliet); Nureyev, Rudolph (Romeo); Blair, David (Mercutio); Doyle, Desmond (Tybalt); Dowell, Anthony (Benvolio); Somes, Michael (Lord Capulet); Farron, Julia (Lady Capulet); Parkinson, Georgina (Rosaline); Larsen, Gerd (Nurse); Hynd, Ronald (Friar Laurence); Newton, Christopher (Lord Montague); Kavanagh, Betty (Lady Montague); and artists of The Royal Ballet.

DISTRIBUTION & AVAILABILITY: *Publisher or responsible agency:* Poetic Films; *Distributor:* NOV, FCM, *Availability:* NOV, B, V \$40; FCM, V, \$39.95.

Romeo and Juliet. **Video/Teleplay**

549. *Romeo and Juliet.* (Series: Play of the Month).

DOCUMENT INFORMATION: *Country:* GB; *Year of first showing:* 1967; *Location of first showing:* BBC. Transmitted 7:50 to 10:05 P.M., Sunday, 3 Dec. 1967.

EDITION, HISTORY, CONTENTS, & EVALUATION: *Edition & history:* Cedric Messina, who was subsequently to play a major role as the first producer of the BBC series, "The Shakespeare Plays," made a preliminary test of the waters with a series of eight Shakespeare plays on British television. This version of *Romeo and Juliet* was one of the first in a cluster that appeared between 1967 and 1975. *Contents & evaluation:* Mike Gambon, who plays the minor role of Gregory, two decades later became famous in North America with his leading role in the television play by Dennis Potter, *The Singing Detective.* More recently he has starred in the title role of the 1988 *Uncle Vanya* in the London West End. Too bad that this earlier work has been consigned to the archives. *Audience:* General use; *Supplementary materials:* "Forthcoming [Publicity Still]." *Times* 4 March 1967: 8; "Program." *RT* 30 Nov. 1967: 21.

MEDIUM INFORMATION: *Medium:* Video; *Sound:* Spoken language; *Color:* No (black & white); *Length:* 120 min. [?]; *Language(s) spoken:* English; *Video type:* Kinescope, 35mm.

AUTHORSHIP INFORMATION: *Producer(s):* Messina, Cedric; *Director(s):* Cooke, Alan; *Composer(s):* Jones, Raymond; *Designer(s):* Diss, Eileen; *Cast:* Markham, Kika (Juliet); Bennett, Hywel (Romeo); Hird, Thora (Nurse); Gambon, Mike (Gregory); Cunliffe, Ronald (Samson); Burnham, Edward (Capulet); Bidmead, Stephanie (Lady Capulet); Gillespie, Robert (Peter); O'Hagan, Michael (Balthasar); Badcoe, Brian (Montague); Austin, Clare (Lady Montague); Pickup, Ronald (Mercutio); Griffin, David (Benvolio); Newlands, Anthony (Friar Laurence); Godfrey, Michael (The Prince); Dennis, Jonathan (Paris); Alba, Julius (Apothecary); Gilbert, Derrick (Friar John); Coburn, Brian (Officer).

DISTRIBUTION & AVAILABILITY: *Publisher or responsible agency:* BBC; *Copy location:* BBC*, archive.

Romeo and Juliet. **Motion Picture/Dance/Scenes**

550. *Romeo and Juliet.*

DOCUMENT INFORMATION: *Country:* GDR (East

Germany); *Year of first showing:* Transmitted 10:50 to 11:10 P.M., Sunday, 3 Dec. 1967.

EDITION, HISTORY, CONTENTS, & EVALUATION: *Edition & history:* A ballet film from East Germany on the theme of Shakespeare's play. *Supplementary materials:* "Program." *RT* 30 Nov. 1967: 21.

MEDIUM INFORMATION: *Length:* 20 min.

AUTHORSHIP INFORMATION: *Producer(s):* Just, Erika; *Composer(s):* Tchaikovsky, Peter; *Choreographer(s):* Chorelli, Juan; *Cast:* Gierth, Romana (Juliet); Lux, Stephen (Romeo).

DISTRIBUTION & AVAILABILITY: *Copy location:* BBC.

Romeo and Juliet. Video/Scenes

551. *Many Faces of Romeo and Juliet, The.*

DOCUMENT INFORMATION: *Country:* USA; *Year of first showing:* 1967; *Location of first showing*: Bell Telephone Hour. Transmitted 10 to 11:00 P.M., Friday, 22 Sept. 1967.

EDITION, HISTORY, CONTENTS, & EVALUATION: *Edition & history:* In this quite extraordinary and imaginative program four versions of the balcony scene as performed in theatre, opera, ballet, and American musicals were presented. The opera was by Gounod; the ballet, Prokofiev; and the musical theatre, *West Side Story. Contents & evaluation:* The critics, who in special dispensation were allowed to preview the program, were enthusiastic. Obviously network executives dislike previews out of fear that a hostile critique will adversely affect ratings. In this case there was no cause for alarm. The show was found to be "a brisk illustration of how a classical theme can inspire contrasting crafts over many years." Claire Bloom came in for particular praise: her "luminous" face with her "subtle mastery of beguiling expressions imparts enormous charm to Juliet's heartrending soliloquies." It sounds like a night on TV to be remembered. One wonders how it could have been packed into a 60-minute time slot. *Supplementary materials:* Gould, Jack. "A Soothing Romeo and Juliet Collage." *NYT* 22 Sept. 1967: 93; see also Raymond Williams in supplementary bibliography.

MEDIUM INFORMATION: *Length:* 60 min.

AUTHORSHIP INFORMATION: *Producer(s):* Lounsbery, Dan; *Director(s):* Jones, Clark; *Cast:* Robards, Jason; Bloom, Claire (Theatre); Konya, Sandor; Moffo, Anna (Opera); Bruhn, Erik; Fracci, Carla (Ballet); Kert, Larry; Lawrence, Carol (Musical theatre).

DISTRIBUTION & AVAILABILITY: *Publisher or responsible agency:* Henry Jaffe Enterprises; *Copy location:* Unknown.

Romeo and Juliet. Motion Picture/Interpretation

552. *Romeo and Juliet.*

DOCUMENT INFORMATION: *Year of release:* 1968.

EDITION, HISTORY, CONTENTS, & EVALUATION: *Awards*: Academy Awards for Costumes and Cinematography; *Edition & history:* Emulating Renato Castellani, who had previously (in 1960) filmed *Romeo and Juliet* on location in an Italian hill city, Franco Zeffirelli, veteran stage and opera director, combined the neorealism of Italian cinema with the unabashed sentimentality of a Puccini opera in making this enormously popular adaptation of Shakespeare's tragedy of young lovers. Moreover he filtered the action through the lens of Leonard Bernstein's *West Side Story* to make the experience totally palatable to the rebellious youth of the late Sixties. What he sacrificed in Shakespeare's language (and perhaps half or more of the text disappeared), he attempted to compensate for with a colorful and visually appealing panorama of life in a northern Italian city. Zeffirelli had previously accomplished much the same results with his filmed 1966 *Taming of the Shrew* (598) starring Richard Burton and Elizabeth Taylor. Moreover he also brought to the venture considerable experience as a director of staged Shakespeare for the RSC and other companies. Hundreds of aspirants were auditioned before Olivia Hussey, then 14-years-old, snapped up the prized role as Juliet. *Contents & evaluation:* Franco Zeffirelli's stunning film of *Romeo and Juliet* like some rich Christmas pudding was almost too much for the world to digest. Its flamboyance, breathtaking energy, brought about a mixed reception and divided critics down the middle: the Bardolaters who thought that it subverted the sacred Shakespearean "text," and the Cineastes who saw it as a triumph in filmmaking. More or less typical of the former point of view was this reaction: "If you keep your mind on the screen credits for Franco Zeffirelli's film *Romeo and Juliet*, 'based on' Shakespeare's play, you may be less irked by it than I was. And perhaps it should be said at once that a Shakespearean actress whom I know found the film 'beautiful' and 'brilliantly directed.' The screenplay by Franco Brusati and Masolino D'Amico seemed to me . . . to distort the original text, and I kept shifting around in my seat, wondering what had happened to various lines one expects to hear. . . . Reading *Romeo and Juliet* is like living for an hour or two before a fragile dawn which—one knows—will not survive into full day. Darkness of many kinds, and night itself, play their important and fulfilling roles in this tale, but within it we are never far from the innocent influence of promise; and what I missed most in Zeffirelli's version . . . was the sense of that 'morning' which alone can bring a 'glooming peace.' No: this *Romeo and Juliet* is a noisy, nervous semipageant whose director seems to have bartered its evanescent grace for the tangibles of elaborate staging" (Armstrong, Marion, "Noisy and Nervous," *TCC* 86 [26 March 1969]: 420-21). Another critic took the opposite tack with the remark that the film "[was] . . . the most satisfactory . . . [that he had] seen this year" (Rapf, Maurice, "Generation Gap in Verona," *Life* 65 [Sept. 1968]): 10). A film so lavish and colorful as this one, however, is obviously much too seductive to resist. Leonard Whiting and Olivia Hussey make an entirely plausible teen-age Romeo and Juliet. The "Catch-22" situation that declares the best actors and actresses (such as Leslie Howard and Norma Shearer) too old to play the lovers is ameliorated by cinema technology. The short take requires that actors speak only a few lines at a time, and editing guarantees that bad performances can be taken out. The film also by filtering Shakespeare's story through *West Side Story* capitalizes on the "generation gap" vogue of the late Sixties in Britain and America. The way that Zeffirelli meshes the brilliant dance and duelling sequences; crams the screen with the costumes, finery, and household goods of Renaissance Italy; creates a memorably manic-depressive Mercutio; and fills the sound track with Nino Rota's sensuous musical score makes for a gripping experience. If there be a flaw, it ironically lies in the movie's genius as a species of the "weepy" genre. Re-screenings sometimes make one think too glibly of *Stella Dallas* (KSR).

Audience: High school (grades 10-12); College and university; General use; *Supplementary materials:* Cirillo, Albert R. "The Art of Franco Zeffirelli and Shakespeare's *Romeo and Juliet.*" *TRQ* 16 (1969): 69-92; Rothwell, K.S. "Z.'s *Romeo and Juliet.*" *LFQ*, 5.4 (1977): 326-31.

MEDIUM INFORMATION: *Medium:* Video; *Sound:* Spoken language; *Color:* Yes; *Length:* 139 min.; *Language(s) spoken:* English; *Video type:* B, CDV, V.

AUTHORSHIP INFORMATION: *Producer(s):* Havelock-Allan, Anthony; Brabourne, John; *Director(s):* Zeffirelli, Franco; *Adaptor/translator(s):* Brusati, Franco; D'Amico, Masolino; Zeffirelli, Franco; *Composer(s):* Rota, Nino; *Choreographer(s):* Testa, Alberto; *Designer(s):* Mongiardino, Renzo; Puccini, Luciano; Carcano, Emilio; *Set designer(s):* Edzard, Christine; *Costume designer(s):* Donato, Danilo; *Other personnel:* De Santis, Pasquale (Camera); Mills, Reginald (Editor); Goodwin, Richard (Asst. prod.); Perino, Nicolo (Fight arranger); Bordogni, Guiseppe (Prod. supervisor); Hopkins, Michael (Dubbing editor); Fisher, Sash (Sound mixer); *Cast:* Whiting, Leonard (Romeo); Hussey, Olivia (Juliet); McEnery, John (Mercutio); O'Shea, Milo (Friar Laurence); Heywood, Pat (Nurse); Stephens, Robert (Prince); York, Michael (Tybalt); Olivier, Laurence (Voiceover Chorus); Robinson, Bruce (Benvolio); Hardwick, Paul (Lord Capulet); Parry, Natasha (Lady Capulet); Pierfederici, Antonio (Montague); Ruspoli, Esmeralda (Lady Montague); Bisacco, Roberto (Paris); with Holder, Ray; Skinner, Keith; Lovell, Dyson; Warwick, Richard; Antonelli, Roberto; Palmucci, Carlo.

DISTRIBUTION & AVAILABILITY: *Publisher or responsible agency:* B.H.E./Verona Prod./Dino de Laurentiis Cinematografica; U.S. Release: Paramount; *Distributor:* FNC, SWA, TWC, BLK, BUD, RCA, TAM, ILL, DCV, FMB*, INM *Availability:* FNC, rental 16mm, $395+; SWA, apply; BLK, CDV $34.98, B,V $66.95; BUD, CDV, $32.98, B,V, $82.95; RCA, 2 discs $34.98; TAM, B,V, $69; ILL, V (S 00541) $24.95; FMB*, apply; DCV, V, $45; INM, V (DS24—Excerpts) $79.95.

Romeo and Juliet. Motion Picture/Adaptation.

553. *Giulietta e Romeo.*

DOCUMENT INFORMATION: *Country:* Italy/Spain; *Year of release:* 1964; United States, 1968.

EDITION, HISTORY, CONTENTS, & EVALUATION: *Edition & history:* "The film was shot on location in Rome, Verona, Avila, and Madrid. Released in Italy in 1964 as *Giulietta e Romeo*; in Spain as *Los amantes de Verona* [Released in United States in Sept. 1968]." (*AFI*). *Audience:* General use; *Supplementary materials:* Parker, *FSF* 19.

MEDIUM INFORMATION: *Medium:* Motion Picture; *Sound:* Spoken language; *Length:* 90 min.; *Language(s) spoken:* Italian; *Dubbed language:* English; *Film type:* 35mm (Cromoscope); 16mm.

AUTHORSHIP INFORMATION: *Producer(s):* Rosson, Angel; *Director(s):* Freda, Ricardo; *Screenplay writer(s):* Freda, Ricardo; *Composer(s):* Tchaikovsky, Pyotr Ilich; Rachmaninoff, Sergei; Nicolai, Bruno; *Designer(s):* Villalba, Teddy; *Set designer(s):* Filippone, Piero; *Lighting designer(s):* Pogany, Gabor; *Cast:* Meynier, Geronimo (Romeo); Dexter, Rosemarie (Juliet); Estrada, Carlos (Mercutio); Raho, Umberto (Friar Laurence); Soler, Toni (Nurse); Della Porta, Antonella (Lady Capulet); Davo, Marco Jose (Paris); Grech, German (Tybalt); De Simone, Mario (Peter); Scipioni, Bruno (Balthasar); Balducci, Franco (Benvolio); Bosic, Andrea (Capulet); Vazzoler, Elsa (Lady Montague); Gradoli, Antonio (Montague).

DISTRIBUTION & AVAILABILITY: *Publisher or responsible agency:* World Entertainment Corp.; *Distributor:* IVY, *Call or copy number:* AFI F6.4150.

Romeo and Juliet. Motion Picture/Documentary

554. *The Teen-Age Lovers of Verona.*

DOCUMENT INFORMATION: *Country:* USA; *Year of release:* 1968.

EDITION, HISTORY, CONTENTS, & EVALUATION: *Edition & history:* A promotion film for the Zeffirelli *Romeo and Juliet* that shows the director rehearsing a scene with Leonard Whiting and Olivia Hussey. *Supplementary materials:* Loughney, Katharine. "Shakespeare on Film and Tape at Library of Congress." *SFNL* 14.2 (Apr. 1990): 4.

MEDIUM INFORMATION: *Length:* 7 min.

AUTHORSHIP INFORMATION: *Director(s):* Zeffirelli, Franco; *Cast:* Hussey, Olivia (Juliet); Whiting, Leonard (Romeo).

DISTRIBUTION & AVAILABILITY: *Copy location:* LCM; *Call or copy number:* FAA 2441.

555. *Romeo and Juliet: The Words of Love.* (Series: Explorations in Shakespeare, X).

DOCUMENT INFORMATION: *Country:* Canada; *Year of release:* 1969.

EDITION, HISTORY, CONTENTS, & EVALUATION: *Edition & history:* Part ten in a series of twelve 23-minute films made in 1969 by the Ontario Educational Communications Authority (see also 18, 40, 65, 124, 162, 257, 322, 465, 488, 617 and 637). *Contents & evaluation:* Not seen. According to the publicity release issued by NBC Educational Enterprises, "the film stresses the social barriers which love has to overcome and the decision made by the lovers who count the world well lost when they reject social mores and give themselves to their love. A balladeer singing about love accompanies these scenes: Romeo's discussion with Mercutio on love; the lover's first meeting; the profession of their mutual love in the balcony scene and finally Romeo's decision to defy all danger for his love. A discussion on contemporary social barriers to love follows the scenes." From this description, it seems that this program emulates the rest of the series in the quest for high relevance. *Audience:* College and university.

MEDIUM INFORMATION: *Medium:* Motion Picture; *Sound:* Spoken language; *Color:* Yes; *Length:* 23 min.; *Language(s) spoken:* English; *Film type:* 16mm.

AUTHORSHIP INFORMATION: *Producer(s):* Reis, Kurt; Moser, Ed; *Screenplay writer(s):* Webster, Hugh; *Composer(s):* Yanovsky, Zal; *Set designer(s):* Adeney, Chris; *Lighting designer(s):* Galbraith, Howard; *Performance group(s):* Ontario Educational Communications/NBC Educational Enterprises.

DISTRIBUTION & AVAILABILITY: *Distributor:* CNU [?].

Romeo and Juliet. Motion Picture/Scenes

556. *Romeo and Juliet,* Prologue; 5.3. (Series: The Shakespeare Series [IFB], X).

DOCUMENT INFORMATION: *Country:* GB; *Year of filming:* 1974.

EDITION, HISTORY, CONTENTS, & EVALUATION: *Edition & history:* Excerpts from *Romeo and Juliet*, Prologue and Act five, scene five. Performed on a reconstruction of an Elizabethan stage to give the impression of rapid movement characteristic (in all likelihood) of the original performances. For others in this series, see also 22, 131, 164, 232, 326, 430, 467, 490, 510, 601 and 619. *Contents & evaluation:* Shows the Chorus delivering the prologue, and the great moments in the fabled tomb scene (5.5.). Unhappily the tomb scene is thriftily managed with only curtains as a backdrop, and a single candle. The camera demands richness of detail, or abstraction. This *mise en scène* is neither. It opens with a long shot of the the Chorus spitting out the prologue on a fake Elizabethan stage. There seems little connection between his body and voice. Compared to most of the films in this series, this one seems not to have found its own identity. On the other hand, Natasha Pyne, the lovely Bianca in the famous 1966 Zeffirelli *Taming of the Shrew*, makes a memorable Juliet. *Audience:* High school (grades 10-12);.

MEDIUM INFORMATION: *Medium:* Motion Picture; *Sound:* Spoken language; *Color:* Yes; *Length:* 8 min.; *Language(s) spoken:* English; *Film type:* 16mm; *Video type:* V, 3/4U (4 per cassette).

AUTHORSHIP INFORMATION: *Producer(s):* Seabourne, John; *Director(s):* Anvil Film and Recording Group; *Cast:* Pennington, Michael (Romeo); Pyne, Natasha (Juliet); Marsden, Roy; Russell, William.

DISTRIBUTION & AVAILABILITY: *Publisher or responsible agency:* Seabourne Enterprises, Ltd.; *Distributor:* IFB, CNU, *Copy location:* FOL; *Call or copy number:* ISBN 0-699-38710-8; FOL, MP 83; *Availability:* CNU rental 16mm, $7; IFB sale 16mm, V, $150, rental $10.

Romeo and Juliet. Video/Musical

557. *Romeo and Juliet in Kansas City.*

DOCUMENT INFORMATION: *Country:* USA; *Year of release:* 1975.

EDITION, HISTORY, CONTENTS, & EVALUATION: *Edition & history:* A performance in the "Cowtown Ballroom" by the Kansas City Philharmonic of Tchaikovksy's music is preceded by a lecture on the musical score and readings from the play. *Supplementary materials:* BUFVC 43.

MEDIUM INFORMATION: *Length:* 27 min.

AUTHORSHIP INFORMATION: *Director(s):* Miller, Alan.

DISTRIBUTION & AVAILABILITY: *Distributor:* KSU.

Romeo and Juliet. Video/Recording

558. *Romeo and Juliet.*

DOCUMENT INFORMATION: *Year of release:* 1976; *Location of first showing:* St. George's Playhouse, London.

EDITION, HISTORY, CONTENTS, & EVALUATION: *Edition & history:* It was the goal of Producer/Director Paul Bosner "to record a live play in performance, bridging the disciplines of theatre and television, in a particular fashion and style and in a prescribed period of time and budget." He had planned to produce the entire canon of Shakespeare's plays as staged in repertory at London's St. George's playhouse. For whatever reasons, perhaps the intense competition from the BBC plays, at this date (March 1990), production of the entire series seems to have been either delayed or abandoned. *Contents & evaluation:* London critics who witnessed the stage production were on the whole favorable. "Movement and quick-silver reaction, often unexpected, make Peter McEnery's Romeo a fine performance, a contemporary victim lost in the pressures of the world outside his own trusted group, quick to realize that he is only 'fortune's fool'," wrote the critic for the *Sunday Telegraph.* She felt that he conveyed the horror of his experience, the "total silence at the news of Juliet's death," without the "too-usual histrionics" often associated with the role (Say, Rosemary, "Review," *ST* 3 June 1976, n.p.). "In the first tape of the series, Peter McEnery and Sarah Badel, with the help of a cast drawn from the St. Georges company, give sensitive portrayals of the two young lovers. Handsomely mounted in color, the production offers greater visual appeal than the *Romeo and Juliet* recorded at the Royal Academy of Dramatic Arts Van Brugh Theatre in 1965. . . . With classroom interest in mind, fidelity to the text gets a high priority; even the often discarded musicians' scene appears on the TV monitor" ("St. Georges *Romeo,*" *SFNL* 1.2 [1977]: 5). *Audience:* High school (grades 10-12); College and university.

MEDIUM INFORMATION: *Medium:* Video; *Sound:* Spoken language; *Color:* Yes; *Length:* 170 min.; *Language(s) spoken:* English; *Video type:* V.

AUTHORSHIP INFORMATION: *Producer(s):* Bosner, Paul; *Director(s):* Bosner, Paul; *Composer(s):* Thorby, Philip; *Costume designer(s):* Robinson, Jane; *Lighting designer(s):* Thomson, Alex; *Other personnel:* de Grunwald, Alexander (Assoc. prod); Murcell, George (Artistic dir.); Thorby, Philip; Westlake, Margaret; Robson, Christopher (Musicians); Wood, John (Prod. designer); Stephenson, Maureen (Make-up); McCutcheon, Jim (Floor manager); de Fries, Loretta (Prod. asst.); Rowe, Anne (Vision mixer); Swan, Dave; Dodd, Barrie; Barber, Dave; Rees, John (Cameramen); *Cast:* McEnery, Peter (Romeo); Badel, Sarah (Juliet); O'Conor, Joseph (Friar Laurence); Hale, Elvi (Nurse).

DISTRIBUTION & AVAILABILITY: *Publisher or responsible agency:* Television and Educational Classics; *Distributor:* TEC*, *Copy location:* FOL; *Call or copy number:* VCR 4.

Romeo and Juliet. Video/Teleplay

559. *Romeo and Juliet.*

DOCUMENT INFORMATION: *Country:* GB; *Year of release:* 1976.

EDITION, HISTORY, CONTENTS, & EVALUATION: *Edition & history:* A "schools production," as the British say, produced by Thames television in eight parts. *Audience:* High school (grades 10-12); College and university; *Supplementary materials:* H&M, 33; *BUFVC* 22.

MEDIUM INFORMATION: *Sound:* Spoken language; *Color:* Yes; *Length:* 180 min. [26 min. each part].

AUTHORSHIP INFORMATION: *Director(s):* Kemp-Welch, Joan; *Cast:* Neame, Christopher (Romeo).

DISTRIBUTION & AVAILABILITY: *Distributor:* TTI*.

Romeo and Juliet. Motion Picture/Documentary

560. *Immortal Passado, The.*

DOCUMENT INFORMATION: *Country:* GB; *Year of release:* 1976.

EDITION, HISTORY, CONTENTS, & EVALUATION: *Edition & history:* Shows how a theatrical repertory company mounts a production in five weeks. *Supplementary materials:* BUFVC 23.

MEDIUM INFORMATION: *Length:* 35 min.

AUTHORSHIP INFORMATION: *Director(s):* Baynes, Jeff.

DISTRIBUTION & AVAILABILITY: *Distributor:* SFL*.

Romeo and Juliet. Video/Documentary

561. *Footnotes to* Romeo and Juliet.

DOCUMENT INFORMATION: *Country:* GB; *Year of first showing:* 1976; *Location of first showing:* Thames Television.

EDITION, HISTORY, CONTENTS, & EVALUATION: *Edition & history:* "Studio discussion between pupils from two different schools and members of the cast and production team of the Thames TV schools version of *Romeo and Juliet.*" A supplement to *Romeo and Juliet* in eight parts (see #559), also produced by

Thames. *Supplementary materials: BUFVC Newsletter* 26 (Feb. 1988): 5.

MEDIUM INFORMATION: *Sound:* Spoken language; *Color:* Yes; *Length:* 25 min.; *Video type:* V.

AUTHORSHIP INFORMATION: *Producer(s):* Thames TV.

DISTRIBUTION & AVAILABILITY: *Publisher or responsible agency:* Thames TV; *Distributor:* TTI.

Romeo and Juliet. **Video/Ballet**

562. *Romeo and Juliet.*

DOCUMENT INFORMATION: *Country:* Italy; *Year of release:* 1977.

EDITION, HISTORY, CONTENTS, & EVALUATION: *Edition & history:* A ballet performance at the famed La Scala Opera. *Supplementary materials:* Novacom Video Inc. catalog.

MEDIUM INFORMATION: *Length:* 128 min.

AUTHORSHIP INFORMATION: *Director(s):* Nureyev, Rudolph; *Cast:* Fracci, Carla; Fonteyn, Margot; Nureyev, Rudolph.

DISTRIBUTION & AVAILABILITY: *Distributor:* NOV, *Availability:* NOV, B, V $78.

Romeo and Juliet. **Video/Teleplay**

563. *Romeo and Juliet.* (Series: The Shakespeare Plays).

DOCUMENT INFORMATION: *Country:* GB; *Year of filming:* 31 Jan.-5 Feb. 1978; *Year of first showing:* 1978; *Location of first showing:* BBC, London; PBS stations, 14 March 1979.

EDITION, HISTORY, CONTENTS, & EVALUATION: *Edition & history:* Shakespearean actors and directors have always had to compete with fabled past performances. David Garrick may have been thinking about James Burbage and Edwin Booth may have been looking over his shoulder at David Garrick. But before the age of mechanical reproduction, past performances remained just that—"fabled" and shadowy. Nowadays film and theatre people work not in the shadow but in the presence of past glories. To produce a *Romeo and Juliet* following the appearance of Franco Zeffirelli's masterpiece is like being asked to sculpture a second "David" after Michelangelo. Nevertheless Director Alvin Rakoff, daring to cast youthful Rebecca Saire as Juliet and working with a small budget, managed to create a tragedy of Verona with its own kind of integrity. Charles Lower's thoughtful review, which follows, generally supports that belief (KSR). *Contents & evaluation:* "From the outset of any evaluation of the BBC

Romeo and Juliet, one must, I believe, appreciate how much tougher an opponent Director Alvin Rakoff tackled than, say, Zeffirelli on film. On the one hand, Rakoff could not eliminate Juliet's 'Gallop apace' soliloquy nor find predominantly visual means suited to film to introduce Romeo (typical Zeffirelli choices in seeking fundamentally a good cinematic experience). For the BBC series has committed itself to minimal cutting. On the other hand, unlike a movie, television—its small screen viewed in the home—greatly restricts both style and camera-work. Television as a dramatic mode and the talkiness of Shakespeare (however beautifully lyrical and articulately revealing) are at war, and BBC chose to encompass the entire battlefield. Decisive victory would be nearly inconceivable. . . . Director Rakoff correctly, I believe, identifies as 'the most important contribution I bring to this production' the close-knit Capulet family unit; and it is what television is most comfortable with. The Capulet household shares the bond of intending only Juliet's best interests, as seen, for example, in III.v. Lady Capulet glows with wifely pride and motherly expectation in saying 'But now I'll tell thee joyful tidings, girl . . . Well, well, thou hast a careful father child.' She sparkles in the prospect of Juliet's own presumed pleasure in wedding Paris . . . to feel for and with the Capulet household is a product of televising: its credible action thrives on intimate facial close-ups. Almost necessarily close-ups tend to equalize. Each line when its speaker dominates the screen implicitly asks our attentiveness to it for its own sake, not subordinated to larger concerns. In effect, television lets everyone upstage everyone with near consistency, thus (with Shakespeare) undermining one's sorting out dramatic priorities" (Lower, Charles B., "Romeo and Juliet," *SFNL* 3.2 [1979]: 6). *Audience:* College and university; General use; *Supplementary materials:* Fenwick, Henry. Introduction. *BSP* 19-25; Videotape (25 min.) from "Shakespeare in Perspective" series with Germaine Greer as lecturer available in U.K. from BBC* (*BUFVC* 22).

MEDIUM INFORMATION: *Medium:* Video; *Sound:* Spoken language; *Color:* Yes; *Length:* 170 min.; *Video type:* B, V, 3/4U.

AUTHORSHIP INFORMATION: *Producer(s):* Messina, Cedric; *Director(s):* Rakoff, Alvin; *Adaptor/translator(s):* Shallcross, Alan; *Composer(s):* Lloyd-Jones, David; Tyler, James and the London Early Music Group; *Choreographer(s):* Stephenson, Geraldine; *Designer(s):* Walker, Stuart; *Costume designer(s):* Barrow, Odette; *Lighting designer(s):* Treays, John; *Other personnel:* Hobbs, William (Fight director); Robertson, Carol (Prod. asst.); Alcock, Dawn (Make-up); Dixon, Colin (Sound); Wilders, John (Literary advisor); *Cast:* Ryecart, Patrick (Romeo); Saire, Rebecca (Juliet); Johnson, Celia (Nurse); Hordern, Michael (Capulet); Gielgud, John (Chorus); O'Conor, Joseph (Friar); Naismith, Laurence (Escalus); Andrews, Anthony (Mercutio); Rickman, Alan (Tybalt);

Hill, Jacqueline (Lady Capulet); Strauli, Christopher (Benvolio); Northey, Christopher (Paris); Henry, Paul (Peter); Davidson, Roger (Balthasar); Paul, John (Montague); Dene, Zulema (Lady Montague); Knight, Esmond (Old Capulet); Sibley, David (Sampson); Carr, Jack (Gregory); Reed, Bunny (Abraham); Dobtcheff, Vernon (Apothecary); Savident, John (Friar John); Schiller, Danny (Musician); Young, Jeremy (First Watch); Chiswick, Jeffrey (Second Watch); Taylor, Gary (Potpan); Arden, Mark; Burbage, Robert (Pages); Bowerman, Alan (First Citizen).

DISTRIBUTION & AVAILABILITY: *Publisher or responsible agency:* BBC/TLF; *Distributor:* AVP, BBC* *Copy location:* UVM; *Availability:* AVP, B, V, 3/4U $450 (1987), sale; BBC* 16 mm or V, apply (*BUFVC* 22).

Romeo and Juliet. Motion Picture/Abridgment

564. *Romeo and Juliet.* (Series: The World of William Shakespeare); *Year of first showing:* 1978.

DOCUMENT INFORMATION: *Country:* USA.

EDITION, HISTORY, CONTENTS, & EVALUATION: *Edition & history:* An abridged version of the play. Made in cooperation with Station WQED Pittsburgh, Carnegie-Mellon University and The Shakespeare Birthplace Trust, Stratford-upon-Avon. A companion film, *Star-Crossed Love* (see 565) offers background material. For others in series, see 137-8, 330-1, 565, and 715. *Contents & evaluation:* There are many deletions made necessary by the brevity of this film. For example, the fight scene at the beginning (it opens with Prince Escalus' speech) and Mercutio's Queen Mab speech are both missing. On the other hand, one becomes completely engrossed in this unpretentious but attractive movie. Juliet is played by an adorable young woman with a little girl voice that simply adds more charm to the role, and her Romeo is sufficiently handsome to be deserving of her favor. The color and music help to make the Capulet ball, the aubade scene in Juliet's bedchamber, and the tomb scene, all come across as neither stagy nor overly cinematic but self-contained. The youthful abandon of the aubade scene, where Romeo and Juliet are seen in bed, comes close to the daring of the Zeffirelli version. When Juliet says "It is the lark," against a background of bird calls, there is a poignant valorisation of the young lovers' commitments to each other. None of this is quite so hyped up as the Zeffirelli version (which makes this NGS production perhaps a better choice for the very young), but it is nevertheless highly charged (KSR). *Audience:* High school (grades 10-12); *Supplementary materials: National Geographic Film Studies Series. Teachers' Guides.* Washington: NGS, 1978; McLean, Andrew. "Educational Films." *SQ* 30 (Summer 1979): 417.

MEDIUM INFORMATION: *Medium:* Motion Picture;

Sound: Spoken language; *Color:* Yes; *Length:* 36 min.; *Language(s) spoken:* English; *Film type:* 16mm; *Video type:* V, 3/4U.

AUTHORSHIP INFORMATION: *Director(s):* Walsh, Bob; *Cast:* Cast not given in print that I screened.

DISTRIBUTION & AVAILABILITY: *Publisher or responsible agency:* National Geographic; *Distributor:* KAR, NGS, *Copy location:* FOL; *Call or copy number:* MP 98, Folger; LC #PN1997.80-706327; *Availability:* NGS, sale, 16mm, $353.50 (50313); V, $69.95 (51194); KAR, rental, $42 + .

Romeo and Juliet. Motion Picture/Documentary

565. *Star-Crossed Love.* (Series: The World of William Shakespeare); *Year of first showing:* 1978. DOCUMENT INFORMATION: *Country:* USA.

EDITION, HISTORY, CONTENTS, & EVALUATION: *Edition & history:* Made in cooperation with Station WQED Pittsburgh, Carnegie-Mellon University and The Shakespeare Birthplace Trust, Stratford-upon-Avon. A companion film, *Romeo and Juliet* (see 564, above), provides an abbreviated version of the play. *Contents & evaluation:* According to publicity, it places *Romeo and Juliet* in the context of the English fascination with Italy in Shakespeare's own time. If it is on the same level as the NGS film on *Macbeth* (330) and its companion film, *Romeo and Juliet* (564), one may comfortably predict its high quality by analogy even without having seen it. *Audience:* High school (grades 10-12); *Supplementary materials: National Geographic Film Studies Series. Teachers' Guides.* Washington: NGS, 1978; McLean, Andrew. "Educational Films." *SQ* 30 (Summer 1979): 417.

MEDIUM INFORMATION: *Medium:* Motion Picture; *Sound:* Spoken language; *Color:* Yes; *Length:* 17 min.; *Language(s) spoken:* English; *Film type:* 16mm; *Video type:* V, 3/4U.

AUTHORSHIP INFORMATION: *Director(s):* Walsh, Bob.

DISTRIBUTION & AVAILABILITY: *Publisher or responsible agency:* National Geographic; *Distributor:* KAR, NGS, *Copy location:* FOL; *Call or copy number:* MP 97, Folger; LC #PR2831. 80-706328; *Availability:* NGS, sale, 16mm, $188.50 (50324); V, $59.95 (51211); KAR, rental, $32 + .

Romeo and Juliet. Video/Documentary

566. *Romeo and Juliet.* (Series: Shakespeare in Perspective).

DOCUMENT INFORMATION: *Country:* GB; *Year of release:* 1978.

EDITION, HISTORY, CONTENTS, & EVALUATION: *Edition & history:* The "Shakespeare in Perspective" series was made to accompany the BBC/Time Life Inc. "The Shakespeare Plays" series. (see also 44, 142, 234, 269, 335, 411, and 624). For overview, see 44. *Contents & evaluation:* According to Germaine Greer, *Romeo and Juliet* is "not at all about" youthful, silly romantic love, as so many of us had naively thought, but about marriage "as an honorable and public estate." Our befuddlement about the true nature of the play comes from overexposure to modern treatments of the story such as *West Side Story*. Dr. Greer goes on to point out some crucial distinctions between the feuding ethnic gangs in New York and the stately Capulets and Montagues of Verona. Shots of young men lounging about the street corners of today's Verona, of the "genuine" balcony of the two lovers, and of the markets in Italian cities give a contemporary look to ancient materials. There are also some fine comments about the role of friars in making secret marriages, and the terrible responsibility that Friar Laurence assumes in joining Romeo and Juliet together. Scenes from the BBC productions illustrate Dr. Greer's points, the balcony scene being particularly useful in underscoring the contrast between the stilted speech of Romeo and the headlong blank verse of Juliet. Somewhere along the way, however, the original idea that the play is less about impetuous young love than about the honorable institution of marriage seems to get lost, or at least so I thought. That's too bad for I personally would like to have had that perspective clarified for me. Dr. Greer speaks intelligently and the excellent visuals prevent the program from degenerating into a mere talking head (KSR).

MEDIUM INFORMATION: *Medium:* Video; *Sound:* Spoken language; *Color:* Yes; *Length:* 25 min.; *Language(s) spoken:* English; *Video type:* 3/4U, V.

AUTHORSHIP INFORMATION: *Producer(s):* Poole, Victor; *Director(s):* Denkow, Barbara; *Other personnel:* Gabell, Steve (Editor); Gatland, John; Dykes, Alan (Sound); Waters, Joe; Sadler, Chris (Camera); Friedman, Liz (Graphics); *Cast:* Greer, Germaine (Commentator).

DISTRIBUTION & AVAILABILITY: *Publisher or responsible agency:* BBC; *Distributor:* BBC*; FNC, *Availability:* Double cassette (w. *Ham.*), Rental $50; Quad cassette (w. *Ham., JC, Mac.*), Rental $75.

Romeo and Juliet. Video/Animated

567. *Rome-O and Julie 8.*

DOCUMENT INFORMATION: *Country:* Canada; *Year of first showing:* 1979.

EDITION, HISTORY, CONTENTS, & EVALUATION: *Edition & history:* The tale of two robots in love in a cosmic parable based on Shakespeare's play. *Supplementary materials:* FCM Catalog.

MEDIUM INFORMATION: *Length:* 25 min.; *Video type:* V.

AUTHORSHIP INFORMATION: *Composer(s):* Sebastion, John.

DISTRIBUTION & AVAILABILITY: *Distributor:* FCM.

Romeo and Juliet. Video/Derivative

568. *Romeu Y Julieta.* [*Romeo and Juliet*].

DOCUMENT INFORMATION: *Country:* Brazil; *Year of release:* 1982; *Country of first showing:* Brazil.

EDITION, HISTORY, CONTENTS, & EVALUATION: *Edition & history:* A free adaptation of Shakespeare's tragedy of young lovers set in Ouro Preto, a mining town in Brazil that has the fragile beauty of the Italian Riviera. The narrator of the film explains, "Ouro Preto like Verona is a perfect setting for a tragedy of love." Although unknown in the United States, the production received enthusiastic reviews when it was shown in London in the National Film Theatre. *Contents & evaluation:* This South American offshoot of Shakespeare's tragic tale of two young lovers combines the spectacle of Renato Castellani's 1954 *Romeo and Juliet*, the operatic flavor of Zeffirelli's and the topicality of Bernstein's *West Side Story*. It is not Shakespeare's play but a re-representation of the play in an idiom that is Brazilian Portuguese, vibrant, topical, and yet, as with all good non-English screen treatments of Shakespeare (such as Kurosawa's and Kozintsev's), curiously and paradoxically faithful to its source. Whatever else can be said, it is first-rate TV entertainment (KSR). *Audience:* High school (grades 10-12); College and university.

MEDIUM INFORMATION: *Medium:* Video; *Sound:* Spoken language; *Color:* Yes; *Length:* 120 min.; *Language(s) spoken:* Portuguese; *Language of subtitles:* English; *Video type:* V.

AUTHORSHIP INFORMATION: *Director(s):* Grisolli, Paulo Afonso; *Cast:* Fábio, Jr., Luciela Santos; de Souza, Ruthe (Juliet); Milani, Francisco; Amayo, Thereza; Danta, Daniel; D'Angelo, J.; Ferraz, Buza; Costa, Claudia; Fayad, Marces.

DISTRIBUTION & AVAILABILITY: *Distributor:* GTV, BFI*, *Availability:* GTV, apply; BFI*, V, 3/4U, hire (*BUFVC* 22).

Romeo and Juliet. Video/Scenes

569. *Life and Adventures of Nicholas Nickleby.*

DOCUMENT INFORMATION: *Country:* GB; *Year of first showing:* 1982; *Location of first showing:* London Channel 4 TV; Mobil Showcase in USA.

EDITION, HISTORY, CONTENTS, & EVALUATION: *Edition & history:* A parody of *Romeo and Juliet* after the style of a nineteenth-century melodrama is mounted by Vincent Crummles in the midst of this Dickensian saga. (I am obliged to Philip Bolton for this reference.) *Supplementary materials: Dickens Studies Newsletter* 14 (1983): 32.

MEDIUM INFORMATION: *Sound:* Spoken language; *Color:* Yes; *Length:* 480 min.; *Video type:* V.

AUTHORSHIP INFORMATION: *Producer(s):* Goddard, Jim; *Director(s):* Nunn, Trevor; Caird, John; *Cast:* Rees, Roger; Petherbridge, Edward.

DISTRIBUTION & AVAILABILITY: *Publisher or responsible agency:* RSC; *Distributor:* CBF.

Romeo and Juliet. Video/Documentary

570. *Le Cid.*

DOCUMENT INFORMATION: *Country:* GB; *Year of release:* 1984.

EDITION, HISTORY, CONTENTS, & EVALUATION: *Edition & history:* Six scenes from Pierre Corneille's *Le Cid* as performed by the Cercle Francais at the Old Rep Theatre, Birmingham, are staged and comparisons are made with Racine's *Berenice* and Shakespeare's *Romeo and Juliet. Supplementary materials: BUFVC* 23.

MEDIUM INFORMATION: *Sound:* Spoken language; *Color:* Yes; *Length:* 50 min.

AUTHORSHIP INFORMATION: *Director(s):* Morby, Paul.

DISTRIBUTION & AVAILABILITY: *Distributor:* UBT*.

Romeo and Juliet. Video/Ballet

571. *Romeo and Juliet.*

DOCUMENT INFORMATION: *Country:* GB; *Year of release:* 1984.

EDITION, HISTORY, CONTENTS, & EVALUATION: *Edition & history:* A videotaping of a dance interpretation of *Romeo and Juliet* at the Royal Opera House, Covent Garden, London. *Supplementary materials:* Novacom Video Inc. catalog.

MEDIUM INFORMATION: *Length:* 128 min.

AUTHORSHIP INFORMATION: *Director(s):* Nears, Colin; *Composer(s):* Prokofiev, Serge; *Choreographer(s):* MacMillan, Kenneth; *Cast:* Ferri, Alessandra; Eagling, Wayne; Drew, David; Jeffries, Stephen; Freeman, Mark.

DISTRIBUTION & AVAILABILITY: *Distributor:* NOV, FCM, *Availability:* NOV, B, V $40; FCM, V, $39.95.

Romeo and Juliet. Video/Documentary

572. *Romeo and Juliet.* (Series: From Page to Stage).

DOCUMENT INFORMATION: *Country:* Canada; *Year of release:* 1985; *Location of first showing:* Stratford Shakespeare Festival, Ontario, Canada.

EDITION, HISTORY, CONTENTS, & EVALUATION: *Edition & history:* One of a series of educational cassettes issued by the Stratford Shakespeare Festival, Ontario, Canada. As of this writing excerpts from five plays have been made available (see also 45, 606, 628, 661). Each play comes in a kit that includes a videotape for classroom viewing, a study guide and the Stratford Festival edition of the play. The study guide and cassette are keyed to specific parts of the play for handy reference. *Contents & evaluation:* Richard Monette, Mercutio in the 1984 Stratford stage production, handles the commentary on this play. His superb, polished diction is difficult to resist, even though the actual scenes from the play suffer from the usual problems associated with *Romeo and Juliet*. The actors are either too young to handle the dramatic side, or too old to represent teen-age exuberance. The latter rather than the former ailment plagues this production. The problem is exacerbated by the close-ups of television. In short the excerpts from the play, as it was produced at Stratford, Ontario, reveal a technically competent performance better suited to stage than to the intimacies of the screen. Still, Richard Monette's Queen Mab speech as Mercutio is a masterpiece, and Seana McKenna's potion speech as Juliet also upholds the high standards of this famous company. Monette's insight, or Elliott Hayes's, that Tybalt's function is to create discord, and the notation of the sense of urgency in the action are helpful in understanding the play. *Audience:* General use; *Supplementary materials:* Kliman, Bernice W. "Video in Review." *SFNL* 12.1 (Dec. 1987): 10; Hayes, Elliott, ed. [Teachers' Committee] *From Page to Stage: Study Guide.* Stratford Shakespeare Festival, 1985.

MEDIUM INFORMATION: *Medium:* Video; *Sound:* Spoken language; *Color:* Yes; *Length:* 30 min.; *Language(s) spoken:* English; *Video type:* B, V, 3/4U.

AUTHORSHIP INFORMATION: *Producer(s):* Roland, Herb; *Director(s):* Dews, Peter (Stage); Schipper, Steven; *Designer(s):* Walker, David; *Cast:* Feore, Colm (Romeo); McKenna, Seana (Juliet); Monette, Richard (Mercutio/Narrator); with, Austin-Olsen, Shaun; Boyes, Derek; Bradbury, Simon; Gibson, Christopher;

Gordon, Lewis; Harrop, Ernest; Johnston, William; Redfern, Damon; Strait, Brent; Zeigler, Joseph.

DISTRIBUTION & AVAILABILITY: *Publisher or responsible agency:* CBC Enterprises; *Distributor:* BEA, *Availability:* B (1-210-5), $120, schools, $96; V (1-209-1), $135, schools, $96; 3/4U (1-211-3), $135, schools, $108.

Romeo and Juliet. Video/Excerpts

573. *Romeo and Juliet.*

DOCUMENT INFORMATION: *Country:* GB/Italy; *Year of release:* 1985.

EDITION, HISTORY, CONTENTS, & EVALUATION: *Edition & history:* A shortened version of the Zeffirelli film with teaching notes prepared by Ina Calvey. For full credits, see the entry under Zeffirelli's *Romeo and Juliet* #552. *Supplementary materials:* BUFVC 22.

MEDIUM INFORMATION: *Length:* 133 min.

AUTHORSHIP INFORMATION: *Director(s):* Zeffirelli, Franco; *Cast:* Hussey, Olivia (Juliet); Whiting, Leonard (Romeo).

DISTRIBUTION & AVAILABILITY: *Distributor:* TSO*.

Romeo and Juliet. Video/Musical

574. *Bernstein Conducts* West Side Story. (Series: PBS Great Performances).

DOCUMENT INFORMATION: *Country:* USA; *Year of release:* 1985.

EDITION, HISTORY, CONTENTS, & EVALUATION: *Edition & history:* Shown on PBS stations in 1985. *Supplementary materials:* Loughney, Katharine. "Shakespeare on Film and Tape at Library of Congress." *SFNL* 14.1 (Dec. 1989): 6.

MEDIUM INFORMATION: *Length:* 90 min.

DISTRIBUTION & AVAILABILITY: *Copy location:* LCM; *Call or copy number:* VBD 2729-2730.

Romeo and Juliet. Motion Picture/Modernization

574.1 *Fire with Fire.*

DOCUMENT INFORMATION: *Country:* USA; *Year of release:* 1986.

EDITION, HISTORY, CONTENTS, & EVALUATION:

Edition & history: A modernized *Romeo and Juliet* in which "the star-crossed lovers" are respectively an inmate in a correctional camp for male delinquents and a student in a convent. *Contents & evaluation:* Not seen. This is apparently another recent exploitation film in the tradition of *China Girl* (574.2). Film critic Tim Brookes describes the plot as "following *Romeo and Juliet* like a drunk following memorized directions across the Bronx." The lovers then have a "secret tryst. A tryst in a crypt, no less." The director's infatuation with music video apparently influenced the big dance number at the convent for the young gentlemen from the work camp, which is of course a transmogrified displacement of the Capulet ball. This peculiar mix of boys and girls may well constitute the world's single most unlikely social event. *New York Times* critic Walter Goodman asks, "Why [did] it [take] four people to write this thing?" *Audience:* Professional; *Supplementary materials:* Brookes, Tim. "Romeo and Ophelia." *Burlington Free Press*, 30 May 1986: n.p.; Goodman, Walter, "Fire with Fire: False Alarm." *NYT* 9 May 1986: C14.

MEDIUM INFORMATION: *Medium:* Motion picture/Video; *Sound:* Spoken language; *Color:* Yes; *Length:* 104 min.

AUTHORSHIP INFORMATION: *Producer(s):* Nardino, Gary; *Director(s):* Gibbins, Duncan; *Screenplay writer(s):* Phillips, Bill; Skaaren, Warren; Boorstin, Paul & Sharon; *Composer(s):* Shore, Howard; *Cast:* Madsen, Virgina (Lisa Taylor); Sheffer, Craig (Joe Fisk); Reid, Kate (Sister Victoria); Polito, Jon (William Dechard).

DISTRIBUTION & AVAILABILITY: *Publisher or responsible agency:* Paramount Pictures; *Distributor:* Unknown. Local video rentals[?].

574.2 *China Girl.*

DOCUMENT INFORMATION: *Country:* USA; *Year of release:* 1987.

EDITION, HISTORY, CONTENTS, & EVALUATION: *Edition & history:* A modernized *Romeo and Juliet* in which "the star-crossed teens" are an Italian girl and Chinese boy on New York's lower east side. For example, the Capulet ballroom gets displaced into a ghetto dance hall. *Contents & evaluation:* As *New York Times* critic Janet Maslin points out the film is "a blatant mixture of *Romeo and Juliet, Mean Streets*, and *West Side Story*." Traces of Director Abel Ferrera's connections with *Miami Vice* also remain in the spastic editing and analytical camera work. If visually the movie has its redeeming moments, the gutter dialogue cancels them out. The once taboo "F-word" becomes a catch-all part of speech that acts as surrogate for noun, verb, adjective, adverb and expletive. The film may well be *prima facie* evidence of the decline of the Republic. Other traces of *Romeo and Juliet* include Capulets and Montagues transmogrified into warring

Chinese and Italian immigrants on New York's lower east side; a balcony scene on a fire escape; and an aubade in a slum bedroom. Mercutio is metamorphosed into Mercury, a thug. As for the rest, perhaps there should be silence. If it exists at all in the Shakespearean orbit, it is on the outer edges, along with such other recent exploitations of Shakespeare as *Fire with Fire* (574.1), and *Blue City* (153.1). *Audience:* Professional; *Supplementary materials:* Maslin, Janet. "Action and Slurs." *NYT* 25 Sept. 1987: C16.

MEDIUM INFORMATION: *Medium:* Motion picture/Video; *Sound:* Spoken language; *Color:* Yes; *Length:* 90 min.

AUTHORSHIP INFORMATION: *Producer(s):* Nozik, Michael; *Director(s):* Ferrara, Abel; *Screenplay writer(s):* St. John, Nicholas; *Composer(s):* Delia, Joe; *Designer(s):* Leigh, Dan; *Costume designer(s):* Hornung, Richard; *Lighting designer(s):* Bazelli, Bojan; *Cast:* Russo, James (Alby); Caruso, David (Mercury); Wong, Russell (Yung Gan); Chin, Joey (Tsu Chin); Hong, James (Gung Tu); Malina, Judith (Mrs. Monte); Chang, Sari (Tye); Panebianco, Richard (Tony).

DISTRIBUTION & AVAILABILITY: *Publisher or responsible agency:* Vestron Pictures Inc.; *Distributor:* FCM, *Availability:* V, $79.98; Rental, commercial video outlets.

Romeo and Juliet. Video/Ballet

575. *Romeo and Juliet.*

DOCUMENT INFORMATION: *Country:* USA; *Year of release:* 1988.

EDITION, HISTORY, CONTENTS, & EVALUATION: *Edition & history:* An American Ballet Theatre production shown "live from Lincoln Center," New York City, on May 7, 1988, from 8 PM to 11 PM on PBS stations nationally. *Contents & evaluation:* Although there were some minor additions, transpositions and omissions, most of the narrative line remained essentially that of Shakespeare. In the opening scene, for example, Romeo is very much a part of the street fight, though of course in Shakespeare's play he appears for the first time after the street brawl. There are also noticeably more women on the street, doubtless to allow the audience to watch the elegant ballerinas. And indeed "elegant," they are. The ability of all the dancers, and especially of course *premiere danseuse,* Natalia Makarova, with the lead male dancer, Kevin McKenzie (a Vermonter), to shape their bodies into incredibly beautiful configurations remains one of the great wonders of the artistic world. The Russian prima ballerina moves as though she were walking on the thinnest air, and manages to capture in the subtlest ways through the stretching and movement of her body the emotional yearning and turmoil in Juliet's heart. The opening street brawl, which must inevitably invite comparison with *West Side Story,* features some of the most highly disciplined duelling patterns imaginable, choreographed by Sir Kenneth MacMillan. The great music by Prokofiev, as conducted by Jack Everly from the glitzy Metropolitan Opera House in New York, completes the evening. If and when this performance becomes available on videocassette, it is highly recommended as an intelligent reworking into another medium of Shakespeare's play (KSR). *Supplementary materials:* Anderson, Jack. "Grandeur and spectacle." *NYT* 5 May 1988: C24.

MEDIUM INFORMATION: *Length:* 160 min.

AUTHORSHIP INFORMATION: *Producer(s):* Goberman, John; *Director(s):* Browning, Kirk; Skogg, Alan; *Composer(s):* Prokofiev, Sergei; Everly, Jack (Conductor); *Choreographer(s):* MacMillan, Kenneth; *Designer(s):* Georgiadis, Nicholas; *Costume designer(s):* Georgiadis, Nicholas; *Lighting designer(s):* Skelton, Thomas; Shelley, Steven; *Other personnel:* Butt, Dan (Prod. manager); Galloway, Alice; Rosecrans, Lori (Stage managers); Lombardo, Gino Aldo (Audio mixer); Shoskes, Michael (Audio); York, Paul C.; Null, Susan (Video); Buchner, Alan; Ten Haagen, Peter (Videotape); *Cast:* Makarova, Natalia (Juliet); McKenzie, Kevin (Romeo); Barbee, Victor (Tybalt); Parkinson, Georgina (Lady Capulet); Jones, Susan (Nurse); Stretton, Ross (Paris); Renvall, Johan (Mercutio); Dunham, Christine (Rosaline); Chapman, Wes (Benvolio); Owen, Michael (Lord Capulet); Taras, John (Escalus/Friar); Schneider, Jurgen (Lord Montague); Hood, Laura (Lady Montague); Fagundes, Christina; Moore, Kathleen; Rose, Amy (Harlots); Katterndahl, Lucette (Rosaline's friend); Adair, Anne; Escoda, Cristine; Hobart, Careen; Kent, Julie; Stackpole, Dana; Vinckier, Greet (Juliet's friends); Collins, Jeremy; Roberts, Keith; Van Fleteren, Roger; Wallace, Robert; Yearsley, Ross; Alfieri, Claudia; Allen, Melissa (Dancers); and four dozen more!

DISTRIBUTION & AVAILABILITY: *Publisher or responsible agency:* Great Performances (Exxon)/PBS/Metropolitan Opera/American Ballet Theatre; *Distributor:* PBS TV [?], *Availability:* Unknown.

Sonnets

Note on the sonnets: The exact time for the composition of the sonnets is unknown, though they initially appeared in the 1609 Thomas Thorpe edition. Presumably before then Shakespeare had worked them over for several years, perhaps in the 1590s, when the plague closed the theatres down. During that same period he was writing the so-called "sonnet plays" to include such lyrical works as *A Midsummer Night's Dream*, *Richard II*, and *The Merchant of Venice*. As a treasure trove for actors' voices, they have been recorded for radio and film, unlike the narrative poems, *The Rape of Lucrece* and *Venus and Adonis*, which so far as I know have never been put on camera (KSR).

Sonnets. **Video/Documentary**

575.1. *The Dark Lady of the Sonnets.*

DOCUMENT INFORMATION: *Country:* GB; *Year of first showing:* 1955; *Location of first showing:* BBC. Transmitted 8:30 to 9:00 P.M., Sunday, 10 Oct. 1955.

EDITION, HISTORY, CONTENTS, & EVALUATION: *Edition & history:* The action takes place on the terrace of the palace at Whitehall in 1600. *Supplementary materials:* "Program." *RT* 2 Oct. 1955: n.p.

MEDIUM INFORMATION: *Length:* 30 min.

AUTHORSHIP INFORMATION: *Producer(s):* Allen, Douglas; *Adaptor/translator(s):* Shaw, George Bernard;

Designer(s): Pemberton, Reece; *Cast:* MacNaughtan, Alan (Shakespeare); Lehmann, Beatrix (Queen Elizabeth); Murray, Barbara (Dark Lady); Woodbridge, George (The Beefeater).

DISTRIBUTION & AVAILABILITY: *Publisher or responsible agency:* BBC; *Copy location:* Unavailable.

575.2. *Ages of Man.*

DOCUMENT INFORMATION: *Country:* USA; *Year of release:* 1965.

EDITION, HISTORY, CONTENTS, & EVALUATION: *Edition & history:* Originally produced by David Susskind as a CBS television program. Part I (Youth) includes passages from *AYL, MND, MV*, and the Sonnets; Part II (Adulthood), from *WT, MM, Tmp.*; Part III (Maturity), from *H5, JC, Ham., Mac.*, and the Sonnets; and Part IV (Death), from *MM, R2, Ham., Rom., Lr., Tmp.*, and *Ado.* Each of the four parts may be rented separately: Part I (Youth) is 23 min; Part II (Adulthood), 29 min; Part III, (Maturity), 25 min; and Part IV (Death), 27 min. *Audience:* High school (grades 10-12); College and university; General use.

MEDIUM INFORMATION: *Medium:* Video; *Sound:* Spoken language; *Color:* Yes; *Length:* 104 min.; *Language(s) spoken:* English; *Film type:* 16mm.

AUTHORSHIP INFORMATION: *Producer(s):* Susskind, David; *Cast:* Gielgud, Sir John.

DISTRIBUTION & AVAILABILITY: *Publisher or re-*

sponsible agency: CBS-TV; *Distributor:* KSU, SYR, *Copy location:* LCL (NCOX 166).

576. *The Sonnets.* (Series: Shakespearean Studies on Video and Film).

ORIGINAL WORK AND PRODUCTION: *Year of first production:* 1590s [?].

DOCUMENT INFORMATION: *Country:* GB; *Year of release:* 1984.

EDITION, HISTORY, CONTENTS, & EVALUATION: *Edition & history:* An educational program that gives an in-depth analysis of fifteen of Shakespeare's sonnets. The sonnets are #8 ("Music to hear, why hears't thou music sadly?"); #18 ("Shall I compare thee to a summer's day?); #25 ("Let those who are in favor with their stars"); #35 ("No more be griev'd at that which thou hast done"); #53 ("What is your substance, whereof are you made?"); #64 ("When I have seen by Time's fell hand defaced"); #65 ("Since brass, nor stone, nor earth, nor boundless sea"); #66 ("Tir'd with all these, for restless death I cry"); #87 ("Farewell, thou art too dear for my possessing"); #91 ("Some glory in their birth, some in their skill"); #94 ("They that have pow'r to hurt and will do none"); #107 ("Not mine own fears, nor the prophetic soul"); #127 ("In the old age, black was not counted fair"); #128 ("How oft when thou, my music, music plays't"); #144 ("Two loves I have of comfort and despair"). Performers include such famous actors as Ben Kingsley, Roger Rees, Claire Bloom and Jane Lapotaire. Critics who comment include A.L. Rowse, Leslie Fiedler, Stephen Spender, Gore Vidal, Arnold Wesker, Nicholas Humphrey and Roy Strong. *Contents & evaluation:* Not seen. From the description in the FFH catalog, summarized above, the omission of so many of the later sonnets, except #144, sidesteps Shakespeare's obsession with the mysterious "dark lady" and his despair and torment over the tyranny of sexual passion. On the other hand that arrangement also makes the program more useful for teachers with younger students (KSR). *Audience:* High school (grades 10-12); College and university.

MEDIUM INFORMATION: *Medium:* Video; *Sound:* Spoken language; *Color:* Yes; *Length:* 150 min.; *Language(s) spoken:* English; *Video type:* B, V, 3/4U.

AUTHORSHIP INFORMATION: *Cast:* Kingsley, Ben; Rees, Roger; Bloom, Claire; Lapotaire, Jane (Performers); Best, Martin (Critic, Sonnet #8); Fiedler, Leslie (Critic, Sonnets #18, #144); Rowse, A.L. (Critic, Sonnets #25, #127); Vidal, Gore (Critic, Sonnets #35, #64); Humphrey, Nicholas (Critic, Sonnets #53, #87);

Spender, Stephen (Critic, Sonnet #65); Wesker, Arnold (Critic, Sonnet #66); Strong, Roy Sir (Critic, Sonnets #91, #107); Mortimer, John (Critic, Sonnet #94); Thomas, D.M. (Critic, Sonnet #128).

DISTRIBUTION & AVAILABILITY: *Distributor:* FFH, GSV*, *Availability:* FFH (814F), B, V, $249, 3/4U $349, Rental $125.

576.1. *Selected Sonnets by Shakespeare.* (Series: Shakespearean Studies on Video and Film).

DOCUMENT INFORMATION: *Country:* GB; *Year of release:* 1984.

EDITION, HISTORY, CONTENTS, & EVALUATION: *Edition & history:* A shortened version of *Shakespeare Sonnets* (see above). Sonnet #65, read by Jane Lapotaire with commentary by Stephen Spender; sonnets #66 and #94, read by Michael Bryant with commentaries by Arnold Wesker and John Mortimer; sonnet #127, read by Ben Kingsley with commentary by A.L. Rowse. Entire program designed to fit into a single class period. *Contents & evaluation:* Not seen. *Audience:* High school (grades 10-12); College and university.

MEDIUM INFORMATION: *Medium:* Video; *Sound:* Spoken language; *Color:* Yes; *Length:* 40 min.; *Language(s) spoken:* English; *Video type:* B, V, 3/4U.

AUTHORSHIP INFORMATION: *Cast:* Kingsley, Ben; Lapotaire, Jane; Bryant, Michael (Performers); Wesker, Arnold; Spender, Stephen; Mortimer, John; Rowse, A.L. (Critics).

DISTRIBUTION & AVAILABILITY: *Distributor:* FFH, *Availability:* FFH (815F) B, V, $149, 3/4U $249, Rental $65.

577. *The Angelic Conversation.*

DOCUMENT INFORMATION: *Country:* GB; *Year of release:* 1985.

EDITION, HISTORY, CONTENTS, & EVALUATION: *Edition & history:* A treatment of the sonnets that from the description seems to stress their male orientation. Director Derek Jarman, an *avant garde* British film director, will be remembered for his 1980 "punk" *Tempest* (622), which was critically acclaimed in England but generally derided or ignored in the United States. *Supplementary materials:* BUFVC 28.

MEDIUM INFORMATION: *Length:* 81 min.

AUTHORSHIP INFORMATION: *Director(s):* Jarman, Derek; *Cast:* Dench, Judi; Reynolds, Paul; Williamson, Philip (Readers).

DISTRIBUTION & AVAILABILITY: *Distributor:* BFI*.

The Taming of the Shrew

ORIGINAL WORK AND PRODUCTION: Farce/
Comedy. *Year performed:* c. 1592; *Site of first production:*
The Theatre in Shoreditch [?]

The Taming of the Shrew. **Motion Picture/Abbreviation**

578. *The Taming of the Shrew.*

DOCUMENT INFORMATION: *Country:* USA; *Year of release:* 1908.

EDITION, HISTORY, CONTENTS, & EVALUATION:
Edition & history: As the work of D.W. Griffith, America's premiere *auteur*, this version of *Shrew* has historical interest. The Biograph pictures logo, "B," appears in many places nested away in the painted sets to identify the maker and to protect against piracy. Only a fragment of the film remains, a reconstruction of a paper roll, in the Library of Congress collection. The best part of the film is Florence Lawrence, the delightful star of so many silent Shakespeare films. Originally known as the "Biograph Girl," she was later ballyhooed by the Carl Laemmle company as the "IMP" (Independent Motion Picture) girl. As the IMP girl, she became the first "free agent" in Hollywood history and thus overturned the economic basis of the industry by making the star system possible. If not much else of Griffith's genius can be detected in the surviving remnant of the film, at least her presence adds further evidence to his reputation for discovering talent. The

Gish sisters were to come later, but in the mean time Florence Lawrence's fresh looks exactly fitted the requirements for a Griffith heroine. *Contents & evaluation:* The lighting is unimpressive. One gets a sense of a flickering, dark interior where curtains economically replace walls and doors. A long-haired shrew (Florence Lawrence) drives Bianca, who is drawing at an easel, out of the room. Kate beats Hortensio over the head with a painting, kicks him, spits at him (it exposes the phoniness of the stereotype of Victorian women as passively genteel). When Petruchio appears he is lucky to be beaten only with a pillow. There is a great deal of wild gesticulating, especially when some seven actors (quite a few in the frame) join Baptista Minola in deploring his harsh fate. A madcap, bizarrely dressed Petruchio then whips poor Grumio and takes Kate off to his retreat in the hills. There are found the usual retinue of cringing servants, who all feel the sting of Petruchio's whip. Overtones of the Mack Sennet tradition take over as the servants madly tumble and dash about in desperate efforts to avoid the master's whip. (One notices on the stairs at this point the Biograph logo, "B.") A starving Kate rushes into the Victorian (!) kitchen in search of food from the servants, but Petruchio snatches it away from her. The film comes to an end with Minola coming to fetch his daughter. But Petruchio and Kate are reconciled and Baptista, thoroughly baffled by the mixed signals he has received from his daughter, departs. Kate and Petruchio are then seen cooing atop a wall. Fade-out. From this brief summary, it can be seen that Griffith

269

privileged the crowd-pleasing slapstick over the play's more serious concern with gender politics. Moreover the Bianca subplot, which introduces interesting phenomenological considerations about the interplay between illusion and reality, has been all but obliterated. As might be expected, this early attempt to accommodate Shakespeare to the tastes of working class Americans sacrificed subtlety for broad farce. Costumes were vaguely Restoration. *Audience:* Professional; *Supplementary materials:* Ball, *SOSF* 62-67.

MEDIUM INFORMATION: *Medium:* Motion Picture; *Sound:* Silent; *Color:* No (black & white); *Length:* 10 min.; *Film type:* 16 mm.

AUTHORSHIP INFORMATION: *Producer(s):* Biograph; *Adaptor/translator(s):* Griffith, David Wark; *Lighting designer(s):* Marvin, Arthur; *Cast:* Lawrence, Florence (Kate); Johnson, Arthur (Petruchio).

DISTRIBUTION & AVAILABILITY: *Publisher or responsible agency:* American Mutoscope and Biograph; *Copy location:* LCM; *Call or copy number:* LC 2786.

The Taming of the Shrew. **Motion Picture/ Abbreviated**

579. *La bisbetica domata.*

DOCUMENT INFORMATION: *Country:* Italy; *Year of release:* 1908.

EDITION, HISTORY, CONTENTS, & EVALUATION: *Edition & history:* Included here as representative of an Italian filmmaker's interest in the play. *Supplementary materials:* Ball, *SOSF* 98; *SIF* 75.

MEDIUM INFORMATION: *Length:* 5 min.

AUTHORSHIP INFORMATION: *Director(s):* Lamberto/ Azeglio.

580. *The Taming of the Shrew.*

DOCUMENT INFORMATION: *Country:* GB; *Year of release:* 1911.

EDITION, HISTORY, CONTENTS, & EVALUATION: *Edition & history:* F.R. Benson, the English theatrical director, made several Shakespeare films in cooperation with Will Barker, the film pioneer, of which this is one. The plays were originally produced at the Shakespeare Memorial Theatre in Stratford, and the company was known as the Co-Operative Cinematograph. *Supplementary materials:* Ball, *SOSF* 84; *SIF* 78.

MEDIUM INFORMATION: *Sound:* Silent; *Length:* 13 min.; *Film type:* 35mm.

AUTHORSHIP INFORMATION: *Director(s):* Barker, Will.

581. *La megere apprivoisee.*

DOCUMENT INFORMATION: *Country:* France; *Year of release:* 1911.

EDITION, HISTORY, CONTENTS, & EVALUATION: *Supplementary materials:* SIF 75; Ball, *SOSF* 129-30.

MEDIUM INFORMATION: *Length:* 10 min.

AUTHORSHIP INFORMATION: *Director(s):* Desfontaines, Henri; *Cast:* Joubé, Romuald; Hervé, Jean; Didier, Cécile.

DISTRIBUTION & AVAILABILITY: *Copy location:* Lost.

582. *La bisbetica domata.*

DOCUMENT INFORMATION: *Country:* Italy; *Year of release:* 1913.

EDITION, HISTORY, CONTENTS, & EVALUATION: *Edition & history:* Arturo Ambrosio may have supervised this film but the scenarist, according to Ball, was Sebastiano Ferraris (a.k.a. Arrigo Frusta). *Supplementary materials:* SIF 75; Ball, *SOSF* 169.

MEDIUM INFORMATION: *Length:* 22 min.

AUTHORSHIP INFORMATION: *Director(s):* Frusta, Arrigo; *Cast:* Rodolfi, Eleuterio.

The Taming of the Shrew. **Motion Picture/ Abridgment**

583. *The Taming of the Shrew.* (Series: Gems of Literature Series).

CURRENT PRODUCTION: *Year:* 1923.

DOCUMENT INFORMATION: *Country:* GB; *Year of release:* 1923; *Country of first showing:* GB.

EDITION, HISTORY, CONTENTS, & EVALUATION: *Edition & history:* A skeletonized British adaptation of *Shrew.* In a stock device of the period, each actor is introduced individually in portrait style at the beginning of the picture, which makes for a marvelous opportunity to verify the cast list and credits. *Contents & evaluation:* More stagy than cinematic, this brief silent version of *Shrew* illustrates the British habit of making movies as though they were stage plays. In its favor is the way in which it develops the thesis that "clothes do not make the person," Petruchio's major reason for showing up at the wedding so badly dressed and for ripping up Kate's new clothing in the subsequent tailor scene. The Bianca plot is nearly all expunged. The sets are mostly dark, poorly lit interiors. In one sequence the light from a rear window is so overwhelming that the actors look like shadows. A title card declares that the production's thesis is to show how "in order to tame Kate, Petruchio determines to be more unreasonable than she in all things." A "Mdlle. Dacia" as Kate and a chubby Lauderdale Maitland as Petruchio give very polished performances to back up this goal. The following title card is typical of the narrative bridges: "After an exhausting journey Petruchio and his tired hungry bride reach his home in Verona." The scenes at Petruchio's country villa are particularly convincing. A title card that reads "[By next day she] began to admire the man whose temper is stronger than her own" tips off the film's controlling concept that women secretly crave domination by men. That idea would not be endorsed by modern feminists, but on the other hand the techniques of filmmaking show some signs of advancement. For one thing, the lost and now dis-used technique of the iris-out is innocently ubiquitous (KSR). *Audience:* General use; *Supplementary materials: SOSF*, 284-86.

MEDIUM INFORMATION: *Medium:* Motion Picture; *Sound:* Silent; *Color:* No (black & white); *Length:* 20 min.; *Film type:* 35 mm.

AUTHORSHIP INFORMATION: *Producer(s):* Godal, Edward; *Director(s):* Collins, Edwin J.; *Adaptor/translator(s):* Stannard, Eliot; *Other personnel:* Kingston, Arthur (Photography); *Cast:* Maitland, Lauderdale (Petruchio); Dacia, Mdlle. [sic] (Katherina); Murray, Gray (Baptista); Murtagh, Cynthia (Bianca); Beard, Ray (Lucentio); Bellamy, Somers (Gremio).

DISTRIBUTION & AVAILABILITY: *Publisher or responsible agency:* Walturdaw; *Copy location:* NFA*, FOL; *Call or copy number:* MP 36 (FOL); *Restrictions:* Archive viewing.

The Taming of the Shrew. Motion Picture/Adaptation

584. *The Taming of the Shrew.*

CURRENT PRODUCTION: *Year:* 1929.

DOCUMENT INFORMATION: *Country:* USA; *Year of release:* 1929/1966.

EDITION, HISTORY, CONTENTS, & EVALUATION: *Edition & history:* Released as a silent in 1929, the film's dialogue was subsequently dubbed in. It was re-released in 1966 with a new music score and sound track. Its historical distinction arises from its status as the first talking Shakespeare film in English. Few actors could match Douglas Fairbanks for swaggering bravado, and his co-starring with Mary Pickford as Kate guaranteed the film's popularity, which is now pretty much out of circulation. The critics, who forgot that *Shrew* is a rollicking farce, not a sacerdotal text like *King Lear*, were very hard on it. Director Sam Taylor was solemnly excoriated for his facetious credit line "with additional dialogue by William Shakespeare." The Library of Congress print that I screened doesn't have this cheeky quip (KSR). *Contents & evaluation:* A farcical, slapstick version of *Shrew* with plenty of physical action. At one point, Fairbanks and Pickford are slash-

ing away at each other with wicked-looking whips. There is a great deal of posturing by Fairbanks and there is also the pixyish personality of Mary Pickford as Kate. According to Peter Morris, she disliked the film so much that she ordered it withdrawn from circulation. A pity, if so, for it is a good entertainment. Certainly Mary Pickford's broad wink at the audience after she utters the famous closing speech on obedience in marriage has gone down in history as one of the slyest and most ironic treatments of this archaic viewpoint about wedlock. The subtle charm of these silent film players surfaces in myriad ways. In an act so simple as munching on an apple during the interpolated wedding scene, which is of course not a part of Shakespeare's text, Douglas Fairbanks shows a world-class talent for maddening insolence (KSR). *Audience:* High school (grades 10-12); College and university; General use; *Supplementary materials:* Morris, *ShOF*, 6.

MEDIUM INFORMATION: *Medium:* Motion Picture; *Sound:* Spoken language; *Length:* 68 min.; *Language(s) spoken:* English; *Film type:* 16mm.

AUTHORSHIP INFORMATION: *Producer(s):* Pickford/Elton Corp.; *Director(s):* Taylor, Sam; *Adaptor/translator(s):* Taylor, Sam; *Designer(s):* Menzies, William Cameron; Irving, Lawrence; *Other personnel:* Struss, Karl (Photography); McNeill, Alan (Editor); Browne, Earl; Humberstone, Lucky; Mayo, Walter (Prod. staff); *1966 re-release staff:* Kemp, Matty; Link, John F.; *Cast:* Pickford, Mary (Katherine); Fairbanks, Douglas (Petruchio); Maxwell, Edwin (Baptista); Cawthorn, Joseph (Gremio); Cook, Clyde (Grumio); Wardell, Geoffrey (Hortensio); Jordon, Dorothy (Bianca).

DISTRIBUTION & AVAILABILITY: *Publisher or responsible agency:* United Artists(1929)/Columbia Pictures (1966); *Distributor:* Not known, *Copy location:* LCM, MOM, FOL, DCV; *Call or copy number:* MP 64 (FOL); *Availability:* DCV, V (#2966), apply.

The Taming of the Shrew. Motion Picture/Travesty

585. *Elstree Calling.*

DOCUMENT INFORMATION: *Country:* GB; *Year of release:* 1930.

EDITION, HISTORY, CONTENTS, & EVALUATION: *Edition & history:* This early British sound musical revue (similar to the American *Show of Shows*) includes a brief sequence in which Donald Calthrop does magic tricks while reciting from Shakespeare's works. Tommy Handley also appears in a travesty of *Taming of the Shrew* with Anna May Wong as Kate Minola throwing furniture at him. Finally Gordon Begg enters as William Shakespeare himself. *Contents & evaluation:* This is "silly" Shakespeare, a precursor to the Monty Python show, screamingly funny if you're in a receptive mood and a bore if you aren't. Historically it is interesting as a very early attempt to speak Shakespeare's words on screen. Moreover there is said to be "interpolated" material by Alfred Hitchcock. *Audience:* General use; *Supplementary materials:* "Review." *Bioscope* 12 Feb. 1930: 30.

MEDIUM INFORMATION: *Medium:* Motion Picture; *Sound:* Spoken language; *Color:* No (black & white); *Length:* 85 min.; *Language(s) spoken:* English; *Film type:* 35mm.

AUTHORSHIP INFORMATION: *Producer(s):* Brunel, Adrian; *Director(s):* Brunel, Adrian; *Cast:* Calthrop, Donald (Petruchio); Wong, Anna Mae (Kate); Begg, Gordon (William Shakespeare).

DISTRIBUTION & AVAILABILITY: *Publisher or responsible agency:* British International Pictures; *Distributor:* Not known, *Copy location:* NFA*.

The Taming of the Shrew. Video/Teleplay

586. *Katherine and Petruchio.*

DOCUMENT INFORMATION: *Country:* GB; *Year of first showing:* 1939; *Location of first showing:* BBC. Transmitted 9:20 to 10:13 P.M., 12 Apr. 1939.

EDITION, HISTORY, CONTENTS, & EVALUATION: *Edition & history:* One of the last transmissions of Shakespeare on television before the BBC closed down for the duration of World War II. This was an acting version of the play prepared by David Garrick in 1754. *Supplementary materials:* TPAB 12 Apr. 1939.

MEDIUM INFORMATION: *Length:* 53 min.

AUTHORSHIP INFORMATION: *Producer(s):* Bower, Dallas; *Cast:* Trevor, Austin (Petruchio); Wheatley, Alan (Hortensio); Barnard, Ivor (Grumio); Scott, Margaretta (Katherine); Webster, Ben (Baptista); Lindsay, Vera (Bianca); Latham, Stuart (Biondello/Joseph); Keir, David (Curtis); Leighton, Will (Nathaniel); Bridge, Cyprian (Nicholas); Dickinson, William (Philip); Chitty, Erik (A Tailor).

DISTRIBUTION & AVAILABILITY: *Publisher or responsible agency:* BBC; *Copy location:* Unavailable.

The Taming of the Shrew. Motion Picture/Derivative

587. *La bisbetica domata.*

DOCUMENT INFORMATION: *Country:* Italy; *Year of release:* 1942.

EDITION, HISTORY, CONTENTS, & EVALUATION: *Supplementary materials:* SIF 76; H&M, 34; Eckert, *SOF* 177.

MEDIUM INFORMATION: *Length:* [?] min.

AUTHORSHIP INFORMATION: *Director(s):* Poggioli, Ferdinand; *Cast:* Silvi, Lilia; Nazzari, Amedeo.

The Taming of the Shrew. Video/Abridgment

588. *The Taming of the Shrew.*

DOCUMENT INFORMATION: *Country:* USA; *Year of first showing:* 1950; *Location of first showing:* ABC Theatre Guild. Transmitted 9:30 P.M., Sunday, 10 April 1950.

EDITION, HISTORY, CONTENTS, & EVALUATION: *Edition & history:* A special continuity was narrated in song by Tom Glazer to bridge gaps between scenes. *Supplementary materials:* "Continuity." *NYT* 10 April 1950: X 9.

MEDIUM INFORMATION: *Color:* No (black & white); *Length:* 60 min. [?]; *Video type:* V.

AUTHORSHIP INFORMATION: *Producer(s):* ABC; *Composer(s):* Levey, Harold; Barnou, Erik (Lyrics); *Cast:* Meredith, Burgess; Redman, Joyce.

DISTRIBUTION & AVAILABILITY: *Publisher or responsible agency:* Theatre Guild on the Air.

589. *The Taming of the Shrew.*

DOCUMENT INFORMATION: *Country:* USA; *Year of first showing:* 1950; *Location of first showing:* Studio One/CBS. Transmitted 10 to 11:00 P.M., 5 June 1950.

EDITION, HISTORY, CONTENTS, & EVALUATION: *Edition & history:* In the early days of North American television, there were several programs devoted to Shakespearean drama but most, as in this instance, seem to have shrunk the plays down to under two hours. Still, these were courageous attempts to confront the dragon of commercialism. On the evening of this performance, the producer competed for audience ratings with such sure-fire entertainments as boxing, "Robert Montgomery Presents," and "Who Said That?" with Ilka Chase and Al Capp. *Supplementary materials:* "On TV." *NYT* 5 June 1950: 40. *Contents and evaluation:* A wonderfully anachronistic interpretation that validates the darkest feminist suspicions about Shakespeare's *Shrew*. Charlton Heston as a macho Petruchio manhandles Lisa Kirk as a subjugated Kate and she sometimes seems to be enjoying it. In "modern" dress (i.e., Fifties hair styles and the ugly suits and dresses of the period), the production has its moments. Despite savage textual cuts, more of the Bianca plot is preserved than is the case in, for example, the Zeffirelli movie version. Although performed "live," there is some interesting camera work with a number of analytical close-ups, mostly involving the service of champagne. The wedding scene is successfully narrated as in Shakespeare's text but the production's budget seems to have put the wedding feast at what looks like a bare kitchen table. Reaction shots of the widow's face during Kate's great speech of capitulation and declaration of obedience allow subversion of the Elizabethan ideology on the need for women's obedience without implicating Kate in the conspiracy. As a document in the history of Shakespeare in performance, the cassette is well worth having (KSR).

MEDIUM INFORMATION: *Color:* No (black & white); *Length:* 60 min. (including Westinghouse commercials); *Video type:* V.

AUTHORSHIP INFORMATION: *Producer:* Miner, Worthington; *Director:* Nickell, Paul; *Costumes:* Russeks; *Designer:* Rychtarick, Richard; *Cast:* Heston, Charlton (Petruchio); Kirk, Lisa (Kate); Sherman, Hiram (Baptista); Chamberlin, Sally (Bianca); Graves, Ernest (Tranio); Barnard, Henry (Lucentio); Gannon, James (Hortensio); Edmonds, Louis (Grumio); Watson, Rudolph (Gremio); Don, Carl (Tailor); Stanley, Florence (Widow); O'Connell, Arthur (Curtis).

DISTRIBUTION & AVAILABILITY: FCM,V, $24.95 (S06987); VID, V, Call.

The Taming of the Shrew. Video/Teleplay

590. *The Taming of the Shrew.*

DOCUMENT INFORMATION: *Country:* GB; *Year of first showing:* 1952; *Location of first showing:* BBC. Transmitted 8:32 P.M., Sunday, 20 April 1952.

EDITION, HISTORY, CONTENTS, & EVALUATION: *Edition & history:* The backstage feuding during rehearsals mostly centered around the director's attempts to locate decent rehearsal space, where the cast would not perish from the cold. With a budget of £1,889, studio executives spoke of the production as "expensive." And indeed with a cast of 20 men and four women, and the usual concern for sets and costumes, the production certainly represented a serious commitment by the studio (WAC TS/502, 25 Feb. 1952). *Supplementary materials:* "Program." *TPAB* 20 Apr. 1952.

MEDIUM INFORMATION: *Length:* 105 min.

AUTHORSHIP INFORMATION: *Producer(s):* Davis, Desmond; *Adaptor/translator(s):* Nixon, Barbara; *Composer(s):* Huntley, John; *Designer(s):* Learoyd, Barry; *Other personnel:* Furness, John (Studio Manager); Seabrooke, Nancy (Stage Manager); *Cast:* Johnston, Margaret (Katherine); Baker, Stanley (Petruchio); Jay, Ernest (Baptista); Shand-Gibbs, Sheila (Bianca); w. Messiter, Eric; Oxley, David; Heslop, Charles; Bowen, Dennis; Siddons, Harold; Fawcett, Peter; Townley, Teke [?]; Mander, Charles; Goolden, Richard; Kelly, Diarmuid; Lindsay, Christine; Munro, Hugh; Lowe, Barry; Grant, Roy; Sherren, Michael; Watson, John; Davis, Noel; Cavallare, Gaylord; Wilson, Jennifer; Errick [?], Anthony.

DISTRIBUTION & AVAILABILITY: *Responsible agency:* BBC; *Location:* Unavailable.

The Taming of the Shrew. Motion Picture/Adaptation

591. *Kiss Me Kate.*

CURRENT PRODUCTION: *Year:* 1953.

DOCUMENT INFORMATION: *Country:* USA; *Year of release:* 1953.

EDITION, HISTORY, CONTENTS, & EVALUATION: *Edition & history:* Musical adaptation by Cole Porter of *The Taming of the Shrew.* A group of actors are engaged in performing the play. The backstage feuding and tension between the two principals, Kathryn Grayson and Howard Keel, mirror the action in Shakespeare's play. In 1988 a revival of this perennial favorite was playing at London's Savoy Theatre to packed houses. *Contents & evaluation:* Universally acclaimed as a work of authentic genius by virtually everyone. Cole Porter's lyrics, especially the catchy "Brush Up Your Shakespeare," have entered into the national consciousness as memorably as some of Shakespeare's own most quotable phrases. While a splendid tonic for students who are timid about plunging directly into the work of Shakespeare, it yet retains its own sparkle and integrity (KSR). *Audience:* High school (grades 10-12); College and university; General use; *Supplementary materials:* [Gene.] "Kate's Great, Get with It." *VAR* 28 Oct. 1953: n.p.

MEDIUM INFORMATION: *Medium:* Motion Picture; *Sound:* Spoken language; *Color:* Yes; *Length:* 109 min.; *Language(s) spoken:* English; *Film type:* 16mm, 35mm.

AUTHORSHIP INFORMATION: *Producer(s):* Cummings, Jack; *Director(s):* Sidney, George; *Screenplay writer(s):* Spewack, Samuel and Bella; *Adaptor/translator(s):* Kingsley, Dorothy; *Composer(s):* Porter, Cole; *Choreographer(s):* Pan, Hermes; *Designer(s):* Gibbons, Cedric; McLeary, Urie; *Costume designer(s):* Plunkett, Walter; *Other personnel:* Rosher, Charles (Camera); Winters, Ralph (Editor); Shearer, Douglas (Sound); *Cast:* Keel, Howard (Fred Graham—Petruchio); Grayson, Kathryn (Killi Vanessi-Katherine); Miller, Ann (Lois Lane—Bianca); Kasznar, Kurt; Fosse, Bob (Bianca's suitors); Wynn, Keenan; Whitmore, James (Hoodlums); Rall, Tommy (Bill Calhoun); Randell, Ron (Cole Porter); Parker, Willard (Callaway, Tex); O'Brien, David (Ralph); Allister, Claud (Paul); Codee, Ann.

DISTRIBUTION & AVAILABILITY: *Publisher or responsible agency:* Metro-Goldwyn-Mayer; *Distributor:* FCM, FMB*; *Copy location:* FOL; *Call or copy number:* MP69; *Availability:* FCM, sale, V $29.95; FMB*, rental 16mm, apply.

The Taming of the Shrew. **Motion Picture/ Derivative**

592. *La megere apprivoisee/La fierecilla domada.*

DOCUMENT INFORMATION: *Country:* France/Spain; *Year of release:* 1955.

EDITION, HISTORY, CONTENTS, & EVALUATION: *Supplementary materials: SIF* 76; Morris, *SHOF* 20; H&M, 34.

MEDIUM INFORMATION: *Length:* 88 min.

AUTHORSHIP INFORMATION: *Director(s):* Román, Antonio; *Cast:* Cordy, Raymond (Baptista); Closas, Alberto (Petruchio); Sévilla, Carmen (Katherina).

DISTRIBUTION & AVAILABILITY: *Distributor:* Vascos [?].

The Taming of the Shrew. **Video/Teleplay**

593. *The Taming of the Shrew.* (Series: Hallmark Hall of Fame).

DOCUMENT INFORMATION: *Country:* USA; *Year of first showing:* 1956; *Location of first showing:* NBC Network. Transmitted 4:00 to 5:30 P.M., Sunday, 18 March 1956.

EDITION, HISTORY, CONTENTS, & EVALUATION: *Edition & history:* Hallmark Hall of Fame television adaptation of *Taming of the Shrew* transmitted originally in color and but now preserved only in black and white. The show was an "Easter program" in Holy Week. In a clever opening device, the characters are presented by means of cue cards. Then Grumio sums up the Sly Induction scene by pointing out that the actors are players. He ends his speech with Sly's words, "Let's let the world slip by." There is then a cut to dancers and jugglers and the plot is mimed, *commedia* style. Quick editing follows in which there is an immediate movement, for example, to the Bianca plot. The lighting occasionally presents problems when characters become difficult to identify. The director himself felt that the colors were 'extraordinary' with a white floor and white set and transitions shot with bright red chiffon scarves floating in front of the lens. All the more pity that it survives only in black-and-white Kinescope. *Contents & evaluation:* In this performance that was taped live, the slickness and polish of modern television is lacking but the raw spontaneity of unedited performance compensates for that. When, for example, Maurice Evans greets Baptista Minola, he fluffs a cue but picks it up quickly. These are not technically polished performances but engrossing enough because of the lively acting. The *commedia* influence results in any number of stylized sequences. One of the most effective is the meeting of Petruchio (obstinately mispronounced as 'Petruk'io' throughout) and Kate. They approach each other to the roll of drums. The tableau has almost the formality of a boxing ring. The dialogue of course has been sanitized and cleaned up so that the excruciatingly vulgar joke about the 'sting in the tale' is expunged. At the end of the boxing match, Kate falls to the floor and her father in effect counts her out as he awards her to Petruchio. Maurice Evans as Petruchio, in another of those endearing fluffs characteristic of early live TV drama, stumbles slightly, and awkwardly, as he attempts to climb back into the ring. The image is hardly that of the swaggering Petruchio of, say, a Douglas Fairbanks. The wedding feast features a ballet of domination and subjugation that mirrors the connection between Kate and Petruchio. The Petruchio figure pushes Kate around, strangles her in jest, playfully whips her, forces her to jump through hoops, and then whirl around the floor. Symbolically the real Petruchio steps in to rescue Kate but symbolically he takes the whip from the hand of the surrogate Petruchio. Obviously in 1956, directors were blissfully unaware of radical feminist theory. At the end when Kate makes her famous speech pledging obedience to Petruchio, she gives no hint of being restless with patriarchal hegemony. There is no attempt to break into the subtext and come up with an interpretation more palatable to modern ideologies (KSR). *Audience:* General use; *Supplementary materials:* Jorgenson, Paul. "Entertainment for TV." *QFRT,* 10 (1956): 391-98; Kliman, B. "Unseen Interpreter: George Schaefer." *FC* 7.3.(1983): 29-37; "Shakespeare Comedy." *NYT* 18 March 1956: X 11.

MEDIUM INFORMATION: *Medium:* Video; *Sound:* Spoken language; *Color:* Yes; *Length:* 90 min.; *Language(s) spoken:* English; *Film type:* 16mm; *Video type:* V.

AUTHORSHIP INFORMATION: *Producer(s):* Evans, Maurice; Cunneff, Joseph; Alberg, Mildred Freed; *Director(s):* Schaefer, George; Hartung, Robert; Luraschi, Adrienne; *Adaptor/translator(s):* Hogan, Michael; Nichols, William; *Composer(s):* Engel, Lehman; *Choreographer(s):* Charmoli, Tony; *Designer(s):* Ter-Arutunian, Rouben; *Costume designer(s):* Ter-Arutunian, Rouben; Glenn, James; *Lighting designer(s):* Knight, William; *Other personnel:* Smith, Dick (Make-up); Adler, Ernest (Hair); Falcone, Phil (Audio); Long, Robert (Technical director); Howard, Brice (Unit manager); *Cast:* Evans, Maurice (Petruchio); Palmer, Lilli (Katherine); Cilento, Diane (Bianca); Bourneuf, Philip (Baptista); Kilty, Jerome (Grumio); Watson, Douglas (Hortensio); Colicos, John (Lucentio); Stone, Robinson (Vincentio); Fletcher, Jack (Tailor); Long, Ronald (Biondello); Able, Will B. (Curtis); Lynn, Mara; Godkin, Paul (Dancers).

DISTRIBUTION & AVAILABILITY: *Publisher or responsible agency:* NBC/Hallmark Hall of Fame; *Copy location:* MOB; *Call or copy number:* Pts. 1&2. T78:0055; *Restrictions:* Archive viewing.

The Taming of the Shrew. **Video/Derivative/Musical**

594. *Kiss Me Kate.* (Series: Hallmark Hall of Fame).

DOCUMENT INFORMATION: *Country:* USA; *Year of first showing:* 1958; *Location of first showing:* NBC. Transmitted 9 to 10:30 P.M., Thursday, 20 Nov. 1958.

EDITION, HISTORY, CONTENTS, & EVALUATION: *Edition & history:* A television version of this perennially popular Cole Porter adaptation of Shakespeare's comedy. This production featured Alfred Drake and Patricia Morison, who had appeared in the original Broadway production. *Supplementary materials:* "Television." *NYT* 20 Nov. 1958: 71; Einstein, Dan. "ATAS/UCLA Archives." *SFNL* 5.1 (Dec. 1980): 1+.

MEDIUM INFORMATION: *Medium:* 16 mm, Kinescope; *Sound:* Spoken language; *Color:* No (black & white); *Length:* 90 min.

AUTHORSHIP INFORMATION: *Producer(s):* Schaefer, George; *Director(s):* Schaefer, George; *Adaptor/translator(s):* Spewack, Sam and Bella; *Composer(s):* Porter, Cole; *Cast:* Drake, Alfred; Morison, Patricia; Wilson, Julie; Klugman, Jack; Lembeck, Harvey; McGrath, Paul; Hayes, Bill.

DISTRIBUTION & AVAILABILITY: *Publisher or responsible agency:* NBC Television Network; *Distributor:* Arch., *Copy location:* UCL.

The Taming of the Shrew. **Motion Picture/Derivative**

595. *Mas fuerte que el amor.* (*Kiss Me Kate*).

DOCUMENT INFORMATION: *Country:* Mexico; *Year of release:* 1959.

EDITION, HISTORY, CONTENTS, & EVALUATION: *Supplementary materials:* SIF 77.

MEDIUM INFORMATION: *Length:* 71 min.

AUTHORSHIP INFORMATION: *Director(s):* Demicheli, Tullio; *Cast:* Mistral, Jorge; Miroslava, Chela Castro.

The Taming of the Shrew. **Video/Recording**

596. *Ukroshchenie stroptivoi.*

DOCUMENT INFORMATION: *Country:* USSR; *Year of release:* 1961.

EDITION, HISTORY, CONTENTS, & EVALUATION: *Edition & history:* Recording of a theatrical performance of the Central Theatre of the Soviet Army. *Supplementary materials:* Morris, *SHOS* 23; SIF 76.

MEDIUM INFORMATION: *Length:* 85 min.

AUTHORSHIP INFORMATION: *Director(s):* Kolosov,

Sergei; *Cast:* Kasatkina, Ludmilla (Katharina); Popov, Andrei (Petruchio).

DISTRIBUTION & AVAILABILITY: *Distributor:* Mosfilm.

The Taming of the Shrew. **Video/Derivative**

597. *Kiss Me Kate.*

DOCUMENT INFORMATION: *Country:* GB; *Year of first showing:* 1964.

EDITION, HISTORY, CONTENTS, & EVALUATION: *Edition & history:* First American musical to be adapted for British television. *Supplementary materials:* "A Gala Show." *RT* 16 April 1964: 23.

MEDIUM INFORMATION: *Length:* 95 min.

AUTHORSHIP INFORMATION: *Director(s):* Gilbert, James; *Cast:* Morison, Patricia (Lilli Vanessi); Keel, Howard (Fred Graham); Martin, Millicent (Lois); Barker, Eric (Harrison Howell).

DISTRIBUTION & AVAILABILITY: *Copy location:* BBC*.

The Taming of the Shrew. **Motion Picture/Adaptation**

598. *The Taming of the Shrew.*

CURRENT PRODUCTION: *Year:* 1966.

DOCUMENT INFORMATION: *Country:* USA/Italy; *Year of release:* 1966.

EDITION, HISTORY, CONTENTS, & EVALUATION: *Edition & history:* With Richard Burton as Petruchio and Elizabeth Taylor as Kate, then reigning king and queen of the cinema world, this lively production by Franco Zeffirelli rivals the Douglas Fairbanks/Mary Pickford pairing in its exploitation of stars. Indeed it can be, and has been, argued that a great deal of Shakespeare's play gets lost along the way. The trade-off lies in the ingenious ways by which Zeffirelli has adapted Shakespeare's play to the needs of the screen. For example, he embeds the Christopher Sly plot within the main plot by conflating Sly with Petruchio, and the drunken Sly remains vestigially as the creature fettered in a cage above the main gate to Padua. This clever transposition also has the unfortunate tendency to degrade Petruchio from his higher social class down to the level of the drunken and lower-class Sly. A raucous movie, it was bound to trigger some doubts, as the words of the following critic illustrate. *Contents & evaluation:* "Don't bother to brush up your Shakespeare when you go to see Elizabeth Taylor and Richard Burton in 'The Taming of the Shrew.' And certainly don't bother to study the Marquis of Queensberry rules, the century-old code of pugilism, which might, for this occasion, have been applied. Both are serenely violated in this totally wild abstraction of the Bard for the purposes of a fast return engagement between the Burtons in a florid and fustian film. . . . Having had at one another very roundly and in a serious dramatic vein in their most recent husband-wife tangle, 'Who's Afraid of Virginia Woolf?', the Burtons are now turned loose with slapsticks for a free-swinging hit-as-hit-can in this forthrightly campy entertainment. . . . They are refereed by Franco Zeffirelli out of the corner of one winking eye. . . . In settings that fairly teem and tumble with lush Renaissance decor, vegetable stands, street singers, heavily robed merchants and clowns, Mr. Burton's hairy Petruchio sweeps grandly onto the operatic scene with the obvious intent of being funny quite as much as that of getting a wealthy wife. And Miss Taylor's powerful Katharina hauls off and swats him with as much desire to set the customers whooping and howling as to discourage his matrimonial quest. . . . In all manner and ways, the text of Shakespeare, and indeed the characters, give way to the shrieking and sweating cornbeef-eaters that Miss Taylor and Mr. Burton devise. And it is in their extravagant overacting and in the evident fun they have that the sheer theatrical gusto and rollicking sport of this film reside. . . . But I find it all grows a bit tedious. After we've examined Mr. Burton's great red beard and Miss Taylor's amazingly revealing and yet deftly restraining decolletage, listened to them toss about the language without much clarity or eloquence, watched Mr. Burton slobber drunkenly through scene after scene, and discovered beneath the finery of Katharina a hint of Gloria in 'Butterfield,' it seems time to have done with clowning and settle down to a bit of comedy—comedy of a slightly adult order. The Burtons never do" (Crowther, Bosley, "Review," *NYT*, 9 March 1967: 43). *Audience:* High school (grades 10-12); College and university; *Supplementary materials:* Harrison, Carey in *FSF* 159-60; Jorgens, *SOF* 66-78; Manvell, *SAF* 99-100.

MEDIUM INFORMATION: *Medium:* Motion Picture; *Sound:* Spoken language; *Color:* Yes; *Length:* 122 min.; *Language(s) spoken:* English; *Film type:* 16mm; 35mm; *Video type:* B, V.

AUTHORSHIP INFORMATION: *Producer(s):* McWhorter, Richard (Exec. prod.); Zeffirelli, Franco; Burton, Richard; Taylor, Elizabeth; *Director(s):* Zeffirelli, Franco; Lastricati, Carol; Ricci, Rinaldo; *Adaptor/translator(s):* Dehn, Paul; D'Amico, Suso Cecchi; Zeffirelli, Franco; *Composer(s):* Rota, Nino; Savina, Carlo; *Designer(s):* De Cuir, John; Mariani, Guiseppi; Webb, Elven; *Set designer(s):* Simoni, Dario; Gervasi, Carlo; *Costume designer(s):* Sharaff, Irene; Donati, Danilo; *Other personnel:* Morris, Oswald; Trasatti, Luciano (Photography); Lohman, Augie (Special effects); Hildyard, David; De Martino, Aldo (Costumes); Ottani, Mario (Sound); Micheletti, Daniele; Cocco, Roberto (Production managers); *Cast:* Burton, Richard (Petruchio); Taylor, Eliza-

beth (Katherina); Hordern, Michael (Baptista Minola); Cusack, Cyril (Grumio); York, Michael (Lucentio); Lynch, Alfred (Tranio); Pyne, Natasha (Bianca); Webb, Alan (Gremio); Spinetti, Victor (Hortensio); Dignam, Mark (Vincentio); Cobelli, Giancarlo (Priest); Dobtcheff, Vernon (Pedant); Holder, Roy (Biondello); Magni, Gianni (Curtis); Bonucci, Alberto (Nathaniel); Capolicchio, Lino (Gregory); Antonelli, Roberto (Philip); Garner, Anthony (Haberdasher); Parry, Ken (Tailor); Valori, Bice (Widow).

DISTRIBUTION & AVAILABILITY: *Publisher or responsible agency:* Royal Films International (N.Y.) F.A.I. Production; *Distributor:* FNC, CWF, SWA, KIT, TWC, RCC, DCV, FCM, FMB*, ILL, INM; *Copy location:* FOL, NFA*; *Call or copy number:* MP44 (FOL); *Availability:* FNC, CWF, SWA, KIT, FMB*, rental, 16mm; TWC, sale, B (SV104B-K6), V (SV104V-K6) TWC, $68.50; RCC, V, $59.95; FCM, sale, V, $59.95; DCV, V (#67127), $58; ILL $59.95; INM $69.95.

The Taming of the Shrew. Video/Derivative

599. *Kiss Me Kate.*

DOCUMENT INFORMATION: *Country:* USA; *Year of first showing:* 1968; *Location of first showing:* Armstrong Circle Theatre/ABC. Transmitted 9:30 to 11:00 P.M., Monday, 25 March 1968.

EDITION, HISTORY, CONTENTS, & EVALUATION: *Edition & history:* Yet another production of the perennial Cole Porter favorite about the backstage trials and tribulations of a Shakespearean company performing Shakespeare's *Shrew. Supplementary materials:* "Television." *NYT* 25 March 1968: 83.

MEDIUM INFORMATION: *Sound:* Spoken language; *Color:* Yes; *Length:* 90 min.

AUTHORSHIP INFORMATION: *Composer(s):* Porter, Cole; *Cast:* Goulet, Robert; Lawrence, Carol; Callan, Michael; Walter, Jessica; Nype, Russell; Munshin, Jules; Ingels, Marty.

DISTRIBUTION & AVAILABILITY: *Publisher or responsible agency:* ABC/Armstrong Theatre.

600. *Man and Woman.* (Series: Great Themes of Literature).

DOCUMENT INFORMATION: *Country:* GB/Italy/USA; *Year of release:* 1972.

EDITION, HISTORY, CONTENTS, & EVALUATION: *Edition & history:* An edited version of Zeffirelli's *The Taming of the Shrew* with excerpts from the film and a narration by Orson Welles. Part of a series, "Great Themes in Literature," the film compares Shakespeare's view of the battle of the sexes with the more somber positions of Henrik Ibsen, Edward Albee, and Tennessee Williams. *Contents & evaluation:* Not seen, but the promise of scenes from a Zeffirelli film and of a narration by Orson Welles sounds enticing. A favorable reviewer noted that "if you are anxious to bring Shakespeare from his scholarly tomb into the eyes and ears of all your students, treat them to this lusty and boisterous look at the relationship between the sexes" (Stocking, David, *EJ* 63 [May 1975]: 96). Others will disagree with this assessment, as after all the Zeffirelli *Shrew* sacrifices virtually all of the Sly induction and the Bianca subplot in favor of underscoring the farcical battles between Kate and Petruchio. The conversion of Petruchio by Burton into a drunken boor, much like Sly, further distorts Shakespeare's play. As a film, however, it often arouses interest in Shakespeare among high school and college students. And the truth is that because this play offers relatively few examples of Shakespeare's brilliant language, it can be adapted by inventive stage and screen directors with a minimum of damage to the original (KSR). *Audience:* High school (grades 10-12); College and university.

MEDIUM INFORMATION: *Medium:* Motion Picture; *Sound:* Spoken language; *Color:* Yes; *Length*: 33 min.; *Language(s) spoken:* English; *Film type:* 16mm.

AUTHORSHIP INFORMATION: *Producer(s):* Learning Corp. of America; *Director(s):* Zeffirelli, Franco; *Cast:* Welles, Orson (Narrator); Burton, Richard (Petruchio); Taylor, Elizabeth (Katherine).

DISTRIBUTION & AVAILABILITY: *Publisher or responsible agency:* Learning Corporation of America; *Distributor:* UIO, *Availability:* UIO, rental, 16mm (50899F), $20.80.

The Taming of the Shrew. Motion Picture/Scenes

601. *The Taming of the Shrew,* 1.2; 2.1. (Series: The Shakespeare Series [IFB], XI).

DOCUMENT INFORMATION: *Country:* Great Britain; *Year of release:* 1974.

EDITION, HISTORY, CONTENTS, & EVALUATION: *Edition & history:* Opens with the trademark shot of an Elizabethan stage and then goes on to give excerpts from *The Taming of the Shrew,* 1.2; 2.1. (For others in this series in which the plays are performed on a replica of an Elizabethan stage, see numbers 22, 131, 164, 232, 326, 430, 467, 490, 510, 556, and 619.) *Contents & evaluation:* This series features a number of outstanding performers from the Royal Shakespeare Company. David Suchet as Petruchio gives a first-rate performance. With his strong masculine presence, he manages to project the inner strength so vital to this role. On the other hand, the actress playing Kate seems miscast, almost spinsterish rather than vigorously alive. While the film is intended to show the staging of the plays, what emerges on screen is not so much Shakespeare on stage as stagy Shakespeare. *Audience:* High school (grades 10-12).

MEDIUM INFORMATION: *Medium:* Motion Picture; *Sound:* Spoken language; *Color:* Yes; *Length:* 13 min.; *Language(s) spoken:* English; *Film type:* 16mm; *Video type:* V, 3/4U (4 per cassette).

AUTHORSHIP INFORMATION: *Producer(s):* Seabourne, John; *Director(s):* Seabourne, Peter; *Cast:* Blakeney, Madeline (Kate); Suchet, David (Petruchio); Marsden, Roy (Hortensio); Kelly, Peter (Grumio).

DISTRIBUTION & AVAILABILITY: *Publisher or responsible agency:* Anvil Film and Recording Group; *Distributor:* IFB, CNU, *Copy location:* FOL; *Call or copy number:* ISBN 0-8354-1592-9; FOL, MP 85; *Availability:* CNU rental 16mm, $8; IFB sale 16mm, $225, V 195, rental $15.

The Taming of the Shrew. Video/Recording

602. *The Taming of the Shrew.*

CURRENT PRODUCTION: *Year:* 1976.

DOCUMENT INFORMATION: *Country:* USA; *Year of release:* 1979; *Location of first showing:* PBS stations/ American Conservatory Theatre, San Francisco. First transmitted on PBS stations 9:00 P.M., Wednesday, 10 November 1976 (included interview with Director William Ball); repeat: Saturday, 9 June 1979.

EDITION, HISTORY, CONTENTS, & EVALUATION: *Edition & history:* A televised recording of the stage play as performed by the American Conservatory Theatre group in San Francisco. Essentially it is a recording of a stage performance but with the theatre audience boldly included, some even sitting on stage. Station WNET/THIRTEEN, New York City, in 1979 repeated the program "back-to-back" with an immediately preceding showing at 8:00 P.M. of the 1953 film *Kiss Me Kate.* The TV/Radio section billed it as, "The Love Comedy Supreme—Two Lively Versions." The opportunity to observe such variations on a theme in a single evening is a rare one. *Contents & evaluation:* "A filmed stage play, not at all 'cinematic' (unless you count editing from close to mid shots), the production does nevertheless show traces of Hollywood influence. 'Mickey Mouse' sound effects—horns, triangles, clackers, cymbals, gongs, slide whistles (and what else?)—punctuate pratfalls and words. And by envisioning the strolling players performing for Christopher Sly as a *commedia dell arte* troupe, the director unites that lost stage tradition with slapstick of the silent era. It must be said, however, that despite the leaping, whirling, somersaulting, and prancing, these are actors who speak crisply and sharply. As so often happens, the Induction gets edited out, with a loss of its subtle commentary on the theme of 'supposings' in the play-within-the-play. But that can be left to classroom exploration. . . . A witty interpolation has the Pedant, zonked out from a Tom-and-Jerry slapstick routine, suddenly recite the opening lines from Gloucester's soliloquy in *R3* (1.1). Right play but wrong day!" (KSR, *SFNL* 1.1 [1976]: 1) *Audience:* High school (grades 10-12); College and university; General use; *Supplementary materials:* "Program." *NYT* 9 June 1979: 22.

MEDIUM INFORMATION: *Medium:* Video; *Sound:* Spoken language; *Color:* Yes; *Length:* 82 min.; *Language(s) spoken:* English; *Video type:* V.

AUTHORSHIP INFORMATION: *Producer(s):* Campbell, Ken; Harrington, Charlene; *Director(s):* Ball, William; Browning, Kirk; *Composer(s):* Holby, Lee; *Designer(s):* Funicello, Ralph; *Costume designer(s):* Fletcher, Robert; *Lighting designer(s):* Engel, Jeff; *Other personnel:* Crawford, Frank (Stage manager); Farmer, Tom (Engineer); Bennewitz, Rick (Technical director); Bhargava, Girish (Videotape); Stephens, Larry (Audio); Sanford, Mark (Video); Brown, Barry; Geving, Hank; Jones, Donovan; Keeler, Mike (Camera); Catonia, James (Make-up); Mei Ling, Jack (Hair styles); Anthes, John (Graphics); *Cast:* Singer, Marc (Petruchio); Olster, Fredi (Kate); Birk, Raye (Gremio); Boen, Earl (Pedant); Boussom, Ronald (Grumio); Hamilton, Rick (Tranio); Kern, Daniel (Biondello); Paterson, William (Baptista Minola); St. Paul, Stephen (Lucentio); Shotwell, Sandra (Bianca); Williamson, Laird (Vincentio); Winker, James R. (Hortensio); and others of the company; *Performance group(s):* American Conservatory Theatre, San Francisco.

DISTRIBUTION & AVAILABILITY: *Publisher or responsible agency:* WNET/THIRTEEN, New York City; *Distributor:* NET, *Copy location:* MOB; *Availability:* NET, V, 3/4U, apply.

602.1. *The Taming of the Shrew.*

DOCUMENT INFORMATION: *Country:* USA; *Year of first showing:* 1978; *Location of first showing:* Delacorte Theatre, Central Park, New York City.

EDITION, HISTORY, CONTENTS, & EVALUATION: *Edition & history:* Recording of the Joseph Papp 1978 *Taming of the Shrew*. There is an archival copy in the TOFT (Theatre on Film and Tape) Collection. For further information, see also *Kiss Me, Petruchio* (605), a documentary based on this production, which is in general distribution; *Supplementary materials:* Barnes, Clive. "Shakespeare in New York City." *SQ* 30.2 (April 1979): 184-5.

MEDIUM INFORMATION: *Sound:* Spoken language; *Color:* Yes; *Length:* 151 min.

AUTHORSHIP INFORMATION: See *Kiss Me Petruchio* (605, below); *Cast:* see 605 below..

DISTRIBUTION & AVAILABILITY: *Publisher or responsible agency:* New York Shakespeare Festival; *Copy Location:* TOFT, LCL (NCOV 83).

The Taming of the Shrew. Video/Teleplay

603. *The Taming of the Shrew.* (Series: The Shakespeare Plays).

DOCUMENT INFORMATION: *Country:* GB; *Year of filming:* 18-24 June 1980; *Year of first showing:* 1980; *Location of first showing(s):* BBC, London; PBS stations, USA, 26 Jan. 1981.

EDITION, HISTORY, CONTENTS, & EVALUATION: *Edition & history:* The most extraordinary thing about this production was Jonathan Miller's assault on stage tradition that saw Petruchio converted from a kind of rollicking swaggerer (e.g., Douglas Fairbanks and Richard Burton) into a rigid, suffocatingly puritanical figure. Miller's Petruchio somehow got cross-hatched with Malvolio. Miller's characteristically brilliant rationale for this apparent absurdity, however, was that Petruchio is actually a puritan. One only has to think of his constant exhortations to Kate that mere outward appearance and fine clothing do not make the man. This point he underscores by showing up at the wedding outfitted in a ridiculous getup. To make the joke even more delicious, Miller selected one of the funniest men alive, John Cleese, of the Monty Python show, to play this solemn Petruchio. It's like casting Woody Allen as Hamlet. Moreover Miller gets away with it. He creates an absorbing show. *Contents & evaluation:* "Enlivened by some fine moments and crushed by some dull ones, this televised *Taming of the Shrew* fails because of the director's culture-bound vision of women. . . . Discarding the incomplete frame of Shakespeare's text—the appearance of Christopher Sly at the start and absence at the close—the TV offering substitutes another frame: the producer's discussion of the play's meaning. So infrequently do we hear a producer's voice—except as we exhume his correspondence after his death or note the excisions and transpositions of scenes in promptbooks—that this new 'frame' offers valuable insights into readings and misreadings of Shakespeare's comedy. For, though Jonathan Miller believes he is presenting a 'liberated' *Taming of the Shrew*, he is still bound by the old cliches. His own words—in conversation with John Cleese, the actor playing Petruchio—betray him. For Miller describes Petruchio's actions as 'bringing a spirited steed under control'(!). This inability to see Kate as a whole person informs and mars the work" (Dash, Irene, "*The Taming of the Shrew*," *SFNL* 5.2 [1981]: 7+). *Audience:* High school (grades 10-12); College and university; General use; *Supplementary materials:* Fenwick, Henry, *The Taming of the Shrew BSP* 19-25; Videotape (25 min.) from "Shakespeare in Perspective" series with Penelope Mortimer as lecturer available in U.K. from BBC* (*BUFVC* 24).

MEDIUM INFORMATION: *Medium:* Video; *Sound:*

Spoken language; *Color:* Yes; *Length:* 125 min.; *Video type:* B, V, 3/4U.

AUTHORSHIP INFORMATION: *Producer(s):* Miller, Jonathan; *Director(s):* Miller, Jonathan; *Adaptor/translator(s):* Snodin, David; *Composer(s):* Oliver, Stephen; *Designer(s):* Lowrey, Colin; *Costume designer(s):* Hughes, Alun; *Other personnel:* Charlesworth, Alan (Prod. asst.); Wilders, John (Literary consultant); Mair, Eileen (Makeup); Anthony, Chick (Sound); Barclay, John (Mixer); Dell, Howard (Editor); Atkinson, Jim (Camera); *Cast:* Cleese, John (Petruchio); Badel, Sarah (Katherina); Chandler, Simon (Lucentio); Pedley, Anthony (Tranio); Franklyn-Robbins, John (Baptista); Thornton, Frank (Gremio); Cecil, Jonathan (Hortensio); Penhaligon, Susan (Bianca); Waters, Harry (Biondello); Kincaid, David (Grumio); Barron, John (Vincentio); Bird, John (Pedant); Hickson, Joan (Widow); Lennie, Angus (Curtis); Willis, Bev (Servant); Webster, Harry (Nathaniel); Morris, Gil (Philip); Sarony, Leslie (Gregory); Deadman, Derek (Nicholas); Gilmore, Denis (Peter); Hay, Alan (Tailor); Kinsey, D.(Haberdasher).

DISTRIBUTION & AVAILABILITY: *Publisher or responsible agency:* BBC/TLF; *Distributor:* AVP, UIO, BBC* *Copy location:* UVM, CTL*; *Availability:* AVP, B, V, 3/4U $450 (1987), sale; UIO, V (72046H), 3/4U (70146V), rental, $22.30; BBC*, 16mm or V, apply (*BUFVC 24*).

The Taming of the Shrew. Video/Recording

604. *The Taming of the Shrew.*

DOCUMENT INFORMATION: *Country:* Canada; *Year of first showing:* 1981.

EDITION, HISTORY, CONTENTS, & EVALUATION: *Edition & history:* A video recording of a summer 1981 stage production of *The Taming of the Shrew* at the Stratford, Ontario, Canada, Festival. A copy is housed in the TOFT (Theatre on Film and Tape) Collection at the New York Public Library. It may be viewed by apppointment (see below). This same production was used also for the excerpts from *Shrew* that appear in the CBC Stratford "From Page to Stage" series (606, below). *Contents & evaluation:* "Len Cariou . . . offered a Petruchio in the current Social Worker mode. On this reading, Petruchio is primarily concerned to save Katharina from herself, and he imparts to her the correct role model. To see the *Shrew* assimilated into homiletic drama is hard for those of us who regard its vital essences as brutality and sexuality. Sharry Flett, after some initial incredulity, acquiesced in this view of matters. She seemed ill suited to the coarse exchanges of II.i, and conveyed that she was placed in the wrong genre. ('I'm really a comedy of manners specialist'; and indeed she played Celimene in the Festival.) The opening scenes with her lacked fire. Had I been refereeing in II.i, I should have stopped the

contest, warned Katharina to show more action, and reprimanded Petruchio for gentlemanly conduct. Things moved on to a more believable level in the second half, when the protagonists agreed to be civilized at everyone else's expense. The suburban bickering of Act V was convincing enough, and the great final speech came over with entire conviction, and why should it not? Naturally it can be delivered with the irony it asks for (and got, from Paola Dionisotti in Bogdanov's RSC production). On the other hand, there's no reason why Katharina shouldn't mean every word in context. The key is that Petruchio has won a bet, and Katharina knows it. . . . The glance that Sharry Flett shot at her groom registered the point fully. ('*Did* you? Good for you! And now you can buy me another gown.') I see no reason why Katharina, alone in Padua, should be untouched by the economic drives sustaining the community. So Kate sang for her supper, and very prettily too" (Berry, Ralph, "Stratford Festival Canada," *SQ* 33.2 [Summer 1982]: 200-1); for a video review, see H.R. Coursen, *SOT* 286-7).

MEDIUM INFORMATION: *Medium:* Video; *Sound:* Spoken language; *Color:* Yes; *Length:* 153 min.; *Language(s) spoken:* English; *Video type:* 3/4U.

AUTHORSHIP INFORMATION: *Producer(s):* Campbell, Norman; *Director(s):* Dews, Peter; *Adaptor/translator(s):* Schonberg, Michael; *Composer(s):* Symonds, Norman; *Designer(s):* Benson, Susan; *Lighting designer(s):* Frehner, Harry; *Cast:* Cariou, Len (Petruchio); Flett, Sharry (Kate); Griffin, Lynne (Bianca); O'Sullivan, Barney (Baptista); Rod, Beattie (Gremio); Ellis, Desmond (Sly); Feore, Colm (Tranio); Gordon, Lewis (Grumio); Helpmann, Max (Lucentio); Hutt, Peter (Lucentio) .

DISTRIBUTION & AVAILABILITY: *Publisher or responsible agency:* Stratford Shakespeare Festival; *Copy location:* LCL TOFT Collection; *Call or copy number:* NCOX 339; *Availability:* By appt.; *Distributor* INM, V (DS26) $99.00.

The Taming of the Shrew. Video/Documentary

605. *Kiss Me, Petruchio.*

DOCUMENT INFORMATION: *Country:* USA; *Year of release:* 1981; *Location of first showing:* USA, PBS stations, 16 Nov. 1981.

EDITION, HISTORY, CONTENTS, & EVALUATION: *Edition & history:* A documentary based on a summer 1978 production by the New York City Shakespeare company at the Delacorte Theatre in Central Park of *The Taming of the Shrew* (see 602.1 above). Behind-the-scenes interviews with Meryl Streep and Raul Julia are intertwined with episodes from the play to provide insights into theatrical art. *Contents & evaluation:* The energy and vitality of Streep and Julia as Kate and Petruchio make for unforgettable performances. Moreover the crowd in the park watching the play adds a further dimension in its demonstration of the dynamic that takes place between live actors and a live audience. Raul Julia, who comments that "Shakespeare is too big to be put in one little way of doing it," brings his own unique personality to the role. Bianca is a nincompoop blonde whom Kate disposes of with a karate chop. Meryl Streep handles the last speech in an ambiguous way, partly straightforward but then toward the end with a definite trend toward farce. Kate in fact drags Petruchio off to bed. In the post-feminist climate of today, one would expect to find a domineering female in the role of Kate. Even so some of the spectators thought that Kate was being over-whelmed by Petruchio. Others commented that "She's [Kate] mad about him, but don't tell him," or "She never met anybody who came up against her before." The metatheatrical experience of watching the audience watching the players (just as Sly watched the performance too) is a tonic (KSR). *Audience:* General use.

MEDIUM INFORMATION: *Medium:* Video; *Sound:* Spoken language; *Color:* Yes; *Length:* 58 min.; *Language(s) spoken:* English; *Film type:* 16mm; *Video type:* V.

AUTHORSHIP INFORMATION: *Producer(s):* Papp, Joseph; *Director(s):* Leach, Wilford; Dixon, Christopher (Film unit); *Composer(s):* Weinstock, Richard; *Costume designer(s):* McGourty, Patricia; *Lighting designer(s):* Tipton, Jennifer; *Other personnel:* Churchill, Jack (Photography); Schopper, Philip (Editor); Stettner, Frank (Sound); *Cast:* Streep, Meryl (Kate); Julia, Raul (Petruchio); Rush, Deborah (Bianca); Gulack, Max (Baptista Minola); Lally, James (Lucentio); Brooke, Joel (Grumio); Pine, Larry (Hortensio).

DISTRIBUTION & AVAILABILITY: *Publisher or responsible agency:* New York City Shakespeare Festival; *Distributor:* FNC, *Copy location:* FOL; *Call or copy number:* VCR; *Availability:* B,V, 3/4U, 16mm, Apply.

The Taming of the Shrew. **Video/Documentary/ Scenes**

606. *The Taming of the Shrew.* (Series: From Page to Stage).

DOCUMENT INFORMATION: *Country:* Canada; *Year of release:* 1985; *Location of first showing:* Stratford Shakespeare Festival, Ontario, Canada.

EDITION, HISTORY, CONTENTS, & EVALUATION: *Edition & history:* One of a series of educational cassettes (see also 45, 572, 628, and 661) issued by the Stratford Shakespeare Festival, Ontario, Canada. For background, see 45. *Contents & evaluation:* Actress Sharry Flett, who plays Kate in the Stratford production (see 604), comments on key scenes in *Shrew* from a script prepared by Elliott Hayes. She is especially

enlightening for today's students when she translates the "taming methods" used by Petruchio from metaphors of hawking into modern theories of "behavior modification." She also attempts to put the patriarchal world of Renaissance Italy into context by explaining Elizabethan attitudes toward marriage. In this way Kate's "submission" speech can be at least understood in its position in history. Its interpretation for modern readers is of course still open. Excerpts from the play include the first act quarrel between Kate and Bianca, the first meeting of Kate and Petruchio, and Kate's "submission" speech. The acting is first rate; and the commentary, intelligent. *Audience:* General use; *Supplementary materials:* Hayes, Elliott, ed. [Teachers' Committee] *From Page to Stage: Study Guide.* Stratford Shakespeare Festival, 1985.

MEDIUM INFORMATION: *Medium:* Video; *Sound:* Spoken language; *Color:* Yes; *Length:* 30 min.; *Language(s) spoken:* English; *Video type:* B, V, 3/4U.

AUTHORSHIP INFORMATION: *Producer(s):* Witmer, Glenn Edward; Campbell, Norman; Levene, Sam; *Director(s):* Dews, Peter (Stage); Campbell, Norman (TV); Cranston, Barry (CBC); *Adaptor/translator(s):* Schonberg, Michael; *Composer(s):* Symonds, Norman; *Designer(s):* Benson, Susan; *Lighting designer(s):* Frehner, Harry; *Cast:* Cariou, Len (Petruchio); Flett, Sharry (Kate/Narrator); Griffin, Lynne (Bianca); O'Sullivan, Barney (Baptista); Beattie, Rod; Christopher, Patrick (Suitors); Austin, Jan; Austin-Olsen, Shaun; Baker, Scott; Bekenn, Anthony; Brand, Arthur; Creed, Wendy; Cross, Stephen; Deakin, Ian; Delabbio, Daniel; Dinicol, Keith; Ellis, Desmond; Feore, Colm; Gordon, Lewis; Helpmann, Max; Henson, Jeremy; Hutt, Peter; Jarvis, Deborah; Keenleyside, Eric; Lightbourn, Arthur; Murphy, Elizabeth; Punyi, Paul; Redfern, Pamela; Sarosiak, Ron; Villa, Walter.

DISTRIBUTION & AVAILABILITY: *Publisher or responsible agency:* CBC Enterprises; *Distributor:* BEA, *Availability:* B (1-170-8) $120, Schools, $96; V (1-179-6) $120, schools, $96); 3/4U (1-180-X) $135; schools, $108.

The Taming of the Shrew. **Television/ Abridgment**

606.1. *The Taming of the Shrew.*

DOCUMENT INFORMATION: *Country:* USA; *Year of release:* 25 Nov. 1986.

EDITION, HISTORY, CONTENTS, & EVALUATION: *Edition & history:* A radically altered version "from an idea by William 'Budd' Shakespeare" performed by the cast of the enormously popular ABC-TV series, "Moonlighting." *Supplementary materials:* Oruch, Jack.

"Shakespeare for the Millions." *SFNL* 11.2 (April 1987): 7.

MEDIUM INFORMATION: *Length:* 30 [?] min.

AUTHORSHIP INFORMATION: *Director(s):* Macken-zie, Will. *Cast:* Willis, Bruce (David/Petruchio); Shepherd, Cybill (Maddie/Kate); MacMillan, Kenneth (Baptista); Beasley, Allyce (Bianca)

DISTRIBUTION & AVAILABILITY: *Publisher or responsible agency:* ABC-TV.

The Tempest

ORIGINAL WORK AND PRODUCTION: Tragi-Comedy. *Year of first production:* 1611; *Site of first production:* Whitehall Palace [?]).

The Tempest. **Motion Picture/Scene**

607. *The Tempest.*

DOCUMENT INFORMATION: *Country:* GB; *Year of release:* 1905.

EDITION, HISTORY, CONTENTS, & EVALUATION: *Edition & history:* A pioneering effort by Charles Urban to record the opening storm scene from Sir Herbert Beerbohm Tree's stage production of *The Tempest,* then enjoying a long run at His Majesty's Theatre, London. Professor Ball's description notes that some prints of the film were tinted, and others even colored. *Supplementary materials:* Ball, *SOSF* 31.

MEDIUM INFORMATION: *Length:* 2 min.

AUTHORSHIP INFORMATION: *Director(s):* Urban, Charles; *Cast:* White, J. Fisher (Gonzalo); Cookson, S.A. (Alonzo); Harding, Lyn (Antonio); Haines, W.A. (Boatswain).

DISTRIBUTION & AVAILABILITY: *Publisher or responsible agency:* Charles Urban.

The Tempest. **Motion Picture**

607.1 *The Tempest.*

DOCUMENT INFORMATION: *Country:* GB; *Year of release:* 1908.

EDITION, HISTORY, CONTENTS, & EVALUATION: *Edition & history:* Because the print at NFA has no credits, it is difficult to identify. It may be the same "Clarendon" film cited in Ball (76). *Contents & evaluation:* The film abruptly opens as Prospero seeks refuge on an island with Miranda. There are then flashbacks showing, as the title cards say, "The discovery of Caliban" and "The fairy spirit Ariel [being] released from a tree by Prospero." Another title card tells us that "Ten years later Ariel protects Miranda from Caliban." Following all this we get to the beginning of Shakespeare's play with "The making of the tempest." Against a backdrop of fraudulent painted boulders, Prospero with the aid of a huge book mixes some arcane nostrum while an admiring Miranda and Caliban look on. The storm erupts in a flurry of Méliès-like special effects: clouds, lightning, flying birds. A model ship founders at sea. Ferdinand walks out of the seas on to the island fully clothed and apparently bone dry. The action comes closer to the Shakespearean source as Prospero interdicts the love match between Ferdinand and Miranda and puts the young man to work lugging logs. Miranda tries to console the exhausted Ferdinand, while in the meantime Ariel tricks Antonio's party. At the end all parties share in a joyous reconciliation, free from any of the lingering darkness of modern Kott-ian interpretations. A genial Prospero forgives all. Ariel is released and all gaily board a ship for Milan, leaving behind a duly repentant Caliban. There is no liberal guilt whatsoever about the possibility of having oppressed native peoples. The movie does make, however, a genuine effort to re-appropriate the text to filmic purposes.

MEDIUM INFORMATION: *Sound:* Silent; *Color:* No (black & white); *Length:* 11 min.; *Film type:* 35mm.

AUTHORSHIP INFORMATION: *Producer(s):* Stow, Percy [?]; *Cast:* Unknown.

DISTRIBUTION & AVAILABILITY: *Publisher or responsible agency:* Clarendon [?]; *Copy location:* NFA.

The Tempest. Motion Picture/Abridgment [?]

608. *The Tempest.*

DOCUMENT INFORMATION: *Country:* USA; *Year of release:* 1911.

EDITION, HISTORY, CONTENTS, & EVALUATION: *Edition & history:* A one-reel Thanhouser silent Shakespeare film that may have been one of his less successful productions. We can never be sure because most of Thanhouser's films were destroyed in a 1917 warehouse conflagration. *Supplementary materials:* Ball, *SOSF* 70.

MEDIUM INFORMATION: *Length:* 10 min.

AUTHORSHIP INFORMATION: *Director(s):* Thanhouser, Edwin.

DISTRIBUTION & AVAILABILITY: *Distributor:* Lost.

The Tempest. Motion Picture/Abbreviation

609. *The Tempest.*

DOCUMENT INFORMATION: *Country:* France; *Year of release:* 1912.

EDITION, HISTORY, CONTENTS, & EVALUATION: *Supplementary materials:* Ball, *SOSF* 150-1; *SIF,* 115; *Length:* 18 min.

AUTHORSHIP INFORMATION: *Director(s):* Eclair.

DISTRIBUTION & AVAILABILITY: *Distributor:* Lost.

The Tempest. Video/Teleplay

610. *Tempest.*

DOCUMENT INFORMATION: *Country:* GB; *Year of first showing:* 1939; *Location of first showing:* BBC. Transmitted 9:07 to 10:48 P.M., Sunday, 5 Feb. 1939.

EDITION, HISTORY, CONTENTS, & EVALUATION: *Edition & history:* The BBC production staff was unhappy with certain technical flaws that marred the production. A prompter was seen in the foreground of a long shot, and a property man walked across a superimposed shot. Moreover one executive grumbled that certain members of the cast were in no position to have accepted their engagements. So apparently all did not go as well as one might have hoped with a cast including such distinguished persons as Peggy Ashcroft. The budget was less than £500, which was skimpy even for those austere years (WAC TS/508, Feb. 1939). *Supplementary materials:* "Program." *TBAP* 5 Feb. 1939.

MEDIUM INFORMATION: *Length:* 90 min.

AUTHORSHIP INFORMATION: *Producer(s):* Bower, Dallas; *Composer(s):* Sibelius; Greenbaum, Hyam (Conductor); *Choreographer(s):* Tudor, Antony; *Designer(s):* Baker-Smith, Malcolm; *Cast:* Ashcroft, Peggy (Miranda); Wheatley, Alan (Alonso); Burt, Oliver (Sebastian); Abbott, John (Prospero); Langton, Basil (Antonio); Ainley, Richard (Ferdinand); Turnbull, John (Gonzalo); Latham, Stuart (Adrian); Payn, Graham (Francisco); Devine, George (Caliban); Goolden, Richard (Trinculo); Farrell, Charles (Stephano); Price, Dennis (Ship's Master); Chitty, Erik (Boatswain); Haggard, Stephen (Ariel); Lindsay, Vera (Iris); Van Praagh, Peggy; Langfield, Therese; Bidmead, Charlotte; Hamilton, Elizabeth; Laing, Hugh; Massey, Guy; Regan, John (Mariners, Nymphs, and Reapers); plus London Ballet.

DISTRIBUTION & AVAILABILITY: *Publisher or responsible agency:* BBC; *Copy location:* Unavailable.

The Tempest. Motion Picture/Derivative

611. *Forbidden Planet.*

DOCUMENT INFORMATION: *Country:* USA; *Year of release:* 1956.

EDITION, HISTORY, CONTENTS, & EVALUATION: *Edition & history:* A science fiction film, which is a very loose adaptation of Shakespeare's *The Tempest. Contents & evaluation:* Part of the fun of watching this film lies in picking up on all the connections with *The Tempest.* Prospero is transformed into a mad scientist, Dr. Morbius (Walter Pidgeon), who has been isolated on the planet Altain-4. Dwelling with him is his daughter, Altaira (Anne Francis), a beautiful young girl who doubles as a kind of Miranda and Ariel. The arrival of a space ship, skippered by Commander Adams (Leslie Nielsen) brings Ferdinand on the scene. A cute little robot seems to correspond to Caliban, and such low-life creatures as Trinculo and Stephano have parallels in members of the enlisted crew. A great, scary amorphous creature, dredged up from Dr. Morbius' subconscious, savagely attacks everyone. Although her father is lost, daughter Altaira safely returns to earth. The *MFB* reviewer called the "Freudian monster from the Id . . . a finely outrageous conception, a King Kong of space!" *Audience:* General use; *Supplementary materials:* [P.H.] "Forbidden Planet, 1956." *MFB* 23. 269 (June 1956): 71-2.

MEDIUM INFORMATION: *Medium:* Motion Picture; *Sound:* Spoken language; *Color:* Yes; *Length:* 96 min.; *Language(s) spoken:* English; *Film type:* 16mm; Cinemascope.

AUTHORSHIP INFORMATION: *Producer(s):* Nayfack, Nicholas; *Director(s):* Wilcox, Fred McLeod; *Screenplay writer(s):* Hume, Cyril; Based on story by Black, Irving and Adler, Allen; *Designer(s):* Gibbons, Cedric; Lonergan, Arthur; *Other personnel:* Folsey, George (Photography); Webster, Ferris (Editor); Barron, Louis and Bebe (Electronic tonalities); Gillespie, A. Arnold; Newcombe, Warren; Ries, Irving G.; Meador, Joshua (Special effects); *Cast:* Pidgeon, Walter (Dr. Morbius); Francis, Anne (Altaira Morbius); Nielsen, Leslie (Commander Adams); Stevens, Warren (Lt. "Doc" Ostrow); Kelly, Jack (Lt. Farman); Anderson, Richard (Chief Quinn); Holliman, Earl (Cook); Wallace, George (Boatswain).

DISTRIBUTION & AVAILABILITY: *Publisher or responsible agency:* Metro Goldwyn Mayer; *Distributor:* FCM, *Copy location:* FOL; *Call or copy number:* MP 67; *Availability:* FCM, V, $59.95.

The Tempest. Video/Teleplay

612. *The Tempest.* (Series: Sunday-Night Theatre).

DOCUMENT INFORMATION: *Country:* GB; *Year of first showing:* 1956; *Location of first showing:* BBC. Transmitted 8:30 to 10:15 P.M., Sunday, 14 Oct. 1956.

EDITION, HISTORY, CONTENTS, & EVALUATION: *Edition & history:* Fortunately a copy of this production on 16mm film is available for study at the NFA in London. The father and son team of Robert and Ian Atkins, long active in the Open Air Theatre in Regent's Park, teamed up to produce the show. The senior Atkins, who began his career at His Majesty's Theatre with Sir Herbert Tree, also plays the role of Caliban. At a budget of £2,826 the production represented a considerable investment, for the times. *Contents & evaluation:* There is a modified, expressionistic studio set that fortunately makes no attempt at literal representation of the island. A dubbed-in filmed sea sequence appears in the background. The studio effects for the opening storm scene gain strength from stirring musi-

cal support, while a Prospero with an incredibly resonant voice easily captures the audience. The Ariel who pops up through some kind of superimposition has a wonderful face—it looks carved. Caliban is a truly horrible, misshapen figure, ape-like with long hair. On the whole the production is reputable, bright, tasteful but not terribly inventive, a little on the stiff side. A talisman of this timidity occurs when Prospero throws away his response to Miranda's "O brave new world." His "'Tis new to thee" is so casual that any sense of his disenchantment, indeed cynicism, over being the "wronged duke of Milan" gets obscured. Then again when Prospero throws away his staff to the accompaniment of Hans Heimler's sensitive musical score, one can cheerfully accept the production for what it is. Here was a *Tempest* literally being produced with everyone looking over the director's shoulder. That was hardly the climate likely to produce bold new visions of a strange new world. *Supplementary materials:* Jones, Elwyn. "The Tempest." *RT* 12 Oct. 1956: 15.

MEDIUM INFORMATION: *Length:* 106 min.

AUTHORSHIP INFORMATION: *Producer(s):* Atkins, Ian; Atkins, Robert; *Composer(s):* Heimler, Hans; *Choreographer(s):* Stephenson, Geraldine; *Designer(s):* Learoyd, Barry; *Costume designer(s):* Harris, Olive; *Cast:* Eddison, Robert (Prospero); Atkins, Robert (Caliban); Barry, Anna (Miranda); Browne, Laidman (Alonso); Wilmer, Douglas (Antonio); Pack, Charles Lloyd (Gonzalo); Pooley, Olaf (Sebastian); Brown, Bernard (Ferdinand); Brooks, Patti (Ariel); Street, Peter (Adrian); Hamelin, Clement (Francisco); Thorndike, Russell (Stephano); Meddings, Jonathan (Trinculo); Kneale, Patricia (Iris); Beamish, Silvia (Ceres); Grayston, Jean (Juno, Vocalist); Deakin, V.; Frankel, R.; Hilton, W.; Kedge, J.; Kenny, M.; Lewis, A.; Crowther, O.; Forest, D.; Gardner, D.; Harmer, J.; Labee, R. (Spirits); Chivers, D.; Moorehead, B. (Mariners); plus musicians.

DISTRIBUTION & AVAILABILITY: BBC; *Copy location:* NFA*, BBC*.

The Tempest. Video/Interpretation

613. *The Tempest.* (Series: Hallmark Hall of Fame).

DOCUMENT INFORMATION: *Country:* USA; *Year of first showing:* 1960; *Location of first showing:* NBC TV. Transmitted 7:30 to 9:30 P.M., 3 Feb. 1960.

EDITION, HISTORY, CONTENTS, & EVALUATION: *Edition & history:* One of the ambitious live telecasts of a Shakespearean play that starred Maurice Evans, this *Tempest* is still well worth viewing. Richard Burton makes an unforgettable Caliban and a youthful Lee Remick as Miranda is absolutely stunning. For other Shakespeare plays in the Hallmark television series, see 102, 126, 305, 309, 484, 593, 594, and 649. *Contents & evaluation:* "Few TV productions of Shakespearean drama have been carried out so successfully as George Schaefer's almost forgotten 1960 Hallmark Hall of Fame *The Tempest*. Although the text was indeed cut and altered to suit the 90-minute format, Schaefer managed to retain his conception of the play as a 'souffle,' something light and airy. . . . This is a light-hearted *Tempest* in which everyone—the characters on screen and the audience—has a good time. . . . Schaefer's camera work was superb. Electronic tricks could make Ariel six inches or six feet high as circumstances dictated. In capturing the joy of the original, the production remains faithful to the spirit of Shakespeare's text. The view of the play is of course remote from the dark, brooding meditation on human depravity revealed in Peter Brook's 1968 production, or in Derek Jarman's 1980 film. Schaefer's *Tempest* may be light as a souffle, but it is substantial enough for the main course" (Vaughan [Carr], Virginia M. "The Forgotten Television *Tempest*." *SFNL* 9.1 [1984]: 3). *Audience:* High school (grades 10-12); General use; *Supplementary materials:* Kliman, Bernice. "An Unseen Interpreter: Interview with George Schaefer." *FC* 7.3 [1983]: 29-37; "TV." *NYT* 3 Feb. 1960: 67.

MEDIUM INFORMATION: *Medium:* Video; *Sound:* Spoken language; *Color:* No (black & white); *Length:* 76 min.; *Language(s) spoken:* English; *Video type:* B, V, 3/4" U.

AUTHORSHIP INFORMATION: *Producer(s):* Schaefer, George; *Director(s):* Schaefer, George; *Designer(s):* Ter-Arutunian, Rouben; *Cast:* Burton, Richard (Caliban); Evans, Maurice (Prospero); McDowall, Roddy (Ariel); Remick, Lee (Miranda); Poston, Tom; Redmond, Liam (Gonzalo).

DISTRIBUTION & AVAILABILITY: *Publisher or responsible agency:* Hallmark Hall of Fame; *Distributor:* FFH, TWC, *Copy location:* MOB; *Call or copy number:* Pts. 1&3. T78:0151; *Availability:* (FFH) Rental: $75; Sale: B, V, $149, 3/4" U, $249; TWC B(CMT 100B-K4), V (CMT 100V-K4), $44.50; *Restrictions:* Viewing by appt. at MOB.

The Tempest. Motion Picture/Abridgment

614. *The Tempest.* (Series: Fair Adventure Series).

DOCUMENT INFORMATION: *Country:* USA; *Year of release:* 1964.

EDITION, HISTORY, CONTENTS, & EVALUATION: *Edition & history:* A four-part abridgment of the play with commentary by Dr. Frank Baxter. For others in the series, see 180, 254, 311, 426, 463, 487, 508, 546, and 653. *Contents & evaluation:* Not seen. The series has not been actively marketed in recent years. *Audience:* Junior High (grades 7-9); High school (grades 10-12).

MEDIUM INFORMATION: *Medium:* Motion Picture;

Sound: Spoken language; *Color:* No (black & white); *Length:* 112 min.; *Language(s) spoken:* English; *Film type:* 16mm.

AUTHORSHIP INFORMATION: *Producer(s):* Hubbard, Ray [?].

DISTRIBUTION & AVAILABILITY: *Publisher or responsible agency:* Westinghouse Broadcasting Company (Group W); *Distributor:* ASF [?], USF [?].

The Tempest. Motion Picture/Documentary

615. *Peter Brook: The Tempest.*

DOCUMENT INFORMATION: *Country:* France; *Year of release:* 1968.

EDITION, HISTORY, CONTENTS, & EVALUATION: *Edition & history:* Peter Brook demonstrates some unorthodox ways of representing *The Tempest* on stage, including the use of tiny ship models for the storm scene while the cast members sit on a kind of trapeze above the turmoil. For a similar documentary in French, see 710, below. *Contents & evaluation:* An excellent opportunity for theatre students to watch an incredibly imaginative and creative director at work. *Audience:* College and university; Professional.

MEDIUM INFORMATION: *Medium:* Motion Picture; *Sound:* Spoken language; *Color:* Yes; *Length:* 27 min.; *Language(s) spoken:* English/French; *Film type:* 16mm.

AUTHORSHIP INFORMATION: *Producer(s):* Wilson, Ian; *Director(s):* Brook, Peter; *Cast:* Actors from RSC for most part.

DISTRIBUTION & AVAILABILITY: *Publisher or responsible agency:* Saga Film, Paris; *Copy location:* FOL; *Call or copy number:* MP 59.

The Tempest. Video/Teleplay

616. *Tempest, The.* (Series: Play of the Month).

DOCUMENT INFORMATION: *Country:* GB; *Year of first showing:* 1968; *Location of first showing:* BBC 1. Transmitted 9:15 to 11:10 P.M., 12 May 1968.

EDITION, HISTORY, CONTENTS, & EVALUATION: *Edition & history:* With Cedric Messina as producer, this production of *The Tempest* marked a step toward what might be called the "modern era" of BBC Shakespeare productions. Mr. Messina was subsequently to capitalize on the experience with these earlier Shakespeare plays when in 1976 he became the first producer of the BBC series, "The Shakespeare Plays." *Supplementary materials:* "The Tempest." *RT* 9 May 1968: 12.

MEDIUM INFORMATION: *Length:* 116 min.

AUTHORSHIP INFORMATION: *Producer(s):* Messina,

Cedric; *Director(s):* Coleman, Basil; *Composer(s):* Leppard, Raymond; *Designer(s):* Abbott, Tony; *Cast:* Redgrave, Michael (Prospero); Wyatt, Tessa (Miranda); Michell, Keith (Caliban); Pickup, Ronald (Ariel); Dennis, Jonathan (Ferdinand); Hardwick, Paul (Antonio); Woodvine, John (Sebastian); Cairncross, James (Alonzo); Eccles, Donald (Gonzalo); Rain, Douglas (Stephano); Macgowran, Jack (Trinculo); Rees, Llewellyn (Francisco); Horton, John (Adrian); Tindall, Hilary (Iris); Kennedy, Ann (Ceres); Moody, Jeanne (Juno); + The Ballet Rambert.

DISTRIBUTION & AVAILABILITY: *Publisher or responsible agency:* BBC; *Copy location:* Unavailable.

The Tempest. **Motion Picture/Documentary**

617. The Tempest: O Brave New World. (Series: Explorations in Shakespeare, XI).

DOCUMENT INFORMATION: *Country:* Canada; *Year of release:* 1969.

EDITION, HISTORY, CONTENTS, & EVALUATION: *Edition & history:* Part eleven in a series of twelve 23-minute films made in 1969 by the Ontario Educational Communications Authority. (See also 18, 40, 65, 124, 162, 257, 322, 465, 488, 555, and 637.) See 18 for overview. *Contents & evaluation:* This eleventh program along with the *Hamlet* episode have provided the basis for the evaluation of the entire series, which is now difficult to obtain. The *Tempest* unit opens with a collage of photographs of corpses in concentration camps, of the KKK on the march, of "Public Enemy" James Cagney pushing a grapefruit into Mae Clarke's face, of a crucified Christ, and, oh yes (this is the Vietnam era), of the face of Lyndon Baines Johnson, then the anti-Christ in the eyes of the peace movement. One might wonder what all this has to do with Shakespeare's play, until the narrator appears on screen to explain that Prospero's problem is how to exclude evil from the world. He may create a Utopia but perhaps at the price of destroying freedom. Prospero can become so obsessed with destroying evil that he himself becomes evil. His choice is "to drown his book" and "break his staff," to cease being a god and become a man. All of this is supported by reasonably well-acted scenes from the play. Jackie Burroughs in a slinky black dress plays Ariel and William Hutt does Prospero, though perhaps the best known in the cast is actor/athlete Roscoe Lee Browne as Caliban. The exploration of Prospero's struggle with the problem of evil is brilliantly handled, and makes whatever flaws there are in the production seem inconsequential (KSR). *Audience:* College and university.

MEDIUM INFORMATION: *Medium:* Motion Picture; *Sound:* Spoken language; *Color:* Yes; *Length:* 23 min.; *Language(s) spoken:* English; *Film type:* 16mm.

AUTHORSHIP INFORMATION: *Producer(s):* Reis, Kurt; Moser, Ed; *Screenplay writer(s):* Webster, Hugh; *Composer(s):* Yanovsky, Zal; *Set designer(s):* Adeney, Chris; *Lighting designer(s):* Galbraith, Howard; *Other personnel:* Oldfield, Michael (Audio); Bates, Don (Tech. dir.); Matteo, Gino (Educational supervisor); Beane, Gerry (Studio director); Farwell, Cathy (Research); *Cast:* Hutt, William (Prospero); Browne, Roscoe Lee (Caliban); Le Blanc, Diane (Miranda); Burroughs, Jackie (Ariel); Petchey, Briain (Ferdinand); *Performance group(s):* Ontario Educational Communications/NBC Educational Enterprises.

DISTRIBUTION & AVAILABILITY: *Distributor:* CNU.

The Tempest. **Video/Adaptation**

617.1. Une tempete.

DOCUMENT INFORMATION: *Country:* France; *Year of first showing:* 1969.

EDITION, HISTORY, CONTENTS, & EVALUATION: *Edition & history:* A video recording of a production of the *Tempest* in Paris by The Compagnie Serreau-Perinetti in October 1969.

AUTHORSHIP INFORMATION: *Director(s):* Serreau, Jean-Marie; *Adaptor/translator(s):* Césaire, Aimé.

DISTRIBUTION & AVAILABILITY: *Copy location:* ASV; *Call or copy number:* A 5.100.035-36.

The Tempest. **Video/Documentary**

618. The Tempest.

DOCUMENT INFORMATION: *Country:* USA; *Year of first showing:* 1973.

EDITION, HISTORY, CONTENTS, & EVALUATION: *Edition & history*: A 1973 television program with discussion and demonstration of *The Tempest* by the Yale Repertory Theatre. A copy is housed in the Theatre on Film and Tape (TOFT) Collection at the New York Public Library. It may be viewed by appointment (see below). *Contents & evaluation:* Not seen. *Audience:* College and university; General use.

MEDIUM INFORMATION: *Medium:* Video; *Sound:* Spoken language; *Color:* No (black & white); *Length:* 30 min.; *Language(s) spoken:* English; *Video type:* V.

DISTRIBUTION & AVAILABILITY: *Publisher or responsible agency:* Yale Repertory Theatre; *Copy location:* LCL TOFT

The Tempest. Motion Picture/Scenes

619. *The Tempest*, 1.2; 3.1. (Series: The Shakespeare Series [IFB], XII).

DOCUMENT INFORMATION: *Country:* Great Britain; *Year of release:* 1974.

EDITION, HISTORY, CONTENTS, & EVALUATION: *Edition & history:* Excerpts from *The Tempest*, 1.2; 3.1. One of twelve programs in a series performed on a reconstruction of an Elizabethan stage to give the impression of the rapid movement that was characteristic in all likelihood of the original performances. For other programs in the series, see 22, 131, 164, 232, 326, 430, 467, 490, 510, 556, and 601. *Contents & evaluation:* Another attempt in "The Shakespeare Series" to record scenes from a stage play. Mostly in close-up or in two shot, the camera is cruel to the actors, whose every weakness is magnified threefold. The production seems static and stagy. Mark Kingston makes a decent Prospero, however. *Audience:* High school (grades 10-12).

MEDIUM INFORMATION: *Medium:* Motion Picture; *Sound:* Spoken language; *Color:* Yes; *Length:* 13 1/2 min.; *Language(s) spoken:* English; *Film type:* 16mm; *Video type:* V, 3/4U (4 per cassette).

AUTHORSHIP INFORMATION: *Producer(s):* Realist Film Unit; *Director(s):* Seabourne, Peter; *Cast:* Kingston, Mark (Prospero); Hall, Elizabeth (Miranda); Gilbert, Derrick (Ferdinand).

DISTRIBUTION & AVAILABILITY: *Publisher or responsible agency:* Realist Film Unit; *Distributor:* IFB, CNU, *Copy location:* FOL; *Call or copy number:* ISBN 0-8354-1596-1; FOL, MP 14; *Availability:* CNU rental 16mm, $9; IFB sale 16mm, $225, V 195, rental $15.

The Tempest. Video/Teleplay

620. *The Tempest*. (Series: The Shakespeare Plays).

DOCUMENT INFORMATION: *Country:* GB; *Year of filming:* 23-28 July 1979; *Year of first showing:* 1979; *Location of first showing(s):* BBC, London; PBS stations, USA, 7 May 1980.

EDITION, HISTORY, CONTENTS, & EVALUATION: *Edition & history:* Director John Gorrie took the Doré illustrations for Dante's *Divine Comedy* as a model for the island settings of his production. The result is a bleak, stark rather arid kind of island, which is curiously lacking in the sounds of the sea. One yearns for the gull cries that make the seacoast scenes in the BBC *Pericles* come aurally alive. The brevity of *The Tempest*, one of Shakespeare's shortest plays, made the need for textual changes minimal. There was some discussion about giving Prospero's speech to Caliban at 1.2.351 to Miranda, which is so harsh in tone as to

seem out of character for Miranda. It was decided, however, to stick with the Peter Alexander text, which is essentially the 1623 Folio version. In Derek Jarman's 1980 film treatment of *The Tempest* (see 622), Toyah Willcox plays a Miranda who might well have been capable of speaking these often disputed lines (KSR). *Contents & evaluation:* "Thus the best lack all conviction and intensity, and the attractions of this *Tempest* tend either to be negative—there are no gross excesses—or external. The rocks and sands of this unoceanic setting are interesting for a while, heightening without distracting. . . . The production tried for a telegenic contemporary fusion of music (some by William Walton), dance, and spectacle with a balletic fairy troupe. Even Inigo Jones would have been surprised by what one New York critic called the 'Fire Island' aspect of the dancers, while Ben Jonson would have chafed at the cutting of the masque's lines. Both of these are laudable in intent, but results are mixed—e.g., the unsuccessful banquet scene in Act IV. There is a seductive, bionic-looking Ariel (David Dixon) who disappears into rocks, and a hairy, gutteral Caliban. Both would be jarring on stage, but they seem familiar on television, as if we already knew them from an earlier episodic cosmology. They, rather than Miranda and Ferdinand (Pippa and Christopher Guard), round out the island family by being its indispensable, sulky teenagers " (Grundy, Dominick, "The Tempest," *SFNL* 5.2. [1981]:3). *Audience:* College and university; General use; *Supplementary materials:* Fenwick, H. Introduction. *The Tempest. BSP* 17-26; Videotape (25 min) from "Shakespeare in Perspective" series with Laurens Vanderpost as lecturer available in U.K. from BBC*; in USA, from FNC (see #624).

MEDIUM INFORMATION: *Medium:* Video; *Sound:* Spoken language; *Color:* Yes; *Length:* 125 min.; *Video type:* B, V, 3/4U.

AUTHORSHIP INFORMATION: *Producer(s):* Messina, Cedric; *Director(s):* Gorrie, John; *Adaptor/translator(s):* Shallcross, Alan; *Composer(s):* Horovitz, Joseph; Lloyd-Jones, David; *Choreographer(s):* Cauley, Geoffrey; *Designer(s):* Joel, Paul; *Costume designer(s):* Hughes, Alun; *Lighting designer(s):* Thomas, Clive; *Other personnel:* Morgan, Brian (Prod. asst.); Wilders, John (Literary consultant); Beveridge, Christine (Make-up); Anthony, Chick (Sound); *Cast:* Hordern, Michael (Prospero); Godfrey, Derek (Antonio); Waller, David (Alonso); Clarke, Warren (Caliban); Hawthorne, Nigel (Stephano); Dixon, David (Ariel); Sachs, Andrew (Trinculo); Nettleton, John (Gonzalo); Rowe, Alan (Sebastian); Guard, Pippa (Miranda); Guard, Christopher (Ferdinand); Gilbert, Kenneth (Boatswain); Brown, Edwin (Master); Greenhalgh, Paul (Francisco); Bramwell, Christopher (Adrian); Lloyd, Gwyneth (Juno); Gardner, Elizabeth (Ceres); Rees, Judith (Iris).

DISTRIBUTION & AVAILABILITY: *Publisher or responsible agency:* BBC/TLF; *Distributor:* AVP, UIO, BBC*

Copy location: NTI, UVM, ITM* [1aSha2] (Archival); *Availability:* AVP, B, V, 3/4U $450 (1987), sale; UIO, V (72047H), 3/4U (70147V), rental, $23.40; BBC*, 16mm or V, apply (*BUFVC* 24).

The Tempest. Video/Documentary

621. *The Stuff of Dreams.*

DOCUMENT INFORMATION: *Country:* USA; *Year of first showing:* 29 April 1979; *Location of first showing:* Vermont Educational Television.

EDITION, HISTORY, CONTENTS, & EVALUATION: *Awards:* First place, New England Film Festival; American Film Festival Finalist; Screened, International Public Television Conference, Milan, Italy, 1979; *Edition & history:* A prize-winning documentary showing the activities of a commune in Guilford, Vermont, whose members conceived of and then mounted an outdoor production of *The Tempest.* Shown on Vermont public television in 1979, the production has since then been kept alive mainly through word of mouth by its admirers. *Contents & evaluation:* The documentary manifestly tells the story of a commune in Vermont at the end of the 1960's whose "hippie" members decide to put on an outdoor performance of *The Tempest* at Sweet's pond near Guilford. Through a brilliantly edited montage by John Scagliotti and Owen Kahn, we see the genesis and incubation of the project: there are shots of Ceres rehearsing in a garden; of John Carroll directing; of a wonderful boat being constructed for the mariners; of a raft on the lake being made over into Prospero's island; of a fund raiser for the performance; of Caliban rehearsing with Prospero; of a woman with strong feminist principles playing the role of old Gonzalo; of music being composed; of an orchestra rehearsing; of dancers listening to their choreographer; of neighboring Vermont farmers voicing their tolerant opinions of the activities of the alien types who have come from the universities and the cities into the peaceful countryside; of oversize peacocks under construction; and of the entire group getting together for a communal supper in the farmhouse kitchen. In its hominess and warmth, the whole scene conjures up recollections of past New England utopias, such as Brook Farm and the Shaker colonies. Toward the end of the film, we also see some well-acted scenes from *The Tempest* played before an enthralled audience of 1500 sitting outdoors on the green Vermont hillside. Scenes from the play include the opening storm scene, the dialogue between Miranda and Prospero, glimpses of Trinculo, and the lovely wedding masque. Audience becomes as much a part of the event as the performers. After all this is an audience that has been willing to venture out into the woods in quest of an unmediated experience. At the end, however, when Prospero breaks his enormous staff, not only has the play come to an end but a whole era has also ended. Just as Prospero sought to banish evil from his island, so have these young people sought to create an idyllic community in Vermont. Thus the film is only manifestly about *The Tempest*; in its deeper significance it is about the lost dreams of yesterday's Sixties generation (KSR).

MEDIUM INFORMATION: *Medium:* Video; *Sound:* Spoken language; *Color:* Yes; *Length:* 77 min.; *Language(s) spoken:* English; *Video type:* 3/4 U.

AUTHORSHIP INFORMATION: *Producer(s):* Carroll, John; Dater, Alan; Dater, Susan; Scagliotti, John; *Director(s):* Carroll, John; Scagliotti, John; *Composer(s):* Hecker, Zeke; McLean, Don; Moyse, Blanche (with Windham Community Orchestra); *Choreographer(s):* Scholl, Virginia; *Costume designer(s):* Peters, Joan; Merton, Sue; *Lighting designer(s):* Dater, Alan; *Other personnel:* Dater, Susan (Sound); Kahn, Owen; Scagliotti, John (Editors); Dater, Alan; Dater, Susan (Additional editing); Light, Chuck; Longston, Warner; Scagliotti, John; Shafnacker, George (Sound); Keller, Dan; Scagliotti, John; Sloan, Steve (Additional photography); Morse, Stacy (Headpieces); Fenwick, Mark (Construction); Williams, Neek (Peacocks); Gens, Jacqueline (Stage manager); *Cast:* Carroll, John (Prospero); O'Sullivan, Sharon (Miranda); Scully, Kevin (Ferdinand); Bronson, Ward (Sebastian); Williams, Marshall B. (Antonio); Rihn, Shoshana (Gonzalo); Gould, Peter (Caliban); Wizansky, Richard (Trinculo); Wilkins, John (Stephano); Baier, Randy (Alonso); Morse, Eric (Ship master); Coutant, Christopher (Ariel); Marr, Joan (Iris); Snyder, Ellen (Ceres); McLean, Evelyn (Juno); plus thirteen dancers and seven musicians.

DISTRIBUTION & AVAILABILITY: *Publisher or responsible agency:* Monteverdi films; *Distributor:* MFV.

The Tempest. Motion Picture/Intepretation

622. *The Tempest: by William Shakespeare, as seen through the eyes of Derek Jarman.* (Series: British Film Now, New York City).

DOCUMENT INFORMATION: *Country:* GB; *Year of release:* 1980; *Year of first showing:* 1 May 1980; *Country of first showing:* GB; *Location of first showing:* London.

EDITION, HISTORY, CONTENTS, & EVALUATION: *Edition & history:* Shown at the New York Film Festival in September 1980, the film opened commercially in the USA at Cinema 3, New York City, on Sept. 28, 1980. In evaluating it, one should note Jarman's subtitle, "as seen through the eyes of." This is a daring and creative appropriation of the subtext of *The Tempest*, not a film for those who prefer that the text on the screen literally capture the text on the page. High school teachers should avoid ordering this R-rated film for student viewing, unless they enjoy sparring with outraged parents. The breast feeding of a full-grown Caliban by his sow of a mother, Sycorax, is surely one of the most revolting spectacles ever filmed. Jarman's most recent film, *The Last of England* (1988), was shown at the National Film Theatre in London and again at the 1988 New York Film Festival. His vision of western civilization on the brink of apocalypse informs not only this film about a decaying Britain but also his treatment of *The Tempest* (KSR). *Contents & evaluation:* "Derek Jarman's screen version of *The Tempest* . . . would be funny if it weren't very nearly unbearable. It's a fingernail scratched along a blackboard, sand in spinach, a 33-r.p.m. recording of 'Don Giovanni' played at 78 r.p.m. Watching it is like driving a car whose windshield has shattered but not broken. You can barely see through the production to Shakespeare, so you must rely on memory. . . . There are no poetry, no ideas, no characterization, no narrative, no fun. The lighting is tacky, and the film's *piece de resistance,* the wedding pageant at the end in which Elizabeth Welch, a black American blues singer out of the 30's, sings 'Stormy Weather,' is a bravura effect gone feeble" (Canby, Vincent, "The Tempest," *NYT* 22 Sept. 1980: c20). "Jarman's film of *The Tempest* comes as an outrageously invigorating breath of fresh air in contrast to the stale, safe atmosphere [of] . . . the BBC's series of INSTITUTIONAL SHAKESPEARES. . . . Although with one notable exception (Arlen's *Stormy Weather*) all the words are Shakespeare's (we get something more than half the text and though it is often rearranged and reassigned, the play's essential plot divisions and developments remain), the film is decidedly Jarman's recreation of the text in his own, highly individualized, cinematic style. Jarman dreams over and through Shakespeare's play in a manner that mixes elements from the work of Cocteau, Welles, Kenneth Anger, and Ken Russell. Dream and nightmare and imprisonment are the key elements in his visual and verbal approach to his Shakespearean material. The tempest itself emanates from Prospero's nightmare, with the mariners' cries of 'we split,' 'hold,' and 'all lost,' echoing through Prospero's disturbed soul repeatedly as he struggles to awake. . . . I found Caliban at his mother's pap intrusive and unnecessary but thought Miss Welch's *Stormy Weather* inspired. Its refrain of 'Keeps rainin' all the time' became a modern equivalent for Feste's corrective to *Twelfth Night's* midsummer madness: 'the rain it raineth every day' (Crowl, Samuel, "A New *Tempest* on Film," *SFNL* 5.1 [1980]: 5+). *Audience:* College and university; General use; *Supplementary materials:* Bies, Werner. "Derek Jarman's *The Tempest:* A Selected Bibliography." *SFNL* 6.2 [1982]: 9+; 7.1.[1982]: 3; see also Collick, John. *Shakespeare, Cinema, and Society.* New York: St. Martin's, 1989: 98-106.

MEDIUM INFORMATION: *Medium:* Motion picture; *Sound:* Spoken language; *Color:* Yes; *Length:* 96 min.; *Language(s) spoken:* English; *Film type:* 16mm; 35mm.

AUTHORSHIP INFORMATION: *Producer(s):* Boyd, Don; Radclyffe, Sarah; Ford, Guy; Schreiber, Mordecai; *Director(s):* Jarman, Derek; *Adaptor/translator(s):* Jarman, Derek; *Composer(s):* Hodgson, Wavemaker-Brian; *Choreographer(s):* Hopps, Stuart; *Designer(s):* Sonnabend, Yolanda; Whittaker, Ian; *Costume designer(s):* Ede, Nicolas; *Other personnel:* Middleton, Peter (Photography); Walker, Leslie; D'Alton, Annette (Editors); Hayes, John (Sound); Vickers, Sarah (Sound editor); *Cast:* Birkett, Jack (Caliban); Williams, Heathcote (Prospero); Johnson, Karl (Ariel); Willcox, Toyah (Miranda); Bull, Peter (Alonso); Warwick, Richard (Antonio); Welch, Elizabeth (Goddess).

DISTRIBUTION & AVAILABILITY: *Publisher or responsible agency:* World Northal Films; *Distributor:* GLB*, KIT; *Availability:* GLB*, apply; KIT, rental 16mm $125; PVG*, sale, B (PVC 2027AB), V (PVC 2027A).

The Tempest. Video/Recording

623. *The Tempest.*

DOCUMENT INFORMATION: *Country:* USA; *Year of first showing:* 1980.

EDITION, HISTORY, CONTENTS, & EVALUATION: *Edition & history:* A performance of the Berkeley Shakespeare Festival *Tempest* presented at the John Hinkel Park Amphitheatre, Berkeley, in repertory 6-31 August 1980, and recorded on video. A copy is housed in the Theatre on Film and Tape (TOFT) Collection at the Billy Rose Theatre Collection of the Library of Performing Arts. *Contents & evaluation:* "Audrey Stanley's direction of *The Tempest* achieved the rare feat of keeping the audience aware that the events and spaces of this play are distinctively Prospero's. The bare, raked circle of the stage became at once Caliban's rough, inhospitable island and the universe of Prospero's imagination. The first scene began at the back of the amphitheatre, using its two side aisles as stage and thus encompassing the audience as well as the mariners in a tempest conducted by Prospero from a promontory on the hillside above the stage with the aid of sinister, shrouded figures under his command. . . . Julian López-Morillas . . . played Prospero. His performance . . . allowed us to hear the arrogance and rigidity in Prospero's undeniable but steel-shod benevolence. His interruption of the masque was as abrupt and theatrically disorienting as it should be. . . . As Caliban Peter Fitzsimmons was costumed as a painted savage; in spite of his begrimed appearance, he was a far-from-formidable "monster," projecting instead the puppy-dog dependency of a naif. Because Miranda and Ferdinand were neither in appearance nor style the ingenuous and superficially attractive mannequins who usually play these roles, the naive wonder and natural deification of the lovers became a more complex triumph of human feeling than it usually is" (Jacobs, Laurence H., "Shakespeare in the San Francisco Bay Area," *SQ* 32.2 [Summer 1981]: 263-64). *Audience:* College and university; General use.

MEDIUM INFORMATION: *Medium:* Video; *Sound:* Spoken language; *Color:* Yes; *Length:* 135 min.; *Language(s) spoken:* English; *Video type:* 3/4U.

AUTHORSHIP INFORMATION: *Director(s):* Stanley, Audrey E.; *Composer(s):* Thewlis, Stephen; *Choreographer(s):* Harris, Joanna G.; *Designer(s):* Angell, Gene; Pratt, Ron; *Costume designer(s):* Russell, Doug; *Lighting designer(s):* Scripps, Sam; *Cast:* Petchey, Briain (Alonso); Sicular, Robert (Antonio); Macfie, Jane (Ariel); Fitzsimmons, Peter (Caliban); Yeuell, D. Paul (Ferdinand); Phillips, J.P. (Gonzalo); Dixon, Lisa Anne (Prospero); López-Morillas, Julian (Prospero); Henry, Steve (Sebastian); Renner, Mike (Stephano); Carniglia, Jerry (Trinculo).

DISTRIBUTION & AVAILABILITY: *Publisher or responsible agency:* Berkeley Shakespeare Festival; *Copy location:* LCL TOFT

The Tempest. Video/Documentary

624. *The Tempest.* (Series: Shakespeare in Perspective).

DOCUMENT INFORMATION: *Country:* GB; *Year of release:* 1980.

EDITION, HISTORY, CONTENTS, & EVALUATION: *Edition & history:* The "Shakespeare in Perspective" series was made to accompany the BBC/Time Life Inc. "The Shakespeare Plays" series. (See also 44, 142, 234, 269, 335, 411, 566. For overview, see 44, above.) *Contents & evaluation:* Novelist Laurens Vanderpost speaks to his viewers from an idyllic island in the Mediterranean, which he thinks would have been an appropriate setting for the action of *The Tempest*. Writer Vanderpost goes in heavily for the older approach that sees *Tempest* as a spiritual autobiography of its author. The play is a "self-exploration," and "a journey of the mind." Scenes from the BBC production starring Michael Hordern support his commentary (KSR).

MEDIUM INFORMATION: *Medium:* Video; *Sound:* Spoken language; *Color:* Yes; *Length:* 25 min.; *Language(s) spoken:* English; *Video type:* 3/4U, V.

AUTHORSHIP INFORMATION: *Producer(s):* Poole, Victor; *Director(s):* Wilson, David; *Other personnel:* Gabell, Steve (Editor); Hore, John (Sound); Friedman, Liz (Graphics); *Cast:* Vanderpost, Laurens (Commentator).

DISTRIBUTION & AVAILABILITY: *Publisher or responsible agency:* BBC; *Distributor:* BBC*; FNC; *Availability:* Double cassette (w. *Lr.*.), Rental $50; Quad cassette (w. *AYL, MND, Lr.*), Rental $75.

The Tempest. Video/Ballet

625. *The Tempest.* (Series: Great Performances [Dance in America]).

DOCUMENT INFORMATION: *Country:* USA; *Year of release:* 1981.

EDITION, HISTORY, CONTENTS, & EVALUATION: *Edition & history:* Performance by San Francisco Ballet company aired on PBS stations in 1981. *Supplementary materials:* Loughney, Katharine. "Shakespeare on Film and Tape at Library of Congress." *SFNL* 14.2 (Apr. 1990): 4 +.

MEDIUM INFORMATION: *Length:* 120 min.

AUTHORSHIP INFORMATION: *Producer(s):* Ardolino, Emile; Kinberg, Judy; *Adaptor/translator(s):* Chihara, Paul Seiko (after Henry Purcell); *Choreographer(s):* Smuin, Michael; *Cast:* Courtney Nigel; Peter Zoltan; McNaughton, David.

DISTRIBUTION & AVAILABILITY: *Copy location:* LCM; *Call or copy number:* VBC 8486-8487.

The Tempest. Video/Adaptation

625.1 *La tempesta.*

DOCUMENT INFORMATION: *Country:* Italy; *Year of first showing:* 1981; *Location of first showing:* Transmitted 14 Dec. 1981 on Radio Televisione Italiana.

EDITION, HISTORY, CONTENTS, & EVALUATION: *Edition & history:* A television adaptation of the production directed by Giorgio Strehler. Taped in 1979.

MEDIUM INFORMATION: *Sound:* Spoken language; *Length:* 90 min.; *Video type:* V.

AUTHORSHIP INFORMATION: *Producer(s):* RAI Productions; *Director(s):* Battistoni, Carlo; *Adaptor/translator(s):* Lombardo, Augustino; *Composer(s):* Carpi, F.; *Designer(s):* Damiani, L.; *Cast:* Gora, Caludio; Virgilio, Luciano; Lazzarini, Giulia.

DISTRIBUTION & AVAILABILITY: *Publisher or responsible agency:* RAI; *Copy location:* ASP.

The Tempest. Motion Picture/Derivative

626. *The Tempest.*

DOCUMENT INFORMATION: *Country:* USA; *Year of release:* 1982.

EDITION, HISTORY, CONTENTS, & EVALUATION: *Edition & history:* This spectacular $13 million movie was filmed variously at Atlantic City, N.J., New York City, Rome, and in Greece. In Atlantic City the abandoned Dunes Casino construction site and the Bally

Park Place Hotel served as a part of the Alonzo enterprises empire. At the construction site stuntman Jerry Hewitt successfully took a ninety-foot high fall. The production next moved to Manhattan for location shots in New York's theatre district on 45th street between Broadway and 8th Avenue, at the Convent of the Sacred Heart on 91st Street which served as Alonzo's palatial residence, on the Westside Highway at the World Trade Center, at MacArthur Airport on Long Island, and an apartment on Horatio Street in Greenwich Village. The company then moved in August first to Athens, Greece, where it shot at the Athenian port of Piraeus as well as the Plastiras Square of downtown Athens. Then six weeks were spent shooting at Gythion, a region of the southeastern Pelopennese known as the Mani. The cast also spent a week on the yacht, "Bluejacket," before traveling to Rome and "Cinecitta" for work on special effects. Altogether a great odyssey! (Producer's PR kit). *Contents & evaluation:* "In Paul Mazursky's new screen version of the "Tempest," . . . Shakespeare's comedy undergoes a remarkable sea change indeed. Prospero becomes Philip [sic], a successful New York architect, who flees his marriage and career by running away to a barren Greek island with his teen-age daughter Miranda; and Ariel, that spirit of air and light, becomes Aretha, a kind of contemporary free-spirit, liberated from the sexual mores and domestic conventions of the past. The storm that shipwrecks Prospero upon the island comes to represent the internal turmoil suffered by Mr. Mazursky's hero; just as his exile in this rocky paradise becomes a metaphor for his own spiritual dislocation . . . the island Philip selects for his self-exile mirrors his own uncompromising state of mind. Here there are none of the amenities, much less luxuries of home—no carpeted apartments, no cars, no black tie parties, and no companionship save that of Kalibanos, the lusty goatherd (Raul Julia). The only food is feta cheese. In fact, what Philip so eagerly embraces as a facsimile of paradise turns out to be a harsh, unfriendly land; if by stripping himself of civilization, he'd hoped to leave its discontents behind, he has also succeeded in losing its comforts and its charms" (Kakutani, Michiko, "'The Tempest' Inspires a Modern Moviemaker," *NYT* 8 Aug. 1982: sec. 2. 1+). "In his updating of the text, Mazursky goes even further than turning it into a contemporary crisis-of-success fable, and in going further has come up with some show business that is not alien to Shakespeare. There are a number of unexpected and delightful song and dance routines on this faraway isle, and Prospero has become an entertainer in a rather John Osborne mood. . . . The particular coup of this interpretation is the casting of Cassavetes— an actor of Greek origin, and a film-maker whose own work (*Shadows, Husbands, Opening Night*), has concerned itself, Prospero-like, with the "reality" of acting, with the stuff that dream and illusion are made of. The subject . . . beneath some of Mazursky's more familiar flummery about the comic dishonesties of sex,

is something that underpins most of Cassavetes' films— the traps and snares of being emotionally honest with oneself and others" (Combs, Richard, "Mid-Life Crises, *Tempest*," *TLS* 25 Feb. 1983:179). *Audience:* General use; *Supplementary materials:* Mazursky, Paul. "*The Tempest:* A Screenplay." *PAJ*, 1982. (BFI #58880).

MEDIUM INFORMATION: *Medium:* Motion Picture; *Sound:* Spoken language; *Color:* Yes; *Length:* 140 min.; *Language(s) spoken:* English; *Film type:* 35mm Metrocolor.

AUTHORSHIP INFORMATION: *Producer(s):* Mazursky, Paul; Bernhardt, Steven; Guzman, Pato; *Director(s):* Mazursky, Paul; Smith, Irby; *Screenplay writer(s):* Mazursky, Paul; Capetanos, Leon; *Composer(s):* Yamashta, Stomu; *Designer(s):* Guzman, Pato; *Set designer(s):* Hefferan, Paul (New York); *Costume designer(s):* Wolsky, Albert; Piazza, Frank; Nichols, Jennifer (New York); Sakovidou, Vicky (Greece); *Other personnel:* McAlpine, Don (Photography); Cambern, Donn (Editor); Ferren, Bran (Special effects); Taylor, Juliet (Casting); Barlia, Lou (Camera); Farley, Bill (Hair stylist); Maitland, Todd (Sound); Eads, Paul (Art director—New York); Cannistraci, Jay (Makeup—New York); Ferrara, Frankie (Stunt coordinator); Lambrou, Aspa (Prod. manager— Greece); Blasetti, Mara (Prod. Manager—Rome); *Cast:* Cassavetes, John (Phillip); Rowlands, Gena (Antonia); Sarandon, Susan (Aretha); Ringwald, Molly (Miranda); Gassman, Vittorio (Alonzo); Julia, Raul (Kalibanos); Robards, Sam (Freddy); Stewart, Paul (Father); Mazursky, Paul (Terry Bloomfield); Mazursky, Betsy (Betsy Bloomfield); Grand, Murray (Pianist); Marolakos, John (N.Y. cafe owner); Moscaidis, George (Athens cafe owner); Lefko, Camille (Guard); Hewitt, Jerry (Stuntman); Mitchell, Barry (Woody Allen lookalike); Cerullo, Al (Heli pilot); Kavalieros, Theodoros (Nightclub MC).

DISTRIBUTION & AVAILABILITY: *Publisher or responsible agency:* Columbia Pictures; *Distributor:* CLC, FCM, DCV, *Copy location:* FOL; *Call or copy number:* MP; *Availability:* FCM, V, $79.95; DCV, V, $75.

The Tempest. Video/Interpretation

627. *The Tempest.*

CURRENT PRODUCTION: *Year:* 1985.

DOCUMENT INFORMATION: *Country:* USA; *Year of release:* 1985.

EDITION, HISTORY, CONTENTS, & EVALUATION: *Edition & history:* Another in the Bard Production video adaptations of Shakespeare's plays. (See also 27, 340, 477, 494.) As has been said before, the producer's big selling point for this series was the use of American rather than British actors, whom American students could more readily identify with their daily lives. In this production, for example, the well-known TV actor, Efrem Zimbalist, Jr., plays Prospero. How successfully this series will compete with the BBC plays remains to be seen. The New York producer, Joseph Papp, writing in *The New York Times* (13 May 1979: 2.32) bitterly complained about the exclusion of American actors from the BBC series, even though the BBC plays were partially underwritten with funds from the USA. *Contents & evaluation:* Not seen. *Audience:* High school (grades 10-12); College and university.

MEDIUM INFORMATION: *Medium:* Video; *Sound:* Spoken language; *Color:* Yes; *Length:* 126 min.; *Language(s) spoken:* English; *Video type:* B, V.

AUTHORSHIP INFORMATION: *Producer(s):* Campbell, Ken; *Director(s):* Woodman, William; *Composer(s):* Serry, John; *Designer(s):* Carra, Lawrence; *Cast:* Zimbalist, Efrem Jr. (Prospero); Bassett, William H. (Alonso); Sorel, Ted (Antonio); Kuter, Kay E. (Gonzalo); Edwards, Edward (Sebastian); Hammond, Nicholas (Ferdinand); Taylor, J.E. (Miranda); Black, Duane (Ariel); Hootkins, William (Caliban); Palillo, Ron (Trinculo); Graf, David (Stephano); Elias, Hector (Boatswain); Pinter, Mark (Adrian); White, Callan (Iris); Friedlander, Gina (Ceres); Farkas, Roberta (Juno); Boatwright, Christopher; Jeschke, Colette; Olson, Reid; O'Rourke, Kevyn (Spirits).

DISTRIBUTION & AVAILABILITY: *Publisher or responsible agency:* Bard Productions Ltd.; *Distributor:* ILL, FCM, TWC, DCV, INM *Availability:* ILL, sale, V (S01593) $89.95; FCM, sale, V $89.95; TWC, sale, apply; DCV, V (82126) $95 (1988); INM, V $99.

The Tempest. **Video/Documentary/Scenes**

628. *The Tempest.* (Series: From Page to Stage).

DOCUMENT INFORMATION: *Country:* Canada; *Year of release:* 1985; *Location of first showing:* Stratford Shakespeare Festival, Ontario, Canada.

EDITION, HISTORY, CONTENTS, & EVALUATION: *Edition & history:* One of a series of educational cassettes issued by the Stratford Shakespeare Festival, Ontario, Canada. As of this writing excerpts from five plays have been made available (see 45, 572, 606, 661). For background, see 45. *Contents & evaluation:* Not seen. Favorable reports about a 1983 Canadian television broadcast of the original stage production as well as screenings of other programs in this series suggest that this production is also of high quality. According to the promotional material, Nicholas Pennell, Stephano in the Stratford production, narrates. Credits below are from the program for the summer 1982 stage production and may include roles that are not represented in the excerpts on the videocassette. *Audience:* General use; *Supplementary materials:* Berry, Ralph. "Review," *SQ* 34.1 (Spring 1983): 95; 1983); Hayes, Elliott, ed. [Teachers' Committee] *From Page to Stage: Study Guide.* Stratford Shakespeare Festival, 1985.

MEDIUM INFORMATION: *Medium:* Video; *Sound:* Spoken language; *Color:* Yes; *Length:* 30 min.; *Language(s) spoken:* English; *Video type:* B, V, 3/4U.

AUTHORSHIP INFORMATION: *Producer(s):* Levene, Sam; *Director(s):* Hirsch, John; *Designer(s):* Heeley, Desmond; *Cast:* Cariou, Len (Prospero); Pennell, Nicholas (Stephano/Narrator); Hazel, Deryck (Ship's Master); Austin-Olsen, Shaun (Boatswain); Curnock, Richard (Alonso); Monette, Richard (Sebastian); Fox, Colin (Antonio); Waisberg, Peter (Adrian); Gordon, Lewis (Gonzalo); Flett, Sharry (Miranda); Deakin, Ian (Ariel); Potter, Miles (Caliban); Mezon, Jim (Ferdinand); Jarvis, John (Trinculo); Neufeld, Irene (Iris); McKennitt, Loreena (Ceres); Noel-Antscherl, Anita (Juno).

DISTRIBUTION & AVAILABILITY: *Publisher or responsible agency:* CBC Enterprises; *Distributor:* BEA, *Availability:* B (1-184-2), V (1-185-0), $120, schools $96; 3/4U (1-186-9), $135, schools $108.

The Tempest. **Video/Recording**

629. *The Tempest.*

DOCUMENT INFORMATION: *Country:* USA; *Year of release:* 1985.

EDITION, HISTORY, CONTENTS, & EVALUATION: *Edition & history:* A videotaping on June 29, 1985 of the Hartford Stage company's *Tempest.* *Audience:* General use.

MEDIUM INFORMATION: *Medium:* Video; *Sound:* Spoken language; *Color:* Yes; *Length:* 123 min.; *Language(s) spoken:* English; *Video type:* V.

AUTHORSHIP INFORMATION: *Producer(s):* Hartford Stage Company; *Director(s):* Lamos, Mark.

DISTRIBUTION & AVAILABILITY: *Publisher or responsible agency:* Hartford Stage Company; *Copy location:* LCL; *Call or copy number:* NCOV 436; *Availability:* Archive.

The Tempest. **Video/Documentary**

630. *Shakespeare: The Tempest, IV.* (Series: Open University Film Library).

DOCUMENT INFORMATION: *Country:* GB; *Year of release:* 1985 [?].

EDITION, HISTORY, CONTENTS, & EVALUATION: *Edition & history:* One of several programs prepared for the Open University television programs in Great Britain. Not seen in the U.S. This program attempts to re-create "the sense of magic" felt by audiences in Shakespeare's own day when confronted with the Act

Four masque scene. *Audience:* College and university; Professional.

MEDIUM INFORMATION: *Medium:* Video; *Sound:* Spoken language; *Color:* Yes; *Length:* 24 min. (each workshop); *Language(s) spoken:* English; *Video type:* V,B.

AUTHORSHIP INFORMATION: *Producer(s):* Hoyle, David.

DISTRIBUTION & AVAILABILITY: *Publisher or responsible agency:* BBC Open University; *Distributor:* GSV*, *Copy location:* BBC; *Availability:* Sale or rental in Great Britain only.

The Tempest. **Video/Recording**

631. *The Tempest.*

DOCUMENT INFORMATION: *Country:* USA; *Year of first showing:* 1986; *Location of first showing:* LCL.

EDITION, HISTORY, CONTENTS, & EVALUATION: *Edition & history:* A videotaping made on March 28, 1986 of a production by the Theatre for a New Audience at CSC of *The Tempest.* Located on East 13th Street in New York City, the CSC company has over the past several years produced memorable work, including an excellent *King Lear, Richard II* and a "cinematic" *Hamlet* that in a reverse motif put on a stage production influenced by cinematic techniques (see "A Cinematic CSC *Hamlet,*" *SFNL* 8.2 [April 1984]: 6). *Audience:* General use.

MEDIUM INFORMATION: *Medium:* Video; *Sound:* Spoken language; *Color:* Yes; *Length:* 135 min.; *Language(s) spoken:* English; *Video type:* V.

AUTHORSHIP INFORMATION: *Producer(s):* Theatre for a New Audience; *Director(s):* Taymor, Julie.

DISTRIBUTION & AVAILABILITY: *Publisher or responsible agency:* Theatre for a New Audience; *Copy location:* LCL; *Call or copy number:* NCOV 493; *Availability:* Archive.

Timon of Athens

ORIGINAL WORK AND PRODUCTION: Tragical Satire. *Year written:* 1607-8; *Year of first production:* 1660s.

Timon of Athens. Video/Interpretation

632. *Timon of Athens.* (Series: The Shakespeare Plays).

DOCUMENT INFORMATION: *Country:* GB; *Year of filming:* 28 Jan.- 3 Feb.1981; *Year of first showing:* 1981; *Location of first showing(s):* BBC, London; PBS stations, USA, 14 Dec. 1981.

EDITION, HISTORY, CONTENTS, & EVALUATION: *Edition & history:* The average person must have had not more than one chance in a lifetime to see even an amateur performance of rarely performed *Timon* before this splendid recording on magnetic tape. Watching Timon gyrate from foolish trust and generosity ("Nev'r speak or think / That Timon's fortunes 'mong his friends can sink" [2.2.230]) to paranoid misanthropy ("I am sick of this false world, and will love nought" [4.3.375]), is exemplary for those who, having given too much, feel the sting of the world's ingratitude. There is much ancient wisdom here about the perils of going from excess to defect that can profitably be reexamined even today (KSR). *Contents & evaluation:* "The BBC Shakespeare series has often seemed more successful with the less frequently performed plays. Thus I looked forward to Jonathan Miller's production of *Timon of Athens*, especially since I had seen Ron

Daniels' production for The Other Place (Stratford) early in January, 1981. But though both productions provided moments of satisfaction, eventually they offered us, like Timon's guests, an empty table . . . once Timon has left Athens, the play seems to come unglued. Jonathan Pryce commented revealingly, in the post-production interview, that he had originally seen the difficulty as being the first half of the play, but found it much easier than he had imagined to play the 'outgoing, giving person' of the first half. The famous poetry comes in the second half but the scenes aren't easier to play—or to vary in tone. In Stratford, the geometrically neat set of the beginning was disarranged, hung with net, strewn with debris, and the Japanese-style costumes gave way to rags. On television the original set was 'changed' from indoors to outdoors by the addition of a small cave and many loudly scrunching rocks. Anyone who came to see Timon announced his or her entrance with strange noises. Only Apemantus against this setting looked neater, and his manner became genial. It was the production's strongest indication of Timon's change; if Apemantus was normal, what should we make of Timon?" (Gilbert, Miriam, "Timon of Athens," *SFNL* 6.2. [1982]: 10). *Audience:* College and university; General use; *Supplementary materials:* Fenwick, Henry. *Timon of Athens. BSP* 19-28; Videotape (25 min.) from "Shakespeare in Perspective" series with Malcolm Muggeridge as lecturer available in U.K. from BBC* (*BUFVC* 25).

MEDIUM INFORMATION: *Medium:* Video; *Sound:*

Spoken language; *Color:* Yes; *Length:* 130 min.; *Language(s) spoken:* English; *Video type:* B, V, 3/4U.

AUTHORSHIP INFORMATION: *Producer(s):* Miller, Jonathan; *Director(s):* Miller, Jonathan; *Adaptor/translator(s):* Snodin, David; *Composer(s):* Oliver, Stephen; *Choreographer(s):* Gilpin, Sally; *Designer(s):* Abbott, Tony; *Costume designer(s):* Lavers, Colin; *Lighting designer(s):* Barclay, Sam; *Other personnel:* Seaborne, Derek (Prod. manager); de Winne, Kezia (Make-up); Miller-Timmins, Derek (Sound); Wilders, John (Literary consultant); *Cast:* Pryce, Jonathan (Timon); Rodway, Norman (Apemantus); Shrapnel, John (Alcibiades); Welsh, John (Flavius); Arthur, Max (Lucilius); Collins, Geoffrey (Flaminius); McGinity, Terence (Servilius); Cossins, James (Lucullus); Gee, Donald (Ventidius); Thomas, Hugh (Lucius); Bailey, John (Sempronius); Shaw, Sebastian (Old Athenian); Fortune, John (Poet); Bird, John (Painter); Kinsey, David (Jeweller); Jay, Tony (Merchant); Neal, David (First Senator); Justin, John (Second Senator); Sharling, Elaine (Phrynia); Dors, Diana (Timandra); Anthony, Michael (Caphis); Manson, Andrew (Servant); Willis, Bev (Servant); Kincaid, David (First Bandit); Deadman, Derek (Second Bandit); Morris, Gil (Soldier); Garrett, Cornelius (Prisoner); Johnson, Karen (Amazon); Lombardi, H.; Indrani, S.; Barton, C.; Reed, C.; Robinson, T. (Lady Amazons); Saipe, Julian (Cupid); w. Finchley Children's Music Group.

DISTRIBUTION & AVAILABILITY: *Publisher or responsible agency:* BBC/TLF; *Distributor:* AVP, UIO, BBC* *Copy location:* UVM, TCL* (Archive); *Availability:* AVP, B, V, 3/4U, sale $450 (1987); UIO, V (72048H), 3/4U (70148V) rental $22.30; BBC*, 16mm or V, apply.

Titus Andronicus

ORIGINAL WORK AND PRODUCTION: Senecan Tragedy. *Year of first production:* 1593-94; *Site of first production:* Rose playhouse, Bankside [?].

Titus Andronicus. Video/Teleplay

633. *Titus Andronicus.* (Series: The Shakespeare Plays).

CURRENT PRODUCTION: *Year:* 1985.

DOCUMENT INFORMATION: *Country:* GB; *Year of first showing:* 1985; *Country of first showing:* GB; *Location of first showing(s):* BBC, London; PBS stations, USA, 19 April 1985.

EDITION, HISTORY, CONTENTS, & EVALUATION: *Edition & history:* This BBC production filters Shakespeare's oddest "tragedy" (actually it's closer to melodrama), through the sharp eye of director Jane Howell. Best known for her work with the minor tetralogy (*1-3H6* and *R3*), Howell in this *Titus* again shows how to work miracles with scarce resources. The spoken words remain those of Shakespeare, but the imaginative visual effects that supplement them are uniquely Howell's. *Contents & evaluation:* "In the BBC-TV production of *Titus Andronicus,* director Jane Howell has chosen Young Lucius, grandson to Titus and eldest son to Lucius, as primary observer of the unfolding of the action. She accomplishes this by overlaying the actual Shakespeare text with a 'video text,' by insert-ing Young Lucius not only more prominently into the scenes in which Shakespeare has written him, but also by featuring him as a visual image in scenes that he is not specifically written into. According to Shakespeare's text, Young Lucius' presence is not required until 3.2. Howell's idea comes partly from her own son's experi-ences with nightmares at the age of nine, and partly from Titus' line at 2.1.251: 'When will this fearful slumber have an end?" Howell's directorial concept is that the story could be the dream of Young Lucius. . . . The costume design reenforces this conception. Howell asked the costumer to create a pair of steel spectacles for young Lucius which immediately attract the video viewer's attention because they are 'out of period,' neither Roman nor Elizabethan but eighteenth centu-ry and these glasses literally punctuate the boy's eyes. . . . In choosing to follow the tale through the eyes of young Lucius, Howell sharpens the central message of the play: who *are* the barbarians? Her interpolation of shots of the boy's face implies a strong corollary statement: How does murder and mutila-tion, ritualized or not, affect the children? The concept also reinforces the 'loss of innocence' motif that con-nects the very name of Young Lucius: light and knowl-edge in the midst of great darkness, awakening at the end of nightmare" (Maher, Mary, "Vision in the BBC's *Titus,*" *SFNL* 10.1 [1985]: 5 +). *Audience:* College and university; *Supplementary materials:* Videotape (25 min.) from "Shakespeare in Perspective" series with An-thony Clare as lecturer available in U.K. from BBC* (*BUFVC* 25).

MEDIUM INFORMATION: *Medium:* Video; *Sound:* Spoken language; *Color:* Yes; *Length:* 150 min.; *Language(s) spoken:* English; *Film type:* 16mm*; *Video type:* B,V,3/4U.

AUTHORSHIP INFORMATION: *Producer(s):* Sutton, Shaun; *Director(s):* Howell, Jane; *Composer(s):* Simpson, Dudley; *Choreographer(s):* Ranson, Malcolm; *Designer(s):* Burrough, Tony; *Costume designer(s):* Lavers, Colin; *Lighting designer(s):* Barclay, Sam; *Other personnel:* Anthony, Chick (Sound); Wilders, John (Literary consultant); Williams, Glenys (Prod. asst.); Garrick, Anthony (Prod. manager); Lowden, Fraser (Prod. assoc.); Edwards, S.; Carver, B. (Floor men); Coward, Shirley (Vision mixer); Tucker, Garth (Camera); Mapson, Colin (Visual effects); Olender, Magda (Properties); Bowman, Ron (Videotape editor); Hay-Arthur, Cecile (Make-up); *Cast:* Davies-Prowles, Paul (Young Lucius); Hardwicke, Edward (Marcus); Brown, Walter (Aemilius); Protheroe, Brian (Saturninus); Gecks, Nicholas (Bassianus); Fuke, Derek (Captain); Aikins, Eileen (Tamora); Searles, Peter (Alarbus); McCaul, Neil (Demetrius); Crompton, Michael (Chiron); Quarshie, Hugh (Aaron); Richards, Gavin (Lucius); Redman, Crispin (Quintus); Hunsinger, Tom (Martius); Packer, Michael (Mutius); Peacock, Trevor (Titus); Calder-Marshall, Anna (Lavinia); Kelly, Paul (Publius); Benfield, John (Messenger); Davies, Deddie (Nurse); Potter, Tim (Clown); Benfield, John (First Goth and Caius); Kelly, Paul (Second Goth); Fuke, Derek (Third Goth and Sempronius); Searles, Peter (Fourth Goth and Valentine).

DISTRIBUTION & AVAILABILITY: *Publisher or responsible agency:* BBC-TV/Time Life Inc.; *Distributor:* AVP, UIO, BBC*; *Copy location:* UVM; *Availability:* AVP, B, V, 3/4U $450 (1987), sale; UIO, V (72072H), 3/4U (70172V), rental, $25.60; BBC* 16mm or V, apply (*BUFVC* 25).

Titus Andronicus. Video/Recording

634. *Titus Andronicus.*

DOCUMENT INFORMATION: *Country:* USA; *Year of release:* 1986.

EDITION, HISTORY, CONTENTS, & EVALUATION: *Edition & history:* A videotaping of the Oregon Shakespeare Festival June 24, 1986 *Titus Andronicus.* TOFT archival copy available at Lincoln Center. *Audience:* General use.

MEDIUM INFORMATION: *Medium:* Video; *Sound:* Spoken language; *Color:* Yes; *Length:* Unknown; *Video type:* V.

AUTHORSHIP INFORMATION: *Producer(s):* Oregon Shakespeare Festival; *Director(s):* Patton, Pat.

DISTRIBUTION & AVAILABILITY: *Publisher or responsible agency:* Oregon Shakespeare Festival; *Copy location:* LCL; *Call or copy number:* NCOV 522; *Availability:* Archive.

Troilus and Cressida

ORIGINAL WORK AND PRODUCTION: Problem Comedy. *Year written:* 1601-2; *Site of first production:* Inns of Court [?].

Troilus and Cressida. **Video/Teleplay**

635. *Troilus and Cressida.*

DOCUMENT INFORMATION: *Country:* GB; *Year of first showing:* 1954; *Location of first showing:* BBC. Transmitted 8:29 to 10:51 P.M., Sunday, 19 Sept. 1954.

EDITION, HISTORY, CONTENTS, & EVALUATION: *Edition & history:* Television and academe combined to produce this *Troilus and Cressida* when Douglas Allen, a former student, encouraged by the studio drama head, Michael Barry, wrote on March 17, 1954, to Prof. George Rylands at Cambridge University asking if he would be interested in helping to produce a Shakespeare play for television. The result was this ambitious production, which went over budget by several hundred pounds but unfortunately drew a largely negative reaction from the public. A BBC survey estimated that the audience "for this broadcast was 7.3% of the adult population of the United Kingdom, equivalent to 27% of the adult TV public, and the smallest audience for a Sunday play since the present system of recording audiences was adopted in 1952." This figure of 27% must be measured against the 64% average for Sunday night plays, which included many plays by authors other than Shakespeare (WAC T5/544, Sept.

1954). *Contents & evaluation:* Adverse criticism took protean shapes but the gist of the complaints was that the audience simply couldn't figure out what was going on, even down to and including being unable to distinguish between Greeks and Trojans. The audience felt "baffled boredom" and found it impossible to follow the dialogue. It is worth recording, though, that there was particular praise for the acting of Mary Watson as Cressida, John Fraser as Troilus, and Richard Wordsworth as Thersites. Some technical difficulties included a "cramped" effect that made the battle scenes seem crowded, though costumes and sets came in for praise. It was obvious that a play so problematical as *Troilus*, which puzzles even the scholars, was ill-suited for a general audience (WAC T5/544, Sept. 1954). *Supplementary materials:* "Program." *TPAB* 19 Sept. 1954; "Production Arranged for TV." *Times* 17 Sept. 1954: 11 d.

MEDIUM INFORMATION: *Length:* 142 min.

AUTHORSHIP INFORMATION: *Producer(s):* Rylands, George; Allen, Douglas; *Other personnel:* Marlowe, Joan (Stage Manager); Adams, Victor (Fight Arranger); *Cast:* Eccles, Donald (Priam); Squire, William (Hector); Fraser, John (Troilus); Lack, Simon (Paris); Homer, Paul (Helenus); Hansard, Paul (Aeneas); Bateson, Timothy (Calchas); Pettingell, Frank (Pandarus); Culliford, James (Servant to Troilus); Malone, Cavan (Servant to Paris); Shingler, Helen (Helen); Balcon, Jill (Cassandra); Watson, Mary (Cressida); O'Conor, Joseph (Agamemnon); Vere, John (Menelaus); Toone,

Geoffrey (Achilles); Brennan, Michael (Ajax); Hudd, Walter (Ulysses); Leigh, Andrew (Nestor); Lucas, Victor (Diomedes); Ciceri, Leo (Patroclus); Wordsworth, Richard (Thersites); + 9 Trojan and Grecian soldiers and attendants.

DISTRIBUTION & AVAILABILITY: *Publisher or responsible agency:* BBC; *Copy location:* Probably not preserved.

636. *Troilus and Cressida.*

DOCUMENT INFORMATION: *Country:* GB; *Year of release:* 1966; *Location of first showing:* BBC. Transmitted in two parts: Part One, 3:25 to 4:25 P.M., Sunday, 25 Sept. 1966.

EDITION, HISTORY, CONTENTS, & EVALUATION: *Edition & history:* Recording of touring production of the National Youth Theatre. *Supplementary materials:* "Program." *RT* 22 Sept. 1966: 15.

MEDIUM INFORMATION: *Length:* 121 min. (58′ + 63′).

AUTHORSHIP INFORMATION: *Producer(s):* Bakewell, Michael (BBC); Hill, Paul (NYT); *Director(s):* Hepton, Bernard (BBC); Croft, Michael (NYT); *Costume designer(s):* Bright, John; *Other personnel:* McKay, Ian (Fight Arranger); *Cast:* Haunton, Tim (Prologue); Godden, Richard (Priam); Block, Timothy (Hector); Murray, Andrew (Troilus); Eschle, Norman (Aeneas); Stockton, David (Pandarus); Womersley, Charlotte (Cressida); Robarts, Leslie (Agamemnon); Wooldridge, Ian (Menelaus); Marks, Dennis (Achilles); Biddle, Haydn (Ajax); Seaton, Derek (Ulysses); Dalton, Tim (Diomedes); Cranham, Kenneth (Thersites); Payne, Mary (Helen).

DISTRIBUTION & AVAILABILITY: *Publisher or responsible agency:* BBC, NYT; *Copy location:* Unavailable.

Troilus and Cressida. Motion Picture/Documentary

637. *Troilus and Cressida: War, War, Glorious War.* (Series: Explorations in Shakespeare, XII).

DOCUMENT INFORMATION: *Country:* Canada; *Year of release:* 1969.

EDITION, HISTORY, CONTENTS, & EVALUATION: *Edition & history:* Part twelve in a series of twelve 23-minute films made in 1969 by the Ontario Educational Communications Authority. (For others in series, see 18, 40, 65, 124, 162, 257, 322, 465, 488, 555, and 617) For background, see 18. *Contents & evaluation:* Not seen. According to the publicity release issued by NBC Educational Enterprises, the play is handled as a "black comedy. Under its savage attack no value survives. Heroic war becomes mere butchery; what passes for love is exposed as lechery; integrity and honour degenerate into deception and treachery. This theme is forcefully supported throughout by ironic ballads,

army songs, posters symbolizing war and lust, and sequences from the play." From this description it seems that writer Hugh Webster and producer Kurt Reis have not hesitated to re-appropriate Shakespeare's vision into the context of the war-torn 1960s. *Audience:* College and university.

MEDIUM INFORMATION: *Medium:* Motion Picture; *Sound:* Spoken language; *Color:* Yes; *Length:* 23 min.; *Language(s) spoken:* English; *Film type:* 16mm.

AUTHORSHIP INFORMATION: *Producer(s):* Reis, Kurt; Moser, Ed; *Screenplay writer(s):* Webster, Hugh; *Composer(s):* Yanovsky, Zal; *Set designer(s):* Adeney, Chris; *Lighting designer(s):* Galbraith, Howard; *Performance group(s):* Ontario Educational Communications/ NBC Educational Enterprises.

DISTRIBUTION & AVAILABILITY: *Distributor:* CNU [?].

Troilus and Cressida. Video/Interpretation

638. *Troilus and Cressida.* (Series: The Shakespeare Plays).

DOCUMENT INFORMATION: *Country:* GB; *Year of filming:* 28 July–5 Aug. 1981; *Year of first showing:* 1981; *Location of first showing(s):* London, BBC; PBS stations, USA, 17 May 1982.

EDITION, HISTORY, CONTENTS, & EVALUATION: *Edition & history:* On the theory that language itself is a major theme of this 'curiously prolix' play, script editor David Snodin and the director elected to retain the Peter Alexander text with only minor cuts and alterations. One fairly major switch is moving the battlefield back to Troy in the last scene on the grounds that it is neater to have the play end where it begins. An interesting casting decision was giving the role of Thersites to The Incredible Orlando (Jack Birkett), the Caliban of the Derek Jarman filmed *Tempest* and a key member of the London-based Lindsay Kemp theatrical group. Birkett, a blind mime and female impersonator, also played Hippolyta/Titania in the Coronado 1984 *Midsummer Night's Dream* (see 416). *Contents & evaluation:* ". . . I much admire the clarity and generosity of this production. Rather than imposing an 'aboutness' on the play, Miller's version works from the inside out, seeming to convey the points of view of the characters themselves; rather than showing us (as in Terry Hands's 1981 RSC production) a handful of moral idiots, caricatures of the great persons of our expectations who wrangle at their empty causes in vain, this version keeps all options open, treating the characters with care and respect, as persons who believe what they say and do has value . . . the major fascination, for me, was Suzanne Burden's wary, chameleon-like Cressida. At first, with Pandarus, we see a witty, slightly bored young woman; alone, she flips to a thoughtful, hesitant cloak of deep privacy in a second, suggesting that she may redeem the already shaky values of this world. But her self-understanding dissolves into awkwardness at Troilus' high naivete and heaven-sent glances in III.ii. [She] enters haltingly, pulled on by Pandarus, and is embarrassed when he pulls off her veil and amazed when Troilus treats her as a holy image, brushing a first clumsy kiss at her fingers. Pandarus' intrusive coaching dirties this innocence, yet when he leaves, Cressida, at a loss, seems a willing if not eager pawn. But Troilus is all made of unspoken lovers' vows, waiting deliverance; his talk gradually overcomes what he reads as Cressida's tongue-tied apprehension, moving her to assume Pandarus' role, to coach herself towards confession" (Hodgdon, Barbara, "Mostly About Cressida?" *SFNL* 7.1.[1982]: 5). *Audience:* College and university; *Supplementary materials:* Fenwick, Henry. *Troilus and Cressida. BSP* 18-28; Videotape (25 min.) from "Shakespeare in Perspective" series with Sir David Hunt as lecturer available in U.K. from BBC* (*BUFVC* 26).

MEDIUM INFORMATION: *Medium:* Video; *Sound:* Spoken language; *Color:* Yes; *Length:* 180 min.; *Language(s) spoken:* English; *Video type:* B, V, 3/4U.

AUTHORSHIP INFORMATION: *Producer(s):* Miller, Jonathan; *Director(s):* Miller, Jonathan; *Adaptor/translator(s):* Snodin, David; *Composer(s):* Oliver, Stephen; *Designer(s):* Lowrey, Colin; *Costume designer(s):* Hughes, Alun; *Lighting designer(s):* Channon, Dennis; *Other personnel:* Lowden, Fraser (Prod. assoc.); Hobbs, William (Fight arranger); Mair, Eileen (Make-up); Miller-Timmins, Derek (Sound); Wilders, John (Literary consultant); *Cast:* Knight, Esmond (Priam); Shrapnel, John (Hector); Lesser, Anton (Troilus); Firth, David (Paris); Garrett, Cornelius (Margarelon); Steedman, Tony (Aeneas); Whitbread, Peter (Calchas); Gray, Charles (Pandarus); Dobtcheff, Vernon (Agamemnon); Brown, Bernard (Menelaus); Haigh, Kenneth (Achilles); Pedley, Anthony (Ajax); Whitrow, Benjamin (Ulysses); Chater, Geoffrey (Nestor); Moriarty, Paul (Diomedes); Cutter, Simon (Patroclus); The Incredible Orlando (Thersites); Burden, Suzanne (Cressida); Pennington, Ann (Helen); Kendall, Merelina (Andromache); Sharling, Elayne (Cassandra); Harvey, Max (Alexander); Kinsey, David

(Servant to Paris); Walmsley, Peter (Servant); Portacio, Tony (Helenus); Cassell, Peter (Deiphobus).

DISTRIBUTION & AVAILABILITY: *Publisher or responsible agency:* BBC/TLF; *Distributor:* AVP, UIO, BBC*, TCL* (Archive only) *Availability:* AVP, B, V, 3/4U $450 (1987), sale; UIO, V (72319H), 3/4U (70319V), rental, $25.40; BBC* 16mm or V, apply (*BUFVC* 26).

Troilus and Cressida. Video/Excerpt

639. *Fortunes of War.*

DOCUMENT INFORMATION: *Country:* GB; *Year of release:* 1987.

EDITION, HISTORY, CONTENTS, & EVALUATION: *Edition & history:* An excerpt from *Troilus and Cressida* appears in this television mini-series when the hero (played by Kenneth Branagh) directs the local British colony in Bucharest, Rumania, in a university production of Shakespeare's play. *Contents & evaluation:* As one might expect when Kenneth Branagh, England's rising young superstar, is involved, the scenes from *Troilus* are carried out with great flair, though pains are taken to preserve the appearance of an amateurish production. The bedsheet costuming, one supposes, is deliberately so. *Audience:* General use; *Supplementary materials:* O'Connor, John J. "Adrift on the Rocky Seas of Adaptation." *NYT* Jan. 17, 1988: H 25.

MEDIUM INFORMATION: *Medium:* V; *Sound:* Spoken language; *Color:* Yes; *Length:* 5 min.

AUTHORSHIP INFORMATION: *Producer(s):* Willingdale, Betty; *Director(s):* Jones, James Cellan; *Adaptor/translator(s):* Plater, Alan; *Cast:* Brudenell, Jeremy (Guy); Thompson, Emma (Harriet); Pickup, Ronald (Prince Yakimov); Clifford, Richard (Clarence); McNamara, Desmond (Galpin); Branagh, Kenneth.

DISTRIBUTION & AVAILABILITY: *Publisher or responsible agency:* WNET/Thirteen (Masterpiece Theatre); BBC; *Distributor:* WNET.

Twelfth Night

ORIGINAL WORK AND PRODUCTION: Festive Comedy. *Year written:* 1602; *Site of first production:* Middle Temple [Inns of Court].

Twelfth Night. **Motion Picture/Abridgment**

640. *Twelfth Night: or, What You Will.*

DOCUMENT INFORMATION: *Country:* USA; *Year of release:* Feb. 3, 1910.

EDITION, HISTORY, CONTENTS, & EVALUATION: *Edition & history:* One of several brief (ten minute) Shakespeare films produced by Vitagraph at the dawn of the American film industry. For some other Vitagraph silents, see 7, 32, 47, 195, 199, 242, 354, 387, 436, 496, and 515. *Contents & evaluation:* How much of Shakespeare's *Twelfth Night* can be squeezed into one reel? One answer is contained in this film that valiantly brings Shakespeare to the unwashed of the Nickelodeon audiences who on the same bill might witness Egyptian dancers and trained seals. Unlike the British silents, which were so often stagy, director Charles Kent paid his camera the respect of using it. Viola actually comes out of the sea, albeit the "sea" may only have been Great South Bay at Bay Shore, Long Island (or so Robert Ball speculates because Vitagraph at one time had a studio in Bay Shore on Union Street). A

lively little Maria effectively torments Malvolio, and Viola remains smiling and vibrant throughout. Much of it is shot out of doors, though camera movements and editing are of course rudimentary. As though to express his displeasure with such crudities, a pouting Malvolio stalks out at the end with a petulant expression that plainly reflects his unspoken exit line: "I'll have revenge on the whole pack of you." The costumes can be described as all-purpose Illyrian. The huddled and tired masses got a lot for their nickels. *Audience:* Professional; *Supplementary materials:* Ball, *SOSF* 56-60; Harrison, Louis Reeves. *Screencraft.* New York, 1916: 114+; "Review." *BIO* 28 Apr. 1910: 37.

MEDIUM INFORMATION: *Medium:* Motion Picture; *Sound:* Silent; *Color:* No (black & white); *Length:* 10 min. [?]; *Film type:* 35mm.

AUTHORSHIP INFORMATION: *Producer(s):* Blackton, J. Stuart; *Director(s):* Kent, Charles; *Cast:* Turner, Florence (Viola); Gordon, Julia Swayne (Olivia); Kent, Charles (Malvolio); Sais, Marin; Storey, Edith; *Performance group(s):* Blackton series of Shakespeare films.

DISTRIBUTION & AVAILABILITY: *Publisher or responsible agency:* Vitagraph; *Distributor:* EMG, JEF, *Copy location:* NFA, LCM, FOL; *Call or copy number:* MP 20 (FOL); *Restrictions:* Archive only.

Twelfth Night. **Video/Teleplay**

641. *Twelfth Night.* (Series: Scenes from Shakespeare).

DOCUMENT INFORMATION: *Country:* GB; *Year of first showing:* 1937; *Location of first showing:* BBC. Transmitted 20 Feb. 1937.

EDITION, HISTORY, CONTENTS, & EVALUATION: *Edition & history:* Part of the "Scenes from Shakespeare" series that appeared in the second year of BBC transmission. During this period there was much writing about Shakespeare in *The Listener* (the BBC house organ). Articles by Tyrone Guthrie, Edith Evans, Harold Child, G.B. Harrison, and J. Dover Wilson appeared in 1937, but little was said directly about these early television programs. *Supplementary materials: TPAB* 20 Feb. 1937.

MEDIUM INFORMATION: *Length:* 15 min.

AUTHORSHIP INFORMATION: *Director(s):* Thomas, Stephen; *Cast:* Atkins, Robert (Sir Toby Belch); Hewitt, Henry (Sir Andrew Aguecheek); March, Nadine (Maria); Percy, Esme (Feste); Swinley, Ion (Malvolio); Lehmann, Beatrix (Viola); Holme, Thea (Olivia).

DISTRIBUTION & AVAILABILITY: *Publisher or responsible agency:* BBC; *Copy location:* Unavailable.

Twelfth Night. **Video/Scenes**

642. *Twelfth Night.* (Series: Play Parade).

DOCUMENT INFORMATION: *Country:* GB; *Year of first showing:* 1937; *Location of first showing:* BBC. Transmitted 9:36 P.M., 14 May 1937.

EDITION, HISTORY, CONTENTS, & EVALUATION: *Edition & history:* One of the very earliest transmissions of Shakespeare on television when the industry was still in its infancy. The credits give Greer Garson as Viola, who was then acting on the London stage and who was subsequently propelled to stardom as Mrs. Miniver (1942). *Supplementary materials: TPAB* 14 May 1937.

MEDIUM INFORMATION: *Length:* 33 min.

AUTHORSHIP INFORMATION: *Producer(s):* O'Ferrall, George More; *Cast:* Wyse, John (Orsino); Garson, Greer (Viola); Pritchard, Hilary (Sea Captain); Black, Dorothy (Olivia); Reach, Edward (Clown/Curio); Blakelock, Alban (Valentine).

DISTRIBUTION & AVAILABILITY: *Publisher or responsible agency:* BBC; *Copy location:* Unavailable.

Twelfth Night. **Video/Recording**

643. *Twelfth Night.*

DOCUMENT INFORMATION: *Country:* GB; *Year of first showing:* 1939; *Location of first showing:* BBC. Transmitted 2 Jan. 1939.

EDITION, HISTORY, CONTENTS, & EVALUATION: *Edition & history:* The television program announced that this play was to be presented "direct from the Phoenix Theatre" in London's West End. One assumes therefore that it was actually recorded on the stage of the theatre rather than in the studio, which must have been quite a technical feat in those early days. Certainly the cast glitters with well known names to include Peggy Aschcroft (Viola) and Michael Redgrave (Sir Andrew Aguecheek). *Supplementary materials: TPAB* 2 Jan. 1939.

MEDIUM INFORMATION: *Length:* 150 min.

AUTHORSHIP INFORMATION: *Producer(s):* St. Denis, Michel; *Cast:* Redgrave, Michael (Sir Andrew Aguecheek); Ashcroft, Peggy (Viola); Knight, Esmond (Orsino); Langton, Basil C. (Sebastian); Devlin, William (Antonio); Rae, John (Sea Captain); Donald, James (Valentine); Whitehead, Peter (Curio); Hayes, George (Malvolio); Heathcote, Thomas (Fabian); Jenkins, Warren (Feste); Bannerman, Alistair (Priest); Lefevre, Pierre (1st Officer); Earle, John (Second Officer); Lindsay, Vera (Olivia); Lisle, Lucille (Maria); Alexander, Mary; Jessel, Genevieve; Salaman, Merula; Acton-Bond, Michael; Blagden, John; Cairncross, James; Dolman, Stephen; Goodwin, Michael; MacMichael, David; Madders, Dennis; Spencer, Norman (Sailors, Lords, Officers, Attendants, Musicians).

DISTRIBUTION & AVAILABILITY: *Publisher or responsible agency:* BBC; *Copy location:* Unavailable.

Twelfth Night. **Motion Picture/Musical**

644. *Noche de reyes.*

DOCUMENT INFORMATION: *Country:* Spain; *Year of release:* 1947.

EDITION, HISTORY, CONTENTS, & EVALUATION: *Edition & history:* An elusive film listed in the Weisbaden filmography, probably a musical version of *Twelfth Night. Supplementary materials: SIF* 95.

MEDIUM INFORMATION: *Length:* [?] min.

AUTHORSHIP INFORMATION: *Director(s):* Lucia, Luis; *Cast:* Fernando, Rey; Fajardo, Eduardo.

Twelfth Night. **Video/Abridgment**

645. *Twelfth Night: or, What You Will.*

DOCUMENT INFORMATION: *Country:* USA; *Year of first showing:* 1949; *Location of first showing:* NBC/TV, Actors Equity/Philco Television Playhouse, 9-10 P.M., 20 Feb. 1949.

EDITION, HISTORY, CONTENTS, & EVALUATION: *Edition & history:* Of historical significance because it is probably the first transmission by a major studio of non-operatic Shakespeare on television in North America. Even before WWII, the British as early as 1937 (see 35) had carried Shakespeare on the BBC. If a record of this 1949 production does remain, it is probably a blurry "Kinescope." It was a joint venture of the Actors Equity and Philco Playhouse. (Earlier, in 1948, Verdi's *Otello* had been televised from the New York Metropolitan Opera (448) but the compelling interest in that instance was doubtless more in the opera than in its source.) *Contents & evaluation:* Jack Gould, the astute *Times* television critic, had mixed feelings about this "pioneering" production. Marsha Hunt, who played Viola, got an excellent notice but for Gould the overall performance was marred by the frantic attempts to make the text conform to the studio clock. "A procession of episodes rather than a piece of integrated theatre," was his judgment. Not surprisingly, given the technical limitations of early television, he also found the lighting unsatisfactory. The set was "deluged with incandescence," he said ("*Twelfth Night*," *NYT* 27 Feb. 1949: x 11). *Audience:* Professional; *Supplementary materials:* "Shakespeare on Video [Still]." *NYT* 20 Feb. 1949: X 11.

MEDIUM INFORMATION: *Medium:* Video; *Sound:* Spoken language; *Color:* No (black & white); *Length:* 60 min.; *Language(s) spoken:* English.

AUTHORSHIP INFORMATION: *Producer(s):* Coe, Fred; *Cast:* Hunt, Marsha (Viola); Carradine, John (Malvolio); Taylor, Vaughan (Sir Andrew Aguecheek); Goode, Richard (Sir Toby Belch); McQuade, John (Feste); *Performance group(s):* Philco Playhouse.

DISTRIBUTION & AVAILABILITY: *Copy location:* Unknown.

Twelfth Night. **Video/Teleplay**

646. *Twelfth Night.*

DOCUMENT INFORMATION: *Country:* GB; *Year of first showing:* 1950; *Location of first showing:* BBC. Transmitted 8:45 to 10:30 P.M., Friday, 6 Jan. 1950.

EDITION, HISTORY, CONTENTS, & EVALUATION: *Edition & history:* Either by sensitivity to the Anglican liturgical calendar or by happy coincidence, the BBC scheduled Shakespeare's *Twelfth Night* for the Feast of the Epiphany (January 6), the day after Twelfth Night. Despite the title, the play alludes only indirectly to its namesake. Even these good intentions, however, could not rescue it from negative reactions within the BBC establishment. One executive thought that the director had removed "all the fun and sparkle" from the play, and another remarked that the casting was "dull" and the tempo "slow." Perhaps comedy was not Mr. Clayton's forte for previously he had directed a successful *Antigone* on television. It is also possible that Mr. Clayton wanted to privilege the sombre side of the play, its identification with Twelfth Night and the Feast of the Epiphany. It's a play, after all, that is set in a context of mourning for the death of Olivia's brother. Because the recording is lost, however, we will never have an opportunity to see if Mr. Clayton's production was justly evaluated or simply misunderstood (WAC T5/547 7 Jan. 1950). *Supplementary materials:* "Program." *RT* 31 Dec. 1949: 43.

MEDIUM INFORMATION: *Length:* 105 min.

AUTHORSHIP INFORMATION: *Producer(s):* Clayton, Harold; *Screenplay writer(s):* Atkins, Robert; *Composer(s):* Robinson, Eric; *Designer(s):* Learoyd, Barry; *Cast:* Lott, Barbara (Viola); Kneale, Patricia (Olivia); Dunn, Geoffrey (Malvolio); Morgan, Terence (Orsino); Tandy, Donald (Curio); Biggerstaff, John (Valentine); Stephenson, Paul (Sea Captain); Logan, Michael (Sir Toby Belch); Evans, Jessie (Maria); Latham, Stuart (Sir Andrew Aguecheek); Gatrell, John (Feste); Sansom, Robert (Antonio); Redington, Michael (Sebastian); Bennett, Peter (Fabian); Jones, Maurice (Priest); Sim, Gerald (First Officer); Rennie, Peter (Second Officer).

DISTRIBUTION & AVAILABILITY: *Publisher or responsible agency:* BBC; *Copy location:* Unavailable.

Twelfth Night. **USA**

647. *This Is Charles Laughton.*

DOCUMENT INFORMATION: *Country:* USA; *Year of release:* 1953.

EDITION, HISTORY, CONTENTS, & EVALUATION: *Edition & history:* Charles Laughton as Orsino reads in a scene from *Twelfth Night*, when Viola is disguised as a page. *Supplementary materials:* Loughney, Katharine. "Shakespeare on Film and Tape at Library of Congress." *SFNL* 14.2 (Apr. 1990): 4.

MEDIUM INFORMATION: *Length:* 15 min.

AUTHORSHIP INFORMATION: *Producer(s):* Gregory, Paul; *Cast:* Laughton, Charles.

DISTRIBUTION & AVAILABILITY: *Copy location:* LCM; *Call or copy number:* FAB 2656.

Twelfth Night. **Motion Picture/Adaptation**

648. Dvenadtsataia noch. [Twelfth Night, or What You Will].

DOCUMENT INFORMATION: *Country:* USSR; *Year of release:* 1955.

EDITION, HISTORY, CONTENTS, & EVALUATION: *Edition & history:* A "Russianized" version of *Twelfth Night* with elaborate sets, costumes and sweeping vistas of the coast line. It is culture shock to hear an Elizabethan ballad sung as though the vocalist were a strolling troubadour at the local Russian Tea Room. What the film lacks in faithfulness to the Elizabethan World Picture, it more than compensates for, however, with its rollicking energy and honest enthusiasm for the subject. *Contents & evaluation:* "Although they have sliced the Bard's comedy to fit it into an an hour-and-a-half running time, Leningrad's filmmakers have done it judiciously. Above all, to judge by the English subtitles, they do not appear to have done injury to the poetry and songs that have lived for 350 years. . . . M. Yanshin, of course, has the fattest, if we may be forgiven a pun, role. A veritable tun of a man, he makes Sir Toby a rambunctious, wine-swilling, devil-may-care mischief maker. As his partners in funny skulduggery, two fellow players, A. Lisyanskava as the capricious Maria, and G. Vipin as the weak-kneed doltish suitor, Sir Andrew, give him noble assists. As the clown, B. Friendlich adds a couple of songs and a comic touch or two" (Weiler, A.H., "Review," *NYT* 5 March 1956: 21). *Audience:* High school (grades 10-12); College and university; *Supplementary materials:* Morris, *ShOF* 19.

MEDIUM INFORMATION: *Medium:* Motion Picture; *Sound:* Spoken language; *Color:* Yes; *Length:* 90 min.; *Language(s) spoken:* Russian; *Language of subtitles:* English; *Film type:* 16mm.

AUTHORSHIP INFORMATION: *Producer(s):* Lenfilm; *Director(s):* Fried, Yakow; *Screenplay writer(s):* Fried, Yan; *Composer(s):* Zhivotov, A.; *Designer(s):* Malkin, S.; *Set designer(s):* Snoinow, I.; *Other personnel:* Shapiro, E.; Ryjow, K. (Photography); Schirkin, G. (Editor); Sound (Hutorianski, B.); *Cast:* Luchko, Katya (Sebastian/Viola); Larionova, Anna (Olivia); Medvediev, V. (Duke Orsino); Yanshin, M. (Sir Toby); Vipin, G. (Sir Andrew Aguecheek); Merkuriev, V. (Malvolio); Lukyanov, S. (Antonio); Freindlich, B. (Clown); Lisyanskava, A. (Maria); Flippov, S. (Fabian); Antonov, A. (Sea Captain)

DISTRIBUTION & AVAILABILITY: *Publisher or responsible agency:* A Lenfilm Production; *Distributor:* COR, *Copy location:* FOL; *Call or copy number:* MP 50; *Availability:* COR, rental, 16mm, apply.

Twelfth Night. **Video/Teleplay**

649. Twelfth Night: or, What You Will. (Series: Hallmark Hall of Fame).

DOCUMENT INFORMATION: *Country:* USA; *Year of first showing:* 1957; *Location of first showing:* NBC-TV, 6:30 to 8:00 P.M., 12 Dec. 1957.

EDITION, HISTORY, CONTENTS, & EVALUATION: *Edition & history:* A Hallmark Hall of Fame television production directed by David Greene and starring Maurice Evans as Malvolio. (For other Hallmark Shakespeare productions, see 102, 126, 305, 309, 484, 593, 594, and 613.) The greeting card commercials framing the production appropriately exploited the play's title, *Twelfth Night.* ("Twelfth Night" is the twelfth day of Christmas, January 5, and the eve of the the Feast of the Epiphany). In Elizabethan times Epiphany was a day especially set aside for gift giving, which is a minor element in the play (e.g, Olivia's ring to Viola). The Museum of Broadcasting copy is marked "out of sync" throughout, though the visual effects, as described below, are often quite spectacular. There are numerous textual deletions, transpositions and alterations. Count Orsino has vanished from the opening along with Viola and the Sea Captain's exchange about her lost brother.

There was serious competition for an audience on the evening that this program was transmitted. The television section of *The New York Times* announced that Hollywood actor Ronald Reagan would be introducing James Stewart on General Electric Theatre in *The Trail to Christmas.* The American people never suspected then that Mr. Reagan was honing his formidable television skills for larger goals. *Contents & evaluation:* The staging is so whimsical as to prefigure the later more famous free-swinging interpretations of Shakespeare by directors such as Peter Brook. Feste becomes a mime who keeps popping in and out of the screen. Maurice Evans sports a kind of Mohawk haircut (this well before the Punk rock craze), and a weird, built-up nose. Viola is outfitted in a white page suit but is nearly rendered invisible by the harsh lighting (this was live television drama with no holds barred if something went awry). The studio set looks and is artificial with its painted backdrops, fake pond and small bridge. Casting Feste as a mime violates Shakespeare's conception of him as a wise rather than a foolish fool. Some clever touches, however, which visualize verbal elements in the Shakespearean text, have Feste inverting an hour glass to signal the passing of time ("the whirligig of time"), and hanging upside down to show the topsy-turviness of this world. The diction, however, of the actors is excellent, despite the flaw of its being "out of sync." Evans affects a lower-class accent for Malvolio. Spectacular dancing and music heighten the sense of Illyria as a far off, exotic place. The eavesdropping scene is done with special flair. When Sir Toby corrects Malvolio's pronunciation of "slough," the steward accepts it but remains oblivious of its clandestine source. At the end of the sequence, in a kind of reverse *deus ex machina,* an ecstatic Malvolio is lifted up to a glittering ballroom. Later, in the madhouse scene, highly subjective avant-garde montages of laughing, mocking masks surround Malvolio. The masks then abruptly enter into a huge, laughing, grinning mouth that appears without warning in the *mise en scène.* The ending is truly spectacular. As Malvolio cries out his famous "I'll be reveng'd on the whole pack of you," the platform he has ascended to explodes and he falls, like Barbaras in *The Jew of Malta,* while everyone expresses pleasure over his demise. No liberal guilt here. In the finale a circular dance pattern reverts to the theme of the "whirligig of time," and Feste comes forward to render his song about the "Wind and the Rain." It is all truly vintage television from the golden era when actors risked everything by appearing live before millions of viewers (KSR). *Audience:* General use; *Supplementary materials:* "[Ad & Still]. *NYT* 15 Dec. 1957: X 17.

MEDIUM INFORMATION: *Medium:* Video; *Sound:* Spoken language; *Color:* No (black & white); *Length:* 90 min.; *Language(s) spoken:* English; *Video type:* Kinescope.

AUTHORSHIP INFORMATION: *Producer(s):* Hartung, Robert; *Director(s):* Greene, David; *Adaptor/translator(s):* Nichols, William; *Composer(s):* Engel, Lehman; *Choreographer(s):* Butler, Paul; *Designer(s):* Ter-Arutunian, Rouben; *Lighting designer(s):* Knight, William; *Cast:* Evans, Maurice (Malvolio); Harris, Rosemary (Viola); King, Dennis (Sir Toby Belch); Elliott, Denholm (Sebastian); Adrian, Max (Aguecheek); Hyland, Frances (Olivia); Morris, Howard (Feste); Ghostley, Alice (Maria); Morton, Gregory (Antonio); Cottrell, William (Sea Captain).

DISTRIBUTION & AVAILABILITY: *Publisher or responsible agency:* NBC Hallmark Hall of Fame; *Copy location:* MOB; *Call or copy number:* Pts. 1&2. T78:0220/221; *Restrictions:* Archive viewing.

Twelfth Night. Video/Teleplay

650. *Twelfth Night.* (Series: Sunday-Night Theatre series).

DOCUMENT INFORMATION: *Country:* GB; *Year of first showing:* 1957; *Location of first showing:* BBC. Transmitted 8:30 to 10:00 P.M., Sunday, 10 March 1957.

EDITION, HISTORY, CONTENTS, & EVALUATION: *Edition & history:* The reliance of British television drama on London's West End theatre is testified to in the program notes that list Newton Blick (Sir Toby Belch) as currently performing at the Vaudeville theatre on the Strand in *Salad Days.* John Moffatt (Malvolio) and Maureen Quinney (Olivia) were also appearing simultaneously at the Adelphi in William Wycherley's Restoration comedy, *The Country Wife. Supplementary materials:* "Program." *RT* 3 March 1957: n.p.

MEDIUM INFORMATION: *Length:* 90 min.

AUTHORSHIP INFORMATION: *Producer(s):* Wrede, Casper; Elliott, Michael; *Composer(s):* Hall, George; *Designer(s):* Taylor, Stephen; *Other personnel:* Dupre, Desmond (Lute); Whittaker, Alec (Hautboy); *Cast:* Hardy, Robert (Orsino); Vieyra, Paul (Curio); Terence, David (Valentine); Hamlett, Dilys (Viola); Skinner, Arthur (Captain); Blick, Newton (Sir Toby Belch); Morgan, Priscilla (Maria); Crowden, Graham (Sir Andrew Aguecheek); Maxwell, James (Feste); Quinney, Maureen (Olivia); Moffatt, John (Malvolio); Thompson, Eric (Antonio); Amer, Nicholas (Sebastian); Hall, George (Fabian); Vieyra, Paul (Officer); Skinner, Arthur (Priest).

DISTRIBUTION & AVAILABILITY: *Publisher or responsible agency:* BBC; *Copy location:* Unavailable.

651. *Was ihr Wollt.*

DOCUMENT INFORMATION: *Country:* German Federal Republic; *Year of release:* 1962.

EDITION, HISTORY, CONTENTS, & EVALUATION: Not seen but listed by Morris. Director Wirth also made another made-for-television movie based on *Hamlet,* starring Maximilian Schell (see 110), which was later released with dubbed-in English. *Supplementary materials:* Morris, *SHOF* 23.

MEDIUM INFORMATION: *Color* No (black & white); *Length:* 166 min.; *Languages spoken:* German; *Dubbed language:* English.

AUTHORSHIP INFORMATION: *Director(s):* Wirth, Franz Peter; *Cast:* Andree, Ingrid (Viola); Vogler, Karl Michael (Orsino).

DISTRIBUTION & AVAILABILITY: *Distributor:* Bavaria Atelier GmbH Production.

652. *Was ihr Wollt.*

DOCUMENT INFORMATION: *Country:* German Democratic Republic; *Year of release:* 1963.

EDITION, HISTORY, CONTENTS, & EVALUATION: Not seen. Listed by Morris. Apparently the East Germans were not to be outdone by their cousins in the West and so a year later there is yet another televised *Twelfth Night. Supplementary materials:* Morris, *SHOF* 24.

MEDIUM INFORMATION: *Color:* No (black & white); *Length:* 97 min.; *Languages spoken:* German.

AUTHORSHIP INFORMATION: *Director(s):* Bellag, Lothar; *Cast:* Wolff, Gerry; Bodenstein, Christel.

DISTRIBUTION & AVAILABILITY: *Distributor:* Unknown.

Twelfth Night. **Motion Picture/Abridgment**

653. *Twelfth Night.* (Series: Fair Adventure Series).

DOCUMENT INFORMATION: *Country:* USA; *Year of release:* 1964.

EDITION, HISTORY, CONTENTS, & EVALUATION: *Edition & history:* A three-part abridgment of the play with commentary by Dr. Frank Baxter. *Contents & evaluation:* Not seen. *Audience:* Junior High (grades 7-9); High school (grades 10-12);.

MEDIUM INFORMATION: *Medium:* Motion Picture; *Sound:* Spoken language; *Color:* No (black & white); *Length:* 84 min.; *Language(s) spoken:* English; *Film type:* 16mm.

AUTHORSHIP INFORMATION: *Producer(s):* Hubbard, Ray [?].

DISTRIBUTION & AVAILABILITY: *Publisher or responsible agency:* Westinghouse Broadcasting Company (Group W); *Distributor:* ASF [?].

Twelfth Night. **Video/Teleplay**

654. *Nichts als Sunde.* [*Twelfth Night*].

DOCUMENT INFORMATION: *Country:* East Germany; *Year of release:* 15 October 1965; *Country of first showing:* East Germany.

EDITION, HISTORY, CONTENTS, & EVALUATION: *Edition & history:* Made for East German television in 1965. Information furnished here is taken from clippings in the Ball collection at the Folger Library. It does not seem to be the same production as number 652 above, though there is a remarkable interest in *Twelfth Night* among the Germans in this decade. *Contents & evaluation:* Not seen. *Audience:* General use.

MEDIUM INFORMATION: *Medium:* Video; *Sound:* Spoken language; *Color:* Yes; *Length:* [?] min.; *Language(s) spoken:* German; *Video type:* V.

AUTHORSHIP INFORMATION: *Producer(s):* Ein DEFA-Musical in Farbe und Totalvision; *Director(s):* Burger, Hanus; *Screenplay writer(s):* Burger, Hanus (from Gunther Deicke and Klaus Fehmel); *Designer(s):* Klein, Helmut; *Set designer(s):* Hirschmeier, Alfred; *Other personnel:* Grewuld, Helmut (Camera); *Cast:* Wyziewski, Arno (Orsino); Burger, Anne Kathrin (Olivia); Graedtke, Herbert (Sebastian); Cockova, Helga (Viola); Hegewald, Hans-Joachim (Uncle Toby); Kiwitt, Peter (Majordomo); Grosse, Herwart (Malvolio).

DISTRIBUTION & AVAILABILITY: *Publisher or responsible agency:* East German TV; *Copy location:* Not known.

Twelfth Night. **Video/Teleplay**

655. *Twelfth Night.*

DOCUMENT INFORMATION: *Country:* USA; *Year of first showing:* 1968; *Location of first showing:* WNET/NY. Transmitted 8:30 to 11:00 P.M., Monday, 15 Jan. 1968.

EDITION, HISTORY, CONTENTS, & EVALUATION: *Edition & history:* A full scale production by a group of performers called the Actors Company assembled by station WNET/Thirteen. *Supplementary materials:* "Program." *NYT* 15 Jan. 1968: 95.

MEDIUM INFORMATION: *Sound:* Spoken language; *Color:* Yes; *Length:* 90 min.

DISTRIBUTION & AVAILABILITY: *Publisher or responsible agency:* WNET.

Twelfth Night. **Motion Picture/Abridgment**

656. *Twelfth Night: An Introduction.* (Series: Shakespeare Series [BHE/BFA], I).

DOCUMENT INFORMATION: *Country:* GB; *Year of first showing:* 1970.

EDITION, HISTORY, CONTENTS, & EVALUATION: *Edition & history:* The first in a series of six abridged versions of the plays (see also 41, 228, 258, 323 and 406). For overview, see 41. *Audience:* High school (grades 10-12); College and university.

MEDIUM INFORMATION: *Medium:* Motion Picture; *Sound:* Spoken language; *Color:* Yes; *Length:* 23 min.; *Language(s) spoken:* English; *Film type:* 16mm.

AUTHORSHIP INFORMATION: *Producer(s):* BHE/Seabourne Enterprises; *Cast:* Not known.

DISTRIBUTION & AVAILABILITY: *Publisher or responsible agency:* BHE/Seabourne; *Distributor:* BFA.

Twelfth Night. **Video/Teleplay**

657. *Twelfth Night: or, What You Will.*

DOCUMENT INFORMATION: *Country:* GB; *Year of release:* 1970; *Location of first showing:* ATV TV.

EDITION, HISTORY, CONTENTS, & EVALUATION: *Edition & history:* Made for British commercial televison, not the BBC, this splendid production has not so far been available on cassette in the United States. *Contents & evaluation:* Shrewd direction by John Dexter and brilliant acting make this British television version of *Twelfth Night* unrivalled for charm. As Viola, Joan Plowright is absolutely in control; as Sir Toby Belch, Ralph Richardson shows his astonishing powers of concentration that allow him to make everything look easy (for example, no one can equal his talent for simultaneously eating and acting—Sir Ralph did the same bit of business in the Olivier *Richard III,* and it's like patting yourself on the head with one hand while describing circles over your tummy with the other); and as Malvolio, Alec Guinness emerges again as the master of protean characterization—his Malvolio is a fussy, ridiculous but nevertheless forlorn creature. *Audience:* General use; *Supplementary materials:* Raynor, Henry. "Magical Viola." *Times* 14 July 1970: 5h.

MEDIUM INFORMATION: *Medium:* Video; *Sound:* Spoken language; *Color:* Yes; *Length:* 105 min.; *Language(s) spoken:* English; *Video type:* Video.

AUTHORSHIP INFORMATION: *Producer(s):* Dexter, John; Clarke, Cecil; *Director(s):* Sichel, John; *Composer(s):* Wilkinson, Mark; Scott, Derek; *Designer(s):* Roden, Peter; Toms, Carl; *Costume designer(s):* Conry-Halley, Kay; *Lighting designer(s):* Hudspith, Tony; *Other personnel:* Bennett, Keith (Editor); Nuttall, Bill (Camera); Evans, Yvonne (Makeup); *Cast:* Guinness, Alec (Malvolio); Steele, Tommy (Feste); Richardson, Ralph (Sir Toby Belch); Plowright, Joan (Viola/Sebastian); Raymond, Gary (Orsino); Corri, Adrienne (Olivia); Moffat, John (Aguecheek); Reid, Sheila (Maria); O'Hara, Riggs (Fabian); Curran, Paul (Sea Captain); Leech, Richard (Antonio); Byron, John (Priest); Timothy, Christopher (Valentine); Christian, Kurt (Curio); Moon, Gerald (Gardener's boy).

DISTRIBUTION & AVAILABILITY: *Publisher or responsible agency:* John Dexter Productions/Precision Video; *Distributor:* TSO*, *Copy location:* FOL; *Call or copy number:* VCR; *Availability:* Archive viewing.

Twelfth Night. Motion Picture/Musical

658. *Viola and Sebastian.*

DOCUMENT INFORMATION: *Country:* Germany; *Year of release:* 1973.

EDITION, HISTORY, CONTENTS, & EVALUATION: *Edition & history:* A musical "pop" version of *Twelfth Night,* perhaps along the lines of *Catch My Soul,* the rock musical based on *Othello. Supplementary materials:* BUFVC, 1st Edition. 50.

MEDIUM INFORMATION: *Length:* 93 min.

AUTHORSHIP INFORMATION: *Director(s):* Guertler, Wilmar R.; *Cast:* Sommer, Inken; Hubner, Karin.

DISTRIBUTION & AVAILABILITY: *Distributor:* GFL*.

Twelfth Night. Video/Teleplay

659. *Twelfth Night.*

DOCUMENT INFORMATION: *Country:* GB; *Year of*

first showing: 1974; *Location of first showing:* BBC TV. Transmitted 14 May 1974.

EDITION, HISTORY, CONTENTS, & EVALUATION: *Edition & history:* Another in the series of eight Shakespeare plays, produced on British television by Cedric Messina, before the advent of "The Shakespeare Plays." North and South Americans may easily confuse them with the BBC "Shakespeare Plays" because so many of the same directors and players were involved. For example, the director of this production, David Giles, later directed the Henriad in 1982 and *King John* in 1984 for "The Shakespeare Plays" series. This *Twelfth Night* was filmed in the marble splendor of Vanbrugh's Castle Howard in Yorkshire, one of England's many spectacular country estates, with the players in Edwardian costumes. *Contents & evaluation:* Writing in the London *Times* (15 May 1974: 8d), critic Michael Ratcliffe saw the production as colorful, energetic, but lacking the requisite undertone of melancholy. The full resources of Castle Howard, as described in the guide books, were not exploited to that end. Instead the play took on a note of violence and slapstick, aided and abetted by Charles Gray as Malvolio, who was, we are told, "superbly funny." So "festive" was this production that all reminders of the outside world's harshness were obliterated, even to include Feste's closing song about "the wind and the rain." *Audience:* General use.

MEDIUM INFORMATION: *Medium:* Video; *Sound:* Spoken language; *Color:* Yes; *Length:* 120 min.; *Language(s) spoken:* English; *Video type:* Video.

AUTHORSHIP INFORMATION: *Producer(s):* Messina, Cedric; *Director(s):* Giles, David; *Cast:* Jones, Nicholas (Aguecheek); Gray, Charles (Malvolio); Suzman, Janet (Viola); Marshall, Bryan (Orsino); Taylerson, Marilyn (Olivia).

DISTRIBUTION & AVAILABILITY: *Publisher or responsible agency:* BBC; *Copy location:* BBC*, archive.

Twelfth Night. Video/Teleplay

659.1. *Twelfth Night: or, What You Will.* (Series: The Shakespeare Plays).

DOCUMENT INFORMATION: *Country:* GB; *Year of first showing:* 1980; *Location of first showing(s):* BBC, London; PBS stations, USA, 27 Feb. 1980.

EDITION, HISTORY, CONTENTS, & EVALUATION: *Edition & history:* The performance is based on the 1951 Peter Alexander edition of Shakespeare's plays, as amended by the director for this television series. *Contents & evaluation:* "John Gorrie's production conveys the best qualities of 'festive' comedy. His actors relish their parts and play them sensitively even to the smallest roles. Illyria is the English countryside, a holiday world away from courtly cares, where swashbuckling cavaliers roam freely. Olivia's mansion resembles Ben Jonson's 'Penshurst'—a lavish and leisured country estate. Here the landed gentry mingle, converse, eat, drink, and enjoy the good life. . . . Malvolio the Puritan is festivity's enemy. In a brilliant performance, Alec McCowen's effeminate sneers and gestures capture Puritan superciliousness, excessive self-regard and vain ambition. . . . Feste is startling in this production. As the household pet, Trevor Peacock is not the usual tense thoroughbred. Instead he seems more like a lumbering and loveable mutt. Peacock's yeoman physique makes Feste manly and substantial. His singing voice is scratchy baritone, his manner down-to-earth. There is nothing of Ariel in this Fool. While he combines a certain wistfulness with his whimsy, Peacock never lets the Fool be alienated or melancholy. Feste's final song, accompanied with the twelve-string lute, is a recapitulation of the play rather than a comment on the human condition. During the second verse, the camera focuses on Fabian, the knave. . . . Feste's conclusion, 'We'll strive to please you everyday,' is aimed directly at the camera and hence the television audience. Shakespeare's lines imply that anyone who wants to be pleased should return for more" (Carr, Virginia M., "*Twelfth Night*," *SFNL* 4.2 [1980]: 5). *Audience:* College and university; *Supplementary materials: Twelfth Night* in *BSP*, 1980; Videotape (25 min.) from "Shakespeare in Perspective" series with David Jones as lecturer available in U.K. from BBC* (*BUFVC* 19).

MEDIUM INFORMATION: *Medium:* Video; *Sound:* Spoken language; *Color:* Yes; *Length:* 130 min.; *Language(s) spoken:* English; *Video type:* B, V, 3/4U.

AUTHORSHIP INFORMATION: *Producer(s):* Messina, Cedric; *Director(s):* Gorrie, John; *Cast:* McCowen, Alec (Malvolio); Hardy, Robert (Sir Toby Belch); Kendal, Felicity (Viola); Crosbie, Annette (Maria); Cusack, Sinead (Olivia); Peacock, Trevor (Feste); Arrindell, Clive (Orsino); Stevens, Ronnie (Sir Andrew Aguecheek); Lindsay, Robert (Fabian); Roeves, Maurice (Antonio); Thomas, Michael (Sebastian); Reynolds, Michael (Valentine); Michael, Ryan (Curio); Morgan, Ric (Sea Captain); Hewlett, Arthur (Priest); Webb, Daniel (Servant); MacLachlan, Andrew; Holt, Peter (Officers).

DISTRIBUTION & AVAILABILITY: *Publisher or responsible agency:* BBC/TLF; *Distributor:* AVP, UIO, BBC*, *Copy location:* UVM, TCL* (Archive); *Availability:* AVP, B, V, 3/4U $450 (1987), sale; UIO, V (72050H), 3/4U (70150V), rental, $22.10; BBC*, 16mm or V, apply (*BUFVC* 27).

Twelfth Night. Video/Teleplay

660. *La nuit des rois.*

DOCUMENT INFORMATION: *Country:* GB/France; *Year of first showing:* 1980.

EDITION, HISTORY, CONTENTS, & EVALUATION: *Edition & history:* Identical to entry 659.1 above except that it has French subtitles.

MEDIUM INFORMATION: *Video type:* 3/4" U.

DISTRIBUTION & AVAILABILITY: *Distributor:* Paris F.R., *Copy location:* VAA; *Call or copy number:* THE 1.27.

Twelfth Night. Video/Documentary/Scenes

661. *Twelfth Night.* (Series: From Page to Stage).

DOCUMENT INFORMATION: *Country:* Canada; *Year of release:* 1985; *Location of first showing:* Stratford Shakespeare Festival, Ontario, Canada.

EDITION, HISTORY, CONTENTS, & EVALUATION: *Edition & history:* One of a series of educational cassettes issued by the Stratford Shakespeare Festival, Ontario, Canada. As of this writing excerpts from five plays have been made available (see 45, 572, 606 and 628). Each play comes in a kit that includes a videocassette for classroom viewing, a study guide and the text of the play. The study guide and cassette are keyed to specific parts of the play for handy reference. (The text furnished in this kit in 1987 was not the Stratford Festival edition but the Pelican, edited by C.T. Prouty.) *Contents & evaluation:* Seana McKenna, who plays Viola in the play, also is the commentator in this program, and has some interesting and agreeable though not earth-shaking things to say about *Twelfth Night*. As with the other scripts, the thrust is more toward understanding than toward interpretation, which is pedagogically defensible. We learn that in *TN* Shakespeare is moving toward "maturity," for example, and that there was a tradition of boy actors playing female roles. The latter point of course helps to explain the cross dressing in the play. *Audience:* General use; *Supplementary materials:* Hayes, Elliott, ed. [Teachers' committee] *From Page to Stage: Study Guide.* Stratford Shakespeare Festival, 1985.

MEDIUM INFORMATION: *Medium:* Video; *Sound:* Spoken language; *Color:* Yes; *Length:* 30 min.; *Language(s) spoken:* English; *Video type:* B, V, 3/4U.

AUTHORSHIP INFORMATION: *Producer(s):* Levene, Sam; Witmer, Glenn Edward; *Director(s):* Giles, David; Erlich, Alan; Mak, Peter; *Composer(s):* Applebaum, Louis; *Designer(s):* Poddubiuk, Christine; *Lighting designer(s):* Whitfield, Michael J.; *Cast:* McKenna, Seana (Viola/Narrator); Pennell, Nicholas (Malvolio); Atienza, Edward (Feste); Feore, Colm (Orsino); Ricossa, Maria (Olivia); Ziegler, Joseph (Sir Andrew Aguecheek);

Blendick, James (Sir Toby Belch); Bricker, Kelly; Campbell, Benedict; Dinicol, Keith; Dunlop, William; Harrop, Ernest; Jennings, Nolan; Kerr, Charles; Khaner, Julie; March, Barbara; McCormack, Eric; McDonald, Elizabeth; Paul, Brian; Pointer, Adam; Renton, David; Rosenstein, Howard; Shepherd, Michael; Stait, Brent; Vickers, William; Zivot, Eric.

DISTRIBUTION & AVAILABILITY: *Publisher or responsible agency:* CBC Enterprises; *Distributor:* BEA, *Availability:* B (1-265-2), V (1-267-9), $120, schools, $96; 3/4U (1-269-5), $135, schools, $108.

Twelfth Night. Video/Documentary

662. *Shakespeare: Twelfth Night: Workshop I.* (Series: Open University Film Library).

DOCUMENT INFORMATION: *Country:* GB; *Year of release:* 1985.

EDITION, HISTORY, CONTENTS, & EVALUATION: *Edition & history:* One of several programs prepared for the Open University television programs in Great Britain. Not seen in the U.S. According to the *BUFVC* catalog, each program features a director leading one of the actors through his/her role. In this program, director Tony Church shows how a group of experienced actors feel their way through a text to achieve the right balance of light-heartedness and seriousness. *Audience:* College and university; Professional; *Supplementary materials:* BUFVC 27.

MEDIUM INFORMATION: *Medium:* Video; *Sound:* Spoken language; *Color:* Yes; *Length:* 24 min. (each workshop); *Language(s) spoken:* English; *Video type:* V,B.

AUTHORSHIP INFORMATION: *Producer(s):* Hoyle, David; *Cast:* Church, Tony (Director); Stewart, Patrick; Johnson, Richard; Allan, Eric; Harrow, Lisa; Lloyd, Bernard.

DISTRIBUTION & AVAILABILITY: *Publisher or responsible agency:* BBC Open University; *Distributor:* GSV*, *Copy location:* BBC; *Availability:* Sale or rental in Great Britain only.

Twelfth Night. Video/Scenes

663. *The Shakespeare Hour.*

DOCUMENT INFORMATION: *Country:* GB/USA; *Year of release:* 1985.

EDITION, HISTORY, CONTENTS, & EVALUATION: *Edition & history:* The series, "The Shakespeare Hour," was shown on national educational television beginning on January 5, 1985 (see also 5, 276, 352 and 417). It was funded by the National Endowment for the Humanities and produced by Station WNET/THIRTEEN,

New York City. *Contents & evaluation:* For general description of "The Shakespeare Hour" series, see 5, above; for information about the 1980 *Twelfth Night* upon which this program is based, see 659.1, above. *Audience:* High school (grades 10-12); College and university; General use; *Supplementary materials:* Quinn, *TSH.*

MEDIUM INFORMATION: *Medium:* Video; *Sound:* Spoken language; *Color:* Yes; *Length:* 180 min.; *Language(s) spoken:* English; *Video type:* V.

AUTHORSHIP INFORMATION: *Producer(s):* BBC-WNET/THIRTEEN; *Director(s):* Gorrie, John; Johnson, Donald; Kieffer, Tom; Bellin, Harvey (WNET); *Screenplay writer(s):* Cavendar, Kenneth; *Other personnel:* Squerciati, Marie Therese (Project director); *Cast:* Matthau, Walter; Cast of BBC/Time Life *Twelfth Night,* directed by John Gorrie, 1980 (659.1).

DISTRIBUTION & AVAILABILITY: *Publisher or responsible agency:* WNET/THIRTEEN; *Distributor:* ALS.

Twelfth Night. Video/Adaptation

663.1 *Twelfth Night.*

DOCUMENT INFORMATION: *Country:* USA [?]; *Year of first showing:* 1986; *Location of first showing:* Playboy Channel, USA, Dec. 1988.

EDITION, HISTORY, CONTENTS, & EVALUATION: *Edition & history:* An "adult" version of *Twelfth Night* that features "slow, soft-porn fantasies" and is used primarily "as an expression of the 'Playboy philosophy' as enunciated years ago *ad infinitum* by Hugh Hefner" (Herbert Coursen, Jr.). Included here as one sample of another sub-subgenre of Shakespeare on screen, the porn adaptation. Information about the film is derived from Professor Coursen's unpublished review.

MEDIUM INFORMATION: *Sound:* Spoken language; *Color:* Yes.

AUTHORSHIP INFORMATION: *Director(s):* Wertheim, Ron; *Cast:* Coolidge, Alan (Sir Andrew); Wilson, Ajita (Antonia); Wertheim, Ron (Feste); Lucas, Yonathan (Malvolglio); Krim, Viju (Maria); Vayann, Greta (Olivia); De Meijo, Carlo (Orsino); Marks, Arthur (Sir Toby); Gentile, Nicky (Viola).

DISTRIBUTION & AVAILABILITY: *Publisher or responsible agency:* Cinderella Productions; *Copy location:* Unknown (Playboy productions [?]).

Twelfth Night. **Video/Recording**

663.2 *Twelfth Night.*

DOCUMENT INFORMATION: *Country:* GB; *Year of first showing:* 1988, Transmitted 13 Dec. 1988.; *Location of first showing:* UK, Channel 4 TV.

EDITION, HISTORY, CONTENTS, & EVALUATION: *Edition & history:* An adaptation to television of Kenneth Branagh's Renaissance Theatre Company production. This theatre company turned out to be the theatrical event of the decade. Branagh since then has gone on to enjoy international fame for his role in *Henry V* (see 182.2). *Contents & evaluation:* "Kafno and Branagh employed a unit set and cameras that kept us in the role of 'audience' facing the set, as opposed to omniscient observers of inner and outer dialogue. The set held the memorial to Olivia's brother, the crypt in which Malvolio was buried alive and left to rot, a mouldy divan, and a stopped clock apparently overlooked by the dustman. Fortunately the acting atoned for the director's pusillanimity in failing to reach for real surrealism. The time was late Victorian, but the set's iron gate was borrowed from Andrew Marvell— a grateful gracenote to coy mistresses. . . . This production should be made available in the U.S. and Canada. The Renaissance Theatre Company should do more plays for TV" (Coursen, Herbert, "The Renaissance Theatre's Television *Twelfth Night," SFNL* 13.2 [April 1989]: 3).

MEDIUM INFORMATION: *Sound:* Spoken language; *Color:* Yes; *Length:* [?] min.

AUTHORSHIP INFORMATION: *Director(s):* Branagh, Kenneth; Kafno, Paul; *Composer(s):* Doyle, Pat; *Cast:* Simmons, James (Andrew); Lesser, Anton (Feste); Briers, Richard (Malvolio); McKern, Abigail (Maria); Langrishe, Caroline (Olivia); Ravenscroft, Christopher (Orsino); Barker, Tim (Captain); Hollis, Christopher (Sebastian); Saxon, James (Toby); Barber, Frances (Viola).

DISTRIBUTION & AVAILABILITY: *Publisher or responsible agency:* Renaissance Theatre Company; *Copy location:* Channel 4 TV, U.K. [?].

Two Gentlemen of Verona

ORIGINAL WORK AND PRODUCTION: Romantic Comedy. *Year written:* 1594; *Site of first production:* Inns of Court [?].

The Two Gentlemen of Verona. **Video/Scene**

664. *The Two Gentlemen of Verona.*

DOCUMENT INFORMATION: *Country:* GB; *Year of first showing:* 1952; *Location of first showing:* BBC. Transmitted 9:22 to 10:04 P.M., 16 July 1952.

EDITION, HISTORY, CONTENTS, & EVALUATION: *Edition & history:* Act One televised from the Old Vic Theatre, London, with a special commentary by Denis Carey. *Supplementary materials: TPAB* 16 July 1952.

MEDIUM INFORMATION: *Length:* 40 min.

AUTHORSHIP INFORMATION: *Producer(s):* Chivers, Alan; *Cast:* Neville, John; Payne, Laurence; Blick, Newton; Blyton, Patricia; Howell, Peter; Tyrrell, Norman; Ure, Gudrun; Aldridge, Michael; Drew, Eleanor; Wilson, Robert; *Musicians:* Slade, Julian; Owen, Myrfyn; Cope, Kenneth.

DISTRIBUTION & AVAILABILITY: *Publisher or responsible agency:* BBC; *Copy location:* Unavailable.

The Two Gentlemen of Verona. **Video/Teleplay**

665. *Zwei Herren aus Verona.*

DOCUMENT INFORMATION: *Country:* German Fed. Republic; *Year of release:* 1963.

EDITION, HISTORY, CONTENTS, & EVALUATION: *Edition & history:* A made for TV film. *Supplementary materials:* Morris, *SOF* 24; H&M, 36; *SIF* 77.

MEDIUM INFORMATION: *Length:* 120 min.

AUTHORSHIP INFORMATION: *Director(s):* Schwarze, Hans Dieter; *Cast:* Hansing, Norbert (Valentine); Becker, Rolf (Proteus); Weis, Heidelinde (Julia); Hoffmann, Katinka (Silvia).

DISTRIBUTION & AVAILABILITY: *Distributor:* Bavaria Atelier GmbH.

The Two Gentlemen of Verona. **Motion Picture/ Documentary**

666. *The Making of a Musical.*

DOCUMENT INFORMATION: *Country:* GB; *Year of release:* 1973.

EDITION, HISTORY, CONTENTS, & EVALUATION: *Edition & history:* How a London West End musical was put together. *Supplementary materials: BUFVC* 27.

MEDIUM INFORMATION: *Sound:* Spoken language; *Color:* Yes; *Length:* 50 min.

AUTHORSHIP INFORMATION: *Director(s):* Guest, Revel.

DISTRIBUTION & AVAILABILITY: *Distributor:* TAF*.

The Two Gentlemen of Verona. Video/ Interpretation

667. *The Two Gentlemen of Verona.* (Series: The Shakespeare Plays).

DOCUMENT INFORMATION: *Country:* GB; *Year of filming:* 25-31 July 1983; *Year of first showing:* 1983; *Location of first showing(s):* BBC, London; PBS stations, USA, 23 Apr. 1984.

EDITION, HISTORY, CONTENTS, & EVALUATION: *Edition & history:* Director Don Taylor saw the 'contemporaneousness' of the play as the single most formidable obstacle to presenting it to twentieth-century audiences (Fenwick, q.v., below). The fashions of Shakespeare's time, particularly the vogue for the 'Italianate,' are hardly the central concerns of modern youths who worship, or at least are professed by the media to worship, rock video, T-shirts, jeans, and Michael Jackson. The social currency of young people in Shakespeare's day dealt in the coinage of the courtly/pastoral tradition: sonnets, bracelets of bright hair about the bone, and shepherdesses. These are lost discourses that must be accommodated to modern audiences. Despite all this surface cynicism, however, the anxieties of the play's youthful lovers will be recognized by many (KSR). *Contents & evaluation:* "The major technical legacy of the BBC Shakespeare series may be its establishment of the two-shot (two heads in the 'frame' conversing) as the basic mode of recording dialogue. When the television screen's borders enclose two heads—shot anywhere from waist-up to relatively tight close-ups—intimacy of expression is enhanced and formal declamation made absurd. The result is increased audience involvement. . . . *Two Gentlemen of Verona,* as an early work of Shakespeare's and relatively primitive in technique, relies heavily on 'duologues,' or 'duets,' as Bernard Beckerman has pointed out. . . . It therefore lends itself especially well to the use of the close-up and the two-shot and, not surprisingly, very effective use is made of these shots in the BBC's television production. The conversations between Valentine and Proteus and the comic dialogues of Launce are given special vitality and charm on the small screen. . . . Surprisingly no subtext was introduced to deal with the notoriously difficult final scene (in which Valentine not only forgives Proteus for his treachery but gives up Silvia to him). The segment was shot in a sequence of close-ups, two-shots, and longer shots which clarified the shifting relations among the characters. Taylor calculated, probably correctly, that he had better play the scene straight and not reveal Silvia's reaction to her lover's extraordinary gesture or convey just what Proteus would have done had Julia's presence not fortuitously been revealed" (Keyishian, Harry, "*Two Gentlemen of Verona,*" *SFNL* 9.1.[1984]: 6). *Audience:* High school (grades 10-12); College and university; General use; *Supplementary materials:* Fenwick, Henry. *Two Gentlemen of Verona. BSP* 19-29; Videotape (25 min.) from "Shakespeare in Perspective" series with Russell Davies as lecturer available in U.K. from BBC* (*BUFVC* 27).

MEDIUM INFORMATION: *Medium:* Video; *Sound:* Spoken language; *Color:* Yes; *Length:* 135 min.; *Language(s) spoken:* English; *Video type:* B, V, 3/4U.

AUTHORSHIP INFORMATION: *Producer(s):* Sutton, Shaun; *Director(s):* Taylor, Don; *Adaptor/translator(s):* Snodin, David; *Composer(s):* Rooley, Anthony; *Designer(s):* Gosnold, Barbara; *Costume designer(s):* Collin, Dinah; *Lighting designer(s):* Barclay, Sam; *Other personnel:* Morgan, Brian (Prod. manager); Moss, Elizabeth (Make-Up); Angel, Ray (Sound); *Cast:* Daneman, Paul (Duke of Milan); Hudson, John (Valentine), Butterworth, Tyler (Proteus); Byrne, Michael (Antonio); Collings, David (Thurio); Barrie, Frank (Sir Eglamour); Kaby, Nicholas (Speed); Haygarth, Tony (Launce); Woodnutt, John (Panthino); Cox, Michael (Host); Peake-Jones, Tessa (Julia); Pearce, Joanne (Silvia); Charnley, Hetta (Lucetta); Flynn, Daniel (Servant); Kurakin, Adam (First Outlaw); Baxter, John (Second Outlaw); Burt, Andrew (Third Outlaw); Richardson, Charlotte; Taylor, Jonathan (Cupids); Badley, Bill; Finucane, Tom; Jeffrey, Robin (Lutenists); Bella (Crab).

DISTRIBUTION & AVAILABILITY: *Publisher or responsible agency:* BBC/TLF; *Distributor:* AVP, UIO, BBC* *Copy location:* UVM (Archive); *Availability:* AVP, B, V, 3/4U $450 (1987), sale; UIO, V (72071H), 3/4U (70171V), rental, $24.10; BBC*, 16mm or V, apply (*BUFVC* 27).

The Winter's Tale

ORIGINAL WORK AND PRODUCTION: Tragi-Comedy. *Year written:* 1609; *Site of first production:* Whitehall Palace [?].

The Winter's Tale. **Motion Picture/Abridgment**

668. *The Winter's Tale.*

DOCUMENT INFORMATION: *Country:* USA; *Year of release:* 1910.

EDITION, HISTORY, CONTENTS, & EVALUATION: *Edition & history:* One of Edwin Thanhouser's silent Shakespeare films. Thanhouser and his wife, who were responsible for the impressive 1916 *King Lear* (246) starring Frederick B. Warde, are regarded as the most serious American producers of silent Shakespeare films. Unhappily no print of this *WT* survives. *Supplementary materials:* Ball, *SOSF* 68.

MEDIUM INFORMATION: *Length:* 10 min.

AUTHORSHIP INFORMATION: *Director(s):* O'Neil, Barry; *Cast:* Rosemond, Anna (Hermione); Faust, Martin (Leontes); Crane, Frank (Polixenes); Barleon, Amelia (Perdita); Hanlon, Alfred (Florizel).

DISTRIBUTION & AVAILABILITY: *Copy location:* Unknown.

669. *Tragedia alla corte di Sicilia.* [*The Winter's Tale*].

DOCUMENT INFORMATION: *Country:* Italy; *Year of release:* 1913.

EDITION, HISTORY, CONTENTS, & EVALUATION: *Edition & history:* An abridgment that retains major elements of both the Shakespearean plot and Robert Greene's *Pandosto, The Triumph of Time* (1588), which was Shakespeare's source. *Contents & evaluation:* This "primitive" Italian silent version of Shakespeare's tale of an insanely jealous husband and of a saintly wife, a "patient Griselda" figure, grows out of the Italian tradition for making films as spectacular as operas. Leontes' palace appears in a vast interior shot, with close to 100 people in the banqueting hall, and huge throngs at the trial of Queen Hermione. Exterior shots depict ships sailing between Sicily and Bohemia. In that classic trope of the silent film era, the film is framed by a representation of William Shakespeare reading to his friends. The lighting in the exterior shots shows heavy shadows from the harsh sun, but there is also an energetic tempo to the rhythm of the editing. The title cards effectively interweave with the action, as with "Leontes orders Camillo to poison Polixenes." The acting is generally at a high level. A close-up of Leontes shows him consumed with jealousy over what he misconstrues as Hermione's flirting with Polixenes. In a memorable tableau, a raven-haired Paulina, eyes blazing, jaw set, glares at Leontes after bringing Hermione's infant to him. At the end of the film, Paulina leads Perdita and Leontes to a *reclining* statue of Hermione for the reconciliation scene. This is a truly ambitious film. Well photographed and edited, it is quite advanced in technique, ambitious in scale (the authentic ships, for example), lavishly costumed, fairly faithful to the main outlines of the plot. It is of course at times somewhat bizarre in its curious accentuations, as, for example, the decision to show Hermione in the finale sleeping supinely rather than having her appear as the traditional free standing statue. And though it begins in bondage to the library by having Shakespeare himself act as the narrator, it soon shows independence by inscribing its own text on Shakespeare's tale (KSR). *Supplementary materials: Bioscope* 23.392 (1914): 303; *Kinematograph* 3 (25 May 1914): 55; Ball, *SOSF* 170-76.

MEDIUM INFORMATION: *Medium:* Motion picture; *Sound:* Silent; *Color:* No (black & white); *Length:* 20 minutes; *Language of subtitles:* English; *Film type:* 16mm.

AUTHORSHIP INFORMATION: *Producer(s):* Milano Films; *Director(s):* Negroni, Baldassare; *Cast:* Fabbri, Pina (Paulina); Cocchi, V. (Leontes).

DISTRIBUTION & AVAILABILITY: *Publisher or responsible agency:* Milano Films; *Copy location:* NFA, FOL; *Call or copy number:* MP 20 (Folger); *Availability:* Archive, viewing by appt.

The Winter's Tale. Motion Picture/Silent

670. *Das Wintermarchen.*

DOCUMENT INFORMATION: *Country:* Germany; *Year of release:* 1914.

EDITION, HISTORY, CONTENTS, & EVALUATION: *Edition & history:* Very little can be found out about this film, except that three reputable filmographies list it. Of the three, apparently the Weisbaden is the first to lay claim to it. Professor Ball says that he could not find out anything about it. I am therefore listing it as "unclassifiable" since I do not know if it was an abridgment, individual scene, a spinoff, or perhaps merely a borrowing of Shakespeare's title (KSR). *Supplementary materials:* Ball, *SOSF* 201; H&M 36; *SIF* 115.

MEDIUM INFORMATION: *Length:* 30 min.

AUTHORSHIP INFORMATION: *Director(s):* Belle Alliance; *Cast:* Soneland, Senta; Paulig, Albert; Senius, Richard.

The Winter's Tale. Video/Teleplay

671. *The Winter's Tale.*

DOCUMENT INFORMATION: *Country:* GB; *Year of first showing:* 1962; *Location of first showing:* BBC. Transmitted April 20, 1962.

EDITION, HISTORY, CONTENTS, & EVALUATION: *Edition & history:* Transmitted in two parts on different evenings. With a cast of 27 principals and 18 extras, it was obviously a major effort. *Supplementary materials:* Morris, *SOF* 23; H&M 36.

MEDIUM INFORMATION: *Length:* 140 min.

AUTHORSHIP INFORMATION: *Director(s):* Taylor, Don; *Cast:* Shaw, Robert (Leontes); Crutchley, Rosalie (Hermione); Smith, Brian (Florizel); Badel, Sarah (Perdita).

DISTRIBUTION & AVAILABILITY: *Publisher or responsible agency:* BBC; *Copy location:* Unavailable.

The Winter's Tale. Motion Picture/Recording

672. *The Winter's Tale.*

CURRENT PRODUCTION: *Year:* 1968.

DOCUMENT INFORMATION: *Country:* GB; *Year of release:* 1968; *Country of first showing:* GB.

EDITION, HISTORY, CONTENTS, & EVALUATION: *Edition & history:* Originally produced for British television, this version of *The Winter's Tale* is a film record of a 'Pop Theatre' production at the 1966 Edinburgh Festival. Later it was released on film for theatrical exhibition. *Contents & evaluation:* "It is difficult to imagine why anyone felt the production (which is not exactly inspired) or the acting (which is of routine standard) worth recording. Further, it is technically crude. The lighting (on the original stage set) is ludicrously inadequate, the colour control varies from shot to shot and close-ups are, to say the least, used inexpertly. Movements and gestures seem wildly overemphatic on the screen" (Morris, *ShOF* 30). *Audience:* College and university.

MEDIUM INFORMATION: *Medium:* Motion Picture; *Sound:* Spoken language; *Color:* Yes; *Length:* 151 min.; *Language(s) spoken:* English; *Film type:* 16mm.

AUTHORSHIP INFORMATION: *Producer(s):* Snell, Peter; *Director(s):* Dunlop, Frank; *Cast:* Harvey, Laurence (Leontes); Asher, June (Perdita); Churchill, Diana (Paulina); Redmond, Moira (Hermione); Dale, Jim (Autolycus); Knight, Esmond (Camillo); Gale, Richard (Polixenes); Weston, David (Florizel/Archimadus); Gray, John (Clown); Maughan, Monica (Lady); *Performance group(s):* Pop Theatre, Edinburgh.

DISTRIBUTION & AVAILABILITY: *Publisher or responsible agency:* Cressida-Hurst Park Prod.; *Distributor:* SCH [?].

The Winter's Tale. Video/Interpretation

673. *The Winter's Tale.* (Series: The Shakespeare Plays).

DOCUMENT INFORMATION: *Country:* GB; *Year of*

filming: 9-15 April 1980; *Year of first showing:* 1980; *Location of first showing(s):* BBC, London; PBS stations, USA, 8 June 1981.

EDITION, HISTORY, CONTENTS, & EVALUATION: *Edition & history:* Except for five cuts, one of which is the Dance of the Twelve Satyrs (4.4), the director elected to use the Peter Alexander script unaltered. The stylized, non-representational sets, described below by Donald Hedrick as 'ice cream cones,' were director Jane Howell's initial step toward the expressionistic *mise en scène* that emerged in her exciting production of the minor tetralogy, which is comprised of the three parts of *King Henry VI* and *King Richard III* (see 186, 187, 193 and 513). In abandoning realism for expressionism, she found an idiom for televised Shakespeare that was to prove powerfully attractive, though in this first experiment it lacked the sparkle of her later work. *Contents & evaluation:* "In its good sense, timidity is restraint; the production is characterized by elegance and clarity. The visually bare setting, defended by Jonathan Miller as apt for this 'fairy tale,' and its symbolic representation of the 'climates of the human heart,' is wintry enough (but do the giant white cones of the backdrop evoke icicles? ice cream cones? horns?). The single tree—bare and white for Sicily, leaved and brown for Bohemia—gives us the play's climates. In general, the use of television for visual effect is, as in most of the series, timid—as if academics were at the camera controls. . . . But in general, the actors, like the bear, have little to do (the opposite of so much contemporary theatre). Too many lines are spoken reverentially. Leontes (red-bearded, bear-coated, Russian-hatted) is quite frightening, and sometimes reduced to a shifty-eyed looney. Perdita's innocence is engaging though unvaried. Florizel mostly moons. Time (why Pierrot-suited?) is more academic than majestic. Where there is little exuberance there is at least a good deal of warmth and geniality (not the easiest of tones to capture in performance). Polixenes sports a mock-ghost voice with Mamillius as he speaks of thoughts that would 'thick his blood'; Hermione jests lovingly in her line asking the boy to be taken from her. . . . But Hermione and Paulina, who should be crisply distinguished, are here blurred. Timidity weakens wonderful Margaret Tyzack's Paulina, whose nobility has far too much of Hermione's propriety to it. Paulina should be more bear-like; her loud verbal attacks, threat of physical violence, and roaring sense of injustice need underscoring, in order to define Hermione's restraint and magnanimity" (Hedrick, Donald, "*The Winter's Tale*," *SFNL* 6.1 [1982]: 4). *Audience:* College and university; General use; *Supplementary materials:* Fenwick, Henry. *The Winter's Tale. BSP* 17-27; Videotape (25 min.) from "Shakespeare in Perspective" series with Stephen Spender as lecturer available in U.K. from BBC* (*BUFVC* 27).

MEDIUM INFORMATION: *Medium*: Video; *Sound*: Spoken language; *Color*: Yes; *Length*: 185 min.; *Language(s) spoken*: English; *Video type*: B, V, 3/4U.

AUTHORSHIP INFORMATION: *Producer(s)*: Miller, Jonathan; *Director(s)*: Howell, Jane; *Composer(s)*: Simpson, Dudley; *Choreographer(s)*: Stephenson, Geraldine; *Designer(s)*: Homfray, Don; *Costume designer(s)*: Peacock, John; *Lighting designer(s)*: Barclay, Sam; *Other personnel*: Sheppard, Val (Prod. asst.); Alston, Cherry (Makeup); Edmonds, Alan (Sound); Wilders, John (Literary consultant); *Cast*: Kemp, Jeremy (Leontes); Stephens, Robert (Polixenes); Calder-Marshall, Anna (Hermione); Tyzack, Margaret (Paulina); Burke, David (Camillo); Welsh, John (Archidamus); Luckham, Cyril (Antigonus); Fulton, Rikki (Autolycus); Dimmick, Jeremy (Mamillius); Kendall, Merelina (Emilia); Kavanagh, Leonard (Lord A); Bailey, John (Lord B); Relton, William (Lord C); Garrett, Cornelius (Servant); Leyshon, E. (Court Official); Benfield, John (Gaoler/Mariner); Curless, John (Cleomenes); McCormack, Colin (Dion); Hewlett, Arthur (Shepherd); Jesson, Paul (Clown); Kermode, Robin (Florizel); Farrington, Debbie (Perdita); Wells, Maggie (Mopsa); Legge, Janette (Dorcas); Howe, George (Third Gentleman); Benson, Peter (Clown's Servant); Broderick, Susan (Second Lady).

DISTRIBUTION & AVAILABILITY: *Publisher or responsible agency*: BBC/TLF; *Copy location*: UVM, CTL* (Archive) *Distributor*: AVP, UIO, BBC* *Availability*: AVP, B, V, 3/4U $450 (1987), sale; UIO, V (72051H), 3/4U (70151V), rental, $24.60; BBC*, 16mm or V, apply (*BUFVC* 27).

The Winter's Tale. Video/Recording

674. The Winter's Tale.

DOCUMENT INFORMATION: *Country*: USA; *Year of first showing*: 1982.

EDITION, HISTORY, CONTENTS, & EVALUATION: *Edition & history*: A recording of scenes from a 1982 Berkeley Shakespeare Festival *The Winter's Tale*. A copy is available in the Theatre on Film and Tape (TOFT) archive at the New York Public Library. *Contents & evaluation*: Not seen. *Audience*: College and university; General use.

MEDIUM INFORMATION: *Medium*: Video; *Sound*: Spoken language; *Color*: Yes; *Length*: 33 min.; *Language(s) spoken*: English; *Video type*: 3/4U.

DISTRIBUTION & AVAILABILITY: *Publisher or responsible agency*: Berkeley Shakespeare Festival; *Copy location*: LCL TOFT Collection; *Call or copy number*: NCOV 309; *Availability*: By appt.

675. *The Winter's Tale.*

DOCUMENT INFORMATION: *Country:* USA; *Year of first showing:* 1985.

EDITION, HISTORY, CONTENTS, & EVALUATION: *Edition & history:* A record of a workshop production of the play presented at the Lincoln Center Institute and videotaped at the Juilliard Drama Workshop Theatre on July 18, 1985. *Audience:* General use.

MEDIUM INFORMATION: *Medium:* Video; *Sound:* Spoken language; *Color:* Yes; *Length:* 136 min.; *Language(s) spoken:* English; *Video type:* V.

AUTHORSHIP INFORMATION: *Producer(s):* Lincoln Center Institute; *Director(s):* Wolk, Andy.

DISTRIBUTION & AVAILABILITY: *Publisher or responsible agency:* Lincoln Center Institute; *Copy location:* LCL; *Call or copy number:* NCOV 446; *Availability:* Archive.

Documentaries and
Unclassifiable Motion Pictures and Videos

Listed chronologically in order of the year of production, "documentaries" include biographies, discussions, commentaries, workshops, travelogues, excerpts and any feature-length movies that cannot be sorted under the heading of a single Shakespearean play. Because of the difficulty of locating older educational films on 16mm, which are rapidly falling into disuse as a result of the video revolution, readers may wish to consult additional sources, such as: Gail Levine's filmography of "Scenes from Shakespeare" beginning in *SFNL* 2.2 (April 1978): 1+; Andrew M. McLean, *Shakespeare: Annotated Bibliographies and Media Guide for Teachers* (Champagne: NCTE, 1980); and the *Educational Film/Video Locator of the Consortium of University Film Centers and R.R. Bowker*, 3rd ed. (New York: R.R. Bowker, 1986).

676. *The Old Actor.*

DOCUMENT INFORMATION: *Country:* USA; *Year of release:* 1912.

EDITION, HISTORY, CONTENTS, & EVALUATION: *Edition & history:* Biograph melodrama about an aging Shakespearean actor. *Supplementary materials:* Loughney, Katharine. "Shakespeare on Film and Tape at Library of Congress." *SFNL* 14.2 (Apr. 1990): 6.

MEDIUM INFORMATION: *Length:* 15 min.

AUTHORSHIP INFORMATION: *Director(s):* Griffith,

D.W.; *Cast:* Miller, Chrystie W.; Bruce, Kate; Pickford, Mary.

DISTRIBUTION & AVAILABILITY: *Copy location:* LCM; *Call or copy number:* FLA 0042.

677. *Life of Shakespeare.*

DOCUMENT INFORMATION: *Country:* GB; *Year of release:* 1914.

EDITION, HISTORY, CONTENTS, & EVALUATION: *Edition & history:* As a silent documentary film about Shakespeare's life, this film is one of the earliest examples of the genre. See Professor Ball's interesting account of this "new aspect of film's Shakespeare industry." *Supplementary materials:* Ball *SOSF* 202-3.

MEDIUM INFORMATION: *Length:* 60 min.

AUTHORSHIP INFORMATION: *Director(s):* McDowell, J.B.; *Cast:* Ward, Albert (Shakespeare).

DISTRIBUTION & AVAILABILITY: *Publisher or responsible agency:* British and Colonial.

678. *Master Shakespeare, Strolling Player.*

DOCUMENT INFORMATION: *Country:* USA; *Year of release:* 1916.

EDITION, HISTORY, CONTENTS, & EVALUATION: *Edition & history:* The director, Edwin Thanhouser, made exceptional contributions to the early films on

Shakespeare. In this documentary/biography he paid special attention to the Shakespeare-Bacon controversy. People never seem to tire of contemplating the possibility that Shakespeare was not Shakespeare but somebody else. This film was a part of the tercentenary commemoration of Shakespeare's death. *Supplementary materials:* Ball *SOSF* 228-29.

AUTHORSHIP INFORMATION: *Director(s):* Thanhouser, Edwin; *Cast:* Swinburne, Lawrence (Shakespeare).

DISTRIBUTION & AVAILABILITY: *Publisher or responsible agency:* Thanhouser; *Availability:* Lost.

679. *Master Will Shakespeare.*

DOCUMENT INFORMATION: *Country:* USA; *Year of release:* 1936.

EDITION, HISTORY, CONTENTS, & EVALUATION: *Edition & history:* A PR spinoff from the 1936 Thalberg/Cukor *Romeo and Juliet* starring Norma Shearer and Leslie Howard, which was a major effort by Hollywood to screen the Bard's work. *Supplementary materials:* SIF 120.

MEDIUM INFORMATION: *Color:* No (black & white); *Length:* 11 min.

AUTHORSHIP INFORMATION: *Director(s):* Tourneur, Jacques; *Adaptor/translator(s):* Goldstone, Richard; *Composer(s):* Stothart, Herbert.

DISTRIBUTION & AVAILABILITY: *Publisher or responsible agency:* MGM.

680. *England's Shakespeare.*

DOCUMENT INFORMATION: *Country:* GB; *Year of release:* 1939.

EDITION, HISTORY, CONTENTS, & EVALUATION: *Edition & history:* An early sound film documentary about Shakespeare's England produced for tourists by a British railroad company. *Audience:* General use.

MEDIUM INFORMATION: *Medium:* Motion picture; *Sound:* Spoken language.

AUTHORSHIP INFORMATION: *Producer(s):* London, Midland and Scottish Railways.

DISTRIBUTION & AVAILABILITY: *Distributor:* Unknown, *Copy location:* MMA; *Call or copy number:* 001191.

681. *Memories of Shakespeare.* (Series: Hoffburg productions).

DOCUMENT INFORMATION: *Country:* Germany; *Year of filming:* 1949.

EDITION, HISTORY, CONTENTS, & EVALUATION: *Edition & history:* A series of 10-minute, 16mm films in three parts comprising a biographical sketch of Shakespeare. They show "his place of birth, where he spent his childhood, and the places which are associated with him." *Contents & evaluation:* Not reviewed. *Audience:* Junior High (grades 7-9); High school (grades 10-12).

MEDIUM INFORMATION: *Medium:* Motion Picture; *Sound:* Spoken language; *Color:* No (black & white); *Length:* 10 min. (each part); *Language(s) spoken:* English ?; *Film type:* 16mm.

AUTHORSHIP INFORMATION: *Producer(s):* Hoffburg Productions.

682. *Shakespeare: England Today.* (Series: Eastin School Films).

DOCUMENT INFORMATION: *Country:* USA; *Year of release:* 1951.

EDITION, HISTORY, CONTENTS, & EVALUATION: *Contents & evaluation:* An agreeable ramble through England of interest to beginning students but probably not to anyone else. Shots of Stratford, Henley, Kenilworth, Warwick, Ann Hathaway's cottage, the Tower of London, London Bridge. Specialists will find the voiceover putting the Globe playhouse in the "general vicinity " of Billingsgate fish market as perhaps a little loose. Most audiences will neither notice nor care. *Audience:* High school (grades 10-12).

MEDIUM INFORMATION: *Medium:* Motion Picture; *Sound:* Spoken language; *Color:* No (black & white); *Length:* 16 min.; *Language(s) spoken:* English; *Film type:* 16mm.

AUTHORSHIP INFORMATION: *Producer(s):* Eastin Pictures; *Director(s):* Soule, Gardner; *Screenplay writer(s):* Soule, Gardner; *Adaptor/translator(s):* Soule, Janee Lee; *Other personnel:* Greenhill, Leslie P. (Photography); Abbott, Gregory (Narration).

DISTRIBUTION AND AVAILABILITY: *Publisher or responsible agency:* Eastin Pictures; *Distributor:* AVI, BLK, *Availability:* Apply.

683. *Shakespeare's Theatre.*

DOCUMENT INFORMATION: *Country:* USA; *Year of release:* 1954.

EDITION, HISTORY, CONTENTS, & EVALUATION: *Edition & history:* Made by Dept. of Theatre Arts at UCLA to show theatrical practices in Shakespeare's playhouse. The sound of Ronald Colman's inimitable voice as narrator adds a reassuring *savoir faire* to the production. *Contents & evaluation:* Using cardboard actors on a model of the Globe playhouse (as envisioned by Dr. J.C. Adams), the narrator gives an excellent summary of the different ways that the inner stage, upper balcony and exits and entrances in the playhouse were probably employed in Shakespeare's time. Brief scenes from *TN, Rom., JC* and *Mac.* offer examples of the uses of stage posts as trees, and ships' masts, and as concealment for eavesdroppers. Trapdoors and the machinery for lowering the gods from the stage roof, and techniques for creating sound effects are demonstrated. There is also an explanation of how dialogue could motivate a logical movement from one part of the stage to another. The opening shots borrow the famous model of Elizabethan London that J. Arthur Rank used for the Olivier *Henry V* to authenticate the occasion. *Audience:* Junior High (grades 7-9); High school (grades 10-12); *Supplementary materials:* SIF 121.

MEDIUM INFORMATION: *Medium:* Motion Picture; *Sound:* Spoken language; *Color:* No (black & white); *Length:* 18 min.; *Language(s) spoken:* English; *Film type:* 16mm.

AUTHORSHIP INFORMATION: *Producer(s):* Jordan, Mildred and Edward R.; *Composer(s):* Jones, Richard; *Other personnel:* Philips, James (Research); Colman, Ronald (Narrator).

DISTRIBUTION & AVAILABILITY: *Publisher or responsible agency:* Univ. of California A/V; *Distributor:* USF.

684. *Introducing Shakespeare.*

DOCUMENT INFORMATION: *Country:* GB; *Year of release:* 1957.

EDITION, HISTORY, CONTENTS, & EVALUATION: *Edition & history:* Background for Shakespeare's life in Stratford and London. *Supplementary materials:* BUFVC 59.

MEDIUM INFORMATION: *Length:* 10 min.; *Film type:* 16mm.

AUTHORSHIP INFORMATION: *Director(s):* Plymouth Films.

DISTRIBUTION & AVAILABILITY: *Distributor:* Formerly EFV*.

685. *The Boyhood of William Shakespeare.*

DOCUMENT INFORMATION: *Country:* USA; *Year of first showing:* 1957; *Location of first showing:* Omnibus/ABC. Transmitted 9 to 10:30 P.M., Sunday, 24 Feb. 1957.

EDITION, HISTORY, CONTENTS, & EVALUATION: *Edition & history:* An advertisement in *The New York Times* proclaimed that the program was to be "a unique journey back through time to relive the exciting era that shaped the future destiny of young William Shakespeare, as reflected in some of his greatest plays." The program was also billed as a "Dramatic Chronicle by Walter Kerr." *Supplementary materials:* "TV Today." *NYT* 24 Feb. 1957: 12 X.

MEDIUM INFORMATION: *Length:* 90 min. [?].

AUTHORSHIP INFORMATION: *Cast:* Karloff, Boris (Narrator); Jones, Henry.

DISTRIBUTION & AVAILABILITY: *Publisher or responsible agency:* Coronet Films; *Distributor:* Formerly EFV*.

686. *English Literature of the Elizabethan Period.*

DOCUMENT INFORMATION: *Country:* GB; *Year of release:* 1959.

EDITION, HISTORY, CONTENTS, & EVALUATION: *Supplementary materials:* BUFVC 31.

MEDIUM INFORMATION: *Length:* 13 min.; *Film type:* 16mm.

DISTRIBUTION & AVAILABILITY: *Publisher or responsible agency:* Coronet Films; *Distributor:* Formerly EFV*.

687. *Shakespeare: Soul of an Age.*

DOCUMENT INFORMATION: *Country:* GB/USA; *Year of first showing:* 1962; *Location of first showing:* WNBC/TV. Transmitted 7:30 to 8:30 P.M., Friday, 30 Nov. 1962.

EDITION, HISTORY, CONTENTS, & EVALUATION: *Edition & history:* Places Shakespeare's words in context of the world that he knew and grew up in around Stratford-upon-Avon. Originally presented on NBC television news. *Contents & evaluation:* Opens with aerial photography shots of English countryside and recitation on the sound track of John of Gaunt's famous deathbed speech from *Richard II* with the words, "This earth, this realm, this England" (often called "Armada rhetoric"). The documentary continues to weave together Shakespeare's language with the sights of the England that Shakespeare knew. Particularly good on Stratford-on-Avon. Actually the program makes an excellent way of introducing American students to the environs of Shakespeare's birthplace (KSR). *Audience:* High school (grades 10-12); College and university; *Supplementary materials:* "Program." *NYT* 30 Nov. 1962: 67.

MEDIUM INFORMATION: *Medium:* V; *Sound:* Spoken language; *Color:* Yes; *Length:* 51 min.

AUTHORSHIP INFORMATION: *Producer(s):* Hazam, Lou; Bingham, Barry Jr.; *Director(s):* Blanchard, Guy; *Screenplay writer(s):* Hazam, Lou; *Composer(s):* Kleinsinger, George; *Other personnel:* McDonough, Loftus (Film editor); Butman, Robert (Research); Gochis, Constantine (Editor); *Cast:* Richardson, Sir Ralph (Starring); Redgrave, Sir Michael; Hudd, Walter; Eddison, Robert; Gwillim, Jack; Sackler, Howard (Narrator).

DISTRIBUTION & AVAILABILITY: *Distributor:* DCV, ILL, *Availability:* DCV, V, $38; ILL (S 00545), V, $29.95.

688. *Shakespeare's World and Shakespeare's London.* (Series: Fair Adventure Series).

DOCUMENT INFORMATION: *Country:* USA; *Year of release:* 1964.

EDITION, HISTORY, CONTENTS, & EVALUATION: *Edition & history:* One in a series of of films that were made in celebration of the Shakespeare Quadricentennial Anniversary (1564-1964). Host for the series was Dr. Frank Baxter, a popular teacher at the University of Southern California. For other documentary films in this series, see 689-693.1. *Contents & evaluation:* Using such props as Visscher's View of London and portraits of celebrated Elizabethans (e.g., Queen Elizabeth), Dr. Baxter gives an introductory lecture on Shakespeare's England. His concept of "the walls were down," meaning that the walls of the medieval cities had been opened up to allow people to move back and forth freely, underscores the new freedom of the age. As "the walls were down," Dr. Baxter says, so was the middle class growing in power. The film is for the most part a "talking head," though Dr. Baxter's firm, authoritative voice and manner (he resembles President Eisenhower just a bit) carries a refreshing certainty in the context of today's passion for uncertainties. Decidedly old-fashioned in style, the material is nevertheless reasonably timeless. Dr. Baxter's "down-home" rhetoric will also appeal to many students ("Lot going on in the Middle Ages. People didn't just vegetate like turnips"). Dated though it is, beginning students can still profit from this sincere film (KSR). *Audience*: Junior High (grades 7-9); High school (grades 10-12).

MEDIUM INFORMATION: *Medium*: Motion Picture; *Sound*: Spoken language; *Color*: No (black & white); *Length*: 29 min.; *Language(s) spoken*: English; *Film type*: 16mm.

AUTHORSHIP INFORMATION: *Producer(s)*: Hubbard, Ray [?].

DISTRIBUTION & AVAILABILITY: *Publisher or responsible agency*: Westinghouse Broadcasting Company (Group W); *Distributor*: USF.

689. *How to Read a Shakespeare Play*. (Series: Fair Adventure Series).

DOCUMENT INFORMATION: *Country*: USA; *Year of release*: 1964.

EDITION, HISTORY, CONTENTS, & EVALUATION: *Edition & history*: A series of films featuring Dr. Frank Baxter of the Univ. of Southern California. In this one Dr. Baxter offers further advice on how to read a play by William Shakespeare. *Contents & evaluation*: Not seen. For description of Dr. Baxter in action, see review of "Shakespeare's World and Shakespeare's London" (688). *Audience*: Junior High (grades 7-9); High school (grades 10-12).

MEDIUM INFORMATION: *Medium*: Motion Picture; *Sound*: Spoken language; *Color*: No (black & white); *Length*: 29 min.; *Language(s) spoken*: English; *Film type*: 16mm.

AUTHORSHIP INFORMATION: *Producer(s)*: Hubbard, Ray [?].

DISTRIBUTION & AVAILABILITY: *Publisher or responsible agency*: Westinghouse Broadcast Company (Group W); *Distributor*: Not known, USF [?].

690. *Kings and Queens*. (Series: Fair Adventure Series).

DOCUMENT INFORMATION: *Country*: USA; *Year of release*: 1964.

EDITION, HISTORY, CONTENTS, & EVALUATION: *Edition & history*: Another in the series of educational films featuring Dr. Frank Baxter of the Univ. of Southern California (see 688-693.1). In this one Dr. Baxter

offers further advice on how to read a play by William Shakespeare. *Contents & evaluation*: Not seen. For a description of Dr. Baxter in action, see review of "Shakespeare's World and Shakespeare's London" (688). *Audience*: Junior High (grades 7-9); High school (grades 10-12).

MEDIUM INFORMATION: *Medium*: Motion Picture; *Sound*: Spoken language; *Color*: No (black & white); *Length*: 29 min.; *Language(s) spoken*: English; *Film type*: 16mm.

AUTHORSHIP INFORMATION: *Producer(s)*: Hubbard, Ray.

DISTRIBUTION & AVAILABILITY: *Publisher or responsible agency*: Westinghouse Broadcasting Company (Group W); *Distributor*: Not known, USF [?].

691. *The Life of William Shakespeare*. (Series: Fair Adventure Series).

DOCUMENT INFORMATION: *Country*: USA; *Year of release*: 1964.

EDITION, HISTORY, CONTENTS, & EVALUATION: *Edition & history*: A series of films featuring Dr. Frank Baxter of the Univ. of Southern California (688-693.1). In this one Dr. Baxter speaks on the life of William Shakespeare. *Contents & evaluation*: Not seen. For a description of Dr. Baxter in action, see review of "Shakespeare's World and Shakespeare's London" (688). *Audience*: Junior High (grades 7-9); High school (grades 10-12).

MEDIUM INFORMATION: *Medium*: Motion Picture; *Sound*: Spoken language; *Color*: No (black & white); *Length*: 29 min.; *Language(s) spoken*: English; *Film type*: 16mm.

AUTHORSHIP INFORMATION: *Producer(s)*: Hubbard, Ray [?].

DISTRIBUTION & AVAILABILITY: *Publisher or responsible agency*: Westinghouse Broadcasting Company (Group W); *Distributor*: Not known, USF [?].

692. *The Printing of the Plays*. (Series: Fair Adventure Series).

ORIGINAL WORK AND PRODUCTION: *Year of first production*: 1964.

DOCUMENT INFORMATION: *Country*: USA; *Year of release*: 1964.

EDITION, HISTORY, CONTENTS, & EVALUATION: *Edition & history*: A series of films featuring Dr. Frank Baxter of the Univ. of Southern California (688-693.1). In this one Dr. Baxter describes the technologies used in an Elizabethan print shop. *Contents & evaluation*: Not seen. For a review of Dr. Baxter in action, see "Shakespeare's World and Shakespeare's London" (688). *Audience*: Junior High (grades 7-9); High school (grades 10-12).

MEDIUM INFORMATION: *Medium*: Motion Picture;

Sound: Spoken language; *Color:* No (black & white); *Length:* 29 min.; *Language(s) spoken:* English; *Film type:* 16mm.

AUTHORSHIP INFORMATION: *Producer(s):* Hubbard, Ray [?].

DISTRIBUTION & AVAILABILITY: *Publisher or responsible agency:* Westinghouse Broadcasting Company (Group W); *Distributor:* Not known, try USF [?].

693. *Shakespeare's Stratford.* (Series: Fair Adventure Series).

DOCUMENT INFORMATION: *Country:* USA; *Year of release:* 1964.

EDITION, HISTORY, CONTENTS, & EVALUATION: *Edition & history:* Yet another of Dr. Baxter's educational films (688-693.1), this one was made in cooperation with the Shakespeare Birthplace Trust in Stratford-upon-Avon and with the Folger Shakespeare Library. An overview of Shakespeare's Stratford, it appeared at the time of the Shakespearean Quadricentennial Celebration (1564-1964). *Contents & evaluation:* Dr. Frank Baxter functions as "the talking head" with the aid of maps, stills, and live shots of the environs of Shakespeare's Warwickshire. Pictures of Holy Trinity Church, Clopton Bridge, Kenilworth Castle and Warwick Castle suggest how it was when Shakespeare was a boy. (No motorcycle gangs from Coventry appear to spoil the pastoral myth.) Dr.Baxter seems especially pleased that Shakespeare was "a country boy." A clever sequence shows Jaques' "Seven Ages of Man" speech re-appropriated into the twentieth century by being illustrated with shots of typical 1960's British subjects going about their business. Dr. Baxter laments, however, that "no mewling and puking infant" could be found. He aptly quotes E.A. Robinson's remark that Shakespeare "filled Rome with deathless Englishman" to underscore how much of England resides in the plays even when ostensibly set in a foreign land. *Audience:* Junior High (grades 7-9); High school (grades 10-12).

MEDIUM INFORMATION: *Medium:* Motion Picture; *Sound:* Spoken language; *Color:* No (black & white); *Length:* 29 min.; *Language(s) spoken:* English; *Film type:* 16mm.

AUTHORSHIP INFORMATION: *Producer(s):* Hubbard, Ray; *Director(s):* Derendorf, Don; *Designer(s):* Spagnolia, Don; *Other personnel:* Volkman, Don (Photography); Pusey, R.E., Jr. (Editor).

DISTRIBUTION & AVAILABILITY: *Publisher or responsible agency:* Westinghouse Broadcasting Company (Group W), in association with KPIX, San Francisco; *Distributor:* USF.

693.1 *Shakespeare's Theatre.* (Series: Fair Adventure Series).

DOCUMENT INFORMATION: *Country:* USA; *Year of release:* 1964.

EDITION, HISTORY, CONTENTS, & EVALUATION: *Edition & history:* A series of films featuring Dr. Frank Baxter (see 688-693.1). This one is on the physical stage in the Elizabethan playhouse. *Contents & evaluation:* Not seen. For a possible duplication, see the undated 744, below. *Audience:* High school (grades 10-12); College and university; *Supplementary materials:* Parker, *TSF* 49; McLean, *SAB* 225.

MEDIUM INFORMATION: *Medium:* Motion picture; *Sound:* Spoken language; *Color:* No (black & white); *Length:* 29 min.

AUTHORSHIP INFORMATION: *Producer(s):* Hubbard, Ray [?].

DISTRIBUTION & AVAILABILITY: *Publisher or responsible agency:* Westinghouse Broadcast Company; *Distributor:* USF [?].

694. *Morning Service from Stratford.*

DOCUMENT INFORMATION: *Country:* GB; *Year of first showing:* 1964; *Location of first showing:* BBC. Transmitted 10:30 to 11:30 A.M., 26 April 1964.

EDITION, HISTORY, CONTENTS, & EVALUATION: *Edition & history:* The BBC overlooked few opportunities to observe the great Shakespeare quadricentennial birthday celebration. This is a religious broadcast that celebrates the 400th christening date of Shakespeare in the Stratford-upon-Avon parish church where the great event took place. The cast of characters assembled on the altar seem reminiscent of the people from one of the English history plays, and the general tone suggests a beatification as much as a commemoration. *Supplementary materials:* "Morning Service." *RT* 23 Apr. 1964: 18.

MEDIUM INFORMATION: *Length:* 60 min.

AUTHORSHIP INFORMATION: *Director(s):* Barrie, Edgar; *Composer(s):* Strickson, John (with parish choir); *Cast:* Purcell, William (Commentator); Bland, Tom the Rev. (Vicar); Archbishop of York (Preacher); Bishop of Coventry.

DISTRIBUTION & AVAILABILITY: *Publisher or responsible agency:* BBC.

695. *The Poet's Eye: Shakespeare's Imagery.*

DOCUMENT INFORMATION: *Country:* GB; *Year of first showing:* 1964; *Released in the USA, 1976 [?].

EDITION, HISTORY, CONTENTS, & EVALUATION: *Edition & history:* "A film tribute to William Shakespeare, made in connection with the quatracentennial celebrations. Spoken extracts from Shakespeare's works blend with visuals of scenes in Britain today to capture the essence of the poet's imagery" (Distributor's blurb). There is also an extract from the Olivier *Henry V.* From descriptions, the production seems to be identical, or nearly so, to the one that was released in the USA in 1976 (see 711).

MEDIUM INFORMATION: *Sound:* Spoken language; *Color:* Yes; *Length:* 16 min.

AUTHORSHIP INFORMATION: *Composer(s):* Dupree, Desmond (Lutenist); *Cast:* Stephens, Robert (Narrator); Murray, Stephen [?].

DISTRIBUTION & AVAILABILITY: *Publisher or responsible agency:* London Television Service; *Distributor:* LTS*, FFH.

Motion Picture. Feature Length/Derivative

696. *Shakespeare Wallah.*

CURRENT PRODUCTION: *Year:* 1965.

DOCUMENT INFORMATION: *Country:* India.

EDITION, HISTORY, CONTENTS, & EVALUATION: *Edition & history:* Indian production about a troupe of itinerant Shakespeare actors in India during the postwar years when the Empire was unravelling. When first shown in New York City in 1966 the film was a critical success but a box office failure. American distributors feared that the public would not flock to see an Indian movie with obscure actors. Since then, with the growing fame of producer Ismail Merchant and director James Ivory, who enjoyed a triumph with their 1985 *Room with a View*, interest in their earlier film has revived. It was shown at the 1987 Montreal Film Festival (*Festival des films du monde*) with Merchant and Ivory both on hand as honored guests, along with cast members and scenarist, Ruth Prawer Jhabvala. With her background as a European married to an Indian, Mrs. Jhabvala was uniquely suited to handling the complicated social issues raised in the film. *Contents & evaluation:* An Anglo-Indian Shakespearean acting troupe led by Mr. and Mrs. Buckingham travels through India. The players are shown in various settings, from a maharajah's palace to a boys' school, putting on scenes from *Ant., Oth., Ham., TN.* The acting, particularly the smothering scene from *Othello*, is superb. Unfortunately not only British economic but also cultural imperialism are on the wane, and the players' audiences are less respectful than they have been in the glory days of empire. Hence the film evokes a nearly unbearable but nevertheless compelling nostalgia for a lost world. In showing the slow demise of the empire, it might even be subtitled *A Passage* from *India.* As Lizzie Buckingham, Felicity Kendal unforgettably plays the daughter of the troupe's director (Geoffrey Kendal), a man forced to watch the decay of a lifetime's work. A young Indian of means falls in love with her, but at the end of the film, Lizzie sails off to England, a country she has in fact never known. With its soft-textured black-and-white photography and deep sensitivity to the curious love/hate affair that existed between the British and Indians, the film is a treasure (KSR). *Audience:* General use; *Supplementary*

materials: Crowther, Bosley, "*Shakespeare Wallah* Opens," *NYT* 23 March 1966: n.p.

MEDIUM INFORMATION: *Medium:* Motion picture; *Sound:* Spoken language; *Color:* No (black & white); *Length:* 115 min.; *Language(s) spoken:* English; *Film type:* 16mm; 35mm.

AUTHORSHIP INFORMATION: *Producer(s):* Merchant, Ismail; *Director(s):* Ivory, James; *Screenplay writer(s):* Jhabvala, Ruth Prawer; Ivory, James; *Lighting designer(s):* Mitra, Subrata; *Other personnel:* Bose, Amit (Film editor); *Cast:* Kapoor, Shashi (Sanju); Kendal, Felicity (Lizzie Buckingham); Jaffrey, Madhur (Manjula); Kendall, Geoffrey (Mr. Buckingham); Liddell, Laura (Mrs. Buckingham).

DISTRIBUTION & AVAILABILITY: *Publisher or responsible agency:* Merchant-Ivory productions; *Distributor:* GLB*; FCM, B,V, $39.95, *Call or copy number:* AFI # F6.4429.

697. *Shakespeare Primer.*

DOCUMENT INFORMATION: *Country:* USA; *Year of release:* 1965.

EDITION, HISTORY, CONTENTS, & EVALUATION: *Edition & history:* According to the distributor's handout, "Hans Conreid excerpts from a number of representative Shakespeare plays including, *Richard III, Romeo and Juliet, Hamlet, As You Like It, Merchant of Venice,* and *King Lear.* The setting is the Shakespeare court at Claremont College, surrounded by famous sculptures illustrating scenes from various plays. Mr. Conreid is in costume for some of his recitations. He comments on facets of Shakespeare's life and on the meanings and interpretations of a number of his writings." *Contents & evaluation:* Not seen. *Audience:* High school (grades 10-12); College and university.

MEDIUM INFORMATION: *Medium:* Motion picture; *Sound:* Spoken language; *Color:* Yes; *Length:* 28 min.; *Language(s) spoken:* English; *Film type:* 16mm.

AUTHORSHIP INFORMATION: *Producer(s):* Bell, David L.; Soltys, Richard; *Cast:* Conreid, Hans.

DISTRIBUTION & AVAILABILITY: *Publisher or responsible agency:* BFA educational media; *Distributor:* ILL, SYR, *Call or copy number:* ISBN 0-699-26380-8.

698. *Shakespeare: A Mirror to Man.* (Series: The Western Civilization Series).

DOCUMENT INFORMATION: *Country:* USA; *Year of release:* 1970 [?].

EDITION, HISTORY, CONTENTS, & EVALUATION: *Contents & evaluation:* Eileen Atkins and Brian Cox play a series of scenes from *Shrew, Romeo, Macbeth,* and *Othello.* Between the acts and costume changes, they lecture the audience on various facets of Shakespearean production. The acting is uneven. In *Othello,* Atkins comes to life as Desdemona, but Cox seems uneasy, as though miscast. When Desdemona says that "she fears him" because "his eyes roll so," Cox isn't looking at her and appears to be sobbing. Desdemona should probably never be smothered in close-up anyway. The rather strident efforts to reassure us of Shakespeare's relevance to the modern world (*West Side Story* is cited) are incongruously uttered by terribly condescending voices. One wonders why this film needed to be made at all, since much of what it does could have been done as well or better on stage. *Audience:* High school (grades 10-12); *Supplementary materials:* "Review." *BKL* (15 Feb. 1970): 724.

MEDIUM INFORMATION: *Medium:* Motion Picture; *Sound:* Spoken language; *Color:* Yes; *Length:* 28 min.; *Language(s) spoken:* English; *Film type:* 16mm.

AUTHORSHIP INFORMATION: *Producer(s):* Secondari, John H.; Secondari, Helen J.; *Director(s):* Brinis, Ian; *Other personnel:* Maher, Terry (Camera); Lanning, Howard (Editor); Rowse, A.L. (Consultant); *Cast:* Atkins, Eileen; Cox, Brian.

DISTRIBUTION & AVAILABILITY: *Publisher or responsible agency:* Learning Corporation of America; *Distributor:* LCA, KSU; *Availability:* Current U.K. distributor in doubt (formerly EFV*); KSU.

699. *Bad Case of Shakespeare.*

DOCUMENT INFORMATION: *Country:* GB; *Year of release:* 1971 [?].

EDITION, HISTORY, CONTENTS, & EVALUATION: *Edition & history:* "John Gielgud, Diana Rigg, and Christopher Plummer present an account of Shakespeare's life and work" (*BUFVC*). *Supplementary materials:* BUFVC 30.

MEDIUM INFORMATION: *Sound:* Spoken language; *Color:* Yes; *Length:* 40 min.

AUTHORSHIP INFORMATION: *Producer(s):* Maskell, Robert.

DISTRIBUTION & AVAILABILITY: *Distributor:* SUX*.

700. *Understanding Shakespeare: His Sources.*

DOCUMENT INFORMATION: *Country:* GB; *Year of release:* 1971.

EDITION, HISTORY, CONTENTS, & EVALUATION: *Edition & history:* A look for beginners at Shakespeare's exploitation of art and nature in his own work. *Supplementary materials:* BUFVC 33.

MEDIUM INFORMATION: *Color:* Yes; *Length:* 20 min.; *Film type:* 16mm.

AUTHORSHIP INFORMATION: *Producer(s):* Gateway Productions.

DISTRIBUTION & AVAILABILITY: *Distributor:* VAV*, CIM.

701. *The Stratford Shakespeare Knew.*

DOCUMENT INFORMATION: *Country:* USA; *Year of release:* 1971.

EDITION, HISTORY, CONTENTS, & EVALUATION:

Edition & history: Another movie showing the familiar tourist sites in and around Shakespeare's birthplace in Stratford-upon-Avon. *Supplementary materials:* Loughney, Katharine. "Shakespeare on Film and Tape at Library of Congress." *SFNL* 14.2 (Apr. 1990): 6.

MEDIUM INFORMATION: *Length:* 20 min. *Motion picture type:* 16mm

DISTRIBUTION & AVAILABILITY: *Copy location:* LCM; *Call or copy number:* FBB 1298.

702. *Shakespeare in Love and War.*

DOCUMENT INFORMATION: *Country:* USA; *Year of first showing:* 1971; *Location of first showing:* WNET. Transmitted 3 to 4:00 P.M., Monday, 22 Nov. 1971.

EDITION, HISTORY, CONTENTS, & EVALUATION: *Edition & history:* Special program: "The Bard by Four." Scenes from Shakespeare in modern dress. *Supplementary materials:* "Program." *NYT* 22 Nov. 1971: 79.

MEDIUM INFORMATION: *Length:* 60 min.

DISTRIBUTION & AVAILABILITY: *Publisher or responsible agency:* WNET.

703. *Feast of Language.* (Series: Feast of Language).

DOCUMENT INFORMATION: *Country:* USA; *Year of first showing:* 1971-72.

EDITION, HISTORY, CONTENTS, & EVALUATION: *Edition & history:* There were eight programs in this series, hosted by Prof. Alan Levitan of Brandeis University. He attempted to show the life and vitality in Shakespeare's works. Through readings and interpretations, he also stressed the language in the plays. The plays covered include: *AYL, 1H4, 2H4, R3, LLL, MM, Lr., Ant.,* and *WT. Audience:* General use.

MEDIUM INFORMATION: *Medium:* Video; *Sound:* Spoken language; *Color:* Yes; *Length:* 30 min.; *Language(s) spoken:* English; *Video type:* Not known.

AUTHORSHIP INFORMATION: *Producer(s):* WGBH; *Cast:* Levitan, Alan (Host).

DISTRIBUTION & AVAILABILITY: *Publisher or responsible agency:* WGBH, Boston; *Copy location:* WGBH, Boston; *Availability:* No longer available.

704. *William: The Life, Works and Times of William Shakespeare.* (Series: ABC After School Special).

DOCUMENT INFORMATION: *Country:* USA; *Year of first showing:* 1973; *Location of first showing:* ABC TV. Transmitted 4:30 to 5:30 P.M., Wed., 3 Jan. 1973.

EDITION, HISTORY, CONTENTS, & EVALUATION: *Edition & history:* An educational television program originally taped in London by Director Ian MacNaughton. This was a gesture by commercial television toward providing meaningful after school programming. There are readings from *Ham., R3, AYL,* and *H5. Contents & evaluation:* "Sir Ralph Richardson, Sir John Gielgud and Miss Lynn Redgrave [appear] in a 'delightful, lighthearted introduction' to William Shakespeare. Sir

John Gielgud, Sir Ralph Richardson, and others give brilliant readings . . . and present modern parallels showing how Shakespeare's words are still part of everyday speech. It's a wonderful way for children to meet the greatest 'friend' the English language ever had [Sponsor: M&M Mars candy]" (*TVG* [2 Jan. 1973]). *Audience:* Junior High (grades 7-9); High school (grades 10-12); *Supplementary materials:* Asimov, Isaac. "'William,' An Introduction to William Shakespeare for Younger Viewers." *TVG* 30 Dec. 1972: 7 + .

MEDIUM INFORMATION: *Medium:* Video; *Sound:* Spoken language; *Color:* Yes; *Length:* 60 min.; *Language(s) spoken:* English; *Video type:* Not known.

AUTHORSHIP INFORMATION: *Producer(s):* Cohen, Alexander H.; *Director(s):* MacNaughton, Ian; *Cast:* Gielgud, Sir John; Richardson, Sir Ralph; Redgrave, Lynn; Ward, Simon.

DISTRIBUTION & AVAILABILITY: *Publisher or responsible agency:* ABC TV; *Copy location:* ABC TV [?].

Motion Picture/Derivative

704.1 Theatre of Blood.

DOCUMENT INFORMATION: *Country:* GB; *Year of first showing:* 1973.

EDITION, HISTORY, CONTENTS, & EVALUATION: *Edition & history:* A frustrated, aging Shakespearean actor, embittered by poor reviews, sets out to avenge himself on the critics who have made his life miserable. *Contents & evaluation:* For Shakespeareans, this fun/horror movie is a kind of gigantic quiz show because each of the offending critics is murdered in a style imitated from one of the plays. One critic goes the way of the stabbing of Julius Caesar; another meets the same fate as Clarence in *Richard III*; another, that of Shylock in *The Merchant of Venice*; another, that of Tamora in *Titus Andronicus*, and so forth. The result is a hilarious entertainment, presided over by a malevolent Vincent Price (as the actor, Edward Lionheart) with assists from his more than slightly balmy daughter, Edwina Lionheart (Diana Rigg). The movie with a distinguished cast that includes Shakespearean actor Michael Hordern deserves to be high on the list of any program of films derived from Shakespeare. *Supplementary materials:* Canby, Vincent. "Review." *NYT* 12 May 1973: 52.

MEDIUM INFORMATION: *Sound:* Spoken language; *Color:* Yes; *Length:* 104 min.; *Video type:* V.

AUTHORSHIP INFORMATION: *Producer(s):* Kahn, John; Mann, Stanley; *Director(s):* Hickox, Douglas; *Composer(s):* Lewis, Michael J.; *Lighting designer(s):* Suschitzky, Wolfgang; *Cast:* Price, Vincent (Edward Lionheart); Rigg, Diana (Edwina Lionheart); Hendry, Ian (Peregrine Devlin); Andrews, Harry (Trevor Dickman);

Browne, Coral (Chloe Moon); Coote, Robert (Oliver Larding); Hawkins, Jack (Solomon Psaltery); Hordern, Michael (George Maxwell); Lowe, Arthur (Horace Sprout); Morley, Robert (Meredith Merridew); Price, Dennis (Hector Snipe).

DISTRIBUTION & AVAILABILITY: *Publisher or responsible agency:* United Artists; *Distributor:* FCM, *Availability:* FCM (SO1559), V $59.95.

705. The Players.

DOCUMENT INFORMATION: *Country:* Canada/Australia; *Year of release:* 1974.

EDITION, HISTORY, CONTENTS, & EVALUATION: *Edition & history:* Documentary film showing players from the Canadian Stratford Shakespeare Festival on tour in Australia. *Contents & evaluation:* Not seen. *Audience:* General use.

MEDIUM INFORMATION: *Medium:* Motion picture; *Sound:* Spoken language; *Color:* Yes; *Length:* 58 min.; *Language(s) spoken:* English; *Film type:* 16mm.

AUTHORSHIP INFORMATION: *Producer(s):* Daly, Tom; *Director(s):* Brittain, Donald; *Lighting designer(s):* Lowe, Ron; Kiefer, Douglas; *Other personnel:* Kramer, John; Merritt, Judith (Editors).

DISTRIBUTION & AVAILABILITY: *Publisher or responsible agency:* National Film Board of Canada/So. Australian Film; *Distributor:* Not known, *Copy location:* National Film Board of Canada, Montreal, Que. [?].

706. William Shakespeare.

DOCUMENT INFORMATION: *Country:* Canada; *Year of release:* 1974.

EDITION, HISTORY, CONTENTS, & EVALUATION: *Edition & history:* Simulated "interview" with William Shakespeare. *Contents & evaluation:* Not seen. *Audience:* General use.

MEDIUM INFORMATION: *Medium:* Motion Picture; *Sound:* Spoken language; *Color:* Yes; *Length:* 25 min.; *Language(s) spoken:* English; *Film type:* 16mm.

AUTHORSHIP INFORMATION: *Producer(s):* Voronka, Arthur; *Director(s):* Voronka, Arthur; *Screenplay writer(s):* Withrow, P.; Wilson, Patrick; *Lighting designer(s):* Capanoss, Ernest; *Other personnel:* Bizio, Andre (Editor).

DISTRIBUTION & AVAILABILITY: *Publisher or responsible agency:* Look Hear Productions, Montreal; McConnell Advertising, Ltd., Canada & Shell Canada Ltd.; Released by Richard Price Assoc.; *Distributor:* Not known.

707. The Shakespeare Murders.

DOCUMENT INFORMATION: *Country:* Canada; *Year of release:* 1974.

EDITION, HISTORY, CONTENTS, & EVALUATION: *Edition & history: The Shakespeare Murders*, a low-budget film completed in fourteen shooting days in and around Toronto, Ontario and Stratford, Canada, is included here mainly because of its title. Backed by the Canada Council, producer/director Dennis Zahoruk sought to create a "murder mystery parody," the clues to the crimes being hidden in references to Shakespeare's plays. The "mystery," we are told, "is not 'Who is the murderer?' but rather what these Shakespearean clues have to do with the film's action.'" It sounds as though the Bard himself would have found all this challenging. *Contents & evaluation:* Not seen. *Audience:* General use; *Supplementary materials:* Hartt, Laurinda. "The Shakespeare Murders." *Cinema Canada* 2.12 (Feb./March 1974): 32-35.

MEDIUM INFORMATION: *Medium:* Motion Picture; *Sound:* Spoken language; *Color:* Yes; *Length:* 55 min.; *Language(s) spoken:* English; *Film type:* 16mm.

AUTHORSHIP INFORMATION: *Producer(s):* Zahoruk, Dennis; *Director(s):* Zahoruk, Dennis; Brough, Don; *Screenplay writer(s):* Zahoruk, Dennis; *Composer(s):* Snook, Michael; *Lighting designer(s):* Sebesta, Josef; *Other personnel:* Clavir, Barry (Production manager); Martin, Ivan (Asst. cameraman); Flower, Richard; Reeve, Susan (Sound); Fisher, Jim; Wolfson, Susan (Gaffers); Leach, David (Grip); Trowsse, Peggy (Props); Hartt, Laurinda (Continuity); Wing, Kathy (Production asst.); *Cast:* Peterman, Gary (David McKay); Raeburn, Alan (Brian Castle); Sharp, Moira (Lilian McKay); Floren, Rita (Julie); Scott, Ron (Richard Beavis); Wild, Arnold ("Junior" Beavis); Murden, Beverly (Wanda Sheridan); Miller, Tony (Henry Foxworth); Jones, Edith (Celia Scofield); Yarwood, Bob (Johnson); Jacobs, Curt (Tom Duncan).

DISTRIBUTION & AVAILABILITY: *Publisher or responsible agency:* Tundra Film Company; *Copy location:* CFI [?].

708. *Elizabethan Lute Song.*

DOCUMENT INFORMATION: *Country:* GB; *Year of release:* 1975.

EDITION, HISTORY, CONTENTS, & EVALUATION: *Edition & history:* Performance and explanation of Elizabethan lute songs for an introduction to the musical background of Shakespeare's plays. *Supplementary materials:* BUFVC 31.

MEDIUM INFORMATION: *Color:* No (black & white); *Length:* 47 min.

AUTHORSHIP INFORMATION: *Cast:* Wells, R.H.; Johnson, Stephen.

DISTRIBUTION & AVAILABILITY: *Publisher or responsible agency:* Univ. of Hull; *Distributor:* UOH*.

709. *Shakespeare et Orson Welles.*

DOCUMENT INFORMATION: *Country:* France; *Year of first showing:* 1975; *Location of first showing:* I.N.A., Paris.

EDITION, HISTORY, CONTENTS, & EVALUATION: *Edition & history:* Orson Welles speaks of Shakespeare in an interview with Richard Marienstras. Through his discussion of the plays, he talks of his own work as an actor, his concept of power, of politics, and his thoughts on the theatre. Includes segments from his films and unedited footage from films of Welles's theatre work before the war. Clips are from *Mac.*, *Oth.*, *Falstaff*, and there are also glimpses of his theatre work in *Mac.* with a black troupe in Harlem (1936) and in *JC* (1937).

MEDIUM INFORMATION: *Color:* No (black & white); *Length:* 60 min.; *Video type:* 3/4U.

AUTHORSHIP INFORMATION: *Producer(s):* Romero, Isidro; *Cast:* Welles, Orson; Marienstras, Richard (Interviewer).

DISTRIBUTION & AVAILABILITY: *Copy location:* VAA; *Call or copy number:* THE 2.8.

710. *Shakespeare et Peter Brook.* **See also 615, above.**

DOCUMENT INFORMATION: *Country:* France; *Year of first showing:* 1975.

MEDIUM INFORMATION: *Sound:* Spoken language; *Color:* Yes; *Video type:* 3/4U.

AUTHORSHIP INFORMATION: *Producer(s):* Romero, Isidro; *Cast:* Marienstras, Richard (Narrator); Benichou, Maurice; Marthouret, Francois; Vincent, Jean-Pierre; Mirren, Helen; Meyers, Bruce.

DISTRIBUTION & AVAILABILITY: *Copy location:* VAA; *Call or copy number:* THE 2.9.

710.1. *Portrait Souvenir Shakespeare.*

DOCUMENT INFORMATION: *Country:* France; *Year of first showing:* 1975.

EDITION, HISTORY, CONTENTS, & EVALUATION: *Edition & history:* Traces the life and works of Shakespeare showing his place in literature, the reponse of the audience, the actors, the directors and producers. Contains scenes from *TN* (directed by Claude Barma), *Oth.* (directed by Claude Barma), *Mac.* (directed by Jean Vilar), and *Ham.* (directed by Laurence Olivier).

MEDIUM INFORMATION: *Sound:* Spoken language; *Color:* Yes; *Video type:* 3/4U.

AUTHORSHIP INFORMATION: *Producer(s):* Demeure, Jacques; *Cast:* Barrault, Jean-Louis; Brook, Peter; Vilar, Jean; Visconti, Luchino.

DISTRIBUTION & AVAILABILITY: *Copy location:* VAA; *Call or copy number:* THE 2.11.

711. *Shakespeare's Imagery: The Poet's Eye.* (Series: Shakespearean Studies on Video and Film).

DOCUMENT INFORMATION: *Year of release:* 1976.

EDITION, HISTORY, CONTENTS, & EVALUATION: *Edition & history:* Brief film that uses "visual quotations" to illustrate Shakespeare's strategies for creating imagery. It may be the same as, or a reworking of,

''The Poet's Eye'' (see 695, above).*Contents & evaluation:* Not seen. *Audience:* High school (grades 10-12).

MEDIUM INFORMATION: *Medium:* Video; *Sound:* Spoken language; *Color:* Yes; *Length:* 16 min.; *Language(s) spoken:* English; *Video type:* B, V, 3/4, 16mm.

DISTRIBUTION & AVAILABILITY: *Distributor:* FFH, *Availability:* FFH (135F), B, V, $139, 3/4U $239, 16mm $325, rental $75.

712. *Shakespeare's Memory.*

DOCUMENT INFORMATION: *Country:* West Germany; *Year of first showing:* 1976.

EDITION, HISTORY, CONTENTS, & EVALUATION: *Edition & history:* Performance documentation of a two-day environmental production which provides an entry into the world that formed Shakespeare's plays: rhetoric, bawdry, the ship of state, etc.

MEDIUM INFORMATION: *Sound:* Spoken language; *Color:* Yes; *Length:* 100 min.; *Language(s) spoken:* German; *Video type:* V, B, 3/4U.

AUTHORSHIP INFORMATION: *Producer(s):* Schaubuhne, Berlin; *Director(s):* Stein, Peter; *Designer(s):* Sabine, Andreas; Gerd, David.

DISTRIBUTION & AVAILABILITY: *Copy location:* GIN, CTL; *Call or copy number:* 792 Sha (GIN); Betamax L370 (CTL).

713. *The Staging of Shakespeare.*

DOCUMENT INFORMATION: *Country:* USA; *Year of release:* 1977.

EDITION, HISTORY, CONTENTS, & EVALUATION: *Edition & history:* Produced by eminent Shakespeare scholar and teacher, Dr. Robert Ornstein, the film shows how Shakespeare's players made use of the Elizabethan stage. *Contents & evaluation:* Unfortunately the camera angles and the actors seem to be at odds so that the result is less dynamic than static. It is the perennial problem of merging a stage with a film performance. The information presented, however, is scholarly, informative, and absorbing (KSR). *Audience:* High school (grades 10-12); College and university; *Supplementary materials:* McLean, Andrew. ''Educational Films.'' *SQ* 30 (Summer 1979): 416. [Generally agrees with above evaluation.]

MEDIUM INFORMATION: *Medium:* Motion Picture; *Sound:* Spoken language; *Color:* Yes; *Length:* 55 min.; *Language(s) spoken:* English; *Film type:* 16 mm.

AUTHORSHIP INFORMATION: *Producer(s):* Ornstein, Robert; *Director(s):* Ornstein, Robert; *Cast:* Webster, Kate; MacKay, Lizabeth; Albers, Ken; Champagne, Michael; Desmond, Dan; Renensland, Howard.

DISTRIBUTION & AVAILABILITY: *Publisher or responsible agency:* Case Western Univ.; *Distributor:* CWU, *Copy location:* FOL; *Call or copy number:* MP 52.

714. *Shakespeare's Verse.*

DOCUMENT INFORMATION: *Country:* USA; *Year of first showing:* 1977.

EDITION, HISTORY, CONTENTS, & EVALUATION: *Edition & history:* A demonstration by Ian Richardson of methods for reading Shakespearean verse. Available in TOFT archive (Theatre on Film and Tape) at the New York Public Library. *Contents & evaluation:* Not seen. *Audience:* College and university; General use.

MEDIUM INFORMATION: *Medium:* Video; *Sound:* Spoken language; *Color:* No (black & white); *Length:* 60 min.; *Language(s) spoken:* English; *Video type:* V, 3/4U.

DISTRIBUTION & AVAILABILITY: *Copy location:* LCL TOFT Collection; *Call or copy number:* NCOW 26; *Availability:* By appt.

715. *Shakespeare of Stratford and London.* (Series: The World of William Shakespeare).

DOCUMENT INFORMATION: *Country:* USA; *Year of release:* 1978.

EDITION, HISTORY, CONTENTS, & EVALUATION: *Edition & history:* Made in cooperation with Station WQED Pittsburgh, Carnegie-Mellon University and The Shakespeare Birthplace Trust, Stratford-upon-Avon. *Contents & evaluation:* The excellent color photography makes this educational film about the life and times of William Shakespeare stand out from many of its pedestrian rivals. Opening shot of Stratford cuts to London and a stirring military band to stress the dichotomy between country and town. It is St. George's Day, April 23rd, and flocks of worshippers come to Trinity, Stratford, bearing flowers in honor of William Shakespeare. A well handled and intelligent commentary explains how the sights and sounds of the Stratford countryside may well have gotten into Shakespeare's plays. ''Light thickens,'' says the commentator as a crow flies overhead. John of Gaunt's famous deathbed speech is spoken against the backdrop of Warwick and Kenilworth castles to underscore the nationalistic fervor of the language. Anne Hathaway's cottage is set against Lorenzo's words from *MV*, ''On such a night . . .'' and there are Falstaff's London taverns with ''the merry clatter of pewter tankards.'' Purists may object to a few liberties but among films about the Shakespearean ''background,'' this one rates very high indeed. *Audience:* High school (grades 10-12); College and university; *Supplementary materials:* McLean, Andrew. ''Educational Films.'' *SQ* 30 (Summer 1979): 415. (McLean agrees with the opinion above: ''one of the best short films available to introduce the man and his times.'').

MEDIUM INFORMATION: *Medium:* Motion Picture; *Sound:* Spoken language; *Color:* Yes; *Length:* 32 min.; *Language(s) spoken:* English; *Film type:* 16mm.

DISTRIBUTION & AVAILABILITY: *Publisher or responsible agency:* National Geographic Society; *Distributor:* KAR, WSU; *Copy location:* FOL (MP 99); *Availability:*

NGS 16mm, sale, $325.50 (50317), Video $69.95 (51119); KAR, rental, $32 +; WSU (Apply).

716. *RSC on Tour.*

DOCUMENT INFORMATION: *Country:* GB; *Year of release:* 1979.

EDITION, HISTORY, CONTENTS, & EVALUATION: *Edition & history:* Another production by London Weekend Television, a commercial TV company in the U.K. Describes the trials and tribulations of going on tour with *Twelfth Night. Supplementary materials:* BUFVC 29.

MEDIUM INFORMATION: *Length:* 52 min.

AUTHORSHIP INFORMATION: *Director(s):* Snell, Andrew; *Adaptor/translator(s):* Bragg, Melvyn.

DISTRIBUTION & AVAILABILITY: *Distributor:* LWT*.

717. *Ian McKellen Acting Shakespeare.*

DOCUMENT INFORMATION: *Country:* USA; *Year of release:* 1982.

EDITION, HISTORY, CONTENTS, & EVALUATION: *Edition & history:* Ian McKellen, the celebrated Shakespearean actor, puts on a one-man show in which he plays scenes from *Hamlet, Richard II,* and *Macbeth.* Originally staged by Sean Mathias, a subsequent television production was re-directed by Kirk Browning. Generously made available to many schools by IBM. *Contents & evaluation:* A brilliant performance, widely acclaimed. *Audience:* High school (grades 10-12); College and university; General use.

MEDIUM INFORMATION: *Medium:* Video; *Sound:* Spoken language; *Color:* Yes; *Length:* 90 min.; *Language(s) spoken:* English; *Video type:* V.

AUTHORSHIP INFORMATION: *Director(s):* Browning, Kirk; *Cast:* McKellen, Ian.

DISTRIBUTION & AVAILABILITY: *Distributor:* UVM, ILE* (BUFVC 35), *Copy location:* FOL; *Call or copy number:* VCR 13; *Availability:* Apply UVM.

718. *Reconstructing the Bankside Theatre.*

DOCUMENT INFORMATION: *Country:* GB; *Year of release:* 1982.

EDITION, HISTORY, CONTENTS, & EVALUATION: *Edition & history:* Documentary film about plans for constructing a replica of the Globe playhouse on London's Bankside under the auspices of Sam Wanamaker's International Shakespeare Globe Centre. *Contents & evaluation:* Dr. Glynne Wickham, the internationally known expert on theatre history, smoothly handles the narration of this informative look at the Bankside theatre project that will one day put a replica of Shakespeare's playhouse nearly on the original site of the Globe, along with a repertory company to go with it. There are colorful shots of the Thames and the surrounding neighborhood and additional dialogue with project architect Theo Crosby, designer John Ronayne, technical advisor Prof. Andrew Gurr, and

general chairman, Sam Wanamaker. Brief scenes are acted on an imitation Elizabethan stage. Because of the recent discovery on Bankside of the foundations of the Rose and Globe playhouses, this documentary takes on a special interest. (Only recently a video about the Rose and Globe excavations has been prepared by the staff of the London Museum.) *Audience:* General use.

MEDIUM INFORMATION: *Medium:* Video; *Sound:* Spoken language; *Color:* Yes; *Length:* 30 min.; *Language(s) spoken:* English; *Video type:* VHS.

AUTHORSHIP INFORMATION: *Producer(s):* Coe, Tony; Clark, Rachel; *Director(s):* Wickham, Glynne; *Screenplay writer(s):* Wickham, Glynne; *Designer(s):* Beaumont, Nick; *Lighting designer(s):* McVean, Andy; *Cast:* Wickham, Glynne (Narrator); Crosby Theo; Ronayne, John; Gurr, Andrew; Powell, Robert.

DISTRIBUTION & AVAILABILITY: *Publisher or responsible agency:* BBC; *Distributor:* GSV*, *Copy location:* UVM.

719. *Shakespeare's Country.*

DOCUMENT INFORMATION: *Country:* GB; *Year of release:* 1983.

EDITION, HISTORY, CONTENTS, & EVALUATION: *Edition & history:* A program developed by the Shakespeare Birthplace Trust in Stratford examines the early years of Shakespeare's life. *Supplementary materials:* BUFVC 32.

MEDIUM INFORMATION: *Sound:* Spoken language; *Color:* Yes; *Length:* 27 min.; *Film type:* 16mm; *Video type:* V.

AUTHORSHIP INFORMATION: *Director(s):* Whiteman, Robin; *Adaptor/translator(s):* Fox, Levi.

DISTRIBUTION & AVAILABILITY: *Distributor:* SCL*, 16mm, V.

720. *Shakespeare's Heritage.*

DOCUMENT INFORMATION: *Country:* GB; *Year of release:* 1983.

EDITION, HISTORY, CONTENTS, & EVALUATION: *Edition & history:* Film about the origins and history of Stratford-upon-Avon. *Supplementary materials:* BUFVC 32.

MEDIUM INFORMATION: *Sound:* Spoken language; *Color:* Yes; *Length:* 27 min.; *Film type:* 16mm; *Video type:* V.

AUTHORSHIP INFORMATION: *Director(s):* Whiteman, Robin; *Adaptor/translator(s):* Fox, Levi.

DISTRIBUTION & AVAILABILITY: *Distributor:* SCL*, 16mm, V.

721. *The Comic Spirit.*

DOCUMENT INFORMATION: *Country:* GB; *Year of release:* 1983.

EDITION, HISTORY, CONTENTS, & EVALUATION:

Edition & history: In a workshop format, scenes from the comedies are acted and analyzed for their comedic effect. *Supplementary materials:* BUFVC 29; TWC Catalog, 13.

MEDIUM INFORMATION: *Color:* Yes; *Length:* 60 min.

AUTHORSHIP INFORMATION: *Producer(s):* Whitworth, David; *Director(s):* Hardy, Noel.

DISTRIBUTION & AVAILABILITY: *Distributor:* CFL*, TWC, *Availability:* TWC, B (MML100B-K4), V (MML100V-K4), $80.

722. *Shakespearean Tragedy.* (Series: Shakespearean Studies on Video and Film).

EDITION, HISTORY, CONTENTS, & EVALUATION: *Edition & history:* Explores the nature of tragedy and the Shakespearean tragic hero. *Contents & evaluation:* According to the 1987 distributor's catalog, this program is "ideal viewing for students before they read any of the tragedies (particularly *Hamlet* and *Macbeth* since it prepares them for Shakespeare's concepts of action, character, and catharsis. After their reading this program helps students understand the relationship between Shakespeare's heroes and their destruction" (*FFH Catalog* 9). *Audience:* High school (grades 10-12); College and university.

MEDIUM INFORMATION: *Medium:* Video; *Sound:* Spoken language; *Color:* Yes; *Length:* 40 min.; *Language(s) spoken:* English; *Video type:* B, V, 3/4U.

AUTHORSHIP INFORMATION: *Producer(s):* Mantell, Stephen.

DISTRIBUTION & AVAILABILITY: *Distributor:* FFH, *Availability:* FFH (764F) B, V, $149, 3.4U $249, rental $75.

723. *Speaking Shakespearean Verse.* (Series: Playing Shakespeare, #1). See also 724-33.

DOCUMENT INFORMATION: *Country:* GB; *Year of release:* 1984.

EDITION, HISTORY, CONTENTS, & EVALUATION: *Edition & history:* Originally shown on London Weekend Television (The South Bank Show) with Mel Bragg as host, this first of eleven programs in the series has since been made available for the educational market. The series was also transmitted on Channel WNYG/31, New York City. *Contents & evaluation:* Three directors (John Barton, Trevor Nunn, and Terry Hands) team up with six actors from the Royal Shakespeare Company in a workshop to explore the speaking of verse in the plays. Clips from past performances by Laurence Olivier, Henry Ainley and Sir Herbert Tree illustrate the various ways that the language has been spoken. Olivier is heard doing a highly rhetorical Agincourt speech from *Henry V*, while other speeches are spoken musically. There is discussion of blank verse as a "norm" of English speech, and an occasion-

al pithy statement such as the pleasure experienced when we hear from an actor "a gleam of nature in the midst of declamation." The level of discussion and the performances by the RSC actors are what one would expect from Briton's best and brightest theatrical talent. *Supplementary materials:* Huffman, Clifford. "RSC Tapes." *SFNL* 14.2 (April 1990): 3.

AUTHORSHIP INFORMATION: Elliott, Nick; *Director(s):* Walker, Peter; Nunn, Trevor; *Designer(s):* Turney, Mike; *Other personnel:* Gavin, Pat (Graphics); Hampton, Trevor (Camera); Fairman, Mike (Sound); *Cast:* Barton, John; Nunn, Trevor; Hands, Terry; McKellen, Ian; Howard, Alan; Lapotaire, Jane; Pennington, Michael; Suchet, David; Stewart, Patrick; *Performance group(s):* Royal Shakespeare Company.

DISTRIBUTION & AVAILABILITY: *Publisher or responsible agency:* London Weekend Television for Channel Four; *Distributor:* FFH; LWT*, *Availability:* FFH (731F), B, V $149, 3/4U $249, Rental $75.

724. *Preparing to Perform Shakespeare.* (Series: Playing Shakespeare, #2). See also 723, 725-33.

DOCUMENT INFORMATION: *Country:* GB; *Year of release:* 1984.

EDITION, HISTORY, CONTENTS, & EVALUATION: *Edition & history:* The second in a series, "Playing Shakespeare on Video," featuring well known directors and actors from the Royal Shakespeare Company exploring various aspects of production. *Contents & evaluation:* John Barton leads the discussion in this program with famed RSC actors David Suchet, Ian McKellen, Michael Pennington, Alan Howard and Patrick Stewart. They rehearse a scene from *Tro.* (4.5). Trevor Nunn speaks interestingly of how actors invent characters as they go along. The actor in this sense is both playwright and actor simultaneously. Ian McKellan reveals something of what goes on in the actor's mind as he works on Macbeth's "Tomorrow and tomorrow" soliloquy, and Patrick Stewart contrasts two different versions of Enobarbus' speech from *Antony and Cleopatra*, 'The barge she sat in. . . .' The program is aimed in general at anyone interested in "performing, reading or watching Shakespeare" and at looking closely at Shakespeare's text for clues as to what the playwright himself intended. *Audience:* High school (grades 10-12); College and university; *Supplementary materials:* Maher, Mary Z. "Video in Review." *SFNL* 8.2 (1984): 6.

MEDIUM INFORMATION: *Medium:* Video; *Sound:* Spoken language; *Color:* Yes; *Length:* 50 min.; *Language(s) spoken:* English; *Video type:* B, V, 3/4U.

AUTHORSHIP INFORMATION: *Producer(s):* Snell, Andrew; Elliott, Nick; *Director(s):* Walker, Peter; Nunn, Trevor; *Designer(s):* Turney, Mike; *Other personnel:* Gavin, Pat (Graphics); Hampton, Trevor (Camera); Fairman, Mike (Sound); *Cast:* McKellen, Ian; Howard, Alan;

Pennington, Michael; Stewart, Patrick; Suchet, David; *Performance group(s):* Royal Shakespeare Company.

DISTRIBUTION & AVAILABILITY: *Distributor:* FFH, *Availability:* FFH (732F), B, V $149, 3/4U $249, rental $75.

725. *The Two Traditions.* (Series: Playing Shakespeare, #3). See also 723-4, 726-33.

DOCUMENT INFORMATION: *Country:* GB; *Year of release:* 1984.

EDITION, HISTORY, CONTENTS, & EVALUATION: *Edition & history:* A third program in a fascinating series, Playing Shakespeare on Video, featuring outstanding actors and directors from the Royal Shakespeare Company practicing their craft. *Contents & evaluation:* John Barton explains how as an academic he came increasingly to see that full understanding of Shakespeare's text could come only through oral interpretation. "Each actor is worth many books," he says. The "Two Traditions" to which the program addresses itself are the Elizabethan and modern approaches to drama, the former somewhat stylized and the latter naturalistic. The problem today lies in bridging the gap between Elizabethan and modern stage conventions. Using Hamlet's advice to the players, Barton and his actors search for clues hidden in Shakespeare's own text that point the way for actors. Ian McKellen does a brilliant job of showing how many different ways one can read the opening line of *MV.* Further examples, come from *Cor.* and *Oth. Audience:* High school (grades 10-12); College and university; *Supplementary materials:* Barton, John. "The Two Traditions," in *Playing Shakespeare.* London: Methuen, 1984. 6-25.

MEDIUM INFORMATION: *Medium:* Video; *Sound:* Spoken language; *Color:* Yes; *Length:* 50 min.; *Language(s) spoken:* English; *Video type:* B, V, 3/4U.

AUTHORSHIP INFORMATION: *Producer(s):* Snell, Andrew; *Director(s):* Carlaw, John; *Composer(s):* Woolfenden, Guy; *Designer(s):* Morley, Christopher; *Costume designer(s):* Formston, Sue; *Lighting designer(s):* Bartlett-Judd, Chris; *Other personnel:* Bragg, Melvyn; Evans, Nick (for London Weekend TV); Davies, Jane (Casting); Cowen, Sabina; Brown, Wendy (Make-up); Middleditch, Lisle; Patterson, Mike (Camera); Fairman, Mike (Sound); *Cast:* Barton, John (Host); with actors selected from the following who appear in the series: Ashcroft, Peggy; Church, Tony; Cusack, Sinead; Dench, Judi; Fleetwood, Susan; Gwilym, Mike; Hancock, Sheila; Harrow, Lisa; Howard, Alan; Kingsley, Ben; Lapotaire, Jane; Leigh-Hunt, Barbara; McKellen, Ian; Pasco, Richard; Pennington, Michael; Rees, Roger; Rodway, Norman; Sinden, Donald; Stewart, Patrick; Suchet, David; Williams, Michael.

DISTRIBUTION & AVAILABILITY: *Publisher or responsible agency:* London Weekend Television for Channel Four; *Distributor:* FFH, IOA, LWT*, *Copy location:* FOL; *Availability:* FFH (753F), B, V $149, 3/4U $249,

Rental $75; IOA, 3/4U (70268V0, rental, $14.70 (restrictions); LWT*, all formats, apply (*BUFVC* 35).

726. *Using the Verse.* (Series: Playing Shakespeare, #4). See also 723-5, 727-33.

DOCUMENT INFORMATION: *Country:* GB; *Year of release:* 1984.

EDITION, HISTORY, CONTENTS, & EVALUATION: *Edition & history:* A fourth in a series of brilliant video programs showing Royal Shakespeare Company members exploring different aspects of producing Shakespeare on stage. *Contents & evaluation:* Host John Barton continues from the previous lesson on "The Two Traditions" and looks at the problem of speaking blank verse. For that reason this program seems to overlap partially with the first program on "Speaking Shakespearean Verse" but the level of discussion is so high that one is willing to overlook it. How should blank verse be spoken? Actress Sheila Hancock recites a sonnet, while Patrick Stewart explores the difference between an end-stopped and run-on line. While all of this may sound forbiddingly technical, it is in fact handled so gracefully and enthusiastically that only the most inert of minds would find it boring. The actors use dialogue from *The Merchant of Venice, King John, Cymbeline, Antony and Cleopatra, Troilus and Cressida, Richard III,* and Sonnet 29. *Audience:* High school (grades 10-12); College and university; *Supplementary materials:* Barton, John. "Using the Verse," in *Playing Shakespeare.* London: Methuen, 1984. 25-47.

MEDIUM INFORMATION: *Medium:* Video; *Sound:* Spoken language; *Color:* Yes; *Length:* 50 min.; *Language(s) spoken:* English; *Video type:* B, V, 3/4U.

AUTHORSHIP INFORMATION: Same as 725, above. *Cast:* Barton, John (Host); Cusack, Sinead; Hancock, Sheila; Harrow, Lisa; Howard, Alan; Lapotaire, Jane; McKellan, Ian; Stewart, Patrick; Suchet, David; Williams, Michael.

DISTRIBUTION & AVAILABILITY: *Publisher or responsible agency:* London Weekend Television for Channel Four; *Distributor:* FFH, UIO, LWT*, *Copy location:* FOL; *Availability:* FFH (754F), B, V $149, 3/4U $249, rental $75; UIO, 3/4U (Restricted), rental, $14.70; LWT*, all formats, apply (*BUFVC* 35).

727. *Language and Character.* (Series: Playing Shakespeare, #5). See also 723-6, 728-33.

DOCUMENT INFORMATION: *Country:* GB; *Year of release:* 1984.

EDITION, HISTORY, CONTENTS, & EVALUATION: *Edition & history:* A fifth program in the excellent "Playing Shakespeare" series in which John Barton conducts a workshop with actors from the Royal Shakespeare Company on problems in production and acting. *Contents & evaluation:* Host John Barton, as engaging as ever, discusses 'words" and the ways that Elizabethans played rhetorical games with them (alliteration, antithesis, etc.). As one example he uses the elaborate wordplay on "remuneration" in *LLL*. Characters, he says, "need language to express situation." He also continues his discussion of how best to strike a balance between Elizabethan and modern stage tradition, which is virtually the common theme of all these programs. Examples are taken from *LLL, H5, JC, Ham., R2, Ant., MV. Audience:* High school (grades 10-12); College and university; *Supplementary materials:* Barton, John. "Language and Character," in *Playing Shakespeare.* London: Methuen, 1984. 47-68.

MEDIUM INFORMATION: *Medium:* Video; *Sound:* Spoken language; *Color:* Yes; *Length:* 51 min.; *Language(s) spoken:* English; *Video type:* B, V, 3/4U.

AUTHORSHIP INFORMATION: Same as 725, above. *Cast:* Barton, John (Host); Cusack, Sinead; Harrow, Lisa; Kingsley, Ben; Pennington, Michael; Rees, Roger; Stewart, Patrick; Suchet, David; Williams, Michael; *Performance group(s):* Royal Shakespeare Company.

DISTRIBUTION & AVAILABILITY: *Publisher or responsible agency:* London Weekend Television for Channel Four; *Distributor:* FFH, UIO, LWT*, *Copy location:* FOL; *Availability:* FFH (755F), sale B, V, $149, 3/4U $249, rental $75; UIO (70270V), rental 3/4U, $14.80 (Restricted); LWT*, standard formats, apply (*BUFVC* 35).

728. *Set Speeches and Soliloquies.* (Series: Playing Shakespeare, #6). See also 723-7, 729-33

DOCUMENT INFORMATION: *Country:* GB; *Year of release:* 1984.

EDITION, HISTORY, CONTENTS, & EVALUATION: *Edition & history:* A sixth program in the fascinating "Playing Shakespeare" series in which John Barton conducts a workshop with actors from the Royal Shakespeare Company on problems in production and acting. There is a tendency as the series unfolds to move to increasingly complex problems. In this program, for example, the question of how to handle such archaisms as set speeches and soliloquies is confronted. *Contents & evaluation:* This workshop is largely devoted to soliloquies, which because they do not involve the interaction of dialogue demand more of actors. For the actor to hold the audience he/she must be specific, not general, and "deeply inside the situation" so as not to lose the sense of spontaneity. Sinead Cusack as Portia does the courtroom speech on the "quality of mercy," and David Suchet plays Shylock. There is a superb rendition of Hamlet's "To be or not to be" as well. Sample passages from *AYL, R3, Tit., 1H4, H5, Tro., 3H6, MND,* and *TN* also are in the program. *Audience:* High school (grades 10-12); College and university; *Supplementary materials:* Barton, John. "Set Speeches and Soliloquies," in *Playing Shakespeare.* London: Methuen, 1984. 86-103.

MEDIUM INFORMATION: *Medium:* Video; *Sound:*

Spoken language; *Color:* Yes; *Length:* 51 min.; *Language(s) spoken:* English; *Video type:* B, V, 3/4U.

AUTHORSHIP INFORMATION: Same as 725, above. *Cast:* Barton, John (Host); Church, Tony; Cusack, Sinead; Dench, Judi; Fleetwood, Susan; Harrow, Lisa; Howard, Alan; Lapotaire, Jane; Leigh-Hunt, Barbara; Pasco, Richard; Pennington, Michael; Sinden, Donald; Stewart, Patrick; Suchet, David.

DISTRIBUTION & AVAILABILITY: *Publisher or responsible agency:* London Weekend Television for Channel Four; *Distributor:* FFH, UIO, LWT*, *Copy location:* FOL; *Availability:* FFH (756F), sale B, V, $149, 3/4U $249, rental $75; UIO (70276V), rental 3/4U, $14.80 (Restricted); LWT*, standard formats, apply (*BUFVC* 35).

729. *Irony and Ambiguity.* (Series: Playing Shakespeare, #7). See also 723-8, 730-3.

DOCUMENT INFORMATION: *Country:* GB; *Year of release:* 1984.

EDITION, HISTORY, CONTENTS, & EVALUATION: *Edition & history:* A seventh program in the delightful "Playing Shakespeare" series in which John Barton conducts a workshop with actors from the Royal Shakespeare Company on problems in production and acting. There is a tendency as the series unfolds to move to increasingly complex problems. In this program, for example, irony and ambiguity become the main topic. *Contents & evaluation:* John Barton leads the workshop in an examination of the ways that irony and ambiguity can be handled on stage. Irony is on the whole even more difficult to manage than the soliloquy since it involves a "double meaning." An excellent example is Marc Antony's funeral oration in the forum over Caesar's body. Also used is King Richard's lengthy speech in Pomfret castle at the end of *R2*. Examples are also taken from *1H4, H5, Tro.,* and Sonnets 69, 138, 151. *Audience:* High school (grades 10-12); College and university; *Supplementary materials:* Barton, John. "Irony and Ambiguity," in *Playing Shakespeare.* London: Methuen, 1984. 120-34.

MEDIUM INFORMATION: *Medium:* Video; *Sound:* Spoken language; *Color:* Yes; *Length:* 51 min.; *Language(s) spoken:* English; *Video type:* B, V, 3/4U.

AUTHORSHIP INFORMATION: Same as 725, above. *Cast:* Barton, John (Host); Church, Tony; Gwilym, Mike; Howard, Alan; Kingsley, Ben; Lapotaire, Jane; Pasco, Richard; Pennington, Michael; Rodway, Norman; Suchet, David; *Performance group(s):* Royal Shakespeare Company.

DISTRIBUTION & AVAILABILITY: *Publisher or responsible agency:* London Weekend Television for Channel Four; *Distributor:* FFH, UIO, LWT*, *Copy location:* FOL; *Availability:* FFH (757F) B, V, $149, 3/4U $249; UIO (70271V), 3/4U rental $14.80 (Restricted); LWT*, standard formats, apply (*BUFVC* 35).

730. *Passion and Coolness.* (Series: Playing Shakespeare, #8). See also 723-9, 731-3.

DOCUMENT INFORMATION: *Country:* GB; *Year of release:* 1984.

EDITION, HISTORY, CONTENTS, & EVALUATION: *Edition & history:* An eighth installment in the ongoing "Playing Shakespeare" series in which John Barton conducts a workshop with actors from the Royal Shakespeare Company on problems in production and acting. This section moves on to even more esoteric problems with a discussion of "passion and coolness" on stage. *Contents & evaluation:* To demonstrate "coolness," Barton has the statue scene from *WT* performed by Patrick Stewart as Leontes, Sinead Cusack as Paulina, and Lisa Harrow as Hermione. They manage to make the scene incredibly moving and gripping. Barton also returns to his major concerns about "balance," "simplicity," and "sharing" of the text. That is to say, he is concerned with balancing the emotional and intellectual demands of the Shakespearean play. In getting at the intentions of Shakespeare, the actors explore Hamlet's famous advice to the players at Elsinore for clues, which would seem to privilege coolness over passion. Other examples come from *Lr., JC, 1H4, Jn., H5, MV, WT,* and Sonnet 129. *Audience:* High school (grades 10-12); College and university; *Supplementary materials:* Barton, John. "Passion and Coolness," in *Playing Shakespeare.* London: Methuen, 1984. 134-50.

MEDIUM INFORMATION: *Medium:* Video; *Sound:* Spoken language; *Color:* Yes; *Length:* 52 min.; *Language(s) spoken:* English; *Video type:* B, V, 3/4U.

AUTHORSHIP INFORMATION: Same as 725, above. *Cast:* Barton, John (Host); Church, Tony; Cusack, Sinead; Fleetwood, Susan; Gwilym, Mike; Hancock, Sheila; Harrow, Lisa; Kingsley, Ben; Leigh-Hunt, Barbara; Pennington, Michael; Sinden, Donald; Stewart, Patrick; *Performance group(s):* Royal Shakespeare Company.

DISTRIBUTION & AVAILABILITY: *Publisher or responsible agency:* London Weekend Television for Channel Four; *Distributor:* FFH, UIO, LWT*, *Copy location:* FOL; *Availability:* FFH (758F), sale B, V, $149, 3/4U $249, rental $75; UIO (70272V), rental 3/4U, $14.80 (Restricted); LWT*, standard formats, apply (*BUFVC* 35).

731. *Rehearsing the Text.* (Series: Playing Shakespeare, #9). See also 723-30, 732-3.

DOCUMENT INFORMATION: *Country:* GB; *Year of release:* 1984.

EDITION, HISTORY, CONTENTS, & EVALUATION: *Edition & history:* The ninth part of the delightful "Playing Shakespeare" series in which John Barton conducts a workshop with actors from the Royal Shakespeare Company on problems in production and acting. This section moves on to consider "macro" elements in presenting a scene from a Shakespearean play, that is to say, not bits and pieces but the overall structure. *Contents & evaluation:* The scene chosen for close analysis of its overall design is from *Twelfth Night.* Barton advises us that if we follow the language of Shakespeare closely enough, it will give us the clues as to how to speak the lines. He also explores the effect of short lines, missing beats and pauses. Richard Pasco as the Duke Orsino and Judi Dench as Viola act the scenes from *TN.* It's all a delight. *Audience:* High school (grades 10-12); College and university; *Supplementary materials:* Barton, John. "Rehearsing the Text," in *Playing Shakespeare.* London: Methuen, 1984. 150-69.

MEDIUM INFORMATION: *Medium:* Video; *Sound:* Spoken language; *Color:* Yes; *Length:* 53 min.; *Language(s) spoken:* English; *Video type:* B, V, 3/4U.

AUTHORSHIP INFORMATION: Same as 725, above. *Cast:* Barton, John (Director); Dench, Judi (Viola); Pasco, Richard (Orsino); Rodway, Norman (Feste); Williams, Michael (Curio); *Performance group(s):* Royal Shakespeare Company.

DISTRIBUTION & AVAILABILITY: *Publisher or responsible agency:* London Weekend Television for Channel Four; *Distributor:* FFH, UIO, LWT*, *Copy location:* FOL; *Availability:* FFH (759F) B, V, $149, 3/4U $249, rental $75; UIO (70271V), 3/4U rental $14.80 (Restricted); LWT*, standard formats, apply (*BUFVC* 35).

732. *Exploring a Character.* (Series: Playing Shakespeare, #10). See also 723-31, 733.

DOCUMENT INFORMATION: *Country:* GB; *Year of release:* 1984.

EDITION, HISTORY, CONTENTS, & EVALUATION: *Edition & history:* The tenth part of the "Playing Shakespeare" series in which John Barton conducts a workshop with actors from the Royal Shakespeare Company on strategies for production and acting. This section moves on to analyze the character of Shylock in *MV.* *Contents & evaluation:* Patrick Stewart and David Suchet take turns portraying Shylock to show how the characterization is affected by the actor's approach. Barton skilfully introduces the question of whether Shylock is an anti-Semitic caricature, or intended to be sympathetic. Shakespeare allows characters to betray themselves by their own words and actions. So-called "inconsistencies" in characterization often turn out to be deliberate enrichment rather than diminishment of the character's personality. The discussion of the alleged anti-Semitism in the play is especially illuminating. This program should be in the hands of every school board or board of trustees that has been urged to ban the play. And the individual performances of Shylock by Suchet and Stewart are superb. *Audience:* High school (grades 10-12); College and university; *Supplementary materials:* Barton, John. "Exploring a Character," *Playing Shakespeare.* London: Methuen, 1984. 169-81.

MEDIUM INFORMATION: *Medium:* Video; *Sound:* Spoken language; *Color:* Yes; *Length:* 51 min.; *Language(s) spoken:* English; *Video type:* B, V, 3/4U.

AUTHORSHIP INFORMATION: Same as 725, above. *Cast:* Suchet, David; Stewart, Patrick (Shylock); *Performance group(s):* Royal Shakespeare Company.

DISTRIBUTION & AVAILABILITY: *Publisher or responsible agency:* London Weekend Television for Channel Four; *Distributor:* FFH, UIO, LWT*, *Copy location:* FOL; *Availability:* FFH (760F), sale B, V, $149, 3/4U $249, rental $75; UIO (70270V), rental 3/4U, $14.80 (Restricted); LWT*, standard formats, apply (*BUFVC* 35).

733. *Poetry and Hidden Poetry.* (Series: Playing Shakespeare, #11). See also 723-32.

DOCUMENT INFORMATION: *Country:* GB; *Year of release:* 1984.

EDITION, HISTORY, CONTENTS, & EVALUATION: *Edition & history:* The eleventh and final installment in the "Playing Shakespeare" series in which John Barton leads an acting and production workshop with actors from the Royal Shakespeare Company. This section moves on to discuss the kind of poetry in Shakespeare that sometimes masquerades as seemingly unpoetic lines. *Contents & evaluation:* As with any other classroom teacher, even Barton begins to repeat himself a bit in the eleventh hour. In response to Ian McKellen's question as to why he left academe to go into theatre, Barton replies that he wanted to see what would happen when a play came alive on stage. He also repeats his observations on the "two traditions" of the opposed Elizabethan and modern styles. He concludes that if we look after sense, "the sound will take care of itself." Polysyllabic lines, he argues, may be lyrical, but it is in the monosyllabic lines that the most powerful thought comes across. A fine cast gives readings from *Lr., AWW, Jn., 2H4, Oth., R3, JC, Tmp., Ham., Tro., Luc.,* and Sonnet 19. *Audience:* High school (grades 10-12); College and university; *Supplementary materials:* Barton, John. "Poetry and Hidden Poetry," in *Playing Shakespeare.* London: Methuen, 1984. 194-211.

MEDIUM INFORMATION: *Medium:* Video; *Sound:* Spoken language; *Color:* Yes; *Length:* 53 min.; *Language(s) spoken:* English; *Video type:* B, V, 3/4U.

AUTHORSHIP INFORMATION: Same as 725, above. *Cast:* Barton, John (Director); Ashcroft, Peggy; Harrow, Lisa; Howard, Alan; Kingsley, Ben; McKellen, Ian; Sinden, Donald; Suchet, David; *Performance group(s):* Royal Shakespeare Company.

DISTRIBUTION & AVAILABILITY: *Publisher or responsible agency:* London Weekend Television for Channel Four; *Distributor:* FFH, UIO, LWT*, *Copy location:* FOL; *Availability:* FFH (761F), sale B, V, $149, 3/4U $249, rental $75; UIO (70275V), rental 3/4U, $14.90

(Restricted); LWT*, standard formats, apply (*BUFVC* 35).

734. *William Shakespeare.* (Series: Famous Authors series).

DOCUMENT INFORMATION: *Country:* GB; *Year of release:* 1984.

EDITION, HISTORY, CONTENTS, & EVALUATION: *Edition & history:* Particularly for students whose first language is not English. *Supplementary materials: BUFVC* 33.

MEDIUM INFORMATION: *Length:* 32 min.

DISTRIBUTION & AVAILABILITY: *Publisher or responsible agency:* Nelson Filmscan; *Distributor:* NFS*.

735. *The Fool in Britain: The Theatrical Figure in His Medieval Background.*

DOCUMENT INFORMATION: *Country:* GB; *Year of release:* 1984.

EDITION, HISTORY, CONTENTS, & EVALUATION: *Edition & history:* Explains the intricacies of the Fool convention for modern audiences. A necessary guide for students puzzled by Yorick and Lear's Fool. *Supplementary materials: BUFVC* 29.

MEDIUM INFORMATION: *Color:* Yes; *Length:* 27 min.; *Video type:* Video.

AUTHORSHIP INFORMATION: *Producer(s):* Billington, Sandra; *Director(s):* Taylor, Joyce; *Adaptor/translator(s):* Billington, Sandra.

DISTRIBUTION & AVAILABILITY: *Distributor:* GAV*.

736. *Shakespeare and the Globe.* (Series: Shakespearean Studies on Video and Film).

DOCUMENT INFORMATION: *Country:* USA; *Year of release:* 1985.

EDITION, HISTORY, CONTENTS, & EVALUATION: *Edition & history:* Acting as both producer and narrator of this program is the distinguished Shakespearean, Prof. Hugh Richmond of the Univ. of California, Berkeley. He reconstructs the Shakespearean milieu by looking at life in London then and now; the historical sources of the plays; theatrical tradition; and Shakespeare's Warwickshire origins. *Contents & evaluation: Shakespeare and the Globe* offers as a guiding principle the concept that the best way to understand Shakespeare's plays is to see them, as well as the visual resources of art, architecture and history surrounding them. The program is ingeniously stitched together from myriad stills and film clips to give a sense of the events and circumstances behind the creation of Shakespearean drama. Thus, there are shots of theatres in modern London, a glimpse of the original site of the Globe playhouse in Southwark, and Roman ruins in Bath (a subtle influence on Shakespeare's Roman history plays perhaps). There are many portrayals of the theatrical history behind Shakespeare's drama: Greek and Roman theatre; Italian *commedia dell'arte;* folk dancing and folkplays; and the medieval theatre. There are clips from the Olivier *Henry V* imaginatively showing the Globe playhouse, and several clips from televised recordings of Shakespearean plays at Berkeley to include *1H4, 2H4*, and *Wiv.* There are even depictions of stock dramatic types such as the Roman braggart warrior and tricky slave. On top of all that is an excursion to Shakespeare's hometown of Stratford, and the tourist sights—Trinity church, the Arden homestead, Hathaway cottage, and so forth. A bore to anyone who has visited Stratford but certainly fresh to most young Americans. More germane perhaps are the scenes of Kenilworth castle, Hampton Court and Warwick, where presumably Shakespeare found the atmosphere for his reconstructions of English history. The most original parts of the presentation are interviews with theatrical luminary, Sam Wanamaker, as he talks about the proposed building of his replica of the Globe on Bankside, and with Prof. Andrew Gurr, a leading authority on the history of the Globe. If there be a flaw in any of this dazzling array, it lies in the sprawling nature of the material. Thirty-one volumes of theatre history are crammed into thirty-one minutes of screen time (KSR). *Audience:* High school (grades 10-12); College and university.

MEDIUM INFORMATION: *Medium:* Video; *Sound:* Spoken language; *Color:* Yes; *Length:* 31 min.; *Language(s) spoken:* English; *Video type:* B, V, 3/4U.

AUTHORSHIP INFORMATION: *Producer(s):* Richmond, Hugh; Shepard, Paul; *Director(s):* Shepard, Paul; *Screenplay writer(s):* Richmond, Hugh; Shepard, Paul; *Other personnel:* Francisco, Mike (Camera—GB); Ichinose, Audrey (Camera—USA); Hawes, Steve (Engineer); Francisco, Mike (Editing).

DISTRIBUTION & AVAILABILITY: *Publisher or responsible agency:* Univ. of California, Berkeley; *Distributor:* FFH, *Copy location:* UC, Berkeley; *Availability:* FFH (931F), B, V $149, 3/4U $249, Rental $75.

737. *Shakespeare Video Workshops: the Roman Tragedies.* (Series: Shakespeare Video Workshop Series).

DOCUMENT INFORMATION: *Country:* GB; *Year of release:* 1985 [?].

EDITION, HISTORY, CONTENTS, & EVALUATION: *Edition & history:* Examines the tyranny, power, and politics in the three major Roman history plays (*Ant., JC,* and *Cor.*) and relates these works to modern political ethics and social values. *Audience:* College and university; Professional; *Supplementary materials:* BUFVC 30.

MEDIUM INFORMATION: *Medium:* Video; *Sound:* Spoken language; *Color:* Yes; *Length:* 65 min.; *Language(s) spoken:* English; *Video type:* B, V.

AUTHORSHIP INFORMATION: *Producer(s):* Hardy, Noel.

DISTRIBUTION & AVAILABILITY: *Publisher or re-sponsible agency:* ILEA Learning Resources Branch for Lloyds Bank; *Distributor:* CFL*, *Availability:* Sale or rental in Great Britain only.

738. *Muse of Fire.* (Series: Story of English).

DOCUMENT INFORMATION: *Country:* GB/USA; *Year of release:* 1986.

EDITION, HISTORY, CONTENTS, & EVALUATION: *Edition & history:* A PBS documentary shown on national television with Robert MacNeil of the MacNeil-Lehrer news team acting as the host. *Contents & evaluation:* An excellent overview of Shakespeare's contribution to the emergence of modern English. Particularly interesting is the discussion of the vocabulary of his native Warwickshire to include such esoteric words as "mobled," which turns up in the First Player's speech in *Hamlet* as the "mobled queen" (2.2.502). Generous excerpts from the BBC Shakespeare plays exemplify patterns of language. They include scenes from *Tmp., Ham., R3, JC, MV,* and *Lr.* In addition Michael Hordern reads unforgettably from the English Bible and such luminaries as John Barton lend further weight to the program (KSR). *Supplementary materials:* McCrum, Robert, William Cran and Robert MacNeil. *The Story of English.* New York: Viking, 1986.

MEDIUM INFORMATION: *Length:* 60 min.

AUTHORSHIP INFORMATION: *Producer(s):* Cran, William; *Director(s):* Pett, John; *Screenplay writer(s):* McCrum, Robert; *Adaptor/translator(s):* MacNeil, Robert; *Composer(s):* Oliver, Stephen; *Other personnel:* Burchfield, Robert; Flexner, Stuart; Quirk, Sir Randolph (Consultants); Goodyer, John (Photography); Mawison, Doug (Sound); Lee, John; Mitchell, Alastair; Perrin, Denise (Editors); *Cast:* MacNeil, Robert (Host); Hordern, Michael (Reader); Barton, John (Speaker); and members of cast from the BBC Shakespeare Plays.

DISTRIBUTION & AVAILABILITY: *Publisher or re-sponsible agency:* BBC/WNET THIRTEEN; *Distributor:* FNC.

739. *Muse of Fire.* (Series: All the World's a Stage).

DOCUMENT INFORMATION: *Country:* GB/USA; *Year of release:* 1988.

EDITION, HISTORY, CONTENTS, & EVALUATION: *Edition & history:* A series shown in the U.S. on public television in the winter of 1988. This segment dealt with the Shakespearean theatre. *Contents & evaluation:* A discussion of Shakespeare's theatrical accomplishments with commentaries by such celebrities as Peter Brook, Peter Hall, Alan Jay Lerner, and Michael Billington. Regrettably the talking is better than the acting of the scenes, which sometimes borders on the amateurish.

MEDIUM INFORMATION: *Length:* 60 min.

AUTHORSHIP INFORMATION: *Director(s):* Langham, Michael (Stage); Slater, William (Film); Williams, Misha (*Johan Johan*); *Screenplay writer(s):* Harwood, Ronald;

Designer(s): Logan, Peter; Young, Michael; *Costume designer(s):* Hearne, John; *Other personnel:* Wickham, Glynne (Advisor); McGlashan, John; Waldeck, Colin; Walters, Nigel (Photography); Chapman, Toni; Winslade, Maureen (Make-up); *Cast:* "Muse of Fire": Eccles, Donald; Irons, Jeremy; Potter, Martin; "Mankind": Mills, Robert; Bryce, James; O'Brien, Terry; Wilde, Philip; "Johan Johan": Bamforth, Ian; Cooper, Trevor; Windsor, James.

DISTRIBUTION & AVAILABILITY: *Publisher or responsible agency:* BBC; *Distributor:* TLF.

740. *Teaching Shakespeare: New Approaches from the Folger Shakespeare Library.*

DOCUMENT INFORMATION: *Country:* USA; *Year of release:* 1988.

EDITION, HISTORY, CONTENTS, & EVALUATION: *Awards:* Golden Apple Award, Ntl. Educational Film & Video Festival; *Edition & history:* "A videotape for any teacher who has ever been daunted by student resistance to Shakespeare. Based on the work of teachers from all parts of the country, who joined with Shakespeare scholars, master teachers, actors, and directors, at the Folger Shakespeare Library's summer teaching institute" (Adv., *SQ,* 39 [Summer 1988]: 269). Not seen. *Supplementary materials:* Learning/Workshop guide by Peggy O'Brien, Education Director of Folger, accompanies tape.

MEDIUM INFORMATION: *Length:* 75 min.

AUTHORSHIP INFORMATION: *Producer(s):* Potts, Robert & Marjory.

DISTRIBUTION & AVAILABILITY: *Publisher or responsible agency:* Vineyard Video Productions; *Distributor:* VVP, FCM *Availability:* VVP, B, V, sale, $179.95, rental, $49.95; FCM, V (SO9264), $179.95.

741. *John Gielgud: An Actor's Life.* (Series: Great Performances).

DOCUMENT INFORMATION: *Country:* GB/USA; *Year of first showing:* 1988; *Location of first showing:* PBS Stations, 9 to 10:30 P.M., Friday, 30 Dec. 1988.

EDITION, HISTORY, CONTENTS, & EVALUATION: *Edition & history:* "A rare and revealing interview with the legendary actor, taped at his country home in Buckinghamshire, England. Many clips are featured" (P.R. handout). Gielgud speaks of coaching Marlon Brando in the MGM *Julius Caesar* (1953), and of playing Romeo. There are clips from the Olivier *Richard III* and *Julius Caesar.*

MEDIUM INFORMATION: *Sound:* Spoken language; *Color:* Yes; *Length:* 90 min.; *Video type:* V.

AUTHORSHIP INFORMATION: *Producer(s):* Miller, John; Williams, Peter; *Director(s):* Heather, David; *Lighting designer(s):* Byde, Robert; *Cast:* Gielgud, John; Miller, John.

DISTRIBUTION & AVAILABILITY: *Publisher or re-*

sponsible agency: TVS/WNET/New York; *Distributor:* NET.

742. *Shakespeare and His Theatre* (I).

DOCUMENT INFORMATION: *Country:* GB; *Year of release:* 198?.

EDITION, HISTORY, CONTENTS, & EVALUATION: *Edition & history:* Part one of a two-part series made for Thames Weekend Television in England, a commercial network in England that offers what in the U.S. would be thought of as "highbrow" public television programs. This cassette examines Shakespeare from the actor's point of view. *Supplementary materials:* BUFVC 32.

MEDIUM INFORMATION: *Length:* 26 min.

AUTHORSHIP INFORMATION: *Director(s):* Thames TV; *Cast:* Neame, Christopher (Narrator).

DISTRIBUTION & AVAILABILITY: *Distributor:* GSV*.

743. *Shakespeare and His Theatre* (II) [Sup.].

DOCUMENT INFORMATION: *Country:* GB; *Year of release:* 198?.

EDITION, HISTORY, CONTENTS, & EVALUATION: *Edition & history:* For part one, see entry 742, above. Narrated by distinguished Shakespeare scholars. *Supplementary materials:* BUFVC 33.

MEDIUM INFORMATION: *Color:* Yes; *Length:* 26 min.; *Video type:* V.

AUTHORSHIP INFORMATION: *Cast:* Hodges, C. Walter; Brown, John Russell; Spencer, Terence (Narrators).

DISTRIBUTION & AVAILABILITY: *Publisher or responsible agency:* Thames TV; *Distributor:* GSV*.

744. *Shakespeare's Theatre.* See also 693.1

DOCUMENT INFORMATION: *Country:* USA; *Year of first showing:* 19[?].

EDITION, HISTORY, CONTENTS, & EVALUATION: *Edition & history:* Not seen but included here because it is listed and described in the Univ. of Connecticut Film Library catalog. Uses the opening sequence from the Olivier *Henry V* to show the hustle and bustle in an Elizabethan playhouse. Then, however, it adds maps and construction details about the playhouse. From the catalog description, this seems to be different from the British study extracts film listed in the *BUFVC* 9. On the other hand, it might also be the same film as 693.1, above. *Supplementary materials:* CNU catalog, 300.

MEDIUM INFORMATION: *Sound:* Spoken language; *Color:* Yes; *Length:* 13 min.; *Film type:* 16mm.

DISTRIBUTION & AVAILABILITY: *Publisher or responsible agency:* Twentieth-Century Fox [?]; *Distributor:* CNU, *Availability:* Rental $7.

745. *The Shakespeare Mystery.*

DOCUMENT INFORMATION: *Country:* GB/USA; *Year*

of first showing: 1989; *Location of first showing:* Public Television Stations, USA, 9:00 P.M., 18 April 1989.

EDITION, HISTORY, CONTENTS, & EVALUATION: *Edition & history:* Shown on public television as a part of the continuing series called *Frontline*. The program warmed over the old argument about whether or not Shakespeare wrote the plays, though judging from the audience reaction the question is so old that it is new to this generation. *Evaluation:* Although the topic may be a bit shopworn to scholars, the television staff made the most out of it. The editing, background and visuals were exceedingly well done. Mr. Charlton Ogburn made his usual plea for the Earl of Oxford as the author of the plays, while Professors S. Schoenbaum and A.L. Rowse, who have been at odds in the past on other issues, denounced his theory as groundless. Mr. Ogburn probably won the sympathy vote for his charge into the valley of death but at the end of the hour Shakespeare the Man of Stratford still was safely ensconced on his pedestal. Perhaps the controversy has a certain PR value in stirring up interest in Shakespeare biography among persons who might otherwise never have bothered to look. *Supplementary materials:* Goodman, Walter. "The Shakespeare Mystery." *NYT* 18 April 1989: C22; "The Shakespeare Mystery on TV." *SFNL* 14.1 (Dec. 1989): 2.

MEDIUM INFORMATION: *Sound:* Spoken language; *Color:* Yes; Length: 60 min.

AUTHORSHIP INFORMATION: *Producer(s):* Fanning, David; Sim, Kevin; *Associate producer:* Rosen, Nick; *Director:* Sim, Kevin; *Cast:* Woodruff, Judy (Hostess); Rowse, A.L.; Schoenbaum, S.; Ogburn, Charlton (Participants).

DISTRIBUTION & AVAILABILITY: WGBH Boston.

Shakespeare's Tragi-Comedies (Romances). Video/Documentary

746. *Peter Hall [on the Late Plays].*

DOCUMENT INFORMATION: *Country:* GB; *Year of first showing:* 1989; *Location of first showing:* Cable network BRAVO. Transmitted 4 June 1989.

EDITION, HISTORY, CONTENTS, & EVALUATION:

Edition & history: "Features interviews with Peter Hall and actors Tim Pigott-Smith, Eileen Atkins, and Sarah Miles as they struggle to produce *Cymbeline, The Winter's Tale,* and *Tempest* for the May 1988 opening at the National Theatre. We get excellent rehearsal footage, particularly of the opening scene of *WT* and Iachimo's observation of Imogen and subsequent report to Posthumous. Particularly interesting are Hall's comments on the half line, where the actor must leave the line at a level that allows the second actor to pick it up, thus completing the line even if two voices speak it. The show [also] gives brief glimpses of Hall's great 1974 production: Denis Quilley and Arthur Lowe as Caliban and Stephano, and John Gielgud's 'This rough magic' speech (Coursen, H.R. "Recently Viewed on TV and Tape." *SFNL* 14.1 [Dec. 1989]: 7).

MEDIUM INFORMATION: *Sound:* Spoken language; *Color:* Yes; *Length:* 55 min.; *Video type:* V.

AUTHORSHIP INFORMATION: *Cast:* Hall, Peter; Pigott-Smith, Tim; Miles, Sarah; Quilley, Denis; Low, Arthur; Gielgud, John.

DISTRIBUTION & AVAILABILITY: *Copy location:* Unknown.

Teaching Shakespeare. Video/Documentary

747. *Teacher Training Series.*

DOCUMENT INFORMATION: *Country:* USA [?]; *Year of first showing:* [?].

EDITION, HISTORY, CONTENTS, & EVALUATION: *Edition & history:* Not seen. This last-minute entry relies for its source on a recent (1990) Facets Multi-Media catalog, which lists five "teacher training" videos devoted to *Hamlet* (SO8766), *Macbeth* (SO8767), *Romeo and Juliet* (SO8768), *Julius Caesar* (SO8769) and *Othello* (SO8770). "Master teachers" give "new or experienced teachers a creative and focused approach to the teaching of great classics in the classroom. Each video includes lesson plans. . . ."

MEDIUM INFORMATION: *Sound:* Spoken language; *Color:* Yes; *Length:* 30 min. [each] ; *Video type:* V.

DISTRIBUTION & AVAILABILITY: *Copy location:* FCM *Distributor:* FCM, V, $39.95 each.

Selected Bibliography

General Reference Works:

American Film Institute Catalog of Motion Pictures Produced in the United States. Ed. Kenneth W. Munden. New York: R.R. Bowker, 1971—. Partial source for supplementary information about Shakespeare films made in the United States.

BBC Television: Author and Title Catalogues of Transmitted Drama and Features 1936-75 with Chronological List of Transmitted Plays. 63 microfiche cards. Cambridge: Chadwick Healey, n.d. Available at British Film Institute Library. Includes BBC Shakespeare transmissions, though information needs to be supplemented by material from the BBC *Programme as Broadcast* (Caversham Park Written Archive, Reading), and *Radio Times*.

Bulman, James and H.R. Coursen, eds. *Shakespeare on Television: An Anthology of Essays and Reviews.* Hanover: UP of New England, 1988. The first full-scale collection of essays and reviews in the emerging field of Shakespeare on television. Includes videographies. Rev.: Berger, Thomas L. "*Shakespeare on TV.*" *SQ* 40.2 (Summer 1989): 237-9; Taylor, Neil. "The Bard in TV Land." *SFNL* 13.2 (April 1989): 5.

Eckert, Charles W. *Focus on Shakespearean Films.* In the Film Focus series. Ed. Ronald Gottesman and Harry M. Geduld. Englewood Cliffs (NJ): Prentice Hall, 1968. Selected essays and a checklist of Shakespeare films.

Eastman, Zita and Kevin Hagopian, eds. *Film Literature Index. Quarterly Author/Subject Index to the International Periodical Literature of Film and Television.* Albany: SUNY, 1973—. Useful tool for locating commentaries on and reviews of films.

Educational Film/Video Locator of the Consortium of University Film Centers and R.R. Bowker, 3rd ed. New York: R.R. Bowker, 1986. Lists educational films on Shakespearean topics, as well as many distributors not listed in this filmography.

Gianakos, Larry James. *Television Drama Series Programming: A Comprehensive Chronicle.* Metuchen N.J.: Scarecrow Press, 1980. Checklist of television dramas, including Shakespeare, transmitted in North America.

Hanson, Patricia K. and Stephen L. Hanson, eds. *Film Review Index.* Phoenix (Ariz.): Oryx Press, n.d. There are over 50 reviews listed for the 1936 George Cukor *Romeo and Juliet* alone.

Holderness, Graham, and Christopher McCullough. "Shakespeare on the Screen: A Selective Filmography." *ShS* 39 (1987): 13-37. Includes 282 "straightforward" versions of Shakespeare's plays on film and video produced in USA, Europe and elsewhere. Data generally includes year of production, producer, director, distributor in UK, and some credits.

Ingber, Nachman, ed. *Shakespeare on Screen.* Tel Aviv, Israel: n.p. 1967. In Hebrew. Ill.

International Index to Film Periodicals: An Annotated Guide. Ed., Francis Thorpe. London: Macmillan, 1978. Published annually since 1972, it offers a quick overview of articles and reviews.

Jorgens, Jack J., comp. "Shakespeare on Film: A Selected Checklist." *LFQ* 4.2. (Spring 1976): 191-3. An excellent survey of the major publications in the field up to 1976.

Katz, Ephraim. *The Film Encyclopedia..* New York: Putnam, 1979. There is no reason whatsoever to dispute the publisher's claim that this is "the most comprehensive encyclopedia of world cinema in one volume." It will answer nearly every question that one can think of about particular actors and directors.

Kliman, Bernice and Rothwell, Kenneth S., eds. *Shakespeare on Film Newsletter,* Univ. of Vermont, Nassau Community College and Shakespeare Globe Centre, London. 1976—. Bi-annual. Furnishes regular updates on Shakespeare in both film and television.

Limbacher, James L. *Feature Films: A Directory of Feature Films on 16mm and Videotape Available for Rental, Sale and Lease.* 8th ed. New York: R.R. Bowker, 1985. Standard reference work for locating films. Rev.: Nesthus, Marie. *SFNL* 10.2 (1986): 7+.

Lipkov, Alexander. *Shakespirovski ekran.* Moscow, 1975. 350 pp. Ill. Even though there is no English translation available, one senses the expertise in this work. Some good illustrations.

Lippman, Max. *Shakespeare Im Film.* Weisbaden: Deutsches Institut fur Filmkunde E.V., 1964. Contains credits for some out-of-the-way films.

Magill, Frank N., ed. *Magill's Survey of Cinema.* Englewood Cliffs N.J.: Salem Press, 1980—. A multi-volumed work that gives ''in-depth analysis'' of some 1500 films and updates with an annual supplement. The Shakespeare films that are included receive conscientious coverage.

McLean, Andrew M. *Shakespeare: Annotated Bibliographies and Media Guide for Teachers.* Urbana: NCTE, 1980. A ''hands-on'' type of book for teachers in search of A/V materials on Shakespeare, though now in some need of updating.

Meserole, Harrison T., *et al.* ed. *Shakespeare Quarterly. Annual Bibliography* 1946—. Annual coverage of Shakespeare in performance to include film and television.

Morris, Peter, ed. *Shakespeare on Film.* Ottawa: Canadian Film Institute, 1972. Also printed in *Films in Review* 24 (1973): 132-63. A filmography that is still useful primarily because of Morris' succinct commentaries.

Moulds, Michael, ed. *International Index to Film Periodicals.* London: FIAF, 1972—. Truly impressive *international* coverage of periodicals in many languages.

Parker, Barry M. *The Folger Shakespeare Filmography: A Directory of Feature Films Based on the Works of William Shakespeare.* Washington (D.C.): Folger Shakespeare Library, 1979. Parker's filmography offers the most original compilation of ''offshoot'' and ''spinoff'' films based on Shakespeare's plays. Rev.: McLean, Andrew M. ''Books in Review.'' *SFNL* 5.2 (May 1981): 10+.

Ross, Harris, comp. ''William Shakespeare and Film.'' *Film as Literature, Literature as Film. An Introduction to and Bibliography of Film's Relationship to Literature.* New York: Greenwood Press, 1987. 209-30. Extensive annotated bibliography covering most of the major publications in the field.

Smith, Gordon Ross. *A Classified Shakespeare Bibliography, 1936-58.* Univ. Park: Pennsylvania State UP, 1963. Includes numerous reviews of films and discs to date. The Garland Shakespeare bibliographies make an excellent supplement, though coverage of film is not so thorough in some volumes as in others.

Terris, Olwen, ed. *Shakespeare: A List of Audio-Visual Materials Available in the UK.* Second edition. London: British Universities Film & Video Council, 1985. Includes listings of film & video distributors in the United Kingdom, as well as many audio aides.

Weiner, David and Michael Atkinson, eds. *The Video Source Book,* 10th ed. Detroit: Gale Research, 1989. Massive listings of videotapes available and places to buy them, though annotations are sometimes slim.

Yutkevich, Sergei. *Shekspir i kino Shakespeare and Film.* Moscow: Nauka, 1973. In Russian. No English translation available. Rev.: Pomar, Mark. *SFNL* 4.1 (1979): 10+.

General Criticism of Shakespeare on Film and Video

Books

Ball, Robert Hamilton. *Shakespeare on Silent Film: A Strange Eventful History.* London: George Allen and Unwin, 1968. Doubtless the most distinguished work of pure scholarship in the field of Shakespeare on film. Professor Ball may indeed have succeeded in saying the last word on this subject, especially as the prints become more and more difficult to locate. A mine of information about the silents.

California, Univ of. at San Diego. Eds. anon. *The Shakespeare Plays: A Study Guide.* San Diego: UC and The Coast Community College District, 1978. Developed by the Univ. of California at San Diego as a text for a television course based on the first season of ''The Shakespeare Plays'' series. Contributors include such prominent Shakespeare scholars as Robert Knoll, Marjorie Garber, John Andrews and Michael Mullin. Rev.: Keating, Martha Hopkins. ''The Shakespeare Plays.'' *SFNL* 5.1. (Dec. 1980): 6+.

Collick, John. *Shakespeare, Cinema and Society.* Manchester and New York: Manchester UP, 1989. The most recent book on the subject of Shakespeare and film appears as a part of a series oriented toward ''cultural politics.''

Davies, Anthony. *Filming Shakespeare's Plays: The Adaptations of Laurence Olivier, Orson Welles, Peter Brook and Akira Kurosawa.* Cambridge: Cambridge UP, 1988. Argues for a radical difference between the spatial configurations of staged and screened Shakespeare.

Dehn, Paul. ''The Filming of Shakespeare.'' *Talking of Shakespeare,* ed. John Garrett. London: Hodder & Stoughton, 1954. 49-72. Early discussion of Shakespeare in talking pictures in ''jolly lecturer'' style.

Hapgood, Robert. ''Shakespeare on Film and Television.'' *The Cambridge Companion to Shakespeare Studies.* Ed. Stanley Wells. Cambridge: Cambridge UP, 1986. 273-86. Surveys history of Shakespeare on film and television.

Jorgens, Jack J. *Shakespeare on Film.* Bloomington : Indiana UP, 1976. Few critics can match Jorgens' dual talents as both a Shakespeare and a film critic. In their recognition of the true relationship between Shakespeare and film, these essays made most prior commentaries seem obsolete. Rev.: Homan, Sidney. ''Books in Review.'' *SFNL* 2.1 (Dec. 1977): 7.

———. ''Shakespeare on Film and Television.'' *William Shakespeare: His World, His Work, His Influence.* Ed. John F. Andrews. Vol. 3. New York: Macmillan, 1985. 681-703. 3 vols. Survey of Shakespeare on film. Rev.: Quinn, Edward. *SFNL* 12.1 (Dec. 1987): 5-6.

Literature/Film Quarterly, ed. James M. Welsh and Thomas Erskine. Salisbury State College, Md. Special issues on Shakespeare and Film. 1.4 (1973). Ed. Thomas Erskine; 4.2 (1976). Ed. James M. Welsh; 5.4 (1977). Ed. Michael Mullin; 11.3 (1983). Ed. Kenneth S. Rothwell.

Manvell, Roger. *Shakespeare and the Film.* 1971. rev. ed.,

Cranbury (NJ): A. S. Barnes & Co., 1979. What Ball did for silent Shakespeare film, Manvell set out to do for the earlier sound films. His interviews with key figures such as Lord Michael Birkett and Sir Peter Hall make the book unique.

———. "Shakespeare on Film." *The Shakespeare Handbook*. Ed. Levi Fox. Boston: G.K. Hall, 1987. 237-58. Brief survey completed just before Professor Manvell's death that updates his 1979 book. Rev.: Schoenbaum, S. "A New Tradition." *SFNL* 13.1 (Dec. 1988): 1+.

———. *Theater and Film: A Comparative Study of the Two Dramatic Forms of Dramatic Art, and of the Problems of Adaptation of Stage Plays into Films*. Rutherford NJ: Fairleigh Dickinson UP, 1979. Trenchant assessment of the problems of putting stage plays into films with heavy stress on Shakespearean drama.

Ritzav, Tue. *Shakespeare po film, en introduktion*. Det Danske Filmmuseums, 1964. Booklet based on a 1964 festival at Det Danske Filmmuseums, Denmark. Discusses several Shakespeare films to include the Olivier *Hamlet*, Castellani *Romeo and Juliet*, and Orson Welles's *Macbeth* and *Othello*. In BFI collection.

Shattuck, Charles H. "Shakespeare's Plays in Performance from 1660 to the Present," *Riverside Shakespeare*, ed. G. Blakemore Evans *et al*. Boston: Houghton Mifflin, 1974: 1799-1825. A fine survey by one of the world's great experts on the history of Shakespeare in performance. Professor Shattuck includes screen as well as stage performances.

Wells, Stanley, ed. *Shakespeare Survey* 39. Cambridge: Cambridge UP, 1987. Issue devoted to Shakespeare on film, television and radio.

Representative Articles

Andrews, John F. "Cedric Messina Discusses the Shakespeare Plays: Interview." *SQ* 30 (Spring 1979): 134-7. Solicits views of the first producer of the important BBC/Time-Life series, "The Shakespeare Plays."

Ball, Robert Hamilton. "If We Shadows Have Offended." *The Pacific Spectator*. 1.1 (Winter 1947): 97-104. A pioneering attack by an eminent authority on those who believed that Shakespeare could not be put into the movies.

Charney, Maurice. "Shakespearean Anglophilia: The BBC TV Series and American Audiences." *SQ* 31 (Summer 1980): 287-92. Discusses the problem of using entirely British casts for American audiences.

———. "Televisionary Shakespeare: Working with *The Shakespeare Hour*. *SQ* 36 (Winter 1985): 489-95. Calls for recognition of the positive role that television can play in attracting students to Shakespeare without necessarily discouraging them from reading or theatergoing.

Felheim, Marvin. "Criticism and the Films of Shakespeare's Plays." *Comparative Drama* 9 (Summer 1975): 147-55. Decries rigidity of conservative Shakespeareans who condemn film without understanding it. Quotes Stanley Kauffmann: ". . . theatre began as a sacred event and eventually included the profane;

the film began as a profane event and eventually included the sacred."

Haun, H. "Touch Up Your Shakespeare, or How Hollywood Has Used, Bruised or Otherwise Abused the Bard." *Films in Review*. 33.9 (Nov. 1982): 522-30. In attacking virtually all attempts to put Shakespeare on screen, the author typifies the position of many who are hostile to putting Shakespeare on film.

Johnson, Ian. "Merely Players: The Impact of Shakespeare on International Cinema." *Films & Filming* 10.9 (April 1964): 41-8. A witty and knowledgeable survey of Shakespeare on film up until 1964. Still worth reading.

Karney, Robyn. "Shakespeare and the Movies: The Bard on Film." *Films and Filming* 421 (Nov. 1989): 14-18. A good survey for beginning scholars but with a wonderful collection of stills that will also appeal to the veteran.

Lillich, Meredith. "Shakespeare on the Screen: A Survey of How His Plays Have Been Made into Movies." *Films in Review*. 7.6 (June/July 1956): 247-60. An intelligent appraisal of Shakespeare films to the year of publication.

"Shakespeare Among the Nations." *Literary Review* 22 (Summer 1979) Fairleigh Dickinson UP. 381-491. Film versions of four of Shakespeare's tragedies are the subject of discussion in this special issue with introductory comments by Jan Kott, Morris Carnovsky, Maurice Charney, and Joan Mellen.

Taylor, John Russell. "Shakespeare in Film, Radio and Television." *Shakespeare: A Celebration 1564-1964*. Penguin: Baltimore, 1964. 97-113. Shakespeare is verbal and therefore not congenial to a pictorial context.

Welles, Orson. "The Third Audience." *Sight & Sound*. 23 (Oct./Dec. 1953): 120-22. A major figure in the history of Shakespeare on film argues that if Verdi can legitimately adapt Shakespeare to opera, then so can a film director adapt the plays to the screen.

Worthen William B. "The Player's Eye: Shakespeare on Television." *CD* 18.3 (Fall 1984): 193-201. Expresses reservations about the capacity of television to handle Shakespeare's plays properly.

Zitner, Sheldon P. "Wooden O's in Plastic Boxes: Shakespeare on Television." *Univ. of Toronto Quarterly* 51 (Fall 1981): 1-12. Despite reservations about the tube as a medium for Shakespeare, author expresses optimism about the future of Shakespeare on television.

Supplementary List of Books and Articles on Individual Screen Treatments of the Plays

(See also main entry in filmography for further items)

All's Well That Ends Well (Nos. 1-5)

All's Well That Ends Well. The BBC TV Shakespeare. Ed. Peter Alexander *et al*. London: BBC, 1980. See entry

#3. One of the companion volumes issued by the BBC to accompany each of the programs in the series known as "The Shakespeare Plays." In general, but not invariably, each volume includes cast credits, a textual note, an introduction by John Wilders, program and/or production notes by Henry Fenwick, illustrations in black and white and in color, and the complete Peter Alexander text of the play with indications of the cuts and additions made for the television adaptation.

Willis, Susan. "Making *All's Well that Ends Well:* The Arts of Televised Drama at BBC." *Shakespeare and the Arts.* Ed. C.W. Cary and H.S. Limouze. Dayton O.: UP of America. 155-63. Analyzes the directorial decisions made in setting up the lighting and design for the BBC production. See entry #3.

Antony and Cleopatra (Nos. 6-29)

Antony and Cleopatra. The BBC TV Shakespeare. Ed. Peter Alexander *et al.* London: BBC, 1981. See entry #23. For description, see also *AWW* above.

Cotton, Ian. "Cleopatra's Real Life Argosy." *TV Times* 8 July 1974: 18-19. Gossipy interview with Janet Suzman and Trevor Nunn about their life styles as compared to those of Shakespeare's fictional characters. Ms. Suzman played an unforgettable Cleopatra in the British television production. See entry #21.

As You Like It. (Nos. 30-46)

As You Like It. The BBC TV Shakespeare. Ed. Peter Alexander *et al.* New York: Mayflower, 1979. See entry #42. See also description under *AWW.*

Halio, Jay L. and Barbara C. Millard, comps. *As You Like It: An Annotated Bibliography, 1940-80.* New York: Garland, 1985. Several entries on the Czinner 1936 version.

[W.F.] "Review" *MFB* 3.33 (1936): 147. "Worth seeing for Elisabeth Bergner's performance as Rosalind." See entry #34.

The Comedy of Errors (Nos. 47-57)

The Comedy of Errors. The BBC TV Shakespeare. Ed. Peter Alexander *et al.* London: BBC, 1984. See entry #55. For description, see also *AWW* above.

Sauvage, Leo "On Stage: Juggling the Bard." *The New Leader* 29 June 1987: 20-21. Detailed analysis of the Vivian Beaumont Theatre "circus" production that was televised nationally on 24 June 1987. See entry #57

Coriolanus (Nos. 58-67)

Coriolanus. The BBC TV Shakespeare. Ed. Peter Alexander *et al.* London: BBC, 1984. See entry #67. For description, see also *AWW* above.

Miner, Worthington. "Shakespeare for the Millions." *Theatre Arts* (June 1951): 58+. An important producer of Shakespeare on television in the earlier days of the industry in the United States discusses problems of performance in the studio. See entry #58.

Cymbeline (Nos. 68-73)

Cymbeline. The BBC TV Shakespeare. Ed. Peter Alexander *et al.* London: BBC, 1983. See entry #73. For description, see also *AWW* above.

Hamlet (Nos. 74-154.1)

Alexander, Peter. *Hamlet: Father and Son.* The Lord Northcliffe lectures, University College, London. Oxford: Oxford UP, 1955. A well known Shakespeare expert finds the Olivier version of *Hamlet* (see entry #98) reductive by reason of its over emphasis on Hamlet's alleged "tragic flaw" of indecisiveness.

Andrews, Nigel. "*Hamlet* 1969." *MFB* 37. 436 (May 1970): 98. Review of the 1969 Richardson production starring Nicol Williamson (entry #123) in which the author finds the camera technique a partial solution to the problem of recording a stage production of a play on camera.

Anon. "*Hamlet*/The Lindsay Kemp Circus." *NFT Programme* Published by B.F.I. May 1980: 27. Describes Celestine Coronado's 1976 *Hamlet* (see entry #132), which was a 67-minute production using video techniques. Helen Mirren doubled as Gertrude and Ophelia and twins, Antony and David Meyer, both played Hamlet. This split vision technique seems to have anticipated the 1987 Cambridgeshire *Hamlet* (see entry #154).

———. "The Filming of *Hamlet:* Interview with Mr. Cecil Hepworth." *Bioscope* 20.354 (24 July 1913): 275-79. Firsthand insight into early film production in Great Britain in dialogue with Mr. Hepworth. See entry #82.

Coursen, Herbert R. "Shakespeare and Television: The BBC-TV *Hamlet.*" *Shakespeare and the Arts.* Ed. C.W. Cary and H.S. Limouze. Dayton O.: UP of America. 127-33. Author admires Derek Jacobi's performance as Hamlet, despite the feeling that Shakespeare on television is too often a "diminished" experience. See entry #140.

Hamlet. The BBC TV Shakespeare. Ed. Peter Alexander *et al.* New York: Mayflower Books, 1980. See entry #140. For description, see also *AWW* above.

Hodgdon, Barbara. "The Mirror Up to Nature: Notes on Kozintsev's *Hamlet.*" *CD* 9: 305-17. A perceptive critic notes that "the camera held up to nature sees more than Shakespeare's mirror, and what it shows us is closer to a lyric meditation than to a drama." See entry #116.

Hopkins, Arthur. "*Hamlet* and Olivier." *Theatre Arts* 32 (1948): 30-31. Included here as a sample of the kind of hostility that putting Shakespeare on film often aroused. The "abortion" of art and a "persistent misconception" in the writer's view. See entry #98.

Kliman, Bernice W. Hamlet *Film, Television, and Audio Performance.* Rutherford N.J.: Fairleigh Dickinson UP; London and Toronto: Assn. UP, 1988. First detailed full-scale study of *Hamlet* in mechanical reproduction. Rev.: Treadwell, T.O. "*Hamlet:* Performance Study." *SFNL* 13.2 (April 1989): 5.

Kozintsev, Grigori. *Shakespeare: Time and Conscience.* Trans. Joyce Vining. New York: Hill & Wang, 1966. A first-hand, introspective account by the director of the emergence of the 1964 Russian *Hamlet*.

Manvell, Roger. "The Film of *Hamlet*." *Penguin Film Review* 8 (1949): 16-14. The late Dr. Manvell attacks "general red herring of whether films should be made from plays" as a "stale issue." Filmmaking and play-making are two different ways of attracting an audience. See entry #98.

McManaway, J.G. "The Laurence Olivier *Hamlet*." *ShAB* 24 (1949): 3-11. An important essay because it was written by a prominent Shakespeare scholar at a time when the idea of putting Shakespeare on film was still new and often anathema. See entry #98.

Schreiber, Flora Rheta. "Television's *Hamlet*." *QFRT* 8 (1953): 150-6). Useful analysis of the 1953 television production starring Maurice Evans (entry #102). Reviewer sees TV as the right medium for scenes of introspection and subjectivity in drama.

King Henry the Fourth, Parts One and Two (Nos. 155-70)

King Henry the Fourth, Parts One and Two. The BBC TV Shakespeare. Ed. Peter Alexander *et al.* 2 vols. New York: Mayflower Books, 1979. See entries #166, #167. For description, see also *AWW* above.

Higham, Charles. *The Films of Orson Welles.* Berkeley: UP of California, 1970. Includes discussions of the Welles *Macbeth* (125-34), *Othello* (135-44), and *Chimes at Midnight* (167-77).

———. *Orson Welles: The Rise and Fall of an American Genius.* New York: St. Martins Press, 1985. An update of the 1970 book.

Leaming, Barbara. *Orson Welles: A Biography.* New York: Viking Press, 1985. Of great interest to students of Welles' film of the Henriad, *Chimes at Midnight* (see entry #161), as well as his other Shakespeare films.

Lyons, Bridget Gellert. Chimes at Midnight. *Orson Welles Director.* New Brunswick N.J.: Rutgers UP, 1988. Includes continuity script for *Chimes,* as well as reviews and commentaries.

King Henry the Fifth (Nos. 171-82.2)

Agee, James. "*Henry V.*" *Agee on Film. Volume I.* New York: Grosset & Dunlop, 1946; reprinted in Gerald Mast and Marshall Cohen. *Film Theory and Criticism. Introductory Readings.* New York: Oxford UP, 1974. 333-6. Thinks that those who made the Olivier film served Shakespeare's language well. See #172.

Branagh, Kenneth, ed. Henry V: *A Screen Adaptation by Kenneth Branagh.* London: Chatto & Windus, 1989. Not seen. Branagh's script for his brilliant movie. By report profusely illustrated with production stills.

King Henry the Fifth. The BBC TV Shakespeare. Ed. Peter Alexander *et al.* New York: Mayflower Books, 1979. See entry #182. For description, see also *AWW* above.

Candido, Joseph and Charles Forker, comps. *Henry V: An Annotated Bibliography.* New York: Garland, 1983. Includes an annotated bibliography of over 200 reviews of and commentaries on film and television versions of *Henry V*, as well as filmographies, videographies and discographies. Admirably thorough.

Garrett, George P., O.B. Hardison, Jr., and Jane R. Gelfman, eds. *Film Scripts.* New York: Appleton-Century-Crofts, 1971. Includes screenplay for Olivier *Henry V.*

Geduld, Harry M. *Filmguide to Henry V.* Indiana Univ. Press Filmguide Series. Bloomington: Indiana UP, 1973. An indispensable guide to anyone seriously interested in Olivier's *Henry V*. Includes history of production, analysis, and an extensive annotated bibliography. See entry #172.

Hutton, C. Clayton. *The Making of* Henry V. London: Ernest Day, 1945. Facts about production. See #172.

Manheim, Michael. " Olivier's *Henry V* and the Elizabethan World Picture." *LFQ* 11.3 (1983): 179-84. Olivier's film and Prof. E.M.W. Tillyard's celebrated reconstruction of "the Elizabethan world picture" stem from a common impetus, though the film has survived more gracefully than the book. See #172.

Silviria, Dale. *Laurence Olivier and the Art of Film Making.* Rutherford N.J.: Fairleigh Dickinson UP, 1985. Includes discussion of Olivier's Shakespeare films.

King Henry the Sixth, Parts One-Three (Nos. 183-93)

Hodgdon, Barbara. "The Wars of the Roses: Scholarship Speaks on the Stage." *Shakespeare Jahrbuch* 108 (1972): 170-84. Not seen but Judith Hinchcliffe's Garland bibliography (New York, 1984) summarizes its examination of the two parts of *The Wars of the Roses*, entitled *Henry VI* and *Edward IV*. See #183, #184.

King Henry the Sixth, Parts One, Two and Three. The BBC TV Shakespeare. Ed. Peter Alexander *et al.* 3 vols. London: BBC, 1983. For the BBC booklets on the three parts of *Henry VI*, see entries #186, #187, #193. For descriptions, see also *AWW* above.

Maher, Mary Z. "The Work of Jane Howell." *SFNL* 13.1 (Dec. 1988): 6. Summarizes results of an important seminar at the 1988 meeting of the Shakespeare Assoc. of America, on the work of Jane Howell, to include her BBC production of the three parts of *Henry VI*.

King Henry the Eighth (Nos. 194-96.1)

Anon. "Cardinal Wolsey." *Bioscope* 15. 287 (11 April 1912): 143. The film is described as an incident in the life of the reign of King Henry the Eighth, without reference to Shakespeare. See entry #195.

King Henry the Eighth. The BBC TV Shakespeare. Ed. Peter Alexander *et al.* New York: Mayflower Books, 1979. See entry #196. For description, see also *AWW* above.

Julius Caesar (Nos. 197-237)

Anon. "Review." *Bioscope* 12 Oct. 1911: 113. Gives high marks to this "wonderful adaptation from Shakespeare's famous drama," which is presumably Guazzoni's *Brutus*. See entry #201.

Harding, Robert, ed. *Julius Caesar and the Life of William Shakespeare.* Introd. John Gielgud. London: Gawthorn Press, n.d. Souvenir booklet of the Mankiewicz film with an introduction by Sir John Gielgud, the text of the play, and an unattributed life of Shakespeare. Most valuable for the splendid stills from the film and Gielgud's introduction in which he praises the director for making adroit use of the camera in filming Shakespeare. See entry #214.

Griffin, Alice V. "Shakespeare Through the Camera's Eye— *Julius Caesar* in Motion Pictures. . . ." *SQ* 4.3 (July 1953): 330-6. Enthusiastic reception of the Mankiewicz *Julius Caesar* as "true to the text, beautifully spoken, and generally well acted." See entry #214.

Houseman, John, *et al.* "Shakespeare in the Mass Media." *QFRT* 8.2 (Winter 1953): 109-50. Collected essays dealing with the Mankiewicz film. #214.

Julius Caesar. The BBC TV Shakespeare. Ed. Peter Alexander *et al.* New York: Mayflower Books, 1979. See entry #233. For description, see also *AWW* above.

L.G.A.. "*Julius Caesar* USA 1953." *MFB* 20. 239 (Dec. 1953): 172-73. Favorable review that has the wit to see that Marlon Brando plays the role of Antony with "such furious compulsion that the effect of authority, power and deadly lack of scruple is most impressively produced," though the critic decided that Gielgud's performance as Cassius was "the best." See #214.

King John (Nos. 238-40)

Ball, Robert Hamilton. "The Shakespeare Film as Record: Sir Herbert Beerbohm Tree." *SQ* 3 (July 1952): 227-36. A reconstruction of Tree's 1899 film of *Jn*, which was the "first" Shakespeare film. See #238. See also "An Addendum." *SQ* 24 (Aug. 1973): 455-9.

King Lear (Nos. 241-280)

Canby, Vincent. "*Ran* Weathers the Seasons." *NYT* 22 June 1986: 21H +. In praise of Kurosawa's film of *King Lear*. See entry #274.

Champion, Larry S., comp. King Lear: *An Annotated Bibliography,* 2 vols. New York: Garland, 1980. Over 100 references to screened treatments of *King Lear*, including 50 to the Kozintsev and about 80 to the Brook versions.

King Lear. The BBC TV Shakespeare. Ed. Peter Alexander *et al.* London: BBC, 1983. See #267. For description, see also *AWW* above.

Griffin, Alice. "Shakespeare Through the Camera's Eye 1953-54." *SQ* 6.1. (Winter 1955): 63-66. With all its faults the Orson Welles/ Peter Brook televised *King Lear* attained at times "the feeling of grandeur and high tragedy." See #250.

Kozintsev, Grigori. King Lear *The Space of Tragedy.* Trans. Mary Mackintosh. Berkeley: UP of California, 1977. Kozintsev's book-length meditation on the production of his film is possibly the finest explanation of the filmmaker's art ever composed by a working director. See #256.

Kurosawa, Akira *et al. Ran: Screenplay.* Boston: Shambhala, 1986. Rev.: Marion D. Perret. "*Caveat Lector:* The Screenplay of *Ran.*" *SFNL* 13.1 (Dec. 198): 1 +. "What appears in print is not always what appears on film." See #274.

Rothwell, K.S., comp. "Godard *Lear:* The Critical Moment." *SFNL* 12.2 (April 1988): 5. Summary of three reviews of the Godard *King Lear*. See #277.

Wadsworth, Frank. "Sound and Fury: *King Lear* on Television." *QFRT* 8 (1954); 254-8. Further discussion of the Welles/Brook 1953 television production. See #250.

Welsh, James M. "To See It Feelingly: *King Lear* Through Russian Eyes." *LFQ* 4.2 (Spring 1976): 153-8. "One is not likely to encounter a more haunting film of Shakespeare for a good many years to come." See #256.

Wilds, Lillian. "One *King Lear* for Our Time: A Bleak Film Vision by Peter Brook." *LFQ* 4.2 (Spring 1976): 159-64. The late Dr. Lillian Wilds correctly points out the cinematic artistry underlying Brook's film of *King Lear*. See #259.

Woods, Alan. "Frederick B. Warde: America's Greatest Forgotten Tragedian." *Educational Theatre Journal.* 29 (Oct. 1977): 333-44. Surveys career of the star of the Ernest Thanhouser 1916 silent *King Lear*. See #246.

Love's Labor's Lost (Nos. 281-83)

Love's Labor's Lost. The BBC TV Shakespeare. Ed. Peter Alexander *et al.* London: BBC, 19? Not seen. See #283. For probable description, see also *AWW* above.

Macbeth (Nos. 284-346.1)

Anderson, Joseph L. and Donald Richie. *The Japanese Film: Art and Industry.* Foreword by Akira Kurosawa.

New York: Grove Press, 1960. Puts Kurosawa's work in the context of the entire Japanese film industry. See #307.

Blumenthal, J. "*Macbeth* into *Throne of Blood*." *Sight and Sound* 34.4 (Autumn 1965); reprinted in Gerald Mast and Marshall Cohen. *Film Theory and Criticism*. New York: Oxford UP, 1974: 340-51. Kurosawa's movie is in the author's view "the only work . . . that has ever completely succeeded in transforming a play of Shakespeare into a film." See #307. For an opposing point of view, see Gerlach, John. "Shakespeare, Kurosawa, and *Macbeth:* A Response to J. Blumenthal." *LFQ* 1.4 (Fall 1973): 343-51.

Jorgens, Jack J. "Kurosawa's *Throne of Blood:* Washizu and Miki Meet the Forest Spirit." *LFQ* 11.3 (1983): 167-73. Kurosawa "traps the characters in severe patterns of symmetry, repeated action, anti-climactic movement, and stage artifice." See #307.

Kiernan, Thomas. *The Roman Polanski Story*. New York: Delilah/Grove Press, 1980. Sensational biography of the cinematic genius who made the "Playboy" film version of *Macbeth*. In fact it does throw light on the genesis of the film. See #324.

Macbeth.The BBC TV Shakespeare. Ed. Peter Alexander *et al*. London: BBC, 1983. See #336. For description, see also *AWW* above.

Mullin, Michael. "*Macbeth* on Film." *LFQ* 1.4 (Fall 1973): 332-42. Surveys movies by Welles, Kurosawa, Schaefer, and Polanski.

Naremore, James. "The Walking Shadow. Welles's Expressionistic *Macbeth*." *LFQ* 1.4 (Fall 1973): 360-66. Welles's often misunderstood film is "arguably the purest example of expressionism in the American cinema." See #297.

Welles, Orson. For commentary on Welles's *Macbeth,* see Higham, above, under *1H4*.

Measure for Measure (Nos. 347-52)

Perret, Marion D. "'To Stage Me to Their Eyes': Visual Imagery in the BBC Production of *Measure for Measure*." *Literature in Performance: A Journal of The Literary and Performing Arts* 2 (April 1982): 12-22. See #350. Not seen.

Measure for Measure. The BBC TV Shakespeare. Ed. Peter Alexander *et al*. New York: Mayflower Books, 1979. See #350. For description, see also *AWW* above.

The Merchant of Venice (Nos. 353-71)

Anon. "Shylock." *Bioscope* 19. 348 (12 June 1913): 835. "Baur's Shylock is an object of ridicule and mirth rather than sympathy. His performance is full of comedy." See #357.

———. "The Broadwest Films Production of *The Merchant of Venice*. Mr. Matheson Lang as Shylock." *Bioscope* 3 Aug. 1916: 451. "Mr. Lang's very popular conception of Shylock has been adopted to a new medium with remarkable skill." But there are complaints about the banality of the title cards. See #359.

———. "Releases for Feb. 1.: *The Jew of Mestri*." *Bioscope* 66 (21 Jan. 1926): 44. See #361. Review of "an elaborate and spectacular German production .. with genuine Venetian interiors."

The Merchant of Venice. The BBC TV Shakespeare. Ed. Peter Alexander *et al*. London: BBC, 1980. See #370. For description, see also *AWW* above.

The Merry Wives of Windsor (Nos. 372-86)

The Merry Wives of Windsor. The BBC TV Shakespeare. Ed. Peter Alexander *et al*. London: BBC, 1983. See #385. For description, see also *AWW* above.

A Midsummer Night's Dream (Nos. 387-419.1)

Anon. "A Midsummer Night's Dream." *Bioscope* 3 March 1910: 47-8. Fulsome praise for this Vitagraph silent. See #387.

A Midsummer Night's Dream. The BBC TV Shakespeare. Ed. Peter Alexander *et al*. London: BBC, 1981. See #412. For description, see also *AWW* above.

W.E.W. "Review." *MFB* 2. 21 (Oct. 1935): 147-8. Favorable review of the Reinhardt/Dieterle film that especially remarks on Mickey Rooney's Puck as "a gamin who chuckles in a raucous tone." See #392.

Much Ado about Nothing (Nos. 420-32)

Much Ado about Nothing. The BBC TV Shakespeare. Ed. Peter Alexander *et al*. London: BBC, 19?. Not seen. See #432. For probable description, see also *AWW* above.

Othello (Nos. 433-81)

Anon. "Carnival." *Bioscope* 66. 749 (19 Feb. 1921): 72. Points out that the play enjoyed great success on the London stage before being made into a film and notes resemblances to Shakespeare's *Othello*. See #441.

———. "A Double Life." *MFB* 15:176 (Aug. 1953): 112. Ronald Colman is a superb actor but "the film achieves little of either artistic or dramatic value." See #446.

Othello. The BBC TV Shakespeare. Ed. Peter Alexander *et al*. London: BBC, 1981. See #472. For description, see also *AWW* above.

Petric, Vlada. "Welles Looks at Himself: Filming *Othello*." *Film Library Quarterly* 13.4 (1980): 21-3. Praises Welles for his excellence as a film teacher as he talks about the making of *Othello* in this rarely seen educational film. See #479.

Welles, Orson. See under *Macbeth* and *Henry IV*.

Pericles (No. 482)

Pericles. The BBC TV Shakespeare. Ed. Peter Alexander *et al.* London: BBC, 19?. Not seen. For probable description, see *AWW* above.

King Richard the Second(Nos. 483-95)

Anon. "Video Rushes in Where Angels Fear." *Life* 8 Feb. 1954: 53-54. Illustrated article on Maurice Evans' television appearance as Richard II. See #484.

Kliman, Bernice W. "The Setting in Early Television: Maurice Evans' Shakespeare Productions." *Shakespeare and the Arts: A Collection of Essays from the Ohio Shakespeare Conference 1981.* Ed. C.W. Cary and H.S. Limouze. Washington D.C.: UP of America, 1982. 135-53. Includes discussion of not only *R2* but also *Ham., Mac.,* and *Shr.* "Shakespeare on television works best when producers do not try to imitate the illusion we expect of movie space, but opt for a semi-illusionist setting like that of the proscenium arch stage." See #484, also #102, #305, and #593.

King Richard the Second. The BBC TV Shakespeare. Ed. Peter Alexander *et al.* New York: Mayflower Books, 1978. See #492. For description, see also *AWW* above.

King Richard the Third(Nos. 496-513)

Brown, Constance A. "Olivier's *Richard III:* A Re-Evaluation." *FQ* 20.4 (1967): 22-32. Already cited under #503, but it is worth repeating here that this is the best single analysis of the film that I have ever found. The analysis of the important shadow and crown tropes leaves little else to be said on the subject.

King Richard the Third. The BBC TV Shakespeare. Ed. Peter Alexander *et al.* London: BBC, 1983. Not seen. See #513. For probable description, see also *AWW* above.

Thorp, Margaret Farrand. "Shakespeare and the Movies." *SQ* 9.3. (Summer 1958): 357-66. Makes an attempt to explore cinematic values in the Olivier *Richard III,* though the author's orientation was more on the literary than on the cinematic side. See #503.

Romeo and Juliet. (Nos. 514-75)

Anon. "Review." *Bisocope* 81.1202 (16 Oct. 1929): 19. Norma Shearer and John Gilbert are "great in a serious and burlesque *Romeo and Juliet.*" See #525.

[A.V.] "*Romeo and Juliet.*" *MFB* 3.34 (Oct. 1936): 176. An early reaction to the 1936 Cukor version, which pointed out that in Hollywood's Verona "nobody is poor and nothing is the slightest degree dirty." See #526.

Dunkley, Chris. "Review." *Financial Times. National Film Theatre Program* London: BFI June 1982: 31. High praise for the Brazilian *Romeo and Juliet,* which "updates the play to a modern context and modern speech." See #568.

Halio, Jay. "Zeffirelli's *Romeo and Juliet:* The Camera and the Text." *LFQ* 5.4 (Fall 1977): 322-5. "However excellent, the film is nonetheless an interpretation which needs to be recognized and weighed." See #552.

[J.M.] "*Romeo and Juliet* GB/Italy 1954." *MFB* 21. 249 (Oct. 1954): 145. "Film attempts to combine some of the elements of Italian neo-realistic filmmaking with Shakespeare." See #538.

Jorgenson, Paul A. "Castellani's *Romeo and Juliet.*" *QFRT,* 10 (1955): 1-10. A defense of the film in terms of Castellani's intentions. See #538.

Kauffmann, Stanley. "*Romeo and Juliet.*" *Figures of Light: Film Criticism and Commentary.* New York: Harper & Row, 1971: 112-14. A critic who generally dislikes filmed Shakespeare declares that Zeffirelli's adaptations show that he [Z.] is not so much an "innovator like Peter Brook" as an "evader." See #552.

Pursell, M. "Zeffirelli's Shakespeare: The Visual Realization of Tone and Theme." *LFQ* 8.4 (1980): 210-18. Sees Z's *The Taming of the Shrew* and *Romeo and Juliet* as "among the most aesthetically successful film adaptations of Shakespeare." See #552.

Romeo and Juliet. The BBC TV Shakespeare. Ed. Peter Alexander *et al.* New York: Mayflower Books, 1978. See #563. For description, see also *AWW* above.

Williams, Raymond. "Some Versions of Shakespeare on the Screen." *TV as Art.* Ed. Patrick Hazard. Champaign Ill.: NCTE, 1966. 117-35. See #551. Calls on teachers to join contemporary artists in struggle to introduce new forms of art, including TV Shakespeare.

The Taming of the Shrew(Nos. 578-606)

[D.W.] "Review." *MFB* 34.399 (Apr. 1967): 57-8. "What emerges is a boisterous, bowlderised version of the play, a Renaissance *Kiss Me Kate.*" See #598.

The Taming of the Shrew. The BBC TV Shakespeare. Ed. Peter Alexander *et al.* London: BBC, 1980. See #603. For description, see also *AWW* above.

The Tempest (Nos. 607-31)

Taylor, Geoffrey. *Paul Mazursky's* Tempest. Written and Ed. by Geoffrey Taylor. New York: Zoetrope, 1982. Screenplay for Mazursky's film. See #626.

The Tempest. The BBC TV Shakespeare. Ed. Peter Alexander *et al.* New York: Mayflower Books, 1980. See #620. For description, see also *AWW* above.

Timon of Athens(No. 632)

Timon of Athens. The BBC TV Shakespeare. Ed. Peter Alexander *et al.* London: BBC, 1981. See #632. For description, see also *AWW* above.

Titus Andronicus(Nos. 633-4)

Titus Andronicus. The BBC TV Shakespeare. Ed. Peter Alexander *et al*. London: BBC, 19?. Not seen. See #633. For probable description, see also *AWW* above.

Troilus and Cressida(Nos. 635-9)

Troilus and Cressida. The BBC TV Shakespeare. Ed. Peter Alexander *et al*. London: BBC, 1981.See #638. For description, see also *AWW* above.

Twelfth Night(Nos. 640-663.2)

Twelfth Night. The BBC TV Shakespeare. Ed. Peter Alexander *et al*. London: BBC, 19?. See #659.1. Not seen. For probable description, see *AWW* above.

The Two Gentlemen of Verona(Nos. 664-7)

The Two Gentlemen of Verona. The BBC TV Shakespeare. Ed. Peter Alexander *et al*. London: BBC, 1984. See #667. For description, see also *AWW* above.

The Winter's Tale(Nos. 668-75)

The Winter's Tale. The BBC TV Shakespeare. Ed. Peter Alexander *et al*. London: BBC, 1981. See #673. For description, see also *AWW* above.

Indexes

Index to Entries

("Number" designates the entry number in the main body of the book, not page number; "Description" gives either the title of production, or origin, series, genre, etc.; "Nation" designates country of origin; "Year" may refer to the date of production or of release and may vary from nation to nation [for full context consult entry in body of text]; all entries have been listed chronologically by titles.)

No.	Description	Nation	Yr
All's Well that Ends Well (AWW)			
1	Royal Shakespeare Company BBC TV	GB	68
2	NY Shakespeare Festival	USA	78
3	BBC: The Shakespeare Plays	GB	80
4	Berkeley Festival	USA	82
5	Shakespeare Hour	USA	85
Antony and Cleopatra (Ant.)			
6	Cleopatra	Fra	1899
7	Vitagraph silent	USA	03
8	Cleopatra	Fra	10
9	Cleopatra	USA	12
10	Marcantonio e Cleo	Ita	13
11	Silent epic	Ita	13
12	Cleopatra	USA	17
13	Stars R. Speiaght	GB	51
14	Spread of Eagle, 7	GB	63
15	Spread of Eagle, 8	GB	63
16	Spread of Eagle, 9	GB	63
17	Carry on Cleo	GB	64
18	Explorations in Shakespeare	Can	69
19	Shaw vs. Shakespeare, 3	USA	70
20	Epic adaptation	GB	72

No.	Description	Nation	Yr
21	Royal Shakespeare Company production	GB	74
22	Scenes: 2.2; 5.2	GB	74
23	BBC: The Shakespeare Plays	GB	80
24	Berkeley Festival	USA	81
25	Making of Antony	GB	82
26	Interview w/ Glenda Jackson	GB	83
27	Bard Video Production	USA	85
28	Workshop: Antony	GB	85
29	Schools: Educational	GB	85
As You Like It (AYL)			
30	Seven Ages of Man	USA	03
31	Pioneer silent	USA	08
32	Vitagraph silent	USA	12
33	Uses title only	GB	16
34	Film/Adaptation	GB	36
35	BBC TV: Scenes	GB	37
36	BBC TV	GB	46
37	BBC TV	GB	53
38	Seven Ages of Man	USA	53
39	BBC TV	GB	63
40	Explorations in Shakespeare	Can	69

No.	Description	Nation	Yr
41	Abridged: Shakespeare series	GB	69
42	BBC: The Shakespeare Plays	GB	78
42.1	French subtitles	GB	78
43	Contemporary Look at Shakespeare	USA	80
44	Shakespeare in Perspective	GB	84
45	Stratford: Page to Stage	Can	85
45.1	Stratford production	Can	85
46	Love: As You Like It	GB	86
The Comedy of Errors (Err.)			
47	Vitagraph silent	USA	08
48	Boys from Syracuse	USA	40
49	Kraft TV Theatre	USA	49
50	BBC Operatic Version	GB	54
51	Komödie Der Irrungen	Ger	64
52	BBC TV: Aldwych	GB	64
53	Rebroadcast of #52	GB	64
54	Royal Shakespeare Company Stage Production	GB	74

No.	Description	Nation	Yr

King Henry the Fifth (H5)

No.	Description	Nation	Yr
171	BBC TV: Scenes	GB	37
172	Film/Adaptation	GB	44
173	Study Extracts	GB	44
174	BBC: Life of H5	GB	51
175	BBC TV	GB	53
176	Excerpt: Omnibus	USA	53
177	Life of H5	GB	57
178	An Age of Kings, 7	GB	60
179	An Age of Kings, 8	GB	60
180	Abridged: Baxter	GB	64
181	Stratford/CBC	Can	67
182	BBC: The Shakespeare Plays	GB	79
182.1	Held Henry	Bel	84
182.2	Branagh Adaptation	GB	89

King Henry the Sixth, Parts One-Three (1-3 H6)

[Inconsistencies in chronology reflect overlaps in adaptations of a three-part play.]

No.	Description	Nation	Yr
183	Wars of Roses, 1	GB	65
184	Wars of Roses, 2	GB	65
185	An Age of Kings, 9	GB	60
186	BBC: *1H6*	GB	82
187	BBC: *2H6*	GB	82
188	An Age of Kings, 10	GB	60
189	Barrymore (*3H6*)	USA	28
190	An Age of Kings, 11	GB	60
191	An Age of Kings, 12	GB	60
192	An Age of Kings, 13	GB	60
193	BBC: *3H6*	GB	82

King Henry the Eighth (H8)

No.	Description	Nation	Yr
194	British silent: Tree	GB	11
195	Cardinal Wolsey	USA	12
196	BBC: The Shakespeare Plays	GB	79
196.1	Parables Power: Documentary	USA	87

Julius Caesar (JC)

No.	Description	Nation	Yr
197	Méliès in JC	Fra	07
198	Silent scene, JC	USA	08
199	Vitagraph silent	USA	08
200	Italian silent	Ita	08
201	Brutus	Ita	10
202	Bruto I and II	Ita	10
203	Silent, one-reeler	GB	11
204	Benson Company	GB	11
205	Giulio Cesare	Ita	14
206	BBC TV: Scenes	GB	37
207	BBC: Modernized	GB	38
208	Scenes, 3.2	GB	45
209	Amherst at Folger	USA	49
210	Studio One TV	USA	49
211	Low budget film	USA	50

No.	Description	Nation	Yr
212	with Robert Speaight	GB	51
213	BBC TV	GB	51
214	Film adaptation	USA	53
215	Old Vic production	GB	55
216	Studio One TV	USA	55
217	Plays in Rehearsal	USA	58
218	BBC TV	GB	59
219	BBC "Schools" production	GB	60
220	Forum scene only	USA	61
221	Spread of Eagle, 4	GB	63
222	Spread of Eagle, 5	GB	63
223	Spread of Eagle, 6	GB	63
224	Four Views Caesar	GB	64
225	TV: National Youth Theatre	GB	64
226	Film adaptation	GB	69
227	BBC TV	GB	69
228	Abridged: Shakespeare series	GB	69
229	Shaw vs. Shakespeare, 1	USA	70
230	Shaw vs. Shakespeare, 2	USA	70
231	Shaw vs. Shakespeare, 3	USA	70
232	Scenes: 2.2; 4.3	GB	74
233	BBC: The Shakespeare Plays	GB	78
234	Shakespeare in Perspective	GB	78
235	NY Shakespeare Festival	USA	79
235.1	TV: Flemish language	Belg.	85
236	Excerpt: Cosby Show	USA	87
237	Giulio Cesara	Ita	[?]

King John (Jn.)

No.	Description	Nation	Yr
238	First Shakespeare film	GB[18]	99
239	BBC TV	GB	52
240	BBC: The Shakespeare Plays	GB	84

King Lear (Lr.)

No.	Description	Nation	Yr
241	German silent	Ger	05
242	Vitagraph silent	USA	09
243	Re Lear	Ita	10
244	Italian silent	Ita	10
245	Le roi Lear au village	Fra	11
246	Thanhouser silent	USA	16
247	Success	USA	23
248	Yiddish King Lear	USA	35
249	BBC TV	GB	48
250	TV: Welles as Lear	USA	53

No.	Description	Nation	Yr
251	Broken Lance	USA	54
252	Scene with Monty Wooley	USA	54
253	Big Show, The	USA	61
254	Abridged: Baxter	USA	64
255	Interview with van Dalsum	Hol	64
256	Karol Lear	USS	69
257	Explorations in Shakespeare	Can	69
258	Abridged: Shakespeare series	GB	69
259	Film/Adaptation	GB	71
259.1	Prospect Theatre	GB	71
259.2	Re Lear, TV adaptation	Ita	72
260	Harry and Tonto	USA	74
261	BBC TV	GB	75
262	Triple Action Theatre	GB	76
263	NY Shakespeare Festival	USA	77
263.1	Re Lear	Ita	79
264	Berkeley Festival	USA	80
265	School version, UK	GB	80
266	Stages: Houseman Directs	USA	81
267	BBC: The Shakespeare Plays	GB	82
268	Carnovsky Performs	USA	82[?]
269	Shakespeare in Perspective	GB	82
270	Koning Lear	Neth.	82
271	Granada TV, Olivier	GB	83
272	Lear and Hoodlums	GB	83
273	The Dresser	GB	85
274	Ran (Chaos)	Jap	85
275	Workshop: Lear	GB	85
276	Shakespeare Hour	USA	85
276.1	Lear: Documentary	USA	85
277	Godard's "Lear"	Fra	87
278	A.K.: Making of Ran	Jap	88
279	Lear Reflections	GB	8?
280	C. L. James on Lear	GB	??

Love's Labor's Lost (LLL)

No.	Description	Nation	Yr
281	Old Vic Production	GB	65
282	TV: Acting Company	USA	80
283	BBC: The Shakespeare Plays	GB	84

Macbeth (Mac.)

No.	Description	Nation	Yr
284	Duel scene	USA	05
285	Italian silent	Ita	09

Index to Series and Genres

(Major series are listed here. For complete data and fuller listings, consult Index to Entries and other indices. Number following the title designates the entry number in the main body of the book, not the page number.)

Index to Films and Videos by Year Produced and/or Released

(Number(s) following the title designates the entry number in the main body of the book, not the page number.)

Name Index:
Actors and Speakers

(Number(s) following the title designates the entry number in the main body of the book, not the page number.)

Name Index:
Producers, Directors, Cinematographers, Designers, Scenarists, Composers, and Other Production Team Members

(Number(s) following the title designates the entry number in the main body of the book, not the page number.)

Name Index:
Authors, Critics, and Editors

(Number(s) following the title designates the entry number in the main body of the book, not the page number.
* = In introduction; ** = In bibliography [check for more than one entry])

Guide to Distributors, Dealers and Archives

AFI
American Film Institute
Kennedy Performing Arts Center
Washington, DC
202-828-4040

ALS
Adult Learning Service
1320 Braddock Pl.
Alexandria, VA 22314
800-257-2578

ASP
Archivo Storico del Piccolo
Via Rovello 2, 20100
Milan, Italy

ASV
Archivo Storico
Bienniale di Venezia
Venice, Italy

AUP
Audio Visual Productions,
Hocker Hill House
Chepstow, Gwent, NP6 5E U.K.
02912-5439

AVG
Alternative Video Group
21 Cockcroft Place
Cambridge CB3 OH U.K.

AVI
Bureau A/V Inst., Univ. of Wis.
1327 Univ. Ave., PO Box 2093
Madison, WI 53701
608-262-1644

AVP
Ambrose Video Publishing
381 Park Ave. So. #1601
New York, NY 10016
800-526-4663
212-696-4545 (NY only)

BBC
British Broadcasting Corporation
6 Royce Road
Peterborough PE1 U.K.
0733-315-315

BBC-S
BBC, Woodlands 80 Wood Lane
London W12 OTT U.K.
01-743-5588

BEA
Beacon Films
1250 Washington Street,
PO Box 575
Norwood, MA 2062
617-762-0811

BFA
BFA Educational Media
2211 Michigan Ave.
Santa Monica, CA 90404
213-829-2901

BFI
British Film Institute
21 Stephen Street
London W1P 1PL U.K.
01-928-3535

BFV
Best Film & Video
Great Neck, NY 11021

BLK
Blackhawk Films
Old Eagle Brewery, Box 3990
Davenport, IA 52808
319-323-9736

BUD
Budget Video
1534 North Highland Ave.
Los Angeles, CA 90029
213-466-2431

BUFVC
British Univ. Film & Video Council
55 Greek St.
London WIV 5LR U.K.
01-734-3687

CBF
CBS Fox Video
333 W. 52nd St.
New York City, NY 10036
212-246-4300

CCA
Cambridgeshire College of
Arts and Technology
East Road
Cambridge CB1 1P U.K.
0223-63271, ext. 2205

CFI
Canadian Film Institute
Institut canadien du film
150 rue Rideau St.
Ottawa, Ontario K1N5X6
Canada
613-232-6727

CFL
CFL Vision
Chalfont Grove, Gerrards Cros
Bucks SL9 8TN U.K.
02407 4433

CIC
CIC Video, 4th Floor, Glenthorne House
5-17 Hammersmith Grove, Hammersmith
London W6 OND U.K.
01 846 9433

CIM
Coronet Instructional Media
65 East South Water St.
Chicago, IL 60601

CLC
Columbia Cinematique
711 Fifth Ave.
New York, NY 10022
212-751-7529

CNU
Center for Institutional Media
Univ. of Connecticut
Storrs, CT 06286
203-486-2350

COR
Corinth Films
34 Gansevoort St.
New York, NY 10014
800-221-4720

CTL
Centrum voor Taal-en
Literatuurwetenschap Vrije
Universiteit Brussel, B 105
Brussels, Pleinlaan 2
Belgium

CVF
Concord Video & Film Council
201 Felixstowe Road
Ipswich IP3 9BJ Suffolk U.K.
0473-715754/726012

CWF
Clem Williams Films
2240 Noblestown Road
Pittsburgh, PA 15205
800-245-1146

CWU
Case Western Univ.
Instructional Support
Cleveland, Ohio 44106

DAR
Darvill Assoc. Ltd.
280 Chartridge Lane
Chesam Bucks HP5 2SG
U.K.
0494 783643

DCV
Drama Classics Video
PO Box 2128
Manorhaven, NY 11050
516-767-7576

DIH
Dorset Institute of Higher Education
Wallisdown Road
Poole, Dorset U.K.
0202 524111

EAS
George Eastman House
East Ave.
Rochester, NY

EAV
Educational Audio-Visual Inc.
17 Marble Ave.
Pleasantville, NY 10570
800-431-2196

EBE
Encyclopedia Britannica
Educational Corp.
425 N. Michigan Ave.
Chicago, IL 60611

EFD
Educational Film Dist. Ltd.
285 Lesmill Road, Don Mills
Ontario M3B 2V1
Canada

EMB
Embassy Home Entertainment
1901 Ave. of the Stars
Los Angeles, CA 90067
213-553-3600

EMG
Em Gee Film Library
16024 Ventura Blvd., Suite 211
Encino, CA 91436
818-981-5506

ERS
Educational Record Sales
157 Chambers Street
New York, NY 10007
212-267-7437

EVI
Educational Video Index
c/o Bucks Film Laboratory,
714 Banbury, Slough, Bucks
U.K.
071 76611

FCM
Facets Multimedia, Inc.
1517 West Fullerton Ave.
Chicago, IL 60614
800-331-6197

FFH
Films for the Humanities
PO Box 2035
Princeton, NJ 08543
800-257-5126

FGF
Fred Goodland Film Service
81 Farmilo Road
London E17 8JN U.K.
01 539 4412

FMB
Filmbank Distributors
Acorn House, Victoria Road
London W3 6XU U.K.
01 993 8144

FMC
New York Filmmakers Co-op
175 Lexington Ave.
New York, NY
212-889-3820

FNC
Films Incorporated
5547 N. Ravenswood Ave.
Chicago, IL 60640-1199
800-323-4222, Ext.43
In Ill.: 312-878-2600, Ext. 43

FOL
Folger Shakespeare Library
201 East Capitol St.
Washington, DC 20003
202-544-4600

GAV
Univ. of Glasgow A/V Service
64 Southpark Ave.
Glasgow G12 8LB U.K.
041-339-8855, ext. 585

GFL
German Film & Video Library
c/o Viscom, Park Hall Road
Trading Estate
London SE21 8EL U.K.
01 761 4015

GIN
Goethe Institute
1014 5th Ave.
New York, NY
212-744-8310

GLB
Glenbuck Films, Ltd.
Glenbuck House, Glenbuck Road
Surrey KT6 6BT U.K.
1-399-0022/5266

GRN
Granada Video
36 Golden Square
London W1R 4AH U.K.
001 734-8080

GSV
Guild Sound & Vision Ltd.
6 Royce Road
Petersborough PE1 5YB U.K.
733-315-315

GTI
Granada Television Intl.
36 Golden Square
London W1R 4AH U.K.
01 734 8080

GTV
Globo TV
909 3rd Avenue
New York, NY 10022
212-754-0440

IAS
Institute for Advanced Studies in the
  Theatre Arts
12 West End Ave.
New York, NY 10023
800-843-8334

ICA
ICA Video, Inst. of Cont. Arts
12 Carlton House Terrace
London SW1Y 5AH U.K.
01 930 0493

IFB
International Film Bureau
332 So. Michigan St.
Chicago, IL 60604
312-427-4545

IFR
Institut Francaise du Royaum-
Uni Service du cinema
15 Queensberry Place
London SW7 U.K.
01 589 6211

ILE
ILEA Learning Resources
275 Kennington Lane
London SE11 5Q2 U.K.
01 633 5972

ILL
Univ. of Illinois Film/Video
1325 So. Oak St.
Champaign, IL 61820
800-367-3456

INM
Insight Media
121 West 85th St.
New York, NY 10024-4401
800-233-9910

IOA (See UIO, below)

ITI
Italian Institute, A/V Service
99 Belgrave Square
London SW1X 8NX U.K.
01 235 1461

ITM
Institut fur Theaterwissenschaft
University of Munich Munich, West
  Germany

IVY
Ivy Films
165 West 46th St.
New York, NY 10036
212 382-0111

JAG
Janus (Germany)
c/o Claus Hellwig
24 Paul Ehrlic Strasse
D 6000
Frankfurt A. Main 70
West Germany
638-055-58

JAN
Janus Films Inc.
888 7th Ave.
New York, NY 10022
212-0753-7100

JEF
JEF Films
143 Hickory Hill C
Osterville, MA 2653
617-428-7198

KAL
Katholieke Universiteit Leuven
Audiovisuele Dienst, Groenveidlaan
3 bus 3, B3030
Leuven, Belgium

KAR
Karol Media, E
22 Riverview Drive
Wayne, NJ 07470
201-628-9111

KIT
Kit Parker Films
1245 Tenth St.
Monterey, CA 93940
800-538-5838

KSC
King Screen Productions
320 Aurora Ave. North
Seattle, WA 98109

KSU
Kent State Univ., A/V Service
330 University Library
Kent, Ohio 44242
216-672-3456

KTV
Kent Ed. TV Centre, Fred
Nartin Studio
Barton Road, Dover
Kent CT16 2ND U.K.
0304-202-827

KUL
Kultur Video
1340 Ocean Ave.
Sea Bright, NJ 07760
201-842-6693

LCA
Learning Corp. of America
16 West 61st Street
New York, NY
212-307-0202

LCL
Lincoln Ctr. Library of Performing Arts
111 Amsterdam Ave.
New York, NY 10023
212-870-1641

LCM
Library of Congress Motion Picture
  Division
Capitol Hill
Washington, DC 20003
202-287-1000

LFM
London Filmmakers Co-Op
42 Gloucester Ave.
London NW1 U.K.
1-586-4806

LFP
London Film Productions
6 Goodwin's Court, St. Martin
London WC2 4LL U.K.
01-836-0576

LTS
London Television Service
Hercules House, Hercules Road
London SE1 7OV U.K.

LWT
London Weekend Television
Seymour Mews House, Wigmore St.
London W1H 9PE U.K.
01-935-9000

MCG
McGraw Hill
1221 Avenue of the Americas
New York, NY
212-512-2000

MFV
Marlboro Film & Video
PO Box 96
Marlboro, VT 05344
802-257-0743

MMA
Museum of Modern Art, Film L 11 W.
  53rd St.
New York, NY 10019
212-708-9433

MOB
Museum of Broadcasting
1 East 53rd St.
New York, NY 10022
212-752-4690

NET
WNET/Thirteen Television
356 West 58th St.
New York, NY 10019
212-560-2000

NFA
National Film Archive
21 Stephen Street
London W1P 1PL U.K.
01-255-1444

NFS
Nelson Filmscan
Mayfield Road, Walton on Thames
Surrey KT12 5PL U.K.
0932 246 133

NGS
National Geographic Society,
17 and M Streets NW
Washington, DC 20036
301-921-1330

NLC
New Line Cinema
853 Broadway
New York, NY 10003
212-674-7460

NOV
Novacom Video Inc.
PO Box 2068
Manorhaven, NY 11050
516-883-0020

NTI
Nederlands Theater Instituut
Herengracht 166-68
Amsterdam Netherlands

NWU
Northwestern Univ. Film Library
PO Box 1665
Evanston, IL 60204
312-869-0602

NYS
New York Shakespeare Festival
425 Lafayette St.
New York, NY 10003
212-598-7109

OPU
Open Univ. Educational Media
110 East 59th St.
New York, NY 10022

OSF
Oregon Shakespeare Festival
Ashland, OR

PCI
Polish Cultural Institute
34 Portland Place
London W1N 4HQ U.K.
01 636-6032

PVG
Palace Video
68 Flempton Road
London E10 U.K.
01 539 5566

PWK
Pickwick Video
Hyde Industrial Estate
The Hyde
London NW9 6JU U.K.
01 200 7000

PYR
Pyramid Film
Box 1048
Santa Monica, CA 90406
800-523-0118

RAI
Cineteca Nostroteca Radiotelevisione
RAI Studios
Torino, Italy

RCA
RCA Radio Videodiscs
7900 Rockville Road
Indianapolis, IN 46244
317-273-3640

RCC
RCA/Columbia
2901 W. Alameda Ave.
Burbank, CA 91505
818-954-4590

REP
Republic Pictures Home Video
12636 Beatrice Street
Los Angeles, CA 90066
213-306-4040

RSC
Royal Shakespeare Co.
RSC Mail Order, RSC
Stratford CV37 U.K.

RVL
Rank Video
PO Box 70, Great West Road
Brentford, Middlesex TW8 9H
U.K.
01 568 9222

SCL
Shakespeare Centre Library
Henley St.
Stratford CV37 U.K.
0789-204016

SFL
Scottish Central Film Library
Dowanhill, 74 Victoria Crescent
Glasgow G12 9JN SC U.K.
041-334-9314

SOV
Soft Video
Via Bettolo, 54
Rome, Italy

SSA
Shakespeare Society of America
Globe Playhouse, 1107 No. King Rd.
Los Angeles, CA 90069
213-654-5623

SSF
Stratford Shakespeare Festival
Stratford, Ontario N5A 6V2
Canada

SSV
Schofield & Sims Video
Dogley Mill, Fenay Bridge
Huddersfield, W. Yorks
484-607080

SUX
Sussex Tapes, Townsend
Poulshot, Devises
Wilts SN10 1SD U.K.
038 082 337

SWA
Swank Motion Pictures
350 Motor Parkway
Hauppage, NY 11788
516-434-1560; 800-645-7501

SYR
Syracuse University
1455 E. Colvin St.
Syracuse, NY 13210
315-432-2631

TAF
Trans Atlantic Films
Albert House, 9 Holland Park
London W11 U.K.
01 727-0132

TAM
Tamarelle's French Film House
1110 Cohasset Stage Road
Chico, CA 95926

TEC
Television and Educ. Classics
Audley House, 9 No. Audley St.
London W7Y 1WF U.K.
01-629-1021

TLF
Time Life Video
100 Eisenhower Drive
Paramus, NJ 07652
800-526-4663

TOFT
Theater on Film and Tape at
Lincoln Center (see LCL)

TSO
Trumedia Study Oxford Ltd.
Oxford Polytech Res. Unit
Wheatley
Oxford OX9 1HX
0865 63097

TTI
Thames Television Intl.
149 Tottenham Court Road
London W1P 9LL U.K.
01-387-9494

TWC
The Writing Company
10,000 Culver Blvd., Room K21
Culver City, CA 90232
800-421-4246

UAC
United Artists Comm.
1620 Broadway
New York, NY
212-333-5690

UBT
Univ. of Birmingham TV & Film
PO Box 363
Birmingham B15 2 U.K.
041 339 88550 Ext. 585

UCL
ATAS/UCLA TV Archives
Dept. of Theatre Arts Melnitz Hall
Los Angeles, CA 90024
213-825-4480

UCN
Univ. of Conn. Film Library Center for
  Instructional Media
Storrs, C T 06268
203-486-2530

UIO
Univ. of Iowa Media Library
C-5 Seashore Hall
Iowa City, IA 52242
319 335-2567

ULA
Univ. of London A/V Centre
North Wing Studios, Malet St.
London WC1E 7J2 U.K.
01 636 8000 Ext. 3809

UNF
United Films
1425 So. Main St.
Tulsa, OK 74119

UNU
Unusual Films
Bob Jones University
Greenville, SC 29614

UOH
Univ. of Hull A/V Centre
Hull HU6 7RX U.K.
0482-497-153

USF
Univ. of South Florida
Educational Resources
Tampa, FL 33620

UVM
UVM Media Service
Nolin House, Univ. of Vermont
Burlington, VT 05405
802-656-1944

UWD
Drama Department
Univ. of Washington
Seattle, WA 98195

VAA
La Videoteque 'Arts du Spectacle'
a la maison Jean Vilar
Avignon, France

VAI
Video Artists International
PO Box 153
Ansonia Station
New York, NY 10023
800-338-2566

VAV
Viewtech A/V Media
161 Winchester Road, Brislington
Bristol BS4 3NJ U.K.
0272 773422

VCT
Videoteca Centro Teatro Ateneo
Rome Italy

VID
Video Yesteryear
Box C
Sandy Hook, CT 06482
800-243-0987

VVP
Vineyard Video Productions
Elias Lane
West Tisbury, MA 02575
617-693-3584

WAC
Written Archives Centre BBC
Caversham Park
Reading RG4 8TZ U.K.
0734 472742 Ext. 280

WCF
Westcoast Films
25 Lusk St.
San Francisco, CA 94107

WFC
Wholesome Film Center, Inc.
20 Melrose St.
Boston, MA 02116

WFG
Winnipeg Film Group
88 Adelaide St.
Winnipeg R3A OW2 MB
Canada
204 942-6795

WGBH TV
125 Western Ave.
Boston, MA 02134
617-492-2777

WSU
A/V Dept.
Wisconsin Univ. at LaCrosse
LaCrosse, WI 54601

Kenneth S. Rothwell is a Professor of English at the University of Vermont. Dr. Rothwell, a specialist in Shakespeare studies, is co-editor of the *Shakespeare on Film Newsletter*. He is the author of numerous articles and reviews on Shakespeare on screen for *Shakespeare Quarterly, Shakespeare Survey,* and *CEA Critic.* His books include: *Questions of Rhetoric and Usage, 2nd Edition* (Boston: Little Brown, 1974) and *A Mirror for Shakespeare* (Burlington: IDC Publications, 1972).

Dr. Annabelle Melzer is a Professor of Theatre at the University of Tel Aviv. She is the recipient of a major grant from the National Endowment from the Humanities to support the compilation of an international database of theatre on film and video produced in the U.S., Canada, and Western Europe.

Book design: Sheldon Winicour
Cover design: Apicella Design
Typography: Roberts/Churcher